USING MICROPROCESSORS AND MICROCOMPUTERS: THE MOTOROLA FAMILY

Second Edition

USING MICROPROCESSORS AND MICROCOMPUTERS: THE MOTOROLA FAMILY

SECOND EDITION

JOSEPH D. GREENFIELD
Rochester Institute of Technology

WILLIAM C. WRAY
Consultant to Microcomputer Division of Motorola, Inc.

JOHN WILEY & SONS, INC.
NEW YORK CHICHESTER BRISBANE TORONTO SINGAPORE

Cover and text design: Karin Gerdes Kincheloe
Cover photo: Fundamental Photographs, New York
Production editors: Laura McCormick
Nancy Prinz

Library of Congress Cataloging in Publication Data:
Greenfield, Joseph D., 1930-
Using microprocessors and microcomputers.
Bibliography: p.
1. Motorola 6800 series microprocessors.
3. Microcomputers. I. Wray, William Ç. II. Title.
QA76.8.M67G75 1988 004.16 87-28020
ISBN 0-471-87954-1
Printed in the United States of America
10 9 8 7 6 4 3 2 1

PREFACE

The goals of this second edition remain the same as in the previous edition except that it has been updated to include many new microprocessors (μPs) and other new material on microcomputer development systems.

The object of the first edition was to explain the uses and operation of the **6800** family of microcomputer components to electronic technology and engineering students. It has been successfully used to provide the basics of microcomputer (μC) design and programming to tens of thousands of students.

The first nine chapters cover the same basic concepts of microcomputer (μC) system design as provided in the first edition. As before, the simple but still current Motorola **6800** μP has been described in detail. These chapters have been slightly reorganized to further simplify them and to put similar subjects together. They serve to introduce beginning students to the world of microcomputers as it exists today.

These basic concepts have not changed dramatically but many new more sophisticated μP and μC "chips" have been introduced and are described in the later chapters. The Motorola family concept started with 8-bit designs such as the **6800** and has grown to include not only many new sophisticated 8-bit types but also 16- and 32-bit μP designs such as the **68030**, which are the most advanced μPs available.

Chapter 1 has been revised to describe the new developments that have occurred and to explain some of the changes in applications that have appeared.

Chapter 2 describes computer number systems as before but now also includes hexadecimal notation.

Chapter 3 describes the basic computer as before but now uses the **6800** instead of a hypothetical rudimentary computer to illustrate the features.

Chapters 4 through 9 are similar to the previous edition, except that Chapter 6 describes more modern Assembler and Linker programs.

Chapter 10 has been revised considerably to describe up-to-date debugging techniques, using simple tools.

Chapter 11 gives many details of the expanded **6801** μC family and introduces the new HCMOS μCs such as the **68HC11**. The low-cost, well-populated **6805** family is discussed and the coverage of the **6809** has been expanded.

Chapter 12 is all new and continues a discussion of debugging methods by introducing several new μC development instruments.

Chapter 13 covers interfacing techniques and is similar to the previous edition except for an added section on computer construction and standard bus concepts.

Chapter 14 describes a real application of a display terminal design but includes a simplified discussion of the **6845** CRT Controller chip.

Chapter 15 is a major addition to the book in that it describes the evolution to the 16-bit **68000** μPs. The programming of the **68000** is thoroughly discussed as well.

Chapter 16 describes the advanced features of the later members of the **68000** family, including the **68010**, **68020**, and **68030**.

We thank the many people who have helped us with the second edition. We must mention the colleagues and students of Joesph Greenfield at Rochester Institute of Technology and the many engineers at Motorola Microsystems (now Motorola Microcomputer Division) who work with William C. Wray, in particular, Jesse Winters, Ken Roehrman, and Jay Hartvigsen, as well as those who reviewed our revision at various stages of development: Richard Rouse, DeVry Institute of Technology, Kansas City, MO; C. P. Johnson, Department of Electronics, Long Beach City College, Long Beach, CA; Rick Burgess, Lewis & Clark College, Godfrey, IL; Everitt Smith, Jr., East Granby, CT, (Univ. of W. Hartford-Ward Technical College); William Moore, Western Kentucky University, Bowling Green, KY; Fred Cleveland, School of Engineering, University of the Pacific, Stockton, CA.

We are grateful for the cooperation of the Motorola Technical Information Center, Phoenix, Arizona, and their managers, Lothar Stern, now retired, and Jeff Gorin, the present manager. With their permission we have reproduced many figures from manuals and other literature. We would like to acknowledge that many of the terms used in the text are trademarks of Motorola Inc. These include EXORciser®, EXbug, Minibug, MIKBUG, JBUG, MICRObug, MDOS, MICROmodule, and HDS. As before, above all, without the help and support of our wives, Gladys and Dorothy, we would not have completed this second edition.

Joseph D. Greenfield

William C. Wray

CONTENTS

CHAPTER 1
INTRODUCTION TO MICROCOMPUTERS 1

CHAPTER 2
COMPUTER ARITHMETIC AND LOGIC OPERATIONS 18

CHAPTER 10 SYSTEM DEBUGGING 311

CHAPTER 11 OTHER 8-BIT MICROPROCESSORS 353

CHAPTER 14
CRT DISPLAY TERMINAL APPLICATION 525

CHAPTER 15
THE 68000 FAMILY 563

CHAPTER 16
ADVANCED FEATURES OF THE NEWER MEMBERS OF THE 68000 FAMILY 640

USING MICROPROCESSORS AND MICROCOMPUTERS: THE MOTOROLA FAMILY

Second Edition

CHAPTER 1

INTRODUCTION TO MICROCOMPUTERS

1-1 INTRODUCTION

The introduction of the digital computer in the early 1950s revolutionized methods of computing, manipulating data, and controlling other devices and systems. The development of the **microcomputer** (one or more semiconductor chips with all the functions of a computer) is now revolutionizing the computer industry and many other industries as well. Because of their low cost, small size, and versatility, microcomputers (μCs) are surely destined to play an increasingly important role in the technologies of the future.

In the past three decades electronics has made tremendous strides, progressing from vacuum tubes to transistors to **integrated circuits** (ICs). ICs are very small electronic components that contain miniature transistors and their associated circuits diffused into a silicon chip. The science of placing large numbers of these electronic components on a tiny (1/4 inch square) semiconductor chip is called *semiconductor technology*. In recent years, highly complex circuits have been fabricated on a single chip. The most complex (and most useful) of these is the μC.

The purpose of this book is to introduce μC integrated circuit components and to help the reader understand how they work and how they can be used. This is not a simple task because many μC families of components are available, each with its own *set of instructions* and *unique hardware configuration*. The first microprocessor (μP) components available were simple devices capable of handling only 4 *bits* of information at a time. They are known as 4-bit μPs. More advanced 8-bit μPs were soon developed, and now μPs are available in up to 32-bit configurations. The 8-bit μPs are the most popular and include the Intel **8080** family, the Zilog **Z80**, and **6502**, and the Motorola **6800** family. If we attempted to describe each type, we could not discuss any one in enough depth to enable the reader to build or use a system containing a specific family. On the other hand, a simple and straightforward μC family can easily be understood and the computer concepts are generally applicable to all other families. Therefore, this book focuses primarily on the popular and extensively used Motorola **6800** family of μC components. The **6800** μP itself, although not included in too many new designs, is still used extensively. It uses the concepts that are common to most μPs (multibyte instructions, interrupts, stacks, clocks, etc.). The reader who understands how these operations work on the **6800** will have little trouble understanding the operation of other μCs. The concepts of the **6800** are used in all the newer μPs and μCs made by Motorola, including the **6801**, **6804**, **6805**, **6809**, and as natural extensions the 16-bit **68000** and **68010** and the 32-bit **68020** and **68030**. This is what is meant by the **6800** family.

One chapter is devoted to other μCs where the emphasis is on the similarities to and differences from the **6800**. We believe that this concept for introducing μCs works well and results in a book that is practical and easily understood.

This introductory chapter presents an overview of μCs, and some material may be difficult for beginners to understand. A detailed explanation of subjects needed to understand μC operation begins in Chapter 2. After reading this chapter, the student should be able to

1. Decide whether to use a μC in a given application.
2. Describe the differences between NMOS, PMOS, CMOS, and HMOS technologies.
3. List the differences between a minicomputer and a μC.

1-2 SELF-EVALUATION QUESTIONS

Watch for the answers to the following questions as you read the chapter. They should help you to understand the material presented.

1. What are the advantages of a μC over a minicomputer? What are the disadvantages?
2. How does programmability give the μC an advantage over hard-wired electronic controllers?
3. What are the most important characteristics of a μC?
4. Explain why displays and switches (the equivalent of a computer front panel) are not required in many μC applications.
5. Why is it important to design connections for test equipment into a μC system?
6. What is the major cost in developing a μC system?
7. What is the major disadvantage of compiler languages for a μC in controller applications?

1-3 HISTORICAL BACKGROUND OF SEMICONDUCTOR TECHNOLOGY

The complexity of electronic circuits that can be incorporated into one integrated circuit chip has been approximately doubling each year for more than a decade.

Since the basic raw materials used in ICs are very inexpensive, and high-volume production has made the cost of digital ICs even lower, the performance/price ratio has increased dramatically.

The first ICs used bipolar technology, which eventually resulted in the availability of families of circuits such as the **7400** transistor-transistor logic (TTL) series. These have been described as *small-scale integration* (SSI). Improvements in this process resulted in bipolar *medium-scale integration* (MSI) devices, which use many gates on each IC and produce complex circuits such as shift registers, which move the bits of a word left or right, and multiplexers, which share the wires and circuits between two functions.

Digital integrated circuits using **Metal-Oxide Semiconductor** (MOS) technology were introduced around 1969. This MOS form of transistor construction is used in many ICs (Section 1-5.2) and has several advantages over bipolar technology:

1. MOS devices require fewer manufacturing steps.
2. MOS gates dissipate less power per gate.
3. MOS gates require less space on the silicon wafer.

Because of these advantages, far more MOS circuitry can be placed on a single IC.

Bipolar TTL integrated circuits continue to dominate in SSI and MSI because of their high speed, wide acceptance, and long history of successful applications. Most *Large-Scale Integration* (LSI) devices, including memories and μPs, which require hundreds or even thousands of gates in a single IC, use MOS rather than bipolar technology.

1-3.1 Developments in Computer Hardware

Many minicomputers and larger computers were built in the 1960s and 1970s using bipolar or TTL ICs. A computer consists of *memory* to hold the program of instructions and data, *input/output* (I/O) *circuits,* a *control section,* and an *arithmetic/logic unit,* which performs the required arithmetic and **logic** operations. The logic uses AND and OR gates to control and coordinate the sequence of operations of the circuits. A computer is different from other electronic circuits because its operation is controlled by a program **(software)**. The operation of the computer can be changed by changing the program instead of rewiring the circuits. A more detailed explanation of computer organization and operation is given in later chapters.

By 1969, when MOS was first introduced, semiconductor technology had progressed to the point where all of the basic μC circuits (gates, registers, arithmetic/logic units, and so forth) existed as individual ICs. At about that time, the IC manufacturers started to combine these individual ICs into a single IC to produce a microprocessor. This chip included most, but not all, of the functions of the complete computer.

The first practical IC μP, the Intel **4004**, appeared in 1971. The **4004** is a 4-bit μP that is, by today's standards, slow and difficult to use. Later in the same year Intel also introduced the **8008**, an 8-bit μP with a more sophisticated instruction set.

Two of the most popular μPs in early systems were the Intel **8080** and the

TABLE 1-1 Microprocessor Types

uP TYPE	MFGR	TCHNGLY	ARCHITECTURE	INTRO DATE	UNIQUE CHARACTERISTICS
4004	Intel	PMOS	4-bit	'71	12-bit multiplxed address
4040	"	"	"		Updated 4004 14 added inst + intrpt
8008	"	"	8-bit	'72	Mltplxed 14 bit addr - 48 instr
8080	"	NMOS	8-bit uP 16-bit addr 16-bit stk ptr	'74	40 pin non-mltplx
8080A	"	"	"		updated 8080
8048	"	"	8-bit uC ROM- RAM I/O-Timer	'78	Sngl chip uC EPROM version unique instr set
8085	"	N chnl depl. load	8-bit uP int clk vect intrpts 5 V Only		8080 compatible
6800	Motor-ola	NMOS	8-bit uP 16-bit addr 16-bit stk 5 V only	'74	40-pin, unlm stack
6802	"	"	6800 uP 128 RAM Int clk	'77	32 byte Lo-pwr RAM for standby. 6800 object compatible
6801			8-bit uC 2K ROM 128 RAM internl clk timer- UART 4- I/O ports	'78	Enhanced instrns faster thruput 6800 object code compatible
6803	"	"	8-bit uC same as 6801 except no ROM	'78	Enhanced instrctns 6800 obj code com-patible
6809	"	"	8-bit uP Int or Ext clk 3 interrupts 2 index regs 2 index/SP regs	'78	Hi-performance uP Enhanced instrns faster thruput 16 bit instrns 6800 source code compatible

Motorola **6800**. They were introduced in 1974, and many are still in use. In 1977 and 1978 several one-chip microcomputers (which included memory and I/O), such as the Fairchild **F8**, the Texas Instruments (TI) **TMS1000**, and the Motorola **6801**, were introduced. Table 1-1 shows the μPs and μCs available in the early days of the computer revolution, their characteristics, technology, and date of introduction.

TABLE 1-1 (continued)

141000 141200	"	CMOS	4-bit static 1K ROM 64x4 RAM 11 or 16 I/O	'77	0-700 kHz clk Sngl chip uC TMS1000 compatible
3870	"	NMOS	8-bit uC 2K ROM 64 bytes RAM Timer-int clk		F8 type map not expandble
IMP-16	Nat.	PMOS	4-bit slice	'73	multi chp 16-bit
SC/MP	"	"	8-bit uP	'75	
PACE	"	"	16-bit uP	'76	1st 16-bit system not TTL cmptbl
2650	Sig- netics	NMOS-I	8-bit uP	'75	
CDP 1801	RCA	CMOS	8-bit uP	'75	
PPS-8	Rock- well	PMOS	8-bit uP	'75	
PPS-4	Rock-	PMOS	4-bit uP	'72	
6502	MOS- tech.	NMOS	8-bit uP int clk	'75	Diffrnt pinouts Like 6800 2nd index reg
F8	Fair child	"	8-bit RAM int clock I/O	'74	
3850	Mostec	"	8-bit uP		F8 type
9900	Texas Inst.	"	16-bit	'76	64 pin pkg
TMS- 1000	TI	PMOS	4-bit uC 1Kx8 ROM 64x4 RAM Int clk 11 I/O lines		28-pin -15 V only
TMS- 1200	TI	PMOS	same except 16 I/O lines		40-pin
Z80	Zilog	NMOS	8-bit CPU 5 V only int clk	'76	Dual register like 8080 175 instructions

Note: NMOS-D denotes depletion load and NMOS-I denotes ion-implantation.

1-4 MICROCOMPUTER FAMILIES

A μC system includes a **microprocessor.** The μP may be a separate IC or part of a more complex chip. In either case, the μP contains within it most of the control and arithmetic functions of a computer. Microprocessors cannot function by themselves and must be augmented by other functions. Random-access memories (RAMs), read-only memories (ROMs), and peripheral drivers for the input and output of data are necessary to form a complete μC. The original μC families used a separate chip for each function, but newer members of the family include RAM, ROM, and I/O sections on the same chip and therefore are complete μCs in one package. These μCs are generally suitable for simple applications and must be augmented by additional ROMs, RAMs, or I/O chips for bigger jobs.

1-4.1 Microprocessors and Microcomputers

Figure 1-1 shows the **6800** μP in a Dual In-line Package (DIP) and also shows a block diagram of the μP and the other functions necessary to complete the μC. These other functions are also available in similar packages. Early μC systems used these packages to assemble an entire computer on a single printed circuit module. Figure 1-2 shows such a module. It contains a **6800** μP plus the associated RAMs, ROMs, clock, and SSI chips required to make a complete functioning μC. Currently, a large selection of single LSI chips are available with all these functions incorporated. Single-chip computers are discussed in Chapter 11.

1-4.2 Microcomputer Memories

Computer memories, which were implemented with magnetic cores in early computers, now are also fabricated using semiconductors and consist of RAMs,

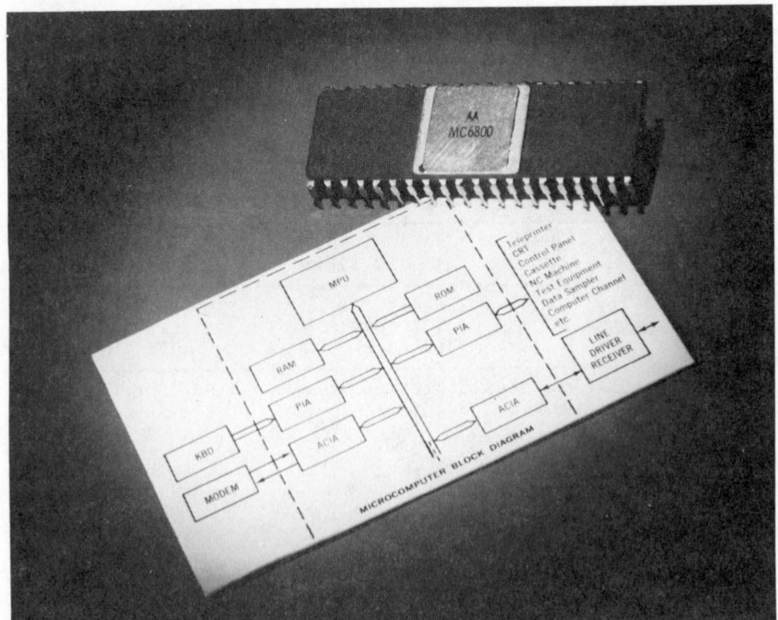

FIGURE 1-1 The **6800** μP and its associated family of ICs.

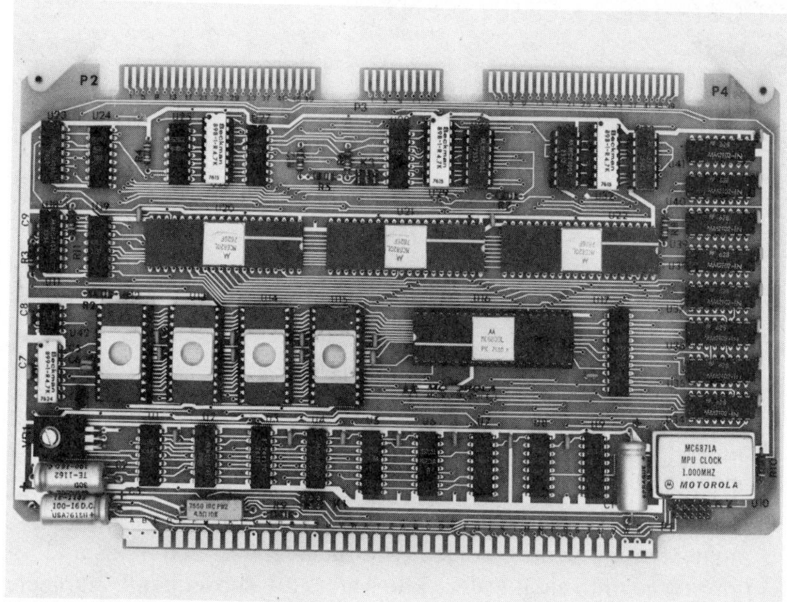

FIGURE 1-2 A **6800** μC system on a single card.

factory-programmed Read-Only Memory (ROM), or field-Programmable Read-Only Memory (PROM). Memory is essential to the operation of any computer and is discussed in detail in Chapter 3. The ROM or PROM is used to store the program instructions permanently, and the RAM temporarily saves all variable data used in the course of program operation. In general, the more functions performed, the more program memory required, but this addition does not affect the cost of the μP chip, the clock, or even I/O functions. Memory ICs are available in a wide variety of configurations, and several of them in the **6800** family are specifically designed for small μC systems. These and other hardware aspects of the **6800** family are discussed in Chapter 7.

1-4.3 Testing of μC Systems

Because test instruments cannot be connected to circuits inside a μP, special instruments have been developed to "see" the register contents. Microcomputer manufacturers introduced these specialized instruments, which are used with their family of μC components for both hardware and software troubleshooting. Intel's first *Microcomputer Development System* (MDS) was called the *Intellec*. Motorola's *EXORciser* was developed in 1974. Other semiconductor manufacturers make similar μC test instruments. A growing number of companies that do not manufacture ICs have introduced a variety of specialized analyzers for general-purpose use in μC system design. The need for these instruments and the techniques for using them are discussed in Chapter 10.

1-5 MICROCOMPUTER COMPONENT MANUFACTURE

This book is concerned primarily with the *use* of μC components. It is important, however, to have a basic understanding of semiconductor manufacture in order to be aware of performance differences, to plan future products, and to anticipate cost trends and future designs.

Semiconductor technology involves photography, chemistry, materials science, metallurgy, physics, and electronics. Progress is being made rapidly in all these disciplines, resulting in continual improvements in the semiconductors themselves.

The first step in the process of making μC family components is to grow *silicon crystals* and slice them into thin *wafers*. The silicon crystals, which in the early days were less than 5 cm (2 inches) across, are now being grown in sizes up to 5 inches. The electrical circuits are then chemically etched into the silicon wafers by treating the wafers with a photosensitive material and exposing the material through a *mask* of the desired pattern. These masks are many feet across when made but are photographically reduced almost 500 times and multiple images are projected onto each wafer. The wafers are subsequently subjected to processes of diffusion or ion implantation and deposition of metal. After many such steps, the wafer is ready to be diced (cut up) into *chips,* which are usually less than 6 mm (1/4 inch) square. The chips are tested to select the good ones, which are then mounted in the familiar plastic or ceramic packages (DIPs). Using presently available techniques, hundreds of dies are now being cut from each wafer. As the technology improves, the yield of good dies per wafer also increases. This has caused the price of ICs to come down to the point where even μCs are inexpensive. The **6800** silicon chip is shown in Fig. 1-3.

1-5.1 Microcomputer Characteristics

Microcomputers are frequently compared on the basis of several main characteristics. Among them are the number of power supplies used, TTL compatibility, and the number of chips needed to form a complete μC. In specialized designs the power dissipation may also be important. The operation of most μCs is controlled by a digital clock (see Chapter 7). If the basic semiconductor technology allows high-speed performance, the clock can be run at a higher frequency. This permits the μC to execute more instructions per second, making it more powerful. The maximum usable clock rate is therefore another comparison factor.

1-5.2 PMOS, NMOS, CMOS, HMOS, and HCMOS Technologies

Metal-oxide semiconductor technology is divided into two basic types: PMOS, which is based on *p*-doped silicon, and NMOS, which is based on *n*-doped silicon. These two types of implementations can be used individually or can be combined to form a third category, known as Complementary MOS (CMOS). These technologies have much in common, but each also exhibits some unique characteristics.

FIGURE 1-3 The **6800** silicon chip.

PMOS was perfected originally and the first μPs were designed using this process. The Intel **4004** and **8008** are examples of PMOS technology. The circuit speed of PMOS was nearly an order of magnitude (one-tenth) lower than that of bipolar devices but, because of the reduced geometry and lower power dissipation per gate, much more complexity was possible on a chip. However, *n*-type silicon is basically three times faster than *p*-type silicon, because the mobility of electrons is three times that of holes. As a result, and because of its TTL-compatible voltage (5 V), NMOS has emerged as the most popular process for μP production. It is the process used for the **6800**, the **8080**, Fairchild's **F8**, and Zilog's **Z80**. Although Intel's process is called NMOS, it still requires three voltages for the **8080**.

The techniques for producing these circuits on silicon have been continually refined, resulting in smaller designs. A smaller geometry has produced many performance improvements. The newest process is called High-density NMOS (HMOS). The high speed of HMOS compared to PMOS or other NMOS types provides a very high performance/price ratio. As a result of HMOS and other techniques, Very Large Scale Integration (VLSI) devices such as the **68000**, **68010**, **68020**, and **68030** have been developed. The **68000** contains about 68,000 transistors, the 32-bit **68020** has nearly 200,000, and the **68030** has nearly 300,000. These are the newest members of the **6800** family (which had about 5000 transistors).

CMOS combines an *n*-channel and a *p*-channel MOS transistor in each gate. It has the advantage of extremely low power dissipation when it is static (not being clocked or switched). CMOS has an added advantage of considerable latitude in supply voltage. Consequently, it is advocated as a good choice for battery operation.

CMOS devices have been used for many years in applications where the primary concerns were low power consumption, wide power supply range, and high noise immunity. The drawback to using the **metal-gate** CMOS was the fact that it was too *slow* for many applications. The logical next step in the CMOS evolution was to introduce a family of devices that are fast enough for most applications and that retain the best features of CMOS. In order to do this, the **silicon-gate** process with a gate length of 3.5 **microns** was developed. The resulting High-speed CMOS (HCMOS) device is a little more than half the size of its metal-gate predecessor. In addition, the silicon-gate process eliminates gate overlaps, which significantly lowers the gate capacities, resulting in higher-speed performance comparable to that of TTL devices.

This HCMOS process is used in a number of inexpensive single-chip μCs in the **M68HC05** family. (The letters HC inside an IC number indicate an HCMOS device.)

New materials such as gallium arsenide are being investigated and, under idealized conditions, can provide an increase in speed of up to seven times.

1-6 MICROPROCESSORS VS HARD-WIRED LOGIC

Industry has made use of industrial controllers to control machines, manufacturing processes, and appliances. The method of building controllers has progressed from electromechanical to electronic (frequently *analog*), to digital ICs, and now to μCs. The original controllers were *hard-wired* devices because their operation was determined by the circuits and wires contained within them. As the ICs became more complex with Large-Scale Integration (LSI), the controllers became smaller and yet more sophisticated. They were capable of performing more diverse operations and responding to a larger number of inputs.

The washing machine is a common example of electromechanical control. Relays, solenoids, and timers within the machine determine the sequence of operations (wash, rinse, spin dry, and so on) and control the time of each operation. More recent designs use power transistors and digital ICs to replace the relays and therefore provide more reliable control.

Any function that can be implemented with hard-wired digital ICs can also be implemented or performed by a μC. The μC is a great leap forward in this evolutionary chain. Its operation is determined primarily by its program instead of the way it is wired. Because of this, μCs are rapidly replacing hard-wired logic in most controllers.

Hard-wired logic still maintains the following advantages over MOS μCs:

1. It is faster. It can execute a function in perhaps 1/10 of the time required by a MOS μC, because the execution time for computer instructions is much longer than for TTL IC logic.

2. For small devices requiring just a few ICs, the hard-wired approach is less costly, because the more complex (and higher cost) chips and their associated connections are not required.
3. No programming costs are incurred.

As the size and complexity of the devices increase, μCs rapidly become more attractive for two reasons:

1. The hard-wired approach requires adding ICs to perform more complex tasks; μCs usually require only a longer program.
2. μCs are more versatile. Any change in a hard-wired system usually involves replacing ICs and rerouting wires.

Most modifications to a μC system are made simply by changing the program. For example, a modification can frequently be accomplished simply by replacing a ROM, which can easily be done in the field by nontechnical users. Where many decisions or calculations are required μCs are very useful. It is easier to use the computational power of a computer than to use discrete logic. One example is TV games, where, for example, the controller must keep track of the position of the ball, determine when a point is scored, and keep score. Most of the controllers for these games include a μC, and different games are selected by replacing the plug-in ROM (or PROM).

Microcomputers are now being considered for many new designs in industrial controller applications and are often used to replace existing mechanical or even digital logic designs, because they are far simpler to use than conventional IC logic. Since the μC approach is programmable (i.e., the operation can be changed by changing only the software), many additional features are possible with little or no added cost. **Programmability** makes possible multiple uses of a common computer hardware assembly (i.e., only the ROM control program needs to be changed).

1-7 COMPUTERS AND MINICOMPUTERS

Large computers (such as the IBM 360 or 370) are used to solve highly sophisticated probems or to handle operations that require large volumes of output data. Most corporations, for example, use large computers to print their payrolls and write their bills.

A minicomputer is a scaled-down version of a larger computer with correspondingly reduced computational power. It is much smaller and less expensive and is an ideal solution for problems of medium complexity. In the early 1970s, minicomputers were used primarily to control industrial processes. Now μCs are replacing minicomputers for these applications. Similarly, minicomputers, which are becoming more sophisticated, are taking over some tasks formerly performed by large computers.

Microcomputer costs are less than those of most minicomputers, but, except for some of the newer 16- and 32-bit μCs, the performance of most μCs is lower than that of a minicomputer. Minicomputers are generally faster than 8-bit μCs. Since minicomputers are often less than fully utilized and many applications do not need their speed, μCs have become a good alternative for many uses. Each year, μC costs drop and performance improves, so more and more applications are being found where the μC is able to substitute for larger computers.

1-7.1 Minicomputers

Minicomputers were the first step in the miniaturization of computers. They are available from a number of manufacturers as basic general-purpose computers that can be adapted for a variety of uses, usually by plugging in various modular cards. These cards usually include a complete function such as an input module, output module, or memory module. The modules are assembled using discrete components as a rule.

1-7.2 Minicomputers vs μCs

A minicomputer usually is equipped with a large RAM and can load and run a variety of programs. It also normally includes displays, registers, entry switches, and plug-in accessory modules. It is a general-purpose package capable of a variety of uses with a minimum of hardware modifications. Practically all minicomputers have only read/write memory, but some units have a small ROM booting program to permit easy loading of the application program into the RAM. Minicomputers usually require either disk, cassette, or similar device to load the programs or to reload the memory in the event of a power interruption. This mass storage unit is either permanently associated with the minicomputer or transported to it to get the minicomputer restarted.

The same configuration can be assembled with a μC, and in fact many μCs are being used in this way as personal computers. This μC configuration can be used to do many of the tasks normally handled by the minicomputer, but the μC does not have the speed for some requirements (see Section 1-9).

On the other hand, because of its small size and low cost, the μC is often designed for a specific task. The real advantage of the μC and its companion LSI components is that they can be assembled with as few or as many parts as needed to do the required task. It is not necessary for example, to include register/display and entry switches or terminal input/output facilities in most systems, because the μC is often built into machinery where the operator is not skilled in computer discipline or the equipment is unattended in normal operation. In these cases, the design, debugging, and maintenance are accomplished by plug-in or transportable test equipment. In some cases, the μC system is designed to accommodate special test equipment. The availability of emulators with most μC development systems makes it possible to test any unique system even if it has no built-in provisions, because the emulator simply replaces the μP or μC. The dedicated μC's memory is often mostly ROM or PROM for program instruction storage with a small RAM for variable data such as scratch pad calculations. Since, in this case, the μC's operating program is nonvolatile (permanent), restarting the program after power has been off is quickly and easily accomplished. If the RAM is equipped with a *battery backup* circuit to keep it operational when the power fails, and the necessary software routines are included in the ROMs, recovery from a power failure without loss of data is possible. This auto-restart capability is one of the μC's most valuable features.

1-8 SOFTWARE CONTROL OF ELECTRONIC SYSTEMS

The technique of substituting software (computer programs) for the actual electronic circuits (i.e., for the **hardware logic**) is largely responsible for the acceptance of μCs. A μC can completely control any system, but it is necessary to provide the appropriate interface. Consider a μC built to control a device that includes motors or solenoid-activated valves. The electronic circuitry external to the μC would consist of solid-state relays or power transistor amplifiers, and the TTL-level signals from the μC I/O lines would control them. (A 5-V ON signal could make a motor run or open a valve, and a 0-V OFF signal would halt the action.) The functions of timing, limiting, and interlocking would be provided in software. This is not always safe, so mechanical limit switches or pressure relief valves, for example, could be added to the hardware, provided that the reliability of the electromechanical devices is adequate. These design decisions are often referred to as hardware/software trade-offs and must be made by the system designer. Mechanical and hydraulic logic devices such as mechanical interlocks or speed-controlling governors are being replaced by appropriately designed μC systems. Electronic control is faster, cleaner, more accurate, and more reliable, and *electronic components do not wear out.* Such systems contain electrical or electronic sensors (transducers) and their outputs are connected to μC input lines so that the information can be processed by the software routines. In the automotive field, for example, ignition spark advance mechanisms, which have been vacuum-controlled, and carburetor controls, which have been universally mechanical, are being replaced by electromechanical devices, which in turn are controlled by μCs. This provides high-speed dynamic adjustments (30 times a second) not previously possible. These advances are possible today because of the low cost of the μC. They can be justified on the basis of the increased reliability, accuracy, or ease with which a feature can be added to a μC controller.

1-9 HOME OR PERSONAL COMPUTERS

One of the prime areas of μC applications has been personal computers for the home. It has been possible for a number of years now to build very practical units with surprising power. Because of their power, low cost, and small size, millions of home computers are now in use and there has been tremendous growth in the development of all aspects of this industry. Not only do personal computers use the latest in μPs or μCs and all other semiconductor products, such as memories, but also this market has resulted in rapid development of accessory items such as disk drives, Cathode Ray Tube (CRT) displays, and printers.

Competition in this business has been fierce and many companies (e.g., Apple and Commodore) have grown dramatically, while others have gone bankrupt. With the growth of home computers there has been a resurgence of time-sharing services, and many systems include a **modem** for communication over telephone lines to other computers, in many cases large computers with access to unlimited information. Communication between home units is also popular.

The information to follow in this book will certainly cover the design of personal-type computers, but the emphasis will be on use of μCs for applications where unique designs are needed. Machinery controllers and robotics are two examples.

1-10 THE FUTURE OF μCS

The technological evolution in microcomputers continues to pack more performance into a smaller space and results in more complex and more powerful semiconductor products. The growth of the **6800** family to the **6809** and on to the 16-bit **68000** family provided outstanding increases of performance, approaching or exceeding that of the mini- and mainframe computer architectures they were originally modeled after.

The increase in performance available in the **68000**, **68010**, and the **68020**s with **68881** *coprocessors* and **68451** or **68851** *memory management units* is resulting in remarkable capabilities for microcomputers. These advanced systems will continue to grow, but it should be noted that *many and perhaps most* applications do not need the higher speed or 32-bit capability. At present the market for 8-bit systems is approximately equal to the 16-bit μC market. The 32-bit market is smaller. The use of 8-bit systems is expected to continue to grow until at least 1990, particularly in the industrial automation area. Industrial control (including *robotics*) does not always need the speed or complexity now possible. Instead, the lower costs due to the reduced die size in 8-bit controller-type processors, with the resultant simplifications in the circuit boards and associated hardware, will lead to many more computerized instruments. When controlling large machinery, *nanosecond* speed is not needed unless many calculations are necessary. Learning about 8-bit μCs thus not only is a good stepping stone to the 32-bit world but also is very worthwhile in its own right.

1-10.1 The Growing Low-End μC Market

The experience gained during the evolution to 32-bit μCs has greatly enhanced the expertise needed in the semiconductor industry to design more powerful low- and midrange devices. The demanding requirements of the midrange control-oriented microprocessor market, for power combined with low cost, has resulted in development of the **M6805** HMOS and **M146805** CMOS families of μCs and μPs. These families are the first to make the software and hardware capabilities of more advanced computers available to the controller market. Previously, designers and manufacturers were required to choose between no processor at all or a processor that functioned more like a calculator than a computer.

Control-oriented μCs have evolved from two different bases: calculator-based and computer-based. The calculator-based design was at first considered a natural building block for controllers since most often a controller was required to be a completely self-contained unit. However, calculator-based control-oriented μPs use a split memory architecture, with separate data paths between the central processing unit (CPU) and peripherals (memory, I/O, and registers). In addition, calculator-based I/O, display, and keypad were separated from program and data storage memory. Separate address maps were required, which forced the inclusion of many special-purpose instructions and resulted in an irregular architecture. As a result, these calculator-based devices required that hardware and software designers remember and consider many special cases in order to perform any task. The software and hardware for the calculator approach became very random, irregular, and difficult to update.

The computer-based design, on the other hand, led to another group of processors like the **6800**, which has many features of larger computers. These devices contain a single data bus that allows access to a single address map, eliminating the need for split memory architecture. In this one-address map design, all I/O, program, and data may be accessed with the same instructions; therefore, there are fewer instructions to remember. The actual number of variations on these instructions is increased by additional addressing modes. For example, the load accumulator (LDA) instruction may *load* the accumulator with data in six different ways, depending on which addressing mode is used. This effectively provides the programmer with more tools to work with but fewer things to remember. These addressing modes generally apply to all registers, memory, or I/O. Because of the regularity of the architecture, the hardware can be implemented more efficiently.

1-10.2 Memory Improvements

Progress in size and speed of memory chips is continuing at a rapid pace with larger and lower-cost RAM and ROM (or PROM) units announced frequently. Today's systems often have up to 64 times as much memory as was commonly used in earlier μC designs, in the same size package (128K vs. 2K).

If the future of μCs is based on projections, it appears that the material cost of the ICs themselves will virtually disappear. Since the raw materials are abundant, it can logically be assumed that the cost of each chip will level off at something less than a few dollars. As more functions are included in each package, the total material costs become insignificant compared with the design and programming costs. With the switchover from hardware to software, new concepts and techniques are necessary to handle the tasks to be performed and therefore new methods of cost analysis must be used. Since the price of each system sold is determined by the cost of the hardware plus the cost of development divided by the number of systems sold, high-volume production can result in a very low-priced equipment. Many people are alarmed at the rising cost of programming, but it should be recognized that it represents just a shift in costs because software is being substituted for hardware.

Software development costs are one-time costs, but the importance of keeping the development costs low should not be overlooked. Selection of a μP that is easy to program and the use of good systems development tools are both advisable. Good development tools include not only software editing and debugging aids but also means of troubleshooting the hardware interface between the μC and its peripherals.

Most μP manufacturers provide support tools for software development, but not all of them provide the necessary hardware debugging assistance. FORTRAN, BASIC, and other high-level languages are used increasingly, but even though program writing is easier than it was in assembly language, the controversy over which is best still continues. High-level languages, in general, are oriented toward simplifying mathematical calculations and are notoriously poor at *bit manipulations*. Bit handling is needed in most control system applications, which are a large segment of μC uses. Some designers feel that the additional debugging time required with high-level languages in some bit-handling I/O designs may outweigh much of the gain and, because of the inherent coding inefficiencies, may result in excessive memory requirements. With these languages compilers are used instead of assemblers to generate the object codes. Improvements in compilers, editors, assemblers, and other development aids continue to be made and should serve to decrease development time and costs.

1-11 SUMMARY

This chapter provided an introduction to μCs, a brief history showing the progress in their development, and a forecast of a bright future for them. The configuration of a μC system and the areas where μCs should and should not be used were discussed.

At this point, you should review the self-evaluation questions (Section 1-2). If any of them seem unclear, you should reread the appropriate sections of the text.

1-12 GLOSSARY

Bit Binary digit (either a 1 or a 0) in the base 2 (or binary) number system.

Clock Fixed-frequency square wave source that synchronizes the operation of a microprocessor.

Controller Device (usually electronic) that controls the operation of a machine or process.

Hardware The actual electronic circuits in a computer.

Integrated Circuit (IC) Small silicon chip that contains many electronic circuits.

Logic Term used to describe various digital circuits (AND and OR gates) that control and coordinate the sequence of operations in computer circuits.

Metal gate Semiconductor construction feature.

Metal-Oxide Semiconductor (MOS) Form of transistor used in an IC.

Microcomputer (μC) Computer consisting of a microprocessor and the associated chips, such as memories, necessary to form a complete computer.

Micron One-hundred millionth of a meter.

Microprocessor (μP) Single integrated circuit containing most of the elements of a computer.

Modem Device used to communicate over telephone circuits between computers or digital terminals.

Multiplex Use the same circuits or wires for several functions, usually on a time-sharing basis.

Programmability Ability to change the operation of a device by changing a program.

Semiconductor Generally silicon doped with *p* or *n* material to form resistors and transistors. Semiconductor material is the basis of transistors and ICs.

Silicon gate Semiconductor construction feature.

Software Programs that control the operation of a computer or microprocessor.

1-13 REFERENCES

Adam Osborne. *An Introduction to Microcomputers,* Vols. 1 and 2, Adam Osborne & Associates, Berkeley, CA, 1976.

Motorola. *High-Speed CMOS Logic Data,* DL129, Phoenix, AZ, 1983.

Motorola. *M6805 HMOS M146805 CMOS Family Microcomputer/Microprocessor User's Manual, M6805UM(AD2),* Phoenix, AZ, 1983.

Motorola. *Motorola Monitor,* Vol. 9, No. 2, October 1971.

CHAPTER 2
COMPUTER ARITHMETIC AND LOGIC OPERATIONS

2-1 INSTRUCTIONAL OBJECTIVES

To understand digital circuits and microcomputers (μCs), the reader must first understand the arithmetic they use. This chapter introduces the binary number system and gives the student some facility in handling binary numbers. The 2s complement system of arithmetic and the logical operations performed by a computer are also introduced. After reading this chapter, the student should be able to

1. Convert binary numbers to decimal numbers.
2. Convert decimal numbers to binary numbers.
3. Find the sum and difference of two binary numbers.
4. Convert negative binary numbers to their 2s complement form.
5. Add and subtract numbers in 2s complement form.
6. Use hexadecimal numbers instead of binary numbers.
7. Add, subtract, and negate hexadecimal numbers.
8. Complement a word.
9. Find the logical AND, OR, and EXCLUSIVE OR of two words.

2-2 SELF-EVALUATION QUESTIONS

Watch for the answers to the following questions as you read the chapter. They should help you to understand the material presented.

1. What are the advantages of digital circuits?

2. What is the difference between a bit and a decimal digit? How are they similar?
3. How are binary addition and subtraction different from decimal addition and subtraction? How are they similar?
4. How are bits, bytes, and words related?
5. What are the advantages of long word lengths? Why do microprocessors use short words?
6. How is the sign of a 2s complement number determined by inspection?
7. What is the major advantage of 2s complement notation?
8. How can the positive equivalent of 2s complement negative numbers be found?
9. What is the advantage of hexadecimal arithmetic?
10. How can binary numbers be converted to hexadecimal and vice versa?

2-3 THE BINARY NUMBER SYSTEM

Computers and microprocessors (μPs) are built from a large number of digital electronic circuits that are carefully interconnected to perform the operations necessary to properly execute each of the computer's instructions. The instructions that a computer understands are numbers in combinations of 1s and 0s. They are numbers in the **binary number system** (see Section 2-4).

As Chapter 1 explained, a μP contains thousands of tiny digital circuits within its package. The output of a digital electronic circuit is an electrical signal that normally is within one of two possible ranges of voltage. These ranges are designated as either **logic 0** or **logic 1**. For example, in Transistor-Transistor Logic (TTL) circuits, any voltage between 0 and 0.8 V is a *logic 0* and any voltage between 2 and 5.25 V is a *logic 1*. Digital circuits also have a range of *undefined* or *forbidden* voltages that separate logic **1s** from logic **0s**. For TTL this range is from 0.8 to 2.0 V. If a circuit should produce an output voltage in the undefined range, it is malfunctioning and should be investigated.

Two advantages are gained by restricting the output of an electronic circuit to one of two possible values. First, it is rarely necessary to make fine distinctions. Whether an output is 3.67 or 3.68 V is immaterial; both voltages correspond to a *logic 1*. Well-designed logic circuits produce voltages near the middle of the range defined for 1 or 0, so there is no difficulty in distinguishing between them. In addition, a digital circuit is very tolerant of any drift in the output caused by component aging or changes. A change in a component would have to be catastrophic to cause the output voltage to drift from a **1** to a **0** or to an undefined value. The second advantage of digital circuits is that it is far easier to remember a 1 or a 0 than to remember an **analog quantity** like 3.67 V that could be any value between ground (0) and 5 V. Since computers are required to remember many bits, this is a very important consideration.

The output of a single digital circuit, a single **bit**, defined as a *single digital quantity,* is enough to answer any question that has only *two* possible answers.

For example, a typical job application might ask, "What is your sex?" A "1" could arbitrarily be assigned to a male and a "0" to a female, so that a single bit is enough to describe the answer to this question. A single bit is all the space a programmer needs to reserve in a computer for this answer.

However, another question on the job application might be, "What is the color of your hair?" If the possible answers are black, brown, blonde, and red, a single bit cannot possibly describe them all. Now several bits are needed to describe all possible answers. We could assign one *bit* to each answer (i.e., brown = 0001, black = 0010, blonde = 0100, red = 1000), but if there are many possible answers to the given question, many bits are required. The coding scheme presented above is not optimum; it requires more bits than are really necessary to answer the question.

It is most economical to use as few bits as possible to express the answer to a question, or a number, or a choice. So the crucial question arises:

What is the minimum number of bits required to distinguish between n different things?

Whether these n things are objects, or possible answers, or n numbers is immaterial. To answer this question, we realize that each bit has two possible values. Therefore k bits would have 2^k possible values. This gives rise to theorem 1.

Theorem 1
The minimum number of bits required to express n different things is k, where k is the smallest number such that $2^k > n$.

A few examples should make this clear.

EXAMPLE 2-1

What is the minimum number of bits required to answer the hair color question, and how could they be coded to give distinct answers?

SOLUTION
There are four possible answers to this question; therefore $2^k = 4$. Since 2 is the smallest number such that $2^2 \geqslant 4$, $k = 2$, and 2 bits are needed. One way to code the answers is 00 = brown, 01 = black, 10 = blonde, 11 = red.

EXAMPLE 2-2

How many bits are needed to express a single decimal digit?

SOLUTION
There are 10 possible values for a single decimal digit (0 through 9); therefore $2^k >$ 10. Since $k = 4$ is the smallest *integer* such that $2^k > 10$, 4 bits are required.

EXAMPLE 2-3

A computer must store the names of a group of people. If we assume that no name is longer than 20 letters, how many bits must the computer reserve for each name?

SOLUTION
To express a name, only the 26 letters of the alphabet, plus a space and perhaps a period, are needed. This is a total of 28 characters. Since $2^k > 28$, $k = 5$, and 5 bits are required for each character. Since space must be reserved for 20 such characters, 100 bits are needed for each name.

2-3.1 Bits and Words

Almost all computers have lines and logic to handle a number of **bits**, or *binary digits,* in *parallel* (i.e., the bits are grouped into **words**). A word is a group of bits that constitute the basic unit of information within the computer. The **word length** of a computer is the *number of bits involved in each data bus transfer* and is always a number equal to a power of two (i.e., 4, 8, 16, and so forth). While word lengths vary from computer to computer, each computer has a definite word length and its registers are built to accommodate words of that length.

Large computers (often called mainframes) generally use long words. The IBM 360/370 series, for example, uses 32-bit words. Minicomputers use intermediate word lengths; 16 bits is the most popular minicomputer word size. Until 1980 almost all μPs used 8-bit words. Since then, 16- and 32-bit μPs have been used in increasingly numbers. These include the Intel **8086**, **80186**, and **80286** and the Motorola **68000**, **68010**, and 32-bit μPs such as the **68020** and **68030**.

There are three advantages to using long word sizes:

1. Larger numbers can be accommodated within a single word.
2. Instruction words are more flexible; they allow the instructions to contain more options.
3. With larger instruction words, each instruction is more powerful; it can do more. Consequently, 16-bit μPs tend to execute the same program faster than 8-bit μPs. Not all 16-bit processors are faster, however, and many other factors are involved.

Presently available μPs can solve complex mathematical problems, such as matrix inversion, but these problems are generally run on large mainframes. Controlling physical processes or handling characters, which do not need the speed of a larger mainframe computer, are the kinds of tasks most often done with μCs. Microcomputers can use shorter word lengths and thus the required hardware is simpler. Data buffers need only be provided for 8 bits, μCs and memories can be simpler, and even the Printed Circuit Boards (PCBs) (see Section 13-6.1) require only eight data lines. This selection of word size allows users to adjust their system to fit their job requirements. Shorter word lengths complicate the programming, however, but the additional effort required to program μPs is offset by the low cost of the hardware.

EXAMPLE 2-4

How many numbers can be represented by

a. A single IBM **360/370** word? (The IBM **360/370** uses 32 bits per word.)
b. An 8-bit μP word?

SOLUTION

a. Since an IBM **360/370** word contains 32 bits, any one of $2^{32} = 4{,}294{,}967{,}296$ numbers may be represented in a single word.
b. For the μP word of **8** bits, 2^8 or 256 numbers may be represented by a single word.

2-3.2 Bytes and Nibbles

A group of 8 bits is called a **byte**. This is a convenient size for storing a single **alphanumeric character** (a letter, a number, or a punctuation mark). For the many μPs that have an 8-bit word size, *byte* and *word* are used interchangeably.

Groups of 4 bits are sometimes called a **nibble**. They also constitute a *hexadecimal digit* (see Section 2-8). Other definitions vary depending on whether the computer is an 8-, 16-, or 32-bit type. Thus we have the following conversion table:

4 bits = 1 nibble
2 nibbles = 1 byte
2 bytes (16 bits) = 1 word (16-bit μP) or half word (32-bit μP)
4 bytes = 1 long word (16-bit μP) or word (32-bit μP)
2 words = 1 mouthful (double word) = 64 bits (for 32-bit computers)

2-4 BINARY-TO-DECIMAL CONVERSION

Because computer operation is based on the *binary* (base 2) number system and people use the *decimal* (base 10) number system, it is often necessary to convert numbers given in one system to their equivalents in the other system. To eliminate any possible confusion, a subscript is used to indicate which number system is employed. Thus, 101_{10} is the decimal number whose value is one hundred and one, while 101_2 is a binary number whose decimal value is five. Of course, in considering these two bases, any number containing a digit from 2 to 9 is obviously not a binary number.

The value of a decimal number depends on the *magnitude* of the decimal digits expressing it and on their *position* in the number. A decimal number is equal to the sum $D_0 \times 10^0 + D_1 \times 10^1 + D_2 \times 10^2 + \cdots$, where D_0 is the least significant digit, D_1 the next significant digit, and so on.

EXAMPLE 2-5

Express the decimal number 7903 as a sum to the base 10.

SOLUTION
Here D_0, the least significant digit, is 3, $D_1 = 0$, $D_2 = 9$, and $D_3 = 7$. Therefore, 7903 equals

$$
\begin{array}{lr}
3 \times 10^0 & 3 \\
+\ 0 \times 10^1 & 0 \\
+\ 9 \times 10^2 & 900 \\
+\ 7 \times 10^3 & \underline{7000} \\
 & 7903
\end{array}
$$

Similarly, a group of binary bits can represent a number in the binary number system. The binary base is 2; therefore the digits can only be 0 or 1. However, the position of the digits is also important and the total value is equal to the sum of the values designated by each bit, namely $B_0 \times 2^0 + B_1 \times 2^1 \cdots$, where B_0 is the least significant bit and so on. The powers of 2 are given in the *binary boat* or table of Appendix A. In this table, n is the exponent and the corresponding positive and negative powers of 2 are listed to the left and right of n, respectively.

A **binary number** is *a group of ones (1s) and zeros (0s)*. To find the equivalent decimal number, we simply add the powers of 2 that correspond to the 1s in the number and omit the powers of 2 that correspond to the 0s in the number.

EXAMPLE 2-6

Convert 100011011_2 to a decimal number.

SOLUTION
The first bit to the left of the decimal point corresponds to $n = 0$, and n increases by one (increments) for each position farther to the left. The number 100011011 has **1s** in positions 0,1,3,4, and 8. The conversion is made by obtaining the powers of 2 that correspond to these n values (using Appendix A, if necessary) and adding them.

n	2^n
0	1
1	2
3	8
4	16
8	256
	283

Therefore $100011011_2 = \mathbf{283_{10}}$.

EXAMPLE 2-7

In the PDP-8 computer each word consists of 12 bits, that is, $k = 12$. How many numbers can be represented by each PDP-8 word?

SOLUTION
Since 12 bits are available, any one of 4096 (2^{12}) numbers can be expressed. These numbers range from a minimum of twelve 0s to a maximum of twelve 1s, which is the binary equivalent of 4095. Therefore, the 4096 different numbers that can be expressed by a single word are the decimal numbers 0 through 4095.

2-5 DECIMAL-TO-BINARY CONVERSION

It is often necessary to convert decimal numbers to binary numbers. Humans, for example, supply and receive decimal numbers from computers that work in binary; consequently, computers are continually making binary-to-decimal and decimal-to-binary conversions.

To convert a decimal number to its equivalent binary number, the following **algorithm** (or procedure) may be used:

1. Obtain N (the decimal number to be converted).
2. Determine whether N is odd or even.
3a. If N is odd, write 1 and subtract 1 from N. Go to step 4.
3b. If N is even, write 0.
4. Obtain a new value of N by dividing the N of step 3 by 2.
5a. If $N > 1$, go back to step 1 and repeat the procedure.
5b. If $N = 1$, write 1.

The number written is the binary equivalent of the original decimal number. The number written first is the least significant bit, and the number written last is the most significant bit.

This procedure can also be implemented by following the flowchart of Fig. 2-1. Computer programmers often use **flowcharts** to describe their programs graphically. For the rudimentary flowcharts drawn in this text, the square box is a command, which must be obeyed unconditionally. The diamond-shaped box is a decision box. Within the decision box is a question that must be answered *yes* or *no*. If the answer is yes, the *yes* path must be followed; otherwise the *no* path is followed. The flowchart of Fig. 2-1 starts with the given number N, and since K equals 0, initially we are writing B_0, the least significant digit. Note that equations in a flowchart are programmer's equations, not algebraic equations. The "equation" $N = N - 1$ makes no sense mathematically. What it means here is that N is *replaced by* $N - 1$.

On the initial pass through the flowchart, B_0, the least significant bit, is written as 0 or 1, depending on whether N is even or odd.

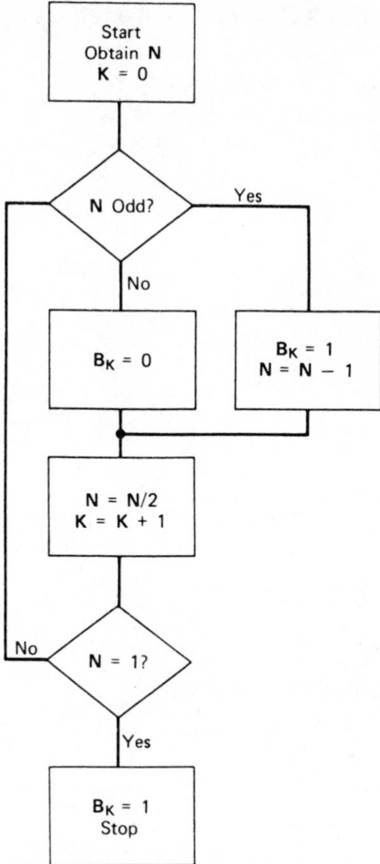

FIGURE 2-1 Flowchart for decimal-to-binary conversion of whole numbers.

Next N is divided by 2 and K is incremented so that on the following pass B_1, the second **Least Significant Bit** (LSB) will be written. We continue looping through the flowchart and repeating the procedure until $N = 1$. Then the **Most Significant Bit** (MSB) is written as a 1, and the process stops. The bits written are the binary equivalent of the decimal number.

EXAMPLE 2-8

Find the binary equivalent of the decimal number 217.

SOLUTION

The solution proceeds according to the algorithm or flowchart. When an odd number is encountered, a 1 is written as the binary digit and subtracted from the remaining number; when the remaining number is even, 0 is written as the binary digit. The number is then divided by 2. The process continues until the number is reduced to 1.

Remaining number		*Binary Digit or Bit*
217	Odd—subtract 1	1
216	Divide by 2	
108	Even—divide by 2	0
54	Even—divide by 2	0
27	Odd—subtract 1	1
26	Divide by 2	
13	Odd—subtract 1	1
12	Divide by 2	
6	Even—divide by 2	0
3	Odd—subtract 1	1
2	Divide by 2	
1	Finish	1

Note that the LSB was written first. Therefore

$$\mathbf{217_{10} = 11011001_2}$$

To check this, convert back from binary to decimal.

$$\mathbf{11011001_2} = 128 + 64 + 16 + 8 + 1 = \mathbf{217_{10}}$$

2-6 ADDITION AND SUBTRACTION OF BINARY NUMBERS

The binary number system is used by computers in the same way that the decimal system is used by humans. Mathematical operations such as addition, subtraction, multiplication, and division can also be performed on binary numbers. In this section the most commonly performed arithmetic operations, addition and subtraction, will be discussed. These are the operations performed by a μP or minicomputer. The reader should consult more specialized texts (Section 2-12) for multiplication, division, squares, square roots, and other arithmetic operations.

2-6.1 Addition of Binary Numbers

The addition of binary numbers is similar to the addition of decimal numbers, except that $1 + 1 = 0$ with a carry out to the next significant place. A carry into a more significant position acts like an additional 1.

EXAMPLE 2-9

Add the binary numbers A = 11101100 and B = 1100110.

SOLUTION

Column	9 8 7 6 5 4 3 2 1	**(decimal addition)**
A	1 1 1 0 1 1 0 0	(236)
B	1 1 0 0 1 1 0	(102)
	1 0 1 0 1 0 0 1 0	(338)

The above addition proceeded as follows:

Column 1	0 + 0 = 0	(least significant digit)
Column 2	0 + 1 = 1	
Column 3	1 + 1 = 0	plus a carry output
Column 4	0 + 1 = 1	plus a carry input from column 3 sums to a 0 and produces a carry out to column 5.
Column 5	0 + 0 = 0	but the carry input from column 4 makes the sum 1.
Column 6	1 + 1 = 0	and a carry output to column 7
Column 7	1 + 1	plus a carry input results in a sum of 1 and a carry output.
Column 8		B does not have an eighth bit; therefore a leading 0 can be assumed. Here 0 + 1 plus a carry input yields a 0 sum plus a carry output.
Column 9		Neither A nor B has a ninth digit so leading 0s are written for both. In column 9 we have 0+0 plus a carry in from column 8 that gives a sum of 1. Since there is no carry out of column 9, the addition is complete.

The sum of Example 2-9 can be checked by converting the numbers to their decimal equivalent. These numbers are shown in parentheses beside the sums.

2-6.2 Subtraction of binary numbers

The rules for the subtraction of binary numbers are

1. 1 − 1 = 0
2. 0 − 0 = 0
3. 1 − 0 = 1
4. 0 − 1 = 1 with a *borrow out*

In order to borrow, change the next 1 in the minuend to a 0 and change all intervening 0s to 1s.

EXAMPLE 2-10

Subtract 101101001 from 100011010011.

SOLUTION

Column	12 11 10 9 8 7 6 5 4 3 2 1	**(decimal subtraction)**
	1 0 0 0 1 1 0 1 0 0 1 1	(2259)
	1 0 1 1 0 1 0 0 1	− (361)
	1 1 1 0 1 1 0 1 0 1 0	(1898)

Column 1	1 − 1 = 0	
Column 2	1 − 0 = 1	
Column 3	0 − 0 = 0	
Column 4	0 − 1 = 1	The 1 in column 5 is changed to a 0 due to the borrow out generated in column 4.
Column 5		This is now 0 − 0 = 0.
Column 6	0 − 1 = 1	The 1 in column 7 is changed to a 0.
Column 7		Due to the borrow from column 6, this now becomes 0 − 1 or 1 with a borrow out that changes the 1 in column 8.
Column 8		This becomes 0 − 0 = 0.
Column 9	0 − 1 = 1	Column 10 and 11 are 0 so the borrow must be from column 12. Columns 10 and 11 contain intervening 0s so they change to 1s and column 12 changes to a 0.
Column 10		This is now 1 − 0 = 1.
Column 11		This is now 1 − 0 = 1.
Column 12	0 − 0 = 0	

The results were checked by converting the binary numbers to their decimal equivalents, which are shown in parentheses beside the numbers.

2-7 2s COMPLEMENT ARITHMETIC

When building hardware such as μCs to accommodate binary numbers, two problems arise:

1. The number of bits in a hardware register is finite.
2. Negative integers must also be represented.

NOTE: These problems do not arise in conventional pencil-and-paper arithmetic. If additional bits are needed, the number can always be extended to the left and negative numbers can always be represented by a minus sign.

Since a hardware register consists of a finite number of bits, the range of numbers that can be represented is finite. An n- bit register can contain one of 2^n numbers. If positive binary numbers are used, the 2^n numbers that can be represented are 0 through $2^n - 1$ (a string of n 1s represents the number $2^n - 1$).

2-7.1 2s Complement Numbers

All modern computers and μCs use the **2s complement** number system to allow them to express both positive and negative numbers.

In this system the *MSB of a 2s complement number denotes the sign* (0 means the number is positive, 1 means the number is negative), but the *MSB* is also a part of the number. In 2s complement notation, positive numbers are represented as simple binary numbers with the restriction that the MSB is 0. Negative numbers are somewhat different. To obtain the representation of a negative number, use the following algorithm:

1. Represent the number as a positive binary number.
2. Complement it (write 0s where there are 1s and 1s where there are 0s in the positive number).
3. Add 1.
4. Ignore any carries out of the MSB.

EXAMPLE 2-11

Given 8-bit words, find the 2s complement representation of

a. 25
b. −25
c. −1

SOLUTION

a. The number +25 can be written as 11001. Since 8 bits are available, there is room for three leading 0s, making the MSB 0.

+25 = 00011001

b. To find −25, complement +25 and add 1.

$$\begin{array}{rcr} +25 & = & 00011001 \\ \overline{(+25)} & = & 11100110 \\ & & +1 \\ \hline \mathbf{-25} & = & \mathbf{11100111} \end{array}$$

Note that the MSB is 1.

c. To write −1, take the 2s complement of +1.

$$\begin{aligned} +1 &= 00000001 \\ \overline{(+1)} &= 11111110 \\ &\quad\ \ \underline{+1} \\ \mathbf{-1} &= \mathbf{11111111} \end{aligned}$$

From this example, we see that a solid string of 1s represents the number -1 in 2s complement form.

To determine the magnitude of any unknown negative number, simply take its 2s complement as described above. The result is a positive number whose *magnitude equals that of the original number.*

EXAMPLE 2-12

What decimal number does 11110100 represent?

SOLUTION

This number must be negative because its MSB is a 1. Its positive equivalent is obtained by 2s complementing the given number.

Given Number	11110100
Complement	00001011
Adding 1	+1
	00001100

This is the equivalent of $+12_{10}$. Therefore $\mathbf{11110100_2 = 12_{10}}$.

2-7.2 Range of 2s Complement Numbers

The *maximum positive* number that can be represented in 2s complement form is a single 0 followed by all 1s, or $2^{n-1} - 1$ for an n-bit number. The *most negative* number that can be represented has an MSB of 1 followed by all 0s, which equals -2^{n-1}. Therefore, an n-bit number can represent any one of $2^{n-1} - 1$ positive numbers plus 2^{n-1} negative numbers plus 0, which is 2^n total numbers. Every number has a *unique* representation.

Other features of 2s complement arithmetic are

1. Even numbers (positive or negative) have an LSB of 0.
2. Numbers divisible by 4 have the two LSBs equal to 0.
3. In general, numbers divisible by 2^n have n LSBs of 0.

EXAMPLE 2-13

What range of numbers can be represented by an 8-bit word (a byte) using 2s complement representation?

SOLUTION
The most positive is $0111111_2 = 127_{10}$.
The most negative 8-bit number is $1000000_2 = -128_{10}$.
Therefore, any number between +127 and −128 can be represented by an 8-bit number in 2s complement form. There are 256_{10} numbers in this range, as expected, since $2^8 = 256_{10}$. Note also that the seven LSBs of −128 are 0, as required, since −128 is divisible by 2^7.

2-7.3 Adding 2s Complement Numbers

Consider the simple equation $C = A$ plus B. Although it seems clear enough, we cannot immediately determine whether an addition or subtraction operation is required. If A and B are both positive, addition is required. But if one of the operands is negative and the other is positive, a subtraction operation must be performed.

The major advantage of 2s complement arithmetic is that

If an addition operation is to be performed, the numbers are added regardless of their signs. The answer is in 2s complement form with the correct sign. Any carries out of the MSB are *meaningless* and should be ignored.

EXAMPLE 2-14

Express the numbers 19 and −11 as 8-bit 2s complement numbers, and add them.

SOLUTION
The number +19 is simply 00010011. To find −11, take the 2s complement of 11.

$$
\begin{aligned}
11 &= 00001011 \\
(\overline{11}) &= 11110100 \\
-11 &= 11110101
\end{aligned}
$$

Now +19 plus (−11) equals

1111 111		Carry
00010011	=	19
11110101	=	−11
00001000	=	+8

Note that there is a carry out of the MSB that is ignored. The 8-bit answer is simply the number +8.

EXAMPLE 2-15

Add −11 and −19.

SOLUTION
First −19 must be expressed as a 2s complement number:

$$\begin{aligned} 19 &= 00010011 \\ (\overline{19}) &= 11101100 \\ -19 &= 11101101 \end{aligned}$$

Now the numbers can be added:

$$\begin{array}{rcll} & & 111111\ 1 & \text{Carry} \\ (-19) & = & 11101101 & \\ +(-11) & = & \underline{11110101} & \\ \mathbf{-30} & = & \mathbf{11100010} & \text{Answer} \end{array}$$

Again a carry out of the MSB has been ignored.

2-7.4 Subtraction of Binary Numbers

Subtraction of binary numbers in 2s complement form is also very simple and straightforward. *The 2s complement of the subtrahend is taken and added to the minuend.* This is essentially subtraction by changing the sign and adding. As in addition, the signs of the operands and carries out of the MSB are ignored.

EXAMPLE 2-16

Subtract 30 from 53. Use 8-bit numbers.

SOLUTION
Note that 30 is the subtrahend and 53 is the minuend.

$$\begin{aligned} 53 &= 00110101 \text{ (minuend)} \\ 30 &= 00011110 \text{ (subtrahend)} \end{aligned}$$

Taking the 2s complement of 30 and adding, we obtain

$$\begin{array}{rcl} (\overline{30}) & = & 11100001 \\ -30 & = & 11100010 \\ +53 & = & \underline{00110101} \\ & & \mathbf{00010111 = 23_{10}} \end{array}$$

EXAMPLE 2-17

Subtract −30 from −19.

SOLUTION
Here

$$\begin{array}{rcll} -19 & = & 11101101 & \text{(see Example 2-15)} \\ +30 & = & 11100010 & \text{(subtrahend)} \end{array}$$

NOTE: −30 is the subtrahend. 2s complementing −30 gives +30 or 00011110.

$$\begin{array}{rl} -19 = & 11101101 \\ +30 = & \underline{00011110} \\ & \mathbf{00001011 = 11_{10}} \end{array}$$

The carry out of the MSB is ignored and the answer, + 11, is correct.

2-8 HEXADECIMAL NOTATION

The binary system uses many 1s and 0s to represent a number but long strings of 1s and 0s are confusing and unwieldy. To condense the representation of numbers, *hexadecimal notation* is used. The hexadecimal number system is a *base 16* arithmetic system. Since such a system requires 16 different digits, the letters **A** and **F** are added to the ten decimal digits (0–9). The advantage of having 16 hexadecimal digits is that each digit can represent a *unique* combination of 4 bits and any combination of 4 bits can be represented by a single hex digit.[1] Table 2-1 gives both the decimal and binary value associated with each **hexadecimal digit**. This notation has been adopted by all μC manufacturers and users.

TABLE 2-1 Hexadecimal-to-Binary Number Conversions

Hexadecimal Digit	Decimal Value	Binary Value
0	0	0000
1	1	0001
2	2	0010
3	3	0011
4	4	0100
5	5	0101
6	6	0110
7	7	0111
8	8	1000
9	9	1001
A	10	1010
B	11	1011
C	12	1100
D	13	1101
E	14	1110
F	15	1111

[1]The word hex is often used as an abbreviation for hexadecimal.

2-8.1 Conversions between Hexadecimal and Binary Numbers

To convert a binary number to hexadecimal, start at the LSB and divide the binary number into groups of 4 bits each. Then replace each 4-bit group with its equivalent hex digit obtained from Table 2-1.

EXAMPLE 2-18

Convert the binary number 110000010111111101 to hex.

SOLUTION
We start with the LSB and divide the number into 4-bit nibbles. Each nibble is then replaced with its corresponding hex digit as shown:

$$\underbrace{0011}_{3}\quad\underbrace{0000}_{0}\quad\underbrace{0101}_{5}\quad\underbrace{1111}_{F}\quad\underbrace{1101}_{D}$$

When the most significant group has less than 4 bits, as in this example, leading 0s are added to complete the 4-bit nibble.

To convert a hex number to binary, simply replace each hex digit by its 4-bit binary equivalent.

EXAMPLE 2-19

Convert the hex number 1CB09 to binary.

SOLUTION
We simply expand the hex number

$$\underbrace{1}_{0001}\quad\underbrace{C}_{1100}\quad\underbrace{B}_{1011}\quad\underbrace{0}_{0000}\quad\underbrace{9}_{1001}$$

Thus the equivalent binary number is

11100101100001001

It is not necessary to write the leadings 0s.

2-8.2 Conversion of Hex Numbers to Decimal Numbers

The hex system is a base 16 system; therefore any hex number can be expressed as

$$H_0 \times 1 + H_1 \times 16 + H_2 \times 16^2 + H_3 \times 16^3 \cdots$$

where H_0 is the least significant hex digit, H_1 the next, and so forth. This is similar to the binary system of numbers discussed in Section 2-4.

EXAMPLE 2-20

Convert 2FC to decimal.

SOLUTION
The least significant hex digit (H_0) is C, or 12_{10}. The next digit (H_1) is F, or 15_{10}, and since it is in the second column it must be multiplied by 16, giving 240_{10}. The next digit (H_2) is 2, which is in column 3 and therefore multiplied by 16^2, giving 256_{10}. Hence, $2FC_{16} = 512 + 240 + 12 = \mathbf{764_{10}}$.

An alternative solution is to convert 2FC to the binary number 1011111100 and then perform a binary-to-decimal conversion.

Decimal numbers can be converted to hex by repeatedly dividing them by 16. After each division, the remainder becomes one of the hex digits in the final answer.

EXAMPLE 2-21

Convert 9999 to hex.

SOLUTION
Start by dividing by 16 as shown in the table below. After each division, the quotient becomes the number starting the next line and the remainder is the hex digit with the least significant digit on the top line.

Number	Quotient	Remainder	Hex Digit
9999	624	15	F
624	39	0	0
39	2	7	7
2	0	2	2

This example shows that $(9999)_{10} = (270F)_{16}$. The result can be checked by converting 270F to decimal, as shown in Example 2-20. By doing so we obtain

$$(2 \times 4096) + (7 \times 256) + 0 + 15 = 9999$$
$$8192 + 1792 + 0 + 15 = 9999$$

2-8.3 Hexadecimal Addition

When working with μCs, it is often necessary to add or subtract hex numbers. They can be added by referring to hexadecimal addition tables, but we suggest the following procedure:

1. Add the two hex digits (mentally substituting their decimal equivalents).
2. If the sum is 15 or less, express it directly in hex (by mentally converting back to hex).
3. If the sum is greater than or equal to 16, subtract 16 and carry 1 to the next position.

The following example should make this procedure clear.

EXAMPLE 2-22

Add D + E.

SOLUTION
D is the equivalent of decimal 13 and E is the equivalent of decimal 14. Together they sum to 27. This is converted back to hex by subtracting 16 (27 − 16 = 11). The 11 is equal to B and there is a carry. Therefore **D + E = 1B.**

EXAMPLE 2-23

Add B2E6 and F77.

SOLUTION
The solution is shown below:

Column	**4 3 2 1**
Augend	B 2 E 6
Addend	F 7 7
Sum	**C 2 5 D**

Column 1	6 + 7 = 13 = D. The result is less than 16 so there is no carry.
Column 2	E + 7 = 14 + 7 = 21 = 5 + a carry, because the result is greater than 16.
Column 3	F + 2 + 1 (the carry from column 2) = 15 + 2 + 1 = 18 = 2 + a carry.
Column 4	B + 1 (the carry from column 3) = C.

Hex subtraction is analogous to decimal subtraction. If the subtrahend digit is larger than the minuend digit, 1 is borrowed from the next most significant digit. If the next most significant digit is 0, a 1 is borrowed from the next digit and the intermediate digit is changed to an F.

EXAMPLE 2-24

Subtract 32F from C02.

SOLUTION
The subtraction proceeds as follows:

Column	**3 2 1**
Minuend	C 0 2
Subtrahend	3 2 F
Difference	**8 D 3**

Column 1 Subtracting F from 2 requires a borrow. Because a borrow is worth 16, it raises the minuend to 18. Column 1 is therefore 18 − F = 18 − 15 = 3.

Column 2 Because column 2 contains a 0, it cannot provide the borrow out from column 1. Consequently, the borrow out must come from column 3, while the minuend of column 2 is changed to an F. Column 2 is therefore F − 2 = 15 − 2 = 13 = D.

Column 3 Column 3 can provide the borrow out needed for column 1. This reduces the C to B and B − 3 = 8.

As in the decimal addition, the results can be checked by adding the subtrahend and difference to get the minuend.

2-8.4 Negating Hex Numbers

The negative equivalent of a positive hex number can always be found by converting the hex number to binary and taking the 2s complement of the result (Section 2-7). A shorter method exists, however:

1. Add, to the least significant hex digit, the hex digit that makes it sum to 16.
2. Add to all other digits the digits that make them sum to 15.
3. If the least significant digit is 0, write 0 as the least significant digit of the answer and start at the next digit.
4. The number written is the negative equivalent of the given hex number.

This procedure works because the sum of the original number and the number is always 0.

EXAMPLE 2-25

Find the negative equivalent of the hex number 20C3.

SOLUTION
The least significant digit is 3. To make 16, D must be added to 3. The other digits are 2, 0, and C. To make 15 in each case, we add D, F, and 3, respectively. The negative equivalent of 20C3 is therefore DF3D. This example can be checked by adding the negative equivalent to the positive number. Since X plus −X always equals 0, the result should be 0

```
  20C3
+DF3D
  0000
```

The carry out of the most significant digit is ignored.

The procedure described above does not work for numbers that end in 0. For these numbers a 0 is also the least significant nibble of the converted word and then the procedure is applied starting at the first nonzero nibble.

EXAMPLE 2-26

Negate 30B00.

SOLUTION
The two least significant nibbles are 00 and the converted number must also end in 00. The first nonzero nibble is B, so the converted value is 5 (B + 5 = 16). The rest are chosen to add to 15 and the answer is **CF500**.

```
Check:   30B00
        +CF500
         00000
```

2-9 LOGICAL OPERATIONS

Besides addition and subtraction, computers must be able to execute a variety of *logical* instructions. These logical operations are performed between words or bytes, on a bit-by-bit basis. There is no interaction (such as a borrow or a carry) betweeen the bits.

2-9.1 The Logical OR Operation

If two words are ORed together, the result, or output word, has a 1 in each bit position where either or both of the input words had a 1. The logical OR of two operands, *A* and *B*, is expressed as **A + B**. Note that this is different from *A plus B*, which means the arithmetic *sum* of *A* and *B*.

EXAMPLE 2-27

Given two words, $A = 10111001$ and $B = 11011010$, find $A + B$.

SOLUTION
The words are lined up as follows:

Bit position	7 6 5 4 3 2 1 0
A	1 0 1 1 1 0 0 1
B	1 1 0 1 1 0 1 0
A + *B*	**1 1 1 1 1 0 1 1**

For all bit positions except position 2, either word *A* or word *B* or both contain a 1. Therefore the logical OR ($A + B$) results in a 1 in all bit positions except position 2.

2-9.2 The Logical AND Operation

When two words are ANDed, the output word is a 1 only in those bit positions where both input words are 1. Since the operation is analogous to multiplication, $Y = AB$ means that *Y* is the logical AND of the two words *A* and *B*.

EXAMPLE 2-28

If the two words of Example 2-27 are ANDed, what is the output word?

SOLUTION
The words are ANDed bit-by-bit:

Bit position	**7 6 5 4 3 2 1 0**
A	1 0 1 1 1 0 0 1
B	1 1 0 1 1 0 1 0
AB	**1 0 0 1 1 0 0 0**

A and *B* are both 1 only in bit positions 3, 4, and 7, as the answer shows.

2-9.3 The EXCLUSIVE OR Operation

Another logical operation that has many uses (parity checking is one example) is the *EXCLUSIVE OR (XOR)* operation. The symbol for the **XOR** operation is $\oplus$. If two words are XORed, the bits of the output word are 1s if *either, but not both,* of the corresponding bits of the input words is a 1.

EXAMPLE 2-29

Find the XOR of words *A* and *B* of Example 2-27.

SOLUTION
The words are XORed on a bit-by-bit basis:

Bit position	**7 6 5 4 3 2 1 0**
A	1 0 1 1 1 0 0 1
B	1 1 0 1 1 0 1 0
$A \oplus B$	**0 1 1 0 0 0 1 1**

The output word is seen to be 1 wherever exactly one of the input words contains a 1.

2-9.4 Complementation

The *complement* of a word is obtained simply by *inverting each bit of the word*. Because **complementation** is often used in computer arithmetic, most μPs contain a complementation instruction.

EXAMPLE 2-30

Complement word *A* of Example 2-27.

SOLUTION
Complementation is obtained simply by inverting each bit of the word.

$$A = 10111001$$
$$\overline{A} \text{ (the complement of } A) = \mathbf{01000110}$$

2-10 SUMMARY

In this chapter, basic binary arithmetic used in computers was introduced. The binary number system was explained and examples of binary addition, binary subtraction, and binary-to-decimal conversion were presented.

The 2s complement system, used in most computers, was introduced and arithmetic examples in this system were presented. The hexadecimal system, which will be used throughout this book, was demonstrated as an extension and condensation of the binary system.

2-11 GLOSSARY

Algorithm Standard procedure or method of computation.

Alphanumeric character A character that may be either an alphabetic, numeric, or punctuation character.

Analog quantity Continuously variable quantity; one that may assume any value, usually within a limited range.

Binary number Number containing only 1s or 0s.

Binary system Number system with 2 as the base.

Bit Single binary digital quantity, a 1 or a 0.

Byte Group of 8 bits.

Complementation Process of inverting each bit of a word.

Digital quantity Variable that has one of two possible values.

Flowchart Graphic representation of a procedure or program.

Hexadecimal digit Number (0 to F) that represents the value of a group of 4 binary bits.

Least Significant Bit (LSB) The bit at the right end of a byte. When set, it adds a value of 1 to the byte.

Most Significant Bit (MSB) The bit at the left end of a byte. When set, it adds a value of 128_{10} to the byte.

Nibble Group of 4 bits.

2s complement Representation of numbers in which negative numbers are obtained by complementing their equivalent and adding 1.

Word Group of bits that constitute the basic unit of information within a computer.

Word length Number of bits involved in each data bus transfer.

2-12 REFERENCES

Greenfield, Joseph D. *Practical Digital Design Using ICs,* Second Edition, Wiley, New York, 1983.

Hill, Frederick J., and Gerald R. Peterson. *Introduction to Switching Theory and Logical Design,* Third Edition, Wiley, New York, 1979.

Kostopoulos, George K. *Digital Engineering,* Wiley, New York, 1975.

Nashelsky, Louis. *Introduction to Digital Computer Technology,* Third Edition, Wiley, New York, 1981.

2-13 PROBLEMS

2-1 How many bits are required to distinguish between 100 different things?

2-2 A major league baseball team plays 162 games a year. Before the season starts, how many bits must be reserved to express the number of games the team will win and the number of games the team will lose?

2-3 A line printer is capable of printing 132 characters on a single line and each character is one of 64 symbols (26 alphabetic symbols plus 10 numbers plus punctuation). How many bits are needed to print an entire line?

2-4 Express the following decimal numbers as a sum.

a. 4507
b. 137,659
c. 8,897,061

2-5 Convert the following binary numbers to decimal.

a. 10111
b. 110101
c. 110001011

2-6 Convert the following decimal numbers to binary.

a. 66
b. 252
c. 5795
d. 106,503

2-7 For each of the following pairs of numbers, find $A + B$ and $A - B$, completing the third and fourth columns below:

	A	B	$A + B$	$A - B$
a.	11011	1001		
b.	1110011	101010		
c.	111000111	100101		
d.	101111011	1000101		

2-8 Find $A + B$ and $A - B$ by converting each number to binary and doing the addition and subtraction in binary. Check the results by converting back to decimal.

	A	B	$A + B$	$A - B$
a.	67	39		
b.	145	78		
c.	31,564	26,797		

2-9 A PDP-11 is a minicomputer with a 16-bit word length. What range of numbers can a single word contain?

2-10 How high can you count in binary using only your fingers?

2-11 Find the 8-bit 2s complement of the following numbers:

a. 99
b. −7
c. −102

2-12 Determine by inspection which of the following 2s complement numbers are divisible by 4.

a. 11011010
b. 10011100
c. 01111000
d. 00001010
e. 01000001
f. 01010100

2-13 A PDP-8 is a computer with a 12-bit word length that uses 2s complement arithmetic. What range of numbers can be expressed by a single PDP-8 word?

2-14 Express each of the following numbers in 9-bit 2s complement form, and add them.

a. $\begin{array}{r} 85 \\ +37 \\ \hline \end{array}$ c. $\begin{array}{r} -85 \\ +37 \\ \hline \end{array}$

b. $\begin{array}{r} 85 \\ +(-37) \\ \hline \end{array}$ d. $\begin{array}{r} -85 \\ +(-37) \\ \hline \end{array}$

2-15 Do the following subtractions after expressing the operands in 10-bit 2s complement notation.

a. $\begin{array}{r} 36 \\ -(23) \\ \hline \end{array}$ c. $\begin{array}{r} -450 \\ -(-460) \\ \hline \end{array}$

b. $\begin{array}{r} 835 \\ -(214) \\ \hline \end{array}$ d. $\begin{array}{r} 316 \\ -(-579) \\ \hline \end{array}$

2-16 A number in 2s complement form can be inverted by subtracting it from −1. Invert 25 using this procedure and 8-bit numbers.

2-17 Convert the following binary numbers to hexadecimal.

a. 11111011
b. 1011001
c. 10000011111100
d. 1001010110001101

2-18 Convert the following hex numbers to binary.

a. 129
b. 84C5
c. 5CF035
d. ABCDE2F

2-19 Perform the following hex additions.

a. $\begin{array}{r} 99 \\ +89 \\ \hline \end{array}$ c. $\begin{array}{r} 15F02 \\ 3C3E \\ \hline \end{array}$

b. $\begin{array}{r} CB \\ DD \\ \hline \end{array}$ d. $\begin{array}{r} 2CFB4D \\ 5DC98B \\ \hline \end{array}$

2-20 Perform the following hex subtractions.

a.	59 F	**c.**	1002 5F8
b.	1CC DE	**d.**	5F306 135CF

2-21 Find the negative equivalents of the following hex numbers.

a. 23
b. CB
c. 500
d. 1F302
e. F5630

2-22 Given 2 bytes:

$A = 10001101$
$B = 01001011$

find

$A + B$
AB
$A \oplus B$
$\overline{A}$
$\overline{B}$

After attempting to solve these problems, try to answer the self-evaluation questions in Section 2-2. If any of them still seem difficult, review the appropriate sections of the chapter to find the answers.

CHAPTER 3
THE BASIC COMPUTER

3-1 INSTRUCTIONAL OBJECTIVES

The basic principles of operation of a microcomputer (μC) are identical to those of any larger computer. In this chapter we discuss the basic parts of a computer and how they work together to execute a simple program. Programming is also introduced and some very elementary programs are presented.

After reading this chapter, the student should be able to

1. List each basic part of a computer and describe its functions.
2. Explain the steps involved in reading or writing a memory word.
3. List the registers and flip-flops required by the control section of a computer and explain their operation.
4. Explain the meaning of the symbols used in flowcharts.
5. Construct a flowchart for a problem.
6. Write programs involving branch instructions and loops.

3-2 SELF-EVALUATION QUESTIONS

Watch for the answers to the following questions as you read the chapter. They should help you to understand the material presented.

1. What are the MAR and MDR? What is their function?
2. Are the contents of a memory location changed when they are written? When they are read?
3. What is the difference between a ROM and a RAM? State an advantage of each.
4. What is the advantage of a PROM over a ROM? When would each be used?

5. What is the PC? Why is it incremented during each instruction?
6. Is there any distinction between data and instructions when they are in memory? How does the computer tell the difference?
7. What decisions must be made during program planning?
8. What instructions allow a computer to make decisions? How does the computer make a decision?
9. How do loop counting and event detection determine when to end a loop?

3-3 INTRODUCTION TO THE COMPUTER

A computer consists of four basic hardware sections, as shown in Fig. 3-1. These are

1. The memory.
2. The arithmetic/logic unit (ALU).
3. The control unit.
4. The input/output (I/O) system.

The difference between a computer and other digital logic is that the computer is controlled by the *bits* in the *instruction decode register* of the control unit. (A register is a hardware device in the μP that holds the bits so they can be evaluated.) These bits are brought into this register in the form of bytes from memory, where they are kept. In order for a computer to do a given task, a

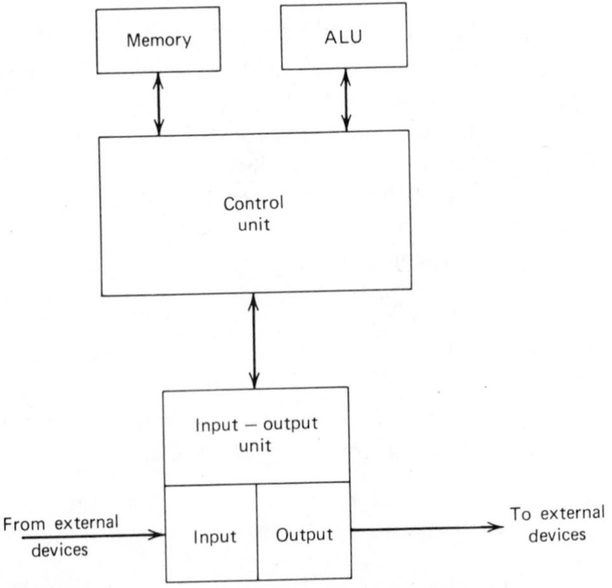

FIGURE 3-1 Block diagram of a basic computer.

program of **instructions** is prepared and the instructions, in the form of 8-bit bytes (for the basic computer we are discussing), are stored in the computer memory. This program is called **software** since it is easily changed.

a. The **memory** holds the *data* used by a program as well as the *instructions* for executing the program. (see Section 3-9)
b. The *arithmetic/logic unit* is the part of the computer that performs the arithmetic and logic operations required by the program and generates the status bits (condition codes) after each instruction is executed. These status bits are the basis of the decision-making capabilities of any computer.
c. The **control unit** consists of a group of logic devices and *registers* (see Section 3-7.1) that regulate the operation of the computer itself. The function of the control unit is to cause the proper sequence of events to occur during the execution of each computer instruction.
d. The **Input/Output (I/O)** system provides communication between the computer and external devices. The computer must receive data and status information from external devices such as sensors, Analog-to-Digital (A/D) converters, keyboards, disk drives, or tape units. It must also produce outputs that depend on its program and the data it receives. If the computer is solving a problem, the output is frequently a printout of the results. In this case, it must issue commands to a printer to cause the results to be printed for the user to read. If the function of the computer is to control a physical process, however, its output will be electronic signals that are translated into *commands* (open a valve, reduce the air flow, etc.) to regulate a process.

The microprocessor (μP) chip contains the ALU and control portions of the computer, while memory and input/output are handled by auxiliary Integrated Circuits (ICs). Some of the newer Metal-Oxide Semiconductor (MOS) ICs also have memory and I/O capability incorporated in them, and manufacturers are calling them single-chip microcomputers (μCs).

In this chapter the construction and operation of the ALU, memory, and control unit are described in detail. A discussion of the input/output system may be found in Chapter 8.

3-4 MEMORY CONCEPTS

A **memory** is an electronic circuit that stores or remembers many bits of electronic information. Even the smallest μP or μC system requires a memory of several thousand bits to store its program and data. Large-scale memories for older computers were constructed of magnetic cores, but modern designs almost exclusively use ICs. A block of memory typically consists of a number of semiconductor memory chips each contained in a Dual In-line Package (DIP), as are the μP and the rest of the semiconductor components of the system.

The binary bits of a block of memory can be organized in various ways. In most computers, the bits are grouped into *words* of 8, 16, or 32 bits each. The **6800** and **6809** are examples of 8-bit μPs, which use an 8-bit (1-byte word). The **68000** is a 16-bit μP and uses a 16-bit (2-byte) data word. The **68020** and **68030** use 32-bit longwords (4 bytes).

Modern computers are *word-oriented* in that they transfer one word at a time by means of the data bus. This bus, the internal computer registers, and the ALU are *parallel* devices that handle all the bits of a word *at the same time*. The memory can be thought of as a post office box arrangement with each location containing a word. The boxes are set up in an orderly sequence so that they can be addressed easily. Each instruction or data word is *written* into a specific location in memory (a word at a selected address) *when it must be preserved* for future use and is *read* at a later time *when the information is needed*. During the interval between writing and reading, other information may be stored or read at other locations.

Eight-bit μC instructions for the **6800** require 1, 2, or 3 bytes (or words) and typical program routines include 5 to 50 instructions. Since IC memories can include thousands of words of data and are physically small and relatively inexpensive, they can be used to provide very comprehensive computer programs.

An 8-bit μC can directly address a maximum memory size of 64K words since it has 16 address lines ($2^{16} = 65{,}536$), but even more memory can be used by employing *bank select logic* to switch in any number of additional 64K blocks of memory. Only specially written software can use the additional memory, however. In dedicated controller applications, the program memory could be as small as 4 or 8K bytes. Unlike standard engineering terminology, where K is an abbreviation for kilo (or 1000), K = 2^{10} or 1024 when applied to memories. This value of K is used because normal memory design leads to sizes that are even powers of 2.

Each word in memory has *two parameters:* its **address**, which locates it within memory, and the *data* that are stored at that location. The process of accessing the contents of the memory locations requires two **registers** (hardware devices that hold a group of related bits) (see Section 3-7.1), one associated with address and one with data. The *Memory Address Register* (**MAR**) holds the *address of the word currently being accessed,* and the *Memory Data Register* (**MDR**) holds the *data being written into or read out of the addressed memory location.* These registers are usually part of the control unit (see Section 3-7).

A block diagram of a small 1K word by 8-bit IC Random-Access Memory (RAM) (see Section 3-5) is shown in Fig. 3-2. The address information in the MAR selects one of the 1024 words in memory.

EXAMPLE 3-1

The 1K by 8-bit memory of Fig. 3-2 is used as part of a μP system with a 16-bit address bus.

a. How many bits are required to address all locations in this IC?

b. How many address bits are used for the whole μP system?
c. How many bits are required in the MDR?
d. How many data bits are contained in this memory IC?

SOLUTION

a. A memory specification of 1K × 8 means 1024 (2^{10}) words of 8 bits each. The MAR must hold an address value between 0 and 1023 (1024 total locations) to select any word in this IC. Thus, 10 bits are needed to address the memory.
b. The μP uses 16 address lines (or bits in the MAR). Since 10 are used to select the locations in this memory IC, the other 6 are available to select other memory ICs.
c. Each memory location contains 8 bits. Consequently, the MDR must be 8 bits long to accommodate one data word.
d. A 1K × 8 memory contains 2^{10} words × 2^3 (8) bits per word = 2^{13} or 8192 bits. For a μC, this is a relatively small memory and several such ICs would typically be used.

In Fig. 3-2 the MAR is shown to contain address 2 and the MDR register contains the value that is in that location.

3-4.1 Reading Memory

Memories operate in two basic modes; READ and WRITE. A memory is read when the information at a particular address is required by the system.

To *read* a memory:

1. The location to be read is loaded into the MAR.

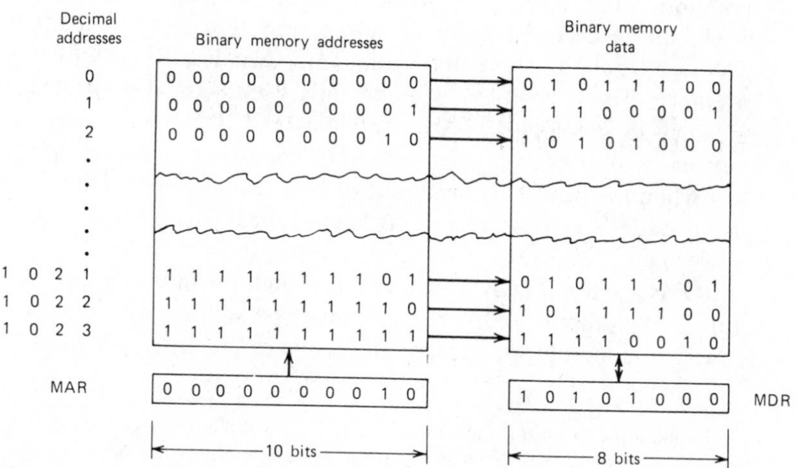

FIGURE 3-2 Typical 1024-word by 8-bit memory.

2. A READ command is given.
3. The data is transferred from the addressed word in memory to the MDR, where it is accessible to the system.

Normally, *the word being read must not be altered by the READ operation,* so the word in a particular location can be *read many times*. This used to be troublesome with older core memory, but it is not a problem with semiconductor memories. The process of reading a location without changing it is called *non-destructive readout.*

3-4.2 Writing Memory

A memory location is written when the data must be preserved for future use. In the process of writing, the information in the specified location is *destroyed* (overwritten).

To *write* into a memory:

1. The address (memory location where the data is to be written) is loaded into the MAR.
2. The data to be written is loaded into the MDR.
3. The WRITE command is then given (by means of the READ/WRITE line), which transfers the data from the MDR to the selected memory location via the data bus.

3-5 SEMICONDUCTOR MEMORIES

Most semiconductor memories in use today are built of MOS circuits. Up until now, most of these have been NMOS, but CMOS memories are growing in use. In addition to the differences in construction, memories consist of two basic types, RAM and ROM. Literally speaking, the term **RAM** means *Random Access Memory,*[1] but that is really a misnomer because ROM is also Random Access Memory. The term **RAM** is universally used, however, to describe a read/write memory (a memory that can both be read and temporarily changed by being written into). RAMs are also said to be **volatile** because the information in them is lost when the power is turned off or fails. Some sophisticated computer systems use a battery backup circuit to keep voltage on the memories when the main power goes off.

ROMs are *Read Only Memories,* in which the data bits are permanently built in during manufacture. Other data cannot be written into them during the normal course of computer operation, and they are therefore *nonvolatile*. Information or

[1]Random access means that any word can be accessed in approximately the same time as any other word. This distinguishes IC memories from nonrandom access memories such as tape or disk, where users must wait until the word they seek is under the read or write head before it can be accessed.

programs that must be present when the power is turned on are placed in ROM.

In most μCs, the memory map consists of two parts, a *ROM* area, used to hold the *program, constants,* and *tables,* and a *RAM* area, used to hold *variable data.*

In some personal computers, the entire operating systems program is stored in ROM, so the computer is ready to execute commands when power is applied. More often, however, the input/output and disk or tape *loader* routines are in ROM ready to load the operating system into a large RAM area. Programs written by the user can be entered into RAM but are lost when power is turned off unless they are preserved (saved) on cassettes or diskettes. RAMs are discussed in this section, and ROMs will be discussed in Section 3-5.4.

3-5.1 Static and Dynamic RAMs

RAMs are subdivided into two types, *static* and *dynamic*. Static RAMs store their information on *Flip-Flops* inside the memory IC. A **Flip-Flop** (FF) can be placed in one of two states (SET or RESET) and remains there until commanded to change states. Thus a single FF function is a 1-bit memory. It remembers whether it was last SET or RESET, as long as it has power applied.

Dynamic memories store their information by charging *capacitors* inside the IC. Unfortunately, the charge on the tiny capacitors tends to leak off and the dynamic RAMs must be *refreshed*[2] at least every 2 ms to retain their information. The refresh circuits are frequently incorporated within them. Dynamic memories are generally less expensive and contain more bits per IC, but static memories are simpler to use. Most μCs use dynamic memories.

The internal structure of the FFs and gates that make up a memory is not considered in this book. Instead, we concentrate on the I/O characteristics that must be understood if one is to use a memory.

3-5.2 Interfacing with a RAM Memory

A semiconductor RAM normally has pins for the following:

1. m data bits.
2. n address bits (for 2^n words).
3. A READ/WRITE line.
4. A CHIP SELECT or ENABLE input.

To read a location in a memory, the address lines for that location are set, the READ/$\overline{\text{WRITE}}$ line is set to the READ level, and the memory chip is then *selected* or *enabled*. This causes the memory contents at the addressed location to be transferred to the data lines and continue to be present until the address, READ/$\overline{\text{WRITE}}$ line, or CHIP SELECT signals change. Reading is *nondestructive*

[2]For a discussion of electronic refresh circuits, see Chapter 15 of Greenfield, *Practical Digital Design Using ICs*. (cited in Section 3-14).

(it does not change the information in the memory cells); the state of the internal memory cells at the selected address is simply brought to the data pins.

Writing into a memory requires that the address of the desired location be in the MAR and the data be in the MDR prior to enabling the memory (see Section 3-7). These registers (MAR and MDR) are connected to the memories by means of bus lines. When the READ/$\overline{\text{WRITE}}$ (R/$\overline{\text{W}}$) line is switched to $\overline{\text{WRITE}}$ and the memory is enabled, the data on the bus lines is then entered into the memory at the addressed location. One must be careful about changing the input data while in the WRITE mode. Any change of data is gated into the memory and overwrites the previous contents of the memory, which are lost.

The CHIP SELECT and ENABLE inputs are used to turn the memory ON or OFF and, more important, to disconnect it from the bus. This allows the μC designer to multiplex several memory or I/O devices onto a common bus.

EXAMPLE 3-2

The **6810** is a RAM that can be used in very small controller-type **6800** μCs. It is a 1024-bit memory organized as 128 bytes (128 words by 8 bits). What input and output lines are required?

SOLUTION

This memory requires

1. Seven address bits to select one of 128 words.
2. Eight data lines, one for each bit of the word.
3. One R/$\overline{\text{W}}$ line.
4. One or more CHIP SELECT or ENABLE lines.
5. Power and ground.

Actually, the **6810** has six CHIP SELECT lines to make decoding simpler, and the data input and output is done on a common bidirectional data bus. Details of the **6810** are given in Section 7-8.

3-5.3 Memory Timing

Memory timing is very important. A READ cycle is limited by the access time of a memory, and a WRITE cycle is limited by the cycle time.[3]

Access time is the time required for the memory to present valid data after the address and select signals are stable. **Cycle time** or WRITE time is the time the address and data must be held constant in order to write to the memory.

[3]A more complete discussion of memory timing is given in Leucke, Gerald, Mize, Jack, and Carr, William, *Semiconductor Memory Design and Application*, Section 9-3, McGraw-Hill, New York, 1973.

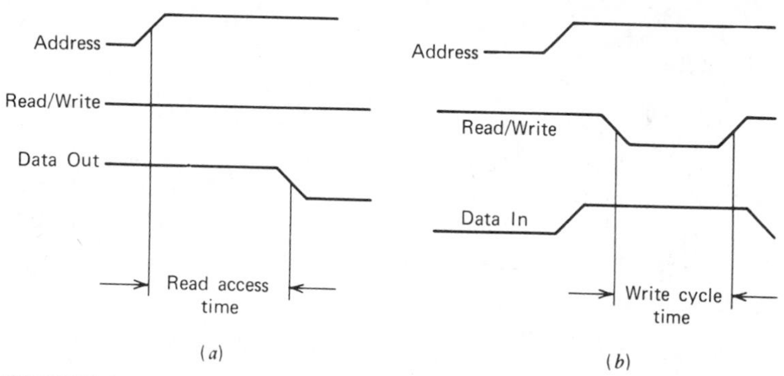

FIGURE 3-3 Memory timing. (a) Read cycle. (b) Write cycle.

Access time and cycle time are illustrated in Fig. 3-3. Similar figures with specific times are supplied by the manufacturers of IC memories.

Figure 3-3a shows the normal situation where the memory is constantly in READ mode. The output data will change in response to an address change and the time for this response, *the access time*, is clearly visible.

Figure 3-3b shows the WRITE cycle. Note that the address and data are firm before the WRITE pulse occurs on the R/$\overline{W}$ line and do not change while the memory is in WRITE mode. This is necessary to prevent spurious writes that could enter unwanted information into the memory.

If a memory has a long access or cycle time, the μP might have to be slowed down to accommodate the memory. This can be done in the **6800 or 6809** systems by use of the Memory Ready feature. See Section 7-7 for details of the **6800** clock and Fig. 11-10 for Memory Ready timing in the **6809**.

3-5.4 Read-Only Memories (ROMs)

As its name implies, a *Read-Only Memory* is read but not written into during the course of computer operation. Data is *permanently written* into a **ROM** when it is manufactured. With its program in ROM, a μC can be **restarted** after a power failure with no need to reload or *boot* its program.

The READ mode of a ROM is identical to the READ mode of a RAM; the μC supplies an address and the ROM provides the data output of the word previously written at that address. Like RAMs, ROMs are organized on an *n* word by *m* bit basis. Supplying the proper address results in an *m*-bit output. Access time for a ROM is the time between the setting of the address input and the appearance of the resulting data word on the output pins.

EXAMPLE 3-3

A memory has dimensions of 8K words by 8 bits. What input and output lines are required if the memory is

a. A RAM?
b. A ROM?

SOLUTION

a. A RAM of this size requires
   1. Eight data bits.
   2. Thirteen address bits ($2^{13} = 8192$).
   3. A R/$\overline{W}$ line.
   4. Chip select line(s).

b. An 8K by 8 bit ROM requires
   1. Eight data bits.
   2. Thirteen address bits.
   3. Chip select line(s).

Since a ROM cannot be written into, the R/$\overline{W}$ line is not required.

3-5.5 Programmable Read-Only Memories

Programmable Read Only Memories (**PROMS**), with the exception of EEPROMs, which are described in Section 3-5.7, are designed to be programmed by the users at their facility, rather than by the manufacturer. At least two types of PROMs are in use. They are both electrically programmable, but one is erasable and re-programmable; it is described in Section 3-5.6. The other is the fusible-link PROM, which comes with all data bits in all bytes at 0. By following the programming procedure specified by the manufacturer, users can change bits at selected locations to a 1. This is done by driving high current through the IC that opens (or blows) the fusible links. Each open link provides a 1 instead of a 0 output. Thus users must open a link for a 1 in every location of their programs. Again, a mistake may cause the PROM to be useless. A 0 can always be changed to a 1, but a 1 cannot be changed back to a 0. If only a small quantity of identical ROMs is required, it is less expensive to use fusible-link PROMs than a custom-masked ROM or EPROM.

3-5.6 Erasable PROMS

Some PROMS can be *erased* and *reprogrammed* in the field if users have the proper equipment. These are called Erasable PROMs (**EPROMs**). EPROMs are made by a number of manufacturers in a variety of sizes. Typical EPROMs are the **68764** (64K bytes) and **27128** (128K bytes). These EPROMS can be erased by exposing them to ultraviolet light. Because they are reprogrammable, they are very popular for developing programs for μPs since programming mistakes are common and changes in the program occur frequently. They also are used in small production runs or until the program has been debugged fully, at which time they may be replaced with maskable ROMs to save production costs.

3-5.7 Electrically Erasable PROMs

One further step in semiconductor memory technology has been the introduction of Electrically Erasable PROMs (**EEPROMs**). This technique provides a non-volatile design that can be electrically reprogrammed in the system in less than 9 ms. One such device is the **MCM2833**, a 4K byte PROM. It is fabricated using Motorola's Floating-gate Electron Tunneling MOS technology (FETMOS). For μP compatibility, on-chip latches are provided for address, data, and controls, allowing the μP to perform other tasks while the **2833** is erasing or programming (writing) itself. The data is thus protected during power-down and power-up cycles. These devices are very popular because they avoid the need to reconfigure multipurpose systems every time they are turned on.

3-6 THE ARITHMETIC/LOGIC UNIT (ALU)

The Arithmetic/Logic Unit (ALU) performs all the arithmetic and logical operations required by the computer. It accepts two operands as inputs (each operand contains as many bits as the basic word length of the computer) and performs the required arithmetic or logical operation on them in accordance with the instruction in process. The ALU function is included within the μP or μC chip.

The ALU included in the **6800** performs the following arithmetic or logical operations:

1. Addition
2. Subtraction
3. Logical OR
4. Logical AND
5. Exclusive OR
6. Complementation
7. Shifting

In the **6800** a 6-bit **Condition Code Register** (CCR) is attached to the ALU and provides status for decisions after every instruction executes. The Condition Code Register is discussed in Section 4-6.

Computers are capable of performing sophisticated arithmetic operations such as multiplication, division, extracting square roots, and taking trigonometric functions; however, in most computers these operations are performed as *software subroutines* (small complete programs). A multiplication command, for example, is translated by the appropriate subroutine into a series of add and shift operations that can be performed by the ALU. A multiplication subroutine is written in Section 5-6.2.

3-7 THE CONTROL UNIT

The function of the *control unit* is to regulate the operation of the computer. It controls the locations in memory and fetches instructions at the proper time. The instructions are then decoded. A group of registers, FFs, and timing circuits are used to keep track of the processor's operation. The registers are the

1. **MAR and MDR.** The memory address register and memory data register are used to control memory.
2. **Program Counter (PC).** This register contains as many bits as the MAR. *It holds the memory address of the next instruction word to be executed.* It is *incremented* during the execution of an instruction so that it contains the address of the next instruction to be executed.
3. **Instruction Register.** This register holds the instruction while it is in the process of being executed.
4. **Instruction Decoder.** This decodes the instruction presently being executed and the various bits control the functions desired. Its inputs come from the instruction register.
5. **Accumulators.** All computers have one or more accumulator registers, each of which contains as many bits as the MDR. In ALU operations where two operands are required and only one accumulator exists, as in the 8080A or Z80 μP, one of the operands is stored in that accumulator as a result of previous instructions. The other operand is then typically read from memory. The **6800** and many other μPs based on it have two accumulators, called A and B, which greatly simplifies many programming problems. In this case, the second operand is typically read from memory into the B accumulator. The two operands form the inputs to the ALU and the result is normally sent back to the A accumulator.

3-7.1 Control Unit FFs

A number of *registers* are included in every μP and peripheral I/O component. A register is frequently implemented as a group of FFs (see Section 3-5.1) that together provide storage for a single unit of information. A single 16-bit number, for example, could be held in a register that consists of 16 FFs.

Individual FFs are used where small quantities of data (several bits) must be remembered and changed frequently.

The control unit usually contains a number of FFs. The status bits or condition codes (see Section 4-6) are stored in FFs. Most μPs also have FETCH and EXECUTE FFs.

The FETCH and EXECUTE FFs determine the state or mode of the computer. The instructions are contained in the computer's memory. *The computer starts by FETCHing the instruction.* This is the FETCH portion of the computer's cycle. *It then EXECUTES, or performs, the instruction.* At this time, the computer is in EXECUTE mode. When it has finished executing the instruction, it returns to FETCH mode and reads the next instruction from memory. Thus *the computer alternates between* FETCH and EXECUTE *modes* and the FETCH and EXECUTE FFS determine its current mode of operation.

3-8 EXECUTION OF A SIMPLE ROUTINE

A μP starts to execute instructions by fetching the byte at the address contained in the PC. Most 8-bit μPs use this first byte as an 8-bit **operation code** or **Op code**. The Op code tells the μP what to do (e.g., add, subtract, load). Since the **6800** has an 8-bit Op code, up to 256 different instructions are possible. Actually, 159 are implemented. (The **6801** has 22 more.) Some of the sophisticated newer 8-bit μPs or μCs, such as the **68HC11**, use 2 bytes for the Op codes and thus have up to four times as many codes.

The Op code includes information on the number of bytes to be used in the instruction. In most cases the μP then executes a second fetch cycle[4] to get the **Operand**, which is usually an address required by the instruction. It then has both the Op code and the address and can execute the instruction. When execution is complete, the μP increments the PC and proceeds to execute the next instruction. The **6800** μP has no HALT instruction as such. Once started, it continues to execute instructions until halted by an external signal. A WAIT instruction can be used to halt the program execution (see Section 9-7.1).

3-8.1 Sample Problem

As a simple example, let us consider what a **6800** μP must do to add two numbers. Before starting this example, both the numbers to be added and the program must be in memory. Suppose we are trying to add the numbers 2 and 3. We can arbitrarily set aside location 80 to hold the number 2 and location 81 to hold the number 3. Location 82 is also set aside to hold the result.

The program, or set of instructions, required to add the numbers would be this:

Location	Op Code	Operand Addr	Comments
10	96	80	First instruction (LOAD A from location 80)
12	9B	81	Second instruction (ADD contents of 81 to the data in A)
14	97	82	Third instruction (STORE A accumulator in location 82)

3-8.2 Hardware Execution of the Routine

The registers and ALU within the μP work together to execute the foregoing program. The instructions must reside at specific locations in memory. As shown in the listing, we have assumed that location 10 is set aside for the start of the

[4]The number of bytes and cycles required for each instruction depends on the instruction mode. This is discussed thoroughly in Chapter 4.

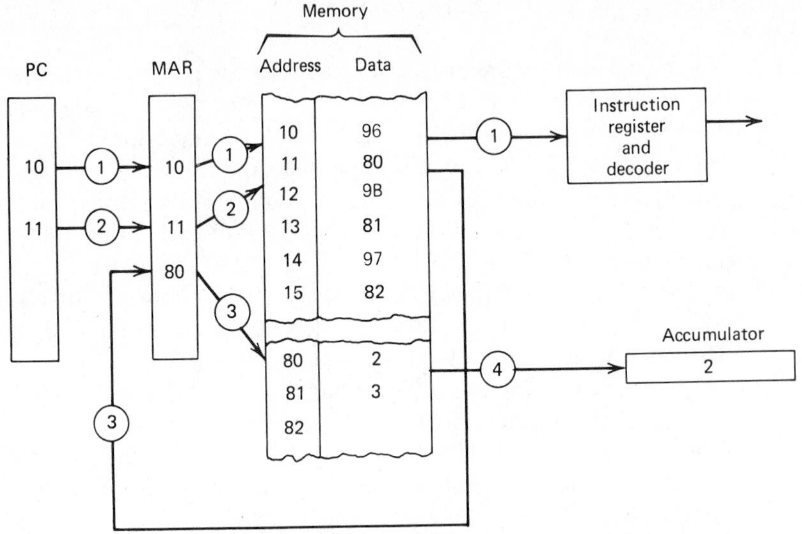

FIGURE 3-4 Execution of a LOAD instruction of a rudimentary μP.

program. Thus, location 10 contains the Op code for the **LOAD** (96) instruction; location 11 contains the address 80, location 12 contains the Op code of the ADD instruction (9B), and so forth. The contents of the registers and memory are shown in Fig. 3-4.

Before starting execution, the starting address of the program (10 in this example) must be written into the PC.

Table 3-1 shows the contents of the registers at each step in the program. It correlates with the following description of the program's progress.

Program execution then proceeds as follows:

1. The 10 is transferred from the PC to the MAR and the 96 is read at memory location 10.
2. Since this is the first part of the FETCH cycle, the data read is placed in the **instruction register** and the instruction decoder determines that it is a LOAD instruction. Note that the μP is not actually reading the word LOAD in location 10. It reads a byte of 1s and 0s (10010110_2 or 96_{16}) that are decoded as a LOAD command.
3. The μP then increments the PC and MAR and reads the contents of 11 (80), which it places in the MAR.
4. The μP is now ready to execute the LOAD instruction. It does so by reading the contents of 80, which are already in the MAR, and placing them in the accumulator. The accumulator now contains the contents of 80 (the number 2).
5. The instruction execution is now finished and the FETCH mode for the next instruction is entered. The PC is again incremented to 12 and placed in the MAR.

TABLE 3-1 Register Changes as the Example of Section 3-8.2 Progresses

PC	MAR	Memory data		Accm Contents	Comments
10	10	96	(LOAD)	X	LOAD instruction
11	11	80		X	
11	80	02		2	
12	12	9B	(ADD)	2	ADD instruction
13	13	81		2	
13	81	03		5	
14	14	97	(STORE)	5	STORE instruction
15	15	82		5	
15	82	05		5	

6. The code for ADD (9B) is fetched from location 12 and decoded.
7. The PC is again incremented and 81 is read from memory and placed in the MAR.
8. The execute phase of the **ADD** instruction is entered. The contents of 81 (3) are read and added to the contents of the accumulator. This uses the ALU within the μP. The results (5) are written to the accumulator and the ADD instruction is complete.
9. The PC is again incremented and transferred to the MAR. The Op code for the STORE instruction (97) is fetched and decoded.
10. The address for the store instruction (82) is fetched from location 15 and placed in the MAR.
11. The **store** instruction (97) is now executed to take the contents of the accumulator (5) and write them to memory at location 82.

3-9 INTRODUCTION TO PROGRAMMING

A program is a group of **instructions** that cause the computer to perform a given task. Each instruction directs the computer to do something specific. An extremely simple program might instruct the computer to add two numbers in its data area; another program might command the computer to subtract the same numbers. Obviously, completely different results can be obtained from the same data by applying different programs. As shown in the previous section, each μP instruction consists of an Op code (a byte that tells the computer what to do) and usually some additional bytes that are a value or specify the address of an *operand.*

3-9.1 Machine Language

The Op codes (combinations of 1s and 0s) are interpreted by the instruction decoder in the control section of the μP and used to perform the internal functions desired. These bytes are called *machine language* because they are the only thing the machine (computer) understands. These 8-bit binary numbers are usually expressed in hexadecimal notation so that humans can easily understand them, as explained in Chapter 2.

Op codes for a given instruction are not the same in all computers because the control unit hardware is different. The **6800** μP machine language is typical, however, and its use here is the most direct way to explain the operation of μPs.

3-9.2 Assembly Language

Machine language is usually used by engineers who must troubleshoot and debug hardware systems containing μPs. Machine language, however, makes programming slow and cumbersome and *assembly language,* which uses mnemonics and is thus easier for humans to understand, has been developed. Programmers prefer to write in *assembly language* or a higher-level language such as BASIC, FORTRAN, or "C."

In assembly language programming, *mnemonics* are used for Op codes, addresses, and labels. Instead of writing 96 80, an assembly language programmer might write

LDA A SAM

where LDA A means *load the A accumulator* and SAM becomes the symbol for an address, 80 in this case. Assembly language programming is used because the programmer does not have to remember the numeric values of Op codes and because it is easier to keep track of variables when calling them by symbolic names.

Assembly language programs cannot be executed directly. The mnemonic program must first be converted to machine language. This is done by using an **assembler** program in another computer. The programmer's mnemonics, called the **source program**, are translated into the 1s and 0s that make up the machine language. This **object program**, as it is also called, can then be loaded directly into the μP's memory.

During development, these programs usually must be changed many times, and they are therefore loaded into RAM for debugging. Once the programs are fully developed and not expected to change, they are usually put into PROMs or a custom-built ROM may be ordered. The manufacturer of the ROM must be given the code each word is to contain. The manufacturer then makes a *mask* that is used to produce the ROM. Because of the custom programming involved, a mask costs more than $1000. Users should be sure of their inputs before they incur the masking charge, because the ROM is normally useless if a single bit is wrong. Once the mask is made, identical ROMs can be produced inexpensively.

Because individual μPs have different machine language Op codes as well as different mnemonics, each μP has an assembler written specifically for it. After deciding which μP to use, the engineer should investigate the assemblers available for that μP.

3-9.3 Higher-Level Languages

In an effort to simplify the programming task, a number of other languages such as BASIC, FORTRAN, Pascal, and C have been developed. With them, it is not necessary to worry about registers and other specific computer details, and *one* high-level language statement can generate *several* machine language instructions. Using them makes it easier for a programmer to write a program. The program necessary to translate these high-level languages to machine code is called a **compiler.** Many μPs do not have compilers for all languages.

There are some objections to using high-level languages with μPs. Some languages are not good when bit manipulation is required or cannot be used to generate precise time delays, and the execution of their code is generally slower than assembly language. They are, however, the most convenient way to write programs. In general, programs written to get answers to problems are written in higher-level languages, whereas programs to control processes and devices, which must operate in *real time,* are written in assembly language.

3-10 FLOWCHARTS

Flowcharts are used by programmers to show the progress of their programs graphically. They are a clear and concise method of presenting the programmer's approach to a problem. They are often used as a part of programming documentation, where the program must be explained to those unfamiliar with it. Since good documentation is essential for proper use of any computer, the rudiments of flowcharts are presented in this section.

3-10.1 Flowchart Symbols

The flowchart symbols used in this book are shown in Fig. 3-5.

1. The *oval* symbol is either a *beginning* or *termination* box. It is used simply to denote the start or end of a program.
2. The *rectangular block* is the *processing* or *command block*. It states what must be done at that point in the program.
3. The *parallelogram* is an *input/output block*. Such commands as READ and WRITE, especially from an external device such as a disk or card reader, are shown on the flowchart by using these boxes.
4. The *diamond box* is a *decision box*. It usually contains a question. There are typically two output paths, one if the answer to the question is yes and the other if the answer is no. When a comparison between two numbers is made, there might be three exit paths corresponding to greater than, less than, and equal.

(a) Beginning or termination block

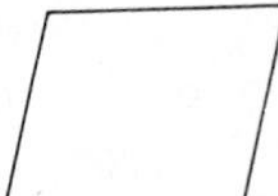

(b) Processing or command block

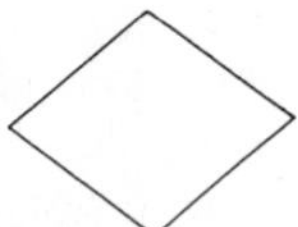

(c) Input/Output block.

(d) Decision block

FIGURE 3-5 The most common standard flowchart symbols. (a) Beginning or termination block. (b) Processing or command block. (c) Input/output block. (d) Decision block

EXAMPLE 3-4

Draw a flowchart to add the numbers 1, 4, 7, and 10.

SOLUTION
The solution is shown in Fig. 3-6. It consists simply of a start box, four command boxes, and a stop box. This is an example of straight-line programming since no decisions were made. It was also assumed that the numbers 1, 4, 7, and 10 were available in the computer's memory and were not read from an external device.

3-10.2 Elementary Programming

To introduce the concepts of programming, we use simple **6800** instructions. The instructions are really binary data words stored in various memory locations. Each instruction is assumed to consist of words that contain the Op code and the address of the data. The Op codes used in this section are ADD, SUBTRACT, LOAD, and STORE.

For example, consider the problem of writing instructions for the flowchart of

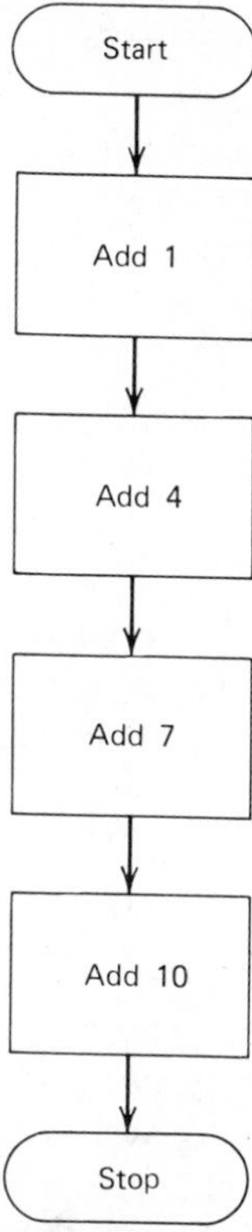

FIGURE 3-6
Flowchart for Example 3-4.

Fig. 3-6. The first problem is to allocate memory areas for the instructions and the data. All these words must be in memory before the program can be started.

To illustrate, we will use the **6800** μP instructions where the first byte is the Op code and the next byte is the address of the data. Again we arbitrarily decide to start the program at location 10 and the data at 80. The program would then be as follows:

Location	Instruction	Op Code
1Ø	96	LOAD
11	8Ø	
12	9B	ADD
13	81	
14	9B	ADD
15	82	
16	9B	ADD
17	83	
18	97	STORE
19	84	
1A	3E	WAIT

The operation of the LOAD, ADD, and STORE instructions was explained in Section 3-8.1.

The data might then be as follows:

Location	Contents
80	1
81	4
82	7
83	10
84	Reserved for result

Once the data areas and all the required constants are written in memory, the code can be executed by starting at location 10. Note that the data could be changed and the same program executed any number of times.

3-11 BRANCH INSTRUCTIONS AND LOOPS

The program of the previous section is extremely simple; indeed, users can compute the answer faster than they can write the program. Suppose, however, the program is expanded so that we are required to add the numbers 1, 4, 7, 10, . . ., 10,000.[5] Conceptually, this could be done by expanding the flowchart of Example 3-4 and the program of Section 3-10.2. However, the program and data areas would then require 3333 locations each, and just writing them would become very tedious. Obviously, something else must be done.

3-11.1 Branch Instructions

Branch instructions provide the solution to the above problem. A **BRANCH** instruction or **JUMP** instruction alters the normal sequence of program execution and is used to create loops that allow the same sequence of instructions to be executed many times.

As we saw in Section 3-8, in the normal course of program execution, the PC is incremented during the execution of each instruction and contains the location of the next instruction to be executed. Assume, however, that the next instruction is

BRA $500

where BRA is the Op code (for branch) and $500 is the branch address (The $ designates hex). This instruction causes the branch address to be written into the PC. Thus the location of the next instruction to be executed is the branch address (500 in this case) rather than the next sequential address. A *branch* instruction can

[5]Since the object of this section is to teach programming and not mathematics, we ignore the fact that this is an arithmetic progression whose sum is given by a simple formula.

therefore be used to cause the program to **loop** back and execute the same instructions again.

There are two types of branch instructions, unconditional and conditional. The **unconditional branch** always causes the program to branch to the specified address. In the **6800** the mnemonic is **BRA**, which stands for BRANCH ALWAYS. The **conditional branch**, which will be explained in the next section, causes the program to branch only if a specified condition is met.

3-11.2 Computer Decisions

As you will recall, in Section 3-6 we described the Arithmetic/Logic Unit (ALU) and the Condition Code Register (CCR).

The bits of the CCR are SET (made equal to 1) or RESET (made equal to 0) by the ALU of the **6800** as each instruction is executed. For example, when one number is subtracted from another, the resulting number is either positive, negative, or zero and the ALU will SET or RESET the bits of the CCR accordingly.

Probably the easiest way to introduce conditional branch instructions is to examine the two instructions that *test* the zero or *Z* bit. These are **BEQ** (**B**ranch if **EQ**ual) and **BNE** (**B**ranch if **N**ot **E**qual to zero). One of these might be used, for example, if the program is deciding whether a number entered is equal to a certain value. That value would be subtracted from the number entered and then tested with one of these instructions. If the test is true, the program branches or skips over part of the program. If it is *not* true, the program continues in sequence. Therefore, when the subtraction instruction previously mentioned is followed by one of these conditional branch instructions, the state of the **Z** bit will determine the path to be taken by the program. This decision-making action is an example of the primary function of a computer and is frequently depicted in flowcharts of programs by a diamond-shaped box with an arrow out of the bottom to show the in-line sequence or out of one side to show a branch.

There are 14 decision-making instructions in the **6800**. Each of the four least significant bits of the CCR (N, Z, V, and C) has two branch instructions associated with it.

EXAMPLE 3-5

A computer is to add the numbers 1, 4, 7, 10, . . ., 10,000.[6] Draw a flowchart for the program.

SOLUTION

The flowchart is shown in Fig. 3-7. We recognize that we must keep track of two quantities. One is the number to be added. This has been labeled *N* in the

[6]For the introductory problem of this section, we have ignored the fact that decimal 10,000 cannot be contained within a single byte.

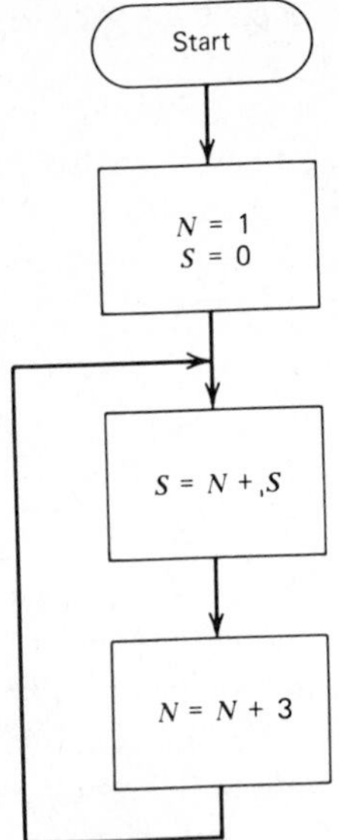

FIGURE 3-7
Flowchart for Example 3-5.

flowchart and progresses 1, 4, 7, 10, · · ·. The second quantity is the sum S, which progresses 1, 1+4, 1+4+7, . . . or 1, 5, 12, ...

The first box in the flowchart is an **initialization** box. It sets N to 1 and S to 0 at the beginning of the program. The next box ($S = N + S$) sets the new sum equal to the old sum plus the number to be added. The number to be added is then increased by 3. At this point the flowchart shows that the program must **loop around** to repeat the sequence. This is accomplished by placing an unconditional branch instruction in the program. The quantities S and N will progress as specified.

3-11.3 Decision Boxes and Conditional Branches

The reader has probably already realized that there is a serious problem with Example 3-5; the loop never terminates. Actually, putting a program into an endless loop is one of the most common programming mistakes.

There are two common ways to determine when to end a loop: *loop counting* and *event detection*. Either method requires the use of decision boxes in the flowchart and corresponding conditional branch instructions in the program. Loop counting is considered first.

Loop counting is done by determining the number of times the loop should be traversed, counting the actual number of times through, and comparing the two.

EXAMPLE 3-6

Improve the flowchart of Fig. 3-7 so that it terminates properly.

SOLUTION

The program should terminate not when $N = 10{,}000$ but when 10,000 is added to the sum. For the flowchart of Fig. 3-7, N is increased to 10,003 immediately after this occurs. At the end of the first loop $N = 4$, the second loop $N = 7$, and so forth. It can be seen here that $N = 3L + 1$ where L is the number of times through the loop. If N is set to 10,003, $L = 3334$. The loop must be traversed 3334 times.

The correct flowchart is shown in Fig. 3-8. The loop counter L has been added and set initially to -3334. It is incremented each time through the loop and tested to see if it is positive. After 3334 loops, it becomes 0. Then the YES path from the decision box is taken and the program halts.

EXAMPLE 3-7

Write the code for the flowchart of Fig. 3-8.

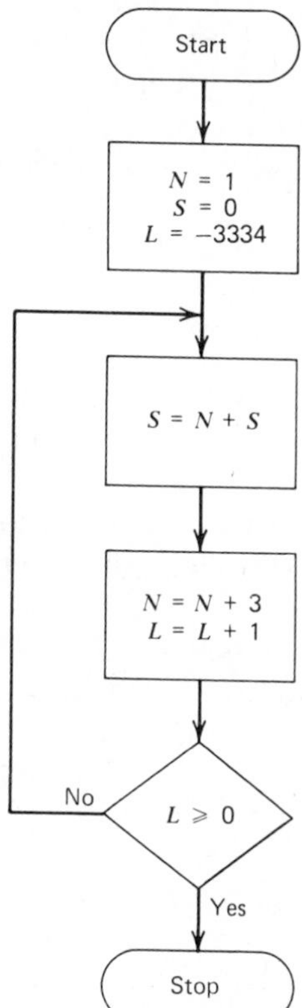

FIGURE 3-8
Flowchart for Example 3-6.

SOLUTION

As in Section 3-10.2, the program is started at location 10 and the data area at location 80. In the data area three variables, *N*, *S*, and *L*, are needed. These should be initialized to 1, 0, and −3334, respectively, before the program starts. In addition, two constants, 1 and 3, are needed during the execution of the program. Before the program starts, the data area should look like this:

Location	Term	Initial Value
8Ø	N	1
81	S	Ø
82	L	-3334
83	Constant	3
84	Constant	1

The program can now be written directly from the flowchart.

Locations	Instructions		Comments
1Ø,11	96 81	LOAD 81	\
12,13	9B 8Ø	ADD	> S = N + S
14,15	97 81	STORE 81	/
16,17	96 8Ø	LOAD 8Ø	\
18,19	9B 83	ADD 83	> N = N + 3
1A,1B	97 8Ø	STORE 8Ø	/
1C,1D	96 82	LOAD 82	\
1E,1F	9B 84	ADD 84	> L = L + 1
2Ø,21	97 82	STORE 82	/
22,23	2B 1Ø	BMI 1Ø	
24	3E	WAIT	

Each instruction takes 2 bytes (except the last), as it could in a typical μP such as the **6800.** Two locations are therefore assigned to each instruction and the addresses are in hex.

Note that the instructions follow the flowchart. The decision box has been implemented by the **B**ranch if **MI**nus **(BMI)** instruction. The program loops as long as *L* remains negative.

Check: As a check on the program, we can write the contents of *N*, *S*, and *L* at the end of each loop as in the following table.

Times through Loop	N	S	L
1	4	1	-3333
2	7	5	-3332
3	1Ø	12	-3331

The chart shows that each time around the loop

$$\frac{N - 1}{3} + |L| = 3334$$

Therefore, when $N = 10{,}003$, L indeed equals 0 and the loop terminates.

Event detection *terminates a loop when an event occurs that should make the loop terminate*. In Example 3-7 that event could be the fact that N is greater than 10,000. Using event detection, locations 1C through 21 could be replaced by

```
1C, 1D     96 82  (LOAD 82)
1E, 1F     90 85  (SUBTRACT 85)
20, 21     01 01  not needed (NOP)
22, 23     2B 10  (BMI 10)
```

where location 85 contains 10,001. This program branches back until $N = 10{,}003$. In this problem, the use of event detection is conceptually simpler and saves one instruction.

3-12 SUMMARY

In this chapter, the operation of a basic computer was described. First, the major parts of the computer were listed and the function of each was explained briefly. In subsequent paragraphs, the operations of the memory, ALU, and control sections were described in detail.

Elementary programming was further explored. Flowcharts and their uses were introduced, and simple problems involving loops and branches were presented.

Finally, an example of the execution of a simple program was presented. We showed how the hardware and software work together in a step-by-step manner to solve a simple problem.

3-13 GLOSSARY

ADD Instruction that adds the contents of an accumulator to those of a specified location.

Access time Time required for a memory to provide valid data after the address and control lines are stable.

Accumulator Register in a computer that holds an operand used by the instructions.

Address Memory location where data is stored.

Arithmetic/Logic Unit (ALU) The part of the computer that performs the required arithmetic and logic operations and indicates the processor status by setting the bits of the Condition Code Register.

Assembler Computer program to translate the programmer's mnemonics to machine language and to provide a program listing.

Assembly language program Program listing of the mnemonics and machine language produced by an assembler.

Branch instruction Instruction that alters the normal sequential course of a program by causing it to skip over or jump to another instruction.

Bus Group of wires; generally a bus carries a set of signals from one group of digital devices to another.

Compiler Computer program that generates machine language from a source program written in a high-level language.

Conditional branch Instruction that branches or transfers the program flow to an address other than the next sequential location but only when a specified condition of the condition codes is met.

Control unit Internal parts of a computer that control and organize its operations.

Cycle time Time the address, data, and control lines must be held stable before valid data is transferred.

EPROM Erasable Programmable Read-Only Memory.

Event detection Using the occurrence of an event to terminate a loop or program.

EXECUTE Portion of an instruction cycle where the instruction is executed.

FETCH MODE Portion of an instruction cycle where the instruction is brought from memory to the instruction register.

Flip-Flop (FF) Electronic circuit that functions as a 1-bit memory.

Flowchart Graphic method used to outline or show the action of a program.

Increment Add 1 to a number.

Initialization Clearing or presetting of RAM locations and the programming of the peripheral adapters (see Chapter 8) prior to program execution.

Input/Output (I/O) system Part of a computer that communicates with external devices.

Instruction Command that directs the computer to perform a specific operation.

Instruction register Register in a computer that holds the instruction currently being executed.

LOAD Instruction that causes data to be brought from memory into an accumulator register.

Loop Return to the start of a sequence of instructions so that the same instructions may be repeated.

Loop counting Counting the number of times a loop is traversed and comparing it to a limit.

MAR Memory *Address* Register. Contains the address of the memory location currently being accessed.

MDR Memory *Data* Register. Contains the data going to or coming from the memory.

Memory Part of a computer used to hold the program or temporary storage of data.

Nondestructive read Readout of data in which the data is not destroyed.

Object program Machine language program of 1s and 0s understood by the computer.

Operation code (Op code) First byte of an instruction that specifies the operation to be performed by the CPU.

Program Group of instructions that control the operation of a computer.

Program Counter (PC) Register in a computer that contains the address of the next instruction to be executed.

RAM Random Access Memory. Memory capable of both READ and WRITE operations.

Register Hardware device in the μP or peripheral device that holds a group of related bits usually containing a character, command, or number.

Restart Act of starting up the computer. A restart is performed when the computer is first turned on and after most power failures.

ROM Read-Only Memory. Memory with a permanent program that can only be read.

Software Programs used to control a computer that are easily changed.

Source program Program written by the programmer using mnemonics.

STORE Instruction that causes data in the accumulator to be moved to memory or a peripheral register.

Subroutine Small program of a complete function.

Unconditional branch Instruction that always jumps the program to an address other than the next sequential location.

Volatility Inability of a memory to retain data when power is interrupted.

3-14 REFERENCES

Bartee, Thomas C. *Digital Computer Fundamentals*, Fifth Edition, McGraw-Hill, New York, 1981.

Greenfield, Joseph D. *Practical Digital Design Using ICs*, Second Edition, Wiley, New York, 1983.

Boillet, Michelle H., Gleason, Gary M., and Horn, Wayne L., *Essentials of Flowcharting*, William C. Brown, Dubuque, IA, 1975.

3-15 PROBLEMS

3-1 The dimensions of a memory are 16K words by 32 bits. How many bits are
a. In the MAR?
b. In the MDR?
c. In the memory?

3-2 Repeat Problem 3-1 for an 8K by 24 bit memory.

3-3 In Problems 3-1 and 3-2, list the input and output lines required for the memory if
a. The memory is a RAM.
b. The memory is a ROM.

3-4 Explain how a memory can be addressed sequentially.

3-5 Write a program to add 50 and 75 and then subtract 25. Select memory areas for your data and instructions. Describe the progression of your program and list the contents of each pertinent memory location before and after its execution.

3-6 Write a program to add 25, 35, 45, and 55 and then shift the results 2 bits to the right. Explain the significance of your answer.

3-7 Prepare a chart similar to Fig. 3-7 for the programs of Problems 3-6 and 3-7.

3-8 Your alarm always goes off at 8 o'clock. You then get up, except on Tuesdays, when you can sleep an extra hour. You then eat breakfast. If it's raining, you take an umbrella. If your car starts, you go to work; otherwise you go back to bed. Draw a flowchart showing this portion of your day's activities.

3-9 Your friends are Alice, George, Cindy, and Arthur in that order. You ask one of them to the ballgame. If it's raining or if none of your friends can make it, you stay home and watch television. Draw a flowchart to show this portion of your activities.

3-10 Write a program to add the numbers 1, 5, 9, 13, . . ., 20,001.

3-11 The number N is in location 40. Write a program to put $N!$ in location 41.

3-12 There are 101 numbers in locations 100 to 200. Some of them are 5. Write a program to count the number of times 5 appears in these locations.

After attempting to solve these problems, try to answer the self-evaluation questions in Section 3-2. If any of them still seem difficult, review the appropriate sections of the chapter to find the answers.

CHAPTER 4

ACCUMULATOR AND MEMORY REFERENCE INSTRUCTIONS

4-1 INSTRUCTIONAL OBJECTIVES

This chapter introduces additional software features of the **6800**, the mnemonics or assembly language concept, and then the accumulator and memory referencing instructions. After reading this chapter, the student should be able to

1. Explain the function of each register in the **6800** μP.
2. Realize the need for mnemonics and assembly language.
3. Write and use instructions that use the immediate, direct, extended, indexed, and implied addressing modes.
4. List each bit in the CCR and explain its function.
5. Perform multibyte additions and subtractions using the carry bit.
6. Use the BRANCH instructions to provide computer decisions.
7. Write programs to add and subtract BCD numbers.
8. Use logic instructions.
9. Use SHIFT and ROTATE instructions.
10. SET or CLEAR specific bits in a register.
11. Test specific bits in a register.

4-2 SELF-EVALUATION QUESTIONS

Watch for the answers to the following questions as you read the chapter. They should help you to understand the material presented.

1. Why are mnemonics easier to use than machine language?
2. What is one advantage of having two accumulators?
3. Which memory locations can be accessed by *direct instructions?* Why can't *all* memory locations be accessed by direct instructions?
4. What is the difference between an ADD and an ADD-WITH-CARRY instruction? Give an example of the proper use of each.
5. Why is it necessary to worry about overflow or underflow?

6. What is the significance of the H bit? Why is it used only in BCD operations?
7. Why doesn't the *carry bit* have any effect on logic operations?
8. Why do INCREMENT, DECREMENT, and CLEAR instructions require many memory cycles?
9. What are the advantages of using the carry bit in conjunction with the SHIFT and ROTATE instructions?

4-3 PROGRAMMING THE 6800 MICROPROCESSOR

The **MC6800,** Motorola's first μP, was introduced in 1974. Millions of them are still in use in existing designs. In Chapter 3 we showed how this μP performs the basic functions of a computer. We used the simpler **6800** instructions to illustrate how it is programmed. The **6800** is a much more powerful computer, and the full operation will now be described from a functional point of view. The diagram of Fig. 4-1 shows the registers contained within the **6800** and identifies the flag bits in the CCR.

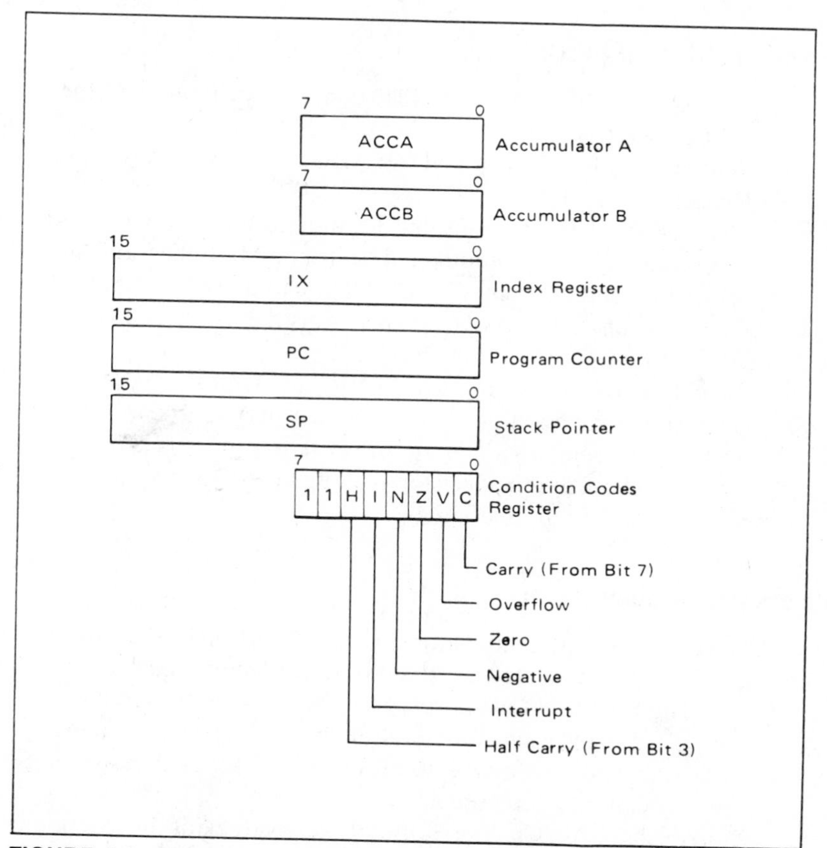

FIGURE 4-1 Programming model of the 6800 microprocessor.

Internally, the **6800** has three 8-bit registers and three 16-bit registers. There are two 8-bit *accumulators* in the **6800,** labeled A and B. These are almost identical in operation. Any arithmetic operation must involve one of them. The accumulator to be used is generally specified by the operation (Op) code. For example, an Op code of 8B specifies an ADD IMMEDIATE to the A accumulator, and an Op code of CB specifies an ADD IMMEDIATE to B.

The 8-bit condition code register contains the *condition codes* or *flags*. It is described in Section 4-6. The three 16-bit registers in the **6800** are the

1. **Program counter (PC).** This is the standard 16-bit PC found in 8-bit μPs. It contains the address of the next instruction to be executed.
2. **Stack pointer.** This register points to an area in memory called the *stack* that is used with PUSHes, PULLs, JUMPs to SUBROUTINEs, and Interrupts. The stack pointer is discussed in Section 5-4.
3. **Index register.** This is used in indexed instructions (see Section 4-5.4).

Most of the functions necessary for total system operation are included in the **6800** IC itself. At this point, the features of the **6800** μP that determine the software characteristics will be described; the hardware aspects will be discussed in later chapters.

4-3.1 Arithmetic/Logic Unit (ALU)

As a complete processor, the **6800** contains within it all of the registers necessary for the operation of a computer, such as the instruction register and decoder, the input and output buffers, and the ALU. These are shown in the expanded block diagram of Fig. 4-2.

The **6800** ALU performs the arithmetic operations of addition, subtraction, complementation, negation, and shifting. Multiplication and division are performed by programs (subroutines) that use these functions (shifts with additions or subtractions). The ALU also performs the Boolean algebra functions of AND, OR, and EXCLUSIVE OR.

The *Condition Code Register* (CCR) is part of the ALU, and its bits are altered as a result of each arithmetic or logic instruction. The bits of this register are then used by the *conditional branch instructions* to select alternative paths for the program. These are the decision-making functions that distinguish a computer and will be described in Section 4-7.

4-3.2 Registers and Accumulators

The registers and accumulators in the **6800** are all 8 bits wide and, as shown in Fig. 4-2, are interconnected by an 8-bit internal bus. The registers in the μP that are associated with addresses [program counter (PC), index (X), and stack pointer (SP)] use 2 bytes each and therefore have a high (H) and a low (L) byte. The **6800** is thus able to generate a 16-bit address, and as a result 65,536 (2^{16}) bytes of memory can be addressed.

As explained in Chapter 3, the PC keeps track of the location in memory where

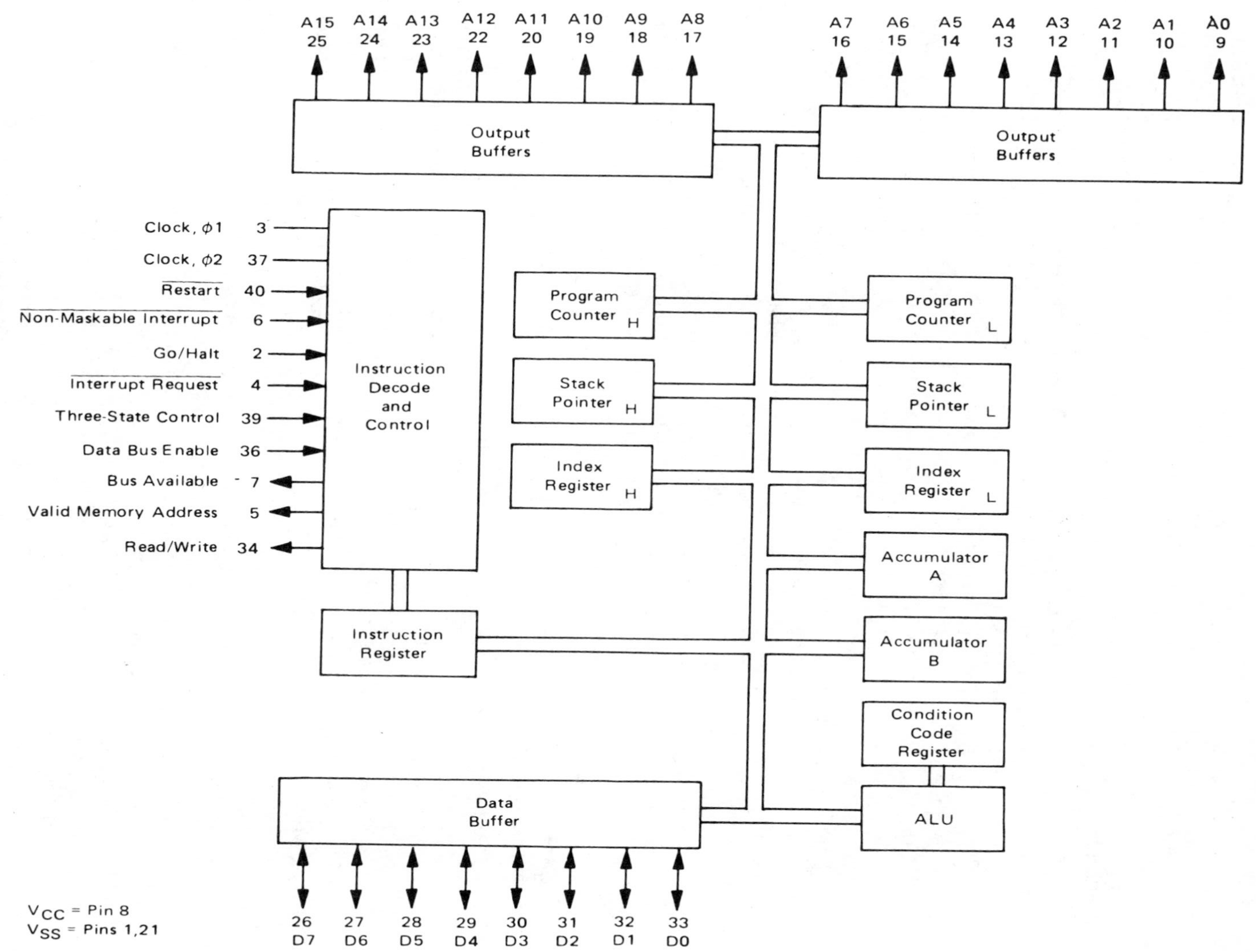

FIGURE 4-2 Expanded block diagram of the **6800**.

the next instruction byte is to be fetched. The bytes are then loaded into the instruction register and the instructions are executed. All **6800** instructions consist of 1, 2, or 3 bytes.

4-3.3 The 6800 Instruction Set

The first byte of each instruction is called the **operation code** (Op code) because its bit combination determines the operation to be performed. The second and third bytes of the instruction (if used) contain address or data information. They are the *operand* part of the instruction. The Op code also tells the μP logic how many additional bytes to fetch for each instruction. There are 197 unique instructions in the **6800** instruction set. Since an 8-bit word has 256 combinations, a high percentage of the possible Op codes are used.

When an instruction is fetched from the location in memory pointed to by the program counter register, and the first byte is moved into the instruction register, it causes the logic to execute the instruction. If the bit combination is 01001111 (or 4F in hex), for example, it CLEARS the A accumulator (RESETS it to all zeros); or if the combination is 01001100 (4C), the processor increments the A accumulator (adds 1 to it). These are examples of *1-byte* instructions that involve only one accumulator. An instruction byte of 10110110 (B6) is the code for the *extended addressing mode* of LOAD A (see Section 4-5.3). It also comands the logic to fetch the *next 2 bytes* and use them as the *address* of the data to be loaded into the A accumulator.

4-3.4 Understanding the 6800 Instructions

When the Op codes for each instruction are expressed in their binary or hex format, as in the previous paragraph, they are known as *machine language instructions*. The bits of these Op codes must reside in memory and be moved to the instruction decoder for analysis and action by the μP.

Writing programs in machine language is very tedious, and trying to follow even a simple machine language program strains the ability of most people. As a result, various techniques have evolved in an effort to simplify the program documentation. The first step in this simplification is the use of *hexadecimal notation* to express the codes. This reduces the digits from 8 to 2 (10100011 = A3, for example) or, in the case of an address, from 16 binary digits (bits) to 4 hex digits. Even this simplification, however, is insufficient, and the concept of using *mnemonic language* to describe each instruction has therefore been developed. *A* **mnemonic** *is defined as a device to help the human memory*. For example, the mnemonics LDA A (load A) and STA A (store A) are used for the LOAD and STORE instructions instead of the hex Op codes of 86 and B7 because the *mnemonics are descriptive and easier to remember*.

Programs and data can be entered into the memory or registers of a μP in machine language by using data switches. It is easier, however, as explained in Chapter 10, to use a control ROM and a terminal to type in the hexadecimal forms of the instructions or data.

4-4 ASSEMBLY LANGUAGE

Not only are mnemonics easy to remember, but the precise meaning of each one makes it possible to use a computer program to translate them into the machine language equivalent that can be used by the computer. A program for this purpose is called an **assembler** and the mnemonics that it recognizes constitute an **assembly language program.** It is possible to have any number of different assemblers for the **6800**, each with its own mnemonics, but the mnemonics described here are used by Motorola for the **6800** μP instruction set. The mnemonic for each machine language instruction code and its hexadecimal equivalent are shown in Table 4-1.

When a program is written in mnemonic or assembly language it is called a *source program*. After being assembled (or translated) by the computer, the machine language codes that are produced are known as the *object program*. An assembler also produces a *program listing*, which is used for debugging the program and is kept as a record of the design.

The programmer must understand the differences between the mnemonics in order to write a program. The following sections and chapters are devoted to describing these differences. A detailed description of the assembler is given in Chapter 6 and debugging is described in Chapter 10.

4-4.1 Numerical Identifications

The **6800** assembler uses several symbols to identify the various types of numbers that occur in a program:

1. A blank or no symbol indicates that the number is a *decimal* number.
2. A $ immediately preceding a number indicates it is a *hex* number. ($24, for example, is 24 in hex or the equivalent of 36 in decimal.)
3. A # sign indicates an *immediate* operand (see Section 4-5.1).
4. A @ sign indicates an *octal* value.
5. A % sign indicates a *binary* number (01011001, for example).

4-5 ADDRESSING MODES

The accumulator and memory instructions available in the **6800** are given in Table 4-2.[1] The leftmost columns indicate their operations and the mnemonic for each instruction. The accumulator and memory instructions can be broken down roughly into these categories:

1. Transfers between an accumulator and memory (LOADs and STOREs).
2. Arithmetic operations—ADDITION, SUBTRACTION, DECIMAL ADJUST ACCUMULATOR.
3. Logical operations—AND, OR, XOR.
4. Shifts and rotates.

[1]The complete **6800** instruction set is given in Appendix A.

TABLE 4-1 Mnemonics and Hexadecimal Values for the **6800** Machine Codes

Code	Mnemonic	Acc	Mode	Code	Mnemonic	Acc	Mode	Code	Mnemonic	Acc	Mode	Code	Mnemonic	Acc	Mode
00	•			40	NEG	A		80	SUB	A	IMM	C0	SUB	B	IMM
01	NOP			41	•			81	CMP	A	IMM	C1	CMP	B	IMM
02	•			42	•			82	SBC	A	IMM	C2	SBC	B	IMM
03	•			43	COM	A		83	•			C3	•		
04	•			44	LSR	A		84	AND	A	IMM	C4	AND	B	IMM
05	•			45	•			85	BIT	A	IMM	C5	BIT	B	IMM
06	TAP			46	ROR	A		86	LDA	A	IMM	C6	LDA	B	IMM
07	TPA			47	ASR	A		87	•			C7	•		
08	INX			48	ASL	A		88	EOR	A	IMM	C8	EOR	B	IMM
09	DEX			49	ROL	A		89	ADC	A	IMM	C9	ADC	B	IMM
0A	CLV			4A	DEC	A		8A	ORA	A	IMM	CA	ORA	B	IMM
0B	SEV			4B	•			8B	ADD	A	IMM	CB	ADD	B	IMM
0C	CLC			4C	INC	A		8C	CPX	A	IMM	CC	•		
0D	SEC			4D	TST	A		8D	BSR		REL	CD	•		
0E	CLI			4E	•			8E	LDS		IMM	CE	LDX		IMM
0F	SEI			4F	CLR	A		8F	•			CF	•		
10	SBA			50	NEG	B		90	SUB	A	DIR	D0	SUB	B	DIR
11	CBA			51	•			91	CMP	A	DIR	D1	CMP	B	DIR
12	•			52	•			92	SBC	A	DIR	D2	SBC	B	DIR
13	•			53	COM	B		93	•			D3	•		
14	•			54	LSR	B		94	AND	A	DIR	D4	AND	B	DIR
15	•			55	•			95	BIT	A	DIR	D5	BIT	B	DIR
16	TAB			56	ROR	B		96	LDA	A	DIR	D6	LDA	B	DIR
17	TBA			57	ASR	B		97	STA	A	DIR	D7	STA	B	DIR
18	•			58	ASL	B		98	EOR	A	DIR	D8	EOR	B	DIR
19	DAA			59	ROL	B		99	ADC	A	DIR	D9	ADC	B	DIR
1A	•			5A	DEC	B		9A	ORA	A	DIR	DA	ORA	B	DIR
1B	ABA			5B	•			9B	ADD	A	DIR	DB	ADD	B	DIR
1C	•			5C	INC	B		9C	CPX		DIR	DC	•		
1D	•			5D	TST	B		9D	•			DD	•		
1E	•			5E	•			9E	LDS		DIR	DE	LDX		DIR
1F	•			5F	CLR	B		9F	STS		DIR	DF	STX		DIR
20	BRA		REL	60	NEG		IND	A0	SUB	A	IND	E0	SUB	B	IND
21	•			61	•			A1	CMP	A	IND	E1	CMP	B	IND
22	BHI		REL	62	•			A2	SBC	A	IND	E2	SBC	B	IND
23	BLS		REL	63	COM		IND	A3	•			E3	•		
24	BCC		REL	64	LSR		IND	A4	AND	A	IND	E4	AND	B	IND
25	BCS		REL	65	•			A5	BIT	A	IND	E5	BIT	B	IND
26	BNE		REL	66	ROR		IND	A6	LDA	A	IND	E6	LDA	B	IND
27	BEQ		REL	67	ASR		IND	A7	STA	A	IND	E7	STA	B	IND
28	BVC		REL	68	ASL		IND	A8	EOR	A	IND	E8	EOR	B	IND
29	BVS		REL	69	ROL		IND	A9	ADC	A	IND	E9	ADC	B	IND
2A	BPL		REL	6A	DEC		IND	AA	ORA	A	IND	EA	ORA	B	IND
2B	BMI		REL	6B	•			AB	ADD	A	IND	EB	ADD	B	IND
2C	BGE		REL	6C	INC		IND	AC	CPX		IND	EC	•		
2D	BLT		REL	6D	TST		IND	AD	JSR		IND	ED	•		
2E	BGT		REL	6E	JMP		IND	AE	LDS		IND	EE	LDX		IND
2F	BLE		REL	6F	CLR		IND	AF	STS		IND	EF	STX		IND
30	TSX			70	NEG		EXT	B0	SUB	A	EXT	F0	SUB	B	EXT
31	INS			71	•			B1	CMP	A	EXT	F1	CMP	B	EXT
32	PUL	A		72	•			B2	SBC	A	EXT	F2	SBC	B	EXT
33	PUL	B		73	COM		EXT	B3	•			F3	•		
34	DES			74	LSR		EXT	B4	AND	A	EXT	F4	AND	B	EXT
35	TXS			75	•			B5	BIT	A	EXT	F5	BIT	B	EXT
36	PSH	A		76	ROR		EXT	B6	LDA	A	EXT	F6	LDA	B	EXT
37	PSH	B		77	ASR		EXT	B7	STA	A	EXT	F7	STA	B	EXT
38	•			78	ASL		EXT	B8	EOR	A	EXT	F8	ADC	B	EXT
39	RTS			79	ROL		EXT	B9	ADC	A	EXT	F9	ADC	B	EXT
3A	•			7A	DEC		EXT	BA	ORA	A	EXT	FA	ORA	B	EXT
3B	RTI			7B	•			BB	ADD	A	EXT	FB	ADD	B	EXT
3C	•			7C	INC		EXT	BC	CPX		EXT	FC	•		
3D	•			7D	TST		EXT	BD	JSR		EXT	FD	•		
3E	WAI			7E	JMP		EXT	BE	LDS		EXT	FE	LDX		EXT
3F	SWI			7F	CLR		EXT	BF	STS		EXT	FF	STX		EXT

Notes: 1. Addressing Modes:

A = Accumulator A
B = Accumulator B
REL = Relative
IND = Indexed
IMM = Immediate
DIR = Direct

2. Unassigned code indicated by "•"

TABLE 4-2 Accumulator and Memory Instructions

The accumulator and memory operations and their effect on the CCR are shown in Table 7. Included are Arithmetic Logic, Data Test and Data Handling instructions.

		ADDRESSING MODES															BOOLEAN/ARITHMETIC OPERATION	COND. CODE REG.					
		IMMED			DIRECT			INDEX			EXTND			IMPLIED			(All register labels refer to contents)	5	4	3	2	1	0
OPERATIONS	MNEMONIC	OP	~	#	OP	~	#	OP	~	#	OP	~	#	OP	~	#		H	I	N	Z	V	C
Add	ADDA	8B	2	2	9B	3	2	AB	5	2	BB	4	3				A + M → A	↕	●	↕	↕	↕	↕
	ADDB	CB	2	2	DB	3	2	EB	5	2	FB	4	3				B + M → B	↕	●	↕	↕	↕	↕
Add Acmltrs	ABA													1B	2	1	A + B → A	↕	●	↕	↕	↕	↕
Add with Carry	ADCA	89	2	2	99	3	2	A9	5	2	B9	4	3				A + M + C → A	↕	●	↕	↕	↕	↕
	ADCB	C9	2	2	D9	3	2	E9	5	2	F9	4	3				B + M + C → B	↕	●	↕	↕	↕	↕
And	ANDA	84	2	2	94	3	2	A4	5	2	B4	4	3				A · M → A	●	●	↕	↕	R	●
	ANDB	C4	2	2	D4	3	2	E4	5	2	F4	4	3				B · M → B	●	●	↕	↕	R	●
Bit Test	BITA	85	2	2	95	3	2	A5	5	2	B5	4	3				A · M	●	●	↕	↕	R	●
	BITB	C5	2	2	D5	3	2	E5	5	2	F5	4	3				B · M	●	●	↕	↕	R	●
Clear	CLR							6F	7	2	7F	6	3				00 → M	●	●	R	S	R	R
	CLRA													4F	2	1	00 → A	●	●	R	S	R	R
	CLRB													5F	2	1	00 → B	●	●	R	S	R	R
Compare	CMPA	81	2	2	91	3	2	A1	5	2	B1	4	3				A − M	●	●	↕	↕	↕	↕
	CMPB	C1	2	2	D1	3	2	E1	5	2	F1	4	3				B − M	●	●	↕	↕	↕	↕
Compare Acmltrs	CBA													11	2	1	A − B	●	●	↕	↕	↕	↕
Complement, 1's	COM							63	7	2	73	6	3				$\overline{M}$ → M	●	●	↕	↕	R	S
	COMA													43	2	1	$\overline{A}$ → A	●	●	↕	↕	R	S
	COMB													53	2	1	$\overline{B}$ → B	●	●	↕	↕	R	S
Complement, 2's (Negate)	NEG							60	7	2	70	6	3				00 − M → M	●	●	↕	↕	①	②
	NEGA													40	2	1	00 − A → A	●	●	↕	↕	①	②
	NEGB													50	2	1	00 − B → B	●	●	↕	↕	①	②
Decimal Adjust, A	DAA													19	2	1	Converts Binary Add. of BCD Characters into BCD Format	●	●	↕	↕	↕	③
Decrement	DEC							6A	7	2	7A	6	3				M − 1 → M	●	●	↕	↕	4	●
	DECA													4A	2	1	A − 1 → A	●	●	↕	↕	4	●
	DECB													5A	2	1	B − 1 → B	●	●	↕	↕	4	●
Exclusive OR	EORA	88	2	2	98	3	2	A8	5	2	B8	4	3				A⊕M → A	●	●	↕	↕	R	●
	EORB	C8	2	2	D8	3	2	E8	5	2	F8	4	3				B⊕M → B	●	●	↕	↕	R	●
Increment	INC							6C	7	2	7C	6	3				M + 1 → M	●	●	↕	↕	⑤	●
	INCA													4C	2	1	A + 1 → A	●	●	↕	↕	⑤	●
	INCB													5C	2	1	B + 1 → B	●	●	↕	↕	⑤	●
Load Acmltr	LDAA	86	2	2	96	3	2	A6	5	2	B6	4	3				M → A	●	●	↕	↕	R	●
	LDAB	C6	2	2	D6	3	2	E6	5	2	F6	4	3				M → B	●	●	↕	↕	R	●
Or, Inclusive	ORAA	8A	2	2	9A	3	2	AA	5	2	BA	4	3				A + M → A	●	●	↕	↕	R	●
	ORAB	CA	2	2	DA	3	2	EA	5	2	FA	4	3				B + M → B	●	●	↕	↕	R	●
Push Data	PSHA													36	4	1	A → M_{SP}, SP − 1 → SP	●	●	●	●	●	●
	PSHB													37	4	1	B → M_{SP}, SP − 1 → SP	●	●	●	●	●	●
Pull Data	PULA													32	4	1	SP + 1 → SP, M_{SP} → A	●	●	●	●	●	●
	PULB													33	4	1	SP + 1 → SP, M_{SP} → B	●	●	●	●	●	●
Rotate Left	ROL							69	7	2	79	6	3				M	●	●	↕	↕	⑥	↕
	ROLA													49	2	1	A } C ← b7 ← b0	●	●	↕	↕	⑥	↕
	ROLB													59	2	1	B	●	●	↕	↕	⑥	↕
Rotate Right	ROR							66	7	2	76	6	3				M	●	●	↕	↕	⑥	↕
	RORA													46	2	1	A } C → b7 → b0	●	●	↕	↕	⑥	↕
	RORB													56	2	1	B	●	●	↕	↕	⑥	↕
Shift Left, Arithmetic	ASL							68	7	2	78	6	3				M	●	●	↕	↕	⑥	↕
	ASLA													48	2	1	A } C ← b7 ← b0 ← 0	●	●	↕	↕	⑥	↕
	ASLB													58	2	1	B	●	●	↕	↕	⑥	↕
Shift Right, Arithmetic	ASR							67	7	2	77	6	3				M	●	●	↕	↕	⑥	↕
	ASRA													47	2	1	A } b7 → b0 → C	●	●	↕	↕	⑥	↕
	ASRB													57	2	1	B	●	●	↕	↕	⑥	↕
Shift Right, Logic	LSR							64	7	2	74	6	3				M	●	●	R	↕	⑥	↕
	LSRA													44	2	1	A } 0 → b7 → b0 → C	●	●	R	↕	⑥	↕
	LSRB													54	2	1	B	●	●	R	↕	⑥	↕
Store Acmltr.	STAA				97	4	2	A7	6	2	B7	5	3				A → M	●	●	↕	↕	R	●
	STAB				D7	4	2	E7	6	2	F7	5	3				B → M	●	●	↕	↕	R	●
Subtract	SUBA	80	2	2	90	3	2	A0	5	2	B0	4	3				A − M → A	●	●	↕	↕	↕	↕
	SUBB	C0	2	2	D0	3	2	E0	5	2	F0	4	3				B − M → B	●	●	↕	↕	↕	↕
Subtract Acmltrs.	SBA													10	2	1	A − B → A	●	●	↕	↕	↕	↕
Subtr. with Carry	SBCA	82	2	2	92	3	2	A2	5	2	B2	4	3				A − M − C → A	●	●	↕	↕	↕	↕
	SBCB	C2	2	2	D2	3	2	E2	5	2	F2	4	3				B − M − C → B	●	●	↕	↕	↕	↕
Transfer Acmltrs	TAB													16	2	1	A → B	●	●	↕	↕	R	●
	TBA													17	2	1	B → A	●	●	↕	↕	R	●
Test, Zero or Minus	TST							6D	7	2	7D	6	3				M − 00	●	●	↕	↕	R	R
	TSTA													4D	2	1	A − 00	●	●	↕	↕	R	R
	TSTB													5D	2	1	B − 00	●	●	↕	↕	R	R
																		H	I	N	Z	V	C

LEGEND:

OP	Operation Code (Hexadecimal);
~	Number of MPU Cycles;
#	Number of Program Bytes;
+	Arithmetic Plus;
−	Arithmetic Minus;
·	Boolean AND;
M_{SP}	Contents of memory location pointed to be Stack Pointer;
+	Boolean Inclusive OR;
⊕	Boolean Exclusive OR;
$\overline{M}$	Complement of M;
→	Transfer Into;
0	Bit = Zero;
00	Byte = Zero;

Note – Accumulator addressing mode instructions are included in the column for IMPLIED addressing

CONDITION CODE SYMBOLS:

H	Half-carry from bit 3;
I	Interrupt mask
N	Negative (sign bit)
Z	Zero (byte)
V	Overflow, 2's complement
C	Carry from bit 7
R	Reset Always
S	Set Always
↕	Test and set if true, cleared otherwise

5. Test operations—bit test and compares.
6. Other operations—CLEAR, INCREMENT, DECREMENT, COMPLEMENT.

To reduce the number of instructions required in a typical program and, consequently, the number of memory locations needed to hold a program, the **6800** features several ways to address them. These are called *addressing modes* and many of them use only 1 or 2 bytes. The following paragraphs and examples illustrate how and when each mode is used.

The instructions of Table 4-2 can be addressed in one or more of the following modes: *immediate, direct, indexed, implied,* and *extended.* Each mode occupies a column in Table 4-2 and the instructions that can be executed in each mode are listed in the appropriate column. The listing contains the Op code, the number of cycles, and the number of bytes required for the instruction. The number of cycles, listed under the ~ symbol, is the number of **clock cycles** each instruction uses. This information is used when analyzing the timing of the μP (Section 9-10). The number of *bytes* is listed under the # symbol and indicates the number of memory locations required by each instruction.

EXAMPLE 4-1

How many cycles and bytes are required by

a. A LOAD IMMEDIATE instruction?
b. A LOAD EXTENDED instruction?

SOLUTION

a. Looking at the load accumulator instructions (LDAA means *load* the A accumulator and LDAB means *load* the B accumulator) in the IMMED column, we find that a LOAD IMMEDIATE takes **two cycles** and requires **2 bytes.**
b. Moving over to the EXTND column, we see that a LOAD EXTENDED takes **four cycles** and the instruction occupies **3 bytes.**

These modes are explained in the following paragraphs and illustrated in Fig. 4-3, where each instruction is assumed to start at location 10. The figure shows the Op code at location 10 and the following bytes. It explains the function of each byte and gives a sample instruction for each mode.

4-5.1 Immediate Addressing Instructions

All the *immediate instructions* in Table 4-2 requires 2 bytes. The first byte is the Op code and the second byte contains the *operand* or *information to be used.* If, for example, the accumulator contains the number 2C and the following instruction occurs in a program:

Location		Example of Code	Instruction and Effect
10	OP Code	8B	ADD A #$33
11	Immediate value	33	Adds $(33)_{16}$ to A.

(a) Immediate addressing

Location		Example of Code	Instruction and Effect
10	OP Code	9B	ADD A $33
11	Direct address	33	Adds the contents of location 0033 to A.

(b) Direct addressing

Location		Example of Code	Instruction and Effect
10	OP Code	BB	ADD A $0133
11	High address byte	01	Adds the contents of location 0133 to A.
12	Low address byte	33	

(c) Extended addressing

Location		Example of Code	Instruction and Effect
10	OP Code	AB	ADD A $06,X
11	Offset	06	Adds the contents of the location given by the sum of the index register +6 to A.

(d) Indexed addressing

Location		Example of Code	Instruction and Effect
10	OP Code	1B	ABA Adds the contents of A to B. The results go into A.

(e) Inherent

FIGURE 4-3 Examples of the various addressing modes of the **6800**.

ADD A #$23

The # indicates that the hex value $23 is to be added to the A accumulator. The immediate mode of the instruction is indicated by the # sign. After the instruction is executed, A contains 4F (23 + 2C).

EXAMPLE 4-2

What does the following instruction do? LDA B #$FF

SOLUTION

The action of this instruction is shown in Fig. 4-4, where the Op code for the instruction LOAD B IMMEDIATE (C6) is in 40 and the immediate operand (FF) is in 41. The instruction places or LOADS the operand into the B accumulator.

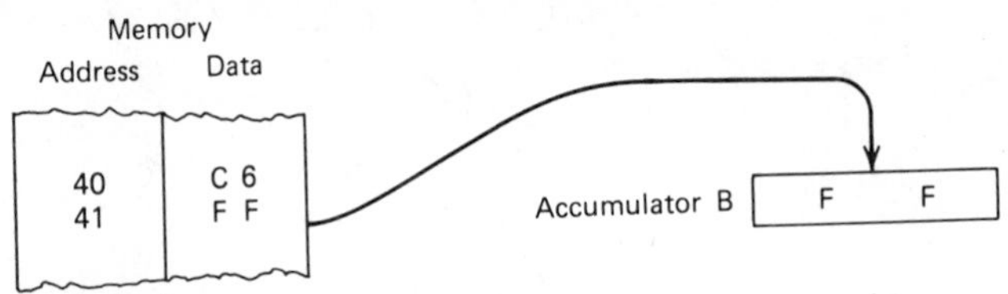

FIGURE 4-4 Action of a LOAD IMMEDIATE instruction.

4-5.2 Direct Instructions

Immediate instructions are used if the variable or operand is *known* to the programmer who is coding. For example, if the programmer wants to add 5 to a variable, it is more efficient to add it *immediately* than to store 5 in memory and do a direct or extended ADD. When one of the operands must reside in *memory*, however, *direct* or *extended* instructions are required.

Like immediate instructions, **direct instructions** require 2 bytes. The *second byte* contains the *address of the operand* used in the instruction. Since the Op code identifies this as a 2-byte instruction, only 8 address bits are available. The μP contains 16 address lines, but for direct instructions the 8 MSBs of the address are effectively set to 0. The memory locations that can be addressed by a direct instruction are therefore restricted to 0000 to 00FF. It is often wise to place variable data in these memory locations because this data is usually referenced frequently throughout the program. The programmer can then make maximum use of direct instructions and reduce memory requirements by up to 25%.

EXAMPLE 4-3

What happens when the instruction

LDA A $55

is encountered in a program? Assume that location 55 contains CA.

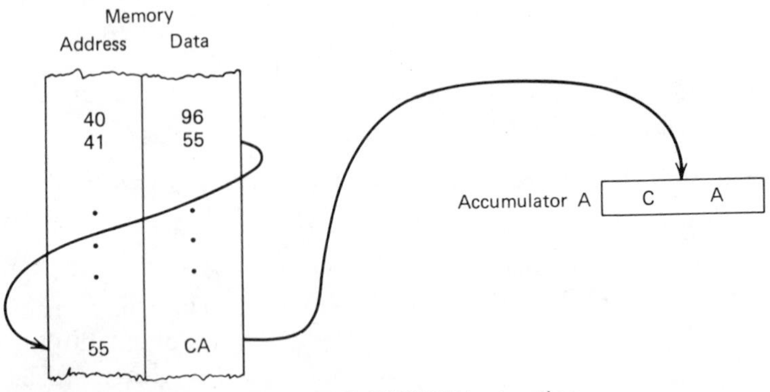

FIGURE 4-5 Action of a LOAD DIRECT instruction.

SOLUTION

This is a direct instruction. The second byte of this 2-byte instruction is the address (0055). The LDA A $55 instruction causes the μP to read location 0055 and load its contents into A. At the end of the instruction, the A accumulator contains CA.

The action of this instruction is shown in Fig. 4-5. The Op code for the LOAD A DIRECT (96) is again in memory location 40 and the operand (55) is in 41. Because this is a direct instruction, the operand is an address (0055) and the contents of that address (CA) are loaded into accumulator A.

EXAMPLE 4-4

If location 55 contains CA and the B accumulator contains 13, what does B contain after execution of the following instructions?

a. ADD B #$55.
b. ADD B $55.

SOLUTION

a. The # indicates the IMMEDIATE mode. Thus, ADD B #$55 causes 55 to be added to 13 and the result is 55 + 13 = **68** (all numbers are hex).
b. Since the address of $55 is less than $100, this is a DIRECT mode instruction. It causes the contents of 55 to be added to B and the result stored in the B register. Since location 55 contains $CA, the result stored is $CA + $13 = **$DD.**

4-5.3 Extended Instructions

Extended instructions are 3-byte instructions. The Op code is followed by 2 bytes that specify the address of the operand used by the instruction. The second byte contains the 8 high-order bits of the address. Because 16 address bits are available, any one of the 65,536 memory locations in the **6800** μP can be selected. Thus, extended instructions have the advantage of being able to select *any* memory locations, but direct instructions require only 2 bytes in the program instead of 3. Direct instructions also require one less cycle for execution, so they are somewhat faster than the corresponding extended instructions.

EXAMPLE 4-5

What occurs when the instruction

STA A $13C

appears in a program?

SOLUTION
Since this operand is a hex address greater than 100, this is an EXTENDED mode instruction. The instruction causes the contents of the A accumulator to be *stored* or written into location $013C.

4-5.4 Indexed Instructions

As its name implies, an **indexed instruction** makes use of the *Index Register* (X)[2] in the **6800** μP. There are two types of instructions and the reader must be able to distinguish between them:

Indexed instructions use the contents of the Index Register to calculate the address of the instruction. *Indexed instructions do not change the contents of the Index Register.*

For any indexed instruction, the address referred to is the *sum* of the number (called the OFFSET) in the second byte of the instruction, plus the contents of X.

Instructions of the second type are those that *do affect* or change the contents of X.

Table 4-3 is a list of instructions that apply to the Index Register and Stack Pointer. Notice that the **6800** provides instructions to LOAD, STORE, INCREMENT, and DECREMENT the stack pointer (SP) as well as X. Under some conditions, the SP can be used as a second index register.

EXAMPLE 4-6

What does the following program accomplish?

```
LDX #$0123
ADD A $A0,X
```

SOLUTION
The first instruction is an immediate LOAD of the index register. It causes the number $0123 to be loaded into X. The second instruction is an INDEXED ADD. In executing this instruction, the μP adds the second byte ($A0) to the contents of X ($0123) to get the data address. Thus, *the contents of memory location $01C3 are added to the A accumulator.*

Note that since the X register is 16 bits wide, an immediate load of the Index Register (LDX #) requires 2 bytes following the Op code, whereas an immediate load of an accumulator (LDAA #) requires only 1 byte (plus the Op code).

Index registers are useful for scanning tables or *relocating* a table or block of data.

[2]Referred to as the X register or simply X.

TABLE 4-3 Index Register and Stack Pointer Instructions

POINTER OPERATIONS	MNEMONIC	IMMED			DIRECT			INDEX			EXTND			IMPLIED			BOOLEAN/ARITHMETIC OPERATION	COND. CODE REG. 5	4	3	2	1	0
		OP	~	#	OP	~	#	OP	~	#	OP	~	#	OP	~	#		H	I	N	Z	V	C
Compare Index Reg	CPX	8C	3	3	9C	4	2	AC	6	2	BC	5	3				$X_H - M, X_L - (M + 1)$	•	•	⑦	↕	⑧	•
Decrement Index Reg	DEX													09	4	1	$X - 1 \rightarrow X$	•	•	•	↕	•	•
Decrement Stack Pntr	DES													34	4	1	$SP - 1 \rightarrow SP$	•	•	•	•	•	•
Increment Index Reg	INX													08	4	1	$X + 1 \rightarrow X$	•	•	•	↕	•	•
Increment Stack Pntr	INS													31	4	1	$SP + 1 \rightarrow SP$	•	•	•	•	•	•
Load Index Reg	LDX	CE	3	3	DE	4	2	EE	6	2	FE	5	3				$M \rightarrow X_H, (M + 1) \rightarrow X_L$	•	•	⑨	↕	R	•
Load Stack Pntr	LDS	8E	3	3	9E	4	2	AE	6	2	BE	5	3				$M \rightarrow SP_H, (M + 1) \rightarrow SP_L$	•	•	⑨	↕	R	•
Store Index Reg	STX				DF	5	2	EF	7	2	FF	6	3				$X_H \rightarrow M, X_L \rightarrow (M + 1)$	•	•	⑨	↕	R	•
Store Stack Pntr	STS				9F	5	2	AF	7	2	BF	6	3				$SP_H \rightarrow M, SP_L \rightarrow (M + 1)$	•	•	⑨	↕	R	•
Indx Reg → Stack Pntr	TXS													35	4	1	$X - 1 \rightarrow SP$	•	•	•	•	•	•
Stack Pntr → Indx Reg	TSX													30	4	1	$SP + 1 \rightarrow X$	•	•	•	•	•	•

EXAMPLE 4-7

A data list that starts at memory location $1000 is to be moved or relocated to start at location $2000. Write a program to accomplish this.

SOLUTION

In this program it is necessary to read a byte from $1000, write it in $2000, read a byte from $1001, write it in $2001, and so forth. Before starting the program, two *pointers,* one for the read addresses and one for the write addresses, must be set up. Let us assume locations $80–$83 are unused and set them aside for the pointers. Note that we are dealing with extended addressing, so the pointer requires 2 bytes to hold its 16 bits. The program is as follows:

Code	Mnemonics	Comments
CE 1000	LDX #$1000	Load pointer 1.
DF 80	STX $80	Store pointer 1.
CE 2000	LDX #$2000	Load pointer 2.
DF 82	STX $82	Store pointer 2.
DE 80 START	LDX $80	Get pointer 1.
A6 00	LDA A 0,X	Get data at X into A.
08	INX	Update pointer 1.
DF 80	STX $80	Store pointer 1.
DE 82	LDX $82	Get pointer 2.
A7 00	STA A 0,X	Store data in new table.
08 INX	INX	Update pointer 2.
DF 82	STX #82	Store pointer 2.
20 F0	BRA START	Loop back for next byte.

The program proceeds by loading pointer 1 into X, doing an indexed LOAD, incrementing X, and restoring the incremented pointer. This leaves the data word in the accumulator. It then loads pointer 2 into X, stores the data in its new location, increments X, and restores pointer 2. It then branches back to get the second data word, and so forth. Of course, this routine, as written, never ends. Methods for terminating loops should be used; they are discussed in Sections 3-11.3 and 4-7.

This program is complex because it really needed two Index Registers, one to point to the source of data and one for the destination, but only one Index Register is available on the **6800**. This resuted in frequent data swapping. More advanced μPs, like the **6809**, have two index registers, which greatly simplifies this type of problem.

The Index Register is often used by programs that are required to perform **code conversions.** Such programs might convert one code to another (ASCII to IBM's EBCDIC, for example) or might be used for trigonometric conversions, where the sine or cosine of a given angle may be required.

EXAMPLE 4-8

If the number in A represents an angle from 0 to 360° in 2° intervals [such that $(01)_{10}$ = 2°, $(15)_{10}$ = $(0F)_{16}$ = 30°, up to $(179)_{10}$ = $(B3)_{16}$ = 358°],[3] write a program to obtain the sine of the angle to the nearest hundredth.

SOLUTION

To solve this problem, a rudimentary sine table must first be written into memory. The base or beginning address is written into X. The sine of any angle can be obtained by going to that location whose address is the sum of the base address plus the angle in A and loading that location with the sine of the corresponding angle. Since 8 bits are available, the values between +127 and −128 can be represented. The numbers +100 and −100 can represent 1.00 and −1.00 and the sine of each angle can be expressed to the nearest 0.01.

To illustrate the use of the table, note that the sine of 60° = 0.866 = 0.87 to the nearest 0.01. If the base address of the table is 500, the 60° value occupies the 30th entry, or location $51E. Since the sine is scaled between +100 and −100, the number 0.87 becomes $(87)_{10}$ = $(57)_{16}$. Therefore the contents of location $51E must be $(57)_{16}$. The table in memory is illustrated in Fig. 4-6.

Once the sine table is in memory, a program for taking an angle in A and producing its sine in B can be written as follows:

Addr	Code	Mnemonic	Comments
100	**CE 04FF LOOP**	**LDX #$04FF**	Place pointer to table in X.
103	**08**	**INX**	Increment index register.
104	**80 01**	**SUBA #1**	Decrement angle in A.
106	**24 FC**	**BCC LOOP**	Branch if carry clear, to LOOP.
108	**E6 00**	**LDA B 0,X**	Load B from address in X (+ 0).

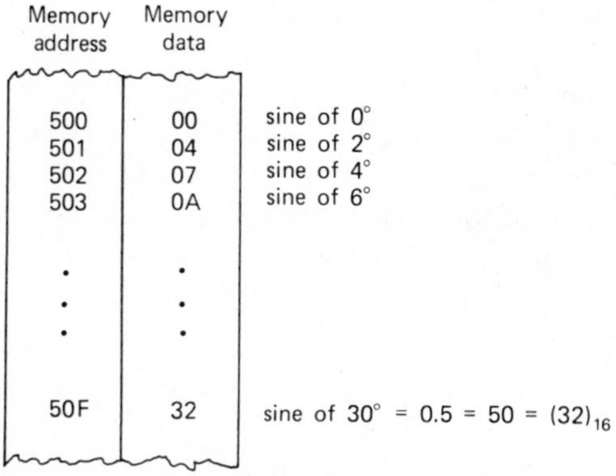

Memory address	Memory data	
500	00	sine of 0°
501	04	sine of 2°
502	07	sine of 4°
503	0A	sine of 6°
⋮	⋮	
50F	32	sine of 30° = 0.5 = 50 = $(32)_{16}$

FIGURE 4-6 The sine table in memory.

[3]Two-degree intervals were used so that all angles from 0 to 360° could be represented within a single byte.

This program uses a common technique of searching a table by incrementing X while simultaneously decrementing the value in A. Numbers larger than 128_{10} in A will use bit 7, and thus we cannot use a conditional branch decision that depends on the negative bit. We must carry the bit (i.e., BRANCH IF CARRY CLEAR). In this type of program DECA is usually used, but it does not set the carry bit, and therefore our program must use a SUBA #1 instruction instead.

To illustrate further, if the sine of 210° is required, A must contain $(105)_{10} = (69)_{16}$. Location \$0569 should contain $(-0.5) = -50$ (on our scale) $= (-32)_{16} =$ \$CE. The program then loads the contents of \$0569, or \$CE, into B.

Modifications and improvements in this program are certainly possible. One obvious possibility is to limit the angle to 90° or less, which could improve the resolution. This example was presented primarily to show how tables can be constructed and used in a **6800** μP.

4-5.5 Implied Addressing

Implied instructions are used when *all* the information required for the instruction is already within the CPU and *no external operands* from memory or from the program (in the case of immediate instructions) are needed. Since no memory references are needed, implied instructions require only 1 byte for their Op code. Examples of implied instructions that affect the accumulators are CLEAR, INCREMENT, DECREMENT, SHIFT, ROTATE, ADD, and SUBTRACT.

EXAMPLE 4-9

What does the following instruction do?

SBA

SOLUTION

This is a 1-byte instruction. SBA is the mnemonic for SUBTRACT ACCUMULATORS. Table 4-2 shows that the operation is $(A) - (B) \rightarrow (A)$. Thus the number in the B accumulator is subtracted from the A accumulator and the results are stored in A. At the end of the instruction, A contains the result (difference), while B contains the original subtrahend and its value is unchanged.

4-6 CONDITION CODES

The **6800** uses six **condition codes,** labeled H, I, N, Z, V, and C. These codes reside in the Condition Code Register (CCR). As shown in Fig. 4-1, the 1s in the two MSBs of the CCR are merely to fill it out to 8 bits.

The function of most of the condition codes is to retain information about the results of the last arithmetic or memory operation for use by the conditional branch instructions. The effect of an instruction on each condition code is shown in the six rightmost columns of Table 4-2. Two symbols dominate this part of the table; the dot (•) means that the instruction *does not* affect the condition codes, and the ↕ symbol indicates that the condition code is SET or CLEARED as a result of the instruction execution.

The I condition code bit is set to enable the μP to be *interrupted*. Its action is discussed in the chapter on interrupts (Chapter 9). None of the accumulator and memory instructions affects the I bit, but CLI and SEI will clear or set it.

4-6.1 The Z Bit

The Z (for zero) bit in the Condition Code Register (CCR) is SET whenever an instruction results in a 0 being entered into the destination register or memory location. The Boolean algebra equation for the Z bit is

$$Z = \overline{R}_7\,\overline{R}_6\,\overline{R}_5\,\overline{R}_4\,\overline{R}_3\,\overline{R}_2\,\overline{R}_1\,\overline{R}_0$$

which means that *Z is 1, only if all 8 bits of the result are 0.*

The major function of the **compare instruction** is to set the Z bit. Compare instructions internally subtract an operand from an accumulator but *do not* change the contents of either. They simply change the bits of the CCR. A μP can determine whether two operands are equal by comparing them. If the Z bit is SET after execution of the compare instruction, it indicates that the two operands are indeed equal. This information is often used by branch instructions (see Section 4-7).

4-6.2 The C Bit

The C or carry bit in the condition code register is mainly set in one of four ways.

1. It is SET during ADD *instructions* when the result of the addition produces a *carry* output.
2. For *subtraction and comparison instructions*, it is SET when the *absolute value of the subtrahend is larger than the absolute value of the minuend*. Generally this implies a *borrow*.
3. It is changed when executing SHIFT and ROTATE instructions. For these instructions the bit shifted out of the accumulator becomes the carry bit and is not lost.
4. It is SET when an SEC instruction is executed.

Some other instructions, such as CLEAR and TEST, affect the carry bit. The careful programmer should consult the notes attached to Table 4-2 when there is any doubt about how an instruction affects the carry bit.

Two instructions, ADD WITH CARRY and SUBTRACT WITH CARRY, use the carry bit as part of the instruction. This simplifies the addition or subtraction of numbers that are longer than 8 bits. If, for example, the least significant bytes are added and produce a carry output, an ADC (add with carry) instruction is used to add the more significant bytes and also adds 1 if the sum of the least significant bytes produced a carry output.

EXAMPLE 4-10

The 16-bit number in memory locations $F2 and $F3 is to be subtracted from the 16-bit number in $F0 and $F1. The result is to be stored in $F4 and $F5. Assume $F0 is the MS byte of the minuend and $F2 is the MS byte of the subtrahend.

a. Write a program to subtract the numbers.
b. Show how the program operates if the minuend is +4 and the subtrahend is −5.

SOLUTION

a. First the least significant bits (LSBs) of the minuend must be loaded into an accumulator; then the LSB of the subtrahend is subtracted. *This may produce a borrow even if the final result is a positive number.* The result is stored and the MSBs of the minuend are loaded into an accumulator. The MSBs of the subtrahend are then subtracted from the accumulator, *with carry*, so that if a borrow had set the carry bit to 1, it is now subtracted from the more significant result. The program is shown in Fig. 4-7a.

b. To check this problem the machine language was written into the memory of a **6800** system equipped with a MINIBUG 3, MICRObug, or BUFFALO monitor program (see Section 10-5.9). These programs have a number of debugging features, including the ability to enter data in memory and to step through the user's program one instruction at a time and display the registers after each step. This is shown in Fig. 4-7b.

The contents of the Condition Code Register are shown in Fig. 4-7b, and Fig. 4-7c shows its interpretation. Note that the two MSBs of the CCR are always 1, and the status of each flag can be determined. For example, the D0 in the first entry of the condition codes means that only 3 bits are set: the two MSBs, as always, and the I bit. All other condition codes are 0 at this point.

After the program has been entered in memory, starting at $1000, as shown at the top of Fig. 4-7a, the data is entered, starting at $F0 as shown at the top of Fig. 4-7b. Note that −5 is entered in its 2s complement form ($FFFB).

The first step of the program loads the least significant byte (04) from $F1 into the A accumulator, as shown in the second line of Fig. 4-7b, and increments the PC to $1002. The data movement is shown pictorially in Fig. 4-7d. The second step subtracts the contents of $F3, that is, the LS byte of the subtrahend. The result (09) is left in the A accumulator. This can produce a borrow, as in this case, and if the $D1 in the CCR is translated, as shown in Fig. 4-7c, the CARRY bit is SET. Step 3 stores the contents of A into location $F5 (LS byte of the result). This is not seen unless the M command is used to display this memory location, as shown at the bottom of Fig. 4-7b. The MS byte of the subtrahend is then subtracted in steps 4 and 5, but this time the

```
ADDR   OBJECT   MNENOMICS     COMMENTS

1000   96 F1    LDA A $F1     Load LS byte of minuend into A
1002   90 F3    SUB A $F3     Subtract [F3] from A
1004   97 F5    STA A $F5     Store A in F5
1006   96 F0    LDA A $F0     Load MS of minuend into A
1008   92 F2    SBC A $F2     Subtrct [F2] from A w/ borrow
100A   97 F4    STA A $F4     Store A in F4
```

a. Subtraction program listing

```
*M 00F0 12 00  lf
* 00F1 2B 04  lf
* 00F2 A3 FF  lf
* 00F3 44 FB  cr

 CC B  A  X    PC   SP
*D0 XX 01 XXXX 1000 A063
*D0 XX 04 XXXX 1002 A063
*D1 XX 09 XXXX 1004 A063
*D1 XX 09 XXXX 1006 A063
*D5 XX 00 XXXX 1008 A063
*D5 XX 00 XXXX 100A A063
*D5 XX 00 XXXX 100C A063

*M 00F4 00  lf
* 00F5 09  cr
```

```
    H I N Z V C
1 1 0 1 0 0 0 0
1 1 0 1 0 0 0 0
1 1 0 1 0 0 0 1
1 1 0 1 0 0 0 1
1 1 0 1 0 1 0 1
1 1 0 1 0 1 0 1
1 1 0 1 0 1 0 1
```

c. Condition Code (CC) binary equivalents

b. Minibug III debug program display (X = unimportant values) (Operator entries are underlined)

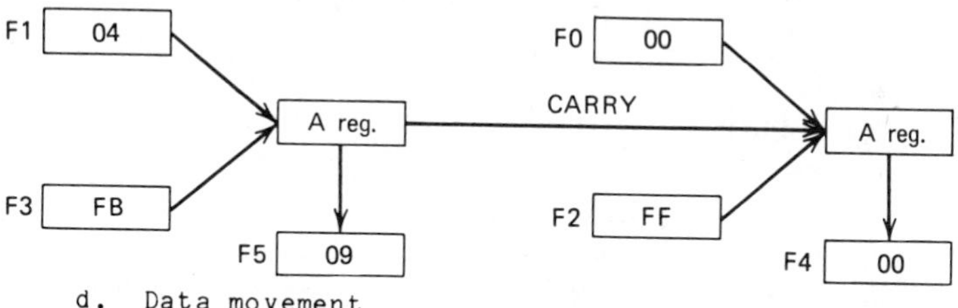

d. Data movement

FIGURE 4-7 Subtraction program for Example 4-10.

carry is included. Step 5 subtracts \$FF from 00, which is the same as subtracting −1 from 0 and will give +1. This is a subtract with carry (borrow), however, and since the carry bit is SET, a 1 is subtracted from the result. Thus, the MS byte of the final result is 00 and the entire result is 0009, which is correct. Note that the carry bit is also SET at the end of the fifth instruction, but this has no effect on this problem. This program works because the carry bit that is SET in step 2 is not affected by the STA A and LDA A instructions (instructions 3 and 4), so it can be used in instruction 5.

As the program progresses it is instructive to follow the condition codes, especially the C and Z flags, which are important here. At the beginning the CCR contains \$D0, indicating both C and Z are 0. The subtraction SETs C and changes the CCR to \$D1. The load of \$F0, which contains 00, SETs Z and changes the CCR to \$D5.

4-6.3 The N Bit

The N (negative) bit of the CCR is SET whenever the results of an operation are negative. That is, the N bit is SET whenever the MSB of the result is a 1 (an MSB of 1 indicates a negative number in 2s complement arithmetic). The Boolean equation for the N bit is $N = R_7$. Note that all accumulator and memory instructions except PSH and PUL affect the N bit.

EXAMPLE 4-11

The numbers $03A4 and $123F are in locations $F0, $F1, $F2, and $F3, respectively.

Write a program to add them and store the results in $F4 and $F5. Make note of which instructions in the program set the N bit.

SOLUTION
The program is shown in Fig. 4-8a. First the LS bytes are added and stored. Then the MS bytes are added (with carry) and stored.

The object program was loaded into memory using the MINIBUG 3 (or MICRObug) debug program and, as described in Example 4-10, was executed a step at a time, as shown in Fig. 4-8b. Figure 4-8d shows the binary equivalent of the hex values in the condition code register (column CC) of Fig. 4-8b. The data movement is also shown in Fig. 4-8c. These three figures show the following.

1. The N bit is set by the first instruction because a negative number (A4) is loaded into A.
2. The second step adds the $3F from $F3. The result in A is seen to be $E3, which also SETs the N bit because bit 7 of that byte is a 1.
3. The result is stored in step 3. The N bit remains SET.
4. The fourth step CLEARS the N bit because a positive number is loaded into A.
5. The N bit remains CLEAR during the fifth and sixth steps because the sum (in A) is a positive number.

Note that the N bit was SET by the first addition. Since this is an intermediate step in the summation, however, the N bit has no significance. At the end of the addition, the N bit is CLEAR, indicating a positive result. Note also that the carry bit was never SET by the numbers used in this program. If it was initially SET, it would have been cleared by the first addition (instruction 2).

4-6.4 The V Bit

The V or *overflow* bit is SET when an arithmetic operation results in a *2s complement overflow* or *underflow*. **Overflow** *occurs when the result of an arithmetic operation produces a number larger than the register can accommodate*

```
STEP  ADDR  OBJECT    MNEMONIC     COMMENTS

1     1000  96 F1     LDA A $F1    LOAD LS BYTE OF AUGEND
2     1002  9B F3     ADD A $F3    ADD LS BYTE OF ADDEND
3     1004  97 F5     STA A $F5    STORE RESULT IN F5
4     1006  96 F0     LDA A $F0    LOAD MS BYTE OF AUGEND IN A
5     1008  99 F2     ADC A $F2    ADD W/C MS BYTE OF ADDEND
6     100A  97 F4     STA A $F4    STORE MS BYTE
```

a. Program listing

```
*M 00F0 29 03   lf
*  00F1 46 A4   lf   augend
*  00F2 49 12   lf
*  00F3 57 3F   cr   addend

 CC   B   A   X     PC    SP          H I N Z V C
*D0  XX  01  XXXX  1000  A078         0 1 0 0 0 0
*D8  XX  A4  XXXX  1002  A078         0 1 1 0 0 0
*F8  XX  E3  XXXX  1004  A078         1 1 1 0 0 0
*F8  XX  E3  XXXX  1006  A078         1 1 1 0 0 0
*F0  XX  03  XXXX  1008  A078         1 1 0 0 0 0
*D0  XX  15  XXXX  100A  A078         0 1 0 0 0 0
*D0  XX  15  XXXX  100C  A078         0 1 0 0 0 0

*M 00F4 15  lf
*  00F5 E3  cr  answer
```

d. Condition codes

b. Execution by steps (Operator entries underlined)

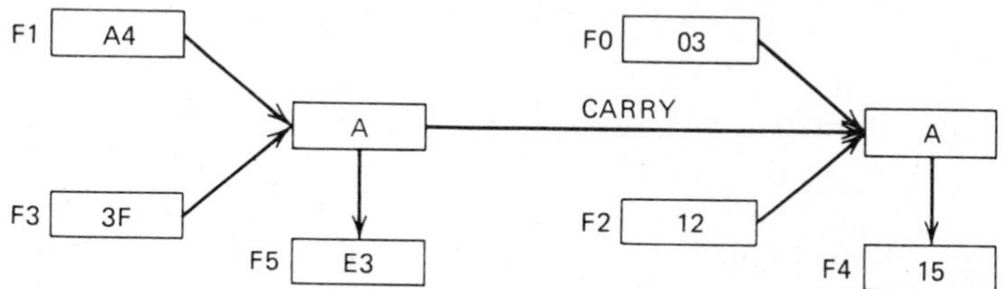

c. Data movement between memory and accumulator

FIGURE 4-8 Program analysis for Example 4-11.

($> 128_{10}$) (i.e., the sign bit is affected). **Underflow** *occurs when the result produces a number more negative than the register can accommodate* (less than 128_{10}). This also affects the *sign* bit.

The limitations on the numbers that can be handled by an n -bit register are $2^{n-1} - 1$ positive numbers and 2^{n-1} negative numbers. A single 8-bit byte is thus restricted to numbers between $+127_{10}$ and -128_{10}.

To illustrate overflow, consider the number 100_{10} expressed as an 8-bit number, 01100100. If an attempt is made to add 100_{10} plus 100_{10}, the result is 200_{10} (11001000). Unfortunately, considered as a 2s complement number, this binary value equals -56. This ridiculous result occurred because the answer, $+200$, was *beyond the range* of numbers that could be handled by a single 7-bit byte ($+200_{10}$ is greater than $+127$).

There are two criteria for overflow and underflow in the **6800**.

1. For **addition instructions** the basic Boolean equation for overflow is

$$V = \overline{A}_7 \overline{B}_7 R_7 + A_7 B_7 \overline{R}_7 \qquad (1)$$

where it is assumed that the operation is A plus $B \rightarrow R$ and A_7 is the MSB of A (the augend), B_7 is the MSB of B (the addend), and R_7 is the MSB of the result. The plus sign in the equation indicates the logical OR.

If the first term of the equation is 1, it indicates that two positive numbers have been added (because A_7 and B_7 are both 0) and the result is negative (because $R_7 = 1$). This possibility was illustrated in the preceding paragraph.

The second term indicates that two negative numbers have been added and have produced a positive result.

EXAMPLE 4-12

Show how the hex numbers 80 and C0 are added.

SOLUTION

80 + C0 = \$40 plus a carry (see Section 2-8.3). Note that \$80 and \$C0 are both negative numbers, but their sum (as contained in a single byte) is positive. This corresponds to the second term of equation 1. Fortunately, this addition sets the V bit to warn the user that overflow (in this case underflow) has occurred.

2. For **subtraction** operations, the Boolean equation is

$$V = A_7 \overline{B}_7 \overline{R}_7 + \overline{A}_7 B_7 R_7 \qquad (2)$$

The assumption here is that $A - B \rightarrow R$. The first term indicates that a positive number has been subtracted from a negative number and produced a positive result. The second term indicates that a negative number has been subtracted from a positive number and produced a negative result. In either case, the overflow bit is set to warn the user.

EXAMPLE 4-13

If the numbers \$23C4 and \$FDAB are added by the program of Example 4-11, what flags are set after the

a. LS bytes are added?
b. MS bytes are added?

SOLUTION

a. First the μP adds the least significant bytes, C4 and AB, to obtain 6F. This addition sets the C and V bits. The V bit is set because two negative numbers were added and the result, 6F, is positive. This position result also clears the N bit.

b. The next part of the program adds the MS bytes, $23 and $FD, and the 1 in the C bit. The result is $21. The C bit is SET, but both N and V are CLEAR. Because numbers of unlike sign were added, overflow is impossible and V is CLEAR.

The significance of the overflow bit depends on the program. In Example 4-13, the V bit was set after the first addition but, because this was an intermediate step, the V bit could be ignored. After the final additon the V bit was CLEAR, indicating that the result was correct.

4-6.5 Manipulation of the Condition Code Register

Table 4-4 shows the instructions that affect the CCR.

		IMPLIED				COND. CODE REG.					
						5	4	3	2	1	0
OPERATIONS	MNEMONIC	OP	~	#	BOOLEAN OPERATION	H	I	N	Z	V	C
Clear Carry	CLC	0C	2	1	0 → C	•	•	•	•	•	R
Clear Interrupt Mask	CLI	0E	2	1	0 → I	•	R	•	•	•	•
Clear Overflow	CLV	0A	2	1	0 → V	•	•	•	•	R	•
Set Carry	SEC	0D	2	1	1 → C	•	•	•	•	•	S
Set Interrupt Mask	SEI	0F	2	1	1 → I	•	S	•	•	•	•
Set Overflow	SEV	0B	2	1	1 → V	•	•	•	•	S	•
Acmltr A → CCR	TAP	06	2	1	A → CCR	(1)					
CCR → Acmltr A	TPA	07	2	1	CCR → A	•	•	•	•	•	•

R = Reset
S = Set
• = Not affected

(1) (ALL) Set according to the contents of Accumulator A.

TABLE 4-4 Condition Code Register Instructions

1. Although the condition codes are normally controlled by the ALU, specific instructions exist to SET or CLEAR the C, V, and I bits.
2. The CCR can be transferred to the A accumulator by a TPA instruction. This would be done if the program had to preserve the present contents of the CCR for future use. The CCR could be transferred to A and then saved in RAM by a STORE A or PUSH A instruction.
3. The contents of accumulator A can be transferred to the CCR by a TAP instruction. This would be done when the contents of the CCR are being restored from memory.

EXAMPLE 4-14

At a point in a program the H, I, and C bits of the CCR should be SET and N, V, and Z bits should be CLEAR. Write a sequence of instructions to set the bits accordingly.

SOLUTION
According to Fig. 4-1, the CCR should look like this:

11110001

It can be forced into this configuration by the following instructions.

Op Code	Mnemonic	Comment
86 F1	**LDA A #$F1**	Load desired contents of CCR into A
06	**TAP**	Transfer A to CCR

4-7 BRANCH INSTRUCTIONS

The major use of the condition codes is with CONDITIONAL BRANCH instructions. As explained in Section 3-11, a BRANCH instruction directs the PC to another address.

Table 4-5 is a partial table of the branch instructions available in the **6800** μP.

The first instruction, BRA, is an **unconditional** branch. The program always jumps or branches when the BRANCH ALWAYS (BRA), instruction occurs. The remaining instructions are **conditional** branches; they take the branch only if the condition codes are set properly. The table shows that there are conditional branches for the N, V, C, and Z condition codes and gives the Op code and condition for each BRANCH instruction. These instructions allow the computer to make the decisions necessary to control the program. (See Section 3-11.2.)

Each branch instruction is accompanied by an *offset*. The offset is a number that is added to the current value of the program counter to determine where the μP will go if it branches. Thus branch instructions skip over part of the program to a location that is *relative* to the program counter. They typically command the PC to "move up 6 locations" or "go back 10 locations."

4-7.1 Calculating Offsets

Branches were originally used in the **6800** and are now used in the same way by many μPs. A BRANCH instruction for the **6800** consists of the BRANCH Op Code in one byte and an 8-bit offset in the following byte. The offset is a 2s complement number that is added to the address.

If N is the location of the branch instruction and T is the target address (the address the program will jump to), then formula (4-1) can be used to calculate the offset.

$$\text{(4-1)} \qquad \text{Offset} = T - (N + 2)$$

Note that both forward and backward branches can be accommodated. Backward branches have negative offsets. The 2 in the formula indicates where the PC would be if a branch did not take place (i.e., at the start of the next instruction).

TABLE 4-5 Partial List of Branch Instructions Available in the 6800 μP

Instruction	Mnemonic	Op Code	Condition
Branch always	BRA	20	—
Branch if carry SET	BCS	25	C = 1
Branch if carry CLEAR	BCC	24	C = 0
Branch if zero	BEQ	27	Z = 1
Branch if not zero	BNE	26	Z = 0
Branch if minus	BMI	2B	N = 1
Branch if plus	BPL	2A	N = 0
Branch if overflow SET	BVS	29	V = 1
Branch if overflow CLEAR	BVC	28	V = 0

EXAMPLE 4-15

The Op code of the branch instruction is in \$011A. What should the offset be if the program must jump to \$0150?

SOLUTION
From (4-1) we obtain

011A + 2 = 011C

Offset = **0150 − 011C = \$34**

Thus the program segment would look like

011A	**XX**	(branch Op code)
011B	**34**	(offset)

EXAMPLE 4-16

The Op code of the branch instruction is in \$011A. What should the offset be if the program must jump to \$00EA?

SOLUTION
From the formula:

011A + 2 = 011C

Offset = **00EA − 011C = FFCE**

For an 8-bit negative offset the \$FF is discarded and the program looks like

011A	**XX**	(branch Op code)
011B	**CE**	(offset)

Note that the offset is a negative number (CE) and the program branches backward from \$11C to \$EA.

EXAMPLE 4-17

a. If the offset for the branch instruction in \$011A is \$39, where will the program branch to?
b. Repeat if the offset is \$93.

SOLUTION

a. Formula 4-1 can be transposed to read

$$T = (N + 2) + \text{offset}$$

Because the Op code is in 011A, $N + 2 = 011C$. Therefore $T = 011C + 39 = 0155$.

b. The procedure can be repeated but \$93 is a negative offset. Negative 8-bit offsets should be preceded by \$FF to convert them to 16-bit numbers.

$$T = 011C + FF93 = 00AF$$

In this case the program will branch backwards to \$AF.

4-7.2 Long and Short Branches

The maximum positive number that can be represented in 1 byte is $7F_{16}$ (or 127_{10}), and the most negative number is 80_{16} (or -128_{10}). Thus the program can branch forward no more than 127 bytes or backward no more than 128 bytes from where it would be if it did not branch (i.e., the start of the next instruction). This range is often sufficient since the destination of most branches is usually nearby. This is a constraint as the programs become larger. In the **6800**, branches to more remote locations must use jumps (see Section 5-3).

Some newer 8-bit μPs, like the **6809**, and all the 16-bit μPs permit *long* branches by allowing the use of a 16-bit offset. This allows the programmer to jump to any location within a 64 K-byte memory.

4-8 BCD ADDITION AND THE H BIT

Although programmers and readers of this book can use hex fluently, most people prefer to communicate with their computers using ordinary *decimal numbers*. Normal input devices such as CRT terminals or hand calculator keyboards have keys only for the numbers 0 through 9, and the displayed outputs, whether on a terminal, printed on paper, or on a seven-segment calculator display, are usually in decimal form.

In applications that deal with money, such as cash registers, it is preferable to keep the numbers in decimal form, rather than converting them to binary or hex. The use of the H bit of the CCR and the Decimal Adjust Accumulator (DAA) instruction makes decimal arithmetic possible.

4-8.1 Expressing Numbers in BCD[4]

Decimal numbers are usually entered into a computer in **Binary Coded Decimal** (BCD) form. The BCD code uses 4 binary bits called a *decade* to represent a single decimal digit (0 to 9). Since numbers greater than 9 are *not* used, the numbers from 10 to 15, which are also possible with 4-bit representation, should *never* appear in a BCD output. The BCD code conversion table is shown in Fig. 4-9.

Decimal Digit	Binary Coded Decimal (BCD) representation
0	0000
1	0001
2	0010
3	0011
4	0100
5	0101
6	0110
7	0111
8	1000
9	1001
X	1010
X	1011
X	1100
X	1101
X	1110
X	1111

FIGURE 4-9 The BCD code conversion table.

When a number consisting of several decimal digits is to be represented in BCD form, each digit is represented by its own group of 4 bits. Therefore, there are four times as many bits in the representation as there are decimal digits in the original number.

EXAMPLE 4-18

Express the number 6309_{10} in BCD form.

SOLUTION

From the code conversion table, we find that

$$\begin{aligned} 6 &= 0110 \\ 3 &= 0011 \\ 0 &= 0000 \\ 9 &= 1001 \end{aligned}$$

The number 6309 is expressed by stringing these bits together:

[4]Readers familiar with BCD may omit this section.

$$(6309)_{10} = \underbrace{0110}_{6}\underbrace{0011}_{3}\underbrace{0000}_{0}\underbrace{1001}_{9}$$

Numbers given in BCD form can be converted into decimal numbers simply by dividing them into 4-bit decades, starting at the least significant bit, and assigning the correct decimal digit to each decade.

EXAMPLE 4-19

Find the decimal equivalent of the BCD number

000101011000011101000

SOLUTION
The given number is divided into groups of 4 bits each and the decimal digit for each decade is identified:

$$\underbrace{0001}_{1}\ \underbrace{0101}_{5}\ \underbrace{1000}_{8}\ \underbrace{0111}_{7}\ \underbrace{0100}_{4}$$

The decimal equivalent of the given BCD number is **15,874**.

4-8.2 Adding BCD Numbers

Since each **6800** memory location contains 8 bits and each BCD decade contains 4 bits, it is natural to store two BCD digits in a single memory location. This is sometimes called *packing*, or *packed BCD*, and is a function of the input/output routine.

Addition and subtraction of BCD numbers are possible, but since all addition and subtraction instructions in the **6800** assume *binary* numbers, the *binary results must be manipulated to convert them to BCD*. This is done by using the H bit and the DAA instruction.

Table 4-2 shows that the H bit is changed only by addition instructions. *It is SET when the addition produces a carry out of bit position 3 and into bit position 4*. For BCD numbers the *H* bit is SET whenever the sum of the two digits, plus carry, is equal to or greater than $(16)_{10}$. Because this carry occurs midway through the byte, the *H* bit is sometimes called the *half-carry* bit.

EXAMPLE 4-20

The A and B accumulators contain the decimal numbers 48 and 79, respectively. They are added by an ADD accumulator (ABA) instruction. What is the result and what are the conditions of the C and H bits after the addition?

```
*M 1100 1B

 CC   B   A   X     PC    SP

*D0  79  48  XXXX  1100  XXXX

*FA  79  C1  XXXX  1101  XXXX
```

a. Results of one instruction step.

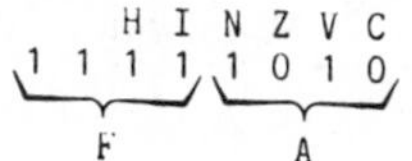

b. Condition Code reg

FIGURE 4-10 Program execution for Example 4-20. (a) Register changes when executed. (b) Condition codes.

SOLUTION
The **6800** adds 48 and 79 as though they were hex digits, placing the sum (C1) in the A accumulator. The results are shown in Fig. 4-10. At the end of the addition the H bit is SET (because the sum of 8 and 9 produces a carry), but the carry bit is CLEAR because the sum of the two most significant digits is less than 16.

4-8.3 The DAA Instruction

The result of Example 4-20 (48 + 79 = C1) is unsatisfactory if decimal arithmetic is being used. Addition instructions must be followed by a **Decimal Adjust Accumulator** (DAA) instruction to convert the hex result to the correct BCD result.

The DAA instruction modifies an answer as shown in Table 4-6. It examines four parts of the result.

1. The lower half-byte.
2. The upper half-byte.
3. The H bit.
4. The C bit.

It then adds 00, 06, 60, or 66 to the answer. This transforms the result to BCD.

TABLE 4-6 Action of the DAA Instruction

State of C bit before DAA (Col. 1)	Upper Half-byte (bits 4–7) (Col. 2)	Initial Half-carry H bit (Col. 3)	Lower Half-byte (bits 0–3) (Col. 4)	Number Added after by DAA (Col. 5)	State of C bit DAA (Col. 6)
0	0–9	0	0–9	00	0
0	0–8	0	A–F	06	0
0	0–9	1	0–3	06	0
0	A–F	0	0–9	60	1
0	9–F	0	A–F	66	1
0	A–F	1	0–3	66	1
1	0–2	0	0–9	60	1
1	0–2	0	A–F	66	1
1	0–3	1	0–3	66	1

EXAMPLE 4-21

What happens if a DAA instruction follows the result of Example 4-20?

SOLUTION
In Example 4-20, the sum was C1. The DAA notes

1. The lower half-byte is 0–3.
2. The H bit is SET.
3. The upper half-byte is A–F.
4. The C bit is CLEAR.

These conditions occur on line 6 of Table 4-6. The table shows that the DAA adds 66 to the result and SETs the C bit. After the DAA, A contains C1 + 66 = 27 and the carry bit is SET, which indicates a carry (a weight of 100 in decimal arithmetic). Therefore the BCD sum is 127, which is correct. The progress of the program is illustrated in Fig. 4-11.

EXAMPLE 4-22

The decimal numbers 2946 and 4957 are in locations $F0, $F1 and $F2, $F3, respectively. Write a program to add them and store the BCD result in locations $F4, $F5.

SOLUTION
The program and its analysis are shown in Fig. 4-12a. Figure 4-12b is the result of executing one instruction at a time with the debug program (MINIBUG III or MICRObug). Figure 4-12ç shows the binary representation of the CCR for each step. The first addition SETs the N and V bits. These bits are both RESET and the carry is SET by the DAA instruction. The last instruction shows how the two adjacent bytes containing the answer can be fetched as a 16-bit or 4 decimal digit number for further manipulation by the program. The result in the X register is the correct answer.

```
*M 1100 1B
   1101 19

 CC   B   A    X      PC     SP          H I N Z V C

*D0  79  48  XXXX   1100   XXXX          0 1 0 0 0 0

*FA  79  C1  XXXX   1101   XXXX          1 1 1 0 1 0

*F1  79  27  XXXX   1102   XXXX          1 1 0 0 0 1

a.  Results of instruction steps       b. Condition Code reg.
```

FIGURE 4-11 Program execution for Example 4-21. (a) Results of instruction steps. (b)Condition codes.

STEP	ADDR	OBJECT	MNEMONIC	COMMENTS
1	1000	96 F1	LDA A $F1	LOAD LS BYTE OF AUGEND
2	1002	9B F3	ADD A $F3	ADD LS BYTE OF ADDEND
3	1004	19	DAA	ADJUST FOR HALF CARRY, IF ANY
4	1005	97 F5	STA A $F5	STORE RESULT IN F5
5	1007	96 F0	LDA A $F0	LOAD MS BYTE OF AUGEND IN A
6	1009	99 F2	ADC A $F2	ADD W/C MS BYTE OF ADDEND
7	100B	19	DAA	ADJUST RESULT
8	100C	97 F4	STA A $F4	STORE MS BYTE
9	100E	DE F4	LDX $F4	LOAD 16 BIT ANSWER INTO X

a) Program listed

```
*M 00F0 XX 29 lf
   00F1 XX 46 lf
   00F2 XX 49 lf
   00F3 XX 57 cr
```

CC	B	A	X	PC	SP
*D0	XX	01	XXXX	1000	A071
*D0	XX	46	XXXX	1002	A071
*DA	XX	9D	XXXX	1004	A071
*D1	XX	03	XXXX	1005	A071
*D1	XX	03	XXXX	1007	A071
*D1	XX	29	XXXX	1009	A071
*F0	XX	73	XXXX	100B	A071
*F0	XX	79	XXXX	100C	A071
*F0	XX	79	XXXX	100E	A071
*F0	XX	79	7903	1010	A071

b) Register changes after each step

		H	I	N	Z	V	C
1	1	0	1	0	0	0	0
1	1	0	1	0	0	0	0
1	1	0	1	1	0	1	0
1	1	0	1	0	0	0	1
1	1	0	1	0	0	0	1
1	1	0	1	0	0	0	1
1	1	1	1	0	0	0	0
1	1	1	1	0	0	0	0
1	1	1	1	0	0	0	0
1	1	1	1	0	0	0	0

c) Condition codes

Figure 4-12 Program and results of execution for Example 4-22.

4-8.4 Subtracting BCD Numbers

BCD subtraction in the **6800** μP can be accomplished by complementation. *Subtraction by complementation* is a method of performing subtraction by addition and works well for decimal numbers. In subtraction by complementation, the subtrahend must be replaced by its 9s complement, which is obtained by taking each decimal digit and replacing it with the difference between itself and 9. The 9s complement of 2, for example, is 7, and the 9s complement of 0 is 9.

EXAMPLE 4-23

Find the 9s complement of the decimal number 399,704.

SOLUTION

The 9s complement is obtained by replacing each digit with its 9s complement as shown:

399,704 (original number)
600,295 (9s complement)

Note that each digit plus its 9s complement adds to 9.

Decimal subtraction can be performed by using the following procedure:

1. Take the 9s complement of the subtrahend and add it to the minuend.
2. Remove the most significant 1, and add it to the least significant digit. This is known as an **end-around-carry**.

EXAMPLE 4-24

Subtract 19,307 from 28,652.

SOLUTION

The 9s complement of 19,307 is 80,692. Adding this to the minuend, we obtain

(minuend)	28,652	(original number)
(subtrahend)	80,692	(9s complement)
	109,344	

Removing the most significant 1 and adding it to the least significant digit yields

109,344	
+ 1	(end-around-carry)
9,345	

This is the correct result.

In the **6800** the H bit is *not* set by subtraction instructions but BCD subtraction can be accomplished by complementing and adding, because addition sets the H bit (if digit total exceeds 9). The **6800** can be programmed for BCD subtraction as follows:

1. Load the **A** accumulator with 99.
2. Subtract the subtrahend (to obtain the 9s complement).
3. Add 1 (to make the 10s complement).
4. Add the minuend (BCD addition).
5. Decimal adjust the accumulator.

In this method, each digit can be subtracted from 9 without "borrows" and thus binary subtraction instructions can be used.

EXAMPLE 4-25

Subtract 35 from 82 using the method described above. Assume 82 is in $F0 and 35 is in $F2.

ADDR	OBJECT	MNEMONICS	COMMENTS
1000	86 99	LDAA #$99	MAKE 9s COMPLEMENT
1002	90 F2	SUBA $F2	GET SUBTRAHEND
1004	4C	INCA	MAKE 10s COMPLEMENT
1005	9B F0	ADDA $F0	ADD OTHER NUMBER
1007	19	DAA	DECIMAL ADJUST

a) Program listing

```
*M 00F0 82 lf
   00F2 35 cr
```

```
*T 0005
 CC   B    A    X     PC    SP
*XX   XX   XX   XXXX  1000  XXXX
*D8   XX   99   XXXX  1002  XXXX
*D2   XX   64   XXXX  1004  XXXX
*D0   XX   65   XXXX  1005  XXXX
*D8   XX   E7   XXXX  1007  XXXX
*D1   XX   47   XXXX  1008  XXXX
```

b) Register changes

```
        H I N Z V C
        X X X X X X
1 1 0 1 1 0 0 0
1 1 0 1 0 0 1 0
1 1 0 1 0 0 0 0
1 1 0 1 1 0 0 0
1 1 0 1 0 0 0 1
```

c) Condition codes

Figure 4-13 Program execution for Example 4-25.

SOLUTION

The program is shown in Fig. 4-13a and the status of the CCR is shown in Fig. 4-13c. The progress of the program is shown in Fig. 4-13b. The correct answer, 47, appears in A at the end of the program. Some adjustments are required in the program if multiple byte subtraction or the possibility of negative results is to be allowed.

4-9 SHIFT AND ROTATE INSTRUCTIONS

Microprocessors can perform a variety of SHIFT and ROTATE instructions. Minicomputers and mainframes have a minor advantage over 8-bit μCs because they can command a multiple shift in a single instruction. For example, it takes only one instruction in a mainframe to shift a register or accumulator 4 bits, whereas it would take four instructions in an 8-bit μP. This advantage does not exist for 16- or 32-bit μCs, however, since they also have multibit shifts (see Chapter 15).

4-9.1 The Shift Operation

The ALU used in the **6800** performs shift and rotate operations. The ASL (arithmetic shift left), ASR (arithmetic shift right), and LSR (logical shift right) instructions are shown in Fig. 4-14. The carry bit that is part of the CCR (see Section 4-6.2) is used in the shift operations.

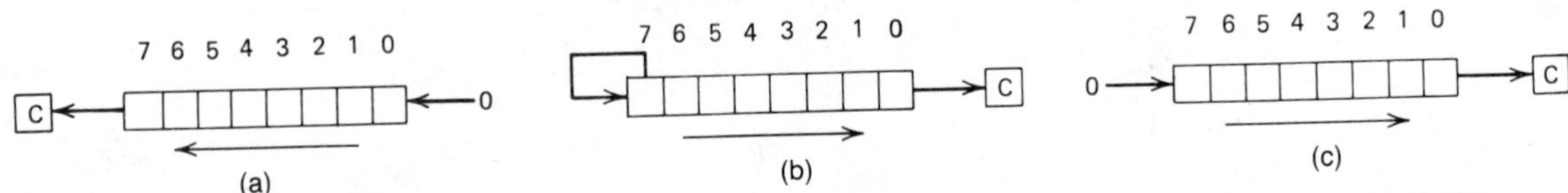

Figure 4-14 The **6800** shift instructions. (a) Arithmetic shift left (ASL). (b) Arithmetic shift right (ASR). (c) Logical shift right.

In the ASL operation, the MSB is shifted out of the data word and into the carry bit. The LSB is filled with a 0. The ASR operation shifts each bit to the right and moves the LSB into the carry bit. The MSB, however, is retained and also shifted into bit 6. If the bits in the register are considered as a 2s complement number, this method of shifting *preserves the sign of the number*. The ASR is equivalent to dividing the number in the register by 2, regardless of the sign of the number.

The LSR operation simply shifts each bit one position to the right. The MSB becomes a 0 and the LSB goes into the carry bit.

EXAMPLE 4-26

An 8-bit word contains the bit pattern 10011010 (hexadecimal 9A).

a. What are the contents of the word after two shifts to the right (ASR, ASR)?
b. What are its contents after three arithmetic shifts to the left (ASL, ASL, ASL)?
c. What are its contents after two logic shifts to the right (LSR, LSR)?

SOLUTION

a. Here every bit is moved two places to the right, except bit 7. Since the rightmost bits are shifted through the carry register, bit 0 is lost and bit 1 becomes the carry bit. After execution of these two instructions, the word is

11100110

Note that bits 7, 6, and 5 are 1s because bit 7 was originally 1.

b. The bits are shifted three positions to the left and the two most significant bits are lost. Since bit 5 was 0, the carry is now 0. The least significant bit positions are filled with 0s; the word is now

11010000

c. After two LSRs the word becomes

00100110

and the carry bit is a 1. Note that 0s are shifted into the MSBs in an LSR.

EXAMPLE 4-27

a. If the number in an accumulator is 50_{10}, show that an ASR is equivalent to a division by 2.
b. Repeat for -50_{10}.

SOLUTION

a. Since +50 = 00110010, an ASR causes the accumulator to become 00011001, or +25.
b. Since −50 = 11001110, an ASR causes the accumulator to become 11100111, or −25. Again, division by 2 has occurred. This would not have been so if a 0 had been shifted into bit 7, instead of a 1.

4-9.2 Rotations

Two additional shifting instructions are ROL (rotate left) and ROR (rotate right), shown in Fig. 4-15. These are special forms of circular shifting where the bits coming off one end of the word are inserted into the carry bit, while the contents of the carry bit are transferred into the vacated bit position.

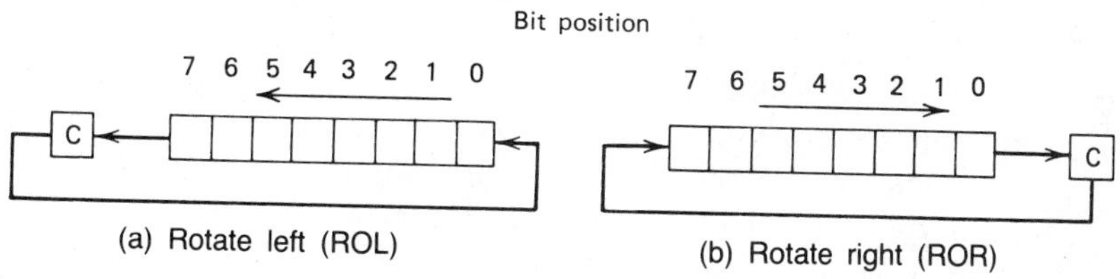

Figure 4-15 The **6800** rotate instructions.

EXAMPLE 4-28

If a computer word is 11011100, what is it after the following commands?

a. Rotate right three times (ROR, ROR, ROR). Assume the carry bit is CLEAR.
b. Rotate left twice (ROL, ROL). Assume the carry bit is SET.

SOLUTION

a. In response to three ROR instructions, the three LSBs are moved through the carry bit to the other end of the word. The word becomes

00011011

and the carry bit contains the 1 that was originally in bit 2.
b. In rotating left twice, the carry now contains the original bit 6 (1) and the 1 that was bit 7 is now the LSB of the word. The result is

01110011

The 1 that was originally in the carry bit has been shifted through bit 0 and appears in bit 1 of the result.

There are many uses for ROTATE instructions. One application is to determine the **parity** of a byte. If the bits of the byte are successively shifted into the carry bit, the number of 1s in the byte can be counted and its parity can be determined.

4-10 LOGIC INSTRUCTIONS

The **6800** contains AND, OR, and EXCLUSIVE OR instructions. They allow the programmer to perform Boolean algebra manipulations on a variable and to SET or CLEAR specific bits in a byte. They can also be used to test specific bits in a byte, but other logic instructions such as BIT, TEST, or COMPARE may be more useful for these tests.

Since logic operations are performed on a *bit-by-bit* basis, the C bit has no effect. It is unchanged by all logic operations. The V bit is cleared by logic operations. The N and Z bits are set in accordance with the result.

4-10.1 Setting and Clearing Specific Bits

AND and OR instructions can be used to SET or CLEAR a specific bit or bits in an accumulator or memory location. This is very useful in systems where each bit has a specific meaning, rather than being part of a number. In the control and status registers of the peripheral interface adapter (PIA) or the asynchronous interface adapter (ACIA) (see Chapter 8), for example, each bit has a distinct meaning.

EXAMPLE 4-29

Bit 3 of A must be SET, while all other bits remain unchanged. How can this be done?

SOLUTION

If A is ORed with 08, which contains 1 in bit position 3, bit 3 of the result will be SET and all other bits will remain as they were. The instruction ORA A #08 (8A 08) accomplishes this.

EXAMPLE 4-30

Bits 3, 5, and 6 of A are to be cleared while all other bits remain unchanged. How can this be done?

SOLUTION
If A is ANDed with 97, which contains 0s in positions, 3, 5, and 6, then these bits of the result are 0 and the rest are unchanged. The instruction 84 97 (AND A #$97) accomplishes this.

4-10.2 Testing Bits

In addition to being able to SET or CLEAR specific bits in a register, it is also possible to *test* specific bits to determine whether they are 1 or 0. In the PIA, for example, a 1 in the MSB of the control register indicates that some external event has occurred. The μP can test this bit and react appropriately. Typically, the result of the test sets the Z or N bit. The program then executes a conditional branch and takes one of two different paths depending on the result of the test.

Accumulator bits can be tested by the AND and OR instructions, but this modifies the contents of the accumulator. If the accumulator is to remain unchanged, the BIT TEST instruction is used. This ANDs memory (or an immediate operand) with the accumulator without changing either.

EXAMPLE 4-31

Determine whether bit 5 of accumulator B is a 1 or a 0, without changing B.

SOLUTION
The instruction BIT B #$20 (C5 20) is a BIT TEST immediate. It ANDs the contents of B with 20, since 20 only contains a 1 in the bit 5 position. The result is 00 if bit 5 of B is 0, and 20 if bit 5 of B is 1. The Z bit is CLEARed or SET accordingly and retains the result of this test.

4-10.3 Compare Instructions

A COMPARE instruction essentially subtracts a memory or immediate operand from an accumulator, leaving the *contents of both memory and accumulator unchanged*. The actual results of the subtraction are discarded; the function of the COMPARE is to SET the condition code bits.

There are two types of COMPARE instructions: those that involve accumulators and those that use the Index Register. Effectively, the two numbers that are being compared are subtracted, but neither value is changed. The subtraction serves to SET the condition codes. In the case of the COMPARE accumulator (CMP A or B) instruction, the carry, negative, zero, and overflow bits are affected and allow us to determine whether the operands are equal or which is greater. The **6800** COMPARE INDEX REGISTER (CPX) instruction sets the Z bit properly, but in the **6800** the N and V bits are often *set incorrectly* and the reader is warned *not* to depend on the N or V after a CPX instruction. This is not true for the **6801** μC, described later.

These instructions are often used to terminate loops (Section 4-7).

EXAMPLE 4-32

Determine whether the contents of location CB are equal to the number $F2.

SOLUTION
One program that does this is

```
C6  F2      LDA  B  #$F2     LOAD B IMMEDIATE
D1  CB      CMP  B  $CB      COMPARE B DIRECT
```

The first instruction loads $F2 into B. The second instruction compares the contents of B ($F2) with the contents of $CB. The Z bit is SET if they are equal, since the result of the subtraction is 0.

EXAMPLE 4-33

Determine whether the contents of $80C0 are greater than, equal to, or less than $2A.

SOLUTION
A program that does this is

```
86  2A      LDA  A  #$2A     LOAD A IMMEDIATE
B1  80C0    CMP  A  $80C0    COMPARE A EXTENDED
```

Three possibilities exist:

1. $2A is greater than the contents of $80C0. In this case, N = Z = 0 after the compare, indicating that the result is not 0 and not negative.
2. The contents of $80C0 equal $2A. In this case, the Z bit is SET.
3. The contents of $80C0 are greater than $2A. Here the subtraction gives a negative result and N is set.

4-10.4 The TEST Instruction

The TEST (TST) instruction subtracts 0 from an operand and therefore does not alter the operand. Its effect, like that of compares or bit tests, is to set the N and Z bits. It differs in that it always CLEARS the overflow and carry bits. It is used to set the condition codes in accordance with the contents of an accumulator or memory location.

EXAMPLE 4-34

Determine whether the contents of location $F0 are positive, zero, or negative.

SOLUTION
This problem is solved by using the TEST instruction. Since $F0 is below $FF it is generally addressed in direct mode, but this mode is not available with the test instruction (see Table 4-2). We can, however, use extended addressing. The instruction

```
TST   $F0          7D   00F0
```

sets the N and Z bits and allows us to determine the sign of the number in $F0.

4-11 OTHER 6800 INSTRUCTIONS

The remaining **6800** instructions listed in Table 4-2 are well described by their name and mnemonics.

4-11.1 CLEAR, INCREMENT, and DECREMENT Instructions

These allow the user to alter the contents of an accumulator or memory location as specified. The instructions referring to memory locations can be executed in extended or indexed modes only. They are simple to write, but they require six or seven cycles for execution because the contents of a memory location must be brought to the CPU, modified, and rewritten to memory.

4-11.2 Accumulator Transfer Instructions

The TAB and TBA instructions allow the transfer of data from A to B and B to A, respectively. These instructions help the user to make use of both accumulators, which simplifies the programming of the **6800**.

4-11.3 COMPLEMENT and NEGATE Instructions

The COMPLEMENT instructions invert all bits of a memory location. They are useful as logic instructions and in programs requiring complementation, such as the BCD subtraction program.

The NEGATE instruction takes the 2s complement of a number and therefore negates it. The negate instruction works by subtracting the operand from 00. Since the absolute value of the operand is always greater than the minuend, except when the operand itself is 00, the negate instruction SETs the carry flag for all cases, except when the operand is 00.

EXAMPLE 4-35

There is a 16-bit number in $F0 (MS byte) and $F1. Write a program to negate the 16-bit number.

SOLUTION

The general method of negating a number is to complement all the bits and add 1. Alternatively, it can be subtracted from zero as the NEGATE instruction does. The simple solution to this problem, negating both \$F0 and \$F1, fails because it effectively adds 1 to both bytes (i.e., if \$F0 and \$F1 contain \$C1D2 and both are negated, the result is \$3F2E, which is *not* −\$C1D2). Negating the LS byte and complementing the MS byte works in all cases *except* the case where the LS byte is 00.

A program that works for all cases is

```
CLR    A
NEG    $F1
SBC    A $F0
STA    A $F0
```

The NEGATE instruction produces a carry for all cases except the case where \$F1 contains 00. Now the SBC subtracts out the carry, complementing the MS byte. If \$F1 contains 00, there is no carry and the SBC instruction negates the MS byte as required (see Problem 4-26).

4-12 SUMMARY

In this chapter the accumulator and memory instructions available in the **6800** μP were introduced. Five modes of addressing were discussed and examples using each mode were given.

The function of each bit of the CCR was explained and the way in which instructions CLEAR and SET these bits was discussed. The addition and subtraction instructions were introduced, and examples of multibyte arithmetic using the carry bit were presented. The effect of the carry bit in Shift and Rotate instructions was described. Finally, logical instructions and miscellaneous instructions, such as transfers, compares, increments, and decrements, were discussed to complete this introduction to **6800** programming.

4-13 GLOSSARY

Binary Coded Decimal (BCD) Use of 4 binary bits to represent a single decimal digit (a number from 0 to 9).

Clock cycles The number of transitions of the square-wave clock signal used to synchronize the operation of the μP.

Code conversion Process of changing the coding of data from one system to another; for example, to change the alphanumeric characters from the ASCII code to IBM's EBCDIC code.

Compare instruction Instruction used to determine whether two operands are the same or whether one is larger. Instructions are provided for either 8 or 16 operations.

Condition Code Register (CCR) Register that contains the ALU status bits or condition codes as set by the last executed instruction. They indicate whether the result was zero, negative, and so forth. In the **6800** the CCR contains six flags (H, I, N, Z, V, C) and two unused bits (always 1).

Condition codes Status or flag bits in the condition code register that are SET or RESET by the ALU as each instruction is executed.

Decimal Adjust Accumulator (DAA) Instruction that adjusts a binary addition to make the results appear as BCD.

End-around-carry Process of adding the most significant 1 to the least significant digit during subtraction by complementation.

Extended instruction Instruction that includes a full 16-bit address as well as the Op code. A 3-byte instruction.

Flags Bits within a μp that retain information about the results of previous operations. Condition codes are also called flags.

Immediate operand Operand that is used directly by the program.

Increment Add one to a number.

Indexed instruction Instruction that uses the contents of the index register plus an offset to calculate the address of the operand.

Index register A 16-bit register in the μP. During indexed instructions an offset (sometimes zero) is added to the specified instruction address to obtain the memory address actually used.

Mnemonic Abbreviated form of a word used as an instruction and designed to be easy to remember.

Overflow Result that is too large to be contained in a single word or byte.

Parity Error checking technique where the number of 1s in a byte are counted. Depending on whether Odd or Even parity is to be used the MSB is made a 1 or a 0.

Program counter (PC) Sixteen-bit register in the μP used to hold the address of the next instruction to be executed.

Stack pointer (SP) Sixteen-bit register in the μP used to hold the address pointer to the next available location in the stack area of memory.

Subtraction instruction Instruction to subtract the contents of one location from another.

Underflow Result that is too negative to be contained in a single word or byte.

4-14 REFERENCES

Greenfield, Joseph. *Practical Digital Design Using ICs,* Second Edition, Wiley, New York, 1983.

Levanthal, Lance. *6800 Assembly Language Programming,* Adam Osborn & Associates, Berkley, CA, 1978.

Motorola. *M68PRM/D 6800 Programming Reference Manual,* Phoenix, AZ, First Edition, 1976, currently 1984 reprint.

Motorola. *M6800 Microcomputer System Design Data,* Phoenix, AZ, 1976.

Southern, Bob. *Programming the 6800 Microprocessor,* Motorola, Phoenix, AZ, 1977.

4-15 PROBLEMS

4-1 Why doesn't the instruction set include a STORE IMMEDIATE instruction?

4-2 If A contains $45 initially, what will it contain after the following instructions?

a. 8A 77	ORA A #$77		f. 4F	CLR A
b. 80 23	SUB A #$23		g. 43	COM A
c. 84 77	AND A #$77		h. 4A	DEC A
d. 8B 77	ADD A #$77		i. 40	NEG A
e. 88 77	EOR A #$77			

4-3 Assume each location in memory between $40 and $4F contains 3 more than its own address ($40 contains $43, $41 contains $44, etc.). If A contains $21 and the index register contains $20, what does A contain after executing each of the following instructions?

a. 88	42	EOR A #$42
b. 9B	42	ADD A $42
c. AB	23	ADD A $23,X

4-4 How many cycles and bytes do *subtract* instructions take in the

a. Immediate mode?
b. Direct mode?
c. Indexed mode?
d. Extended mode?
e. Implied mode?

4-5 Show that the instruction 88 FF is equivalent to the instruction 43.

4-6 Show how the program of Example 4-8 operates if the angle is

a. 44°
b. 144°
c. 244°
d. 344°

What memory locations are accessed and what do they contain?

4-7 Write a program to add the 32-bit number in $F3–$F0 to the 24-bit number in $F6–$F4. Place the results in $FF–$FC.

4-8 If the two numbers in Problem 4-7 are

F35C2472 and CC8142

show the results in the accumulator and the state of the H, V, Z, N, and C bits after each step in your program.

4-9 Show that 20 00 is an NOP.

4-10 The instruction in locations $012D and $012E is BRA XX. Where will the program branch to if XX equals

a. F2?
b. E5?
c. 26?
d. 05?

4-11 The Op code of a BRANCH instruction is located in \$0110. What offset is needed for the following destinations?

a. C0
b. D5
c. 0153

4-12 Write a program to add the decimal numbers

4972 and 3729

Use BCD arithmetic. Show the status of the accumulator and H, V, N, Z, and C after each instruction.

4-13 Write a program to subtract 016359 from 242214. Use BCD arithmetic. Show the status of the accumulator and H, V, N, Z, and C after each instruction.

4-14 Write a program to SET bits 2, 4, 6, and 7, leaving all other bits unchanged.

4-15 A 16-bit computer contains the following word in its accumulator:

1011100111000111

What will the accumulator contain after the following instructions?

a. Shift left 2 bits.
b. Shift right 4 bits.
c. Rotate left 5 bits.
d. Rotate right 3 bits.

4-16 Write a program to add \$50 and \$75 and then subtract \$25. Select memory areas for your data and instructions. Describe the progression of your program and list the contents of each pertinent memory location before and after its execution.

4-17 Write a program to add \$25, \$35, \$45, and \$55 and then shift the results 2 bits to the right. Explain the significance of your answer.

4-18 Write a program to CLEAR bits 2, 4, 6, and 7, leaving all other bits unchanged.

4-19 Compare the bytes in \$F0 and \$F1 to determine whether they are equal.

a. Use the COMPARE instruction.
b. Use the EXCLUSIVE OR (XOR) instruction.

4-20 Test the contents of \$F3 to determine whether bit 4 is a 1.

a. Use an AND instruction.
b. Use a BIT Test instruction.

How do the condition codes indicate whether the bit is a 1 or a 0?

4-21 a. What does each instruction of the following program do?

```
96 40     C9 00     97 42
D6 41     8B 05     98 43
48        C9 00
```

b. If the numbers in \$40 and \$41 initially are \$7E and \$23, what numbers appear in \$42 and \$43 at the end of the program?

4-22 Suppose Y is an integer ($0 < Y < 10$) in the A accumulator and we must calculate $20Y^3 - 10Y^2 + 5$. This is to be done by table lookup, rather than making the μP do the calculations. Construct the table and a program to write the correct result into location $D0 and $D1.

4-23 When two numbers are added the result is positive when the N bit and V bit are both CLEAR or both SET. Explain. Give an example of each case using numbers.

4-24 Explain why the N and V bits are SET in Fig. 4-7.

4-25 A 16-bit number is in location $F0 (MS byte) and $F1. Write a program to shift it 2 bits to the left. Bring 0s into the vacated positions. Ignore the two MSBs.

4-26 Consider the three programs:

```
NEG $F1        NEG $F1        CLR A
NEG $F0        COM $F0        NEG $F1
                              SBC A $F0
                              STA A $F0
```

What is the result of each program if $F0 and $F1 contain

a. 1357?
b. 1300?

In which cases do each of these programs correctly negate the number?

After attempting to solve these problems, try to answer the self-evaluation questions in Section 4-2. If any of them still seem difficult, review the appropriate sections of the chapter to find the answers.

CHAPTER 5
STACKS, SUBROUTINES, AND OTHER INSTRUCTIONS

5-1 INSTRUCTIONAL OBJECTIVES

This chapter continues the presentation of the **6800** instruction set by introducing the STACK, and the BRANCH and JUMP instructions that allow the use of subroutines. After reading this chapter, the student should be able to

1. Use any BRANCH or JUMP instructions in a program.
2. Compare numbers in signed or absolute form and branch accordingly.
3. Use instructions involving stacks, such as PUSH, PULL, and JUMP TO SUBROUTINE.
4. Use indirect jumps.
5. Write programs using subroutines and preserve the contents of the main program's registers during subroutine execution.
6. Write multiply and divide routines.

5-2 SELF-EVALUATION QUESTIONS

Watch for the answers to the following questions as you read the chapter. They should help you to understand the material presented.

1. Explain why branch instructions are said to be in the *relative* mode. What are they relative to?
2. What is the difference between a jump and a branch?
3. Why must a JUMP instruction be used when the object of the jump is more than +129 or −126 locations away?
4. What is the difference between a BRANCH GREATER THAN OR EQUAL instruction and a BRANCH IF PLUS instruction?

5. What is the function of the stack pointer (SP) register? Why must it be initialized if it is going to be used?
6. Explain why instructions that write to the stack (i.e., PUSH), decrement the SP, while instructions that read from the stack (i.e., PULL), increment the SP.
7. In a jump or branch to subroutine, how and why are the program counter (PC) contents preserved?

5-3 BRANCH AND JUMP INSTRUCTIONS

Some of the basic **6800** BRANCH instructions were introduced in Section 4-7. Table 5-1 shows *all* the BRANCH and JUMP instructions available in the **6800** μP. They complete the **6800** instruction set and allow programs requiring *decisions, branches, and subroutines* to be written.

Table 5-1 also contains several other instructions that will be discussed later. RTS is discussed in Section 5-5.2; RTI, SWI, and WAI are discussed in Chapter 9.

5-3.1 Jump Instructions

One of the simplest instructions in Table 5-1 is the **JUMP** instruction. It loads the

TABLE 5-1 Jump and Branch Instructions

		RELATIVE			INDEX			EXTND			IMPLIED				COND. CODE REG. 5	4	3	2	1	0
OPERATIONS	MNEMONIC	OP	~	#	OP	~	#	OP	~	#	OP	~	#	BRANCH TEST	H	I	N	Z	V	C
Branch Always	BRA	20	4	2										None	•	•	•	•	•	•
Branch If Carry Clear	BCC	24	4	2										C = 0	•	•	•	•	•	•
Branch If Carry Set	BCS	25	4	2										C = 1	•	•	•	•	•	•
Branch If = Zero	BEQ	27	4	2										Z = 1	•	•	•	•	•	•
Branch If ≥ Zero	BGE	2C	4	2										N ⊕ V = 0	•	•	•	•	•	•
Branch If > Zero	BGT	2E	4	2										Z + (N ⊕ V) = 0	•	•	•	•	•	•
Branch If Higher	BHI	22	4	2										C + Z = 0	•	•	•	•	•	•
Branch If ≤ Zero	BLE	2F	4	2										Z + (N ⊕ V) = 1	•	•	•	•	•	•
Branch If Lower Or Same	BLS	23	4	2										C + Z = 1	•	•	•	•	•	•
Branch If < Zero	BLT	2D	4	2										N ⊕ V = 1	•	•	•	•	•	•
Branch If Minus	BMI	2B	4	2										N = 1	•	•	•	•	•	•
Branch If Not Equal Zero	BNE	26	4	2										Z = 0	•	•	•	•	•	•
Branch If Overflow Clear	BVC	28	4	2										V = 0	•	•	•	•	•	•
Branch If Overflow Set	BVS	29	4	2										V = 1	•	•	•	•	•	•
Branch If Plus	BPL	2A	4	2										N = 0	•	•	•	•	•	•
Branch To Subroutine	BSR	8D	8	2										See Special Operations	•	•	•	•	•	•
Jump	JMP				6E	4	2	7E	3	3				See Special Operations	•	•	•	•	•	•
Jump To Subroutine	JSR				AD	8	2	BD	9	3				See Special Operations	•	•	•	•	•	•
No Operation	NOP										01	2	1	Advances Prog. Cntr. Only	•	•	•	•	•	•
Return From Interrupt	RTI										3B	10	1		①	①	①	①	①	①
Return From Subroutine	RTS										39	5	1	See Special Operations	•	•	•	•	•	•
Software Interrupt	SWI										3F	12	1	See Special Operations	•	•	•	•	•	•
Wait for Interrupt*	WAI										3E	9	1	See Special Operations	•	②	•	•	•	•

*WAI puts Address Bus, R/W, and Data Bus in the three-state mode while VMA is held low.

① (All) Load Condition Code Register from Stack. (See Special Operations)

② (Bit 1) Set when interrupt occurs. If previously set, a Non-Maskable Interrupt is required to exit the wait state.

PC with a new address that causes the program to fetch the next instruction from a location that is not in sequence.

The JUMP instruction can be specified in one of two modes, indexed or extended. The JUMP INDEXED (JMP 0,X) is a 2-byte instruction; the second byte or *offset* is added to the Index Register and the sum is loaded into the PC.

EXAMPLE 5-1

What does the following program accomplish?

```
LDX   #$5234      CE   5234
JMP   $2D,X       6E   2D
```

SOLUTION

The functioning of the two modes of the jump instruction is shown in Fig. 5-1. Figure 5-1a shows the indexed mode. In this example the first instruction, LDX #$5234, is an immediate load and loads $5234 into the Index Register (X). The second instruction is an indexed jump. It adds the second byte, $2D, to the contents of X and loads the sum, $5261, into the PC. Thus the next Op code to be executed is in location $5261. If the offset byte had been zero (0,X), the destination of the jump would have been the same as the address in the index register.

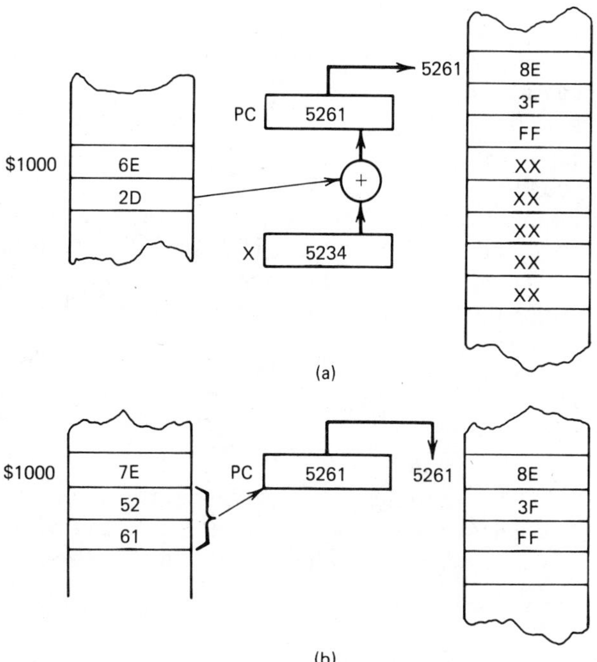

Figure 5-1 The two modes of the JMP instructions. (a) Indexed mode. (b) Extended mode.

Extended jumps are 3-byte instructions, where the last 2 bytes are a 16-bit address. Their action is shown in Fig. 5-1b. Since a 16-bit address is available, they allow the program to jump to any location in memory. They are very easily understood because they require no calculations.

5-3.2 Indirect Jumps

Many programmers make use of **indirect jumps**, where the program must jump to an address that is stored in a memory location, rather than to the memory location itself.

EXAMPLE 5-2

Assume the address to which we wish to jump is contained in locations 40 and 41. How can an indirect jump be performed in the **6800** μP?

SOLUTION
First the 2 bytes are placed in the X register with an LDX direct instruction (LDX $40). Then the JMP 0,X indexed instruction is used, which transfers X to the PC, effectively completing the indirect jump while using only 4 bytes.

5-3.3 Branch Instructions

BRANCH instructions have been explained in Sectioons 3-11 and 4-7. Both BRANCH and JUMP instructions cause the program to start executing instructions at the branch or jump address, rather than continuing to the next sequential location. (As explained in Sections 3-11 and 4-7 conditional branches are taken only when the condition is true.)

In the **6800**, although conditional branch instructions can *branch* only within the range of a 1-byte 2s complement offset (+129 or −126 from the location of the branch instruction), a combination of branch and jump instructions can be used to effectively conditionally branch anywhere in the 64K map. For example, consider the following two program segments:

```
1. 26   XX    BNE   START         2. 27   03     BEQ   *+5
   ..   ..    ...   .....            7E   XXXX   JMP   START
                                     ..   ..     ...   .....
```

The programs will both go to the next instruction in sequence when the condition is true (Z = 1). When Z = 0, they will go to the location of START, which, in the first program, must be within branching range. In the second program, START can be anywhere in memory.

Branches are often preferred because they use only 2 bytes and can be used in **relocatable programs**, where the entire program can be moved to a different area of memory without changing the BRANCH instructions. In addition, assemblers calculate branch values (see Section 6-7) and relieve the programmer of the task.

5-3.4 Other Conditional Branch Instructions

The unconditional branch instruction BRA and the conditional branch instructions that depend on the C, V, N, and Z bits were discussed in Section 4-7. When writing programs, it often happens that two numbers are compared and a branch must be taken, depending on which number is greater. The term *greater* may also depend on whether we are using *unsigned numbers* (all numbers considered positive) or *signed* (2s complement) *numbers*. Table 5-1 shows that the **6800** has six additional BRANCH instructions (not shown in Table 4-5) that can be executed after a COMPARE instruction to compare numbers in signed or absolute form and to branch accordingly. They are

1. **Branch if Greater than or Equal to zero (BGE)**. We have already seen that it is possible to add two positive numbers and get a negative result if overflow occurs (Section 4-6.4). The BGE instruction takes the branch if the result of the last operation was positive or 0, *even if the N bit is 1*. It is often used after subtraction or compare instructions and branches only if the minuend is greater than or equal to the subtrahend. The logic equation is $N \oplus V = 0$.
2. **Branch if Greater Than zero (BGT)**. This instruction is very much like BGE. It branches only if the result of the last operation was positive and not equal to 0. The logic equation is $Z + N \oplus V = 0$.
3. **Branch if HIgher (BHI)**. This instruction is meant to be executed after a compare or subtract instruction (CBA, CMP, SBA, or SUB). It branches if the minuend, considered as an unsigned binary number, is greater than the subtrahend. The logic equation is $C + Z = 0$, so the instruction will not branch if C is 1 (indicating that the result of the subtraction is negative; see Section 4-6.2) or if Z is 1 (indicating that the minuend and subtrahend are equal and the result of the subtraction is 0).
4. **Branch if Less Than or Equal to zero (BLE)**. This instruction branches if the result of the last operation is less than or equal to 0. It allows for the possibility that $N = 0$ due to overflow.
5. **Branch if Less Than zero (BLT)**. Similar to the BLE, but no branch is taken if the last result is 0.
6. **Branch if Lower or the Same (BLS)**. This instruction complements the BHI. It is also meant to be executed after a compare or subtract instruction and causes a branch if the subtrahend is greater than or equal to the minuend. Since the logic equation is $C + Z = 1$, the branch is taken if the result of the subtraction is negative ($C = 1$) or 0 ($Z = 1$).

The BGE, BGT, BLE, and BLT instructions treat the numbers as *signed numbers*, but BHI and BLS are for *absolute numbers*.

EXAMPLE 5-3

Assume that A accumulator contains 60 and B contains 90.

a. Which number is higher?

b. With which of the following programs will it branch?

1. CBA	**2.** CBA	**3.** CBA
BHI	BGT	BPL

SOLUTION

a. Considered as unsigned numbers B > A; but if signed numbers are being used, the 60 is positive and 90 is negative, therefore A > B.

b. CBA is the mnemonic for COMPARE accumulators. The result of the compare is 60 − 90 = D0, with the C, N, and V bits all SET. The contents of the A and B accumulators remain 60 and 90, however, because they are not affected by a COMPARE instruction.

Program 1 will not branch because 90 is higher (in absolute value) than 60, and the subtraction SETs the C bit so that $C + Z = 1$.

Program 2 will branch because the BGT considers signed numbers and A > B. Note that the logic equation $Z + N \oplus V = 0$ is satisified because $Z = 0$ and both N and $V = 1$.

Program 3 will not branch because the result SETs the N bit and the **6800** considers the result as negative.

The results of this program show that the BHI instruction should be used when comparing *absolute* numbers but, when comparing 2s complement signed numbers, the BGE or BGT instructions are correct.

EXAMPLE 5-4

If the following program is executed, what numbers must be in the B accumulator for the program to branch?

```
LDA A  #$FD
CBA
BHI
```

SOLUTION

The first instruction loads \$FD into A and the second instruction compares the accumulators. Unless B contains \$FF, \$FE, or \$FD, the minuend is higher than the subtrahend and the program will branch.

5-4 STACKS

In **6800** μPs and many larger computers, memory is divided into three distinct areas: the program and data areas that we have already considered, and the stack. *The* **stack** *is an area of memory used for the temporary storage of important information or data that is changed frequently*. Subroutines (see Section 5-5) and interrupts (see Chapter 9) make use of the stack. Since it must be written to as well as read, the stack must be in RAM.

5-4.1 The Stack Pointer

The system designer must determine the area of memory allocated to the stack during initialization. The **stack pointer** (SP) is a register within the μP that contains the *address of the next location available for the stack.* The **6800** internal logic causes the SP to decrement automatically when data or return addresses are stored in the stack and to increment when they are removed. Therefore, the SP must initially be set to the highest address in the stack area. This location is often called the *top of the stack* and is pointed to when nothing is stored in the stack. The following instructions pertain to the stack pointer:

Mnemonic	*Description*
DES	Decrement stack pointer.
INS	Increment stack pointer.
LDS	Load stack pointer. (This instruction can be executed in the immediate, direct, indexed, or extended mode.)
STS	Store stack pointer. (This instruction can be executed in the direct, indexed, or extended mode.)
TXS	Transfer the contents of the index register (minus 1) to the stack pointer register.
TSX	Transfer the contents of the stack pointer register (plus 1) to the index register. (See Table B-2 in Appendix B.)

EXAMPLE 5-5

The stack is to occupy locations $0200 to $02FF. What instructions are required at the beginning of the program to initialize the SP?

SOLUTION
The SP points to the highest vacant location in the stack. At the beginning of the program the entire stack is empty so the SP must point to $02FF. The single instruction,

```
LDS   #$2FF          (8E   02FF)
```

is a LOAD IMMEDIATE that loads $02FF into the SP register. This instruction is said to *initialize* the stack so that it starts at $02FF. Whenever the stack is used the SP is decremented. The stack must not be allowed to become so large that it invades memory area set aside for programs or data, or it will overwrite them. One common programming mistake is to do something that causes the stack pointer to decrement and to fail to increment it later. This can cause the stack to overflow and destroy the program.

5-4.2 Push and Pull

Two memory instructions that were not discussed in Chapter 4 because they involve the stack are **PUSH** and **PULL**.[1] These are implied instructions that refer to the A and B accumulators.

A PSH A (or B) takes the contents of the specified accumulator and *writes* it in the stack at the SP location. It then *decrements* the SP because the original stack location is no longer vacant; it contains the *pushed byte*.

EXAMPLE 5-6

If A contains CB, what do the following instructions accomplish?

```
LDS   #$2FF
PSH   A
```

SOLUTION
The first instruction loads $02FF into the SP, as in Example 5-5. The second instruction pushes A onto the stack. After execution, location $02FF contains $CB and the SP contains $02FE, which points to the highest vacant location in the stack.

A PULL instruction first *increments* the SP, then *transfers* the contents of the stack at the new address of the SP to the accumulator. Note that once the contents of a stack location have been pulled, the location is considered vacant although the byte is still there. It will be overwritten by the next PUSH or other usage of the stack.

EXAMPLE 5-7

If the SP contains $200, location $200 contains $CB, and $201 contains $CC, what happens in response to a PUL B instruction?

SOLUTION
The SP is incremented to $201 and the stack is read. At the end of the instruction, B contains $CC and the SP contains $201. Now $200 and $201 are both considered to be vacant.

Note that the stack acts as a LAST-IN-FIRST-OUT (LIFO) register. *A PULL retrieves the information that was last PUSHed onto the stack.*

[1]The word POP is often used instead of PULL by other manufacturers.

5-5 SUBROUTINES

When the same function is required more than once in a program, it is frequently written as a **subroutine,** that is, a subprogram that can be used any number of times by the main program. This capability is provided by three of the instructions listed in Table 5-1 (JSR, BSR, and RTS). Subroutines to do multiplications, 16-bit adds, and square roots are typical. In Section 4-5.4 a program to obtain the sine of an angle was given. If the sine had to be calculated more than once during the execution of the main program, the sine program would surely be a subroutine.

Figure 5-2 illustrates the use of the same subroutine by two different parts of the main program. The subroutine located at $200 can be entered from either location $0011 or $00CC by placing a JUMP TO SUBROUTINE (JSR) (Op codes of $AD, $BD, or $8D, depending on the mode) in these addresses. The PC actions, as a result of the subroutine jump at $0011, are identified by the *a* in Fig. 5-2, and *b* identifies jumps from $00CC.

After the subroutine is complete, the program resumes from the instruction following the location where it called the subroutine (see Section 5-5.2). Because the subroutine must return to one of *several* locations, depending on which one caused it to be entered, the *original contents of the PC must be preserved* so the subroutine knows where to return.

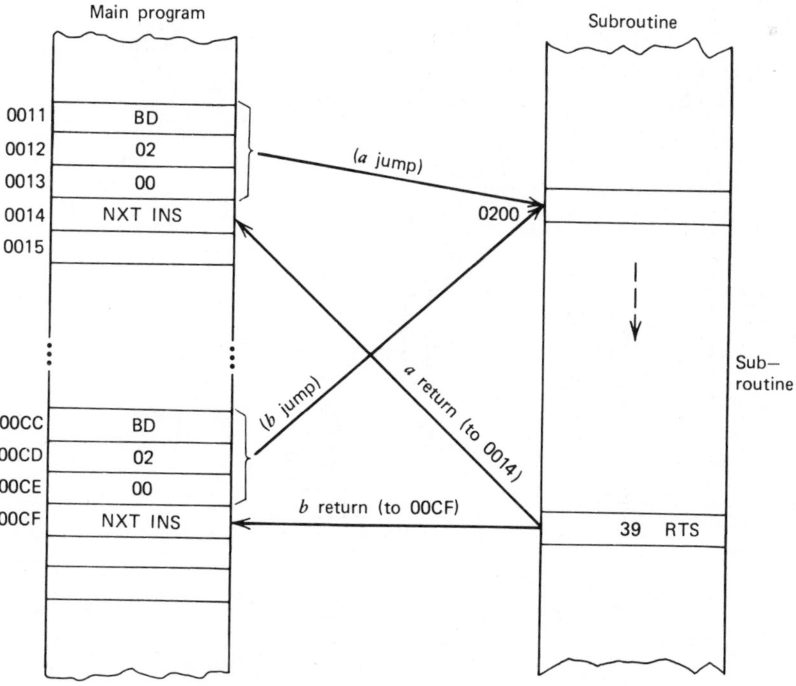

Figure 5-2 Use of a subroutine.

5-5.1 Jumps to Subroutines

The JUMP TO SUBROUTINE (JSR) instruction remembers the 16-bit address of the next main instruction by *writing it to the stack* before it takes the jump. The JSR can be executed in the indexed or extended mode. There is a BRANCH TO SUBROUTINE (BSR) instruction that can be used if the starting address of the subroutine is within +129 to −126 locations of the program counter. The advantage of the BSR is that it uses an 8-bit offset and therefore needs one less byte in the main program.

The actions of the subroutine instructions are illustrated in Fig. 5-3. In each case they store the address of the next instruction on the stack before taking the jump.

EXAMPLE 5-8

If the SP and X registers both contain $0200, what happens when the instruction

JSR $20,X

in location $30 is executed?

SOLUTION

This is the indexed mode of the instruction JSR. Since the Op code for the JSR ($AD) occupies location $30, and $20 (the offset) occupies location $31, the address of the next instruction, $0032, is written to the stack. Location $0200 then contains $32 and location $01FF contains 00. The SP has been decremented twice and contains $01FE. The program then jumps to $0220 (the sum of the contents of X and the offset), which should be the starting location of the subroutine.

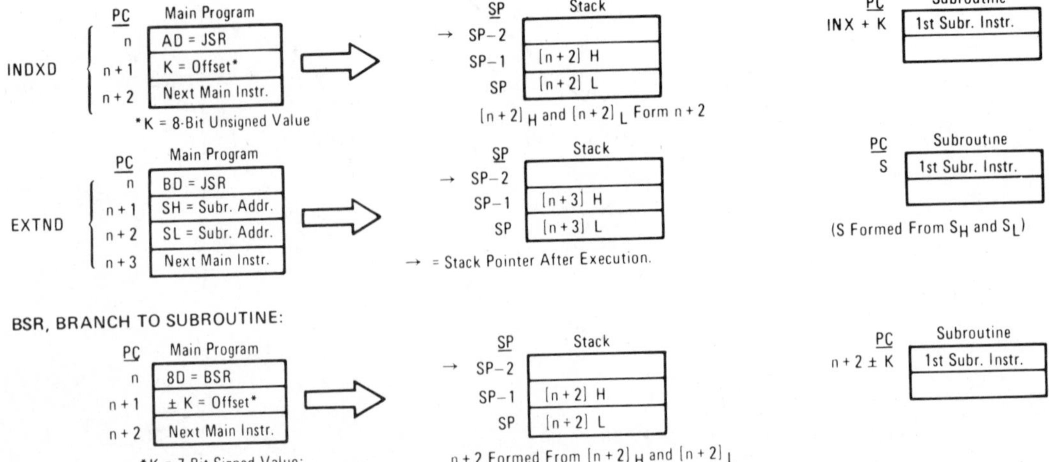

Figure 5-3 Jumps and branches to subroutine in the **6800** μp.

5-5.2 Return from Subroutine

The JSR and BSR instructions preserve the contents of the PC on the stack, but a *RETURN FROM SUBROUTINE* (RTS) instruction is required to properly return. The RTS is the last instruction executed in a subroutine. Its action is shown in Fig. 5-4. It places the contents of the stack in the PC and causes the SP to be incremented twice. Because these bytes contain the address of the next main instruction in the program (put there by the JSR or BSR that initiated the subroutine), the program resumes at the place where it left off before it entered the subroutine.

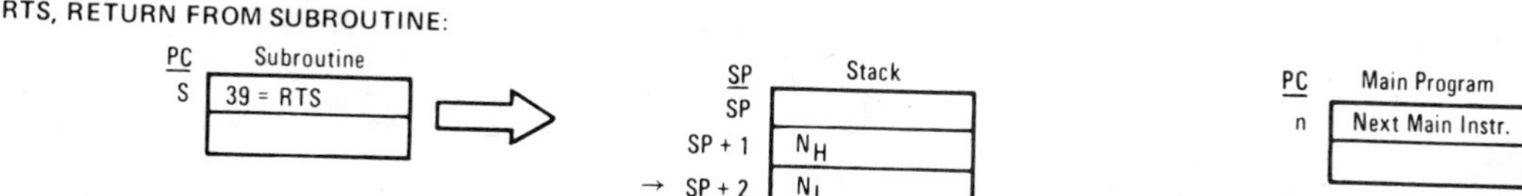

FIGURE 5-4 Action of the return-from-subroutine (RTS) instruction.

5-5.3 Nested Subroutines

In some sophisticated programs the main program may call a subroutine, which then calls a second subroutine. The second subroutine is called a **nested subroutine** because it is used by and returns to the first subroutine.

The situation is shown graphically in Fig. 5-5. The main program does a JSR (JUMP TO SUBROUTINE) extended at address $40. This puts $0043 on the stack. The first subroutine does a JSR at $01C3, placing $01C6 on the stack and jumping to the second subroutine. When the second subroutine is complete, an RTS returns it to $01C6 and increments the SP twice. Now the first subroutine picks up where it left off. When the first subroutine finishes, it ends with an RTS that causes a return to the main program. By making use of the stack as shown, there can be any number of nested subroutines, limited only by the stack size.

5-5.4 Use of Registers during Subroutines

During the execution of a subroutine, the subroutine will use the accumulators; it may use X and it changes the contents of the CCR. When the main program is reentered, however, the contents of these registers must often be as they were before the jump to the subroutine.

The most commonly used method for preserving register contents during the execution of a subroutine is to write the subroutine so that it PUSHes those registers it must *preserve* onto the stack at the beginning of the subroutine and then PULLs them off at the end of the subroutine, thus *restoring their contents* before returning to the main program.

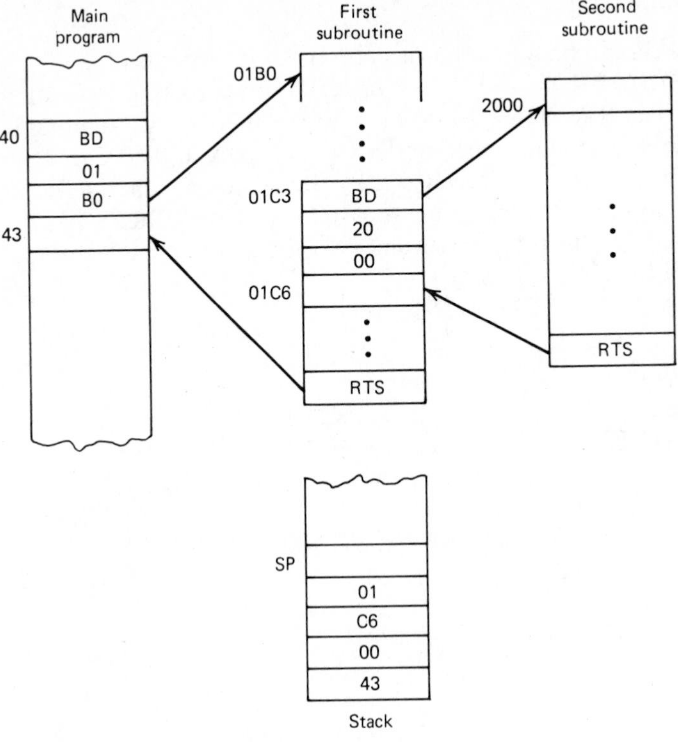

FIGURE 5-5 Nested subroutines.

EXAMPLE 5-9

A subroutine uses the A and B accumulators and the CCR. How can the main program contents of these registers be preserved?

SOLUTION
To preserve the contents of these registers for the main program, the first four instructions of the subroutine should be

Op Code	*Mnemonic*
36	**PSH A**
37	**PSH B**
07	**TPA**
36	**PSH A**

This puts the contents of A, B, and the CCR on the stack as shown in Fig. 5-6.
To restore these registers before returning to the main program, instructions

that are converse to those at the beginning must be executed in *reverse* order. The last five instructions of the subroutine must be

Op Code	*Mnemonic*
32	**PUL A**
06	**TAP**
33	**PUL B**
32	**PUL A**
39	**RTS**

Note that the A register had to be preserved. It is also used by the TPA and TAP instructions. Thus its contents are overwritten and will be lost unless it is first pushed onto the stack.

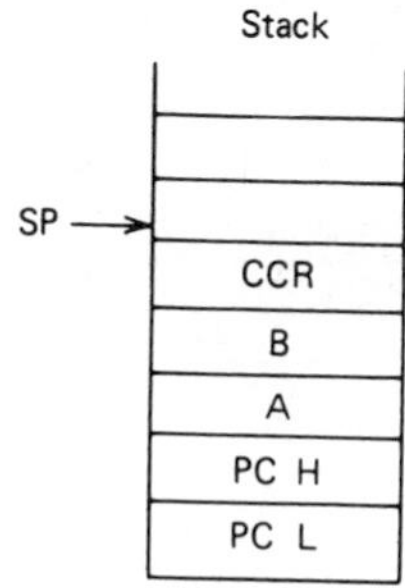

Figure 5-6 Contents of the stack after entering the subroutine of Example 5-9 and executing the first four instructions.

5-6 MULTIPLICATION

In a μC, multiplication and division are performed far less often than addition, subtraction, and logical operations. There are no multiply and divide instructions in the **6800** μP, and therefore these operations must be done using software subroutines. In this section a subroutine for multiplying 2 bytes is developed.

5-6.1 The Multiplication Algorithm

Multiplication starts with a multiplier, multiplicand, and product register. The product register, which is initially 0 and eventually contains the product, must be as long as the number of bits in the multiplier and multiplicand added together. In computers, the multiplier and multiplicand are typically one n-bit word each, and two n-bit words must be reserved for the product.

Multiplication can be performed in accordance with the following algorithm:

1. Examine the least significant bit of the multiplier. If it is 0, shift the product register 1 bit to the right. If it is 1, add the multiplicand to the MSB of the product register and then shift.
2. Repeat step 1 for each bit of the multiplier.

At the conclusion the product should be in the product register.

It is common to shift the multiplicand 1 bit left for each multiplier bit and then add it to the product register. This is analogous to multiplication as taught in grade school. The algorithm presented here, however, holds the position of the multiplicand constant by shifts the product register right. This algorithm is more easily implemented in a μP.

EXAMPLE 5-10

Multiply 22 × 26 using the above algorithm.

Note: All numbers are decimal.

SOLUTION

The solution is shown in Fig. 5-7. The multiplier bits are listed in a column with the least significant bit (LSB) on top. The multiplication proceeds in accordance with these bits as the leftmost column shows.

Consider line 5 as an example. Since the multiplier bit is 1, the 5- bit multiplicand (26) is added to the 5 most significant bits (MSBs) of the product register that appear on line 4 as 13. The result, 39, appears on line 5. The product moves steadily to the right. The final product appears on line 9 and is a 10-bit number in this case. Note that the MSB of the product register is reserved for carries that may result from the additions.

5-6.2 Multiplication Subroutines

Multiplication can be performed in accordance with the above algorithm by using the **6800** μP. A routine for a 1 byte by 1 byte multiplication is shown in Table 5-2. Before the program starts, these assumptions are made:

Multiplier = 22 = 1 0 1 1 0

Multiplicand = 26 = 1 1 0 1 0

Line Number		Product		Multiplier Bit	
1		0 0 0 0 0			Initial product
2		0 0 0 0 0	0	0	Shift product register
3		1 1 0 1 0	0	1	Add multiplicand
4		0 1 1 0 1	0 0		Shift product register
5	1	0 0 1 1 1	0 0	1	Add multiplicand
6		1 0 0 1 1	1 0 0		Shift product register
7		0 1 0 0 1	1 1 0 0	0	Shift product register
8	1	0 0 0 1 1	1 1 0 0	1	Add multiplicand
9		1 0 0 0 1	1 1 1 0 0		Shift – final product

Figure 5-7 Multiplying 22 × 26.

1. The multiplicand is in location \$80.
2. Locations \$82 and \$83 are reserved for the 16-bit product. Actually, the partial products will be in the A accumulator and location \$83. At the end of the program, A, which contains the MS byte of the product, is stored in \$82.
3. Location \$84 contains the multiplier.

TABLE 5-2

Location	Machine Code	Mnemonic	Comments
20	C6 08	LDA B #8	Put 8 in B register
22	D7 81	STA B \$81	Save shift count in \$81
24	D6 80	LDA B \$80	Load multiplicand into B
26	4F	CLR A	Clear A
27	74 0084	LSR \$84	Shift multiplier right
2A	24 01	BCC \$2D	Skip to \$2D if carry clear
2C	1B	ABA	Add accumulators
2D	46	ROR A	Shift product MS byte Rt.
2E	76 0083	ROR \$83	Shift product reg LS byte
31	7A 0081	DEC \$81	Decrement count
34	26 F1	BNE \$27	Branch back to 27 if not 0
36	97 82	STA A \$82	Is 0. Done. Store MS byte
38	20 FE	BRA \$38	HALT program by looping
		END	
	Reserved locations		
80	Multiplicand		
81	Count		
82	Product Register (MS byte)		
83	Product Register (LS byte)		
84	Multiplier		

The program starts by storing the required number of shifts into $81 and storing the multiplicand into B. It then shifts the multiplier right. If the bit of the multiplier that is shifted into the carry FF is a 1, the multiplicand is added to the product register (A). The reader may have noticed that a 1 is sometimes carried out of the product register in the illustrative example. Fortunately, this 1 goes into the carry FF and is preserved.

The two ROR instructions then shift A and location $83. This is essentially a 16-bit shift of the product register. Location $81 keeps track of the number of shifts and the program halts when it decrements to a 0. Multiplying larger numbers requires 16-bit adds and 32-bit shifts but can proceed in accordance with the same general algorithm.

5-6.3 Parameter Passing in Subroutines

In order to use subroutines correctly, several conditions must be observed:

1. If any constants change during the execution of the subroutine, they must be *reinitialized* whenever the subroutine is used again. In the multiplication subroutine, location $81, the shift count, is an example. It is decremented to zero during the course of the subroutine. Therefore it must be reinitialized every time the subroutine is started. This is done by the first two instructions of the subroutine.
2. The calling routine must know where to put the parameters. In the multiplication subroutine the calling routine must place the multiplicand in location $80 and the multiplier in $84 before it can call the subroutine.
3. The calling routine must know where to find the result of the subroutine. In the multiplication subroutine the results are always stored in $82 and $83.

The last two conditions are called **parameter passing**. The calling routine must provide the subroutine with the proper input parameters (i.e., multiplier and multiplicand) and the subroutine must make its results available to the calling program (i.e., store them in locations $82 and $83).

EXAMPLE 5-11

There are numbers in $A1, $A2, $B1, and $B2. Describe a program to find the sum of the two products

$$S = (A1)(B1) + (A2)(B2)$$

Store S in $C1 and $C2.

SOLUTION
The first decision is to use the multiply routine of Section 5-6.2 as a subroutine to obtain both of the required products. Once this decision is made the program can start at location $100, for example, to keep out of the way of the multiply subroutine and the data. The stack can start at $200 to keep it out of the way of everything else. The program then proceeds as follows:

1. Load the stack pointer. Whenever a program requires use of the stack (and subroutines use the stack) the SP must be initialized before it is used. Otherwise the SP may be pointing to a random location and the jump or branch to subroutine may overwrite the program or data.
2. Move $A1 to $80 and $B1 to $84. This sets up the multiplier and multiplicand for the subroutine. This is an example of parameter passing.
3. Jump to $20 to enter the multiply subroutine.
4. Move the product in $82 and $83 to $C1 and $C2.
5. Move $A2 and $B2 to $80 and $84, for the second product.
6. Jump to the multiply subroutine again.
7. Add the contents of $82 and $83 with $C1 and $C2 to get the sum of the two products. Store the results in $C1 and $C2. This completes the program.

5-7 A BCD-TO-BINARY CONVERSION PROBLEM

As a final practical example that uses lists, indexed instructions, subroutines, and stacks, let us consider the problem of converting BCD information to binary. BCD was introduced in Section 4-8. BCD information can be entered into a μC system from the terminal keyboard. Each ASCII (see Section 8-7.1) number must be ANDed with a $0F to remove the four MSBs. This leaves a BCD digit. Other peripherals may also supply BCD information.

BCD numbers must often be converted to binary before computations can be made using the number. One way to convert from BCD to binary[2] is to assign a weight to all the BCD bits and then add the weights for all bits that are 1 in the BCD representation of the number. The weights are assigned in accordance with the value represented by each BCD bit, that is, 1, 2, 4, 8, 10, 20, 40, 80, 100, 200, ... A table of the decimal numbers and binary weights corresponding to each BCD bit is given in Fig. 5-8.

EXAMPLE 5-12

Convert the decimal number 169 to binary using the add algorithm.

SOLUTION

The number 169 is expressed in BCD form as

$$\underbrace{0001}_{1}\underbrace{0110}_{6}\underbrace{1001}_{9}$$

where the LSB is on the right. There are 1s in positions 1, 4, 6, 7, and 9. The weights corresponding to these numbers are (from Fig. 5-8)

[2]A thorough discussion of BCD-to-binary and binary-to-BCD conversion is given in Greenfield, *Practical Digital Design Using ICs* (cited in Section 5-10).

Bit Position	Decimal Number	Binary Number
1	1	1
2	2	10
3	4	100
4	8	1000
5	10	1010
6	20	10100
7	40	101000
8	80	1010000
9	100	1100100
10	200	11001000
11	400	110010000
12	800	1100100000
13	1000	1111101000
14	2000	11111010000
15	4000	111110100000
16	8000	1111101000000

FIGURE 5-8 Tables of weights for BCD-to-binary conversion.

0001
1000
10100
101000
1100100

Simple addition of these binary numbers yields 10101001, which is the binary equivalent of decimal 169.

Computers, which generally have binary adders, often use the add algorithm to convert from BCD to binary.

Now that the method of converting from BCD to binary has been explained, a conversion program using the **6800** can be written.

EXAMPLE 5-13

A four-digit BCD number is in locations \$F0 and \$F1, with the least significant digit in \$F1, bits 3–0, and the most significant digit in \$F0, bits 7–4. Write a routine to convert this number to binary.

SOLUTION

First we start with a vague general idea of how to perform the conversion; add the proper number wherever a 1 appears in the given BCD number. Each bit can be tested by performing a shift right and testing the carry bit.

We also realize now that the list of Fig. 5-8 must be placed in memory so that the proper number can be added to the sum. Figure 5-8 shows that smaller binary values can be included in 1 byte but the larger values need 2 bytes. For uniformity, it is wise to allocate 2 bytes for each binary entry. It will soon become clear that this simplifies the programming. The list is arbitrarily started at location \$100, so \$100 and \$101 contain the binary equivalent of 1 (hex 0001); the list continues to \$11F, where locations \$11E and \$11F contain the binary equivalent of 8000_{10}, which is $1F40_{16}$ or

$$11E \quad \underbrace{0001}_{1}\underbrace{1111}_{F} \qquad 11F \quad \underbrace{0100}_{4}\underbrace{0000}_{0}$$

The result can be no larger than $(9999)_{10}$, which means it can be represented by a 14-bit binary number. Let us reserve \$F2 and \$F3 for this number. We also assume that the addition is done by a subroutine so the stack pointer is arbitrarily initialized to 200. The flowchart can now be drawn and is shown in Fig. 5-9.

The flowchart assumes that the list and the numbers to be converted are already in memory. The program proceeds in the following way.

1. The sum is initialized to 0, the index register (X) to \$100, and the SP to \$200.
2. The first word (two least significant digits) is loaded into the A accumulator and shifted out. After each shift, the carry bit is tested.
3. The X register is then incremented twice to point to the next 2-byte numbers in the list. It should now be apparent that if the list contained both 1- and 2-byte entries, additional programming would have been required to determine the starting address of the next item. This is why 2 bytes were allocated to each item in the list whether they were required or not.
4. X is tested for the HALT condition. The program should halt after 16 shifts or when the list is exhausted. Since the list contains 16 two-byte numbers, it is exhausted when X equals $(120)_{16}$.
5. The second word to be converted must be loaded into A after eight shifts or 16 increments of X. This occurs when the number in X = \$0110. Note that in this program the X register is performing the dual function of selecting the appropriate number in the list and determining whether or not branches are to be taken.
6. When C = 1 the add subroutine is entered. Since the A accumulator is used by both the main program and the subroutine, it is immediately pushed onto the stack to save it for the main program.
7. The proper number in the list (as determined by X) is added to the LSBs of the sum in \$F3.
8. The MSBs of the list are added (with carry) to \$F2. This completes a 16-bit addition.
9. The A accumulator is restored to its original value and the main program is reentered.

Using the detailed flowchart of Fig. 5-9, the coding is straightforward and is shown in Table 5-3. Before coding can begin, a starting address must be assigned arbitrarily to the main program (\$20) and the subroutine (\$80). The only caution is

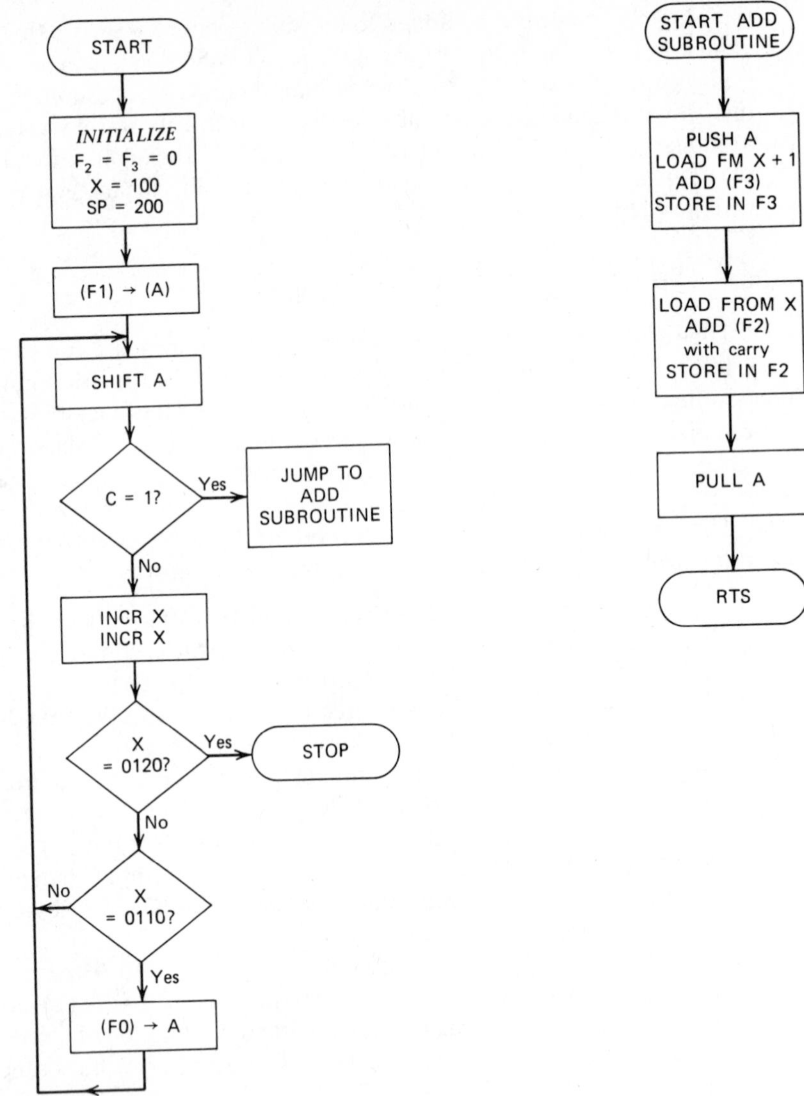

Figure 5-9 Flowchart for Example 5-13.

that these areas must not overlap each other, the data, the list, or the stack area.

The student may have observed that this program is not optimum. There is no real need for a subroutine (it could have been included in the main program) and some instructions could have been saved by using the B accumulator. The program was used because it demonstrates many of the features available in the **6800** software.

TABLE 5-3 Program for Example 5-13

MAIN PROGRAM

ADDRESS	CODE	MNEMONICS	COMMENTS
20	4F	CLR A	Clear A
21	97 F2	STA A $F2	Clear F2
23	97 F3	STA A $F3	Clear F3
25	8E 0200	LDS #$200	Initialize Stack Pointer
28	CE 0100	LDX #$100	" Index Register
2B	96 F1	LDA A $F1	Load LS BCD digit into A
2D	47	ASR A	Shift A right
2E	24 02	BCC $32	Skip to $32 if C = 0
30	8D 4E	BSR $80	To Add subroutine if C = 1
32	08	INX	Increment X twice to
33	08	INX	point to next entry
34	8C 0120	CPX #$120	Reached end of list ?
37	27 09	BEQ $42	Yes - branch to HALT at $42
39	8C 0110	CPX #$110	Is word 1 finished ?
3C	26 EF	BNE $2D	No, loop back & shift again
3E	96 F0	LDA A $F0	Yes, load MS digits into A
40	20 EB	BRA $2D	Loop to $2D & shift MS digit
42	20 FE	BRA $42	Repeat and HALT prog.

* ADD SUBROUTINE

ADDRESS	CODE	MNEMONICS	COMMENTS
80	36	PSH A	Save A on stack
81	A6 01	LDA A 1,X	Load from list-LS byte
83	9B F3	ADD A $F3	Add LS byte of sum
85	97 F3	STA A $F3	Update LS byte of sum
87	A6 00	LDA A 0,X	Load MS byte from list
89	99 F2	ADC A $F2	Add MS byte w/ carry
8B	97 F2	STA A $F2	Update MS byte of sum
8D	32	PUL A	Restore A
8E	39	RTS	Return to main prog.

5-8 SUMMARY

This chapter introduced the BRANCH and JUMP instructions available in the **6800** μP. The conditions that caused the branches were explained, as were the methods of calculating the branch locations.

The stack was then introduced. Its use in conjunction with PUSH and PULL instructions and subroutines was explained. Finally, a multiplication program and a BCD-to-binary conversion program were presented as examples that used many of the features of the **6800**.

5-9 GLOSSARY

BRANCH Jump where the location jumped to can be specified by a 1-byte offset from the current value of the PC.

Indirect jump Jump to an address stored in memory rather than directly to the memory location itself.

JUMP Instruction that loads the PC with a new address that causes the program to fetch the next instruction from a location that is not in sequence.

Nested subroutine Subroutine called by another subroutine. It is used by the first subroutine and, when it completes, the program returns to the first subroutine.

Parameter passing Placing data in prescribed locations so the subroutine and main program can share them.

PULL Instruction that copies into an accumulator the contents of the location in the stack pointed to by the SP.

PUSH Instruction that copies the contents of the accumulator to the stack at the current SP location.

Relocatable program Program of instructions containing only relative branching. Thus, it can be located anywhere in memory (i.e., it is relocatable).

Stack Area of memory reserved for subroutine return addresses and saving register contents during an interrupt. Also, other parameters can be saved and retrieved.

Stack Pointer (SP) Register that contains the address of the highest vacant location in the stack.

5-10 REFERENCES

Bishop, Ron. *Basic Microprocessors and the 6800,* Hayden, Rochelle Park, NJ, 1979.

Greenfield, Joseph D. *Practical Digital Design Using ICs,* Second Edition, Wiley, New York, 1983.

Leventhal, Lance. *6800 Assembly Language Programming,* Adam Osborn & Associates, Berkeley, CA, 1978.

Motorola. *M6800 Programming Reference Manual,* M68PRM(D), Phoenix, AZ, 1976.

5-11 PROBLEMS

5-1 Write a program to write the number $C2 into all locations between $0250 and $02FF.

5-2 Write a program to transfer the contents of locations $0100 to $0120 to locations $0110 to $0130. Hint: Start by moving $120 to $130, then $11F to $12F, etc.

5-3 The Boolean equation for BGE is $(N \oplus V) = 0$. Explain what it implies.

5-4 If the SP contains $021C and X contains $022C, write the contents of the stack and the starting address of the subroutine if the instruction in location $40 is

a. **JSR $30,X**	**AD 30**
b. **JSR $C2,X**	**AD C2**
c. **JSR $15F**	**BD 015F**
d. **BSR *+$25**	**8D 23**
e. **BSR *−6**	**8D F8**

5-5 Write a program to convert a 13-bit binary number to BCD. The algorithm is to subtract from the given number the highest number in Fig. 5-8 that is less than the given number, and write 1s in all positions where these subtractions are performed.[3]

5-6 Your receivables are positive numbers in locations $0100 to 01FF. Your expenses are positive numbers in locations $0200 to 02FF. Write a program to determine your net worth.

5-7 Describe in words what the following program does.

Location	*Machine Code*	*Mnemonic*
40	CE 0130	LDX #$130
43	8E 01D0	LDS #$1D0
46	A6 00	LDA A 0,X
48	36	PSH A
49	09	DEX
4A	8C 0100	CPX #$100
4D	26 F7	BNE $46
4F	20 FE	BRA $4F

5-8 Using the multiplication routine of Table 5-2, multiply 127_{10} by 75_{10}. Show the contents of the accumulator after each step.

5-9 Write a divide routine. Reserve 1 byte for the quotient and 1 byte for the remainder.

5-10 Write the code for Example 5-11.

5-11 A business deals in a series of items. If the price of each item is listed in locations $A0 to $BF and the corresponding number of items sold is in locations $C0 to $DF, write a program to determine the gross receipts.

After attempting to solve these problems, try to answer the self-evaluation questions in Section 5-2. If any of them still seem difficult, review the appropriate sections of the chapter to find the answers.

[3]A more complete description is given in Greenfield, *Practical Digital Design Using ICs*, Chapter 10 (cited in Section 5-10).

CHAPTER 6
ASSEMBLY LANGUAGE FOR THE 6800

6-1 INSTRUCTIONAL OBJECTIVES

The purpose of this chapter is to acquaint the **6800** system designer with standard methods of writing and documenting software and to expand on the use of mnemonics for ease of programming. The assembler and editor programs are presented to handle the mechanics of program development.

After reading this chapter, the student should be able to

1. Translate flowcharts or other program concepts into the assembly language mnemonic statements of a source program.
2. Write the program and save it on tape or disk.
3. Specify the assembler directives needed to properly assemble the program.
4. Assemble and reedit the source program until it assembles without errors.
5. Obtain the program listing and object code output tapes or disk files needed to load the program into memory for testing.

6-2 SELF-EVALUATION QUESTIONS

Watch for the answers to the following questions as you read the chapter. They should help you to understand the material presented.

1. How are mnemonics used to express addressing modes and addresses?
2. What is the difference between a source program and an object program?
3. What is an assembler program?
4. What is the function of the program comments?
5. What is the difference between an instruction and an assembler directive?
6. What steps are required to assemble a source program using a **6800** μP system and a tape terminal?

7. Why does the assembler editor program version number have to be different for a floppy disk system and a tape system?

6-3 ASSEMBLY LANGUAGE PROGRAMMING

The use of mnemonics as the basis of assembly language programming was described briefly in Chapter 4. In this chapter we show how these expressions are used to write programs and how the *assembler* (see Section 6-3.2) and *editor* (see Section 6-6) *programs* are used.

The mnemonic operator (Op) codes of the Motorola **6800** assembly language (shown in Table 4-1 of Chapter 4) all use three letters and are followed by an operand (or dual operand), that modifies each Op code according to the addressing mode. The various addressing modes and some examples of how they apply to the LoaD Accumulator (LDA) instruction are shown below:

Addressing Mode	*Mnemonic*	*Machine Code*
1. Extended addressing	**LDA A $A0F3**	**B6 A0F3**
2. Direct addressing	**LDA A $F3**	**96 F3**
3. Immediate addressing	**LDA A #$F3**	**86 F3**
4. Indexed addressing	**LDA A 3,X**	**A6 03**

The above instructions are in *assembly language format* (see Section 6-4). The $ sign denotes a hexadecimal value, and the # sign indicates an immediate operand.

In analyzing these instructions the following points should be noted:

a. The **6800** μP assembler recognizes addresses below $100 $(256)_{10}$, as **direct addresses**. As shown in line 2 above, the assembler generates instructions that are 2 bytes in length (the Op code plus one 8-bit address byte). Three-byte **extended addressing** instructions, as shown in line 1, are used to reference addresses above 00FF.

b. The **immediate addressing** instruction of line 3 loads the value $F3 into the A accumulator, instead of loading the contents of location $F3 as would be the case for the direct mode shown in line 2 above.

c. The 3 shown in the **indexed addressing** instruction (line 4) is an example of an **offset** value that is added to the index register when this instruction is executed. The offset is limited to 1 byte and is considered to be positive. It is expressed in the machine language as the second byte of that instruction (03 in this case).

d. When referencing either accumulator, the space after the Op code is optional, as shown in line 4 above.

Below are several other addressing modes that were not shown because they are not applicable to the LDA instruction.

Addressing Mode	*Mnemonic*	*Machine Code*
5. Relative addressing	**BPL *+5**	**2A 03**
6. Inherent addressing	**ABA**	**1B**
7. Accumulator addressing	**ASL A**	**48**

Here, the * is interpreted as the value of the program counter (PC) at the *beginning* of the instruction, and the second byte adjusts the PC *relative* to the value it would have, after this instruction is executed (i.e., the original PC+2+3). A minus sign could have been used, and the second byte would be the 2s complement of the minus number, also adjusted by the 2 bytes of the instruction. The second byte therefore can represent a maximum offset of $+127_{10}$ ($7F) or -128_{10} ($80) bytes relative to the address of the first byte of the *following* instruction.

The last two instructions are **inherent** instructions. They need only *one* byte because all the information needed for their execution is already within the μP and no memory locations or immediate operands are required.

6-3.1 Use of Mnemonics to Express Addresses

Mnemonics can be used to express *addresses* as well as Op codes. When used in this way they are called **labels**. For example, a program to add three numbers and then branch back to itself might be

```
BEGIN       LDA A   FIRST
            ADD A   SECOND
            ADD A   THIRD
            STA A   SUM
            BRA BEGIN
```

Here the operands that represent addresses were given the *symbolic* names of FIRST, SECOND, THIRD, BEGIN, and SUM. These are the names of the locations in memory from which the contents are fetched (in the case of the first three instructions) and in which the results (in A) are stored (in the fourth instruction). The *symbols* chosen are usually whatever pops into the programmer's mind, and they are considered to be **mnemonic** because they are usually English-like expressions that give some clue to what they represent. Note that the program starts with a label called BEGIN and it is referenced in the operand of the branch instruction.

6-3.2 Source and Object Programs

When several mnemonic or assembly language statements are written to form a program as in the BEGIN routine above, the result is known as a **source program** or *assembly language* program. To make this program intelligible to a μC, it must be processed by an **assembler** program. This is a program that runs in a computer and converts the source program into machine language (also called the **object program**). The object program can be expressed in a number of ways, but the assembler being described here assigns *hexadecimal* digits to the Op codes and addresses. The assembler also produces a *program listing*, which shows both the *object codes* and the *mnemonics*.

Most assembler programs are written in the language of the computer for which the program being assembled is intended. In some cases the user may want to use a minicomputer or time-sharing computer because printers or other facilities are already available. Assemblers that run in one type of computer and generate code for another type are called **cross-assemblers**. Chapter 10 includes descriptions of **6800** μP development systems, which are generally used to do these assemblies in all but very large companies where multiple usage of the larger systems can economically justify them.

EXAMPLE 6-1

If the program of Section 6-3.1 was assembled and the addresses were assigned to the labels as FIRST = \$40, SECOND = \$41, THIRD = \$42, SUM = \$43, and BEGIN = \$20, what would the assembler produce as an object program?

SOLUTION

To illustrate, a simplified program listing is shown below:

Addr	*Object*	*Label*	*Mnemonic*		*Comments*
20	96 40	BEGIN	LDA A	FIRST	Load A from location 40.
22	9B 41		ADD A	SECOND	Add contents of 41 to A.
24	9B 42		ADD A	THIRD	Add contents of 42 to A.
26	97 43		STA A	SUM	Store contents of A to 43.
28	20 F6		BRA BEGIN		Branch back to begin.

Note that the assembler substitutes the appropriate machine code or address for each part of the mnemonic statement [i.e., \$96 = LDA A (direct), \$40 = FIRST, etc.]. In the last statement the assembler program calculated the offset value for the branch (−10 = \$F6). This is not a practical program since it results in an endless loop, but it could be used as a test program. When using assemblers, programmers are not required to calculate the offset values for branch instructions. The assembler will do it for them.

6-4 PROGRAM LISTINGS

A source program consists of a number of lines of *source statements,* and each line must be written in a *specific format* so that it can be interpreted by the assembler. These lines can have one or more mnemonics and possibly a comment, terminated by a carriage return. All must be printable ASCII characters (except line feed, carriage return, and spaces).

When the *source program* is processed by the assembler program, it produces two outputs: the *program listing* and the machine language *object listing*. The program listing is normally printed on the operator's terminal of the software development system or on a line printer that is part of that system. The object program, or machine code output, is usually put on *tape* or in a *disk* file so that it can be loaded into the computer for which it is intended and tested. This process is described in detail in Chapter 10.

A program listing of a sample program is shown in Fig. 6-1. This is *not* a real program. It is *only* intended to demonstrate the many features of the assembler and to show the distinctions between the various mnemonic expressions. The comments on each line explain the feature involved. Examples of several useful programs are given later in this chapter. Figure 6-1 shows that the assembler formats the listing into seven *columns* or fields:

1. Line number
2. Addresses
3. Object codes
4. Labels
5. Operators
6. Operands
7. Comments

```
LINE  ADDR  CODE      LABEL  OP     OPERAND       COMMENTS
 1     2     3          4     5        6              7

00001                        NAM    PGM
00002                 * REVISION 1
00003                        OPT    O,S           OBJECT + SYMBOLS OPTIO
00004 0100                   ORG    256
00005       000A      COUNT  EQU    @12           @ INDICATES OCTAL
00006 0100 8E 0132    START  LDS    #STACK        LOAD STACK POINTER
00007 0103 FE 0136           LDX    ADDR          LOAD X EXTENDED
00008 0106 C6 0A             LDA B  #COUNT        IMMEDIATE ADDRESSING
00009 0108 96 0A      BACK   LDA A  10            DIRECT ADDRESSING
00010 010A A1 02             CMP A  2,X           INDEXED ADDRESSING
00011 010C 27 05             BEQ    FOUND         RELATIVE ADDRESSING
00012 010E 09                DEX                  INHERENT ADDRESSING
00013 010F 5A                DEC B                ACCUMULATOR ONLY ADDR
00014 0110 26 F6             BNE    BACK          LABEL REFERENCE
00015 0112 3E                WAI                  WAIT FOR INTERRUPT

00017 0113 BD 0119    FOUND  JSR    SUBRTN        JUMP TO SUBROUTINE
00018 0116 7E 0100           JMP    START         EXTENDED ADDRESSING
00019                 * COMMENT STATEMENT NOTE TRUNCATION 012345678
00020 0119 16         SUBRTN TAB                  COMMENT FIELD TRUNCATI
00021 011A BA 0133           ORA A  BYTE          SET MST SGNIFICNT BYTE
00022 011D 39                RTS                  RETURN FROM SUBROUTINE

00024 011E 0014              RMB    20            AREA FOR STACK
00025 0132 0001       STACK  RMB    1             START OF STACK
00026 0133 80         BYTE   FCB    $80           FORM CONSTANT BYTE
00027 0134 10                FCB    $10,%10010111  % IS FOR BINARY
      0135 97
00028 0136 0138       ADDR   FDB    DATA          FORM DOUBLE BYTE
00029 0138 53         DATA   FCC    'SET' FORM CONSTANT CHARACTERS
      0139 45
      013A 54
00030                        END

COUNT  000A START  0100 BACK   0108 FOUND  0113 SUBRTN 0119
STACK  0132 BYTE   0133 ADDR   0136 DATA   0138

TOTAL ERRORS 00000
```

Figure 6-1 Sample program to show assembler features.

The mnemonic expressions in columns 5 and 6 are translated by the assembler into the machine code shown in column 3. This code resides at the addresses in column 2. Some of the lines (1, 3, 4, 5, 24, 26, 29, and 30) of Fig. 6-1 include statements that are not listed as instructions in Table 4-1. These mnemonic statements are **assembler directives** and are listed in Table 6-1 (see Section 6-5). Some of these directives produce object code (lines 26, 27, 28, and 29 of Fig. 6-1), but those that do not are used to control the assembler or to format the listing. Each column of Fig. 6-1 will now be described.

6-4.1 Line Numbers (Column 1)

Each line in the listing is numbered and the line numbers appear in column 1. When the programmer writes source statements, *line numbering* is *optional*. If the source program has line numbers, they will be printed as each line is assembled. If numbers were not originally used, the assembler will provide them. Line numbers are decimal, and 65536 is maximum.

6-4.2 Addresses (Column 2)

The addresses correspond to the location in memory for each byte. Addresses are listed as four-digit hexadecimal numbers and are automatically incremented by the number of bytes required for each instruction by the assembler. The starting address is determined by the ORG statement (described in Section 6-5) specified by the programmer.

6-4.3 Object Codes (Column 3)

Each instruction is translated into machine language and the codes are printed on each line in hexadecimal format. These instructions can be 1, 2, or 3 bytes in length, depending on the instruction and addressing mode involved. Section 6-9 gives details on the object code output of the assembler.

6-4.4 Labels (Column 4)

In Section 6-3.1 we explained that mnemonics could be assigned to *addresses* as well as *Op codes*. Mnemonics that apply to addresses are called **labels**. The labeled addresses can be operands, but they can also refer to the location of program steps. Labels that are program locations are listed in column 4 of the assembled program.

Both types of labels are used on line 6 of Fig. 6-1. The label START in column 4 refers to the starting address of the program. Column 2 shows that the starting address of the program is $0100 or that START = $0100.

Line 6 also contains the label STACK, whose address is loaded into the stack pointer (SP) by the *immediate* instruction. Note that the second and third bytes of column 3 are 0132, which is the value of STACK. STACK is used as a label on line 25, where it is further defined (Section 6-5.1).

EXAMPLE 6-2

a. What is the address of the instruction on line 8?
b. How can it be expressed symbolically?

SOLUTION

a. The location of the LOAD instruction in line 8 is at $0106 as given on the assembler printout (column 2). It could have been calculated by realizing that this instruction occurs after two 3-byte instructions from START ($0100).
b. This location can be expressed symbolically as START + 6, or the programmer can assign a mnemonic to it.

Labels are generally used for program locations that are the objects of branch instructions. In Fig. 6-1 the labels FOUND and BACK are used this way. The branch instruction on line 14 (BNE BACK), for example, returns the program to BACK (location $0108) if the branch is taken. The use of labels here eliminates the problem of *calculating offsets*. The assembler calculates the proper value for the second byte of a branch instruction and inserts it into the offset ($F6 in this case).

Specific rules apply when writing labels. The **6800** assembler has the following requirements:

1. A label consists of 1 to 6 alphanumeric characters.
2. The first character of a label must be alphabetic.
3. A label must begin in the first character position of a statement.
4. All labels within a program must be unique.
5. A label must not consist of any one of the single characters A, B, and X. (These characters are reserved for special syntax and refer to accumulator A, accumulator B, and the index register X, respectively.)

The EQU directive is used to assign *values* to labels. Line 5, for example, reads COUNT EQU @12. This sets the value of COUNT to octal 12 (or hex 000A).

Here are some typical labels:

START   START2   E3   W   B120   SUBRTN

6-4.5 Operators (Column 5)

The operation codes (Op codes) appear in column 5. Mnemonics that are not in Table 5-1 are assembler directives; these are discussed in Section 6-5.

6-4.6 Operands (Column 6)

The operand field of an instruction contains a *value*, an address, or a label that references one of them. Inherent instructions do not need an operand (see line 12). Operands can also reference a label. In line 8 of Fig. 6-1 the value (000A) (which has been given to COUNT by the EQU statement on line 5) is used by the assembler. The EQU assumes the number can be up to 16 bits long. Since the number involved is less than 256, it does not overflow when loaded into the 8-bit accumulator by the instruction in line 8 of Fig. 6-1. This instruction is an example in which the label is preceded by the # sign to indicate the *immediate* mode of addressing. An operand can also contain an expression such as *+5 that will be evaluated algebraically by the assembler. (This operand is interpreted as the current value of the program counter plus 5.)

Examples of statements with various operands are

LDA A #$F3	Immediate load of hex value F3.
LDX SUZY,X	"X" indicates indexed instruction. Offset equals the *value* of SUZY.
JMP $1200	Jump to 1200 (hex).
BRA EXIT	Branch to label called EXIT.
BEQ *+5	Branch to the address of this instruction plus 5.

Numbers can be expressed in several ways in all operands but, except for decimal, must be preceded by a symbol as follows:

1. Hexadecimal	**$**
2. Octal	@
3. Binary	%
4. Decimal	(none)

EXAMPLE 6-3

What do the instructions on lines 9 and 10 of Fig. 6-1 do?

SOLUTION

Line 9 contains LDA A 10. It loads the contents of location 10_{10} ($A in hex) (not defined in this printout) into the A register.

Line 10 compares the contents of A with the contents of the address in the index register plus 2. Since X contains $138 (see lines 7 and 28), A is compared with the contents of $013A, which are seen to be $54 (see line 29). Thus the instruction in line 10 compares the contents of A with $54 and sets the flags.

6-4.7 Comments (Column 7)

Comments are used to explain what each line or each section of the program is doing. They can be added to any statement by separating it from the operand (or operator if no operand is used) with one or more spaces. A comment can also be used on a line by itself, if preceded by an * in the first character position of the line. Comments do not generate machine code but are simply copied from the source to the program listing (verbatim). *Comprehension* of the program is aided immeasurably by use of proper comments. Comments are *required* if the program is to be understood by someone other than the programmer.

Good comments should indicate the function of the instruction in the program. For example, "JUMP TO SUBROUTINE AT LOC 20" and "STORE EXTENDED" are poor comments because they do not tell what the instruction is doing in the *context* of the program. The program flow can be understood more readily if these are replaced by comments such as "JUMP TO MULTIPLICATION SUBROUTINE" and "STORE ADDEND."

The comments in Fig. 6-1 are poor because this is not a normal program that does something. They can be contrasted with those in Fig. 6-3, which contains good comments.

6-5 ASSEMBLER DIRECTIVES

When writing a program, options are available to enable the programmer to reserve memory bytes for data, specify the starting address of the program, and select the format of the assembler output. These options are called *assembler directives* and are listed in Table 6-1.

Assembler directives are all three-letter mnemonics (with the exception of PAGE); they are written into the source program in the same way as instructions and are interpreted during the assembly process. Three of the directives generate object code in the form of data, but others only control the assembler. Table 6-1 shows that the *assembler directives* are divided into three major categories:

1. **Assembly control**, which names the program, defines its starting address, and tells the assembler when to stop processing the source program.
2. **Listing control**, which specifies the output format of the assembly and the options to be used.
3. **Data definition**, which specifies the type of data and where it will be stored in memory.

Reference to the program listing of Fig. 6-1 shows how the directives are used. The NAM statement must be the first line of the program, and the name used (up to eight characters) is printed at the top of each page along with the page number during assembly. Other directives such as OPT and ORG are also used. Certain options are selected by the assembler by default and are identified in Table 6-1 (these differ with various versions of the assembler).

6-5.1 The RMB Directive

The reserve memory byte (RMB) directive reserves a location in memory or a group of locations where data is to be stored. If several areas are required for different types of data, several RMBs can be used.

TABLE 6-1 Assembly Directives

Directive	Function
Assembly control	
NAM XXXXXXXX[a]	Program name (8 letters maximum)
ORG nnnn[b]	Origin (any number base)
END	Program end
Listing control	
PAGE	Top of page
SPC n	Skip "n" lines
OPT NOO	No object tape
OPT O	The Assembler will generate an object tape (selected by default).
OPT M	The Assembler will write machine code to memory.
OPT NOM	No memory (selected by default).
OPT S	The Assembler will print the symbols at the end of Pass 2.
OPT NOS	No printing of symbols (selected by default).
OPT NOL	The Assembler will not print a listing of the assembler data.
OPT L	The listing of assembled data will be printed (selected by default).
OPT NOP	The Assembler will inhibit format paging of the assembly listing.
OPT P	The listing will be paged (selected by default).
OPT NOG	Causes only 1 line of data to be listed from the assembler directions FCC, FCB, and FDB.
OPT G	All data generated by the FCC, FCB, and FDB directions will be printed (selected by default).
Data definition storage allocation	
FCC "MESSAGE"	Character string data } Generates data
FCB XX, YY, ZZ, etc.	One-byte data } Generates data
FDB XXXX, YYYY, ZZZZ, etc.	Double-byte data } Generates data
RMB nnnn	Reserve n memory bytes } No data generated
Symbol definition	
EQU nnnn	Assign permanent value } No data generated

[a]X's indicate alphanumeric characters.
[b]n's refer to any number base: 65420, $F100, @7756. We usually show 4 n's since the number we use is often a 4-digit hex number.

EXAMPLE 6-4

In Fig. 6-1, where is the stack located and how is it specified by the assembler?

SOLUTION

The RMB directive on line 24 specifies that 20 decimal or 14 hex locations are to be reserved. The RMB on line 25 specifies the top or start of the stack (since it decrements when used). The programmer merely writes RMB 20 and RMB 1 for the start of the stack. The assembler then reserves 14 hex locations for the stack plus 1 location for the start of the stack. In this example the assembler has thus assigned 21 locations, from \$011E to \$0132 inclusive, for the stack.

6-5.2 The FCB, FDB, and FCC Directives

The Form Constant Byte (FCB) and Form Double Byte (FDB) directives are used to define data used by the program. These mnemonics must be followed by a decimal, hex, octal, or binary number, or a label. The byte on line 26 is labeled BYTE and used by the instruction on line 21. The FCB is used on lines 26 and 27 of Fig. 6-1. Note that on line 27 two operands are defined, one written in hex and one written in binary. They occupy locations $134 and $135 in memory. Many bytes can be defined by a single FCB or FDB, provided that the data values are separated by commas and do not overflow the line.

A 2-byte constant, labeled ADDR, is defined by the FDB directive on line 28. The operand of the FDB is the label DATA. The assembler assigned an address to DATA and thereby defined 0138 as the FDB reference.

The Form Constant Characters (FCC) directive (used on line 29) is useful for formating ASCII expressions or messages that are to be printed by a program. This directive generates the machine language equivalents for the ASCII characters included between the delimiters (apostrophes in this case). Here the word SET is translated to its hex equivalent of 53, 45, and 54, respectively.

If a large number of operands or a longer message is used, the directives FCB, FDB, and FCC take a lot of room to print. For this reason the OPT NOG directive is generally used to inhibit all but the first line of each of these statements. The object tape or floppy disk file is not affected, however, and contains all the data bytes.

6-5.3 The EQU Directive

The EQU directive is used to assign a permanent value to a label. For example, the statement on line 5 of Fig. 6-1,

```
COUNT        EQU        @12
```

assigns the value octal 12 (000A in hex) to the label COUNT, and that value is used in line 8. This directive is used to assign absolute values to a label. The addresses of the registers in the hardware peripheral devices used in a system are absolute numbers and the EQU directive is often used to identify them (see Chapter 8).

6-5.4 Other Directives

The other directives listed in Table 6-1 are NAM, ORG, END, PAGE, SPC, and the various OPT directives. Table 6-1 clearly explains the functions of the NAM, PAGE, and END directives, and examples of all but PAGE can be seen in Fig. 6-1. The SPC directive will not show in an assembly listing such as Fig. 6-1 because it just creates blank lines, but it is entered in the source program in the same way as the other directives.

The SPC directive is used when the programmer wants to insert blank lines in the program. This may be done to separate various sections of the program and is often used after returns from subroutines (RTS) or jumps (JMP).

The ORG directive is used to define the starting address of the program or a section of a program. Line 4 of Fig. 6-1, for example, is

ORG 256

This statement causes the program to start at location 256_{10} (hex 100).

The OPT directive is used to give the programmer various options in the way the output is presented. Table 6-1 defines the options.

6-5.5 The Symbol Table

When OPT S is specified, the assembler will print a **symbol table** at the end of the program listing. The symbol table lists each symbol used by the program and the address or value of that symbol. In a large program this can be very helpful in finding a particular symbol (or label) location. The symbols are listed across the page in the order of their occurrence.

In Fig. 6-1 nine symbols are used. They are listed in the symbol table immediately below the END statement.

EXAMPLE 6-5

In the assembly of Fig. 6-1, what is the starting address of the subroutine?

SOLUTION

We find that the label for the subroutine is SUBRTN. Its address can be found by examining the code, but in a long program it can be found more easily by going directly to the symbol table, which in this case shows that SUBRTN equal $0119.

6-6 WRITING A PROGRAM

Several assembler programs have been written for the **6800**. All those written by Motorola have the same mnemonics but do have slightly different directives. Before writing a source program, the user should consult the manual for the particular assembler. Section 6-13 contains references to several such manuals. The user must understand the directives and rules that apply to the assembler actually being used, or errors will occur.

As an example of assembly language programming, let us write the source program for the BCD-to-binary program of Section 5-8. It starts with the NAM directive that provides the name at the top of each page. Comment lines can be used at any time after the NAM statement but must be preceded by an * in the first character position. When typing the source program, an **editor** program is used because its features help to get the lines in the proper format. After each carriage return, for example, it inserts a line feed and four nulls. The nulls provide a delay to allow time for the carriage to return (see Chapter 10 for more detail). When writing and correcting long programs, the *search* and *change* features of the editor are very useful. Figure 6-2 shows the source program as it appears when finished. The instructions are the same as the program for Example 5-13. Notice that all labels and the asterisks are in the first character position of each line. If a statement is an instruction or directive *without* a label, it must have *one or more spaces* at the *start* of the line. One space between each field is sufficient. Blank lines are not allowed, but if one or more are desired in the assembly printout, either an * followed by a CR or the SPC directive can be used. To provide multiple blank lines, the SPC is followed by a number to indicate the number of blank lines desired. SPC 5 is an example. The required space between the C and the 5 illustrates the need for proper formatting. Line 23 of Fig. 6-1 is an SPC 2.

The programmer must also specify where every block of code will start so that it coincides with the hardware locations of memory. To do this, the ORG statement is used and is followed by the desired address. Labels are assigned for all data locations and destinations of jumps or branches that will not be known until the assembly is done. This is a convenience since it eliminates any requirement for calculations on the part of the programmer. Section 6-7 describes how the assembler determines the location of the labels.

For the data locations, let us specify

a. WORD1 and WORD2 (the BCD number to be converted to binary).
b. SUM1 and SUM2 (the locations holding the binary equivalent of the BCD word).

The RMB directive is usually used to provide a place to store data such as this, but by using the FCB directive it is possible to *create a location and preset it to a prescribed value* at the same time. This avoids the necessity of writing an initialization routine (the value of 169 for the BCD digits to be converted was chosen arbitrarily in this example). Here, the FCB 0 takes the place of the first three instructions of Example 6-13, whose purpose was to initialize the SUM to zero.

Next, the program locations that are to be referenced can be labeled. The program entry is called START1 and the first statement of the subroutine is called START2. Other labels are added as required. For example, the program loops back to the address labeled SHIFT2. The SPC directive is used to format the listing for easy reading. Skipping a line after each branch or jump instruction usually clarifies the flow of the program. The ORG statement and options such as OPT NOL and OPT L can be repeated as often as necessary, and ORG is used again in this program to locate the lookup table at $100. An END statement must be used to tell the assembler when to stop inputting data and to terminate the processing. It then returns program control to the system monitor ROM or disk executive programs (see Chapter 10). The **monitor** is a μP system control program, usually in ROM, that provides I/O routines and routines to load or dump object programs and to test them. It also allows memory and register contents to be viewed or changed.

An absolute address for the location of the stack is specified in the START1 line. This is usually done as shown in Fig. 6-1 to be sure that the stack is separate from the program and data areas and does not overwrite them. Remember that the stack decrements when used. Also note that the X register is initialized, in effect,

```
 NAM BCDBIN
*PROGRAM TO CONVERT BCD NUMBERS TO BINARY
*WORD1 & WORD2 CONTAIN THE BCD WORDS
*SUM1 &SUM2 CONTAIN THE BINARY EQUIVALENT
*WRITTEN BY J. D. GREENFIELD 1/24/78
 OPT O OUTPUT OBJECT PGM
 OPT S OUTPUT SYMBOL TABLE
*
 ORG $20
WORD1 FCB 1 MSB BCD NUMBER
WORD2 FCB $69 LSB  PACKED BCD NUMBER
SUM1 FCB 0 BINARY RESULT
SUM2 FCB 0 2ND BINARY BYTE
 SPC 1
START1 LDS #$200 SET STACK
 LDX #LIST
 LDA A WORD2 GET LSB WORD TO BE CONVERTED
SHIFT2 ASR A SHIFT RIGHT
 BCC INCR
 BSR START2 GO TO ADD SUBROUTINE
INCR INX
 INX
 CPX #$120 LIST COMPLETED?
 BEQ HALT YES-GO INTO LOOP ON SELF
 CPX #$110 TEST FOR WORD1
 BNE SHIFT2 LOOP FOR NEXT BIT
 SPC 1
 LDA A WORD1 LOAD MSB BCD WORD
 BRA SHIFT2
 SPC 1
HALT BRA * LOOP BACK 2 BYTES
 SPC 1
* ADD ALGORITHM SUBROUTINE
 SPC 1
START2 PSH A
 LDA A 1,X LOAD LSB FROM LIST
 ADD A SUM2 ADD LSB OF SUM
 STA A SUM2 UPDATE SUM
 LDA A 0,X LOAD MSB FROM LIST
 ADC A SUM1 ADD MSB OF SUM
 STA A SUM1 UPDATE SUM
 PUL A
 RTS RETURN TO MAIN PROGRAM
 SPC 2
 ORG $100
LIST FDB 1
 FDB 2
 FDB 4
 FDB 8
 FDB 10
 FDB 20
 FDB 40
 FDB 80
 FDB 100
 FDB 200
 FDB 400
 FDB 800
 FDB 1000
 FDB 2000
 FDB 4000
 FDB 8000
 SPC 1
 END
```

Figure 6-2 Source program for Example 5-13.

by referencing it to the immediate value (#) of the LIST label (i.e., its address). The value of LIST is $100 because of the ORG statement immediately preceding it.

To summarize, the source program of Example 5-13 is shown in Fig. 6-2 as written in the assembly format using the following steps:

1. The name BCDBIN was assigned to the program on the top line by the NAM directive.
2. Four lines of comments were added. (Comments should be used for every program.)
3. The options desired (those not selected by default) were added by using OPT O and OPT S directives.
4. The program was set to start at address $20 by the ORG statement and initialization of the data locations was accomplished by using the FCB directive to set initially the BCD words to 169 and the sum to 0.
5. The program continues until the HALT label is encountered. This "branch-on-self" instruction locks up the PC in a loop. Note the use of labels such as SHIFT2 for all instructions that are the object of branches or jumps. Note also that blank lines were used after each branch by means of the SPC directive.
6. The subroutine is located outside the main program flow but is referenced by the START2 label.
7. The list table was written as a string of FDB directives because each one should be a 16-bit number. Decimal numbers are used for convenience and the assembler converts them to hex.
8. The END statement completes the source program.

The assembled program is shown in Fig. 6-3. It should be carefully compared with the source listing of Fig. 6-2. Note the formatting into fields and blank lines. One can also see how the decimal values and offset address were calculated by the assembler. The blank lines are created by the SPC directive.

6-7 THE TWO-PASS ASSEMBLER

To convert a source program to an object program, this Motorola assembler must read the source program twice. It is known as a *two-pass* assembler. When it reads through the program the first time (called the first pass or pass 1), the number of bytes required for each instruction is determined and the PC is incremented accordingly. As each label or symbol is encountered its address is stored away in the symbol table but nothing is printed (except errors if they occur). During the second reading (pass 2), the values of these labels are inserted in the object code and the offsets are calculated by the assembler for each branch instruction. It then prints the assembly listing as shown in Fig. 6-3. It also produces the object code in a form that allows it to be entered into the μC (see Section 6-9).

```
                        NAM    BCDBIN
                 *PROGRAM TO CONVERT BCD NUMBERS TO BINARY
                 *WORD1 & WORD2 CONTAIN THE BCD WORDS
                 *SUM1 &SUM2 CONTAIN THE BINARY EQUIVALENT
                 *WRITTEN BY J. D. GREENFIELD 1/24/78
                        OPT    O        OUTPUT OBJECT PGM
                        OPT    S        OUTPUT SYMBOL TABLE
                 *
0020                    ORG    $20
0020 01          WORD1  FCB    1        MSB BCD NUMBER
0021 69          WORD2  FCB    $69      LSB  PACKED BCD NUMBER
0022 00          SUM1   FCB    0        BINARY RESULT
0023 00          SUM2   FCB    0        2ND BINARY BYTE

0024 8E 0200     START1 LDS    #$200    SET STACK
0027 CE 0100            LDX    #LIST
002A 96 21              LDA A  WORD2    GET LSB WORD TO BE CONVERTED
002C 47          SHIFT2 ASR A           SHIFT RIGHT
002D 24 02              BCC    INCR
002F 8D 12              BSR    START2   GO TO ADD SUBROUTINE
0031 08          INCR   INX
0032 08                 INX
0033 8C 0120            CPX    #$120    LIST COMPLETED?
0036 27 09              BEQ    HALT     YES-GO INTO LOOP ON SELF
0038 8C 0110            CPX    #$110    TEST FOR WORD1
003B 26 EF              BNE    SHIFT2   LOOP FOR NEXT BIT

003D 96 20              LDA A  WORD1    LOAD MSB BCD WORD
003F 20 EB              BRA    SHIFT2

0041 20 FE       HALT   BRA    *        LOOP BACK 2 BYTES

                 * ADD ALGORITHM SUBROUTINE

0043 36          START2 PSH A
0044 A6 01              LDA A  1,X      LOAD LSB FROM LIST
0046 9B 23              ADD A  SUM2     ADD LSB OF SUM
0048 97 23              STA A  SUM2     UPDATE SUM
004A A6 00              LDA A  0,X      LOAD MSB FROM LIST
004C 99 22              ADC A  SUM1     ADD MSB OF SUM
004E 97 22              STA A  SUM1     UPDATE SUM
0050 32                 PUL A
0051 39                 RTS             RETURN TO MAIN PROGRAM


0100                    ORG    $100
0100 0001        LIST   FDB    1
0102 0002               FDB    2
0104 0004               FDB    4
0106 0008               FDB    8
0108 000A               FDB    10
010A 0014               FDB    20
010C 0028               FDB    40
010E 0050               FDB    80
0110 0064               FDB    100
0112 00C8               FDB    200
0114 0190               FDB    400
0116 0320               FDB    800
0118 03E8               FDB    1000
011A 07D0               FDB    2000
011C 0FA0               FDB    4000
011E 1F40               FDB    8000

     0000               END
WORD1  0020 WORD2  0021 SUM1   0022 SUM2   0023 START1 0024
SHIFT2 002C INCR   0031 HALT   0041 START2 0043 LIST   0100

TOTAL ERRORS 00000
```

FIGURE 6-3 Assembly listing for BCDBIN program.

6-8 ERROR INDICATION

If the source program is not written in accordance with the rules specified for each type of statement, error lines will be printed. A list of these errors is shown in Table 6-2. Note that each error has a number. The manual provides an explanation of each type of error as an aid to debugging. The most common causes of errors are improper spacing and the use of illegal characters.

Most of the errors are printed during pass 1 and allow the operator to abort the assembly in order to make corrections. If there are only a few errors and they are not serious, he or she may elect to let the assembler complete the listing anyway so that an object machine code file can be obtained and tested. Usually, other revisions are also required. In addition to the printing of an error number, which identifies the type of error, the original line is reprinted (unformatted) so that the programmer can find any mistake. Often the error is not obvious, and the rules may have to be reviewed before the reason for it is found. Some errors, such as error 208 (out-of-range), are not encountered until pass 2 is in progress. This occurs in pass 2 because the relative addressing offsets cannot be calculated by the assembler until the label table is completed during pass 1. An error total is printed at the end of each assembly.

The assembler listing of a program to provide communication through an Asynchronous Communications Interface Adapter (ACIA) is shown in Fig. 6-4a. This device is described in Chapter 8.

Errors were discovered on line 15 during assembly of the program. This resulted in two errors being printed during pass 1 (Fig. 6-4b) and three during pass 2 (in the listing of Fig. 6-4a). Table 6-2 indicates that 216 is an operand error. A study of line 13 shows a similar instruction, and it appears that the errors were caused by an omitted space following the binary number in the operand. This is obviously also a syntax error (204 error). The 211 error was listed because the assembler thought it found a new undefined label. Note also that the machine code was incorrectly calculated (10 instead of 11). The total error count is the total for both passes. Figure 6-4c is explained in Section 6-9. Other errors, not related to spacing or improper syntax, frequently occur in new programs because of label conflicts. If a label is omitted a 211 error (undefined symbol) is printed, and the label, followed by FFFF, is printed during pass 1. If a label is used twice a 206 error (redefined label) is printed, and all references to the label are printed during pass 1. In each case, a line number is also printed, which makes it easy to find.

6-9 OBJECT CODE OUTPUT

All Motorola assembler programs, whether on a larger computer or resident in the μP Development System, produce object tapes (or files) in an ASCII-hex format, as shown in Table 6-3. This format includes three types of lines: the S0 or *name* line, the S1 or *data* line, and the S9 or *terminating* line. Figure 6-4*c* shows the object output for the ACIA1 program.

Each line starts with either S0, S1, or S9, which identifies the type of line. This

TABLE 6-2 Assembler Error Messages

201 NAM DIRECTIVE ERROR
MEANING: The NAM directive is not the first source statement, or it occurs more than once in the same source program (Applies only to version 1.2)

202 EQU DIRECTIVE SYNTAX ERROR
MEANING: The EQU directive requires a label (Applies only to version 1.2)

204 STATEMENT SYNTACTICALLY INCORRECT
MEANING: The source statement is syntactically incorrect.

205 LABEL ERROR
MEANING: The statement may not have a label or the label is syntactically incorrect.

206 REDEFINED SYMBOL
MEANING: The symbol has been previously defined.

207 UNDEFINED OPCODE
MEANING: the symbol in the operation code field is not a valid operation code mnemonic or directive.

208 BRANCH ERROR
MEANING: The branch count is beyond the relative byte's range. The allowance is
$(*+2) - 128 \leq D \leq (*+2) + 127$
where D = address of the destination of the branch
where D = instruction.
* = address of the first byte of the branch instruction.

209 ILLEGAL ADDRESS MODE
MEANING: The mode of addressing is not allowed with the operation code type.

210 BYTE OVERFLOW
MEANING: A one-byte expression has been converted to a value greater than 255_{10} or less than -128_{10}.

211 UNDEFINED SYMBOL
MEANING: The symbol does not appear in the label field.

213* EQU DIRECTIVE SYNTAX ERROR
MEANING: The EQU directive requires a label.

216 DIRECTIVE OPERAND ERROR
MEANING: The directive operand field is in error.

218 MEMORY ERROR
MEANING: The memory option was used and the object code was directed to overwrite the assembler/editor or into nonexistent memory.

(a)

```
00001                           NAM     ACIA1
00002                   *PROGRAM FOR AN ACIA IN SYSTEM NOT REQUIRNG
00003                   *ERROR CHECKING OR WIRED INTERRUPTS

00005          8008     ACIACS EQU     $8008      CONTROL/STATUS REG ADDR
00006          8009     ACIAD  EQU     $8009      DATA REGISTERS ADDR
00007                          OPT     O,S        SELECT OBJECT & SYMBOLS

00009 0100                     ORG     $100

00011                   *INITIALIZATION

00013 0100 86 03       INIT    LDA A   #%00000011  =HEX 3
00014 0102 B7 8008             STA A   ACIACS     MASTER RESET
****ERROR  216
****ERROR  204
****ERROR  211
00015 0105 86 10        LDA A #%00010001= 8 BITS+2 STOP+DVD BY 16
00016 0107 B7 8008             STA A   ACIACS     PROGRAM THE ACIA
00017 010A 39                  RTS                RETURN TO OTHER SYSTEM INIT.

00019 010B B6 8008 INPUT       LDA A   ACIACS     GET STATUS WORD
00020 010E 47                  ASR A              SHIFT RDRF INTO CARRY
00021 010F 24 FA               BCC     INPUT      LOOP TIL BIT SET
00022 0111 B6 8009             LDA A   ACIAD      BRING IN CHARACTER

00024 0114 F6 8008 OUTPUT      LDA B   ACIACS     GET STATUS
00025 0117 C5 02               BIT B   #2         TX BIT SET?
00026 0119 27 F9               BEQ     OUTPUT     NO LOOP TIL READY
00027 011B B7 8009             STA A   ACIAD      PRINT CHARACTER
00028 011E 39                  RTS
00029                          END
ACIACS 8008
ACIAD  8009
INIT   0100
INPUT  010B
OUTPUT 0114

TOTAL ERRORS 00005
```

(b)

```
 ****ERROR  216
 ****ERROR  204
0015 0105 86 10      LDA A #%00010001= 8 BITS+2 STOP+DVD BY 16

        FFFF
```

(c)

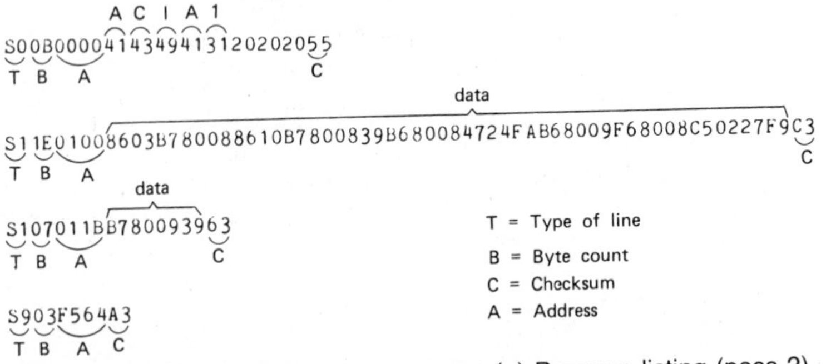

Figure 6-4 Assembler output showing an error. (a) Program listing (pass 2). (b) Printout for pass 1. (c) Printout of object code output.

TABLE 6-3 Object Code ASCII-Hex Format

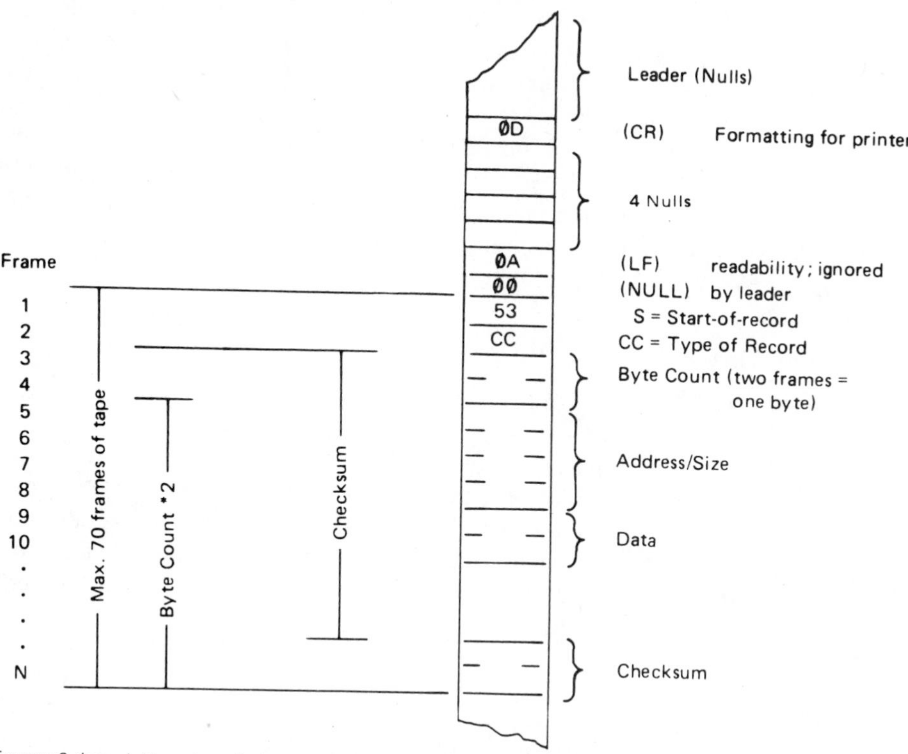

Frames 3 through N are hexadecimal digits represented by a 7-bit ASCII character. Two hexadecimal digits are combined to make one 8-bit byte

The checksum is the one's complement of the summation of 8-bit bytes.

Frame	CC = 30 Header Record		CC = 31 Data Record		CC = 39 End-of-File Record	
1. Start-of-Record	53	S	53	S	53	S
2. Type of Record	30	0	31	1	39	9
3. Byte Count	31	12	31	16	30	03
4.	32		36		33	
5. Address/Size	30	0000	31	1100	30	0000
6.	30		31		30	
7.	30		30		30	
8.	30		30		30	
9. Data	34	48-H	39	98	46	FC (Checksum)
10.	38		38		43	
.	34	44-D	30	32		
.	34		32			
.	35	52-R	41	A8 (Checksum)		
.	32		48			
.						
N. Checksum	39	9E				
	45					

is followed by a *byte count* (two hexadecimal characters) that defines the number of bytes in the remainder of the line. The *address* where the data will go is then listed, followed by the data bytes themselves. The line ends with a checksum byte. The **checksum** is used by the loader routine to verify that no errors were made. As Table 6-3 shows, *the checksum is the 1s complement of the summation of all of the data,* including the *byte count* and *the address bytes*. It is calculated by the assembler and is recorded on the tape as the last byte of each line. The loading function of the monitor program used in the development system (see Chapter 10) recalculates the sum as it loads the program and prints an error message if it is wrong. This avoids wasting time with a faulty program.

6-9.1 The S0 Line

The three types of lines produced by the assembler for the ACIA1 program are shown in Fig. 6-4*c*. The top line is the S0 line. S0 is followed by the byte count (0B), indicating that there are 11 bytes following. The next 2 bytes are not used and are set to 0000 for the S0 line. The remaining bytes are the ASCII codes for the letters of the program name. The 20s are ASCII spaces and indicate that the assembler will accept up to eight characters in the name. If the bytes following the 0B are added, it will be found that they total $AA. The 1s complement is $55, as shown in the checksum.

6-9.2 The S1 Line

The S1 line contains the object codes of the program. There may be many S1 lines since the largest number of data bytes for each line is 27_{10}. This varies with different assemblers or monitors, which also generate this format. Some programs provide 16 bytes of data per line. The last line can be anything less, even only 1 byte of data.

Figure 6-4*c* shows two S1 lines. Note that the address of the first line is $0100, which corresponds to the ORG statement as the starting address. The bytes of data then follow (i.e., 86 03 37 80 etc.). The address in the second line is $011B, which is the address of the 28th byte of data.

6-9.3 The S9 Line

The S9 line signifies the end of the object code. The byte count and checksum for this terminating line are calculated in the same way as for the other type lines. The address is shown as 0000 in most assemblers, but later versions have an option to include the starting address for the program in the S9 line as shown in Fig. 6-4*c*.

6-10 ASSEMBLER OPERATION USING A TAPE-EQUIPPED TERMINAL

With the original ASR33 teletypewriters (TTYs), the most common way to store and load programs was to use punched paper tapes, where each character is determined by the hole pattern punched into the tape. Figure 6-5 shows such a tape and the hole pattern for each ASCII character (a hole is equivalent to a "1"). This ASR33 (automatic send–receive) teletypewriter terminal was very popular because it combined the following features:

1. Keyboard entry
2. Hard copy (printed paper) output
3. Tape punch (to save programs)
4. Tape reader (to load programs)

The TTY has been replaced in almost all laboratories by newer devices because it is noisy and slow. Equivalent functions can be had in the newer, quieter, and faster ASR733 terminal made by TI, but even it has been superseded by CRTs and disk systems. The ASR733 uses magnetic cassettes in place of paper tape. Since both the ASR33 and ASR733 tape terminals respond to the standard ASCII control characters (DC1, DC2, DC3, and DC4) to start and stop the tapes [i.e., to read or record (punch) the tapes], the same basic version of the assembler (and editor) can be used. It must be selected so that the I/O addresses match the monitor ROM in use, however.

Although these systems are now largely obsolete, a few still exist, and because of their simplicity they are good models for explaining how the assembler works. The reader is encouraged to work with the newer equipment now being used, however, which is described in later sections of this chapter.

Here are the steps in the development of software using the coresident tape assembler:

1. The assembler/editor programs are loaded into memory from tape using the LOAD routine of the system monitor program (e.g., EXBUG, MIKBUG, MINIBUG).
2. Once loaded, the editor program is entered (at $103 for this version of the tape editor) and prints the editor heading.
3. If the terminal uses cassettes, a blank tape is placed in the record side of the terminal. (With a TTY, it is only necessary to see that paper tape is in the punch.)
4. The source statements are then typed on the terminal and are transferred to tape by the editor. (See the editor manual referenced in Section 6-13 for full instructions.)
5. After the source tape has been run through edit until it is fully corrected and

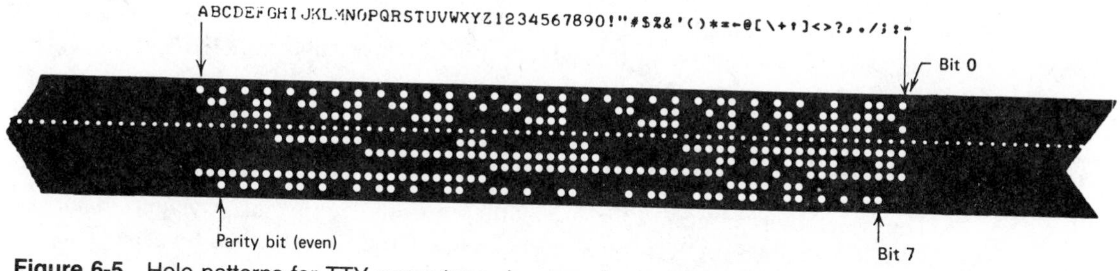

Figure 6-5 Hole patterns for TTY paper tape showing all printable characters.

complete, it is rewound and set up in the reader. Another blank cassette is installed if an object tape is desired.

6. The assembler program is entered (at $100) and prints the assembler heading.
7. The pass number is entered on the terminal keyboard. Enter 1P or 1S for pass 1 (with or without clearing the symbol table), or 2L, 2T, or 2P for pass 2 to request a listing, an object tape, or both.
8. The assembler outputs a reader ON command (ASCII DC1) to start the tape.
9. The characters of each line are stored in the assembler's buffer until the carriage return (CR) is detected.
10. After the carriage return and line feed characters are sent, the reader OFF character (DC3) is transmitted and the reader stops.
11. The assembler scans its buffer and processes each instruction. OP codes are looked up in a table and stored temporarily. The line number and PC counters are incremented as required. If pass 1 is in progress, the labels and their address are stored in the symbol table. Nothing is printed unless an error is detected. When the END statement is encountered, the assembler heading is printed again. The tape is then rewound and step 7 is repeated.
12. When pass 2 is executed, steps 8 through 11 are repeated. After the Op codes are processed, the PRINT routine of the assembler is entered. This routine prints the line number, program counter, and machine codes previously stored. It looks up all references in the symbol table and inserts the proper values for each label. It formats these properly (inserting the necessary spaces or lines) and then prints the contents of the line buffer, which was read from the source tape, exactly as the programmer wrote it (except for added spaces). Any comments that follow on the same line are also printed but are limited to 29 characters since the assemblers are set for a maximum of 72 characters on a line.
13. When the assembler begins pass 2, it reads the first source statement, which is the NAM line, and prints the page number and program name at the top of a page. It then outputs a line of code to the output tape. This line is formatted as described in Section 6-9. After about five source lines have been read, processed, and printed, enough bytes have been saved to output another object code line to the record cassette.
14. The succeeding lines are then read and processed as described until the END statement is reached. The remaining object codes are then put on the tape as shown in line 3 of Fig. 6-4*c*. The tape is terminated by an end-of-file record (or line), which begins with an S9 (last line of Fig. 6-4*c*).
15. The program prints the assembler header message again as described in step 2 and waits for another command. If an "X" is typed at this point, the program control is returned to the system monitor program (e.g., EXBUG or MIKBUG).

6-10.1 Assembler Operation Using Floppy Disk Storage

The assembler programs for use with Motorola floppy disk systems (such as EXORciser and EXORset) are nearly identical to that described for tape. The I/O routines are different, however, because the source program must be read from a file on the disk rather than from a tape, and the object code is written into another disk file. The assembly operation is also similar except that both passes are performed when only one command is typed. The program control returns to the disk executive when assembly is completed. The command line includes the names of the input and output files and the options that specify whether an object file, program listing, or both are required. (Refer to the disk operating system manuals available with the product.)

6-10.2 Coresident Assembler/Editor Memory Requirements

This assembler editor is really two programs that can be resident in memory at the same time. This was desirable since it took up to 25 minutes to load the assembler when using paper tape. With the disk version this is not important, since the disk assembler can be loaded in a few seconds. When using the coresident tape assembler in a μP development system a minimum of 8K of RAM is required. The assembler occupies memory from $300 to $1610, as shown in the memory map of Fig. 6-6. The area from $100 to $300 is used for I/O routines, and the symbol (label) table extends above 1D00. The area of memory below $100 is used for scratch (RMBs). It will also be seen that the editor program (which is used to write the source program) can be in memory simultaneously between $1610 and $1D05.

In the course of program development, it is not uncommon to reedit a source program and reassemble it several times before all errors are eliminated. The editor uses the same I/O routines and scratch memory area. It also uses the memory between the top of the editor ($1D05) and the end of an 8K RAM module ($1FFF) for the edit buffer (755 bytes). The assembler uses the same area for a symbol table. This provides for 93 symbols. If a larger symbol table is required, this area can be extended at either end. Selecting the editor overwrite feature increases the area to accommodate up to 312 symbols, since the area then starts at $1610, but it is necessary to reload the editor to use it again. The assembler overwrite flag can be used to extend the edit buffer, but if more than 8K of RAM is available in the software development system, the table can be extended to the end of available memory by modifying the end-of-memory vector without overwriting either program.

6-11 ASSEMBLERS FOR VARIOUS HARDWARE CONFIGURATIONS

Various assembler programs are provided by Motorola and other companies to generate **6800** system software. Most are designed to be used with one of the standard μP development systems (see Chapters 10 and 12). Some of these systems are specialized **6800 family** systems such as the Motorola EXORciser and EXORset and have *monitor control* programs in integrated circuit ROMs. The older coresident assemblers were intended to be used with these systems and the

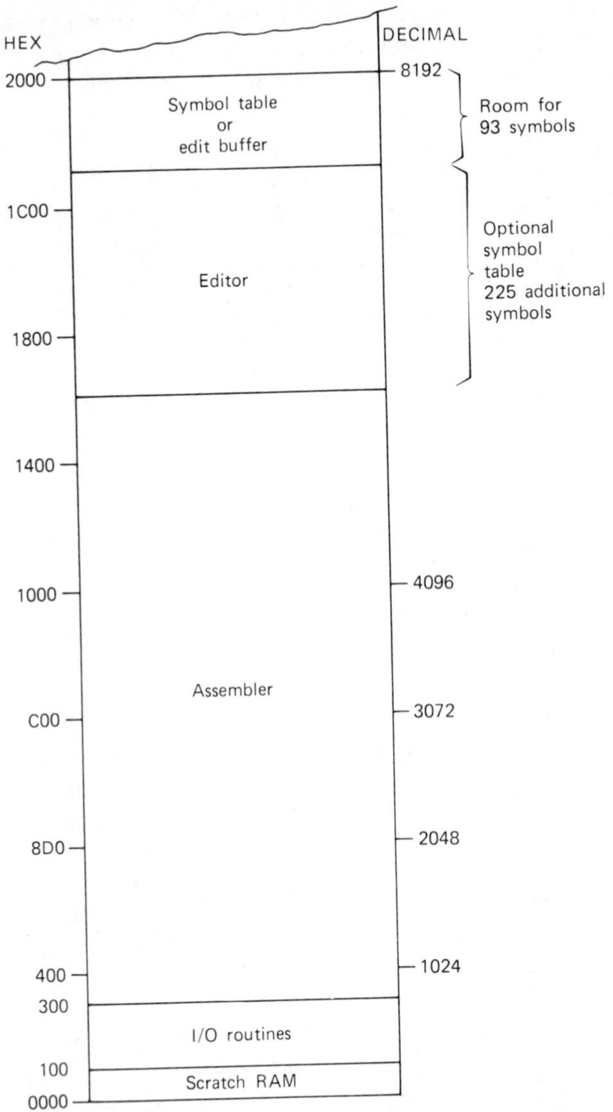

Figure 6-6 Coresident assembler/editor memory map (tape version).

ROMs contain the I/O routines to work with terminals that use paper tape or cassettes and respond to the ASCII control codes (e.g. DC1). Other 8-bit assemblers were intended to work with disk operating systems such as EDOS (now obsolete), MDOS, and XDOS (for the EXORset). Thousands of EXORciser, both **6800** and **6809**, versions have been shipped but are now also obsolete. The EXORset is still in production in the European division of Motorola Microsystems. It is a **6809** system using $5\frac{1}{4}$-inch disks. One of the functions of these systems is to serve as a software development station to write, edit, assemble, and debug **6800 family** programs (**6800**, **6801**, **6805**, and **6809** μPs and μCs are supported). Various versions of the monitor programs used with this early hardware are in use under the names EXBUG, EXORbug, MIKBUG, MINIBUG, MICROBUG, and JBUG. Each one requires a different version of the assembler/editor programs, primarily because of the different addresses for the I/O routines. Disk versions were available only for EXBUG (for the EXORciser) and EXORbug (for the EXORset).

Through the years there has been growing use of cross-assemblers, and Motorola and others provide a complete line of them for the **6800 family** that run on the **68000** computers. These are used with the μC development systems described in Chapter 12. Versions of assemblers were also available to run on IBM 370, DEC PDP-11, and IBM or other microcomputers. Radio Shack provides a **6809** assembler for use with its color computer that uses the Z80 processor. When these nondevelopment systems are used to generate software, new problems arise and other equipment is needed to download the object programs and to debug them. This is discussed in Chapters 10 and 12.

6-11.1 Advanced Assemblers

Up to now, the descriptions of the assembler functions have been limited to those provided by the *coresident assembler* in order to keep things simple. There are, however, several newer assemblers for the 8-bit μPs with dramatically improved capability. These assemblers are generally known as *macro assemblers,* but they also include other features:

1. Linking
2. Relocation
3. Macro operations
4. Conditional assembly

Generally it can be said that these concepts make it easier to write large programs.

6-11.2 Linking Object Modules

The linking scheme used with the macro assemblers is a means of modularizing the source program into *sections* and was developed to provide the following capabilities:

1. Parallel program development by a team
2. Program relocation
3. Multiple program linking
4. Easy development of programs for a RAM/ROM environment
5. Easy specification of any addressing mode
6. Specification of uninitialized areas of memory called *blank common*
7. Specification of initialized areas of memory called *named common*

The word **initialize** is used by programmers to indicate that memory locations or registers are given a value initially, to allow the program to start up properly. This value could be zero or could be made equal to some constant, depending on the instructions used by the programmer. The RAM in a certain area may be cleared (zeroed), for example.

Program sections provide the basis of the relocation and linking scheme. In the Motorola Macro assembler there are five different sections:

> ASCT, or *absolute* section, is a nonrelocatable section. There may be a limited number of absolute sections in a user's program. These sections are used to allocate or initialize memory locations that are assigned by the programmer rather than by the **6800** Linking Loader (explained below). For example, ASCT can be used to define the locations of PIAs or ACIAs.
>
> BSCT, or *base* section, is a relocatable section. There is only one base section. The **6800** linking loader assigns portions of the base section to each module that requires space in the BSCT. The base section is generally used for variables that are to be accessed using the direct addressing mode. BSCT is restricted to memory locations 0–255 inclusive (decimal).
>
> CSCT, or *blank common,* is a relocatable section. There is only one blank common section. CSCT is similar to blank common used in Fortran. The blank common section cannot be initialized.
>
> DSCT, or *data* section, is a relocatable section. There is only one data section. The **6800** linking loader assigns portions of this section to each program that requires space in DSCT. DSCT is generally used to contain variables that are in RAM and are to be accessed using the extended addressing mode.
>
> PSCT, or *program* section, is a relocatable section. There is only one program section. PSCT is similar to DSCT. However, it is generally used to contain program instructions. Use of DSCT and PSCT facilitates creation of programs that reside in ROM but access variables in RAM.

Uninitialized blank common is placed in CSCT as described above. At times, however, it is convenient to have several common areas, each of which may be initialized. Therefore, the concept of *named common* was included in the relocation and linking scheme. Named common can be specified in either BSCT, DSCT, or PSCT. The size of the named common area that is allocated will be the largest of the named common sizes, from the program modules that reference it. A named common block must reside wholly within a single section.

The *load map* shown in Fig. 6-7 illustrates a typical memory map that might be produced by loading two program modules. EX1 and EX2. The module EX1 requires memory to be reserved in BSCT, CSCT, DSCT, and PSCT, although the only space necessary in DSCT is for the named common area NCOM1. The module EX2 requires that memory be allocated in BSCT, CSCT, DSCT, and PSCT. Neither module defines any ASCT blocks.

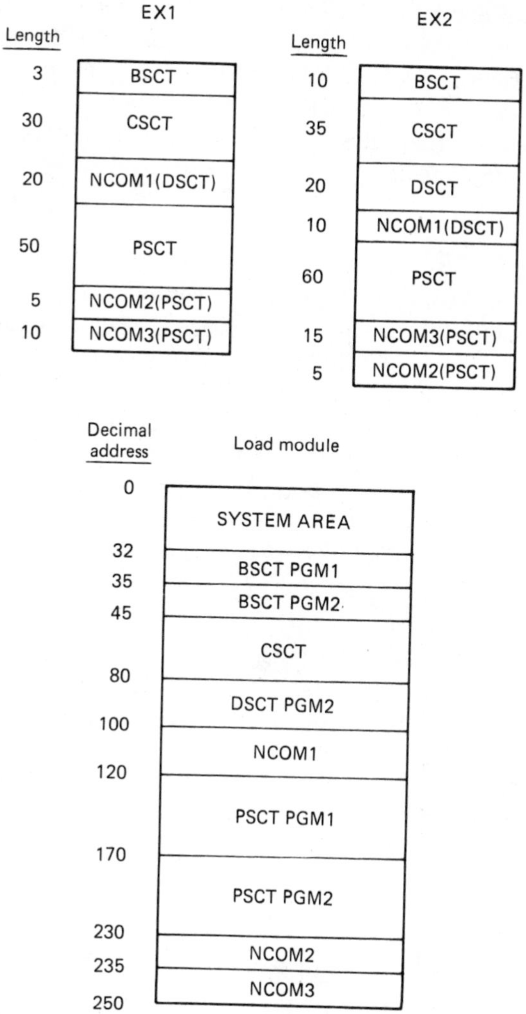

EX1

Length	
3	BSCT
30	CSCT
20	NCOM1(DSCT)
50	PSCT
5	NCOM2(PSCT)
10	NCOM3(PSCT)

EX2

Length	
10	BSCT
35	CSCT
20	DSCT
10	NCOM1(DSCT)
60	PSCT
15	NCOM3(PSCT)
5	NCOM2(PSCT)

Decimal address	Load module
0	SYSTEM AREA
32	BSCT PGM1
35	BSCT PGM2
45	CSCT
80	DSCT PGM2
100	NCOM1
120	PSCT PGM1
170	PSCT PGM2
230	NCOM2
235	NCOM3
250	

Figure 6-7 Load maps showing memory section assignments.

The BSCTs for both EX1 and EX2 are allocated memory within the first 256 bytes of memory. As shown, the first 32 ($20 hex) bytes of BSCT are reserved by the loader for use by the disk operating system, unless otherwise directed. After BSCT, space for blank common is allocated, followed by space for the EX2 DSCT. Since EX1 requires no DSCT for its exclusive use, none will be allocated. The named common block NCOM1 within DSCT is assigned memory at the end of DSCT. Finally, the PSCTs for EX1 and EX2 are allocated along with the PSCT common blocks NCOM2 and NCOM3.

The loader assigns memory within sections in the order in which the modules are specified. Named common blocks are allocated memory at the end of their corresponding section, in the order in which they are defined. Figure 6-8 shows a load map produced by loading EX2 followed by EX1. This map is different from the map in Fig. 6-7, where EX1 was loaded first.

For a complete description of the linking loader, the reference manuals listed in Section 6-13 should be consulted.

6-11.3 Relocation

Relocation refers to the process of binding a program to a set of memory locations at a time other than during the assembly process. For example, if subroutine "ABC" is to be used by many different programs, it is desirable to allow the subroutine to reside in any area of memory. One way to reposition the subroutine in memory is to change the "ORG" directive's operand field at the beginning of the subroutine and then reassemble the routine. A disadvantage of this method is the expense in time and effort of reassembling ABC. An alternative to multiple assemblies is to assemble ABC once, producing a **relocatable object module** that

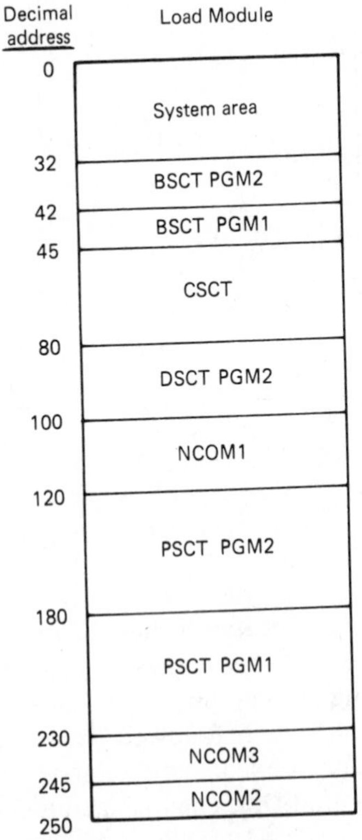

Figure 6-8 Load map showing memory assignments when EX2 loaded first.

contains enough information so that another program (the **6800 linking loader**) can easily assign a new set of memory locations to the module. This scheme offers the following advantages:

1. Reassembly is not required.
2. The object module is substantially smaller than the source program.
3. Relocation is faster than reassembly.
4. Relocation can be handled by the linking loader (rather than editing the source program and changing the ORG directive).

In addition to program relocation, the linking loader must resolve interprogram references. For example, the other programs that are to use subroutine ABC must contain a jump-to-subroutine instruction to ABC. However, since ABC is not assembled at the same time as the calling program, the assembler cannot put the address of the subroutine into the operand field of the subroutine call. The linking loader, however, will know where the calling program resides and, hence, can resolve the reference to the call to ABC. This process of resolving interprogram references is called "linking."

6-11.4 Macros

Programming applications frequently involve coding a repeated pattern of instructions. These patterns frequently also require variable entries at each iteration. A shorthand notation for handling this is called a **macro**. Having determined the iterative pattern, the programmer can, within the macro, designate fields of any statement as variable.

When the pattern is defined, it is given a name. This name becomes the mnemonic by which the macro can be invoked. (It can be called from various places in the program.) The programmer can use the entire pattern as many times as needed, substituting different parameters for the designated variable portions of the statements (substitutable arguments).

The macro causes source statements to be generated by the assembler. The statements may contain *substitutable arguments*. They can also be any processor instruction, almost any assembler directive, or any previously defined macro.

Once a macro is debugged, it simplifies coding just as a modular subroutine does.

To invoke a macro, the macro mnemonic must appear in the Op code field of a source statement. Any arguments are placed in the operand field. By suitably selecting these arguments, the programmer causes the assembler to produce in-line coding variations of the macro definition.

The effect of a macro call is the same as an open subroutine, in that it produces in-line code to perform the macro function. The code is inserted in the normal flow of the program so that the generated instructions are executed in-line with the rest of the program each time the macro is called.

The following example applies to all **6800 family** assemblers except for the **M6805** Macro Assembler (because it does not have a B accumulator).

If the following three code patterns were used in a program:

```
ADDA   LA+5        ADDA   LU          ADDA   LW+LX
ADCB   LB+5        ADCB   LV          ADCB   LY+LZ
SUBA   LC          SUBA   ALPHA       SUBA   GAMMA
SBCB   LD          SBCB   BETA        SBCB   DELTA
```

then the following macro definition could be used:

```
LDM     MACR
        ADDA   \0
        ADCB   \1
        SUBA   \2
        SBCB   \3
        ENDM
```

with \0, \1, \2, and \3 as the substitutable arguments.

In each case, the previous coding examples could be replaced as follows:

```
LDM     LA+5, LB+5, LC, LD
 .
 .
LDM     LU, LV, ALPHA, BETA
 .
 .
LDM     LW+LX, LY+LZ, GAMMA, DELTA
```

The LDM calls the macro, and the substitutable arguments are the operands that follow. They substitute in the macro for the appropriate backslash character, \0, \1, etc. The assembler recognizes these substitutable arguments by the presence of the backslash (\).

6-11.5 Conditional Assembly

Conditional assembly allows the programmer to write a comprehensive source program that can cover many conditions. Assembly conditions may be specified through the use of arguments in the case of macros and through definition of symbols via the SET and EQU directives. Variations of parameters can then cause assembly of only those parts or instructions necessary for the specified conditions.

For example,

```
*
* DEVTYP = 0   MEANS DISK I/O
* DEVTYP = 1   MEANS TAPE I/O
*
                .
                .
                IFEQ DEVTYP
                .
                .  DISK I/O STATEMENTS
                .
                .
```

```
ENDC
IFNE DEVTYP
.
.   TAPE I/O STATEMENTS
.
ENDC
```

When the program above is assembled, one of the I/O sections will be included and one will be excluded based on the assembly time value of the symbol DEVTYP.

If the statement DEVTYP = 0 is placed in the source file prior to any references, the disk I/O will be included. If DEVTYP = 1, the disk I/O will be excluded and the tape I/O will be included. Other conditional directives could have been used (e.g., "greater than" or "less than"). The conditional assembly feature makes it possible to have one source file that will accommodate any number of different hardware "conditions." Having one file makes it easier to keep the performance the same for all versions.

6-11.6 Modern Macro Assemblers

The features just described are included in a group of assembler programs that are available to develop assembly language programs for Motorola **6800**, **6801**, **6804**, **6805**, **6809**, and **68HC11** microprocessors. The programs are so similar that only one manual is required to describe them all. This reference manual contains the rules, examples, and guidelines to help programmers, system designers, analysts, and software engineers to write and understand the software. Throughout this manual, these microprocessors are referred to as the **6800 family.** The information contained in the manual pertains only to the operation of the assemblers. Detailed information on individual members of the **6800** family μPs or μCs can be found in their reference manuals and some of them will also be described in chapter 11 of this book. Section 6-11.7 contains a list of appropriate manuals for members of the **6800** family.

The assemblers are used to translate assembly language source programs into object modules for **6800** family systems and are referred to in these manuals as relocatable assemblers (RASMs) and structured cross-assemblers (XASMs). The RASM family of assemblers are all nearly identical with one exception (an ASM assembler is provided for the **6804** μP).

Listed below are the items that perform together:

Category	*OP System*	*Hardware Required*
RASMs (and ASM04)	MDOS	EXORciser Development System
	XDOS	EXORset Development System
XASMs	VERSAdos	EXORmacs Development System
		VMC 68/2 Microcomputer System
		VME/10 Microcomputer Development System
		Any VME-based μP system with Versados (VME101, VME110, VME115, VME120, etc.)

6-11.7 Scope

The M68XRASM/D1 (or later) manual provides assembler information on two product groups: EXORciser-MDOS/ EXORset-XDOS, and VERSAdos. The list below shows the assembler for each product group.

EXORcisers-MDOS and EXORset-XDOS products

RASM	(**6800/6801** Relocatable Assembler)
RASMHC01	(**68HC01** Relocatable Assembler)
ASM04	(**6804** Assembler)
RASM05	(**6805** Relocatable Assembler)
RASM09	(**6809** Relocatable Assembler)
RASMHC11	(**68HC11** Relocatable Assembler)

VERSAdos products (run in a 68000 system)

XASM00	(**6800/6801** Structured Cross-Assembler)
XASMHC01	(**68HC01** Structured Cross-Assembler)
XASM04	(**6804** Structured Cross-Assembler)
XASM05	(**6805** Stuctured Cross-Assembler)
XASM09	(**6809** Structured Cross-Assembler)
XASMHC11	(**68HC11** Structured Cross-Assembler)

6-11.8 6800 Family Structured Cross-Assemblers

The assemblers listed in the last part of the table above are cross-assemblers and run on **68000**-type computers. They perform in the same way as the RASM assemblers. They translate source statements written in the appropriate 8-bit assembly language into relocatable object code, assign storage locations to instructions and data, and perform auxiliary assembler actions designated by the programmer. The assemblers include macro and conditional assembly capabilities and implement certain structured programming control constructs.

RASMs produce object information in Motorola S-record format, memory image format (binary), absolute MDOS/XDOS object files, and relocatable MDOS/XDOS object files. The relocatable MDOS/XDOS object files are compatible with the MDOS linking loader or the XDOS linking loader. The outputs produced by the individual RASM assemblers are indicated in Table 6-4.

TABLE 6-4 RASM Assembler Object Outputs

	Assemblers					
	RASM	RASM HC01	ASM 04	RASM 05	RASM 09	RASM HC11
Motorola S-record format	X	X	X	X	X	X
Absolute MDOS/XDOS loadable object file	X	X	X	X	X	X
Memory image format	X			X	X	
Relocatable MDOS/XDOS object file	X	X		X	X	X

The XASMs (except for XASM04) produce relocatable object code that is compatible with the 8-bit Cross-Linkage Editor. The XASM04 assembler produces object information in Motorola S-record format and in absolute MDOS/XDOS loadable object format.

The MDOS Linking Loader, XDOS linking loader, and 8-bit Cross-Linkage Editor will all be referred to simply as the linkage editor in this manual.

6-12 SUMMARY

Because of its mnemonic nature, assembly language is used for programs far more than is machine language. This chapter explained how to write an assembly language source program and how to translate it to machine language. Detailed printouts of assembler programs were shown and their features presented in detail. Directives, symbol tables, and error messages were demonstrated to help the user write and debug programs. Finally, we described the techniques of linking, relocation, and conditional assembly and the use of macros. These features are now used in the assemblers for the **6800** family of μPs and μCs.

6-13 GLOSSARY

Assembler directive Instruction-like mnemonic that controls the assembler. Some directives produce object code but others affect the formatting of the listing.

Checksum byte Byte calculated by the assembler to be the 1s complement of the sum of the bytes on each line and appended to each line of the object program. It is checked by the loader to verify that no error occurred in loading.

Conditional assembly Assembler feature that includes or excludes certain instructions at will.

Cross-assembler Assembler program that runs on one type of computer and generates object code for a different type of computer. It also produces a program listing.

Direct address Address below $100 that permits 2-byte instructions to be used.

Editor Progam used to write or edit source programs and save them on tape or disk.

Extended addressing Instruction addressing mode that references addresses above $FF using 3-byte instructions.

Immediate addressing Instruction mode that uses the value of the second byte of an instruction instead of treating it as an address as is done for the *direct addressing mode*. In some cases, it uses the value of the second and third bytes as a 16-bit operand.

Indexed addressing Instruction mode that uses the address in the index register (X) for the operand. In some cases it uses this address plus an *OFFSET*.

Inherent instruction Instruction that needs only 1 byte because all the information needed for its execution is already within the μP and no memory locations or immediate operands are required.

Initialize Assign values to memory locations or registers that allow the program to start up properly.

Label Mnemonic word used to reference an address or value.

Linking loader Program to combine relocatable object modules into an absolute load module (for a specific address).

Macro instructions Instruction-like mnemonic that the Macro Assembler replaces with a sequence of assembly language statements.

Monitor Control program, usually in ROM, which provides routines to load or dump programs and to test them. Also allows memory and register contents to be viewed or changed.

Offset Value in the second byte of indexed mode instructions that is added to the index register to get the address of the operand.

Relocatable object module Object code module produced by an assembler intended for use with a linking loader.

Symbol table List of each symbol used by a program and the address or value of that symbol. Symbols are also called labels.

6-14 REFERENCES

Motorola Assembler Manual M68CRA (D), November 1976.

Resident Software Supplement, Third Edition, 1975.

6800, 6801, 6805, 6809 Macro Assembler Reference Manual M68MASR (D2), September 1979.

MDOS Linking Loader Reference Manual M68LLD (D4), September 1979.

M6800 Programming Reference Manual M68PRM (D), November 1976.

M6800 Co-Resident Editor Reference Manual M68CRE (D), January 1977.

M68XRASM/D M6800 Family Macro Assemblers Reference Manual, Motorola Microsystems, May 1984.

These manuals can be purchased from Motorola Semiconductor Products Inc., Literature Distribution Center, P.O. Box 20924, Phoenix, AZ 85036.

6-15 PROBLEMS

6-1 In Fig. 6-3, what are the locations of the following?

a. SUM1
b. START2
c. LIST
d. SHIFT2

6-2 In Fig. 6-3, why aren't lines 27, 30, 32, and 34 printed?

6-3 Which of the following are satisfactory labels?

SAM

SUZY Q

SUZYQ

2SUZY

SUZY2

BILLANDJOE

X

Y

Z

6-4 Verify the relative offset value in location 30 of Fig. 6-3 by adding it to the location of the PC.

6-5 Write an assembly language source program for the program of Table 5-2.

6-6 Write an assembly language source program for the program of Table 5-3.

6-7 What would have happened to the listing of Fig. 6-3 if line 7 (the options) had been omitted?

6-9 Explain how each byte of the second S1 line in Fig. 6-4*c* was obtained.

After attempting to solve these problems, try to answer the self-evaluation questions in Section 6-2. If any of them still seem difficult, review the appropriate sections of the chapter to find the answers.

CHAPTER 7
HARDWARE CONFIGURATION OF THE 6800 SYSTEM

7-1 INSTRUCTIONAL OBJECTIVES

This chapter introduces the student to the hardware components of the **6800** system and examines some of the problems encountered when interconnecting them. After reading this chapter, the student should be able to

1. List each component of the **6800** system and explain its function.
2. Explain the functions of the address and data buses and each line of the **6800** control bus.
3. Determine the number of clock cycles and the number of data bytes required by each instruction.
4. Determine the exact data that appears on the address and data buses at the end of each instruction.
5. Allocate memory space to the various components of a system.

7-2 SELF-EVALUATION QUESTIONS

Watch for the answers to the following questions as you read the chapter. They should help you to understand the material presented.

1. What are the three states of a three-state driver?
2. Why do memories need three-state driver/receivers on their data lines but only receivers on their address lines?
3. What is the purpose of the "memory ready" circuit in the clock module?
4. Are the μP data bus drivers enabled when the R/W line is in READ or WRITE mode? Explain.
5. Explain why BA does not go HIGH as soon as HALT goes LOW.

6. What is the relationship between the access time of the memory used and the clock frequency? Why is it important?
7. Why is it advantageous to have many chip select lines on a component?

7-3 INTRODUCTION TO THE 6800 SYSTEM

When introduced in 1974, the basic **6800** family of microcomputer components consisted of five parts:

1. The **MC6800** microprocessor (μP).
2. **MC6830** masked programmable read-only memory (ROM) (1024 bytes of 8 bits each).
3. **MC6810** static random-access memory (RAM) (128 bytes of 8 bits each).
4. **MC6820** peripheral interface adapter (PIA) (for parallel data input/output).
5. **MC6850** asynchronous communications interface adapter (ACIA) (for serial data input/output).

As shown in Figure 7-1, a complete μC can be built today using the components listed above (with the exception of the 6820, which has been replaced by the 6821) plus a clock, which is needed to control the timing of the system. Several clock devices, such as the **MC6871A** and the **MC6875**, are available. These are *crystal-controlled oscillators* that provide the necessary two-phase nonoverlapping timing pulses and are equipped with output circuits suitable for driving metal-oxide semiconductor (MOS) circuitry.

Since 1974, when these components were first introduced, there have been dramatic improvements in technology and in the amount of circuitry that can be included in MOS integrated circuits (ICs), particularly memories, and thus many new components have been added to the family. Because higher-speed circuits are more easily achieved, the **6830** ROM has been replaced with the faster **68A30**. The **6820** PIA has also been superseded by a later design. It is noteworthy, however, that 10 years later the other basic components are still used in many systems. After these basic parts are described, the newer designs will be introduced.

Figure 7-1 shows that other components are being added to this basic family periodically. Some are to interface various peripheral devices to the **6800** bus, but many are larger single-chip memories. The basic units have also been redesigned to incorporate depletion loads and other technological improvements but are functionally equivalent and physically interchangeable with the older parts. Faster (up to 2 MHz) and wider temperature range units are now available as a result.

Although the **6800** is still manufactured and used in many existing systems, newer designs may, for example, specify the **6802**, which has an identical μP unit but also includes in the single chip a 128-byte RAM (equivalent to the **6810**) and a clock circuit similar to the **6875**. Replacing these three ICs with the **6802** significantly reduces the cost of a system. The **6802** and other enhanced μCs are described in Chapter 11. They are all based on the **6800** instruction set and bus structure, which will be described in the remainder of this chapter.

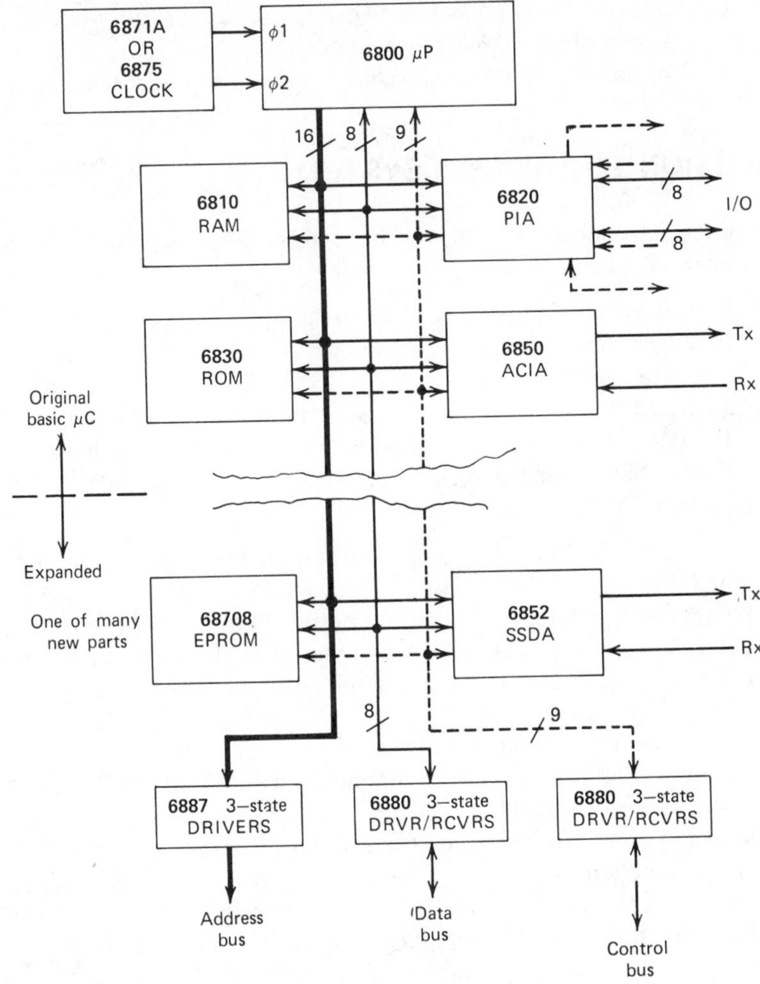

Figure 7-1 The **6800** family components.

7-4 6800 SYSTEM HARDWARE FEATURES

The suitability of the **6800** family of components as elements of a μC system depends on a number of factors. First, *all elements of a computer must be present,* and second, they must be partitioned in the various packages so that they are *modular* and a variety of configurations can easily be assembled. Finally, there is a need for a simple way to interconnect them.

In the system of Fig. 7-1, the program instructions for the system would typically be stored in the **68A30** ROM or the **68764** erasable programmable ROM (EPROM) (or their larger counterparts) and all variable data would be written into or read from the **6810** RAM. Other byte-wide RAMs with up to 2048 bytes are available and might be substituted. The input/output (I/O) of data for the system would be done via the PIA, ACIA, or Synchronous Serial Data Adapter (SSDA).

To understand the ways these units work together, it is necessary to know the hardware features of each part. Figure 7-1 also shows that the system components are interconnected via a 16-wire address bus, an 8-wire data bus, and a 9-wire control bus. For a component to be a member of the **6800** μC family and to ensure compatibility, it must meet specific system *standards*. The standards must also make it convenient for external devices to interface (or communicate) with the **6800** μP. These standards, which apply to all **6800** components, are as follows:

1. 8-bit bidirectional data bus
2. 16-bit address bus
3. Three-state bus switching techniques
4. TTL/DTL level compatible signals (see Section 7-4.4)
5. 5-volt N-channel MOS silicon gate technology
6. 24-, 28-, and 40-pin packages
7. Clock rate 100 kHz to 2 MHz
8. Temperature range 0° to 70°C

7-4.1 The Data Bus

Since the basic word length of the **6800** is 8 bits (1 byte) it communicates with other components via an 8-bit data bus. The data bus is *bidirectional,* and data is transferred into or out of the **6800** over the same bus. A read/write line (one of the control lines) is provided to allow the μP to control the direction of data transfer.

An 8-bit data bus can also accommodate ASCII (American Standard Code for Information Interchange) characters and packed binary coded decimal (two BCD numbers in 1 byte).

7-4.2 The Address Bus

A 16-bit address bus was chosen for these reasons:

1. For programming ease, the addresses should be multiples of 8 bits.
2. An 8-bit address bus would provide only 256 addresses but a 16-bit bus provides 65,536 distinct addresses, which is adequate for most applications.

7-4.3 Three-State Bus Concepts

A typical digital line is normally either HIGH (at the "1" level), or LOW (at the "0" level). A technique has been developed for using **three-state** output devices to interface a number of components, which is advantageous when they must communicate with each other (as in a μC) on a common bus. The concept depends on the ability of all the interconnected components to be switched to a third state that presents a very *high impedance* to the bus. In this way *one, and only one, component is selected* to drive the bus at one time. The selected **6800** system component causes a 1 or a 0 to be placed on each line of the bus in accordance with the data word being transmitted. *All unselected components* must place their bus drivers in the *high-impedance* state. Simultaneously, one of the other components on the bus is enabled to read the data, thus transferring or transmitting it in one direction. This three-state switching (or selection) is controlled by the μP's read/write (R/W) and valid memory address (VMA) lines, along with the address bus. The transfer of information via the data bus can therefore be *bidirectional* over the same eight-line bus. All components of the **6800** family include this three-state capability in their data circuits.

External devices, not part of the family, can be connected to the bus via three-state driver/receivers that are available in dual in-line (DIP) packages. The **MC6880/MC8T26** is a three-state bus driver/receiver whose pin configuration is shown in Fig. 7-2a. The bus **driver/receiver** is a quad IC with four lines connected to the bus, four receiver outputs from the bus, and four driver inputs to the bus. A typical bus application for the **MC6880** is shown in Fig. 7-2b.

The receiver gates are enabled by a LOW (ground) signal on the $\overline{\text{Receiver Enable}}$ (pin 1). These gates invert the data and transfer the information on the bus to the TTL devices connected to the receiver outputs. When $\overline{\text{Receiver Enable}}$ is HIGH, the four receiver outputs are in the high-impedance state and are effectively disconnected from the bus. The **6800** drives the bus whenever its Driver Enable input (pin 15) is HIGH. The state of the four driver inputs determines the state of the four bus lines, and the data is again inverted. If Driver Enable is LOW, the bus outputs of the **6880** are in the high-impedance state, allowing another device to drive the bus.

An inverted data bus presents no problem since the data is reinverted by the following receiver. The **8T28** is a similar device for use where a noninverted bidirectional data bus is desired. It has greater propagation delay, however.

Each of the **6800** components has outputs capable of driving ten MOS inputs or one TTL load, and directional switching is very simple in a small system because it is determined by internal logic in both the μP and the RAMs. The R/W line controls the RAM so that either the μP or the RAM output circuits are ON, depending on whether the μP is writing or reading.

When the system is larger, however, driver/receivers such as the **6880** are used. Care must be taken in this case to provide external logic for proper operation (i.e., in addition to selecting the RAM for a read or write, the data path must be switched for the direction needed).

If the **6880** is arranged as shown in Fig. 7- 2*c*, with a jumper from pin 12 to pin 14, the drivers and receivers are connected so that the direction of transmission is determined by the R/W line. This line is connected to the Driver Enable and Receiver Enable inputs (pins 1 and 15). The Driver Enable input is enabled when the μP is reading memory (R/W = 1), and the $\overline{\text{Receiver Enable}}$ input is enabled when the μP is writing to memory (R/W = 0).

EXAMPLE 7-1

Which component drives the bus when

a. The μP is reading memory?

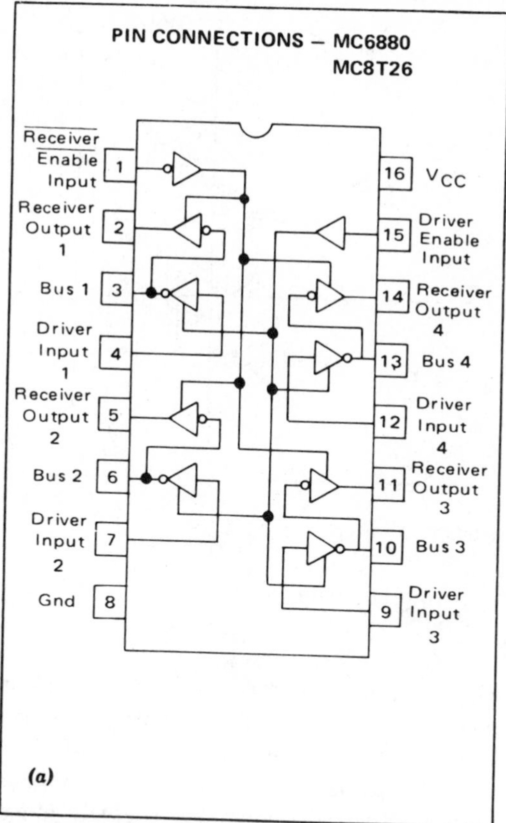

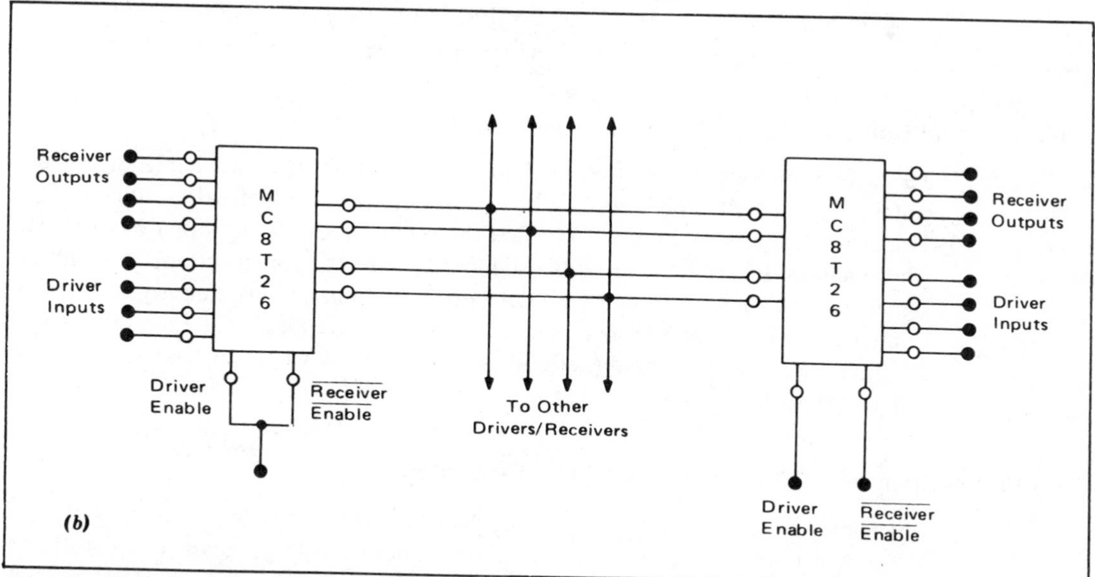

FIGURE 7-2 The **6800** family three-state bus driver/receiver. (a) Pin configuration. (b) Typical bidirectional bus application.

(c)

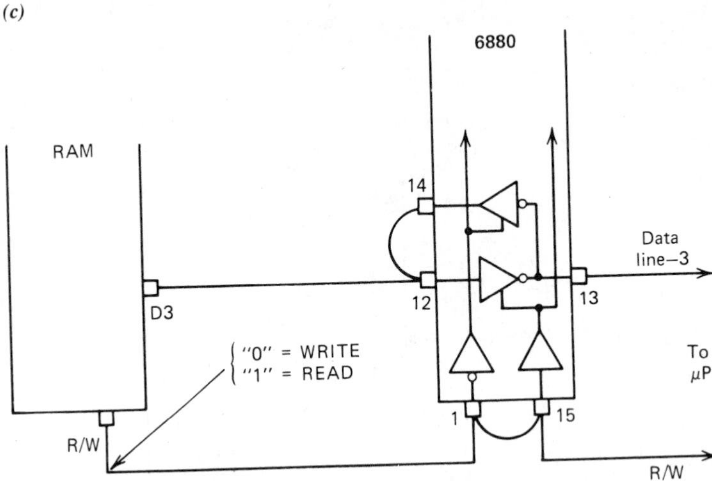

(c) Signal flow diagram.

b. The μP is writing to memory?

SOLUTION

a. When the μP is *reading* memory it must receive information that is in memory. The memory must drive the data bus with that information so that the μP can read it. All other devices must be in their *high-impedance state*.

b. When *writing*, the μP is sending information to the memory. Therefore the μP bus drivers are active. The memory receivers must be ON and all other bus drivers (including the receiving memory) must be in the *high-impedance state*.

7-4.4 TTL Signal Compatibility

The **6800** components are designed to be compatible with available digital circuitry. At present, the **7400** TTL series dominates the field of digital ICs. Transistor–Transistor Logic (TTL) and the older Diode–Transistor Logic (DTL), whose names describe the circuits used in their internal construction, have similar signal characteristics (voltages and currents at the pins). Consequently, the design standard chosen for the **6800** series of components requires that each output will drive one standard TTL load (defined as 1.6 mA at 0.4 V) plus a capacitive load of 130 pF (at 1 MHz).

7-4.5 5-Volt N-Channel MOS Silicon Metal Gate Technology

The **6800** was one of the first μPs to use NMOS technology that requires only +5 V for its operation. The use of a single standard voltage gave it a significant advantage over other μPs and MOS devices that required several different voltages for their operation. Those devices are now mostly obsolete.

7-4.6 24-, 28-, and 40-Pin Packages

The **6800** μP uses a 40-pin DIP package. This allows for 38 input/output connections (plus power and ground) so that it can simultaneously present the information on its 16 address lines, 8 data lines, and the various control lines. Other components in the **6800** series (the ACIA and memories) do not require full 16-bit addressing and use a smaller 24-pin DIP package. Some of the newer large memory devices such as the **68764** EPROMS use 28 pins to allow for the increased number of address lines needed.

7-4.7 Clock Rate

The clock rate determines the speed at which the μP executes instructions. Many **6800** family parts are now available in three clock rates. The **6800** can be driven by a clock up to 1 MHz, the **68A00** up to 1.5 MHz, and the **68B00** up to 2 MHz (see Section 7-7).

7-4.8 Temperature Range

Since most μPs operate in a controlled environment (comfortable rooms or laboratories), they are not subjected to extreme temperature variations. The temperature range chosen for the plastic-encased **MC6800P** (0° to 70°C) is adequate for almost all industrial and commercial applications. This temperature range is also the same as the standard TTL temperature range. The **MC6800CP** has a wider range of −40° to +85°C. Military versions are also available for operation from −55° to +125°C.

It should be recognized that all operating temperatures are measured at the device location in the housing. The system must not generate so much heat that it causes the temperature in the vicinity of any of the components to exceed specifications. If necessary, cooling fans can be placed in a system housing to dissipate excessive heat.

7-5 THE 6800 MICROPROCESSOR UNIT

Figure 7-3 shows the block diagram of a **6800** μP. An 8-bit internal bus interconnects the various registers with the instruction decode and control logic. The nine control lines that communicate with the external devices can be seen on the left, with the address bus at the top and the data bus at the bottom of the figure.

These are the features of the **6800** μP that will be discussed in the following chapters:

Vectored interrupts

Nonmaskable interrupt

Software interrupt

I/O treated like memory (addressable)

16-bit index register

16-bit program counter register

16-bit stack pointer register

Two 8-bit accumulators

Direct memory access and multiprocessing capability

Halt/go and single step capability

Dynamic logic and two-phase clock

Wait instruction

7-5.1 Hardware Aspects of the 6800 ALU and Registers

The Arithmetic/Logic Unit (ALU) included in the **6800** is an 8-bit, parallel processing, 2s complement device. It includes the *condition code* (or processor status) *register*. The functions of the ALU and the various registers were described in Sections 4-3.1 and 4-3.2. The clock hardware is described later in this chapter (Section 7-7). Interrupt functions, Direct Memory Access (DMA), and various hardware design features are described in later chapters.

7-5.2 Registers and Accumulators

As explained in Section 4-3.2 the **6800** system has a 16-bit address bus, but as seen in Fig. 7-3, the internal bus is 8 bits wide and the index and stack pointer registers (and the address buffers) are implemented with a high (H) and a low (L) byte. The two 8-bit accumulators, A and B, speed up program execution by allowing two operands to remain in the μP. Instructions that can be performed using both accumulators (e.g., ABA and SBA) are very fast because they do not require additional cycles to fetch the second operand.

7-5.3 Other Features of the 6800

Five of the six condition codes (H, N, Z, V, and C in Fig. 7-3) were described in Section 4-6. The action of the sixth condition code register bit (I), or interrupt mask, and DMAs are discussed in Chapter 9. The clock hardware and HALT modes are discussed in Section 7-6.

7-5.4 Vectored Interrupts

An **interrupt** is a signal to the μP that causes it to stop execution of the normal program and to branch (or jump) to another location that is the beginning address of an interrupt service routine. These routines are written to provide whatever action is necessary to respond to the interrupt. Four types of interrupts are provided in the **6800**, and each has its unique software service routine and vector. Three of them also are implemented by pins on the **6800**. They are

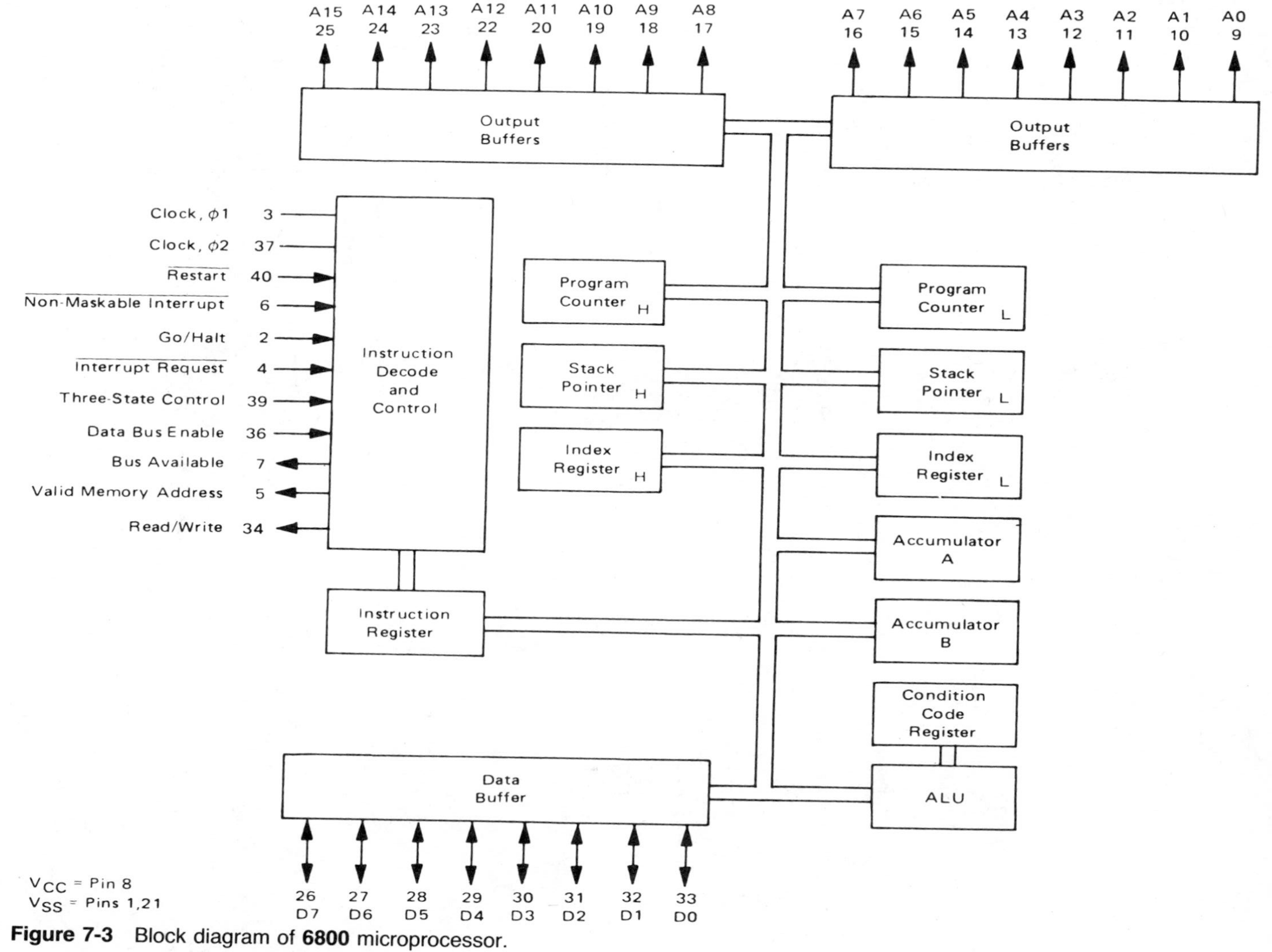

Figure 7-3 Block diagram of **6800** microprocessor.

RESTART (RST)

NONMASKABLE INTERRUPT (NMI)

SOFTWARE INTERRUPT (SWI)

INTERRUPT REQUEST (IRQ)

For the program to be branched to the appropriate routine, the top eight locations of the ROM or PROM that is highest in memory are reserved for these interrupt vectors. The contents of these locations contain the 16-bit addresses where the service routines begin. When activated, the program is "vectored" or pointed to the appropriate address by the μP logic. This is called a **vectored interrupt**. The details of these interrupts are discussed in Chapter 9.

7-6 6800 CONTROL LINES AND THEIR FUNCTIONS

The hardware aspects of system design involve interconnecting the components of the system so that the data is properly transferred between them and to any external hardware that is being used. In addition to the obvious requirement for power and ground to each component, the address bus, and the bidirectional data bus, numerous control signal lines are required. These control lines are in effect a third bus called the *control bus*. The lines are shown in Fig. 7-1 and are identified in Fig. 7-3, which also shows their pin numbers.

To design a system that performs properly, it is necessary to understand each signal's characteristics and function. These are described in the following paragraphs.

7-6.1 Read/Write (R/W)

This output line is used to signal all external devices that the μP is in a READ state (R/W = HIGH) or a WRITE state (R/W = LOW). The normal standby state of this line is HIGH. This line is three-state. When Three-State Control (TSC) (see Section 7-6.8) goes HIGH, the R/W line enters the high-impedance mode.

7-6.2 Valid Memory Address (VMA)

The **Valid Memory Address** output line (when in the HIGH state) tells all devices external to the μP that there is a valid address on the address bus. During the execution of certain instructions, the address bus may assume a random address, because of internal calculations. VMA goes LOW to avoid enabling any device under those conditions. Note also that VMA is held LOW during HALT, TSC, or during the execution of a WAIT (WAI) instruction. VMA is not a three-state line and therefore DMA cannot be performed unless VMA is externally opened (or gated).

7-6.3 Data Bus Enable (DBE)

The **Data Bus Enable** (DBE) signal enables the data bus drivers of the μP when it is in the HIGH state. This input is normally connected to the phase 2 ($\phi 2$) clock but is sometimes delayed to ensure proper operation with some memory devices. When HIGH, it permits data to be placed on the bus during a WRITE cycle. During a μP READ cycle, the data bus drivers within the μP are disabled internally. If an external signal holds DBE LOW, the μP data bus drivers are forced into their high-impedance state. This allows other devices to control the I/O bus (as in DMA).

7-6.4 Interrupt Request, Nonmaskable Interrupt, and Reset

An active signal on the IRQ, NMI, or RESET lines initiates an interrupt sequence. The action of these lines is discussed in Chapter 9, where interrupts are considered in detail.

7-6.5 Phase One (ϕ1) and Phase Two (ϕ2) of the Clock

These two pins are used for a two-phase nonoverlapping clock. This clock runs at a frequency up to 1 MHz for the **M6800** and up to 2 MHz for the depletion load versions of the **6800 (MC68B00)**.

7-6.6 HALT and RUN Modes

When the HALT input to the **6800** is HIGH, the μP is in the RUN mode and is continually executing instructions. When the HALT line goes LOW, the μP halts after completing its present instruction. At that time the μP is in the **HALT mode**. Bus available (BA) goes HIGH, VMA (Section 7-6.2) becomes a 0, and all three-state lines enter their high-impedance state. Note that the μP does not enter the HALT mode as soon as HALT goes LOW; it does so only when the μP has finished execution of its current instruction. It is possible to stop the μP while it is in the process of executing an instruction by stopping or "stretching the clock," as described in Section 7-7.

7-6.7 Bus Available (BA)

The **Bus Available** (BA) signal is a normally LOW signal generated by the μP. In the HIGH state it indicates that the μP has stopped and that the address bus is available. This occurs if the μP is in the HALT mode or in a WAIT state as the result of the WAI instruction.

7-6.8 Three-State Control (TSC)

Three-State Control (TSC) is an externally generated signal that effectively causes the μP to disconnect itself from the address and control buses. This allows an external device to assume control of the system. When TSC is HIGH, it causes the address lines and the READ/WRITE line to go to the high-impedance state. The VMA and BA signals are forced LOW. The data bus is not affected by TSC and has its own enable (DBE). TSC is used in DMA applications discussed in Chapter 9.

7-7 CLOCK OPERATION

The μP is a dynamic IC that must be periodically refreshed by its own clocks. Phase 1 should not be stopped longer than 9600 ns ($PW\phi_H$) or the μP may lose some of its internal data.

The **6800** utilizes a **two-phase** clock to control its operation. The waveforms and timing of the clock are critical for the proper operation of the μP and the other components of the family. The timing requirements are shown in the waveforms and table of Fig. 7-4. The two phases of the clock must be nonoverlapping and conform to the timing table (Fig. 7-4b).

The clock synchronizes the internal operations of the μP as well as all external devices on the bus. The program counter, for example, is advanced on the falling edge of $\phi 1$ and data is latched into the μP on the falling edge of $\phi 2$. All operations necessary for the execution of each instruction are synchronized with the clock.

Certain components and functions of the system affect the clock requirements. If dynamic memories are used, slow memories are involved, or DMA is required, the clock may have to be stopped momentarily, or stretched. If the memory is slow, for example, phase 2 has to be long enough to allow the memory to complete its READ or WRITE operation. Since a memory that is too slow to operate with a 1-MHz clock (such as an Intel 1702A EPROM) may only be addressed periodically, there is no need to slow the clock for the entire system, provided a **memory ready** feature can be included in the clock.

The **MC6875** shown in Fig. 7-5 is a 16-pin IC that includes all the features necessary to control the timing of a **6800** system. It includes an internal oscillator whose frequency can be determined by an external crystal or *RC* network connected to pins X1 and X2. (An inexpensive 3.59-MHz crystal made for color TVs can be used.) Alternatively, an external timing signal can be connected to the Ext. In pin. The oscillator frequency is divided by four and shaped to provide $\phi 1$ and $\phi 2$, the two-phase nonoverlapping clock required by the **6800** μP. If the system contains slow memories, $\phi 2$ can be stretched by holding Memory Ready low until the data is transferred. The **6875** also contains a Schmitt trigger input that controls $\overline{\text{Reset}}$. A capacitor to ground (power ON reset) and/or a reset switch may be used. DMA or dynamic memory refresh can also be accommodated. These will be discussed in Chapter 9.

7-7.1 Evolution of Clock Circuits

The unique two-phase clock signals required for the **6800** can be provided by other means, such as the **6871A** hybrid clock circuit or even a simple oscillator followed by a number of discrete components to provide the two nonoverlapping phases (as done on the EXORciser MPU module described in Chapter 10). As will be seen in Chapter 11, however, all of the newer members of the **6800** family of μC components have an internal oscillator on the chip. This circuit includes everything needed except for an external crystal and two small capacitors. An internal divide by 4 circuit is also provided so that a 4-MHz (or 8-MHz) crystal can be used. It is therefore much smaller and cheaper than the one needed for the **6800**. The **6802**, for example, is one of these newer μPs with the internal clock circuits. It has a processor that is identical to the **6800** (see Chapter 11 for details).

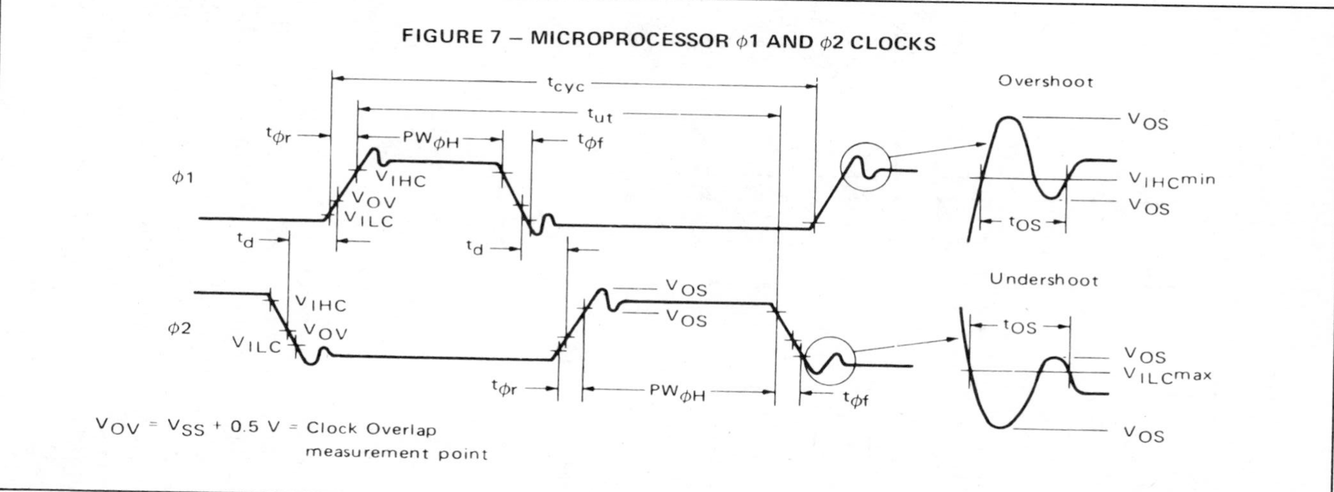

(a) Waveforms

Frequency of Operation	f	0.1	–	1.0	MHz
Clock Timing (ϕ1 and ϕ2)					
Cycle Time	t_{cyc}	1.0	–	10	μs
Clock Pulse Width (Measured at V_{CC} - 0.3 V) ϕ1	$PW_{\phi H}$	430	–	4500	ns
ϕ2		450	–	4500	ns
Clock Up Time	t_{ut}	940	–	–	ns
Rise and Fall Times ϕ1, ϕ2 (Measured between V_{SS} + 0.3 V and V_{CC} - 0.3 V)	$t_{\phi r}$, $t_{\phi f}$	5.0	–	50	ns
Delay Time or Clock Separation (Measured at V_{SS} + 0.5 V)	t_d	0	–	9100	ns
Overshoot Duration	t_{OS}	0	–	40	ns

(b) Timing table

Figure 7-4 **6800** clock timing. (a) Waveforms. (b) Timing table.

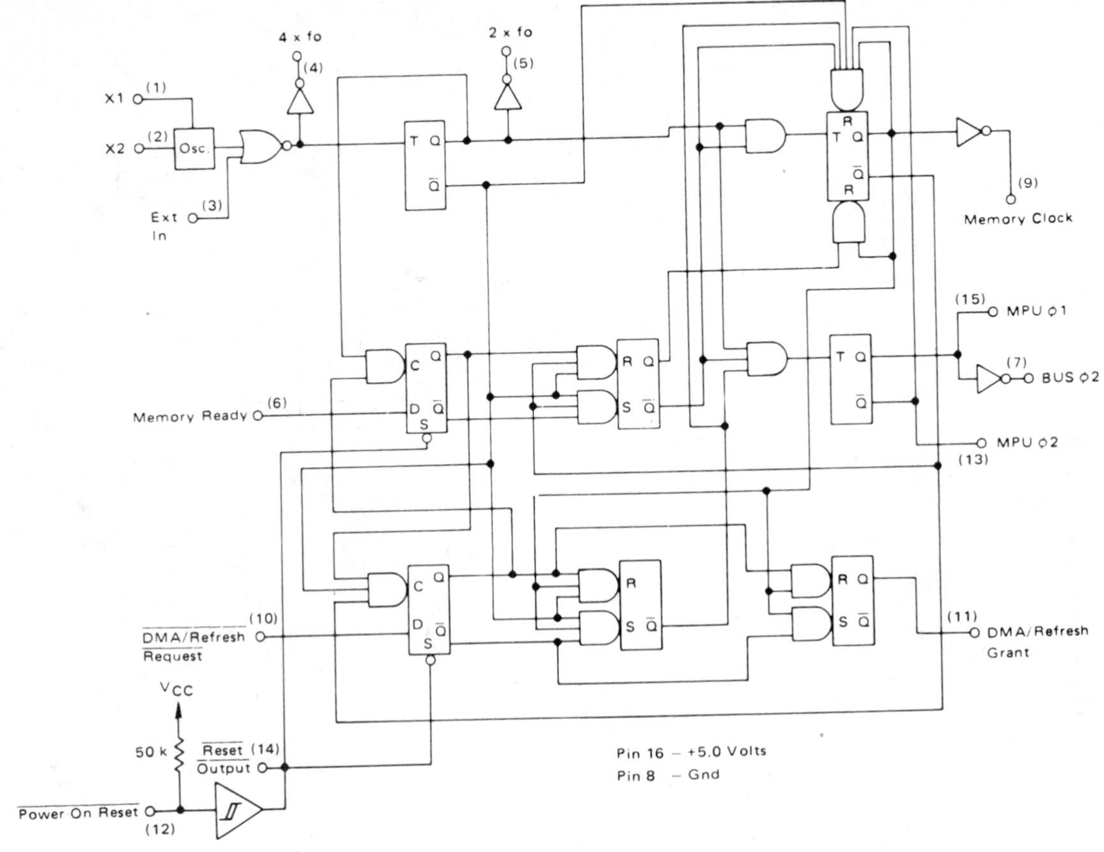

Figure 7-5 **6875** block diagram.

7-7.2 Instruction Bytes and Clock Cycles

In the **6800** instruction table (Appendix B), the number of bytes and the clock cycles are listed for each instruction. The number of bytes for each instruction determines the size of the memory and the number of cycles determines the time required to execute the program. LDA A $1234 (which is the extended addressing mode), for example, requires 3 bytes, one to specify the operation (Op) code and two to specify the address, but requires four cycles to execute. Often an instruction requires the processor to perform internal operations in addition to the fetch cycles. Consequently, for any instruction the number of cycles is generally larger than the number of bytes.

EXAMPLE 7-2

How long does it take to execute a LDAA 0,X (indexed) instruction if a 1-MHz oscillator is used as the system clock?

SOLUTION
From Appendix B, we find that a LDAA 0,X instruction requires 2 bytes and five cycles. The 2 bytes are the Op code and the offset address. The μP must add the offset to the contents of its index register. This accounts for the large number of clock cycles required for this instruction. Since the instruction takes five cycles, it takes 5 μs to execute at a clock rate of 1 MHz.

Note that Chapter 11 describes the **6801** μC with an augmented instruction set (22 additional Op codes) that uses one less cycle for most instructions, and yet the augmented instructions are functionally compatible with the **6800**.

7-8 THE 6810 RANDOM-ACCESS MEMORY (RAM)

Figure 7-6 shows the **6810**. It is a 1024-bit (128 words by 8 bits per word) memory in a 24-pin package. It provides 128 bytes of read/write memory and is designed for use in the **6800** system. The 8-bit word organization makes it uniquely applicable for small μP systems since many such systems only need 128 or 256 bytes of RAM.

The **6810** bus interface of Fig. 7-7 shows how a typical IC would be connected to the three buses. The pins include

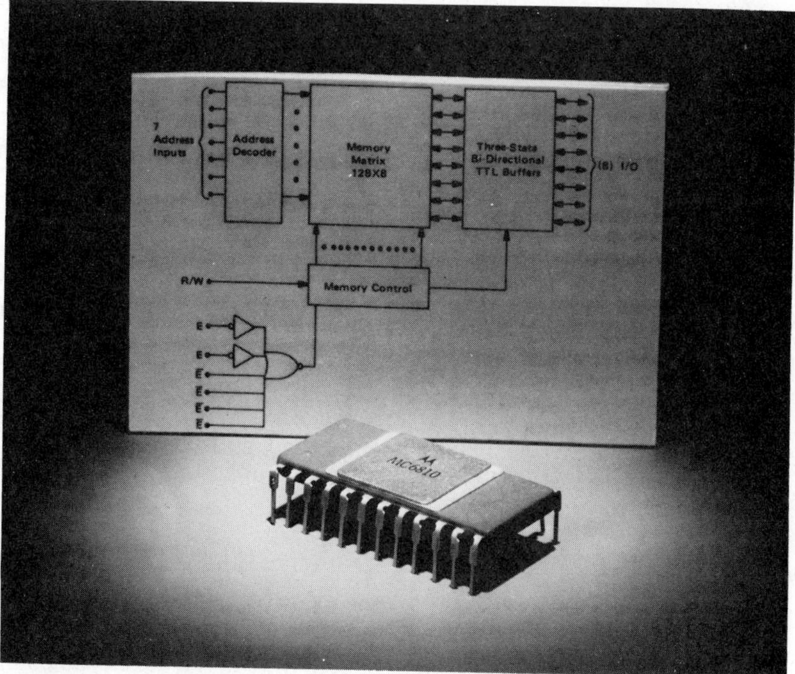

Figure 7-6 The **6810** random access memory (128 8-bit words).

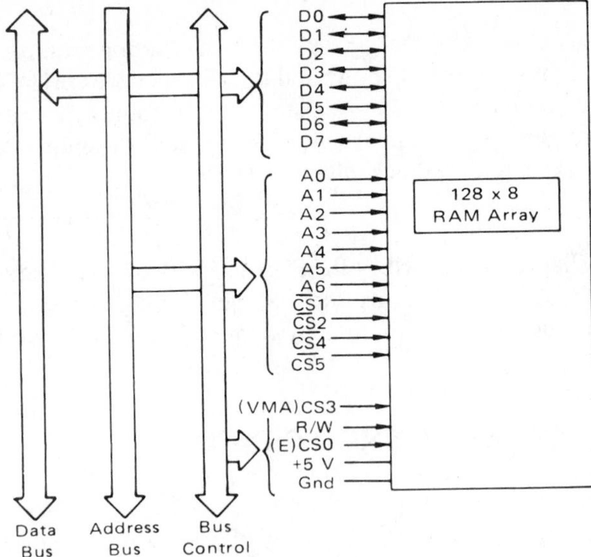

Figure 7-7 **6810** RAM bus interface.

1. Eight data lines (D0–D7). These are three-state bidirectional lines for compatibility with the **6800** data bus.
2. Seven address lines.
3. Six chip select lines.
4. An R/W line.

The **6810** is a static RAM, which requires only one power supply (+5 V). It has four LOW-level and two HIGH-level **chip select pins**. These pins can be directly connected to address lines or voltage levels, as shown in Fig 7-7, to select the chip without additional decoders. When selected and R/W is HIGH, the output buffers are turned ON to drive the data bus (see Section 7-14 for details). The use of E and VMA connected to the CS lines is discussed in Section 7-14.

Fifteen versions of **6810**s were manufactured at one time (see Table 7-1). They differ in clock rate, environmental requirements, or packaging. A plastic package and two types of ceramic packaging, CERDIP and SIDEBRAZE, are used. The latter two are hermetically sealed.

The A and B in the middle of the type designations in Table 7-1 denote the 1.5- and 2-MHz depletion load versions. The L denotes ceramic and the P is for a plastic package. The ceramic versions of the last two types are also available in commercial and military temperature ranges, −40° to +85°C and −55° to +125°C, respectively.

EXAMPLE 7-3

What is the maximum memory access time that a **6810**-type component may have when used in a **6800** system with a 1-MHz clock?

SOLUTION
Reference to the **6810** data sheet (see References, Section 7-17) shows that the time from the point in the cycle where the *address* lines become stable (all 1s are above 2.0 V and all 0s are less than 0.8 V) until the *data* become stable is defined as the *memory read access time* (Tacc) and that the data will remain stable a minimum of 10 ns after the end of the cycle. The **6800** data sheet READ timing figure shows that the time from the beginning of the cycle until all address, R/W, and VMA lines are stable is a maximum of 300 ns, and the minimum length of time the data must be available (on the bus) is 100 ns. The clock timing waveform shows that, at 1 MHz, the total time from where $\phi 1$ starts setting the address until $\phi 2$ cuts off the data (Tut) is 940 ns. Therefore, the access time for the memory is

$$\text{Tacc} = 940 - (300 + 100) = 540 \text{ ns}$$

This shows that all the newer **6810**s meet the requirements. These calculations assume that a minimum configuration system is involved and therefore no additional delays are incurred in bus drivers or TTL decoders.

7-9 THE 68A30 READ-ONLY MEMORY (ROM)

The **6830** (now **68A30**) was the ROM designed originally for use in the **6800** system and it introduced several interesting concepts. Like the **6810**, it comes in a 24-pin DIP package and features three-state outputs capable of driving the data bus.

TABLE 7-1 Types of 6810 RAMS

Type	Clock Frequency	Temperature Range[a]	Package
MCM6810L	1	1	Ceramic
MCM6810CL	1	2	
MCM68A10L	1.5	1	
MCM68B10CL	2	2	
MCM68B10L	2	1	
MCM6810P	1	1	Plastic
MCM6810CP	1	2	
MCM68A10P	1.5	1	
MCM68A10CP	1.5	2	
MCM68B10P	2	1	
MCM6810S	1	1	Cerdip
MCM6810CS	1	2	
MCM68A10S	1.5	1	
MCM68A10CS	1.5	2	
MCM68B10S	2	1	

[a] Range 1 is equivalent to 0° to 70°C; range 2 is equivalent to −40° to +85°C.

The **68A30** contains 1024 bytes of ROM. Its bus organization is shown in Fig. 7-8. Note that there are 10 address lines, 8 data lines, and 4 chip select lines. Because this is a ROM, no read/write line is needed. If this IC is selected, the byte at the addressed location will appear on the data bus. When the IC is not selected, its output drivers are in the high-impedance state, allowing another device to drive the I/O bus. The access time of the **68A30A** is 350 ns and is fast enough for any **6800** system running up to 1.5 MHz.

The **6830** is no longer made, but two faster versions of it with the same pinouts (the **68A30** and **68B30**) are still available. A new family of ROMs with similar capability but larger capacity and with different pinouts has been introduced. They are known as **MCM68A308**, **MCM68A316**, **MCM68A332**, **and MCM68A664** and are all in the same 24-pin package. The four sizes are basically pin-compatible with each other and, more important, are also compatible with equivalent EPROMs. The desirability of this feature will be explained shortly in Section 7-10. As the part numbers indicate, these byte-wide ROMs are sized from 8K bit (1024 bytes) up to 64K bit (8092 bytes). Other parts, such as the **63128** 128K bit (16K byte) or even the **63256** 256K bit (32K byte) are also now available in 28-pin ICs.

7-9.1 Mask-Programmed ROMs

Manufacturers' specification sheets give instructions on how to submit the program. A *mask* is created from the program and is then used to manufacture the customized ROMs. The user should be very sure of the program before ordering a custom ROM, because masked ROMs are not reprogrammable and one erroneous bit generally makes a program useless. It is necessary to avoid human error when

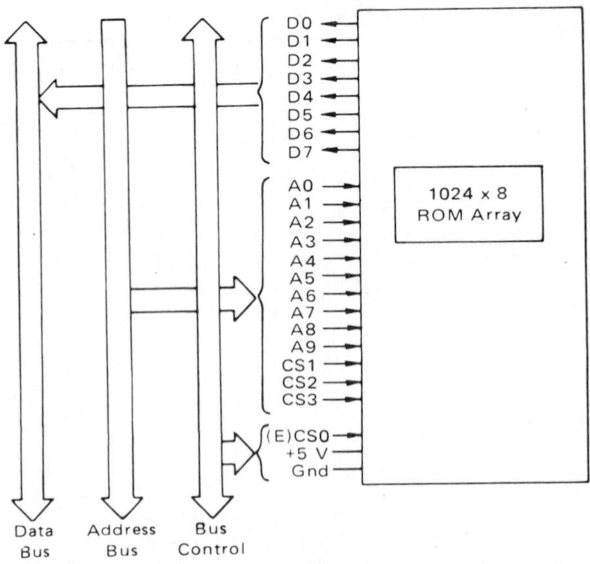

Figure 7-8 **6830** ROM bus interface.

transmitting the program to the factory. Different methods are used by various manufacturers, but currently at Motorola there are two approved ways to do this:

1. EPROMs—with the program installed
2. Magnetic tape—nine track, 800 bits per inch (bpi), odd parity written in EBCDIC character code. Motorola's R.O.M.S. format.

Typically, up to four pins are used for chip selects in this type of ROM. These are defined as 1-level or 0-level enables by the customer when the mask for the ROM is specified.

7-10 PROMS AND EPROMS

It is usually necessary for μP designers to determine the program for the ROM in their own laboratory. This can be accomplished by using a *Programmable Read-Only Memory* (PROM). Several types are used. One type is an Erasable Programmable Read-Only Memory (EPROM). EPROMs can be erased by ultraviolet light and reprogrammed any number of times. They therefore are extremely valuable for program and system development. Custom maskable programmable ROMs, which are pin-compatible with these EPROMs, are available. This makes it possible for designers to build their hardware in final form (with sockets for memories) so that the testing and program revisions can continue, using EPROMs, even after the first models of the product are shipped. Ultimately, a mask-programmable ROM can be installed, either in the field or in future production. This would be done in high-volume production systems because the mask-programmable ROMs are approximately ½ to ⅓ of the price of EPROMs.

Fusible-link PROMs are often used in μCs. One type of these PROMs comes from the manufacturer with a fusible link in each bit of each word and thus presents an output pattern of all 0s. The user then puts them into a **PROM programmer**, an electronic device that allows the user to overdrive the bits corresponding to the 1s in the program, blowing the fuses to open each bit. Since the manufacturer of PROMs of this type is not required to program them individually, they are produced in large quantities and are inexpensive. Several manufacturers produce 1024 × 8 or 2048 × 8 bit fusible-link PROMs that can be used directly in **6800** systems.

7-11 6820 or 6821 PERIPHERAL INTERFACE ADAPTER (PIA)

The **6820** PIA, shown in Fig. 7-9, provides a simple means of interfacing peripheral equipment on a parallel or byte-wide basis to the **6800** μC system. This device is compatible with the **6800** bus interface on the μP side and provides up to 16 I/O lines and 4 control lines on the peripheral side, for connection to external units. The **6820** outputs are TTL or CMOS compatible.

In April 1977 an augmented version of the **6820** was introduced (called the **MC6821**). It is identical to the **6820** except that it can drive two TTL loads on all A

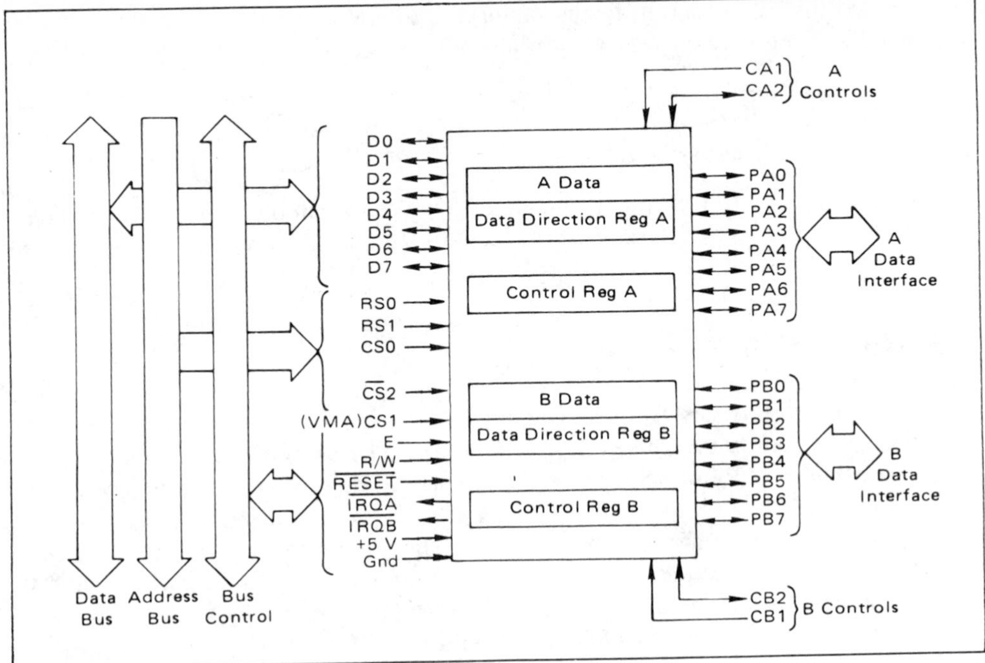

Figure 7-9 PIA bus interface and registers.

and B side buffers and is capable of static operation (no clocking required). Because of these enhancements, the **6820** is no longer manufactured.

7-12 ASYNCHRONOUS COMMUNICATIONS INTERFACE ADAPTER (ACIA)

The **6850** ACIA is a 24-pin IC similar to all the others in the **6800** family. It provides the circuitry to connect serial asynchronous data communications devices, such as a teletypewriter (TTY) or a CRT terminal, to bus-organized systems such as the **6800** μC system.

The bus interface includes select, enable, read/write, and interrupt signal pins in addition to the 8-bit bidirectional data bus lines. The parallel data of the **6800** system is serially transmitted and received (simultaneously) with proper ASCII formatting and error checking. The *control register* of the ACIA is programmed via the data bus during system initialization. It determines word length, parity, stop bits, and interrupt control of the transmit or receive functions. The operation of the **6850** is discussed in detail in Section 8-10.

The PIA and ACIA are the most used I/O components in the **6800** family, but Table 7-2 shows the many other I/O components that are currently available for 8-bit systems. The reader should consult the manufacturer's literature for information on these products.

TABLE 7-2 Other I/O Devices That Are Available

6852 Synchronous Serial Data Adapter (SSDA)
6854 Advanced Data Link Controller (ADLC)
68488 General Purpose Interface Adapter (IEEE 488-1975 bus)
6845 CRT Controller (CRTC)
6843 Floppy Disk Controller
6844 Direct Memory Access Controller (DMAC)

7-13 MEMORY SPACE ALLOCATION

The I/O devices in the **6800** system (e.g., the PIA, ACIA, and SSDA) all have internal registers that contain the I/O data or control the operation of the device. In the Motorola design concept each of these registers is allocated a unique address on the address bus and is communicated with just as if it were memory. This technique is called **memory-mapped I/O** and, in addition to allowing the use of all memory-referencing instructions for the I/O functions, it eliminates the need for special I/O instructions.

The process of addressing a particular memory location includes not only selecting a cell in a chip but also selecting that chip from among all those on the same bus. *The low-order address lines are generally used to address individual memory bytes or registers within the chips, and the high-order lines are available to single out the desired chip.* These high-order lines could be connected to a decoder circuit with one output line used to enable each chip, but since most of the **6800** family devices have several chip select pins available, these are frequently connected directly to the high-order address lines (A15, A14, A13, etc.) and separate decoders are not needed, particularly in simple systems.

Table 7-3 shows the number of addresses required and the number of chip select (CS) pins available for typical **6800** family components.

A component is selected only if all its CS lines are satisfied. The **6810**, for example, is enabled only if it sees a HIGH level on two of its select lines (CS0, pin 10, and CS3, pin 13) and a LOW level on its four negative select pins ($\overline{CS1}$, $\overline{CS2}$, $\overline{CS4}$, and $\overline{CS5}$). When unselected, a component places its outputs in a high-impedance state and is effectively disconnected from the data bus.

When setting up a **6800** system, each component must be allocated as much memory space as it needs and must be given a *unique* address so that *no address*

TABLE 7-3 Addresses Required and Chip Select Pins Needed

Component	Addresses Required	Positive CS Pins	Negative CS Pins
6810 RAM	128	2	4
68A30 ROM	1024	3	1
6821 PIA	4	2	1
6850 ACIA	2	2	1
6852 SSDA	2	0	1

selects more than one component. In addition, one component (usually a ROM) must contain the vector interrupt addresses (see Chapter 9).

7-14 ADDRESSING TECHNIQUES

Most systems do not use all 64K bytes of available memory space. Therefore, not all of the address lines need to be used, and **redundant addresses** will occur (i.e., components will respond to two or more addresses). It is important, however, to choose the upper-address lines used so that no two components can be selected by the same address. Since the chip selects serve to turn ON the bus drivers (for a μP READ), only *one* component should be on at any time or ON may be damaged.

For proper system operation, most memory and peripheral devices should transfer data only when φ2 and VMA are HIGH. Consequently, one CS line on each component is usually connected to each of these signals or a derivative of these signals. The **6820** PIA, for example, must have its E pin connected to φ2 or it will not respond to an interrupt and can lock up the system following the receipt of a WAI instruction. (The **6821** does not need to be clocked and therefore does not need φ2.)

When allocating memory, it is wise to place the **scratch pad** RAMs at the bottom of the memory map, since it is then possible to use the direct address mode instructions throughout the program when referencing these RAM locations. Because 2-byte instead of 3-byte instructions are used, a savings of up to 25% in total memory requirements is possible.

In summary, the following rules should govern the assignment of address bus lines to the various chip select pins:

1. Not all address bus lines need to be used for chip selection. **Partial decoding** is acceptable provided that precautions are taken to avoid two or more chips responding to the same address.
2. φ2 must be included in the selection so that the bus drivers in each chip are ON only at the proper time.
3. VMA must be included to avoid chip selection by the chance state of the address bus during non-memory-referencing cycles.
4. When an address line is used as a positive enable on one chip, the same line should go to negative enables on all other chips, if possible. This prevents any two chips from being selected at the same time regardless of the state of the address bus.
5. One ROM (or PROM) should contain the interrupt vector addresses and should respond to FFF8 through FFFF either directly or redundantly. (It also can respond to other redundant addresses.)
6. RAMs should respond to addresses 0000 through 00FF (256 bytes) to permit direct addressing mode instructions to be used. (Only one **6810** is needed in small systems.)
7. PIAs and ACIAs must have φ2 connected directly to E (the enable pin) in order to respond properly to interrupts. **6821**s do not require this since they are static parts.

EXAMPLE 7-4

How many address lines are available to select

a. A **6810**?
b. A **68A30**?

SOLUTION

a. A **6810** is a 128-word RAM that requires 7 bits to select a specific address ($2^7 = 128$). Thus the seven LSB address lines are connected to the **6810** address pins for word selection, leaving 9 bits available for chip selection.
b. A **68A30** is a 1024-word ROM. It requires 10 bits ($2^{10} = 1024$) to select a word, which leaves 6 bits available to select the chip.

Example 7-4 shows that there are more address lines for chip selection than there are CS pins on each component. For large systems where most of the available 64K of memory is used, it may be necessary to use all of the lines and some address decoding to provide a unique location in the memory map for each block. Most systems, however, use only a fraction of the available memory space. For these smaller systems, a judicious choice of memory locations to avoid interference between redundancies reduces the need for added TTL decoding.

A memory map, shown in Fig. 7-10, helps keep track of the memory space allocations. For convenience the space is shown divided into 64 blocks of 1K (1024) bytes each. A **68A30** occupies an entire block but eight **6810**s can fit into one block. If, for example, we assign a **68A30** ROM to address C4XX, the required binary states of the six most significant address lines are as shown in the lower right of Fig. 7-10. This corresponds to position 50 in the map. The 10 LSBs of the address are shown as "X" since they may take on a value of either 1 or 0 depending on which word in the ROM is selected.

EXAMPLE 7-5

a. Which address does each component in the system configuration of Fig. 7-11 respond to?
b. Which component must contain the Restart and the other vector addresses?

SOLUTION

a. Figure 7-11 shows a small system where only address bits 13 and 14 are used for the decoding. In addition to address lines A14 and A13, VMA and $\phi 2$ are also tied to all of the components being addressed. These signals are HIGH when a "Valid Memory Address" is present and when the data is to be transferred (during $\phi 2$). They therefore contribute to selection of the component that has the right combination of A14 and A13. It can be seen that ROM-1

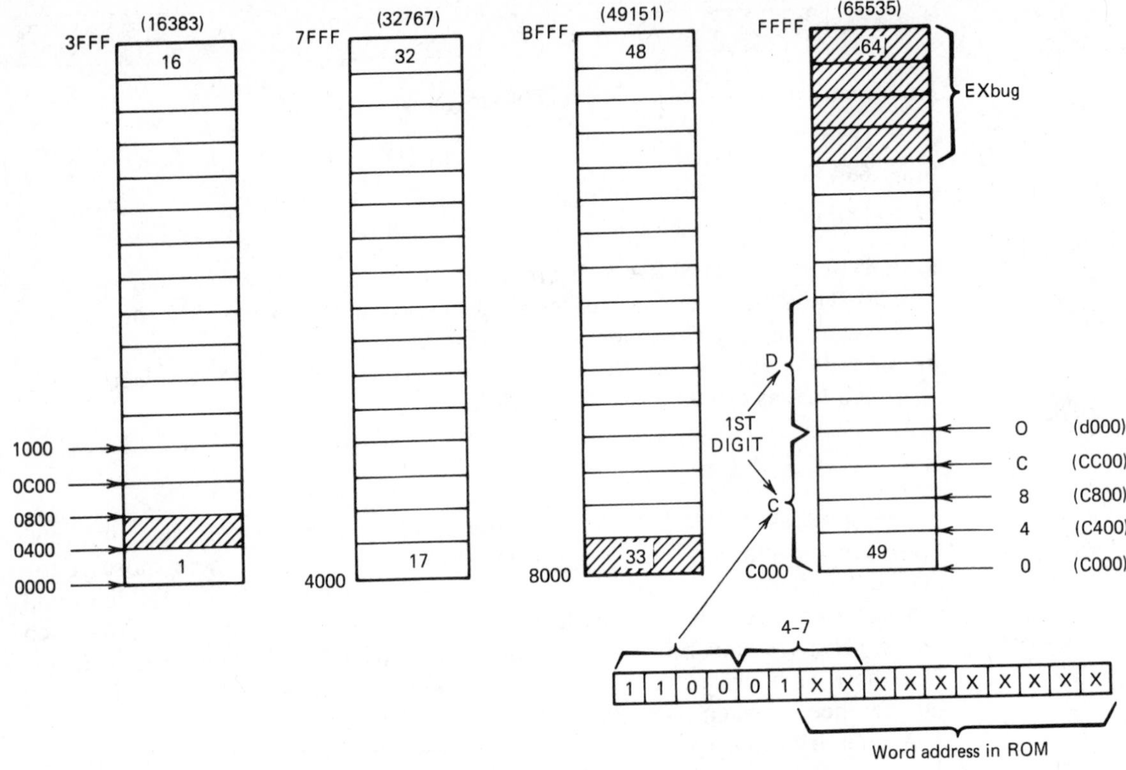

Figure 7-10 Memory map, showing address bits needed to select an address in block 50.

contains three positive and one negative CS inputs. Since one of its positive CS inputs (CS2) is tied to $\phi 2$ and another (CS3) is connected to VMA, it responds to any address that satisfies its other two CS inputs. The positive input (CS0) is connected to A14 and the negative input ($\overline{CS1}$) is connected to A13. Therefore, ROM-1 responds to any address of the binary form X10X XXXX XXXX XXXX (X means either 1 or 0) or any address whose most significant hex digit is 4, 5, C, or D.

ROM-2 has all its inputs programmed for active HIGH and responds to X11X XXXX XXXX XXXX or any address whose most significant hex digit is 6, 7, E, or F.

The RAM has two of its negative $\overline{CS}$ bits connected to A13 and A14. It therefore responds to X00X, XXXX XXXX XXXX or any address whose most significant digit is 0, 1, 8, or 9.

The PIA input requires A13 (CS1) to be a 1 and A14 ($\overline{CS2}$) to be a 0. It responds to any address of the form X01X XXXX XXXX XXXX or any address that has a most significant digit of 2, 3, A, or B.

Note: Each component in this system has a set of addresses that pertain uniquely to itself, since each responds to a different set of most significant digits of the address.

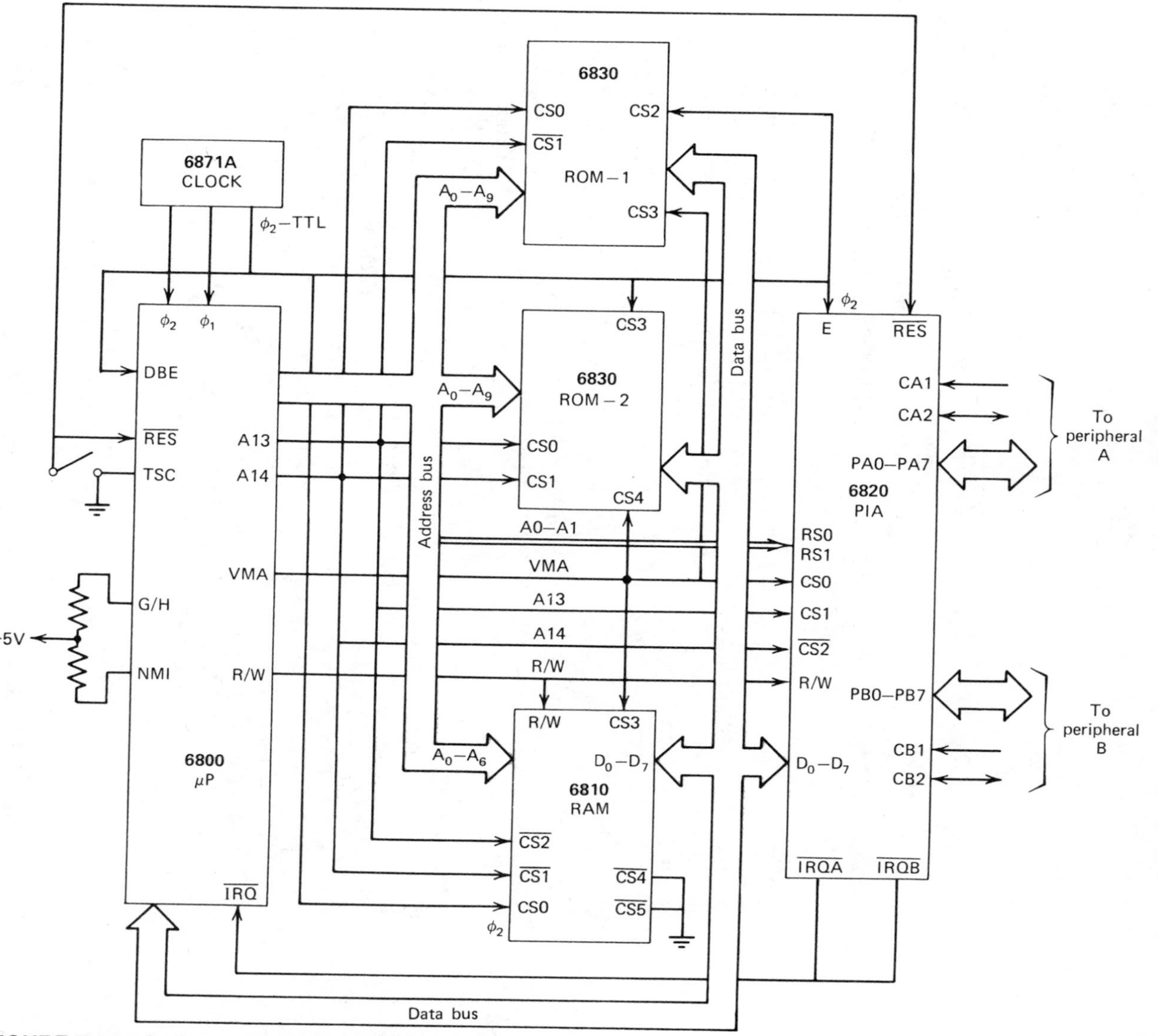

FIGURE 7-11 System configuration for Example 7-5.

b. ROM-2 must contain the restart and other interrupt vector addresses since this is the only component that responds to addresses whose most significant digit is F.

EXAMPLE 7-6

A **6800** system consists of the μP, two ROMs (**68A30**s), eight RAMs **6810**s), an ACIA (**6850**), and a PIA (**6821**). Allocate memory space to each component. Use TTL logic gates as required.

SOLUTION

In this problem, the number of elements that can be accommodated with the chip selects available is exceeded. By combining some of the signals that are common to a number of components with simple TTL gates, each component can be uniquely addressed.

First, to discriminate between the types of components the assignments of Table 7-4 are made.

They satisfy all requirements for the ROMs but do not separate the RAMs from each other or distinguish the ACIA from the PIA.

There are several ways to select a particular RAM. There are two unused CS lines on the RAMs ($\overline{CS4}$ and $\overline{CS5}$) and these can be selected by IC decoders. For an alternative selection method, however, proceed as follows:

1. VMA can be combined with $\overline{A15}$ to provide a negative chip select that is common to all RAMs and I/O. The ROMs do not need this since they already have VMA included. This takes two **7400** gates, as shown in Fig 7-12.
2. Then A9, A8, and A7 can be used to represent the binary numbers 0 through 7. Unfortunately, this does not work well because 000 requires three negative inputs and 111 requires three positive inputs. In both cases, only two are available. In addition, we need a positive input for $\phi 2$.
3. If, however, $\phi 2$ and A7 are put through inverters, as in Fig. 7-12, so that their complements are also available, pin assignments can be made as shown in Table 7-5.

Table 7-6 summarizes the selections and shows the range of addresses in hexadecimal notation. The Xs indicate address lines that are not connected and

TABLE 7-4 Preliminary Chip Select Signal Requirements

	A15	A14	VMA	Ø2
ROM1	CS	CS	CS	CS
ROM2	CS	$\overline{CS}$	CS	CS
RAMX	$\overline{CS1}$	$\overline{CS2}$	CS0	CS3
ACIA	$\overline{CS2}$	CS0	CS1	E
PIA	$\overline{CS2}$	CS0	CS1	E

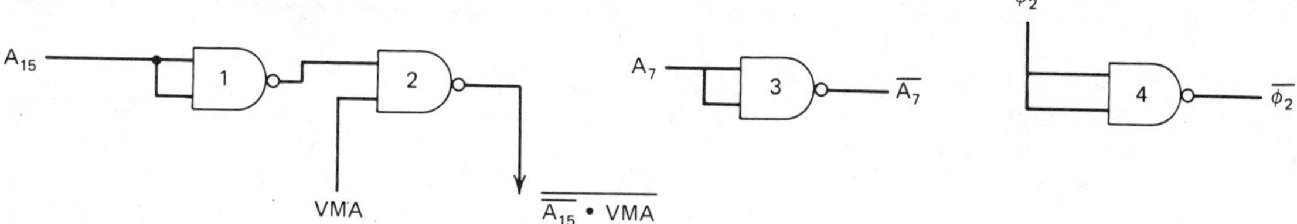

Figure 7-12 Connections for the **7400** IC used in Example 7-6.

are referred to as "don't care" bits. The Ys indicate bits that select the various locations in the chip. The upper range of addresses is the range covered by Y if we assume all Xs are 1s. The lower line is the range of Y if we assume all Xs are 0s.

If the Xs are assumed to be 0s, the top ROM is addressed at C000 to C3FF for programming purposes, but will respond to FC00 through FFFF when the interrupt or restart vectors are fetched (see Chapter 9).

The RAM is contiguous from 0000 to 03FF. This system therefore meets all the requirements of the rules and requires only the addition of one **7400** TTL IC.

7-15 SUMMARY

This chapter introduced the hardware components of the **6800** system. The μP, clock, and memory were discussed in detail. The function of each signal on the I/O bus was explained. Finally, we explained methods of allocating memory space among the system components and gave an example.

TABLE 7-5 Completed Chip Select Assignments for Example 7-6

	$\overline{A15 \cdot VMA}$	A14	A9	A8	A7	$\overline{A7}$	Ø2	$\overline{Ø2}$
RAM0	$\overline{CS1}$	$\overline{CS2}$	$\overline{CS4}$	$\overline{CS5}$		CS0	CS3	
RAM1	$\overline{CS1}$	$\overline{CS2}$	$\overline{CS4}$	$\overline{CS5}$	CS0		CS3	
RAM2	$\overline{CS1}$	$\overline{CS2}$	$\overline{CS4}$	CS0	$\overline{CS5}$		CS3	
RAM3	$\overline{CS1}$	$\overline{CS2}$	$\overline{CS4}$	CS0	CS3			$\overline{CS5}$
RAM4	$\overline{CS1}$	$\overline{CS2}$	CS0	$\overline{CS4}$	$\overline{CS5}$		CS3	
RAM5	$\overline{CS1}$	$\overline{CS2}$	CS0	$\overline{CS4}$	CS3			$\overline{CS5}$
RAM6	$\overline{CS1}$	$\overline{CS2}$	CS0	CS3	$\overline{CS4}$			$\overline{CS5}$
RAM7	$\overline{CS1}$	$\overline{CS2}$	CS0	CS3		$\overline{CS4}$		$\overline{CS5}$
ACIA	$\overline{CS2}$	CS1			CS0		E	
PIA	$\overline{CS2}$	CS1				CS0	E	

TABLE 7-6 Final Address Line and Chip Select Assignments

	MS digit	Third digit	Second digit	LS digit	
ROM2	11XX	XXYY	YYYY	YYYY	FC00–FFFF C000–C3FF
ROM1	10XX	XXYY	YYYY	YYYY	BC00–BFFF 8000–83FF
RAM0	00XX	XX00	0YYY	YYYY	3C00–3C7F 0000–007F
RAM1	00XX	XX00	1YYY	YYYY	3C80–3CFF 0080–00FF
RAM2	00XX	XX01	0YYY	YYYY	3D00–3D7F 0100–017F
RAM3	00XX	XX01	1YYY	YYYY	3D80–3DFF 0180–01FF
RAM4	00XX	XX10	0YYY	YYYY	3E00–3E7F 0200–027F
RAM5	00XX	XX10	1YYY	YYYY	3E80–3EFF 0280–02FF
RAM6	00XX	XX11	0YYY	YYYY	3F00–3F7F 0300–037F
RAM7	00XX	XX11	1YYY	YYYY	3F80–3FFF 0380–03FF
ACIA	01XX	XXXX	1XXX	XXXY	7FFE–7FFF 4080–4081
PIA	01XX	XXXX	0XXX	XXYY	7F70–7F73 4000–4003

7-16 GLOSSARY

Bus Available (BA) Signal generated by the μP to tell an external device when the μP is halted.

Bus driver/receiver Integrated circuit (IC) capable of driving and receiving information from a bidirectional I/O bus.

Chip Select pins Signal lines (or pins) that enable (or disable) a memory or peripheral IC.

Clock oscillator Component or circuit that provides the two-phase nonoverlapping timing pulses suitable for driving the MOS circuits of the **6800** μP.

Crystal control Use of a small quartz crystal that has been precisely ground to provide a stable fixed frequency for the timing pulses.

Data Bus Enable (DBE) Signal to the μP allowing it to activate its data bus drivers.

Diode–Transistor Logic (DTL) Older circuitry for use in IC logic components.

Direct Memory Access (DMA) Ability to communicate directly with memory without using the μP.

HALT mode Mode in which the processor has stopped executing instructions.

Interrupt Signal from an external device that causes the processor to stop executing its program and branch to a routine that will service the interrupt.

Memory-mapped I/O Technique whereby I/O device registers are treated just like memory. It eliminates the need for special I/O instructions as used in other μPs (i.e., the 8080).

Memory-ready signal Line to the clock circuit that stops the clock with phase 1 low and phase 2 high to permit operation with slow memory devices without slowing the system all the time.

Partial decoding Technique where not all address lines are used; it is acceptable if precautions are taken to avoid two or more chips responding to the same address.

PROM programmer Electronic device that will change the bits in the PROM from all 1s to 1s and 0s as required to correspond to the machine language program being installed. Most PROM programmers will work with fusible-link PROMs or EPROMs. Fusible-link PROM programming consists of "blowing" the fusible links for each bit that must be changed to a 1.

Redundant addresses Addresses that are the same except for some bits (or lines) that are not connected to the memory chip (IC) involved.

Reset Interrupt that causes the program to restart.

RUN mode Mode in which the processor is continually and normally executing instructions.

Scratch pad RAM RAM memory used for miscellaneous calculations or storage by various routines in a program.

Three-state bus Data bus configured with driver/receiver ICs capable of a third high-impedence state as well as the normal TTL levels of 1 and 0. This permits many devices to be placed on the same bus and bidirectional transmission to be possible over the same eight lines.

Three-State Control (TSC) Signal to the processor that, when HIGH, causes it to disconnect the address bus and R/W line drivers.

Transistor–Transistor Logic (TTL) Standard method of construction for internal circuits of **7400** family IC logic components.

Two-phase clock Two nearly identical clock signals called $\phi1$ (phase 1) and $\phi2$ (phase 2), but one is the inverse of the other and they are nonoverlapping. Used to drive the logic inside the 6800 μP.

Valid Memory Address (VMA) Signal generated by the processor which indicates that there is a valid address on the address bus.

Vectored interrupt Interrupt that sets the program counter to the address of the appropriate service routine.

7-17 REFERENCES

Greenfield, Joseph D. *Practical Digital Design Using ICs,* Second Edition, Wiley, New York, 1983.

Motorola Programming Manual M68PRM (D), 1976, reprinted 1984.

Motorola Monitor, Vol. 9, No. 2, October 1971.

M6800 Microcomputer System Design Data, Document No. 9701-5, February 1976.

Motorola MC6800 8-Bit Microprocessing Unit (MPU) Data Sheet, DS9471-R2, 1984.

Motorola MC6810 128 × 8-Bit Static Random Access Memory, DS9487-R3, 1984.

Motorola MC6850 Asynchronous Communications Interface Adapter, DS9493-R3, 1984.

Motorola MC6821 Peripheral Interface Adapter, DS9435-R4, 1984.

7-18 PROBLEMS

7-1 How many bytes and how many cycles are required for each of the following instructions?

AND IMMEDIATE

LOAD EXTENDED

STORE DIRECT

STORE INDEXED

ROTATE LEFT EXTENDED

JSR EXTENDED

7-2 What information appears on the address and data buses at the conclusion of each instruction of the following program? Make a table as shown for Example 7-6.

Address	*Program*
20	96
21	C2
22	8B
23	AB
24	97
25	C3
26	20
27	F8

7-3 How long does it take to execute each loop in the program of Problem 7-2?

7-4 A system using several **68A30**s should have only one that responds to positive levels on all its CS lines. Explain why this is so.

7-5 A **6800** system has its components connected to the address bus as given by the following table.

Address bits	*ROM1*	*ROM2*	*RAM1*	*RAM2*	*PIA1*
A15	**CS1**	**CS1**	$\overline{\text{CS1}}$	$\overline{\text{CS1}}$	**CS1**
A14	**CS2**	**CS2**	$\overline{\text{CS2}}$	$\overline{\text{CS2}}$	$\overline{\text{CS2}}$
A13	**CS3**	$\overline{\text{CS3}}$	$\overline{\text{CS4}}$	$\overline{\text{CS4}}$	**CS0**
A7			**CS0**	$\overline{\text{CS5}}$	

Which addresses does each component respond to? Which component contains the vector addresses?

7-6 A **6800** system consists of four ROMs, eight RAMs, two PIAs, and an ACIA. Allocate the memory space for each IC. Give the addresses that affect each component. Use **7400** series ICs as required as in Example 7-10.

7-7 If a **6800** system's memory space is to be filled entirely with **6810**s, how many **6810**s can be accommodated? How many **6810**s can be accommodated without resorting to external decoding?

After attempting to solve these problems, try to answer the self-evaluation questions in Section 7-2. If any of them still seem difficult, review the appropriate sections of the chapter to find the answers.

CHAPTER 8
INPUT/OUTPUT

8-1 INSTRUCTIONAL OBJECTIVES

The object of this chapter is to introduce those components which control the Input/Output (I/O) operations of the **6800** system. After reading this chapter, the student should be able to

1. Explain how a μC can control an external device using PIAs and/or Digital-to-Analog (D/A) and Analog-to-Digital (A/D) converters.
2. Explain the function of each signal connected to the PIA.
3. Explain the function of each bit in the PIA's Control and Direction Registers.
4. Utilize the PIA to transmit data.
5. Utilize the PIA to communicate with a peripheral, by using CB1 and CB2 lines to control the data flow.
6. Explain the function of each register and I/O line in the ACIA.
7. Write a program to transmit asynchronous serial data using the ACIA.
8. Connect an ACIA to a data terminal or modem.

8-2 SELF-EVALUATION QUESTIONS

Watch for the answers to the following questions as you read the chapter. They should help you to understand the material presented.

1. What are the two basic methods of I/O?
2. Explain the difference between control words and status words.
3. What is the function of A/D and D/A converters?
4. What is initialization?
5. What is the difference between the control lines and the other I/O lines on the PIA?

6. Why is the B side of the PIA better suited for outputting data and the A side better suited for receiving data?
7. What is the function of START and STOP bits?
8. Explain the interaction in a **6850** ACIA between the Transmit Data Register and the Transmit Shift Register and the interaction between the Receive Shift Register and the Receive Data Register.

8-3 INTRODUCTION TO INPUT/OUTPUT

The bus-structured organization of the **6800** system discussed in Chapter 7 provides an efficient way for the components of the computer to communicate with each other. The *purpose of a μC, however, is to control an external device* such as a line printer or a drill press. The μC exercises this control by sending commands to the device. Usually these commands are based on comparisons between desired and actual conditions existing in the external system. It may be necessary, for example, to stop the drill press if its motor temperature or speed exceeds a certain predetermined limit. The system must monitor these crucial conditions and send this information to the μP. *The communications that allow the μC to receive information from an external system* (Input) *and present data and commands to the external system* (Output) *are referred to as* Input/Output (I/O).

8-3.1 Methods of Input/Output (I/O)

Two basic methods are used to perform I/O functions between the bidirectional internal bus of the μC and the lines associated with the external devices. The fastest and most popular is the *parallel interface,* where many lines can be used to transfer data simultaneously in one step. A second method is to use *serial transmission* of the bits of each byte over one signal path (for each direction). This is done either **asynchronously** or **synchronously** (**synchronous** means in step with a clock or timing signal). The need for only two transmission paths makes the serial method attractive when the device being controlled is some distance away. These methods are implemented in the **6800** system by several unique parts:

1. The **6821** Peripheral Interface Adapter (PIA) or the **68488** General Purpose Interface Adapter (GPIA) is used for *parallel transfer.*
2. The **6850** Asynchronous Communications Interface Adapter (ACIA), the **6852** Synchronous Serial Data Adapter (SSDA), or the **6854** Advanced Data Link Controller (ADLC) is used for *serial* transfer.

All of these Metal Oxide–Semiconductor (MOS) Large-Scale Integrated Circuits (LSI ICs) include *control, status,* and *data* registers that are accessible from the μC buses because they are *addressable*. The mode of operation of each IC is determined by storing one or more control words in the IC's **control registers**. The **status registers** are accessed by the μC to sense the condition of the external device as determined by signals from the device.

8-3.2 Control Words and Data Words

The **6800** communicates with external devices via the PIA, ACIA, SSDA, ADLC, or GPIA. The μP can send out either *data words* or *control words* and receive either *data words* or *status words*. The **control word** selects the mode of operation of the interface component and determines whether the I/O lines are to operate as inputs or outputs. It also selects the polarity sensed by the control lines. Once the interface is properly programmed, the data registers can then be used to transmit commands or data to the external device.

Command words are commands to the external device. They tell it what to do (or control it). If command words are used, the external hardware is often designed so that each bit controls a different function. For example, bit 0 could control a solid-state relay, bit 1 could be connected to a solenoid, and bit 2 could drive an indicator light for the operator.

Data words are used to represent either a *code* or a *magnitude*. As a code, for example, 1 byte could tell a teletypewriter which alphanumeric character to print. As a magnitude, it might tell a drill press how fast to rotate or determine the cutting depth of a lathe.

The **6800** can receive either *data* words or *status* words. *Data* words typically represent system parameters such as the position of a tool or the temperature of a motor. **Status words** give the μC the state of the system (e.g., whether a relay is ON or a tape is rewinding).

8-3.3 Digital-to-Analog (D/A) Conversion[1]

If the μC is sending out a word designed to control something like the cutting depth of a lathe, the bits in the output word must, in many systems, be converted to an analog quantity, typically a voltage. The magnitude of this voltage is determined by bits of the output word.

To convert the output bits of a μC to a voltage, a **Digital-to-Analog (D/A) converter** is used. Thus, to control the lathe's cutting depth, the following steps are necessary:

1. The μC must determine the desired cutting depth and present this as a digital word to the interface IC. (The PIA is assumed in this case.)
2. The digital output of the PIA must be connected to the input of a D/A converter.
3. The voltage output of the D/A converter then drives a mechanical converter, which sets the cutting depth of the lathe.

A block diagram of this system is shown in the upper part of Fig. 8-1. The wide arrow represents eight or more digital input lines to the D/A converter, depending on the resolution required, and the single output line carries the output voltage of the converter.

[1]D/A and A/D converters are discussed further in Section 12-6.

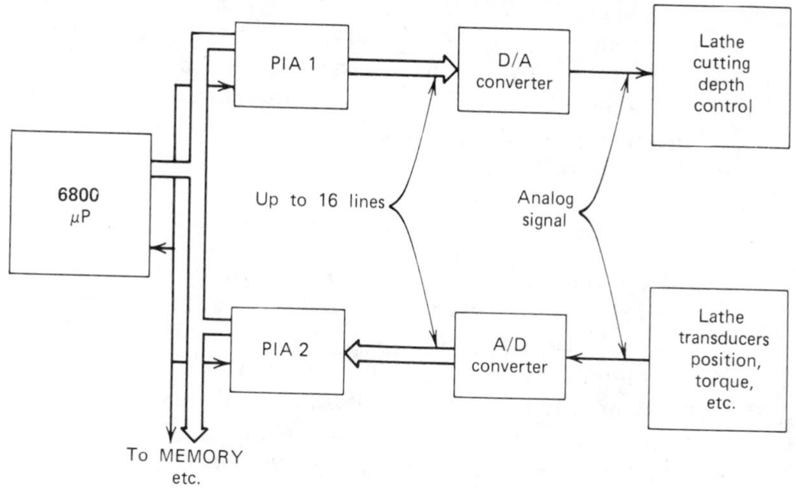

FIGURE 8-1 A typical μP Analog INPUT/OUTPUT system.

EXAMPLE 8-1

The cutting depth of the lathe can vary from 0 to 16 cm. If the D/A converter has an 8-bit input, how close to the desired value can the cutting depth be set?

SOLUTION

Since an 8-bit input allows for 256 (2^8) different numbers, each digital increment corresponds to 16 cm/256 = **0.0625 cm**. This is the *resolution* of the converter. If greater resolution is required, more than eight lines must be used in the converter. This requires a somewhat more sophisticated hardware system.

8-3.4 Analog-to-Digital (A/D) Conversion

In order to control an external system, a μC must be able to monitor it. This monitoring is usually accomplished by using *sensors, transducers,* and **Analog-to-Digital (A/D) converters.**

Sensors and **transducers** convert physical quantities to voltages. *Sensors* are generally used to sense relatively static quantities, such as the temperature at a particular point or the weight of the liquid in a fuel tank. *Transducers* generally convert more dynamic physical quantities, such as pressures or velocities, to voltages.

The output voltages of the sensors or transducers must be in digital form before being sent to the μC. An A/D converter accomplishes this.[2] It accepts a voltage as

[2]Many transducers and sensors have direct digital outputs.

its input and produces a corresponding digital output. A/D converters with 8-, 10-, and 12-bit outputs are readily available. The more bits provided, the higher the resolution of the converter, as shown in Example 8-1 above. Any size digital word can be accommodated by multiplexing it (dividing it in 8-bit bytes that are brought in sequentially), but if the resolution is adequate it is simplest to use a byte-size converter. A block diagram of the μC input system is shown in the lower part of Fig. 8-1.

Thus, the functions of computer-controlled systems generally are as follows:

1. The operation of the system is monitored by sensors and transducers.
2. The outputs of the sensors and transducers are converted to digital quantities by an A/D converter, if they are not already in digital form.
3. The outputs are sent to the μC via the PIA.
4. The computer program examines the inputs to determine whether the system is operating properly.
5. If the μC determines that adjustments are required, it sends commands out via the PIA.
6. The outputs are converted by a D/A converter to voltages that adjust the system and restore optimal operation.

8-4 THE PIA IN DETAIL

The PIA is a 40-pin Large-Scale Integration (LSI) IC designed to control *parallel* data transfers between the **6800** system and external devices. PIAs are used to transfer data or commands when the equipment to be controlled is nearby and the many lines are easily accommodated. Sections 8-7 through 8-11 describe the uses of the serial interfaces, which are more often used for distant control.

A block diagram of the **6821** PIA that is used for parallel data transfer in **6800** systems is shown in Fig. 8-2. The figure shows the registers within the PIA, the interface to the **6800** data, address, and control buses on the left, and the interface connections to external devices on the right.

8-4.1 The PIA Registers

Figure 8-2 shows that the PIA is a dual I/O port unit (a **port** is defined as an 8-bit parallel interface) with two similar sides labeled *A* and *B*. This drawing from Motorola literature shows that each side contains three registers and identifies them as:

1. **The Control Register.** This controls the operation of its side of the PIA.
2. **The Data Direction Register.** This register determines the direction of data flow (in or out) on each I/O line.
3. **The Data Register.** This holds the I/O data going between the external system and the PIA.

To reduce confusion and to be a bit more accurate for this book we prefer to refer to the first two registers as follows:

1. **The Control/Status Register.** This has 6 bits used to control the PIA and 2 bits of status.
2. **The Direction Register.** This register determines the direction of data flow (in or out) on each I/O line.

The action of these registers is discussed in detail in Sections 8-5 and 8-6.

8-4.2 The PIA/6800 Interface

The PIA registers are treated as a *set of memory locations* by the **6800** system. The system reads and writes these registers as it would any memory location. The user must assign these PIA addresses in the same way as other memory addresses, as described in Chapter 7.

The lines connecting the PIA to the **6800** I/O bus are shown on the left side of Fig. 8-2. This interface consists of

1. **Inputs D0–D7.** The 8-bit data bus.
2. **Inputs RS0, RS1 and CS0, CS1, and $\overline{\textbf{CS2}}$.** These lines are normally connected to the **6800** address bus. RS0 and RS1 are usually connected to A0 and A1 and determine, along with a bit in the Control Register, which of the six registers within the PIA is selected. The chip select lines CS0, CS1, and $\overline{\text{CS2}}$ are used to select the particular PIA (see Section 7-14).
3. **Enable (E).** The E pin of the **6821** PIA, unlike its earlier predecessor, the **6820**, need not be clocked continuously, since the **6821** is a static part. The **6820** was a dynamic part and therefore the E pin was generally connected to a signal

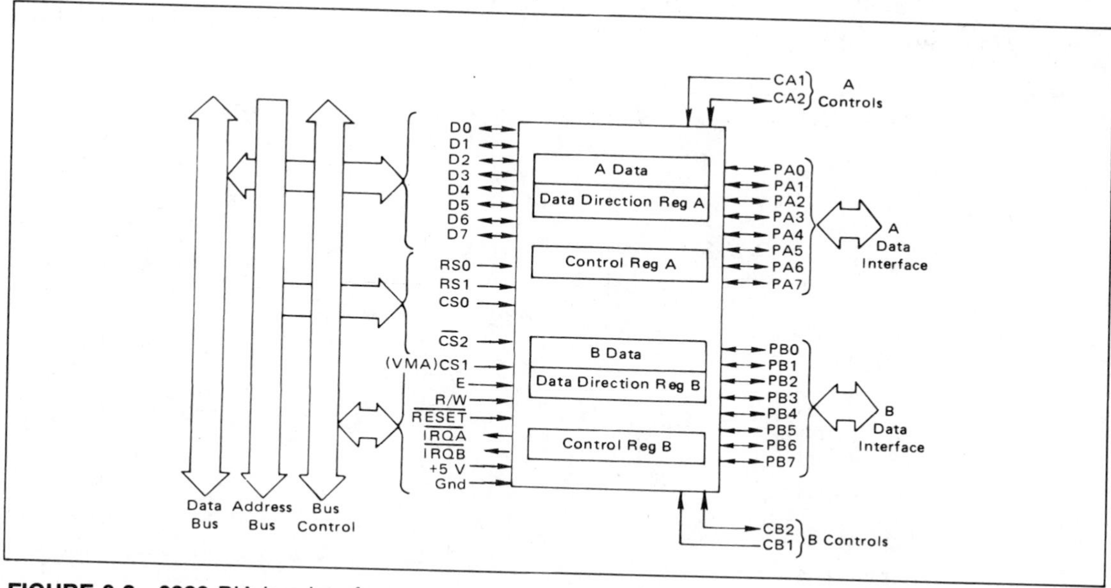

FIGURE 8-2 **6820** PIA bus interface.

derived from the $\phi 2$ clock. The **6821** will work in the same circuit but, since clocking is not needed, the E pin can be used as another Chip Select.

4. **PIA Read/Write (R/$\overline{\text{W}}$).** This signal is generated by the μP to control the direction of data transfers on the data bus. A LOW state on the PIA R/$\overline{\text{W}}$ line enables the input buffers. Data is transferred (or written) from the μP to the PIA when enabled by the E signal if the device has been selected. A HIGH on the R/$\overline{\text{W}}$ line sets up the PIA for a transfer of data *to* the μP (a read) via the bus. The PIA output buffers are enabled when the proper address and the E pulse are present.
5. **$\overline{\text{RESET}}$.** This active low RESET line is used to reset all register bits in the PIA to a logical 0 (LOW). This pin of the PIA is normally connected to the RESET line of the μC system and is usually activated (taken LOW) by a momentary switch or automatic restart circuit during POWER ON.
6. **$\overline{\text{IRQA}}$ and $\overline{\text{IRQB}}$.** These are the PIA interrupt lines. They are designed for **wire-OR** operation and are generally tied together and wired to the interrupt input on the **6800**. A LOW signal on either of these lines causes the **6800** to be interrupted. Details of this operation are described in Section 9-5.

8-4.3 The Interface between the PIA and External Devices

The connections between the PIA and the external devices are shown on the right side of Fig. 8-2. There are two groups of eight bidirectional data lines (PA0–PA7 and PB0–PB7) and two control lines (CA1 and CA2, or CB1 and CB2) for each side. The control lines are used to regulate communication between the PIA and the external devices.

Figure 8-3 shows the output port circuitry for ports A and B of the **6821** PIA. Note that they have greatly different characteristics. The A side is designed to drive CMOS logic to normal 30 to 70% levels and incorporates an internal pull-up

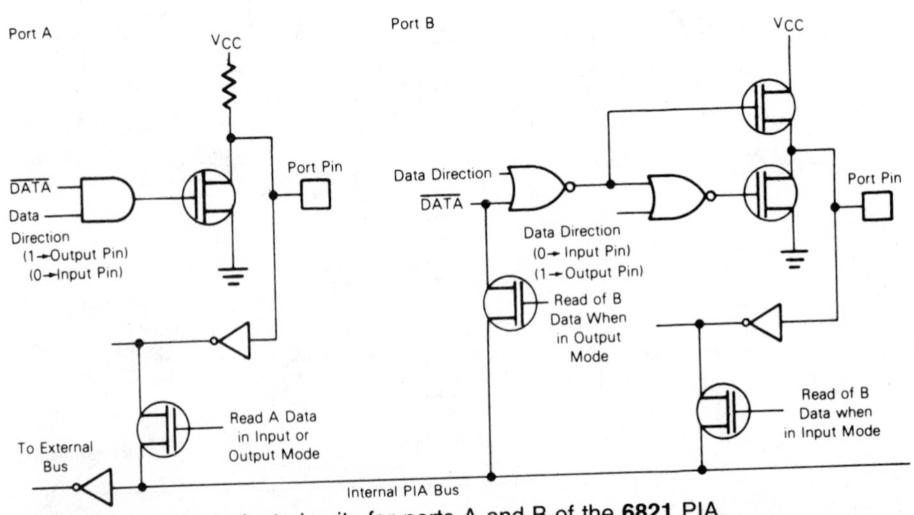

FIGURE 8-3 Equivalent circuits for ports A and B of the **6821** PIA.

device that remains connected even in the input mode. Because of this, the A side requires more drive current in the input mode than port B. In contrast, the B side uses a normal three-state NMOS buffer, which cannot pull up to CMOS levels without external resistors. The B side can drive extra loads such as **Darlingtons** without difficulty. (Darlingtons are a pair of transistors in a single package connected internally so as to provide the output capabilities of a power transistor with high enough gain to permit control by a PIA.) After the PIA is reset, the bits of the A port are configured as inputs with pull-up resistors, whereas the B side (also in input mode) will float high or low depending on the external load.

Notice also the difference between port A and port B read operations for the PIA when in the output mode. When reading port A, the actual pin is read, whereas the B side read comes from an output latch ahead of the actual pin.

These port differences mainly affect the external circuitry and do not otherwise affect functionality.

8-5 DATA TRANSFERS BETWEEN THE PIA AND EXTERNAL DEVICES

Before any data transfers can take place via the PIA, its Control/Status Registers and Direction Registers must be set up (or *programmed*) to determine the mode of operation and the direction of the data transfer (in or out of the PIA). This is known as **initialization**. Once initialized, these registers generally remain unchanged unless they are reset, although one of the PIA's outstanding capabilities is its programmable nature and ability to change system function during the operation of a program. This permits many unique features to be implemented in special programs with a minimum of external hardware and also permits the same PIA to be used in many applications (see Example 8-8).

8-5.1 The Direction Register

The Direction Register, called the Data Direction Register or DDR in Motorola diagrams, determines the direction of each bit of data being transferred on the PIA's bidirectional data lines. The DDR is 8 bits long, so there is a one-to-one correspondence between its bits and the PA0–PA7 or PB0–PB7 lines. A 1 in any bit of the DDR causes the corresponding PA or PB line to act as an output, whereas a 0 causes it to become an input. Typically, direction registers contain 00 or FF so that an entire byte is transferred in or out, but some bits of either side of a PIA can act as inputs and some as outputs, as shown in Example 8-3.

8-5.2 The Data Register (DR)

The Data Register contains the data being transferred into or out of the PIA. The Data and Direction Registers have the same address, but whether a word to that address reaches the Data Register (DR) or the Direction Register (DDR) depends on bit 2 of the Control Register.

Table 8-1a shows the addressing scheme for the PIA registers. When RS1 is a 0, the A registers are addressed, and when it is a 1, the B side is accessed. Since RS0 is generally connected to A0 and RS1 to A1, the Control/Status Registers for both sides are located at an odd address and the Data/Direction Registers are at the prior even address. Although there are six registers, only four addresses are used, as shown in Table 8-1b. If bit 2 of the Control Register for the A or B side (CRA2 or CRB2) is a 1, the Data Register is accessible, whereas if bit 2 is a 0, only the Direction Register can be accessed. Thus, if the PIA receives a write command at the Data/Direction register address, it will use bit 2 of the control register to determine which register is to be written into. Bit 2 is sometimes called the *steering* bit because it steers reads or writes to either the Direction or the Data Register.

8-5.3 Initializing the PIA

The PIA must always be initialized by a system reset. When the RESET line of the PIA is taken LOW, it clears (or zeros) all registers. This sets up the PA0–PA7, PB0–PB7, CA2, and CB2 lines as inputs and disables all interrupts. Since bit 2 is also 0 the Direction Registers are set to be accessed. The PIA RESET line is normally connected to the μP RESET, and therefore a RESTART program routine is automatically accessed whenever RESET is activated. The desired PIA configuration is *programmed* into the chip during the execution of this RESTART (or initialization) program routine.

If the PIA needs to be reconfigured without using the RESET line, it must be done in the following sequence:

1. Clear the Control/Status Register (including bit 2).
2. Rewrite the Direction Register.

TABLE 8-1 PIA Addressing

(a) Internal Addressing

RS1	RS0	CRA2	CRB2	Registers
0	0	1	X	Data Register A
0	0	0	X	Direction Register A
0	1	X	X	Control/Status Reg. A
1	0	X	1	Data Register B
1	0	X	0	Direction Register B
1	1	X	X	Control Register B

(b) Memory Location

Address	Registers
XXX11	B Control/Status (1 register)
XXX10	B Data/Direction (2 registers)
XXX01	A Control/Status (1 register)
XXX00	A Data/Direction (2 registers)

3. Rewrite the Control Word with bit 2 SET to select the Data Register.
4. Write or read data.

EXAMPLE 8-2

Write a program to send the contents of locations $40 and $41 to a peripheral device. Assume the Control/Status Register is at address $8009 and the Direction Register and Data Register are both at address $8008.

Note that because bit 1 of the address is 0, the A side of the PIA is being used.

SOLUTION

The steps of the solution are listed below. The coding has been omitted to save space.

1. Accumulator A is cleared and stored in $8009. This clears all the bits of the Control/Status Register; in particular, it clears bit 2.
2. Accumulator A is loaded (Immediate) with $FF and stored in $8008. Because bit 2 of the Control/Status Register is now a 0, when $FF is written to address $8008, it enters the Direction Register and causes all the data lines to act as outputs.
3. An 04 is now loaded (LDA A Immediate) into the accumulator and stored in $8009. This changes bit 2 of the Control Register to a 1, which latches the Direction Register and allows the Data Register to be accessed.
4. The contents of location $40 are loaded into the accumulator and stored at $8008. Because bit 2 of the Control/Status Register is now a 1, these bits go to the Data Register and are output on the I/O lines.
5. After the first word has been read by the peripheral and sensed by reading the status bits (usually signaled by one of the control lines, as described later), the contents of location $41 are loaded in A and stored at $8008. This places that data on the I/O lines.

Note that once the Control and Direction Registers have been set up, data can be sent out repeatedly without reinitializing those registers.

EXAMPLE 8-3

Write a program to read the state of four switches and send the data out to a hexadecimal display.

SOLUTION

One solution is shown in the circuit of Fig. 8-4, where the four switches are connected to lines PA0 through PA3 and the display inputs are connected to peripheral lines PA4 to PA7. The program for the solution proceeds.

1. During initialization, $F0 is written into the Direction Register. This configures the 4 LSBs as inputs and the 4 MSBs as outputs.

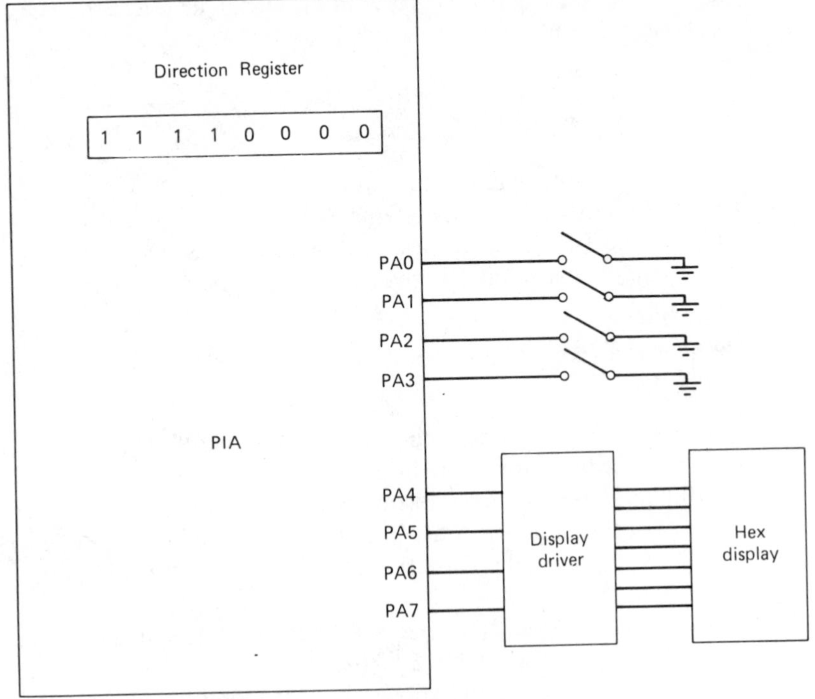

FIGURE 8-4 The PIA connectors for Example 8-3.

2. The Control Register is then rewritten to make bit 2 a 1. The instruction LOAD A (from) $8008 reads the switch contents into the 4 LSBs of the accumulator.
3. Four LEFT SHIFT instructions shift the switch settings into the MSBs of the accumulator.
4. Now a STORE A at $8008 places the switch settings on the output lines (PA4–PA7), where they can drive the display.

8-6 THE PIA CONTROL LINES

When an external device has information for the μC, it must send the PIA a signal (often called DATA READY). When the PIA has read the byte, it typically acknowledges receipt of the information by sending an ACK (for acknowledge) signal to the device. A similar situation exists when the PIA is transmitting information *to* the device. The protocol and signals that control the exchange of information are called **handshaking**.

In Section 8-5 we concentrated on the data lines and ignored the CA1 and CA2 (or CB1 and CB2) lines, which control the interchange of information. The operating mode of these control lines is determined by the bits in the A and B Control/Status Register. The control lines, in turn, affect the contents of bits 6 and 7 of the Control/Status Registers, as will be explained.

The configuration of the Control/Status Register is shown in Table 8-2. The upper register (CRA) is for the "A" side of the PIA, and the lower one (CRB) is an identical register used to control the "B" side. The function of bit 2 (Direction Register access) was described in Section 8-5.2. Bits 0, 1 and 3, 4, 5 of the Control/Status Register are used to select the functions of the control lines. Status bits 6 and 7 are SET by the transitions of the CA1 and CA2 (CB1 and CB2) lines. Bits 6 and 7 are *read only* bits that cannot be changed by writing into the Control/Status Register but are reset indirectly by a read data operation, as explained in Section 8-6.1.

8-6.1 Control Lines CA1 and CB1

Control lines CA1 and CB1 are *input only* lines that function identically. As shown in Table 8-2, they are controlled by bits 0 and 1 of the Control/Status Register, and their action can be determined from Table 8-3. Table 8-3 shows the following:

1. If CRA1 (CRB1) is a 0, status bit 7 of the Control/Status Register is set HIGH whenever there is a negative transition (↓) on the CA1 (CB1) line. These lines are typically connected to an external device that causes a transition whenever it requires attention. If CRA1 (CRB1) is a 1, a positive transition (↑) on CA1 (CB1) SETs status bit 7 of the corresponding Control/Status Register.
2. If CRA0 (CRB0) of the Control/Status Register is a 0, the interrupt line $\overline{IRQA}$ ($\overline{IRQB}$) is disabled and $\overline{IRQA}$ ($\overline{IRQB}$) remains HIGH, even when status bit CRA7 (CRB7) goes HIGH as a result of the CA1 line transitions. If CRA0 (CRB0) is a 1, the $\overline{IRQA}$ (or $\overline{IRQB}$) pin is pulled down each time the status bit is set. If these pins are wired to the μP chip, the **6800** can be interrupted (see Section 9-5).

These bits can be reset only by reading the corresponding *data* register. The reason for this operation is that the manufacturer assumes that a transition on CA1 (CB1) sets CRA7 (CRB7) and indicates that the peripheral has data available for the μP. The μP accepts the data by *reading its input port,* the PA or PB data register, which transfers the data to an accumulator. This also resets CRA7 (CRB7) because the data has now been taken by the μP.

TABLE 8-2 PIA Control Word Format

	7	6	5	4	3	2	1	0
CRA	IRQA1	IRQA2	CA2 Control			DDRA Access	CA1 Control	
	7	6	5	4	3	2	1	0
CRB	IRQB1	IRQB2	CB2 Control			DDRB Access	CB1 Control	

TABLE 8-3 Control of Interrupt Inputs CA1 and CB1

CRA-1 (CRB-1)	CRA-0 (CRB-0)	Interrupt Input CA1 (CB1)	Interrupt Flag CRA-7 (CRB-7)	MPU Interrupt Request $\overline{IRQA}$ ($\overline{IRQB}$)
0	0	↓ Active	Set high on ↓ of CA1 (CB1)	Disabled — $\overline{IRQ}$ remains high
0	1	↓ Active	Set high on ↓ of CA1 (CB1)	Goes low when the interrupt flag bit CRA-7 (CRB-7) goes high
1	0	↑ Active	Set high on ↑ of CA1 (CB1)	Disabled — $\overline{IRQ}$ remains high
1	1	↑ Active	Set high on ↑ of CA1 (CB1)	Goes low when the interrupt flag bit CRA-7 (CRB-7) goes high

Notes: 1. ↑ indicates positive transition (low to high)

2. ↓ indicates negative transition (high to low)

3. The Interrupt flag bit CRA-7 is cleared by an MPU Read of the A Data Register, and CRB-7 is cleared by an MPU Read of the B Data Register.

4. If CRA-0 (CRB-0) is low when an interrupt occurs (Interrupt disabled) and is later brought high, $\overline{IRQA}$ ($\overline{IRQB}$) occurs after CRA-0 (CRB-0) is written to a "one".

EXAMPLE 8-4

A PIA is in locations \$8004–\$8007 (all addresses are hex).

a. How can the user determine whether a transition has occurred on CB1?
b. If bit 7 of control register B is set, how can it be cleared?

SOLUTION

a. If a transition has occurred on CB1, then CRB7 will be set. Therefore reading CRB (location \$8007) will set the N flag in the Condition Code Register. This is the usual way to test bit 7 of the Control Register.
b. If CRB7 is set, it can be cleared only by reading the corresponding data register. Here we need an LDAA \$8006 to clear the bit in \$8007. The fact that one location (\$8006) has to be read in order to clear a bit in another location (\$8007) is sometimes confusing. The user must also be sure that the LDAA \$8006 is reading the Data Register and not the Direction Register. Reading the Direction Register will not reset CRB7.

Many systems do not use or need interrupts, and a number of examples of these systems will be described in the remainder of this chapter. The use of interrupts is a complex subject and much of the next chapter is devoted to it.

8-6.2 Control Line Monitoring

The **6800** system has two ways of responding to any of the control line transitions that indicate that an external device is requesting attention:

1. By continuously *polling* status bits. (**Polling** means that the system program periodically reads the Control/Status Registers of *all* I/O devices to determine whether the flag bit of one of them has been SET.)
2. By electronically responding to the hardware *interrupt* request lines (see Chapter 9 for interrupt details).

EXAMPLE 8-5

What happens if 06 is written into Control/Status Register A?

SOLUTION

A control word of 06 results in the conditions specified on line 3 of Table 8-3. Bit 7 is SET by a positive transition of the CA1 line. $\overline{\text{IRQA}}$ is disabled. The Direction Register is unaffected because bit 2 is also SET. If 06 is written to the Control/Status Register and read back before a positive transition on CA1 occurs, the μP reads it back as 06, but if a transition occurs between the writing and reading, the μP reads it back as an $86 because CRA7 is now SET. Once SET, CRA7 can be cleared only by reading Data Register A, as stated in the footnotes to Table 8-3.

EXAMPLE 8-6

Write a program to monitor the CA1 line constantly and to take action when a transition occurs. Assume the Control/Status Register's address is $8009.

SOLUTION

First the Control/Status Register must be initialized to select the proper transition (↓ or ↑) and disable interrupts. Then the program can proceed as shown in Table 8-4.

The instruction at location $1000 loads the contents of the Control/Status Register into the A accumulator, and it is tested by the following instruction (at $1003) to see if bit 7 (the interrupt flag bit) is SET. If not, the contents of the register at $8009 are positive and the instruction branches back to $1000 and fetches the status again. It continues to loop in this fashion until bit 7 goes HIGH. Since the resulting byte is then negative, the program falls through to the following instruction. The PIA's Data Register at $8008 is then read to reset CRA7 and get the data. Note that this is a very tight loop; that is, the computer did nothing but

TABLE 8-4 Program for Example 8-6

Addr	Data	Mnemonic	Comment
1000	B6 8009	LDA A $8009	Get status
1003	2A FB	BPL *−3	If plus, branch back to 1000 and repeat.
1005	B6 8008	LDA A $8008	Get data.
Etc.	. . . .	. . . .	

monitor the PIA. Interrupts, described in Chapter 9, allow the computer to perform other tasks while waiting for the transition.

EXAMPLE 8-7

A PIA is located at \$8004–\$8007. A debounced switch is connected to CA1 and the outputs PA0–PA6 drive a seven-segment display, as shown in Fig. 8-5. Write a program to increment the number in the seven-segment display every time the switch is thrown. When the number reaches 9 the display must return to 0 after the next switch throw.

SOLUTION
The program is shown in Table 8-5. It starts by initializing the A port for outputs. It then monitors Control/Status Register A. A switch throw causes a transition on CA1 and causes CRA7 to go HIGH. When this occurs, the program falls through to location \$35, where it

1. Reads the A Data Register to reset CRA7.
2. Increments X and resets it to 0 if X has gone beyond 9.
3. Jumps to a table to get the proper codes to drive the seven-segment display.

In this program the table starts at location \$A0. To show a 0 on the display, the data must cause all segments except g (see Fig. 8-5) to light. The code in \$A0 must therefore be \$3F. If \$A1 is accessed, a 1 should appear by lighting segments B and C, so that \$A1 should contain 06. (Figure 8-5 shows the segments with their PIA interconnections).

Many μC systems that use seven-segment displays drive their displays directly by using similar tables. Note that this program provides a way for the μP to count and display external events as they occur.

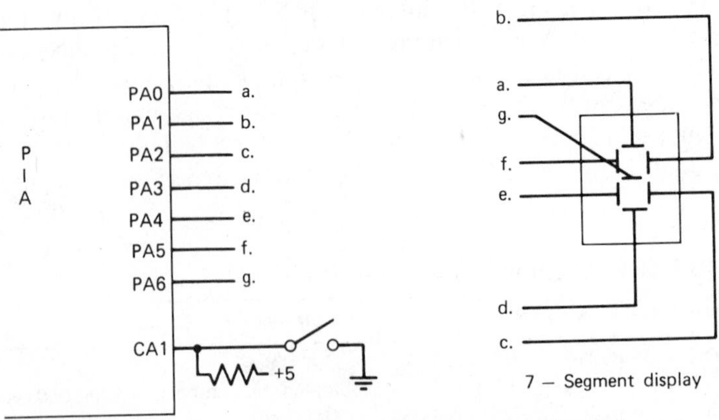

FIGURE 8-5 Control of a 7-segment display using the PIA.

TABLE 8-5 Program and Data Table for Example 8-7

(a) Program

Addr	Code		Mnemonic	Comments
2Ø	CE ØØØØ		LDX #Ø	CLEAR X
23	7F 8ØØ5		CLR $8ØØ5	CLR BIT 2 TO SELECT DIR REG
26	86 FF		LDA A #$FF	SET TO ALL 1S
28	B7 8ØØ4		STA A $8ØØ4	SET DIRECTION FOR OUTPUTS
2B	86 Ø4		LDA A #$4	GET WORD FOR NEG GOING CA1 &
2D	B7 8ØØ5		STA A $8ØØ5	SET CRA2 TO SELECT DATA REG
3Ø	B6 8ØØ5	LOOP	LDA A $8ØØ5	GET STATUS
33	2A FB		BPL LOOP	WAIT FOR CRA7 TO BECOME 1
35	B6 8ØØ4		LDA A $8ØØ4	CLEAR BIT 7
38	Ø8		INX	INCREMENT X
39	8C ØØØA		CPX #$A	IS IT > 9 ?
3C	26 Ø3		BNE *+5	NO-SKIP NEXT INSTRUCTION
3E	CE ØØØØ		LDX #Ø	YES-CLEAR X
41	A6 AØ		LDA A $AØ,X	GET THE 7-SEGMENT CODE
43	B7 8ØØ4		STA A $8ØØ4	OUTPUT IT TO DISPLAY
46	2Ø E8		BRA LOOP	RETURN TO 3Ø AGAIN

(b) Data Table

Location	Contents	Decimal Number to be Displayed
AØ	3F	Ø
A1	Ø6	1
A2	5B	2
A3	4F	3
A4	66	4
A5	6D	5
A6	7D	6
A7	Ø7	7
A8	7F	8
A9	6F	9

One of the interesting features of the PIA is its programmability. Its function can be changed dynamically during operation, as illustrated in the following example.

EXAMPLE 8-8

Write a program that will input characters from a keyboard using a PIA. They will be displayed on the screen and kept in a buffer. This is a program that could be part of a word processor system. In this example, the keyboard has a line that goes LOW whenever a key is depressed. It stays low as long as the key is held. Use the CA1 line to set the CRA6 flag when a character is ready. Using the same line, provide a character repeat feature when the key is held down.

SOLUTION

Table 8-6 shows a program to meet the requirements. This was developed as part of a word processor program that uses a CRT display. It serves to bring in characters from a keyboard whenever keys are pressed and display them on the screen. They also go into a buffer or are acted on if they are control characters. This is all done by the CHOUT routine and will not be shown now. A *repeat character* feature is included such that if a key is kept down for more than a selected time (count of $6000), the character will be repeated. The *rate* of repetition is determined by the smaller count ($A00). This works by first programming the CA1 line so that it looks for a negative-going signal from the keyboard; but once the character is fetched, the CA1 line is reprogrammed to look for a positive-going signal so that the *release* of the key can be sensed. If the key is held down beyond the time-out period, the character is repeated on the screen.

Since the PIA must be reinitialized each time this input character routine is entered, and not by the RESET routine, it has a unique INIT routine. Note that the registers are reset by first clearing the control word and then reprogramming them again. The AECHO flag is used to allow or inhibit the display on the screen. As long as the AECHO flag is zero, the character is "echoed" (displayed). Also, a toggled byte labeled RPT is used to change the duration of the delay. The values of these delays were chosen by cut and try to provide action that was comfortable to the operator. (They will vary from this if the clock rate is different.)

The PIA's base address is $EB04 for this program but can be changed to any convenient value to match other hardware. The program could be in ROM, but AECHO and RPT must be in RAM since they are changed by the program.

8-6.3 Control Lines CA2 and CB2

Lines CA2 and CB2 can be used as either input or output control lines, and they are controlled by bits 3, 4, and 5 of the Control/Status Register. If bit 5 of the Control/Status Register is a 0, the lines function as interrupt inputs as shown in Table 8-7. Table 8-7 reveals that these lines function exactly as CA1 and CB1 do except that transitions caused by the external devices set bit 6 instead of bit 7 of the Control/Status Register.

EXAMPLE 8-9

Assume a tape drive is connected to a **6800** system, and it must send the **6800** either data or status information on the same I/O lines. The data is the words read from the tape, and the status information tells the system what the tape is doing (e.g., running forward, rewinding, at end of tape). How can the system distinguish between data and status information?

SOLUTION
One solution is to connect both CA1 and CA2 to the tape drive. If the tape drive is sending data, it raises CA1 every time it has a byte to send, whereas if it is sending status information, it raises CA2. The μP system can distinguish between status and data requests by examining bits 6 and 7 of the PIA's Control/Status Register.

TABLE 8-6 Input Character Routine with Repeat for Example 8-8

```
Addr   Code               Mnemonics            Comments

1000   8E 1FFF   INIT     LDS #$1FFF           SET STACK POINTER
1003   BD 0400            JSR  INITS           DO OTHER INIT
1006   20 18              BRA RETURN           SCAN KEYBOARD

                 * INITIALIZE KEYBOARD PIA
1008   4F        CTST1    CLR A
1009   B7  EB05           STA A  PIA+1         UNLATCH DIRECTION REG
100C   B7  EB04           STA A  PIA           SET DIRECTION = INPUT
100F   B7  EB07           STA A  PIA+3         UNLATCH DIRECTION REG
1012   B7  EB06           STA A  PIA+2         SET DIRECTION = OUT
1015   86  06             LDA A  #6            GET CW
1017   B7  EB07           STA A  PIA+3         SET "B" SIDE
101A   86  36             LDA A  #$36          SET CA1 FOR NEG GOING
101C   B7  EB05           STA A  PIA+1
101F   39                 RTS
                 *
1020   8D  E6    RETURN   BSR CTST1            RESET PIA EACH TIME
1022   8D  02    CLP      BSR INCH             GET CHARACTER
1024   20  FC             BRA CLP              LOOP
                 *
1026   B6  EB05  INCH     LDA A  PIA+1         NEG TRANSITION?
1029   2A  FB             BPL INCH             NO - LOOP
102B   B6  EB04           LDA A  PIA           YES - GET CHARACTER
102E   84  7F             AND A  #$7F          RESET BIT 7
1030   C6  34    IN2      LDA B #$34           PROG TO DETECT RELSE
1032   F7  EB05           STA B  PIA+1         SET CW
1035   7F  2001           CLR RPT              CLEAR REPEAT FLAG
1038   7D  2000           TST AECHO            SET TO ECHO?
103B   27  0E             BEQ OUTCH            YES
103D   B6  EB04  IN1      LDA A PIA            CLEAR INTR BIT
1040   84  7F             AND A #$7F           RESET MSB
1042   C6  36             LDA B #$36
1044   F7  EB05           STA B PIA+1          RESTORE CA1 NEG-GOING
1047   7F  2000           CLR  AECHO           RESET ECHO FLAG
104A   39                 RTS                  RETURN TO LOOP
                 *
104B   36        OUTCH    PSH A                SAVE A ON STACK
104C   BD  3000           JSR  CHOUT           DISPLAY CHAR ON SCRN
104F   32                 PUL A                RESTORE CHARACTER
1050   CE  6000           LDX   #$6000         SET START DELAY
1053   7D  2001           TST   RPT            WHICH DLY IN EFFECT?
1056   27  03             BEQ   *+5            SKIP IF REPT CLEAR
1058   CE  0A00           LDX   #$A00          SET REPT DELAY
105B   F6  EB05  OT1      LDA B PIA+1          GET STATUS
105E   2B  DD             BMI   IN1            RELEASED YET?
1060   09                 DEX                  NO- DECRMT DLY COUNT
1061   26  F8             BNE   OT1            TIMEOUT?
1063   7C  2001           INC   RPT            SET FOR SHORT DELAY
1066   20  E3             BRA   OUTCH          YES - DISPLAY AGAIN
```

8-6.4 Use of CB2 as an Output in the Handshake Mode

The action of the CB2 line as an output is described in Table 8-8. Note that the CB2 line goes LOW after a WRITE to the Data Register. This simplifies the programming and therefore makes it preferable for the B section of the PIA to be used to send data to external devices (output).

TABLE 8-7 Control of CA2 and CB2 as Interrupt Inputs; CRA5 (CRB5) is Low

CRA-5 (CRB-5)	CRA-4 (CRB-4)	CRA-3 (CRB-3)	Interrupt Input CA2 (CB2)	Interrupt Flag CRA-6 (CRB-6)	MPU Interrupt Request $\overline{IRQA}$ ($\overline{IRQB}$)
0	0	0	↓ Active	Set high on ↓ of CA2 (CB2)	Disabled — $\overline{IRQ}$ remains high
0	0	1	↓ Active	Set high on ↓ of CA2 (CB2)	Goes low when the interrupt flag bit CRA-6 (CRB-6) goes high
0	1	0	↑ Active	Set high on ↑ of CA2 (CB2)	Disabled — $\overline{IRQ}$ remains high
0	1	1	↑ Active	Set high on ↑ of CA2 (CB2)	Goes low when the interrupt flag bit CRA-6 (CRB-6) goes high

Notes: 1. ↑ indicates positive transition (low to high)
2. ↓ indicates negative transition (high to low)
3. The Interrupt flag bit CRA-6 is cleared by an MPU Read of the A Data Register and CRB-6 is cleared by an MPU Read of the B Data Register.
4. If CRA-3 (CRB-3) is low when an interrupt occurs (Interrupt disabled) and is later brought high, $\overline{IRQA}$ ($\overline{IRQB}$) occurs after CRA-3 (CRB-3) is written to a "one".

The top line of Table 8-8 illustrates a mode of operation commonly called the handshaking mode. This case is illustrated in Figure 8-6 and the sequence of events is as follows:

1. The control word to the B side is written as shown. Note that CRB 5, 4, and 3 are 100, respectively.
2. When the system must send data out it writes the data to Data Register B. This causes CB2 to go LOW.
3. The peripheral device acknowledges receipt of the data by placing an acknowledge pulse on CB1. The negative transition of this pulse causes CB2 to return HIGH and raises the CRB7 flag.
4. The **6800** system responds to a HIGH on CRB7 as an indication that the data has been accepted by the peripheral, and the next byte can be written to the PIA.
5. Before the next output byte can be written to the PIA, Data Register B must be *read* to reset CRB7.

EXAMPLE 8-10

The data between memory locations \$1000 and \$104F must be sent to a peripheral using the system of Fig. 8-6. Draw a flowchart to show how this is accomplished.

SOLUTION

The solution is shown in Fig. 8-7 and proceeds as follows:

TABLE 8-8 Control of CB2 as an Output; CRB5 Is High

CRB-5	CRB-4	CRB-3	CB2 Cleared	CB2 Set
1	0	0	Low on the positive transition of the first E pulse following an MPU Write "B" Data Register operation.	High when the interrupt flag bit CRB-7 is set by an active transition of the CB1 signal.
1	0	1	Low on the positive transition of the first E pulse after an MPU Write "B" Data Register operation.	High on the positive edge of the first "E" pulse following an "E" pulse which occurred while the part was deselected.
1	1	0	Low when CRB-3 goes low as a result of an MPU Write in Control Register "B".	Always low as long as CRB-3 is low. Will go high on an MPU Write in Control Register "B" that changes CRB-3 to "one".
1	1	1	Always high as long as CRB-3 is high. Will be cleared when an MPU Write Control Register "B" results in clearing CRB-3 to "zero".	High when CRB-3 goes high as a result of an MPU Write into Control Register "B".

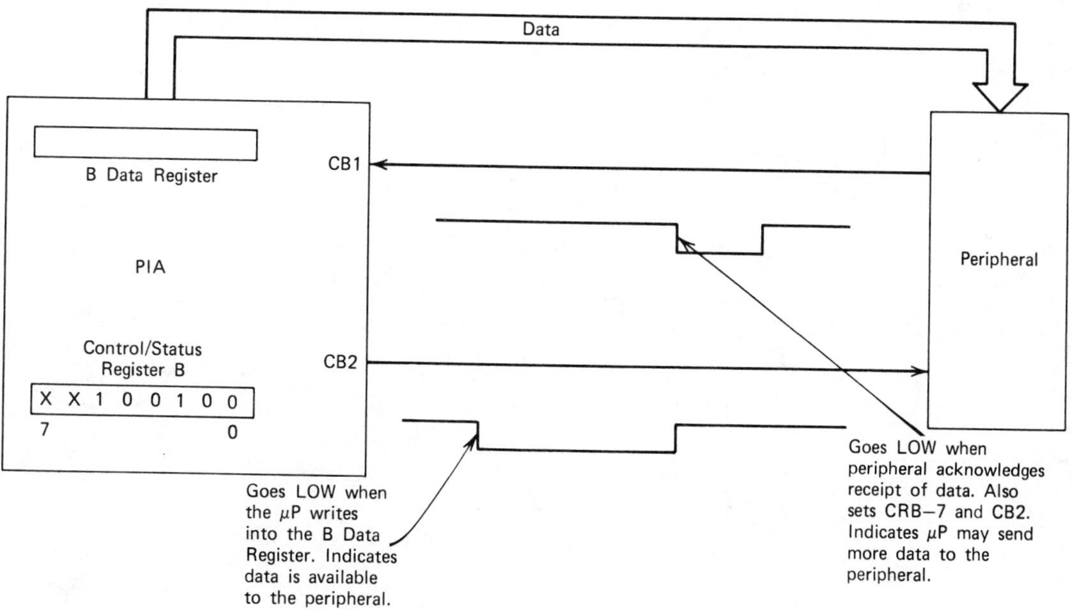

FIGURE 8-6 Handshaking with the B side of the PIA.

1. The Control/Status Register is set to 00 (or the PIA is RESET).
2. Direction Register B is initialized to FF (all bits to be outputs) and then the Control/Status Register is set to 24 (hex) to initialize the handshaking procedure described above.
3. The index register is set equal to $1000 and the first memory word to be transmitted is loaded from that location into the accumulator and stored in Data Register B. This causes CB2 to go LOW.
4. The program goes into a loop until the peripheral accepts the data and causes a negative transition (↓) on CB1. This SETS CRB7 and CB2. Before the transition, the result is positive (MSB = 0) and the program continues to loop. After the transition the result is negative and the program exits from the loop.
5. The program reads the B Data Register to reset CRB7. It then tests to

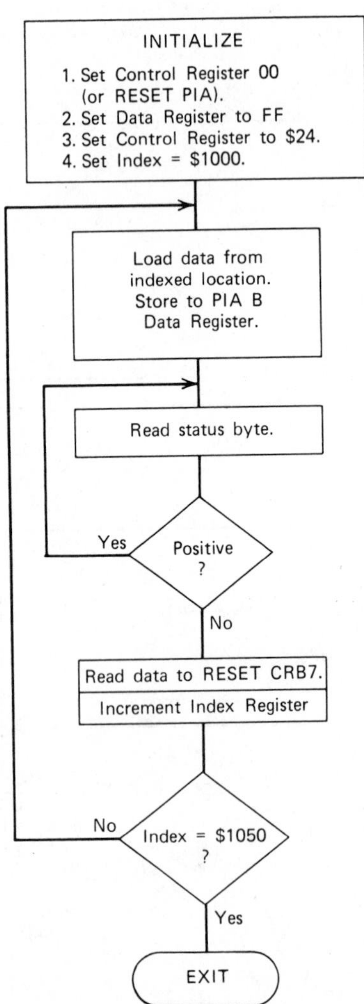

FIGURE 8-7 Flowchart for Example 8-10.

determine whether it has exhausted its data area by comparing the index register with $1050 after each time it has been incremented. If it has exhausted its data area, it stops; if it has not, it loads the next data word, causing CB2 to go LOW again, and repeats the above steps.

8-6.5 Use of CB2 in the Pulse Mode

If a peripheral device is connected to a PIA as shown in Fig. 8-8, and bits 5, 4, and 3 of the Control/Status Register are 101 as also shown, the CB2 line will be pulsed LOW whenever data is written into the "B" data register. This line can be used to inform the peripheral that new data is available on the PIA output lines. If the peripheral can accept the data without fail, in the few microseconds that it takes before the program can output the next byte there is no need for an acknowledgement. The pulse mode of the PIA is outstanding for its simplicity of programming. Every WRITE into the B Data Register causes CB2 to be pulsed. This mode is capable of very fast operation and is best used for high-speed peripherals such as a floppy disk system.

EXAMPLE 8-11

Show how the pulse mode can be used on the B side to output data to a high-speed device like a floppy disk system. Give an example of a program. Assume that the base address of the PIA is $8004 and the PIA has been initialized with a Control Word of $2C.

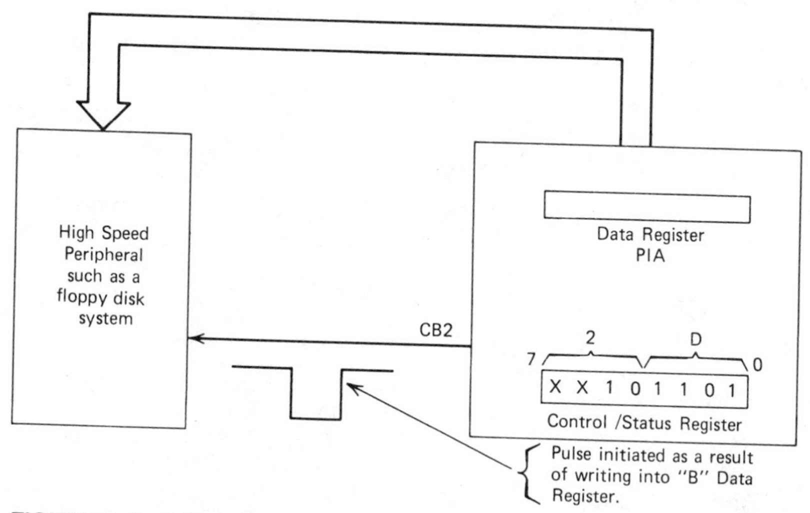

FIGURE 8-8 Pulse Mode of the PIA used with B side.

SOLUTION

Refer once more to Fig. 8-8 and to the program shown in Table 8-9. Again, this pulse mode assumes that data can be accepted as fast as it is put out by the program. The CB2 line can be used to strobe a data latch or to increment an address counter so that the data can be stored in the register of the peripheral, for example. The program shown in Table 8-9 is written to reside at $1000 and assumes that the data to be transmitted is in memory at $2000–$20FF (256 bytes).

The first instruction sets the **6800**'s Index Register (X) to the starting address of the data. The instruction at $1003 loads the A accumulator from the location specified by the Index Register. This byte is then stored to the PIA Data Register (or output), which informs the peripheral by pulsing the CB2 line. The program then increments the μP's Index Register to the address of the next byte. The compare Index (immediate) instruction is used to determine whether all of the data has been sent out. This is done by the instruction at location $1009 to see whether the Index Register has gone past the end address of the data and, if not, to loop back for the next byte.

8-6.6 ON–OFF Control of CB2

The last two lines of Table 8-8 specify a mode of operation in which the level of CB2 can be directly programmed. If CRB5 and CRB4 are both 1s, the CB2 line assumes the same level as CRB3. This allows the program to control the length of time CB2 is LOW or HIGH.

8-6.7 Control of CA2 as an Output (Handshaking Mode)

CA2 can be used as an output line to regulate the flow of data from the peripheral to the PIA in the same way that CB2 does (see Example 8-9), except that the CA2 line is taken LOW on the negative transition of E instead of the positive transition and after a READ of the A Data Register instead of a WRITE of B (see Table 8-10). Use of CA2 is therefore to be preferred when data input is involved.

EXAMPLE 8-12

A **6800** system must read several words from a disk. To do so, it must first send

TABLE 8-9 Program for Example 8-11

Addr	Data	Label	Mnemonics	Comments
1000	CE 2000		LDX #$2000	Get pointer to data.
1003	A6 00	LOOP	LDA A 0,X	Get data.
1005	B7 8006		STA A $8006	Store to B data register.
1008	08		INX	Increment pointer.
1009	8C 2100		CPX #$2100	End of data ?
100C	26 F5		BNE LOOP	No. Get next byte.
100E	. . . .		etc.	

TABLE 8-10 Control of CA2 as an Output; CRA5 is HIGH

CRA-5	CRA-4	CRA-3	CA2 Cleared	CA2 Set
1	0	0	Low on negative transition of E after an MPU Read "A" Data operation.	High when the interrupt flag bit CRA-7 is set by an active transition of the CA1 signal.
1	0	1	Low on negative transition of E after an MPU Read "A" Data operation.	High on the negative edge of the first "E" pulse which occurs during a deselect.
1	1	0	Low when CRA-3 goes low as a result of an MPU Write to Control Register "A".	Always low as long as CRA-3 is low. Will go high on an MPU Write to Control Register "A" that changes CRA-3 to "one".
1	1	1	Always high as long as CRA-3 is high. Will be cleared on an MPU Write to Control Register "A" that clears CRA-3 to a "zero".	High when CRA-3 goes high as a result of an MPU Write to Control Register "A".

the disk controller several bytes of information that tell it, for example, the disk address and the number of words to be read. Describe how the transfer can be accomplished.

SOLUTION

1. The Direction Register (B side) is set up for output (FF), and the A side Direction Register is set up for input (00).
2. The **6800** sends commands to the disk controller via data lines PB0 through PB7, using the handshaking procedure discussed in Section 8-6.4. CB2 controls the flow of commands as shown in Fig. 8-6.
3. When the first word is ready, the controller causes a transition on CA1, which SETS CRA7 and CA2 (see Fig. 8-9).
4. The **6800** system now reads the first word from the PIA and places it in memory. This RESETS CA2, which requests new data from the disk. The read also RESETS CRA7.
5. This procedure continues until the required number of bytes have been transferred from the disk to the μC's memory.

8-6.8 Pulse Mode for CA2

If CRA5, 4, and 3 are 101, respectively, the A side of the PIA operates in a Pulse Mode identical to that described for the B side, but it is triggered by a READ instead of a WRITE data operation.

8-6.9 ON–OFF Mode for CA2

When CRA5 and CRA6 are both 1s, the state of CA2 will be the same as that of bit CRA3, and therefore CA2 can be set HIGH or LOW as desired. This gives the program total control of CA2.

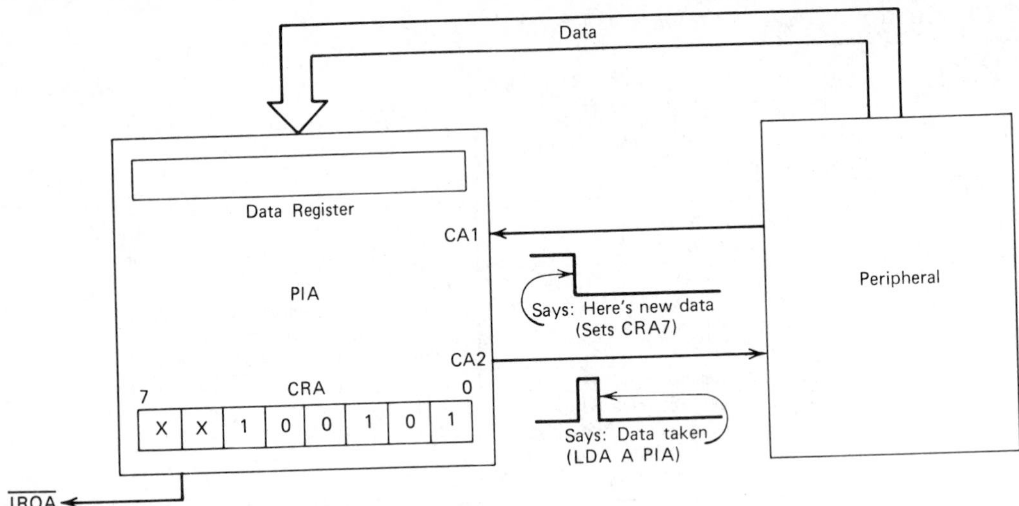

FIGURE 8-9 Handshaking with a peripheral on the A side.

EXAMPLE 8-13

A PIA is to be used to interface a High-Speed Paper Tape Reader to a **6800** system. The reader has eight TTL output lines (one for each bit) and a sprocket hole output for a *ready* signal. The tape is advanced a character at a time by a stepper motor that requires a negative-going pulse. What are the Control Words for the ON/OFF mode of the PIA? Give an example of a program. Assume a base address for the PIA of $8004.

SOLUTION

As shown in Fig. 8-10, the eight data lines from the reader's photocell outputs are connected to PA0–PA7 of the PIA, and the sprocket hole output is connected to CA1. CA2 is connected to the stepper motor pulse circuit in such a way that a negative-going pulse will step the tape. Reference to Table 8-10 shows that the Control Word should be $3C initially and is changed to a $34 in order to strobe the stepper motor. The program in the form of a subroutine to control this circuit is shown in Table 8-11.

The first instruction is a dummy READ operation to clear CRA7. The A accumulator is loaded with the value in the next (Immediate) byte ($34) and it is output to the PIA Control Register. This causes CA2 to go LOW, thus starting the strobe pulse. The next two instructions repeat this action, except the Control Word is $3C and bit CRA3 is now brought HIGH, which causes CA2 to return HIGH, terminating the strobe pulse to the stepper motor. The mechanical design is such that one pulse moves the tape one frame (to the next character). The next step is to watch for the spocket hole signal to SET the interrupt flag status bit CRA7. This is determined by testing the word loaded into A to see if it is positive (bit 7 is a 0). If it is positive, the program is branched back to input the word again and test it. This loop is repeated until the status goes negative.

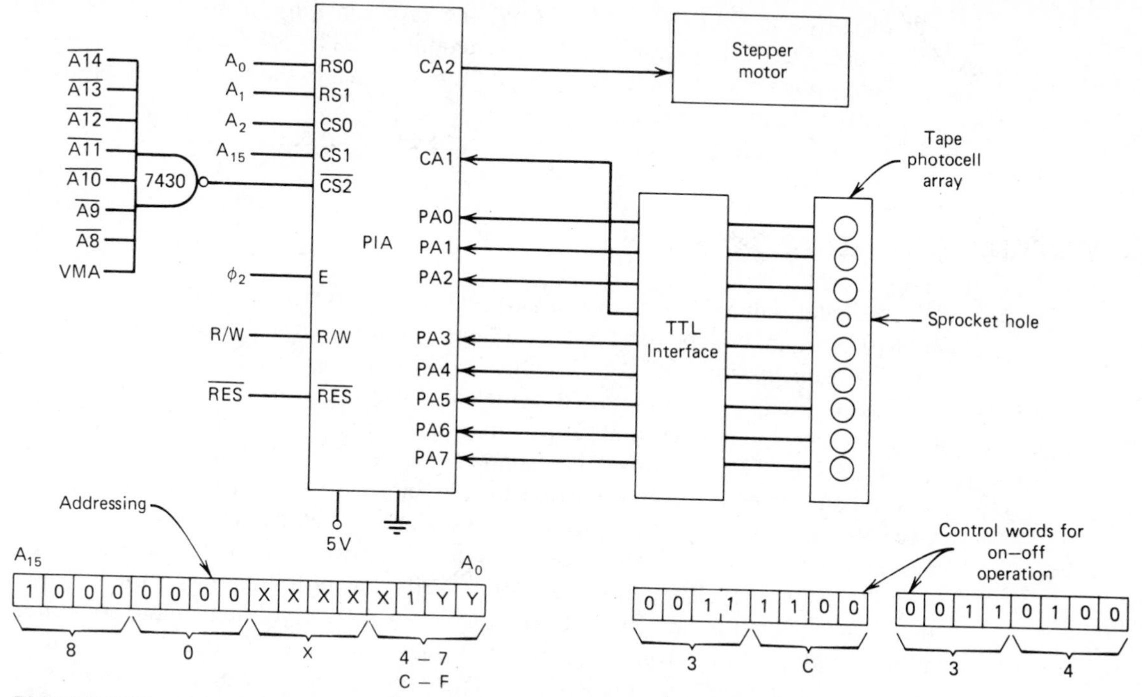

FIGURE 8-10 PIA circuit for a High-Speed Tape Reader (for Example 8-13).

Since this program is controlling a mechanical tape reader that reads about 100 characters per second, it takes 10 ms to move the tape to the next character. The μP will loop back about 1250 times before the tape *arrives* at the new position as sensed by the sprocket hole photocell. In a real system it would be advisable to include a time-out loop at this point to generate an error message if the tape does not advance in a reasonable time. Once the tape has reached the sprocket hole, as

TABLE 8-11 Program for Example 8-13

Addr	Data	Mnemonic	Comments
1000	B6 8004	LDA A #$8004	Read A Data Reg to
*			clear interrupt (CRA7)
1003	86 34	LDA A #$34	Load A with 34
1005	B7 8005	STA A $8005	Store Control Word to
*			turn on pulse
1008	86 3C	LDA A #$3C	Load A with 3C
100A	B7 8005	STA A $8005	Store Control Word to
*			end pulse
100D	B6 8005	LDA A $8005	Load A with Status Reg
*			contents
1010	2A FB	BPL *-5	If plus, branch back 5
*			bytes to 100D
1012	B6 8004	LDA A $8004	Load A from Data Reg
1015	39	RTS	Return to the main prog

indicated by the CA1 line going LOW, the program *falls through* the decision point and LOADS the data into the A accumulator. The RTS instruction causes the main program to be resumed, and it stores or prints the data (in A) before it returns for the next character.

8-7 SERIAL DATA TRANSMISSION

When digital data is being transmitted or transferred between components in a **6800** μC system, it is moved 1 byte at a time by means of the 8-bit data bus. This is *parallel transmission,* and it is synchronized by the system clock. When signals are sent to equipment not located in the same cabinet or over cables longer than about 10 feet, the long ground return circuit creates problems of noise or interfering signals in TTL circuits (see Chapter 13). Extraneous current pulses and alternating current (AC) are carried by the same ground wires and can induce unwanted pulses or glitches into the digital signals. To alleviate these problems, parallel digital signals are often converted to *serial* form on a single line, translated to RS232 signal levels (see Section 8-9.2), and transmitted *1 bit at a time*. When the distance is more than 50 or 100 feet, as in a system involving a main computer and several satellite terminals, this serial digital signal is frequently changed to audio tones by means of a **modem** (modulator–demodulator) and transmitted over telephone circuits. Most modems provide for duplex operation (one serial path in each direction) over one telephone circuit. Obviously, serial transmission with only one pair of wires is simpler and cheaper than parallel transmission with eight or more lines and with the RS232 or modem interface is less likely to cause errors since the grounding problems are eliminated. The operation of a full duplex data transmission system that transmits serial data in both directions simultaneously is shown in Fig. 8-11.

In the transmit part of the modem, the digital information modulates an audio tone that is then transmitted to the distant device (usually over telephone circuits). The receive part of the remote modem demodulates the audio signals and sends them on to the remote equipment as digital data.

8-7.1 Asynchronous Transmission

Most serial systems use **asynchronous** (unclocked) data transmission. The characters are sent in a standard format or code so that equipment made by different

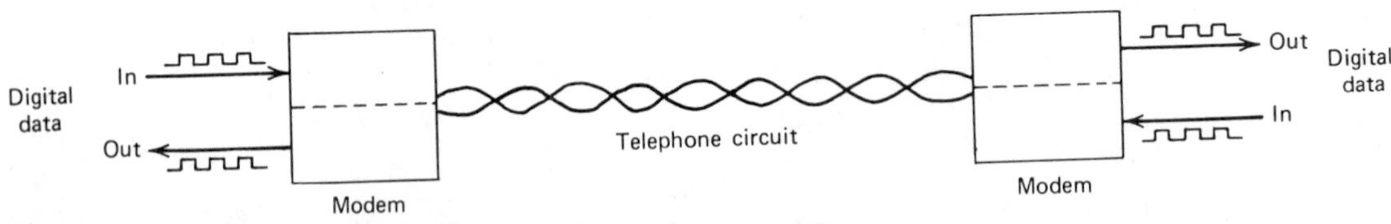

FIGURE 8-11 A full duplex data transmission system.

manufacturers can be used together in a system. The most common code for asynchronous data transmission is the American Standard Code for Information Interchange (ASCII). As used originally in the Model 33 and Model 35 teletypewriters (TTYs), it is an 11-bit START–STOP code. This code has been adopted by the computer industry and is used in almost all data terminals and μCs that use terminals. The basic pattern for this standard is shown in Fig. 8-12. When the line is quiescent (transmitting no data), it is constantly in the MARK or 1 state. The start of a character is signaled by the **START bit**, which drives the line to the 0 or SPACE state for 1-bit time. The 7 bits immediately following the START bit are the data bits of the character. The bits are sent with the Least Significant Bit (LSB) first. The ASCII code (see Appendix E) uses 7 bits to generate 128 unique

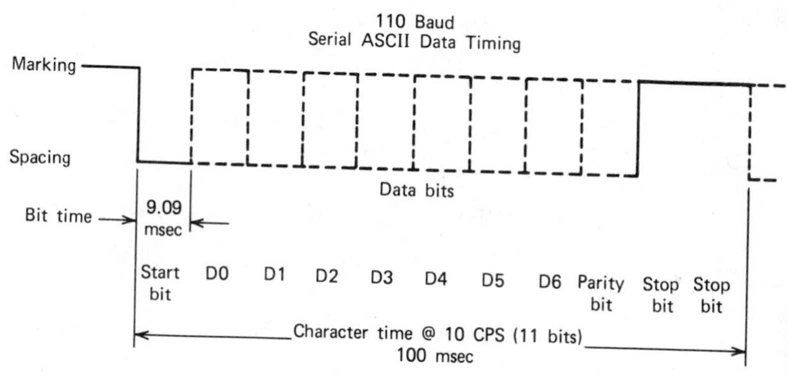

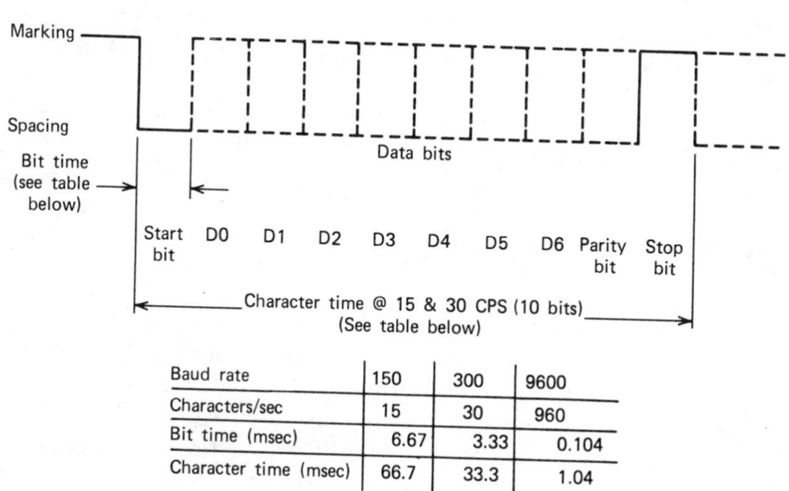

Baud rate	150	300	9600
Characters/sec	15	30	960
Bit time (msec)	6.67	3.33	0.104
Character time (msec)	66.7	33.3	1.04

$$\text{Bit time} = \frac{\text{sec}}{\text{Baud rate}}$$

FIGURE 8-12 ASCII character bit timing.

codes. These include upper- and lowercase letters A to Z, numbers 0 to 9, plus many punctuation and mathematical symbols. Many nonprintable control characters are also provided. The character consists of 7 data bits and a parity bit. The state of the parity bit depends on whether even, odd, or no parity is desired.

Frequently, *even* parity is used in the incoming direction because most TTY keyboards originally were connected to generate *even*-parity characters (the number of 1s in each character is even). The TTY does not check parity on data to be printed, but many high-speed data terminals do.

After the last data and parity bit, the transmission line must go HIGH for either 1- or 2-bit times. These are the **STOP bits**. TTYs use 2 STOP bits, but terminals operating above 150 baud use only one. If no further data is to be transmitted, the line simply stays HIGH (marking) until the next START bit occurs. This data pattern thus uses 10 or 11 bits as follows:

a. One START bit (always a space or 0).
b. Eight data bits (including parity).
c. One or two STOP bits (always a mark or 1).

EXAMPLE 8-14

a. What is the bit pattern of the character shown in Fig.8-13?
b. Is the parity odd or even?

SOLUTION

a. As shown in Fig. 8-13, the waveform bits are 00001001011. The first 0 is the START bit and the next eight are the character (including the parity bit). Since the LSBs are transmitted first, they must be reversed to correspond to the convention used in most μP literature and in this book. Therefore the character is 01001000 (48 hex, or ASCII "H"). The two 1s following the last data bit are STOP bits. Any additional 1s following the STOP bit merely indicate that the line is idle.
b. Since the character contains an even number of 1s, the parity bit is zero and therefore this is an even-parity character.

8-8 THE ACIA

In the **6800** system, serial data transmission is implemented by the **6850** Asynchronous Communications Interface Adapter (ACIA). The ACIA is designed to accept parallel data from the μC system data bus, 1 byte at a time, and to send the bits serially to an asynchronous serial data device such as a TTY, CRT terminal, line printer, or modem. At the same time, other circuits in the ACIA can accept serial data characters from a keyboard, a modem, or a tape reader and place them on the μC bus as parallel bytes. Figure 8-14 shows the block diagram of the ACIA.

The left side of the diagram shows the lines that connect to the data, address,

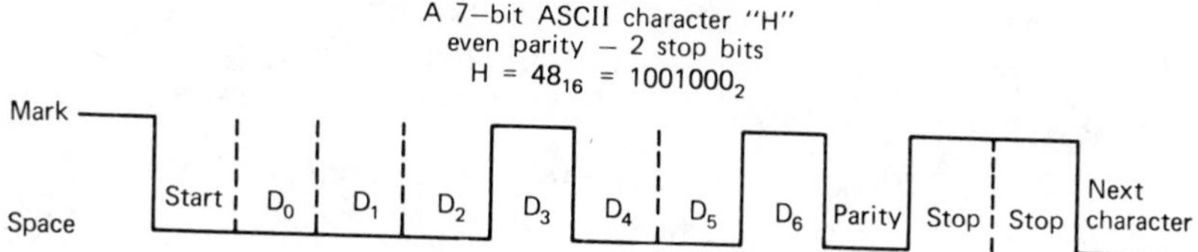

FIGURE 8-13 Character pattern for Example 8-14.

and control bus lines of the μP. The right side shows the lines used for the serial interface with external hardware.

The ACIA appends start, stop, and parity bits to the 7 or 8 data bits used for each character. The data could be a standard 7-bit ASCII character of any other 7- or 8-bit code such as EBCDIC, or even binary. The resulting character is either 10 or 11 bits long, depending on whether the character has 1 or 2 stop bits. Since the

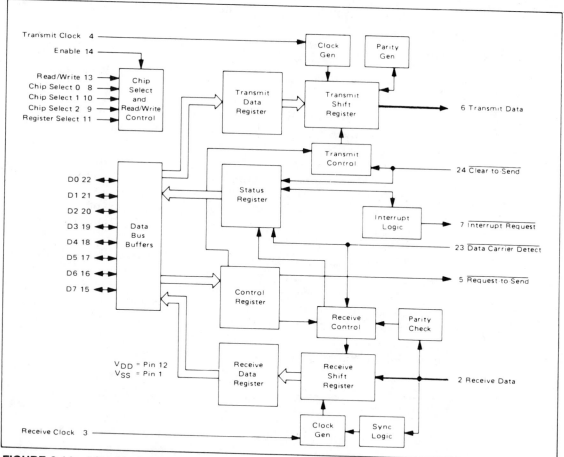

FIGURE 8-14 ACIA block diagram.

characters can be sent asynchronously, the time between each character can be from zero up. The ACIA is programmed during initialization via the μP data bus for the desired data configuration. It thus provides the following functions:

1. Parallel-to-serial and serial-to-parallel conversions of data (simultaneously).
2. Asynchronous transmission by means of start and stop bits.
3. Error control by means of parity, framing, or overrun error detection.

8-8.1 Parallel-to-Serial and Serial-to-Parallel Conversion

The ACIA block diagram shown in Fig. 8-14 includes TRANSMIT and RECEIVE shift registers. The transmit shift register is loaded in parallel from the data bus and then shifted right to send the bits out serially on one line. The receive shift register accepts serial data as input and sends it to the data bus in 8-bit bytes. The wide arrows in Fig. 8-14 indicate the parallel side of the device (eight lines). The externally generated receive and transmit bit rate clocks are used to shift these registers at the appropriate standard serial data rate (e.g., 110, 300, 2400, etc. bits per second). Note that these serial clock inputs are completely independent and can be used simultaneously at different rates if desired.

8-8.2 ACIA Registers

Figure 8-15 is a programming model of the ACIA. It shows the μP bus connections and the internal registers. Here is a list of the registers:

1. **Transmit Data Register (TDR).** The byte to be transmitted is written in parallel to the TDR by the μP. It is transferred to the Transmit Shift Register, if it is empty. The byte is then shifted out serially. While one byte is being shifted out, a second byte can be loaded into the TDR. It is automatically loaded into the Transmit Shift Register when transmission of the first byte is completed.
2. **Receive Data Register (RDR).** Information from external devices enters the ACIA serially via the Receive Shift Register, which strips off the start and stop bits and sends the byte in a parallel transfer to the RDR. The μP must read the RDR while the second byte is being received. If it is not read in time, the ACIA loses data and causes the Receiver Overrun bit in the Status Register to be set (Section 8-8.6).
3. **Control Register.** This register controls the format of both the transmitted and received data. It is discussed in detail in Section 8-8.4.
4. **Status Register.** The Status of the progress of data transmission and reception is available in this register and is used by programs to control the ACIA. It is discussed in detail in Section 8-8.6

EXAMPLE 8-15

A standard 110 bits per second TTY is sending 11-bit characters continuously to the ACIA. How much time does the μP have to read each character?

SOLUTION
Since each character consists of 11 bits, the data rate is 10 characters per second. This allows the μP 0.1 s to read each character before the next character is assembled in the Receive Data Register.

8-8.3 ACIA Signal Lines

The lines connected to the ACIA are shown in Fig. 8-15. The IC pin number for each line is also shown. The lines and their functions are as follows.

1. Eight bidirectional data lines. These are connected to the **6800** data bus.
2. Three Chip Select lines (CS0, CS1, and $\overline{CS2}$). Like the PIA, the ACIA occupies specific locations in the address map. The Chip Select lines and the Register Select (RS) line are connected to the address bus to select the ACIA and its registers. (See Sections 7-13 and 7-14.)
3. Read/Write (R/$\overline{W}$) and Register Select (RS). The combination of these two inputs selects one of the four major registers. The Transmit Data Register and Control Register are write only; the μP cannot read them. If R/$\overline{W}$) is HIGH

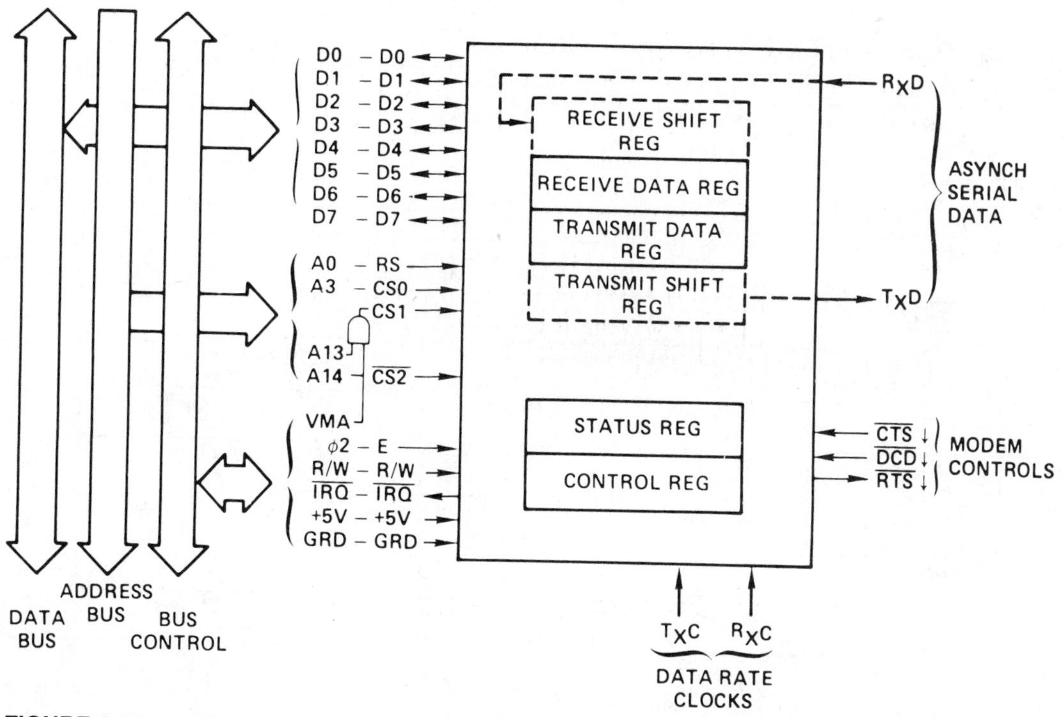

FIGURE 8-15 ACIA Bus Interface and Register Configuration.

(for read) the Receive Data or Status Register is *read* (depending on whether the Register Select (RS) pin is high or low, respectively). If R/$\overline{W}$ is low, a word is *written* to either the Transmit Data Register or the Control Register, depending on whether RS is high or low, respectively.

8-8.4 ACIA Control Register

Table 8-12 shows the contents of the ACIA registers. The Boolean statements at the top of the table are the signals required to address each register. The Control Register, for example, has the equation $\overline{RS} * \overline{R/W}$. This means the Control Register is addressed only if both the RS and R/$\overline{W}$ inputs to the ACIA are 0.

The functions of the Control Register are complex. They are explained in the following paragraphs.

The function of counter divide bits (CR0 and CR1) is shown in Table 8-13 and allows three choices; it divides the incoming clock by either 1, 16, or 64.

The divide-by-1 mode can be used only if the Receive Clock is synchronized with the data being received and a bit is available at every positive transition of the Receive Clock. Most systems using an ACIA are asynchronous, however, and the arrival of the byte is signaled by a START bit that can occur at any time. For these cases, the divide-by-16 or divide-by-64 option must be used.

TABLE 8-12 Definition of ACIA Register Contents

Data Bus Line Number	Buffer Address: RS • $\overline{R/W}$ Transmit Data Register (Write Only)	RS • R/W Receive Data Register (Read Only)	$\overline{RS}$ • $\overline{R/W}$ Control Register (Write Only)	$\overline{RS}$ • R/W Status Register (Read Only)
0	Data Bit 0*	Data Bit 0*	Counter Divide Select 1 (CR0)	Receive Data Register Full (RDRF)
1	Data Bit 1	Data Bit 1	Counter Divide Select 2 (CR1)	Transmit Data Register Empty (TDRE)
2	Data Bit 2	Data Bit 2	Word Select 1 (CR2)	$\overline{\text{Data Carrier Detect}}$ ($\overline{DCD}$)
3	Data Bit 3	Data Bit 3	Word Select 2 (CR3)	$\overline{\text{Clear-to-Send}}$ ($\overline{CTS}$)
4	Data Bit 4	Data Bit 4	Word Select 3 (CR4)	Framing Error (FE)
5	Data Bit 5	Data Bit 5	Transmit Control 1 (CR5)	Receiver Overrun (OVRN)
6	Data Bit 6	Data Bit 6	Transmit Control 2 (CR6)	Parity Error (PE)
7	Data Bit 7***	Data Bit 7**	Receive Interrupt Enable (CR7)	Interrupt Request (IRQ)

* Leading bit = LSB = Bit 0
** Data bit will be zero in 7-bit plus parity modes.
*** Data bit is "don't care" in 7-bit plus parity modes.

TABLE 8-13 Counter Divide Select Bits

CR1	CR0	Function
0	0	÷ 1
0	1	÷ 16
1	0	÷ 64
1	1	Master Reset

EXAMPLE 8-16

An ACIA operates using the divide-by-16 mode.

a. If the bit frequency is 100 bps, what receive clock frequency is required?
b. At what point after the START bit begins should the data be sampled?

SOLUTION

a. Since the clock is divided by 16 the receive clock frequency must be 1600 bps to accept data at a rate of 100 bps.
b. The START bit can be thought of as occupying counts 1 to 16, the first data bit counts 17 to 32, etc. For maximum accuracy, each bit should be sampled, or clocked into the Receive Shift Register in the middle of its time slot or at counts 8, 24, 40, etc. This is automatically accomplished by the internal logic of the ACIA (see Fig. 8-16).

Bit synchronization in the divide-by-16 and divide-by-64 modes is initiated by the leading mark-to-space transition of the start bit. The start bit on the receiver data input sampled during the positive transitions of the external clock is shown in Fig. 8-16b. If the input remains at a LOW level for a total of eight separate samplings in the divide-by-16 mode or 32 samplings in the divide-by-64 mode, which is equivalent to 50% of a bit time, the bit is assumed to be a valid start bit. This start bit is shifted into the ACIA circuitry on the negative edge of the internal clock. Once a valid start bit has been detected, the remaining bits are shifted into the Shift Register at their approximate midpoints.

If the receiver input returns to a mark state during the start bit sampling period, this false start bit is ignored and the receiver resumes looking for the mark-to-space transition or a valid start bit; this technique is called *false bit detection.*

Divide-by-1 mode selection will not provide internal bit synchronization within the receiver. Therefore, the external receive clock must be synchronized to the data under the following considerations. The sampling of the start bit occurs on the positive edge of the external clock, and the start bit is shifted into the shift register on the negative edge of the external clock, as shown in Fig. 8-16a. For higher reliability of sampling the positive transition of the external clock (sampling point) should occur at the approximate midpoint of the bit interval. There is no

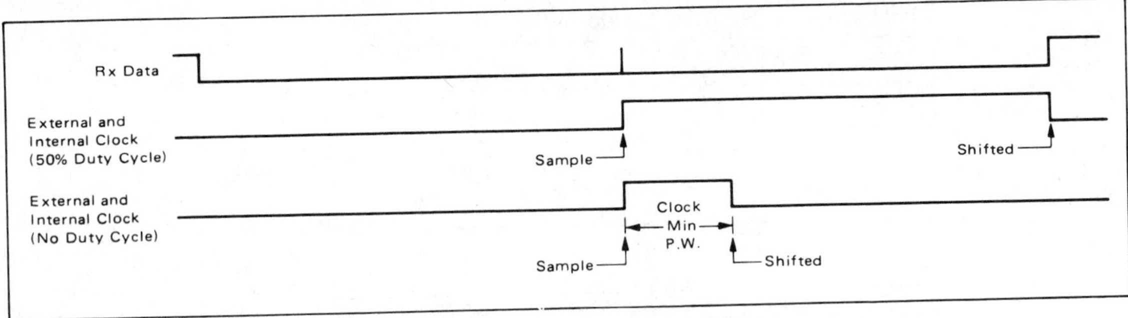

(*a*) Divide – by – 1

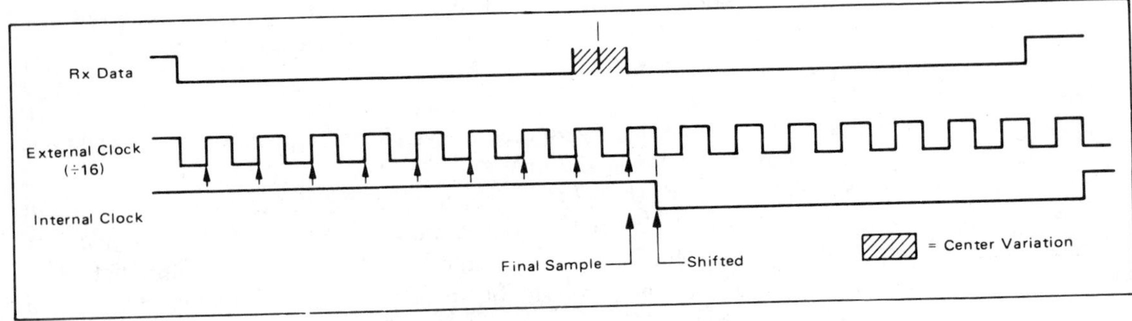

(*b*) Divide – by 16

FIGURE 8-16 Relation of the data and sampling clock in an ACIA.

requirement on the duty cycle of the external receive clock except that the clock must meet the minimum pulse width requirement, as noted on the ACIA data sheet.

Bits CR2, CR3, and CR4 of the Control Word are written to the ACIA during initialization and determine the configuration of the words being transmitted and received. The user can choose the number of data bits transmitted in each character (7 or 8), the parity (odd, even, or no parity), and the number of stop bits (1 or 2). The options are given in Table 8-14. Note that when transmitting with parity, the user need not be concerned with the parity of the data sent to the ACIA. It calculates the correct parity and inserts the proper bit.

Bits CR5 and CR6 provide Transmit Interrupt Control as well as control of RTS, as shown in Table 8-15. (RTS is the Request-To-Send signal used with modems.) If CR6 and CR5 are 0 and 1, respectively, the ACIA interrupts the μP (if IRQ is connected to the μP) whenever the Transmit Data buffer is empty. This maximizes the data transmission rate since it causes the system to send the ACIA an output character as soon as it can accept one. If CR5 and CR6 are both 1s, the ACIA transmits a constant 0 level, called a *break*. A break is used as a control signal in some communications systems. Bit CR7 is the Receive Side Interrupt

TABLE 8-14 Word Select Bits

CR4	CR3	CR2	Function
0	0	0	7 Bits + Even Parity + 2 Stop Bits
0	0	1	7 Bits + Odd Parity + 2 Stop Bits
0	1	0	7 Bits + Even Parity + 1 Stop Bit
0	1	1	7 Bits + Odd Parity + 1 Stop Bit
1	0	0	8 Bits + 2 Stop Bits
1	0	1	8 Bits + 1 Stop Bit
1	1	0	8 Bits + Even Parity + 1 Stop Bit
1	1	1	8 Bits + Odd Parity + 1 Stop Bit

Enable. If CR7 is a 1, the ACIA interrupts whenever the Receive Data Register is full or the Overrun or Data Carrier Detect (DCD) conditions occur.

EXAMPLE 8-17

What are the characteristics of a transmission system if the Control Register contains C2?

SOLUTION

CR7 is a 1, so Receive Interrupts are enabled, but Transmit Interrupts are disabled because CR6 and CR5 are 1 and 0, respectively. Bits CR4, 3, and 2 are all 0s, so the data word consists of 7 bits + even parity + 2 stop bits. Finally, because CR1 is 1 and CR0 is 0, the frequency of the input clock must be 64 times the bit rate of the data.

8-8.5 ACIA Power-ON Reset

The ACIA does not have a RESET pin but it contains an internal power-ON reset circuit to detect the 5-V turn-on transition and to hold the ACIA in a RESET state until initialization by the μP is complete. This prevents any erroneous output transitions from occurring. In addition to initializing the transmitter and receiver sections, the power-ON reset circuit holds the CR5 and CR6 bits of the Control

TABLE 8-15 Transmitter Control Bits

CR6	CR5	Function
0	0	$\overline{RTS}$ = low, Transmitting Interrupt Disabled.
0	1	$\overline{RTS}$ = low, Transmitting Interrupt Enabled.
1	0	$\overline{RTS}$ = high, Transmitting Interrupt Disabled.
1	1	$\overline{RTS}$ = low, Transmits a Break level on the Transmit Data Output. Transmitting Interrupt Disabled.

Register at a logic 0 and logic 1, respectively, so that the RTS output is held HIGH and any interrupt from the transmitter is disabled. The power-ON reset logic is sensitive to the shape of the V_{DD} power supply turn-on transition. To ensure correct operation of the reset function, the power turn-on must have a positive slope throughout its transition. The conditions of the Status Register and other outputs during power-ON reset or software master reset are shown in Table 8-16.

The internal ACIA power-ON reset logic must be released prior to the transmission of data by performing a *software Master Reset,* followed by a second control word. During Master Reset, Control Register bits CR0 and CR1 are set to 1s, which releases the latch condition of bits CR5 and CR6, allowing them to be programmed in the following control word. In recent production the processes have produced faster parts and this release may occur during master reset. To guard against the possibility of RTS going LOW, it is advisable to use a master reset word of 43 (hex). This retains the preset conditions of CR5 and CR6. The final condition can then be determined in the second control word without any false or momentary shifts in the RTS level. This also applies to Receiver Interrupt Enable (RIE), which is controlled by bit CR7. The $43 will ensure that the interrupt is inhibited until its state is specified in the second control word.

After Master Reset of the ACIA, the programmable Control Register must be set to select desired options such as the clock divider ratios, word length, 1 or 2 stop bits, and parity (even, odd, or none). Bits CR5 and CR6 of the Control Register are no longer inhibited and can now be programmed for the options defined in Table 8-15.

8-8.6 The ACIA Status Register

The status of the ACIA and what has happened to the data being handled are determined by examining the Status Register at the proper time in the program.

The function of each bit is given in Table 8-12.

TABLE 8-16 ACIA Initialization Sequence

ACIA Initialization Sequence

	POWER-ON RESET	MASTER RESET (Release Power-On Reset)	MASTER RESET (General)
	b7 b6 b5 b4 b3 b2 b1 b0	b7 b6 b5 b4 b3 b2 b1 b0	b7 b6 b5 b4 b3 b2 b1 b0
Status Register	0 0 0 0 X X 0 0	0 0 0 0 X X 0 0	0 0 0 0 X X 0 0
$\overline{\text{IRQ}}$ Output	1	1	1
$\overline{\text{RTS}}$ Output	1	1	X
Transmit Break Capability	Inhibit	Inhibit	Optional
Internal: RIE	0	X	X
TIE	0	0	X

Held by Power-On Reset (RTS Output, Transmit Break Capability, TIE in Master Reset (Release Power-On Reset) column)

Defined by Control Register (RTS Output, Transmit Break Capability, RIE, TIE in Master Reset (General) column)

(X-Independent of Reset function)

Bit 0. Receive Data Register Full (RDRF) This bit is set when a character has been received by the ACIA and should be read by the μP.

Bit 1. Transmit Data Register Empty (TDRE) This bit indicates that a character to be transmitted can be sent to the ACIA.

Bits 2 and 3. Data-Carrier-Detected (DCD) and Clear-to-Send (CTS) These bits will be HIGH only if the pins on the chip are not held LOW by the external circuitry (normally the RS232C interface). This could be the case if a modem is connected to the port and not ready for transmission or operating improperly, or if the signals are not properly jumpered when a terminal rather than a modem is being used.

Bit 4. Framing Error (FE) A framing error indicates loss of character synchronization, faulty transmission, or a break condition. If one of these conditions is present, the internal receiver transfer signal will cause the FE bit to go HIGH. The next internal transfer signal will cause the FE status bit to be updated for the error status of the next character. A HIGH on the $\overline{\text{DCD}}$ input or a Master Reset will disable and reset the FE status bit.

Bit 5. Overrun Error (OVRN) A HIGH state on the OVRN status bit indicates that a character was received but not read from the Receive Data Register, resulting in the loss of one or more characters. The OVRN status bit is set when the last character prior to the overrun condition has been read. The read data command forces the RDRF and OVRN status bits to go HIGH if an overrun condition exists. The next read data command causes the RDRF and OVRN status bits to return to a LOW level. During an overrun condition, the last character in the Receive Data Register that was not read subsequent to the overrun condition is retained since the internal transfer signal is disabled. A HIGH state on the $\overline{\text{DCD}}$ input or a Master Reset disables and resets the OVRN status bit.

Bit 6. Parity Error (PE) If the parity check function is enabled, the internal transfer signal causes the PE status bit to go HIGH if a parity error condition exists. The parity error status bit is updated by the next internal transfer signal. A HIGH state on the $\overline{\text{DCD}}$ input or a Master Reset disables and resets the PE status bit.

Bit 7. Interrupt Request (IRQ) A HIGH level on the IRQ status bit may be generated from three sources:

a. Transmitter—if the Transmit Data Register is Empty (TDRE = 1), and TIE is SET (bit CR6 = 0 and CR5 = 1).
b. Receiver—if the Receive Data Register is Full (RDRF = 1), and RIE (CR7) is SET.
c. Data Carrier Loss—a loss of carrier (a HIGH level) on the $\overline{\text{DCD}}$ input generates an interrupt, as indicated by the IRQ bit, if the RIE bit (CR7) is SET.

EXAMPLE 8-18

The Status Register of an ACIA reads A3. What is the status of the ACIA?

SOLUTION
The data indicates that bits 0, 1, 5, and 7 are SET. Table 8-12 shows that

a. The Receive Data Register is full.
b. The Transmit Data Register is empty.
c. A Receive Overrun Error has occurred.
d. An Interrupt Request is pending. (Interrupts are explained in Chapter 9.)

The Receive Data Register has overrun, indicating that the μP did not fetch the last character during the time available, there is another character in the Receive Data Register waiting to be read, and the ACIA is trying to interrupt. The Transmit Data Register is available to accept any data for transmission. Essentially these conditions mean that the μP is not paying attention to the ACIA. They probably indicate that a timing problem (either hardware or software) has caused the system to malfunction.

8-9 HARDWARE INTERFACES TO THE ACIA

The ACIA serial inputs and outputs are TTL-level signals. Two standard interfaces have evolved, and each requires additional hardware to make the signals compatible with the external device. Both interfaces are often included in general-purpose computers.

8-9.1 The TTY Interface

A standard teletypewriter has several interface options. The most popular is the 20-mA current loop. This is characterized by a steady 20 mA of Direct Current flowing in the keyboard and printer circuits when no data is being transmitted. This is called the *mark* signal and coincides with the logic 1 TTL level of the ACIA. The current flow is interrupted (called a *space* signal) when a logic 0 TTL level is sent, such as the START bit. Many higher-speed data terminals including some CRTs use a 20-mA option. Figure 8-17 shows the TTY interface and the way 20-mA current loops can be generated using an optical coupler.

Optical couplers are suggested for electrical signal isolation because the contacts in the TTY frequently produce serious noise spikes, and if the wire or cable to the terminal is very long, it can be exposed to interference from AC power lines, other TTYs, or radio signals. When such an isolation circuit is built, it is important to keep the wires associated with the digital side separated or shielded from those carrying the 20-mA currents to avoid electrostatic coupling of the noise spikes, which can defeat the purpose of the optical coupling. Common ground returns are to be avoided also since extraneous current flow can produce noise

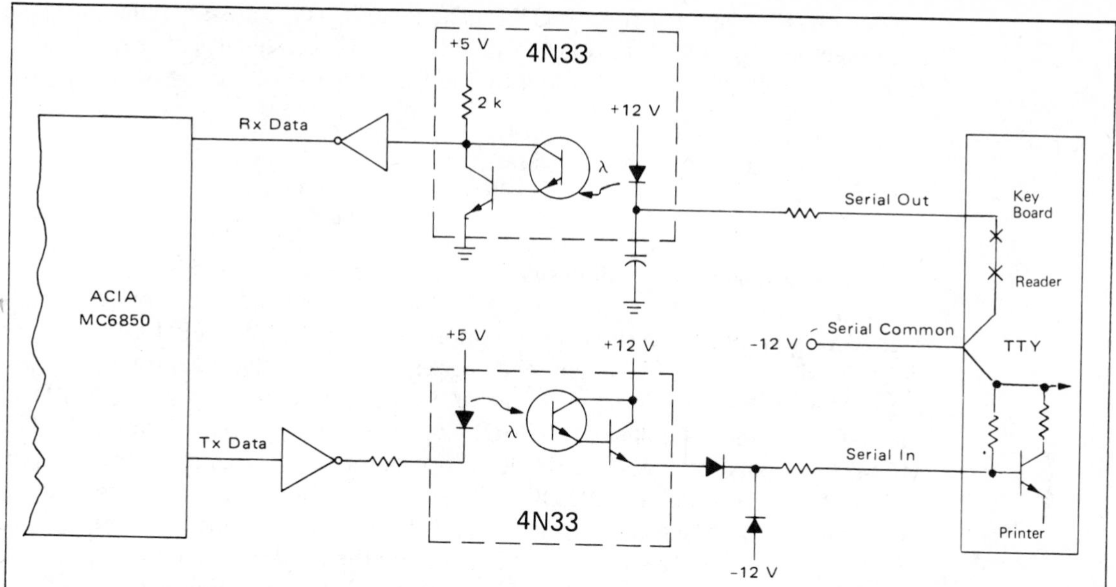

FIGURE 8-17 Teletypewriter 20 mA Interface Circuit.

voltage differences that are effectively in series with the digital signals (see Section 13-4.1).

The path of the signal transmitted from the ACIA to the TTY is shown in the lower half of Fig. 8-17. The transmitted data output of the ACIA is coupled to a Light-Emitting Diode (LED) within the optical isolator via a TTL inverter. In the *mark* state the diode is lit and turns on the photosensitive Darlington pair of transistors. This drives 20 mA into the printer. When a character is being shifted out of the ACIA, the 0s of the character turn off the LED, interrupting the current path. These 1s and 0s are mechanically latched in the TTY, and when all bits are received the TTY printer types the character.

Note the use of the plus and minus 12 V in the TTY circuits. These voltages are desirable because they put a total of 24 V across the TTY keyboard or reader contacts. These contacts are designed to work with up to 130 V and will not work reliably with very low voltages (such as 0.7 or even 5 V), since insulating oxides or even particles of dirt will form on the contacts in time. The higher voltages will break through the oxides and provide reliable performance.

When a key is depressed on the keyboard, the TTY transmits its code to the ACIA, as shown in the upper half of Fig. 8-17. Here the bits of each character selected by the keys cause the receive LED to be turned ON and OFF as they are sent. The phototransistor detects the light changes and transmits the bits to the data input via a TTL inverter.

8-9.2 RS232C Interface

For data transmission to remote terminals, modems and telephone lines are used. The ACIA is connected to modems in accordance with Electronic Industry

Associates (EIA) specification RS232C. The RS232C is the most popular interface to connect to a local TTY or other terminal. All RS232C signals at the terminal or modem connector can be described by the following notation:

Data binary state	1	0
Signal condition	Mark	Space
Function	OFF	ON
Voltage	−3 to −15	+3 to +15

The transmit and receive data signals must be between +3 and +15 V for a 0 or *space condition*, or between −3 and −15 V for a 1 or *mark*. The control signals seem reversed, but since the *true* condition for these TTL lines is LOW or 0, for these steady-state control signals, they agree. Consequently, level translators are required between the TTL levels of the ACIA and the modems. Two popular level translators are the **MC1488** and the **MC1489**, both manufactured by Motorola. The **MC1488** is a quad TTL-to-RS232C level translator for data going *to* the modem, and the **MC1489** is a quad RS232C-to-TTL level translator for data coming *from* the modem to the ACIA. Unfortunately, level translators require additional power supplies (typically −12 and +12 V) to generate the required signal voltages. The connections between the ACIA and a modem are shown in Fig. 8-18.

For asynchronous transmission, the following five signals go between the ACIA and the modem:

1. **Transmitted Data**—from the digital device to the modem. This is the data to be transmitted.
2. **Received Data**—from the modem to the digital device. This is the data received from the remote modem.
3. **Request To Send**—from the digital device to the modem. This signal should be a 0 (ON) whenever data is to be transmitted. In *half-duplex* communications, it is used to control the direction of transmission. When switched to a 1, the

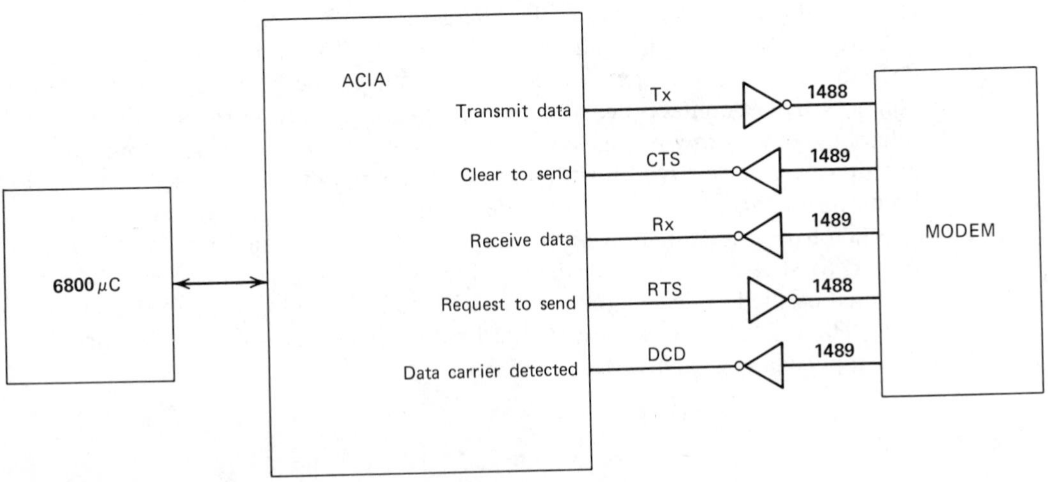

FIGURE 8-18 An RS232C Interface between the ACIA and a modem.

local modem carrier is turned off, which tells the distant end that it can start sending data. In *full-duplex* operation RTS remains in the 0 state.

4. **Clear To Send**—from the modem to the digital device. This signal is a response to Request To Send and indicates that the modem can accept data for transmission. In full-duplex operation, it is normally always active and presents a 0 level to the digital device.
5. **Data Carrier Detected (DCD)**—from the modem to the digital device. A 1 on this line indicates that the data carrier is not being received. For half-duplex systems, this would be the signal to turn on the local carrier and begin transmission. In full-duplex systems it indicates an abnormal condition. This line must be in the 0 state for reception of data.

8-10 USES OF THE ACIA

Typical applications using an ACIA are illustrated in Fig. 8-19.

System 1 shows how a terminal is connected to a μC. The interface box between the ACIA and the terminal is required to match the ACIA output voltages and the terminal's input voltage or current requirements. The most common interface at present is the RS232C discussed in Section 8-9.2. Some terminals use the 20-mA current loop described in Section 8-9.1.

System 2 shows a remotely located terminal, which can be in the next building or thousands of miles away. Here data transmission takes place via modems. A number of standard modems are available for various speeds of operation, up to 9600 bits per second. Any modem that is faster than 4800 bps usually requires two telephone circuits in order to transmit and receive simultaneously in full-duplex (one for each direction). They usually will transmit over dial-up telephone lines, but for high reliability they may require dedicated lines, which must be rented from the telephone company at considerable expense.

System 3 shows a possible way for computers to exchange data using modems. The degree of automation depends on the ingenuity and capability of the designer.

EXAMPLE 8-19

An ACIA is to transmit and receive data over a modem from a remote data terminal as described in system 2. The data will be sent in both directions simultaneously, while the μC controls the characters from both channels. The data to be transmitted is in memory starting at location $1000 (hex), and the received data is to be stored in consecutive locations starting at $2000. Explain how to set up the ACIA and write the program to control the data transfer.

SOLUTION

Table 8-17 shows subroutines that could be used. The main program is not shown. It would bring the data into a buffer from the input subroutine and send data to the output subroutine.

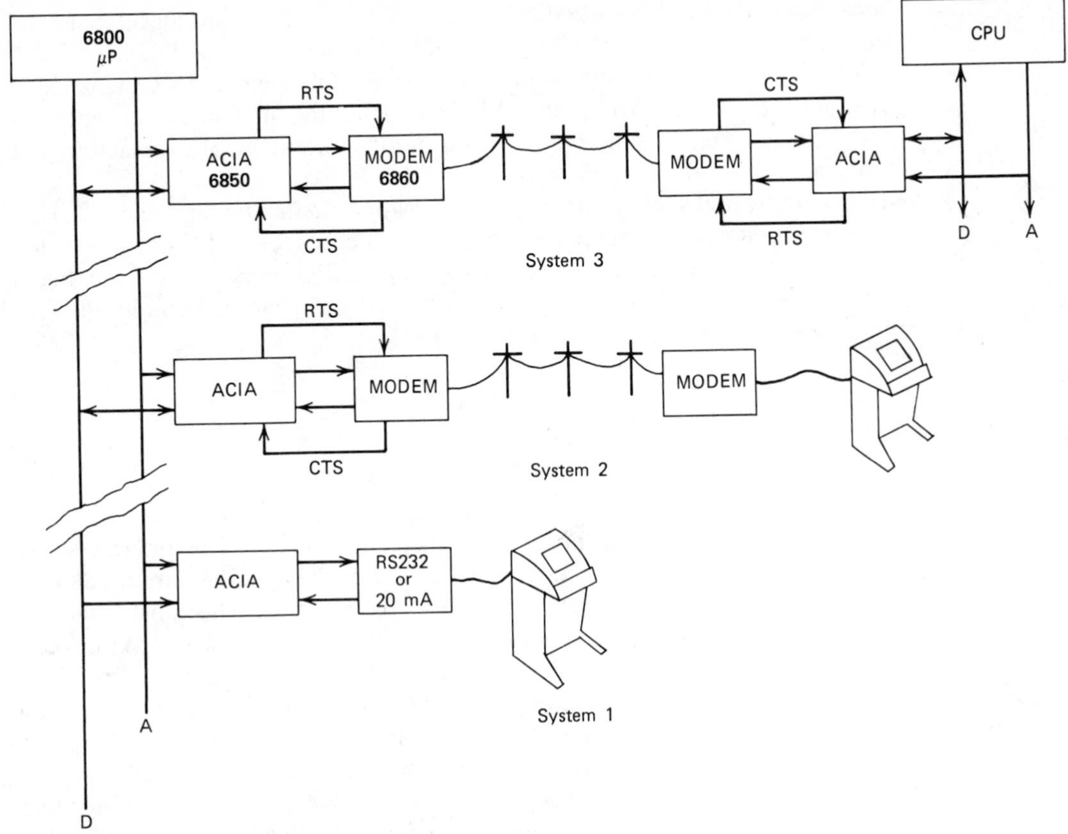

FIGURE 8-19 System applications of the ACIA.

The routines shown consist of an initialization routine to set up the ACIA, an input character routine, an output character routine, an error print routine, and routines to turn RTS ON and OFF. The RTS line and its uses are explained in Section 8-9.2.

First the hardware must be assembled to provide the proper features, and then the program must be written. A clock 16 times the baud rate would typically be used with the ACIA in the divide-by-16 mode to produce a baud rate compatible with the modem and data terminal. Typically this might be 300 or 1200 baud to work with a standard 212 type modem.

Since polling is to be used, interrupts are inhibited and the control register must be initialized to $49. This does the following:

a. Bits CR1 and CR0 are 01 selecting the divide-by-16 mode.
b. Bits CR2, CR3, and CR4 are 0, 1, and 0, respectively, selecting a word format of 7 bits + even parity + 1 stop bit. This is a format typically used by standard terminals working at 300 baud or higher.
c. Bits CR6 and CR5 are 1 and 0, respectively, programming RTS HIGH and disabling transmit interrupts.

TABLE 8-17 Program for Example 8-19

```
                              NAM     ACIA2
                    * ACIA PROGRAM FOR USE WITH A MODEM
                    *
           8008     ACIASC    EQU     $8008     ACIA STATUS/CONTROL REG
           8009     ACIADA    EQU     $8009     ACIA TX & RX DATA REGS
      0200                    ORG     $200
      0200 0001     ECHO      RMB     1         ECHO FLAG

                    *  INITIALIZATION
      0201 86 43    INIT      LDA A   #$43
      0203 B7 8008            STA A   ACIASC    MASTER RESET - RTS=0
      0206 86 49              LDA A   #$49      CONTROL WORD -
      0208 B7 8008            STA A   ACIASC
      020B 7F 0200            CLR     ECHO      MAKE IT ECHO
      020E 39                 RTS               RTN TO OTHER SYSTEM INIT

      020F B6 8008  INPUT     LDA A   ACIASC    GET STATUS
      0212 47                 ASR A             CHAR RCVD?
      0213 25 08              BCS     IN1       YES -GO ON
      0215 84 04              AND A   #4        NO - CTS SET?
      0217 27 02              BEQ     *+4       NO - SEND MSG
      0219 20 F4              BRA     INPUT     YES - TRY AGAIN
      021B 20 35              BRA     PRNT      PRNT CTS ERR MSG
      021D 47       IN1       ASR A             SKIP TX RDY BIT
      021E 47                 ASR A             SKIP DCD BIT
      021F 47                 ASR A             SKIP CTS BIT
      0220 47                 ASR A             FRAMING ERROR?
      0221 24 04              BCC     IN2       NO -
      0223 86 33              LDA A   #$33
      0225 20 1D              BRA     OUTPUT    YES - RETURN #3 ERROR
      0227 47       IN2       ASR A             OVERRUN ERROR?
      0228 24 04              BCC     IN4       NO -
      022A 86 32              LDA A   #$32
      022C 20 16              BRA     OUTPUT    YES - RETURN #2 ERROR
      022E 47       IN4       ASR A             PARITY ERROR?
      022F 24 04              BCC     IN3       NO -
      0231 86 3F              LDA A   #$3F      YES - PRNT "?"
      0233 20 0F              BRA     OUTPUT
      0235 B6 8009  IN3       LDA A   ACIADA    GET CHARACTER
      0238 84 7F              AND A   #$7F      REMOVE PARITY BIT
      023A 7D 0200            TST     ECHO      ECHO INHIBITED?
      023D 27 01              BEQ     OUTPUT    NO - DO IT
      023F 39                 RTS

      0240 F6 8008  OUTPUT    LDA B   ACIASC    GET STATUS
      0243 57                 ASR B
      0244 57                 ASR B             TRANSMIT BIT SET ?
      0245 24 F9              BCC     OUTPUT    NO - LOOP
      0247 B7 8009            STA A   ACIADA    YES - SEND IT
      024A 7F 0200            CLR     ECHO      CLEAR ECHO FLAG
      025D 39                 RTS

      025E CE XXXX  PRNT      LDX     #MSG      GET POINTER TO MSG
      0261 BD XXXX            JSR     PRINT     PRINT CTS MSG
      0264 39                 RTS

      0265 86 41    RTSOFF    LDA A   #$41
      0267 B7 8008            STA A   ACIASC    TURN OFF RTS
      026A 39                 RTS

      026B 86 09    RTSON     LDA A   #$9
      026D B7 8008            STA A   ACIASC    TURN ON RTS
      0270 39                 RTS
                              END
```

d. Bit CR7 is 0, disabling receive interrupts. (Interrupt techniques are explained in Chapter 9.)

The initialization is done as shown in Table 8-16.

A master reset control word ($43) is sent to the Control Register. As explained in Section 8-8.5, this latches the IRQ and RTS internal bits so that neither line can go to its active state (LOW). This is followed by the Control Word required to set up the system as desired ($49 for 7 bits, even parity, 1 stop bit). The ECHO flag is then cleared so the character received will be *echoed* back to the terminal by the input character routine (see lines 41 and 42 of Table 8-17).

The input character routine of Table 8-17 is next, and it works as follows:

1. The ACIA status register is read.
2. The status word is shifted right 1 bit. This puts the Receive Data Register Full (RDRF) flag into the carry bit.
3. The carry flag is tested. If it is 0, the receive buffer is empty (refer to Table 8-11). To be sure the modem is ready we also test the CTS bit by ANDing it with a 4 to see if it is a "1" (false). If the carry is equal to 1 the program will "fall through" the BEQ instruction and loop back to INPUT for another status word.
4. If the carry is equal to 1, the Receive Data Register is full and the program jumps to IN1. IN1 then shifts the status word until the Framing Bit is in the carry register. It is tested, and if the carry is clear it branches to IN2. The program continues to check the overrun and parity bits. If no error exists it goes to IN3, where the data character is fetched from the Data Register. If any of these error bits are set, an appropriate error number is sent to the output routine for transmission back to the terminal. If the character is fetched by line 39, it has the MSB stripped off. The ECHO flag is then tested, and if it is a 0 the data is echoed back to the terminal by the output routine. When the RTS at the end of the output routine is finally reached, the program returns to the main program with the character in the A accumulator, where it is stored or printed.
5. The OUTPUT routine tests bit 1 after ignoring bit 0. If it is 0, it loops back until this transmit bit is set, indicating that the Tx register is empty and ready to accept a new character. Note that the B accumulator is used to hold the Status Word so that the character in A is not disturbed.
6. If bit 1 equals 1, the transmit data register is empty. The character in A is then "stored" to the Data Register, which then transmits it to the terminal.
7. Return to step 1 of this explanation and repeat.

This program checks all of the ACIA status bits (except DCD) for errors and echoes an error number back to the remote terminal. Another ACIA program is shown in Chapter 6 (Fig. 6-4), but since it is for a local terminal it is much simpler and does not check for errors. Although routines are shown for turning RTS ON and OFF, this is left for the reader. The RTS signal is used by some modems to reverse the channel. (See the reference to the Bell 202 type modem in Section 8-14.)

8-11 SYNCHRONOUS COMMUNICATIONS

Asynchronous communications via the ACIA are used primarily with low-speed terminals where information is generated on a keyboard (manually) and the communication is not necessarily continuous. Synchronous communications are usually encountered where high-speed continuous transmission is required. This information is frequently read to modems, disk, or tape systems at 1200 bps or faster. Synchronous systems transmit a steady stream of bits even when no characters are available (a *sync* character is substituted). Because there are no start and stop bits to separate the characters, care must be taken to synchronize the receiving device with the transmitted signal so that the receiver end of the circuit can determine which bit is bit 1 of the character.

Synchronous systems usually use a preamble (all 1s, for example) to establish synchronization between the receiver and transmitter and then maintain sync by transmitting a sync pattern until interrupted. Because start and stop bits are not needed, the efficiency of transmission is 20% better for 8-bit words (8 instead of 10 bits per character).

Synchronous transmission is illustrated in Fig. 8-20. The top line is the clock that is used in most systems to control the data. In this figure, all data changes occur on the positive edge of the clock. For maximum reliability, data should be sampled in the middle of the bit. Note that after the preamble, the data flows continuously.

8-11.1 The 6852 Synchronous Serial Data Adapter (SSDA)

The SSDA is a 24-pin MOS LSI IC that provides a bidirectional serial interface for synchronous data information interchange with bus-organized systems such as the **6800** μP. It is a complex device containing seven registers. Although it is primarily designed for synchronous data communications using a "Bi-sync" format, several

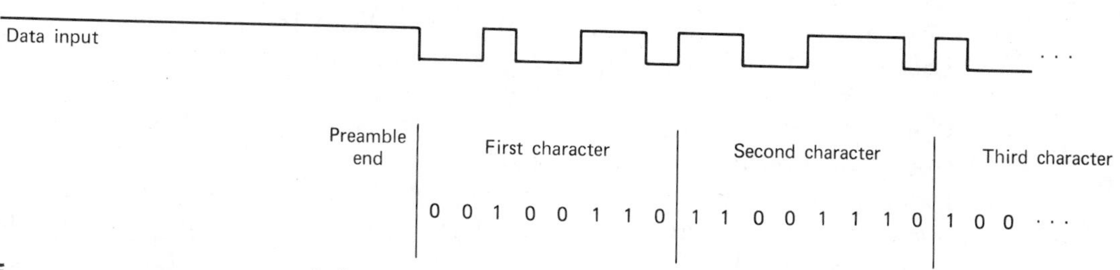

F

FIGURE 8-20 Synchronous transmission.

of the **6852**'s features, particularly the First In, First Out (FIFO) buffers, make it useful in other applications where data is to be transferred between devices that are not being clocked at precisely the same speed, such as tape cassettes, ape cartridges, or floppy disk systems. Because the SSDA is so complex, space does not permit a detailed discussion of it. The reader is referred to the manufacturers' literature. (See the references in Section 8-14).

8-12 SUMMARY

This chapter dealt with interfacing and communications between the **6800** μP and peripheral devices. The two most popular interfacing ICs, the PIA and the ACIA, were discussed in detail. The operation of their internal registers and the programs necessary to make them function properly were explained. The differences between parallel, serial synchronous, and serial asynchronous transmission were explained so that the designer can use the proper interface ICs.

Other **6800** family devices generally known as peripheral controllers, such as the **6854** Advanced Data Link Controller (ADLC) and the **6844** Direct Memory Access Controller (DMAC), are manufactured to perform specific functions in μC systems (see Section 9-9.4). They are like the PIA because they are bus-compatible and addressable. They also have programmable control registers, data registers, and status registers. These devices are very complex and cannot be explained thoroughly in this book, but readers who have absorbed the principles of PIA and ACIA operation should be able to understand these special-purpose ICs after consulting the manufacturers' literature.

8-13 GLOSSARY

ACIA (MC6850) **6800** family Asynchronous Communications Interface Adapter component.

American Standard Code for Information Interchange (ASCII) Serial data communications code used by the majority of data terminals and computers.

Analog-to-Digital (A/D) converter Device that converts analog signals to digital signals.

Asynchronous Independent of a clock (i.e., random).

Command Words Words (bytes) sent to a peripheral device to tell it how to act.

Control Register Register where bits are entered to configure or control a peripheral IC device.

Control Word Group of bits written to a peripheral device such as a PIA or ACIA register that controls the mode of operation.

Darlington transistor Consists of a pair of transistors in a single package interconnected so as to provide a power transistor output with high enough gain that it can be controlled by a PIA.

Data word Group of bits (usually 8) that is moved from one device to another in a μC system.

Digital-to-Analog (D/A) converter Device that converts digital information to analog for control of external devices.

Direction Register Register within the PIA that controls the direction of data flow on each of the I/O lines.

EBCDIC Extended Binary Coded Decimal Interchange Code (IBM).

Handshaking Interchange of signals between devices to acknowledge or authorize communication.

Initialization Process of programming the registers to configure a PIA or ACIA or other device for the required application.

Interrupt Signal that informs the μP that a peripheral device is requesting service. It generally causes the μP program to jump to a service routine for the requesting device.

Modem Device that uses digital signals to *mod*ulate audio tones in one direction and *dem*odulate similar tones to obtain digital signals for transmission in the other direction.

PIA, Peripheral Interface Adapter (MC6821) **6800** family parallel data interface IC component.

Polling Interrogating the Status Register of each peripheral device in turn to determine if it has data for the μP.

Resolution Voltage represented by the smallest change in the output when one bit is added or deleted.

Sensor Device that senses an analog quantity and typically converts it into a voltage that is proportional to the magnitude of the quantity.

START bit Bit that signals the start of a character in an asynchronous communication system.

Status Register Register that contains status bits.

Status Word Bits in a PIA or ACIA register that indicate what is currently happening in that device.

STOP bit(s) One or two bits (always 1s) that indicate the end of an asynchronous character.

Subroutine nesting Incorporation of subroutines within subroutines.

Synchronous In step with a clock signal.

Transducer Device that converts a dynamic quantity, such as velocity, into a voltage.

Wire-OR circuits Circuits that can be connected together so that any one of them can pull down the interrupt line to activate the **6800** μP interrupt function.

8-14 REFERENCES

Direct Connect 1200 BPS Asynchronous Data Modem Model 202S, Universal Data Systems, Huntsville, AL, July 1982.

Direct Connect 212A Modem, Rev. A, Universal Data Systems, Huntsville, AL, May 1980.

IBM. *Binary Synchronous Communications (Bi-sync)*, IBM File No. TP-09, Form GA-27-3004-1, Third Edition, October 1970.

Microprocessor Interfacing Techniques, Second Edition, Austin Lesea & Rodney Zaks SYBEX Inc., Berkeley, CA, 1978.

Motorola. *MC6830L7 MIKBUG/MINIBUG ROM*, EN100, SPD Inc., Phoenix, AZ, 1980.

Motorola. *MC6854 Advanced Data-Link Controller (ADLC)*, DS9495-R2, Motorola SPD Inc., Phoenix, AZ, 1984.

Motorola. *MC6852 Synchronous Serial Data Adapter (SSDA)*, DS9494-R4, Motorola SPD Inc., Phoenix, AZ, 1984.

Motorola. *MC6850 Asynchronous Communications Interface Adapter*, (ACIA), DS9493-R3, Motorola Inc., Phoenix, AZ, 1984.

Motorola. *MC6821 Peripheral Interface Adapter*, (PIA), DS9435-R4, Motorola, Inc., Phoenix, AZ, 1984.

USA Standard Character Structure and Character Parity Sense for Serial-by-Bit Data Communication in the USA Standard Code for Information Interchange (ASCII), USAS X3.4-1968, American National Standards Institute, Washington, DC.

8-15 PROBLEMS

8-1 A D/A converter has 8 input bits. If its output ranges from 0 to 5 V, how much voltage does each digital step require?

8-2 Repeat Problem 8-1 if the output range is from −7 to +7 V.

8-3 An A/D converter is required to have an output range of 0 to +20 V. It must have an input resolution of 0.01 V or more. How many bits are required on the digital input?

8-4 Write a program to configure Direction Register A of a PIA so that lines 6 and 7 are inputs and to configure Direction Register B so that lines 1 and 2 are inputs. All other lines should be outputs.

8-5 Write the coding for Example 8-2.

8-6 Write the instruction for the program of Example 8-9 if the data between locations 100 and 150 are to be sent to the peripheral controller.

8-7 If a PIA Control Register reads \$3F, what is the PIA doing?

8-8 A peripheral has two control lines, A and B. If it SETs A, it wants to read the data in location \$100. If it SETs B, it wants to read the data in location \$200. Write a program to initialize the PIA to allow this to happen. Assume that both control lines are not SET simultaneously.

8-9 Write a program so that a peripheral can write data into memory sequentially, starting at location \$100.

8-10 The Status Register of an ACIA reads \$81. What action should the program take?

8-11 Write a program to transmit the contents of locations \$100 to \$1FF to a peripheral using an ACIA.

8-12 If a peripheral is transmitting serial data to a μP via an ACIA, write a program to store the data in sequential locations, starting at $100.

8-13 A TTY is sending data. The μP must "echo" by transmitting the same data it is receiving so that the TTY operator sees the data being sent. Write the ACIA program to accomplish this.

8-14 Every time a person enters a room, a TTY is to type the word "hello." Describe the equipment and the program required to make this happen.

8-15 The following program uses a PIA at locations $8020–$8023:

```
Addr              Mnemonic
20                LDX #$100
23                CLR $8021
26                CLR $8020
28                LDA A #$24
2B                STA A $8021
2E         QQ     LDA A $8021
31                BPL *-3
33                LDA A $8020
36                STA A $20,X
38                INX
39                CPX #$200
3B                BNE QQ
3D                BRA *
```

a. Is the data flow in or out of the μP? Which side of the PIA is being used?
b. What area of memory is reserved for data? How many bytes?
c. Is CA1 or CB1 being used? If so, how?
d. Is CA2 or CB2 being used? If so, how?
e. What is QQ?
f. Explain what the program is doing.

8-16 Modify Example 8-7 so that the seven-segment display shows the hex digits (0–9 and A–F).

After attempting to solve these problems, try to answer the self-evaluation questions in Section 8-2. If any of them still seem difficult, review the appropriate sections of the chapter to find the answers.

CHAPTER 9

INTERRUPTS, TIMING, AND DIRECT MEMORY ACCESSES

9-1 INSTRUCTIONAL OBJECTIVES

This chapter introduces two methods whereby a peripheral device can communicate with a computer: *interrupts* and *direct memory accesses*. After reading this chapter, the student should be able to

1. Write a *restart* routine to initialize a **6800** μP system.
2. Write an *interrupt service routine* for a device that uses the IRQ or NMI interrupt.
3. Use the SWI and WAI instructions.
4. Use the **6828** Peripheral Interrupt Controller (PIC).
5. Design software and hardware timing circuits.
6. Design controllers that use DMA.

9-2 SELF-EVALUATION QUESTIONS

Watch for the answers to the following questions as you read the chapter. They should help you understand the material presented.

1. What is an *interrupt?* What advantages does it give a μP system?
2. How is the interrupt mask set and cleared?
3. In a system that allows several devices to interrupt on the same line, how is the interrupting device identified?
4. Why is the NMI a higher-priority interrupt than the IRQ?
5. What is the difference between a WAI and an SWI?
6. What does the RTI instruction do? Why is it important?
7. In doing DMA, why can TSC not be held LOW longer than 9.5 μs?
8. What are the advantages of a hardware timer over software timing routines? What are the disadvantages?

9-3 INTRODUCTION TO INTERRUPTS

One of the most important features of a μC is the ability to act on feedback from peripheral devices such as line printers or machinery controllers and control the devices accordingly. The μC must be able to sense the operation of the system under its control and respond quickly with corrective commands when necessary.

When conditions that require fast response arise, the system is wired so as to send a signal called an *interrupt* to the μP. An **interrupt** *causes the μP to stop execution of its main program and jump to a special program, an interrupt service routine,* that responds to the needs of the external device. The main program resumes when the interrupt service routine is finished.

Although a computer can perform many useful tasks without using or responding to an interrupt, the ability to do so is a necessary function for many system designs. The **6800** includes a powerful interrupt structure. Important aspects of this are the *stack concept*, the use of *vectored interrupts*, and the *interrupt priority scheme* provided by the μP logic.

9-3.1 The Stack Concept

As described in Chapter 5, the **stack** is an area in memory pointed to by the Stack Pointer (SP) register. The stack has three basic uses:

1. To save return addresses for subroutine calls.
2. To save and retrieve data using PUSH and PULL instructions.
3. To save register contents during an interrupt.

Use of the stack during interrupts is discussed in this chapter.

9-3.2 Vectored Interrupts

The **6800** uses four different types of interrupts: *Reset* (RST), *NonMaskable* (NMI), *SoftWare* (SWI), and *Interrupt ReQuest* (IRQ). Unique interrupt servicing routines must be written by the system designer for each type of interrupt used, and these routines can be located anywhere in memory.

When one of the four types of interrupts occurs, the μP logic fetches the contents of 2 bytes from a specific address for each interrupt. Those bytes contain the address of the service routine and they are loaded into the Program Counter (PC). This causes the program to jump to the proper interrupt routine. The fetched addresses are commonly called **vectors** or *vector addresses* since they *point to* the software routine used to service the interrupt.

Three of the interrupts (RST, NMI, and IRQ) are activated by signals on the pins of the μP, and the fourth (SWI) is initiated by an instruction.

The eight locations that contain the vector addresses for the four interrupt types are at the top of the memory map as follows:

1. Reset (RST) $FFFE–$FFFF
2. NonMaskable Interrupt (NMI) $FFFC–$FFFD

3. SoftWare Interrupt (SWI) $FFFA–$FFFB
4. Interrupt Request (IRQ) $FFF8–$FFF9

These are shown in the memory map of Fig. 9-1.

It should be noted (as explained in Sections 7-14, 7-15, and 7-16) that the actual ROM (or PROM) accessed for these vectors may contain a program that runs at some lower address as long as it also responds to the addresses shown above. These interrupts have similar but different sequences of operation and each will be described.

9-4 RESET (RST)

A **reset** is used to start the main program. The RESET line is pulled LOW by the restart button or as a result of an auto-restart circuit. The LOW pulse on the RESET pin of the μP causes the logic in the μP to be reset and also causes the starting location of the main program to be fetched from the *reset vector* locations at $FFFE and $FFFF. The vector address is picked up on the data bus by the μP and transferred to the PC.

9-4.1 Reset Timing

The μP's response to a reset signal is similar to its response to an interrupt. When the RESET line is pulled down and held, the following conditions exist:

1. The interrupt mask (the I bit in the Condition Code Register) is SET.
2. VMA is LOW.
3. The data bus is high-impedance.

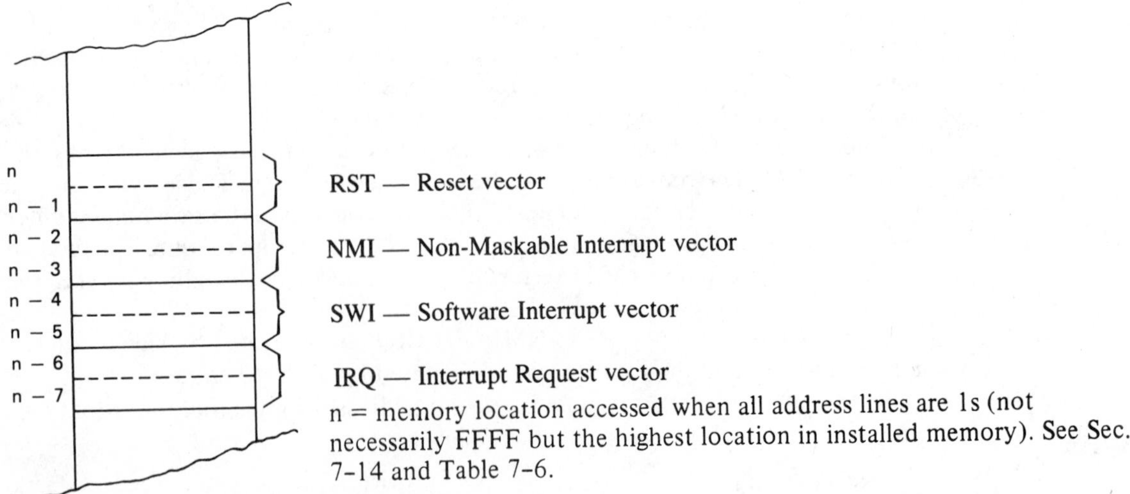

FIGURE 9-1 Restart and Interrupt Vector locations in memory.

4. BA is LOW.
5. $R/\overline{W}$ is HIGH.
6. The address bus contains $FFFE.

Figure 9-2 illustrates the system responses to the RESET line. When the voltage reaches 4.75 V, after the power is turned ON, and the clock oscillator stabilizes, it is necessary to wait at least eight cycles for the μP logic to clear before the program can be started.

During these eight cycles, $\overline{\text{RESET}}$ should be held LOW since the μP's VMA signal can be indeterminate. Any device such as a battery-backed RAM should also be inhibited by $\overline{\text{RESET}}$ since it could experience a false write.

$\overline{\text{RESET}}$ can go HIGH asynchronously with the system clock any time after the eighth cycle. When the $\overline{\text{RESET}}$ line is allowed to go HIGH, it will fetch the *restart vector* and jump to it, as shown in Fig. 9-2.

The $\overline{\text{RESET}}$ line is also connected to any hardware devices that have a hardware reset and need to be initialized, such as the Peripheral Interface Adapter (PIA) (see Chapter 8). Grounding the $\overline{\text{RESET}}$ line clears all registers in the PIA, and the restart service routine reprograms the PIA Control and Direction Registers before allowing the main program to start. The Asynchronous Communications Interface Adapter (ACIA) has no RESET pin and depends on software initialization. All software flags, or constants in RAM, must also be preset. If the system includes power-failure sensors and associated service routines, additional steps will be needed in the restart service routine to provide the automatic restart function (see Example 9-4).

EXAMPLE 9-1

The program starts at location 123 (hex). What must be done to ensure a proper start?

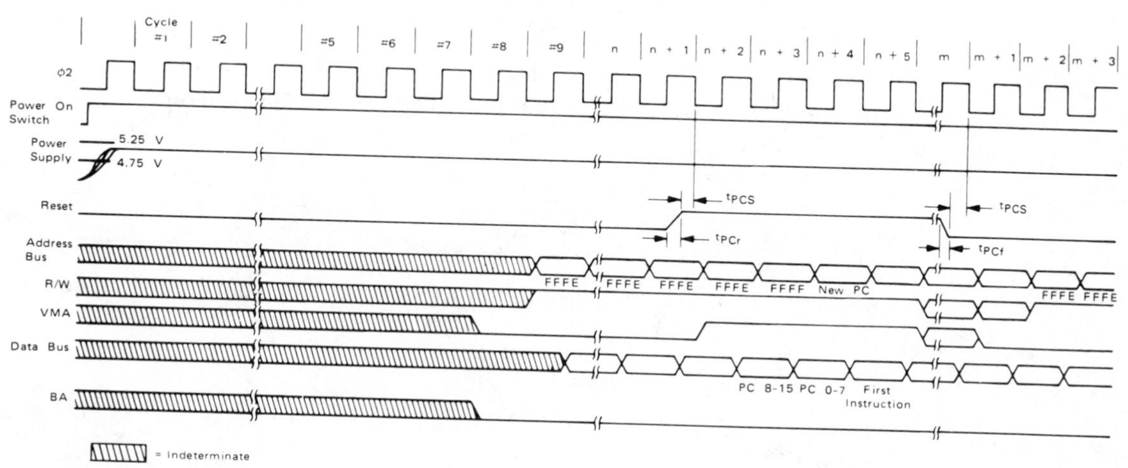

FIGURE 9-2 Reset timing.

SOLUTION
Before a program can be started automatically, the RESET vector must be in place. In this case a 01 must be stored in a location that is accessed when $FFFE is on the address bus and a $23 must be in the following location.

When the reset line is grounded (perhaps by a restart timer or by a pushbutton switch), the **6800** fetches the vector in two steps by outputting $FFFE and then $FFFF. When the bytes appear on the data bus (01, followed by $23), they are loaded into the Program Counter in the high and low bytes, respectively, and the program starts in the proper place.

This automatic start is possible only if the vector and the main program are in ROM (or EPROM). If a test system has RAM at the top of memory, a small test program can be loaded, perhaps by hardware switches, and can be started by entering the program address into the restart vector and operating the reset switch. Preferably, a μP Development System (see Chapter 10) will be used and the program can be loaded and entered directly by routines in the ROM Monitor program.

9-5 THE IRQ INTERRUPT

The **IRQ** interrupt is typically used when peripheral devices must communicate with the μP. It is activated by a LOW signal on the $\overline{\text{IRQ}}$ pin (pin 4) of the μP. Both the ACIA and PIA have $\overline{\text{IRQ}}$ pins that can be connected to the μP when the system design requires it. Even though this line is pulled LOW, the $\overline{\text{IRQ}}$ interrupt does not occur if the I bit of the Condition Code Register (CCR) is SET. This is known as **masking** *the interrupt*.

The I bit is SET in one of three ways:

1. By the hardware logic of the μP as part of the restart procedure.
2. Whenever the μP is interrupted by a LOW on the NMI or IRQ lines.
3. By an SEI (set interrupt mask) instruction.

Once SET, the I bit can be cleared only by a CLI (clear interrupt mask) instruction. Therefore, if a program is to allow interrupts while it runs, it must have a CLI instruction near its beginning.

EXAMPLE 9-2

What conditions must be satisfied for an ACIA or PIA to interrupt the processor?

SOLUTION
All of the following are required.

1. The $\overline{\text{IRQ}}$ output of the PIA or ACIA must be connected to the $\overline{\text{IRQ}}$ input of the μP.
2. The I flag of the μP must be CLEAR.

3. The control register in the ACIA or PIA must be programmed to enable interrupts.
4. There must be a transition on one of the control lines (CA1 or CA2, for example) of the PIA, entry of a word into the ACIA shift register, or the TDRE flag going true. These last two must also be enabled.

9-5.1 Interrupt Action

When an interrupt is initiated, *the instruction in progress is completed before the μP begins its interrupt sequence*. The first step in this sequence is to save the program status by storing the PC (2 bytes), X (2 bytes), A, B, and CC registers on the stack in the order shown in Fig. 9-3. These 7 bytes are written into memory, starting at the current location in the Stack Pointer (SP) register. It is decremented on each write. When completed, the SP is pointing to the next empty memory location. The condition of the stack before and after accepting an interrupt is shown in Fig. 9-4. The μP next sets the interrupt mask bit (I), which allows the service program to run without being interrupted. Next, the μP fetches the *address* of the interrupt service routine from the IRQ vector location, by placing \$FFF8 and \$FFF9 on the address bus, and inserts it into the PC. The μP then fetches the first instruction of the service routine from the location now designated by the PC.

9-5.2 Return from Interrupt (RTI)

The interrupt service routine must end with an **RTI** (return from interrupt) instruction. The action of the RTI is shown in Fig. 9-5. It reloads all the μP registers with the values they had before the interrupt and, in the process, moves the stack pointer to SP+7, where it was before the interrupt. The RTI uses 10 clock cycles to write the contents of the 7 bytes currently on the stack back into the μP registers. The program resumes at the address restored to the PC (which is the next instruction that would have been executed before the interrupt occurred).

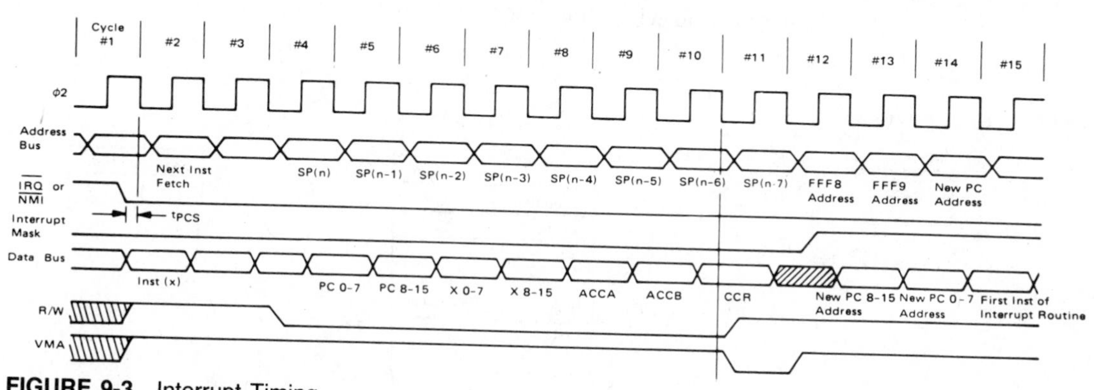

FIGURE 9-3 Interrupt Timing.

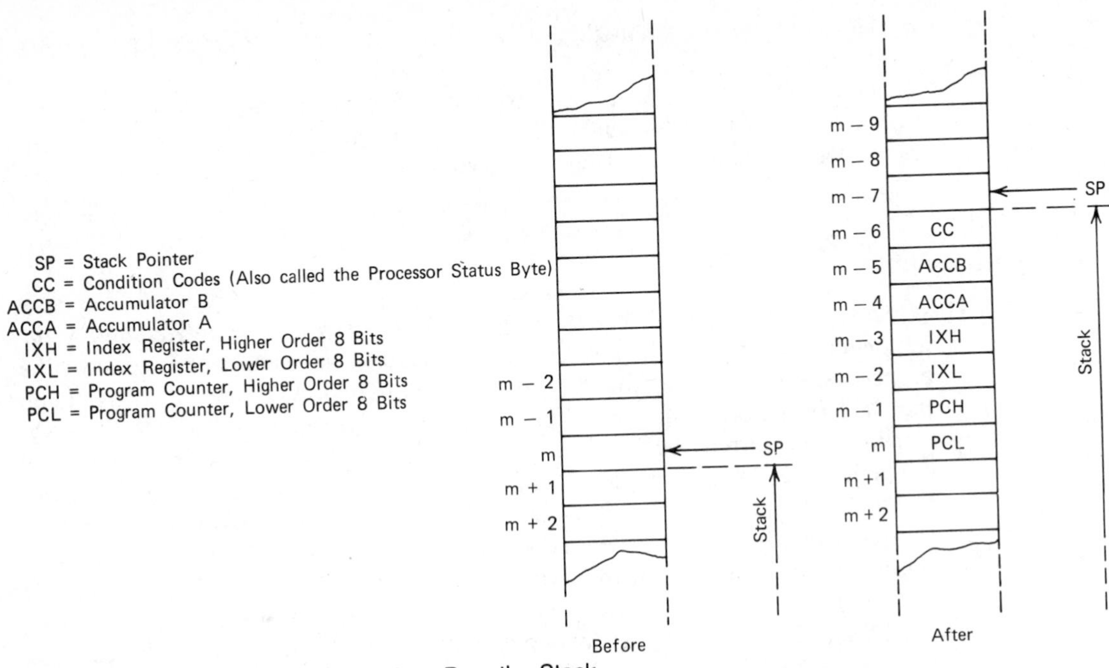

FIGURE 9-4 Saving the Status of the μP on the Stack.

9-5.3 Nested Interrupts

Normally an interrupt service routine proceeds until it is complete without being interrupted itself, because the I flag is SET automatically by the μP when servicing an interrupt. If it is desirable to recognize another IRQ interrupt (of higher priority, for example) before the servicing of the first one has been completed, the interrupt mask can be cleared by a CLI instruction at the beginning of the current service routine. This allows "an interrupt of an interrupt," or **nested interrupts**. It is handled in the **6800** by stopping the execution of the original service routine and storing another sequence of registers on the stack. Because of the automatic decrementing of the stack pointer by each interrupt and subsequent incrementing by the RTI instruction when the second interrupt is complete, the first interrupt

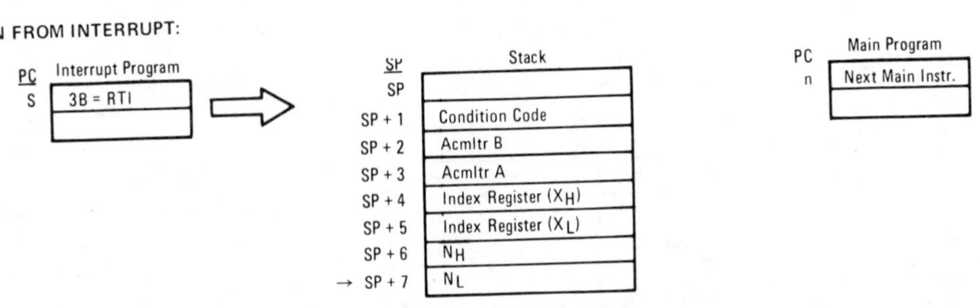

FIGURE 9-5 Operation of RTI—the Return from Interrupt instruction.

service routine is resumed and the interrupts are serviced in the proper order. Interrupts can be nested to any depth, limited only by the amount of memory available for the stack.

9-5.4 Interrupt Initialization

For successful interrupt handling, the interfaces that communicate with peripheral devices, such as the PIA or ACIA, must be properly initialized at the start of the main program. In the preceding chapter, a number of examples were given using the PIA without using interrupts. Now it will be shown how some of the same functions can be done using the interrupt capabilities of the PIA. The advantage is that the processor does not have to be dedicated to scanning for an input but instead can do other useful tasks while waiting for each interrupt to occur.

EXAMPLE 9-3

Show how to program a system to use the A side of the PIA for inputs (from a keyboard, for example) and the B side for outputs (to a printer, perhaps). Use the IRQ line to interrupt the processor and indicate how the proper interrupt service routine is selected to input or output a character.

SOLUTION

Figure 9-6 shows the interface connections to the PIA for this systems application.

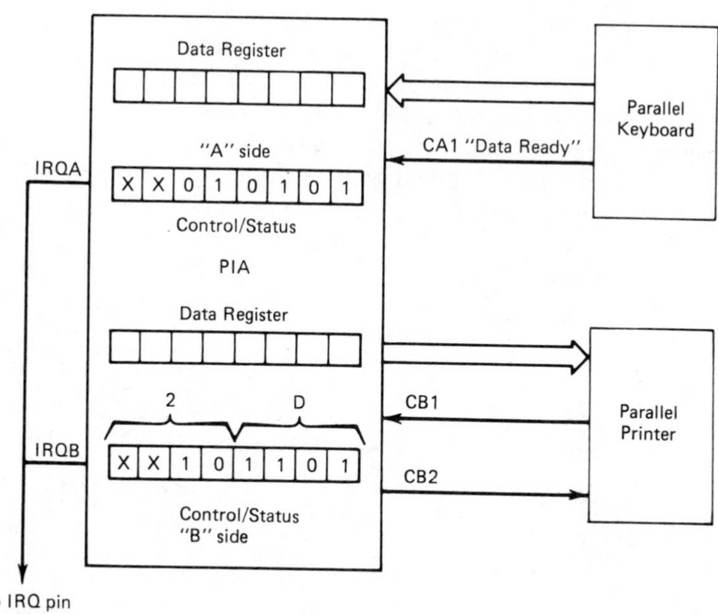

FIGURE 9-6 Hardware configuration for Example 9-3.

Note: This is a common way to connect a printer to a computer. The CB1 line is used as a *request data* signal, and the CB2 line is used as a *data strobe*, to cause the printer to read the data on the output lines of the PIA. In practice, additional *paper out* and *printer selected* lines are used, but these will be ignored in this example.

This program consists of three basic parts. The first part is shown in Fig. 9-7 and is an initialization or restart routine for the PIA. It is normally included with other initialization routines for other parts of the system and is executed whenever the RESET signal line is activated. This is done either by the RESTART hardware, which automatically pulls down and releases the RST pin of the μP when power is applied to the system, or by a START pushbutton. Assuming that the PIA RESET pin is connected to the RESET line (as it should be), all I/O lines in the PIA are initialized as inputs and interrupts are disabled because all registers are cleared. The initialization program shown in Fig. 9-7 then sets the registers, as required for this application.

Note that bit 2 of Control Register A (CRA2), when set, latches the A-side Direction Register with the I/O lines selected as inputs, and bit 2 of CRB latches the B-side lines as outputs. The latter occurs because the COM A instruction inverted the 00 it found in the A accumulator to FF (all 1s), and it is stored in the B-side Direction Register before bit 2 is SET.

In Control Register A, the CA1 line is programmed to interrupt on negative-going transitions (bits 1 and 0 are 0 and 1, respectively), and the line is connected to external circuitry so that the keyboard produces a negative-going pulse whenever a key is pressed. The B-side control word is set up so that the CB2 line will strobe the printer when a character is put into the Data Register by the output character routine. This will cause the printer to read the data on the output lines. The CB1 line is programmed to cause an interrupt whenever the printer requests new data, which it will do as soon as it finishes printing the previous character.

Bits 5, 4, and 3 of the CRA are 0, 1, and 0, respectively, and, as described in Table 8-7, this programs the PIA so that the CA2 line cannot cause an interrupt unless taken HIGH. It could be wired to ground to prevent this.

The reading or writing of the data registers is done by the other parts of the

```
Addr   Code                 Mnemonics        Comments

1000   4F          INIT     CLR A            SET A TO ZEROS
1001   B7 2001              STA A $2001      CLEAR "A" CONTROL REG
1004   B7 2003              STA A $2003      CLEAR "B" CONTROL REG
1007   B7 2000              STA A $2000      SET "A" SIDE FOR INPUTS
100A   43                   COMA             GET $FF
100B   B7 2002              STA A $2002      SET "B" SIDE FOR OUTPUTS
100E   86 15                LDA A #$15       GET KEYBOARD CONTROL WORD
1010   B7 2001              STA A $2001      STORE CW IN CRA
1013   86 2E                LDA A #$2D       SET CW FOR STROBE & RQST
1015   B7 2003              STA A $2003      STORE CW IN CRB
1018   .....                etc.
```

FIGURE 9-7 Initialization Routine for Example 9-3.

program. As seen in line 2 of Table 8-8, the WRITE to the B Data Register by the *output character* routine takes CB2 LOW, which causes the printer to read the character data on the output lines.

9-5.5 Polling

In a system that allows several devices to interrupt, it is necessary to use either a hardware or software method to identify the interrupting device. A hardware device is described in Section 9-8. The software method is called *software* **polling** and in this case, the IRQ pins are usually connected together and to the μP's IRQ pin as in the system of Fig. 9-6. When the CA1 line is pulled LOW by the keyboard circuits (each time a key is pressed), or the CB1 line is pulled LOW by the printer, the resulting interrupt will *vector* the processor to the polling routine of Fig. 9-9.

A flowchart of the polling sequence for Example 9-3 is shown in Fig. 9-8, and the corresponding program is shown in Fig. 9-9. With this interrupt routine, the contents of the PIA's A-side Control/Status register are loaded into the A accumulator by the first instruction of the program shown in Fig. 9-9 and tested by the following BPL (Branch-if-PLus) instruction, to see if status bit 7 of CRA is SET. If it is, an interrupt has occurred, and since the resulting byte is a negative number the program falls through to the *input character*-handling routine. If bit 7 is not SET, the word is positive and the BPL instruction branches to the POLL2 routine at address \$120. If bit 7 of CRB (address \$2003) is SET, the *output* interrupt has occurred, the BPL (2A) instruction at location \$123 does not branch, and the *output character*-handling routine is entered. Each of these character-handling routines ends with an RTI instruction. They serve to return the processor from the interrupt sequence and the main program is resumed at the point where it was interrupted.

9-5.6 Other Interrupt Service Routines

In response to each type of interrupt, a routine must be written to service that interrupt. The polling sequence of Section 9-5.5 is an example of the **interrupt service routine** for an IRQ interrupt. The main program must also be written to allow or prevent interrupts at the proper time, as explained at the end of part b of Example 9-12.

9-6 NONMASKABLE INTERRUPT

A NonMaskable Interrupt (**NMI**) is initiated by placing a LOW level on the NMI pin (pin 6) of the **6800**. When an NMI occurs, the program counter is loaded with the vector accessed from \$FFFC and \$FFFD. This causes the μP to jump to the start of the NMI service routine.

As its name implies, the NMI is not affected by the I bit of the CCR and an interrupt occurs whenever the NMI pin is pulled LOW. Consequently, NMI

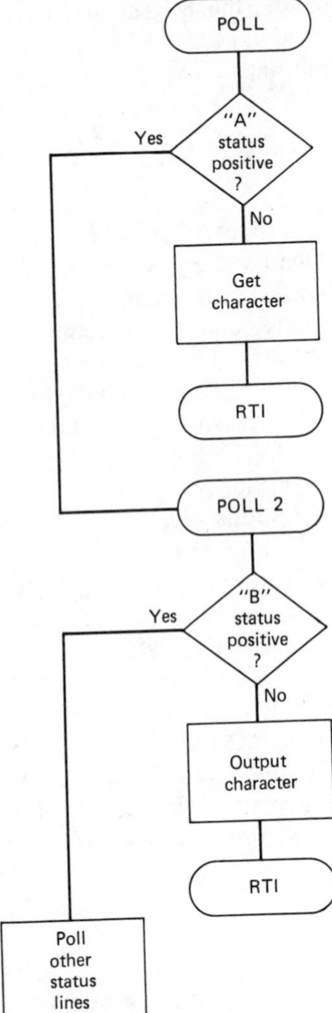

FIGURE 9-8 Polling sequence flowchart.

```
ADDR    DATA     LABEL    MNEMONICS          COMMENTS

100     B6 2001  POLL     LDA A $2001        GET "A" STATUS
103     2A 1D             BPL POLL2          BRANCH IF + TO POLL2

                 *  INPUT CHARACTER ROUTINE
...     B6 2000           LDA A $2000        GET DATA
...     XX                ETC
11F     3B                RTI                RETURN FROM INTERRUPT
                 *
120     B6 2003  POLL2    LDA A $2003        GET "B" STATUS
123     2A 1D             BPL POLL3          BRANCH IF + TO OTHERS
                 *  OUTPUT CHARACTER ROUTINE (PRINT)
...     B7 2002           STA A $2002        OUTPUT DATA
...     XX                ETC
...     3B                RTI
                          END   RETURN FROM INTERRUPT
```

FIGURE 9-9 Polling program for Example 9-3.

functions as a *very high priority interrupt*. It is usually reserved for events such as a power failure in the μP or in a peripheral, which could be catastrophic if the μP did not recognize them and take immediate action. It is also sometimes used for keeping a clock updated, since any failure to respond can cause the clock to lose time.

EXAMPLE 9-4

Assume a system like that in Fig. 9-10 is being used as part of a financial terminal where transactions involving customer bank accounts are being handled and the information must be preserved in the event of a power failure. Describe the interrupt service routines required.

SOLUTION

Since it is necessary, in this type of system, to save all calculations and status, a nonvolatile RAM is needed with a *power fail* detector as shown in Fig. 9-10.

The function of the battery shown in Fig. 9-10 is to act as a backup source of energy for the RAM so that the RAM will not lose information when the main power fails.

When a power failure occurs, the NMI line is pulled down by the power fail logic, the main program is interrupted at the end of the current instruction, and the registers are stored in the stack. (The power supply will take many milliseconds before the voltage is too LOW to operate the system, and this routine takes only microseconds). The vector for the power fail routine is fetched and the processor starts its execution. This routine's main function is to save, in nonvolatile memory, all relevant information, such as the contents of the PIA and ACIA registers, and partial products of any calculations that may be in process. (The stack should also be in nonvolatile memory.) The program should then use a PIA to pull down the HALT line to prevent any false operation of the μP while the voltage is marginal.

Figure 9-10 also includes the RESET circuitry necessary to resume operation when the power comes on again. The box labeled "Reset logic" must decide when the voltage is normal, and it then initiates a RESET pulse. The RESET routine fetched by the RESET vector must not only reconfigure the PIAs and the ACIAs as they were but also reload all interim products or data into the appropriate registers (the RTI restores the μP registers). The program then resumes from the address restored to the PC register, without loss of any vital data.

9-7 THE SOFTWARE INTERRUPT (SWI)

An interrupt activated by an instruction is available in the **6800** and serves several interesting purposes. One use is as an aid in debugging systems, but it can be used for error indications or other uses. The **SWI** instruction, when encountered in a

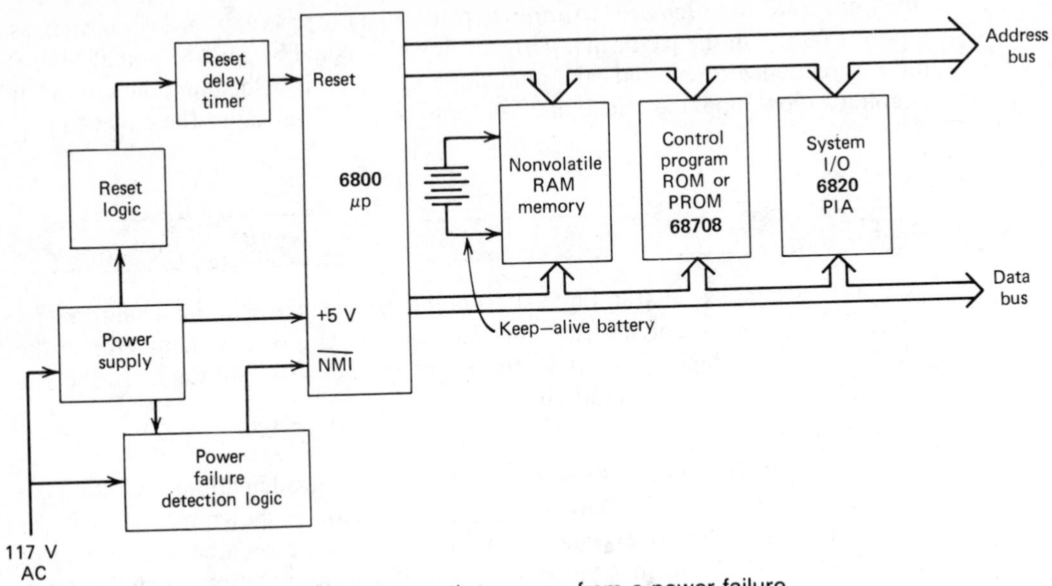

FIGURE 9-10 A **6800** system for automatic recovery from a power failure.

program, causes the registers to be put away on the stack and a vector to be fetched, just as for other interrupts. The vector for SWI is located at address $FFFA and $FFFB. Monitor programs such as BUFFALO found in the **68HC11EVB** system (see Section 10-4) use an SWI to store the register contents on the stack, where they can be read out to the user.

9-7.1 The WAI Instruction

The **6800** μP also incorporates a WAit-for-Interrupt (**WAI**) instruction. Figure 9-11 is the timing diagram for a WAI. It is similar to an interrupt sequence but provides a way to speed the response to an interrupt. In Fig. 9-11, a WAI instruction has been executed in preparation for an interrupt:

1. The WAI instruction initiates the interrupt sequence one cycle after it is decoded. It stores the 7 bytes of μP register contents in the stack.
2. After cycle 9, the μP goes into a *metamorphic* state by placing the address, data, and R/W lines in their high-impedance mode with VMA held LOW and BA HIGH.
3. The μP remains this way until an interrupt (IRQ or NMI) occurs.
4. In the fourth cycle following the interrupt line transition, the appropriate vector is fetched and the service routine is started during the sixth cycle.
5. The interrupt mask bit (I) of the CC register must be clear if an IRQ is expected; otherwise the system will hang up indefinitely.
6. When the interrupt does occur, it is processed more quickly since the registers have already been moved to the stack (6 cycles are required until the service routine starts, instead of 14).

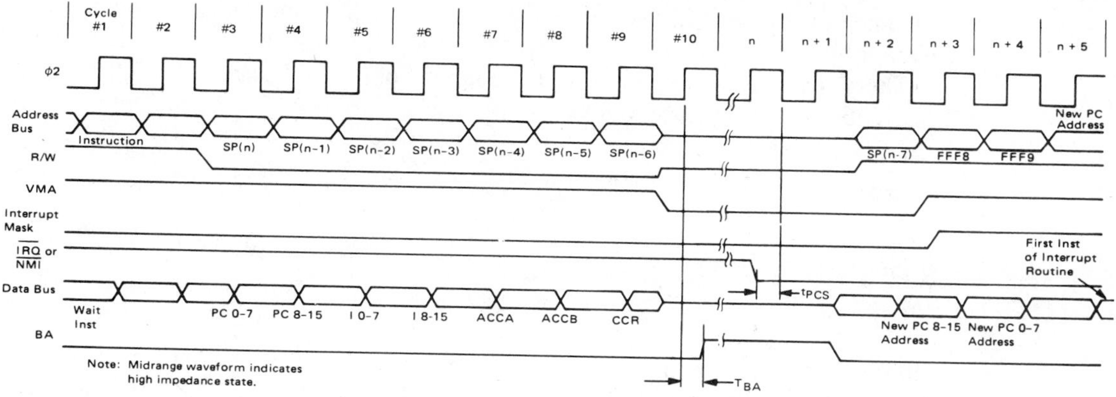

FIGURE 9-11 WAI (WAIT) instruction timing.

EXAMPLE 9-5

What does the following program accomplish?

(a) Main Program

Addr	Label	Mnemonic	Comments
0FFE		...	
0FFF		...	
1000		SWI	Go to SWI service routine
1001		LDA B #3	Resume program by loading B
		...	with 3,etc.

(b) SWI Service Routine

Addr	Label	Mnemonics	Comments
2000	SWISRV	INS	Increment stack pointer
2001		LDA A $40	Load A direct
2003		PSH A	Put A on stack
2004		RTI	Return to main program

SOLUTION

The main program encounters an SWI instruction that places the contents of the registers in the stack and then branches to the SWI service routine. The INS instruction increments the stack pointer so that it points to the Condition Code byte rather than the highest vacant stack location. The A accumulator is then loaded and pushed on the stack, causing the contents of memory location $40 to overwrite the contents of the CCR, as stored in the stack. The PSH A instruction also restores the stack pointer to the value it had after the SWI. The RTI now causes the 7 bytes following the stack pointer to be restored to the μP registers. At the end of the program, everything is exactly as it was when the program started, except that the CCR has been replaced by the contents of location \$40.

There are easier ways to change the contents of the CCR, such as using the TAP instructions, but this program has been presented to demonstrate the operation of the SWI and RTI instructions

9-8 THE 6828 PRIORITY INTERRUPT CONTROLLER (PIC)

In Section 9-5.5 we described a polling routine that is used to identify the interrupting device when an interrupt occurs. This is necessary since the interrupt pins for the peripheral ICs are connected together to the one IRQ pin. If a number of peripherals are involved, this polling could take a lot of time (for a μC system). For a system requiring faster response to any interrupt, the **6828** *priority interrupt controller* (**PIC**) is available. It generates a *modified address vector to point to the correct service routine* in response to prioritized interrupt lines. This hardware device is faster than the software polling routines it replaces. The block diagram and function table for the PIC are shown in Figs. 9-12a and 9-12b. Eight devices that are capable of interrupting can be connected to the designated lines ($\overline{\text{IN0}}$ through $\overline{\text{IN7}}$). When any device interrupts, by pulling one of these lines LOW, the $\overline{\text{IRQ}}$ line goes LOW and the vector addresses are translated by the PIC, as shown in Fig. 9-12c and explained in Example 9-6, to fetch the start location of the proper interrupt service routine.

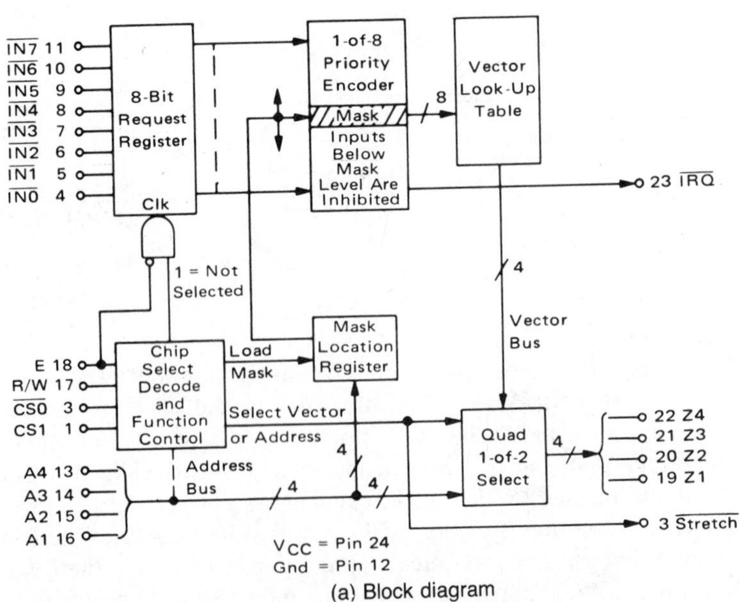

(a) Block diagram

FIGURE 9-12 The **6828** Priority Interrupt Controller (PIC).

Active Input		Output When Selected Z4	Z3	Z2	Z1	Equivalent to Bits 1-4 of B0, B1 . . . , B15 Hex Address	Address ROM Bytes Contain Address of:
Highest	$\overline{IN7}$	1	0	1	1	F F F 6 or 7	Priority 7 Routine
	$\overline{IN6}$	1	0	1	0	F F F 4 or 5	Priority 6 Routine
	$\overline{IN5}$	1	0	0	1	F F F 2 or 3	Priority 5 Routine
	$\overline{IN4}$	1	0	0	0	F F F 0 or 1	Priority 4 Routine
	$\overline{IN3}$	0	1	1	1	F F E E or F	Priority 3 Routine
	$\overline{IN2}$	0	1	1	0	F F E C or D	Priority 2 Routine
	$\overline{IN1}$	0	1	0	1	F F E A or B	Priority 1 Routine
Lowest	$\overline{IN0}$	0	1	0	0	F F E 8 or 9	Priority 0 Routine
	None	1	1	0	0	F F F 8 or 9	Default Routine*

*Default routine is the response to interrupt requests not generated by a prioritized input. The default routine may contain polling routines or may be an address in a loop for an interrupt driven system.

(b) Address vector for each interrupt line

FIGURE 9-12 (continued).

The use of the PIC in a system is shown in Fig. 9-13. The PIC is enabled by NANDing together the address lines required to address the top memory chip in the system and connecting the NAND gate output to $\overline{CS0}$ of the PIC. Note that lines A1 through A4 of the highest memory are connected to the Z outputs of the PIC, rather than directly to the address bus. When the PIC is enabled, it transforms the addresses as shown in the truth table of Fig. 9-12b. This effectively creates *eight new vector addresses* (located from $FFE8 to $FFF6). *A unique vector address points to the start of the service routine for each of the interrupting devices.*

If several devices interrupt at once, the PIC responds according to their priority. The interrupt lines from the various external devices are connected in order of importance. The device having the highest priority is connected to $\overline{IN7}$. Priority is usually determined by how much time is available to respond to an interrupt

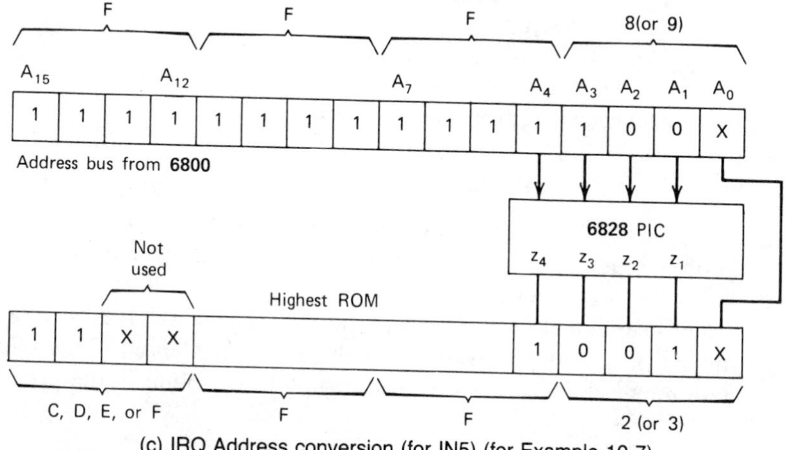

(c) IRQ Address conversion (for IN5) (for Example 10-7)

FIGURE 9-12 (continued).

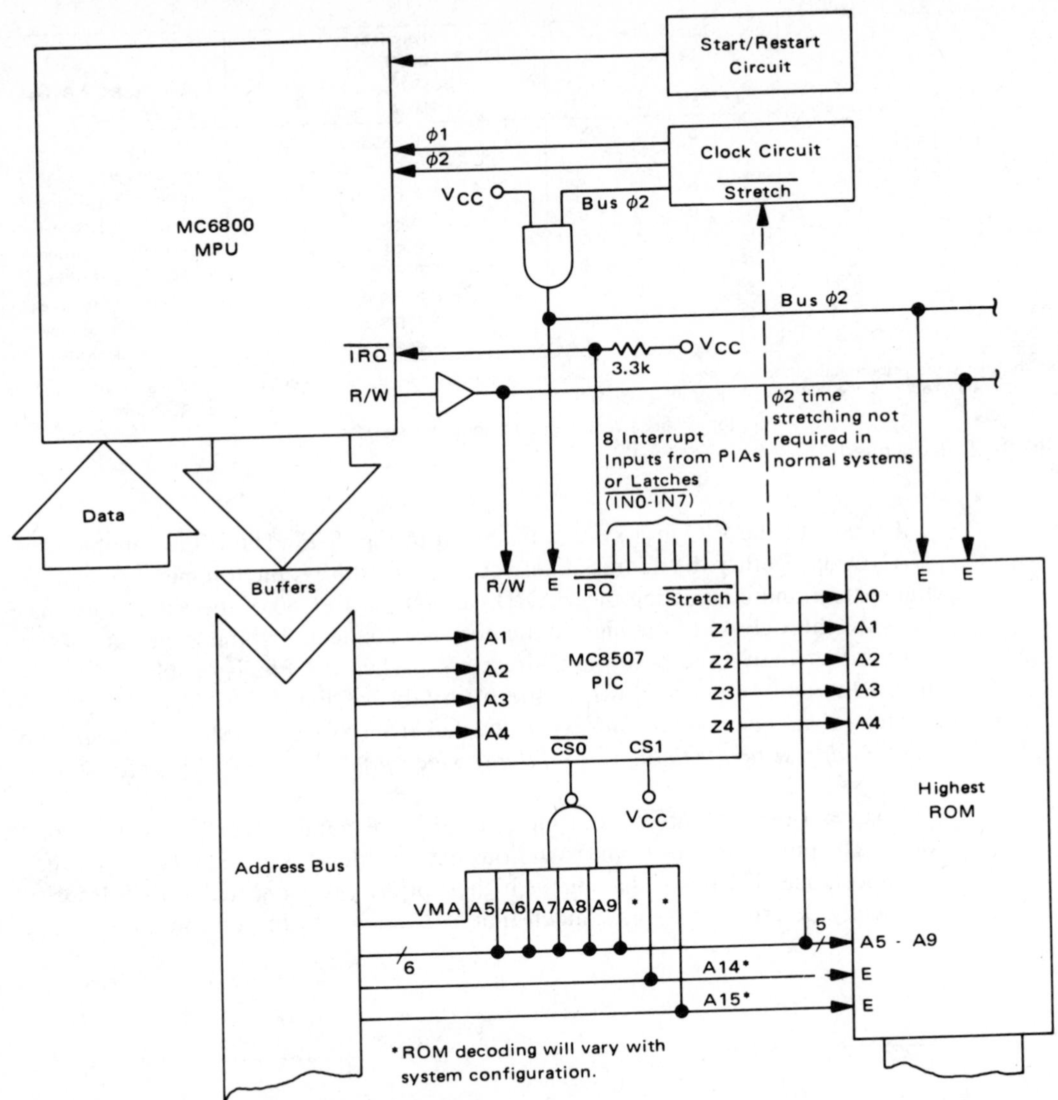

FIGURE 9-13 Typical **6800** system configuration (with **6828**).

before any data is lost. For example, a floppy disk that puts out data at 32 kilobytes per second must be serviced much more quickly than a TTY, which takes 100 ms per character.

The user can also set a mask in the PIC. If SET, devices with lower priority than the mask cannot interrupt until the mask is cleared. This allows the user to determine which devices may interrupt at any point in the program.

EXAMPLE 9-6

A device's interrupt line is connected to $\overline{IN5}$ (pin 9) of the PIC. What happens when the device interrupts?

SOLUTION
If the PIC mask allows this device to interrupt, it brings $\overline{IRQ}$ LOW. If the I bit of the CC register is clear (unmasked), the μP system responds by placing $FFF8 on the address bus. The PIC is enabled and translates bits A4, A3, A2, and A1 from 1100 to 1001. Since IN5 is LOW, as shown in Fig. 9-12c, the Z outputs place an address of $FFF2 on the lines of the highest ROM. (Note that bit 0 is not changed by the PIC and thus selects the odd or even byte of the vectors.) On the next cycle, $FFF9 is converted to $FFF3 by the PIC. Thus the interrupt vector is fetched from $FFF2 and $FFF3 to initiate the service routine for this device.

9-9 SOFTWARE TIMING LOOPS

It is often necessary for μPs to send timing signals at precise intervals to devices they control. These intervals can vary from a few microseconds to minutes or even hours.

Timing sequences and intervals can be controlled very precisely by a μP because it, in turn, is controlled by the highly accurate *quartz* crystal clock that generates its $\phi 1$ and $\phi 2$ signals. It must be noted, however, that software loops require the μP to be dedicated to the timing and this method will not work in a system that uses interrupts for other devices. An interrupt would, in effect, stop the count until the interrupt is serviced.

9-9.1 Construction of a Basic Timing Loop

The basis for μP timing control is the **timing loop**, which is simply a program loop that is designed to take a specific time for completion.

Since the number of cycles required by each instruction and the clock frequency are known, the time to traverse the loop can be calculated. Timing loops are generally constructed by loading the Index Register, an accumulator, or a memory location with the number of times the loop is to be traversed, decrementing it each time around the loop, and leaving the loop when it equals 0. A memory location or the accumulator allows up to 256 counts, but since X is a 16-bit register, it will handle up to 65,536 loops. Still longer times can be generated using a combination of the two.

EXAMPLE 9-7

Set up a program for a 0.1-s delay. Assume the basic μP clock is 1 MHz.

SOLUTION
The program for a 0.1-s delay is

Code	Mnemonic	Cycles	
CE 2710	**LDX #10000**		
09	**DEX**	4	timing loop
01	**NOP**	2	
26 FC	**BNE *−2**	4	
.. ..	**etc.**		

This timing program was constructed by realizing that the DEX and BNE had to be in the loop. Each of these requires four cycles. The NOP (two cycles) was added simply to pad the loop so it would contain a convenient number of cycles. This loop takes 10 cycles or 10^{-5} seconds, if a 1-MHz clock is used. Since the required delay is 10^{-1} seconds, the loop must be traversed 10,000 times. Therefore the number $(2710)_{16}$, which is the hex equivalent of the decimal 10,000, is loaded into X at the start of the program. The program branches back to the DEX instruction 10,000 times before reducing X to 0 and falling through. Note that the timing can easily be changed by changing the number loaded into X.

EXAMPLE 9-8

In Example 9-7, can the stack pointer be used instead of X?

SOLUTION
The SP cannot be used instead of X because Table 4-3 shows that decrementing the SP does not set the Z bit. Again, one must carefully determine which instructions set the flags for correct operation.

9-9.2 Longer Delays

Longer delays can be obtained by combining several loops. This can be done by using one timing loop as a subroutine and having a second timing loop jump to it during its execution. It is very convenient to have the subroutine take exactly 1 second, because this is often used as a timing base.

EXAMPLE 9-9

Write a 1-second timing loop subroutine.

SOLUTION

If the timing loop takes only 10 cycles as in Example 9-7, a 1-second delay using the X register alone is impossible because the largest number that can be loaded into X is 65,535. If, however, the timing loop is increased to 20 cycles, a 1-second delay is possible and the subroutine can be written as shown in Table 9-1.

The first step in the subroutine is to store X, in case the Index Register (X) is used by both the main program and the subroutine. Next X is loaded with the proper timing value and the main loop is entered. This loop has been padded so that it takes exactly 20 cycles, and it effectively decrements X once. When X becomes 0, the subroutine restores the value of X originally saved and exits. For a 1-second delay the 20-cycle loop should be traversed 50,000 times, minus provision for overhead.

The cycles in the subroutine that are not in the main loop are *overhead*. The overhead cycles have also been padded so that they also take exactly 20 cycles. These 20 cycles of overhead are compensated for by reducing the original X value by one, or from $(50{,}000)_{10}$ to $(49{,}999)_{10}$ or $(C350)_{16}$ to $(C34F)_{16}$.

Note: In order to keep the overhead to exactly 20 cycles the direct mode of STX is used, as is the extended mode of LDX. Both use five cycles. The program will have to be changed if the storage for X is at an adddress above $FF since the direct mode instruction cannot be used.

EXAMPLE 9-10

Set up a circuit to turn a light on for 1 hour and off for ½ hour cyclically.

TABLE 9-1 Program for Example 9-9

Code		Mnemonic	Cycles	
DF FØ		STX $FØ	5	
CE C34F		LDX #49999	3	
Ø8	LOOP	INX	4 \	20 cycle timing loop
Ø9		DEX	4	
Ø9		DEX	4	
Ø1		NOP	2	
Ø1		NOP	2	
26 F9		BNE LOOP	4 /	
FE ØØ FØ		LDX $ØØFØ	5	
Ø1		NOP	2	
39		RTS	5	

SOLUTION
One way to do this is to use the CA2 or CB2 line as an output to control the light. The program proceeds as follows.

1. Set CA2 HIGH, turning on the light.
2. Delay for 1 hour.
3. Set CA2 LOW, turning off the light.
4. Delay for ½ hour.
5. Return to step 1.

Table 9-2 shows the program. It starts at location \$10 and the PIA is at \$8000.

The 1-second timing routine (DLY1) can be used as described in Example 9-10. By loading $(3600)_{10}$ into X we achieve a 1-hour delay and with $(1800)_{10}$ we achieve a half-hour delay. Note that far more complex timing patterns can be generated by this method, and the timing can be changed in response to input signals to the μP by modifying the program.

9-9.3 Traffic Light Controllers

The program of Example 9-10 can obviously be adjusted to control traffic lights at road intersections where the lights must be alternately red and green. If the traffic lights merely cycle repetitively, electromechanical devices can do as well as μPs. Traffic flow, however, can be optimized using algorithms that consider the volume and speed of the traffic on the intersecting roads, the time of day, and other factors. Traffic control algorithms are becoming more complex and require the computational ability of the μP. Therefore, when traffic control goes beyond just switching the lights on and off and attempts to adjust the lights for optimum control, the intelligence and programmability of the μP are indispensable.

9-9.4 Real-Time Clocks

In many applications the μC must keep track of the time when certain events occurred or cause external events to occur at specific times. This timing can be

TABLE 9-2 Program for Example 9-10

Location	Code	Label	Mnemonic	Comments
10	86 3C	START	LDA A #3C	Store Control Word
12	B7 8001		STA A \$8001	to make CA2 go HIGH
15	CE 0E10		LDX #3600	Set hour delay
18	BD XXXX	LOOP1	JSR DLY1	JSR to 1-sec delay
1B	09		DEX	Decrement X
1C	26 FA		BNE LOOP1	Loop back to addr 18
1E	86 34		LDA A #34	Store Control Word
20	B7 8001		STA A #8001	to make CA2 go LOW
23	CE 0708		LDX #1800	Set half-hour delay
26	BD XXXX	LOOP2	JSR DLY1	JSR to 1-sec delay
29	09		DEX	Decrement X
2A	26 FA		BNE LOOP2	Rtn to location 26
2C	20 E2		BRA START	Rtn to location 10

generated internally by using software, by an external real-time clock, or by a timer IC such as the **6840** (discussed in the following sections.)

To generate a real-time clock using software, a timing loop (see Section 9-9.2) should be written with the time interval set to a value appropriate to the particular problem. One second and one minute are typical time values. Each time the timing loop expires, it increments a memory location or pair of memory locations. The numbers in the memory locations can be used as elapsed time or, if the locations are preset to the current time, the numbers will remain current and thus provide a real-time clock.

EXAMPLE 9-11

It is necessary to record the time a person passes through a gate, such as at an airport, during the course of an hour. The time of each entry is to be recorded in memory, starting at $A0. Two memory locations are used for each event. The 8 bits of the upper location are divided into two BCD digits that represent the minutes of the hour and the lower location has two BCD digits that represent the seconds. Describe how to implement this sytem.

SOLUTION

The following steps are necessary:

1. A photocell and light beam detector can be used to determine when a person enters the gate. Every time the light beam is interrupted, the photocell puts a pulse on the CA1 or CB1 line of the PIA, which sets bit 7 of the PIA Control/Status register.
2. The X and SP registers and the PIA control register must be initialized before the program can start.
3. Since the time storage is 16 bits long, a pair of memory locations must be reserved for the clock.
4. A 1-second subroutine must be written (see Example 9-9). Each time it expires, it increments the locations that represent the clock. Note that the clock must be set up so that each time the Least Significant Digit (LSD) of the seconds reaches 10, it must return to 0 and increment the Most Significant Digit (MSD) of the seconds, and when the MSD of the seconds reaches 6, it must increment the LSD of the minutes, etc.
5. Bit 7 of the PIA Control Register can now be monitored or polled. This can be done within the 1-second timing loop.
6. Each time bit 7 goes HIGH the contents of the clock can be transferred to memory starting at $A0.
7. At the end of the hour, memory will contain a list of the times people entered the gate.

The code for this program is too long to be presented here, but the student should be capable of writing it.

9-9.5 Hardware Real-Time Clocks

If hardware *counters* such as the **14566B** IC or programmable timer-counters such as the **6840** are used, they remove or greatly reduce the involvement of the μP in time-keeping and thus the μP can do other tasks. Interrupts can then also be used without affecting the time.

Hardware real-time clocks can be fabricated in many ways and interfaced to the μC so that the time information is available as needed. One way is to use an electric clock motor that closes a mechanical contact every minute. This obviously can be connected to CA1 of a PIA and used to increment a software routine. In these days of solid-state electronics, a more reliable method would be to use digital counter ICs that are driven by the 60-Hz power line. A variety of circuits is possible using divide-by-60 counters, one of which is shown in Fig. 9-14; the resulting binary words must be brought into the μC system and processed with some type of clock program.

9-9.6 The 146818A Real-Time Clock IC (RTC)

A more appropriate way for μC designers to make a clock is to use one of the many large-scale integrated (LSI) timer circuits that are proliferating in the industry. These devices are simple to use because they are self-contained and connect directly to the μC bus. Outside the LSI IC itself, a quartz crystal is all that is needed. One such device is the **MC146818A** real-time clock/RAM. It generates seconds, minutes, hours, days, date, month, and year as well as alarms or periodic rates. Since it uses low-power CMOS technology, it can also be battery powered to keep time in the event of power failures. A 64-byte RAM is included with 14 bytes for the clock and 50 bytes for the user's data. The time data is simply picked up in byte form on the data bus by a suitable program. This timer is thus very much like any peripheral chip in the **6800** family and is easily incorporated in a system. [See Application Note 894 (AN894) and the **146818A** Data Sheet referenced in Section 9-15.]

EXAMPLE 9-12

Each time an event occurs (a switch being thrown or a person entering a room, for example) the time of this event must be recorded in three consecutive locations in memory in the following format:

HH MM SS

where HH are two decimal digits (in one memory location) that represent the hour of the event, MM represents another byte for minutes, and SS is for seconds. Assume the event interrupts the μP. Describe the routine required to service this event

a. If a real-time clock, such as that shown in Fig. 9-14, is available.

b. If a real-time clock is not available.

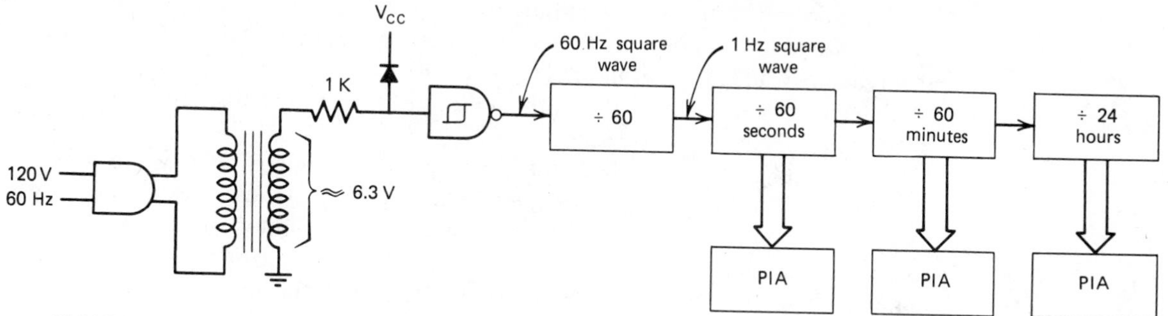

FIGURE 9-14 A real-time clock (using 60 Hz).

SOLUTION[1]

For either case, an area in memory must be set aside to hold the time data, and a pointer to this area must also be stored at a given location in memory. The starting address of the interrupt service routine is written into $FFF8 and $FFF9 and the program branches to it when the interrupt occurs.

a. With a real-time clock available, the interrupt routine does the following:

1. Loads the pointer into X.
2. Reads the PIA ports sequentially and stores seconds, minutes, and hours in memory (incrementing the pointer each time).
3. Stores the incremented pointer back in memory to await the next interrupt.
4. Returns from interrupt.

Note that we are not concerned about the fact that the Index Register has been used by the interrupt routine. It is restored to the value it had before the interrupt by the RTI instruction.

b. If a real-time hardware clock is not available and interrupts are not used, the main program can generate a 1-second timing loop (see Example 9-9). This timing loop must control three locations in memory that each contain two decimal digits (packed BCD) that represent the real-time equivalent of seconds, minutes, and hours. When the timing loop expires, the program must

1. Increment the seconds locations.
2. Execute a Decimal Adjust Accumulator (DAA) instruction (to keep the byte in BCD).
3. If seconds = 60, clear seconds and increment minutes location.
4. DAA.
5. If minutes = 60, clear minutes and increment hours.
6. DAA.
7. If hours = 24, clear hours.

[1]Part b of this example was run as a laboratory exercise at R.I.T. A debounced switch was connected to a PIA, and each switch throw became an event.

The main program is shown in the flowchart of Fig. 9-15. When an interrupt occurs the main program stops and the interrupt routine loads the real time from memory and stores it in the list area. The list pointer is incremented and the interrupt routine terminates with an RTI. (See Section 9-10.10 for a similar program.)

One subtle point remains. If the main program is interrupted while it is incrementing the time, it may be interrupted when it has just finished incrementing the seconds but has not yet incremented the minutes. If the interrupt routine stores the time, the minutes and seconds will not match. Note that numbers like 4A could also be stored in the list if the interrupt occurred between the increment and the DAA instructions.

To prevent these possibilities when using IRQ, one can use an SEI to *mask* interrupts before the incrementing part of the routine and then *clear* the interrupt flag (CLI) to permit interrupts when returning to the timing loop, as shown in Fig. 9-15. This, however, is not a practical solution for software clocks if any other IRQ interrupt (to service a printer, perhaps) is allowed. This would cause the software clock to lose time. Therefore, to implement a reliable clock it is necessary to avoid all interrupts or use a hardware clock as described in Section 9-9.6, or in the following section.

9-10 INTERRUPTS AND TIMING

The difficulty with software timing loops as used in part b of Example 9-12 is that they use the processor continuously and do not allow the computer to do other useful work. One simple solution to this problem is to construct a hardware clock that interrupts the computer periodically (once a second, for example). The computer can respond to this interrupt by incrementing a set of memory locations that maintain clock time as in Example 9-12 and then return to its main program. In this way, the main program has real time always available but does not have the task of updating the clock. This is discussed in detail in Section 9-9.6. Another solution is to use a special *counter/timer* IC such as the **6840** described in the next section. This IC can be used to keep track of time intervals since it counts without the μP being involved and only has to interrupt the μC periodically. It uses the system clock instead of a dedicated quartz crystal. It also has other uses besides time-keeping. Most μC manufacturers produce such an IC.

9-10.1 The 6840 Programmable Timer Module (PTM)

The **6800** family of components includes the 28-pin **MC6840** NMOS IC. It consists of three independent software-controllable 16-bit timing counters. They can be used to cause precise delays, count events, or produce timing signals based on the internal ($\phi 2$) or an external clock signal. Figure 9-16 is the block diagram of the **MC6840** PTM.

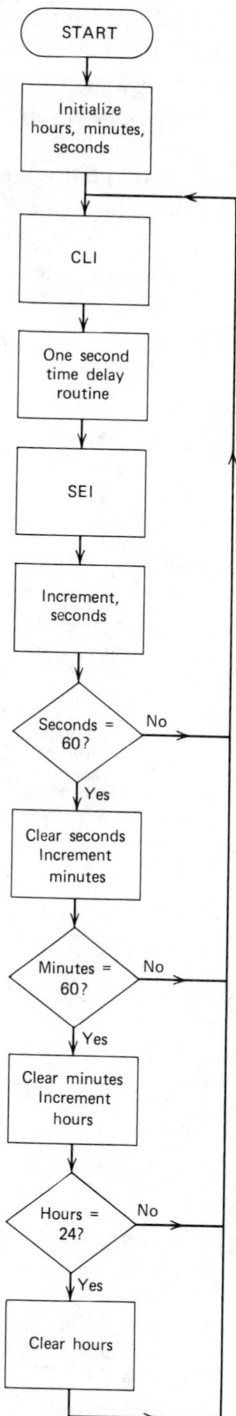

FIGURE 9-15 Flowchart for the timing routine of Example 9-12b.

Figure 9-16 shows that each section has an external clock input ($\overline{C}$), a gate input ($\overline{G}$), and an output ($\overline{O}$). Each section can be used alone or cascaded (by connecting the output of one section to the input of the next) for longer time delays. When used for timing (or delays), the cascading produces intervals, which can be measured in days or even years.

The three counter/timers are identical except for a divide-by-8 prescaler that is part of timer 3 and a minor difference in the function of bit 0 of the control words.

Each timer has three 8-bit registers associated with it: a control register and two 8-bit counter/latches. The PTM has a total of 15 registers including a common STATUS register. These are addressed as shown in Table 9-3.

The bits of the control register select the following:

1. Modes
2. Choices of internal ($\phi 2$) or external clock
3. IRQ (masked or unmasked)
4. Output (enabled or not)
5. Square wave or variable duty cycle

Because of all these options, many applications for this device are possible.

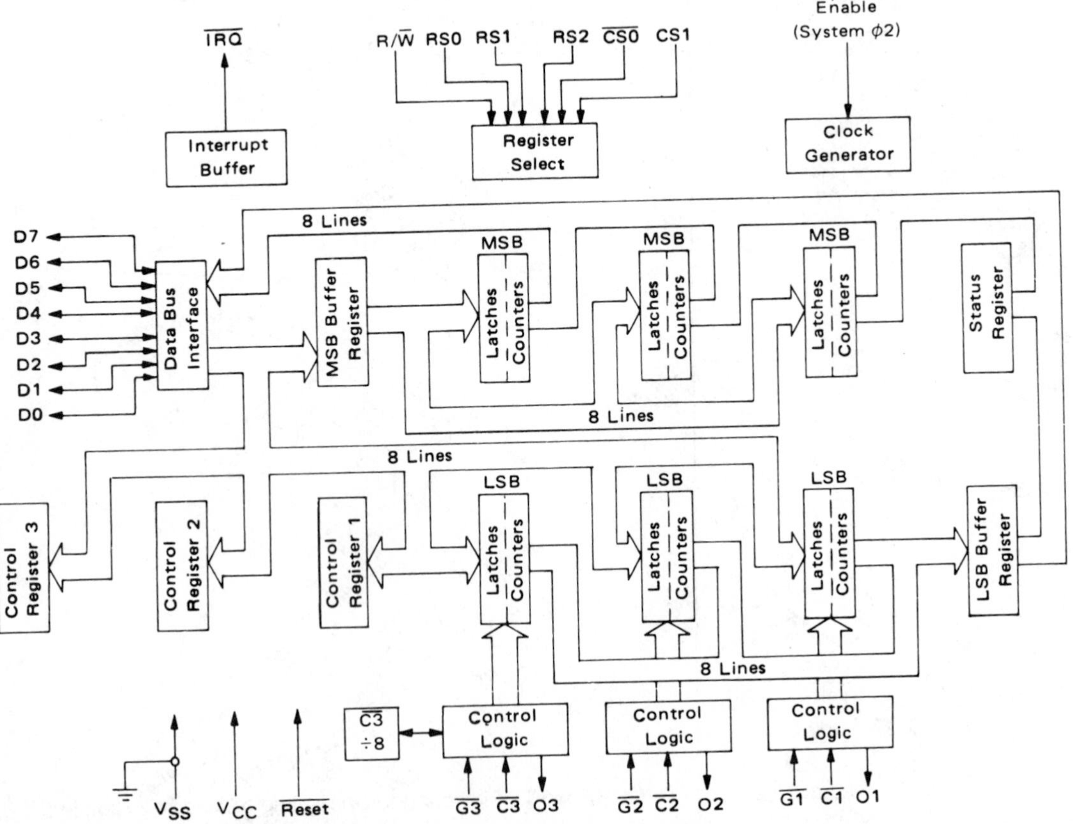

FIGURE 9-16 6840 Programmable Timer Module (PTM) Block Diagram.

TABLE 9-3 The **6840** PTM Register Selection

Register Select Inputs			Operations	
RS2	RS1	RS0	$R/\overline{W} = 0$	$R/\overline{W} = 1$
0	0	0	CR20 = 0 Write Control Register #3 CR20 = 1 Write Control Register #1	No Operation
0	0	1	Write Control Register #2	Read Status Register
0	1	0	Write MSB Buffer Register	Read Timer #1 Counter
0	1	1	Write Timer #1 Latches	Read LSB Buffer Register
1	0	0	Write MSB Buffer Register	Read Timer #2 Counter
1	0	1	Write Timer #2 Latches	Read LSB Buffer Register
1	1	0	Write MSB Buffer Register	Read Timer #3 Counter
1	1	1	Write Timer #3 Latches	Read LSB Buffer Register

9-10.2 The Hardware Interface to the 6840

Figure 9-17 shows the pinout of the **6840** PTM and how it is connected to a **6800.** Its interface consists of:

1. An 8-bit bidirectional data bus, D0–D7.
2. Three Register Select inputs (RS0, RS1, RS2). These select the register being accessed. Generally they are connected to A0, A1, and A2, the three LSBs of the address lines.
3. A READ/WRITE ($R/\overline{W}$) line.
4. Two Chip Select lines ($\overline{CS0}$ and CS1). The **6840** is selected only when $\overline{CS0} = 0$ and $CS1 = 1$. Two CS lines simplify chip selection.
5. The enable clock. This is usually the system's $\phi 2$ clock. The enable pin must be pulsed HIGH during a READ or WRITE to the **6840**.
6. A RESET input. A LOW signal on this pin resets the timer IC. It is usually connected to the system reset line.
7. An IRQ. This is an output from the **6840** that can be used to interrupt the μP controlling it.

The pins listed above communicate with the μP. In addition, there are the CLOCKS, GATES, and OUTPUTS for each timer (C1, C2, C3; G1, G2, G3; and O1, O2, O3).

9-10.3 General System Operation

Table 9-3 relates the nine system registers to the eight combinations of register select inputs. The **6840** generally operates as follows:

1. The Control Registers are set up by the initialization routine for the required function (see Section 9-10.4).
2. The most significant byte of the count is entered into the MSB buffer register.
3. The least significant byte of the count is entered into the timer latches. This action enters the entire 16-bit count into one counter/timer of Fig. 9-16.

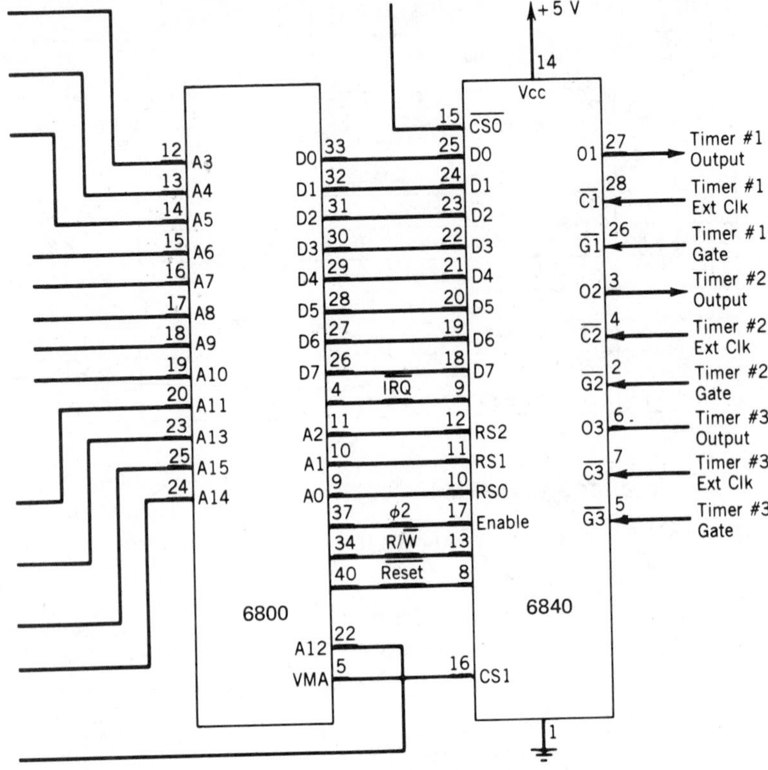

FIGURE 9-17 A PTM (**6840**) connected to a **6800**μP.

4. When the **6840** starts operation, each counter counts down from the number in its latches to 0. When 0 is reached, the number in the latches is reloaded into the counter and the down-counting continues.

EXAMPLE 9-13

A μP system has no devices in the address range of \$4000–\$7FFF. How can a **6840** be added to this system?

SOLUTION

Since these addresses all have A15 = 0 and A14 = 1, A15 can be connected to $\overline{\text{CS0}}$ and A14 to CS1. RS0, RS1, and RS2 would then be connected to A0, A1, and A2, respectively. Adding the R/$\overline{\text{W}}$ line and connecting ϕ2 to the enable pin completes the interface. The **6840** will then respond to any set of eight contiguous addresses in the range. Most commonly the addresses \$4000–\$4007 will be used to select the registers.

EXAMPLE 9-14

The 16-bit number $2ABC is to be loaded into the counter/latches for timer 2. How can this be done? Assume the **6840** is at addresses $4000–$4007.

SOLUTION
Examination of Table 9-3 shows that the MSB for register 2 is at $4004 and the timer 2 latches are at $4005. The writing can be accomplished by the following program:

```
LDA A   #$2A
STA A   $4004
LDA A   #$BC
STA A   $4005
```

Note that the MSB buffer must be written first, followed by the timer 2 latches, or nothing will get in.

A simpler program is

```
LDX  #$2ABC
STX  $4004
```

9-10.4 Programming the Control Registers

Each of the three counter/timers has an 8-bit control register associated with it. The bits in the control register determine the action of the counter/timer. Table 9-3 shows the function of each bit. Bit 0 of each control register has a slightly different function.

In Control Register 1, bit 0 determines whether the counters are held preset (see Section 9-10.5) or are allowed to operate.

Bit 0 of Control Register 2 is a *steering* bit. Table 9-3 shows that Control Register 2 has a unique address (RS0 = 1, RS1 = RS2 = 0), but Control Registers 1 and 3 have the same address (RS0 = RS1 = RS2 = 0). A WRITE to this address will access Control Register 1 if bit 0 of Control Register 2 is a 1, but will address Control Register 3 if bit 0 of Control Register 2 is a 0. This allows the **6840** to place nine registers within eight addresses.

Bit 0 of Control Register 3 determines whether the input to Control Register 3 is *prescaled* by a divide-by-8 counter. If bit 0 of Control Register 3 is 1, it takes eight clock pulses to produce one output on register 3.

All the other bits of the control registers have identical functions, as shown in Table 9-4. They are as follows.

Bit 1. Internal/external clock This bit determines whether the internal clock (coming in on the E pin) or an external clock (tied to the input of the counter) will pulse that counter.

TABLE 9-4 Function of Each Bit in the **6840** Control Register

CR10 Internal Reset Bit	CR20 Control Register Address Bit	CR30 Timer #3 Clock Control
0 All timers allowed to operate	0 CR#3 may be written	0 T3 $\overline{\text{Clock}}$ is not prescaled
1 All timers held in preset state	1 CR#1 may be written	1 T3 $\overline{\text{Clock}}$ is prescaled by ÷8

Bit	Function
CRX1*	Timer #X $\overline{\text{Clock}}$ Source
0	TX uses external clock source on $\overline{\text{CX}}$ input
1	TX uses Enable clock
CRX2	Timer #X Counting Mode Control
0	TX configured for normal (16-bit) counting mode
1	TX configured for dual 8-bit counting mode
CRX3 CRX4 CRX5	Timer #X Counter Mode and Interrupt Control (See Table 3).
CRX6	Timer #X Interrupt Enable
0	Interrupt Flag masked on $\overline{\text{IRQ}}$
1	Interrupt Flag enabled to $\overline{\text{IRQ}}$
CRX7	Timer #X Counter Output Enable
0	TX Output masked on output OX
1	TX Output enabled on output OX

*Control Register for Timer 1, 2, or 3, Bit 1.

Bit 2 This bit determines whether the counter operates in 16-bit or dual 8-bit mode (see Section 9-10.7).

Bits 3 and 4 If bit 3 is a 0, bit 4 determines whether a WRITE into the timer latches will initialize them. If bit 4 is a 0, the timers will initialize on a WRITE to the counter/latches, but if bit 4 is a 1, a WRITE will not initialize it. If bit 3 is a 1, the timer operates in either frequency comparison or pulse width comparison modes, depending on bit 4. These modes are seldom used and will not be discussed further.

Bit 5. Single-shot/continuous mode This bit determines whether the counter will count down to 0 and then stop (single-shot mode) or reinitialize itself immediately and resume counting (continuous mode).

Bit 6 This bit determines whether interrupts are enabled. If enabled, the **6840** will interrupt when the count reaches 0.

Bit 7 This bit determines whether the outputs are masked or enabled.

9-10.5 Resets

There are two types of RESETS on the **6840**, a hardware RESET and a software RESET.

A *hardware* RESET occurs when the RESET pin on the **6840** is brought to ground. A hardware RESET causes the following events:

1. All bits of all control registers will be 0, except for bit 0 of Control Register 1, which will be 1 (counters held preset).
2. All counters and latches will be loaded with the maximum count ($FF).

The **6840** will be completely frozen in this position until the hardware RESET is removed.

A *software* RESET is caused by setting bit 0 of Control Register 1 to a 1. The counters and latches can be written to and read during a software RESET, but they will not count. The RESET condition can be removed by changing bit 0 of Control Register 1 to a 0.

9-10.6 Counter Initialization

A counter is initialized by transferring data from the latches into the counter. This can happen in one of four ways:

1. The counter is released and allowed to count by changing bit 0 of Control Register 0 from 1 to 0, with the gate LOW.
2. The gate associated with the counter is opened by placing a HIGH-to-LOW (↓) transition on it (bit 0 of CR0 = 0).
3. A write to the latches will initialize the counter if bits 3 and 4 of the Control Register are 0.
4. The counter is counted down to 0 in continuous mode. It then reinitializes itself.

9-10.7 The 16-Bit and Dual 8-Bit Modes

Each counter of the **6840** can operate in either 16-bit mode or dual 8-bit mode, depending on bit 2 of its Control Register. The top part of Fig. 9-18 (CRX2 = 0)

CONTINUOUS MODE
(CRX3 = 0, CRX5 = 0)

Control Register			Initialization/Output Waveforms
CRX2	CRX4	Counter Initialization	*Timer Output (OX) (CRX7 = 1)
0	0	$\overline{G}$↓+W+R	(N+1)(T) (N+1)(T) (N+1)(T); V_{OH}, V_{OL}; t_o TO TO TO
0	1	$\overline{G}$↓+R	
1	0	$\overline{G}$↓+W+R	(L+1)(M+1)(T) (L+1)(M+1)(T); V_{OH}; (L)(T) (L)(T) V_{OL}; t_o TO TO
1	1	$\overline{G}$↓+R	

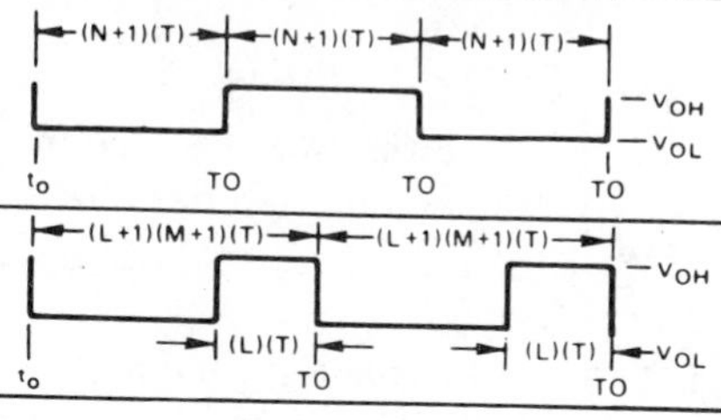

$\overline{G}$↓ = Negative transition of $\overline{Gate}$ input.
W = Write Timer Latches Command.
R = Timer Reset (CR10 = 1 or External $\overline{Reset}$ = 0)
N = 16-Bit Number in Counter Latch.
L = 8-Bit Number in LSB Counter Latch.
M = 8-Bit Number in MSB Counter Latch.
T = Clock Input Negative Transitions to Counter.
t_o = Counter Initialization Cycle.
TO = Counter Time Out (All Zero Condition).

*All time intervals shown above assume the the $\overline{Gate}$ ($\overline{G}$) and $\overline{Clock}$ ($\overline{C}$) signals are synchronized to Enable (System $\phi 2$) with the specified setup and hold time requirements.

FIGURE 9-18 Continuous Operating Mode of the **6840**.

shows the operation in 16-bit mode, where N is the 16-bit number entered into the counter/latches. If the counter/latches are divided into a Most Significant Byte M and a Least Significant Byte L, then N = 256 × M + L.

EXAMPLE 9-15

A counter has the number $0403 set into its latches. How does it count down in 16-bit mode?

SOLUTION
The counter counts down as follows:

```
0403
0402
0401
0400
03FF
03FE
 .
 .
 .
0001
0000
0403
 .
 .
 .
```

Note that when the counter gets to 0 it will then be reloaded with the number in the counter latches ($0403).

In dual 8-bit mode, the L counter resets to the LSB value of L rather than to $FF. The output waveform for dual 8-bit mode is shown in the lower part of Fig. 9-18 (CRX2 = 1).

EXAMPLE 9-16

Repeat Example 9-15 if the counter is in dual 8-bit mode.

SOLUTION
The counter now counts

```
0403
```

0402

0401

0400

0303

0302

.

.

.

0001

0000

0403

EXAMPLE 9-17

If counter 3 has 0403 loaded into its latches and it is driven by a 1-MHz clock on its E line, sketch the output if the Control Word for Register 3 is

a. \$83.
b. \$86.

SOLUTION
(See Fig. 9-24 for a similar solution.)

a. A Control Register containing \$83 means that

1. The outputs are enabled.
2. The divide-by-8 prescaler is on (since this is counter 3).
3. The internal clock (1 MHz) is selected.
4. The counter is in the 16-bit mode.

In 16-bit mode $N = 256_{10} \times M + L = 256_{10} \times 4 + 3 = 1027_{10}$.

Figure 9-18 shows that the output is down for N + 1 counts and up for N + 1 counts. Because of the prescaler it takes eight inputs to produce one count, so each count takes 8 μs. Thus the counter is up and down for $(N + 1)T = 1028 \times 8\ \mu s = 8.224$ ms. This output is shown in Fig. 9-19a.

b. If the Control Word contains \$86, it means

1. The prescaler is not invoked.
2. The internal clock is again selected.
3. The counter operates in dual 8-bit mode.
4. The outputs are enabled.

From Fig. 9-18 we see that the total output time is $(M + 1)(L + 1)T = 5 \times 4 \times 1\ \mu s = 20\ \mu s$ and the output is HIGH for $L \times T$ or 3 μs. The output waveform is shown in Fig. 9-19b.

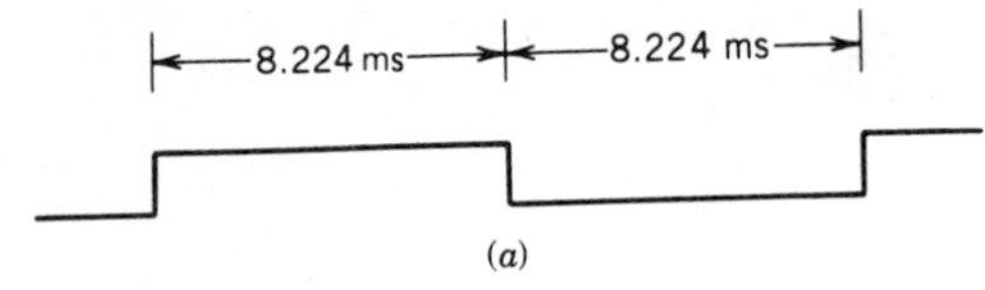

(a)

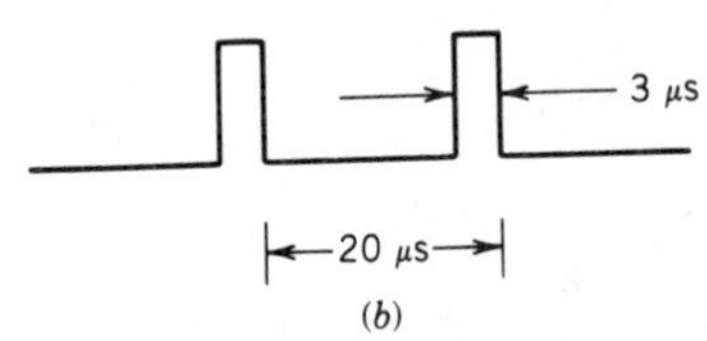

(b)

FIGURE 9-19 Waveforms for Example 9-17.

9-10.8 Single-Shot Mode

In single-shot mode (Control Register bit 3 = 0, Control Register bit 5 = 1), the **6840** acts like a monostable multivibrator or one shot; in response to a trigger or initialization pulse, it produces a single output pulse for a predetermined time period.

The single-shot waveforms are shown in Fig. 9-20. In 16-bit mode the output is LOW for one clock pulse following initialization and HIGH for N clock cycles thereafter. It then stays LOW until another trigger or initialization event occurs. In dual 8-bit mode, Fig. 9-20 shows that the output is LOW for (L + 1) (M + 1) − L pulses and HIGH for L pulses. The output will then stay LOW until initialization occurs.

Initialization or triggering occurs when

1. The RESET is released.
2. The gate goes LOW.
3. Bit 4 of the Control Register is 0 and there is a WRITE into the counter/latches. The initialization conditions are also shown in Fig. 9-20.

A negative-going signal on the gate input initializes the **6840**, but the gate need not remain LOW in single-shot mode. It can go HIGH without affecting the output.

EXAMPLE 9-18

A **6840** is located at addresses $4000–$4007. How should it be initialized to provide a 520-μs pulse in response to a trigger on gate 1? Assume the internal clock is being used and is 1 μs.

SOLUTION

Since 520 pulses are required and $(520)_{10} = (0208)_{16}$, the counter can be initialized by the following program:

```
LDA A  #1        Set up register 2 to point to register 1.
STA A  $4001
LDA A  #$A2      Send the control word (output enabled, single-shot
                 16-bit mode, internal clock) to Control Register 1.
STA A  $4000
LDX    #$208     Store the count in register 1's latches.
STX    $4002
```

The counter will now produce a 520-μs pulse in response to a negative edge on the gate.

9-10.9 Other Applications of the 6840 PTM

The **6840** PTM can be used to provide timed interrupts for clocking or other uses, and while the timer is counting, thousands or even millions of other instructions can be executed. The interrupt features of the **6840** in conjunction with those of μPs or μCs in the **6800** family (e.g., **6801**, **6805**, or **6909**) make this possible since the PTM time-out function can be serviced at precisely the right time while only briefly interrupting other tasks.

EXAMPLE 9-19

Provide a real-time clock function for use in a control system to display the time each second or to provide scheduling for industrial processes. Use the **6840** PTM and show its connections as well as programs to provide these functions.

SOLUTION

Single-shot mode
(CRX3 = 0, CRX7 = 1, CRX5 = 1)

Control register		*Initialization/output waveforms*	
CRX2	*CRX4*	*Counter initialization*	*Timer output (OX)*
0	0	$\overline{G}\downarrow + W + R$	(L + 1)(M + 1)(T); (L + 1)(M + 1)(T); (L)(T); t_0; TO; TO
0	1	$\overline{G}\downarrow + R$	
1	0	$\overline{G}\downarrow + W + R$	(N + 1)(T); (N + 1)(T); (N)(T); t_0; TO; TO
1	1	$\overline{G}\downarrow + R$	

FIGURE 9-20 Single-shot Operating Mode.

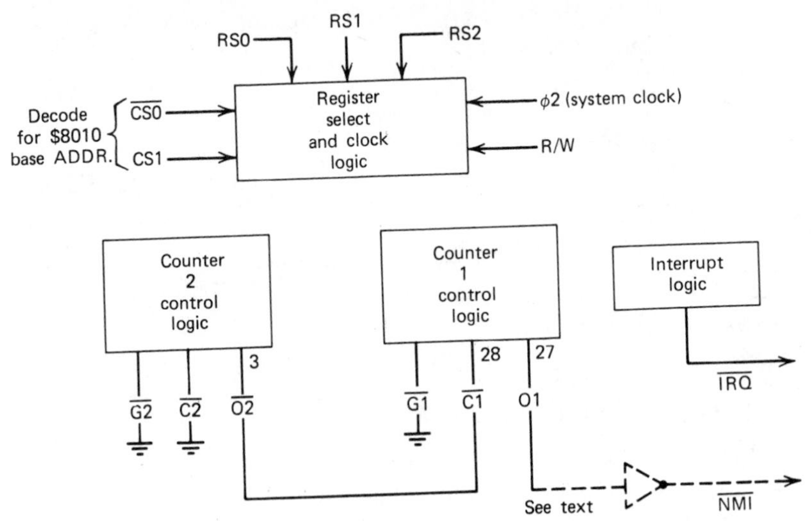

FIGURE 9-21 Connections for the **6840** PTM as a 1-second timer.

Figure 9-21 shows a block diagram of the **6840** with two counter sections connected in cascade to provide an interrupt (IRQ) every second. The assembly language routine needed to initialize the timers for this application is shown in Fig. 9-22. Since counter 2 is programmed to use the internal phase 2 enable signal generated by the system crystal clock, the only connection required is to its output (φ2—pin 3). This output is connected to the clock input (C1—pin 28) of counter 1. Counter 1 is programmed for external clocking to use that signal and provides the interrupt when it times out.

Note that 32 bits are available (two 16-bit sections) for this application. The 1-second time delay is provided by writing the proper counts into the counters. The product of these is equal to the frequency of the φ2 clock.

The following example will help the reader to understand several of the continuous-mode timing functions, however. Figure 9-23 shows the purpose of each bit in the control registers. The formatting of the two control words used in this example is shown in Fig. 9-24.

As explained in the **6840** Data Sheet (see Section 9-15), the control registers and latches must be written in the prescribed sequence, as shown in the routine of Fig. 9-22. Register 2 bit 0 must be set to 1 so that Control Register 1 is addressable (at

```
                   *
F039 86 83         INIT    LDA A   #$83       SET OUTPUT,INT CLK, SLCT REG
F03B B7 8011               STA A   $8011      WRITE TO REG 2
F03E CE 270F               LDX     #10000-1
F041 FF 8014               STX     $8014      SET COUNT FOR CTR 2
F044 CE 0031       INIT1   LDX     #50-1      "     "     "    "  1
F047 FF 8012               STX     $8012
F04A 86 40                 LDA A   #$40
F04C B7 8010               STA A   $8010      UNMASK IRQ AND ENABLE CTRS
F04F 39                    RTS
                   *
```

FIGURE 9-22 Initialization routine for the PTM in Example 9-19.

7	6	5	4	3	2	1	0		Register 1	Register 2	Register 3
X	X	X	X	X	X	X	↕	0	All Timers Operate	Reg #3 May Be Written	T3 $\overline{\text{Clk}}$ $\div 1$
								1	All Timers Preset	Reg #1 May Be Written	T3 $\overline{\text{Clk}}$ $\div 8$

7	6	5	4	3	2	1	0		
X	X	X	X	X	X	↕	X	0	External Clock ($\overline{\text{CX}}$ Input)
								1	Internal Clock (Enable)
X	X	X	X	X	↕	X	X	0	Normal (16 Bit) Count Mode
								1	Dual 8 Bit Count Mode
X	X	X	↕	0	X	X	X	0	Write To Timers Will Initialize
								1	Write To Timers Will Not Initialize
X	X	X	↕	1	X	X	X	0	Frequency Comparison
								1	Pulse Width Comparison
X	X	↕	X	0	X	X	X	0	Continuous Operating Mode
								1	Single-Shot Mode
X	X	↕	X	1	X	X	X	0	Interrupt If Less Than Counter Time Out
								1	Interrupt If Greater Than Counter Time Out
X	↕	X	X	X	X	X	X	0	Interrupt Flag Masked ($\overline{\text{IRQ}}$)
								1	Interrupt Flag Enabled ($\overline{\text{IRQ}}$)
↕	X	X	X	X	X	X	X	0	Timer Output Masked
								1	Timer Output Enabled

FIGURE 9-23 **6840** Control register programming.

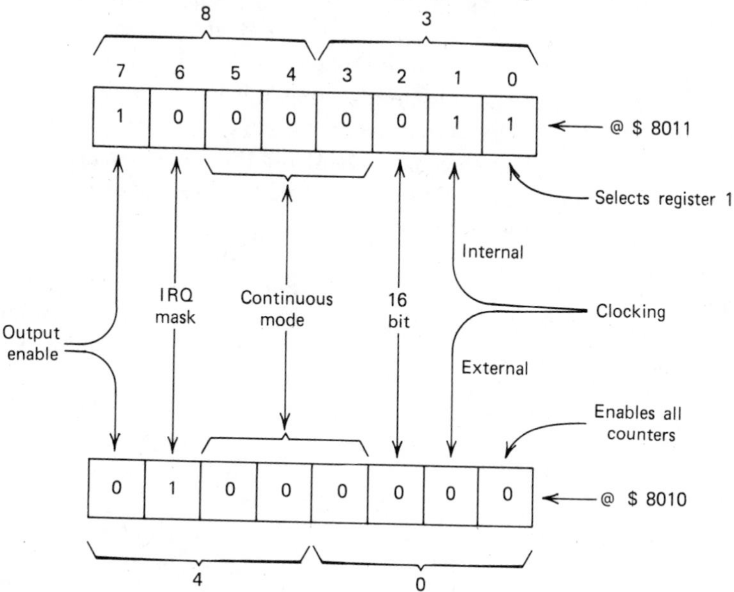

FIGURE 9-24 Control word formats

$8010). Register 1 bit 0, when reset to 0, *enables* all counters. The counters are initialized in some cases by writing to the latches as determined by bit 4. It is interesting to note how the values in the MSB and LSB registers determine the timer's count. When a number is entered and decrementing starts, it will count down to zero (called time-out) and, in the continuous mode, will reinitialize (reload the latches) and continue. This requires one cycle, so the number used must be one less than required. Another factor in this application is that the clock input (C1) of counter 1 decrements only after it sees a negative-going edge of the output signal from counter 2. This means that counter 2 must time-out twice before each counter 1 decrement occurs. It does not matter which of the two values is placed in the first counter, but in the program of Fig. 9-22 the larger number was used in counter 2. Since a "divide by" 1,000,000 is required with a 1-MHz crystal clock, it was elected to divide by 10,000 and then by 100. Hex 2710 is equal to 10,000. This was decreased by 1 to 270F. As explained above, this actually requires two time-outs and results in a negative-going signal on C1 every 20 ms (see Fig. 9-25). Therefore, instead of dividing by 100 ($64) in counter 1, a ratio of 50 (− 1) is used (which the assembler converts to $31). This results in an interrupt every second and has crystal-controlled accuracy just as available in "quartz" watches.

9-10.10 Real-Time Display

In the previous example, we showed how an interrupt is generated every second and now we show how to use it. One way is shown in the complete program of Fig. 9-26.

This program includes an *interrupt service routine* that updates and *prints* the time every second. The program is started at the "SET" routine, which first prints "HH:MM:SS AM" and then provides for the correct time to be entered. It then initializes the timer. Note also that the IRQ vector is written into location $FFF8 and $FFF9. This was done in this case since the program was debugged in a development system that used RAM for the **6800** vectors. In a typical system, the vector would be in ROM and the initialization might be a subroutine called by the main initialization routine.

Another typical application might not require a continuous display and the updated time values would be used to schedule events. The time would be kept in memory and updated every second or sooner if desired. This scheduler program would scan a table each update time and implement scheduled tasks.

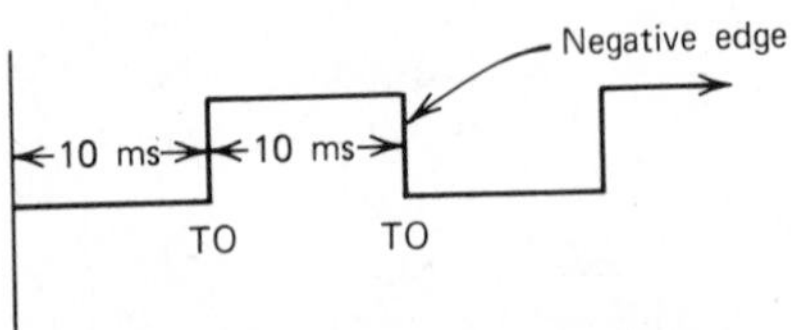

FIGURE 9-25 Output of counter 2.

```
PAGE   001    TIMER


00001                         NAM     TIMER
00002                    *  PROGRAM TO DISPLAY TIME ON CRT
00003                    *  4/16/79 WCWRAY
00004                    *  USES 6840 PTM TO DIVIDE DOWN THE 1 MHZ CLK
00005                    *  INTERRUPT (IRQ) USED ON COUNTER 1
00006                    *  02 CONNECTED TO C1
00007                    *  DIVIDES BY 1,000,000
00008                    *
00009          E14B      PDATA1 EQU     $E14B      MINIBUG 3 OUTPUT STRING
00010          E126      OUTCH  EQU     $E126      MINIBUG 3 OUTPUT CHAR
00011          E133      INCH   EQU     $E133      INPUT CHARACTER ROUTINE
00012                    *
00013 F000                      ORG     $F000
00014                           OPT     O
00015                    *
00016 F000 0D            MSG1   FCB     $D
00017 F001 48                   FCC     /HH:MM:SS AM/
      F002 48
      F003 3A
      F004 4D
      F005 4D
      F006 3A
      F007 53
      F008 53
      F009 20
      F00A 41
      F00B 4D
00018 F00C 04                   FCB     4
00019                    *
00020                    *  PROGRAM TO DISPLAY TIME
00021                    *
00022 F00D 8E A07F       SET    LDS     #$A07F     SET STACK
00023 F010 CE F000              LDX     #MSG1      GET MSG1 POINTER
00024 F013 BD E14B              JSR     PDATA1     PRINT PROMPT
00025 F016 CE F001              LDX     #MSG1+1    GET MSG POINTER
00026 F019 86 0D                LDA A   #$D        GET CR
00027 F01B BD E126              JSR     OUTCH      PRINT IT
00028 F01E BD E133       LOOP1  JSR     INCH       GET TIME TO SET
00029 F021 A7 00                STA A   0,X        PUT IN LINE
00030 F023 8C F00A              CPX     #MSG1+$A   DONE?
00031 F026 27 03                BEQ     CONF       YES- START COUNTING
00032 F028 08                   INX                NO- GET NEXT NUMBER
00033 F029 20 F3                BRA     LOOP1
00034                    *
00035 F02B CE F050       CONF   LDX     #IRQ       GET SUBROUTINE ADDR
00036 F02E FF FFF8              STX     $FFF8      PUT VECTOR IN RAM
00037 F031 BD F039              JSR     INIT       INITIALIZE PTM
00038 F034 01                   NOP
00039 F035 0E                   CLI                ALLOW INTERRUPT
00040 F036 01            LOOP2  NOP
00041 F037 20 FD                BRA     LOOP2      LOCK UP TIL INTRRUPT
00042                    *
00043 F039 86 83         INIT   LDA A   #$83       SET OUTPUT,INT CLK, SLCT REG
00044 F03B B7 8011              STA A   $8011      WRITE TO REG 2
```

FIGURE 9-26 Display time program for the **6840** PTM.

It will be found in using the continuous mode to generate maskable interrupts (IRQs) that two problems exist. First, it is necessary to reinitialize counter 1 each time-out to clear the $\overline{\text{IRQ}}$ signal (see line 53 in Fig. 9-26). Second, it may not be possible to use other interrupts or to mask the IRQ without destroying the accuracy of the time (i.e., interrupts will be missed).

It therefore is advisable to use the NMI instead of IRQ for this timer function.

```
PAGE  002    TIMER

F03E CE 270F          LDX     #10000-1
F041 FF 8014          STX     $8014      SET COUNT FOR CTR 2
F044 CE 0031  INIT1   LDX     #50-1      "    "    "    "  1
F047 FF 8012          STX     $8012
F04A 86 40            LDA A   #$40
F04C B7 8010          STA A   $8010      UNMASK IRQ AND ENABLE CTRS
F04F 39               RTS
              *
F050 8D F2    IRQ     BSR     INIT1      RELEASE IRQ LINE
F052 CE F000          LDX     #MSG1      GET POINTER TO TIME STORAGE
F055 86 39            LDA A   #$39       SETUP UPDATE INFO
F057 C6 30            LDA B   #$30
F059 A1 08            CMP A   8,X        REACHED 9 ?
F05B 27 04            BEQ     SKIP2      YES - UPDATE
F05D 6C 08            INC     8,X        NO - INCREMENT SECONDS
F05F 20 5E            BRA     DISPLY     PRINT EVERYTHING
F061 E7 08    SKIP2   STA B   8,X        CLR LSB
F063 86 35            LDA A   #$35       GET MAX 10S DIGIT
F065 A1 07            CMP A   7,X        REACHED 59 YET ?
F067 27 04            BEQ     SKIP3      YES- UPDATE
F069 6C 07            INC     7,X        NO - INCREMENT AGAIN
F06B 20 52            BRA     DISPLY     PRINT RESULTS
F06D E7 07    SKIP3   STA B   7,X        CLR MSB SECONDS
F06F 86 39            LDA A   #$39       LAST NO. ?
F071 A1 05            CMP A   5,X        REACHED 9 ?
F073 27 04            BEQ     SKIP4      YES - UPDATE
F075 6C 05            INC     5,X        NO - INCR LSB MIN.
F077 20 46            BRA     DISPLY     PRINT RESULTS
F079 E7 05    SKIP4   STA B   5,X        CLR LSB MINUITS
F07B 86 35            LDA A   #$35       59 MINUITS ?
F07D A1 04            CMP A   4,X
F07F 27 04            BEQ     SKIP5      YES - UPDATE
F081 6C 04            INC     4,X        NO - INCR
F083 20 3A            BRA     DISPLY     PRINT IT
F085 E7 04    SKIP5   STA B   4,X        CLR DIGIT
F087 86 32            LDA A   #$32       LOOK FOR 2 OF 12
F089 C6 39            LDA B   #$39
F08B A1 02            CMP A   2,X        12 ?
F08D 27 08            BEQ     SKIP6      YES - POSSIBLY
F08F E1 02            CMP B   2,X        NO - 9 YET ?
F091 27 24            BEQ     SKIP8      YES - UPDATE
F093 6C 02            INC     2,X        NO - INCR
F095 20 28            BRA     DISPLY     PRINT IT
F097 86 31    SKIP6   LDA A   #$31
F099 A1 01            CMP A   1,X        LOOK FOR 1 OF 12
F09B 27 04            BEQ     SKIP7      YES - UPDATE
F09D 6C 02            INC     2,X        NO - INCR
F09F 20 1E            BRA     DISPLY     PRINT IT
F0A1 A7 02    SKIP7   STA A   2,X        CHNG 11 TO 12
F0A3 86 20            LDA A   #$20       GET SPACE
F0A5 A7 01            STA A   1,X        CLR MSB HOUR
F0A7 A6 0A            LDA A   $A,X
F0A9 81 41            CMP A   #'A        IS IT AM?
F0AB 26 04            BNE     AM         YES- PRINT IT
```

FIGURE 9-26 (continued).

Since the NMI is not normally connected to the **6840** and the output goes HIGH instead of LOW, it is necessary to install an inverter and connect it to the counter 1 output pin (O1—pin 27) as shown in the dashed circuitry of Fig. 9-21. This requires only minor revisions to the program. One is a change to the Control Word of counter 1 ($80 instead of $40). It is not necessary to reinitialize the counter in this case since it just generates a 1-cycle-per-second square wave. This means that

```
---

PAGE  003   TIMER

FOAD 86 50              LDA A  #'P       NO- SWITCH TO PM
FOAF 20 02              BRA    AM1
FOB1 86 41    AM        LDA A  #'A
FOB3 A7 0A    AM1       STA A  $A,X      UPDATE DISPLAY
FOB5 20 08              BRA    DISPLY    PRINT IT
FOB7 86 30    SKIP8     LDA A  #$30
FOB9 C6 31              LDA B  #$31
FOBB A7 02              STA A  2,X       9 TO 10
FOBD E7 01              STA B  1,X       "
FOBF CE F000  DISPLY    LDX    #MSG1
FOC2 BD E14B            JSR    PDATA1    PRINT NEW DISPLAY
FOC5 3B                 RTI              RETURN FROM INTERRUPT
              *
                        END

TOTAL ERRORS 00000
```

FIGURE 9-26 (continued).

the NMI remains LOW for 1/2 s, but since it is an edge-sensitive signal instead of a level-sensitive signal, as in the case of IRQ, it will not interfere with other interrupts. Since NMI is "nonmaskable" and has highest priority, nothing will interfere with the accuracy of the time. When IRQ is used an interrupt occurs after each time-out, while NMI will respond only on negative-going edges. Therefore the count value of one of the latches must be cut in half as compared to the interrupt (IRQ) implementation in order to get the 1-s update.

9-11 DIRECT MEMORY ACCESS (DMA)

We previously discussed input/output techniques using the PIA, ACIA, or SSDA LSI packages. These functional components, when properly programmed, make data communications between the μP data bus and the outside world possible. Using them results in a maximum transfer rate of approximately 40,000 bytes per second.

Another method of I/O commonly used in all computers is **Direct Memory Access** (DMA); this is a way to connect an input or output device directly to the memory of a μC via the address and data buses. It allows the transfer of data without using the **6800**. To cause a DMA, an external device must be capable of taking over the bus and supplying the proper memory address and R/$\overline{W}$ signal. It must also have a data register to receive data on a READ memory cycle and provide data on a WRITE cycle. DMA is made possible in the **6800** system by the availability of internal logic, which is associated with several pins on the μP itself. These pins are TSC, DBE, HALT, and BA.

There are two basic methods of DMA in a **6800** system (see Figs. 9-27 and 9-29): using the HALT line, and using the TSC line.

9-11.1 DMA Using the HALT Line

The simplest way to execute a DMA is to have the peripheral device place a LOW on the $\overline{\text{HALT}}$ line and wait for the μP to respond by setting Bus Available (BA) HIGH. This is shown in Fig. 9-27. When BA is asserted the address bus, data bus, and R/$\overline{\text{W}}$ line from the μP are in their HIGH-impedance state and VMA is forced LOW. The peripheral device can now access memory (VMA is not a three-state signal and must be gated to allow it to be raised while the μP is halted). When it completes its memory cycle it releases the $\overline{\text{HALT}}$ line and the μP resumes normal operation.

EXAMPLE 9-20

Design a circuit to allow DMA via the $\overline{\text{HALT}}$ line. Assume VMA is used along with the addresses to enable the system's memories.

SOLUTION

One solution is shown in Fig. 9-28. The peripheral makes a memory request by setting the DMA REQUEST FF. This causes the $\overline{\text{HALT}}$ line to go LOW via the NOR gate. When BA is received from the μP, the DMA one-shot fires, which does four things:

1. It clears the DMA REQUEST FF.
2. It enables the three-state drivers from the peripheral to control the address and data buses and the R/W line.
3. It holds the $\overline{\text{HALT}}$ line LOW.
4. It forces VMA HIGH, enabling the memory.

The pulse time of the one-shot should be equal to the cycle time of the memory,

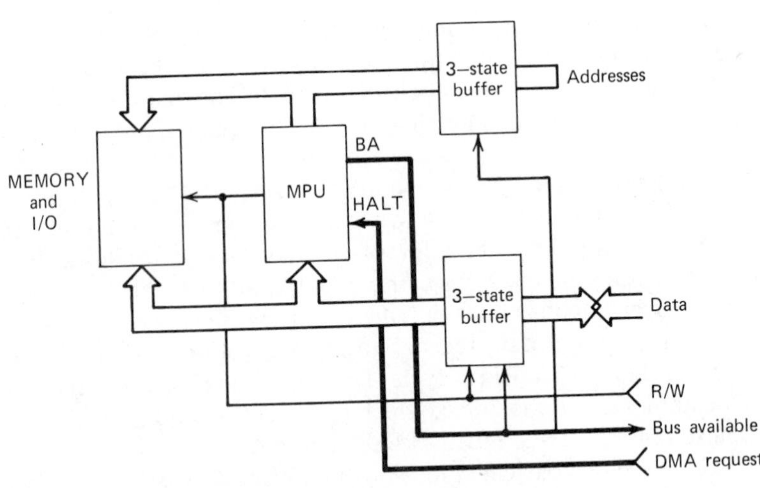

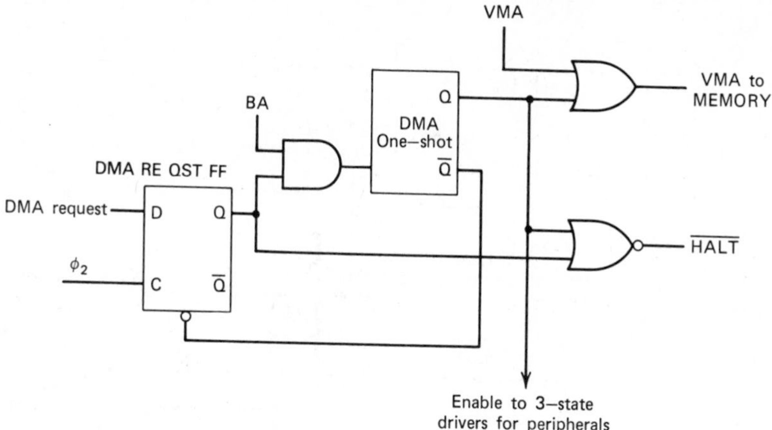

FIGURE 9-28 DMA Request circuit

plus any gate delays. When the one-shot pulse expires, the $\overline{HALT}$ line returns HIGH and the μP resumes normal operation.

VMA is controlled by the VMA OR gate. In normal operation the DMA one-shot is CLEAR, effectively connecting the μP's VMA to the memory. During DMA, VMA is LOW, but the DMA one-shot forces VMA to the memory HIGH so that a valid memory request can be made.

9-11.2 DMA Using TSC and DBE

When using the $\overline{HALT}$ line, the DMA must await the completion of the current instruction, as signaled by a 1 on BA, before it can take control. This could mean a delay of 2 to 13 μs. When high-speed data transfers are required where the data must be handled instantly (within 1 or 2 μs), the TSC method of Fig. 9-29 is required. To appreciate the timing problems involved, the TSC signal characteristics must be carefully analyzed. Figure 9-30 shows the Three-State Control (TSC) timing requirements.

When the TSC line is HIGH, the address bus and the R/$\overline{W}$ line are placed in a high-impedance state by the **6800**. VMA and BA are forced low whenever TSC is HIGH to prevent false reads or writes on any device enabled by VMA. While TSC is held HIGH, the $\phi 1$ and $\phi 2$ clocks must be held HIGH and LOW, respectively, in order to stop program execution. Figure 9-30 shows that the transitions of TSC must occur within 40 ns after the positive-going edge of $\phi 1$. VMA is forced LOW and the address and R/$\overline{W}$ line will reach the high-impedance state after a delay of 700 ns (max) for the **MC6800** or 270 ns for the **MC68A00**. This is identified as t_{TSD}. (See the data sheets on **MC68A00** and **MC68B00** in Section 9-15). In this example, the data bus is also in the high-impedance state while $\phi 2$ is being held LOW since DBE is connected to $\phi 2$. A DMA transfer can now occur on cycles 3 and 4. When TSC is returned LOW, the μP's address and R/$\overline{W}$ line drivers are reconnected to

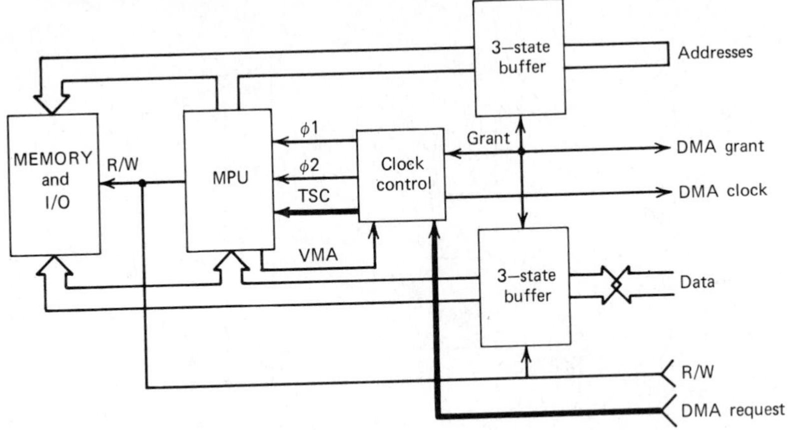

FIGURE 9-29 Direct Memory Access (DMA) using the TSC line.

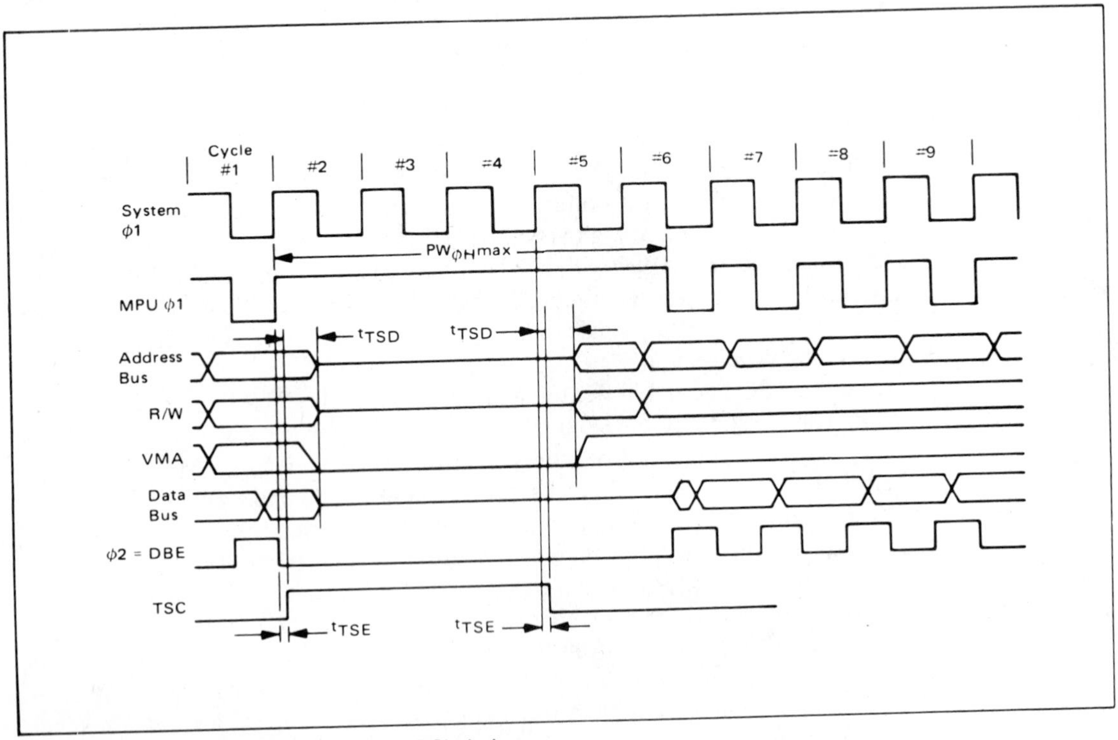

FIGURE 9-30 Three-State Control (TSC) timing.

the bus. Because it is too late in cycle 5 to access memory, this cycle is dead and used for synchronization. Program execution resumes in cycle 6.

The **6800** uses dynamic logic and must be clocked periodically. Since TSC stops the clocks, it must not hold up the μP for more than 9.5 μs or data may be lost. This is $PW_{\phi Hmax}$ in Fig. 9-30 (9.5 μs is also allowed for **MC68A00** and **MC68B00** μPs).

9-11.3 DMA by Cycle Stealing

A very nice way to perform DMAs is to use the **MC6875** as the clock generator (see Section 7-7). This IC provides nonoverlapping $\phi 1$ and $\phi 2$ clock signals, and internal logic allows for stretching these clocks with $\phi 2$ HIGH for slow memories or with $\phi 1$ HIGH for DMA or dynamic memory refresh. If properly interconnected with the μP's TSC as shown in Fig. 9-30, a DMA cycle-stealing circuit can be built.

9-11.4 The 6844 Direct Memory Access Controller (DMAC)

When DMA is used in a system, it usually requires the addition of considerable hardware to keep track of memory addresses and byte counts, as well as other logic requirements during a DMA transfer. A **6800** family component called the **MC6844** Direct Memory Access Controller (DMAC) contains all the registers and logic to provide for four DMA channels. It is intended to be used with a clock generator such as the **6875** and eliminates the need for most, if not all, additional TTL ICs. This device uses the μP HALT and/or the TSC function of the μP to provide three modes of operation:

1. HALT burst
2. HALT steal
3. TSC steal

The HALT burst mode uses the HALT line to stop the μP and then performs a data transfer of any number of bytes. In the HALT steal mode, the μP is restarted after each byte of data is transferred.

In the TSC steal mode, the TSC line is used to control the system buses. Hence, only 1 byte can be transferred in one DMA cycle because of the limitation on the stretching of $\phi 1$ (9.5 μs max). Maximum data transfer rates are 1 megabyte for the HALT burst mode, 70K byte for the HALT steal mode, and 250K byte for the TSC steal mode (with a 1-MHz clock). This component is a 40-pin device with 16 registers that are accessible to the user. They are divided as follows:

Four Status Registers (8 bits each)
Four channel Control Registers (8 bits)
Four Byte-Count Registers (16 bits)
Four Address Registers (16 bits)

Bit 3 of the channel Control Register determines whether the Address Registers are incremented or decremented after each DMA transfer.

9-12 MULTIPROCESSING

In some computer systems the amount of work required exceeds the capabilities of a single μP. Since μPs are small and inexpensive, it is often feasible to add a second μP to share the load. The use of two or more processors working semi-independently, but simultaneously, on parts of the same task is called **multi-processing**.

If the two (or more) μPs can be connected so that they can perform separate tasks at the same time, a real increase in throughput can occur. In such a system it is necessary to transfer data between subsystems, but this may take only a small percentage of the time.

One of the most time-consuming tasks in μC systems is the input or output of data. If the data is being printed by a teletypewriter, for example, it takes 100 ms for each character. A processor can run 100,000 cycles (30,000 to 50,000 instructions) during that time. Consequently, if the external printer requires any degree of intelligence to perform its task, it could be practical to provide a dedicated μP for that purpose.

9-12.1 Master–Slave Systems

In many multiprocessing systems, one μP is designated as the *master*. It controls the operation of the system and apportions tasks between itself and the other μPs, which are called *slaves*. In the system described above, for example, the master μP might sense that data for the printer is located in a certain area of memory. It can then inform the slave μP that controls the printer, and it becomes the slave's task to send this information to the printer while the master μP does other things. Typically, master and slave μPs share common memory. Because of coordination problems, programming master–slave or other multiprocessor systems is often complex.

One clever method that allows the computers to share memory is shown in Fig. 9-31. The two μPs run on opposite clocks (ϕ1 of μP1 is ϕ2 of μP2). Since each μP enables memory only on its own ϕ2, they never access memory at the same time. This system requires fast memory. Normal-speed memories require a priority circuit to avoid conflicts when both μPs need to access the same memory location.

9-13 SUMMARY

In this chapter we described the response of the μP system to an interrupt (storing the registers on the stack, executing the interrupt service routine, restoring the registers, and resuming the main program). Each type of interrupt that occurs in the **6800** system and the events associated with it were discussed. In addition, timing loops and timer ICs were described. Finally, I/O transfers using DMA and multiprocessing were explained. These features facilitate communication between the **6800** system and its peripherals.

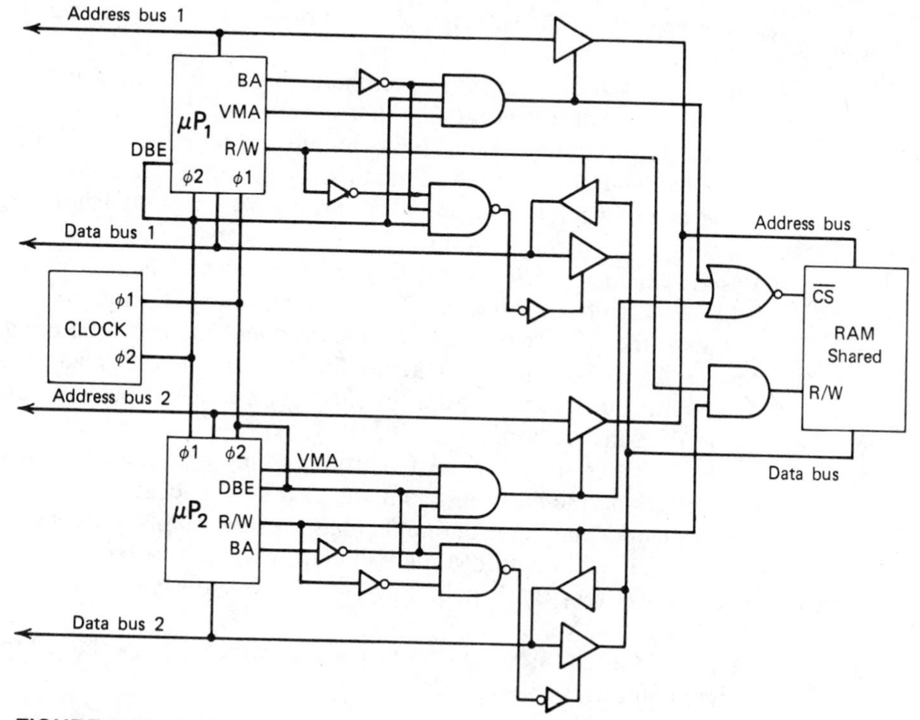

FIGURE 9-31 Multiprocessing circuit using transposed clock and shared memory.

9-14 GLOSSARY

Direct Memory Access (DMA) Communication between a device and memory without going through a computer.

Interrupt Signal to the computer which causes it to halt execution of its normal program and branch to a service routine for the interrupting device.

Interrupt service routine Software routine that clears or initializes registers or directs a peripheral device to take action to remove the need for its interrupting action.

IRQ A normal interrupt request.

Mask bit Bit in the Condition Code Register which, when SET, inhibits the IRQ action.

Masking Setting bits in Control Registers of the μP or its peripheral ICs, to inhibit them from activating their interrupt lines.

Multiprocessing Using two or more computers to work simultaneously on the same problem.

Nested interrupt Interrupt of the processing of a previous interrupt service routine.

NMI NonMaskable Interrupt. A high-priority interrupt which is not affected by the interrupt flag.

PIC Peripheral Interrupt Controller. An IC that determines which devices may interrupt, determines their interrupt priority, and assigns each device a separate interrupt vector.

Polling Act of querying each peripheral device to determine if it has data for the computer or if it was the one that interrupted.

Reset Action used to start up a computer. Grounding the RESET line will reset the hardware logic of the μP and its peripheral ICs, and the action also fetches the restart vector that jumps the program to an initialization routine prior to entering the main program.

Restart Signal which causes the computer to start its program at the beginning.

RTI ReTurn from Interrupt. The last instruction in an interrupt subroutine that causes the μP's registers to be restored and the previous program to resume.

Stack Area of memory assigned to hold subroutine return addresses, μP register contents during an interrupt, or data that has been "pushed" onto the stack by the PSH instruction.

SWI SoftWare Interrupt. An instruction that acts as an interrupt by storing the registers on the stack and jumping to a vector location.

Timing loop Software routine that has the total number of cycles adjusted so that a prescribed amount of time will elapse when it is executed.

Vector Address that "points to" a software routine for servicing interrupts or reset.

WAI WAit for Interrupt. An instruction which causes the μP to store its registers and await an interrupt.

9-15 REFERENCES

Ferguson, Bob. *The 6800 Handles Clock Stealing, Digital Design,* M6800 Microcomputer System Design Data, Motorola Semiconductor Products, Inc., Phoenix, AZ, October 1978.

Greenfield, Joseph D. *Practical Digital Design Using ICs,* Second Edition, Wiley, New York, 1983.

Motorola. *M6800 Microprocessor Applications Manual,* Motorola Semiconductor Products, Inc., Phoenix, AZ, March 1975.

Motorola. *M6800 Microcomputer System Design Data,* (9701–9), Motorola Semiconductor Products, Inc., Phoenix, AZ, November 1976.

Motorola. *User Considerations for MC146818 Real Time Clock Applications,* AN894A, Motorola SPD Inc., Austin, TX, 1986.

Motorola. *Advance Information, MC146818A Real-Time Clock Plus RAM,* Motorola SPD Inc., Austin, TX, 1982.

Motorola. *Low Power Considerations for MC146818 Real Time Clock Applications,* Applications Note AN856, Motorola SPD Inc., Austin, TX, 1982.

Motorola. *Programmable Timer Fundamentals and Applications, MC6840,* MC6840UM (AD-1), Second Edition, Austin, TX, 1981.

Motorola. *8-Bit Microprocessor and Peripheral Data, Series C,* Austin, TX, 1983.

9-16 PROBLEMS

9-1 If a system responds to both high- and low-priority interrupts, why must each low-priority service routine have a CLI instruction near its beginning?

9-2 If a system uses a 1-μs clock, what is the minimum time that reset may be held low?

9-3 A program consists of a main program and an interrupt routine. In addition, a portion of the main program must not be interrupted. Describe where each SEI and CLI instruction should go in the program.

9-4 A low-priority device interrupts the program and is then interrupted by a high-priority device. With reference to the original Stack Pointer, what are the contents of SP-3? Of SP-12?

9-5 A μP system stores an equivalent of real time as a 16-bit number in locations $100 and $101. The μP is interrupted once a second by a clock and must increment the 16-bit number in those locations. Assume it is interrupted by a positive transition on a line.

a. Bring the line in via the PIA and write the initialization routine for the PIA.
b. Write the interrupt service routine.
c. Design the hardware to cause the interrupt. Assume the 1-second pulse is achieved by counting down the 60 cycle from the AC power lines.

9-6 A μP uses an ACIA. Whenever the Transmit Data Register is empty, it interrupts. If the address of the Transmit Data Register is $8011, write an interrupt routine to transfer the contents of location $40 to the ACIA.

9-7 An ACIA, whose data register is at 8011, interrupts each time it receives a character. The first character received should go into location 0100, the second into 0101, etc. When location 01FF is used, the program should execute an SWI and go to 0500. Write the interrupt routine. (All addresses are hex.)

9-8 A device is connected to IN2 of the PIC. Where are its interrupt vectors?

9-9 List the parts a controller must have if it is to make DMAs using the TSC line. Describe the function of each part.

9-10 Explain the following statement: "Whenever the flags are stored by an IRQ interrupt, the I flag is always 0." Is this statement true for NMI and SWI interrrupts?

9-11 An ACIA is to communicate with a TTY as in Example 9-23. If the system is to use interrupt rather than polling, write the interrupt service routine.

9-12 In response to a switch closure, a signal line should be on for 300 μs, off for 100 μs, on for 500 μs, and then off. Write a program to do this using the PIA.

9-13 A **6840** has Ø3 C3 loaded into one of its registers. If the clock is 50 kHz and the register is using the internal input, sketch the output if the register is operating in

a. 16-bit continuous mode.
b. Dual 8-bit continuous mode.
c. Single-shot dual 8-bit mode.

Show specific times on your sketch.

9-14 A **6840** is being driven by a clock whose input period is 1.25 μs.

a. Write a program to set up register 3 for a 1-second output.
b. Using registers 1 and 2, produce a pulse that is high between 45 and 55 seconds of the first minute of each hour. Show your program. (Hint: Use register 1 to gate register 2.)

9-15 The basic clock of a system is 500 kHz. When an input line goes high, a computer (the **6800**) is to read in the time from a PTM into two memory locations. The time is to be read in seconds and hundreds of seconds.

Write a program in assembly language to

a. Set up counter 1 or the PTM to produce a 10-ms output.
b. Set up counters 2 and 3 to count hundredths of seconds and seconds as necessary.
c. Design the hardware to allow the PTM to interrupt after each second.

After attempting to solve these problems, try to answer the self-evaluation questions in Section 9-2. If any of them still seem difficult, review the appropriate sections of the chapter to find the answers.

CHAPTER 10
SYSTEM DEBUGGING

10-1 INSTRUCTIONAL OBJECTIVES

The preceding chapters have covered the design of a microcomputer (μC) using the **6800** family of components. This chapter will cover the development of testing procedures as they have evolved since microprocessors (μPs) and μCs were first introduced. Many methods necessary to perfect the design will be discussed. After reading this chapter, the student should be able to

1. Assemble the hardware and software needed for a specific design and test to see whether they work together properly.
2. Make the hardware/software trade-offs by evaluating performance.
3. Understand the purpose of Microcomputer Development Systems (MDSs).
4. Select the best methods for his or her situation to perfect the system under development.
5. List the features of the various debugging systems.
6. Explain how firmware debug programs (Monitor ROMs) can be used.
7. Use breakpoints in a program.
8. Save programs and load them during development.
9. Determine trade-offs of time saved and ease of use against the cost of MDSs.
10. List the steps necessary in the development of a μP system using the EXORciser.

10.2 SELF-EVALUATION QUESTIONS

Watch for the answers to the following questions as you read the chapter. They should help you to understand the material presented.

1. What is the lowest-cost method for analyzing the operation of a μC?
2. Why does low initial cost not necessarily provide the best method for developing a μC system?

3. Why is it necessary to know the register contents in debugging a μC?
4. How do breakpoints speed the location of faults in μC systems?
5. Which μP signals should be monitored during debugging?
6. Why are three-state drivers necessary in switch and light monitoring systems?
7. What are the features of ROM Monitor systems?
8. What are pseudoregisters? What is their function?
9. What advantages does a Microcomputer Development System (MDS) have over a MINIBUG III or a BUFFALO Monitor system?
10. How does a logic analyzer help test μC systems?
11. How does a Hardware Development Station (HDS) reduce development costs?

10-3 INTRODUCTION TO SYSTEM DEBUGGING

When a computer program is written, it is necessary not only to choose the proper instructions but also to properly format each instruction statement. Assemblers and compilers will generate *syntax errors* when processing source program statements that are improperly written, but even when these programs are edited to eliminate all syntax errors, there is no guarantee that the program will run successfully or function properly. The program's logic can be tested only by executing the instructions. A newly written program is likely to have mistakes and therefore must be tested carefully before attempting to let it run by itself. A **Microprocessor Development System** (MDS) with its many debugging features, is usually used so that the problems can be analyzed. With this tool, the program can be stopped and corrected when something is wrong. System **debugging** is the name given this process. It verifies not only that the program does calculations and handles data correctly but also that the external hardware is properly controlled by the software.

This chapter and some of the chapters to follow describe various debugging methods. They progress from very simple debugging tools such as switches and lights and *Monitor ROMs*, to MDSs such as the EXORciser, and then to present-day Hardware Development Stations (HDSs). The HDS-200 and HDS-300, for example, are powerful testing stations built specifically for system development and debugging for the whole family of μPs from the 8-bit **6800** to the 32-bit **68020**.

10-3.1 Rudimentary Debugging Systems

The most basic methods for testing and debugging μC systems are described first. More sophisticated debugging systems are described in Section 10-4 and beyond.

Any method of testing and debugging a μC system must include at least the ability to

1. Read or write into memory at any location.
2. Run and HALT the program.

To be really useful and easy to use, a development system should also have the ability to

3. Display or change the registers.
4. Set "breakpoints."
5. Single-step a program (run the program one instruction at a time) and observe its effect.

The most elementary method for observing the operation of a μC is to use *lights*, typically Light-Emitting Diodes (LEDs), to show the state of the lines of the address and data buses and *switches* to control the buses.

A typical switch control circuit is shown in Fig. 10-1. Switches are needed to control the Read/Write (R/$\overline{W}$) line and to run or halt the program. Typically, three-state buffers are used to transfer control of the memory from the μP to the switches when reading or writing new data.

When the WRITE switch is depressed a short pulse pulls down the R/$\overline{W}$ line (0 = Write), and the three-state gates transfer the data from the data switches to memory at the address set on the address switches. When not activated, these gates present a high impedance to the lines and do not interfere with normal μP operation. The three-state receivers are left connected to the lines at all times to drive the LED displays since their inputs are always high-impedance and do not load down the buses.

If this data and address display circuit is combined with the single-step switch circuit described in the following section, the functions of a *basic* μP hardware analyzer are provided. After manually entering the machine codes of the user's program with the switches, the program can be executed at full speed in the RUN

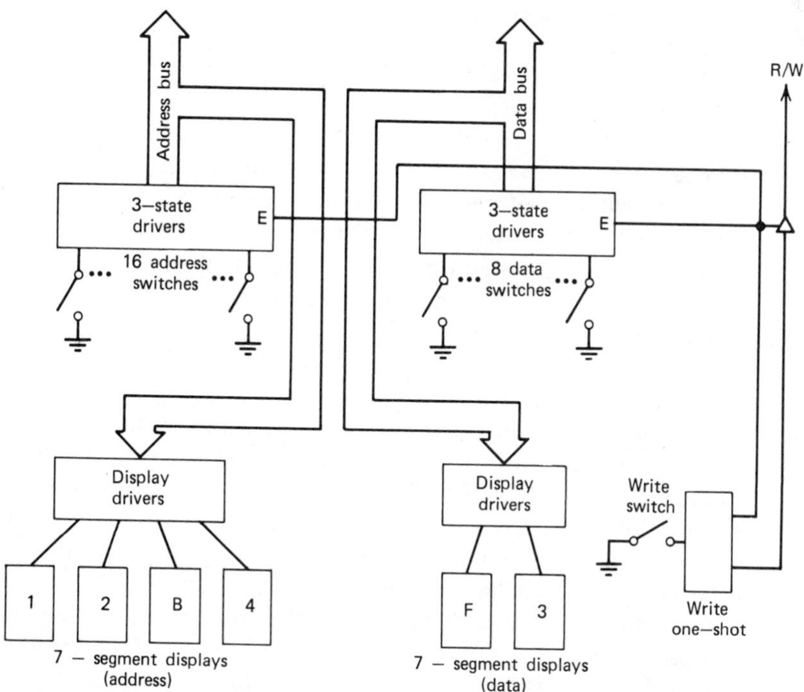

FIGURE 10-1 Light and switch monitoring of a μP.

mode or stepped *one instruction at a time* by using the STEP switch. These hardware techniques have severe limitations, but because of their low cost they are used by some experimenters or hobbyists. Better methods are discussed later in this chapter.

10-3.2 Single-Step Operation

In order to understand a computer's functioning as it executes a program, it is customary to step it *one instruction at a time* and observe the status of many signals and the contents of the registers and memory.

The information required includes

1. The address on the bus.
2. The data on the bus.
3. The state of each line of the control bus (i.e., HALT, BA, TSC, VMA, NMI, IRQ, and $R/\overline{W}$).
4. The contents of the μP registers (i.e., PC, X, A, B, and CC).
5. The contents of any memory location.

It used to be common practice to allow hardware **single-step** operation. In this mode, the clock is stopped and the computer is stepped through a program one instruction at a time by a momentary contact switch. Some older large computers and minicomputers may still permit this. These computers usually had front panel displays and switches and hardware registers so that the address bus, data bus, and contents of the CPU registers could be examined and/or changed while the processor was halted. This method of analysis was slow and tedious but was sometimes used when a program failed to perform as expected. Most μPs, however, are *dynamic* devices and the clock cannot be stopped for more than 5 or 10 μs without losing data. Also, since the lines within the μP package are not accessible, it is not possible to use this method to look at the data in the various registers within the chip. Most μP systems have no built-in display. For these reasons a number of more sophisticated debugging methods have evolved, and they are described later in this chapter.

The **6800** can be halted for an indefinite time with the clock still running and the internal registers will retain their information, but it is not possible to examine or change them with the processor halted.

The timing requirements for single-stepping a **6800** system are complex and are shown in Fig. 10-2.

The instruction illustrated is a 1-byte, two-cycle instruction such as CLR A. When $\overline{\text{HALT}}$ goes LOW, the μP halts after completing execution of the current instruction. The transition of $\overline{\text{HALT}}$ must occur at least 200 ns (t_{PCS}) before the positive edge of $\phi 2$ in the last cycle of that instruction (point A of Fig. 10-2). If $\overline{\text{HALT}}$ is HIGH at point A but goes LOW during $\phi 2$ of that cycle, the μP halts after completion of the next instruction. BA (Bus Available) goes HIGH by t_{BA} (Bus Available delay time) after $\phi 1$ of the next cycle. At this time, **Valid Memory Address** (VMA) is LOW and $R/\overline{W}$, the Address Bus, and the Data Bus are in the high-impedance state. To step through programs instruction by instruction,

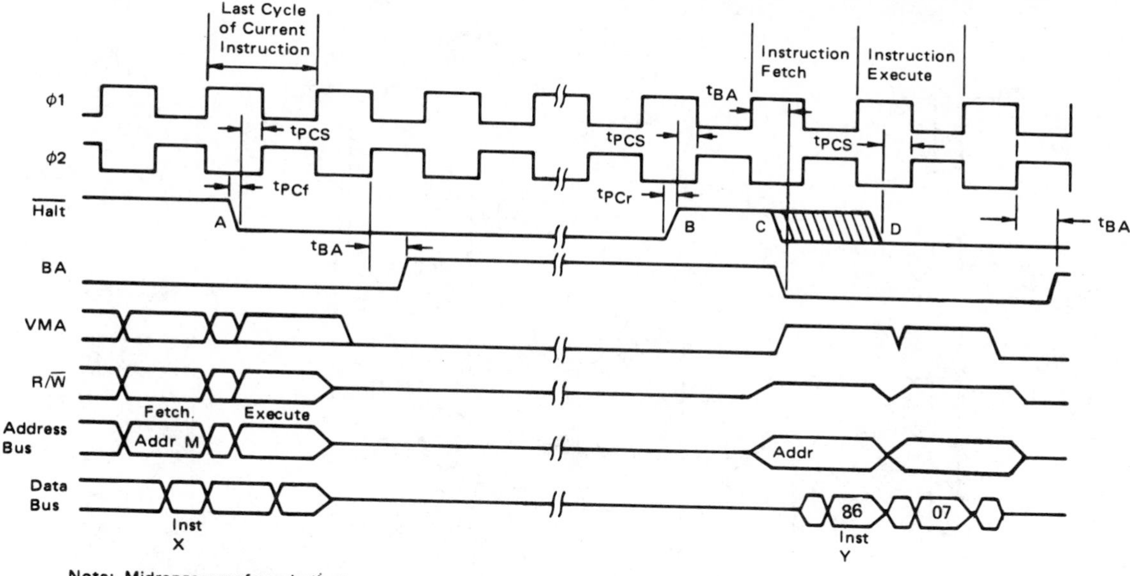

FIGURE 10-2 HALT and single-step operation.

$\overline{\text{HALT}}$ must be brought HIGH, as shown at point B, and then returned LOW, as shown, at some point between C and D of Fig. 10-2. Again, the transition of $\overline{\text{HALT}}$ must occur t_{PCS} before the positive edge of $\phi 2$. BA will go LOW at t_{BA} after the positive edge of the next $\phi 1$, indicating that the Address Bus, Data Bus, VMA, and R/$\overline{\text{W}}$ lines are active again. During the first cycle of this instruction (LDA A #7) the Op code (86) is fetched, and even though the $\overline{\text{HALT}}$ line has been taken LOW again, the second byte (07) is also fetched. Since the $\overline{\text{HALT}}$ line was taken LOW more than 200 ns prior to the positive edge of $\phi 2$, the processor halts after the end of the cycle and the data and address lines all go to their high-impedance state. BA returns HIGH at t_{BA} during the next cycle of the clock, indicating that the μP is off the bus. If this instruction had used three cycles, the length of the BA LOW time would have been increased by one cycle.

EXAMPLE 10-1

Design a circuit to control a **6800** μP. Provide two momentary contact switches for RESET and STEP and one toggle switch for RUN/HALT.

SOLUTION

One solution is shown in Fig. 10-3. The switches at the left are each followed by cross-coupled **7404** gates to provide debouncing. If the RUN/HALT toggle switch is in the HALT position when the system is first turned ON, the D input of flip-flop 2 (FF2) is LOW. Therefore, on the first positive-going edge of the $\phi 1$ clock, FF2 resets. This in turn causes the Q output of FF2 and the D input of FF1 to be

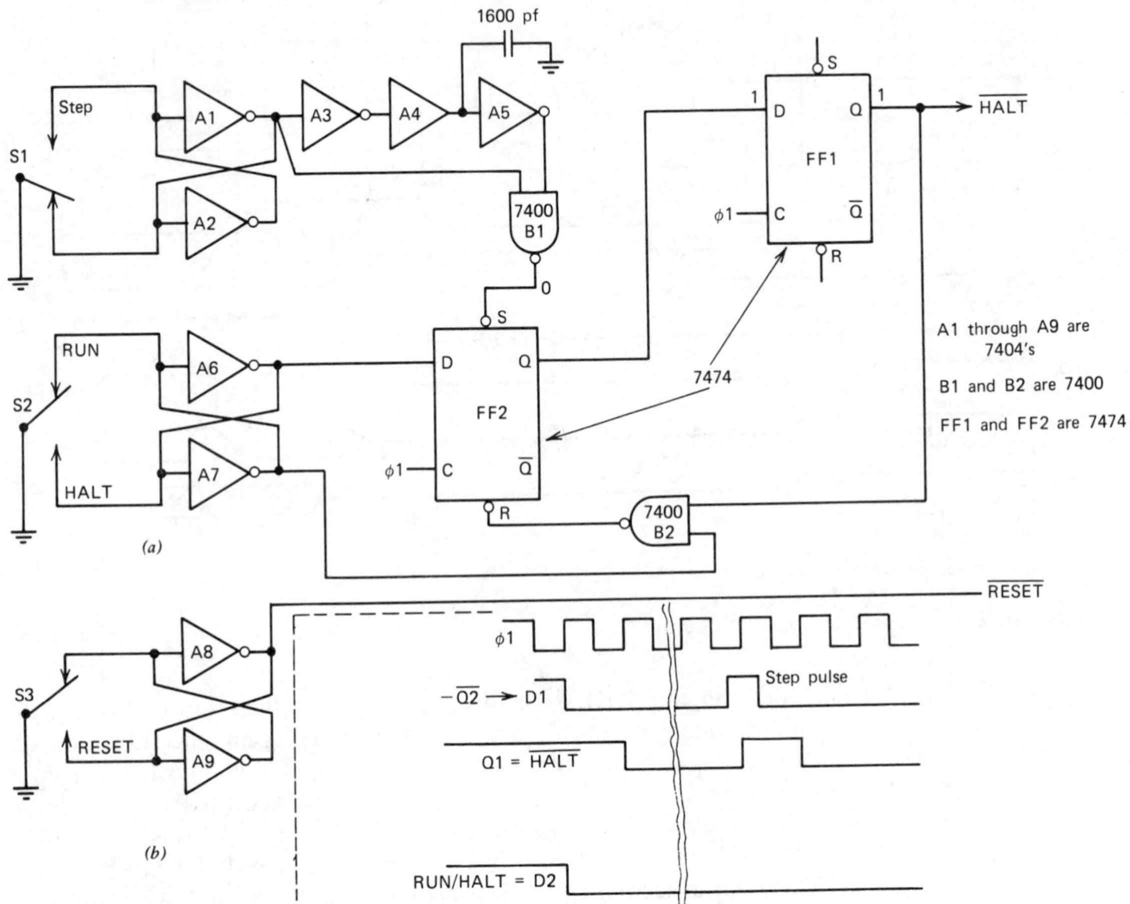

FIGURE 10-3 Single-step circuit. (a) Circuit. (b) Timing.

LOW. On the next leading edge of the clock, FF1 will reset and its Q output will hold the $\overline{\text{HALT}}$ line LOW, preventing program execution by the μP.

In the RUN position, the D input of flip-flop 2 (FF2) is HIGH. When the $\phi 1$ clock input sees the next positive-going edge, it sets FF2. FF1 sets on the next positive-going edge of the $\phi 1$ clock, and its Q output, which is connected to the HALT line of the μP, will be HIGH, allowing the system to RUN.

With the limitations described in Section 10-3.1 in mind, we can use the circuit of Fig. 10-3 to step through a program.

When the RUN/HALT switch is in the HALT position, the Step switch can be used to advance the μP one instruction at a time as follows. Normally, the output of A1 is LOW, and the output of A5 is therefore HIGH. Gate B1 (**7400**) sees one HIGH input and one LOW, B1's output will be HIGH, and the SET input to FF2 will be disabled. When the Step switch is depressed, the output of A1 goes HIGH instantly, and A4 attempts to go HIGH but is held down until the capacitor can be charged. Since one input of B1 is already HIGH and the other one goes HIGH when the capacitor reaches a "1" level, B1's output goes LOW, setting FF2. This takes approximately 100 ns with the parts shown. When A5's input reaches its threshold it switches and removes one HIGH input from B1, thus allowing the SET input of FF2 to return HIGH. The circuit just described ensures that a single 100-ns pulse will be provided to SET FF2 regardless of how fast the Step switch is operated or released. (A typical minimum time for the manual operation of this switch would be 25 ms.) When FF2 is SET by this pulse, it will remain SET until the next positive edge of $\phi 1$. While FF2 is SET it holds the D input of FF1 HIGH, and therefore, when the next positive edge of $\phi 1$ occurs, it simultaneously SETS FF1 and RESETS FF2. Since it is not possible, with the time constants of the step circuits as they are, for FF2 to be SET again for many milliseconds, FF1 will be RESET by the next positive edge of $\phi 1$. Thus, the $\overline{\text{HALT}}$ line of the μP is HIGH for exactly one clock cycle. Reference to Fig. 10-2 shows that this is the ideal way to single-step the μP.

The RESET switch of Fig. 10-3 is connected directly to the μP (via the debounce circuit) and must be used initially to get the μP system started at the correct address. The details of the RESET function are described in Chapter 9.

10-3.3 Step-by-Step Program Tracing

Appendix C shows a table of cycle-by-cycle operation for each instruction in the **6800** repertoire. It gives the information that appears on the address and data buses during each cycle of each instruction. This information can be very helpful when examining a program in single-step mode. Note, however, that the program is only halted after each instruction, not after each cycle of an instruction. Therefore, the user can only examine the Address and Data Buses at the *end of each instruction,* but this information is sometimes enough to indicate the status of the program. Methods of determining the cycle-by-cycle operation of the instruction and other advanced debugging aids are discussed later in this chapter.

When the μP is halted, the Address and Data Buses are in their high-impedance state and cannot be examined. Therefore, systems that use single-cycle operation often gate the address and data buses into hardware registers on each $\phi 2$ clock when VMA is high. These registers drive displays. This type of debugging system is shown in Fig. 10-1. Thus the information in the displays, while the μP is halted, shows the status of the Address and Data Buses during the last instruction cycle when the μP was running.

EXAMPLE 10-2

What information appears on the Address and Data Buses at the end of each instruction in the program shown in Table 10-1, and what can we deduce about the operation of the program?

TABLE 10-1 Program for Example 10-2

Addr	Data	Mnemonic	
20	86	LDA A #$7B	LOAD A accumulator with "immediate" value
21	7B		of Hex 7B.
22	48	ASL A	SHIFT A left.
23	8B	ADD A #3	ADD (to A) the "immediate" value of 3.
24	03		
25	2B	BMI * − 2[a]	BRANCH (if number in A is negative) back
26	FC		to previous instruction (−4 bytes).
27	20	BRA *	BRANCH back 2 bytes unconditionally
28	FE		(repeats same instruction).

*[a]The asterisk is used to denote the current location of the PC counter at the beginning of this instruction.

SOLUTION

If a chart is kept of the information displayed and the contents of the A accumulator are calculated after each step (as shown in Table 10-2), it is possible to follow the program. The operation performed during each instruction is explained at the right in the chart. If this problem involved the B accumulator or index register, the chart would have to be more complex.

The first instruction (LDA A #$7B) is a 2-byte, two-cycle *immediate* (#) mode instruction. From Appendix C it is seen that the immediate value (#$7B) is LOADED into the A accumulator during these two cycles. The displayed values, as latched at the end of the second cycle, are as shown on the step 1 line of Table 10-2.

Appendix C shows that on the last cycle of an LDA A or LDA B instruction, the Operand address and operand data appear on the Address and Data Buses.

TABLE 10-2 Results of Single-Stepping Program of Example 10-2

Step	Address Bus (Displayed)	Data Bus (Displayed)	"A" ACC (Calculated)	Operation (Performed)
STRT	20	XX	XX	
1	21	7B	7B	7B LOADed in A.
2	23	8B	F6	A SHIFTed left.
3	24	03	F9	3 ADDed to A.
4	23	8B[a]	F9	Result NEGATIVE-BRANCHed back.
5	24	03	FC	3 ADDed again.
6	23	8B[a]	FC	BRANCHed back.
7	24	03	FF	3 ADDed again.
8	23	8B[a]	FF	STILL NEG-BRANCH.
9	24	03	02	3 ADDed
10	26	FC	02	POSITIVE did not branch
11	28	FE	02	BRANCH always back 2 bytes.
12	28	FE	02	Again.

[a]Data may vary depending on bus capacitance.

Therefore, we expect to see \$21 on the Address Bus and \$7B on the Data Bus.

The next instruction is an ASLA, an *inherent* instruction (since memory references are not required). The chart shows that the Operand address + 1 (\$23) and the Op code of the next instruction (\$8B) are on the Address and Data Buses. This is an example of the *look-ahead* feature of the **6800**. The A register value of \$7B becomes \$F6 when shifted left, but this cannot be seen when the μP is halted because we cannot see the register contents in this hardware step mode. If, however, the values in the registers are calculated as shown in Table 10-2, the progress of the program can be seen. (Section 10-5 describes a better method for debugging with ways to display the registers.) The add 3 immediate (ADD A #3) results in an Address Bus value of \$24 and a Data Bus value of 03 (the Op code address + 1 and the operand data). The A accumulator becomes F9.

Step 4 executes the conditional Branch-on-MInus (BMI * − 2) instruction. Since the result of the last instruction was negative, the program branches back 4 bytes (\$FC = −4) and displays the branch address (\$23) at the end of its fourth cycle. The Data Bus value may vary. Since no operation other than a change in the Program Counter (PC) has taken place, the A accumulator remains the same.

Step 5 adds 3 again and A is now equal to \$FC. The following steps are identical as the program loops back and adds 3 until step 9. At this point, our calculations show that A will equal 02, which is a positive number, and as seen in step 10 the Address Bus has gone forward (did not branch) to a displayed value of \$26. The last instruction (BRA *) branches to itself and thus halts further execution.

10-3.4 Software for the Single-Step Tester

If a test system incorporates lights and switches to control the Address and Data Buses and other hardware to HALT and STEP the μP, as described in Example 10-2, several software techniques can be used to find problems. One is to use a branch-on-self instruction (BRA *) or 20 FE. In this case, after the program is manually entered in memory with the switches, it is started and is then stopped by the RUN/HALT switch. The contents of the various storage locations in memory can then be examined by means of the address switches and data bus lights. If the program failed to store the right results in the reserved locations, it can be assumed that it did not get to the end or did the wrong thing. In that case the branch instruction is moved to occur sooner in the program and the routine retried. Another way is to insert a JMP to a convenient location where a routine stores the registers in memory and then executes a branch-on-self instruction so that the μP can be halted and memory examined as above. Of course, many other useful routines and methods are provided in the variety of Monitor ROMs described in Section 10-5, and they are easier to use.

EXAMPLE 10-3

Assume that an error occurred in Example 4-25 (the BCD subtraction problem of Chapter 4). The error can be traced by examining the contents of the accumulator and the Condition Code Register (CCR) at each step in the program. How can this be done?

SOLUTION
The easiest way is to use MIKBUG 2.0 or an equivalent Monitor program. This displays the contents of the registers after each step, as shown in Fig. 4-13.

If a control program is not available, however, the contents of A and the CCR can still be preserved in memory. One way would be as follows:

1. Initialize the X and SP registers.
2. Place a JSR after each LOAD, ADD, or DAA instruction.
3. Write a subroutine as shown in Table 10-3.

This subroutine stores the contents of A and the CCR each time it is used and leaves the result in memory, starting at the initial value of X. Note that the contents of A are destroyed by the TPA instruction because it writes the CCR into A. Therefore the program "backs up" to reload A and then adjusts X to point to the next vacant location before exiting via the RTS instruction.

10-3.5 Hex Switches and Seven-Segment Displays

Considerable improvement can be made in this HALT and STEP method of system monitoring by replacing the individual address and data switches with hexadecimally coded switches. These deal with four lines at a time and provide easier interpretation. Still greater improvement can be made by using software and a keyboard, as will be explained in the following sections.

10-3.6 Deficiencies of Hardware Debuggers

Total reliance on lights and switches to debug a program has three major drawbacks.

TABLE 10-3 Subroutine for Example 10-3

Instructions	Comments
STA A 0,X	Store the contents of A
INX	Increment X
TPA	Transfer CCR to A
STA A 0,X	Store A at X
DEX	Decrement X
LDA A 0,X	Reload the contents of A
INX	Increment X
INX	" "
RTS	Return from subroutine

1. Since the data cannot be seen on the lights unless the processor is halted, the program must be stepped from one halted state to the next. This, of course, is not the way a μC works and the system might not run properly at full clock speed because of timing problems even though it executes the instructions correctly in this circuit.
2. It is slow and tedious. It is unwise to use this method for programs longer than about 100 lines because stepping through the program and keeping track of everything will be very difficult.
3. The main shortcoming is that the μP registers can not be directly observed.

10-4 A MICROCOMPUTER SYSTEM FOR SOFTWARE DEBUGGING

As we have suggested many times in the last nine chapters, it is possible to use a μC for many tasks. Two of those tasks can be the *development* and *testing* of software. An alternative to the *lights and switches* system is to use a μC system that is controlled by a unique software program to perform the various debugging tasks. Motorola has developed such a system to work with most of their μPs. One of them has been designed for use with one of the newer members of the **6800** family, the **M68HC11A8** μC. This is a μP-type IC, like the **6800**, but because of the dramatic improvements in technology, it not only has an enhanced **6800** μP but also includes the clock oscillator, various kinds of memory, and I/O peripherals, all on the same chip. This complete *computer on a chip* (called a μC) is described in detail in Chapter 11. The **68HC11** Evaluation Board (EVB) shown in Fig. 10-4 is introduced here to illustrate the use of Monitor (or debugger) programs in ROM (or EPROM) for systems analysis.

This EVB has been specifically designed to test the **68HC11**. It is also **6800**-compatible. The **6800** instruction set is a subset of the **68HC11** instruction set and **6800** programs will execute without difficulty. The **68HC11A8** that is used in this EVB has an extra index register, called the Y register, that can be ignored while running **6800** programs or instructions. The other registers are the same as those in the **6800**.

The debugger program in the EVB is called *BUFFALO*. It must be used with a terminal that allows the designer to enter commands into BUFFALO and to display the results. The BUFFALO debugger/Monitor program contains many features for program development and analysis. One of its best features is a One-Line Assembler/Disassembler. This is an EVB *command* (or routine) that can be used to manually assemble instructions from mnemonics or disassemble them (to mnemonics) from previously loaded machine code. Other commands can then execute the instructions and observe their effects on memory and the registers.

FIGURE 10-4 The MC68HC11EVB EValuation Board

This system therefore makes an excellent tool for studying any of the **6800** example programs or instructions described in the previous chapters.

Many other features of the enhanced **68HC11** μC can also be evaluated by this EVB but these will not be needed until the μC is studied in Chapter 11.

The Block Diagram of this EVB system is shown in Fig. 10-5 and includes

1. A **68HC11A8** μC that incorporates
   - **a.** An enhanced **6800** type of processor.
   - **b.** An oscillator circuit, requiring only an external inexpensive crystal, and two small capacitors.
   - **c.** A 256-byte RAM.
   - **d.** A 512-byte EEPROM.
   - **e.** Other built-in peripheral features equivalent to a PIA, an ACIA, and a TIMER (see Chapter 11 for details).
2. A separate **6850** ACIA for serial output with an RS232C terminal interface.
3. An **HC4040** baud rate generator to supply clocks for the ACIA.
4. An optional 8K RAM or EPROM.
5. An 8K byte EPROM with the BUFFALO program.
6. An **MC68HC24** Port Replacement Unit (PRU), which allows the EVB to *emulate* a **68HC11** with true I/O characteristics.

The EVB can be purchased by universities or individuals from the Training Department of the Semiconductor Products Sector of Motorola in Phoenix, Arizona. It requires a user-supplied +5, +12, and −12 V DC power supply.

The EVB is used with a data terminal such as a TTY, a TI 733, or a CRT and can optionally be connected to a *host* computer as shown in Fig. 10-5. For small programs, the object code that is to be analyzed is entered on the terminal in machine language or assembled on the EVB using the one-line assembler. For large programs a *host* computer is used to write and assemble a new object program that is then downloaded to the EVB RAM using Motorola S-records (see Sections 10-5.2, 10-5.4, 6-9 or 12-10.3). Other routines in the BUFFALO monitor are then used to debug the user's program.

Thus, overall evaluation/debugging control of the EVB is provided by the monitor program residing in EPROM (external to the μC) via terminal interaction. The RS232C terminal/host I/O port interface circuitry provides communication and data transfer operations between the EVB and the external terminal/host computer (as described in Section 12-10). Independent baud rate selection capabilities are provided for the terminal and host I/O ports. Baud rates for the ACIA terminal port are selectable (300–9600) by changing a jumper.

The EVB is not intended to take the place of more powerful and flexible tools such as the Motorola **M68HC11EVM** Evaluation Module or the Development systems described in Chapter 12.

10-4.1 The EVB Memory Map

The memory map for the **68HC11** EVB is very similar to a typical **6800** system map, but certain differences should be noted. The **68HC11** has 256 bytes of internal RAM that normally occupy locations 0 to $100. Also, as will be seen in Chapter 11, these μCs with many on-chip peripherals require a number of registers, similar to those in the PIA or ACIA, to control them. In the **68HC11A8**, these registers normally reside between $1000 and $103F (see Section 11-8.9). As explained in Section 11-8.9, these default locations can be changed. The **68HC11A8** normally also includes a ROM from $E000 to $FFFF. When the *ROMON* bit of the *configuration register* (at $103F) is *OFF*, the internal ROM is disabled and that map space is available for external use. The BUFFALO EPROM uses the space from $E000 to $FFFF. It also uses part of the RAM from $40 to $FF. Thus, the other part of the internal RAM ($00 to $3F) is available for the user. A separate RAM chip for user programs is also provided and resides at $C000 to $DFFF. An optional RAM or EPROM can be installed to occupy the space from $6000 to $7FFF. The space from $B600 to $B7FF is occupied by an EEPROM, which is another feature of the **68HC11** μC (see Section 11-8.8).

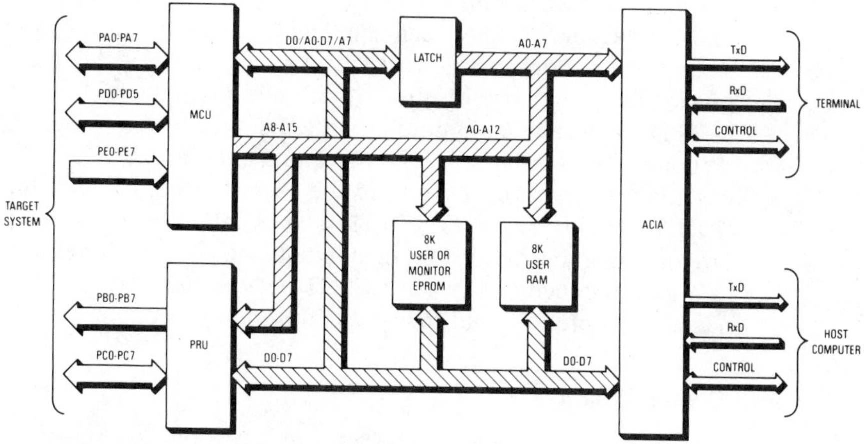

FIGURE 10-5 MC68HC11EVB block diagram.

10-5 THE BUFFALO MONITOR PROGRAM

The complete listing of the BUFFALO program is included in the **68HC11** EVB User's manual cited in Section 10-11 and can be used to fully understand the program descriptions to follow. Studying a program such as this is an excellent way to learn programming and how the hardware and software work together. The various commands will be described in the following paragraphs.

Debug program routines such as those provided in the BUFFALO monitor IC usually include several utility functions, such as LOAD or VERIFY (**S-records**). When this EPROM is included in the system, it must reside at the top of memory so that the RESET vector will be properly fetched. The RESET vector directs the μP to start executing the initialization routine at $E000. It then enters the *command loop,* called MAIN, where the prompt is issued, and waits for input from the keyboard.

Typically, the program to be analyzed is put into memory by one of the methods described in Section 10-5.2 or 10-5.4 and then tested by the other functions provided in the BUFFALO EPROM. The desired debug functions are selected by means of commands entered on the CRT or TTY operator terminal. The commands for BUFFALO are shown in Fig. 10-6. The operator can access or change data, registers, or instructions and, in effect, communicate in machine language (hexadecimal) with the system under development.

The use of EPROM monitor programs and a software approach to debugging is faster and cheaper than switches and lights, and many times easier, thus saving a great deal of time in debugging larger programs.

10-5.1 RESTART

RESTART is not a command to be entered on the keyboard but is an action required to start up the system. When the power is turned on or the RESET button is pressed, the RESET vector is fetched and the initialization routine at $E000 is entered. The routine first tests the position of the K4 jumper, and if it is positioned between pins 1 and 2 (as shipped) the initialization routine will continue. If the jumper is between pins 2 and 3 the program will jump to the EEPROM and allow its program to direct the μC. Obviously, if this memory has not been previously programmed, this would not be done. The initialization of the **68HC11**'s internal configuration is then set up by the program as it writes predetermined values to the *options* and *Timer Mask* registers. This process is described in Section 11-8 and in the **68HC11A8** Advanced Information manual (ADI 1207) cited in Section 10-11. This is followed by setting the stack pointer, programming the ACIA, and then initializing the other internal serial port. As far as a user is concerned, when RESET occurs, the BUFFALO program prints its name and a prompt, and then waits for an input command.

10-5.2 Memory Display/Change

A new program can be loaded into memory by downloading from a *host* (described in Section 10-5.4), or entered manually, as described here. This EVB

Command	Description
ASM [<address>]	Assembler/Disassembler
BF <addr1> <addr2> <data>	Block Fill Memory with Data
BR [-] [<address>] . . .	Breakpoint Set
BULK	Bulk Erase EEPROM
BULKALL	Bulk Erase EEPROM + CONFIG Register
CALL [<address>]	Execute Subroutine
G [<address>]	Execute Program
HELP	Display Monitor Commands
LOAD <host download command>	Download S-Records via Host Port
LOAD <T>	Download S-Records via Terminal Port
MD [<addr1> [<addr2>]]	Dump Memory to Terminal
MM [<address>]	Memory Modify
MOVE <addr1> <addr2> [<dest>]	Move Memory to New Location
P	Proceed/Continue from Breakpoint
RM [p,y,x,a,b,c,s]	Register Modify
T [<n>]	Trace \$1-\$FF Instructions
TM	Enter Transparent Mode
VERIFY <host download command>	Compare Memory to Download Data via Host Port
VERIFY <T>	Compare Memory to Download Data via Terminal Port

FIGURE 10-6 BUFFALO Monitor program commands.

system has RAM memory from $C000 to $DFFF. If the user types an "MM" (upper- or lowercase), followed by an address and a carriage return <cr>, BUFFALO will display the contents of that location, as shown in Fig. 10-7. If, after opening the location in this way and observing the 8-bit data, it is desired to change the data, the new data is entered from the keyboard (one or two hex characters) followed by a line feed <lf>. The system stores the byte and displays the next address and its contents. It then waits for the next operator response. A line feed will display the next location, or an uparrow (↑) will back up to the previous location. A carriage return terminates the memory display/change routine and returns to the prompt, ready for the next command. The last line of the display in Fig. 10-7 shows an alternative way to display the data with the MM command. If, after entering the MM and address (followed by the <cr>), a space is used instead of a line feed, the next location is displayed on the same line. Any number of spaces can be entered to space across the page. This command is also used to view or change bytes after a program is downloaded from the host as described in Section 10-5.4

```
>mm c1ØØ<cr>

C1ØØ F7 44<lf>
C1Ø1 33 <lf>
C1Ø2 1B <lf>
C1Ø3 BA <^>
C1Ø2 1B <lf>
C1Ø3 BA <lf>
C1Ø4 41 <cr>

>mm c1ØØ<cr>

C1ØØ 44 _33 _1B _BA _41<cr>  (spaces entered between bytes)

>

(all operator entries are underlined)
<lf> is the linefeed key or a control-J
<cr> is the return or enter key
```

FIGURE 10-7 Memory display/change using the MM command.

10-5.3 Display of μP Registers

In analyzing programs, registers must be displayed and changed as well as memory. The Register Modify command (RM) is provided for that purpose. When RM is entered, followed by a <cr>, it displays all of the registers as shown in Fig. 10-8, and waits, after repeating the P register, for another entry. If a *space* is entered, the next register is displayed below the first, on the next line. Another space displays the next register and so on, as shown. If any register must be changed, the new data is entered prior to entering the space, as shown for the Y register. If a <cr> is entered at any time, even after the first display, it terminates the Register Display and returns to the command loop. This is indicated by the prompt in column 1.

10-5.4 LOAD Function

The BUFFALO monitor includes a LOAD function that will download an object program in S-record format (see Section 6-9 or 12-10.3), from a Host computer. It is necessay to connect the Host port of the EVB to that computer with the proper RS232C cables (see Section 12-10.2) and then enter the necessary commands. The

```
>rm <cr>
P-C166 Y-FFFF X-FFFF A-1Ø B-ØØ C-C4 S-DFFF
P-C166 <space>
Y-FFFF 3344 <space>
X-FFFF <space>
A-1Ø   <space>
B-ØØ   <space>
C-C4   <space>
S-DFFF <space> or <cr>
>

(operator entries are underlined)
```

FIGURE 10-8 The Register Modify (RM) command.

path could be through *modems*. The Host then sends the file and the EVB puts the machine code into its RAM. The methods used will vary, depending on the Host. One typical way is shown in Fig. 10-9. We first enter the *transparent mode* (the command is TM), in order to communicate with the Host to prepare it for the download of a file. The file would contain the S-record object program that has been previously assembled on the Host. We can verify that the file is present by entering a command such as "type hc11.lx." This will use the hosts *type* command to display the S-records on the EVB's terminal. Once that communication is possible, (assuring that the baud rates and other port parameters are correct), the TM mode is exited (using control-A) and, after getting the EVB's prompt, the *load* command is then entered on the EVB's terminal (e.g., as shown in Fig. 10-9). A typical entry would be *load type hcll.lx* (in the case where the Host is a CPM or IBM PC system). This *load* command sets up the BUFFALO program to receive S-records, is ready to put them in memory, and sends the rest of this command to the Host. The *type* command causes the host to start listing the *hcll.lx* object file to the serial port. When the S9 record is received, the EVB exits from the load routine, and sends the word *done* to the EVB's terminal. The prompt is then displayed, ready for another command. This assumes that no errors occurred in loading into the right locations or in the checksum. If an error occurs the "error addr xxxx" message is displayed.

Once the *done* appears, the user should check to see whether the program is actually in the proper memory locations. The last three commands shown in Fig. 10-9 show the use of the MD command to display portions of the memory where it will be seen that the bytes are actually in place.

The program must have been properly assembled on the Host with the ORG

```
>tm <cr>               (EVB's Transparent Mode command)

A> C:<cr>              (Host's prompt, assumming it is ON and ready)

C> type hcll.lx        (Host's command to list the S-record file)

S10B00020860FB700307EC160B9
S109C1608EDFFFBDC200EA
S106C2004C5C3956
S9030000FC

C>  ^A                 (TM's exit command)

>load type hcll.lx <cr>    (Download command)
done
>md 20 27 <cr>

0020 86 0F B7 00 30 FF FF FF FF FF FF FF FF FF FF FF
>md c160 c166 <cr>

C160 8E DF FF BD C2 00 FF FF FF FF FF FF FF FF FF FF
>md c200 c202 <cr>

C200 4C 5C 39 FF FF FF FF FF FF FF FF FF FF FF FF FF
>
```

FIGURE 10-9 A typical download procedure.

statement set to an address that matches the RAM locations. The bytes received from the port are stored in the locations specified by the addresses in each S-record.

10-5.5 Breakpoints and Program Tracing Methods

As explained in Chapter 9, the μP register contents are placed on the stack whenever the processor is interrupted. The interrupt can be any of the internal or external hardware interrupts or a software interrupt. Both hardware and software interrupts are used in the **68HC11** EVB to implement the debugging routines.

The contents of the μP registers associated with the user's program are kept in locations called *Pseudoregisters* in the monitor program RAM. In the case of the EVB, those addresses are $9E through $A6 (9 bytes). They are updated each time an interrupt is encountered and the service routine also redisplays the register's content.

The *TRACE* or *T command* operates by setting the Output Compare 5 (OC5) interrupt to time out after the first cycle of the first Op code fetched. To use this feature to examine a program's operation, the PC is set to the instruction to be tested (using the RM command), and a T command is then entered to execute that instruction, as shown in Fig. 10-10b. A portion of the user's program is shown in Figure 10-10a. This monitor program command (t) serves to set up the OC5 timer count values and enable its interrupt to occur after a prescribed number of clock cycles. This is the exact time required to run through the monitor routines and start executing the users instruction. The μP will run the instruction pointed to by the PC at normal clock speed and then stop to service the OC5 interrupt. The service routine gets the register contents from the stack, stores them in the pseudoregisters, and then displays them. It then reenters the BUFFALO command loop, displays the prompt (>), and awaits the next command. This processing is mostly transparent to the operator. Figure 10-10 shows the trace command repeated for 5 instructions. It is possible to see the effect on the registers for each instruction traced.

This debug routine is known as the **run-one-Instruction** or TRACE command. It is a convenient way to step through a program one instruction at a time. The logic of the user's program instructions can be observed by studying the display of the registers before and after each instruction is executed.

This T command should not be confused with HALT and STEP operation, since in this case running one instruction actually runs the user program instruction at full clock speed and simply does an interrupt afterward to return to the display register routine and print out the registers. The processor is not HALTed at any time.

The T command is probably the most useful of all commands for finding errors, since the program can easily be stepped through a program segment while observing the register changes and the effect on the program branching due to the Condition Codes. The method is slow but the program logic is much easier to understand than when using the hardware step circuit previously described because the register contents can also be observed.

```
0020 86 0F          LDAA   #$F
0022 B7 0030        STAA   $30
0025 7E C160        JMP    $C160

C160 8E DFFF        LDS    $DFFF
C163 BD C200        JSR    $C200
C166 .. ...         ....

C200 4C             INCA
C201 5C             INCB
C202 39             RTS

a)   User's program partial listing
```

```
>rm
P-FFFF Y-FFFF X-FFFF A-0F B-FF C-FF S-FFFF
P-FFFF C160<cr>

>t<cr>

OP- 8E
P-C160 Y-FFFF X-FFFF A-0F B-FF C-C8 S-DFFF
>t<cr>

OP- BD
P=C163 Y-FFFF X-FFFF A-0F B-FF C-C8 S-DFFD
>t<cr>

OP- 4C
P-C200 Y-FFFF X-FFFF A-10 B-FF C-C8 S-DFFD
>t<cr>

OP- 5C
P-C201 Y-FFFF X-FFFF A-10 B-00 C-C4 S-DFFD
>t<cr>

OP- 39
P-C166 Y-FFFF X-FFFF A-10 B-00 C-C4 S-DFFF
>

b) EVB responses
```

FIGURE 10-10 Use of the TRACE command. (a) User's program partial listing. (b) EVB responses.

To attempt to trace one instruction at a time, through the hundreds of thousands of instructions that would normally be executed in a second, would probably take many days, so **breakpoints** are used. The breakpoint routines temporarily insert a SoftWare Interrupt (SWI) instruction in place of a user's program instruction, and provide an *interrupt service routine* that displays the contents of the pseudo-registers. With breakpoints, the program can be interrupted, at will, after any number of instructions have executed and the register contents can then be examined. This is known as *running to a breakpoint,* or simply *using a breakpoint*. The breakpoint is placed in the program at some point between sections or segments of instructions, such as after an initialization routine or after the RAM is cleared. (It is actually put at the beginning address of the next instruction of the next segment.) These segments of the user's program are run at normal clock speed, and the breakpoint is used to stop it at any desired instruction. This is done by a series of commands that permit insertion of these temporary breakpoints in a table or removal of them, as desired. Each time a breakpoint is installed in the table, and the program is started, the user's instruction at that address is saved and replaced with an SWI instruction.

The program will run up to the SWI instruction, display the contents of the μP registers, and return to the debug programs command loop. Memory and registers can then be examined to see if they contain the expected data. If so, the P command is entered and the program will *proceed* to the next breakpoint. Thus, it is possible to execute portions of the user's program using breakpoints until a bad segment is found. The bad program segment can then be examined in detail by using the TRACE routine. Breakpoints are the fastest way to find problems in a program and are therefore frequently used to troubleshoot μP systems.

Note also that the use of SWI in this way requires that the user's program be in RAM. This is not undesirable however, since it is then easily possible to change the instructions (known as patching the program) to the correct ones where required (see Section 12-4.9). Since RAM is used, this also means that the user's program must be loaded after the system is turned on, either from disk (using S-records) or manually from the keyboard as described in Section 10-5.2. Later, in the study of the EXORciser, it will be shown that other methods can be used to trace through programs in ROM.

In BUFFALO, up to four breakpoints can be stored at one time. They are kept in a *breakpoint table*. It is only necessary to enter the BR command, followed by an address, to enter them in the table (called *inserting a breakpoint*), or to enter BR, followed by a − (minus) and the address, to remove a breakpoint. A BR followed by a − will remove all breakpoints. The BR command alone will print the addresses of all breakpoints in the table.

EXAMPLE 10-4

A segment of a user's program is shown in Fig. 10-10a. It starts at location \$20 but jumps to other areas of memory. Describe the methods used with the BUFFALO program to perform breakpoint testing of this user's program and system. Location \$C160 was chosen for the first breakpoint, with location \$C200 as the second, and \$C166 as the third.

SOLUTION

The user's program shown in Fig. 10-10a can be loaded into memory using the MM command as described in Section 10-5.2, or assembled on a Host and downloaded as described in Section 10-5.4. Figure 10-11 shows the BUFFALO commands required, and their responses, to analyze or debug the program. The steps are as follows.

```
>br c160 <cr>

C160 0000 0000 0000
>br c200 <cr>

C160 C200 0000 0000
>br c166 <cr>

C160 C200 C166 0000
>g 20 <cr>

P=C160 Y=FFFF X-FFFF A-0F B-FF C-D0 S-004A
>p <cr>

P-C200 Y-FFFF X-FFFF A-0F B-FF C-C8 S-DFFD
>p <cr>

P-C166 Y-FFFF X-FFFF A-10 B-00 C-C4 S-DFFF
>
```

FIGURE 10-11 Breakpoint operation for Example 10-4.

a. The first breakpoint is entered using the BR command. This displays the breakpoints on the next line, and $C160 is shown. The second breakpoint is then entered, and both breakpoints are then displayed along with the zeros for the other two unused breakpoints.
b. The third BR is then entered and all three are displayed.
c. The Go command is used to start the program (G 20).
d. When the breakpoint is encountered, the register contents are displayed with no perceptible delay, since the execution up to the SWI is at full clock speed. Note that accumulator A has changed to $0F as a result of the first instructions of the user's program, and the SP is $004A, which is the default value used by the EVB.
e. The P command is entered to *proceed* to the next breakpoint and this causes the next register display. Note that the PC is at $C200 as it should be and the SP is $DFFD. This may seem strange, but note that the SP is set to $DFFF by the fourth instruction and the breakpoint is at the beginning of the subroutine. Therefore the return address has been put on the stack.
f. Another P command will *proceed* to the last breakpoint.

Note that the A and B accumulators are no longer the same as they were. This is a result of the instructions executed by the routine at $C200.

Obviously, if the program does not reach the SWI it is because some instruction in that segment did not perform as expected. If this should occur, the operator may then have to reload the program (since it probably ran away and may have altered some of the instructions). The program is then executed again, up to the last SWI that was properly executed, and the run-one-instruction command is then used until the incorrect or omitted instruction is found.

Monitor ROMs, like BUFFALO, provide these various features to help the designer to debug the systems. They enable the testing of software and any hardware that may be included on the same μP bus.

A common problem is the programmer's failure to set the Stack Pointer at the beginning of the program. In a typical program, if the SP is not set to the planned area, the program will attempt to "stack" things wherever it is and this will usually cause the program to "bomb out" because some of the code or variables will be overwritten. The EVB's use of a *default* stack (at $004A) avoids trouble when debugging but the problem may still exist when attempting to run the program in the system under development.

When a Breakpoint is reached, or a Trace completed, the registers are first stored in the stack area by the interrupt, moved to the pseudoregisters, and then displayed on the terminal by the *interrupt service routine*. All this can be seen in Fig. 10-12. The MD command was used as shown in Fig. 10-12b to display the area of Monitor RAM from $40 to $AF. Note that there is both a monitor and a user's stack area. The monitor stack (at $68) is never displayed by BUFFALO, but reference to the Monitor program listing in the user's manual will show that the addresses of $E4E7, $E7FB, and $E18C in that stack are legitimate return addresses for the MD function of the Monitor program. The Register Modify display in Fig. 10-12a shows that the user's stack is at $DFFF. Another MD display of the area at $DFF0 to $DFFF (Fig. 10-12c) shows that these register values are in the user's *real stack* and the pseudoregister locations at $9E to $A8 contain the same information.

```
>rm <cr>
P-C166 Y-FFFF X-FFFF A-10 B-00 C-C4 S-DFFF
P-C166 <cr>

>

a) Register display after reaching last breakpoint.


>md 40 af <cr>

0040 FF FF C0 FF 0F FF FF FF FF C1 60 FF E4 E4 E4 E4
0050 95 E3 C6 00 E4 E4 E4 95 E3 C6 00 E4 95 E3 C6 00
0060 B4 00 20 E4 E7 E7 FB E1 8C 6D 64 20 34 30 20 61 p a       md 40 a
0070 66 0D 32 30 32 0D 31 2E 6C 78 0D FF FF FF FF FF f 202 1.lx
0080 FF FF FF FF FF FF FF FF FF FF FF FF 4D 44 20 44             MD D
0090 20 FF FF FF 00 AF C1 60 C2 00 C1 66 00 00 C1 66            f   f
00A0 FF FF FF FF 10 00 C4 DF FF 01 01 01 00 02 00 40                @
>

b) Memory Dump of the EVB's Monitor RAM area.


>md dff0 dfff <cr>

DFF0 AE F1 D3 B1 E9 C0 FF C4 00 10 FF FF FF FF C1 67                g
>

c) Memory Dump of the User's stack area.
```

FIGURE 10-12 Display of Pseudoregister and Stacks.

10-5.6 GO to User's Program

The G command is used to start program execution. It picks up the operand value entered with the G command and installs it in the proper place in the pseudoregisters. It then places the pseudoregisters on the monitor stack and executes an RTI. This puts the monitor stack contents into the μP registers and starts executing from the address in the PC.

Normally, once the program has been started with the G command, the P command is used (think of it as "proceed"), since it simply continues the program execution with all the pseudoregister contents as they are.

10-5.7 Servicing a User's Interrupts

Many systems under development need the ability to test response to interrupts. Some way must be provided to change the vectors to accommodate different user's programs. This is done in the BUFFALO monitor by having the vectors (at locations $FFD6 through $FFFF) in ROM set to access locations in RAM (at $C4 through $FD). Those RAM locations contain a jump instruction that can be changed to point to the desired service routine. For example, the three locations starting at $EE are used to store the user's IRQ vector. These RAM locations are initialized during RESET to jump to a routine called STOPIT, which executes a **68HC11** STOP instruction. This effectively HALTS the μP and requires a RESET to recover. In other words, if an IRQ occurs and you have not set the vector to point to the IRQ service routine, it will STOP and the EVB will have to be RESET. When the *interrupt service routine's* address is entered in these locations (preceded by a $7E) and an interrupt occurs, the μP will jump to the service routine *indirectly* through these vectors. If the IRQ interrupt is involved, the IRQ mask bit must not be *set* for it to respond. These **interrupt vectors** include those for SWI that is used by BUFFALO as well as some for the **68HC11A8** internal peripherals, such as the timer and I/O ports.

10-5.8 Developing Programs

The BUFFALO program and the EVB are used to debug and patch programs until they work (see Section 12-4.9). When several program *bugs* have been corrected (by using MM to change the instructions), the program should be updated and reassembled in the host and downloaded again for further testing. This may be necessary after only one serious bug is found where it is too difficult to patch the program.

It can be seen that this **68HC11** EVB system is about the simplest possible software development tool that can be used effectively. The features of BUFFALO allow software and hardware debugging, although they are not as easily done as with the development systems to be described later in this chapter and in Chapter 12.

10-5.9 Other Monitor Systems

Since the introduction of the **6800** in 1974, many versions of these ROM-based debug programs have been developed, starting with one called MINIBUG. It was only 256 bytes long and was included in the same ROM with the first version of MIKBUG. MIKBUG is a 512-byte second generation debugger/monitor program also released in 1974. A PIA was used for serial I/O (by doing the serial-to-parallel, and parallel-to-serial conversions in software) because the ACIA was not yet available when this was written. These two programs were provided for many years in a ROM called **MC6830L8**, but it is now obsolete. It is described and listings are included in Engineering Note 100 (EN100) as cited in Section 10-11.

Table 10-4 shows some of the other monitor/debug programs that have been developed for the **6800**.

MINIBUG III and MICRObug are identical programs but are located at different addresses. They are similar to MIKBUG 2.0 and BUFFALO because they also have commands (functions 10, 11, and 12) to trace user programs (run-one-instruction), continue after a breakpoint, and insert, display, or remove breakpoints. They were used in Chapter 4 to illustrate instruction operation. BUFFALO can also be used.

10-6 TERMINAL REQUIREMENTS FOR ROM MONITOR PROGRAMS

All of the monitor ROMs described so far have been written to work with a keyboard/printer/terminal equivalent to the ASR33 teletypewriter (TTY). This terminal was the standard of the industry for many years, and its ASCII protocol is still used in most data communications and computer equipment. The 20-mA interface (described in Section 8-9.1) is also still used in some systems. Through the years, however, several alternative terminals have been offered. One hard-copy (next generation) terminal is the TI 733ASR, which has equivalent functions to the TTY, including program storage on tape. (Digital cassettes are used in place of paper tape.) Since it uses a heat-sensitive paper to print, it is quieter and faster than the TTY.

Users (particularly hobbyists) have tried to find less expensive ways to control or operate μP systems. The most popular device today is the Cathode Ray Tube (CRT) terminal. Most computers now either include a CRT or work with a separate CRT terminal. Several of the least expensive personal computers are designed to work with a commercial TV set. Liquid crystal displays are also being used in portable terminals.

All data terminals, with the exception of some IBM types, use the ASCII code and have an RS232C interface. These standards are explained in Chapter 8 and in Section 12-10.

When a CRT terminal is used in place of TTY or a TI type of tape terminal, saving programs from on-board RAM is not possible. To overcome this disadvantage, several techniques have been used. One is to use an audio cassette recorder/

TABLE 10-4 ROMs Available for **6800** Showing Functions Included

	MEX68EX12	MCM6830L7		MEC68MIN2	MEC68MIN3	In MEK6800D2 Kit Only	M68MM08A
Function	**Exbug 1.2 (F000-FBFF)**	**Minibug (FE00-FEFF)**	**Mikbug (E000-E1FF)**	**Minibug II (E000-E3FF)**	**Minibug III (E000-E3FF**	**J-Bug (E000-E3FF)**	**Microbug (FC00-FFFF)**
1. Load programs	X	X	X	X	X	X	X
2. Print contents of memory (ASCII)	X		X	X	X		X
3. Punch contents of memory on tape (ASCII)	X		X	X	X		X
4. Display and/or change memory	X	X	X	X	X	X	X
5. Display and/or change MPU registers	X	X	X	X	X	X	X
6. Reinitialize	X	X	X	X	X	X	X
7. Run user program	X	X	X	X	X	X	X
8. Use coresident assembler/editor	X		X	X	X		X
9. Change terminal speed	X			X	X		X
10. Trace user program	X				X		X
11. Continue user program after trace or breakpoint	X				X	X	X
12. Insert, display, and/or remove breakpoints	X				X	X	X
13. Search tape for specific title	X						
14. Verify program loaded into memory	X						
15. Stop on address	X						
16. Calculate offset for relative branches	X					X	
17. Provide scope trigger at selected address	X						

(*Continued on next page.*)

player. Several low-cost computers offer this feature. Also, a number of Motorola Applications Notes (including AN-788, cited in Section 10-11) have been written to show low-cost ways to use cassettes.

Another method for storing and retrieving data is on a floppy or hard disk system. Disk systems have been growing in popularity and becoming less expensive, so they are universally used now for both professional and personal systems. The added cost can often be justified by the dramatic improvement in operating speed. An assembler program that took about 25 minutes to load from paper tape can be loaded in about 5 seconds with the disk system.

A floppy disk subsystem can be added to a Monitor ROM system but requires a disk controller and a Basic Input Output System (BIOS) program (usually in ROM) to control it. It, in turn, loads a Disk Operating System (DOS). The more sophisticated EXORciser system to be described in Section 10-7.2 includes a

TABLE 10-4 *Continued.*

Function	MEX68EX12	MCM6830L7		MEC68MIN2	MEC68MIN3	In MEK6800D2 Kit Only	M68MM08A
	Exbug 1.2 (F000-FBFF)	Minibug (FE00-FEFF)	Mikbug (E000-E1FF)	Minibug II (E000-E3FF)	Minibug III (E000-E3FF	J-Bug (E000-E3FF)	Microbug (FC00-FFFF)
18. Abort from user program	X					X	
19. Disk interface	X						
20. Use macro-assembler	X						
21. Decimal, octal, hex conversions	X						
22. Search for specific bit pattern	X						
23. Trace to specified address	X						
24. Execute specified number of instructions	X						
25. Start user program from autostart	X						
26. 1200 or 2400 Baud TI operation	X						
27. Stop after encountering breakpoint "N" times	X						
28. Punch/load binary formatted tapes				X			
29. Test selected portion of memory				X			
30. Load memory from tape	X				X	X	X
31. Store memory on tape	X				X	X	X
32. Trace one instruction	X				X	X	X
Device marking	SCM44507,8,9	MCM6830L7,8		SCM44506	SCM44503	SCM44520	SCM37501
ACIA or PIA addresses required	FCF4-5	FCF4-5	8004-8007	8008-9	8008-9	8008-9	8408-9
RAM addresses required	FF00-FFFF	FF00-FF7F	A000-A07F	A000-A07F	A000-A07F	A000-A07F	380-3FF

Motorola Disk Operating System (MDOS). Most personal computers available today have disk systems, and that is why they are popular as Hosts for EVBs as described above.

10-7 μP SYSTEM DEVELOPMENT AND TESTING INSTRUMENTATION

Because of the unique problems of designing and debugging μP systems, special concepts in test instrumentation have evolved. In digital logic design, we are usually concerned with only one or two signals at a time. In the case of a μP, however, changes in the state of signals occur on 8 data lines, 16 address lines, and several control lines at the same time. Several separate instruments have been created specifically for μP system testing. Most can be separated into two classes:

Logic Analyzers and μP development systems. *Microcomputer Development Systems* are used throughout the product design cycle from the early stages of software development, when very little hardware exists, to the final debugging, where hardware/software interfacing and emulation with the complete target system are involved. Logic analyzers are used when the prototype is first turned ON but will not run for some reason (such as shorted address lines). They are also useful for performance analysis or for finding intermittent problems, which may be due to a *glitch* (see Section 10-8.14) in the hardware signals. Many analyzers do not provide much help in software analysis. Some MDSs can do the whole job when equipped with an emulator (see Chapter 12). Likewise, some logic analyzers are versatile enough to be able to perform software debugging as well. Logic Analyzers are described in Section 10-8.

10-7.1 μP Development Systems (MDSs)

The monitor ROM systems previously described all have limitations that make some tasks difficult. For example, they cannot readily be used to emulate the user's system hardware, which would minimize time and effort in early development.

The problem of getting the system running with new untried hardware is sometimes overwhelming. Once the system is running the Debug or Monitor program, the routines in it can be used to test the user's system software and I/O hardware.

The amount of help a Debug program provides is related to the size of the program. The original MINIBUG had 512 bytes and MINIBUG 3 has 1024 bytes. MIKBUG 2.0 has 2048 bytes. MDSs provide added capability through larger debug programs and added hardware features. These greatly enhance the ability to debug both software and hardware and to further simplify the development process.

MDSs have been created to overcome the problems presented by earlier evaluation kits and modules. Some of them use debug programs that are loaded into RAM rather than being resident in ROM, but are similar to the MIKBUG and MINIBUG systems previously described. As a minimum, a development system must have a loader routine in ROM so that the debugger can be brought into memory from a tape or disk file.

Since most development systems are complete operational systems to which the user's system can be attached, the problems of getting the user's system running are greatly reduced. The major manufacturers of μPs have introduced such instruments for their products, and most MDSs will support several different μP types. Although all μP development systems provide the ability to develop and debug software, not all of them provide a full hardware emulation capability or the ability to evaluate prototype or production hardware.

10-7.2 The EXORcisers

In 1974, when the **6800** μP was first introduced, a Motorola μC development system called the EXORciser was also produced. EXORciser I is a modularized expandable development system that contains all the common ingredients of a microcomputer and offers a versatile means of emulating any **6800** system. It consists of six basic module types:

- Debug module
- MPU module
- Memory modules
- Parallel I/O module
- Serial I/O module
- Wirewrap module (for custom circuitry)

The Debug module and the MPU module can be operated by themselves, but the concept introduced here is that the other modules can also be installed in the same card cage (on the same bus) to *emulate* any conceivable **6800** system. Figure 10-13 shows a block diagram of EXORciser I. It shows how the user and debug systems share the same MPU. They use it alternately.

The *Debug module* includes a monitor or control program (called EXbug) in ROM (3092 bytes), along with several hardware circuits that provides debugging features not possible with software alone.

EXORciser I's memory map is not configured in the same way as a conventional **6800** system. The very top of memory is 256 bytes of RAM, in contrast to ROM or PROM, which would normally be used. This is done so that the interrupt vectors can be changed during the system development. (A small PROM that contains the EXbug RESTART vector is switched in to get EXbug started.) The initialization routine then sets the interrupt vector locations to values used by EXbug. IRQ is not used by EXbug and is always masked when running in that program.

In EXORciser I, the top 4096 bytes of the 65,536 bytes available are used by the debug system, which leaves 61,440 bytes for the user. Because user systems almost never need to use the entire memory area, this configuration permits almost any user's complete system to be assembled and debugged.

10-7.3 System Address Selection

To understand how the EXORciser can be used to develop a system, consider the system shown in Fig. 10-14. It contains only an EPROM, a RAM, and a PIA. Not all 16 address lines are needed in most **6800** systems. Usually, as few lines as possible are used in order to keep the decoding simple. Here, only lines A15 and A14 are used for chip selection and only A15 is really required for the PROM. The addressing scheme is shown at the right of each IC. The starting address of the RAM (when all Ys are 0) can be an address starting with 0, 1, 2, or 3, a second digit of 0 to F, and a third digit of 0 or 8 (for example, 0000, $0080, $1A00, or $3F80). PIA addresses would start with 4, 5, 6, or 7 and the PROM address with C, D, E, or F (when A14 is also used). Note that the PROM can be programmed to run at $CXXX and still respond to $FXXX. This makes it possible to test the program (running at $CXXX) without interfering with EXbug, and yet in a final

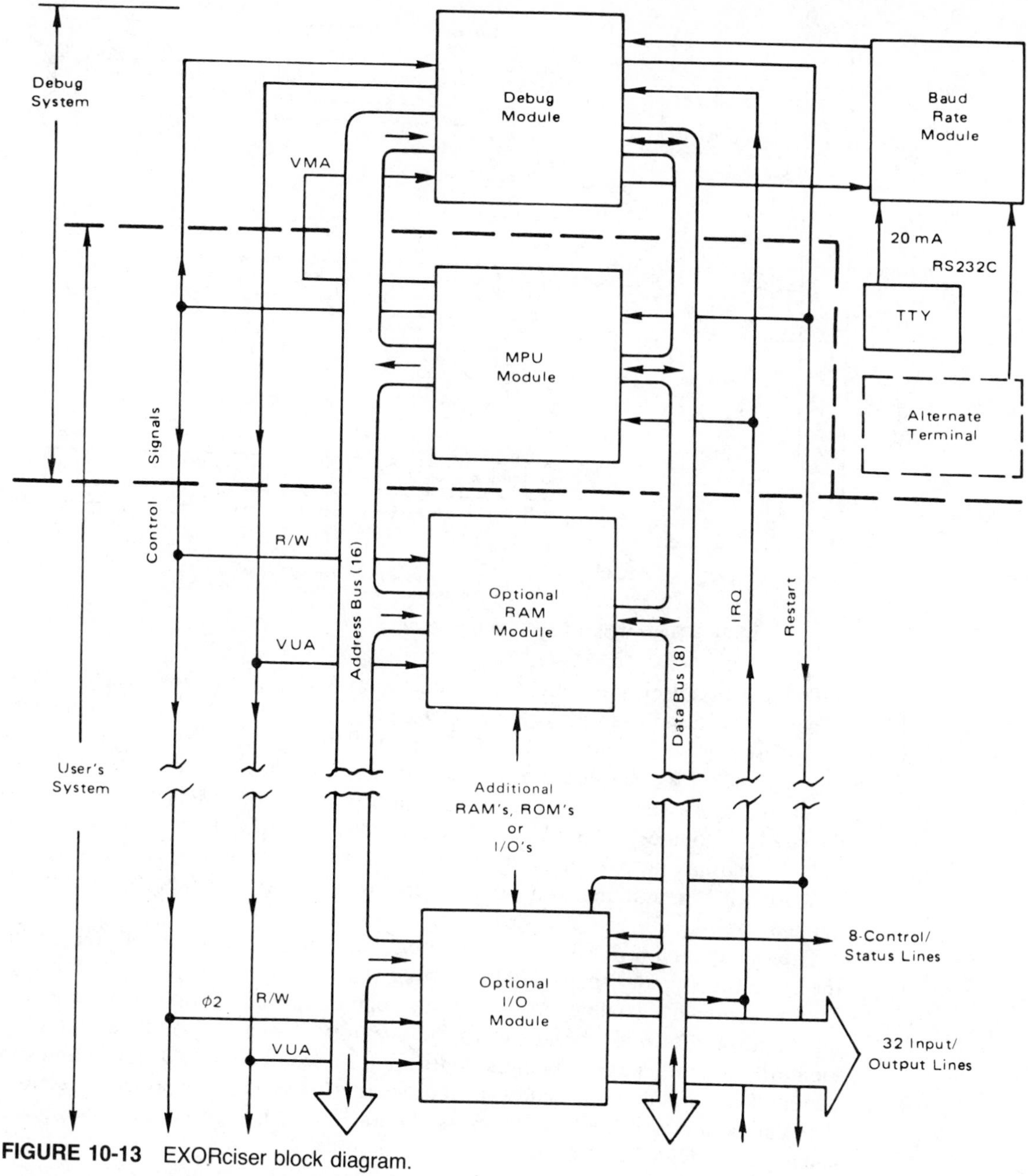

FIGURE 10-13 EXORciser block diagram.

system configuration, where the PROM will actually have rebundant decoding, the top eight locations ($FFF8–FFFF) *will be* accessed by the **6800** μP interrupt functions.

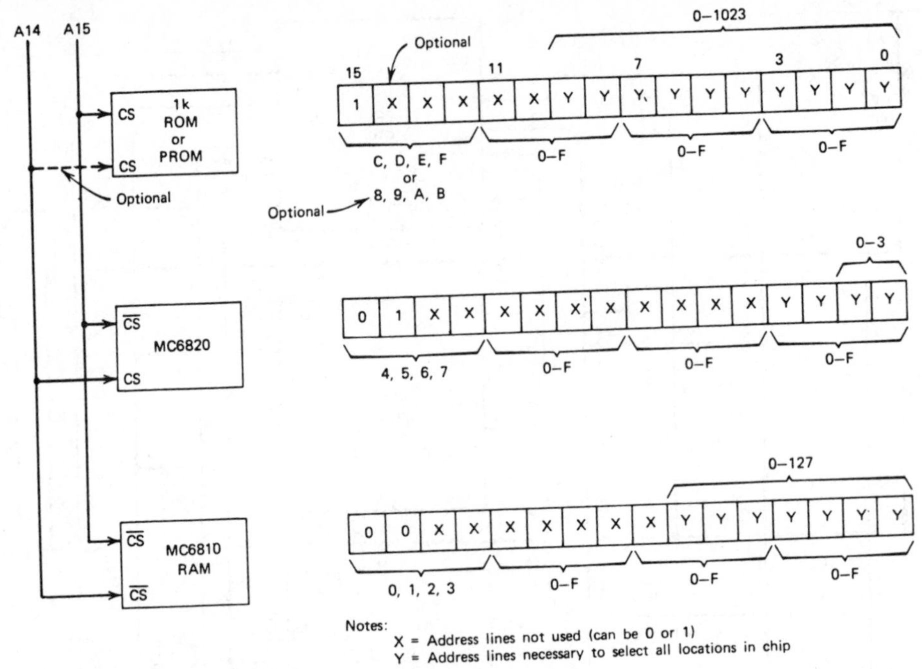

FIGURE 10-14 Typical small system addressing.

The first EXORciser was built to support the 1-MHz versions of the **6800** family of parts. These included the original versions of the **6801**, **6802**, **6805**, and **146805** μPs or μCs. (See Chapter 11 for details of these μCs.) Separate plug-in modules for use in the EXORciser were provided for each of these newer μCs.

When 2-MHz versions of the μPs began to appear, EXORciser II was introduced. The modules and motherboard were redesigned to work at the higher clock rate. It also has new features such as a dual memory map to avoid one of the EXORciser I limitations that some users found confusing (see the following explanation).

The Debug module hardware and EXbug program occupy the top 4096 bytes of the available memory map, with 256 bytes of RAM at the very top of memory. This is somewhat troublesome to many people when they first learn that the interrupt vectors *must be* at the top of memory. Once they realize that their memories and other system components *do not* have to be fully decoded and can be redundantly addressed as described in Section 7-14 and in the previous section, they can understand the techniques used with EXORciser I to design a standard **6800** system (with ROM at the top of the map).

EXORciser II simplifies the process, however, since it includes a map-switching technique that provides a second 65,536-byte map for the user's system. That map is not occupied by any of the development system hardware, and thus the user's program (that will be put in ROM) can be located at \$F000 to \$FFFF, in the USER map of EXORciser II. This map is shown in Fig. 10-15.

EXORciser II is shown in Fig. 10-16. Like EXORciser I, it is a complete μC system with hardware-debugging features and therefore is more expensive than

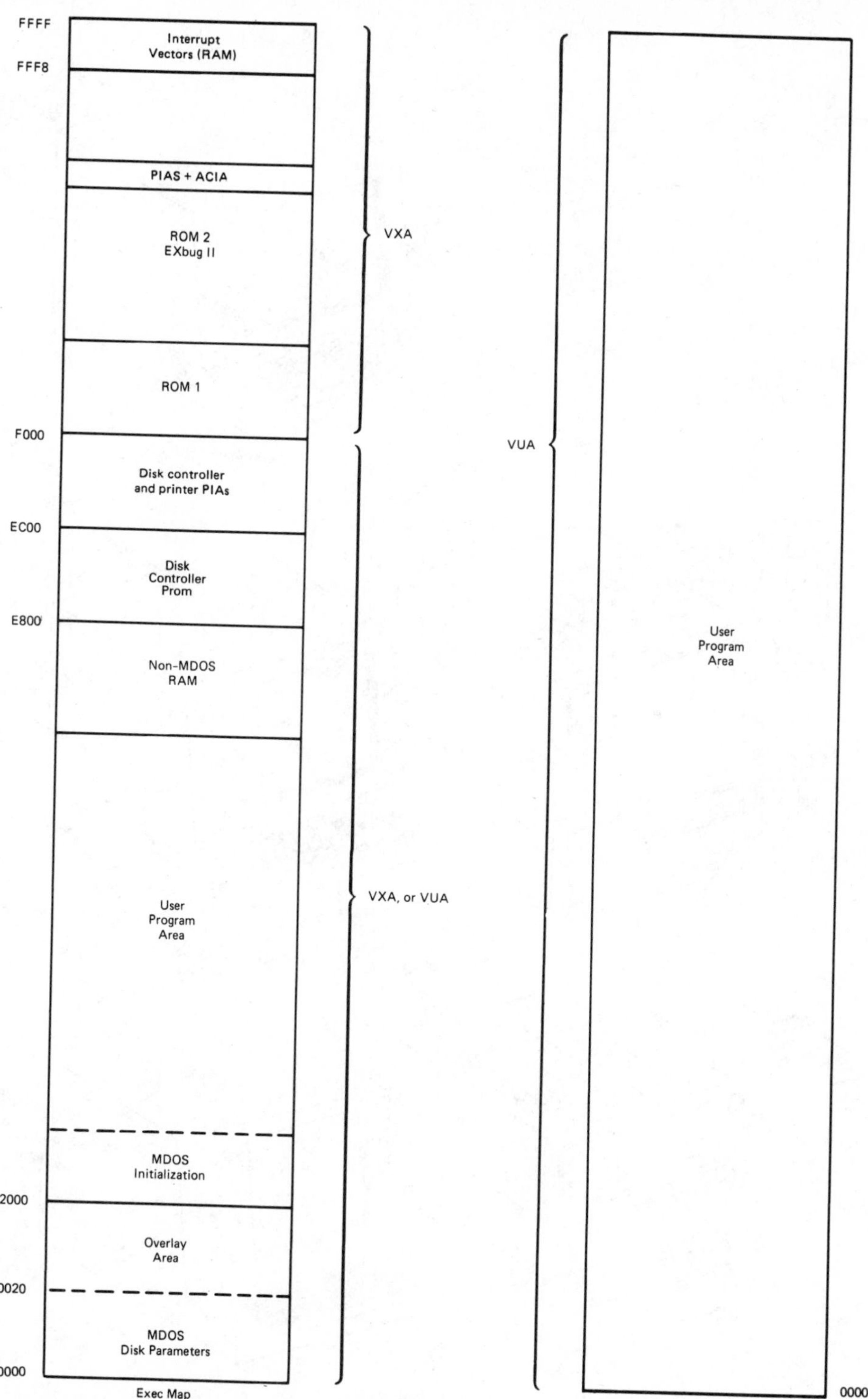

FIGURE 10-15 EXORciser II, dual memory map for User System.

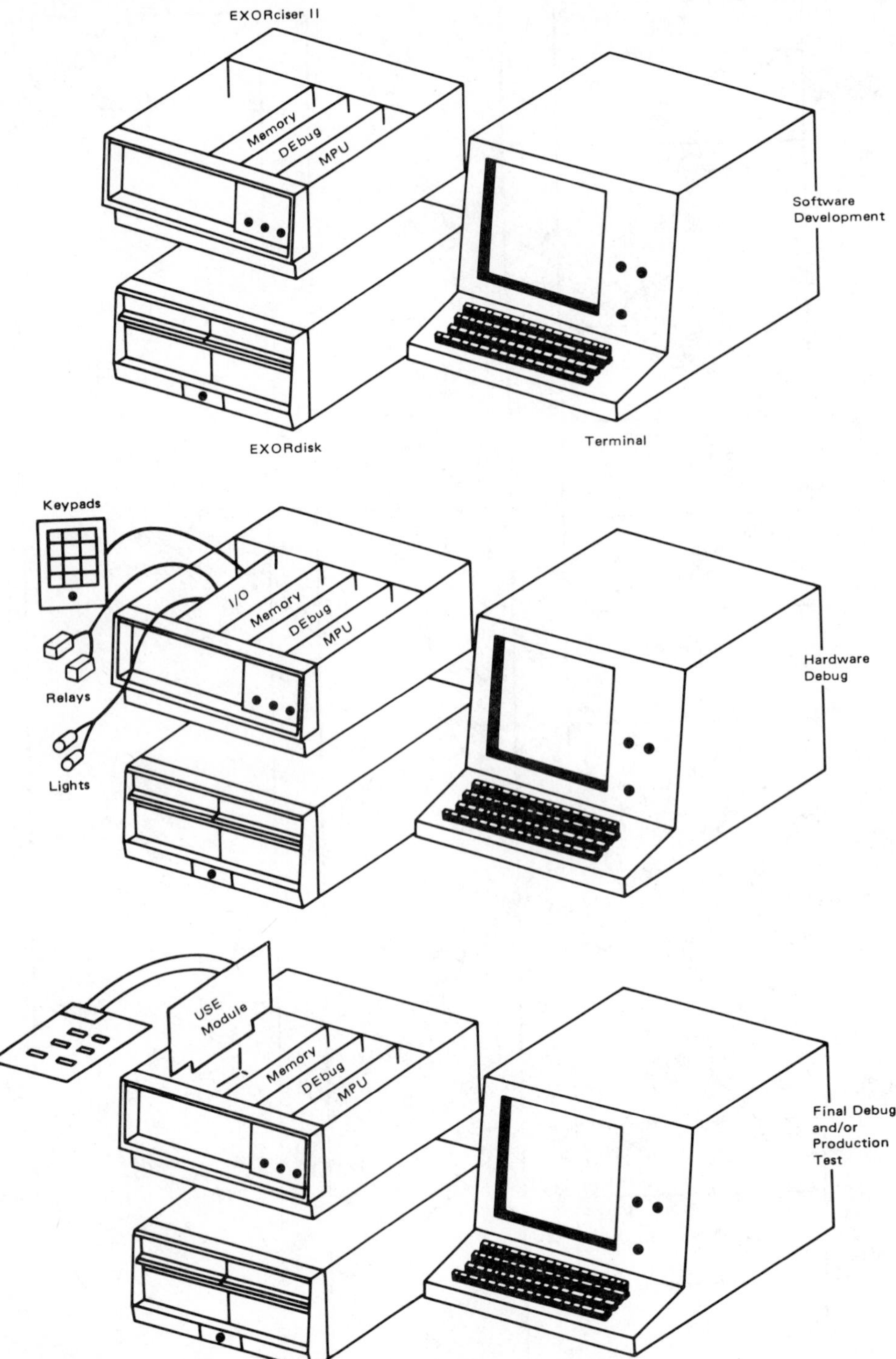

FIGURE 10-16 EXORciser II, the development tool.

the monitor systems of Section 10-5, but so much engineering time can be saved by using its many features that it effectively pays for itself and is therefore economical in the long run.

10-7.4 The EXBUG Program

EXBUG is a *monitor* program with all of the features previously described for MINIBUG or MIKBUG 2.0 but also includes routines to control hardware circuits on the Debug module of the EXORciser. EXbug is 3K in length and is stored in ROMs in both versions of the EXORciser. Several of EXbug's features also serve to debug the hardware.

The EXORciser was originally developed to use a data terminal such as a TTY or its more modern equivalent, the TI ASR733 terminal, to communicate with the Debug system and with the system under development. All addresses and data are entered via the keyboard, and all status or data are printed (or displayed) in ASCII-hex characters. Bytes and words are used rather than 1s and 0s. The TTY and the TI733 are very useful terminals because, in addition to providing a keyboard and printer, they provide a means of saving the software programs on paper or cassette tape and loading them back into memory when required. Coresident Editor/Assembler programs that run in the EXORciser were originally programmed for use with these tape terminals. A CRT terminal is universally used today but because it lacks the tape features, an MDOS floppy disk subsystem is also required. This combination is more expensive than a TTY or TI terminal but provides greater speed and flexibility. The disk operating systems provide LOAD and SAVE routines for handling object programs.

10-7.5 Microcomputer Development Trends

The advent of 16- and 32-bit μPs and high-level languages has caused a shift in the role of the MDS. The trends are to divorce the software development from the hardware testing, and as a result software is being developed on larger mainframe computers or on lower-cost personal computers. The hardware development has gravitated into stand-alone emulators. This split is becoming even more popular because of the increasing trend toward common high-level languages for all different types of μPs.

The EXORcisers are no longer manufactured, but their functions are now provided by these new types of Motorola development tools and are described in Chapter 12.

10-8 USE OF LOGIC STATE ANALYZERS

As mentioned in Section 10-7, new Logic Analyzers have also been designed to troubleshoot μP systems. They are an expansion of the multichannel Cathode Ray Oscilloscope (CRO) and provide simultaneous displays of the data and address lines. Rather than displaying the data in a voltage versus time mode, it is often more useful to have data expressed as digital words in either 1s and 0s or, even better, as hexadecimal digits. μPs require the analysis of combinations of signals rather than of one or two.

10-8.1 The Tektronix 1240/1241 Logic Analyzers

The Tektronix **1240/1241** Logic Analyzers are portable units that provide features for analyzing **6800** family μC systems. The **1241** color chassis with its Liquid Crystal Color Shutter (LCCS) and the **1240** monochrome chassis provide rapid setup and operation. Use of either instrument is made simple through a straightforward menu-oriented approach combined with four-level operation and touch-screen soft keys. Multilevel operation allows the user to select the level best matched to the user's skill level and the task at hand. Touch-screen soft keys provide high-level commands at a keystroke, keeping operator selections simple and well labeled. The **1240/1241** Analyzer is shown in Fig. 10-17.

10-8.2 Hardware Analysis

For hardware analysis, the **1240/1241** offers up to 36 channels of acquisition at sampling rates of 100 MHz asynchronous and 50 MHz synchronous. Detection of *glitches* (see Section 10-8.14) as small as 6 ns is also possible.

Standard memory depth is 512 bits per channel and can be extended to a maximum of 2048 bits per channel by using a special memory-chaining feature. This feature allows one card's memory to be chained to another, trading channel width for memory depth.

Hardware triggering capabilities include data and glitch triggering for isolating the problem area, clocked and unclocked triggering for capturing events that might not coincide with sample points, and counters, timers, and duration filters for triggering on the characteristics of a signal as well as its occurrence.

Auto-run capability allows the user to track intermittents through continuous acquisitions, change parameters on the system under test, and dynamically monitor their effects.

10-8.3 Software Analysis

Software analysis is supported by up to 72 data channels at sampling rates of 50 MHz synchronous/asynchronous. A flexible clocking scheme includes data demultiplexing without double probing.

Fourteen software triggering capabilities are provided so that program flow can be tracked. Included are conditional branching, counters, timers, and both program flow and data flow qualification. These functions are implemented in two independent event recognizers.

Other features that assist in software analysis are flexible channel groupings for display, standard display radices (including ASCII and EBCDIC), and an eight-level pattern search and memory compare with highlighting.

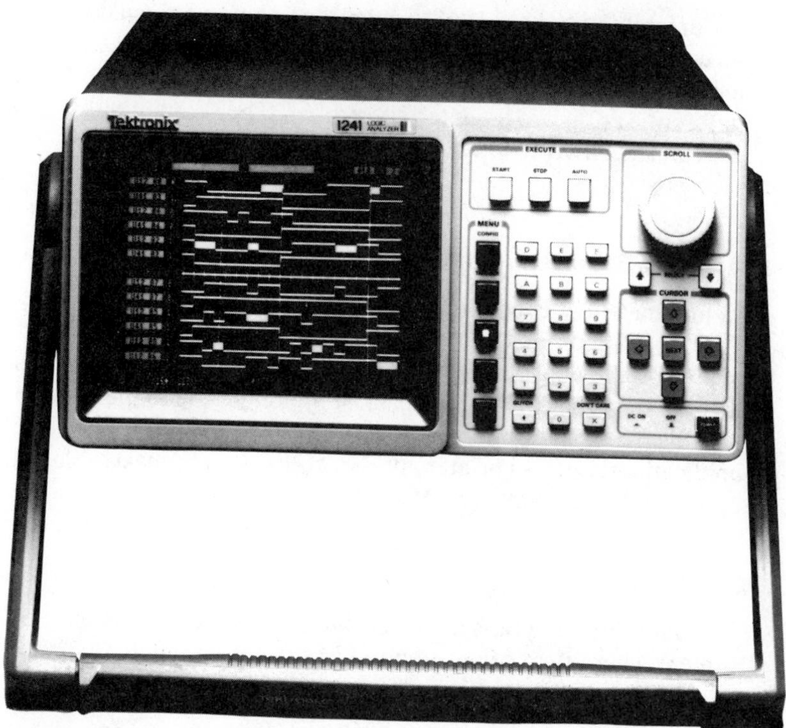

FIGURE 10-17 Tektronix **1240/1241** Logic Analyzer. (Courtesy of Tektronix, Inc.)

10-8.4 Hardware/Software Integration

The **1240/1241** offers a dual time base system that integrates all the hardware and software analysis capabilities. The dual time base system greatly speeds the hardware–software integration process by tying together the acquisition, triggering, and display of two independent time bases. The user can fully monitor the interaction between hardware and software or the relationship of two interdependent systems. All data displays are time-aligned and completely correlated. The dual time base allows the user to integrate functional modules, an increasingly important design task.

The power of the **1240/1241** stems from the configurable architecture of the chassis. Features can be selected that meet the current application needs, and later, when increased performance is needed, the chassis can be further upgraded.

10-8.5 Selectable Acquisition Cards

Data processing capabilities can be added by inserting *ROM packs* into the ROM port on the side of the chassis. These ROM packs provide the capability to capture data that is very specific to the problem at hand, and they assist in analyzing the data by processing and presenting it in the most useful manner.

Currently, there are ROM packs supporting performance analysis (12R01) and mnemonic disassembly (12RMXX) of most popular μPs including the **6800**, **6801**, **6802**, and **6809**. The version of the ROM (designated by the XX) is different for the different μPs, as are the interface probes. The standard 8-bit system configuration also includes two 1240D2 18-channel data acquisition cards, each with two P6480 probes.

10-8.6 COMM Packs for External Communications

Communication capabilities can be added by inserting *COMM packs* into a communications port on the rear of the chassis. These COMM packs act as adapters, allowing the **1240/1241** to function in different communication environments. The 1200C01 COMM pack supports RS232C, the 1200C02 supports GPIB, and the 1200C11 supports the parallel printer interface. Special communication applications, such as printer support (12RC01) and master/slave (12RC02), require both ROM pack and COMM pack.

10-8.7 Menu Operation and Soft Keys

Menu displays and on-screen soft keys make it easy to make setup choices on the screen, where the user's attention is already directed. Distraction by the need to look elsewhere on the instrument is avoided.

10-8.8 Multiple Operation Levels

Another major feature of the menu operating system is user-selected operation levels. The **1240** and **1241** provide four operation levels, ranging from basic operation for simple applications to full operation for complex jobs. The sophistication of system features increases with the operation level.

10-8.9 Configurable from the Front Panel

The **1240** and **1241** are completely configurable from the front panel, thus eliminating the need to switch boards and reconnect probes when changing from hardware to software applications. The keyboard has a simple layout with single-function keys. A knob is included on the keyboard for data scrolling. This knob and the extreme smoothness of the data scrolling make the **1240/1241** displays easier to read and manipulate.

10-8.10 Automatic Nonvolatile Storage

A battery-backed CMOS memory stores two complete instrument setups, including the last setup used before the **1240** or **1241** is powered down. This facilitates quick instrument start-up when returning to work and eliminates the problem of losing a setup as a result of power system interruptions.

In addition to its usefulness in the engineering environment, the **1240/1241** is well suited for manufacturing and service tasks. It transfers easily from one environment to another and helps facilitate communications between the different groups through its portability, remote control, mass storage, and remote servicing (see Section 10-8.12) capabilities.

10-8.11 Other Features

The **1241/1240** weighs only about 28 pounds and is therefore quite portable. The 1200C01 RS232C and 1200C02 GPIB COMM packs provide an automated test capability through remote control. Mass storage of setups, acquisition memories, and reference memories is achieved through RAM and EPROM Packs. Storage and retrieval of information from the 12RS01 8K RAM pack and the 12RS02 64K RAM pack is accomplished via menu soft keys. The 12RS11 32K EPROM pack (no EPROMs included) and the 12RS12 32K EPROM pack (EPROMs included) provide a permanent storage medium for setups and memories. To store files on these EPROM packs, the setups and memories are uploaded from the **1240/1241** to a host computer via GPIB or RS232C and then burned into EPROMs. Menu soft keys are used to retrieve files.

10-8.12 Remote Servicing

By means of the 12RC02 Master/Slave ROM pack, a 1200C01 RS232C COMM pack, and a modem, one **1240/1241** can remotely control another over a telephone line. This greatly eases troubleshooting, since service specialists can get to the problem via the telephone rather than having to travel to the problem site.

10-8.13 Other Models

In addition to the many options for these **1240/1241** analyzers, (described in Section 10-8.5), Tektronix offers two other digital analysis systems, the DAS9100 and the DAS9200. These are more expensive units with higher performance but are not portable.

10-8.14 The Hewlett-Packard Logic Analyzer

Hewlett-Packard also makes a number of logic state analyzers, such as the 1630G shown in Fig. 10-18. This unit is of particular interest to **6800** family users because it has preprocessor/interface, that is, *personality modules,* that make interconnection very simple and tailor the instrument to display the mnemonics of the processor selected. Modules are available for several Motorola μPs as well as for those made by other manufacturers. One is provided for **6800** system designers. The analyzer connects into the user's system either by a 40-pin clothespin-type clip or by replacing the μP with a 40-pin Dual In-line Package (DIP) plug and cable. The **6800** is reinstalled in the probe body. Up to 1024 cycles of address,

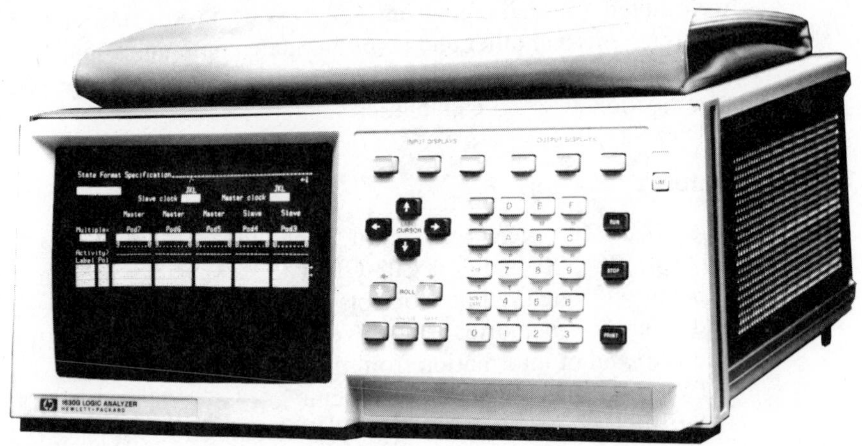

FIGURE 10-18 Hewlett-Packard 1630G Logic Analyzer. (Courtesy of Hewlett-Packard.)

data, and control information are captured. A triggering circuit is set up from the instrument's keyboard to trigger when a selected address, data, or external data event occurs. Hexadecimal, octal, or binary display of the captured cycle-by-cycle program flow is possible. Of particular interest is the ability to convert the Op codes into mnemonics, as shown in Fig. 10-19. Although only a screenful of information is displayed at a time, the window can be scrolled so that all 1024 steps are seen. The trigger point is identified by inverting the video. It is possible to delay the trigger a prescribed amount and to calculate execution times between two selected events. This instrument is really three different analyzers and can be used for State, Timing, or System Performance Analysis. It has the ability to switch modes during an analysis.

The timing waveform diagrams provide simultaneous display of up to 16 channels. A *glitch* display (see the following section) and direct readout of time between cursors let the user quickly adjust parameters to match the application. State analysis allows the hardware designers to window on a problem and then use the resolution of timing and waveform analysis to solve the problem. Many hardware problems are intermittent, recurring when the μP performs a specific function. The **HP 1631A/D,** with independent state triggering and four user-defined resource terms, can monitor the millions of bus transactions that occur per second and then trigger precisely on the one event that is causing the hardware problem.

State analysis also aids in integrating systems by either tracing program flow or performing cross-domain measurements.

10-8.15 Glitch Problems

In a digital system, a **glitch** refers to a momentary impulse that occurs on a signal line. In most cases, energy impressed on the line by an unexpected source causes glitches. The source could be outside the system, such as electromagnetic radiation from a switching device or a power line surge caused by large motors or welding equipment. Most often, however, the glitch source lies within the system itself; for example, it may be due to undersized V_{cc} or ground trace lines, where the current levels reached by simultaneously switching a high number of gates may create an excessive pulse in other circuits, or to a circuit board design where two lines run very close together over a long distance and the distributed capacitance between them couples energy from one line to the other (see Chapter 13 for details).

Since many situations like these occur in a typical design and can cause glitches, a number of problems can arise. Fortunately, not all glitches cause problems; in fact, many go unnoticed because the momentary toggling of a single line may do no harm. On the other hand, when a glitch toggles an additional gate at a time when a set of logic gates are switched, the control function instruction or data generated by that set of gates is altered—often with bizarre and possibly catastrophic results. False data may be transferred, the wrong device may turn ON, or the μP may poll the wrong peripheral. When the μP receives invalid or unintelligible information, the results can include anything from an erroneous output to a self-imposed shutdown.

10-8.16 Glitch Detection

Two forms of glitch detection are common. The latch method captures glitches and displays each glitch as a data bit, one sample period wide. Glitch detection for Hewlett-Packard logic analyzers defines a glitch as more than one transition across the voltage threshold within a single clock period. Glitches are stored in a separate memory and can be displayed uniquely on the analyzer screen.

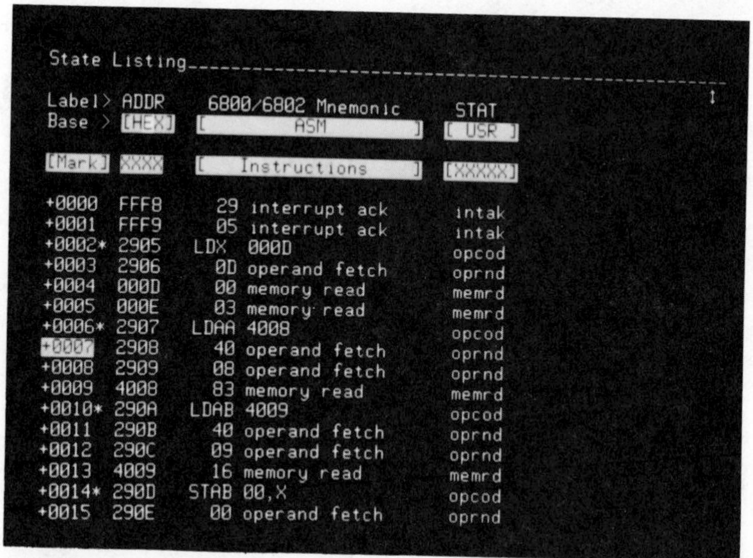

```
State Listing_____________________________________________

Label> ADDR    6800/6802 Mnemonic       STAT
Base > [HEX]  [         ASM         ]  [ USR ]

[Mark] XXXX   [    Instructions     ]  [XXXXX]

+0000  FFF8      29 interrupt ack       intak
+0001  FFF9      05 interrupt ack       intak
+0002* 2905   LDX  000D                 opcod
+0003  2906      0D operand fetch       oprnd
+0004  000D      00 memory read         memrd
+0005  000E      03 memory read         memrd
+0006* 2907   LDAA 4008                 opcod
+0007  2908      40 operand fetch       oprnd
+0008  2909      08 operand fetch       oprnd
+0009  4008      83 memory read         memrd
+0010* 290A   LDAB 4009                 opcod
+0011  290B      40 operand fetch       oprnd
+0012  290C      09 operand fetch       oprnd
+0013  4009      16 memory read         memrd
+0014* 290D   STAB 00,X                 opcod
+0015  290E      00 operand fetch       oprnd
```

FIGURE 10-19 Hewlett-Packard 1630G screen display showing **6800** mnemonics. (Courtesy of Hewlett-Packard.)

The glitch-latch approach has the disadvantage that it frequently results in the same display whether the glitch occurred one or two sample periods before the data transition or one sample period after the data transition. Glitches that occur in the same sample period as a data transition are not detected at all with the latch method; unfortunately, these can be some of the most troublesome glitches.

The Hewlett-Packard glitch detection method uses twin overlapping continuous monitors to identify glitches and stores this information in a separate memory. Glitches on specified control lines can be used as part of trigger conditions, separately, or logically ANDed with synchronous or asynchronous triggers.

Once glitches have been discovered by these methods, the designer must use the techniques described in Chapter 13 to get rid of them, or, better yet, the methods described should be used when first designing any μC system to minimize this possibility.

10-9 SUMMARY

The problems of designing and testing μPs were described and the evolution of the ROM monitor program concept for μP debugging was shown. Two classes of instrumentation, the Logic Analyzer and the μP Development System, were defined. The EXORciser and its EXbug program were described to illustrate how μP designers use this type of instrument to emulate and later test prototypes or production versions of their design. Finally, Logic Analyzers and their application were explained.

10-10 GLOSSARY

68HC11A8 An enhanced **6800**-type μP that includes a clock and 256 bytes of RAM, 512 bytes of EEPROM, and 8K bytes of ROM.

Bipolar PROM TTL-type device that is programmed by blowing out fuse-type links.

Breakpoint Software technique for halting a program at a specified address; used for Debugging.

Carriage return (CR) Data terminal character used to shift the cursor to the left end of a line.

Coresident programs Noninterfering programs resident in memory at the same time (e.g., Editor/Assembler).

CRT terminal Data terminal that uses a Cathode Ray Tube (CRT), or TV tube, instead of printing.

Debugging Troubleshooting or analyzing programs or hardware.

Firmware ROM or PROM.

Glitch Momentary impulse on a signal line usually causing false operation; due to unwanted coupling between lines or from external sources.

Interrupt vector Address pointing to the interrupt service routine.

Line feed (LF) Data terminal character that moves cursor down one line.

Memory map Diagram of the full addressable range of memory locations.

Microprocessor Development System (MDS) Instrument designed to aid in the design of μP systems.

Module Printed circuit card of standard size with specific functions implemented in TTL or MOS ICs.

Monitor program Program to display registers or memory contents. Also to load, dump, change, or debug a user's program. Usually in ROM or PROM.

Real Time Executing at the normal clock rate of 1 or 2 MHz (not slowed down).

Run-one-instruction Software technique whereby a single instruction is executed in real time and the registers are then displayed; also called TRACE or single-step.

S-Records Motorola standard method of formatting a machine language object program by converting bytes that are in binary form to their two-character hexidecimal equivalent. These ASCII characters plus adresses, byte count, and checksum are included on each S1 line. An S9 record terminates each program.

System debugging Verifying not only that the software does calculations and handles data properly but also that the external hardware is properly controlled by the software.

TI terminal Automatic Send/Receive model 733 Texas Instruments data terminal with cassettes.

Transparent Mode (TM) Command to allow the terminal to communicate directly with the Host (transparently through the evaluation system).

TTY Western Electric Model 33 Teletypewriter.

Valid Memory Address (VMA) Signal line on the **6800** μP that tells devices when to accept the address on the bus.

10-11 REFERENCES

M68HC11EVB Evaluation Board, Brochure BR278, Motorola LDC, 1986.

M68HC11EVM Evaluation Module, Brochure BR266, Motorola LDC, 1986.

M68HC11EVB/D1 Evaluation Board User's Manual, Motorola LDC, 1986.

MC68HC11A8 HCMOS Single-Chip Microcomputer, ADI 1207, Motorola LDC, 1986.

Hewlett-Packard. *Functional Analysis of the Motorola M6800 μP System,* Applications Note 167-9, Hewlett-Packard, Palo Alto, CA, 1981.

Hewlett-Packard. *The Role of Logic State Analyzers in μP Based Designs,* Applications Note 167-13, Hewlett-Packard, Palo Alto, CA, 1981.

Motorola. *M6800 EXORciser User's Guide,* Second Edition, M68PRMD (D) Motorola Semiconductor Products, Phoenix, AZ, 1977.

Motorola. *M68MM01A Monoboard Microcomputer IA,* Motorola Microsystems, Phoenix, AZ, 1977.

Motorola. *MINIBUG III Operating Procedures,* Preliminary Information, Motorola Microsystems, Phoenix, AZ, 1977.

Motorola. *MICROBUG Operating Procedures,* Preliminary Information, Motorola Microsystems, Phoenix, AZ, 1977.

Motorola. *MC6830L7 MIKBUG/MINIBUG ROM,* EN 100, 1980.

Wray, William C. *The EXORciser and Its Uses,* WESCON paper, presented in San Francisco, September 16–19, 1975.

Tektronix. *1240/1241 Logic Analyzer,* Tektronix, Beaverton, OR, 1987.

Tektronix. *Debugging a μP Based Process Control System,* Applications Note 57K3-1, Tektronix, Beaverton, OR, 1977.

Tektronix. *Troubleshooting a μP,* Applications Note 57K1.0, Tektronix, Beaverton, OR, 1977.

Note: All Motorola literature is available from Motorola Literature Distribution Center (LDC), P. O. Box 20912, Phoenix, AZ 85036.

10-12 PROBLEMS

10-1 The following program is written into a **6800** μC:

```
10  LDA A $20
12  ADD A #$BB
14  INC A
15  STA A $21
17  BRA   $F7
```

If location 20 contains $32, what are the contents of the registers and what is on the address and data lines after each cycle?

10-2 Rewrite Example 10-3 using the stack instead of the index registers.

10-3 A program is halted at location $10 by the instruction

```
$50   20 FE        BRA  *
```

Add instructions prior to $50 so that before the program halts, it stores the contents of A at $3E, B at $3F, and X at $3A and $3B.

10-4 In Fig. 10-5, list the components associated with

a. The HOST RS232 interface.

b. The terminal RS232 interface.

10-5 A program starts at $C020 and does not use the stack. A breakpoint must be put in at $C040 to save all the registers in locations $20–$28. You may add an LDS at $C01D and start the program there. How do you put the breakpoint in at $C040?

After attempting to solve these problems, try to answer the self-evaluation questions in Section 10-2. If any of them still seem difficult, review the appropriate sections of the chapter to find the answers.

CHAPTER 11

OTHER 8-BIT MICROPROCESSORS

11-1 INSTRUCTIONAL OBJECTIVES

Since the **6800** was introduced in 1974, many newer and more sophisticated μPs have been designed and built. This chapter introduces the newer 8-bit μPs and describes their features. As we have taken most of this book to describe the **6800**, you will realize that space limitations prevent us from describing all of the other μPs in equal detail. We hope to give you a grasp of the functions and capabilities of some of these new μPs, as well as the details of some of the new features, such as the timer, the Serial Communications Interface (SCI), and the Serial Peripheral Interface (SPI).

The objective of this chapter, therefore, is to introduce the newer μPs that are derived from the **6800**, so that the best μP for a planned system can be selected. You are then advised to consult the manufacturer's literature for more detailed information on the μP chosen.

11-2 SELF-EVALUATION QUESTIONS

Watch for the answers to the following questions as you read the chapter. They should help you to understand the material presented.

1. What is the Y register? Which μPs use a Y register?
2. On the **6801**, what is the difference between $\overline{IRQ1}$ and $\overline{IRQ2}$?
3. What are the differences between the single-chip mode and the multiplexed mode?
4. What **6801** registers are associated with the timer and the SCI? Where are they located and what is their function?
5. What is a "wake-up" feature?

6. What is an $\overline{LTR}$? What is an $\overline{LIC}$? On what μCs are they used? What good are they?
7. In a **6802** system, what functions are performed by the **6802** and what functions by the **6846**?
8. What are the advantages of CMOS? Of HCMOS? How do you tell if a **6805** is manufactured by using HMOS, CMOS, or HCMOS?
9. How do you tell if a **6805** contains ROM or EPROM?
10. What additional registers are in the **6809**? What is their function?
11. What is a postbyte? What **6809** instructions take postbytes?
12. What is the advantage of indirect addressing? Of program counter relative addressing?
13. On an RTI, with the **6809** what determines how many registers will be pulled from the stack?

11-3 INTRODUCTION

Since the introduction of the **6800** in 1974, the *packaging density*, or the ability to put more gates on an IC, has improved dramatically. This has resulted in two different types of improved μPs. One type is the *single-chip controller*, which has ROM, RAM, I/O, Timers, and sometimes other functions such as an analog-to-digital (A/D) converter on the chip as well as the μP. This type of IC has all the functions of a computer and is called a microcomputer (μC). It is used in small systems that do not require extensive programs to control processes or as the nucleus of a larger system with additional memory or I/O ICs. The second type of μP, exemplified by the **6809**, remains strictly a processor (and a clock). The additional gates on the IC are used to provide more registers and other instructions. This results in a μP with a more powerful instruction set than the **6800**.

The newer Motorola μPs or μCs are divided into four different *families* and all are related to the **6800**. There are several members of each family; each member has the same basic family number plus some other numbers to differentiate it from the other family members.

Figure 11-1 shows the newer μPs. The chart shows the year of their introduction and their performance compared to the **6800**. Performance generally refers to the speed with which tasks are completed. High-performance μPs often have powerful instructions that accomplish in one instruction tasks that require three or four **6800**-type instructions. On the chart the letters A and B generally refer to the μPs that are functionally identical to the generic μP but operate at higher speeds. The **68A00**, for example, uses a 1.5-MHz clock, and the **68B00** is for use with 2.0-MHz clocks. A μP number containing the letters HC indicates that the IC uses *high-speed* CMOS gates rather than NMOS gates. The HCMOS μCs operate up to 2.1 MHz, like their NMOS predecessors, but HCMOS consumes less power.

The four new families of μPs or μCs shown in Fig. 11-1 are (from bottom to top) the **6805**, **6801**, **6802**, and **6809**. The **6805** family contains a simplified version of the **6800** μP, and Fig. 11-1 shows that its performance in terms of speed in processing is less than that of the **6800**. Each **6805** version, however, has a variety

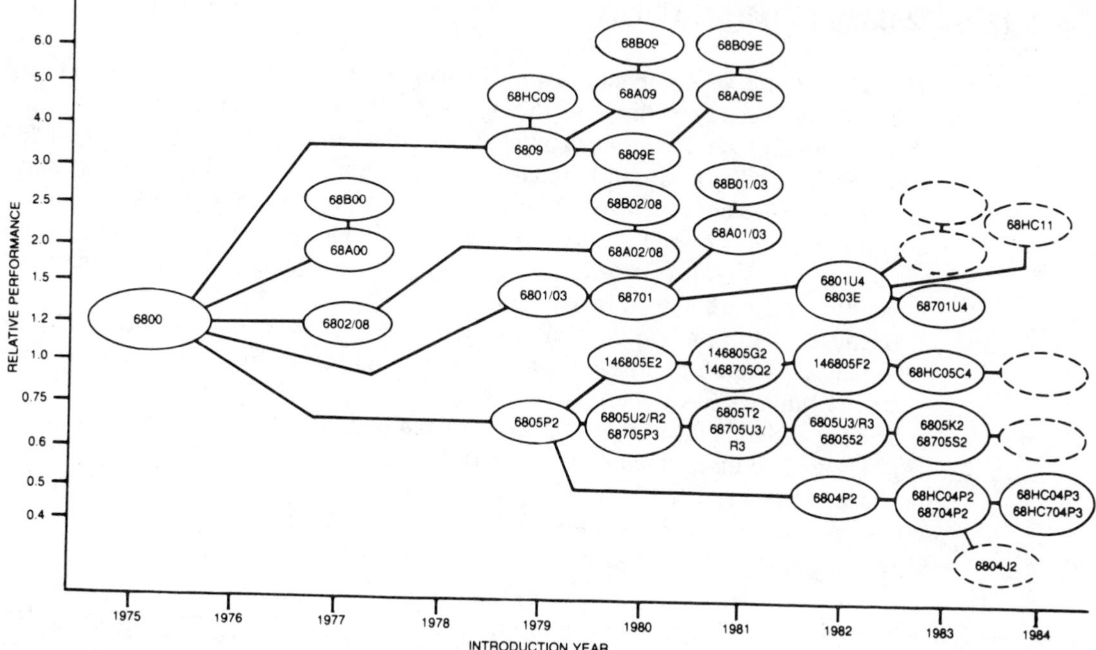

FIGURE 11-1 Geneology of the **6800** μP/μC family.

of peripherals included within the IC. They are used for single-chip controller applications. The **6805** family is discussed in Section 11-10.

All members of the **6801** family contain an enhanced **6800** processor. They also contain RAM, ROM, or EPROM, a timer, and serial and parallel I/O similar to an ACIA and PIA. Other members of the **6801** family include the **6803**, which has no ROM and thus can only be operated in some of the **6801** modes, the **68701**, which contains an on-board EPROM rather than ROM, and the **68HC11**, with its powerful peripheral features. The **6801** is discussed in Section 11-5 and the **68HC11** in Section 11-8.

The **6802** and the **6808**, which is the same chip without a working ROM, were the first μPs designed after the **6800**. They contain a **6800** μP, a clock oscillator circuit, and some RAM. When used in conjunction with a second IC (the **6846**) that included a timer, some I/O, and a ROM, a complete computer was provided. Manufacturing of the **6846** was discontinued in March 1986. The **6802**, however, is still being widely used. The **6802/6846** combination was a two-chip μC and is included here only to show that it was the first step toward the newer single-chip μCs like the **6801**.

The **6809** is one of the highest-performance 8-bit μPs that Motorola manufactures. There are no peripheral functions in the **6809** (except the clock), but its additional registers and enhanced instruction set make it very powerful. It is used in many new designs. The **6809** is discussed in Section 11-12.

11-4 THE 6802/6846 COMBINATION

The **6802** μP and its companion chip, the **6846** ROM-I/O-Timer, were introduced late in 1977. These two chips together formed a *complete* μC since they combined the functions of six of the original **6800** family members (Fig. 11-2a). The **6802** includes an oscillator circuit (similar to the **6875**), 128 bytes of RAM (the equivalent of a **6810**), and a μP with functions identical to those of the **6800**. The **6846** contains 2K bytes of ROM (like two **6830**s), a timer (one-third of a **6840**), and a parallel I/O port (half of a **6821**, see Section 8-4). The interconnections between these two chips are shown in Fig. 11-2b.

Because of the on-board clock and RAM in the **6802**, the system costs are reduced and therefore this chip has become the basis for many high-volume systems. Millions have been used by the automotive industry alone.

The pin assignments of the **6802** are very similar to those of the **6800** as shown in Fig. 11-2c. The direct memory access (DMA) feature of the **6800** was sacrificed because of the need for additional pins to accommodate the on-board RAM and clock. A comparison of pinouts shows that TSC, DBE, and φ1 were removed and RAM enable (RE), EXtal (EX), Xtal (X), memory ready (MR), Enable (E),

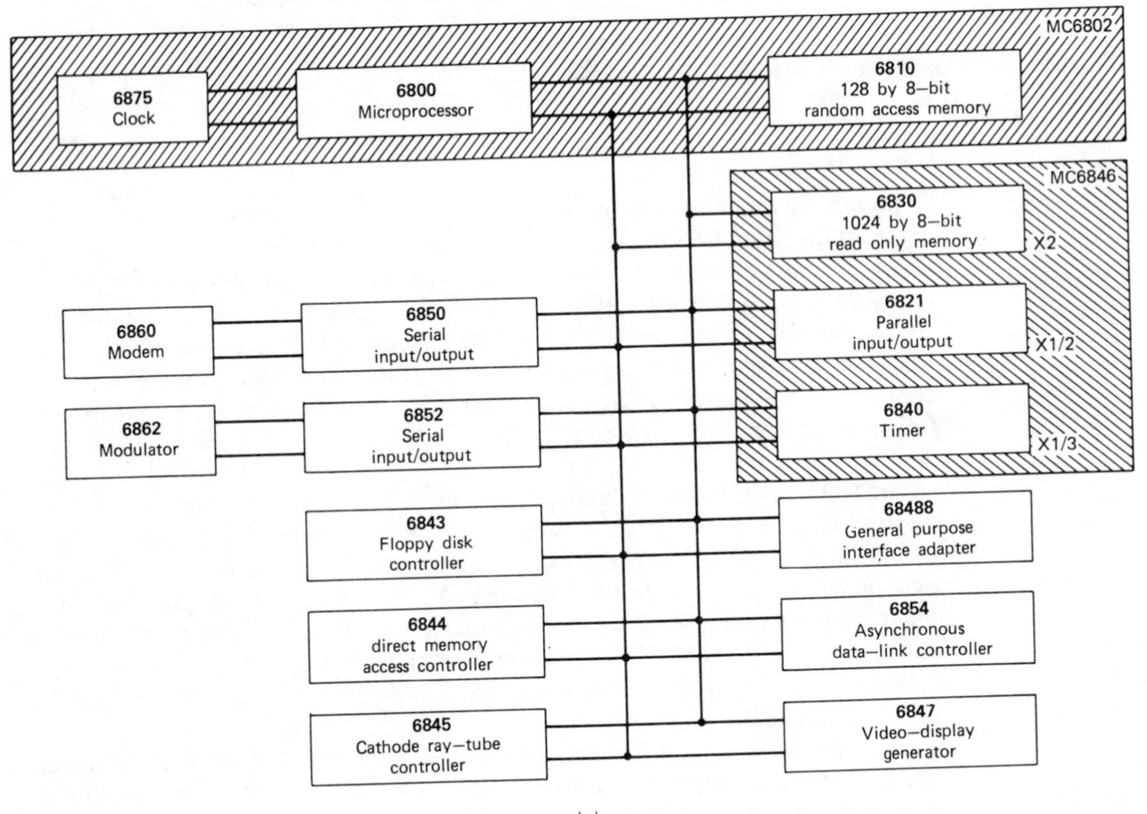

FIGURE 11-2a The **6802/6846** two-chip μC showing functions.

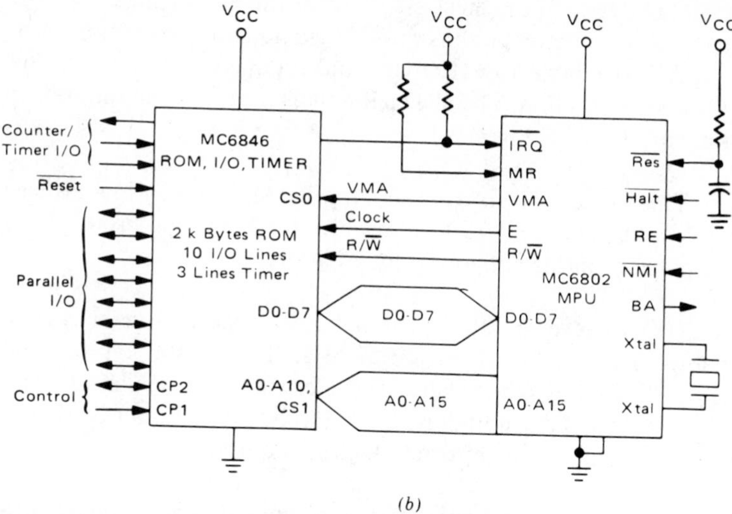

(b)

FIGURE 11-2b Two-Chip μC interconnections.

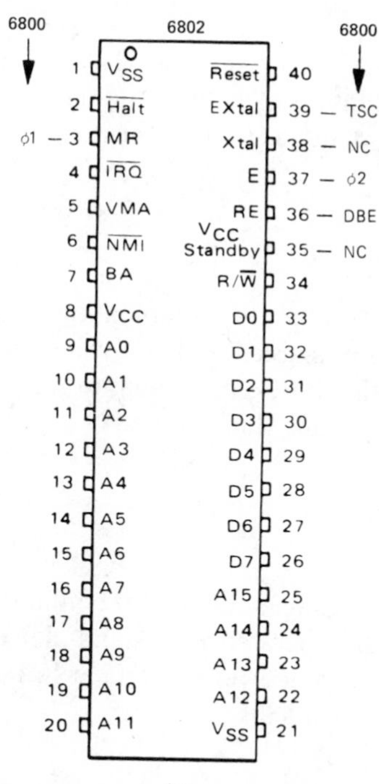

(c)

FIGURE 11-2c **6802/6800** pinouts.

and V_{CC} Standby were added. In the **6802**, 32 bytes of the RAM can be used to retain information (by using a battery), thus providing a nonvolatile memory. The **6802/6846** system was expandable to 64K bytes and retained all the other **6800** features such as 5-V-only operation. The **6802** μP signals (or pins) that differ from those of the **6800** μP are listed below:

RAM Enable (RE) This signal controls the on-chip RAM. If taken low at least three cycles before V_{CC} falls below 4.75 V, it disables the RAM and protects any data in the 32-byte portion that is supported by a battery.

EXtal (EX) and Xtal (X) These are for a parallel resonance quartz crystal to control the internal oscillator. A 4-MHz (or 3.59-MHz TV) crystal can be used since the frequency is divided by 4 internally. These crystals are smaller and less expensive than the 1-MHz crystal normally used. Pin 39 (EXtal) can be driven from an external TTL oscillator if a separate clock is required.

Enable (E) This is the output of the divide-by-4 clock and is a single-phase TTL-compatible signal used to drive the rest of the system. It is equivalent to the **6800** $\phi 2$ clock. This signal is stretched by the Memory Ready signal.

Memory Ready This is used as described in Section 7-7 to stretch the $\phi 2$ clock integral multiples of half-periods to allow use of slow memories. It is a TTL signal and allows normal operation when high.

V_{CC} Standby This pin supplies the DC voltage (battery or V_{CC}) to the 32 bytes of RAM. When properly used with the RE signal, retention of data during power down is guaranteed. The student should study the data sheets cited in Section 11-15 for more details.

11-4.1 The 6846 ROM-I/O-TIMER

The **6846** provided three important features for this two-chip, μC combination. As seen in Fig. 11-2a, it included 2K bytes of mask-programmable ROM equivalent to two of the original **6830** components, an 8-bit bidirectional I/O port similar to the B side of a **6821**, and a timer-counter function similar to one-third of a **6840**.

11-5 THE 6801 μC FAMILY

The **6801** was introduced in 1979 and is Motorola's first single-chip μC. It contains all the elements of a complete computer and can be operated in a stand-alone mode with very little external circuitry (a few resistors and port interface ICs). The following system components are contained in each **6801** μC:

1. An enhanced **6800** μP
2. A RAM
3. A ROM or EPROM

4. A Timer
5. Three 8-bit I/O ports (plus a 5-bit port)
6. A Serial Communications Interface (SCI)

Since 1979, several variations or enhancements of the basic **6801** have been introduced. The μPs or μCs in the **6801** family as of 1987 are shown in Table 11-1.

The differences between the various members of this family are mostly explained in Table 11-1. The **68120 and 68121** are classed as Intelligent Peripheral Controllers (IPCs) and provide the interface between a **6800** or **68000** family μP and a peripheral device. System bus data is transferred to and from the IPC via dual-ported RAM. All of the μCs shown in Table 11-1 include an enhanced **6800** μP with additional instructions (see Section 11-5.10). The **68HC01** and **68HC11** are enhanced additionally and are described in Section 11-8. The student is referred to the specific Data Sheets cited in Section 11-15 for added details.

Because these μCs are all based on the original **6801**, we will describe it in detail. Its internal configuration is shown in Fig. 11-3. This chip contains all elements of a μC, including 2K bytes of ROM, 128 bytes of RAM, a clock, a 16-bit timer, a serial I/O port, 29 parallel programmable I/O lines, and an improved **6800** μP. The **6801** is architecturally compatible with the **6800** family, so it works with any of the **6800** peripheral components.

11-5.1 The 6801 Modes and Ports

The **6801** operates in one of eight different *modes*. Depending on the mode, it can operate by itself as a stand-alone one-chip controller or can serve as a central processor and control external memory and peripheral devices.

The **6801** contains four I/O *ports* as shown in Fig. 11-3. There are three 8-line ports (1, 3, and 4) and one 5-line port (port 2). All ports can be used as general-purpose I/O ports under control of their Data Direction registers in the **6801** μC. Most ports also have special-purpose functions, depending on the operating mode of the **6801**. The function of each port is as follows:

Port 1. This is strictly an eight-line port that is independent of the mode. It is always an I/O port.

TABLE 11-1 The **6801** Family of μCs

μP/μC	Pins	I/O Pins	RAM	ROM	EPROM	EEPROM
6801	40	29	128	2K	—	—
6803	40	13	128	—	—	—
68701	40	29	128	—	2K	—
6803E	40	13	128	—	—	—
6801U4	40	29	192	4K	—	—
6803U4	40	13	192	—	—	—
68701U4	40	29	192	—	4K	—
68120	48	21	128	2K	—	—
68121	48	5	128	—	—	—
68HC01	40	29	128	4K	—	—
68HC11A8	52	40	256	8K	—	512

Port 2. This is a five-line multipurpose port. In addition to its general-purpose I/O capability, it provides for *timer* I/O and for *serial* I/O through the SCI interface. It is also used for setting the **6801** operating modes during RESET, as explained in Section 11-5.2.

Port 3. In the *single-chip* mode (see Section 11-5.3), it is used as a general-purpose I/O port. Data can be strobed into it using the *Input Strobe* (IS) line. On output, an *Output Strobe* (OS) can be generated to load data from port 3 into an external device. (A *strobe* is a pulse on a signal line at a specific time, usually used to read or latch data.) This provides a *handshake* capability between μPs. In the expanded non-multiplexed mode (see Section 11-5.4) port 3 functions as the data bus, and in the *expanded multiplex mode* (Section 11-5.5) it is used for both address and data. An *address strobe* samples the address at the proper time, preventing any conflict between address and data. These lines are said to be *multiplexed,* since they switch functions during the execution of an instruction.

Port 4. This port is also used for I/O in the single-chip mode. In the nonmultiplexed mode it is used as the low 8 bits of the address bus, and in the multiplexed mode it is used as the high 8 bits of the address bus.

Each line of Fig. 11-3 is marked with the two or three identities it may have when the various modes are chosen. For example, the line in the upper right of the figure, connected to port 2, is either I/O line 0 or Tin (Timer in). The upper left line, connected to port 3, can be either address line A7, data line D7, or I/O line 37 (pin 30), depending on the mode selected.

11-5.2 Setting the Operating Modes

The eight **6801** operating modes are shown in Table 11-2. Depending on the mode, the **6801** can stand alone as a one-chip controller or can serve as a central processor controlling external memory or peripheral devices. The mode is determined at RESET. When a RESET pulse occurs, port 2 pins 0, 1, and 2 become inputs, and the binary number on these three pins determines which of the eight modes the **6801** will operate in until the mode is changed by another RESET pulse.

TABLE 11-2 The **6801** Operating Modes

MODE	I/O 22(7) PC2	I/O 21 PC1	I/O 20 PC0	ROM	RAM	Interrupt Vectors	Bus Mode	Operating Mode
7	H	H	H	I	I	I	I	Single Chip
6	H	H	L	I	I	I	MUX(6)	Multiplexed/Partial Decode
5	H	L	H	I	I	I	NMUX(6)	Non-Multiplexed/Partial Decode
4	H	L	L	I(2)	I(1)	I	I	Single Chip Test
3	L	H	H	E	E	E	MUX(4)	Multiplexed/No RAM or ROM
2	L	H	L	E	I	E	MUX(4)	Multiplexed/RAM
1	L	L	H	I	I	E	MUX(4)	Multiplexed RAM & ROM
0	L	L	L	I	I	I(3)	MUX(4)	Multiplexed Test

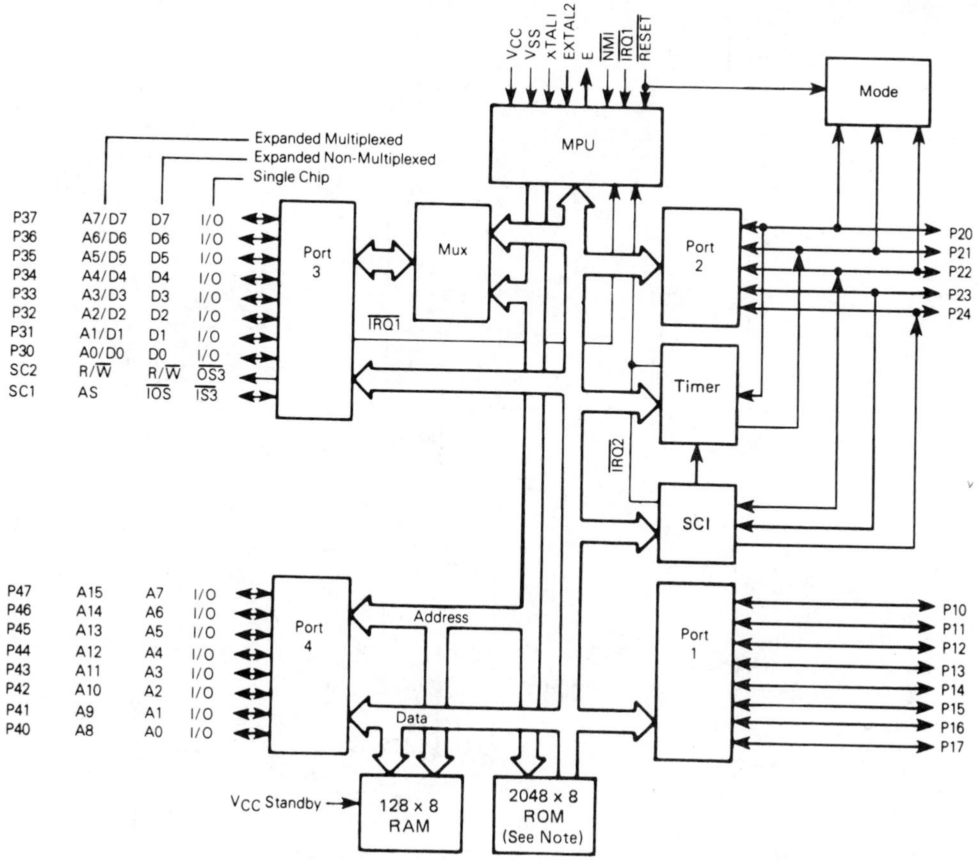

NOTE: No functioning in MC6803

FIGURE 11-3 **6801** microcomputer family block diagram.

Figure 11-4 is a simple *mode programming circuit*. The user selects a mode by setting the switches appropriately and then pushing RESET. When RESET is low, the capacitor discharges and the inputs to pins P20, P21, and P22 of port 2 are determined by the switches. When RESET is high, the capacitor charges toward V_{CC} and reverse-biases the diodes, effectively removing the switches from the circuit. The selected mode values are also entered into bits 5, 6, and 7 of the Data Register for port 2 (location $0003), which makes the mode available to the program. After RESET has occurred, port 2 is configured as a 5-bit data input port.

The **6801** μC uses an internal Schmitt trigger circuit to guarantee proper start-up. The designer need only use a simple *RC* pull-up on the reset pin.

Although the **6801** has eight operating modes, it really operates in one of three major modes: single-chip, nonmultiplexed, and multiplexed. These modes are described in the following paragraphs.

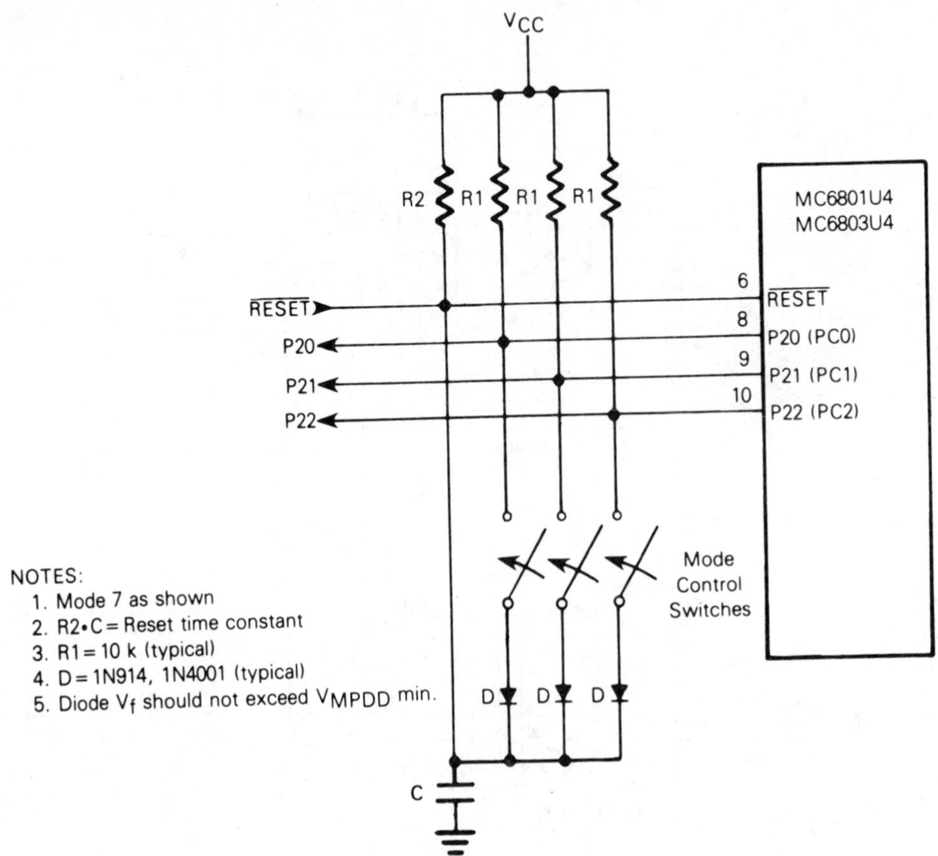

FIGURE 11-4 Typical mode programming circuit.

11-5.3 The Single-Chip Mode

Mode 7 is the basic *single-chip* mode. In single-chip mode the **6801** is the entire μC, and no additional memory or I/O is used. The address and data buses are not available externally. Figure 11-5a shows the hardware configuration of the single-chip mode and Fig. 11-5b shows its memory map. In single-chip operation only the internal RAM and ROM are used. Therefore, systems that require more than 128 bytes of RAM or 2K of ROM cannot operate in single-chip mode. (The **6801U4** provides 192 bytes of RAM and 4K bytes of ROM.)

Ports 1 and 2 are I/O in all modes. In single-chip operation ports 3 and 4 also become I/O ports. The operation of port 3 is controlled by SC1 and SC2 (the Strobe Control lines), which function as two additional control lines. In this mode, SC1 functions as an input, called $\overline{IS3}$ (Input Strobe 3). $\overline{IS3}$ is used by an external device to indicate that it has data for the μC or to acknowledge that it has accepted data from the μC.

SC2 functions as an Output Strobe, $\overline{OS3}$. The strobe is generated by a read or a write to data register 3. The operation of $\overline{IS3}$ and $\overline{OS3}$ is further controlled by the

Port 3 Control and Status register, as shown in Fig. 11-6. This is one of the internal registers and is at address $000F.

11-5.4 The Expanded Nonmultiplexed Mode

The expanded nonmultiplexed mode is mode 5 and it allows the user to add 256 bytes of RAM to the user system. In this mode ports 3 and 4 become the data and address bus that enables the μC to communicate with the additional memory, and thus these ports can no longer be used for I/O.

Figure 11-7a shows the hardware configuration for the nonmultiplexed model and Fig. 11-7b is the memory map. It shows that the additional memory occupies locations $0100 to $01FF. Port 3 functions as a bidirectional data bus for this memory, and port 4 provides the least significant byte (LSB) of the address. [The Most Significant Byte (MSB) is $01.] In this mode Strobe line 1 functions as an Input/Output select ($\overline{\text{IOS}}$) strobe that goes low only when the external memory is selected. This line can be used to enable the external memory. Strobe line 2 functions as the R/$\overline{\text{W}}$ line. On RESET, the Data Direction Register for port 4 configures it as an input port. This must be changed to enable it to function as an address bus.

11-5.5 Expanded Multiplexed Mode

When the **6801** system requires more memory or peripheral devices than are provided in the chip, it is used in the *expanded multiplexed mode*. In this mode port 3 *multiplexes* its 8-bit bus adddress lines A0–A7 with data line D0–D7 (see

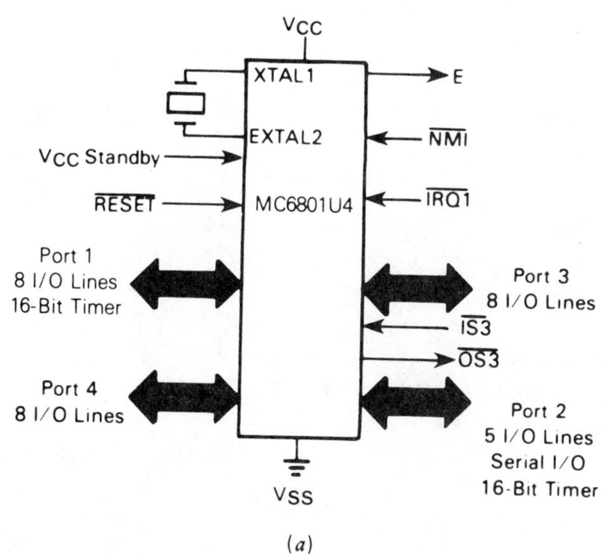

(*a*)

FIGURE 11-5 The **6801** single-chip mode.
(a) **6801** hardware connections.

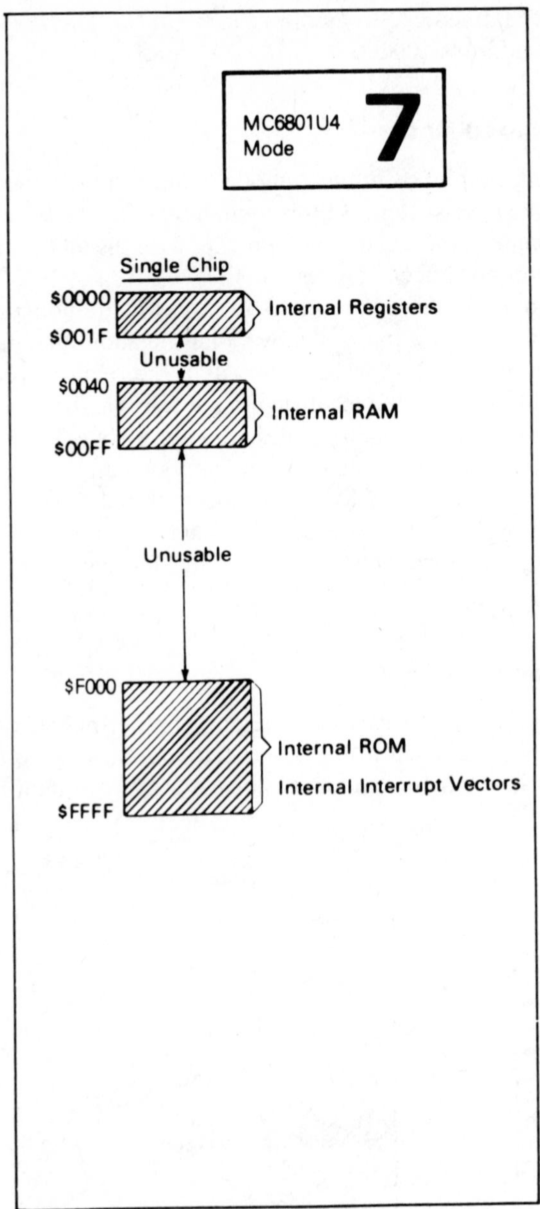

FIGURE 11-5 (*Continued*). (b) Memory map.

PORT 3 CONTROL AND STATUS REGISTER

7	6	5	4	3	2	1	0	
IS3 Flag	IS3 $\overline{\text{IRQ1}}$	X	OSS	Latch Enable	X	X	X	\$0F

Bits 0-2 Not used.

Bit 3 **Latch Enable** – This bit controls the input latch for port 3. If set, input data is latched by an IS3 negative edge. The latch is transparent after a read of the port 3 data register. Latch enable is cleared during reset.

Bit 4 **OSS (Output Strobe Select)** – This bit determines whether OS3 will be generated by a read or write of the port 3 data register. When clear, the strobe is generated by a read; when set, it is generated by a write. OSS is cleared during reset.

Bit 5 Not used.

Bit 6 **IS3 $\overline{\text{IRQ1}}$ Enable** – When set, an $\overline{\text{IRQ1}}$ interrupt will be enabled whenever the IS3 flag is set; when clear, the interrupt is inhibited. This bit is cleared during reset.

Bit 7 **IS3 Flag** – This read-only status bit is set by an IS3 negative edge. It is cleared by a read of the port 3 data register or during reset.

FIGURE 11-6 Port 3 control and status register.

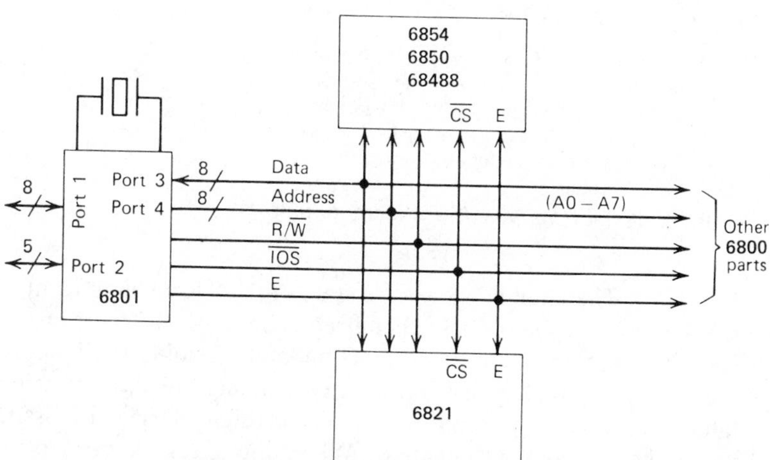

FIGURE 11-7 The **6801** expanded nonmultiplex mode.
(a) Hardware configuration.

MC6801U4 Mode **5**

Non-Multiplexed/Partial Decode

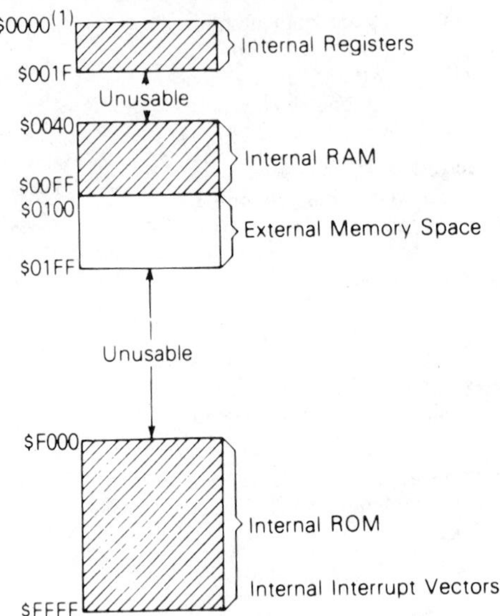

NOTES:

1) Excludes the following addresses which may not be used externally: $04, $06, and $0F (no $\overline{\text{IOS}}$).
2) Address lines A0 to A7 will not contain addresses until the data direction register for port 4 has been written with "1s" in the appropriate bits. These address lines will assert "1s" until made outputs by writing the data direction register.

FIGURE 11-7 (*Continued*). (b) Memory map.

Fig. 11-8). The **latch** IC stores the state of the 8 least significant address bits when the Address Strobe (AS) line is pulsed. The fourth I/O port provides address lines A8–A15. With the addition of this 8-bit latch, a stable 16-bit address is provided at the right time. Figure 11-9 shows a typical latching circuit, using a **74LS373** 8-bit latch. The AS latching pulse is asserted (high) during the first half of the cycle when the E clock is negative. When the E clock goes positive the data is transferred between the μC and the memory. The direction depends on the R/W line.

Thus, at the expense of some I/O capability, the designer has all 64K of address space available, except for sections that are occupied by internal functions. The first and second ports are always used for I/O functions.

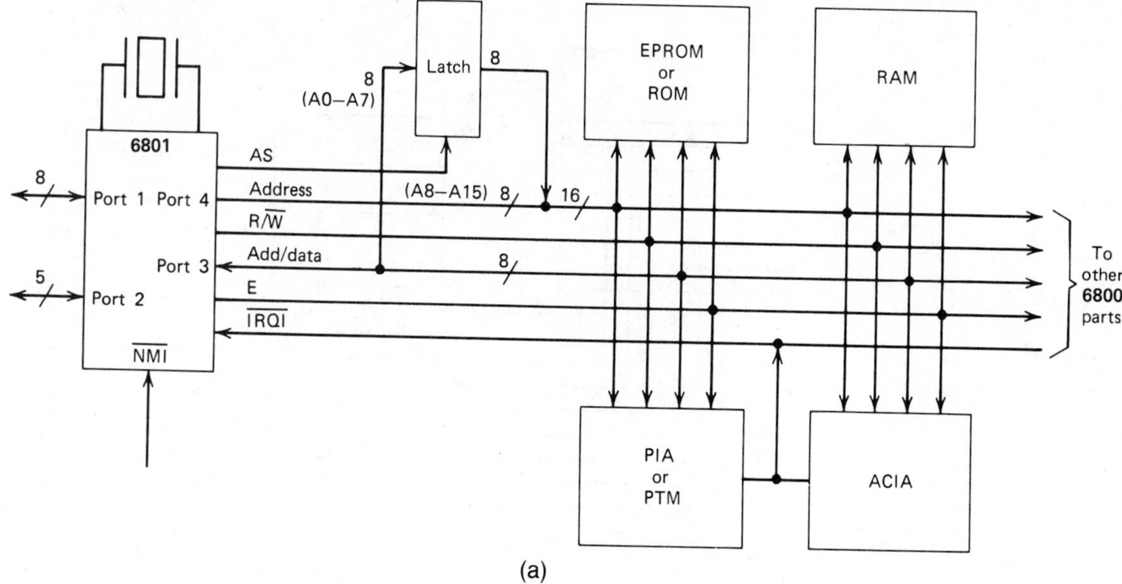

(a)

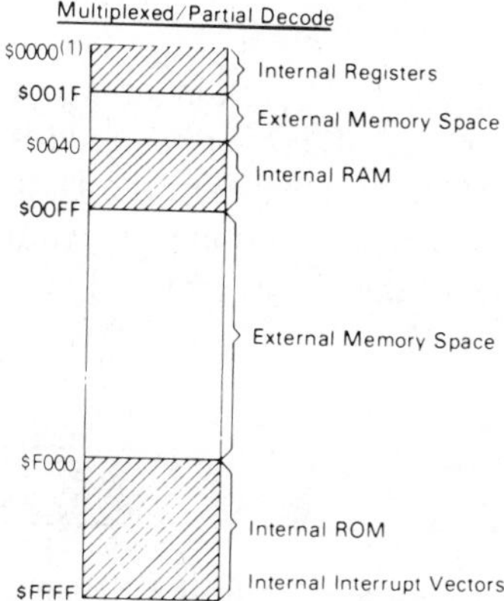

NOTES:

1) Excludes the following addresses which may be used externally: $04, $06, $0F.
2) Address lines A8-A15 will not contain addresses until the data direction register for port 4 has been written with "1s" in the appropriate bits. These address lines will assert "1s" until made outputs by writing the data direction register.

(b)

FIGURE 11-8 The **6801** expanded multiplexed mode. (a) Hardware configuration. (b) Memory map.

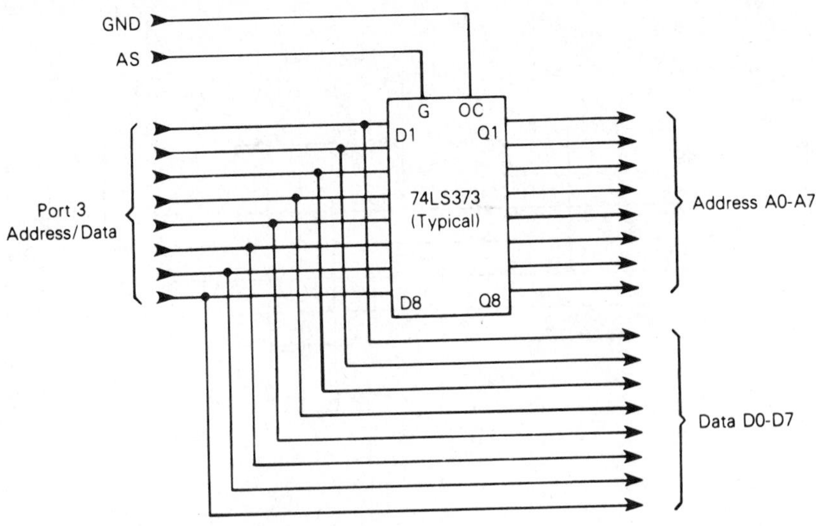

FIGURE 11-9 Typical latch arrangement

To start a data transfer, the 16-bit address is put out on ports 3 and 4. The LSB of that address on port 3, however, must be externally *latched,* because it will change to data in the last half of the instruction cycle.

11-5.6 Memory Allocation and Registers

Most versions of the **6801** have similar *memory maps,* with certain areas of memory allocated to specific functions. Locations $0000 to $001F are reserved for internal registers as shown in Table 11-3. Addresses $0000 to $0007 are the Data and Data Direction Registers (DDRs) for the four ports. These function as they do in the PIA (see Section 8-4.1). The other registers control the Timer and SCI (see Sections 11-5.12 and 11-6).

EXAMPLE 11-1

Port 3 must be configured so that its four MSBs are inputs and its four LSBs are outputs. How can this be done?

SOLUTION

The constant $0F must be written into the port 3 Data Direction Register (DDR), which is at location $0006 as shown in Table 11-3. The instructions to do this are

```
LDAA  #$F
STAA  $6
```

Table 11-1 shows that most **6801**s have 128 bytes of internal RAM that reside at locations $0080 to $00FF. They also have 2K bytes of ROM (or EPROM) that are normally located at $F800 to $FFFF. These locations can be specified, at mask

TABLE 11-3 Register Locations in a **6801**

Hex Address	Register
00	Data direction 1
01	Data direction 2
02	I/O port 1
03	I/O port 2
04	Data direction 3
05	Data direction 4
06	I/O port 3
07	I/O port 4
08	TCSR
09	Counter high byte
0A	Counter low byte
0B	Output compare high byte
0C	Output compare low byte
0D	Input capture high byte
0E	Input capture low byte
0F	I/O port 3 C/S register
10	Serial rate and mode register
11	Serial control and status register
12	Serial receiver data register
13	Serial transmit data register
14	RAM/EROM control register
15-1F Reserved	

time, to be at $C800, $D800, or $E800. This ROM normally includes the interrupt and restart vectors from $FFF0 to $FFFF (see Table 11-4), but these can be external as determined by the mode of operation (see Table 11-2, note 3).

11-5.7 Interrupts on the 6801

The **6801** also has a powerful interrupt capability. Eight interrupts are provided, with one being under software control. There are three types of externally generated interrupts, $\overline{\text{NMI}}$, $\overline{\text{IRQ1}}$, and $\overline{\text{IRQ2}}$. $\overline{\text{NMI}}$ and $\overline{\text{IRQ1}}$ come in on pins 4 and 5, respectively. $\overline{\text{IRQ2}}$ is an internal interrupt generated by the timer or SCI. Because both of these are within the **6801**, no external signal is required to cause an $\overline{\text{IRQ2}}$ interrupt. $\overline{\text{NMI}}$ is the highest-priority interrupt, followed by $\overline{\text{IRQ1}}$ and $\overline{\text{IRQ2}}$.

Table 11-4 gives the interrupt vectors for the **6801**. They are similar to the **6800** interrupt vectors, except that the timer and SCI generate one of four vectors, depending on the cause of the interrupt.

11-5.8 The 6801 Clock Circuit

The **6801** contains an internal oscillator that includes a divide-by-4 circuit. This permits the use of a higher-frequency quartz crystal, which is therefore smaller

TABLE 11-4 Interrupt Vectors in a **6801**

	Vector		Interrupts Description
Highest priority	FFFE	FFFF	Restart
	FFFC	FFFD	Nonmaskable interrupt
	FFFA	FFFB	Software interrupt
	FFF8	FFF9	Interrupt request ($\overline{IRQ1}$)
	FFF6	FFF7	Timer input capture (IRQ2)*
	FFF4	FFF5	Timer output compare (IRQ2)
	FFF2	FFF3	Timer overflow (IRQ2)
Lowest priority	FFF0	FFF1	Serial I/O (IRQ2)

*IRQ2 is an internal interrupt.

and less expensive. A mask option **(6801E)** allows the chip to be driven from an external TTL-compatible clock source. The internal clock circuit also supplies the E signal for any devices on the external buses.

11-5.9 The 6801 Timer

The **6801** also has three 16-bit timers. Typically, one controls inputs, one is for outputs, and the third serves as a 16-bit overflow. All functions are performed with the aid of an internal 16-bit free-running counter that may be read by the **6801** μP. The timers operate under software control.

11-5.10 6801 Instruction Improvements

The **6801** instruction set is both source and object *compatible* with current **6800**s, and **6800** programs will run on the **6801** *without* modification. The registers of the **6801** are identical to those of the **6800** and are shown in Chapter 4 (Fig. 4-1). The **6800** instruction set has been augmented, however, by 10 new instructions (21 OP codes), as shown in Table 11-5.

Additions to the **6801** instruction set include six 16-bit operations on the double accumulator (D). The double accumulator is a 16-bit accumulator made up of the A accumulator (which forms the 8 MSBs of D) and the B accumulator (the 8 LSBs). Instructions using the double accumulator are LOAD, STORE, ADD 16 bits, SUBTRACT 16 bits, and shift the double accumulator right or left. Three other new instructions manipulate the index register (X) as follows:

1. Push X register (onto the stack).
2. Pull X register (from the stack).
3. Add B accumulator to X register.

The push and pull of the index register enhance the **6801**'s ability to handle *reentrant* as well as *position-independent* code and allow quick temporary storage of the index register.

TABLE 11-5 Additional Instructions for the **6801**

ADDED INSTRUCTIONS

In addition to the existing M6800 instruction set, the following new instructions are incorporated in the MC6801 microcomputer.

ABX	Adds the 8-bit unsigned accumulator B to the 16-bit X-Register taking into account the possible carry out of the low order byte of the X-Register.	IX←IX + ACCB
ADDD	Adds the double precision ACCD* to the double precision value M:M+1 and places the results in ACCD.	ACCD←(ACCD) + (M:M+1)
ASLD	Shifts all bits of ACCD one place to the left. Bit 0 is loaded with zero. The C bit is loaded from the most significant bit of ACCD.	
LDD	Loads the contents of double precision memory location into the double accumulator A:B. The condition codes are set according to the data.	ACCD←(M:M+1)
LSRD	Shifts all bits of ACCD one place to the right. Bit 15 is loaded with zero. The C bit is loaded from the least significant bit of ACCD.	
MUL	Multiplies the 8 bits in accumulator A with the 8 bits in accumulator B to obtain a 16-bit unsigned number in A:B. ACCA contains MSB of result.	ACCD←ACCA * ACCB
PSHX	The contents of the index register is pushed onto the stack at the address contained in the stack pointer. The stack pointer is decremented by 2.	↓ (IXL), SP←(SP) − 1 ↓ (IXH), SP←(SP) − 1
PULX	The index register is pulled from the stack beginning at the current address contained in the stack pointer +1. The stack pointer is incremented by 2 in total.	SP←(SP) + 1; Msp → IXH SP←(SP) + 1; Msp → IXL
STD	Stores the contents of double accumulator A:B in memory. The contents of ACCD remain unchanged.	M:M + 1←(ACCD)
SUBD	Subtracts the contents of M:M + 1 from the contents of double accumulator AB and places the result in ACCD.	ACCD←(ACCD) − (M:M + 1)

*ACCD is the 16 bit register (A:B) formed by concatenating the A and B accumulators. The A-accumulator is the most significant byte.

The ComPare indeX register (CPX) instruction is also modified to properly set all of the condition code bits, so that *less than* or *greater than* decisions can be made. The instruction ADD ACCUMULATOR B to X greatly reduces the time to modify addresses in the index register. Perhaps the most interesting new instruction for the **6801** is an 8-by-8 bit *unsigned multiply* that multiplies the A and B registers and provides a 16-bit result in the D register in only 10 ms. This instruction is 20 times faster than an implementation in **6800** software. The multiply instruction, along with the instruction for adding accumulator B to the index register, makes real-time table lookup and interpolation three to four times faster than before.

Table 11-6 gives the timing (in cycles) for the **6801** instruction set. It shows that modifications have also been made to *shorten* the execution of many existing instructions. Many **6801** instructions therefore execute about 25% faster than similar **6800** instructions.

11-5.11 The 6801 Pin Assignments

The basic **6801** is a 40-pin IC. The pinout for the **6801** is shown in Fig. 11-10, and consists of 29 port pins and 11 other pins. The 11 pins are as follows.

Power Pins These are V_{CC} (+5 V), V_{SS} (GND), and V_{CC} standby. The latter pin is used to provide battery power to the internal RAM in systems where its contents must be preserved.

Clock Pins These are XTAL1, EXTAL2, and E (enable). A crystal to control the operating frequency of the **6801** is connected between XTAL1 and EXTAL2. The E pin is an output clock that is 1/4 of the crystal frequency. The timing for all external devices on the buses is referenced to this clock.

Interrupt Pins RESET, IRQ, and NMI. These are essentially equivalent to the corresponding pins on the **6800**.

Strobe Control Pins SCI and SC2. These have different functions, depending on the mode, and are discussed in Section 11-5.3.

I/O Pins There are 29 I/O pins on the **6801**, divided into three 8-bit ports and one 5-bit port.

11-5.12 The Counter/Timer

The **6801** has an internal 16-bit counter that is continuously clocked by the E clock. Its block diagram is shown in Fig. 11-11. The value in the counter can be read continuously from locations $09 and $0A (low byte). These registers are read-only with one exception; a write to $09 will set the count to $FFF8, regardless of the data written.

TABLE 11-6 Timing (in Cycles) for the **6801** Instructions

	ACCX	Immediate	Direct	Extended	Indexed	Inherent	Relative
ABA	•	•	•	•	•	2	•
ABX	•	•	•	•	•	3	•
ADC	•	2	3	4	4	•	•
ADD	•	2	3	4	4	•	•
ADDD	•	4	5	6	6	•	•
AND	•	2	3	4	4	•	•
ASL	2	•	•	6	6	2	•
ASLD	•	•	•	•	•	3	•
ASR	2	•	•	6	6	2	•
BCC	•	•	•	•	•	•	3
BCS	•	•	•	•	•	•	3
BEQ	•	•	•	•	•	•	3
BGE	•	•	•	•	•	•	3
BGT	•	•	•	•	•	•	3
BHI	•	•	•	•	•	•	3
BIT	•	2	3	4	4	•	•
BLE	•	•	•	•	•	•	3
BLS	•	•	•	•	•	•	3
BLT	•	•	•	•	•	•	3
BMI	•	•	•	•	•	•	3
BNE	•	•	•	•	•	•	3
BPL	•	•	•	•	•	•	3
BRA	•	•	•	•	•	•	3
BSR	•	•	•	•	•	•	•
BVC	•	•	•	•	•	•	3
BVS	•	•	•	•	•	•	3
CBA	•	•	•	•	•	2	•
CLC	•	•	•	•	•	2	•
CLI	•	•	•	•	•	2	•
CLR	2	•	•	6	6	2	•
CLV	•	•	•	•	•	2	•
CMP	•	2	3	4	4	•	•
COM	2	•	•	6	6	2	•
CPX	•	4	5	6	6	•	•
DAA	•	•	•	•	•	2	•
DEC	2	•	•	6	6	2	•
DES	•	•	•	•	•	3	•
DEX	•	•	•	•	•	3	•
EOR	•	2	3	4	4	•	•
INC	2	•	•	6	6	•	•
INS	•	•	•	•	•	3	•

TABLE 11-6 *(Continued)*

	ACCX	Immediate	Direct	Extended	Indexed	Inherent	Relative
INX	•	•	•	•	3	•	
JMP	•	•	•	3	•	•	
JSR	•	•	5	6	•	•	
LDA	•	2	3	4	•	•	
LDD	•	3	4	5	•	•	
LDS	•	3	4	5	•	•	
LDX	•	3	4	5	5	•	•
LSLD	•	•	•	•	•	3	•
LSL	•	•	•	6	6	2	•
LSR	2	•	•	6	6	2	•
LSRD	•	•	•	•	•	3	•
MUL	•	•	•	•	•	10	•
NEG	2	•	•	6	6	2	•
NOP	•	•	•	•	•	2	•
ORA	•	2	3	4	4	•	•
PSH	3	•	•	•	•	3	•
PSHX	•	•	•	•	•	4	•
PUL	4	•	•	•	•	4	•
PULX	•	•	•	•	•	5	•
ROL	2	•	•	6	6	2	•
ROR	2	•	•	6	6	2	•
RTI	•	•	•	•	•	10	•
RTS	•	•	•	•	•	5	•
SBA	•	•	•	•	•	2	•
SBC	•	2	3	4	4	•	•
SEC	•	•	•	•	•	2	•
SEI	•	•	•	•	•	2	•
SEV	•	•	•	•	•	2	•
STA	•	•	3	4	4	•	•
STD	•	•	4	5	5	•	•
STS	•	•	4	5	5	•	•
STX	•	•	4	5	5	•	•
SUB	•	2	3	4	4	•	•
SUBD	•	4	5	6	6	•	•
SWI	•	•	•	•	•	12	•
TAB	•	•	•	•	•	2	•
TAP	•	•	•	•	•	2	•
TBA	•	•	•	•	•	2	•
TPA	•	•	•	•	•	2	•
TST	2	•	•	6	6	2	•
TSX	•	•	•	•	•	3	•
TXS	•	•	•	•	•	3	•
WAI	•	•	•	•	•	9	•

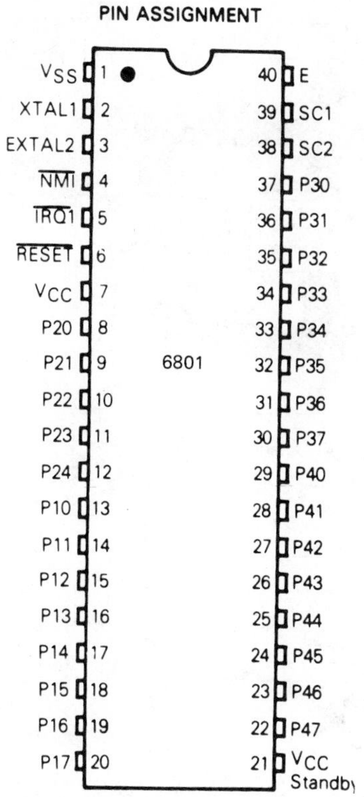

PIN ASSIGNMENT

Signal	Pin		Pin	Signal
V_{SS}	1		40	E
XTAL1	2		39	SC1
EXTAL2	3		38	SC2
$\overline{NMI}$	4		37	P30
$\overline{IRQ1}$	5		36	P31
$\overline{RESET}$	6		35	P32
V_{CC}	7		34	P33
P20	8		33	P34
P21	9	6801	32	P35
P22	10		31	P36
P23	11		30	P37
P24	12		29	P40
P10	13		28	P41
P11	14		27	P42
P12	15		26	P43
P13	16		25	P44
P14	17		24	P45
P15	18		23	P46
P16	19		22	P47
P17	20		21	V_{CC} Standby

FIGURE 11-10 The **6801** Pinouts.

The counter is controlled by the Timer Control and Status Register (TCSR) at \$08. Figure 11-12 gives the function of each bit in this register. Bits 0–4 can be written; the others are read-only.

The *Output Compare Register* (at \$0B and \$0C) can be written with any desired 16-bit number. When the number in the counter equals the number in the OCR, a pulse is generated that sets the Output Compare Flag (OCF) in the status register and also clocks Output Level (OLVL) into the output level flip-flop (FF). If bit 1 of the Data Direction Register (DDR) for port 2 has been set (it is cleared during RESET), this output level will appear at P21. This can be used as a signal to external devices that a compare has occurred.

EXAMPLE 11-2

One of a system's requirements is that P21 go high 20 ms after the instruction in location \$100 is executed. Describe how the program and hardware can do this. Assume the E clock is running at 1 μs.

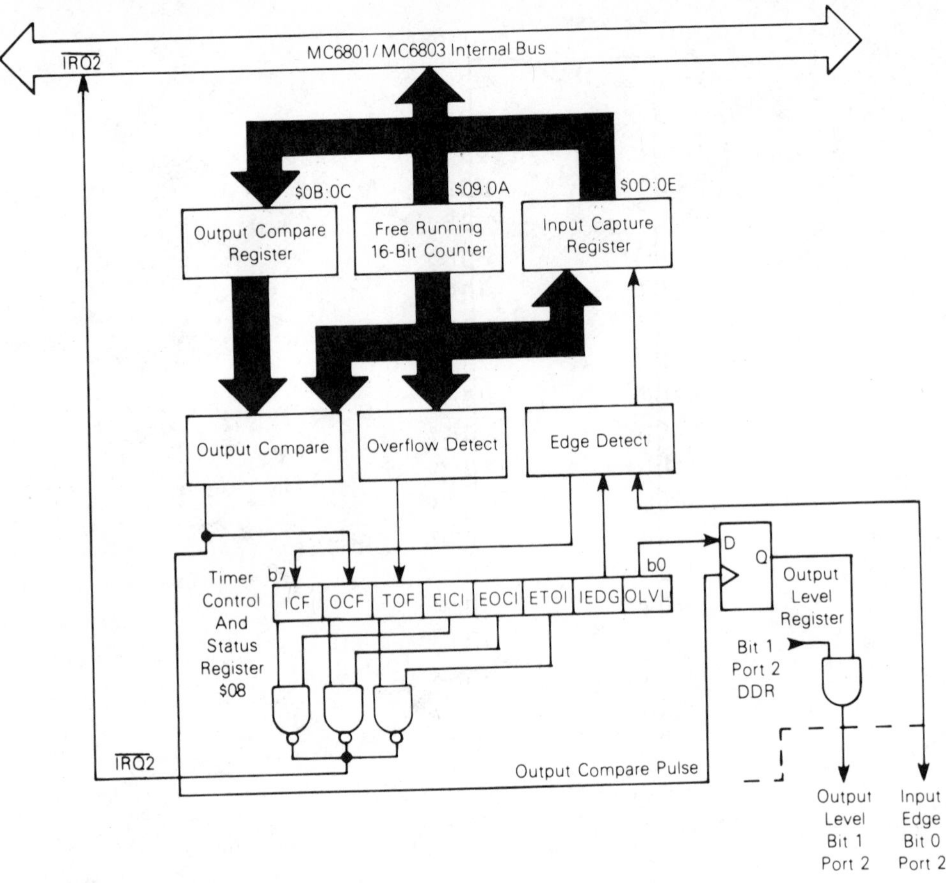

FIGURE 11-11 Block diagram of the **6801** programmable timer.

SOLUTION

During initialization, bit 1 of the DDR for port 2 (at $01) must be set. Bit 0 (OLVL) of the Timer Control and Status Register must be cleared, and a compare must be caused to clock OLVL into the flip-flop and onto P21. This causes P21 to be low.

After the instruction at $100 is executed the contents of the timer can be read. Because 20 ms is 20,000 E clocks, the timer register contents plus 20,000 (minus overhead if extreme accuracy is required) can be calculated by a program and written into the Output Compare Register. After 20 ms a compare will be generated. OLVL will be changed to a 1 and clocked into the FF, which in turn raises pin P21 to a 1.

As Fig. 11-11 shows, the **6801** timer also contains an **Input Capture Register** (at $0D and $0E) that is controlled by the action on pin P20. When a transition occurs on P20 the value of the counter is transferred to the Input Capture Register and the Input Capture Flag (ICF) in the TCSR is set. The direction of the transition is controlled by the Input Edge (IEDG) bit in the TSCR.

TIMER CONTROL AND STATUS REGISTER (TCSR)

7	6	5	4	3	2	1	0	
ICF	OCF	TOF	EICI	EOCI	ETOI	IEDG	OLVL	\$0008

Bit 0 OLVL — Output Level. OLVL is clocked to the output level register by a successful output compare and will appear at P21 if bit 1 of the port 2 data direction register is set. It is cleared during reset.

Bit 1 EIDG — Input Edge. IEDG is cleared during reset and controls which level transition will trigger a counter transfer to the input capture register:
IEDG = 0 Transfer on a negative-edge
IEDG = 1 Transfer on a positive-edge.

Bit 2 ETOI — Enable Timer Overflow Interrupt. When set, an $\overline{\text{IRQ2}}$ interrupt is enabled for a timer overflow; when clear, the interrupt is inhibited. It is cleared during reset.

Bit 3 EOCI — Enable Output Compare Interrupt. When set, an $\overline{\text{IRQ2}}$ interrupt is enabled for an output compare; when clear, the interrupt is inhibited. It is cleared during reset.

Bit 4 EICI — Enable Input Capture Interrupt. When set, an $\overline{\text{IRQ2}}$ interrupt is enabled for an input capture; when clear, the interrupt is inhibited. It is cleared during reset.

Bit 5 TOF — Timer Overflow Flag. TOF is set when the counter contains all ones. It is cleared by reading the TCSR (with TOF set) then reading the counter high byte (\$09), or during reset.

Bit 6 OCF — Output Compare Flag. OCF is set when the output compare register matches the free-running counter. It is cleared by reading the TCSR (with OCF set) and then writing to the output compare register (\$0B or \$0C), or during reset.

Bit 7 ICF — Input Capture Flag. ICF is set to indicate a proper level transition; it is cleared by reading the TCSR (with ICF set) and then the input capture register high byte (\$0D), or during reset.

FIGURE 11-12 Timer control and status register (TCSR).

The input capture register can be used to determine the frequency or pulse width of an external signal or event. If the external signal is connected to pin P20, the time of the first transition will be stored in the register and the ICF is set. If the program reads the TSCR and then reads the input capture register, the ICF flag will clear. The time of the next transition will be set into the input capture register, and the time between transitions can be calculated by finding the time difference between the two transitions.

The timer has three ways to interrupt the μC:

1. The output compare register finds a comparison.
2. The timer overflows.
3. The ICF flag is set by a transition on P20.

Each of these events sets a bit in the TCSR. Each event also has a masking bit in the TCSR that will allow or disable the interrupt. As Fig. 11-11 shows, if an interrupt is generated it will be an $\overline{\text{IRQ2}}$.

EXAMPLE 11-3

The pulse widths used in timing operations are sometimes critical. Show how to measure them with the **6801** timer.

SOLUTION
The IEDG bit of the TCSR determines which edge causes the counter contents to be transferred to the Input Capture Register. When it is 0, the transfer occurs on the negative-going edge. If the IEDG bit is set properly to sense the leading edge and then changed when it is read, the trailing edge is timed. Once the rising and falling edge times are captured, a software routine is used by the **6801** μP to compute the pulse width. The input transition-detector may also generate an interrupt to the μP to inform it that new data is available.

11-5.13 The 6803 μC

The **6803** μC is a **6801** without a ROM and therefore can be operated only in the extended multiplexed modes.

11-6 THE SERIAL COMMUNICATIONS INTERFACE (SCI)

The **6801** also contains an SCI, whose functions are similar to those of an ACIA (see Section 8-8). The SCI can transmit or receive data in an asynchronous format, like the ACIA (see Section 8-7.1), or as *biphase* data. Serial data enter the SCI at port 2, pin 3, or P23. Transmitted data leave at P24, and an external clock, if used to synchronize the data, is brought in on P22.

Like the ACIA, the SCI contains a receive data register (at address $12), a transmit data register (at $13), and a control and status register (at $11). The SCI also contains a mode and control register (at $10) that determines the bit rate and whether asynchronous or biphase data are being used.

The SCI is now used in many other μCs, such as the **68HC11**, and in some versions of the **6805** family. It is a full-duplex asynchronous interface that can send and receive data in standard Non-Return-to-Zero (NRZ) format, for use with an ASCII terminal, or in biphase format for communications with other μCs. It can operate at a variety of baud rates. The SCI transmitter and receiver are functionally independent but use the same data format and bit rate. Both formats provide 1 start bit, 8 or 9 data bits, and 1 stop bit. "Baud" and "bit" are used synonymously in these descriptions.

11-6.1 Wake-Up Feature

In a typical serial loop multiprocessor configuration, such as that shown in Fig. 11-19, any messages sent by one processor will be present on the inputs to all the others. The software protocol must identify the desired addressee(s) at the beginning of a message in order to permit uninterested μCs to ignore the messages not directed to them. For μPs that are not addressed, all further SCI signal processing is inhibited until this **wake-up feature** is invoked when the data line returns to the idle state. An SCI message starts after a string of at least 11 consecutive 1s. Software for the transmitter must provide for the required idle string between consecutive messages and prevent it from occurring within messages.

11-6.2 Programmable Options

The following features of the SCI are programmable:

- Format: standard mark/space (NRZ) or biphase
- Clock: external or internal bit rate clock
- Baud: one of four per E clock frequency, or external clock (8 × desired baud)
- Wake-up feature: enabled or disabled
- Interrupt requests: enabled individually for transmitter and receiver
- Clock output: internal bit rate clock enabled or disabled to P22

11-6.3 Serial Communications Registers

The SCI includes four addressable registers as depicted in Fig. 11-13. It is controlled by the Rate and Mode Control Register and the Transmit/Receive Control and Status Register. Data is transmitted and received using a write-only transmit register and a read-only receive register. The shift registers are not accessible to software.

11-6.4 Rate and Mode Control Register (RMCR)

The rate and mode control register controls the SCI bit rate, format, clock source, and, under certain conditions, the configuration of P22. The register consists of 4

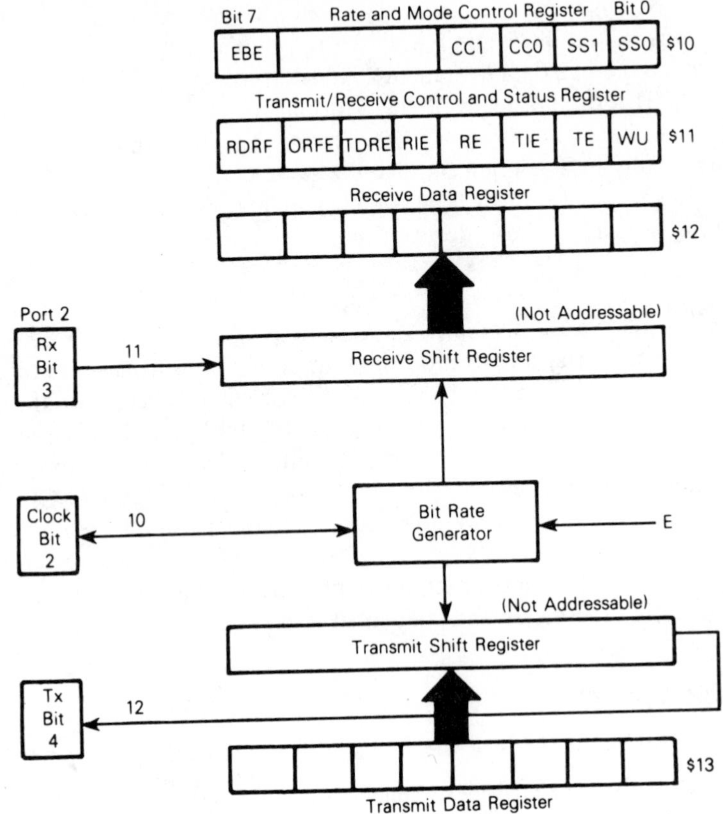

FIGURE 11-13 SCI registers.

write-only bits, which are cleared during reset. The 2 least significant bits control the bit rate of the internal clock and the remaining 2 bits control the format and clock source.

11-6.5 Baud Rate Bits

The baud rate bits, SS1 and SS0, provide the means for selecting different baud rates for the transmitter and receiver when using the internal clock. Four rates may be selected which are a function of the μC clock frequency.

11-6.6 Enhanced Baud Rates for the 6801U4

The **6801U4** μC has an additional feature called Enhanced Baud Enable (EBE), which is controlled by a bit 7 that has been added to the rate and mode control register. For the **6801U4**, when this bit is clear, the standard **6801** baud rates are selected as shown in the top four lines of Table 11-7. When the bit is set, the additional baud rates shown in the lower half of the table are selected. This bit is cleared by reset and is a write-only control bit.

TABLE 11-7 Bit Times and Rates for Three Crystal Frequencies

	EBE	SS1:SS0		4 f_o →	2.4576 MHz		4.0 MHz		4.9152 MHz		
					614.4 kHz		1.0 MHz		1.2288 MHz		
				E	Baud	Time	Baud	Time	Baud	Time	
6801	0	0	0	÷16	38400.0	26 μs	62500.0	16.0 μs	76800.0	13.0 μs	6801U4
6801	0	0	1	÷128	4800.0	208.3 μs	7812.5	128.0 μs	9600.0	104.2 μs	6801U4
6801	0	1	0	÷1024	600.0	1.67 ms	976.6	1.024 ms	1200.0	833.3 μs	6801U4
6801	0	1	1	÷4096	150.0	6.67 ms	244.1	4.096 ms	300.0	3.33 ms	6801U4
	1	0	0	÷64	9600.0	104.2 μs	15625.0	64 μs	19200.0	52.0 μs	6801U4
	1	0	1	÷256	2400.0	416.6 μs	3906.3	256 μs	4800.0	208.3 μs	6801U4
	1	1	0	÷512	1200.0	833.3 μs	1953.1	512 μs	2400.0	416.6 μs	6801U4
	1	1	1	÷2048	300.0	3.33 ms	488.3	2.05 ms	600.0	01.67 ms	6801U4
	External (P22)*				76800.0	13.0 μs	125000.0	8.0 μs	153600.0	6.5 μs	

*Using maximum clock rate

EBE = 0 standard **6801** baud rates
EBE = 1 additional baud rates

Table 11-7 lists bit times and rates for three specific crystal frequencies.

11-6.7 Clock Control and Format Select Bits

The CC1 and CC0 bits of the RMCR control the format (NRZ or biphase) and select the serial clock source (internal or external). If CC1 is clear, the source is internal with no external connection and the status of CC0 determines whether the format is NRZ or biphase. If CC0 is also clear, biphase is selected. If CC1 is set, it means that the clock will be connected to port 2 bit 2, and then if CC0 is 0 the internal clock will be sent out on that line. If CC0 is 1, an external clock will be brought in on the line. Thus, the Data Direction Register (DDR) value for port 2 line 2 is forced to the value typically needed in these PIA-like circuits for output or input. The DDR bit happens to be the complement of CC0 and cannot be altered until CC1 is cleared. If CC1 is cleared after having been set, its DDR value is unchanged. Table 11-8 defines the formats, clock source, and use of P22.

If both CC1 and CC0 are set, an external TTL-compatible clock must be connected to P22 at eight times (8×) the desired bit rate, but not greater than E, with a duty cycle of 50% (±10%). If CC1:CC0 = 10, the internal bit rate clock is provided at P22 regardless of the values for TE or RE.

Note: The source of SCI internal bit rate clock is the timer free-running counter. A write to the counter by the μC can disturb serial operations.

TABLE 11-8 Clock and Format Control for an SCI

CC1:CC0	Format	Clock Source	Port 2 Bit 2
00	Bi-Phase	Internal	Not Used
01	NRZ	Internal	Not Used
10	NRZ	Internal	Output
11	NRZ	External	Input

11-6.8 Transmit/Receive Control and Status Register

The transmit/receive control and status register is also shown in Fig. 11-13. It controls the transmitter, receiver, wake-up feature, and two individual interrupts and monitors the status of serial operations. All 8 bits are readable and bits 0 to 4 are also writable. The register is initialized to \$20 by $\overline{\text{RESET}}$. Refer to the data sheet on the **6801** cited in Section 11-15 for details of the functions of these bits.

EXAMPLE 11-4

Show how to use the SCI for an RS232C interface to a data terminal.

SOLUTION

The example discussed here uses two I/O lines from port 2 as the serial input and output lines. Figure 11-14 is a schematic diagram of an RS232 interface for serial I/O. The baud rate selection (Table 11-7) shows the required register bit values for SS1 and SS0 to obtain the standard baud rates of 300, 1200, 4800, and 9600. These cannot be obtained unless the μC crystal frequency is as shown in Table 11-7. The baud rates are determined by the divide down internal logic in the μC and

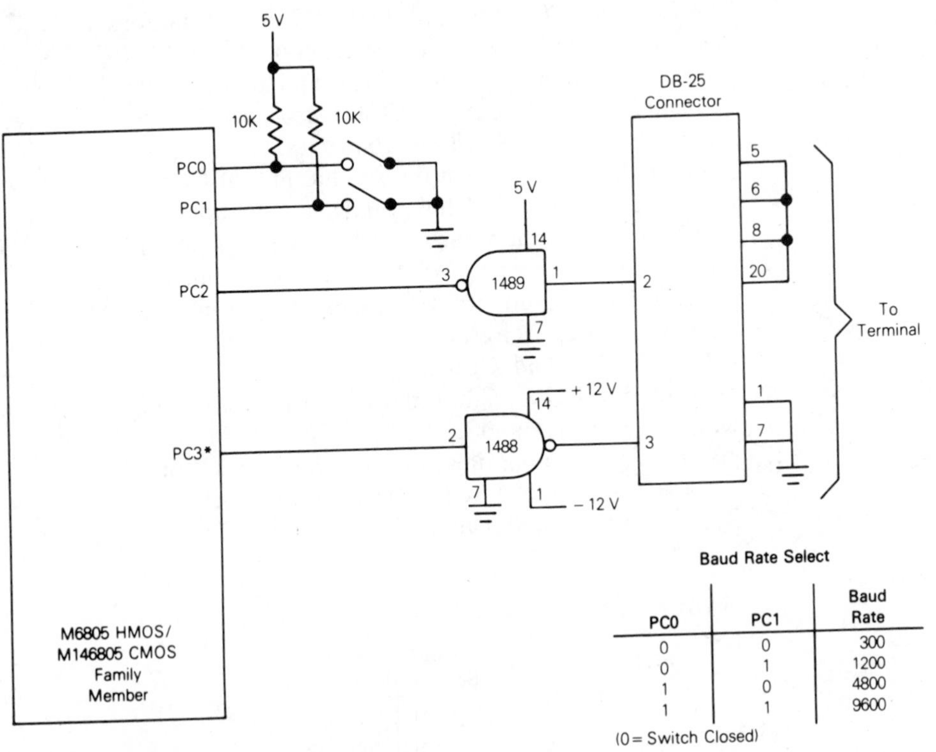

PC0	PC1	Baud Rate
0	0	300
0	1	1200
1	0	4800
1	1	9600

(0 = Switch Closed)

* For devices which have port C as input-only, use PB7

FIGURE 11-14 Schematic diagram of RS232 interface for serial I/O via I/O port lines.

therefore the crystal frequency (f_{osc}) must be within 5% of 4.915200 MHz (maximum tolerance for the typical ASCII/RS232 serial data link). The SCI is used in a number of other μCs, such as the **68HC05C4** and the **68HC11A8**. The software driver subroutine required is similar to the ACIA program shown in Fig. 6-4. This program in **6800** code will have to be modified, however, to adjust for the generally fewer cycles per instruction of the **M146805** CMOS family members. A similar subroutine is used in all **6805** HMOS/**146805** CMOS family evaluation programs where an ASCII terminal interface is needed.

Unfortunately, space limitations preclude detailed discussion of all the bits in the SCI registers and all the modes of operation. The reader should refer to a 1984 (or later) **6801** Data Sheet or the Motorola single-chip microcomputer data manuals for the **68HC05C4** or **68HC11A8** (for further information see Section 11-14).

11-6.9 SCI Operations

The SCI is initialized by writing control bytes first to the Rate and Mode Control Register and then to the Transmit/Receive Control and Status Register. When the Transmit Enable (TE) bit is set (see Fig. 11-13), the output of the transmit serial shift register is connected to P24 and serial output is initiated by transmitting a 9-bit preamble of 1s.

At this point, one of two situations exists:

1. If the transmit data register is empty (TDRE = 1), a continuous string of 1s will be sent, indicating an idle line.
2. If a byte has been written to the transmit data register (TDRE = 0), it will be transferred to the output serial shift register (synchronized with the bit rate clock), TDRE will be set, and transmission will begin.

The start bit (a 0), 8 data bits (beginning with bit 0), and a stop bit (a 1) will be transmitted. If TDRE is still set when the next byte transfer should occur, 1s will be sent until more data is provided. In *biphase* format, the output toggles at the start of each bit and at half-bit time when a 1 is sent. Receive operation is controlled by the Receive Enable (RE) bit, which configures P23 as an input and enables the receiver. The two SCI data formats are illustrated in Fig. 11-15.

11-6.10 Data Format

The NRZ data format is compatible with the asynchronous data format discussed in Section 8-7.1 for the ACIA and is shown in Fig. 11-16. It must meet the following criteria:

1. A high level indicates a logic 1 and a low level indicates a logic 0.
2. The idle line is in a high (logic 1) state prior to transmission/reception of a message.
3. A start bit (logic 0) is transmitted/received, indicating the start of a message.

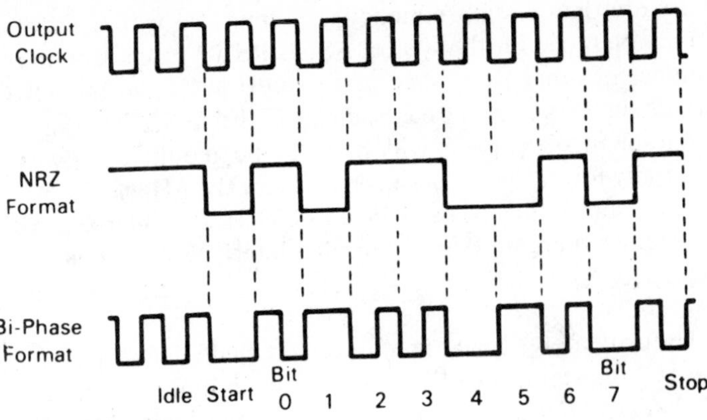

Data: 01001101 ($4D)

FIGURE 11-15 SCI data formats

4. Data is transmitted and received with the least significant bit first.
5. A stop bit (a high in the 10th or 11th bit position) indicates that the byte is complete.
6. A **break** is defined as the transmission or reception of a low (logic 0) for some multiple of the data characters (more than one character without stop bits).

It will be noticed that the ACIA can be programmed to be compatible with the SCI (see Section 8-8), and therefore they can "talk" to each other. In fact, they can be used with interface circuits such as the RS232 **1488**s and **1489**s and separated by distances up to 60 feet.

11-6.11 Multiprocessor Applications

For multiprocessor applications, the **6801** architecture allows operation in several ways: programmable peripheral control, handshaking, and serial I/O. Each method allows the μPs to communicate at a different speed and has advantages and disadvantages depending on the hardware configuration.

As a multiprocessor programmable peripheral controller (shown in Fig. 11-17), the **6801** interconnects directly to any **6800**-type μP bus (**6800**, 6802, or **6809**) or to another **6801**, simply as a peripheral device. Here the **6801** acts as a slave, communicating through the third I/O port on the master processor bus. Through this port, the processors can be made to talk to each other and interrupt each other for the purpose of **handshaking** (or testing when ready). The other peripheral I/O

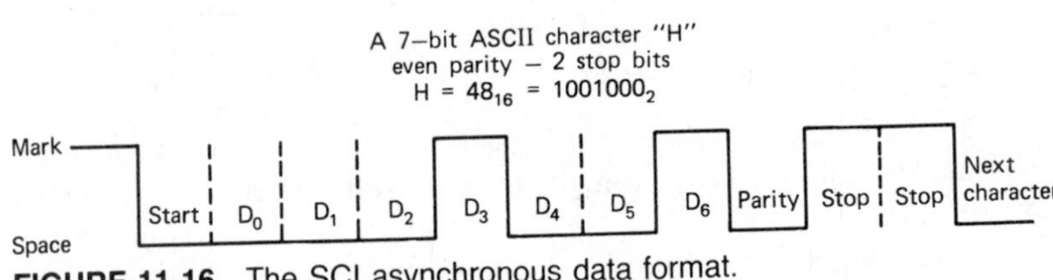

FIGURE 11-16 The SCI asynchronous data format.

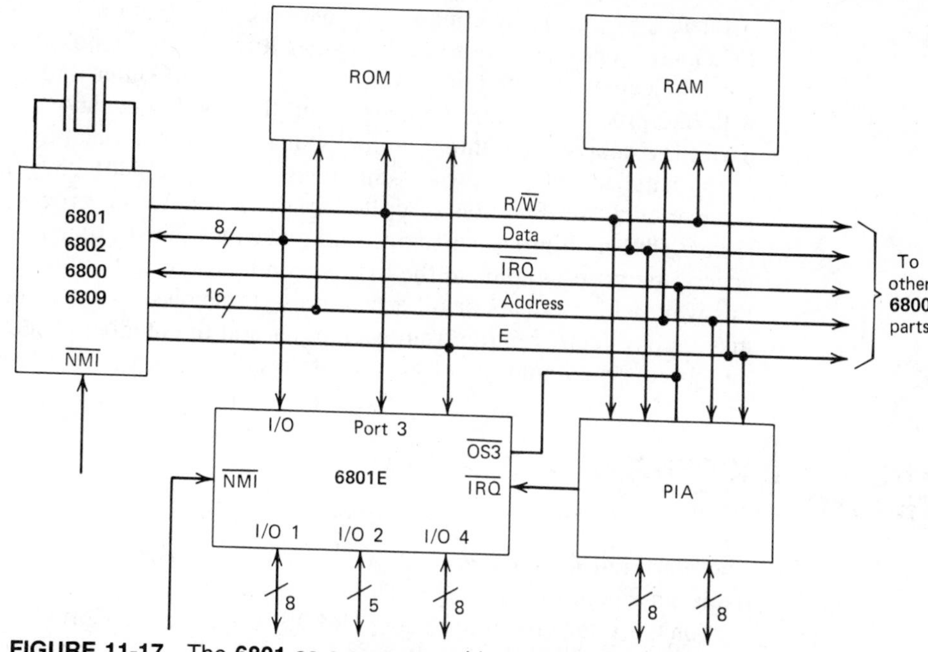

FIGURE 11-17 The **6801** as a programmable peripheral controller.

ports (the first, second, and fourth) are available for peripheral control functions.

In the *multiprocessor handshaking mode*, shown in Fig. 11-18, two independent **6801**s may communicate over the 8-bit parallel bus from the third I/O port. The input strobe (IS) and output strobe (OS) may be used for *handshake* control. Since this port is the only one used for this mode, the other 21 I/O lines are still available for local functions, along with the $\overline{\text{IRQ}}$ and $\overline{\text{NMI}}$ interrupts.

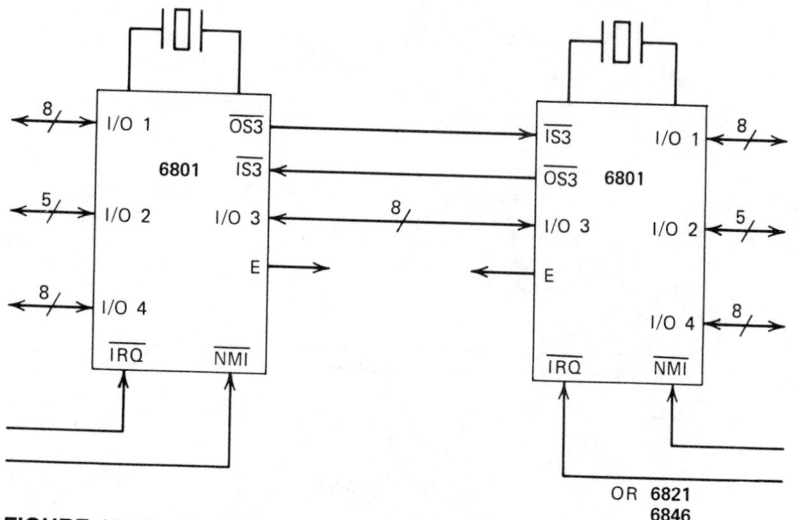

FIGURE 11-18 The **6801** in a handshaking arrangement.

Finally, by interconnecting several **6801**s, 68HC11s, or 68HC05C4s, using serial I/O, multiprocessor operation (shown in Fig. 11-19) is possible. The μCs can communicate with each other over the single-wire I/O lines (bits 3 and 4 of port 2), with one processor being the master and the rest being slaves. Bit 2 of port 2 is used for clocking if the internal-clock-out and external-clock-in options are used. I/O is handled with hardware shift registers on the **6801** chip; it is possible to achieve data transfer rates of up to 76 kilobaud between processors. This is the *fastest* **6801** multiprocessor mode and makes the most efficient use of the **6801**s general-purpose I/O pins in the first, second, and third I/O ports. When linked in this way, with modems or other low-noise transmission links, the **6801** locations may be physically remote from each other and the number of locations is limited only by the minimum data transfer rate required for a particular application.

11-7 NEW PROCESSING AND CIRCUIT TECHNOLOGIES

The **6800** and **6801** μP and μC were fabricated using NMOS (*n*-channel metal oxide on silicon) technology. The newer μCs, to be discussed in the following sections, are manufactured using HMOS, CMOS, or HCMOS.

11-7.1 HMOS Features

HMOS (high-density NMOS) is an improved version of NMOS and some of the μCs produced in the past few years use this process. When compared to PMOS or

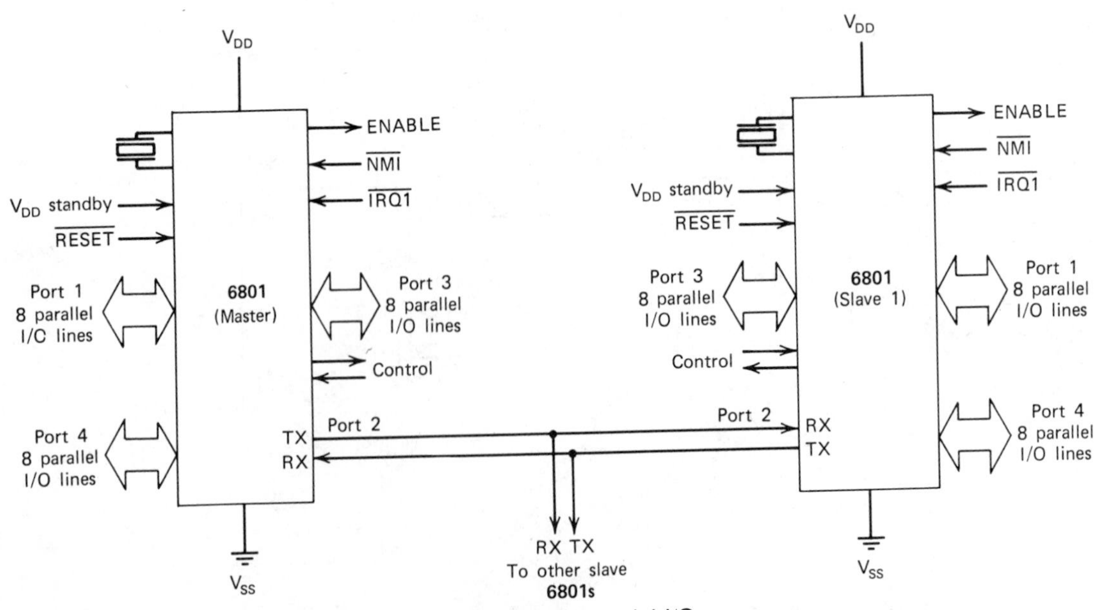

FIGURE 11-19 Multiprocessing interconnections using serial I/O.

other NMOS processes, the high speed of HMOS and the small size of an HMOS gate are outstanding advantages.

11-7.2 CMOS Features

CMOS (Complementary MOS, i.e., using both *p*- and *n*-channel devices) is a very popular technology because CMOS gates use very little power. The unique properties of CMOS are increasingly attractive. Some applications for μCs are simply not feasible with PMOS, NMOS, or HMOS, primarily because of heat or excessive current requirements.

Maximum power consumption of CMOS parts ranges from 1/15 to 1/200 of that of an equivalent HMOS part. Low power consumption is important in several classes of applications:

a. **In portable equipment.** Hand-held and other portable units are operated from self-contained batteries. Battery drain is frequently important in such applications.
b. **For battery backup.** CMOS is appropriate in AC-powered applications when some or all system functions must continue during a power outage. A small rechargeable battery keeps a CMOS μC operable.
c. **With storage batteries.** Automotive equipment and telephone equipment operate from larger batteries. Automobile battery drain must be low when the engine is not running. Telephones must operate independent of AC power.
d. **For low heat dissipation.** Packaging constraints sometimes preclude dissipating electronics-generated heat, or the heat is costly to dissipate. In addition, heat directly affects device reliability.

The CMOS technology inherently operates over a wide range of supply voltages, which is to be expected in battery-powered equipment. If line power is available, a lower-cost, loosely regulated supply may be used.

An additional advantage of CMOS is that the circuitry is fully *static* (as opposed to dynamic logic, which must be clocked periodically). CMOS μCs may be operated at any clock rate less than the guaranteed maximum. This feature may be used to conserve additional power, since power consumption decreases with lower clock frequencies. Static operation may also be advantageous during product development, where the clock is sometimes stopped for testing.

11-7.3 HCMOS Features

By shrinking the CMOS circuitry in the same way as HMOS, significant increases in performance are realized. The HCMOS technology emerged in 1984 and 1985. It permits a high level of integration on an extremely small chip. At the same time, the CMOS structure gives it low power and the fully static design. It has features that seem to be the best of both worlds. An increasing number of μCs are being built using this process.

11-7.4 Electrically Erasable Programmable ROM (EEPROM)

The electrically erasable programmable read-only memory is one of the recent developments in semiconductor technology. Once it is programmed it is like any ROM with similar access times, and it will retain the program indefinitely or until reprogrammed. The advantage of an EEPROM is that it can be erased electrically. This allows in-circuit programming to permit storage of semipermanent information, as in configuring a program for use with a specific terminal, or to allow operators to select their preferred options when running a machine. The disadvantage of EEPROM is that the programming or erasing is relatively slow in terms of normal IC access times because it takes 10 ms to program each byte. See the manuals listed in Section 11-15 for details of the programming and erasure processes. EEPROM is being included in a growing number of μCs. See details of its use in the **68HC11A8** in Section 11-8.8 and in the **68HC805C4** in Section 11-11.3.

11-7.5 Added Circuit Features

With newer technologies it is possible to put more circuitry on an IC chip. Therefore the complexity of the μPs themselves has increased and many additional circuit functions have been added. In addition to the obvious inclusion of memory and I/O, other system components have been developed. These include analog circuits such as A/D converters and Phase-Locked Loops (PLLs) and many digital devices such as timers. Another area of expansion has been to provide additional digital communications circuits to allow processors to exchange data with external peripheral devices or other processors. This allows engineers to design multiprocessor systems with a variety of specialized μCs communicating with each other. The SCI was described in Section 11-6, and another important addition, the SPI, will be explained in Section 11-11.

11-8 THE 68HC11 μC

The **68HC11A8** is a single-chip μC that uses HCMOS technology. It is an enhanced addition to the **6801** family of μCs. It was introduced in 1985 and reflects the advances in technology that occurred between 1979 (when the **6801** was introduced) and 1985. On-chip memory includes an 8K byte ROM, 512 bytes of EEPROM, and 256 bytes of static RAM. The **68HC11A8** μC also provides highly sophisticated on-chip peripheral functions, including an 8-channel A/D converter, an SCI subsystem (see Section 11-6), an SPI subsystem (Section 11-11), and an advanced timer circuit. The timer system is similar to the **6801** timer (Section 11-5.12) but provides three input capture lines and a real-time interrupt circuit.

Other **68HC11A8** features include

1. A pulse accumulator that can be used to count external events (event counting mode) or measure an external period.
2. A Computer Operating Properly (COP) *watchdog* system that helps protect against software failures.

3. A clock monitor system that causes generation of a system reset in case the clock is lost or running too slow.
4. An illegal Op code detection circuit that provides an unmaskable interrupt if an illegal Op code fetch is detected.
5. Two power-saving standby modes, STOP and WAIT.

Many of these features were formerly provided in external circuitry. Of these, the **Computer Operating Properly (COP)** or **watchdog circuit** is probably least known. It is a technique that has been used in some systems to monitor the operation of the computer, and to alert someone or make automatic corrections if the computer stops executing in its normal program sequence for any reason. The COP usually is implemented by requiring that the program reset a counter periodically. The counter is not incremented by processor action but by direct clock pulses and, if not reset before the limit, will cause an interrupt. This starts the processor executing the service routine (which restarts the processor in the regular program).

11-8.1 The 68HC11A8 Hardware Configuration

The **68HC11A8** comes in a 48-pin Dual In-line Package (DIP) or a 52-lead quad pack. Its hardware configuration, shown in Fig. 11-20, includes five 8-bit ports

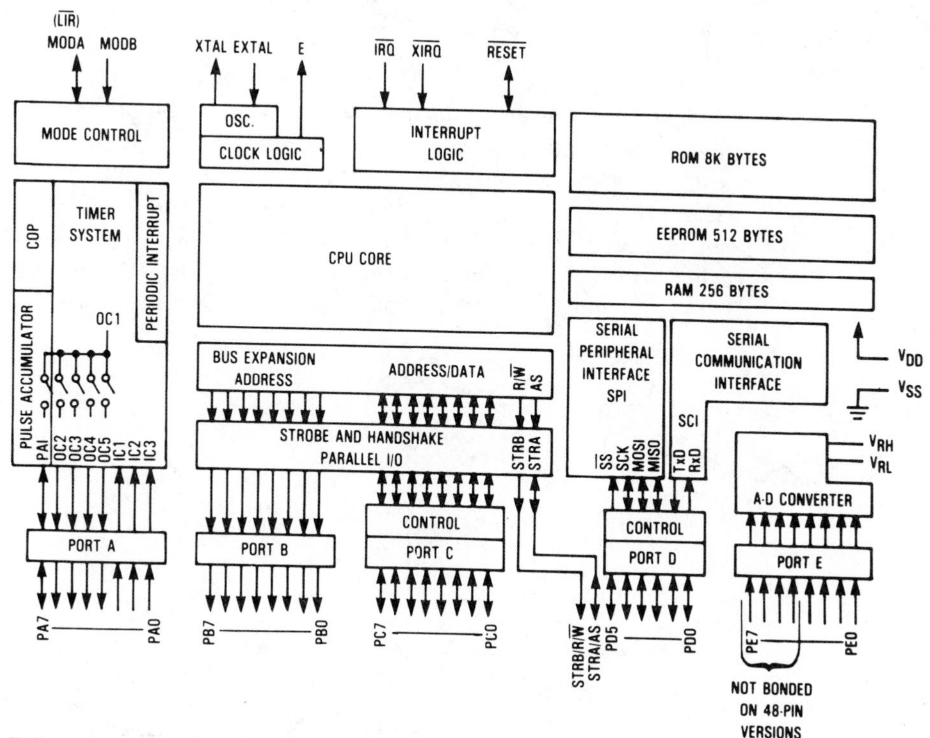

FIGURE 11-20 Block diagram of the **68HC11A8** μC.

(see Section 11-8.4). There are also several new signals. $\overline{XIRQ}$ is a new interrupt signal, MODA and MODB are mode input signals, and V_{RH} and V_{RL} provide the reference voltages for the A/D converter. All of these signals are discussed in the following paragraphs.

The RESET pin is an active LOW *bidirectional* control pin used to initialize the **68HC11A8** to a known start-up state and as an *open-drain output* to indicate that an internal failure has been detected in either the COP or the clock monitor circuit. Figure 11-21 shows a typical RESET circuit, and Fig. 11-22 shows the RESET timing for this circuit.

11-8.2 Power-On Reset

When the power is turned ON, a second type of RESET, known as the *power-on reset* (POR), occurs. When a positive transition is detected on V_{DD} as shown in Fig. 11-23, the power-on circuitry provides for a 4064-cycle time delay from the time of the first oscillator operation. In a system where E = 2 MHz, POR lasts about 2 ms. If the system power supply rise time is more than 2 ms, an external reset circuit should be used. If the external RESET pin is low at the end of the power-on delay time, the processor remains in the reset condition until the RESET pin goes high. The power-on reset is used strictly for power turn-on conditions and should not be used to detect drops in power.

11-8.3 Interrupts

The $\overline{IRQ}$ pin function of the **68HC11** is similar to that of the **6801** and is set for level-sensitive triggering during reset. It can be programmed after reset to be either level-sensitive or negative edge-sensitive. The $\overline{IRQ}$ pin requires an external resistor to V_{DD} and should be used in a wire-OR circuit.

The $\overline{XIRQ}$ pin is for requesting asynchronous nonmaskable interrupts. During reset, the X bit of the Condition Code Register is set and the $\overline{XIRQ}$ interrupt is masked to preclude interrupts on this line until μP operation is stabilized. The $\overline{XIRQ}$ is a level-sensitive pin and requires an external resistor to V_{DD}.

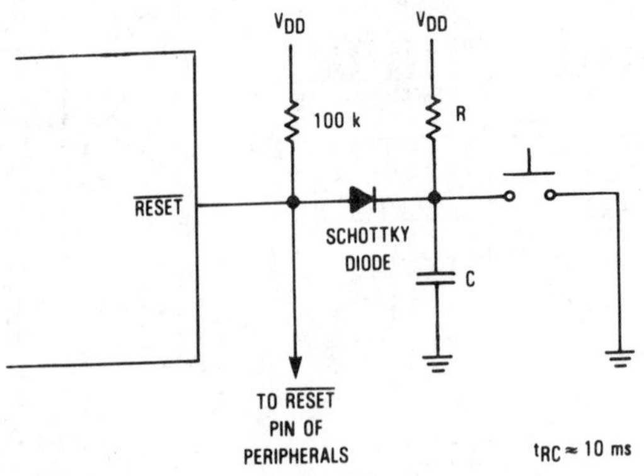

FIGURE 11-21 Typical reset circuit.

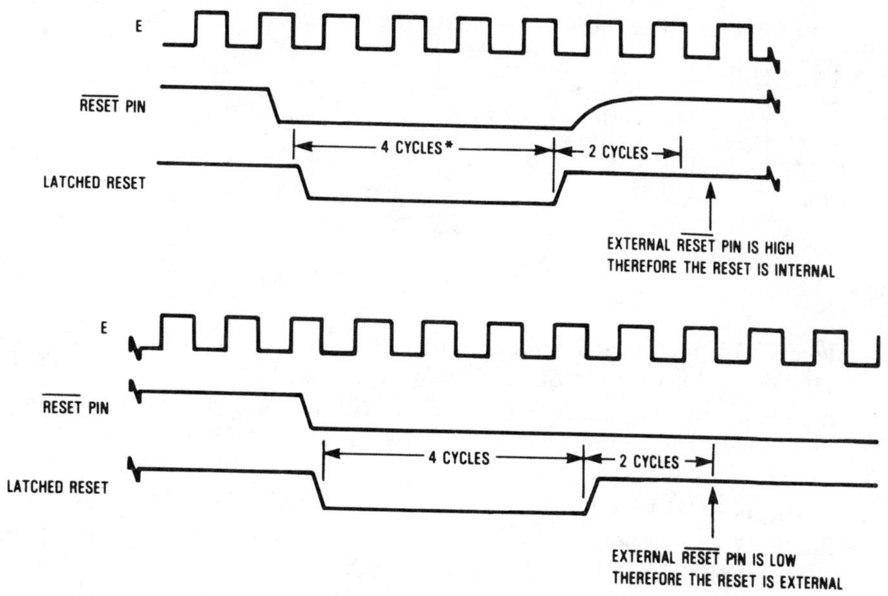

*The RESET pin will never be low for less than four cycles because an internal device will hold it low even if it is only driven for a short time.

FIGURE 11-22 Reset timing.

11-8.4 Operating Modes

The **6801** has eight different operating modes (see Section 11-5.2) but the **68HC11A8** has only four. These are shown in Table 11-9. During RESET, the voltage levels on the MODA and MODB pins determine which mode is selected. Note that for the special modes, the early versions of the **68HC11A8**s required a non-TTL signal level of at least 1.8 times V_{DD}. Later parts use standard TTL

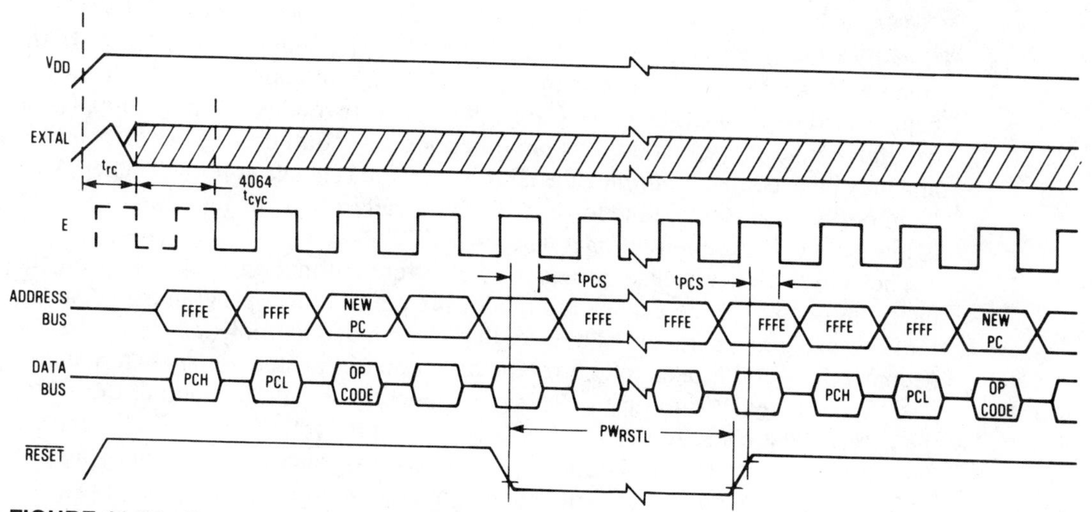

FIGURE 11-23 Power-on reset and RESET timing diagram.

TABLE 11-9 The **68HC11A8** Operating Modes

MODB	MODA	Mode Selected
1	0	Single-Chip (Mode 0)
1	1	Expanded Multiplexed (Mode 1)
#	0	Special Bootstrap
#	1	Special Test

NOTE:
1 = Logic High
0 = Logic Low
# = 1.8 Times V_{DD} (or Higher)

levels with the special voltage replaced by a logic 0 signal. After $\overline{\text{RESET}}$, the MODA pin becomes an output signal called Load Instruction Register ($\overline{\text{LIR}}$), and it goes low during the first E clock of each instruction and remains low for the duration of that cycle to indicate an Op code fetch. MODB does not have a second function.

The **68HC11A8** operates in one of four modes. In the single-chip mode it functions as a monolithic μC without external address or data buses. Internally, it contains 8K of ROM and 256 bytes of RAM.

In the expanded multiplexed mode, the **68HC11A8** has the capability of accessing a full 64K byte address range. This total range includes the on-chip memory addresses as used in the single-chip mode but also covers external peripheral and memory devices.

The **68HC11A8** bootstrap mode is a special mode distinguished from the normal operating single-chip mode. In bootstrap mode, 192 bytes of ROM are enabled as internal memory space at $BF40–$BFFF. This ROM contains a small boot loader program that reads a 256-byte program into on-chip RAM ($0000–$00FF) via the SCI. After the character for address $00FF is received, control is automatically passed to that program at memory address $0000.

The test mode is used for factory testing.

The two special pins AS/STRA (Address Strobe/STRobe A) and R/$\overline{\text{W}}$/STRB (Read/$\overline{\text{Write}}$/Strobe B) provide different functions depending on the mode. In the single-chip mode, the AS/STRA pin acts as a programmable input strobe, which can be used with STRB and port C for full handshake modes of parallel I/O. In the expanded multiplexed mode, this pin functions as an output *Address Strobe* (AS) and may be used to *demultiplex* the address and data signals at port C. When AS is high, port C is presenting the lower 8 bits of the address on its lines, and when AS is low port C is the bidirectional data bus.

The R/$\overline{\text{W}}$/STRB pin also provides two different functions depending on the operating mode. In the single-chip mode, the pin acts as a programmable strobe for handshake to a parallel I/O device. In the expanded multiplexed mode, the line becomes R/$\overline{\text{W}}$ and is used to control the direction of transfers on the external data bus. A low level (Write) on the R/$\overline{\text{W}}$ pin connects the data bus output drivers to the external data bus. A high level (Read) on this pin forces the output drivers to a high-impedance state and data is read from the external bus. R/$\overline{\text{W}}$ will stay low during consecutive data bus write cycles, as in a double-byte store.

11-8.5 Ports

There are five 8-bit ports on the **68HC11A8** μC. Three of these ports serve more than one purpose, depending on the mode configuration of the μC. A summary of the pins versus function and mode is provided in Table 11-10, and these are discussed in the following paragraphs.

Port A contains three input lines (PA0, PA1, and PA2), four output lines (PA3–PA6), and one bidirectional line (PA7). Depending on the mode, these lines can be used as data input lines or can be connected to the three input capture registers in the internal timer of the μC. The four output lines can be used for general-purpose outputs or can be connected to the four output compare registers in the timer. PA7 is a bidirectional line. On input it can be connected to the

TABLE 11-10 Pin Fractions for the **68HC11A8**

Port-Bit	Single-Chip Modes 0 and Bootstrap Mode	Expanded Multiplexed Mode 1 and Special Test Mode
A-0	PA0/IC3	PA0/IC3
A-1	PA1/IC2	PA1/IC2
A-2	PA2/IC1	PA2/IC1
A-3	PA3/OC5/and-or OC1	PA3/OC5/and-or OC1
A-4	PA4/OC4/and-or OC1	PA4/OC4/and-or OC1
A-5	PA5/OC3/and-or OC1	PA5/OC3/and-or OC1
A-6	PA6/OC2/and-or OC1	PA6/OC2/and-or OC1
A-7	PA7/PAI/OC1	PA7/PAI/OC1
B-0	PB0	A8
B-1	PB1	A9
B-2	PB2	A10
B-3	PB3	A11
B-4	PB4	A12
B-5	PB5	A13
B-6	PB6	A14
B-7	PB7	A15
C-0	PC0	A0/D0
C-1	PC1	A1/D1
C-2	PC2	A2/D2
C-3	PC3	A3/D3
C-4	PC4	A4/D4
C-5	PC5	A5/D5
C-6	PC6	A6/D6
C-7	PC7	A7/D7
D-0	PD0/RxD	PD0/RxD
D-1	PD1/TxD	PD1/TxD
D-2	PD2/MISO	PD2/MISO
D-3	PD3/MOSI	PD3/MOSI
D-4	PD4/SCK	PD4/SCK
D-5	PD5/SS	PD5/$\overline{\text{SS}}$
D-6	STRA	AS
D-7	STRB	R/$\overline{\text{W}}$
E-0	PE0/AN0	PE0/AN0
E-1	PE1/AN1	PE1/AN1
E-2	PE2/AN2	PE2/AN2
E-3	PE3/AN3	PE3/AN3
E-4	PE4/AN4 ##	PE4/AN4 ##
E-5	PE5/AN5 ##	PE5/AN5 ##
E-6	PE6/AN6 ##	PE6/AN6 ##
E-7	PE7/AN7 ##	PE7/AN7 ##

- not bonded in 48-pin variations

internal *pulse accumulator*. This is an 8-bit register that can be used to count external events and is incremented by a transition on the PA7 line.

Port B is strictly for outputs. In single-chip mode it functions as an output port and can be used as a strobed output where the STRB output pin pulses each time port B is written. In multiplexed mode, port B provides the high-order 8 bits of the 16-bit memory address.

In single-chip mode, port C is an 8-bit bidirectional port whose direction is controlled by the data direction register in the register control block that starts at location $1000. Port C may be used in handshake mode (similar to the PIA) where STRA and STRB act as the control lines. In multiplexed mode, port C carries the lower 8 bits of the address and the memory data. Here STRA is the Address Strobe (AS) and STRB is the R/$\overline{W}$ line.

Port D is independent of the operation mode. Bits 0–5 may be used for general-purpose I/O or with the SCI and the SPI (see Section 11-10.6) subsystems. As shown in Fig. 11-20, bit 0 is the receive data input (RXD) and bit 1 is the transmit data output (TXD) for the SCI. Bits 2 through 5 are used by the SPI. Bits 6 and 7 are STRA and STRB, respectively. They are used to control ports B and C, as discussed in the preceding paragraphs.

Port E is an input port. Its pins can be used as general-purpose input or as input to the internal A/D converter. There are four or eight inputs, depending on whether the 48-pin package or the 52-pin package is being used (see Section 11-9).

11-8.6 68HC11A8 CPU Registers

The Programming Model of the registers, shown in Fig. 11-24, is identical to that of the **6801** except for the additional Y register and the top 2 bits of the Condition Code Register. The stack operation (pointer writes and then increments) and the

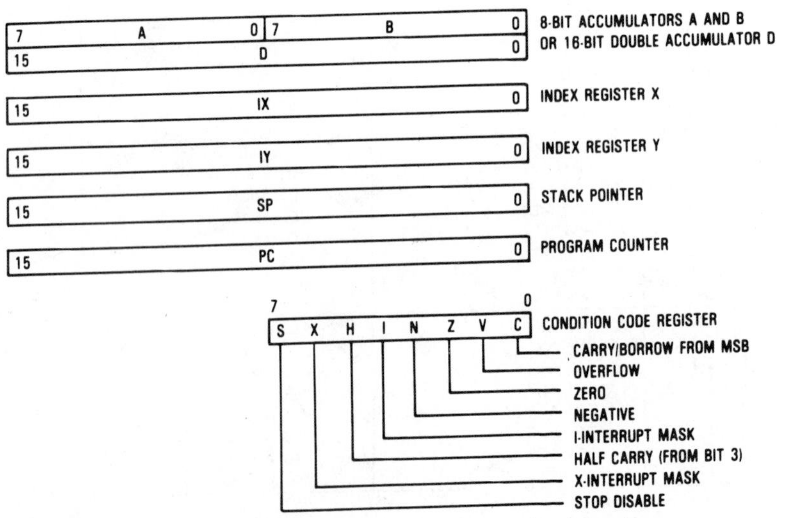

FIGURE 11-24 68HC11A8 programming model (registers).

interrupt stacking order are the same except for the additional 2 bytes needed for the Y register. These differences do not affect execution of either **6800** or **6801** programs.

The 16-bit Y index register is used with indexed mode instructions in almost the same way as the X register. However, all instructions using the Y register require an extra byte of machine code and an extra cycle of execution time since they are 2-byte Op codes.

The X interrupt mask bit of the condition code register is set only by hardware ($\overline{\text{RESET}}$ or $\overline{\text{XIRQ}}$ acknowledge). After minimum system initialization, the X bit may be cleared by a TAP instruction, thus enabling $\overline{\text{XIRQ}}$ interrupts. Thereafter, software cannot set the X bit. Since the operation of the I bit-related interrupt structure has no effect on the X bit, the $\overline{\text{XIRQ}}$ pin remains effectively nonmasked. An RTI (return from interrupt) instruction restores the X and I bits to their preinterrupt request status.

The STOP DISABLE bit (S) is set to disable the STOP instruction. The S bit is program-controlled. The STOP instruction is treated as a NOP (no operation) if the S bit is set.

11-8.7 68HC11A8 Instruction Set

The μP in the **68HC11A8** is basically an enhancement of the μP in the **6801**. Major functional additions include a second 16-bit index register (Y register), two types of 16 bit by 16 bit divide instructions, STOP and WAIT instructions, and bit manipulation instructions (see the following subsection).

In addition to its ability to execute all **6800** and **6801** instructions, the **68HC11A8** μC uses 2- byte Op codes for several groups of new instructions, thus providing 91 new Op codes. A *prebyte* has been added to certain Op codes.

A complete list of **68HC11A8** instructions is given in Appendix F. It shows that the **68H11A8** instructions associated with the Y register have a prebyte of $18 and a second Op code byte that is the same as the one used for the X register. For example, the Op code for ABX is 3A and the one for ABY is 18 3A. It should also be noted that almost every instruction has an additional *indexed with Y* instruction, such as ANDA 0,Y (18 A4). (ANDA 0,X is A4.) This alone accounts for 52 of the new instructions.

Bit Manipulation Instructions Another new group of instructions that have been added to the basic **6801** core are identified as *bit manipulation* instructions. These were originally added to the **6805** family μCs and their characteristics will be explained in detail in Section 11-10.2. The implementation for the **68HC11** family is slightly different, however, and will be described briefly here.

Bit manipulation is an important and often used function in microcontroller μCs. Because many of the I/O lines are frequently connected to indicators or electrically activated devices, such as solenoids or relays, a large percentage of the program is devoted to turning on or off these individual lines. These instructions provide this ability with considerably fewer bytes of machine code.

The bit manipulation instructions are

BSET	**Set a bit.**
BCLR	**Clear a bit.**
BRSET	**Branch on bit set.**
BRCLR	**Branch on bit clear.**

Bit manipulation consists of two different addressing modes: BIT SET/CLEAR and BIT TEST AND BRANCH. The BIT SET/CLEAR mode allows individual memory and I/O bits to be set or cleared under program control. The BIT TEST AND BRANCH mode allows any bit in memory to be tested and, depending on the instruction, to conditionally execute a branch as a result. Each of these addressing modes is described below.

BIT SET/CLEAR Addressing Mode Direct byte addressing and bit addressing are combined in instructions that set and clear individual memory and I/O bits. In the BSET and BCLR instructions, the memory address location (containing the bit to be modified) is specified either as a direct address in the location following the Op code or, in the case of indexed instructions, by the 8-bit positive **offset** byte (0 to $FF) that is added to the index register. With the direct addressing mode, only the first 256_{10} memory locations can be addressed, but the indexed instructions permit access to any location in memory. These instructions operate on any individual bit in the word accessed whether the memory is RAM or I/O. Because the **6800** family uses memory-mapped I/O, the bit instructions can operate directly on the I/O registers, thus directly controlling the I/O pins.

The actual bit or bits to be modified, within the byte, is (are) specified by a **mask byte**. The bit set and clear instructions are 3-byte instructions (except for those using the Y register which are four-byte): one (or two) for the Op code, another to address the byte that contains the bit(s) of interest, and one to specify which bit(s).

EXAMPLE 11-5

Show the instructions necessary to clear bit 2 of a flag that is located at an offset of 3 from $C300.

SOLUTION

Two programs, one for the **68HC11A8** and one for the **6800**, are shown in figure 11-25, a and b respectively. Note that the programs are the same except that one instruction of Fig. 11-25a (at $103) replaces the three instructions needed in Fig. 11-25b.

The **68HC11A8** Instruction Set in Appendix F shows the BCLR instruction operation as $M \cdot \overline{mm} \rightarrow M$. This is interpreted as *ANDing* the value in memory at $C303 (CD) with the complement of the *mask* byte ($06 = \overline{F9}$) to get a new memory value of C1.

In the **68HC11** instructions of Fig. 11-25a, the $1D is the Op code, and $03 is the

```
Ø1ØØ CE C3 ØØ        LDX   #$C3ØØ   Set index register

Ø1Ø3 1D Ø3 Ø4        BCLR  3,X 4    Clr bits 2

C3ØØ                 FCB   ...
C3Ø1                 FCB   ...
C3Ø2                 FCB   ...
C3Ø3                 FCB   $CD

  C3ØØ= X-register contents (added to offset)
```

(a)

```
Ø1Ø3 A6 Ø3           LDA   3,X      GET PRESENT STATUS
Ø1Ø5 85 FB           BITA  #$FB     CLEAR BIT 2
Ø1Ø7 A7 Ø3           STAA  3,X      SEND TO OUT
```

(b)

FIGURE 11-25 Two types of BIT CLEAR instructions for Example 11-5.

offset to be added to the index register that locates the byte to be modified. The 06 defines the bits (2 and 3) to be cleared. Although not shown, the value in location $C303 would then be $C1.

Figure 11-25a shows that the BCLR instruction takes only 3 bytes, compared to 6 bytes for the same function using conventional instructions (Fig. 11-25b). A similar savings will result for the BRSET, BRCLR, and BSET instructions. This shows the *byte efficiency* comparison that is important in μCs with their limited-size ROMs.

EXAMPLE 11-6

Illustrate the preferred **68HC11A8** instruction needed to turn ON lines 2 and 3 of the B side of a PIA located at $4000.

SOLUTION

Because the address of the PIA is not in the direct addressing range, an indexed BIT SET instruction is used as shown in Fig. 11-26.

The example uses an indexed Y instruction at $1004 to illustrate a 4-byte example. Bytes 1 and 2 are the Op code and byte 3 is the offset (pointing to the B-side data register). Byte 4 is the mask byte, which, according to the *operation* formula from Appendix F, is *ORed* with the existing data at this location to set bits 2 and 3 high (to a 1).

```
      4000         PIAB      EQU  $4000
       ...                   ...  .....
1000   18 CE 40 00           LDY  #PIAB
1004   18 1C 02 06           BSET PIA1  Y,02 06    SET bits 2 & 3
```

FIGURE 11-26 BIT-SET indexed instruction for Example 11-6.

11-8.8 The 68HC11 EEPROM

The **68HC11A8** includes 512 bytes of EEPROM located in the area $B600 through $B7FF, which has the same read cycle time as the internal ROM. The programming of the EEPROM is controlled by the PPROG register shown in Fig. 11-27. This register is at location $x038 (see Section 11-8.9) and is cleared during RESET.

The operating modes for the 512-byte EEPROM are

Normal read

Programming

Erase

Read Mode In this mode the ERASE bit in the PPROG register must be clear (not erase mode) and the EELAT bit must be clear (not programming mode). While these two bits are cleared, the ROW and EEPGM bits in the PPROG register have no meaning or effect and the 512-byte EEPROM may be read as if it were a normal ROM.

Programming The bits of each byte of the EEPROM can be forced to a 0 or left as a 1 during the programming process. (The erased state of all EEPROM cells is logic 1.) The data is written to the desired address and the programming voltage is then coupled to the EEPROM array by setting the EEPGM bit to a 1. Programming (and erasure) takes up to 10 ms. Details of this process should be obtained by referring to the Data Sheets for the part as listed in Section 11-14.

Erase The CSEL bit in the OPTION register must be set when erasing the EEPROM. The EEPROM has three erase modes:

1. Full 512-byte simultaneous erase.
2. Row—where only one row (16 bytes) is erased at a time.
3. Byte—where a single specified byte is erased.

Again, refer to the manuals listed in Section 11-15 for full details.

B7	B6	B5	B4	B3	B2	B1	B0
ODD	EVEN	-	BYTE	ROW	ERASE	EELAT	EEPGM

FIGURE 11-27 The EEPROM programming control register PPROG.

11-8.9 The 68HC11A8 Internal Control Registers

There are 64 internal registers that are used to control the operation of the **68HC11A8** μC. These are shown in Table 11-11. These registers can be remapped (or moved around) in the internal memory space on 4K boundaries using the INIT register. The default location of this block of registers is $1000 (the INIT register is set to 01 during RESET). The functions of most of the registers are explained throughout this text.

11-8.10 The Configuration Register (CONFIG)

The last register in the block of internal control registers is the Configuration Register. It has only 3 bits that are used. This register is implemented with EEPROM cells and is shown in Fig. 11-28. It can be written to or erased, like the other bytes of the EEPROM. Each bit controls one of three internal features, the COP function, the ROM, and the EEPROM. When a bit is set to a 1, the feature is ON or operational. When 0 or clear, it is OFF or disabled (i.e., the 512-byte EEPROM is disabled when the EEON bit in the CONFIG register is clear). Because this register is EEPROM, the system retains the selected configuration even after power is turned OFF and then ON again.

11-9 ANALOG-TO-DIGITAL CONVERTER

The **68HC11A8** includes eight input lines (port E) that are connected to an A/D converter. (Only four A/D inputs are available in the 48-pin package version of the **68HC11A8**.) An internal multiplexer determines which line (or channel) is connected to the converter. The A/D converter uses *successive approximations* with a *sample and hold* circuit to minimize conversion errors caused by rapidly changing input signals. Two dedicated pins, V_{RL} and V_{RH}, are provided for the reference supply voltage inputs. These pins may be connected to a low-noise power supply to ensure full accuracy of the A/D conversion. The 8-bit A/D converter has a linearity error of $\pm 1/2$ LSB and accepts analog inputs that range from V_{RL} to V_{RH}. Normally, V_{RL} is connected to ground and V_{RH} is connected to +5 V, but smaller analog input ranges can also be obtained by adjusting V_{RH} and V_{RL} to the desired upper and lower limits.

11-9.1 Clocking the A/D Converter

The A/D converter is synchronized by a clock. The clock *select* flag (bit 6 of the OPTION register) determines whether the system E clock or a 1.5-MHz *RC* oscillator controls the converter. When CSEL (bit 6) is cleared, the A/D uses the system E clock. When the system clock is slower than 1 MHz, CSEL is set, so the A/D uses the internal clock. Each conversion is accomplished in 32 clock cycles. The Configuration Options Register (OPTIONS) is used during initialization to configure internal system options; it is discussed in Advance Information Booklet 1207 or later literature, as cited in Section 11-14.

TABLE 11-11 The Internal Registers in the **68HC11A8**

Address	Bit 7	6	5	4	3	2	1	Bit 0	Register	Description
$i000	Bit 7	–	–	–	–	–	–	Bit 0	PORTA	I/O Port A
$i001									Reserved	
$i002	STAF	STAI	CWOM	HNDS	OIN	PLS	EGA	INVB	PIOC	Parallel I/O Control Register
$i003	Bit 7	–	–	–	–	–	–	Bit 0	PORTC	I/O Port C
$i004	Bit 7	–	–	–	–	–	–	Bit 0	PORTB	I/O Port B
$i005	Bit 7	–	–	–	–	–	–	Bit 0	PORTCL	Alternate Latched Port C
$i006									Reserved	
$i007	Bit 7	–	–	–	–	–	–	Bit 0	DDRC	Data Direction for Port C
$i008			Bit 5	–	–	–	–	Bit 0	PORTD	I/O Port D
$i009			Bit 5	–	–	–	–	Bit 0	DDRD	Data Direction for Port D
$i00A	Bit 7	–	–	–	–	–	–	Bit 0	PORTE	Input Port E
$i00B	FOC1	FOC2	FOC3	FOC4	FOC5				CFORC	Compare Force Register
$i00C	OC1M7	OC1M6	OC1M5	OC1M4	OC1M3				OC1M	OC1 Action Mask Register
$i00D	OC1D7	OC1D6	OC1D5	OC1D4	OC1D3				OC1D	OC1 Action Data Register
$i00E	Bit 15	–	–	–	–	–	–	Bit 8	TCNT	Timer Counter Register
$i00F	Bit 7	–	–	–	–	–	–	Bit 0		
$i010	Bit 15	–	–	–	–	–	–	Bit 8	TIC1	Input Capture 1 Register
$i011	Bit 7	–	–		–	–	–	Bit 0		
$i012	Bit 15	–	–		–	–	–	Bit 8	TIC2	Input Capture 2 Register
$i013	Bit 7	–	–		–	–	–	Bit 0		
$i014	Bit 15	–	–		–	–	–	Bit 8	TIC3	Input Capture 3 Register
$i015	Bit 7	–	–		–	–	–	Bit 0		
$i016	Bit 15	–	–		–	–	–	Bit 8	TOC1	Output Compare 1 Register
$i017	Bit 7	–			–	–	–	Bit 0		
$i018	Bit 15	–			–	–	–	Bit 8	TOC2	Output Compare 2 Register
$i019	Bit 7	–			–	–	–	Bit 0		
$i01A	Bit 15	–			–	–	–	Bit 8	TOC3	Output Compare 3 Register
$i01B	Bit 7	–			–	–	–	Bit 0		
$i01C	Bit 15	–			–	–	–	Bit 8	TOC4	Output Compare 4 Register
$i01D	Bit 7	–		–	–	–	–	Bit 0		
$i01E	Bit 15	–		–	–	–	–	Bit 8	TOC5	Output Compare 5 Register
$i01F	Bit 7	–		–	–	–	–	Bit 0		

TABLE 11-11 *(Continued)*

Address	Bit 7	6	5	4	3	2	1	Bit 0	Name	Description
$i020	OM2	OL2	OM3	OL3	OM4	OL4	OM5	OL5	TCTL1	Timer Control Register 1
$i021			EDG1B	EDG1A	EDG2B	EDG2A	EDG3B	EDG3A	TCTL2	Timer Control Register 2
$i022	OC1I	OC2I	OC3I	OC4I	OC5I	IC1I	IC2I	IC3I	TMSK1	Main Timer Interrupt Mask Register 1
$i023	OC1F	OC2F	OC3F	OC4F	OC5F	IC1F	IC2F	IC3F	TFLG1	Main Timer Interrupt Flag Register 1
$i024	TOI	RTII	PAOVI	PAII			PR1	PR0	TMSK2	Misc Timer Interrupt Mask Register 2
$i025	TOF	RT1F	PAOVF	PAIF					TFLG2	Misc Timer Interrupt Flag Register 2
$i026	DDRA7	PAEN	PAMOD	PEDGE			RTR1	RTR0	PACTL	Pulse Accumulator Control Register
$i027	Bit 7	–	–	–	–	–	–	Bit 0	PACNT	Pulse Accumulator Count Register
$i028	SPIE	SPE	DWOM	MSTR	CPOL	CPHA	SPR1	SPR0	SPCR	SPI Control Register
$i029	SPIF	WCOL		MODF					SPSR	SPI Status Register
$i02A	Bit 7	–	–	–	–	–	–	Bit 0	SPDR	SPI Data In/Out
$i02B	TCLR		SCP1	SCP0	RCKB	SCR2	SCR1	SCR0	BAUD	SCI Baud Rate Control
$i02C	R8	T8		M	WAKE				SCCR1	SCI Control Register 1
$i02D	TIE	TCIE	RIE	ILIE	TE	RE	RWU	SBK	SCCR2	SCI Control Register 2
$i02E	TDRE	TC	RDRF	IDLE	OR	NF	FE		SCSR	SCI Status Register
$i02F	Bit 7	–	–	–	–	–	–	Bit 0	SCDR	SCI Data (Read RDR, Write TDR)
$i030	CCF		SCAN	MULT	CD	CC	CB	CA	ADCTL	A to D Control Register
$i031	Bit 7	–	–	–	–	–	–	Bit 0	ADR1	A to D Result Register 1
$i032	Bit 7	–	–	–	–	–	–	Bit 0	ADR2	A to D Result Register 2
$i033	Bit 7	–	–	–	–	–	–	Bit 0	ADR3	A to D Result Register 3
$i034	Bit 7	–	–	–	–	–	–	Bit 0	ADR4	A to D Result Register 4
$i035									Reserved	
$i036									Reserved	
$i037									Reserved	
$i038									Reserved	
$i039	ADPU	CSEL	IRQE	DLY	CME		CR1	CR0	OPTION	System Configuration Options
$i03A	Bit 7	–	–	–	–	–	–	Bit 0	COPRST	Arm/Reset COP Timer Circuitry
$i03B	ODD	EVEN		BYTE	ROW	ERASE	EELAT	EEPGM	PPROG	EEPROM Programming Control Register
$i03C	RBOOT	SMOD	MDA	IRV	PSEL3	PSEL2	PSEL1	PSEL0	HPRIO	Highest Priority I-Bit Interrupt and Misc.
$i03D	RAM3	RAM2	RAM1	RAM0	REG3	REG2	REG1	REG0	INIT	RAM–I/O Maping Register
$i03E	TILOP		OCCR	CBYP	DISR	FCM	FCOP	TCON	TEST1	Factory TEST Control Register
$i03F						NOCOP	ROMON	EEON	CONFIG	COP, ROM, & EEPROM Enables (EEPROM Cells)
	Bit 7	6	5	4	3	2	1	Bit 0		

```
  B7      B6       B5        B4        B3        B2       B1       BØ
-----------------------------------------------------------------------
|  -  |   -  |    -   |    -   |    -  | NOCOP| ROMON| EEON   |
-----------------------------------------------------------------------
```

FIGURE 11-28 The CONFIG register.

11-9.2 The Conversion Process

The A/D converter is **ratiometric**. An input voltage equal to V_{RL} converts to $00 and an input voltage equal to V_{RH} converts to $FF (full scale), with no overflow indication. For ratiometric conversions, the source of each analog input should use V_{RH} as the supply voltage and be referenced to V_{RL}.

11-9.3 Channel Assignments

A multiplexer within the **68HC11A8** allows the single A/D converter to select one of 16 analog signals (or channels) for conversion. When in the multichannel mode, these channels are subdivided into four *groups* of four channels. Eight of these channels correspond to port E input pins to the μC, four are for internal reference points or test functions, and four are reserved for future use. There are four *channel select control bits,* which are used to select a particular channel. Table 11-12 shows the signals selected by the four channel select control bits and the grouping of the channels.

11-9.4 Conversions

The A/D converter is controlled by the A/D control/status register located at $x030 of the internal register block (see Table 11-11). All bits in this register may be read or written, except bit 7, which is a read-only status indicator, and bit 6, which always reads as a zero. Conversion is started by writing into this register. Bit 7 is cleared at RESET but the other bits are not affected.

There are two modes of operation, *single* and *continuous*. In single mode, a write to the A/D Control/Status register (called the ADCTL register) starts *four* consecutive conversions. The results of these four conversions are sent to four *A/D result registers*. In continuous mode, the result registers are continuously updated by repeated conversions.

Conversions are also performed on either a *single* channel or a *group* of channels. In single-mode, single-channel operations, four consecutive conversions are performed on a specified single channel to fill the result registers. In *multiple* mode, one conversion is performed on each of the *four* channels in a specific *group,* and the results fill the registers.

11-9.5 Control/Status Register (ADCTL)

The A/D control status register controls the converter. It is shown in Fig. 11-29. The four channel select bits (CD, CC, CB, and CA) specify the channel or group to be converted. The function of the other bits is described in the following paragraphs.

Bit 7. CCF Conversions Complete Flag This read-only status indicator bit is set when all four A/D result registers contain valid conversion results. Each time the ADCTL register is written, this bit is automatically cleared and a conversion sequence is started. In the continuous modes, conversions are repeated and the result registers continue to be updated with current data even though the CCF bit remains set.

Bit 6 Not implemented. Reads as zero.

Bit 5. SCAN When this control bit is cleared, the single mode is selected. The four requested conversions are performed once to fill the four result registers. When this control bit is set, conversions continue in a round-robin fashion with the result registers being updated as data become available.

Bit 4. MULT—MultiChannel/Single-Channel Control When this bit is cleared, the A/D system is configured to perform four consecutive conversions on the single channel specified by the four channel select bits CD through CA (bits 3–0 of ADCTL). When this bit is set (multichannel mode), the A/D system is configured to perform a conversion on each of the four channels in a group. The two least significant channel select bits (CB and CA) have no meaning and the CD and CC bits specify which group of four channels are to be converted. The signals selected by the four channel select control bits are shown in Table 11-12.

11-9.6 Single-Channel Operation

There are two variations of single-channel operation. In the first (SCAN = 0), the selected channel is converted four consecutive times with the first result being stored in the ADR1 result register and the fourth result being stored in the ADR4 register. After the fourth conversion is complete, all conversion activity is halted until a new conversion command is written to the ADCTL control register. In the second variation (SCAN = 1), conversions continue to be performed on the selected channel with the fifth conversion being stored to the ADR1 register (overwriting the first conversion result), the sixth conversion overwriting ADR2, and so on continuously.

11-9.7 Four-Channel Operation

There are two variations of multiple-channel operation. In the first (SCAN = 0), the selected group of four channels are converted, one time each, with the first result being stored in the ADR1 result register and the fourth result being stored in the ADR4 register. After the fourth conversion is complete, all conversion activity halts until a new conversion command is written to the ADCTL control register. In the second variation (SCAN = 1), conversions continue to be performed on the

B7	B6	B5	B4	B3	B2	B1	BØ
CCF	-	SCAN	MULT	CD	CC	CB	CA

FIGURE 11-29 A/D control/status register (ADCTL).

TABLE 11-12 The Function of the Channel Control Bits in the A/D Converter of the **68HC11A8**

CD	CC	CB	CA	Channel Signal	Result in ADRx if Mult = 1
Group Ø					
Ø	Ø	Ø	Ø	ANO	ADR1[b]
Ø	Ø	Ø	1	AN1	ADR2
Ø	Ø	1	Ø	AN2	ADR3
Ø	Ø	1	1	AN3	ADR4
Group 1					
Ø	1	Ø	Ø	AN4[a]	ADR1
Ø	1	Ø	1	AN5[a]	ADR2
Ø	1	1	Ø	AN6[a]	ADR3
Ø	1	1	1	AN7[a]	ADR4
Group 2					
1	Ø	Ø	Ø	Reserved	ADR1
1	Ø	Ø	1	Reserved	ADR2
1	Ø	1	Ø	Reserved	ADR3
1	Ø	1	1	Reserved	ADR4
Group 3					
1	1	Ø	Ø	V_{RH} pin	ADR1
1	1	Ø	Ø	V_{RL} pin	ADR2
1	1	1	Ø	$(V_{RH})/2$	ADR3
1	1	1	1	Reserved	ADR4

[a] Not available in 48-pin package versions.
[b] Refer to the following paragraph.

selected group of channels with the fifth conversion being stored in the ADR1 register (replacing the earlier conversion result for the first channel in the group), the sixth conversion overwriting ADR2, and so on continuously.

EXAMPLE 11-7

The A/D control register reads B4. What is the A/D doing? What data is going into the A/D result registers?

SOLUTION

The B in the most significant nibble means that the CCF is set, and the converter is continuously scanning in multichannel mode. The 4 indicates that channel group 1 is being converted because CD = 0 and CC = 1. Thus, the converted result of the input on channel AN4 is going into result register 1 (ADR1), the input on channel AN5 is going into ADR2, and so forth. Because the conversions are continuous, we would expect CCF to be set.

11-9.8 Operation of the A/D in the Stop and Wait Modes

If a conversion sequence is still in process when the **68HC11A8** enters the STOP or WAIT mode, the conversion of the current channel is suspended. When the μC resumes normal operation, that channel will be resampled and the conversion sequence resumes. As the μC exits the WAIT mode, the A/D circuits are stable and valid results can be obtained on the first conversion. However, in STOP mode, all analog bias currents are disabled and it becomes necessary to allow a stabilization period when leaving the STOP mode. If the **68HC11A8** exits the STOP mode with a delay, there will automatically be enough time for these circuits to stabilize before the first conversion. If the **68HC11A8** exits the STOP mode with no delay (DLY bit in OPTION register equal to zero), the user must allow sufficient time for the A/D circuitry to stabilize to avoid invalid results.

11-9.9 A/D Power Up

A/D power up is controlled by bit 7 (ADPU) of the OPTION register. When ADPU is cleared, power to the A/D system is disabled. When ADPU is set, the A/D system is enabled. A delay of typically 100 μs is required after turning on the A/D converter to allow the analog bias voltages to stabilize.

11-10 THE 6805 FAMILY OF μCS

There is a large and still growing industrial demand for *microcontrollers*. A **microcontroller** is a small, low-cost, special-purpose system designed to monitor or control a specific process or machine. In addition to the customized I/O interface to the machine, the system often consists of a minimal μP, a small RAM, some ROM to hold the special-purpose program, a timer, and perhaps an A/D converter or a phase-locked loop (PLL). Each member of the **6805** family of μCs includes some or all of these features on a single chip, and because of the simplified design of the μP and timer, they are easier to manufacture. This in turn accounts for the low cost of the **6805** and is the principal reason for using it in place of **6801**s or **68HC11**s.

The declining costs of microcontrollers make it possible to automate smaller and lower-cost machines and have led to an increase in the number of applications.

At least 30 different types of **6805** μCs exist at the time of this writing and more are being developed. They have a variety of I/O features and use different technologies. Table 11-13 gives the features of 15 of these μCs. All versions of the **6805** family contain a simplified **6800** type μP.

The μCs in Table 11-13 have 64 or 112 bytes of RAM and 1.1K to 3.8K bytes of ROM or EPROM. They have between 20 and 30 bidirectional I/O lines. All these μCs contain a timer. The μCs with an R in their designation contain an A/D converter, and the **6805T2** contains a phase-locked loop. Thus the user can select the μC that best satisfies particular requirements from a wide variety of available **6805**s without incurring unnecessary costs for unused features. In some high-volume applications, such as intelligent toys, the low selling price is crucial.

Figure 11-30 is a block diagram of the basic **6805**, which is identical for all members of the family, including the CMOS **146805E2**. One main difference between family members is in the size of the stack pointer and program counter registers. Since the size of these two registers is determined by the amount of memory that must be addressed, they vary from 11 to 13 bits.

Each family member contains peripheral I/O such as a timer, some bidirectional I/O lines, RAM, and an on-chip oscillator that provides the processor timing, plus reset, and interrupt logic. All family members except the **146805E2** also include an on-chip ROM. The peripherals and memory are placed in similar locations throughout the family; therefore, a user who is familiar with any family device is familiar with all of them. It is likely that new devices will be incorporated in the family by adding to and/or subtracting from the peripheral blocks associated with the CPU in the basic configuration. These peripheral blocks could include additional I/O lines, more RAM, EPROM, EEPROM, SCI, SPI, A/D converter, phase-locked loop, or an external bus. Details of these optional functions are discussed starting in Section 11-10.3.

The **6805** family of μCs, like all **6800** family devices, are implemented using a single address map with memory-mapped I/O. Figure 11-31 shows the memory map for the **6805P2**, which is one of the smaller units.

Peripheral I/O devices (A/D, timer, etc.) are controlled by entries in the control and/or data registers located in the low end of the address map. The key to using the **6805** family I/O features is in learning how the peripheral registers affect the device operation.

11-10.1 The 6805 μP

The μP (or CPU) in the **6805** is a simplified version of the **6800** μP, whose register architecture is shown in Fig. 11-32. The differences between the **6805** and the **6800** follow:

1. The program counter and stack pointer (SP) registers are each 11, 12, or 13 bits long, instead of 16 bits, depending on whether the size of the usable memory (both RAM and ROM) is 2, 4, or 8K bytes.
2. The B accumulator has been eliminated (this also eliminates all instructions that referenced the B accumulator).

TABLE 11-13 Features of the **6805** Family of μCs

M6805 HMOS Family MCUs

Features	MC6805P2	MC6805P4	MC6805P6	MC6805R2	MC6805R3	MC6805T2	MC6805U2	MC6805U3
Technology	HMOS	HMOS	HMOS	HMOS	HMOS	HMOS	HMOS	HMOS
Number of Pins	28	28	28	40	40	28	40	40
On-Chip RAM (Bytes)	64	112*	64	64	112	64	64	112
On-Chip User ROM (Bytes)	1.1K	1.1K	1.8K	2K	3.8K	2.5K	2K	3.8K
External Bus	None	None	None	None	None	None	None	None
Bidirectional I/O Lines	20	20	20	24	24	19	24	24
Unidirectional I/O Lines	None	None	None	6 Inputs	6 Inputs	None	8 Inputs	8 Inputs
Other I/O Features	Timer	Timer	Timer	Timer, A/D	Timer, A/D	Timer, PLL	Timer	Timer
External Interrupt Inputs	1	1	1	2	2	2	2	2
EPROM Version	MC68705P3	MC68705P3	MC68705P3	MC68705R3	MC68705R3	None	MC68705U3	MC68705U3
STOP and WAIT	No	No	No	No	No	No	No	No

*Indicates standby RAM.

M6805 HMOS/M146805 CMOS Family EPROM MCUs

Features	MC68705P3	MC68705R3	MC68705U3	MC1468705G2
Technology	HMOS	HMOS	HMOS	CMOS
Number of Pins	28	40	40	40
On-Chip RAM (Bytes)	112	112	112	112
On-Chip User ROM (Bytes)	1.8K EPROM	3.8K EPROM	3.8K EPROM	2K EPROM
External Bus	None	None	None	None
Bidirectional I/O Lines	20	24	24	32
Unidirectional I/O Lines	None	6 Inputs	8 Inputs	None
Other I/O Features	Timer	Timer, A/D	Timer	Timer
External Interrupt Inputs	1	2	2	1
EPROM Version	—	—	—	—
STOP and WAIT	No	No	No	Yes

M146805 CMOS Family MPU/MCUs

Features	MC146805E2	MC146805F2	MC146805G2
Technology	CMOS	CMOS	CMOS
Number of Pins	40	28	40
On-Chip RAM (Bytes)	112	64	112
On-Chip User ROM (Bytes)	None	1K	2K
External Bus	Yes	None	None
Bidirectional I/O Lines	16	16	32
Unidirectional I/O Lines	None	4 Inputs	None
Other I/O Features	Timer	Timer	Timer
External Interrupt Inputs	1	1	1
EPROM Version	None	None	MC1468705G2
STOP and WAIT	Yes	Yes	Yes

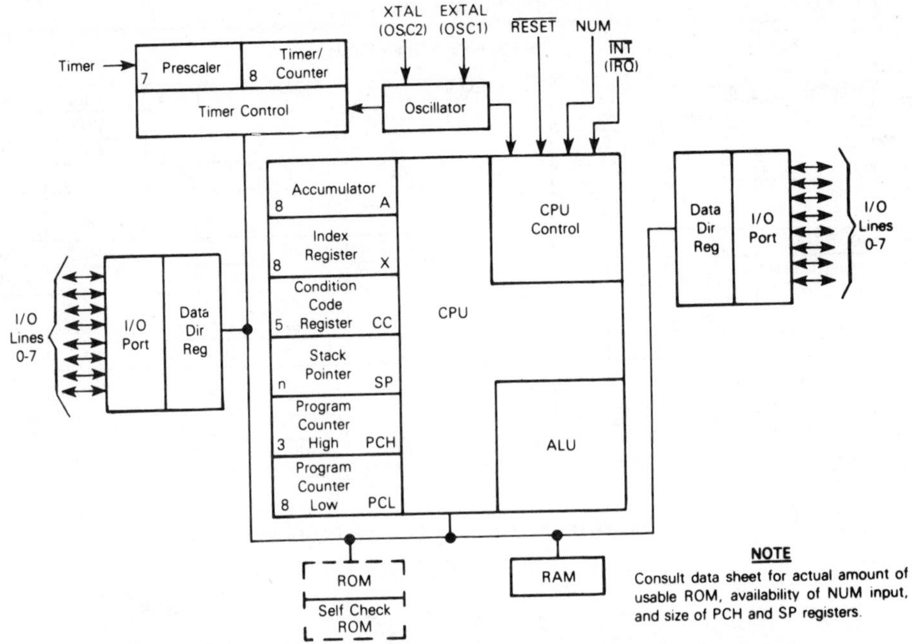

FIGURE 11-30 6805 HMOS/**M146805** CMOS family basic μC block diagram.

3. The index register is only 8 bits long.
4. The V bit has been deleted from the Condition Code Register.

The **6805** instruction set is similar to the **6800** set, but some instructions have been deleted or changed because of the elimination of the B register and the use of an 8-bit X register. At the same time, a number of instructions have been added that are specifically designed for byte-efficient program storage. Table 11-14 shows the **68HC11** Instruction Set. It includes all of the instructions typically used in the **146805** CMOS family plus an additional multiply (MUL) instruction. Both have the STOP and WAIT instructions since both processors are implemented using **CMOS**.

The **6805** executes its instructions in the inherent, immediate, direct, extended, indexed, and relative addressing modes. Except for the indexed mode, all modes are identical to the **6800** modes. The indexed mode consists of three submodes:

1. The no-offset (or 0 offset) mode. In this mode there is no offset and the index register contains the Effective Address (EA) of the instruction. Therefore the addresses are restricted to the range $0000 to $00FF.
2. The 8-bit offset mode. In this mode the EA is the sum of the *offset* (the second byte of the instruction) and the contents of X.
3. The 16-bit offset mode. In this mode the EA is the sum of the second and third bytes (read as a 16-bit number) of the instruction and X. This is the only indexed mode that allows access to the entire memory space.

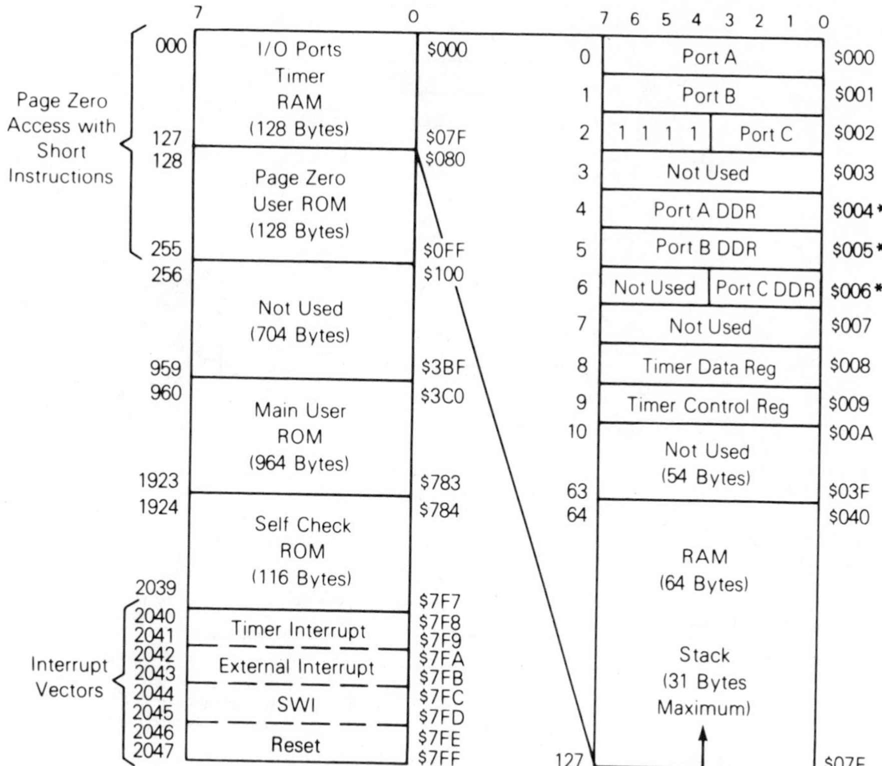

*Caution: Data direction registers (DDRs) are write-only; they read as $FF.

FIGURE 11-31 MCU address map.

Each indexed instruction (LDA 0,X for example) has three different Op codes to tell the μP which submode to use. No-offset instructions are single-byte instructions (only the Op code is needed), 8-bit offset instructions require 2 bytes, and 16-bit offset instructions require 3 bytes.

EXAMPLE 11-8

Write a program to move a block of data $20 bytes long from $1500 to $1700. Use indexed instructions.

SOLUTION

A possible program is shown in Fig. 11-33. Each time through a loop the accumulator is loaded with the contents of memory, starting at $1520, and then it is stored in the new location. The program is smaller if we start at the last byte and decrement X each time through the loop since we simply test for a minus number to see when we are done. In that way, a compare instruction is unnecessary.

Now, if X is 20 the first time through the loop, 1F the second time, etc., the

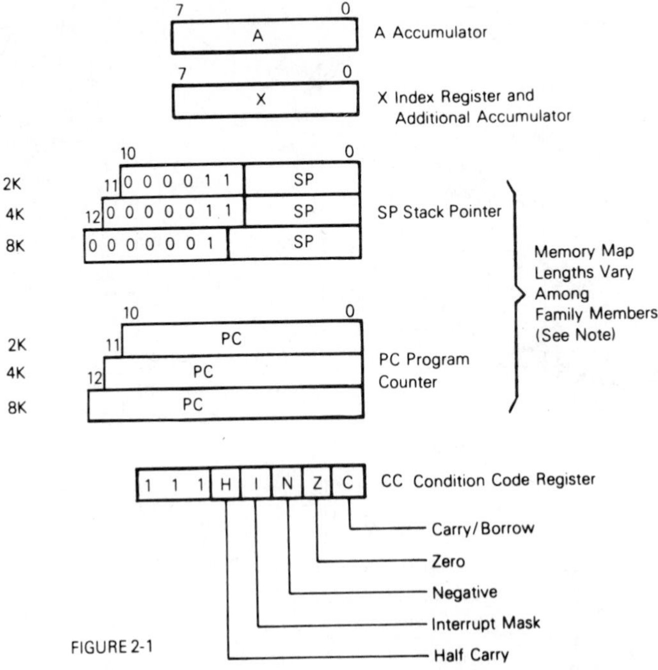

FIGURE 11-32 **6805** HMOS/**M146805** CMOS family register architecture.

contents of 1520 will be loaded and stored at 1720, then the contents of 151F at 171F, and so forth until X goes negative.

11-10.2 Bit Manipulation

New instructions created for the **6805** family include some for bit test and bit manipulation. The benefits of these for μCs were explained in Section 11-8.7. The **6805** family has a very byte-efficient implementation that is slightly different from that previously described for the **68HC11** family. The same functions are provided (i.e., to set or clear a bit and to branch on a set or clear bit), but the **6805** implementation generally has one less byte for the same function. Only direct

```
100 AE 20             LDX #$20       Preset the X register
102 D6 15 00   LOOP   LDA $1500,X    Fetch the data
105 D7 17 00          STA $1700,X    Store it
108 5A                DEX            Decrement the X register
109 26 F7             BPL LOOP       Loop until X is minus
```

FIGURE 11-33 Block move using indexed instructions, Example 11-8.

TABLE 11-14 The 68HC11 Instruction Set

	Bit Manipulation		Branch	Read/Modify/Write					Control		Register/Memory						
	BTB	BSC	REL	DIR	INH	INH	IX1	IX	INH	INH	IMM	DIR	EXT	IX2	IX1	IX	
Low \ Hi	0 0000	1 0001	2 0010	3 0011	4 0100	5 0101	6 0110	7 0111	8 1000	9 1001	A 1010	B 1011	C 1100	D 1101	E 1110	F 1111	Hi \ Low
0 0000	BRSET0 3 BTB 5	BSET0 2 BSC 5	BRA 2 REL 3	NEG 2 DIR 5	NEG 1 INH 3	NEG 1 INH 3	NEG 2 IX1 6	NEG 1 IX 5	RTI 1 INH 9		SUB 2 IMM 2	SUB 2 DIR 3	SUB 3 EXT 4	SUB 3 IX2 5	SUB 2 IX1 4	SUB 1 IX 3	0 0000
1 0001	BRCLR0 3 BTB 5	BCLR0 2 BSC 5	BRN 2 REL 3						RTS 1 INH 6		CMP 2 IMM 2	CMP 2 DIR 3	CMP 3 EXT 4	CMP 3 IX2 5	CMP 2 IX1 4	CMP 1 IX 3	1 0001
2 0010	BRSET1 3 BTB 5	BSET1 2 BSC 5	BHI 2 REL 3		MUL 1 INH 11						SBC 2 IMM 2	SBC 2 DIR 3	SBC 3 EXT 4	SBC 3 IX2 5	SBC 2 IX1 4	SBC 1 IX 3	2 0010
3 0011	BRCLR1 3 BTB 5	BCLR1 2 BSC 5	BLS 2 REL 3	COM 2 DIR 5	COMA 1 INH 3	COMX 1 INH 3	COM 2 IX1 6	COM 1 IX 5	SWI 1 INH 10		CPX 2 IMM 2	CPX 2 DIR 3	CPX 3 EXT 4	CPX 3 IX2 5	CPX 2 IX1 4	CPX 1 IX 3	3 0011
4 0100	BRSET2 3 BTB 5	BSET2 2 BSC 5	BCC 2 REL 3	LSR 2 DTR 5	LSRA 1 INH 3	LSRX 1 INH 3	LSR 2 IX1 6	LSR 1 IX 5			AND 2 IMM 2	AND 2 DIR 3	AND 3 EXT 4	AND 3 IX2 5	AND 2 IX1 4	AND 1 IX 3	4 0100
5 0101	BRCLR2 3 BTB 5	BCLR2 2 BSC 5	BCS 2 REL 3								BIT 2 IMM 2	BIT 2 DIR 3	BIT 3 EXT 4	BIT 3 IX2 5	BIT 2 IX1 4	BIT 1 IX 3	5 0101
6 0110	BRSET3 3 BTB 5	BSET3 2 BSC 5	BNE 2 REL 3	ROR 2 DIR 5	RORA 1 INH 3	RORX 1 INH 3	ROR 2 IX1 6	ROR 1 IX 5			LDA 2 IMM 2	LDA 2 DIR 3	LDA 3 EXT 4	LDA 3 IX2 5	LDA 2 IX1 4	LDA 1 IX 3	6 0110
7 0111	BRCLR3 3 BTB 5	BCLR3 2 BSC 5	BEQ 2 REL 3	ASR 2 DIR 5	ASRA 1 INH 3	ASRX 1 INH 3	ASR 2 IX1 6	ASR 1 IX 5		TAX 1 INH 2		STA 2 DIR 4	STA 3 EXT 5	STA 3 IX2 6	STA 2 IX1 5	STA 1 IX 4	7 0111
8 1000	BRSET4 3 BTB 5	BSET4 2 BSC 5	BHCC 2 REL 3	LSL 2 DIR 5	LSLA 1 INH 3	LSLX 1 INH 3	LSL 2 IX1 6	LSL 1 IX 5		CLC 1 INH 2	EOR 2 IMM 2	EOR 2 DIR 3	EOR 3 EXT 4	EOR 3 IX2 5	EOR 2 IX1 4	EOR 1 IX 3	8 1000
9 1001	BRCLR4 3 BTB 5	BCLR4 2 BSC 5	BHCS 2 REL 3	ROL 2 DIR 5	ROLA 1 INH 3	ROLX 1 INH 3	ROL 2 IX1 6	ROL 1 IX 5		SEC 1 INH 2	ADC 2 IMM 2	ADC 2 DIR 3	ADC 3 EXT 4	ADC 3 IX2 5	ADC 2 IX1 4	ADC 1 IX 3	9 1001
A 1010	BRSET5 3 BTB 5	BSET5 2 BSC 5	BPL 2 REL 3	DEC 2 DIR 5	DECA 1 INH 3	DECX 1 INH 3	DEC 2 IX1 6	DEC 1 IX 5		CLI 1 INH 2	ORA 2 IMM 2	ORA 2 DIR 3	ORA 3 EXT 4	ORA 3 IX2 5	ORA 2 IX1 4	ORA 1 IX 3	A 1010
B 1011	BRCLR5 3 BTB 5	BCLR5 2 BSC 5	BMI 2 REL 3							SEI 1 INH 2	ADD 2 IMM 2	ADD 2 DIR 3	ADD 3 EXT 4	ADD 3 IX2 5	ADD 2 IX1 4	ADD 1 IX 3	B 1011
C 1100	BRSET6 3 BTB 5	BSET6 2 BSC 5	BMC 2 REL 3	INC 2 DIR 5	INCA 1 INH 3	INCX 1 INH 3	INC 2 IX1 6	INC 1 IX 5		RSP 1 INH 2		JMP 2 DIR 2	JMP 3 EXT 3	JMP 3 IX2 4	JMP 2 IX1 3	JMP 1 IX 2	C 1100
D 1101	BRCLR6 3 BTB 5	BCLR6 2 BSC 5	BMS 2 REL 3	TST 2 DIR 4	TSTA 1 INH 3	TSTX 1 INH 3	TST 2 IX1 5	TST 1 IX 4		NOP 1 INH 2	BSR 2 REL 6	JSR 2 DIR 5	JSR 3 EXT 6	JSR 3 IX2 7	JSR 2 IX1 6	JSR 1 IX 5	D 1101
E 1110	BRSET7 3 BTB 5	BSET7 2 BSC 5	BIL 2 REL 3						STOP 1 INH 2		LDX 2 IMM 2	LDX 2 DIR 3	LDX 3 EXT 4	LDX 3 IX2 5	LDX 2 IX1 4	LDX 1 IX 3	E 1110
F 1111	BRCLR7 3 BTB 5	BCLR7 2 BSC 5	BIH 2 REL 3	CLR 2 DIR 5	CLRA 1 INH 3	CLRX 1 INH 3	CLR 2 IX1 6	CLR 1 IX 5	WAIT 1 INH 2	TXA 1 INH 2		STX 2 DIR 4	STX 3 EXT 5	STX 3 IX2 6	STX 2 IX1 5	STX 1 IX 4	F 1111

Abbreviations for Address Modes

INH	Inherent
A	Accumulator
X	Index Register
IMM	Immediate
DIR	Direct
EXT	Extended
REL	Relative
BSC	Bit Set/Clear
BTB	Bit Test and Branch
IX	Indexed (No Offset)
IX1	Indexed, 1 Byte (8-Bit) Offset
IX2	Indexed, 2 Byte (16-Bit) Offset

LEGEND

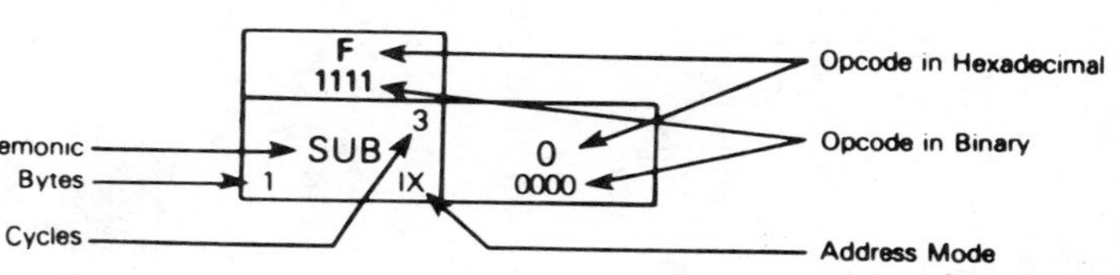

addressing is supported, however, so these instructions operate only on any individual bit in the first 256_{10} bytes of address range, whether the memory is RAM, ROM, or I/O. As in the **68HC11A8**, the instructions can work directly on I/O registers (because they are memory mapped) and thus directly control the I/O pins.

Note, however, that on some **6805** family HMOS devices the Data Direction Registers are write-only registers and will read as $FF. Therefore, the bit set/clear instructions (or read/modify/write instructions) should not be used to manipulate the DDR.

In the **6805**, the bit set and clear instructions are 2- byte instructions: one for the Op code (includes the bit number) and the other to address the byte that contains the bit of interest. Analysis of the instructions in Table 11-14 will show that the actual bit to be modified in the byte is specified within the low nibble of the Op code. Bits 1 to 3 of this nibble contain the bit number and the LSB determines whether the bit involved is set or cleared. If it is a 0, it is set, and a 1 indicates that it is to be cleared. Thus, this is the complement of what actually happens to the bit.

EXAMPLE 11-9

Explain the following instruction:

```
                        PORTB   EQU $01
XXXX   15 01                    BCLR 2, PORTB
```

SOLUTION

BCLR is the Op code for BIT CLEAR instruction. The bit to be cleared is bit 2 of port B, which is at location $01, as the EQU directive specifies. This instruction translates to machine language as 15 01. In the first nibble of the Op code, the 1 designates this instruction as a BCLR. The next 3 bits (010 in binary) indicate that bit 2 is to be cleared. The 1 in the LSB indicates that the bit is to be cleared rather than set. The second byte, 01, is the memory location that contains the bit that is to be cleared.

EXAMPLE 11-10

Show an example that compares the bit manipulation instructions of the **6805** HMOS/**14605** CMOS family to the conventional instructions. Use the bit manipulation instruction to turn off a light-emitting diode (LED) (using bit 2 of port B) and conventional instructions to turn the LED on.

SOLUTION

The example polls the timer control register interrupt request bit (TCR, bit 7) to determine when the LED should turn on, and this is shown in the assembly listing of Fig. 11-34.

```
         0001        PORTB  EQU   $01            Define Port B Addr
         0009        TIMER  EQU   $09            Define TCR Address

                   BIT MANIPULATION INSTRUCTIONS

058F     15 01              BCLR   2,PORTB        Turn Off LED
0591     0F 09 FD   REPT    BRCLR  7,TIMER,REPT   Check Timer status
                                                  Repeat if not timed
                                                  out
0594     14 01              BSET   2,PORTB        Turn ON LED if Timer
                                                  times out

                     CONVENTIONAL INSTRUCTIONS

0596     B6 09      AGAIN   LDA    TIMER          Get Timer status
0598     A5 80              BIT    #$80           Mask out proper bit
059A     26 FA              BNE    AGAIN          Test-turn On if Timer
*                                                   times out
059C     B6 01              LDA    PORTB          Get Port B data
059E     A4 FB              AND    #$FB           Clear proper bit
05A0     B7 01              STA    PORTB          Save modified data
*                                                    to turn OFF LED
05A2     .. ..              ...    ....           Continue
```

FIGURE 11-34 Program to illustrate the efficiency of the **6805** instructions.

The bit manipulation routine shown in Fig. 11-34 uses a bit test and branch instruction to poll the timer, that is,

REPT BRCLR 7,TIMER,REPT

The first REPT is a label and is followed by the Op code mnemonic of the instruction. Here the BRCLR means to branch if the bit being tested (bit 7) is clear. TIMER is a symbol for the address of the byte being tested. The last REPT is the object of the branch. This instruction causes timer bit 7 to be tested repeatedly until it is set, at which time the program falls through to turn on an LED. Figure 11-35 illustrates this loop by showing both the branch and no branch status. Note that if timer bit 7 is clear (timer not timed out), a backward branch is taken, the offset byte $FD is added to $0594 and it branches back to $0591. When the timer times out, timer bit 7 is *set* (the C bit is also *set)* and the program falls through to $0594. The condition codes are unaffected by this instruction except for the C bit, which is set to the state of the bit being tested.

Notice that in the program example shown in Fig. 11-34, conventional bit test and branch instructions require three separate instructions and 6 bytes to perform the same function that BRCLR does with 3 bytes. This *bit test and branch mode* is a combination of direct, relative, and bit set/clear addressing. The data byte to be tested is located via a direct address in the location following the Op code. The actual bit to be tested in the byte is specified within the low-order nibble of the Op code (bits 1–3). The relative offset address for branching is in the byte following the direct address (second byte following the Op code). Thus, the bit test and branch instructions are 3-byte instructions (Op code byte, direct byte, and relative

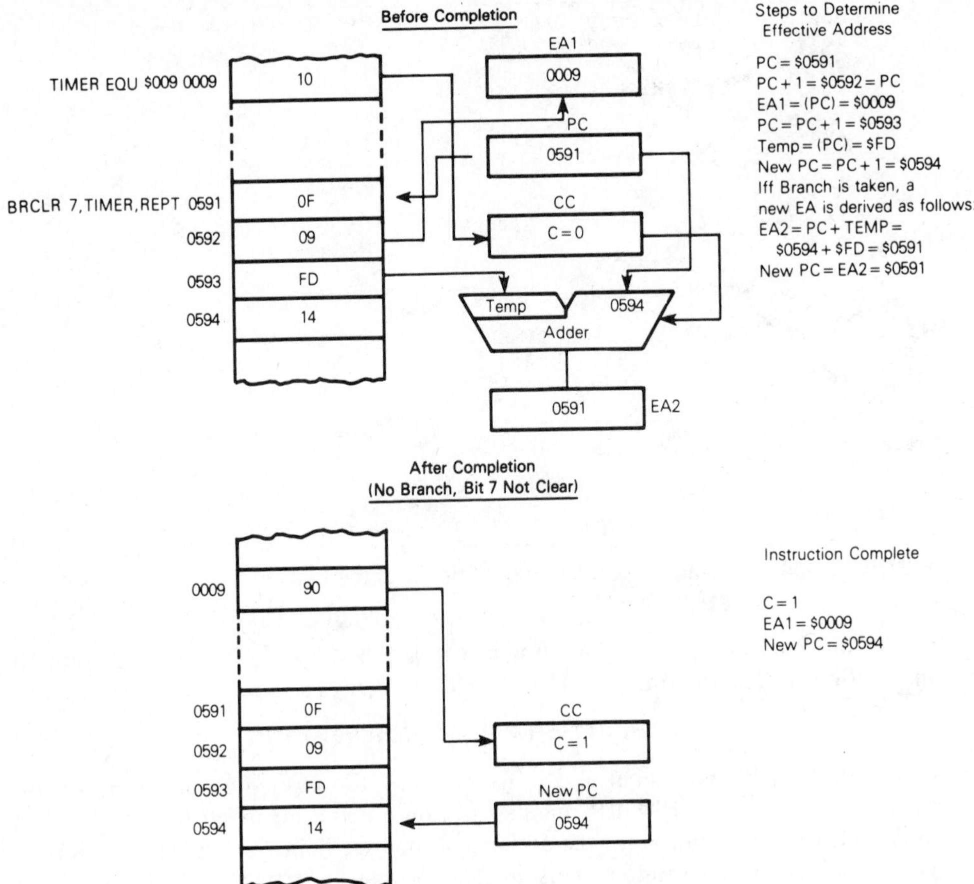

FIGURE 11-35 Bit test and branch addressing mode example.

byte). A bit test and branch has a relative addressing range of PC − 125 to PC + 130 from the beginning of the instruction.

Reference to the bit set/clear instruction at address $58F and to its equivalent in conventional code (starting at $59C) shows that 2 bytes do the work of 6 in this case.

An alphabetical listing of the **6805** instruction set is given in Appendix H. Further details, such as the cycle-by-cycle operation of each instruction, can be found in the manufacturer's literature (see Section 11-14).

11-10.3 The 6805 Timer

All **6805**s contain an internal timer. Most of them are based on an 8-bit down-counter and a 7-bit prescaler. The prescaler can divide the input count by any multiple of 2^n up to 2^7. The prescale option is set by the user at the same time he specifies the ROM mask. Figure 11-36 is a block diagram of the timer found in most CMOS versions of the **(14)6805**. The Timer Data Register (TDR) is an 8-bit decrementing counter that can be used as a clock or can be used to interrupt the **6805** periodically.

There is a single TIMER IN pin on the **6805**. Figure 11-36 shows that the signal on TIMER IN can either come directly into the TDR or be gated with the internal clock. In the former case the timer acts as a counter and counts the pulses on the TIMER IN pin. In the latter case, the clocks count only when the level on the TIMER IN pin is high. This can be used to determine the width of a pulse applied to TIMER IN. The timer in the HMOS versions of the **6805** is slightly different. A mask option allows the user to select the gated or straight-through option for the timer input. Also, as described in Section 11-10.7, the HCMOS versions of the **6805**s, such as the **68HC05C4**, include a more complex and capable timer.

11-10.4 The SCI and SPI

As shown in Table 11-15, some members of the **6805** family have a Serial Communications Interface (SCI) and a Serial Peripheral Interface (SPI). The SCI functions in the **6805**s are similar to those in the **6801** (see Section 11-6).

11-11 SERIAL PERIPHERAL INTERFACE (SPI)

The SPI is a second serial interface built into a number of the newer μCs that allows several of them or a whole family of CMOS interface chips to be interconnected within a single assembly or on the same printed circuit board. These TTL signals are very high-speed and therefore cannot be transmitted very far because of grounding and coupling problems and the subsequent noise (see Section 13-4). The CMOS interface chips make it possible to connect other peripherals to a

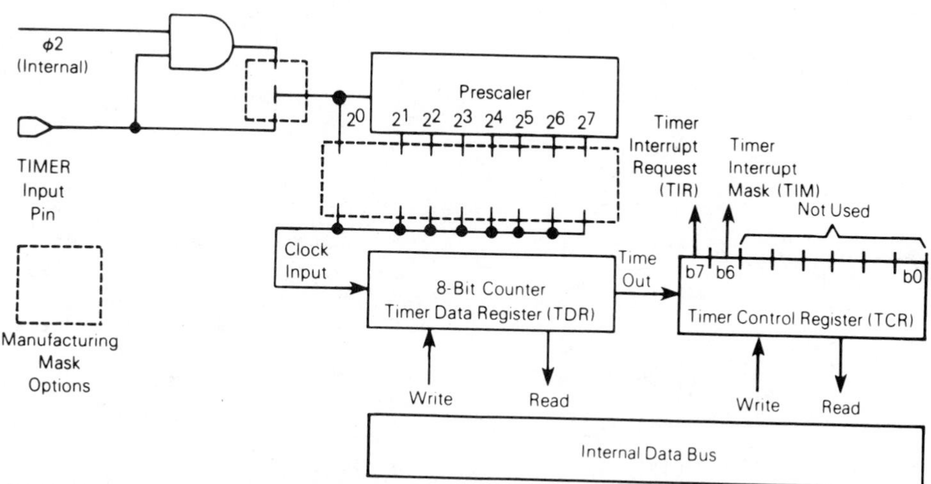

FIGURE 11-36 Timer block diagram.

system. One important advantage of SPI over SCI is the 2.1-MHz data bit rate. Table 11-15 shows some of the devices that have the SPI interface.

11-11.1 SPI System Considerations

In a Serial Peripheral Interface (SPI), separate wires (signals) are required for data and clock. In the SPI format, the clock is not included in the data stream and must be furnished as a separate signal. In an SPI system some μCs are designated as masters and some as slaves.

Figure 11-37 illustrates two different system configurations. These are identified as **6805** μCs in the figure but the functions can be implemented with any of the μCs that have the SPI interface. Figure 11-37 also shows that the SPI bus contains four lines:

> **Slave Select (SS)**. A low on this input designates the device as a slave. It also allows the slave to transmit on the MISO lines. If SS is high, the slave's MISO lines must be held in the high-impedance state.

TABLE 11-15 μCs Using SCIs and SPIs

Part Type	SCI	SPI	Comments
A. uPs and uCs			
68Ø1	x		Introduce SCI
68Ø1U4	x		
687Ø1/U4	x		
68HC11A8	x	x	
68HC8Ø5C4	x	x	EEPROM
68HCØ5C4	x	x	Introduce SPI
68HCØ5C8	x	x	8K ROM
68Ø5S2/S3		x	
68Ø5K2/K3		x	UV erasable EPROM
B. Peripherals			
68HC68A1		x	ADC; 8-bit accuracy; 1Ø-bit resolution
68HC68R1/R2		x	SRAM; 128/256 bytes
68HC68T1		x	RTC; RAM; with PS + control
MC145ØØØ/Ø1		x	LDC drivers, master/slave
MC145Ø4Ø/41		x	ADC; 11 channels, 8-bit SAT
MC145157/58		x	PLL;
MC14411Ø/11		x	DAC; 6-bit, four-channel

Master-Out-Slave-In (MOSI). This is a serial data line for transmission from a master to a slave μC.

Master-In-Slave-Out (MISO). This is a serial data line for transmission from a slave to a master μC.

SCK. This is the clock that synchronizes the data byte on the line. The clock rate can be as high as 2.1 MHz.

Figure 11-37a shows a system where there is one master μC and four slaves. The master μC generates the SCK clock and the slaves all receive it. The master also controls the MOSI and MISO lines, writing data to the slave devices on the MOSI lines and reading data from the slave devices on the MISO lines. The SS pins to the slaves are connected to an output port on the master. Thus the master can enable the slaves selectively by pulling down the SS inputs to the proper slaves. To ensure proper data transmission, the master μC may have the slave respond with a previously received data byte. (This data byte could be inverted or differ in some other prescribed way from the last one sent by the master.) Other transmission security methods might be defined using ports for handshake lines or data bytes with command fields.

A multimaster system may also be configured by the user. A system of this type is shown in Fig. 11-37b. An exchange of master control could be implemented by using a handshake method through the I/O ports or by an exchange of code messages through the SPI system. The major device control that plays a part in this system is the MSTR bit in the serial peripheral control register and the MODF bit in the serial peripheral status register.

More detailed information on the SPI is available in the **6805** technical data manuals (see Section 11-14).

11-11.2 SPI Features

- Full duplex, three-wire synchronous transfers
- Master or slave operation
- 1.05 MHz (maximum) master bit frequency
- 2.1 MHz (maximum) slave bit frequency
- Four programmable master bit rates
- Programmable clock polarity and phase
- End-of-transmission interrupt flag
- Write collision flag protection
- Master–master mode fault protection capability

11-11.3 More Advanced 6805 μCs

The **68HC05C4** μC is one of the HCMOS (High-density CMOS) versions of the **6805** family. This 8-bit μC contains an on-chip oscillator, CPU, RAM, ROM, I/O, two serial interface systems (SCI and SPI), and a timer. The fully static design allows operation at clock frequencies down to zero, thus further reducing its

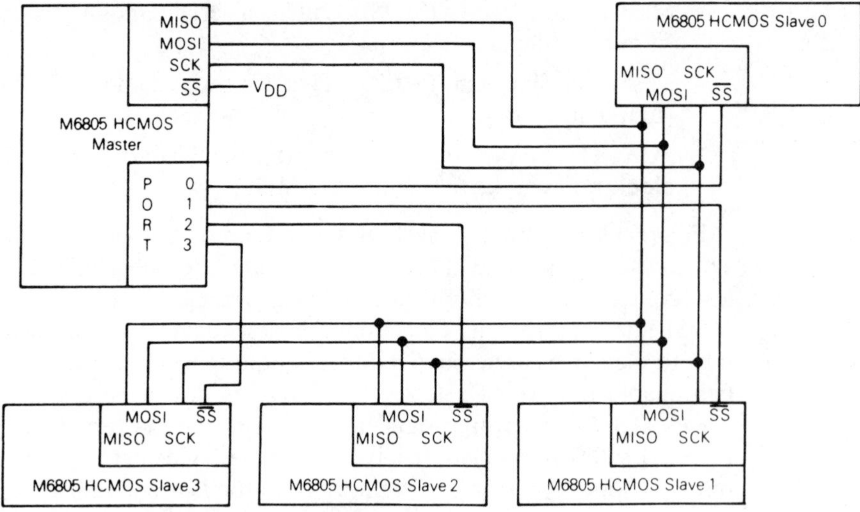

a. Single Master, Four Slaves

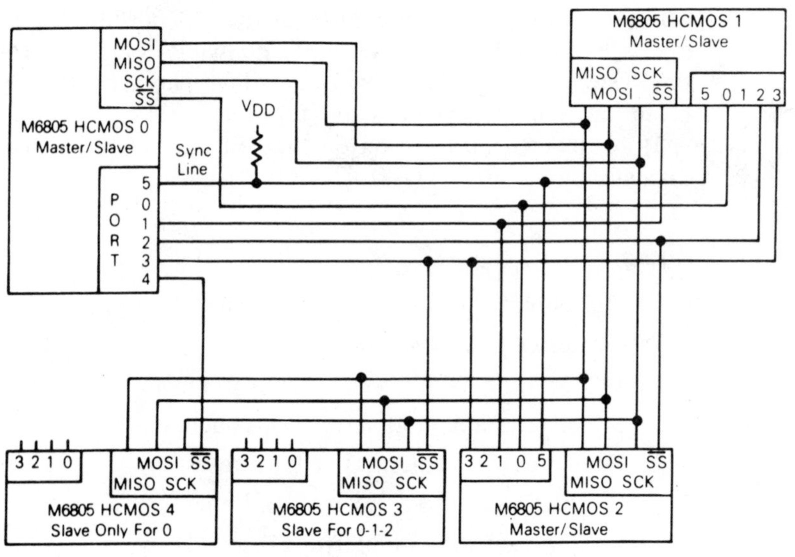

b. Three Master/Slave, Two Slaves

FIGURE 11-37 Master–slave system configuration.

already low power comsumption. The small size of the HCMOS die allows the use of larger memories as well as the addition of functions such as the SPI and a timer as in the **6801.**

The **68HC05C8** is similar to the **68HC05C4** version except that the user ROM is

7744_{10} bytes instead of 4096_{10} bytes. The memory map is actually the same, but the area from 4362_{10} to 7935_{10} is now used.

The **68HC805C4** μC is also similar to the **68HC05C4** except that the ROM is replaced with 4160_{10} bytes of EEPROM, a bootstrap programming ROM is provided, and program/breakpoint/IRQ registers have been added. Note that the 8 in the part number designates EEPROM instead of ROM.

It should also be noted that the use of EEPROM and the other modifications make the μC very useful to *emulate* the 68HC05C4 for early testing. Since the EEPROM version is more complex it is more expensive than the ROM version, but it can be used in early systems to *prove out* the design. When no more program changes are expected and the designers are satisfied that the program is working properly, the **68HC805C4** can be replaced with a mask-programmed version of the **68HC05C4**, which will reduce production costs.

These HCMOS versions all include a timer similar to the one in the **6801**. This more capable timer has a 16-bit architecture. Pulse widths can vary from several microseconds to many seconds. A block diagram of the **68HC05C4** timer is shown in Fig. 11-38.

11-12 THE 6809 HIGH-PERFORMANCE μP

The **6809** is an upgraded version of the **6800** and was introduced in the fall of 1978. Although the **6800** features are retained, many improvements make it one of the most powerful 8-bit μPs available today. The architecture remains basically the same as in the **6800**, but enhancements such as additional registers and new instructions with more addressing modes are included. They simplify the software development and offer greater *throughput,* improved *byte efficiency,* and the ability to handle new software methods. These include the use of *position independent, reentrant, recursive* codes, and high-level language features. Note that the "relative performance" is at the top of the chart in Fig. 11-1.

The **6809** is bus-compatible with the **6800** peripherals and is software-compatible with the **6800** at the source (mnemonic) level. The **6809** object codes are not the same, but a Macro Assembler is provided that will generate **6809** machine codes from a **6800** source program. New instructions and more addressing modes have been added. The following sections point out the improvements inherent in the **6809**.

11-12.1 Programming Model

The programming model of the **6809** is shown in Fig. 11-39. It is similar to the **6800** but three additional registers are provided in the **6809**: the Direct Page register (DP), User stack pointer (U), and a second index register (Y). Much greater flexibility of register usage is also provided by new addressing modes. In particular, the addition of indirect addressing and enhancements of the indexed and relative addressing modes have increased the power of many instructions. These improvements are described in the following paragraphs.

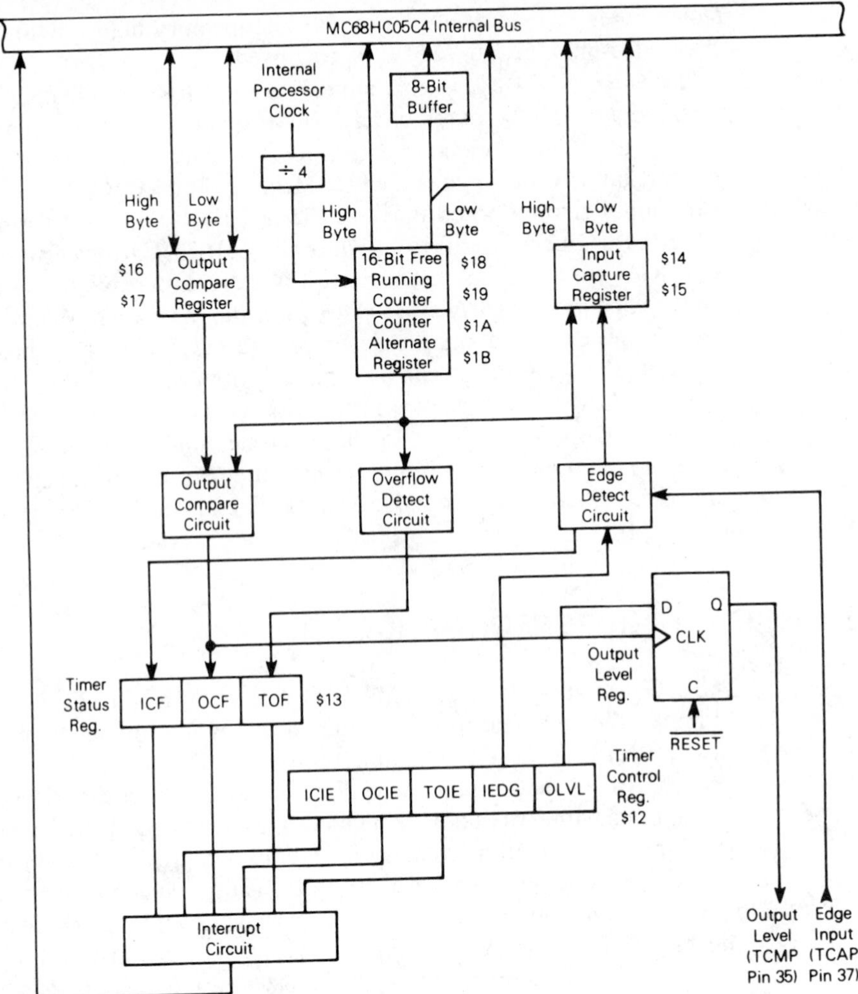

FIGURE 11-38 Programmable timer block diagram.

11-12.2 Accumulators

As in the **6800**, the A and B registers are general-purpose 8-bit accumulators used for arithmetic and data manipulations. In general, the two registers are identical in the **6809**, although some special-purpose instructions apply to the A register only. Certain new instructions allow the A and B registers to be used together (concatenated), as shown in Fig. 11-39, to form a 16-bit accumulator known as the D (double) register. The A accumulator is the most significant byte. A number of 16-bit instructions (including loads, stores, compares, adds, subtracts, transfers, exchanges, pushes, and pulls) have been added. These double accumulator instructions have been provided with all the expanded addressing modes.

The increased power of these instructions can be seen in the following example.

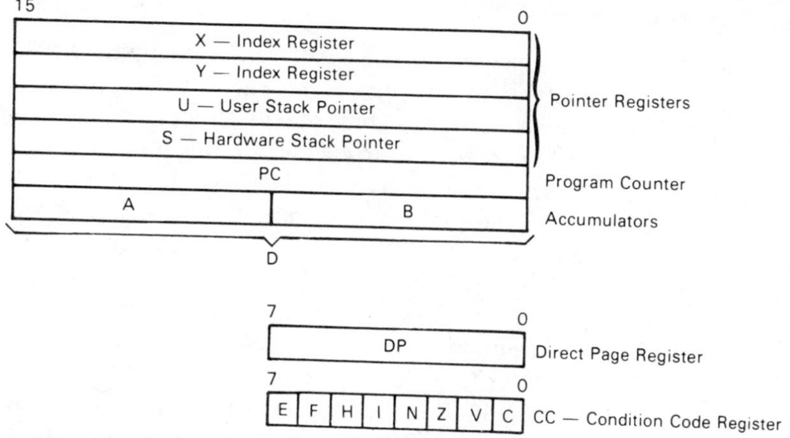

FIGURE 11-39 Programing model of the **6809** μP.

EXAMPLE 11-11

a. Two 16-bit numbers are in memory locations $F0, $F1, $F2, and $F3. Write a **6809** program to add them and store the results in $F4 and $F5.
b. Compare the number of bytes and cycles required by this program with those of the program in Example 4-11.

SOLUTION

a. The program is shown in Table 11-16.
b. The **6800** program uses twice as many bytes (12 vs 6) and requires 20 cycles instead of 16.

Note that the **6809** program is much simpler and faster.

11-12.3 Index Registers

The **MC6809** has a second index register, referred to as the Y register. Several additional indexing modes have also been added. The use of an X and a Y index register and the additional indexing modes gives the **6809** much more flexibility. Indexing is discussed further in Section 11-12.11.

TABLE 11-16 **6809** Program to Add Two 16-Bit Numbers

Addr	Code	Mnemonics	Cycles
1000	DC F0	LDD $F0	5
1002	D3 F2	ADDD $F2	6
1004	DD F4	STD $F4	5

11-12.4 Direct Page Register

The direct addressing mode of the **6800** is enhanced in the **6809** by use of the DP register. The contents of this register appear as the high-order bits (A8–A15) of *direct addressing* instructions, which allows direct addressing *anywhere* in memory. All bits of this register are cleared during RESET to ensure **6800** compatibility. An assembler directive (SETDP) is employed to make use of this feature. Table 11-17 shows the application of the directive as well as its effect on the assembly of typical instructions. For example, when the directive is acted on by the assembler, the statements on lines 7 and 9 are assembled in the direct addressing form (2 bytes) since they are in the $1A page, while line 8 is assembled as an extended instruction (3 bytes). In lines 9–13, the > and < symbols are used to force the assembler to generate extended or direct addressing modes. Direct addressing is forced in lines 9, 10, and 13 (by <), as is extended addressing in lines 11 and 12 (by >). The forcing of line 10 to assemble as a direct instruction is of dubious value since the DP register has not been previously set (to $1B), as indicated by the assembler warning message. Line 14 is a repeat of the SETDP directive (to set the page to $1B).

This directive can be used as many times as desired during an assembly. (This information is covered in detail in the **6809** Macro Assembler reference manual listed in Section 11-15). Note that if the programs of Example 11-11 were changed, for example, to use locations at $10F0 through $10F5 for the data storage, the **6800** version would take 18 bytes, and if the DP register of the **6809** was set to $10, the **6809** program would still take only 6 bytes. Proper use of the DP Register can provide a considerable reduction in the number of bytes used and thus improve *byte efficiency*.

11-12.5 Condition Code Register

Bits 0 through 5 of the CCR are identical to those of the **6800**, but bits 6 and 7 have been added (see Fig. 11-39) for interrupt handling. Bit 6 (F) is the mask bit for FIRQ and bit 7 (E) controls the ReTurn from Interrupt (RTI) instruction to ensure that the proper number of registers are pulled from the stack by the RTI instruction.

11-12.6 Stack Pointers

There are two stack pointers in the **6809**. The *hardware stack pointer (S)* is used to automatically store machine states during execution of subroutines and interrupts in the same way as in the **6800** (with a minor difference that is explained below). An additional *user stack pointer (U)* is provided in the **6809** and is controlled by the user program, thus allowing instructions such as PUSH and PULL to be used with the U stack without interfering with the return addresses on the S stack. Both S and U have the same indexed mode addressing capabilities as the X and Y registers, which allows the **6809** to be used effectively as a stack processor, greatly enhancing its ability to support higher-level languages and to move **argu-**

TABLE 11-17 A Typical **6809** Program Listing

```
PAGE  001  DIRPGE   SA:0  DIRPGE

00001                             *     SET DIRECT PAGE DIRECTIVE
00002                             *THIS PROGRAM SHOWS THE EFFECT OF
00003                             *THE DIRECT PAGE DIRECTIVE IN ASSEMBLY
00004                             *OF A PROGRAM.
00005                                     NAM     DIRPGE
00006                001A     A           SETDP   $1A
00007A 0000 96       00       A           LDA     $1A00
00008A 0002 B6       1B00     A           LDA     $1B00
00009A 0005 96       00       A           LDA     <$1A00
****WARNING   002--00000
00010A 0007 96       00       A           LDA     <$1B00
00011A 0009 B6       1A00     A           LDA     >$1A00
00012A 000C B6       1B00     A           LDA     >$1B00
00013A 000F 9E       FF       A           LDX     <$1AFF
00014                001B     A           SETDP   $1B
00015A 0011 96       00       A           LDA     $1B00
00016                                     END
TOTAL ERRORS 00000--00000
TOTAL WARNINGS 00001--00010
```

ments (mathematical variables) from one routine to another. To facilitate use of the stack pointers in indexed mode addressing, the registers always point to the last byte placed on the stack instead of the next available byte as in the **6800**, as shown in Fig. 11-40.

11-12.7 The 6809 Instruction Set

The complete instruction set for the **6809** is given in Table G-1 through G-5 of Appendix G. The instructions that are identical to **6800** instructions have the same Op codes. An $86, for example, is an immediate load of the A accumulator for either μP. Some instructions that do not exist for the **6800** have been assigned new Op codes. LoaD the Double register (LDD) is an example. Other instructions that use the added registers or addresssing modes take a 2-byte Op code. All instructions that require a 2-byte Op code have a 10 or 11 as the first byte. Finally, a few **6800** Op codes have a different mnemonic for the **6809**.

EXAMPLE 11-12

What are the Op codes for LDX and LDY (LoaD X and LoaD Y) immediate?

SOLUTION

Table G-6 in Appendix G shows that the Op code for LDX is 8E. This is the code for LDS in the **6800**. The table also shows that the Op code for LDY, an instruction that does not exist on the **6800**, is 10 8E. Thus LDY has a 2-byte Op code and the first byte is 10.

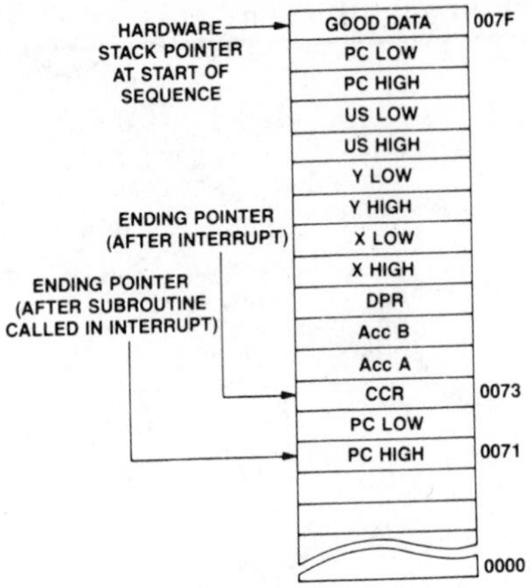

FIGURE 11-40 **6809** stack operation.

11-12.8 The Postbyte

Many instructions take a **postbyte**, which is a byte that immediately follows the Op code and further defines the instruction. The format of an instruction with a postbyte is

Op code
Postbyte
Additional bytes (if required)

Instructions and modes that require a postbyte include

Indexed instructions
Exchanges
Pushes
Pulls
Indirect instructions

The configuration of the postbyte will be defined when the instructions that use them are discussed. Assemblers generate postbytes automatically, and programmers using assemblers need not be concerned with them. They should be aware, however, that postbytes take up space in memory and are a necessary part of the instructions.

11-12.9 Addressing Modes

Three basic new categories have been added to the addressing modes of the **6800**, making a total of nine for the **6809**. These are

Immediate
Inherent
Direct
Extended
Indexed
Relative
Extended indirect
Indexed indirect
Long relative

11-12.10 Immediate, Inherent, Direct, and Extended Modes

These modes are effectively the same as in the **6800**. The power of Direct addressing instructions has been enhanced by the addition of the DP register. (See Section 11-12.4.)

11-12.11 Indexed Modes

In the **6800**, the indexed mode of addressing provides for adding an offset to the index register to form an *Effective Address* (EA), and this effective address is used to access memory locations. In the **6809** the same feature exists, but several additional methods are available to generate the EAs. For example, the offset can be up to 16 bits and can be an expression (such as a symbol plus a constant). The student is again referred to the assembler manual for a complete definition of the possible forms.

Five basic types of indexing are available. A postbyte is used to specify the basic type as well as the pointer register to be used. Table 11-18 gives the assembler form as well as the number of bytes and cycles added to the basic values for each variation of the postbyte.

11-12.12 The Zero-Offset Mode

In the zero-offset indexed mode, a selected pointer register contains the effective address. The pointer registers are X, Y, S, and U. This is the fastest indexing mode.

Examples are

```
LDD 0,X
LDA 0,U
```

The Macro Assembler will allow the 0 and comma to be omitted (i.e., LDD X).

11-12.13 The Constant Offset Mode

The constant offset indexed mode adds a 2s complement offset to the contents of

TABLE 11-18 The Format of the 6809 Indexed Instructions

Type	Forms	Non Indirect				Indirect			
		Assembler Form	Postbyte OP Code	+ ~	+ #	Assembler Form	Postbyte OP Code	+ ~	+ #
Constant Offset From R (2's Complement Offsets)	No Offset	,R	1RR00100	0	0	[,R]	1RR10100	3	0
	5 Bit Offset	n, R	0RRnnnnn	1	0	defaults to 8-bit			
	8 Bit Offset	n, R	1RR01000	1	1	[n, R]	1RR11000	4	1
	16 Bit Offset	n, R	1RR01001	4	2	[n, R]	1RR11001	7	2
Accumulator Offset From R (2's Complement Offsets)	A Register Offset	A, R	1RR00110	1	0	[A, R]	1RR10110	4	0
	B Register Offset	B, R	1RR00101	1	0	[B, R]	1RR10101	4	0
	D Register Offset	D, R	1RR01011	4	0	[D, R]	1RR11011	7	0
Auto Increment/Decrement R	Increment By 1	,R +	1RR00000	2	0	not allowed			
	Increment By 2	,R + +	1RR00001	3	0	[,R + +]	1RR10001	6	0
	Decrement By 1	, − R	1RR00010	2	0	not allowed			
	Decrement By 2	, − − R	1RR00011	3	0	[, − − R]	1RR10011	6	0
Constant Offset From PC (2's Complement Offsets)	8 Bit Offset	n, PCR	1xx01100	1	1	[n, PCR]	1xx11100	4	1
	16 Bit Offset	n, PCR	1xx01101	5	2	[n, PCR]	1xx11101	8	2
Extended Indirect	16 Bit Address	—	—	—	—	[n]	10011111	5	2

R = X, Y, U or S
x = Don't Care

RR:
00 = X
01 = Y
10 = U
11 = S

+ ~ and + # indicate the number of additional cycles and bytes for the particular variation.

the pointer registers to form the effective address. Three sizes of offsets are available: 5-bit (-16 to $+15$), 8-bit (-128_{10} to $+127_{10}$), and 16-bit (-32768_{10} to $+32767_{10}$). The 2s complement 5-bit offset is included in the postbyte and therefore is the most efficient in use of bytes and cycles. The 2s complement 8-bit offset value is in a single byte following the postbyte, and a 16-bit offset requires an additional byte. The assembler calculates the size of this offset. This mode is similar to the **6800** index mode except that several different indexing registers are available in the **6809.**

Examples of constant-offset indexing are

```
LDA   23,X     (8-bit offset)
LDX   -2,S     (5-bit offset)
LDY   300,X    (16-bit offset)
LDU   CAT,Y    (depends on the value of CAT)
```

Note that the machine language could be up to 5 bytes for this instruction as follows:

Op code—1 or 2 bytes (two for some less used instructions)
Postbyte—one
Offset—one (for 8-bit) or two (for 16-bit)

EXAMPLE 11-13

What does LDX −2,S do? What numbers are in the postbyte and the offset?

SOLUTION

The instruction subtracts 2 from the address in the S register and loads the contents of that location into the X register. That is, if S = $210, then the instruction would load the contents of $20E and $20F into the X register.

This instruction could be coded in three different ways:

```
1. AE   Op code for LDX indexed
   7E   (postbyte specifying a 5-bit offset of -2)     01111110₂.

2. AE   Op code
   E8   (postbyte specifying an 8-bit offset)          11101000₂.
   FE   (offset of -2)

3. AE   Op code
   E9   (postbyte specifying a 16-bit offset)          11101001₂.
   FF   \
   FE   /(offset of -2 as a 16-bit number
```

Note that the binary value of the postbyte would be as shown on the right. Bits 5 and 6 specify the register. In this case 11 = S. The first way is obviously the most economical and would be selected by the assember.

11-12.14 The Accumulator Offset Mode

The *accumulator offset* is a new indexing mode. It is similar to the previous mode except that a 2s complement value in one of the accumulators (A, B, or D) is added to the pointer register value to form the Effective Address. The postbyte shows which accumulator is used and no additional bytes are needed. This mode is useful because the value of the offset can be calculated at run time. Some examples are

LDA B,Y

LDX D,Y

LEAX B,X

11-12.15 Autoincrementing and Decrementing

The **6809** pointer registers can be automatically incremented or decremented each time they are accessed. In the *autoincrement* mode the contents of the pointer register are read first; then the register is incremented by 1 or 2 bytes, depending on whether an 8- or a 16-bit operand is being fetched. This is sometimes called *postincrementing* because the register is incremented after it is read. When *autodecrementing* is used, the register is first decremented and then read. This is also known as *predecrementing*.

Autoincrementing and autodecrementing are useful for work with tables of single or double bytes (16 bits). The preincrement, postdecrement nature of these modes allows X and Y to be used for stacks that behave identically to those using the U or S registers.

Autoincrementing and autodecrementing can also be used when a pointer register is used as a loop counter.

Examples of the assembler mnemonics are

```
LDA  ,X+
STD  ,Y++
LDB  ,-Y
LDX  ,--S
```

The **6809** assembler mnemonics are used here with the + and − indicating an increment or decrement (+ + is a double increment). For an example of autoincrementing and its use with the double accumulator, see the program shown in Table 11-19. Refer to the macro-assembler manual identified in Section 11-15 for details on the proper instruction syntax.

EXAMPLE 11-14

Explain specifically how the program of Table 11-19 works.

SOLUTION
The program operates as follows:

1. The instructions on lines 112, 113, and 114 load the address of Tables A, B, and C (the table for the results) into the X, Y, and U registers. At this point, X contains \$108E, Y contains \$10B6, and U contains \$10DE, as shown on lines 124, 128, and 132.
2. The instructions on lines 116, 117, and 118 cause the first two bytes of X (0001) to be added to the first two bytes of Y (9998). The result (9999) is stored in Table C. Note the use of the double registers for 16-bit addition.
3. Because of the autoincrement mode, X now contains \$1090 (108E + 2), Y contains \$10B8, and U contains \$10E0.
4. Because Table A contains 20 entries of 2 bytes each, X is now compared to

$$\begin{aligned} 2*20 + \text{Table A} &= (40)_{10} + 108\text{E} \\ &= (28)_{16} + 108\text{E} = 10\text{B}6_{16} \end{aligned}$$

If they are equal, Table A is exhausted and the program stops. Otherwise it branches back and continues. Autoincrementing has taken care of properly incrementing the registers.

11-12.16 Indexed Indirect Addressing

Indirect addressing can be used in conjunction with indexing. It is usable in all but the autoincrement/decrement (by one) modes. The *Effective Address* (EA) is contained at the location specified by the index register plus any offset. In the example below, the A accumulator is loaded indirectly using an EA calculated from the index register and an offset. Note that the square brackets indicate indirect addressing.

TABLE 11-19 Program for Example 11-14

```
M6800-M6809 CROSS-ASSEMBLER  2.2

                          ********** VECTOR ADDITION / 16-BIT **********
                          *
                          *      PERFORM AN ELEMENT-BY-ELEMENT ADDITION ON
                          *      TWO VECTORS OF N 16-BIT ELEMENTS EACH.
                          *      PLACE THE RESULT IN A DIFFERENT VECTOR.
                          *      LET N BE 20.
                          *
                          *      SETUP:          3 LN, 10 BY,  10 CY
                          *      OPERATION:      5 LN, 11 BY, 32*20=640 CY
                          *      TOTAL:          8 LN, 21 BY, 650 CY
                          *
                          ***********************************************

1077 8E    108E      3 ANBNCN LDX    #TABLEA
107A 108E  10B6      4        LDY    #TABLEB
107E CE    10DE      3        LDU    #TABLEC

1081 EC    81        8 AN1    LDD    ,X++
1083 E3    A1        9        ADDD   ,Y++
1085 ED    C1        8        STD    ,U++
1087 8C    10B6      4        CMPX   #2*20+TABLEA
108A 26    F5        3        BNE    AN1

108C 20    FE        3        BRA    *

108E       0000        TABLEA FDB    $00,$01,$02,$03,$04
1098       0005               FDB    $05,$06,$07,$08,$09
10A2       0010               FDB    $10,$11,$12,$13,$14
10AC       0015               FDB    $15,$16,$17,$18,$19
10B6       0099        TABLEB FDB    $99,$98,$97,$96,$95
10C0       0094               FDB    $94,$93,$92,$91,$90
10CA       0089               FDB    $89,$88,$87,$86,$85
10D4       0084               FDB    $84,$83,$82,$81,$80
10DE       0000        TABLEC FDB    0,,,,,,,,,,,,,,,,,,,0
```

EXAMPLE 11-15

Show how the A accumulator is loaded indirectly using an EA calculated from the index register and an offset.

Before execution

A = XX (don't care)
X = $F000

SOLUTION
The following locations are assumed to contain the given data:

$0100	**LDA**	**($10,X)**	EA is now $F010
$F010	**$F1**		$F150 is now the new EA
$F011	**$50**		
$F150	**$AA**		

After execution:

A = \$AA Actual data loaded
X = \$F000

Some other examples of indexed indirect instructions are

```
LDA  [,X]
LDD  [10,S]
LDA  [B,Y]
LDD  [,X++]
```

11-12.17 Relative Mode

Relative addressing involves adding a signed constant to the contents of the Program Counter. When used in conjuntion with a branch instruction, this sum becomes the new program counter content if the branch is taken. (If the branch is not taken, the PC advances to the next instruction.)

Relative addressing differs from that in the **6800** because of two important additions. The first is that the constant offset (which is a signed number) can be either 7 bits ($+128_{10}$) or 15 bits ($+32{,}768_{10}$). In the latter case, the program can branch to any location in the memory field, since the addresses wrap around (0000 is next after \$FFFF or \$FFFF is one less than 0000), and any location is therefore always less than $32{,}768_{10}$ bytes away one way or the other. Branch instructions that use a 2-byte offset are called *long-branch* instructions.

EXAMPLE 11-16

A program is to branch from address $(1200)_{16}$ to address $(995)_{16}$. Find the correct offset.

SOLUTION
Using the formula

$$\text{Target} = (\text{PC} + 2) + \text{offset}$$

we have

$$\begin{array}{rr} \text{Offset} = & 0995 \\ - & \underline{1202} \\ & \text{F793} \end{array}$$

Thus the first byte of the offset will be \$F7 and the second byte will be \$93.

Some examples of relative addressing using an assembler are

BEQ CAT	(short)
BGT DOG	(short)

```
CAT   LBEQ   RAT      (long)
DOG   LBGT   RABBIT   (long)
```

11-12.18 Program Counter Relative Addressing

In addition to the normal function, the **6809** provides a mode allowing the program counter to be used as an index register. It is called Program Counter Relative (PCR) and, as in relative addressing, the 8- or 16-bit signed offset is added to the current PC to create the effective address. Program counter relative addressing is used for writing *position-independent* programs. Tables related to a particular routine will maintain the same relationship after the routine is moved, if referenced relative to the program counter.

Examples are

```
LDA  CAT,PCR
LEAX TABLE,PCR     (where CAT and TABLE are labels)
```

Since program counter relative is a form of indexing, an additional indirect addressing level is available as follows:

```
LDA [CAT,PCR]
LEAX [TABLE,PCR]
```

EXAMPLE 11-17

If CAT = $0100, what does the instruction 0010 LDA CAT,PCR do?

SOLUTION

The effective address for this instruction is $0110 (i.e., CAT + PC). The A register is loaded from location $0110.

11-12.19 Relative Indirect Mode

This addressing mode is, in effect, *indexed indirect* with the program counter used as an index register. One or two bytes (optionally) following the postbyte are used to provide a 7-bit or 15-bit offset. This signed number is added to the contents of the program counter, forming a pointer to consecutive locations in memory that contain the new effective address, for example,

```
LDA  [CAT,PCR]
LDU  [DOG,PCR]
```

11-12.20 Extended Indirect Mode

This addressing mode is actually another option of indexed indirect addressing. In this case, the 2 bytes following the postbyte are used as a pointer to consecutive locations in memory that contain the new Effective Address.

11-12.21 Absolute Indirect Mode

This mode is exclusively used for restart and interrupt vectoring. Servicing of these conditions involves fetching the contents of a dedicated location in memory to be loaded into the program counter, and thus it is not available for any locations other than the interrupt vectors.

11-13 UNIQUE 6809 INSTRUCTIONS

Some of the more unique instructions include Load Effective Address (LEA), synchronization with interrupt (SYNC), and EXchanGe registers (EXG). These, along with others not available on the **6800**, are detailed in the following paragraphs.

11-13.1 Pushes and Pulls (PSHU/PSHS and PULU/PULS)

The push instructions have the capability of pushing onto either the hardware stack (S) or the User stack (U), any single register or set of registers with a single instruction.

The pull instructions have the same capability of the push instruction, except in reverse order. The postbyte immediately following the PUSH or PULL Op code determines which register or set of registers is to be pushed or pulled. The actual PUSH/PULL sequence is fixed; each bit defines a unique register to push or pull, as shown in Fig. 11-41.

EXAMPLE 11-18

If it is necessary to push A, B, X, and CC onto the user's stack, what does the instruction look like? What does the postbyte look like? In what order are they placed on the stack?

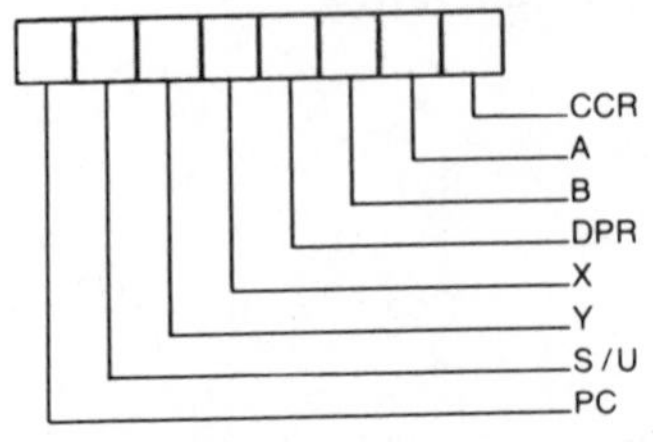

FIGURE 11-41 Push (PSH) or pull (PUL) instruction postbyte.

SOLUTION
The instruction to do this looks like: PSHS A, B, X, CC. The postbyte (00010111) uses a "1" to represent registers that are to be pushed. The stacking order would be CC, A, B, and X.

11-13.2 TFR/EXG Instructions

Within the **6809**, any register may be transferred to or exchanged with another of like size, that is, 8 bit to 8-bit or 16-bit to 16-bit. Bits 4–7 of the postbyte define the source register, while bits 0–3 represent the destination register as shown in Fig. 11- 42.

Note: All other combinations are undefined and invalid, although there is an obvious link between 8-bit and 16-bit registers through the 16-bit D accumulator.

EXAMPLE 11-19

How can a user load the Direct Page (DP) register with $1C?

SOLUTION
There is no instruction that loads the DP register, but the user may load A and then transfer it into the DPR.
The program might be

```
LDA   #$1C
TFR   DP,A
```

Figure 11-42 shows that the postbyte on the transfer instruction would be $8B.

11-13.3 LEAX/LEAY/LEAU/LEAS Instructions

The Load Effective Address (LEA) instruction works by calculating the Effective Address used in an indexed instruction and stores that address value, rather than

TRANSFER/EXCHANGE POST BYTE

SOURCE	DESTINATION

REGISTER FIELD (Source or Destination)

0000 = D (A:B)	0101 = PC
0001 = X	1000 = A
0010 = Y	1001 = B
0011 = U	1010 = CCR
0100 = S	1011 = DPR

FIGURE 11-42 Exchange (EXG) or transfer (TRF) instruction postbyte.

the data at that address, in a pointer register. This makes all the features of the internal addressing hardware available to the programmer. The LEA instruction also makes use of a postbyte (see Table 11-18).

The LEA instruction allows the user to access data and tables in a position-independent manner. For example,

```
        LEAX  MSG1,PCR
        LBSR  PDATA (print message routine)
        .
        .
MSG1    FCC   "MESSAGE"
```

This sample program prints: MESSAGE. By writing MSG1, PSCR, the assembler computes the distance between the present address and MSG1. This result is placed as a constant into the X register, which will be indexed from the PC value at the time of execution. No matter where the code is located, when it is executed the computed offset from the PC will put the absolute address of MSG1 into the X pointer register. This code is totally position-independent.

The LEA instructions are very powerful and use an internal holding register (temp). Care must be exercised when using the LEA instructions with the autoincrement and autodecrement addressing modes because of the sequence of internal operations.

The LEA internal sequence is outlined as follows:

LEAa ,b+ (any of the 16-bit pointer registers X, Y, U, or S may be substituted for a and b)

1. b → temp (calculate the EA)
2. b + 1 → b (modify b, postincrement)
3. temp → a (load a)

LEAa ,−b

1. b → temp (calculate EA with predecrement)
2. b − 1 → b (modify b, predecrement)
3. temp → a (load a)

Autoincrement-by-two and autodecrement-by-two instructions work similarly. Note that LEAX ,X+ does not change X. LEAX, −X, however, does decrement X. LEAX 1,X should be used to increment X by one.

Some examples of LEAX instructions are shown in Fig. 11-43.

EXAMPLE 11-20

What does LEAX ,S+ do?

SOLUTION

This is an example of the LEAa ,b+ instruction discussed above. This instruction loads the value in S into X, then increments S. Symbolically,

$$(X) \leftarrow (S)$$
$$(S) \leftarrow (S+1)$$

11-13.4 Multiply (MUL) Instruction

MUL multiplies the unsigned binary numbers in the A and B accumulators and places the unsigned result in the 16-bit D accumulator. This unsigned multiply also allows multiple-precision multiplications.

11-13.5 Synchronize with Interrupt (SYNC)

The SYNC instruction causes processing to discontinue until an interrupt input (NMI, IRQ, or FIRQ) is activated. When an interrupt occurs, and the associated mask is clear, the processor services the interrupt normally. If the interrupt mask is SET when the interrupt occurs, the processor exits the sync state by continuing to the next instruction. The Bus Available (BA) output is activated during the sync state. The instruction is particularly useful for synchronizing the program with a peripheral that uses or supplies data.

Stacking of registers during an interrupt is accomplished in the following order:

PC, U, Y, X, DP, B, A, CC

Note that the CCR is the last register pushed. This means that it is the first one pulled, and the E bit of that register then determines whether to pull just one more byte or the whole set of registers.

11-13.6 Sign Extend

This Sign EXtend (SEX) instruction causes all bits in the A register to take on the value of the most significant bit of the B register so that a 16-bit number in the D register is created from an 8-bit number in the B register. The SEX instruction preserves the sign of the original number.

Instruction		*Operation*	*Comment*
LEAX	10,X	X+10−X	Adds 5-bit constant 10 to X
LEAX	500,X	X+500−X	Adds 16-bit constant 500 to X
LEAY	A,Y	Y+A−Y	Adds 8- bit accumulator to Y
LEAY	D,Y	Y+D−Y	Adds 16-bit D accumulator to Y
LEAU	−10,U	U−10−U	Subtracts 10 from U
LEAS	−10,S	S−10−S	Used to reserve area on stack
LEAS	10,S	S+10−S	Used to "clean up" stack
LEAX	5,S	S+5−X	Transfers as well as adds

FIGURE 11-43 Effective addressing examples.

11-13.7 CWAI

This instruction is similar to the wait for interrupt used with the **6800**, but includes an immediate byte to clear condition codes if desired. The CWAI instruction can be used with any of the three interrupt lines, even though CWAI stacks all registers (except S). After stacking is complete, BA is activated and the processor idles until an interrupt occurs.

11-13.8 Missing Instructions

Those familiar with the **6800** will note that some instructions are missing from the set available with the **6800**. Provisions have been made to perform such operations in alternative ways when required. An example might be decrement X. This will not often be needed with the **6809** because of the autodecrement option with indexed addressing. If needed, however, the operation can be accomplished with an LEAX −1,X instruction. Likewise, the **6800** instructions to clear/set various condition codes are replaced with ANDCC/ORCC. In this manner, the **6809** uses fewer instruction mnemonics (59 vs 72) than the **6800**, yet is fully software-compatible as well as being considerably more powerful.

11-14 HARDWARE FEATURES OF THE 6809

The **6809** is similar to the **6800** in that it is also a 40-pin NMOS IC with the same basic bus architecture. An internal clock has been added similar to those used in the **6801** and **6802** μC and μP. Four of the pins are reassigned (XTAL, EXTAL, E, and Q). For the **6809** pinout diagram, see Fig. 11-44.

11-14.1 XTAL and EXTAL Pins

These inputs are used to connect the on-chip oscillator to an external parallel-resonate quartz crystal. Alternatively, the pin EXTAL may be used as a TTL-level input from an external clock source. XTAL must be grounded in this case.

11-14.2 The E and Q Signals

E is similar to the **6800** bus timing signal $\phi 2$; Q is a quadrature clock signal that leads E. Q has no parallel on the **6800** but provides two additional timing edges at the 1/4 and 3/4 points in the cycle. Addresses from the μP will be valid with the leading edge of Q. Data is latched on the falling edge of E. Timing relationships between E and Q are shown in Fig. 11-45.

11-14.3 Memory Ready (MRDY)

The pin assignments also include five other new signal names. A memory ready (MRDY) signal inhibits transitions of the on-chip clock, an integral multiple of

Pin	Signal	Pin	Signal
1	V_{SS}	40	$\overline{HALT}$
2	$\overline{NMI}$	39	XTAL
3	$\overline{IRQ}$	38	EXTAL
4	$\overline{FIRQ}$	37	$\overline{RESET}$
5	BS	36	MRDY
6	BA	35	Q
7	V_{CC}	34	E
8	A0	33	$\overline{DMA}/\overline{BREQ}$
9	A1	32	R/$\overline{W}$
10	A2	31	D0
11	A3	30	D1
12	A4	29	D2
13	A5	28	D3
14	A6	27	D4
15	A7	26	D5
16	A8	25	D6
17	A9	24	D7
18	A10	23	A15
19	A11	22	A14
20	A12	21	A13

6809

FIGURE 11-44 6809 pin assignments.

quarter (1/4) bus cycles, as also shown in Fig. 11-45. (This line can be held low a maximum of 10 μs to extend the data access time for slow memory applications.) It can also be seen that if MRDY is pulled low a minimum of 60 ns before the end of a normal E cycle, it will prevent any level changes in either Q or E until the next quarter-cycle after it is released.

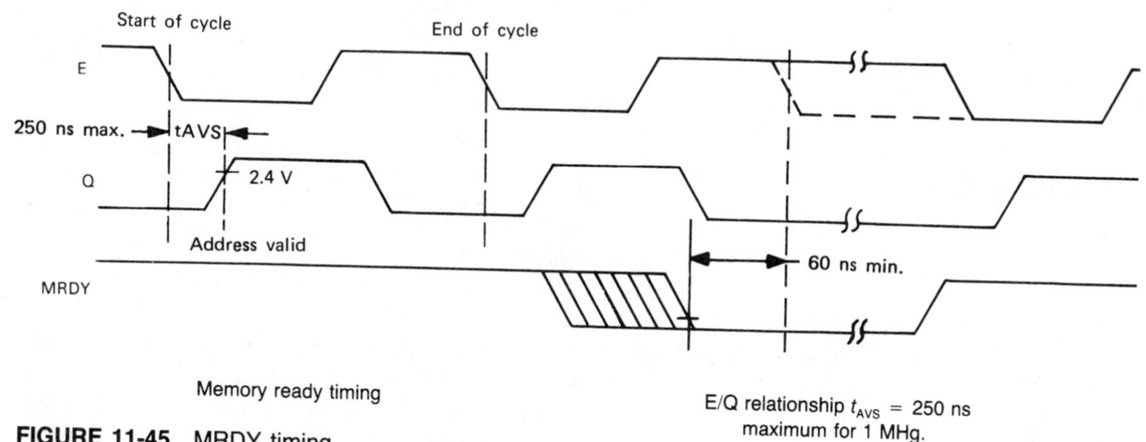

FIGURE 11-45 MRDY timing.

11-14.4 DMA/BREQ

A new bus request input (DMA/BREQ) provides for DMA and dynamic memory refresh. The DMA/BREQ input provides a method of suspending program execution and acquiring the μP bus for another use, such as DMA and dynamic memory refresh.

Transitions of DMA/BREQ should occur during Q as shown in Fig. 11-46a. A low level on this pin will stop instruction execution at the end of the current cycle unless preempted by self-refresh. The μP will acknowledge DMA/BREQ by setting BA and BS to a 1. The requesting device will now have up to 15 bus cycles before the μP retrieves the bus for self-refresh. Self-refresh requires one bus cycle with a leading and trailing dead cycle. The self-refresh counter is cleared only if DMA/BREQ is inactive for two or more μP cycles.

The **self-refresh** condition happens whenever the DMA/BREQ line is held for enough time to put the μP in a mode where it needs to refresh itself, or lose data. The **6809**, like the **6800**, is a dynamic device. This means that if the clock stops, only a short time may pass before certain parts of the μP will cease to function properly. To guard against this condition, the **6809** will automatically keep up with the number of clock cycles it needs. In the DMA/BREQ mode the μP must be refreshed once every 15 cycles.

Typically, the DMA controller will request to use the bus by setting the DMA/BREQ pin low on the leading edge of E. When the μP replies by setting BA and BS to a 1, that cycle will be a dead cycle, which should be used to transfer bus mastership to the DMA controller.

False memory access may be prevented during any dead cycles by generating a system DMA/VMA signal that is low in any cycle when BA has changed.

When BA goes low (as a result of either DMA/BREQ being high or a μP self-refresh), the DMA device should be taken off the bus. Another dead cycle will elapse before the μP accesses memory, to allow transfer of bus mastership without contention. As shown in Fig. 11-46b, a self-refresh feature will automatically refresh internal dynamic registers whenever DMA/BREQ is held longer than 14 cycles, by executing one μP cycle. It will repeat every 15th cycle until DMA/BREQ is released.

The VMA signal and its need for additional gating in chip selection have been eliminated in the **6809**.

11-14.5 RESET

A low level on this Schmitt-trigger input for greater than one bus cycle will reset the μP. The Reset vectors are fetched from locations $FFFE and $FFFF when interrupt acknowledge is true. During initial power-on, the RESET line should be held low until the clock oscillator is fully operational.

Because the **M6809** RESET pin has a Schmitt-trigger input with a threshold voltage higher than that of standard peripherals, a simple *RC* network may be used to reset the entire system. This higher threshold voltage ensures that all peripherals are out of the reset state before the μP.

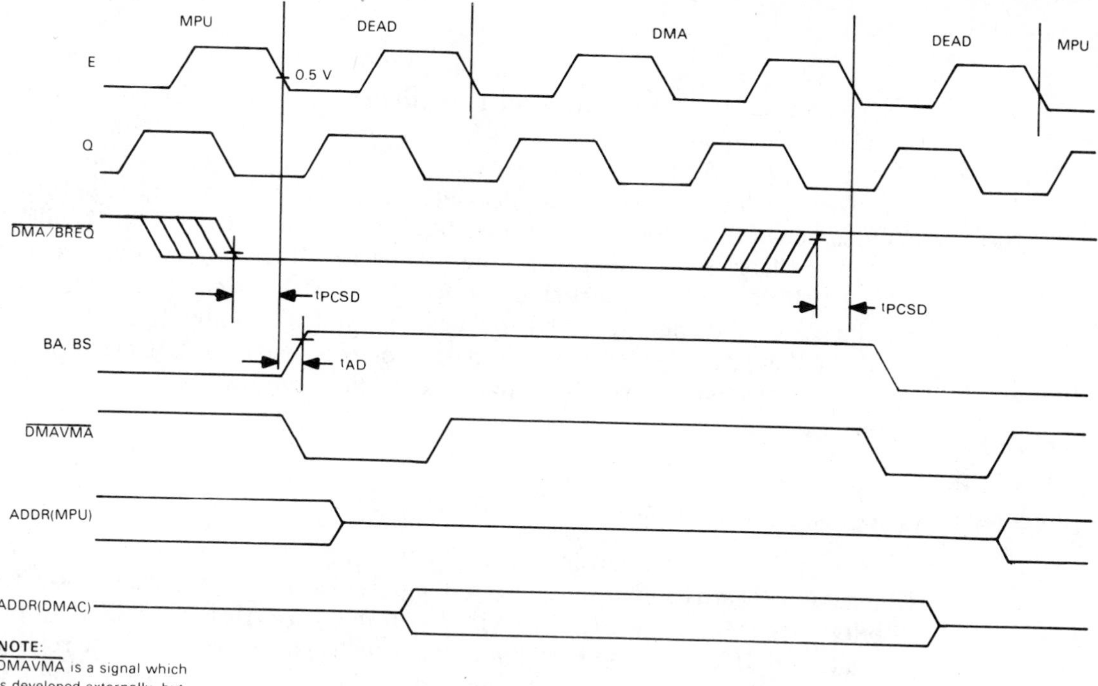

(a)

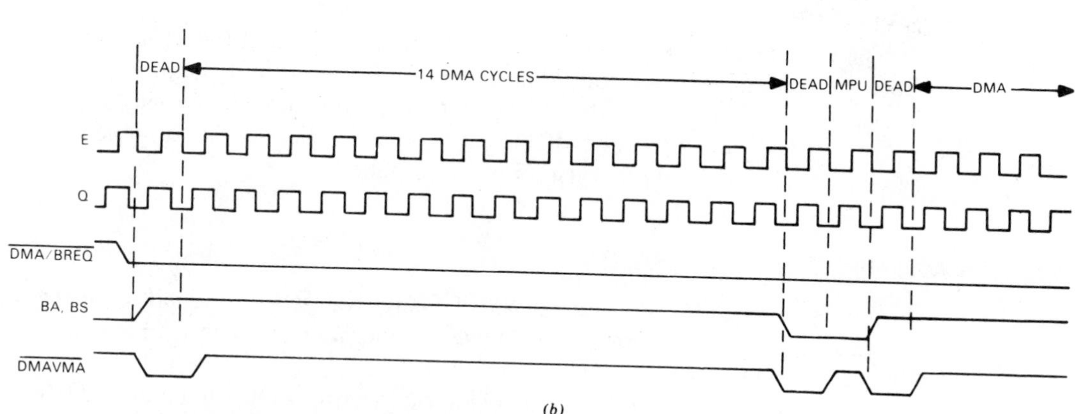

(b)

FIGURE 11-46 Auto-refresh DMA timing.
(a) Typical DMA timing (<14 cycles).
(b) Auto-refresh DMA timing (>14 cycles.)

11-14.6 HALT

A low level on this input pin will cause the μP to stop running at the end of the present instruction and remain halted indefinitely without loss of data. When halted, the BA output is driven high, indicating that the buses are high-impedance. BS is also high, which indicates that the processor is in the Halt or Bus Grant state. While halted, the μP will not respond to external real-time requests (FIRQ, IRQ), although DMA/BREQ will always be accepted and NMI or RESET will be latched for later response. During the Halt state, E and Q continue to run normally. If the MPU is not running (in RESET or DMA/BREQ), a halted state may be achieved by pulling HALT low while RESET is still low. If DMA/BREQ and HALT are both pulled low, the processor will reach the last cycle of the instruction (by reverse cycle stealing). The machine will then enter the HALT state.

11-14.7 Fast Interrupt Request (FIRQ)

A third interrupt, Fast Interrupt ReQuest (FIRQ), has been added, so that NMI, IRQ, and FIRQ are the hardware interrupt inputs available on the **6809**. FIRQ has priority over the standard IRQ and is fast in the sense that it stacks only the contents of the CCR and the Program Counter (PC). The interrupt service routine should clear the source of the interrupt before doing an RTI. When a logic 0 is recognized at the FIRQ input, the **6809** places only the Program Counter and Condition Code Registers on the stack prior to accessing the FIRQ vector (it also resets the E flag of the CCR). See Section 11-12.5. The IRQ or NMI still put the contents of all registers on the stack (same as **6800**), and *sets* the E flag of the CCR. Two software interrupts (SWI2 and SWI3) are also added. The interrupts in order of priority have NMI the highest followed by SWI, IRQ, FIRQ, SWI2, and SWI3.

When the microprocessor encounters an RTI instruction (necessary to return from the interrupt service routine), the CC is recovered first. If the recovered E bit is clear, it indicates that a FIRQ occurred and only the Program Counter address is additionally pulled. If the bit is set, it indicates that a standard IRQ sequence occurred and all registers must be pulled.

11-14.8 Bus Available, Bus Status (BA, BS)

Two lines on the **MC6809** and **MC6809E** microprocessors are used to determine which of four possible states the **M6809** is operating in. These four states are shown in Table 11-20.

The BA output is an indication of an internal control signal that makes the MOS buses of the μP high-impedance. This signal does not imply that the bus will be available for more than one cycle. When BA goes low, a dead cycle will elapse before the μP acquires the bus.

The BS output signal, when decoded with BA, represents the μP state (valid with the leading edge of Q).

TABLE 11-20 Bus Condition Signals

BA	BS	
0	0	Normal (running)
0	1	Interrupt or Reset Acknowledge
1	0	Sync Acknowledge
1	1	HALT or Bus Grant Acknowledge

An Interrupt ACKnowledge function (IACK) can be decoded from the BS and BA signals, as shown in Table 11-20, to indicate when a vector is being fetched for any of the interrupts (i.e., RESET, NMI, SWI, IRQ, FIRQ, SWI2, or SWI3).

Similarly, Sync Acknowledge can be detected to provide a hardware feedback, perhaps to a peripheral, to indicate when the IRQ responded to terminate the waiting condition started by the SYNC instruction. This allows hardware devices to be synchronized with the IRQ, hence the name. HALT/BUS GRANT is true when the **6809** is in a Halt or Bus Grant condition. In this condition other devices may make DMA requests to the **6809**'s memory.

11-15 THE 6809E μP

The **6809E** is a version of the **6809** that has some differences that make it more suitable for some system configurations. It uses an external clock, which makes it easier to do multiprocessing or DMA. The **6809E** pinout diagram is shown in Figure 11-47. The E and Q pins become inputs rather than outputs and, since the clock is external, pins 39, 38, 36 and 33 have new uses. These are TSC, LIC, AVMA, and BUSY, respectively. Except for these pins and the differences just described, the **6809E** and the **6809** are identical. These special signals are described in the following praragraphs.

11-15.1 Tri-State Control (TSC)

A LOW signal on TSC will cause the address, data, and R/W buffers to assume a high-impedance state. The other control signals (BA, BS, BUSY, AVMA, and LIC) will not go to the high-impedance state. TSC is intended to allow a single bus to be shared by other masters (processors or DMA controllers).

11-15.2 Advanced Valid Memory Address (AVMA)

A high signal on the AVMA pin indicates that the μP will use the bus on the next cycle. The predictive nature of this signal allows efficient shared-bus multiprocessor systems to be built.

11-15.3 Last Instruction Cycle (LIC)

A high occurs on the LIC pin during the last cycle of every instruction. Its transition from high to low indicates that the first byte of an Op code will be

Signal	Pin		Pin	Signal
V_{SS}	1		40	$\overline{\text{HALT}}$
$\overline{\text{NMI}}$	2		39	TSC
$\overline{\text{IRQ}}$	3		38	LIC
$\overline{\text{FIRQ}}$	4		37	$\overline{\text{RESET}}$
BS	5		36	AVMA
BA	6	6809E	35	Q
V_{CC}	7		34	E
A0	8		33	BUSY
A1	9		32	R/$\overline{\text{W}}$
A2	10		31	D0
A3	11		30	D1
A4	12		29	D2
A5	13		28	D3
A6	14		27	D4
A7	15		26	D5
A8	16		25	D6
A9	17		24	D7
A10	18		23	A15
A11	19		22	A14
A12	20		21	A13

FIGURE 11-47 6809E pin assignments.

latched at the end of the present bus cycle. LIC will be high when the μP is halted at the end of an instruction (i.e., not in CWAI or RESET), in SYNC state, or stacking registers during interrupts. This also provides information useful in multiprocessing systems.

11-15.4 BUSY

BUSY will be high for the read and modify cycles of a read–modify–write instruction and during the access of the first byte of a double-byte operation (e.g., LDX, STD, ADDD). BUSY is also high during the first byte of any indirect or vector fetch (jump extended, SWI indirect, etc.). In a multiprocessor system, BUSY indicates the need to defer the rearbitration of the next bus cycle to ensure the integrity of the above operations. This difference provides the indivisible memory access required for a "test-and-set" primitive, using any one of several read–modify–write instructions. BUSY does not become active during PSH or PUL operations.

11-15.5 Applications

Because of its increased versatility and new operating modes, the **6809** is used for many new applications requiring 8-bit μPs. For example, it is used in the Radio Shack color computer. The user can also purchase an assembler for the **6809** from Radio Shack and several other software suppliers, as well as from Motorola, that simplifies the assembling and debugging of **6809** programs.

11-16 SUMMARY

The **6801**, **6802**, **6805**, **68HC05C4**, **68HC11**, and **6809** μPs and μCs were described and it was shown that the previous chapters on the **6800** are applicable to these upward compatible components. The instruction sets are similar. The software and hardware features of each μP were discussed. The new and unique features of each μP such as the SCI, SPI, A/D converter, and timer were explained in some detail.

11-17 GLOSSARY

Arguments Mathematical variables associated with one routine that must be transferred to another.

Bit manipulation Process of changing one or more bits in a byte, usually associated with flags or I/O registers.

Byte efficiency Achieving more tasks or functions with fewer bytes of machine code.

Computer operating properly (COP) Special function of the **68HC11A8** to check for possible noncontinuous program operation.

Handshaking Process in which devices test signals from each other to determine readiness.

Input capture register One of the registers in the timer of a μC.

Latching Technique of retaining a signal condition after the pulse has stopped; usually done with an FF.

Mask byte Byte that is effectively ANDed with another byte to ensure that only the desired bits are kept in the high state.

Microcontroller Simple low-cost μC.

Multiplexing Using one signal line for two purposes; usually at different times.

Offset Byte following a branch Op code that determines the relative address that will be accessed next; usually a 2s complement 8-bit number.

Output compare register One of the registers in a μC timer.

Position-independent code Object code written with relative branch instructions such that it will operate correctly when located at any address.

Postbyte Byte immediately following an indexed, PSH, PUL, TFX, or EXG instruction Op code that specifies type or registers involved.

Ratiometric Expression describing the relationship of the hexadecimal numbers in the result registers with the voltage on each A/D channel input.

Recursive code Code in which each routine is capable of calling itself.

Reentrant code Technique of writing a subroutine such that the status can be saved while it is used by a higher-priority program and then the original can be continued.

Self-refresh Circuit within the **6809** to restore the register contents periodically.

Static Retaining its state indefinitely as long as power is applied; refers to circuitry.

Strobe Pulse on a signal line at a specific time, usually used to read or latch data.

Throughput Speed of processing data.

Wake-up feature SCI feature to decode and alert a specific μC when several are connected on the same serial data line.

Watchdog circuit Circuit that must be reset periodically or it will interrupt or restart the program; the COP circuit.

11-18 REFERENCES

8-Bit Microprocessor and Peripheral Data, Motorola, Phoenix, AZ, 1983.

HCMOS Single-Chip Microcomputer, Motorola Semiconductor Technical Data, Motorola, Phoenix, AZ, 1985.

Motorola, *M6805UM(AD2), M6805 HMOS, M146805 CMOS Family User's Manual,* Prentice-Hall, Englewood Cliffs, NJ, 1983.

Motorola's New High Technology Seminar, Microprocessors, Arrays, Systems, Motorola Semiconductor Products, Austin, TX, 1983.

Single-Chip Microcomputer Data, Motorola, Phoenix, AZ, 1984.

Systems on Silicon, Motorola Microcomputer Components, Integrated Circuits Division, Mesa, AZ.

MC6801/6803 Data Sheet DS 9841-R1, Motorola Semiconductor Products, Austin, TX, 1984.

MC6801U4 Advance Information Sheet ADI 896, Motorola Semiconductor Products, Austin, TX, 1982.

MC6809 Advance Information Sheet ADI-804-R1, Motorola, Phoenix, AZ, 1980.

MC6809E 8-Bit Microprocessor ADI 847, Motorola Semiconductor Products, Austin, TX, 1984.

MC6809 Macro Assemblers Reference Manual, M68MASR (D), Austin, TX, December 1978.

MC6809 Motorola Microcomputer—Technical Training Manual, Motorola Semiconductor Products, Phoenix, AZ, 1983.

MC6846 *Advance Information* ADI-473, Motorola, Phoenix, AZ, 1978.

MC68HC11A8 HCMOS Single-Chip Microcomputer, Advance Information Sheet ADI 1207, Motorola Literature Distribution, Phoenix, AZ, 1985.

MC68HC05C4, MC68HC05C8, MC68HC805C4, 8-Bit Microcomputers, ADI 991R2, Motorola Literature Distribution, Phoenix, AZ, 1985.

M6805 HMOS, M146805 CMOS Family, Microcomputer, Microprocessor User's Manual, Second Edition, Prentice-Hall, Englewood Cliffs, NJ, 1983.

11-19 PROBLEMS

11-1 a. Describe how to implement a circuit to use the 32 bytes of RAM in the **6802** μP with a battery to provide power failure recovery. Assume the **6846** combination shown in Fig. 11-2b.

b. Write a routine for power failure detection as well as one for recovery.

11-2 a. Describe the connections needed to use the timer of the **6846** to provide a real-time clock with 1-s updates. Use the μP crystal as a source.

b. Write the initialization routines to set up the timer.

11-3 a. Assuming a **6801** system as shown in Fig. 11-8, describe the mode to be selected and how its done.

b. Assuming the ROM is really an EPROM, write a program to use the internal serial port to talk to an RS232 duplex terminal at 9600 baud. Assume a 4.9152-MHz crystal. Include the initialization and I/O routines. Include external vectors in the top of the EPROM. Assume the EPROM resides at $E800.

11-4 a. Write the software to implement the **6801** timer. Connect pin 9 (timer out) to pin 4 (NMI) (with a 3.3K pull-up), and program it to respond to periodic interrupts when the timer is enabled.

b. Set up the output compare register to interrupt the system when a value is entered. What location is used for the service routine vector?

11-5 Write a routine to move a block of data using the ABX instruction. Write the same thing in **6800** language and compare the number of bytes as well as the cycle times.

11-6 How does the **6809** RTI instruction know when to restore only the PC and CC registers?

11-7 What happens when the DMA/BREQ line is pulled down while a program is being executed and is held down indefinitely?

11-8 What is the **6809** equivalent instruction for the **6801**'s ASLD? How would the function be done in the **6809**?

11-9 For the **68HC11A8**, write a program segment to command the control/status register to convert the input on channel AN5. Check CCF to see when conversions are complete and then average the results of the four conversions.

11-10 For a **68HC05C4**, write the code to set bit 3 of port A, if port A is at address $EE.

11-11 In a system that uses a **1468052**, write instructions that will branch to a new routine when the tested bit (3) is set (a bit manipulation instruction).

11-12 What is the difference between the **6800** TSX and the **6809** TFR, S,X instructions? What has the change in the operation of the stack to do with it?

11-13 What **6809** instruction is equal to **6800**'s INX?

11-14 How can a ROM be programmed for a **6809** μP so that the ROM will execute properly when located at any absolute address?

11-15 A **6809** with register contents as shown in Fig. 11-48 has just encountered an RTI instruction. Show the contents of the registers after execution of the RTI.

11-16 The **6809** shown in Fig. 11-49 has just encountered an RTI. Show the contents of the registers after execution of the RTI.

11-17 Using a figure like 11-49, show the register contents after executing the instructions below. Use the instruction set summary or the **6809** data sheet to determine the address modes.

Hex Address	*Hex Contents*
1FB	1C
1FC	00
1FD	8E
1FE	02
1FF	0A
200	A6
201	1F
202	EE
203	0F
204	02
205	09
206	10
207	EE
208	98
209	02
20A	10
20B	8E
20C	02
20D	08
20E	1F
20F	8B
210	D6
211	03

After attempting to solve these problems, try to answer the self-evaluation questions in Section 11-2. If any of them still seem difficult, review the appropriate sections of the chapter to find the answers.

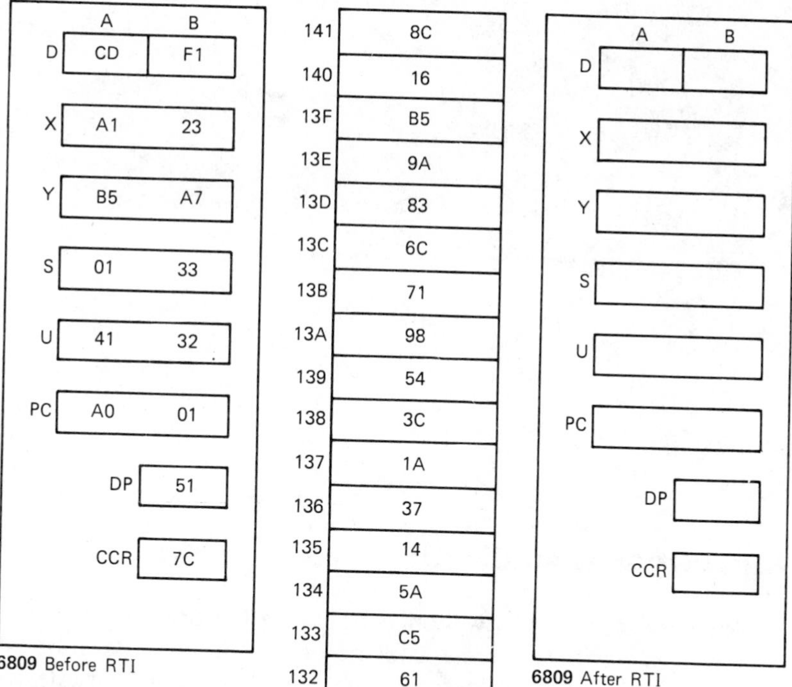

FIGURE 11-48 Register contents for Problem 11-15.

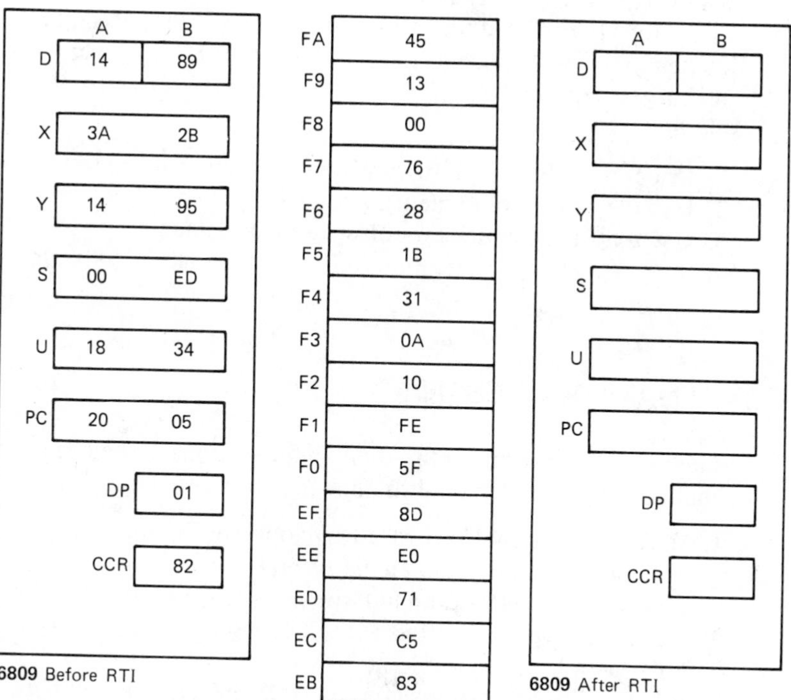

FIGURE 11-49 Register contents for Problem 11-16.

CHAPTER 12

NEW CONCEPTS IN MICROCOMPUTER DEVELOPMENT SYSTEMS

12-1 INSTRUCTIONAL OBJECTIVES

Prior to Chapter 11, we concentrated on the **6800** μP and its peripheral chips because its bus structure and instruction set are the basis for all of the newer μPs and μCs designed by Motorola and it is a straightforward design that is easy to understand. Once this basic μP has been mastered, it is easy to understand other μPs or μCs, particularly those in the **6800** family.

Chapter 11 described the growing families of 8-bit μPs and μCs. This chapter is devoted to the new concepts in Microcomputer Development Systems (MDSs) for this burgeoning family of μCs. After reading this chapter, the student should be able to

1. Understand how a Hardware Development Station (HDS) works.
2. Use the new development systems described.
3. Use a host computer for software development.
4. Set up the communications circuits to enable "downloading" the object programs.

12-2 SELF-EVALUATION QUESTIONS

Watch for the answers to the following questions as you read the chapter. They should help you understand the material presented.

1. Why has the new Hardware Development Station (HDS) concept of Control Modules and individual emulator pods become desirable?
2. How can personal computers be used to build μC systems?
3. What two types of software are necessary to allow use of an existing computer as a host?
4. What additional features does an HDS-300 have as compared to an HDS-200?

12-3 NEW CONCEPTS FOR μC DEVELOPMENT

A **Microprocessor Development System (MDS)** is a tool to help develop the hardware and software of a microprocessor-based computer system. An MDS contains a microcomputer that controls it, a disk or tape system used to save or reload programs, debug programs and other utilities that are totally or partially in ROM, and other hardware aids to facilitate the development and refinement of the system being built. The MDS package includes programming utilities such as editors and assemblers or compilers to produce the necessary user system software. The user controls the development system from a data terminal, which is typically a cathode ray tube (CRT) or printer/terminal.

Much of the cost of an MDS is in the disk system, the printer, and the terminal. Because these peripherals are frequently available from previous design efforts or in small Personal Computers, they are not duplicated in the new development system. The software development can be done on any computer for which communications and cross-assembly software is available, such as the many Personal Computers (PCs) now in use. In this way, very little additional investment is necessary to do the software development.

Motorola's first MDS was the EXORciser, which was introduced in 1974 and is described in Chapter 10. It used the concept that a system could be constructed from the modular pieces supplied that could act as a model for a proposed user's system. It included a **6800** or **6809** μP module, which served as the processor for both the Development System and the user's system under development. It was possible to connect a user's external system components such as motors or solenoid valves to the various I/O modules and actually have a complete operational industrial control (or other) system. The EXbug program made it possible to debug all the software and to exercise the user's external system components.

Because of the proliferation of 8-bit μCs (over 40 types are built by Motorola alone), it has become desirable to change the concept of the development systems and, if possible, reduce the cost. The *dual processor* concept, as used in the first MEX6805 plug-in modules for the EXORciser, worked well and led to the concept that the system should be divided into two parts, with the common circuitry such as the power supply, serial ports, and emulation memory assembled in one box or *Control Station* and the *processor-dependent hardware* with its own μP built into an *Emulator* or *Personality Pod*. It was found advantageous to have a *different* Pod assembly for each of the different target μPs or μCs. It is then only necessary to supply a new emulator pod and some new software when a new type of processor is introduced.

Analysis of all these factors has led to the concept of a stand-alone μP development system. This **Hardware Development Station** or HDS, as it is called, was first introduced as the HDS-200. Figure 12-1 shows two typical HDS configurations and Fig. 12-2 is a photograph of the HDS-200. The Control Module is the low flat box in the background. The Emulator Pod and its output plug are in the foreground.

Currently two types of HDSs are being built: the HDS-200 and the HDS-300. The **6801** and **6809** Emulators for the HDS-300 now replace those made for the EXORciser.

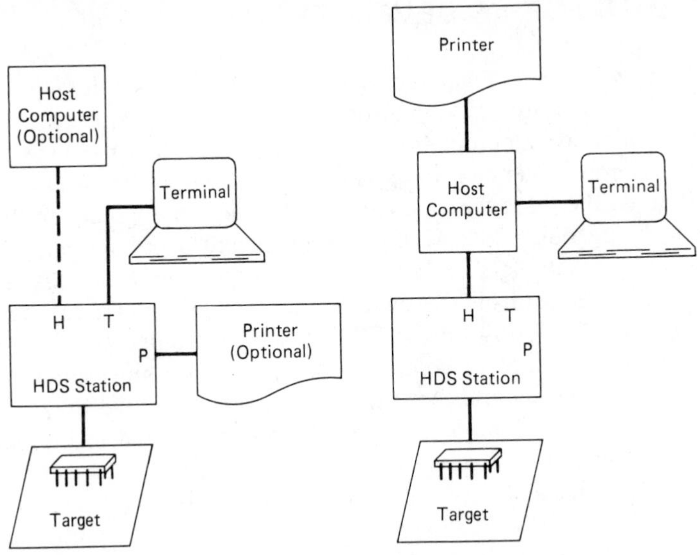

FIGURE 12-1 Typical HDS configurations.

A complete HDS-type Emulator/Analyzer is illustrated functionally in Fig. 12-3. The control module contains:

1. The μP that controls the system.
2. The debug PROM.
3. A **Family Interface Module (FIM)**. The FIM contains the circuitry that is common to all of the emulators of the family and serves as the interface for data transfers betweeen the HDS circuits on the control module and those in the emulator pod. It also serves as the path for the user code passed between processor systems.
4. An **emulation RAM**. This is provided as a substitute for the user's ROM during program development or until the memory on the user's system prototype is operational.
5. Two RS232C ports. One connects to the terminal and the other to a host computer. These are marked T and H in Fig. 12-1.

The cables out of the front of the HDS are connected to the rear of an Emulator Module. This module contains another μC that is identical to the one that will be used in the user's system. Thus there is a different emulator pod for every type of μC. These pods are also called *personality modules*. The emulator pod shown in the foreground of Fig. 12-2 is for the **6804P2** μC. The short cable coming out the front of the module is designed to plug into the μC socket of the user's system. The μC in the pod thus replaces the user's μC, but its operation can now be monitored by the HDS and allows efficient debugging.

The control module for the HDS-200 is a Micromodule 17 with a **68B09** μP. The control module for the HDS-300 uses a **68008** μP that is part of the **68000** family and has 32-bit architecture. It has an 8-bit data bus and a 20-bit address bus (see Chapter 15).

FIGURE 12-2 The HDS-200.

Both systems use FIMs, but they are of different design and not interchangeable. The HDSs are constructed differently and have differences in the command syntax and display of the results. The HDS-300 is the most recent design and has more features, such as the **Bus State Monitor (BSM)**. The BSM is similar to a logic analyzer in that it can display or record the state of each bus cycle. It captures this information when the trigger events are met and the bus states can then be displayed. The BSM is a very powerful debugging tool and is described in Section 12-8.4.

A photograph of the HDS-300, Fig. 12-4, shows the control module and emulator pods for the **68HC11** μC and the **6809** μP.

12-3.1 Communications with an HDS

An HDS contains two RS232C ports. One is for use with a CRT terminal and is all that is needed in the early stages of development. The second port is for communication with a host computer (a minicomputer, PC, or a mainframe), when it is time to develop a user's program foı the system. The object program in the form of S-records (see Section 6-9) is then downloaded to the HDS through this second serial port. The HDSs are said to be terminal and host-independent because they can work with a great variety of terminals and host sytems. They are supported by Motorola with cross-software for use with other Motorola software development systems such as the EXORciser, EXORset, VME10, or the EXORmacs. These

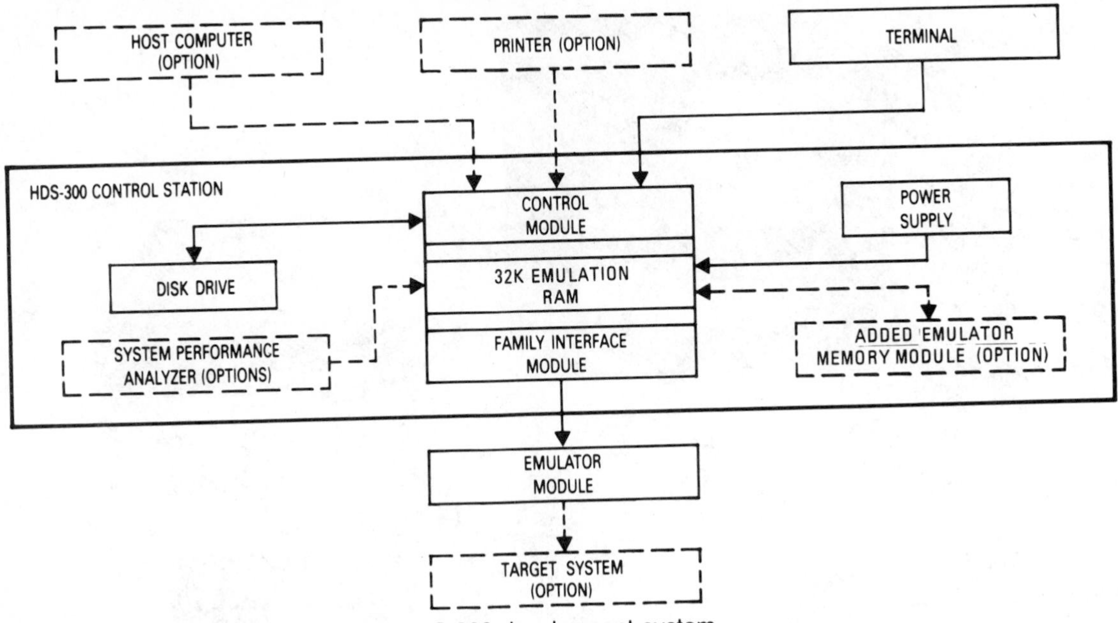

FIGURE 12-3 Block diagram of the HDS-300 development system.

combinations of HDSs and hosts provide complete hardware/software development systems for the Motorola families of μPs. Other computers, such as CPM-80 systems, certain Radio Shack models, and IBM–PCs or their equivalents, can also serve as hosts, but their usefulness will depend on cross-software availability. Motorola provides several communications software packages for the IBM-PC for use with the HDS-300. Third-party software is also available.

12-3.2 HDS Advantages

Three major factors contribute to the usefulness of the HDS as a systems development tool. The first is the ability to serve as a fully functional substitute for the selected μC in the target system. By plugging the emulator cable into the μC socket on the prototype hardware, it is easy to test the hardware as well as the software. It then performs the functions of the μC being emulated exactly as the μC would have performed were it still in the circuit being tested. The emulator provides the amount of memory and I/O ports normally on the chip and operates at the same speed as the emulated μC. There are no wait states in the emulator to confuse circuit functions, and there are no restrictions on the use of emulator memory that are not imposed by the μC itself.

The second factor is its list of analysis commands. These easy-to-use, plain language commands enable the user to rapidly debug and integrate the software with the hardware to produce prototype systems.

The third feature is the ability to interface to a host computer, and the combination, with its added features, constitutes a powerful Microcomputer Development System (MDS).

12-3.3 Using the HDS for System Emulation

The initial stages of development for a μC-based system normally involve two parallel, rather independent, efforts. These are *hardware* design and programming or *software* design. They are often done by two different teams. Before long, however, the software must be integrated with the new hardware being designed. The HDS has features that make it useful in all of these tasks.

The HDS can be used in a stand-alone configuration (without a Host) and without a target system, for initial evaluation of the selected μC, as follows:

a. Using the Memory Mapping (MAP) selection command, set up the emulation RAM to match the locations required for EPROM or ROM in the selected μC map. Be sure to select the top of memory so that the RESET vector can be properly accessed. Some of the emulation memory will be needed for scratch RAM also.
b. Set the HDS to use the emulator clock since no target is used.
c. Determine the clock frequency to be used in the user system, and set the HDS clock circuits accordingly.
d. Connect the terminal to the RS232C HDS terminal port. The host is not needed until the system software is designed and is ready to be written.

Test programs can now be entered manually from the terminal into the emulation memory and debugged. As explained in more detail later, evaluation of the μC's I/O will require that the HDS be plugged into a target system. It can be as simple as a handmade *wirewrap* target system that provides interconnections to the external system hardware (see Fig. 12-5). The HDS can be used to examine this interface and determine what is needed to update and expand the user's system.

FIGURE 12-4 The HDS-300.

Most of the debugging techniques described in Chapter 10 can be used with the HDS but are enhanced with several new features not previously available. These new features are

1. **HELP command.** This results in a list of commands being displayed that make the system easy to learn and it reduces dependence on the manuals.
2. **One-line Assembler/Disassembler.** This reduces the dependence on machine language.
3. **Transparent communications mode.** This mode permits conversations with the host computer via the RS232C link and facilitates downloading (or uploading) *S-record* versions of the object code (see Sections 6-9 and 12-10.3).
4. **Macro capability.** One macro command automatically executes a series of commands. Macros allow custom commands to be devised by the user.
5. **Breakpoint feature.** One of the most powerful debugging features of any development system is the breakpoint feature. This was described in Chapter 10. The HDS has the same feature but also has the ability to insert temporary breakpoints at selected locations in the program. Breakpoints in the HDS also allow additional qualifiers such as running a macro after the second encounter of the breakpoint address.
6. **Emulation Memory.** HDSs provide RAM that can be placed in the memory map or "mapped" as a substitute for the ROM that will ultimately hold the user's program. The use of RAM permits patching or changing instructions in a program as it is being tested.

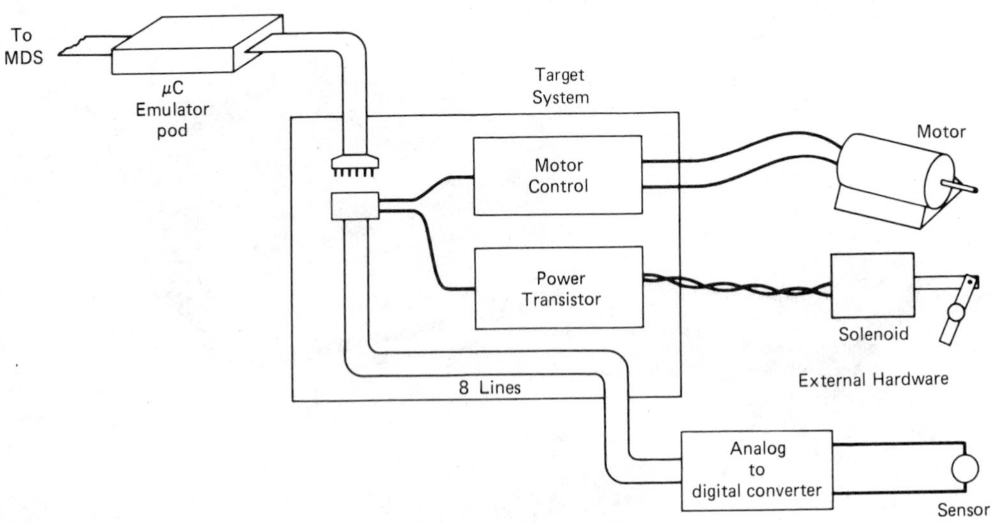

FIGURE 12-5 User's target system.

12-3.4 Host Interfacing

The **Transparent Mode (TM)** command causes the data to and from the terminal to be connected through the HDS's second RS232 port directly to the host computer. The host computer is operated as though the HDS were not present (transparently). In this mode, source programs can be written or modified with the host's editor and assembled or compiled on the host. The operator does not have to change consoles, plugs, or components. Returning to HDS operation is accomplished simply by depressing the exit character on the terminal keyboard. The object program can then be downloaded to the HDS from the host by using S-records (see Section 6-9) that employ byte counts and checksums to detect transmission errors. Thus all transactions in writing and modifying software, up- and downloading, memory manipulation, and so forth can be accomplished at a single console. If modems are used, the host can be remote from the HDS. Refer to Selection 12-10 for more details of host communications.

12-3.5 HDS Operation

The HDS is an instrument that speeds development of μC systems by accelerating the hardware and software debugging process. Many features help to isolate and correct problems in a newly designed user's system. This combination hardware/software instrument replicates all functions (including timing) of the target chip in its hardware and software environment. The HDS performs in a **noninvasive** manner, which means that the emulator does not use the target system resources and target code need not be modified to support emulation.

Up until now we have described the HDS features that are common to the HDS-200 and HDS-300 Development Systems. We would like to note at this point that the HDS-300 has additional features. One of these is the **windows** concept.

In addition to the emulation support, the HDS-300 provides the user with a **window** that allows a look into the target system operation to a degree not possible with other instruments such as logic analyzers. The *window* concept is created by the development system's menu display capability. The fundamental method of starting and stopping target code execution by means of breakpoints, trace, or BSM triggering has been expanded by individual window displays for each of these techniques. This makes it easier for the user to verify that the newly developed programs really perform as designed. The user may examine or alter target memory or processor registers when target execution is stopped. When in the *DEBUG window,* other windows are opened by some of the subcommands, such as *Memory Edit* (ME). With *trace,* the target code instructions are *stepped through,* one instruction at a time, to examine execution results. Alternatively, when a *breakpoint* or *trigger condition* is specified, the processor is instructed to continue running under emulation until the specified condition is reached.

This stop–examine–continue method is an effective mechanism for hardware and software debugging. It provides an efficient and timesaving way to isolate and resolve problems typical in early system development.

The HDS-200 provides the same functional performance but without the windows.

12-4 SYSTEM DEVELOPMENT USING AN HDS

An HDS is primarily designed to test the hardware. It does so by exercising the hardware with software. In the later stages of development it *tests the hardware with the system software*. This is called *system testing*.

12-4.1 Peripheral Interfacing

The external system hardware typically has functions that need to be controlled and sensors that need to be monitored (see Fig. 12-5). The μCs described in Chapter 11 contain I/O lines, Timers, Serial Communications Interfaces (SCIs), and other inputs or outputs that can be used to sense or control the external hardware. Once the emulator pod is plugged into the μC socket on the user's system, the user can test the hardware interfaces by using the Memory Display (MD) and/or the Memory Modify (MM) commands. **6800** family I/O devices are *memory mapped*, and thus these HDS system commands can be used to input or output data through the μC ports simply by reading or writing to the I/O registers.

If a parallel output port in one of the μCs is involved, for example, it may be used to cause a motor to run, a solenoid valve to open, or a relay to close. To do this, it is necessary to understand how the μC's I/O circuitry is controlled and how it is interfaced to the hardware devices it must control. When a new μC system design is started, the first steps might be to build up a wirewrap board with a μC socket on it and connect the pins to the external hardware that is part of the product to be controlled (level conversions or power transistors may be needed).

After the circuitry is connected between the pins of the μC socket and the external hardware, it can be controlled in the same way as a PIA (see Section 7-11). A byte with the appropriate bits set must be sent to the direction register to set it for output. A data word is then sent to the output data register to raise or lower the correct pin. If the expected results do not occur, a scope or meter can be used to observe changes on the output lines and/or peripheral devices and the wires moved or the control word changed to correct the problem.

Once the proper control words have been determined, a similar analysis is made where sensors are involved. After setting the direction register for inputs, a data byte is read from the input data register. The bits of this byte should match the data levels on the lines from the sensor hardware.

When both the control and status words are correct, a routine to exercise the external hardware can be entered into memory. This can be done in machine language, using the Memory Modify (MM or MS) command, or with the one-line assembler using mnemonics. The routine can be tried and modified until a complete I/O driver routine for this particular peripheral is developed.

The same technique is repeated for any other subsystems and their peripheral units and finally for the main system software, until a whole system is assembled. This entire process is shown in Fig. 12-6. Each step in the figure has feedback paths so that the hardware or software can be improved any number of times until the desired performance is reached.

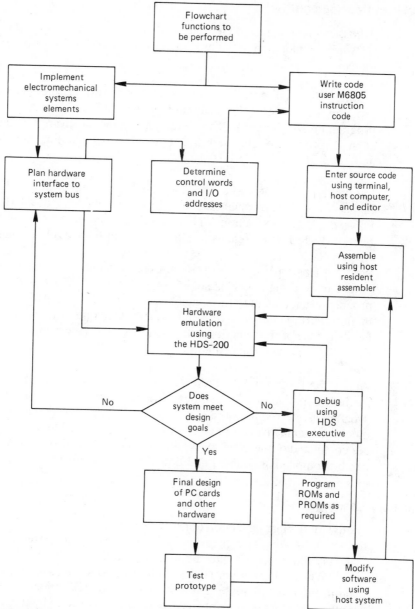

FIGURE 12-6 System designing and verifying procedure.

The engineer now has an operating model of the user system using HDS and wirewrap hardware, with a minimum amount of time spent on prototype construction. The programmer can now finalize the software routines. The advantages of the HDS to the programmer are that the I/O programming steps can be verified by testing them before a formal source program is written and the resulting object code can be debugged in real time.

12-4.2 Software Development

A host can be connected (see Fig. 12-1) and the testing programs written on that software development system. Software is developed on the host computer as follows:

Program Requirements The first step in software development is to define the program requirements. This cannot be done until the hardware is defined and the program details cannot be completed until some hardware testing has been done as in the procedures shown in Fig. 12-6. This specification should be as complete and detailed as possible.

Language Selection The program can be written in assembly language or a higher-level language such as "C," if it is available. Not all Hosts have them, however. Refer to Section 6-11 for more details on the Macro Assembler or to Section 12-13 for references to information on high-level language compilers.

Program Design After the program requirements have been defined, the program can be designed. This step is very important. The completed design of the program is equivalent to the schematic for the hardware. This design may be done in flowchart, *metacode,* or some other technique with which the designer is familiar. One of the benefits is that memory and the processor registers are more likely to be properly allocated.

Writing the Program Once the design is complete, the program is written using the host computer's edit facilities. The program can then be saved on disk. This program is referred to as the *source program*. If the program is written in modular blocks, they may be compiled or assembled and linked together for testing as they are completed. Otherwise, the complete program will have to be entered before it can be compiled/assembled and downloaded for testing.

12-4.3 Memory Loading

Hardware debugging can be done by writing into the I/O registers and observing the results. As testing progresses, a short read/write loop routine might be entered manually into memory with the Memory Modify or the one-line assembler command. When the program is more fully developed, it can be assembled or compiled in the host computer and downloaded to HDS memory. The user must be sure the memory assignments have been properly set up by the MAP environment before starting the memory loading process.

It should be possible to run the parts of the program devoted to calculations or moving data without having the target board in place. When it is necessary to test the I/O functions, however, this will not be true.

Once the user program is loaded into memory and debugging is started, the Memory Modify and/or one-line assembler command can be used to modify or *patch* the memory contents. The patched program can be stored back on the disk by using the SAVE command. After several errors have been collected, the source can be reedited and reassembled or compiled and the updated object redownloaded.

12-4.4 Debugging Techniques

The HDS control program provides three different methods of controlling program execution to assist in locating hardware and software problems. The methods are

a. Breakpoints
b. Trace
c. Stop-on-address

Each method has its advantages and restrictions. Combined, they provide very powerful and flexible techniques for testing and debugging. The user can begin to debug both hardware and software, once the following three functions are performed:

The memory is properly assigned.

The program and data are in memory.

The μP signals are appropriately enabled.

After a test program has been downloaded successfully to memory, the Disassembly (MM; DI or DASM) command or the Memory Display (MD) command can be used to show that the proper code is in memory.

12-4.5 Breakpoints

Breakpoints are probably the most useful of the three debugging techniques. It is not likely that a new program will run properly the first time, so it is wise to try it a little at a time. Breakpoints or Stop-On-Address are usually used to find any segments that do not work properly.

The first step in debugging would be to go through the program and set a **breakpoint** after each modular section of the program. The program is then executed in real time until the breakpoint is reached. This stops the user's program and the registers are displayed. If a fault occurs and the breakpoint is not reached, or incorrect actions result, trace is then used to pinpoint the actual instruction responsible in the segment.

Breakpoints can be set in emulation RAM, the user's RAM, or ROM. Section 12-6.1 describes the breakpoint installation, chaining, and macro calling for the HDS-200, as does Section 12-7 for HDS-300.

Breakpoints are also useful in testing the execution of program loops (i.e., a *count* can be specified to cause a break after that number of times through the loop).

12-4.6 Trace

When a section of program fails to reach the breakpoint or exhibits other problems, it can be tested with the Trace feature to isolate the missing or improper instructions. **Trace** provides single-step execution of a program to allow examination of the updated register contents after each instruction. Multiple-step trace does not give real-time operation, but it shows the register changes after each instruction is executed. See Section 12-6.3 for more details of this function for the HDS-200. Similarly, Section 12-7 describes the HDS-300 implementation. In the HDS-300, by enabling the Bus Slate Monitor (BSM) during this single-instruction execution, it is possible to see the actual state of the buses and control inputs.

12-4.7 Stop-On-Address or Halt on Trigger

This function for the HDS-200 is similar to Breakpoints except that the Stop-On-Address (SOA) logic examines the address bus all the time rather than just during Op code fetches. See Section 12-6.4.

In the HDS-300 the same function is available but it has a different name. It is a function of the BSM called *Triggering on an event.*

12-4.8 I/O Testing

The three techniques described in Section 12-4.4 may be used for testing many parts of the program. However, if the equivalent I/O devices for the final system are not in place in the HDS, the routines that handle these devices and the corresponding I/O cannot be tested easily. If these routines are to be tested at all without the corresponding hardware, then software routines must be written to simulate the I/O.

12-4.9 Program Patching

There are two ways to correct bugs (or programming errors). If the bug is relatively minor, such as loading the wrong register or accessing the wrong address, it may be patched—that is, corrected in memory by changing a few bytes. With this type of patch, a written record should be made of the patch so that the program source may be corrected at a later time. It is also a good idea to save the patched program on disk so that the program, with its corrections, can be restored in memory in the event of a runaway or *program crash* while pursuing the next bug.

Debugging a machine language program usually results in correcting inverted logic (BNE where BEQ is needed), replacing the value of an offset to branch to a different place, or inserting omitted statements. In the first two cases a 1-byte code is simply replaced with another, but in the last case, no room exists for the addition. This requires the other form of *program patching* where additional instructions are needed. The patch to add the instructions consists of a jump from the main program to a vacant area of memory. The additional instructions plus the instructions in the main program that were written over by the jump are written in this area. The patch is completed by jumping back to the main program.

After several patches have been collected, the source program should be edited and the bugs corrected. Then the program can be recompiled or reassembled, and testing can continue with the new version of the object program. If the program bug is major, such as an error in program organization, it may be necessary to go directly to the reedit, recompile, or reassemble procedure.

EXAMPLE 12-1

Assume that the stack pointer had to be initialized at the start of the multiplication routine (Table 5-2). How can this be done?

a. Assume the addresses before location $20 are available.
b. Assume the addresses before location $20 contain information that cannot be changed.

SOLUTION
We cannot use addresses at the bottom of memory for programs in most of the **6801**, **6805**, or **146805** systems because they would interfere with the I/O registers. The following solution assumes that we are using a **6800** or **6809** μP system.

a. If the locations before $20 are available, we can write the 3-byte machine codes for the LDS IMMEDIATE instruction into location $1D, $1E, and $1F. Then the starting address of the program (the contents of $FFFE and $FFFF) can be changed to $001D and the program will operate correctly.
b. If locations $1D, $1E, and $1F are unavailable, a jump patch must be made. The contents of locations $20, $21, and $22 are replaced by a JMP $0040 (assuming $40 is a vacant memory area). At $40 we can write

```
40  8E xxxx    LDS    #$xxxx    Set the stack pointer to xxxx.
43  C6 08      LDA B  #$8       Replace overwritten
45  D7 81      STA B  $81         instructions.
47  7E 0024    JMP    $24       Return to main program.
```

This completes the patch, which includes the main program instructions that were overwritten by the jump to the patch plus the necessary additional instruction.

If, after a program is written, an instruction is found to be unnecessary, it can be replaced by a NOP (or several NOPs). This removes the instruction without causing the entire program to be rewritten. If a group of instructions are found to be unnecessary, they can be skipped by inserting a jump following the last useful instruction to the point where the program must resume.

All of the above changes are made only during program development. The program should be "cleaned up," eliminating useless NOPs and awkward jumps, before it is finalized and written to a ROM.

The example shows that it is unwise to start a program at 0000. If a program is started at 100 instead and the need arises to add instructions at the beginning of the program, locations 0000 to 00FF can be used instead of having to patch by jumping. This also allows room for variables in the direct addressing range as in the program above, so simpler programs can be written (2-byte instructions instead of 3).

12-4.10 Testing Prototype or Production Systems

Once the designer has emulated the user system with the HDS plugged into a *wirewrap board* and it is operating properly, construction of a *prototype* Printed Circuit Board (PCB) is the next step. By emulation, the user now knows exactly how many output ports or lines are required, what interface circuitry is needed, what the clock circuit should be, and, if any external memory is used, what decoding scheme must be employed. This information allows the user to design a PC prototype that is reasonably close to the final production units. The need for a prototype has not been eliminated altogether, but probably several iterations have been bypassed.

When construction is complete, the user must test the prototype in the same way and determine whether it performs as well as the emulation system did.

It is still possible to operate and test the prototype system using the emulation RAM of the HDS in place of the μC's RAM, ROM, or PROM. The program can be tested with the HDS debugging routines until the user is satisfied that the system is firm enough for the program to be put into PROM or EPROM. The user must be certain that the proper restart vector is in the EPROM.

12-4.11 Procedure for Design

To better understand the use of the HDS in the design and development of any μC system, let us review the procedure followed by a typical engineer in developing such a system and see how the HDS simplifies the design (see Fig. 12-6).

a. The user system is defined, using flowcharts or other means, and the software and hardware functions to be performed are determined.
b. The HDS is set up to emulate the user system hardware. Any special circuitry to interface to the peripherals is built.
c. After testing the hardware required to accomplish the intended function and determining the addresses and control words, the software programs are prepared on the host and downloaded to the HDS.
d. The HDS control program is used to debug both the hardware and software until the user system is working.
e. A preproduction model of the user system is built.
f. The preproduction hardware is substituted for the wirewrap version and tested with the user system software previously developed.

g. Using the HDS control program and the emulator module, the hardware and software are debugged and fixed.
h. At this point, the program may be stored in PROMs and the user system extensively tested and evaluated in an actual working environment.
i. The final prototype of the user system is built.
j. The production hardware is combined with the system software and the final adjustments are made to the user system. The HDS may again be used in evaluating the user system by means of the emulator module.
k. The system is released to production.
l. Problems in production hardware are also analyzed with the HDS.

12-5 THE HDS-200 HARDWARE/SOFTWARE DEVELOPMENT STATION

In this section the features that are unique to the HDS-200 will be discussed. The specific HDS-200 emulator modules for the various μC family members, along with the pins, RAM size, ROM/EPROM size, and I/O lines for each applicable μC type, are shown in Table 12-1.

TABLE 12-1 HDS-200 Emulators for the **6805/6804** MCU Family

MCU TYPE NUMBER		EMULATOR MODEL PART NUMBER	BYTES OF ON-CHIP USER ROM
HMOS	MC6804J2	M6804P2HM	1024
	MC6804P2	M6804P2HM	1024
	MC6805P2	M6805P234HM	1092
	MC6805P4	M6805P234HM	1092
	MC6805P6	M6805P234HM	1796
	MC6805R2	M6805RU23HM	2040
	MC6805R3	M6805RU23HM	3768
	MC6805S2	MC6805S2HM	1500
	MC6805T2	M6805T2HM	2500
	MC6805U2	M6805RU23HM	2040
	MC6805U3	M6805RU23HM	3768
	MC68705P3	M6805P234HM	1796
	MC68705R3	M6805RU23HM	3768
	MC68705U3	M6805RU23HM	3768
	MC68705P5	M6805P234HM	1796
CMOS	MC146805E2	M146805E2HM	—
	MC146805F2	M146805F2HM	1070
	MC146805G2	M146805G2HM	2096
	MC1468705F2	M146805F2HM	1070
	MC1468705G2	M146805G2HM	2096
HCMOS	MC68HC05C4	M68HC05C4HM	4096

12-5.1 HDS-200 Control Station

The control station contains an internal power supply, a Micromodule 17 (MM17) control module, and a Family Interface Module (FIM) to interface via a cable to the associated outboard Emulator Pod Module. The MM17 includes logic circuits, a clock, and a **6809** μP that runs the debug ROM and works with the two RS232 ports (one for the terminal and one for the host.) Paired with each Emulator Pod is a small cartridge that is plugged into the front of the HDS-200 station. This cartridge contains the necessary programs in PROM to enable the HDS-200 to adapt to the specific "personality" of the selected μC type. (See Fig. 12-2.)

To demonstrate the versatility and effectiveness of the HDS-200, a few of the system's development capabilities are described in the following paragraphs.

12-5.2 The HDS-200 Command Format

The general syntax for commands in the HDS-200 is

> [NO]<name> [<parameters>] . . . [;<option>]

where

>	is the prompt.
[. .]	is optional.
[NO]	is the negative (opposite) of some primitive commands.
<name>	is the primitive command name (two to five letters).
<parameter>	is a number representing an address, data, etc.
<option>	is one of the command's options.

Most options have *default* values that are used when a command is given without entering the choice of options or data. The command is activated by entering a Carriage Return (CR). A complete list of available commands is given in Tables 12-2 through 12-5. It is not necessary, however, to continually refer to these printed tables because the command set can be displayed on the screen of the terminal simply by calling HELP. The command HE causes the first page of the command set to be displayed together with a variety of options for the commands (see Fig. 12-7). Sequential pages can be called up by striking any character key on the terminal keyboard. Should more information on a specific command be required, the command HE xx, with the x's equal to the selected command, brings up a more detailed description (see Fig. 12-8).

EXAMPLE 12-2

What command is needed to set a breakpoint at $0100 the fifth time this location is reached?

SOLUTION

TABLE 12-2 System Control Commands

CODE	COMMAND NAME AND DESCRIPTION	SYNTAX
TM	ENTER TRANSPARENT MODE Enables terminal and host computer to communicate directly with each other. HDS-200 ignores data passing through its RS-232C ports until it detects the termination character which causes it to exit the Transparent Mode.	TM [‹char›]
LO	LOAD EMULATOR FROM PORT (DOWNLOAD) Causes "S" records from host or terminal to be loaded in emulator memory. Additional "text" material may be sent to the port before downloading. Includes the option to display "S" records on terminal, to ignore checksum errors, or to authorize continuing loading after memory load error causes loading interrupt.	LO ‹port› [;{‹option›}][= ‹text›]
DU	DUMP EMULATOR MEMORY TO PORT (UPLOAD) Causes the specified portion of emulator memory to be transmitted out of the indicated port, as "S" records.	DU ‹port› ‹low› ‹high› [= ‹text›]
HE	PRESENT INFORMATION ON COMMAND (HELP) If no command is specified, entire list of commands is displayed together with its syntax. If a specific command is given, a more detailed description of the command and its use is presented.	HE [‹command›]
DE	SET/DISPLAY DEFAULTS Allows user to examine or change default options for input and output format of data. (Hex, ASCII, Binary or Decimal)	DE [{‹defopt›}]
MA	DEFINE/DISPLAY MACRO Displays each macro and its definition, and allows user to add new macros to library. An individual macro text may contain other macro cells.	MA [‹macro name›]
NOMA	DELETE MACRO Allows user to delete all or specified macros from library.	NOMA [‹name›]
PF	PORT FORMAT Enables user to establish alternate flow control characters to establish load and dump compatibility with foreign host. It also allows for the changing of the serial data format ("8-bits," "7-bits," "Parity" or "No-Parity," etc.). This may be done for either port.	PF ‹port›
★	STAR COMMAND Transmits one line of text to host port without entering the transparent mode.	★ ‹TEXT›

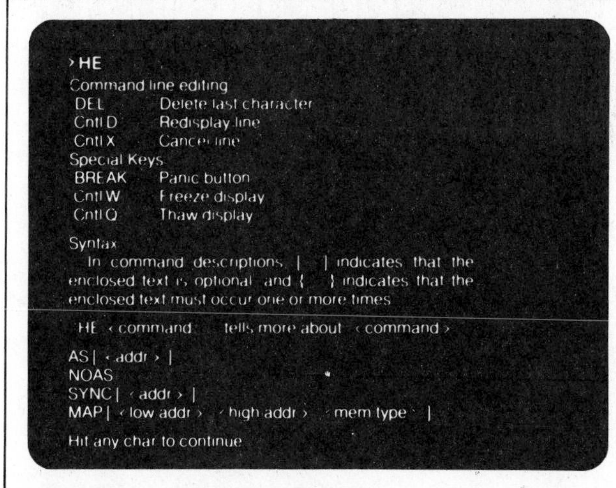

FIGURE 12-7 Command listing.

TABLE 12-3 Memory/Register Commands

CODE	COMMAND NAME AND DESCRIPTION	SYNTAX
MD	MEMORY DISPLAY Displays memory contents. If instructions, specified number of instructions are shown in disassembled form; otherwise the specified number of bytes are shown in both Hex and ASCII form.	MD ‹addr› [‹count›]
MM	MEMORY MODIFY With the aid of a number of subcommands, user can modify memory at specific locations in optional format.	MM ‹addr›
MS	MEMORY SET Deposits given data in memory starting at address specified.	MS ‹address› {‹data›}
RD	REGISTER DISPLAY Displays all or selected register contents in optional format.	RD [‹reg›]
RM	REGISTER MODIFY Specified register contents are displayed, one at a time, in optional format allowing user to modify as required.	RM [‹reg›]
BF	BLOCK FILL MEMORY All memory between specified low and high addresses is filled with entered data consisting of specified number of bytes.	BF ‹low› ‹high› ‹data›
BS	BLOCK SEARCH User specifies a given bit pattern and memory range. Memory is then searched from low address to high address specified and the address of each location where the given bit pattern is found will be displayed.	BS ‹low› ‹high› ‹data› [‹mask›]
BSN	BLOCK SEARCH — NEGATIVE Same as BS except displays addresses where specified bit pattern is not found.	
BM	BLOCK MOVE MEMORY The block of memory between given low and high memory addresses is copied to new location starting at specified address.	BM ‹low› ‹high› ‹new›
BT	BLOCK TEST MEMORY Causes the specified address range of the emulator RAM to be tested. Current contents are destroyed. A message indicates success or failure of test.	BT ‹low› ‹high›

Figure 12-8 explains how to set up the command. It is BR 100,5. The 100 is the hex address and the 5 is the count option.

With these commands, the contents of all registers or selected individual registers can be displayed or modified. Mass block memory moves, data updates, address modifications, and memory scans (to locate a specific data address) are among the many operations available.

12-5.3 Memory Manipulation—MAP Display

The MAP command displays the memory map allocations, as shown in Fig. 12-9. It is also used to change the assignments. The various commands for register and memory manipulation are listed and described in the memory/register commands table (Table 12-3).

12-5.4 Memory Display/Modify with Disassembly

The Memory Display (MD) command displays a portion of the memory for the user. A typical (MD) sequence is illustrated in the upper portion of Fig. 12-10. In

TABLE 12-4 Program Control Commands

CODE	COMMAND NAME AND DESCRIPTION	SYNTAX
G	GO FROM ADDRESS Starts execution of program, restarting at specified address. If no address is given, program will start at point currently in program counter.	G [‹address›]
GT	GO TILL BREAKPOINT Sets a temporary breakpoint at address specified. When a breakpoint is encountered, the temporary breakpoint is deleted.	GT ‹address›
DF	SET/SHOW DISPLAY FORMAT Specifies what registers and memory locations are to be displayed when a breakpoint is encountered, or after each instruction during tracing. Format of display is optional.	DF [‹name›]
NODF	DELETE DISPLAY FORMAT The specified register or memory location is removed from display format. If not specified, format is reset to default form.	NODF [‹name›]
T	TRACE INSTRUCTIONS Causes program execution, one step at a time, for specified number of steps. Displays contents of registers and memory specified by DF command. Format is also specified by DF. After the execution of each instruction, the processor registers are displayed and the instruction disassembled.	T [‹count›]
TT	TRACE TO BREAKPOINT Sets a temporary breakpoint at address specified and starts trace. Trace stops when breakpoint is encountered and the temporary breakpoint is deleted.	TT ‹address›
BR	SET BREAKPOINT The breakpoint table can be displayed and new breakpoints established. A counter can be started allowing the program to ignore the breakpoint for a specified number of times. Another option allows the emulator to be restarted automatically when all breakpoint processing has been finished.	BR [‹address› [{‹BP option›}]]
NOBR	REMOVE BREAKPOINT(S) Deletes specified breakpoint. If no address given, deletes all BPs.	NOBR [‹address›]
ARM	ARM BREAKPOINT Will arm all or specified breakpoints.	ARM [{‹address›}]
NOARM	DISARM BREAKPOINT(S) Disarms breakpoints specified. If none are specified, all breakpoints are disarmed.	NOARM [{‹address›}]
CHAIN	CHAIN BREAKPOINTS When a specified breakpoint address is reached in the program, and the breakpoint counter zeros, a special group of breakpoints can be prioritized. That is, certain selected breakpoints can be selected from breakpoint table and armed. Nonselected breakpoints will be disarmed.	CHAIN ‹BP address› [{‹address›}]
S	STOP PROCESSOR Halts processor in reset user code.	S
RESET	RESET PROCESSOR Places processor in reset condition. Initiates execution from processor's reset vector.	RESET

the example, the memory listing starts at address \$100 and continues for the next five instructions. The DI option adds disassembly. Each line of data includes the address of the Op code, the hexadecimal instruction code, the instruction mnemonic, and the operand.

The Memory Modify (MM) command causes memory at a specified address to be displayed. It may be shown in either hexadecimal or mnemonic (disassembled) form. If the disassembled form is selected, a new source line may be entered at that address (one-line assembly) to correct the program, if necessary.

The lower portion of Fig. 12-10 shows the implementation of the MM command (MM 108.DI). The first line shows existing data at the \$0108 address. The follow-

TABLE 12-5 Special Commands

CODE	COMMAND NAME AND DESCRIPTION	SYNTAX
AS	ENABLE STOP ON ADDRESS Causes the emulator to halt when the specified address appears on address bus. Command is used to trace through code in ROM. This command disables the SYNC feature.	AS [‹address›]
SYNC	SYNC ON ADDRESS Causes an oscilloscope or other instrument sync pulse to be generated when the specified address appears on the address bus. This command disables the AS command.	SYNC [‹address›]
IROM	ENABLE INTERNAL ROM Configures the MCU to use its internal ROM.	IROM
READ	MOVE ROM TO RAM Moves the memory between a given low and high address from the processor ROM into the same portion of the emulator RAM. This allows a program originally in ROM to be debugged.	READ ‹low› ‹high›
MAP	CONFIGURE/DISPLAY MEMORY MAP In the configure mode, command allows user to allocate emulator memory among different types of memory (RAM, EPROM and peripherals). The display mode shows current allocation.	MAP [‹low address› ‹high address› ‹memory type›]

ing line shows existing data at the \$0108 address. The next line is the new data to be loaded at \$0108. The memory modification is completed with the entry of a Carriage Return (CR). Since an "=" sign is used, the new data (at the same address) is then disassembled and displayed on the following line. After the next prompt (?), another CR increments to the next address and its contents are displayed.

EXAMPLE 12-3

Using the Disassembly/assembly mode of MM (MM;DI), show how to add instructions to the listing of Fig. 12-10 to OR the contents of A with 15_{10} (immediate mode), and store the results in location \$45.

SOLUTION

The Commands and resulting HDS outputs are shown in the following Listing—starting with the last instruction of Fig. 12-10:

```
>MM 10A;DI
$010A    $C7 $40C2          STA  >$40C2
?   (CR)
$010D  $9D                  NOP
?ORA  #15=       (CR)
$010D    $AA $0F            ORA  #&15
?   (CR)
$010F  $9D                  NOP
?STA  $45=       (CR)
$010F    $B7 $45            STA      $45
?
```

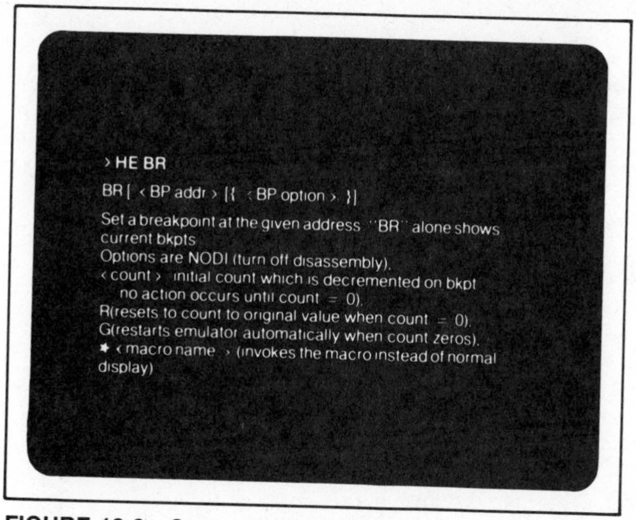

```
>HE BR
BR [ <BP addr> [{ <BP option> }]
Set a breakpoint at the given address "BR" alone shows
current bkpts
Options are NODI (turn off disassembly).
<count> initial count which is decremented on bkpt
   no action occurs until count = 0).
R(resets to count to original value when count = 0).
G(restarts emulator automatically when count zeros).
* <macro name> (invokes the macro instead of normal
display)
```

FIGURE 12-8 Command description.

When the MM 10A;DI is entered, the code at that address is diassembled, and a "?" is displayed. A Carriage Return is then entered to display the next instruction. When the next "?" is seen, the ORA #15 instruction is then entered. If it is followed with an "=" sign as in this case, the machine language and mnemonic of the entered instruction is displayed on the next line but the PC is not incremented. If the "=" is not used, the next location is disassembled and displayed. The last instruction is then entered. The "=" feature is used to read and modify I/O registers. This capability is handy for toggling a bit in a parallel output device, or repetitively viewing an input device. Also the numerical values entered without a $ sign are displayed in decimal but the machine language bytes are converted to hex for installation in memory. The & sign indicates a decimal number.

12-5.5 Command Diagnostics

The HDS-200 has diagnostic capability that enables it to detect various types of errors. When an error is encountered, such as a bad command with extra parameters, an appropriate error message is displayed (see Table 12- 6).

12-5.6 Macro Commands

A **macro** is a sequence of commands that can be defined and saved in memory. They will automatically be executed when the macro name is entered as a command. Macros allow custom commands to be devised by the user. The text of a macro can include the name of another macro (nesting). Macros can be nested to 10 levels deep.

```
HDS-200 Monitor 1.0
Copyright 1982 by Motorola
Self-Test begins
Self-Test ends
6805 P2, 3, 4, 5 Cartridge 1.0
Address Range      I/O     RAM     INTERNAL     EPROM     UNUSED
0000   0007         *
0008   000F                           *
0010   003F                                                  *
0040   007F                           *
0080   00FF                  *
0100   03BF                                                  *
03C0   0787                  *
0788   07F7                                                  *
07F8   07FF                  *

Type HE for help
>
```

FIGURE 12-9 The map display.

12-5.7 Selective Display Format

In many commands, instructions and data can be entered or displayed in a choice of hex, decimal, binary, or ASCII format.

12-6 DEBUGGING WITH THE HDS-200

In the HDS-200, breakpoints, trace, and stop-on-address all use the software interrupt instruction (SWI) to stop program execution. Since an interrupt pushes the contents of the processor registers on the stack, the Stack Pointer (SP) must

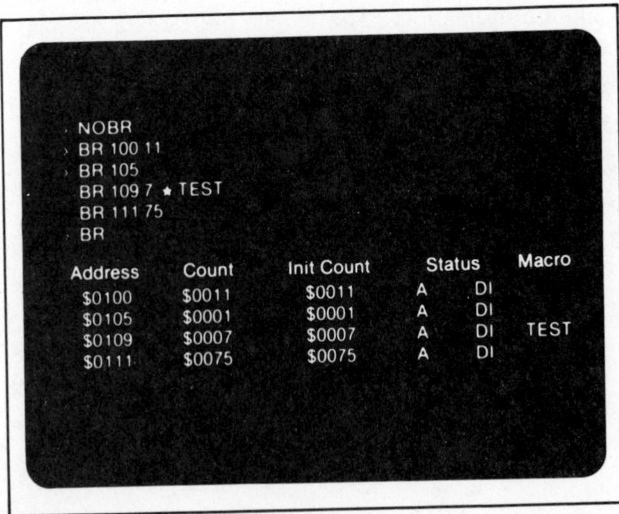

FIGURE 12-10 Memory display modify.

TABLE 12-6 Error Messages

No cartridge	No number
Bad command	Bad digit?
No command	Bad register
Extra parameters	Bad option
String expected	No option
Number expected	Breakpoint exists
Address out of range	Bad place holder
Table full	Library overflow
Too many digits	No such breakpoint

be pointing at a valid stack area in RAM when the interrupt occurs. The SP is set to the top of its range by a RESET or the RSP instruction. Most of the earlier **6805**s use a 7-bit register that defines the address range of the stack. The stack thus occupies the area of memory from $0060 to $007F. Some of the newer **6805**s, such as the **68HC05C4**, have a larger stack area ($C0 to $FF) and also a larger memory area.

12-6.1 Breakpoints

A maximum of 16 breakpoints can be active at any given time. They can be used to check program flow (i.e., a breakpoint can be put in each path of a branch instruction if it is uncertain whether it will branch). Breakpoints can be set at various locations throughout the program; then, when the program reaches a breakpoint, execution of the user's program is stopped and the processor registers are displayed.

An example of setting breakpoints and the resulting display is shown in Fig. 12-11. The first entry, NOBR, causes all existing breakpoints to be deleted. New breakpoints are set at addresses $100, $105, $109, and $111. At $100, $109, and $111 a counter is set at 11, 7, and 75, respectively. The counter is decremented by one each time the breakpoint is passed. When the counter reaches zero, the breakpoint will be executed. Address $109 calls for a macro named "TEST" to be executed after seven cycles. As shown in Fig. 12-11, BR followed by a CR causes a listing of the newly established breakpoints to be displayed.

12-6.2 Prioritized Selected Breakpoints

The breakpoint features of the HDS-200 are extremely versatile. When creating a breakpoint, the user may select a number of options to control what occurs when the breakpoint is reached. Here are some of the actions that may occur.

1. Program halts when it sees an SWI. It determines whether it was a breakpoint or part of the user's program. If the latter, execution is restarted at the address in the SWI vector.
2. Terminal displays user-selected register/memory or other specified information.

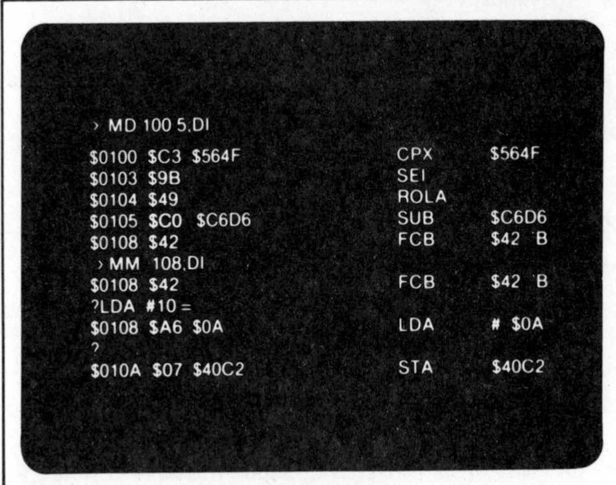

› MD 100 5,DI
$0100 $C3 $564F CPX $564F
$0103 $9B SEI
$0104 $49 ROLA
$0105 $C0 $C6D6 SUB $C6D6
$0108 $42 FCB $42 B
› MM 108,DI
$0108 $42 FCB $42 B
?LDA #10 =
$0108 $A6 $0A LDA # $0A
?
$010A $07 $40C2 STA $40C2

FIGURE 12-11 Breakpoint definition.

3. Specified BRs may be armed or disarmed for a specific number of passes or set to activate on reaching a specified address.
4. One or more user-defined macros (see Section 12-5.6) may be executed.
5. A temporary BR can be used to initiate a one-shot action (e.g., subroutine call, skip forward). After completion of this action it is deleted from the BR table.
6. A chain of selected BRs may be defined and implemented.

12-6.3 Trace Commands

Trace or *run-one-instruction,* as it was previously described, is an effective and commonly used debugging aid. Trace commands cause instructions to be executed, one at a time, starting at any selected program step. After each line of instruction, the processor register contents are displayed and instructions are disassembled, allowing analysis and modifications to be made as required.

The trace feature for the HDS-200 comes in two options:

1. Trace a given number of instructions with a register display after each one.
2. Trace with the display turned off (;NODI).

Both methods are useful for examining the μP registers during program execution. Care must be exercised while using trace, however, since it is easy to generate more register printout than one can reasonably digest. Since the trace feature uses a hardware-generated interrupt, programs in ROM as well as RAM can be traced. The restriction on trace is that the program execution is not in real time. The HDS control program interrupts the program after each instruction so that it can provide a register printout. This is done by substituting SWI for the next instruction to be executed, causing the μP to vector to shared RAM, where it reads the stack, prints the registers, and returns to the user via an RTI instruction.

12-6.4 Stop-On-Address

The Stop-On-Address (SOA) function is useful in determining how a location is inadvertently being changed. SOA substitutes an SWI when the specified address appears on the address bus. It is not necessarily associated with the execution of a specific instruction, as are the two previous techniques. Since it is a function of address, the SOA can also be used as a single breakpoint for a program in ROM. Because it watches the address bus at all times, rather than just during Op code fetches, the SOA will stop the program on fetches of data as well as instructions, but it also halts the μC when the instruction prefetch **(look-ahead)** accesses a selected address.

The restrictions on the use of the SOA are that the μP is not interrupted until after completion of the instruction that accessed the specified location and that unexpected halts may occur due to the operation of certain instructions. The first restriction causes the program counter to indicate the next instruction to be executed after the instruction that accessed the specified location. In most cases, this does not cause a problem. However, if the instruction that caused the halt also caused a change in program flow (such as a branch, JMP, JSR, RTS, or RTI), it may be difficult to determine which instruction caused the halt.

12-6.5 Scope Sync

Associated with the SOA function is a *scope sync* function, which is enabled and disabled by the same HDS control program commands as the SOA. A pulse is generated at the scope trigger point on the rear panel when the addresses match. The scope sync feature triggers an oscilloscope to allow monitoring the waveforms associated with a particular point in the program. The restriction on the scope sync is that unexpected trigger pulses may result. This happens for the same reason as the unexpected stops—the specified address appearing on the bus because of a preceding single-byte instruction.

If a real-time signal is required for monitoring, the **SYNC** command may be used. For example, if the user wants to verify a specific I/O operation at location $0100, a scope is connected to the SYNC terminal on the rear panel and the following is entered: >SYNC 100. If the program is going through a read or write instruction operation at location $0100, a pulse is displayed on the scope. Should the user wish to know if the signal is a read or a write (high or low), the other scope channel can be used to monitor the R/W line of the processor on the emulator module.

12-7 THE HDS-300 HARDWARE DEVELOPMENT SYSTEM

The HDS-300 was introduced in 1985 to support the **6801** and **6809** chips that were formerly supported by the EXORciser as well as the more powerful HCMOS chips that were introduced in 1985. The μPs and μCs initially supported were

a. MC68HC11.
b. MC6809, 6809E.
c. MC6801, 6801U4, 6803, 68120, 68701, 68701U4.
d. MC68705C4 and MC68705C8.

In 1986, support for the **68000** family μPs (**68000, 68010, and 68020**) was added to the HDS-300. These chips were formerly supported by the HDS-400 Emulator System. The emulator modules (pods) for these μPs were slightly redesigned to work on the HDS-300 and new software was developed. Chapter 15 describes these more powerful 16- and 32-bit μPs.

The HDS-300 has the following features:

1. The dual processor concept discussed in Section 12-3, with a **68008** in the control module for the user interface (debugging and host communications) and another μP, of the same type as used in the target, in the emulator pod dedicated to user emulation.
2. Built-in local disk storage, enhancing stand-alone operation.
3. Host and terminal independence, as in the HDS-200.
4. Assembler/Disassembler.
5. Sophisticated macro capability and Macro Edit (ME) command.
6. Input/Output connectors provided for external synchronization of multiple HDS systems.
7. Built in real-time Trace—1K × 64-bit Bus State Monitor (BSM) with the following features:
   a. Disassembly of trace buffer.
   b. Pre- and posttrigger trace capability.
   c. Trigger on 64-bit-wide maskable bit pattern where address can be =, <, or >.
   d. External trigger in/out for operation with other analysis tools.
   e. Trace including multiple user inputs.
   f. Trigger and no halt mode.
   g. Record-only mode.
   h. Histogram performance analysis capability.
   i. Any BSM lines not used by the emulated processor available as probes.

The **68008** chip is part of the 16-bit **68000** family (see Chapter 15). It has an 8-bit data bus and a 20-bit address bus. It provides the benefits of a 32-bit μP architecture for execution of the HDS control program. The **68008** has full code compatibility with the **68000**.

The HDS-300 also has a $5\frac{1}{4}$-inch floppy disk for local storage of the debug monitor programs as well as for saving user's files. Once programs have been developed by the one-line assembler or downloaded from the host, they can be saved and reloaded without redownloading. Thus, while a program is being debugged, the system can be operated independently of the host.

The built-in BSM function adds considerable debugging capability to the HDS-300. This formerly required a separate instrument that was at least as expensive as the emulator itself. Disassembly of the trace buffer is an added capability.

The macro command capability is similar to that provided by the HDS-200 but is more sophisticated. Macro commands can be generated and stored for use throughout the development cycle.

12-7.1 System Functional Description

The HDS control unit interfaces with a host computer, a terminal, and an emulator module. The VME/10, EXORmacs, or EXORcisor development system or almost any other computer such as an IBM-PC may serve as the host computer as long as cross-assembly or cross-compiler software is available. The VME/10 and the IBM-PC can be used as either the terminal or the host computer or both when equipped with the proper software. The terminal provides visual display of command functions as well as entry of data into the HDS-300 through the terminal port. In the transparent mode of operation, the terminal communicates directly with the host computer. The user's program is downloaded into the emulator memory or to the local disk from a host computer.

The control module allows the user to control the operation of the HDS-300 system by use of the HDS-300 executive program. The HDS-300 executive is partially contained in ROM and the remainder is in the software that is loaded from a program diskette. The diskette is unique to the processor being used and the I/O being emulated. Thus, the emulator module and program diskette function together to allow the user to emulate specific HMOS, CMOS, or HCMOS processor parts in the target system.

12-7.2 Integrated Bus Analyzer

Real-time trace is provided in addition to emulation. The HDS-300 user often saves the *trace* activity of the executing target processor in memory. This is done while the user's system is operating in real time so that the information can then be analyzed. The bus analyzer function is enhanced by providing triggering capability based on user-selected conditions (or events) on the processor bus and by disassembly of the traced information. Both hardware and software faults are quickly isolated using the analyzer.

Flexible triggering methods may

a. Initiate or terminate a bus activity trace.
b. Cause emulation to continue or stop as desired.
c. Provide a synchronizing signal to an external instrument.

This function is provided by the integrated BSM. Refer to Section 12-8.4 for a full discussion.

12-7.3 Emulation Memory

Emulation RAM is provided to initially replace the target system's proposed ROM (or EPROM). Assignment of emulation memory in blocks is specified by the user. The standard product has 32K bytes of emulation RAM. Optional memory modules can be used to increase the memory to 64K, 128K, or even 256K bytes. In the process of "mapping" memory, the user may designate blocks of contiguous memory as *write-detected*. This feature applies to emulation RAM only and has no effect on target memory. It allows the detection of writes to locations that will be ROM or EPROM in the final system and should thus be forbidden during testing. The size of the memory blocks depends on the emulator. For the **6801**, **6809**, and **68HC11**, the blocks are 2K bytes.

12-7.4 Local Assembly/Disassembly

The HDS-300 can disassemble the object code in memory, providing the equivalent of assembly language source statements. The instruction cycles captured by the BSM can also be disassembled, making it easier for the programmer to detect problems. Object code can easily be *patched* using the one-line assembler function or the MM command. The assembler and disassembler both can use user-defined local symbols that can be saved in a macro file for later use.

12-7.5 User Interface

Commands, entered by the user, control the HDS-300. The commands are processed and the results are displayed on the terminal screen. The user interface is command line-oriented. All HDS-300 commands have the following format:

command mnemonic [parameters/options]

Some commands require a large number of parameters. For these commands, the full screen editor provided in the HDS-300 is very useful. The commands can be entered in the appropriate places on the various screens.

A **screen** is divided into three regions: the common region, the command region, and the active region. The common region consists of the status line (at the top of the screen), while the command region consists of the last four lines on the screen. Figure 12-12 shows the MENU screen with the elements of the status line identified and the possible options shown. The four command region lines are also explained.

The command region is divided as follows:

a. Error line.
b. Command line.
c. Two lines of available command mnemonics or common syntax.

The status line at the top of the screen shows the status of five basic elements of the HDS-300:

Environment (Env:)

Emulator: (including the μC mode)

Bus State Monitor (BSM:)

Collections:

Macros:

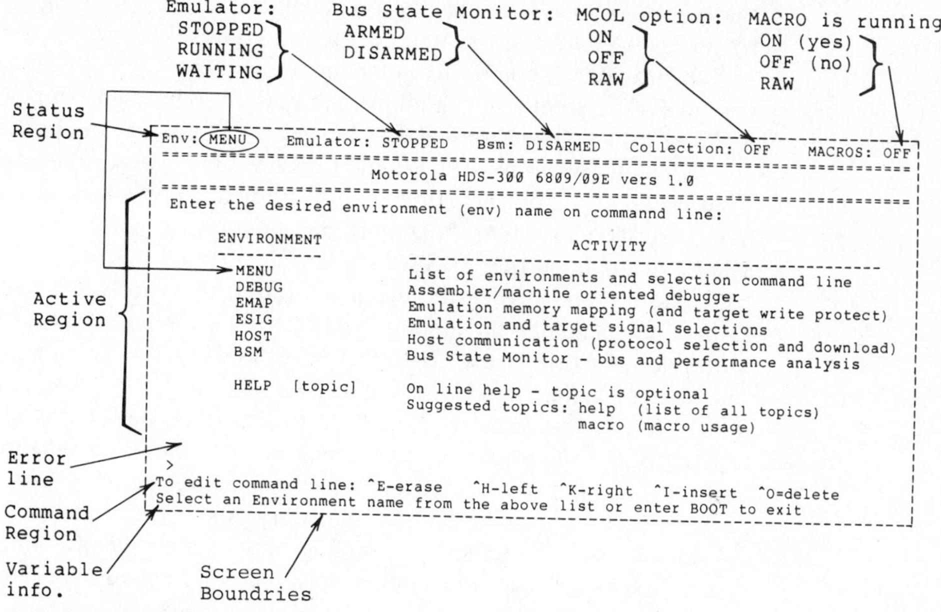

FIGURE 12-12 The menu screen.

The rest of the screen is the *active* region. This area is used for displays responding to the user's commands, such as HELP information, register displays, or bus analysis histograms. For commands using the screen editor, the active region is the area in which the editor operates.

HDS-300 commands are logically grouped into *operating environments* according to the command functions. Each environment controls a specific user activity. The list of environments follows:

MENU	HELP	DEBUG	BSM
MAP	ESIG	HOST	

The BSM in turn is subdivided into the following environments:

BDIS PAN PDIS BCOL

These will all be explained in the following paragraphs. The user enters an environment by typing one of the above mnemonics. The appropriate screen is displayed for each environment, and the associated commands can then be entered.

12-7.6 Control Module Communications

The Control Module includes two fully implemented RS232C serial communications ports. Jumpers are provided so that they can be configured as a DTE (terminal) or a DCE (host). All of the "handshaking" signal lines can be connected for standard interfacing with another RS232 device or they can be internally jumpered "ON" so that they will work with almost any terminal or host. In the HDS-300, the communication parameters for the terminal port are controlled by an eight-section dip switch on the back of the control station cabinet. This switch provides for selection of baud rate, parity, 7 vs 8 bits, or diagnostics ON/OFF. The eighth switch allows the system to be used with either one or two RS232C cables. The terminal and host can be separate devices or combined to communicate over one port. When only one cable is used, the visual feedback on what is happening during a download is limited. The two-cable setup is therefore more user-friendly. The host port parameters are software-controlled by the selections made on the HDS-300s HOST screen.

In one method of design, the proposed system software is developed on a suitable host and downloaded to the HDS-300 for debugging (see Section 12- 10). Motorola S-records are used to transmit the data (see Section 6-9 and 12-10.3). The object program can be loaded into emulation memory and later *saved* on the floppy disk or downloaded directly to the disk. To do the download, the HOST environment is entered, the communications parameters compatible with the host are selected, and a method of *flow control* is determined. The parameters are initially set for 9600 baud, 8-bits, no parity, and 1 stop bit.

Flow control is a method of stopping transmission when a buffer is full or the disk is not ready. The flow control selected will depend on a number of factors, mostly hardware-related.

In the HDS-300, the HOST screen references four methods of flow control:

a. ACK/NAK
b. X-ON/X-OFF
c. CTS/RTS
d. DTR/DSR

The first two use ASCII characters with appropriate software and the last two use hardware connections to the CTS pin of the serial communications chip. In one case the RTS line is connected to the CTS pin, and in the other DTR is connected to that pin. These hardware methods depend on the logic in the communications chip or driver software to inhibit transmission when CTS is not true. The hardware methods will not work with modems because CTS is not transmitted through to the other end. In the HDS-300, flow control is initially set for ACK/NAK.

The four methods of flow control are as follows:

ACK/NAK This makes use of the ASCII control characters designated for this function (see Section 12-10.1). As each S-record is received, it is checked for the proper checksum. If it checks, an ACK is returned. Otherwise, a NAK is sent. A special program must be written for the host to provide this protocol. The manual lists a Pascal and a **68000** assembly language version of a compatible ACK/NAK program called SACK.

X-ON/X-OFF This protocol also uses ASCII control characters. These characters are commonly used in many systems to stop and start transmission of data. Most often they are used to stop the scrolling of the CRT displays when dumping a file to the screen. If the host is properly equipped to respond to the X-OFF (and X-

ON), S-records can be transmitted at rates up to 9600 baud (or more) without error.

CTS/RTS This is a hardware method of flow control and uses the RS232C standard feature that stops data transmission when the CTS signal line is taken false. Either the host hardware must use a communications chip like the **6850** ACIA that has built-in logic to inhibit transmission when CTS is not TRUE, or the software must be written to sense that condition and stop transmission. This CTS method reacts quickly but cannot be used over modem circuits because the CTS status is not transmitted to the distant end of a telephone circuit.

DTR/DSR This is the same as CTS/RTS but it uses different wires to carry the signal. It must still connect to the communications chip in the same way. Most likely it will also connect to the CTS pin in the host serial port circuitry.

12-8 SYSTEM PREPARATION

When starting a development, the prototype hardware, if any exists, and the HDS-300 system with the appropriate emulator are connected together. To prepare the HDS-300 for use it must first be configured for the terminal and host that have been selected. This includes the hardware jumpering for the proper RS232C interfaces as well as menu selections. The terminal port is entirely controlled by switches and jumpers, while the host port parameters, except for the RS232C jumpering, are software-selectable on the HOST screen. Other menus are selected and typed entries are used to set up the desired address map, enable the desired μP control inputs, and determine the BSM collection parameters.

12-8.1 The MAP Environment

The MAP environment is used to enable emulation memory in place of the user's system RAM or ROM before the user's system is functioning. During the development stage, emulation memory can be very useful. It can be employed to write small test programs for performing READ/WRITE tests of the I/O or other special routines. Emulation RAM can be write-protected to emulate ROM. Termination of code execution on write detection can be enabled. A write to target or user's system RAM can be detected, but the memory cannot be protected. If the system hardware is complete, the emulation memory can take the place of the user's ROM for program development. Emulation memory is not in the user's final product.

12-8.2 ESIG (Enable Signals)

The **ESIG** environment is used to disable or enable the control inputs to the μP being emulated. Disabling may be necessary during the development stage. For instance, before or during the debug of an interrupt routine, the interrupt line may have to be disabled.

The ESIG environment allows the user to specify whether the clock source is from the emulator or the target system. When the program moves data from emulation memory to the target I/O, or vice versa, separate clocks cannot be used. One or the other must be enabled. Other special emulator-specific selections are also made. For example, when using the **6809** emulator pod, the **6809** μP or the **6809E** μP must be specified.

The inputs to the μP are enabled only while executing the user's code. When execution is stopped, all inputs are disabled. This may tend to produce some unusual results in the user's system. For example, disabling the RESET input disconnects it from the emulator μP, but the rest of the user's system still responds when RESET is asserted.

12-8.3 Macros

The HDS-300 development system is greatly enhanced by its powerful macro capability. This enhancement is important in hardware development. Macros can be used to execute repetitive events, to create special commands, or to produce output in the user's specified format. Macros are created from scratch by using the Macro EDit (MED) command or by turning on the *Macro COLlection* (MCOL) capability during normal emulator operation. During the course of a debug session each typed command is temporarily listed on the debug screen. If the MCOL feature is turned on prior to a debug session, these commands are automatically *collected* and placed in a file on the disk for later retrieval. The file can be edited for more orderly operation and used in later debugging sessions.

12-8.4 Bus State Monitor (BSM)

The BSM is a highly useful HDS-300 feature. It allows the user to examine the state of the buses on a cycle-by-cycle basis but does not show signal setup and hold times. The BSM monitors 63 lines that include the address, data, and control lines of the μP being emulated. Eight of the 63 lines are available to connect into the user's system at various points that the user may want to monitor.

A **trigger** event is established when the inputs on the 63 lines match a pattern determined by using the BCOL and Bus EVent (BEV) screens. The BEV screen concerns bus event definitions. The template allows the use to specify three areas: signal selection, address, and data. Each line can be selected to be 1, 0, or don't care (X) to cause the trigger event.

The HDS-300 contains a 1K word by 63 bit memory and acts like a logic analyzer. It can be set up to record or halt when a trigger event occurs. It records the status of the 63 lines for each of 1024 processor cycles. The BCOL screen allows the trigger point to be exactly specified anywhere in the 1024-cycle range.

Two counters are used to position the trigger event in the execution of the user's code. The *Event Counter* is initialized to select the occurrence of the trigger event to be viewed. The *PostTrigger counter* is then used to position the trigger event inside the 1K-deep Trace History RAM. Thus, the trigger event can be placed at the beginning of the display, anywhere in the middle, or at the end.

This allows the user to examine the status of the μP and its program operation in the vicinity of the trigger address. The BSM can also be used to HALT the execution of the program on detecting a specific condition so that the user can enter the DEBUG environment and examine registers or memory. The trace mode can also be used to examine the program on a step-by-step basis.

The BSM is set up while in the Bus COLlection (**BCOL**) environment, and the Trace History RAM is viewed through the Bus DISplay (**BDIS**) environment. BDIS has many codes of display: raw, disassembled, or mixed. They are selected by appropriate subcommands. The Search Filter Pattern (SFP) and Set Search Pattern (SSP) subcommands allow selection of a filter pattern (masking certain bits) and searching with it.

12-8.5 System Debugging

In testing the hardware, it is necessary to determine the proper control words and addresses as well as the correct wiring. The HDS-300 is very useful in helping to verify that these items are correct. This can be illustrated by the following example for the **6801** emulator.

EXAMPLE 12-4

Port 3 of the **6801U4** has an Input Strobe line called IS3. It can be programmed to cause an interrupt when strobed by an external device. The interrupt is then used to input the data to the port. Write a test program to confirm the operation.

SOLUTION
The program follows:

```
F810 0E         CLI                 Clear the interrupt mask
F811 86 40      LDAA    #$40        Get the control word
F813 97 0F      STAA    $0F         Write it to the register
F815 CE F800    LDX     #$F800      Get the vector address
F818 FF FFF8    STX     $FFF8       Put it in the IRQ1 vector location
F81B 20 FE      BRA     $F81B       Branch on self

                ORG     $F800
F800 7E F000    JMP     $F000       Go to service routine

                ORG     $F000
F000 4A         DECA
F001 20 FD      BRA     $F000       Give it a little work looping
```

The HDS-300 is set up as follows:

a. Select the **6801U4** and enable IRQ in the ESIG environment.
b. Enter RESET command to establish the correct memory map.
c. Enter MAP to verify the memory locations.
d. Enter the program using the ASM command of the DEBUG environment.
e. Set a breakpoint at $F000.

f. GO to address $F810 (screen shows "RUNNING").
g. Ground the IS3 line (pin 39) of target plug. (Connect the BSM black clip to it.)
h. Program stops at breakpoint.
i. Clear the interrupt by reading the Status Register at $0F and then reading the port 3 Data Register.

When the RESET command is entered, after the **6801U4** is selected, it selects the proper memory map and write-protects the area from $F000 to $FFFF. Thus this program will not work since it will be unable to write the vector at $FFF8. Because this is just a test program, however, the write detect flag on the ESIG screen can be disabled. Alternatively, the vector can be entered manually using the ME command and the appropriate lines deleted from the program.

When the program is executed by the GO command it sets up (initializes) the proper conditions and then loops on itself indefinitely until the IS3 line is grounded. When that occurs, the processor fetches the vector address ($F800) and goes there. It in turn JMPs the program to the "service routine" at $F000 and the breakpoint is triggered. The screen displays it.

12-8.6 Performance Analysis (PAN)

After the more obvious software faults are corrected by patching the object code as described in Section 12-4.9 or reediting the source and redownloading a revised program, it may be necessary to use the *trace capture* or *histograms* to refine the program. To do this requires setting up the *events* on the BEV screen and viewing the results on the BDIS or PDIS screen. The BSM is also used to provide performance analysis data, as described in the next section.

Thus, it can be seen that almost all of the various *environments* will be used in the course of a μC system development, and the features provided are all very helpful in finding and correcting the problems typically found.

The **Performance ANalysis (PAN)** feature of the HDS-300 provides a tool for optimizing user code by showing graphically where the code is spending its time and thus highlighting bottlenecks. When the PAN screen (or environment) is called up, as shown in Fig. 12-13, it allows specification of the parameters for a *memory activity analysis session*. For details of this feature, the reader is advised to study the manuals cited in Section 12-13.

12-8.7 Invasive versus Noninvasive Analysis

Memory activity analysis is performed using the BSM. While user code is executing, the BSM records bus cycles of interest for the analysis. The user can choose **noninvasive** mode, which means that the user code continues to execute between BSM samples (i.e., does not interfere with normal operation), or **invasive** mode, which means that the user code is halted between samples. Noninvasive mode provides a snapshot view of target execution, whereas invasive mode provides a comprehensive analysis.

```
Env: PAN      Emulator: STOPPED  Bsm: ARMED      Collection: OFF    MACROS: OFF
================================================================================
                        Memory Activity Analysis Setup
================================================================================

     ----------------- Address Ranges and Divisions --------------------
                       (up to 16 divisons in total)

Saddr Eaddr Div     Saddr Eaddr Div     Saddr Eaddr Div     Saddr Eaddr Div
0000  0000  04      0000  0000  04      0000  0000  04      0000  0000  04
----  ----  --      ----  ----  --      ----  ----  --      ----  ----  --
----  ----  --      ----  ----  --      ----  ----  --      ----  ----  --
----  ----  --      ----  ----  --      ----  ----  --      ----  ----  --

Halt the emulator between samples: ( @ ) No ( - ) Yes

Analyzed cycles: ( @ ) Instructions    ( - ) Use BEV event definition

        Select PDIS environment before issuing G (go) command

 >
Commands:  ^U=up (to edit)   UNDO [;d]     PROC
Marked (inverse video or asterisked) fields have been edited, but not processed
```

FIGURE 12-13 The PAN screen.

12-8.8 The PDIS Screen

The **PDIS** screen (shown in Fig. 12-14) displays the results of PAN memory activity analysis. As user code is executing, it is analyzed in the mode specified in the PAN subenvironment, and the results are displayed as a **histogram**. Module address ranges are listed along the vertical axis. The total number of samples for each module is displayed as an absolute number and as a percentage of the total samples. The percentage is also displayed graphically as a histogram along the horizontal axis.

12-9 SOURCE LEVEL DEBUGGING

A new concept in software debugging introduced with the HDS-300 is called *Source Level Debugging* (SLD). With the stand-alone version of the HDS-300 and other recent development systems, the option of using *disassembly* was provided so that programmers could see the program displayed in assembler mnemonics instead of machine language. Now, with so many programs being written in higher-level languages such as "C," it is appropriate to display them as *C language source statements*. Unfortunately, the art has not progressed to the point where the machine language can be disassembled into these statements directly, but a technique has been developed whereby the statements can be downloaded along with the machine language and displayed together. In fact, one mode (the FD mode) is provided in which the disassembled machine language instructions are displayed along with the associated C language source statements. The limitation of this method is that, once a program bug has been found and the machine language is patched, the source statements will no longer match.

```
Env: PDIS     Emulator: STOPPED    Bsm: ARMED      Collection: OFF     MACROS: OFF
================================================================================
  Range    Samples   %  0    10   20   30   40   50   60    70    80    90   100
0000 0FFF     5120 100  **********************************************************
1000 1FFF        0   0
2000 2FFF        0   0
3000 3FFF        0   0
4000 4FFF        0   0
5000 5FFF        0   0
6000 6FFF        0   0
7000 7FFF        0   0
8000 8FFF        0   0
9000 9FFF        0   0
A000 AFFF        0   0
B000 BFFF        0   0
C000 CFFF        0   0
D000 DFFF        0   0
E000 EFFF        0   0
F000 FFFF        0   0
  Total       5120 100% of    5120 samples

 >      SO   CLR
To edit command line: ^E-erase   ^H-left  ^K-right  ^I-insert  ^O=delete
```

FIGURE 12-14 The PDIS screen.

The solution is that if the patched code fixes the problem, the high-level C source should be corrected and recompiled and then redownloaded to continue the debugging.

Another innovation is the use of the HDS-300 with Motorola's release of AT&T's **UNIX** Operating System 5. This software product is available for use with the EXORmacs, VME10, and PC68000 products. The latter is a plug-in module for the IBM-PC that is used with the System V/68 software to provide a high-performance dual processor system for software development. Any of the three systems can be used as a host for the HDS-300 with the software described in the following paragraphs.

Combined with a System V/68 host, the HDS-300 provides high-level software development as well as hardware emulation and development support for a large range of Motorola μPs. Full control over the target processor is provided from the System V/68 host. Full symbolic debug, in both assembly language and C language, is supported. This is accomplished through use of a high-speed communication protocol between the hosted software and the HDS-300 station. The execution of the HDS-300 software will appear to be very similar to the standalone execution described in the HDS-300 Hardware Development Station Operations Manuals (see Section 12-13).

The term **hosted** describes the use of a host computer to control the HDS-300 rather than just a terminal. The two systems are linked via a standard RS232C serial cable. The terminal is connected directly to the host. The *hosted* software is then loaded into the user's host computer, and an SLD diskette is booted by the HDS-300 when its power is turned on. After the terminal configuration and initialization files have been executed, the main menu appears and commands can be entered.

12-9.1 Features of SLD

Among the features of the hosted version of the HDS-300 is the *Source Level Debug (SLD)* environment. This high-level tool is a window-based debugging aid that allows full symbolic debug of source code written in the C language. Assembly language is also fully supported symbolically. The FD command will simultaneously show the C statement and the corresponding machine language code.

The features of SLD include the following:

Set breakpoints at source line, function, or physical address.

Examine variables in a window. Set variables.

Single-step execution, free-running execution.

Restart execution from beginning of application.

Display dynamic function nesting.

Scroll source windows.

Display intermixed source and disassembly.

Escape to system.

These features are additions to the capabilities of the stand-alone version of the HDS-300. The capabilities of the stand-alone version are fully supported, with the exception of several of the off-line utilities such as Format and Backup. Refer to the HDS-300 hardware development station operations manual for a description of the off-line utilities.

12-9.2 Requirements

To use the SLD and the hosted version of the HDS-300, certain hardware and software requirements exist. The hardware requirements are

a. A **68000**-based host computer with at least 512K user memory. The HDS-300 program requires at least 350K of user memory to run. The user's system must be able to support programs using this amount of memory.
b. Approximately 1/2 Mb of disk space to store the HDS-300 program and its associated files.
c. An HDS-300 with emulator.
d. An RS232C cable to connect between the host computer and the station.
e. A terminal that meets the HDS-300 minimum requirements.
f. One serial port on the host computer, configured as follows: 8 data bits, 1 stop bit, no parity, and 9600 baud.

The software requirements are

a. System V/68 Release 2 Version 1.0 or later.
b. A C compiler, assembler, and linker capable of generating a Common Object File Format (COFF) file for the target processor.
c. The hosted software package consisting of seven files.

12-9.3 General Description

SLD is a window-based debugger that allows a user to view and manipulate the target system via source language. Single lines may be stepped, breakpoints set, and variables displayed and set. These functions may be accomplished using the source level language syntax. The windowing feature is supported on any terminal that can be used with the HDS-300.

12-9.4 Windows

The context of the execution is always on display within the source window. This allows the user to maintain a perspective on the execution that is unattainable with a debugger that shows only the next line to be executed. In addition, the user may choose to view other files (i.e., header files where constants have been defined). Any textual file may be viewed from within the SLD.

Within the source window, two cursors may be displayed: an *execution* cursor, which indicates the next source line to be executed, and a *browse* cursor, which indicates the current line of interest.

In addition to the source window, two other windows may be opened. One window displays the values of user-specified variables. A command log window displays the results of several of the commands.

All of the three possible windows (source, variable, and command log) may be scrolled. This allows a larger viewing area than can be displayed on the screen at any one time.

12-9.5 Variables

Variables can be displayed at any time to check on the state of the program being debugged. In addition to viewing a variable a single time, the SLD provides a variable display window that permits an updated display of selected variables. This means that the user need not be constantly requesting a display of a particular variable; its updated value is displayed every time the user target program halts.

Variables may be viewed in any manner acceptable to the source language. For example, in C a character can be displayed as an integer (in hex, octal, decimal, or binary). Conversely, an integer can be viewed as a character. Structured variables and multidimensional arrays are displayed in their entirety with the elements labeled appropriately. Variables with variable indices may also be displayed. When viewing objects of pointers, if the pointer value changes, the display reflects the new object value.

12-9.6 Source Code References

References to positions within the source code (as in setting a breakpoint or moving the browse cursor) can be made by line number or address, or by referring to a function name or a source module with a line number.

12-10 HOST COMPUTER COMMUNICATIONS

The advent of hardware development systems like the HDS-200 and HDS-300 has placed new emphasis on communications between computers. The HDS can be operated in a stand-alone mode (without a host) to execute instructions and exercise the target hardware, but all test programs must be written in machine language or generated by the one-line assemblers. Some complete user programs may be written in this way, but full-size programs are usually produced on a *host* computer and *downloaded* to the HDS. Motorola provides software to do this with certain Motorola hosts. There is a need to communicate with a growing number of non-Motorola computers, primarily those classed as personal computers or PCs, and in some cases with PCs or mainframes via modems.

To be useful as a host, a computer must be able to generate the μC's object code and have a communications program available to transmit it to the HDS. This program must be more than a terminal emulator because the object program to be transmitted is usually in a disk file. The communications program must be able read the disk and send the object file to the HDS via its serial port.

A number of third-party suppliers are now making assemblers or compilers that run on PCs or mainframe computers. These programs will produce object code for many Motorola processors. Fortunately, the Motorola S-record concept can be used to download the object codes to the HDSs. Also, since S-records are implemented in ASCII-hex characters, most systems have a terminal program that will transmit them.

The two HDS systems both have two RS232C ports for communicating with a terminal and a host computer. They also have a Transparent Mode (TM) command similar to that in other Motorola Monitor ROMs for use with the two-port configuration. This is shown for the HDS-300 in Fig. 12-15 as configuration #1. It is also possible to communicate and download through the host port with one cable, as shown in configuration #2, but the feedback on the screen is not as helpful.

A number of items are involved in this communication process:

1. The ASCII standard.
2. The RS232 standard.
3. The Motorola S-Record standard.
4. Methods of Flow Control.
5. Transmission protocols.
6. Baud rate conventions.
7. The host's communication port requirements.
8. Terminal communications programs.

12-10.1 The ASCII Standard

The ASCII standard is described in Section 8-7.1 and the character codes are shown in Appendix E. The American Standard Code for Information Interchange (ASCII) has been adopted by nearly all computer and terminal manufacturers.

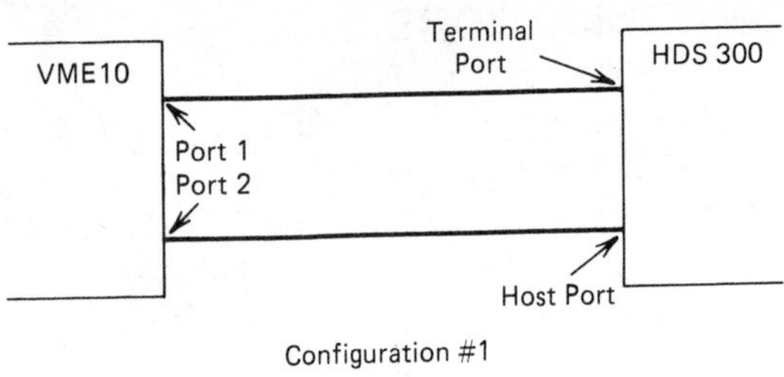

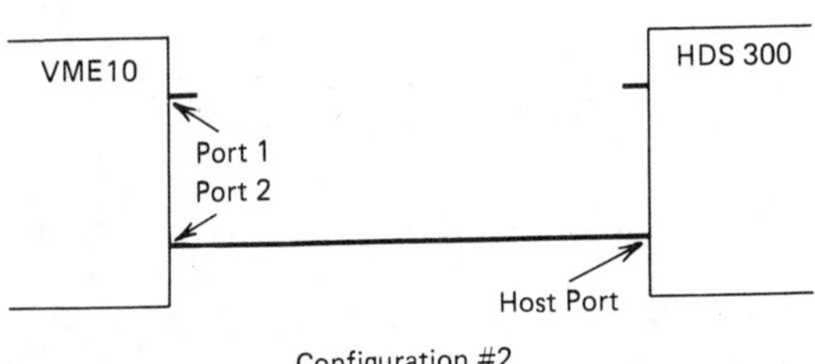

FIGURE 12-15 HDS-300/VME10 system configuration.

Some characters of special interest for communications use are ACK, NAK, DC1, and DC3. They are specifically for use in data transmission and flow control. **Flow control** is the name given to methods used to stop and restart transmission to avoid overflow of the buffers and/or disk files and consequent loss of data.

12-10.2 The RS232C Standard

RS232C describes the hardware interface that has been adopted as the standard for use between terminals and computers (see Section 8-9.2). It is also used for computer-to-computer communications. RS232C defines cable pin numbers and signal levels. A de facto standard connector has also been adopted. Originally this standard was designed to work with modems, and thus several *handshaking* signals are involved. These signals can be a source of confusion, particularly when modems are not needed.

The standard specifies two interfaces: Data Terminal Equipment (DTE) and Data Communications Equipment (DCE). The use of DTE to describe a terminal should be easily understood, but it should be noted that any device that is intended to talk to a terminal must be connected as a DCE (i.e., a *modem* or a *host* computer). Also, when one computer talks to another directly (without modems), one must be connected as a terminal (DTE) and the other as a modem (DCE).

Figure 12-16 shows the full implementation (for asynchronous systems). It is seen that terminals normally send signals on the Request To Send (RTS) and Data Terminal Ready (DTR) lines and receive signals on Clear To Send (CTS), Data Carrier Detect (DCD), and Data Set Ready (DSR) lines. Both configurations have a Transmit Data (TD) line and a Receive Data (RD) line. A signal ground between the devices is also necessary, but a chassis ground through the cable is not because all equipment of this type requires grounds through the power cord. Thus the RS232C cable for asynchronous communications only needs wires on pins 2, 3, 4, 5, 6, 7, 8, and 20.

Not all signals are implemented in many systems; in fact, the only ones really necessary are TD, RD, and a ground. However, many systems use some or all of the other lines to provide helpful error messages or to control the system. This is known as **handshaking**. CTS, for example, is intended to inhibit transmission of data when false, and a false DCD inhibits reception in proper RS232C implementations. DTR is sometimes used to "disconnect" calls. DSR is required by some driver software but is not always used.

With such a variety of ways to connect equipment, most good systems either use all signals or provide a way to force them to be *true* with jumpers so the system will work. This is the case with the HDS-300. For example, CTS, DSR, DCD, and even RI (Ring Indicator) can be jumpered to be *true* in case the signal is

DTE (Terminal)			DCE HOST or MODEM
2	**TXD**	→	2
3	**RXD**	←	3
4	**RTS**	→	4
5	**CTS**	←	5
8	**DCD**	←	8
7	**GROUND**		7
6	**DSR**	←	6
20	**DTR**	→	20

A Terminal		A Host	
Sends	**RTS**	Sends	**CTS**
	DTR		**DCD**
			DCR
	TxD		**RxD**
Senses	**CTS**	Senses	**RTS**
	DCD		**DTR**
	DSR		**TxD**
	RxD		

CTS inhibits transmission when false.
DCD inhibits reception when false.
DSR is seldom used by most systems.

FIGURE 12-16 RS232C standard.

not implemented from the other end. Ring Indicator is used only in automatic answering systems.

Lines other than 2, 3, 4, 5, 6, 7, 8, and 20 need not and probably should not be connected, since some equipment uses them for nonstandard purposes. Many of these other lines do have RS232C standard uses in synchronous systems.

12-10.3 The Motorola S-Record Standard

The S-Record concept has been used by Motorola since the days of MIKBUG (1974) to move data between systems (this is described in Section 6-9). The binary 8-bit data is converted into printable ASCII-hex characters since they can be transmitted through any serial link even though it is only capable of handling 7-bit transmissions. Both *byte counts* and *checksums* are used to ensure integrity. The S-record concept has been used in almost all Motorola Monitor ROMs, assemblers, compilers, and linkers. Unfortunately, some differences exist in the various implementations of S-records. The standard is shown in Appendix A of the HDS-300 operations manual (M68HDS30M/D2) as well as in most Motorola software manuals. All of the versions are consistent in the use of the 1s complement checksum on each S-Record and the use of the address to load the data in the proper place. Differences exist in the treatment of the "S9" record and carriage returns and linefeeds. The proper implementation, as done in EXbug and all of the MDOS 8-bit software, was to use byte count and checksum in the S9 record also (i.e., l/f S9030000FC c/r). Some assemblers replace the four 0s in the S9 record with the program entry address, in which case the checksum is appropriately calculated.

Note that the S-record concept uses two ASCII characters to generate each 8-bit byte of (binary) data, so 7-bit transmission (with or without parity) will work. Eight-bit transmission (with bit 8 = 0) is also usable.

Because of the lack of standardization in some S-record programs, it may be necessary to edit them or write a conversion program to add or delete carriage returns or linefeeds on each line. Generally a CR is required after each checksum. Linefeeds are not required but they help to make the records readable on the screen or printer. The loader programs will generally ignore all characters after a CR until the next capital S, but characters can be edited out if they are not included in the byte count or checksum.

12-10.4 Methods of Flow Control

With disks and finite-sized buffers involved, the need for flow control should be obvious. In some cases, if the data rate is slowed below 2400 baud, the download may be successful without flow control. This lower rate is automatic when using most modems since they operate at 300 or 1200 baud. Modems for 4800 or 9600 baud are rarely used because they are expensive and synchronous protocol is necessary.

Many large systems such as UNIX, CPM, MSDOS, and VERSAdos 4.4 use X-ON/X-OFF (also known as control-Q and control-S or DC1 and DC3). The

HDS-200 can be configured to use it, as can VERSAdos 4.3. In most systems X-ON/X-OFF stops and starts the data (which solves the buffer overflow problem) but the loader does not always test the checksum. On the other hand, ACK/NAK, as implemented in the HDS-300, also does a checksum on each record. The software for both X-ON/X-OFF and ACK/NAK is built into the HDS-300 but in the case of ACK/NAK it is necessary to provide software in the host to work with it. The HDS-300 Operations Manual includes two program listings (in Appendix C) for a program called SACK. This is provided in Pascal and in **68000** assembly language and can be added to VDOS 4.3 or any other computer. This ACK/NAK is not compatible with the XMODEM program described below.

12-10.5 Baud Rate Conventions

The standard baud rates go from 50 to 38,400, but not all systems are equipped with all these rates. 110 baud is used for teletypewriters (TTYs), but 300, 1200, 2400, 4800, and 9600 are now the most common. The lower rates are normally used only when modems are involved. 9600 is the most common for local (in the same room) systems. These circuits also use asynchronous transmission. When modems are used at rates above 1200 or 2400 baud, synchronous operation is necessary. This requires special software not commonly used in any Motorola products.

12-10.6 The Host's Communications Port Requirements

When setting up a link for downloading it is necessary to make sure the host can satisfy all the requirements. Typically all computers have RS232C ports and can be configured for the proper baud rates, parity, bits per character, and stop bits. (The TTY is the only terminal that uses 2 stop bits.) Parity is not necessary, but is added insurance against errors, and 7-bit *even* parity is quite common. UNIX uses it by default, for example. Typically, IBM or DEC computers, as well as those with CPM, UNIX, or even VERSAdos, can handle X-ON/X-OFF, so it is the preferred flow control method.

Whether the host uses CTS, DCD, DSR, or combinations of them varies with the driver program in use. VERSAdos, for example, communicates (using CONNECT) without DSR being true, but the COPY command requires it.

12-10.7 Terminal Communications Programs

Most computer systems are equipped with *Terminal Emulation* software so that they can be used as a terminal to talk to a remote system. Not all of them can dump out files from the disk or read them into the disk, however. Some of the better known programs are

1. CONNECT for VERSAdos.
2. The VERSAdos Tool Kit (includes CONNECT for UNIX).
3. CU for UNIX.
4. TRANSFER for EXORset.

5. DOWNLOAD PROMs for EXORcisers.
6. XMODEM for CPM or MS-DOS systems.
7. KERMIT for IBM-PC and others.
8. MITE for KAYPRO (with XModem).

The last three are not Motorola programs but are used by many other computer systems.

It is usually necessary for a communications program to be able to do two things in order to *download* object code for use in an HDS. First, it must be able to *emulate* a terminal to talk to the HDS for the purpose of setting up and testing the communications path and setting up the remote system to send the object files. Second, it must be able to read the file from the disk and transmit S-records with some method of flow control. These two functions are frequently done with separate programs, but some terminal software does both.

CONNECT was originally developed for VERSAdos and can be used in the VME10 for HDS systems. It causes the keyboard and screen of the VME10 to be connected to one port of the VME400 Serial Module and allows the other port to remain connected to the VERSAdos Operating System. The CONNECT command provides only communications, and the COPY command of VERSAdos must be used to move data through the port (i.e., COPY filename.ext,#).

For UNIX-based VEM10s the VERSAdos Tool Kit contains the BUILDS program for generating S-records from COFF files. CONNECT provides communications and terminal emulation. The UNIX command *cat* can be used by redirecting it to the files (i.e., cat < filename) for downloading.

KERMIT is a terminal emulation and file transfer program provided by Columbia University Center for Computing Activities. It is placed in the public domain for free use (it cannot be sold). It has been adapted to many different computers. A copy for use with the IBM-PC is available. Kermit can be used as a terminal communications program with a separate ACK/NAK routine (written in BASIC) for downloading. Because it is written in BASIC, this routine is easily adaptable to other computers. For file transferring with KERMIT's protocol, a copy of KERMIT is required in both the sending and receiving computers; since this is not available for the HDS-300, only terminal emulation is provided in this case.

XMODEM is a universal standard program used by thousands of CPM systems since 1977. It employs a specific protocol known as "Ward Christensen's Protocol" for actual data transfer. It includes terminal emulation to allow control of file transferring. It uses the standard ACK/NAK characters but also does block numbering and checksum or Cyclical Redundancy Checking (CRC) on each 128-byte block. It does retries in the event of error, so it is extremely reliable. Perfect results are easily achieved. Many other systems such as Kaypro's MITE also use this protocol, and it is available in several programs for the IBM-PC using MS-DOS.

XMODEM cannot be used with HDS-300 because the built-in ACK/NAK for that system does not do block counting or checksum on blocks.

12-11 SUMMARY

The new concept of the Hardware Development System (HDS) was introduced and the two models by Motorola were described. This included explanations of Bus State Monitors, the new techniques of Source Level Debugging, and the new emphasis on computer communications brought on by these new products.

12-12 GLOSSARY

ACK An ASCII character ($06) assigned to ACKnowledge a correct transmission.

Assembler Program used to convert programmer's mnemonics to machine language.

BCOL Screen or environment for the HDS-300 used to define the collection of bus data into a macro file.

BDIS Screen or environment for the HDS-300 used to display the data collected by the BSM.

Breakpoint Feature of debugging systems used to stop the execution of a program at a specific address.

Bus State Monitor (BSM) Device to record the status of all the signal lines of the μP buses for each cycle of instructions.

Capture Process of recording or saving the status of signals or data in memory.

Command Instruction to a computer.

Configuration Description, software selection, or diagram defining the selections of options in a computer system.

CRT (Cathode Ray Tube) terminal Data terminal with a TV-like screen.

Debugging Process of finding and eliminating "bugs" in hardware or software.

Diagnostics Type of program used to test hardware or systems.

Disassembler Program that converts machine language back into the mnemonics that were used to generate it.

Download Move a file via a transmission path from a remote computer to the local computer.

Edit Use an editor utility program to create or modify another program.

Emulation RAM Memory in an emulator system used to hold programs while testing newly developed hardware.

Emulator Device or software used to duplicate the operation of another device.

Environment Situation or condition created to allow certain activities. It is set up by entering a command such as DEBUG in the HDS-300. This then permits Memory Display (MD), Register Display (RD), or many other subcommands to be entered.

ESIG Screen or environment in the HDS-300 where the external signals can be enabled or disabled (i.e., made active or not active).

Event Something that occurs when conditions are correct.

EXBUG ROM-based control program for the EXORciser that contains debugging and utility subroutines.

EXORciser Microcomputer Development System (MDS) built by Motorola to aid in the development of μP systems using the **6800** or **6809** μPs.

EXORMACS **68000** microcomputer system built by Motorola.

Family interface module (FIM) Module that contains all of the common circuitry for a family of emulator pods.

Flow control Technique of stopping and starting the transmission of data to avoid overflowing a buffer or exceeding the rate of acceptance of a disk system.

Handshaking Use of signal lines to enable or control the transfer of data between two data storage devices.

Hardware development station (HDS) System concept to aid in the development of μC systems. It uses personality pods to accommodate the different μC types.

HELP One of the screens or environments of an HDS system.

Histogram Graphics-displayed bar chart commonly used in μC development systems to show the relative amounts of time used to perform tasks.

Host Computer used for software development or as a source of data for another.

Hosted Version of software that allows one computer to be controlled by another.

Invasive Interfering with or delaying the normal operation of a computer; term used to describe software or functions.

Language Term to distinguish between a group of expressions or methods used to generate machine language for a computer. BASIC, PASCAL, C, and FORTRAN are examples of high-level languages; ASSEMBLY language is provided by the μP manufacturer for each μP.

Linker Program used with compilers and assemblers to combine object modules and generate a load module for specific addresses.

Look-ahead Feature of the **6800** family μPs in which the instruction at the next address is fetched while the current one is being processed. Also known as Instruction Prefetch.

Macro Collection of instructions that can be customized and executed like a single instruction.

Map Screen or environment where the μP memory map to be used can be selected.

MDS Microcomputer Development System.

MENU Screen or environment that can be called up by a command.

Metacode Shorthand method of defining a program.

Mnemonics English-like instructions used by the programmer to specify the functions of a software program.

MODEM (MOdulator/DEModulator) Device used to convert digital signals to audio tones for transmission over a telephone channel, or vice versa. Most modems are full duplex and convert signals in both directions simultaneously.

NAK An ASCII character ($15 hex) used to indicate an error in transmission (“Not AcKnowledged”).

Noninvasive Not interfering with the normal operation of a computer system.

One-line assembler Command that permits entries of mnemonics and deposits the appropriate machine language in memory.

PAN Performance ANalysis. Screen or environment that permits specification of the parameters for a memory activity analysis (see PDIS).

Patching Method of modifying the machine language of an object program without reassembling or recompiling it.

PC Personal Computer, Printed Circuit board, or Program Counter.

PDIS Screen or environment that displays the results of memory activity analysis. Code is analyzed in the mode specified by the PAN screen, and the results are displayed as a histogram (see PAN).

Performance analysis Display of relative times for user code to perform tasks.

Personality pod Another name for an Emulator Module for a specific μC.

Protocol Format or prescribed procedure.

Prototype Hand-made model of a system destined for production.

Screen CRT display that is formatted in a prescribed way.

Source Level Debugger (SLD) Technique used to display a program in mnemonic form and allow single-statement execution.

STOP Emulator command used to stop execution of a user's program.

SYNC Command in the HDS-200 used to set up an address to trigger an external device.

Template Screen format displayed when a screen or environment command is entered; it shows the options for various parameters and has some options selected by default.

Terminal emulation Program that makes one data terminal or computer look and act like another specific terminal.

Transparent Mode (TM) Command Command that connects the Terminal Port to the Host Port so that the keyboard and screen display data is transmitted between the terminal and the host as if they were directly connected.

Trace Command that causes one instruction to be executed and updates the register's display information. The registers are not displayed automatically in the HDS-300 but can be requested.

Trigger Signal or condition that causes an action. The condition can be a combination of events.

UNIX Operating system developed by AT&T that is noted for its ability to be ported to many different computers. It is written in a high-level language called C. Compilers are available for a variety of processors. Motorola released the first **68000** version of System V, which is called System V/68.

Upload Move a program file from the local computer to a remote computer via the serial transmission link.

VERSAdos Operating system developed by Motorola for its **68000** family of μPs.

VME10 Desktop computer built by Motorola that uses a **68010** μP and includes a 15-inch CRT, keyboard, 15- or 40-Mb hard disk, and $5\frac{1}{4}$-inch floppy disk. It also has slots for other VME modules.

Window Software technique whereby temporary information overlays a display on a CRT screen that is later restored.

Wirewrap Technique for constructing a prototype model of an electronic circuit that uses patented tools for wrapping wires around posts instead of soldering them.

12-13 REFERENCES

Motorola. *HDS-300 Hardware Development Station Operations Manual,* M68HDS3OM/D1, Motorola Semiconductor Products, Inc., Phoenix, AZ, 1985.

Motorola. *HDS-200 Hardware Development Station User's Manual,* M68HDS2UM/D1, Motorola Semiconductor Products, Inc., Phoenix, AZ, 1983.

Motorola. *HDS-200 Hardware Development Station Operations Manual,* M68HDS2OM/D2, Motorola Semiconductor Products, Inc., Phoenix, AZ, 1983.

Motorola. *M6805/M6804 Microcomputers from Design Idea to Prototype,* BR144, Motorola Semiconductor Products, Inc., Phoenix, AZ, 1984.

Motorola. *HDS-200 Microcomputer Hardware/Software Development Station,* DS4082 Issue B, Motorola Semiconductor Products, Inc., Phoenix, AZ, 1987.

Motorola. *8-Bit MPU and MCU Families,* BR261, Motorola Semiconductor Products, Inc., Phoenix, AZ, 1985.

Relms. *HDSMDS Cross-Support Package,* BR240, Relms Relational Memory Systems, San Jose, CA, 1984.

Motorola. *BLU-200 Interface Package,* BR239 3501, Austin, TX, 1983.

Relms. *Intel to Motorola MCU Conversion,* BR239, Relms Relational Memory Systems, San Jose, CA, 1985.

Motorola. *MC68HC05C4 HDS-200 Emulator Module User's Manual,* M68HC05C4HM/D1, Motorola Semiconductor Products, Inc., Phoenix, AZ, 1984.

Motorola. *MC6805R2, MC6805U2, MC68705R3, MC68705U3, HDS-200 Emulator Module User's Manual,* M6805RU23/D1, Motorola Semiconductor Products, Inc., Phoenix, AZ, 1983.

Motorola. *MC146805E2 HDS-200 Emulator Module User's Manual,* MC146805E2/D2, Motorola Semiconductor Products, Inc., Phoenix, AZ, 1983.

Motorola. *HDS-300 Hardware Development Station User's Manual,* M68HDS3UM/D1, Motorola Semiconductor Products, Inc., Phoenix, AZ, 1985.

Motorola. *M68HC11 HDS-300 Emulation Module User's Manual,* M68HC11HM3/D1, Motorola Semiconductor Products, Inc., Phoenix, AZ, 1985.

Motorola. *M6809 HDS-300 Emulation Module User's Manual,* 0M6809HM3/D1, Motorola Semiconductor Products, Inc., Phoenix, AZ, 1985.

Motorola. *M6801 HDS-300 Emulation Module User's Manual,* M6801HM3/D1, Motorola Semiconductor Products, Inc., Phoenix, AZ, 1979.

Motorola. *HDS-300 Source Level Debugging User's Manual,* M68HDS3SLD/D1, Motorola Semiconductor Products, Inc., Phoenix, AZ, 1986.

Motorola. *Customer Letter for HDS-300 Source Level Debugging (SLD) on System V/68,* Motorola Semiconductor Products, Inc., Phoenix, AZ, 1986.

Motorola. *M68HC11 Cross C Compiler User's Manual,* M68KXCURM/D2, Motorola Semiconductor Products, Inc., Phoenix, AZ, 1985.

CHAPTER 13

REAL-WORLD APPLICATIONS AND INTERFACING TECHNIQUES

13-1 INSTRUCTIONAL OBJECTIVES

This chapter considers the problems of connecting or interfacing external system components to a μC. This may involve both digital and analog signals. Particular attention is paid to interfacing in an electrically noisy environment, as is often found in industry. (*Electrical noise* is unwanted pulses or voltage variations on the power or signal lines that causes false operation.) This is a very important aspect of *real-world* requirements, and even when the internal design of the μC system is well done, the overall performance will not be acceptable unless the μC is properly interfaced to the external system components.

After reading this chapter, the student should be able to

1. Use noise reduction techniques such as twisted pair wiring or electrostatic shielding where necessary.
2. Properly protect systems from electrical noise or damage.
3. Use input and output modules to isolate μCs from high-power systems.
4. Use A/D and D/A converters to enable the μC to communicate with the analog world.
5. Explain the *successive approximation* technique for converting analog signals to their digital equivalents.

13-2 SELF-EVALUATION QUESTIONS

Watch for the answers to the following questions as you read the chapter. They should help you to understand the material presented.

1. Why should the grounds for circuits meet at only one common point?
2. What are the advantages of *twisted pair* wiring?

3. What are the advantages of input modules over direct TTL coupling? Under what circumstances must input modules be used?
4. What advantages do differential amplifiers have for the transmission of digital or analog signals?

13-3 USES OF μCS

Although the use of μCs for *business applications* is rapidly increasing, the majority are still used to control *industrial processes*. Automotive use alone could become a yearly market of approximately 10 million μCs.

Larger computers known as *mainframes* have been used for business applications for some time, but many μC-based designs have been introduced in recent years. These business μCs are complete stand-alone systems (the IBM-PCs, Radio Shack computers, and Apple's Macintosh are examples) with many software options. Some μC business or hobbyist systems use BASIC as their programming language and have their own proprietary Disk Operating System (DOS).

As opposed to those systems that work with bytes and the BASIC language, most *industrial control* applications use *bit manipulation* and assembly language programming. Each bit sent by the μP is a command to turn ON or OFF external devices, such as motors, solenoids, and relays. The bits received represent the *status* of the input sensors, such as mechanical limit switches, ON/OFF operator controls, or pressure transducers. Because most industrial applications are unique, they present more difficult and challenging problems for the designer.

Systems for turning devices ON or OFF as a result of discrete events can easily be implemented by TTL or CMOS logic. They may even use external mechanical movement devices, such as a *shaft angle decoder,* that generate digital signals. When *decisions* must be based on a calculated result of inputs, the computing power of a μC is needed. Many μC systems must also accept a variable analog input signal or must output a similar variable control signal.

13-3.1 Real-World Electrical Interference

The internal bus structure of many μC systems has been discussed, but the real-world connections to external equipment have not been described in detail. This interfacing is an important aspect of computer design.

In a laboratory or business environment where the μC is less than 20 or 30 feet away from the devices it is controlling and no large power-operated devices are used, there are usually few problems with electrical interfacing. Frequently, however, this is not the case, and electrical noise can cause false operation. In *process control* applications, for example, the equipment being controlled is often powered by high-current DC or, more likely, high-power AC sources. Because of the inductive nature of wiring and the use of motors or solenoids, large *voltage or current pulses* can be generated. Unless proper design techniques are used to interconnect the μC system to the power equipment, these pulses can be induced into the μP or other digital circuits and cause system malfunctions. In some cases, the pulses may be so powerful that the interfacing parts are damaged. Since externally powered control equipment may produce transient voltages exceeding several thousand volts, it is obvious that semiconductor devices, designed for 5- or even 12-V operation, can be damaged permanently.

13-3.2 Overvoltage Protection

The most devastating event for an IC component is excessive voltage. In industrial installations, when dealing with long signal lines that go outside the equipment cabinets, additional precautions are necessary. These lines are usually not TTL digital circuits. Low-level analog lines (see Section 13-9) that must be connected to remote sensors can easily come in contact with abnormal voltages. Therefore all inputs must be protected from damage from unexpected sources, including lightning or power transients. However, the protection technique must not affect the accuracy of the voltage measurement in the normal range. This is usually done using a circuit similar to that shown in Fig. 13-1. Here the maximum range of voltages is limited by diodes that conduct whenever their reverse bias is exceeded. To protect the diodes from damage in the event of an installation error or lightning stroke, a limiting resistor and a fuse are used. The series resistance must be low compared to the amplifier's input impedance so as not to degrade accuracy.

13-4 NOISE REDUCTION IN DIGITAL INTERFACING

The I/O devices discussed in previous chapters were mostly TTL-compatible, and therefore an interfering voltage pulse greater than about 1.2 V can cause false operation by changing a 1 to a 0 or vice versa. CMOS devices are less susceptible to these interfering pulses but still can fail when pulses exceed 2.5 or 3 V. These induced pulses are usually termed *noise, spikes* or *glitches*. When a μC is operated in an electrically noisy environment, special shielding and grounding precautions must be taken to prevent the introduction of interfering pulses (noise) into the μC signal lines.

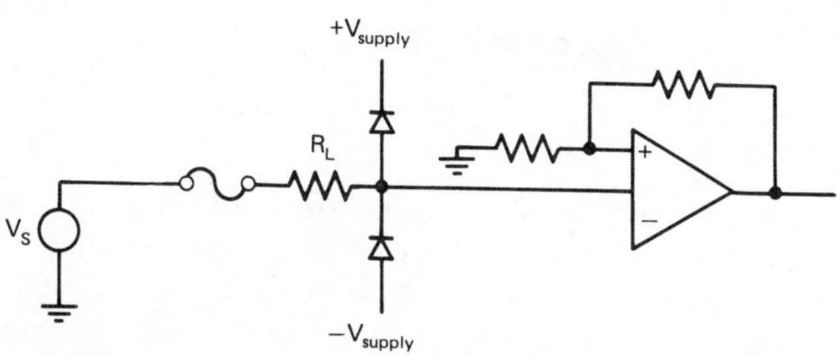

FIGURE 13-1 Overvoltage protection circuit for analog lines.

13-4.1 Ground Coupling

Improper grounding of digital circuits is one of the principal causes of severe problems. Depending on how circuits are wired, currents from several different circuits can flow through the same ground path and, even if there is only a fraction of an ohm resistance in that path, can cause unwanted coupling. If the currents are large enough (a current of 12 A through 0.1 ohm produces a potential difference of 1.2 V), false operation can result in a typical TTL circuit. Figure 13-2a shows an example of improper grounding. The circuit of Fig. 13-2a uses two transistors to amplify the input signal, V_{IN}. The problems occur because the ground line of transistor B is improperly connected to the ground of transistor A rather than directly to the system ground. Assume that the wire from the emitter of transistor A to the signal ground has a resistance of 0.1 ohm. If transistor B draws 12 A when it is ON, the emitter of A will be raised to 1.2 V, which will change its biasing dramatically and probably cause improper operation. Figure 13-2b shows the correct way to connect the grounds in order to eliminate any coupling due to the common ground path. If all grounds for a system are brought to *only one point* so that mutual resistance paths are avoided, coupling from this source is eliminated.

13-4.2 Capacitive and Inductive Coupling

Capacitive or inductive coupling between lines not actually connected to each other can also result in interference. Since digital signals are pulses and have changing levels like AC, capacitive coupling can cause interfering voltages to be induced.

Two lines parallel to one another on a printed circuit (PC) card or in a ribbon cable, or a metallic cabinet close to the interconnecting wiring, can act like a capacitor. Since the input impedance of some IC gates is as high as 100 kohm, a capacitance of only a few picofarads (pf) can result in a signal large enough to cause trouble. This coupling between lines is called **crosstalk**. It is particularly troublesome when the coupling is to a line or surface that is hundreds of volts above ground, which can be the case if the chassis and/or power supply grounds are not properly connected. Similarly, whenever there are large currents in wires, strong magnetic fields result, which inductively produce currents in nearby wires and thus lead to unwanted pulses.

13-4.3 Engineering Techniques for Reduction of Noise

Several techniques are used to avoid interference resulting from capacitive, inductive, or ground circuit coupling.

1. Capacitively coupled noise voltages are reduced greatly by using an **electrostatic shield**. This consists of a grounded wire (or metallic screen) between the two circuits or surrounding one of them. A coaxial cable (which is a wire surrounded by a grounded braid) is frequently used to carry digital signals whenever it is necessary to avoid possible capacitive interference. Most

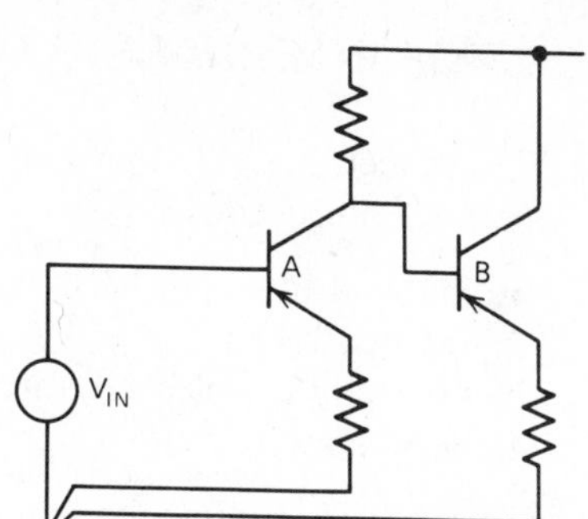

(a) (b)

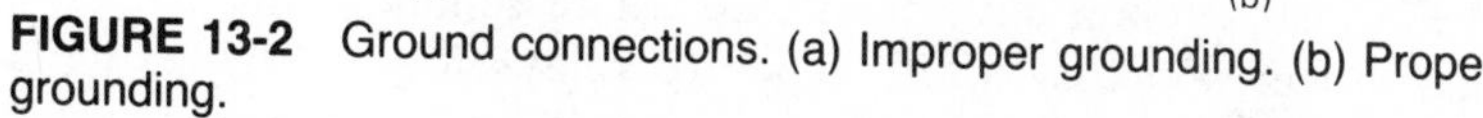

FIGURE 13-2 Ground connections. (a) Improper grounding. (b) Proper grounding.

oscilloscope probes, for example, use coaxial cable. A grounded line is frequently used between two signal lines on PC boards (see Section 13-6.1) or in a flat ribbon cable to provide this type of shielding.

2. Magnetic coupling between adjacent circuits can be reduced by using **twisted pair wires**. This technique is commonly used in telephone lines and other audio systems to eliminate audible hum. If two lines are carrying equal and opposed-polarity signals, such as a signal line and its return line, proper twisting of these two wires (so that they are transposed several times) causes the magnetic fields to nearly cancel each other and thus greatly reduces inductively generated interfering voltages. When combined with proper (right-angle) separation, this can effectively eliminate magnetic coupling. Twisting a ground wire with a signal wire can also reduce capacitive coupling since it serves to provide electrostatic shielding and therefore reduces this form of crosstalk.
3. Optical coupling, described below, is one of the most effective means of minimizing ground problems.

13-4.4 Optical Coupling

As shown in Fig. 13-3, an **optical coupler** consists of a *Light-Emitting Diode* (LED) and a *phototransistor*. Because the information is transmitted optically (i.e., light from the LED shines on the phototransistor to turn it ON), the input circuit is electrically isolated from the output and separate power sources or ground returns are possible. When optical couplers are properly installed, common ground and capacitive coupling are both avoided. One disadvantage is that the response time of *some* devices is very slow compared to that of standard TTL gates. Various types of optical couplers are now available to provide this circuit isolation, and some of them feature the ability to withstand up to 7500 V (RMS) between input and output.

13-5 METHODS OF INTERFACING DIGITAL DEVICES

To connect the TTL signals of a μC to external control equipment, the following methods are used:

1. Direct TTL or CMOS.
2. Relays.
3. Optically coupled DC circuits.
4. Solid-state relays.

A direct TTL connection can be used only if external power or grounds are very carefully connected and in a low-noise environment such as a laboratory or office.

For years, relays have been used where isolation was needed between grounds and power sources. Many types of relays are available, including a growing number of types that can be mounted on PC cards. Figure 13-4 shows two types of relays, an electromechanical relay (commonly called just a "relay") and its semiconductor equivalent, the Solid-State Relay. Figure 13-4a shows that the isolation qualities of the electromechanical relay are excellent because the coil circuit is not electrically connected to the contacts, but these relays are mechanical devices and will wear out or require adjustment in time. Converting to electronic switching is an answer to this problem, but care must be taken to avoid the coupling problems mentioned in Section 13-4.2.

Optically coupled DC circuits are functionally equivalent to relays, and DC optical coupling is available in single transistor or dual-transistor **Darlington** types. They can be used in many applications where ground isolation is needed and large DC voltages or currents are involved.

Solid-state relays are optically coupled circuits that usually include TRIACS or Silicon-Controlled Rectifiers (SCRs) to switch AC circuits. A Solid-State Relay circuit is shown in Fig. 13-4b, and its similarity to the electromechanical relay can be seen. These circuits can also include *zero-crossing* detection circuits (the circuit is opened or closed only when the AC voltage is at the zero point of the cycle) to minimize the generation of transient noise signals.

All the previous devices are used as output ON/OFF switches where isolation

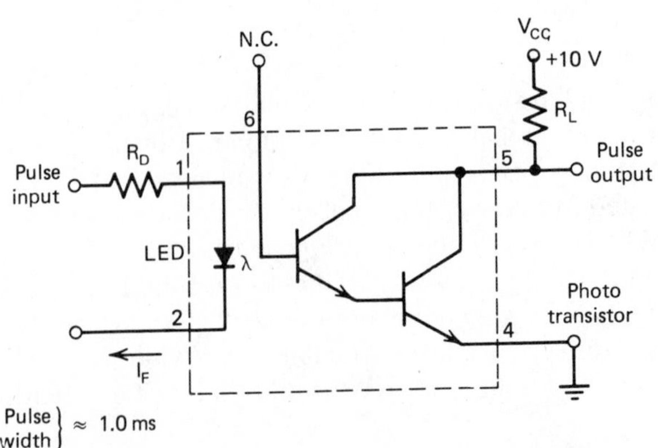

FIGURE 13-3 An optical coupler.

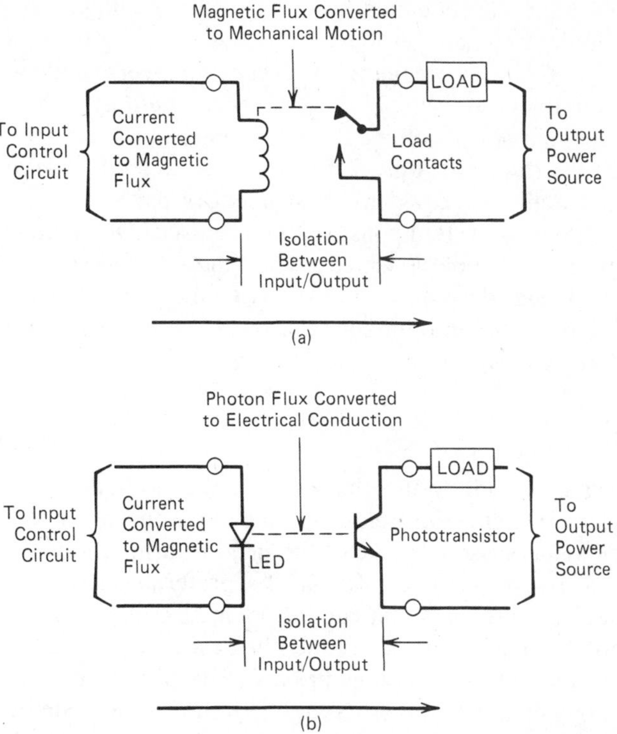

FIGURE 13-4 Two types of relays. (a) Electromechanical relay. (b) Solid-state relay.

between the μC circuits and the controlled equipment is required. All except the AC versions of solid-state relays can also be used to connect input signals into the μC.

13-6 METHODS OF CONSTRUCTION FOR μC SYSTEMS

The various hardware components that are needed to assemble a μC system were described from a functional or electrical point of view in previous chapters, but not much has been said about the mechanical construction. The parts can be put together in an unlimited number of ways, but certain methods have evolved that are reasonably well standardized. The ICs themselves are designed to be soldered into plated-through holes in an insulated board that is approximately 1/16 inch thick. In some cases the ICs are plugged into sockets that are soldered to the board. Sockets are more expensive, but it is much easier to remove or replace an IC plugged into a socket than to unsolder an IC attached to a board.

The connections between components are made by copper strips that are also plated onto the insulated board. The board material is usually fiberglass. Originally these boards were made by copper-plating one or both sides of a 1/16-inch fiberglass sheet and then chemically etching away the unwanted material, leaving only the desired paths between pins.

Today these *PC* boards are made with very thin layers sandwiched together and about 1/16 inch thick overall. They are called *multilayer boards* and provide multiple *ground planes* or voltage levels anywhere on the board. Up to 10 layers are possible, but typically only 2 to 4 are used. Adding layers increases the expense but also allows very dense placement of parts.

Two basic styles of system construction are used. One is to place all the parts on one specialized PC board, which is then mounted in some sort of protective case. The other method is to divide the ICs and associated discrete parts (like capacitors and resistors) into functional groups that are placed on separate boards and called *modules*.

13-6.1 Printed Circuit Modules

The designer may decide to use the single-board method, but if devices such as optical couplers or solid-state relays are included on the same board as the μC, noise problems may arise because of the need to bring the high-power lines into the same area as the μC lines. It may be preferable to place the high-power devices on separate modules that can be shielded. The modular construction has another important feature. It is frequently desirable to use the same types of computer system modules to connect to a variety of different machines. This can easily be done by changing the programmed ROMs to accommodate the different external system peripherals.

The μC itself, with a clock circuit and some bus driver ICs, may turn out to be a module that is used with several different combinations of memory configurations or interface modules. Thus, designers have the option of selecting the functions needed for their systems.

These modules are connected together to form a complete computer by plugging them into a *motherboard*. The motherboard is also a PC board and has many connectors that are linked by other printed circuit lines. These lines are used to tie together the address, data, and control pins of the connectors. The same pins are used for the same purpose on each connector, so the modules can be plugged into any position. For 8-bit μCs there are 16 address lines, 8 data lines, and various control lines that run parallel between connectors. They form a *bus*.

13-6.2 Standard μC Buses

A *bus standard* defines the electrical characteristics of the interconnecting signal lines, which pins are connected to which lines, the type of connectors, and the mechanical dimensions of the modules that are expected to work together. These factors must all be compatible so that the modules of each family can be assembled into various combinations to form different systems. Unfortunately, each family is different.

The methods of construction for μC systems have been evolving for years, so several standard module families have been designed by various manufacturers.

One of the first such standards was the *EXORbus* as used in the EXORciser (see Chapter 10). Later, a *chassis* (or card cage) like the EXORciser chassis was designed and used in assembling other combinations of modules. These chassis are made to be mounted in a standard 19-inch rack of a type that is frequently used in many industrial installations. Motorola also produced a line of EXORbus Micromodules that were used in constructing systems with the Motorola **6800** family of IC components. In 1986, Motorola sold that line to Micro Industries of Cleveland (see the References section). Many Control Systems manufacturers are still using Micromodules in new equipment.

Other manufacturers, notably Intel, have developed similar bus products for their 8-bit components. Intel called their bus the *Multibus*.

Recently, μP manufacturers have developed new bus standards to work with their newer 16- and 32-bit μPs (see Chapter 15). Motorola and four other manufacturers collaborated to develop the *VMEbus,* while Intel developed *Multibus II*. These buses have become very popular and dozens of companies are busy designing new modules. Not all types of modules are provided by the semiconductor companies, however, and particularly in the area of interfacing to external peripherals such as machinery, other companies, including Analogic and Burr-Brown, have provided modules for use on these popular buses. Some of the modules provide an isolated digital interface and others do the same for analog signals. Descriptions of digital modules follow, and the A/D and D/A modules are discussed in Section 13-11.

Not enough space is available in this book to explore the advantages or disadvantages of the various buses. Instead, we will show some examples of the types of systems that can be assembled, with emphasis on the problems of interfacing the μC's internal data bus to the external system components.

13-7 DIGITAL MODULES

Digital modules are used to interface digital lines between external system devices and μCs. They provide isolation to prevent the problems described in Sections 13-3 and 13-4. Two types of modules are described: output modules, which transfer signals from the μC to the external system components, and input modules, which transfer signals from the remote system peripherals to the μC circuits.

13-7.1 Digital Output Modules

Figure 13-5 shows a Burr-Brown **MP701/702** digital output module for use in *EXORbus* systems (see Section 13-6.2). These modules use relays or optical couplers to provide the necessary circuit isolation. This module was sold for years as an **M68MM13A** (or **B**) Motorola *Micromodule* but is now available only from Burr-Brown. This output module is physically compatible with the EXORciser bus (EXORbus) and other Micromodules. It uses miniature Dual In-Line package (DIP) reed relays to provide up to 600 V isolation protection. Figure 13-6 shows a

FIGURE 13-5 Digital output module. (Reproduced by permission of Burr-Brown.)

block diagram. The address decoding and control logic cause the registers on these modules to appear as memory locations when they are plugged into the μC buses (memory-mapped).

Address bits A0 and A1 on **MM13A** and A0 on **MM13B** (which connect into the control logic) select which of the four sets of eight outputs are to be controlled. The rest of the address lines are used to select the board itself. When data is written to the resulting address, the 1s turn ON the appropriate relays and the 0s turn them OFF. Specifications for these modules can be found in the references in Section 13-14.

13-7.2 Digital Input Modules

Figure 13-7 shows a similar module (Burr-Brown **MP710** or Motorola **M68MM13C** and **D**) that is used for input of **digital** (ON/OFF) signals. As shown in the block diagram of Fig. 13-8, these modules provide 24 isolated inputs using optically coupled circuits and can withstand voltages up to 600 V between the external wires and ground. The input circuits can also work with up to 84 V DC or 168 V AC (peak to peak) between the wires. The circuit also provides the **wetting voltage** to work with external contacts, typically used in limit, pressure, thermostat, or other similar switches. These modules also plug into the EXORbus and are addressed in the same way as the output module described above.

13-8 APPLICATIONS OF DIGITAL MODULES

The previously described modules are used in a wide variety of applications. Several examples of their use are described in the following paragraphs.

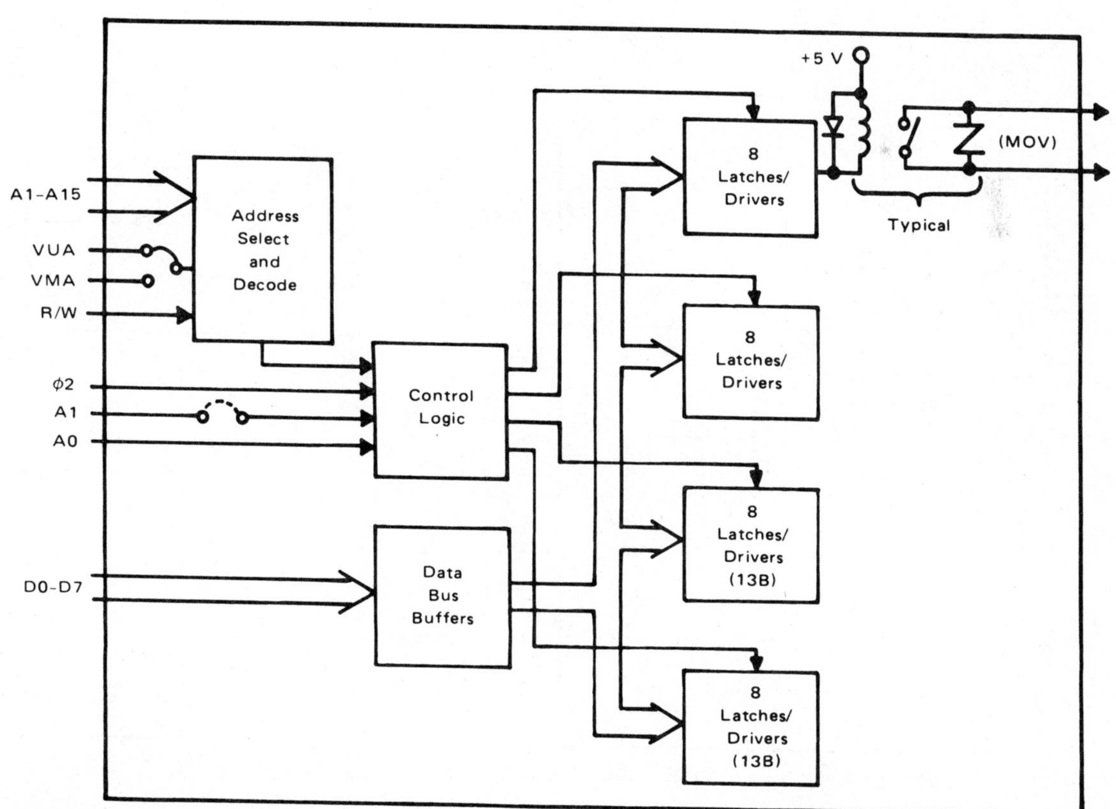

FIGURE 13-6 MP701/MP702 isolated digital output module block diagram. (Redrawn from information supplied by Burr-Brown.)

FIGURE 13-7 Digital input module. (Reproduced by permission of Burr-Brown.)

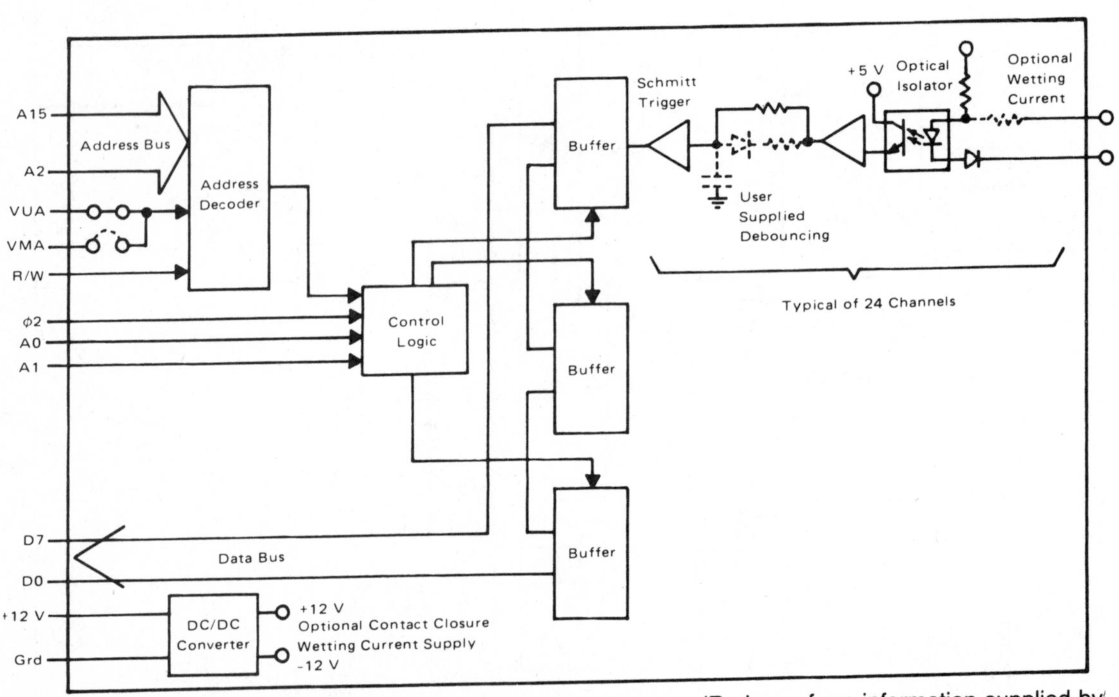

FIGURE 13-8 MP710 isolated digital input module block diagram. (Redrawn from information supplied by Burr-Brown.)

13-8.1 Temperature Controller Application of Digital Modules

Figure 13-9 shows a simplified temperature controller subsystem using a μC that can be assembled with many standard bus modules. This example uses modules with optically isolated digital inputs and reed-relay outputs. Temperature limit switches are used to provide the contact closures. Limit switch B1 closes when the temperature exceeds the HIGH limit, and switch B0 closes when the temperature is too LOW, in accordance with Table 13-1 (page 510).

Figure 13-10 (page 511) shows the flow diagram of the system functions to be implemented in software.

Note that this is an extremely simple example and could easily have been implemented in discrete TTL logic. A μC might be used, however, because it can simultaneously perform other functions. It gives the designer a great deal of flexibility, and modifications of the functions can easily be made by changing the program.

13-8.2 Mixture Controller Application Using Digital Modules

Figure 13-11 shows a mixture-control subsystem. Two solenoid valves control the flow of liquids into a vat. Two float switches close their contacts whenever levels A or B are reached. The μC starts a sequence with the vat empty. Valve A is opened until level switch A closes. Valve B is then opened until level B switch closes. The two liquids are then mixed and drained out by devices not shown in the figure. Level C is monitored at all times, and if it is ever reached both valves are turned OFF and an alarm is sounded.

Again, this is a simple example just to show the application of the input/output modules. You can use your imagination to elaborate on the design. For example, several more float sensors could be added and a high- and low-speed flow could be used by switching to low speed for "topping off" when a level just under the desired level is reached. Alternatively, the mixture "recipe" could be changed by an operator entry to a control terminal that selects different sensors.

13-8.3 Solid-State Relays

Figure 13-12 (page 512) shows a solid-state relay capable of controlling motors or heaters or other AC-operated devices. The functional block diagram is shown in Fig. 13-12a, and a picture of several typical units is shown in Fig. 13-12b. Solid-state relays are just another form of optically coupled semiconductors, where the DC input to the LEDs controls TRIACs or SCRs to turn AC-powered devices ON or OFF. Basic units are available that control up to 25 A with an isolated DC input of 1 to 10 mA. Depending on the sensitivity, they can be directly operated from a **6821** PIA. (The **6821** is rated at 3.2 mA.) Three-phase AC motors of considerable power can be controlled with one TTL PIA output when connected to the paralleled DC inputs of three solid-state relays (a driver transistor capable of up to 30 mA may be required). The three output circuits would be connected in series with each of the three AC power wires to the motor.

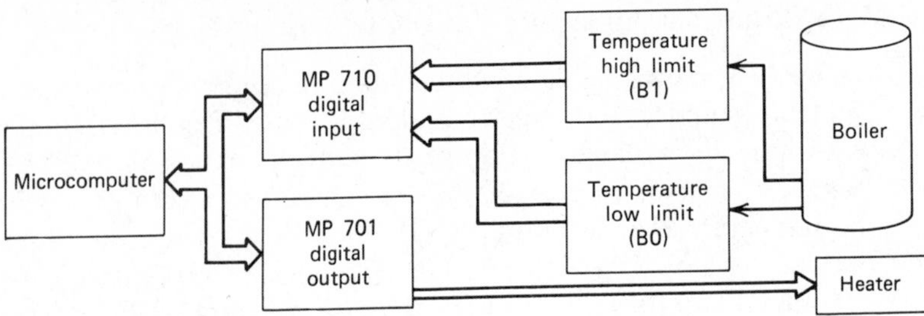

FIGURE 13-9 Temperature control subsystem. (Redrawn from information supplied by Burr-Brown.)

13-9 ANALOG INPUT/OUTPUT (I/O) for μC SYSTEMS

Microcomputer systems often must *generate* analog (or variable) control voltages and must read or *sense* variable input voltages with high accuracy (possibly as high as 0.01%). In the fields of process control, industrial instrumentation, and medical electronics, a variety of physical parameters must first be converted to electrical analog signals and then translated to a digital equivalent in order to be compatible with and controllable by a μC system. Devices that perform these functions are called **transducers**. They convert heat, motion, and position, for example, to (or from) an electrical signal proportional to their magnitude. For example, a pressure transducer may consist of a diaphragm connected to a strain gauge whose resistance varies as the diaphragm is deflected by the pressure. Using the strain gauge as one arm of a resistance bridge, a voltage proportional to the pressure is obtained. This voltage is used as an input to an analog interface.

The output of an analog transducer can range from millivolts to volts and can also be in the form of a varying current. Fortunately, some standardization exists, and most transducers have outputs falling within five major voltage/current categories: high- and low-level voltages and three current ranges.

High-level voltage outputs may range up to several volts, generally not exceeding 10 V. Low voltages may be up to a few tens of millivolts, either positive or negative. Current ranges of most transducers are 0–20 mA, 4–20 mA, or 10–50 mA.

Frequently, it is possible to set up a typical analog input system that includes a number of transducers having similar output signal levels. In this case it is possible to use a **multiplexer** to switch the various transducers to the same input

TABLE 13-1 Operation of Temperature Limit Switches

Input			
B1	B0	Process Status	Control Action
0	0	Temperature acceptable	No change required
1	0	Temperature too high	Turn OFF heater
0	1	Temperature too low	Turn ON heater
1	1	Controller malfunction	Sound alarm

Closed contacts = 1.

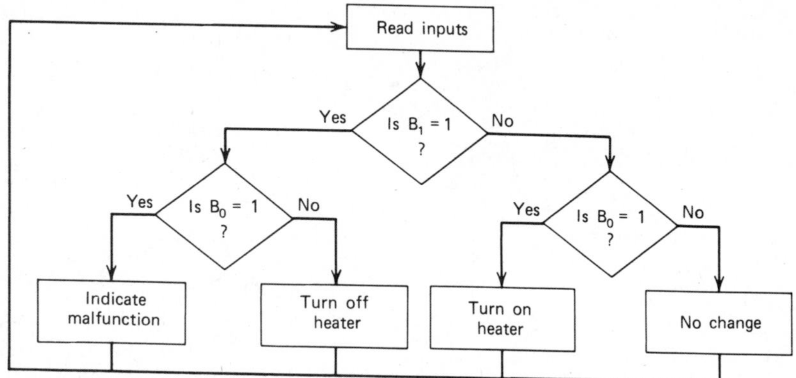

FIGURE 13-10 Flow diagram for temperature control system software. (Redrawn from information supplied by Burr-Brown.)

circuit (rather than using a duplicate amplifier and analog-to-digital converter for each channel).

Each of the components used in a data acquisition system has unique characteristics that must be understood before specifying or constructing an interface. Overall speed, accuracy, and noise immunity must all be considered in any system.

13-9.1 Interface Problems with Analog Signals

All the noise problems that affect digital inputs also affect analog signals. Since most analog signals are smaller than TTL digital signals, interference effects may be more severe. If a single wire and ground is used to input an electrical analog signal to an amplifier, the presence of noise is amplified by the same factor as the desired signal. This is shown in Fig. 13-13a (page 513).

Amplifiers with *differential* inputs are used extensively to separate the two signals. A differential amplifier is designed so that the noise signal impressed *in*

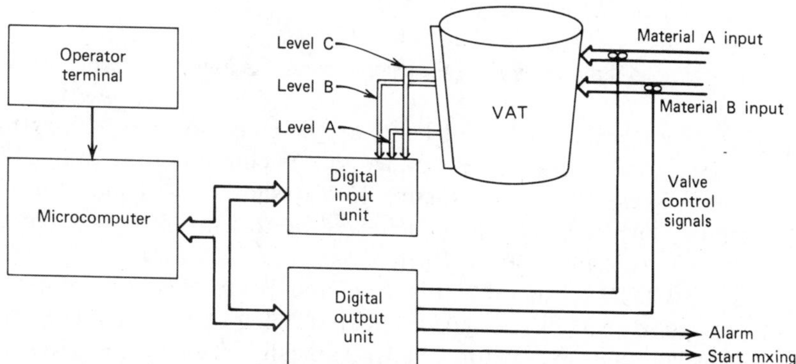

FIGURE 13-11 Mixture control system. (Redrawn from information supplied by Burr-Brown.)

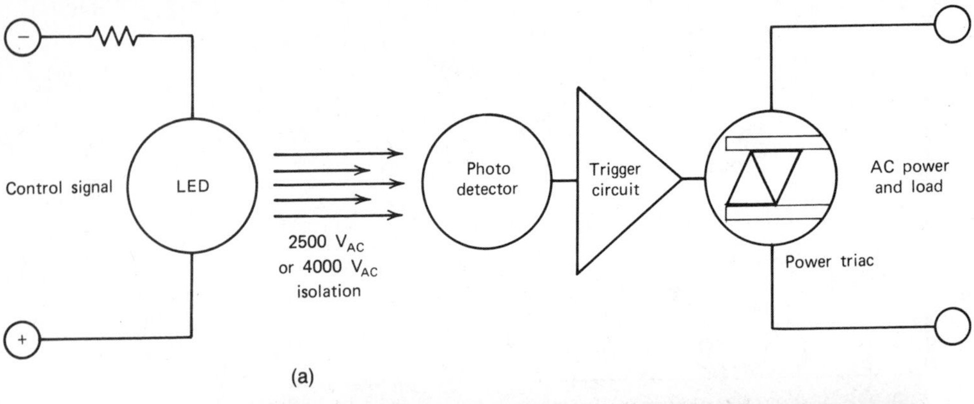

(a)

(b)

FIGURE 13-12 Typical solid-state relays. (a) Functional block diagram. (b) Solid-state relays.

phase on both inputs will be rejected. Only voltages *across* the input (out of phase) are amplified. The voltage that is common to both lines is known as the *common-mode* voltage. Figure 13-13b shows the connections for *differential* inputs. The noise reduction achieved by this means is considerable and is measured by the ratio of the *Differential-Mode Gain* (DMG) to the *Common-Mode Gain* (CMG). Generally this *Common-Mode Rejection* Ratio (CMRR) is expressed in decibels (dB) and is equal to 20 log DMG/CMG. (See the article by Don Aldridge cited in Section 13-14.) Typically, values of CMRR range from 70 to 120 dB.

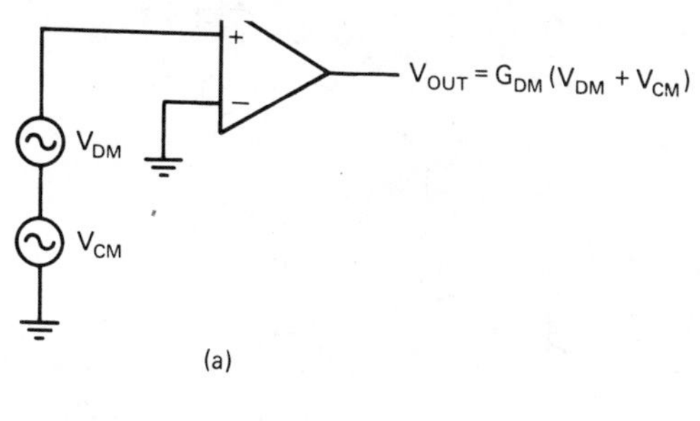

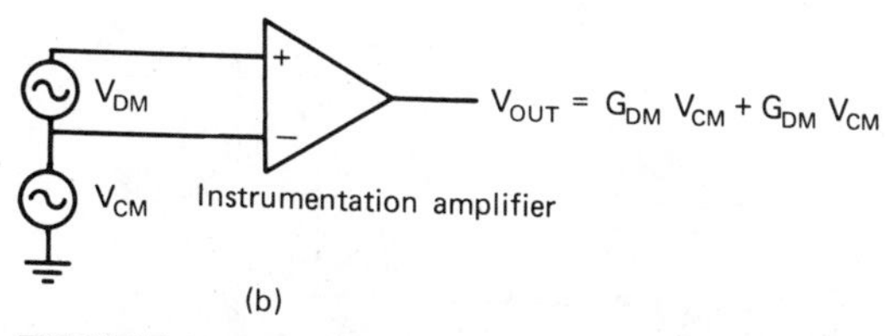

FIGURE 13-13 Single-ended versus differential input connections. (a) Single-ended analog connection. (b) Use of differential input amplifiers.

13-10 ANALOG-TO-DIGITAL (A/D) CONVERSION TECHNIQUES

An Analog-to-Digital converter is used to change analog (continuously varying amplitude) signals, such as the output of temperature or pressure transducers, to a digital signal that can be accepted by μCs. A typical A/D converter has

1. An analog input.
2. Digital outputs that represent the analog input signal voltage in digital form.
3. A start-of-conversion (SOC) input from the μC that tells the A/D converter to start converting its analog input into a digital value.
4. An end-of conversion (EOC) output that tells the μC that the converter has finished and the data is available.

Several techniques are used to convert analog transducer outputs to digital signals. To perform a fast conversion at a moderate price, **successive approximation** converters are almost always the choice. A block diagram of a simple 4-bit successive approximation circuit is shown in Fig. 13-14a. It shows the *comparator* (usually an *operational amplifier)* that adjusts a D/A converter until its output voltage closely approximates the analog input signal value. When the closest match is found (the comparator output is close to 0 volts), an EOC signal is activated (not shown) and the digital inputs to the D/A converter are used to represent the unknown analog signal. This is shown in the graph of Fig. 13-14b for this 4-bit converter.

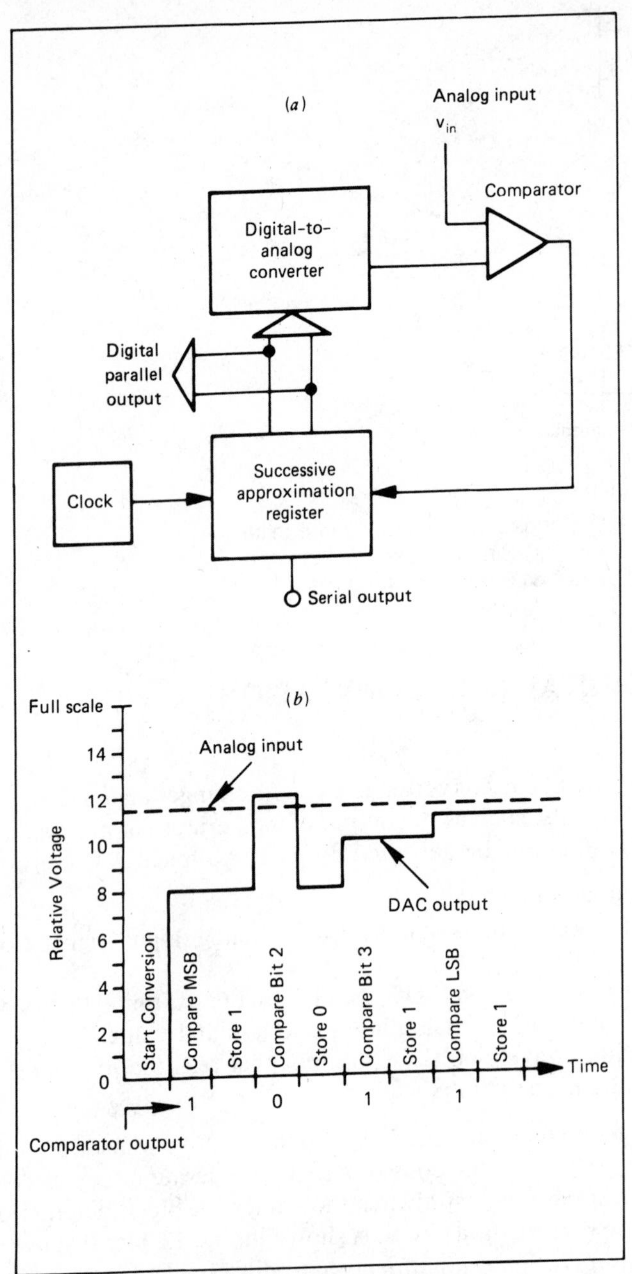

FIGURE 13-14 Four-bit successive approximation converter. (a) Block diagram. (b) Waveforms.

13-10.1 A/D Converters For the 6800 Family

An A/D converter for use in a **6800** system can be assembled as shown in Fig. 13-15. The **Digital-to-Analog Converter (DAC)** used is the **MC1408L-8** IC. This chip contains the Flip-Flops (FFs) and ladder network necessary to produce the binary values of current used by the comparator. The 8-bit digital word is input by the DAC from the A side of the PIA. An internally compensated *operational amplifier* **(MC1741)** is used as a buffer for the input voltage and provides the proper current source to match the current output of the **1408** (through R1 and R2). The comparator is an **MLM301A**. This amplifier's output saturates if the input currents of the buffer and **1408** are mismatched even slightly, thus toggling the comparator. The comparator's output is sensed by PB7 of the PIA so that the software can readjust the DAC to obtain the desired match. The program needed for this hardware setup is shown in Fig. 13-16.

A similar A/D converter can be assembled using a Burr-Brown **MP11** DAC unit as shown in Fig. 13-17. The MP11 contains two channels. Each channel has an 8-bit D/A converter, two operational amplifiers, a precision voltage reference, and a thin film network. Laser trimming for gain and offset errors is used, and therefore no external adjustments are needed to obtain an absolute accuracy of ±0.2% over a +10 V output range. Moreover, the analog output remains linear to within ±1.22 mV, when using the 10-V output range (with 12-bit resolution). It also takes less than 25 μs for the output to settle to within ±1.22 mV of the long-term value. A program similar to Fig. 13-16 would be used.

13-10.2 Interfacing A/D Converters

In any A/D converter system, the method of handling the A/D conversion must be considered. The simplest method, after the process has been started, is for the program to continually check the *end of conversion* signal to determine when the conversion is finished. This is inefficient, however, and wastes valuable μP time since nothing else is accomplished during this period.

A better method uses the μP's *interrupt* system to report the end of conversion. During the conversion time, other segments of the program can be executed until the end-of-conversion signal interrupts the μP. Although this approach may appear efficient, caution should be used when interfacing very fast analog systems to digital systems. The overhead time associated with servicing the interrupt may take the μP longer than the time required for the conversion. The net effect is that the overall throughput is slower than when looping and waiting for the end-of-conversion signal.

The analog system can be connected in such a way that it places the μP in a WAIT state during the conversion process. This provides the highest throughput speed for programmed data transfers while considerably reducing the electrical noise generated by the digital system. An additional benefit can be found in processors, such as the **6800**, that can be halted in midcycle to wait for slow memory. With the **6800**, the entire conversion process is carried out during the course of a single memory read instruction with the timing of the operation totally

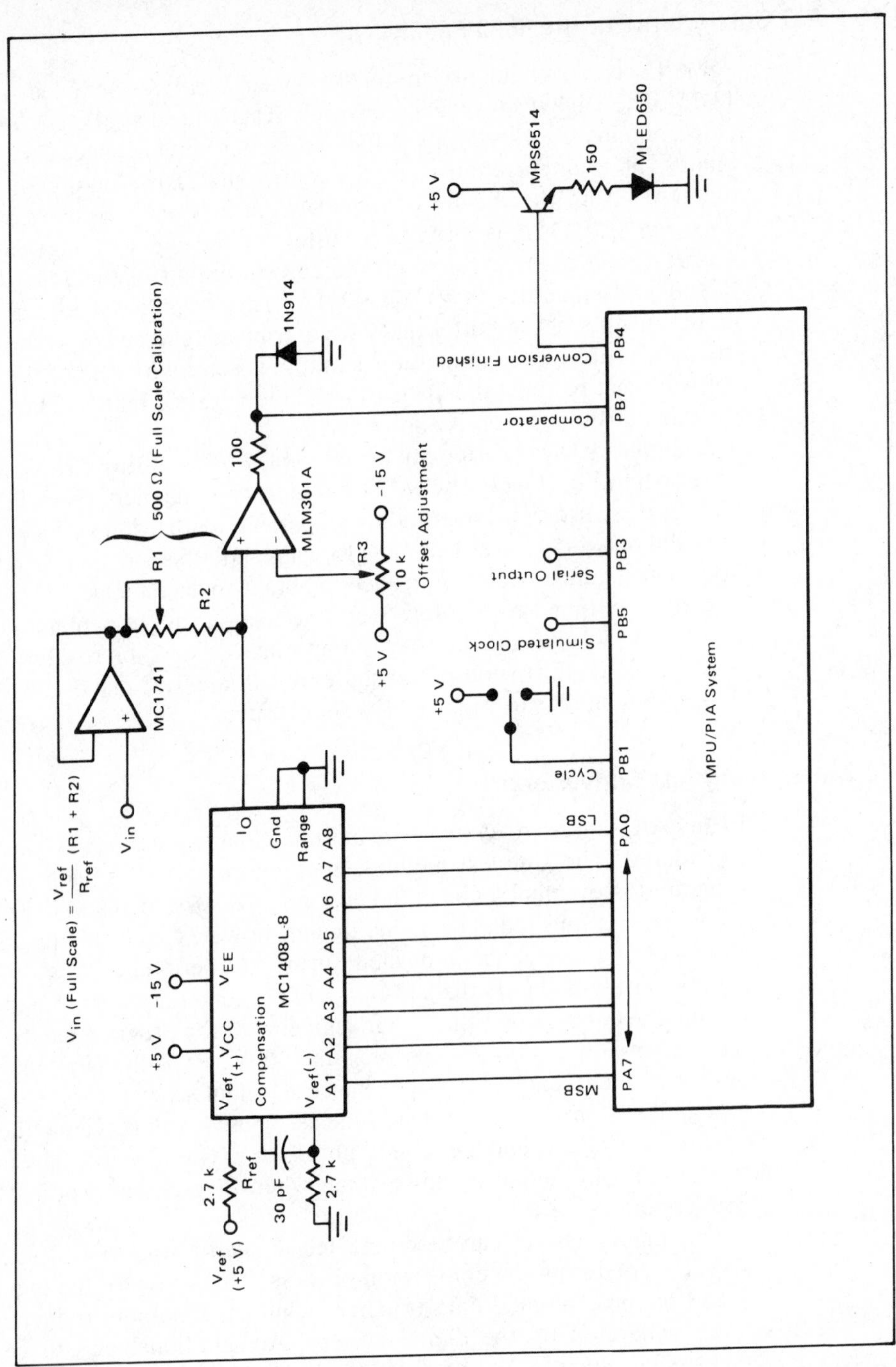

FIGURE 13-15 An 8-bit successive approximation A/D converter for the 6800 system.

```
PAGE  001    DWA12

                             NAM    DWA12
                             OPT    0
                      *  8 BIT SUCCESSIVE APPROXIMATION A/D
                      *  WRITTEN BY DON ALDRIDGE - MODIFIED BY W C WRAY
                      *
0020                         ORG    $20
0020 0001             ANS    RMB    1          FINAL ANSWER MEMORY LOCATION
0021 0001             POINTR RMB    1          TEMP MEMORY LOCATION
                      *
4004                         ORG    $4004      PIA MEMORY ADDRESS ASSIGNMENT
4004 0001             PIA1AD RMB    1          A SIDE - DIRECTION/DATA REGIS
4005 0001             PIA1AC RMB    1          A SIDE - CONTROL/STATUS    "
4006 0001             PIA1BD RMB    1          B SIDE - DIRECTION/DATA    "
4007 0001             PIA1BC RMB    1          B SIDE - CONTROL/STATUS    "
                      *
                      *  PIA1AD IS USED FOR DIGITAL OUTPUT TO THE DAC
                      *  PIA1BD IS USED FOR A/D CONTROL
                      *
                      *             PIABD PIN ASSIGNMENTS
                      *  PB7    PB6    PB5    PB4    PB3    PB2    PB1
                      * COMP    NC     SC     CF     SO     NC    CYCLE
                      *
                      * COMP = COMPARATOR - NC = NO CONNECTION - SC = SIMU
                      * SO = SERIAL OUTPUT - CF = CONVERSION FINISHED
                      *
1200                         ORG    $1200      BEGINNING ADDRESS
                      *
                      *      PIA INITIALIZATION
1200 7F 4005                 CLR    PIA1AC     SELECT DIRECTION REGISTER
1203 7F 4007                 CLR    PIA1BC     "          "          "
1206 86 7D                   LDA A  #$7D       SET B DIRECTION FOR CONTROL S
1208 B7 4006                 STA A  PIA1BD
120B 86 FF                   LDA A  #$FF
120D B7 4004                 STA A  PIA1AD     SET ALL LINES AS OUTPUTS ON A
1210 86 04                   LDA A  #4
1212 B7 4005                 STA A  PIA1AC     LATCH DIRECTION AND DISABLE I
1215 B7 4007                 STA A  PIA1BC     "      "      "      "      "
                      *
1218 86 10            RSTART LDA A  #$10
121A B7 4006                 STA A  PIA1BD     SET CONVERSION FINISHED BIT
                      *
                      *     CYCLE TEST
                      *
121D B6 4006          CYCLE  LDA A  PIA1BD     GET B STATUS
1220 84 02                   AND A  #2         TEST BIT 1
1222 27 F9                   BEQ    CYCLE      IF ZERO, LOOP TIL PULSED
                      *
1224 7F 4004                 CLR    PIA1AD     CLEAR OUTPUT REGISTER
1227 7F 0021                 CLR    POINTR     CLEAR TEMP LOCATION
                      *
122A 7F 4006                 CLR    PIA1BD     RESET CONVERSION FINISHED BIT
122D 0D                      SEC
                      *
122E 76 0021          CONVRT ROR    POINTR     MOVE CARRY INTO MSB
```

FIGURE 13-16 Program for successive approximation A/D converter.

```
PAGE  002   DWA12

1231 25 E5              BCS    RSTART   IF CARRY SET - SET CONV FINIS
1233 B6 4004            LDA A  PIA1AD   RECALL PREVIOUS DIGITAL OUTPU
1236 9B 21              ADD A  POINTR
1238 B7 4004            STA A  PIA1AD   SET NEW DIGITAL OUTPUT
                  *
                  *     DELAY FOR COMPARATOR
                  *
123B 01                 NOP
123C 01                 NOP
123D 01                 NOP
123E 01                 NOP
123F B6 4006            LDA A  PIA1BD   GET B STATUS
1242 2B 10              BMI    YES      IF BIT 7 SET GO TO YES
                  *
                  *  LOW COMPARATOR LOOP
                  *
1244 B6 4004            LDA A  PIA1AD   GET VALUE IN DATA REG
1247 90 21              SUB A  POINTR
1249 C6 20              LDA B  #$20     SERIAL OUT OF "0" - CLOCK SET
124B F7 4006            STA B  PIA1BD
124E 5F                 CLR B
124F F7 4006            STA B  PIA1BD   CLOCK RESET
1252 20 10              BRA    END      FINISH
                  *
                  *  HIGH COMPARATOR LOOP
                  *
1254 B6 4004 YES        LDA A  PIA1AD   GET DATA
1257 01                 NOP
1258 01                 NOP             DELAY
1259 01                 NOP
125A C6 28              LDA B  #$28     SERIAL OUTPUT OF "1" - CLOCK
125C F7 4006            STA B  PIA1BD
125F C6 08              LDA B  #8
1261 F7 4006            STA B  PIA1BD   CLOCK RESET
                  *
1264 B7 4004 END        STA A  PIA1AD   OUTPUT TO DAC
1267 97 20              STA A  ANS      PLACE OUTPUT VALUE IN ANSWER
1269 20 C3              BRA    CONVRT   GO AROUND AGAIN
                  *
                        END

TOTAL ERRORS 00000
```

FIGURE 13-16 *(Continued).*

transparent to the programmer. For all of its merits, this method has one serious drawback. The μP is completely blind to any other outside events during the conversion. Where μP response times (for external events) are required to be shorter than the conversion time, this method cannot be used.

When several channels are to be converted before the data is processed or a block of channels must be continually scanned, direct memory access (DMA) should be considered as the interfacing method. Although more complicated from a hardware point of view, this method maximizes channel throughput with a minimum of software. In one mode of operation, a segment of memory can be continually updated by continuous automatic operation of the analog system and the transfer of digital data performed between processor cycles. Only a slight

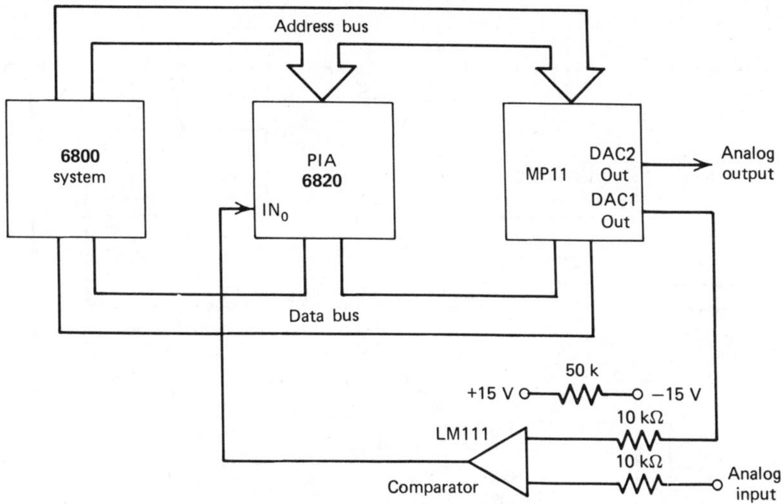

FIGURE 13-17 A simple A/D converter.

reduction in software execution speed is noticed, and the data is fetched from memory without regard to the details of operating the analog interface. Another mode of operation might allow several channels to be processed and then an interrupt generated to signal the software that the block of data is available.

13-11 ANALOG I/O MODULES

Block diagrams for two A/D modules that are designed to work with a **6800** system are shown in Figs. 13-18 and 13-19. These are Micromodules made by Analogic Corporation for Motorola (see References, Section 13-14). They are no longer sold by Motorola but can still be obtained from Analogic. The **M68MM15A/15A1** analog *input* module block diagram is shown in Fig. 13-18. It accepts analog input signals, converts them to digital, and makes the value available on the μP bus. The data sheets and manuals cited in Section 13-14 provide detailed specifications and programming information. The **M68MM15CV** and **M68MM15CI** are similar analog *output* modules, and their block diagram is shown in Fig. 13-19. Each module has DACs; the difference between them is that the CI module has a *current* output of 4 to 20 mA whereas the CV module provides various ranges of output *voltage*.

Two programming examples for Micromodule 15A/15A1 are shown in Table 13-2. They illustrate some of the considerations described in the preceding paragraphs. Details of these modules are given in the References, Section 13-14.

13-11.1 Boiler Control with Analog Modules

An example of a typical μC application might be found in a large process control facility. Large computers direct the overall operation of the plant through the activities of μC systems placed strategically through the plant. As shown in Fig.

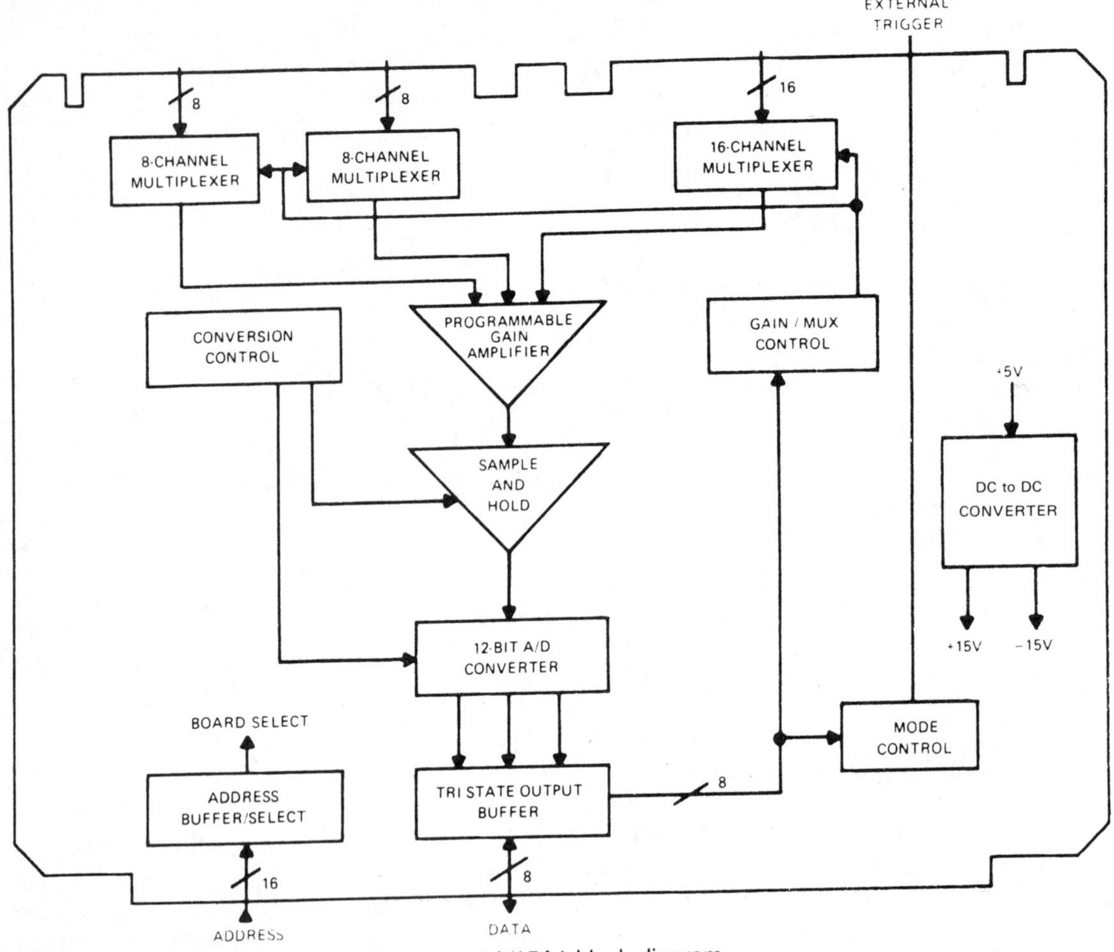

FIGURE 13-18 Analog input Micromodule 15A/15A1 block diagram.

13-20, one such μC system might be assigned the sole task of monitoring the combustion in a boiler. Inputs would originate from flame-temperature transducers, effluent-gas analyzers, and fuel-flow meters. Outputs would control fuel and oxygen flow and drive a small strip-chart recorder to make a permanent record of the burner's operation. The main plant supervisory computer would direct the μC system to set the burner for a specified (desired) flame temperature. With this information, the μC's control algorithm would make the necessary adjustments to fuel flow and mixture to attain the required temperature while maintaining minimum combustion pollutants and maximum fuel economy.

At the analog interface, the signals must undergo an A/D conversion before they are suitable for processing. Since there is more than one input, either multiple A/D converters are used or, if all transducers provide the same range of output, all inputs are connected to a single A/D converter through a multiplex switch. The latter method is currently the least expensive and is almost universally used.

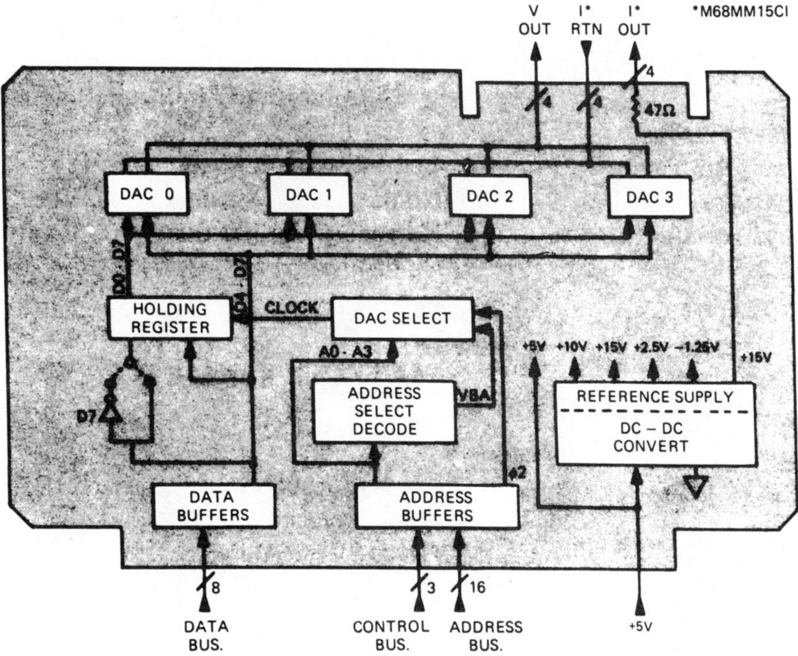

FIGURE 13-19 Block diagram of the **68mm15CV** analog output module.

TABLE 13-2 Programming Examples for the MM15A Analog Module

a. Software Start-of-Conversion with busy test for End-of-Conversion.

```
        LDA   A   #%01000001       SELECT CHAN  1 - GAIN = 2
        STA   A   $9D00            OUTPUT TO GMAR  REG.
        LDA   A   #%00000100       START CONVERSION NO IRQ OR HALT
        STA   A   $9D01            OUTPUT TO CONTROL/STATUS REG.
TEST    BIT   A   $9D01            TEST BUSY BIT
        BNE   TEST                 LOOP TILL BUSY = 0
        LDX   $9D02                LOAD X REG WITH DATA
```

b. External Trigger starts conversion - with IRQ at End-of-Conversion.

```
        LDA   A   #%10000010       SELECT CHAN 2 - GAIN = 4
        STA   A   $9D00            OUTPUT TO GMAR REG.
        LDA   A   $%01010100       ARM BUSY - ALLOW EXT TRIG TO STRT
        STA   A   $9D01            CONVERSION - ALLOW IRQ AT E-O-C

        (Run other program until an interrupt occurs)

IRQ     LDA   A   $9D01            SERVICE IRQ - READ STATUS
        BMI   ADATA                IF IRQF SET, READ DATA
        ...   .....                OTHER INTERRUPT POLLING
        RTI

ADATA   LDA   A   $9D02            LOAD  A  ACCUM WITH DATA HI
        LDA   B   $9D03            LOAD  B  ACCUM WITH DATA LOW
```

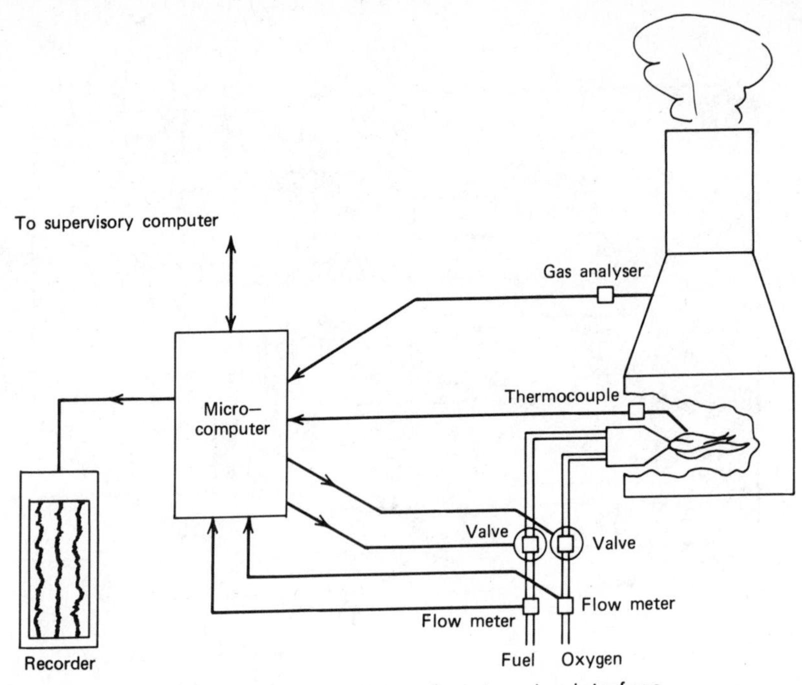

FIGURE 13-20 Boiler control with a μC and analog interface.

However, before these low-level signals can go through the conversion process, they must be amplified. All modern A/D converter designs require inputs of several volts. A differential-input instrumentation amplifier is used for this purpose. Not only is amplification performed but also, through the return of both signal lines from the transducers as a differential connection, high common-mode noise rejection can be attained (see Section 13-9.1). Electrically operated, proportionally controlled fuel and mixture valves are adjusted through their voltage inputs. The analog output modules produce these voltages through a separate D/A converter for each transducer.

13-11.2 Remote Operation

When it is not convenient to locate the computer at the remote site but the distance is too far to run low-level analog signals (more than 100 feet), it is possible to use a system like the one shown in Fig. 13-21. Here, the digital information is transmitted *serially* over twisted pair telephone lines by converting it to 20-mA current loop circuits. Similar 20-mA converter circuits would be used at both ends of the lines and the **6850** Asynchronous Communication Interface Adapters (ACIAs) would send and receive data at 2400 bps or more. This method can be used over lines up to several thousand feet long. The ACIA at the distant end would be used to convert the data back to parallel for connection to the analog modules.

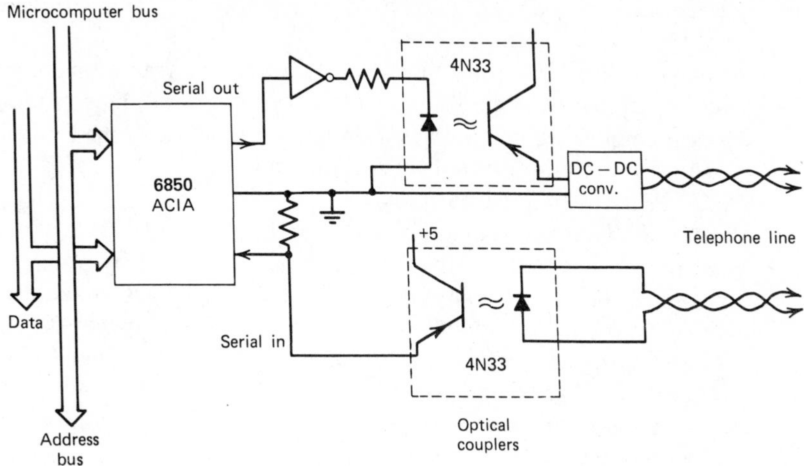

FIGURE 13-21 Serial digital transmission.

13-12 SUMMARY

This chapter has shown how μCs should be interfaced to real-world industrial control equipment for proper operation. The problems of electrical interference or possible equipment damage in industrial environments were discussed and design methods to avoid them were described. ON/OFF (digital) signals were covered as well as cases where analog signals are needed. Methods of hardware construction were described and bus standards were discussed. Several typical system applications that use analog modules were also described.

13-13 GLOSSARY

AC Alternating current.

ACIA Asynchronous Communication Interface Adapter, the **6850** serial data component.

A/D Analog to digital conversion.

Analog Resembling the original. In electronics, it usually refers to a voltage that varies in direct relation to some physical property.

DAC Digital-to-Analog Converter.

Darlington transistor A pair of transistors in a single package interconnected so as to provide a power transistor output with high enough gain that it can be controlled by a PIA.

DC Direct current.

Digital Having two states: HIGH and LOW, 1 and 0, ON and OFF, etc.

Dual In-Line Package (DIP) Standard package for integrated circuits with pins on a 0.1-inch grid pattern.

Electrostatic shield Conductive screen placed between or around an electrical circuit to drain off unwanted charges.

Ground Earth potential, the point to which the frame or chassis is connected.

Multiplexer Electronic switch to select any of a number of inputs or outputs.

Optical coupler Semiconductor device that uses a Light-Emitting Diode (LED) whose output is detected by a phototransistor.

PCB Printed Circuit Board.

Picofarad Unit of capacitance equal to 10^{-12} farad.

Reed relay Vacuum-encapsulated contacts operated by a magnetic field.

Solenoid valve Electrically operated valve using a DC magnetic actuator.

Solid-state relay Semiconductor device connected so that the optically coupled output turns on a TRIAC or Silicon-Controlled Rectifier (SCR) for control of AC motors, lights, and so on.

Successive approximation Technique for determining equality by comparing with progressively smaller values.

Transducer Converter to change physical parameters to electrical signals, or vice versa.

TRIAC Semiconductor device that can be ''triggered'' ON or OFF for control of AC-powered units.

Wetting voltage Voltage impressed across contacts to break through any oxides or dirt to ensure a low contact resistance.

13-14 REFERENCES

Aldridge, Don. *Analog-to-Digital Conversion Techniques with the* **M6800** *Microprocessor System,* Application Note AN-757, Motorola Semiconductor Products, Inc., Phoenix, AZ, 1975.

Burr-Brown. *Digital Output (Contact Closure) Microperipherals for Motorola Microcomputers,* MP701, MP702, PDS 381, Burr-Brown Research Corp., Tucson, AZ, 1977.

Burr-Brown. *Microcomputer Digital Input System,* MP710, PDS 386, Burr-Brown Research Corp., Tucson, AZ, 1978.

Greenfield, Joseph D. *Practical Digital Design,* Second Edition, Wiley, New York, 1983.

Kostopulos, George K. *Digital Engineering,* Wiley, New York, 1975.

Morrison, Robert. *Data Acquisition and the Microcomputer,* Burr-Brown Research Corp., Tucson, AZ, 1977.

Motorola. *M68MM15A/15A1 High-Level A/D Module,* First Edition, Motorola Microsystems, Phoenix, AZ, 1979.

Motorola. *M68MM15C Analog Output Module,* Micromodule 15C, M68MM15C (D), First Edition, Motorola Microsystems, Phoenix, AZ, 1978.

Teeple, C. R. *Isolated Digital Input/Output Microcomputer Peripherals Solve Industrial Problems,* Burr-Brown Research Corp., Tucson, AZ, 1977.

CHAPTER 14
CRT DISPLAY TERMINAL APPLICATION

14-1 INSTRUCTIONAL OBJECTIVES

The major function of a CRT display terminal is to display alphanumeric information on the screen of a Cathode Ray Tube (CRT). This chapter discusses the principles of a display terminal. Motorola's popular Cathode Ray Tube Controller (CRTC) IC, the **6845**, is described in detail and the total design of a display terminal using the **6845** is also presented.

After reading this chapter, the student should be able to

1. Understand CRT display terminal fundamentals and the functions of the CRTC and of a character generator.
2. Design a video display circuit using **6800** family components.
3. Use the **6845** CRTC and set up its registers.
4. Write the software necessary to provide the features expected in an operator terminal.
5. Use serial communications in distributed processing systems.

14-2 SELF-EVALUATION QUESTIONS

Watch for answers to the following questions as you read the chapter. They should help you to understand the many uses of μCs.

1. Why should a display terminal include a serial communications interface?
2. What makes a terminal "intelligent"?
3. What are the advantages of a CRT terminal over a TeleTypewriter (TTY) or other "hard-copy" devices?
4. How does the **MC6845** CRT controller IC simplify the design and improve performance of a display terminal?

5. Why is the access time of the **6800** memories so important in a terminal design?
6. What are the advantages of programmable screen formatting and software cursor control?

14-3 THE 6800 μP IN DATA HANDLING APPLICATIONS

Large central computers have been used extensively to implement data processing and even some industrial process control systems. With the advent of μPs, however, the concept of *distributed processing* is being used more and more. The central processor (in some cases also a μP) is still used to direct the overall system operation, but several μPs are frequently used together to perform the individual tasks. Operator control points are usually required and a human–machine interface is involved.

14-3.1 The CRT Terminal

Probably the most popular Input/Output (I/O) device for communications between humans and computers is the *CRT terminal*. It consists of a CRT (see Section 14-3.2) that displays alphanumeric or graphic information, either read from a computer's memory or received over a line from a distant system; a keyboard similar to a typewriter; and an interface for data transfer from the memory to the CRT. Figure 14-1 shows a typical CRT terminal. Most business systems use CRT terminals for entering and examining data files and other information exchange. In large companies a number of CRTs are often interconnected within a plant or even

FIGURE 14-1 Typical CRT terminal.

between several plants in different cities using modems and telephone circuits. Airline reservation systems, for example, make extensive use of CRT terminals. Sophisticated CRT terminals have editing and graphics capabilities.

The CRT terminal provides essentially the same functions as a teletypewriter but has several advantages. It is quiet, very fast, and generates no printed record (called hard copy) of the transactions. Sometimes a printed record of the data is required, but files are often accessed just for information and the hard copy is unnecessary. Furthermore, the nuisance of constantly feeding paper into the machine is avoided.

CRTs can be used with μC Development Systems (MDSs) for debugging or editing programs and *hard copy* is not needed. Where it is required, as for assembly listings, a printer is provided. A CRT terminal of this type contains several subsystems, including a *keyboard encoder, video display circuitry,* and a *serial communications interface*. In the past these subsystems were interconnected on a common bus and used discrete logic to provide the necessary functions. A μP can provide the same functions, and many new ones such as editing commands or graphics are easily added.

14-3.2 CRT Fundamentals

A **Cathode Ray Tube (CRT)** is an evacuated glass tube that produces images by focusing an electron beam on phosphors that coat the screen area of the device. The brightness of the display is determined by the current in the beam. The beam is directed by either electrostatic or magnetic deflection circuits built around the neck of the CRT. A display is created by systematically sweeping the beam across the entire surface of the screen while varying the intensity of the beam. This will produce a line on the screen if left on for a time or perhaps only a dot if rapidly switched on and off. In a typical CRT data terminal or in a home TV set, an electron beam starts in the upper *left-hand* corner and moves horizontally across the screen. This action is called a *horizontal scan*. The beam is then *blanked* (or turned OFF) to avoid interference with the display on the screen and returned to the left side to start another scan. The time for this *horizontal retrace* is much shorter than the scan time. The horizontal scan rate for American TV and some of the early data terminals is 15,750 Hz.

During the horizontal scan the beam is also slowly moving down the screen, and each scan is one line below the previous one. Eventually the scans reach the bottom. At this point the beam has made many *horizontal scans* and one *vertical scan*. The beam is then blanked and rapidly returned to the top to start another vertical scan or *field*.

Two types of raster scanning are used in CRTs, *interlaced* and *noninterlaced*. Interlaced scanning is used in broadcast TV and on some data monitors where high-density data must be displayed. Two trips, or *fields,* are made down the screen for one single picture or *frame*. One field starts in the upper left corner and the second in the top center, overlapping or interlacing the two fields into a single frame. This is shown in Fig. 14-2, where the solid line indicates the visible trace for field 1 and the dotted line is the return. The second field is indicated by the

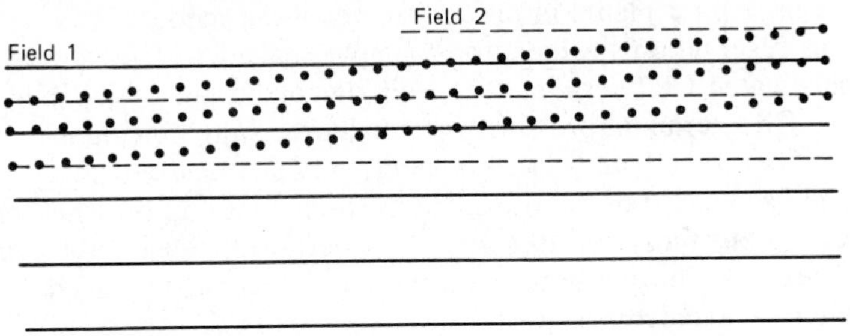

FIGURE 14-2 Interlaced scan.

dashed lines. There are 262.5 horizontal lines per field and a total of 525 lines per frame. The field rate is 60 Hz and the frame rate 30 Hz. The interlace method works well in TV applications, where colors and shadings change gradually. In the display of characters, however, noninterlace scanning is more commonly used. In noninterlaced scanning the beam starts on the same scan line each time so that the frame refresh rate is 60 Hz.

EXAMPLE 14-1

A standard CRT has a horizontal sweep frequency of 15,750 Hz and presents 60 fields per second. Find

a. The time for each horizontal sweep.
b. The time for each vertical sweep.
c. The number of horizontal sweeps (scan lines) per field.

SOLUTION

a. The time for each horizontal sweep is

$$t_h = 1/15{,}750 = 63.5\ \mu\text{/scan line}$$

b. The time for each vertical sweep is

$$t_v = 1/60\ \text{Hz} = 16.667\ \text{ms/field}$$

c. The number of scan lines per field is

$$\frac{16{,}667\ \mu\text{s/field}}{63.5\ \mu\text{s/scan}} = 262.5\ \text{scans/field}$$

Higher-density displays are needed for some of the more advanced terminals, and future developments will undoubtedly use new methods. To get more characters on the screen and/or clearer characters by increasing the number of dots per character, data CRTs use a higher sweep frequency. The horizontal oscillator frequency can range from 15,720 Hz, which gives 262 scan lines per field, to 68,850 Hz (338 scan lines) or higher.

As the beam is sweeping the screen, its horizontal position is controlled by a *horizontal oscillator* (typically running at 15,750 Hz), and the vertical position is similarly controlled by a *vertical oscillator* (operating at 60 Hz). These oscillators must be kept in step with each other and with the displayed information. This is accomplished by generating a *horizontal sync* and a *vertical sync* signal. Fig. 14-3 shows the display and its controlling signals. Each of these causes its oscillator to be reset and starts the beam over again at precisely the right time. As the beam scans off the edge of the screen, it must be turned off until it returns to a position where data is to be displayed to avoid producing a streak during retrace in both the horizontal and vertical directions. This is called **Blanking** and the signal which turns the electron beam ON and OFF is called *the Blanking signal* or, conversely, the *display enable* signal.

14-3.3 Character Generation

The most common method of generating characters is to create a matrix of dots, "x" dots (or columns) wide and "y" dots (or rows) high. Each character is created by selectively filling in dots. As "x" and "y" become larger, a more detailed character can be created. Two common dot matrices are 5×7 and 7×9. Characters require some space between them, so they are placed in a character block that is larger than the character as shown in Fig. 14-4. As the electron gun of the CRT scans one line across the screen, it displays the first row of dots for each character on that character line. On the next scan, the second row of dots and

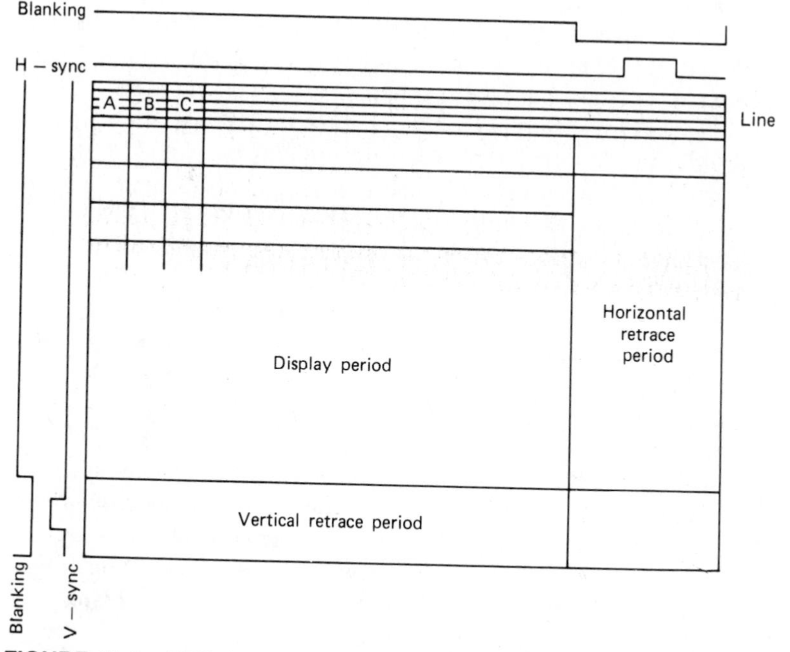

FIGURE 14-3 CRT display controlled by Hsync, Vsync, and blanking.

ROW SELECT
TRUTH TABLE

RS3	RS2	RS1	RS0	OUTPUT
0	0	0	0	R0
0	0	0	1	R1
0	0	1	0	R2
0	0	1	1	R3
0	1	0	0	R4
0	1	0	1	R5
0	1	1	0	R6
0	1	1	1	R7
1	0	0	0	R8
1	0	0	1	R9
1	0	1	0	R10
1	0	1	1	R11
1	1	0	0	R12
1	1	0	1	R13
1	1	1	0	R14
1	1	1	1	R15

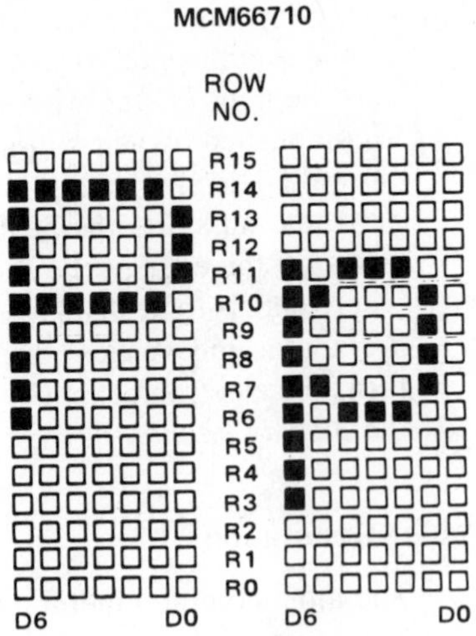

MCM66710

ROW NO.

R15 R14 R13 R12 R11 R10 R9 R8 R7 R6 R5 R4 R3 R2 R1 R0

D6 D0 D6 D0

FIGURE 14-4 A 7 × 9 dot matrix character in a 9 × 16 character block.

spaces for each character are displayed. This process continues until all "y" rows of the character have been displayed, as shown in Fig. 14-5. The row-by-row scanning is then repeated for every line of characters on the screen.

This method of scanning is implemented by use of a *character generation* ROM, which converts an ASCII-encoded character into the dots required to display that character. The inputs to the ROM are the ASCII code of the desired character and the row address being scanned. The lines of ASCII codes (1 byte for each character) are normally stored in the display RAM and retrieved repeatedly as the rows of dots are being refreshed.

Figure 14-6 shows one of many patterns that are available in one type of these ROMs, the Motorola **MC66750**. It contains the full ASCII set of 128 character codes in a 7×9 format. These consist of both upper- and lowercase letters, numbers from 0 to 9, punctuation marks, and 32 control characters. Other simpler character generators are also available, such as the Signetics **2513** for 5×7 format systems.

Control characters such as NUL (00) and EOT ($04) are used to control messages and are not normally displayable, but a feature of full complement ROMs like the **66750** is the ability to display a symbol or a dual character (as shown in the top two rows of Fig. 14-6) for each of the control codes if desired. The *carriage return* ($0D) and *line feed* ($0A) also have those symbols but are really "displayable" characters since their actions can be seen.

These ROMs are usually used in the more advanced *intelligent* CRT terminals and software is used to select whether the control codes are sent or a display is generated. This option is valuable when testing communications systems. Most of the simpler ROMs like the Signetics **2513** or other 5×7 Character Generators do not display lowercase letters or control codes.

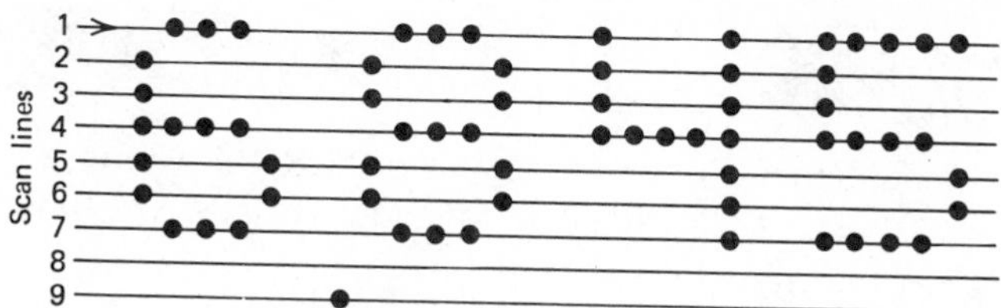

FIGURE 14-5 Dot matrix scanning using 5 × 7 characters.

As seen in the boxes along the top and sides of Fig. 14-6, the seven address lines (A0–A6) select the character. The four Row Select inputs (RS0–RS3) select the row of dots that make up the character. This is shown in more detail in Fig. 14-4.

Note: This character ROM has a feature to shift some characters down by three rows (see the note at the bottom of Fig. 14-6). This allows the tails of the y's and other characters to descend below most characters and produces a more realistic and readable display.

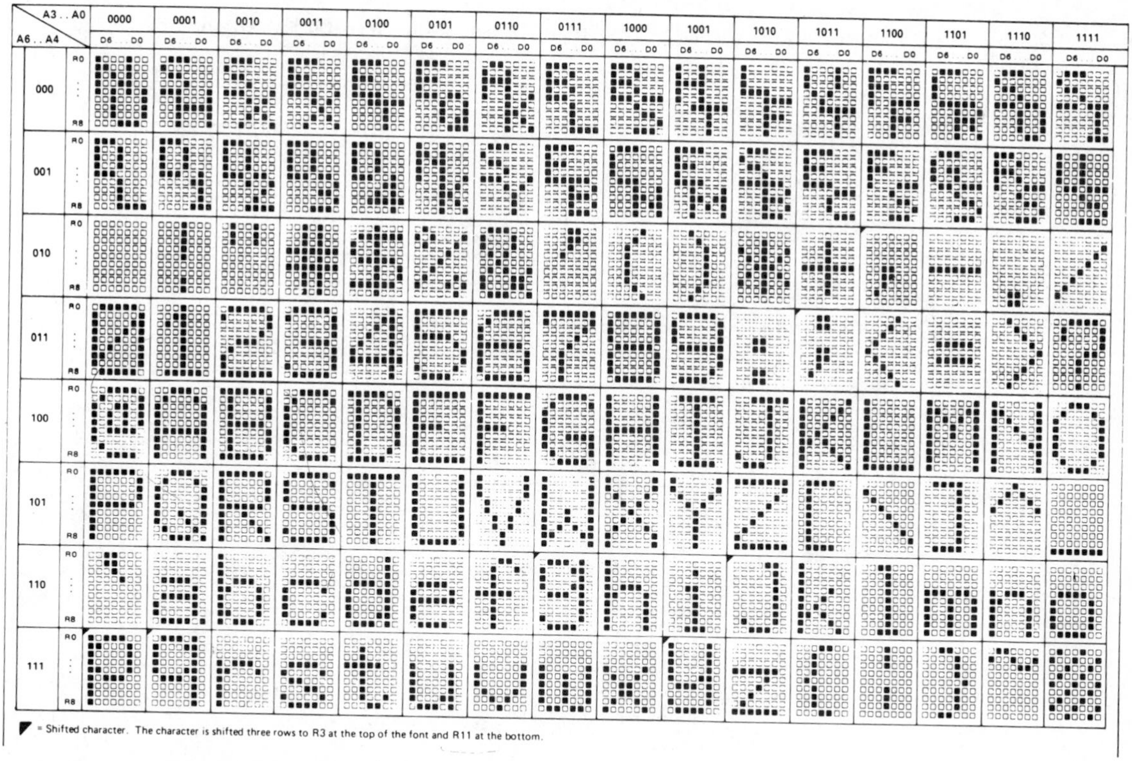

◤ = Shifted character. The character is shifted three rows to R3 at the top of the font and R11 at the bottom.

FIGURE 14-6 **MCM66750** pattern.

EXAMPLE 14-2

What output is obtained from a **66750** character ROM when the ASCII character \$41 (or A6.....A0) is 1000001 and the row address (RS3..RS0) is 0000?

SOLUTION
Figure 14-6 shows that for A3..A0 = 0001 the character is in the second column, and for A6, A5, A4 = 100 (the fifth row down) the character is "A." If the row select pins are all 0, the top row is selected. The ROM output code is **0011100**.

Figure 14-7 shows a typical character generator circuit. The 7-bit ASCII code is applied to pins A0 to A6 of the character ROM and the row count of the character is applied to pins RS0 to RS3. The character ROM then outputs dots for the selected row of the selected character. The output dots (0011100 for Example 14-2) are sent to a parallel-to-serial converter, where they are shifted out to the CRT beam circuit to produce dots on the screen in the right place. Here two **7495**s shift registers are used in series to accommodate the 7 bits of each character row. Of course, the row and character selection must be synchronized with the scanning beam. When the entire row of dots has been displayed, the row counter is incremented and the next row of dots for each character is displayed.

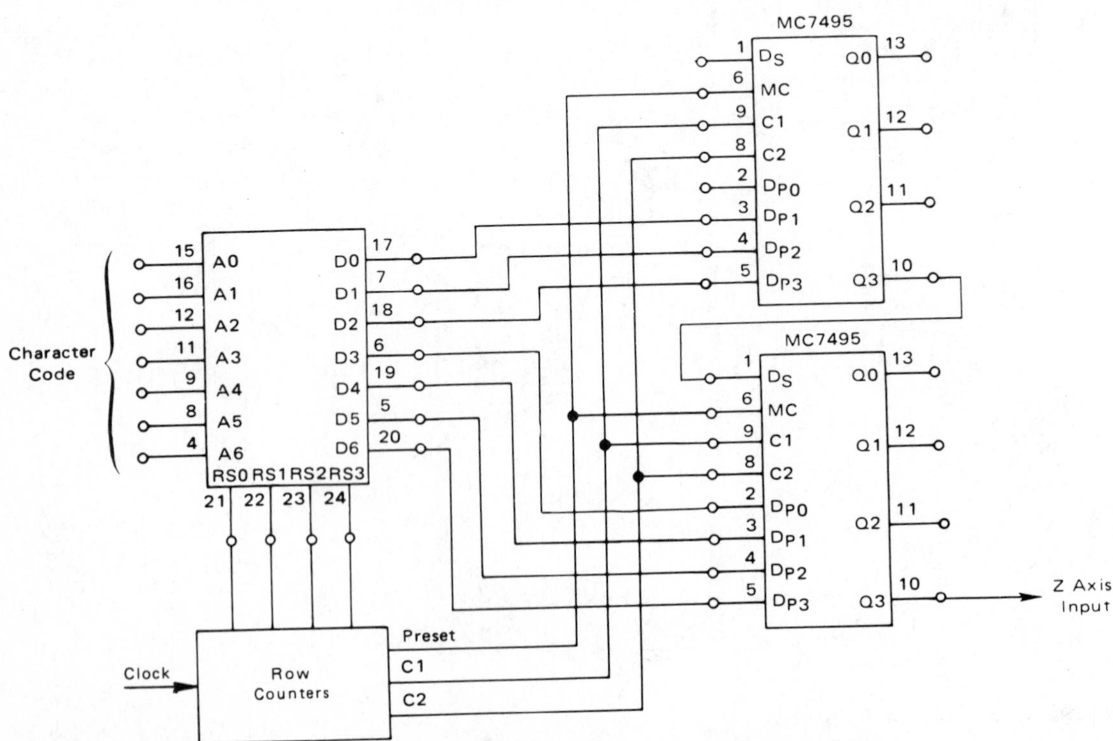

FIGURE 14-7 Character generator circuit showing method of serializing the dots.

EXAMPLE 14-3

Using a 5 × 7 character embedded in an 8 × 10 field, how many character lines can be written on a CRT screen if standard timing is used? Assume the characters are not interlaced.

SOLUTION

At this point, we must make a distinction between *rows* and *lines*. We define a *row* as a *single horizontal sweep of the beam,* where typically dots are displayed. A *line* is a *line of characters* such as those you are reading here, which requires several *rows* of dots for its presentation.

Example 14-1 showed that there are 262.5 rows per field on an ordinary TV screen. Subtracting the time required for Vertical Sync and Retrace and for leaving adequate margins on the top and bottom of the display leaves about 200 usable rows per frame. Therefore, if 10 rows are used for each character, 20 lines of characters can be displayed.

14-3.4 The Dot Rate

The time required to go from dot to dot as the beam scans across the screen is called the *dot rate*. It is the highest frequency used in the character generator circuitry. The maximum dot rate is about twice the bandwidth or upper frequency response of the video circuitry driving the CRT. The bandwidth of a commercial TV set is about 3.5 MHz, which limits the dot rate clock to about 7 MHz. Monitors, which are CRT devices built specifically for the purpose of displaying alphanumeric information, have higher bandwidths and can display more characters on a line.

EXAMPLE 14-4

If the dot rate for a display is 5 MHz, how many characters can be displayed on a CRT? Assume the character is 8 dots wide (including blanks) and 40 μs is available for each line.

SOLUTION

Since the dot rate is 5 MHz, each dot requires 0.2 μs for display. The number of dots that can be displayed on a single line is therefore 40 μs/0.2 μs per dot = 200 dots. The number of characters per line is 200 dots/8 dots per character = 25 characters.

Example 14-4 explains why CRT circuits that use commercial TVs usually do not have a large number of characters per line. If about 80 characters per line are required, a CRT monitor should be used rather than a TV set. A commercial TV set is the least expensive display one can buy. Hobbyist or homebuilt CRT systems using a TV set usually display 32 characters per line.

The Apple II computer uses a **2513**-character generator and produces a 5 × 7 dot matrix embedded in a 7 × 8 grid. The dot clock of an Apple II is 7.159 MHz, or 140 ns per dot.

EXAMPLE 14-5

An Apple II computer in text mode uses 24 lines of 40 characters each.

a. How long does it take to display each line?
b. How long does it take to display each frame?

SOLUTION

a. The time each line is displayed is

140 ns/dot × 7 dots/character × 40 characters/line = 39.1 μs/line

b. The Apple II uses 24 lines times 8 rows per line, or 192 rows. It therefore requires 192 rows × 63.5 μs/row or 12.2 ms. Thus the Apple display is ON for 39.1 of the 63.5 μs on each horizontal line and for 12.2 ms of the 16.7 ms for each frame. The remaining time is used for vertical and horizontal retrace. Note that an alphanumeric display does not use the entire available time because it cannot completely fill up the screen the way a TV picture does. Alphanumeric displays require margins.

14-4 THE 6845 CRT CONTROLLER

Complex circuitry is required to put each character on the screen in its proper place and to generate the synchronizing and blanking signals. Fortunately, these functions have been incorporated into a Large-Scale Integrated (LSI) μP peripheral IC known as a *CRT Controller*. The Motorola device for this purpose is the **6845** CRTC and it is used as the interface from the μP bus to the video monitor (detailed information can be found in the **6845** Data Sheet cited in Section 14-10).

A block diagram of a system that uses this CRT controller is shown in Fig. 14-8. In the figure, all the system components associated with the video display and character generation are shown below the μP bus lines, and the components that make up the rest of the computer system are shown at the top of the diagram. Several EPROMs might be used to provide sufficient memory for the controlling program (depending on the number of features implemented). The RAM may also have to be increased to 1K byte or more. The I/O components shown allow parallel keyboard input and serial communication (perhaps via modems from a remote site). If desired, a **6852** Synchronous Serial Data Adapter (SSDA) might be substituted for the ACIA.

One of the requirements of a CRT data terminal is that the characters must be rewritten on the screen every frame time. This is called *screen refresh*. In the implementation shown in Fig. 14-8, this is done by using a RAM array, which stores the characters in the format specified by the **6845**. This RAM is called the *display* or *refresh* RAM. The screen formats are programmable in the **6845** and almost any configuration can be provided [24 lines of 80 characters (80 × 24), 64 × 16, 72 × 64, 132 × 20, etc.]. The number of characters capable of being stored depends on the display RAM size. As shown in Fig. 14-8, the primary functions of the CRTC are generating *refresh addresses*, generating *row selects* for the character ROM, and video monitor timing **(Hsync, Vsync)**. The internal cursor register generates a *cursor output* when its contents compare to the current refresh address. *The cursor position indicates to the operator where the next character will be written.*

EXAMPLE 14-6

A CRT displays 54 characters per line, and there are 10 rows per line. Describe how the screen RAM is read as the scan progresses.

SOLUTION

In a normal CRT, the ASCII codes for the first line would be stored in RAM locations 0 to 53, the second line would be stored in locations 54 to 107, and so forth. As the beam sweeps through the first row of the first line of characters, it must access locations 0 to 53 successively. The beam then retraces to write the second row of the first line. It must again access locations 0 to 53 (the row counter has been incremented, however, and this selects the next row of dots from the character generator ROM). This continues for each row of the first line. Therefore locations 0–53 are accessed 10 times before the first line is completed. Then the second line is written by accessing locations 54–107 ten consecutive times. This procedure continues until the entire screen is written.

Obviously, generating this sequence of memory addresses is complex. Fortunately the **6845** generates these addresses properly, and the user need not be concerned with the problem.

The **6845** CRTC contains 18 internal registers that must be initialized by the μP. The μP communicates with the **6845** registers through a buffered 8-bit data bus. These **6845** registers hold the basic system parameters such as the number of horizontal lines for each character row, number of lines per field, cursor location, and whether interlaced or noninterlaced scan is desired (see Section 14-4.2).

EXAMPLE 14-7

Sixty-four characters must be displayed on each line of a CRT. If the standard TV

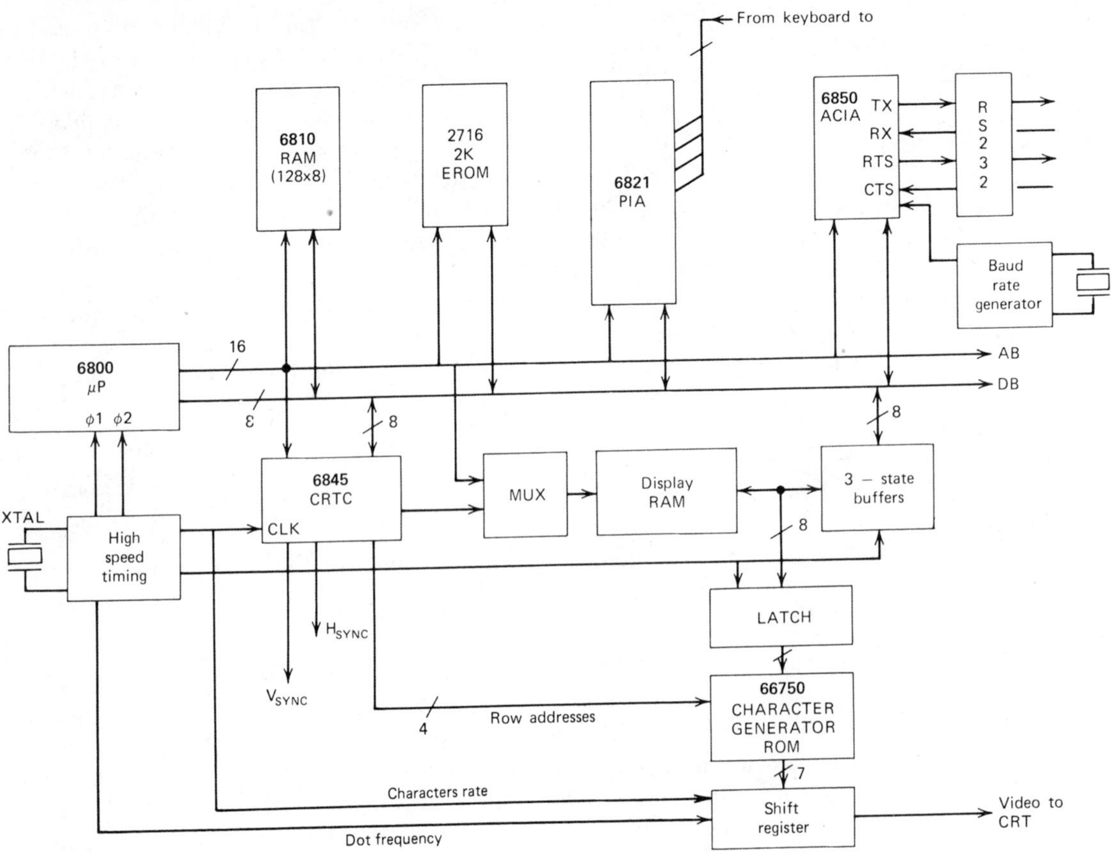

FIGURE 14-8 CRT terminal block diagram.

sweep frequency is used and 20% of the line is allowed for horizontal blanking and retrace, how much of the time is allowed for each character?

SOLUTION
The standard TV display scan frequency is 15,750 Hz. This means that each sweep takes 1/15,750 = 63.49 μs. If 20% of this time is used for blanking and retrace, the displayable part of the line takes 50.79 μs. The time to display each character is therefore 50.79/64 = 0.79 μs or a rate of 1.267 MHz.

If there are 80 characters on the line the rate must be 1.58 MHz. Unless multiplexing is used, the display RAM must be accessed at this rate.

All **6845** timing is derived from the CLOCK (CLK) input. In alphanumeric terminals this corresponds to the character rate and is divided down from the video dot rate by a high-speed external counter. The video signal to the display is the row of bits shifted out of the output shift register by the DOT high-speed timing (see Fig. 14-8).

To summarize, the **6845** CRTC is a Very Large Scale Integrated (VLSI) component that replaces several counters in a more primitive display terminal. The **6845** does the following:

1. It generates horizontal and vertical sync pulses for the video output.
2. It generates the row addresses needed by the character generator.
3. It generates the proper addresses for the refresh RAM.
4. It generates a display enable signal when the display is active.
5. It generates a cursor signal when the cursor should be displayed.
6. It has an input for a light pen strobe and will store the position of a light pen in a set of registers.

14-4.1 The 6845 Signals

Figure 14-9 shows the pin assignments for the **6845**. The processor interface consists of

1. The μP data bus signals D0–D7.
2. Chip Select $\overline{CS}$. This signal must be active (LOW) when the μP is communicating with the **6845**. When $\overline{CS}$ is HIGH, however, the **6845** will continue to

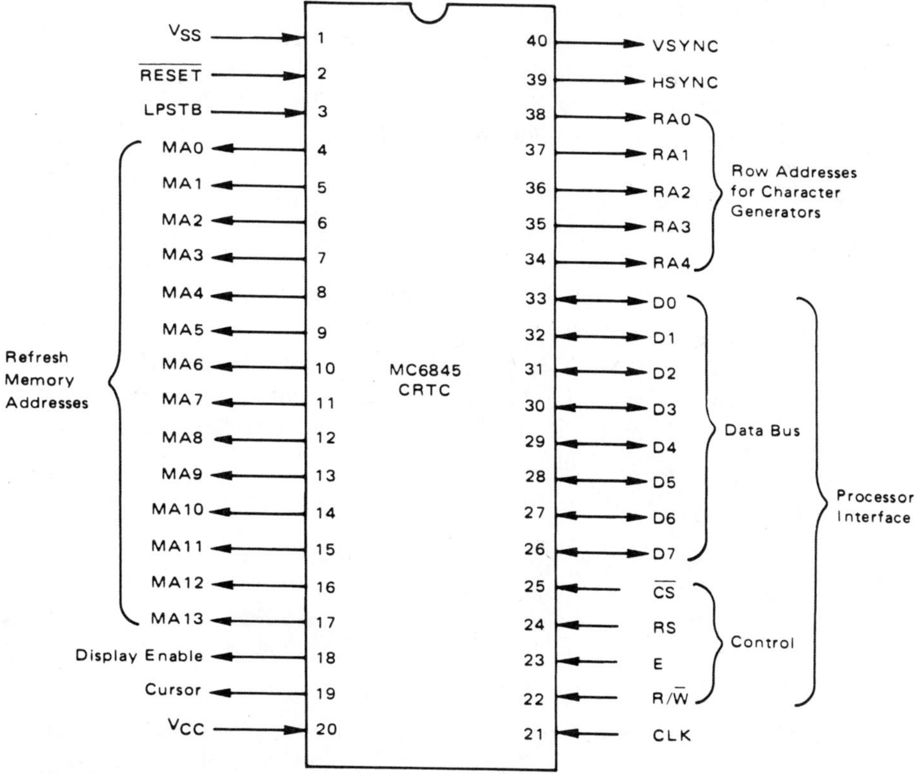

FIGURE 14-9 **6845** pin assignment.

generate row addresses and refresh RAM addresses, so the display can be updated without any action by the μP.

3. Register Select ($\overline{RS}$). When $\overline{RS}$ is LOW, a WRITE to the **6845** writes the address register (see Section 14-4.2). When $\overline{RS}$ is HIGH, a READ or WRITE to the **6845** reads or writes data.
4. Enable (E). This signal is meant to be tied to the μP's clock signal to synchronize data transfers between the μP and the **6845**.
5. Read/$\overline{\text{Write}}$ (R/$\overline{W}$). As in all **6800** ICs, a LOW on this line indicates that the μP is *writing* data into the **6845**.

The other signals on the **6845** are vertical and horizontal sync, the row addresses for the character generator, the refresh RAM addresses, light pen strobe, reset, display enable, cursor, and CLK. The clock signal is at the character rate (not the dot rate) of the display.

14-4.2 The 6845 Registers

There are 18 control/status registers and one address register in the **6845** that are used to control the display and perform other peripheral functions, such as indicating the cursor position. A block diagram of the **6845** is shown in Fig. 14-10 and an illustration of the CRT screen format that is controlled by the CRTC is shown in Fig. 14-11.

Table 14-1 lists the 18 internal registers in the CRTC and gives their functions. The READ and WRITE columns of Table 14-1 show that registers R0 to R13 are write-only (they cannot be read). The number of bits to be written into each register is also given in the table.

EXAMPLE 14-8

How many bits are written into the address register?

SOLUTION
Table 14-1 shows that bits 7, 6, and 5 are crossed out, so 5 bits are written to the address register. The address register must address one of 18 registers, so only 5 bits are required. The address of each register is given in the address register columns of Table 14-1.

The function of each register in the **6845** is described in the rest of this section.

The address register holds the address of the control register to be written into. Addresses are written into the address register when $\overline{CS}$ = R/$\overline{W}$ = $\overline{RS}$ = 0. Control registers are written when $\overline{CS}$ = R/$\overline{W}$ = 0 and $\overline{RS}$ = 1. A typical way to write the control register is to

1. Set $\overline{RS}$ to 0 and write a zero into the address register.
2. Change $\overline{RS}$ to 1 and write the data into R0.
3. Change $\overline{RS}$ to 0 and write 1 into the address register.
4. Change $\overline{RS}$ to 1 and write the data into control register 1.

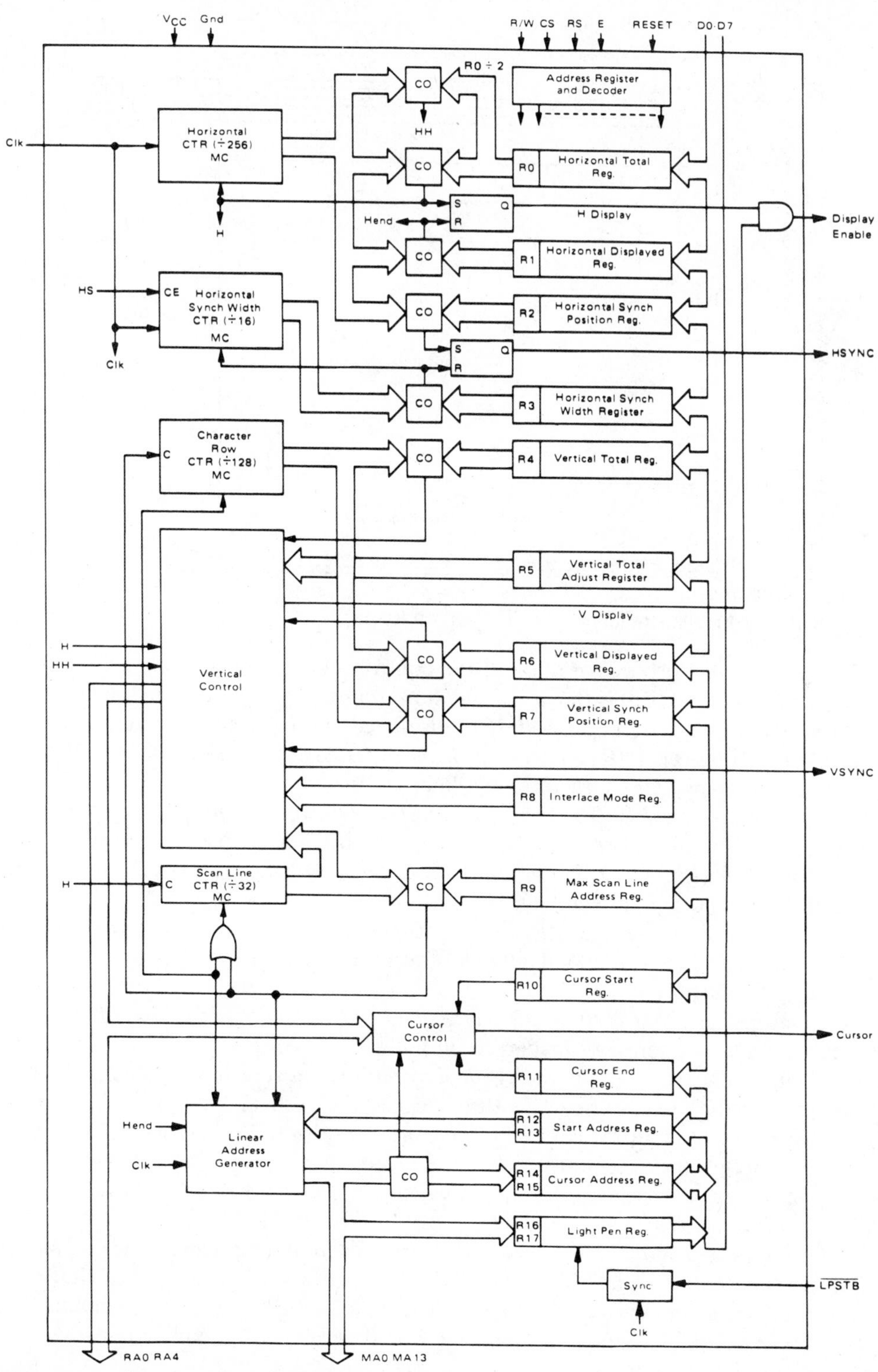

FIGURE 14-10 CRTC functional block diagram.

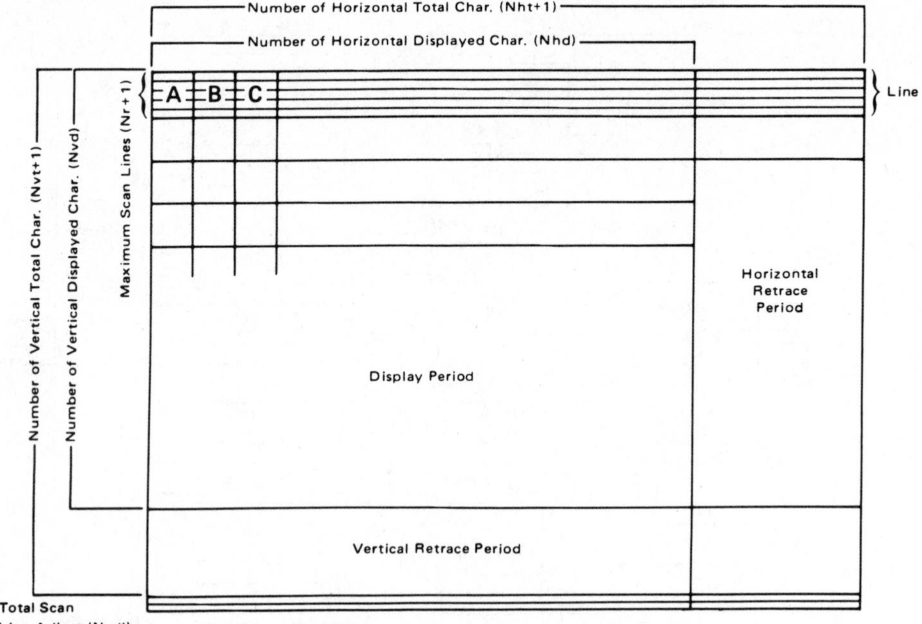

FIGURE 14-11 Illustration of the CRT screen format.

Continue this procedure until all the control registers have been written into. Control register 0 (R0) is the *horizontal total register*. It contains the total number of horizontal characters on each line (displayed and nondisplayed) minus 1.

Control register 1 (R1) is the *horizontal displayed register*. It contains the number of displayed characters on a line.

Control register 2 (R2) is the *horizontal sync position register*. It controls the position of the displayed characters relative to the horizontal sync pulse.

Control register 3 (R3) is the *horizontal sync width register*. It determines the width of the horizontal sync pulse.

Control registers R4 and R5 are the *vertical total* (R4) and *vertical total adjust* (R5) registers. This is the total number of rows (R4) and fractional rows (R5) in the field of the display.

Control register 6 (R6) is the *vertical displayed register*. It determines the number of character rows displayed on the CRT screen.

Control register 7 (R7) is the *vertical sync position register*. It determines the position of the displayed rows with respect to the vertical sync pulse.

Control register 8 (R8) is the *interlace mode register*. This 2-bit register determines whether the screen display is interlaced.

Control register 9 (R9) is the *maximum scan line address register*. It determines the number of scan lines per character row.

Registers R10 and R11 are the *cursor start* and *cursor end* registers. Bits 5 and 6 of the cursor start register determine whether the cursor blinks and its blink rate (or period), as shown in Fig. 14-12a. The other bits in the register define the starting row of the cursor and register R11 determines the cursor end row, as shown in Fig. 14-12b.

Registers R12 and R13 are the *start address registers*. They consist of a 14-bit refresh RAM starting address. The 6 higher-order bits are in R12 and the 8 lower-order bits in R13.

Registers R14 and R15 are the *cursor position registers*. They constitute a 14-bit register that determines the cursor location. These are the only registers in the **6845** that can be both read and written into.

Registers R16 and R17 are the *light pen registers*. When a light pen strobe occurs, the beam address is stored in these registers. They constitute a 14-bit read-only address register and give the μP the address of a light pen's position on the screen.

14-4.3 Setting Up a CRTC System

To set up a CRTC system, the following are required:

1. The hardware components shown in Fig. 14-8 must be in place.
2. The μP must write the data to be displayed into the refresh RAM. The

TABLE 14-1 CRTC Internal Register Assignments

		Address register					*Register*		*Program*			*Number of bits*							
$\overline{CS}$	*RS*	*4*	*3*	*2*	*1*	*0*	*#*	*Register file*	*unit*	*READ*	*WRITE*	*7*	*6*	*5*	*4*	*3*	*2*	*1*	*0*
1	X	X	X	X	X	X	X	—	—	—	—								
0	0	X	X	X	X	X	X	Address register	—	No	Yes								
0	1	0	0	0	0	0	R0	Horizontal total	Char.	No	Yes								
0	1	0	0	0	0	1	R1	Horizontal displayed	Char.	No	Yes								
0	1	0	0	0	1	0	R2	H. sync position	Char.	No	Yes								
0	1	0	0	0	1	1	R3	H. sync width	Char.	No	Yes								
0	1	0	0	1	0	0	R4	Vertical total	Char. row	No	Yes								
0	1	0	0	1	0	1	R5	V. total adjust	Scan line	No	Yes								
0	1	0	0	1	1	0	R6	Vertical displayed	Char. row	No	Yes								
0	1	0	0	1	1	1	R7	V. sync position	Char. row	No	Yes								
0	1	0	1	0	0	0	R8	Interlace mode	—	No	Yes								
0	1	0	1	0	0	1	R9	Max scan line address	Scan line	No	Yes								
0	1	0	1	0	1	0	R10	Cursor start	Scan line	No	Yes		B	P			(Note 1)		
0	1	0	1	0	1	1	R11	Cursor end	Scan line	No	Yes								
0	1	0	1	1	0	0	R12	Start address (H)	—	No	Yes								
0	1	0	1	1	0	1	R13	Start address (L)	—	No	Yes								
0	1	0	1	1	1	0	R14	Cursor (H)	—	Yes	Yes								
0	1	0	1	1	1	1	R15	Cursor (L)	—	Yes	Yes								
0	1	1	0	0	0	0	R16	Light pen (H)	—	Yes	No								
0	1	1	0	0	0	1	R17	Light pen (L)	—	Yes	No								

Note 1: Bit 5 of the Cursor Start Raster Register is used for blink period control, and Bit 6 is used to select blink or non-blink.

Example of cursor display mode:

Bit 6	Bit 5	of Cursor Start Register
Ø	Ø	Nonblink
Ø	1	Cursor nondisplay
1	Ø	Blink, 1/16 field rate
1	1	Blink, 1/32 field rate

←blink period 16 to 32 × field period

(a)

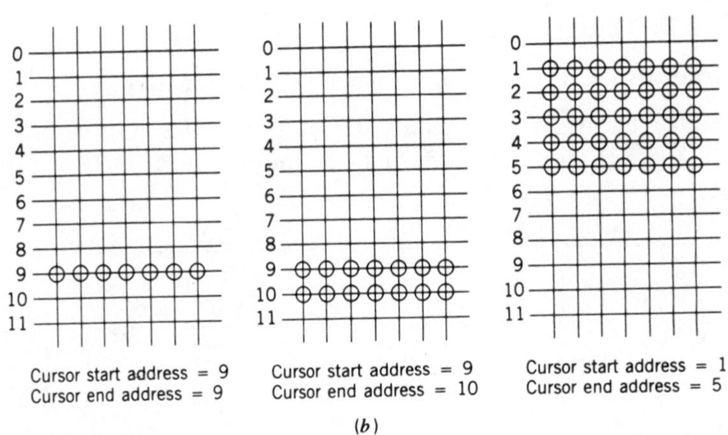

FIGURE 14-12 Example of cursor display mode. (a) Cursor start register. (b) Cursor control.

multiplexer in Fig. 14-8 determines whether the μP or the CRTC controls the addresses of the refresh RAM. Normally, the CRTC controls, but when the μP needs to read or write the RAM, it must control the addresses. In some sophisticated systems, the μP has access when a clock is HIGH and the CRTC has access when the same clock is LOW.

3. The CRTC registers must be initialized to properly control the displays. This requires both a program and a hardware interface to the μP. A CRTC worksheet, as shown in Table 14-2, greatly aids the designer.

This procedure is best illustrated by the example given in the next section.

14-4.4 Example of a CRTC Design

This section presents a very simple example of a video display system using the CRTC. We chose to have 16 displayed lines of 32 characters each.[1] The characters were chosen to be a 5 × 8 matrix embedded in a 7-column by 10-row block. This is compatible with a **2513** character generator.

The display was designed to operate at standard TV-type CRT specifications,

[1] This example was tried in the laboratory at Rochester Institute of Technology.

TABLE 14-2 CRTC Format Worksheet

Display Format Worksheet

1.	Displayed Characters per Row		______	Char.
2.	Displayed Character Rows per Screen		______	Rows
3.	Character Matrix	a. Columns	______	Columns
		b. Rows	______	Rows
4.	Character Block	a. Columns	______	Columns
		b. Rows	______	Rows
5.	Frame Refresh Rate		______	Hz
6.	Horizontal Oscillator Frequency		______	Hz
7.	Active Scan Lines (Line 2 × Line 4b)		______	Lines
8.	Total Scan Lines (Line 6 ÷ Line 5)		______	Lines
9.	Total Rows Per Screen (Line 8 ÷ Line 4b)		____ Rows	and ____ Lines
10.	Vertical Sync Delay (Char. Rows)		______	Rows
11.	Vertical Sync Width (Scan Lines (16))		16	Lines
12.	Horizontal Sync Delay (Character Times)		______	Char. Times
13.	Horizontal Sync Width (Character Times)		______	Char. Times
14.	Horizontal Scan Delay (Character Times)		______	Char. Times
15.	Total Character Times (Line 1 + 12 + 13 + 14)		______	Char. Times
16.	Character Rate (Line 6 × 15)		______	Hz
17.	Dot Clock Rate (Line 4a × 16)		______	Hz

CRTC Registers

		Decimal	Hex
R0	Horizontal Total (Line 15 − 1)	______	______
R1	Horizontal Displayed (Line 1)	______	______
R2	Horizontal Sync Position (Line 1 + Line 12)	______	______
R3	Horizontal Sync Width (Line 13)	______	______
R4	Vertical Total (Line 9 − 1)	______	______
R5	Vertical Adjust (Line 9 Lines)	______	______
R6	Vertical Displayed (Line 2)	______	______
R7	Vertical Sync Position (Line 2 + Line 10)	______	______
R8	Interlace (00 Normal, 01 Interlace, 03 Interlace, and Video)		______
R9	Max Scan Line Add (Line 4b − 1)	______	______
R10	Cursor Start	______	______
R11	Cursor End	______	______
R12, R13	Start Address (H and L)	______	______
R14, R15	Cursor (H and L)		______

Display Format Worksheet

1 Displayed characters per row		32	Char.
2 Displayed character rows per screen		16	Rows
3 Character matrix	**a** Columns	5	Columns
	b Rows	8	Rows
4 Character block	**a** Columns	7	Columns
	b Rows	10	Rows
5 Frame refresh rate		60	Hz
6 Horizontal oscillator frequency		15,750	Hz
7 Active scan lines (line 2 × line 4b)		160	Lines
8 Total scan lines (line 6 ÷ line 5)		262	Lines
9 Total rows per screen (line 8 ÷ line 4b)		26 Rows	and 2 lines
10 Vertical sync delay (char. rows)		0	Rows
11 Vertical sync width (scan lines (16))		16	Lines
12 Horizontal sync delay (character times)		10	Char. times
13 Horizontal sync width (character times)		10	Char. times
14 Horizontal scan delay (character times)		10	Char. times
15 Total character times (Line 1 + 12 + 13 + 14)		62	Char. times
16 Character rate (line 6 × 15)		976.5	KHz
17 Dot clock rate (line 4a × 16)		6.836	MHz

	CRTC Registers	**Decimal**	**Hex**
R0	Horizontal total (Line 15–1)	61	3D
R1	Horizontal displayed (Line 1)	32	20
R2	Horizontal sync position (Line 1 + Line 12)	42	2A
R3	Horizontal sync width (Line 13)	10	A
R4	Vertical total (Line 9–1)	25	19
R5	Vertical adjust (Line 9 Lines)	2	2
R6	Vertical displayed (Line 2)	16	10
R7	Vertical sync position (line 2 + line 10)	16	10
R8	Interlace (00 normal, 01 interlace, 03 interlace, and video)		0
R9	Max scan line add (line 4b − 1)	9	9
R10	Cursor start	0	0
R11	Cursor end	9	9
R12, R13	Start address (H and L)	—	—
R14, R15	Cursor (H and L)		—

FIGURE 14-13 CRTC format worksheet.

which are 60 frames/s and a horizontal oscillator frequency of 15,750 Hz. These specifications determine the first nine entries in the display format worksheet (Table 14-1).

To complete the display format worksheet, the vertical sync delay was chosen as 0 rows, and the horizontal sync delay, horizontal sync width, and horizontal scan delay were all chosen as 10 character times. This gave a total of 62 characters per line at a 15,750-Hz horizontal frequency, or a 976.5-Hz character rate.

Figure 14-13 shows the display format worksheet for this example and the contents of the CRTC registers as derived from the specifications.

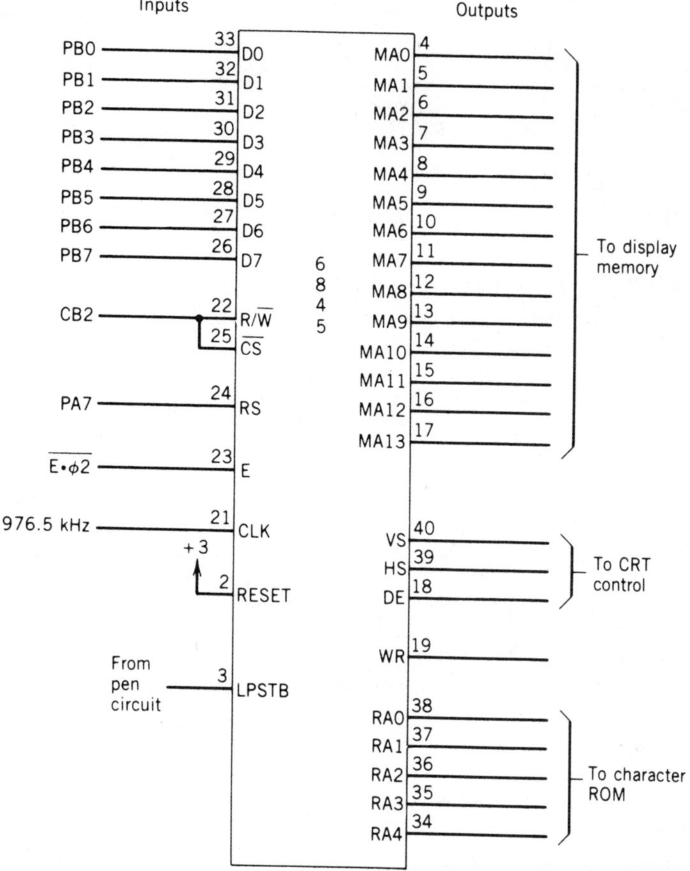

FIGURE 14-14 Schematic diagram showing the connections to the **6845.**

The **6845** was connected to a **6809** μP[2] (see Chapter 11) via a PIA (see Section 8-4), as shown in Fig. 14-14. The data bus on the **6845** was connected to the PB lines and the PIA was placed in pulse mode so that each time data was written to data register B, CB2 went LOW, causing a LOW on R/$\overline{\text{W}}$ and $\overline{\text{CS}}$. The $\overline{\text{RS}}$ input to the **6845** was connected to PA7.

Figure 14-15 shows a program to initialize the **6845**. After initialization, the program writes register 0, repeats with register 1, and so on. The contents of each control register are shown in Fig. 14-16.

Many more sophisticated CRTC display drivers and terminals are described in Motorola's literature. Space limitations preclude discussing them, but the simple CRTC circuit presented here should give the reader a firm grasp of the fundamentals required to successfully use a **6845** CRTC in a display terminal. A complete design of a practical terminal that uses the **6845** is given starting in Section 14-6.

[2] The **6809** was part of the **6809-D4** kit manufactured by Motorola.

```
                                 OPT   S,O,L
           E0FD          CRA     EQU   $E0FD       INIT NAMES FOR THE PIA
           E0FC          DRA     EQU   $E0FC
           E0FF          CRB     EQU   $E0FF
           E0FE          DRB     EQU   $E0FE
           000F          REGNUM  EQU   $0F
           0240          REGTAB  EQU   $240
0200                             ORG   $200        START AT $200
0200 7F    E0FD          START   CLR   CRA
0203 7F    E0FF                  CLR   CRB
0206 96    FF                    LDA   $FF         INIT PIA
0208 B7    E0FC                  STA   DRA
020B B7    E0FE                  STA   DRB
020E 86    3C                    LDA   #$3C
0210 B7    E0FD                  STA   CRA
0213 86    2C                    LDA   #$2C
0215 B7    E0FE                  STA   DRB
0218 5F                          CLRB
0219 8E    0240                  LDX   #REGTAB     GET START OF TABLE

021C 4F                  REGINT  CLRA
021D B7    E0FC                  STA   DRA         SET RS LINE LOW
0220 F7    E0FE                  STB   DRB         WRITE REG NUM INTO ADDRESS
0223 86    80                    LDA   #$80
0225 B7    E0FC                  STA   DRA         SET RS HIGH
0228 A6    80                    LDA   0,X+        LOAD REG CONTENTS
022A B7    E0FE                  STA   DRB         STORE IN REG
022D 5C                          INCB              NEXT REG
022E C1    10                    CMPB  #REGNUM+1   DONE?
0230 26    EA                    BNE   REGINT      DO IT AGAIN
0232 3F                          SWI
                                 END

TOTAL ERRORS:   0      TOTAL WARNINGS:   0

SYMBOL TABLE

CRA    E0FD  CRB    E0FF  DRA    E0FC  DRB    E0FE  REGINT 021C
REGNUM 000F  REGTAB 0240  START  0200
```

FIGURE 14-15 A **6809** program to initialize the **6845.** (From *The Microprocessor Handbook,* edited by Joseph D. Greenfield. Copyright © 1985 by John Wiley & Sons. Reprinted by permission of John Wiley & Sons, Inc.)

14-5 MEMORY ACCESS TECHNIQUES

The display RAM must be read and its output sent to the character ROM whenever the screen needs refreshing, but the RAM must also be accessed by the μP to enter or delete data from the screen. One way to handle any contention in doing this is to refresh the screen from the RAM during $\phi 1$ of the μP cycle and to allow R/$\overline{\text{W}}$ access to the RAM by the μP during $\phi 2$, just as normally done with any **6800** system memory. This provides a transparent access (i.e., no flicker).

Figure 14-8 showed the block diagram for a CRT terminal. A similar terminal can be designed using a standard CRT monitor (or a modified TV set), a **6800** μP, and a **6845** CRT controller. The **6800** has a two-phase clock with a constant-length cycle, in contrast to that of other μPs. During $\phi 1$ the **6800** presents the address to the bus, and during $\phi 2$ the data is either written to or read from any addressed device. By using faster memory devices, it is possible for the **6845** to separately access memory during the time when $\phi 1$ is high without interfering with the normal $\phi 2$ access by the μP.

The display timing is shown in Fig. 14-17. The Apple computer uses a similar scheme; it shares computer memory accesses with screen refresh accesses on alternate phases of the system clock.

If a 1-MHz **6800** system is to use the timing shown in Fig. 14-17, the memory must have an access time of 350 ns or better to complete the access during one phase of the clock.

At the higher data rates necessitated by 80 characters on a line, two characters must be read from the memory during $\phi 1$ to keep memory access times in the range of 300–500 ns. To accomplish this, the display memory is split into two blocks and *interleaved* to form an array 8 bits wide to the μP and 16 bits wide to the CRTC. A block diagram of this type of system is shown in Fig. 14-18.

During the *first* character time of a scan, the CRTC accesses the first two memory locations. At the end of this character time 16 bits of data are latched into two 8-bit latches. This data represents the character generator addresses of the characters to be displayed. During the *second* character time the data from the **even** memory block is applied to the character generator. At the end of the *second* character time the character generator's output data is loaded into the shift register. Also during the *second* character time, the memory is available to the μP for access. Not until the *third* character time is the data for the *first* character shifted out onto the screen. This delay through the memory requires the blanking and cursor outputs to also be delayed by two character times. During the *third* character time the data in the *odd* memory latch is applied to the character generator, and the CRTC is simultaneously accessing the next two memory locations. This sequence of events continually repeats itself.

Location	*Register*	*Contents*	
240	R0	30	
241	R1	20	
242	R2	2A	
243	R3	0A	
244	R4	19	
245	R5	02	
246	R6	10	
247	R7	10	
248	R8	00	
249	R9	09	
24A	R10	00	
24B	R11	09	
24C	R12	-	
24D	R13	-	
24E	R14	-	USER DEFINED
24F	R15	-	

FIGURE 14-16 Register location contents. (From *The Microprocessor Handbook*, edited by Joseph D. Greenfield. Copyright © 1985 by John Wiley & Sons. Reprinted by permission of John Wiley & Sons, Inc.)

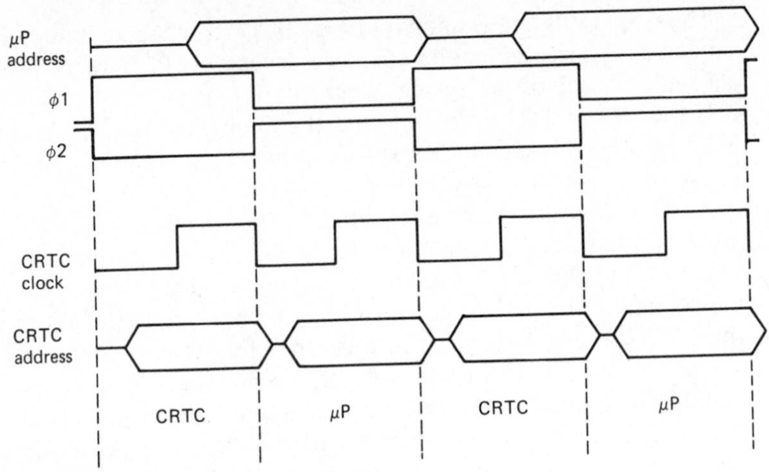

FIGURE 14-17 Display memory timing.

14-6 A PRACTICAL CRT DESIGN USING THE 6845

Figure 14-19 is the actual implementation of the previous block diagram. This CRT data terminal system uses the character generator circuit, the **6845** CRT controller, and memory access techniques previously described. It includes an ACIA with RS232 interface and selectable baud rates for serial I/O and a PIA for use with a keyboard. Reference to the figure shows that the display memory access is implemented using three **74LS157**s to form a single multiplex bus switch for the RAM address lines. DBE (which is the same as $\phi 2$) controls this switch and selects the CRTC during $\phi 1$ and the μP during $\phi 2$. Three **MC3449**s form a bidirectional data bus switch to the μP bus with the A0 line used to select the even/odd bank of memory. The $R/\overline{W}$ line controls the direction of the bidirectional buffers. Two **74LS374**s are used to latch the 16-bit data flowing to the CRT. The outputs of these latches are three-state and are controlled by address line MA0. The *even* block of data is routed to the character generator when MA0 is low and vice versa. Data in the latches is delayed by one character time, so MA0 is also delayed by the **74LS174**.

The timing relationships for this CRT system are shown in Fig. 14-20. All signals are derived from a central 18-MHz oscillator. The frequency of this oscillator is at the **DOT clock** rate and is determined by the required system parameters. The DOT clock is divided by nine (seven dots + two spaces) to generate the *character clock* (nine dots per character block). A three-input AND gate decodes the seventh count, which is delayed 1/2 clock time by the **74S74** and used to load the shift register (Fig. 14-20). Clocking for the **6800** is created by dividing the Q3 output of the counter by two. A nonoverlapping clock is generated by the series of gates shown above the oscillator in Fig. 14-19. The ROM at $C000 contains the CRTC program and all initialization.

14-7 SOFTWARE FOR THE 6845 CRT CONTROLLER

The program written to work with the hardware described in the previous section is shown in Appendix D.

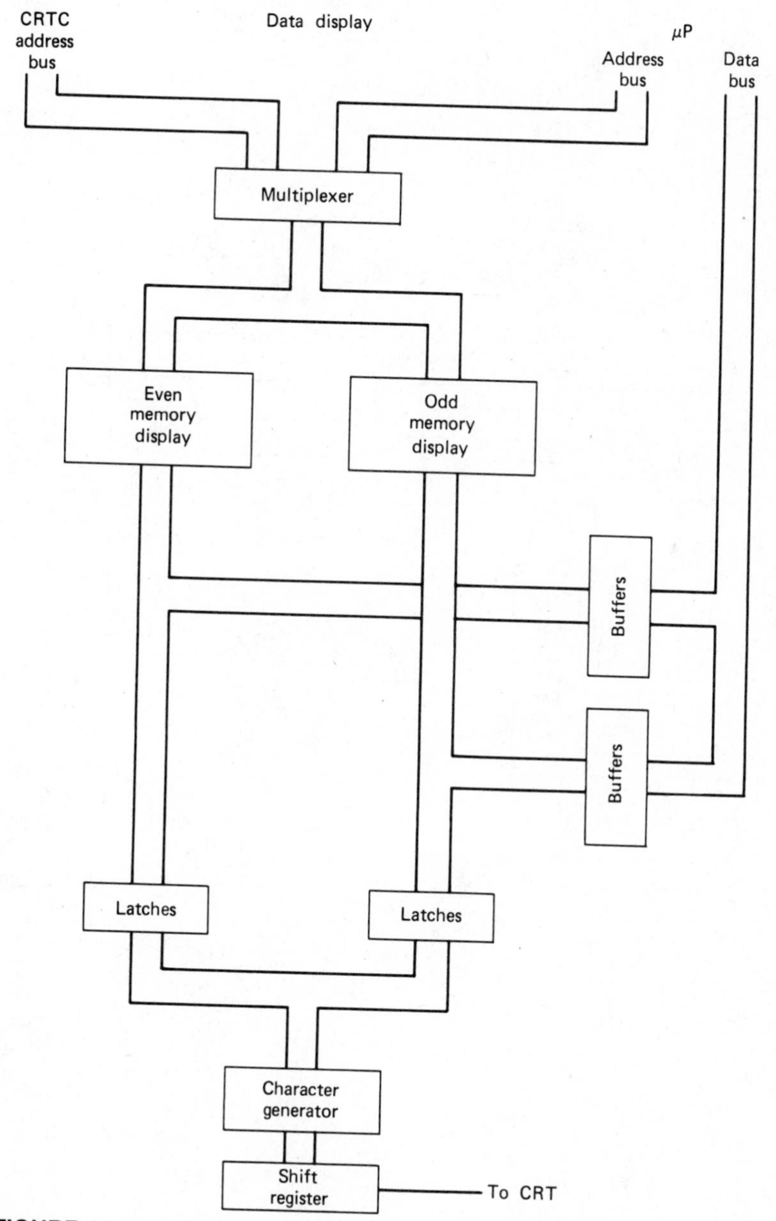

FIGURE 14-18 Block diagram showing interleaved memory.

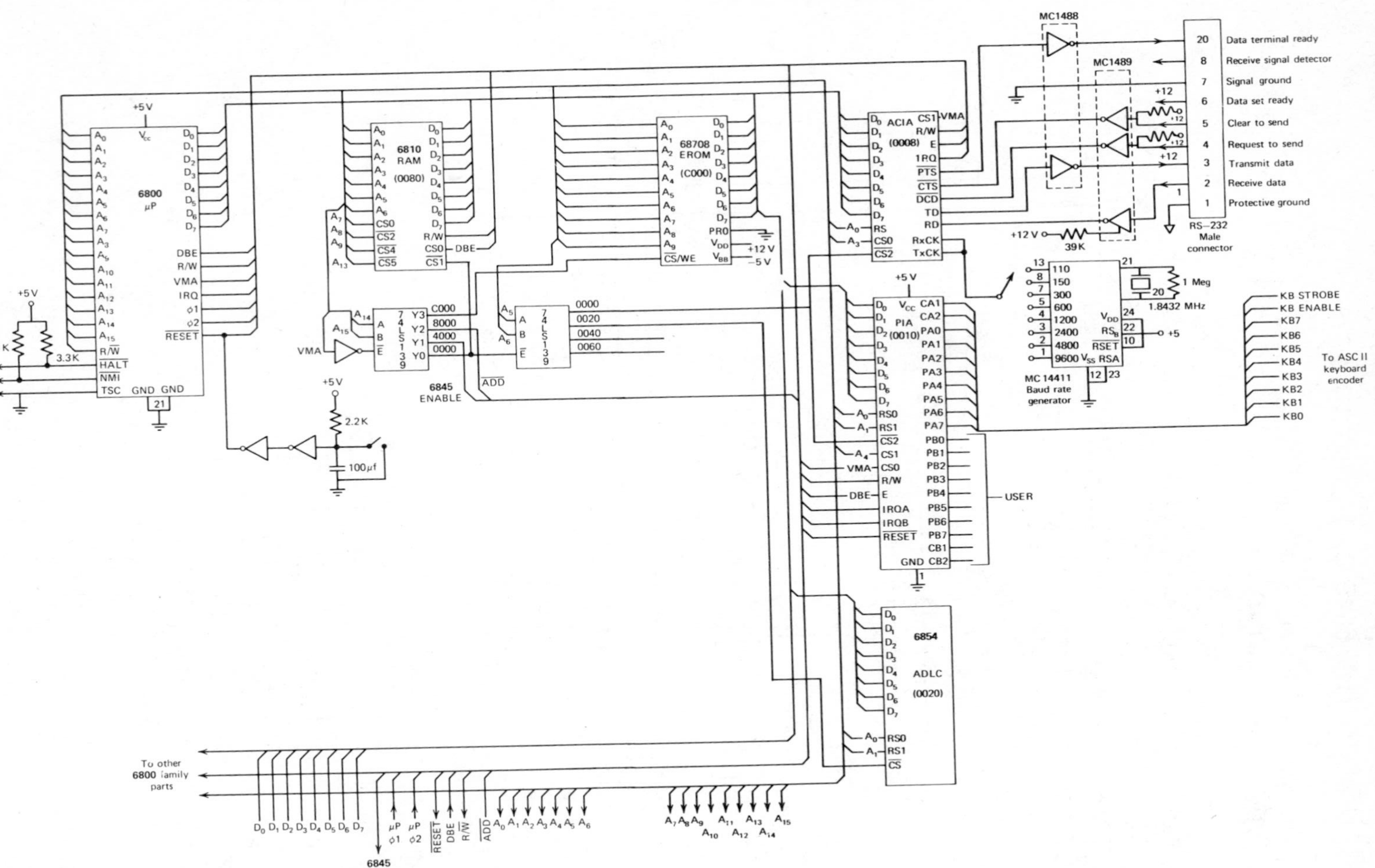

FIGURE 14-19 Schematic of complete μP controlled CRT data terminal. Note that all unmarked inverters are type **7404.**

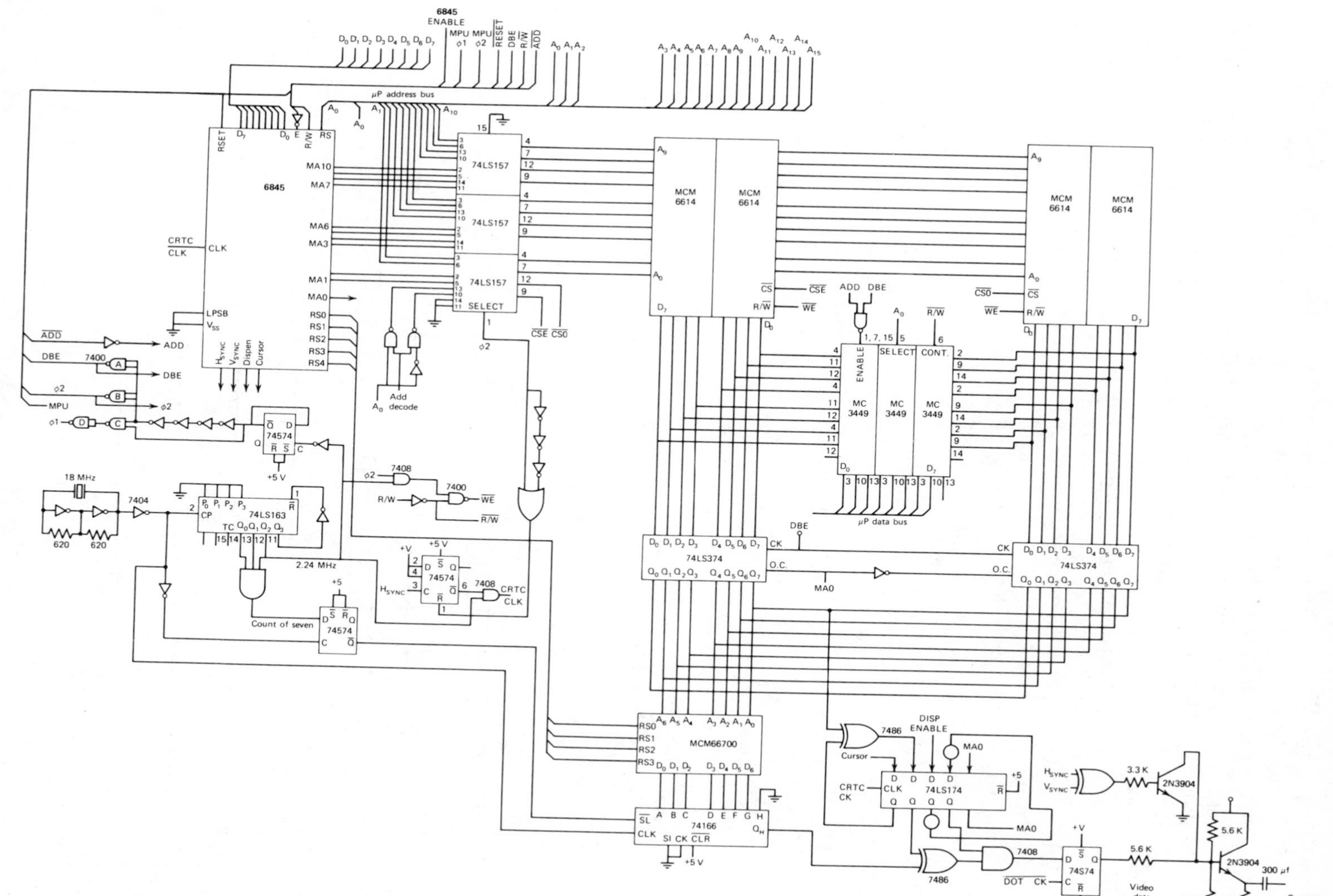

FIGURE 14-19 *(Continued)*.

The **6845** CRTC is an example of how an LSI IC plus software can do many of the functions previously done in hardware alone. It formerly required almost 100 ICs to accomplish what the **6845** will do with only 25 ICs. The secret, of course, is the use of a *programmable* IC and the use of a μP such as the **6800**. Together, they provide the user with a basic CRT terminal. For instance, all keyboard functions, data movement, cursor movement, and editing are under processor control, whereas the CRTC provides video timing, display memory addressing, hardware scrolling and paging, and light pen detection. Because of the CRTC, such things as a software routine for block moves (to scroll and page the display) are not needed. In addition, powerful driver routines can be generated in a few hundred bytes of memory.

The software provides the following features:

User-defined display format
Carriage return
Line feed
Scroll up
Scroll down
Page up
Page down
Character decode
Memory clear
Keyboard input
Serial I/O
CRTC initialization

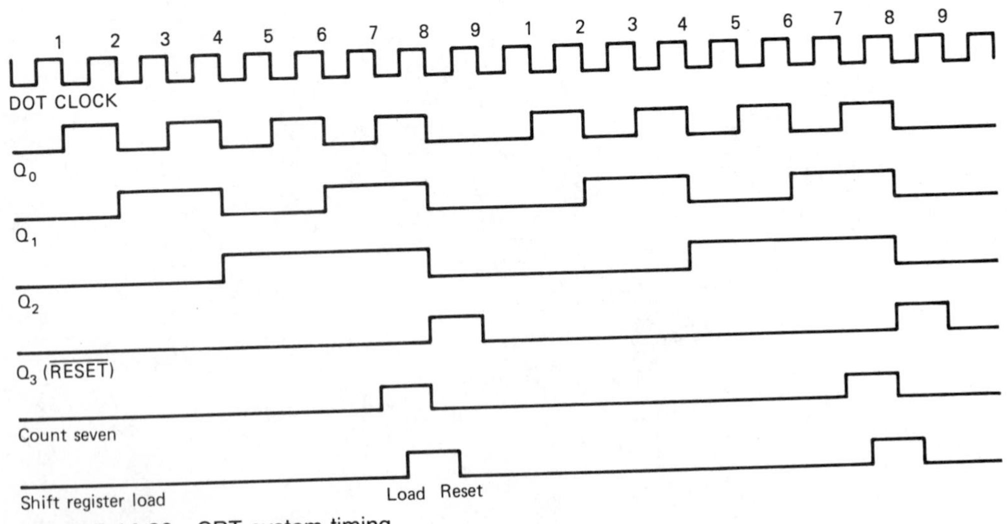

FIGURE 14-20 CRT system timing.

To maintain software flexibility, most of the commands were written as subroutines. A small control loop combines these subroutines into a useful terminal function. Other commands and subroutines may be added by expanding the command search table. Equate statements are given at the end of the listing and must be in accord with the hardware addresses used.

Figure 14-21 is an overall flowchart for the program shown in Appendix D. After reset, the ACIA (serial interface) and PIA (keyboard interface) are initialized. The display memory should be cleared before the CRTC is initialized to eliminate a flash of false data on the screen. The CRT initialization routine loads the contents of the CRT table (CRTTAB) into the 18 CRTC registers and clears the character and line counters.

The CRTC allows up to 165 displayed characters per line and up to 105 displayed character rows per field. (See the **6845** Data Sheet.) CLINE equals the number of displayed characters per line and LSCREN equals the number of displayed character rows per screen, minus one. These two parameters and the other CRT initialization values determine the display format. They have been initially set for an 80 × 24 display but can easily be changed to accommodate any format.

On completing the initialization, the processor enters a subroutine that checks for a *keypress* and, if it finds one, reads the keyboard. It then enters a control loop that recognizes the *control* characters and, if any are found, calls the appropriate subroutines to implement the basic terminal functions. This is accomplished in the software routine by examining the state of bits 5 and 6 of the character. If they are zero, then the character is a control character; otherwise it is a *displayable* character. Referring to the program in Appendix D, page 2, lines 00064 and 00065 show that this testing for a control character is done by ANDing the character with $60; if the result is zero, the program is branched to DECOD1. If the character was not a control character it is transmitted via the serial interface to a computer, another nearby RS232 terminal, or perhaps via a modem to a distant terminal. Normally the system is operated in full duplex, which means that the information typed is sent to the distant processor, where it is echoed back so that the operator can see what he or she typed.

A keyboard encoder circuit is used to generate the ASCII codes, which are then transferred into the system via the PIA. The encoder also provides the keypress signal to the PIA. After checking the PIA for a keypress, the ACIA (which provides the serial interface to the outside world) is checked to see if a remote character has been received. In this control loop routine, the PIA and ACIA inputs are scanned alternately and continuously until a character is received.

To keep track of where the next character is to be placed, several parameters must be retained. Since the CRTC requires binary addresses, two 16-bit binary numbers for both the *cursor position* and *starting address* are saved in RAM. Labels for these two are CURPOS and STARAD, respectively. In addition, the number of characters per line must be retained to ensure that a carriage return and line feed are performed if the entered characters exceed the line length. The number of lines per screen must also be counted to determine if Scroll Up must be

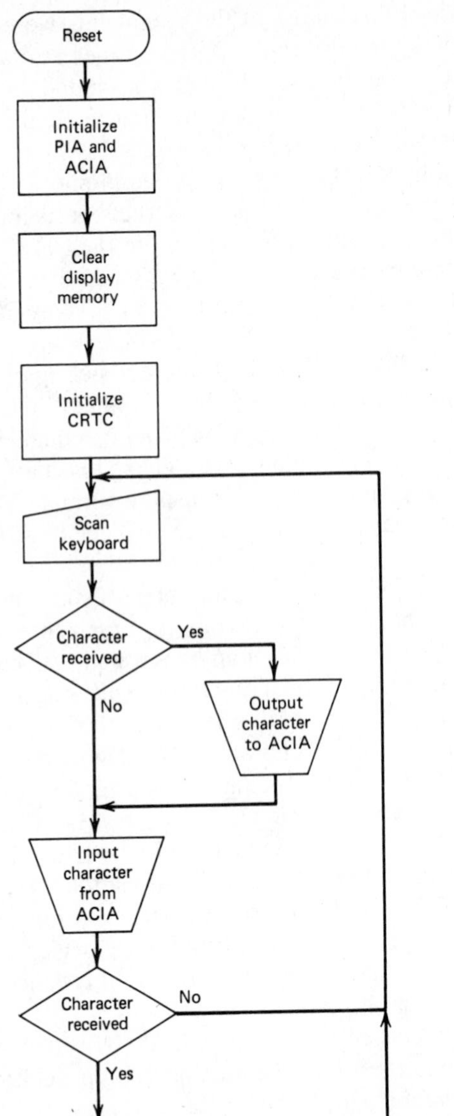

FIGURE 14-21 Flowchart for CRT program.

performed. Labels for the line counter and character counter are CCOUNT and LCOUNT, respectively.

When a displayable character is received, it is stored in the memory location pointed to by CURPOS. However, CURPOS is a 16-bit counter and not an absolute memory location. Therefore, first the higher-order address bits must be masked to the display memory size, and then the correct high-order address bits must be "ORed" to correctly position the character in the μP memory map. The cursor position counter (CURPOS) must be incremented as well as the characters-per-line counter (CCOUNT). If CCOUNT is equal to the line length, then a

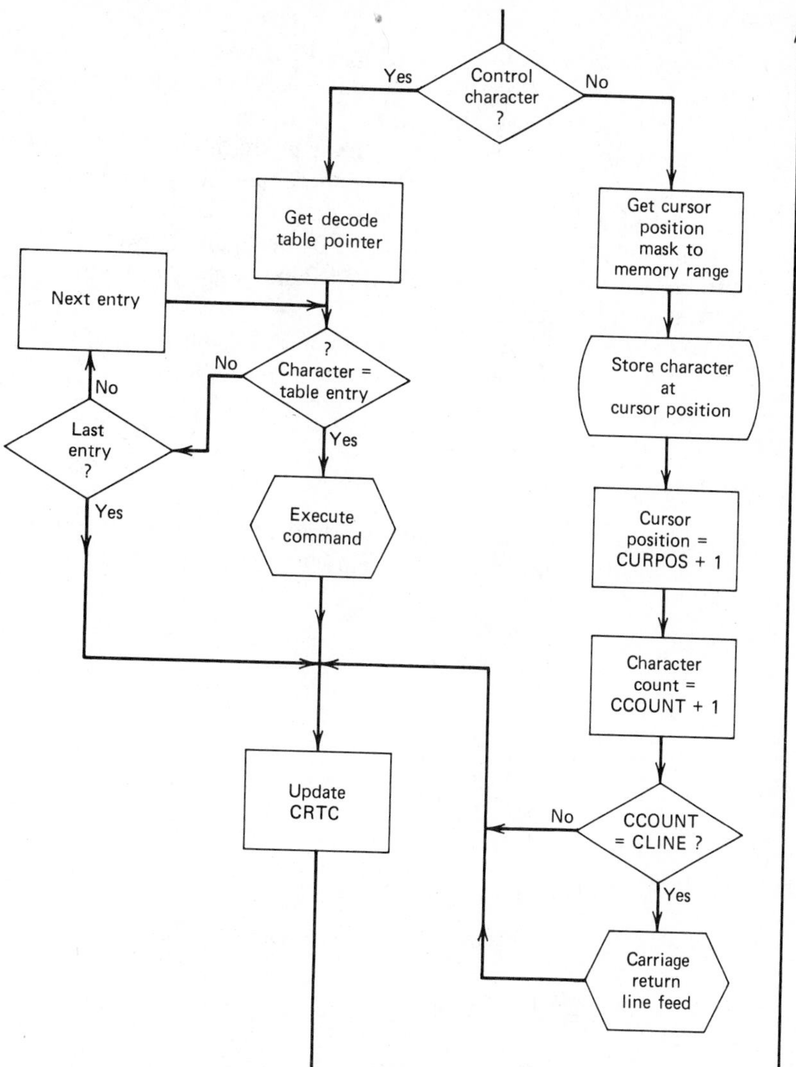

FIGURE 14-21 (*Continued*).

carriage return/line feed must be performed. After all the counters are updated the CRTC Start Address and Cursor Address Register are updated.

If the input character is a control character, it must be examined to determine the command. This is accomplished by stepping through a decode table (DECTAB), comparing the character with table entries, and counting the entries. If a match is found, the count equals the table entry. Another table containing addresses of each command routine (DECADD) is entered by stepping through entries and decrementing the entry count until it reaches zero. The address of the correct subroutine is available and the subroutine can be executed. Again, the CRTC must be updated before returning to the control loop. Each of the subroutines will now be described.

14-7.1 Line Feed

The Line Feed subroutine (see Fig. 14-22) moves the cursor down to the same position in the next line. If the current line is the last line on the screen, a line feed will also cause a Scroll Up.

To perform a Line Feed, the cursor position counter (CURPOS) and current line starting address pointer must be incremented by the number of characters per line (CLINE). This subroutine must be fast if the terminal is to run at 9600 baud. At this baud rate the characters are 1.04 ms apart. However, the ACIA is double-buffered so that for a short burst the μP has slightly more than one character time to execute a line feed.

The line counter must also be checked to see if a scroll up is required. If not, the line counter is incremented. Otherwise a scroll up is performed and the CRTC is updated.

14-7.2 Carriage Return

The Carriage Return subroutine (see Fig. 14-23) moves the cursor to the beginning of the current line, clears the character counter (CCOUNT), and updates the CRTC.

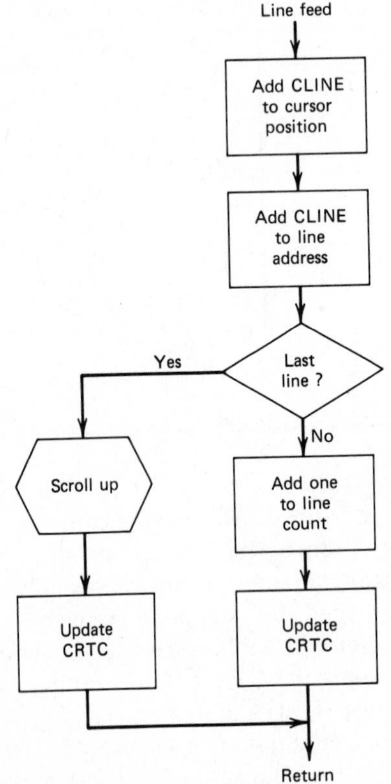

FIGURE 14-22 Flowchart for the line feed subroutine.

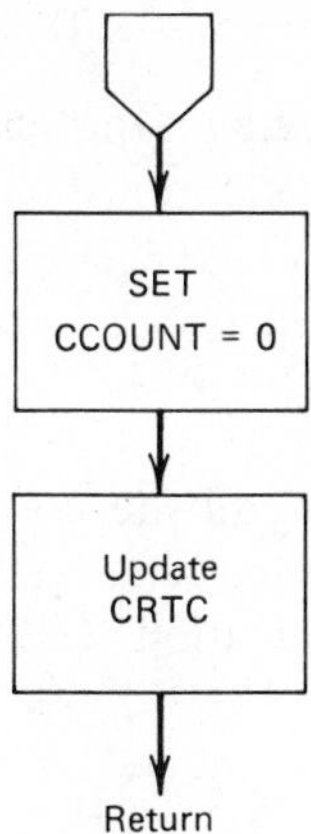

FIGURE 14-23 Carriage return software flowchart.

14-7.3 Memory Clear

The Memory Clear routine (see Fig. 14-24) stores an ASCII space (hex 20) in the memory address pointed to by memory start (MEMSTR), increments the pointer, loops back to store another space, and continues until the pointer reaches the memory end (MEMEND).

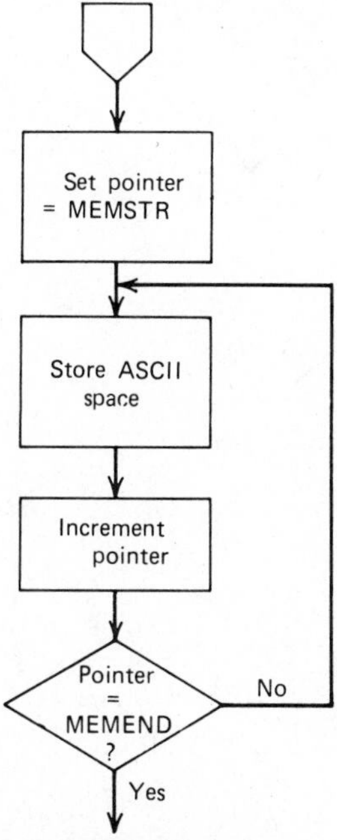

FIGURE 14-24 Memory clear subroutine.

14-7.4 Scroll Up

The Scroll Up subroutine (see Fig. 14-25) moves all data on the screen up one line and adds a new line to the bottom. The new line is not cleared. The cursor remains in the same character position.

14-7.5 Scroll Down

The Scroll Down subroutine (see Fig. 14-26) moves all the data on the screen down one line and adds a new line to the top of the screen. The new line is not cleared. The cursor remains in the same character position.

14-7.6 Page Up

The Page Up subroutine (see Fig. 14-27) calls the scroll up subroutine enough times to shift all the lines off and new ones on. The new lines are not cleared and the cursor remains in the same character position.

14-7.7 Page Down

The Page Down subroutine (see Fig. 14-28) calls the scroll down subroutine enough times to shift all existing lines off the screen and new ones on. The new lines are not cleared and the cursor remains in the same character position.

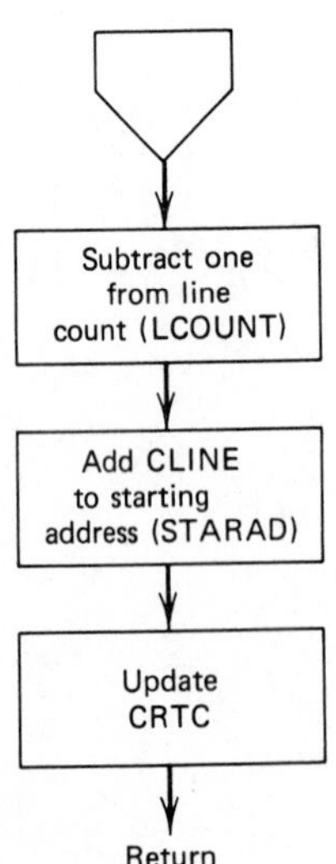

FIGURE 14-25
Scroll up subroutine.

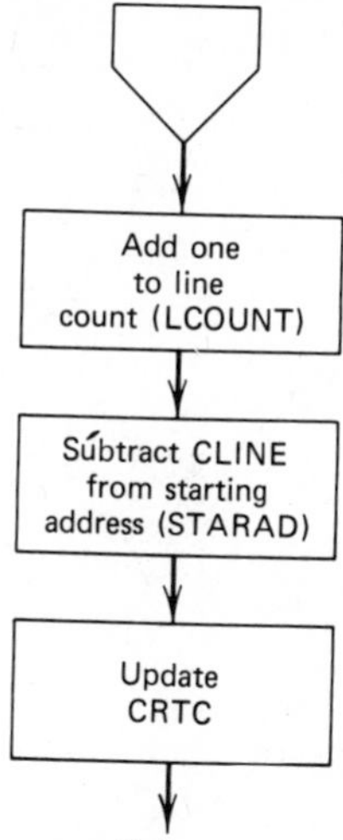

FIGURE 14-26
Scroll down subroutine.

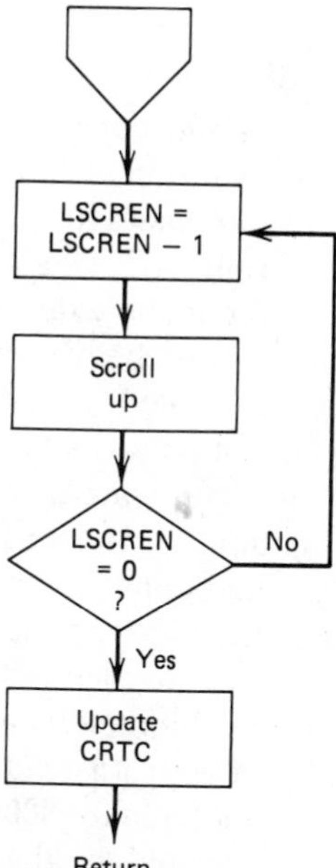

FIGURE 14-27
Page up subroutine.

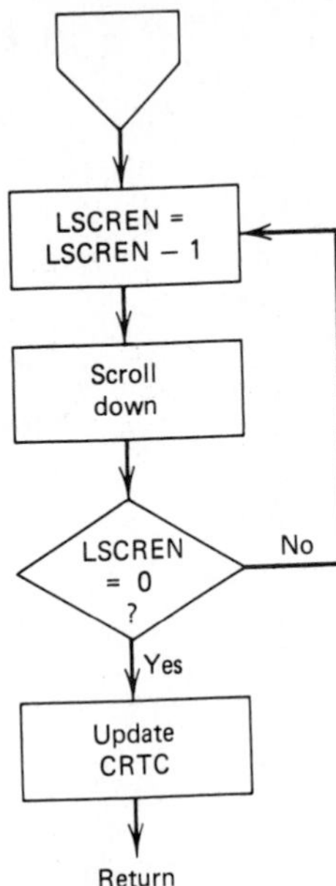

FIGURE 14-28
Page down subroutine.

14-8 SUMMARY

This chapter introduced the CRT display terminal and considered its uses and operation. The fundamental components of a display terminal, such as the circuits for the scanning process, the display RAM, and the character generator ROM, were discussed. The **6845**, a complex CRT controller IC, was discussed and a simple example of its use was developed. Finally, a complete design of a practical CRT terminal was given to illustrate applications of the various **6800** family components. This included not only the hardware needed to generate the video signal for display of alphanumeric data on the CRT monitor but also the software to complete the system design. The software and hardware also allow for keyboard input and serial data communications functions. Unfortunately, some portions of the design may appear overly complex, and complete details cannot be included in the space available. Many of the new IC peripherals fall in this category, and a full chapter would be needed to explain them adequately.

We regret that we could not have given additional complete system examples but, as seen in this chapter, this would have been difficult. Instead, in the previous chapters we tried to present basic principles of individual **6800** μP component applications and gave examples so that the readers should, by the time they reach this chapter, be able to assemble a system of their own design. It is strongly recommended that students procure the manufacturers' literature and applications notes cited in the References in each chapter for more complete understanding.

14-9 GLOSSARY

Alphanumeric Including both letters and numbers.

Blanking Inhibiting a portion of the scan line because it is out of the displayable area or is a retrace line.

Cathode Ray Tube (CRT) Special vacuum tube that produces images on its screen area.

Character generator A ROM (usually NMOS) that serves as a lookup table for characters. With an input of the character code and the row address, it will provide the dot bits for each row of the character matrix.

DOT clock Timing signal that indicates the point on each scan line where a dot can be located.

Hsync Horizontal oscillator's synchronization pulse.

MODEM MOdulator/DEModulator, used to translate signal parameters from data to audio and vice versa.

Shift register An IC (usually containing Flip-Flops) in which the bits can be loaded in parallel and shifted out serially.

Video Signal intended for display on a CRT (TV) monitor.

Vsync Vertical oscillator's synchronization pulse.

14-10 REFERENCES

Greenfield, J. D. *Practical Digital Design Using ICs*, Second Edition, Wiley, NY, 1983.

Kister, Jack E. *CRT Concepts and Implementations*, unpublished application note, Motorola Semiconductor Products, Inc., Phoenix, AZ, 1978.

Motorola. *MC6845 CRT Controller Data Sheet DS9838-R1*, Motorola Semiconductors, Austin, TX, 1984.

Motorola. *MEX6845 (D) CRTC Support Module User's Guide*, Motorola, Inc., Integrated Circuits Division, Microsystems, Phoenix, AZ, 1978.

14-11 PROBLEMS

14-1 Repeat Example 14-1 for a terminal that has a horizontal scan frequency of 20 KHz and displays 50 fields per second.

14-2 What is the output of a **66750** if row 3 of the character **1000110** is the input?

14-3 A 5 × 5 dot matrix is embedded in a 6 × 6 grid. How many character lines can be written to the screen if

a. The refresh rate is 60 Hz?

b. The refresh rate is 50 Hz?

Assume that the display can show 240 lines. Also assume that 80% of the rows are available for display.

14-4 Repeat Problem 14-3 for a 5 × 7 dot matrix embedded in a 6 × 8 grid.

14-5 What is the maximum number of horizontal characters that can be displayed if the frequency response of the CRT limits the input to 8 × 10^6 bps. The horizontal oscillator runs at 15,750 Hz. Assume that

a. The characters are 8 bits wide.
b. The characters are 6 bits wide.
c. 42 μs is available for displaying each line.

14-6 Design a CRT driver for 20 lines of 48 characters. Assume each line can be displayed for 40 μs. Each character is in an 8 × 10 matrix and uses a **2513** character generator.

a. What is the frequency of the dot clock?
b. How many memory words do you need in the refresh RAM?
c. Sketch vertical sync, horizontal sync, and composite sync, with specific times.
d. What are the range of RAM addresses for

  1. Line 2, row 2?
  2. Line 2, row 5?
  3. Line 3, row 2?

14-7 A CRT is to display 18 lines of 40 characters. The characters matrix is 7 × 9 and the block is 9 × 11. Fill out the **6845** form provided. Where values have not been specified, use the values in the book.

14-8 Draw the flowcharts for adding the following routines and, if time permits, write the assembly language program:

a. Insert character.
b. Delete character.
c. Insert line.
d. Delete line.

14-9 What happens to the top line when the screen is scrolled up?

14-10 What would be required to use the scroll feature in a word processing system?

14-11 Why is the terminal described called an intelligent terminal?

14-12 How much additional memory space is available with the address decoding shown in the circuit of Fig. 14-19 for additional routines?

14-13 If a suitable CRT tube could be obtained, what would be the advantage of using interlaced scan?

14-14 **a.** What data would you save if a power failure feature were added?
b. Which routines would need modification?
c. Which routines would have to be added?
d. What hardware additions are needed to add power failure recovery?

After attempting to solve these problems, try to answer the self-evaluation questions in Section 14-2. If any of them still seem difficult, review the appropriate sections of the chapter to find the answers.

CHAPTER 15

THE 68000 FAMILY

15-1 INSTRUCTIONAL OBJECTIVES

This chapter introduces the newer, more powerful 16-bit microprocessors. The features and operation of the **68000**, Motorola's basic 16-bit μP, are explained. More advanced versions of the **68000** family are discussed in Chapter 16. After reading this chapter, the student should be able to

1. List the advantages and disadvantages of a 16/32-bit μC as compared to the 8-bit versions.
2. Describe the advantage of a 24- or 32-bit address bus over a 16-bit bus.
3. List the registers in the **68000** and explain their function.
4. Calculate the effective address of an instruction in all modes.
5. Write program segments to demonstrate **68000** features.
6. Define the function of each pin on the **68000**.
7. List the error conditions that cause exception processing in **68000** family systems.

15-2 SELF-EVALUATION QUESTIONS

Watch for the answers to the following questions as you read the chapter. They should help you to understand the material presented.

1. A **68000** has 23 address pins but addresses 16 Mbytes of memory, which requires a 24-bit address. How is this possible?
2. Why can the data registers be used as accumulators, but not the address registers?
3. How does the **68000** determine which of the two registers labeled A7 is the stack pointer?
4. What is a privileged instruction? What types of instructions are privileged?

5. What are the limitations of QUICK instructions? What are their advantages?
6. What are the differences between a MOVE-TO-ADDRESS-register instruction and a MOVE-TO-DATA-register instruction?
7. Why is it desirable to increase the word size in a computer system?
8. What new hardware techniques are used in the new generations of 16/32-bit μPs?
9. What new programming techniques are supported by the 16/32-bit μPs?

15-3 INTRODUCTION TO THE 68000 FAMILY

At the same time that semiconductor designers were improving the 8-bit μPs and creating the 8-bit μCs, Motorola launched a project called Motorola Advanced Computer Systems on Silicon (MACSS) to design and fabricate enhanced microprocessors. Several possible architectures and design strategies were investigated. The **MC68000** μP family resulted from this work. (The MC designates the Motorola part, but since other manufacturers are licensed to make these μPs, the generic term **68000** will be used.) The major goal of these studies was to provide improved μP performance and to do so in an *expandable* way. One of the decisions was to use increased word sizes because larger words allow more powerful instructions. Since many of the desired hardware goals were not immediately attainable, it was extremely important that the first designs use software that would be *upwardly compatible* with the designs envisioned. Software compatibility was considered to be a vital factor because of the very great time and expense required to develop programs. Another consideration was the need to have usable peripheral chips as quickly as possible after the release of a new μP, so a method of using existing 8-bit peripheral ICs was devised.

In 1979 Motorola introduced the first implementation of a new 16/32-bit μP architecture—the **68000**. With its 16-bit data bus and 24-bit address bus, this μP was only the first in a family of processors that implement a comprehensive extendable computer architecture. It was soon followed by the **68008**, with an 8-bit data bus and 20-bit address bus.

The **68008** allows the design of cost-effective systems using the less expensive 8-bit peripherals and byte-wide memories, while providing the benefits of a 32-bit μP architecture. The performance of the **68008** is comparable to that of the 8-bit **6809** μP and superior to that of several 16-bit units. Complete compatibility with the **68000** instruction set is maintained by the **68008**, with 56 instruction types.

The **68010** is the third member of the family and was first available in the spring of 1983. It is object code-compatible with the **68000** and has the same pinouts. However, it has new instructions, new registers, and several other enhancements that will be described in Chapter 16.

In 1984 the **68020**, with its full 32-bit Arithmetic Logic Unit (ALU), 32-bit address and data buses, an on-chip instruction *cache memory,* and a *coprocessor interface,* was added to the family, implementing the next stage of the **68000** family architecture.

Another family member, the **MC68030**, was announced in September 1986. This μP, described as the industry's second-generation *mainframe computer on a chip,* has twice the performance of the **68020** while maintaining 100% upward software code compatibility with the existing 16/32-bit family μPs. About 300,000 transistors are included on a 3/8-inch square of silicon. An average speed of about 8 million instructions per second is achieved. This is nearly double that of some recent mainframe computers and about 10 times that of current popular high-performance personal computers.

The **68000**, which forms the basis for all of Motorola's 16/32-bit μPs, will be discussed first. The **68010**, **68020**, and **68030** and their advanced features will be covered in the next chapter. The emphasis of this book has been to teach *systems design*, so the hardware features of the μPs are covered as well as the programming.

15-3.1 Eight-bit vs 16-bit vs 32-bit μCs

The previous chapters showed how the 8-bit μC has become a very sophisticated and popular computer system. However, its performance is limited as compared to 16-bit μPs. Data bytes and ASCII characters or even individual bits can be handled with little difficulty in an 8-bit system, but mathematical operations are time-consuming because it is necessary to handle larger, multibyte values a byte at a time. This slower *processing time* of the 8-bit μPs can also cause trouble in *multiuser* systems, because one user has to wait while the system is processing inputs for another user. These *waits* may be imperceptible in many cases, but as additional users are added the delays become annoying.

One of the outstanding features of the **68000** architecture is the use of 32-bit registers so that operations with larger numbers are much faster. The **68000** uses a 16-bit ALU and I/O data path, so it is properly called a 16-bit μP. However, the 32-bit registers (see Section 15-5) and associated instructions provide many advantages when compared to other 16-bit μP designs. Also, the internal 32-bit architecture uses software that is *upwardly compatible* with the full 32-bit design of the **68020** and **68030**. Another limitation in an 8-bit system is in *addressable memory*. Typical 8-bit systems are limited to 64K bytes unless bank switching is used, and this is also slow. In modern computers, where high-level languages are increasingly being used, larger memory sizes are desirable. Sixteen-bit μPs use address buses of 20 or 24 bits and can therefore address 1 to 16 megabytes of memory. The **68020** and **68030** have a full 32-bit addresss bus and can address 4 gigabytes.

When an 8-bit Op code is increased to 16 or 32 bits, more functions can be performed simultaneously inside the processor. Multiply and divide instructions for 16- or 32-bit numbers are also provided instead of subroutines. This saves considerable time.

The availability of 16-bit Op codes in 16-bit μPs means that many more instructions, modes, and options are possible. Figure 15-1 shows a comparison of the Op codes for the ADD instruction in the **6800** and **68000** μPs. The number of bits in a

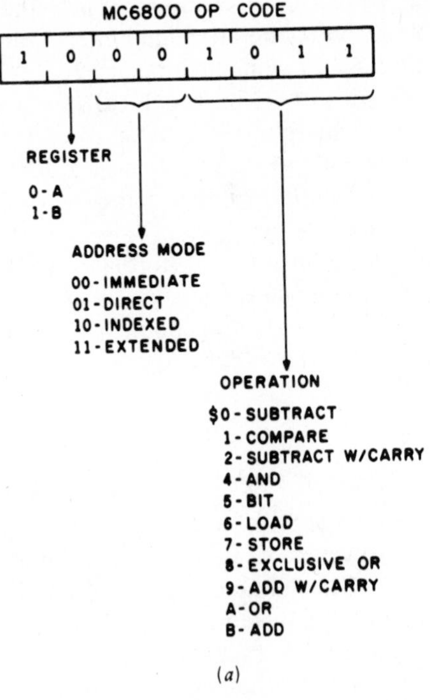

(a)

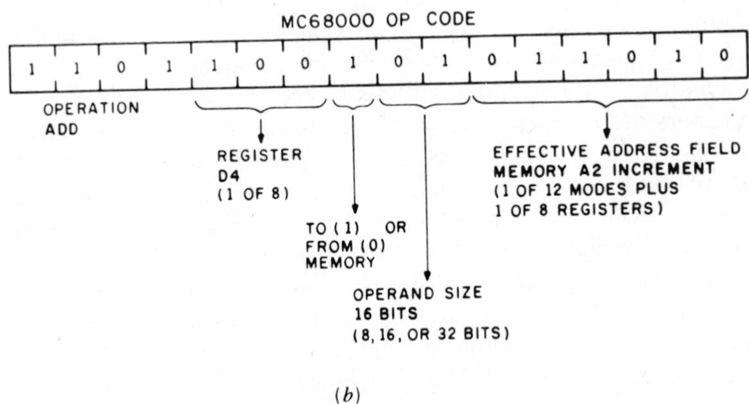

(b)

FIGURE 15-1 Comparisons of 8 vs 16 bits. (a) OP code organization for the **6800.** (b) The **68000** ADD instruction OP code.

6800 Op code is limited to 8. One bit of the Op code is needed to specify which of the two accumulators is used. If four different addressing modes are used for accessing the data, 2 more bits are required. The last 5 bits are used to encode the *operation* (ADD in this case), so a total of only 32 different operations can be performed. It is obvious that the 16-bit Op codes for the **68000**, with their ability to use so many more registers and address modes, are much more powerful.

The 16-bit μPs are used where their increased computational power is important, such as in controllers where high-speed Analog-to-Digital conversions are necessary, in multiuser systems, in robotics, and in artificial intelligence. They also have been found to be desirable in all of the newer personal computers where customer appeal depends on the power of their μPs. The Macintosh, Amiga, and Atari computers all use the **68000**.

There are also some disadvantages to 16-bit μPs. Their larger word size requires more memory, more gates in the IC buffers, and more address and data lines on the Printed Circuit Boards (PCBs).

The 8-bit μPs and μCs are less expensive, and the amount of computing power for the dollar is still very high. Where faster performance is not a requirement, a low cost 8-bit system may be the best choice. It can be used very effectively in many smaller industrial or process control systems. In fact, in the majority of computer applications (some engineers estimate at least 90%), the increased speed of the 16- or 32-bit instructions is not necessary and the added power of the larger word size systems is not needed. The market for 8-bit systems was approximately equal to that of the 16/32 bit market in 1986, and according to a published current analysis (see the Dataquest reference in Section 15-17), the world-wide 8 bit board market will continue to grow at a compound annual rate of 10% from 1986 to 1990. Dataquest also states that by 1989, the 8-bit market will be driven by the Industrial Automation applications segment which will require at least half of the systems produced. At present, a whole PCB assembly using an 8-bit μC can be built for less than the cost of a 32-bit μP.

15-3.2 New Features of the 68000 Family

The knowledge the reader has acquired by studying the **6800** family is directly applicable to the 16-bit μPs. But there are also many new and unique features in the **68000** family of μPs. These include

1. Asynchronous data bus and Bus Arbitration.
2. User and Supervisory processing states.
3. Internal eight-level Priority Interrupt system.
4. Interface with **6800** peripherals.
5. Virtual memory/machine concepts.
6. HCMOS process with 200,000 transistors per wafer.
7. Cache memory.
8. Coprocessors.
9. Pipelining.

The first four of these will be explained in this chapter and the more advanced features (5 through 9) will be covered in the next chapter.

One of the most important features of the **68000** family is that the basic instructions are the same for all members of the family and programs written for a **68000** will run on all of the advanced processors (currently three) and those planned. The **68000** and the **68008** are identical from the point of view of the programmer, except that the **68000** can directly access 16 megabytes (24 bits of address) and the **68008** can directly access 1 megabyte (20 bits of address).

15-4 PROCESSING STATES

In addition to the many hardware differences between the 16-bit μPs and the 8-bit μPs described in previous chapters, the **68000** family has many differences in internal operation. One difference is the use of *processing states*. The **68000** is always in one of three processing states: Normal, Exception, or Halted.

The *Normal* processing state occurs when the program is proceeding in normal sequence through the instructions, including the bus cycles to fetch instructions or operands or to store the results.

A special case of the normal state is the *stopped state,* which the processor enters when a STOP instruction is executed. In this state, no further memory references are made until an interrupt occurs that restarts the processor.

The *Exception* processing state is associated with resets, interrupts, trap instructions, tracing, and other *exceptional* conditions. (This expression has been shortened throughout the **68000** family literature to the word *exception.)* This state may be internally generated by an instruction or by an unusual condition arising during the execution of an instruction. Exception processing is described in Section 15-12.

The *Halted* processing state is an indication of catastrophic hardware failure. For example, if a bus error occurs it causes the **68000** to jump to the *bus error vector* and start an exception process (see Section 15-12.2). If another bus error occurs during the execution of this routine, the processor assumes that the system is unusable and halts. Only an *external RESET* can restart a halted processor. Note that a processor in the stopped state is not in the halted state, nor vice versa.

15-4.1 Privilege Levels

Another innovation in the **68000** operation is the use of *privilege levels*. The processor operates at one of two levels of privilege: the *User* or the *Supervisor* level. The supervisor level is a higher level of privilege. Not all processor instructions can be executed in the lower-privileged user state, but all are available in the supervisor state.

The register set of the **68000** is described in Section 15-5. It contains two stack pointers, a *Supervisory Stack* Pointer and a *User Stack* Pointer. The User Stack Pointer register is called A7 and the Supervisor Stack Pointer register is called A7′. The privilege level is used internally by the processor to choose between the *User Stack Pointer* and the *Supervisor Stack Pointer* during operand references, and it can be used by external memory management devices to control and translate addresses for memory accesses (also see Chapter 16).

The privilege level is a mechanism for providing security in a computer system. This is achieved in two ways, through the *Supervisor–User* distinction and through the allocation of separate memory for *data* and *instructions*. These allocations are controlled by an external *Memory Management Unit* (MMU) in conjunction with the Function Control pins (see Sections 15-4.4 and 15-11 and Chapter 16). For example, in a multiuser system, the executive or **operating system program** that controls the computer operates in the *Supervisor* mode while the users operate in the more restricted *User* mode, so that their programs cannot interfere with the system operation or the programs of other users. In addition, all programs access only their own data areas of memory and are prevented from accessing information that they do not need and must not modify. The techniques for doing this are discussed in detail in Chapter 16.

15-4.2 Supervisor State

The **Supervisor State** is the more privileged of the normal processing modes. For instruction execution, the Supervisor state is selected by *setting* the *S* bit of the Status Register (see Section 15-5.4). All instructions can be executed in the Supervisor State. The bus cycles generated by instructions executed in the Supervisor State are classified as *supervisor references*. While the processor is in the supervisor privilege state, instructions that use either the Supervisor Stack Pointer implicitly or Address Register seven (A7) explicitly access the Supervisor Stack Pointer. All *exception processing* is done in the Supervisor State, regardless of the setting of the *S* bit. All stacking operations during exception processing use the Supervisor Stack Pointer (see Section 15-12).

15-4.3 User State

The **User state** is the lower state of privilege. The *S* bit of the Status Register is negated (LOW) when the processor is executing instructions in the User State. Most instructions execute identically in the User state and the Supervisor state. However, some instructions that have important system effects are made *privileged* (i.e., they will work only in the Supervisor mode). User programs are not permitted to execute the *STOP* instruction or the *RESET* instruction. To ensure that a user program cannot enter the Supervisor state except in a controlled manner, the instructions that modify the *S* bit of the Status Register are privileged. To aid in debugging programs that are to be used as operating systems in the Supervisor mode, the MOVE User Stack Pointer (MOVE USP) instruction is provided.

While the processor is in the user state, instructions that use either the system stack pointer implicitly or address register seven (A7) explicitly access the User Stack Pointer.

15-4.4 Function Codes and Address Space Types

There are three **Function Code** (FC) pins on the **68000** μP (see Section 15-11). The processor indicates the cycle type being executed during each bus cycle by setting the state of these pins. Table 15-1 lists the types of access and their respective address space encoding. The bus cycles generated by an instruction executed in

TABLE 15-1 Function Codes for Classification of Address Space

Function Code Output			Cycle Type
FC2	FC1	FC0	
Low	Low	Low	(Undefined, Reserved)
Low	Low	High	User Data
Low	High	Low	User Program
Low	High	High	(Undefined, Reserved)
High	Low	Low	(Undefined, Reserved)
High	Low	High	Supervisor Data
High	High	Low	Supervisor Program
High	High	High	CPU Space

the User state, for example, are classified as *user references* (Function Codes 1 and 2). Referencing the state of these pins allows external translation of addresses, control of access to different areas of memory, and differentiation of special processor states such as CPU space (includes *interrupt acknowledge*). This allows an external *memory management* device to translate the address and control access to protected portions of the address space (see Chapter 16).

15-5 THE 68000 REGISTERS

One of the major features of the **68000** is its large register set. Because most of the registers can be used in more than one way, the **68000** has much more flexibility and versatility than any 8-bit μP. Even in single-precision operations, the **68000** data registers can handle numbers between $\pm 2^{31}$.

These features greatly simplify the writing of programs and make the computer more powerful. The registers in the **68000** are shown in Fig. 15-2.

The User mode of all **68000** family devices has

Eight 32-bit Data registers (D0–D7).

Seven 32-bit Address registers (A0–A6).

One User Stack Pointer (USP) register (A7).

A 32-bit Program Counter (PC).

An 8-bit Condition Code Register (CCR).

When the **68000** and **68008** μPs are in the Supervisor mode, the registers shown crosshatched in Fig. 15-2 are also provided. The *Supervisor Stack Pointer* (SSP) is substituted for the *User Stack Pointer* (USP) and the upper or *system* byte of the status register is made available.

15-5.1 The Data Registers

The top eight registers shown in Fig. 15-2 are the Data registers (D0–D7). They are used as accumulators or as Index registers. The vertical dotted lines show their ability to handle byte (8-bit), word (16-bit), and **long-word** (32-bit) operations. Byte operands occupy the low-order 8 bits of the register, word operands occupy the low-order 16 bits, and long-word operands occupy the entire 32 bits. The Least Significant Bit (LSB) is bit 0 and the Most Significant Bit (MSB) is bit 31.

15-5.2 The Address Registers

The second set of eight registers in Fig. 15-2 comprises the seven Address registers (A0–A6) and, depending on whether the processor is in the User or Supervisor mode, the USP or the SSP. They hold the memory addresses of operands or data and may be used as additional software stack pointers or base address registers. The Address registers may be used for word and long-word operations. If a word is used as a source operand, it occupies the low-order bits of the register. Address registers do not support byte-sized operands. All seven of the Address registers may also be used as Index registers.

15-5.3 The Program Counter

The **68000** contains a 32-bit Program Counter (PC) that holds the address of the next instruction to be executed. The **68000** instructions occupy one to five words in memory. All instructions must start at even addresses. The **68000** Op codes are always 16 bits wide, and any arguments the **68000** requires are always stored as one or more additional 16-bit words (even if the argument is only a byte quantity).

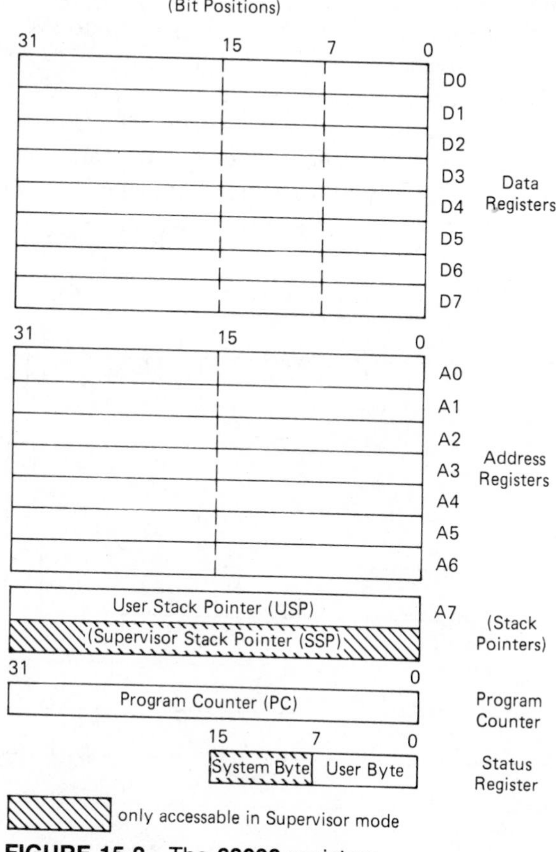

FIGURE 15-2 The **68000** registers.

Because of this, code that starts on an even-byte boundary will stay on an even-byte boundary and thus will be accessed at the highest rate possible.

15-5.4 The Status Register

The Status Register, shown in Fig. 15-3, contains 2 bytes. The lower or *user byte* includes the condition code bits; the N (negative), Z (zero), V (overflow), and C (carry) flags that are similar to the **6800** flags; and the X (extend) bit that is used to accommodate the 8-, 16-, and 32-bit data. The X bit is similar to the carry bit with some differences. Most instructions affect the X and C bits in the same way. The differences are:

1. LOGIC, MOVE, MULTIPLY, and DIVIDE instructions clear the C bit but do not affect X.
2. X and C behave differently for some SHIFT and ROTATE instructions.
3. ADD-with-carry and SUBTRACT-with-carry in the **6800** have become ADD-with-extend (ADDX) and SUBTRACT-with-extend (SUBX) in the **68000**.

The MS byte of the Status Register is the **System Byte**. It contains the *interrupt mask* (eight levels available; see Section 15-13.1), the *Trace* (T) bit, which will cause the program to single-step if it is set (see Section 15-14), and the *Supervisor state bit (S),* which selects the User or Supervisor mode. When it is set, the system is in the Supervisor state.

The System Byte is accessible only in Supervisor mode. Proper computer systems design must allow only a supervisor to control the system. If the system byte were available in the User mode, a user could change the *S* bit and then execute any privileged instruction, thus taking control of the entire system.

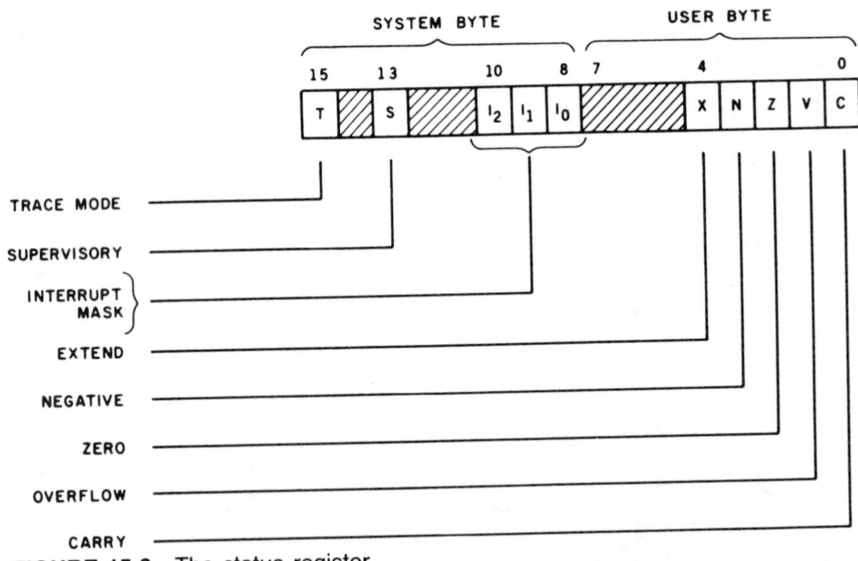

FIGURE 15-3 The status register.

15-6 DATA ORGANIZATION AND ADDRESSING

Memory for the **68000** is organized in words. Bytes can be addressed with the high-order byte having an even address the same as the word address, as shown in Fig. 15-4. The low-order byte has an odd address that is one count higher than the word address. Instructions and multibyte data are accessible only on word (even-byte) boundaries. If a long word is located at address n (n even), then the second word of that long word is located at address n + 2.

Five basic data types are supported:

- Bits
- Binary Coded Decimal (BCD) digits (4 bits)
- Bytes (8 bits)
- Words (16 bits)
- Long words (32 bits)

Each of these types is put into memory as shown in Fig. 15-5. The numbers indicate the order in which the data would be accessed by the processor. Note that addresses increase in a downward direction. Figure 15-5a shows bit data, addressed as bit n of the byte at location m. Figure 15-5b shows byte addressing in a long word. The MSB is byte 0. The sequence of addressing three words is shown in Fig. 15-5c, and the addressing of three long words is shown in Fig. 15-5d.

15-6.1 BCD Data in Memory

The organization of Binary Coded Decimal (BCD) data is shown in Fig. 15-5e. In the **68000**, BCD digits are encoded two to a byte. This is called *packed* BCD. The BCD instructions operate on 1 byte (two BCD digits) at a time. In a byte, BCD0 is the Most Significant Digit (MSD), followed by BCD1. Figure 15-5e shows the arrangement of eight BCD digits in a long word. Here BCD0 is the MSD and BCD7 is the LSD.

15-7 THE 68000 EDUCATIONAL COMPUTER BOARD

Motorola has produced an Educational Computer Board (ECB), shown in Fig. 15-6, for use as a training aid in colleges and universities. The ECB is capable of

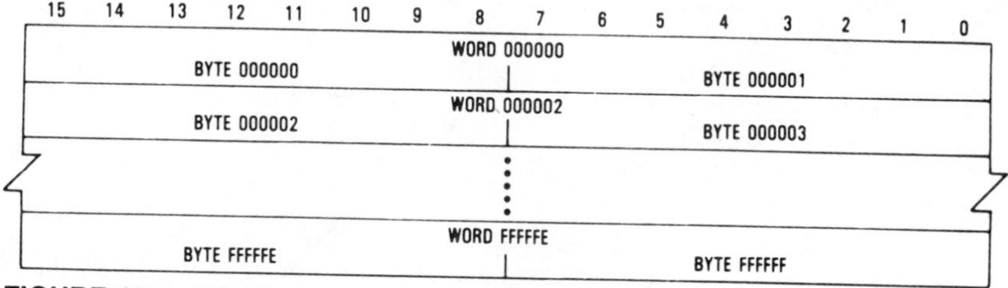

FIGURE 15-4 Word organization in memory.

(a)

7	6	5	4	3	2	1	0

(b)

1 byte = 8 bits

Address	15 … 8	7 … 0	
Address = N[a]	Byte 0	Byte 1	N + 1
N + 2	Byte 2	Byte 3	N + 3

(c)

1 word = 16 bits

Address	15 … 0	
Address = N	Word 0	N + 1
N + 2	Word 1	N + 3
N + 4	Word 2	N + 5

(d)

1 long word = 32 bits

Address	15 … 0	
Address = N	Long word 0 (H)	N + 1
N + 2	Long word 0 (L)	N + 3
N + 4	Long word 1 (H)	N + 5
N + 6	Long word 1 (L)	N + 7
N + 8	Long word 2 (H)	N + 9
N + 10	Long word 2 (L)	N + 11

[a] N is an even number.

(e)

Decimal Data
2 Binary Coded Decimal Digits = 1 Byte

15 14 13 12	11 10 9 8	7 6 5 4	3 2 1 0
MSD BCD 0	LSD BCD 1	BCD 2	BCD 3
BCD 4	BCD 5	BCD 6	BCD 7

MSD = most significant digit
LSD = least significant digit

FIGURE 15-5 Data organization in memory. (a) Bits. (b) Bytes. (c) Words. (d) Long words. (e) BCD.

FIGURE 15-6 MC68000 Educational Computer Board.

examining memory or registers and is therefore very helpful in creating and debugging **68000** programs. It provides an excellent way to understand the makeup and operation of the **68000** and its instructions. The student is encouraged to try out each of the **68000** instruction features as they are presented. The board contains a **68000** μP, 32K of RAM, a debugger program in ROM called TUTOR, and several types of peripheral I/O ICs. It needs only to be connected to a display terminal and a power supply (+5, +12, and −12 V) to become an operational computer.

The major features of the TUTOR program are the ability to

1. Set and display all the registers in the **68000**.
2. Write to and display sections of memory.
3. Run or trace (single-step) a program.
4. Set breakpoints.
5. Use a one-line assembler or disassembler.

One of the most important features of TUTOR is its Assembly/Disassembly feature. This allows the user to write programs in Assembly mnemonics and TUTOR converts them to machine language and stores them in memory. The user can also *download* a program from a host computer, Disassemble the machine language, and display it in Assembly language (mnemonics).

Figure 15-7a shows the use of the Display Formatted (DF) registers command in TUTOR. In response to the DF command, the first line lists the contents of the

Program Counter (PC), the Status Register, and the Supervisory and User Stack pointers. The Status Register contents are shown in hex and also in ASCII format. The ASCII format displays the Status Register in the following order: trace bit, status bit, interrupt vector, and X, N, Z, V, and C bits of the Condition Codes. Dots indicate that the bit is 0 or not set.

EXAMPLE 15-1

In Fig. 15-7 what are the contents of the Status Register in both hex and ASCII?

SOLUTION

The translation of the system and user bytes into ASCII letters or numbers is shown in Fig. 15-7b. The figure shows that the status register contents are:

2704 = . S7 . . Z . .

The hex value is $2704. This corresponds to .S7..Z.. in an ASCII format. The dots indicate that the T, X, N, V, and Z bits are *off*. The S and Z bits are *set* and the interrupt mask bits are 111.

The contents of the eight Data Registers and eight Address Registers are then displayed. Because the **68000** is in Supervisory mode, A7 is the Supervisor Stack Pointer. The last line lists the instruction pointed to by the PC in both machine language and its disassembled form.

Details on the setup and use of the board and on TUTOR are given in the *Educational Computer Board User's Manual* (see References, Section 15-17).

```
TUTOR  1.3 > DF
PC=00001000 SR=2704=.S7..Z.. US=00002000 SS=00000F00
D0=FFFFFFFF D1=00000000 D2=00000000 D3=00000000
D4=B0000018 D5=0000003F D6=00000000 D7=00000000
A0=00010040 A1=00000638 A2=00001000 A3=00000542
A4=00000544 A5=0000053A A6=0000053A A7=00000F00
---------------------001000     0C000030          CMP.B   #48,D0
```

(*a*)

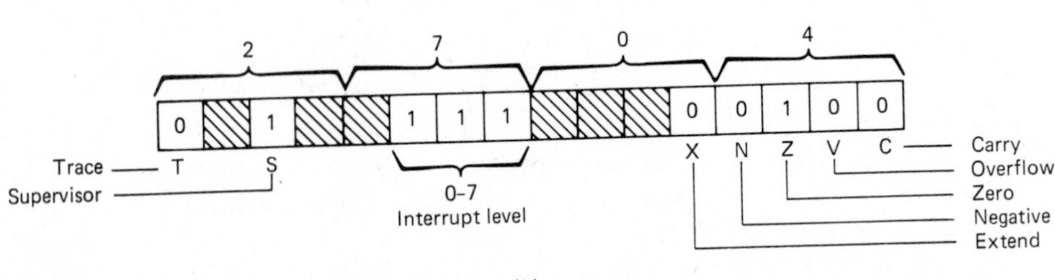

(b)

FIGURE 15-7 (a) TUTOR'S register display. (b) Translation of status register to ASCII.

15-8 68000 INSTRUCTION FEATURES

Many new software techniques have been developed to work with the advanced register set and instruction modes of the **68000**. Among these are methods for organizing and moving data. All of the old LOAD, STORE, PUSH, PULL, POP, and I/O instructions from other μPs were combined into one very powerful and flexible MOVE instruction in the **68000**. The MOVE instruction can move 8-, 16-, or 32-bit data from any location to any other. Data from the top of the stack can be moved to or from any register, another stack, a queue,[1] or any I/O location, all in one simple operation.

Another advantage of the **68000** is its ability to use any one of the eight Address Registers as a Stack Pointer; this allows as many as eight different stacks to be used without having to swap out registers.

Direct memory-to-memory moves are also possible. There are 10 different memory-addressing modes (see Section 15-9) to select from for the source operand and seven for the destination. Each addressing mode can use any of the eight Address Registers, further increasing the versatility of these MOVE instructions.

15-8.1 The 68000 Instruction Format

Each **68000** instruction has a one-word Op code, followed by extension words, if necessary, to specify absolute addresses, immediate data, and so on. This is shown in Fig. 15-8. The Op code defines the instruction, its length (B, W, or L), the source field, and the destination field.

Instructions for the **68000** contain two kinds of information: the type of function to be performed and the location of the operand(s) on which to perform the function.

Instructions specify an operand location in one of three ways:

- Register specification—the number of the register is given in the register field of the instruction.
- Implicit reference—the definition of certain instructions implies the use of specific registers.
- Effective Address—use of the different address modes.

The first two methods are easily understood but the last needs further explanation (see Section 15-9).

The various instructions are described in the following sections, and a detailed description of each instruction is also given in the **68000** *Microprocessor Programmer's Reference Manual,* cited in Section 15-17. Figure 15-9 is a page of this manual that defines the ADD instruction.

A typical manual page consists of four major parts, as shown in Fig. 15-9:

[1] A *queue* is a programming technique for a special type of buffer where data is added at the end (pointed to by one pointer) and read from another location pointed to by another pointer. The concept is similar to the normal meaning of standing in line while waiting to be served. In a multiuser program, for example, queues are frequently provided to properly sequence the use of a common routine.

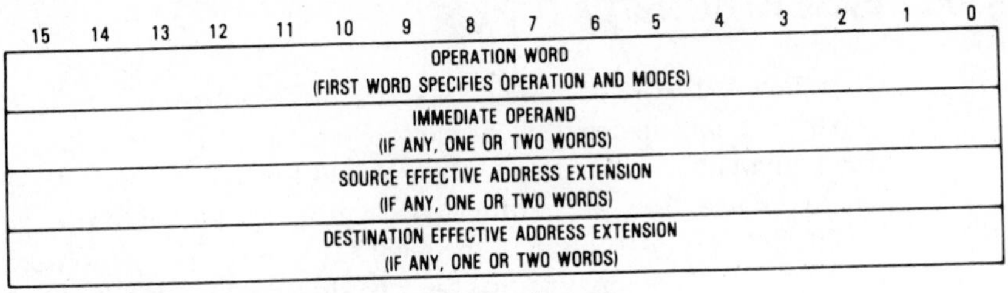

15 14 13 12 11 10 9 8 7 6 5 4 3 2 1 0
OPERATION WORD (FIRST WORD SPECIFIES OPERATION AND MODES)
IMMEDIATE OPERAND (IF ANY, ONE OR TWO WORDS)
SOURCE EFFECTIVE ADDRESS EXTENSION (IF ANY, ONE OR TWO WORDS)
DESTINATION EFFECTIVE ADDRESS EXTENSION (IF ANY, ONE OR TWO WORDS)

FIGURE 15-8 The **68000** μP instruction format.

1. A description of the instruction.
2. The effect of the instruction on the Condition Codes or flags.
3. The format of the instruction word.
4. Definitions of the fields in the instruction format.

15-8.2 Register Notation

To understand the operation of the **68000** instructions, a standard *register notation* has been adopted. This is used in the description of the instruction operation and in the Assembler syntax. It shows the various logic operations. The following mnemonics are used to identify the registers:

An—Address register (n is register number)

Dn—Data register (n is register number)

Rn—Any register, Address, or Data (n is register number)

Xn—Any Index register: can be address or data (n is register number)

PC—Program Counter

SR—Status Register

CCR—Condition Code Register

SP—Stack Pointer

USP—User Stack Pointer

SSP—Supervisor Stack Pointer

d—Displacement value

N—Operand size in bytes (1, 2, 4)

As described in Section 15-8.1, all **68000** instructions must specify a word length, the source operand, and then the destination operand. The instruction ADD.B would be used to designate a byte-sized operand, ADD.W would designate a word operand, and ADD.L a long-word operand.

Use of the ECB helps clarify the operation of these instructions. It is educational to enter the byte option (.B) and observe the resulting machine language code and then enter the word option (.W) to see the difference. It is also interesting to run the instruction to see the effect on the registers. Even more clarification of the μP operations can be seen if negative numbers are used. This will demonstrate how the various-sized entries are *sign* extended.

ADD — Add — ADD

Operation: Source + Destination → Destination

Assembler Syntax: ADD <ea>,Dn
ADD Dn,<ea>

Attributes: Size = (Byte, Word, Long)

Description: Add the source operand to the destination operand using binary addition, and store the result in the destination location. The size of the operation may be specified to be byte, word, or long. The mode of the instruction indicates which operand is the source and which is the destination as well as the operand size.

Condition Codes:

X	N	Z	V	C
*	*	*	*	*

N Set if the result is negative. Cleared otherwise.
Z Set if the result is zero. Cleared otherwise.
V Set if an overflow is generated. Cleared otherwise.
C Set if a carry is generated. Cleared otherwise.
X Set the same as the carry bit.

The condition codes are not affected when the destination is an address register.

Instruction Format:

15	14	13	12	11	10	9	8	7	6	5	4	3	2	1	0
1	1	0	1	Register Dn			Op-Mode			Effective Address Mode			Effective Address Register		

Instruction Fields:

Register field — Specifies any of the eight data registers.
Op-Mode field —

Byte	Word	Long	Operation
000	001	010	<ea> + <Dn> → <Dn>
100	101	110	<Dn> + <ea> → <ea>

Effective Address Field — Determines addressing mode:
a. If the location specified in a source operand, the all addressing modes are allowed as shown:

Addr. Mode	Mode	Register
Dn	000	reg. number:Dn
An*	001	reg. number:An
(An)	010	reg. number:An
(An)+	011	reg. number:An
−(An)	100	reg. number:An
(d_{16},An)	101	reg. number:An
(d_8,An,Xn)	110	reg. number:An

Addr. Mode	Mode	Register
(xxx).W	111	000
(xxx).L	111	001
#<data>	111	100
(d_{16},PC)	111	010
(d_8,PC,Xn)	111	011

*Word and Long only.

b. If the location specified is a destination operand, then only alterable memory addressing modes are allowed as shown:

Addr. Mode	Mode	Register
Dn	—	—
An	—	—
(An)	010	reg. number:An
(An)+	011	reg. number:An
−(An)	100	reg. number:An
(d_{16},An)	101	reg. number:An
(d_8,An,Xn)	110	reg. number:An

Addr. Mode	Mode	Register
(xxx).W	111	000
(xxx).L	111	001
#<data>	—	—
(d_{16},PC)	—	—
(d_8,PC,Xn)	—	—

Notes: 1. If the destination is a data register, then it cannot be specified by using the destination <ea> mode, but must use the destination Dn mode instead.
2. ADDA is used when the destination is an address register. ADDI and ADDQ are used when the source is immediate data. Most assemblers automatically make this distinction.

FIGURE 15-9 The **68000** ADD instruction page from the programming manual.

EXAMPLE 15-2

What does the **68000** instruction ADD.W D1,D3 do?

SOLUTION
This instruction can be entered into memory at any location ($2000, for example) using the ECB's Assembler/Disassembler command (MM $2000;DI). If ADD.W D1,D3 is entered and then executed (by placing $2000 in the PC and entering T to run one instruction), it causes the 16 LSBs of D1 to be added to the 16 LSBs of D3, and the result is placed in the 16 LSBs of D3. The Condition Codes are set in accordance with the 16-bit results. All of D1 and the 16 MSBs of D3 are unchanged. Even if there is a carry out of the addition it will not affect the MSBs of D3, but it will affect the Condition Codes.

EXAMPLE 15-3

What does the machine language instruction D019 do?

SOLUTION
The instruction is disassembled as shown in Fig. 15-10. Bits 12–15 are a hexadecimal D, which indicates an ADD instruction. Bits 9–11 determine that Data Register 0 is the data register involved in this instruction. The Op mode is also 0. This Op mode indicates that

1. The data length is a byte.
2. Register 0 is one of the operands. The contents of the byte referenced by the Effective Address is the other operand, and register 0 is also the destination, or where the results will reside.

Bits 0–5 determine the address and mode of the other operand. The operand mode in this case is 011 (see Table 15-2 in Section 15-9) and the address register involved is Address Register 1.

The effect of this instruction is to ADD the number in data register 0 to the number in the memory location pointed to by Address Register 1. The results go to data register 0. Also, the mode is autoincrementing so that Address Register 1 is incremented at the end of the instruction. Thus the disassembled instruction is

ADD.B (A1)+,D0

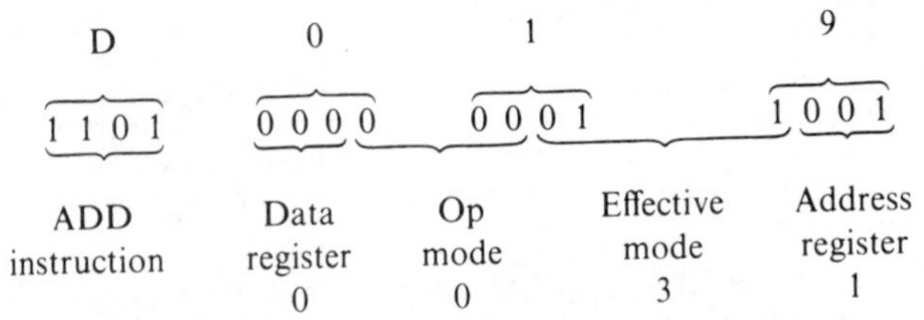

D	0		1		9
1 1 0 1	0 0 0	0 0 0		0 0 1 1	0 0 1
ADD instruction	Data register 0	Op mode 0		Effective mode 3	Address register 1

FIGURE 15-10 Disassembling the OP code D019.

15-8.3 Assemblers

The reverse of the disassembly procedure of Example 15-3 is called *hand assembly*. It requires the user to look up the machine language code for every instruction used. This manual process is so tedious and laborious that it is rarely done. Some hand assembly may be necessary during the hardware debug phase of a project, to determine whether the signals on the various data and address lines are correct, but software for the **68000** is rarely written in machine language.

Much of the labor in Example 15-3 is eliminated by using an Assembler. **68000** Assemblers are available from Motorola and many other software vendors. In addition to making programming easier, they will detect and flag invalid instructions and addressing modes. We recommend that the programmer use one of these Assemblers or the ECB (see Section 15-7) to ensure the correctness of the code before attempting free-running execution in the processor itself. Note that when dealing with addresses and data, most Assemblers require a distinction between decimal and hex numbers. Motorola uses the $ (dollar sign) to mean hex. Some commands of the ECB and some Assemblers assume the number is decimal unless the $ is included.

15-9 ADDRESS MODES

Most instructions specify the location of an operand by using a 6-bit field within the instruction word that is called the *Effective Address (EA) field*. Three bits are used to specify the addressing mode and 3 bits are used to specify a register, as shown in Fig. 15-11. The address mode and register are used together to calculate the actual address of the data or operand. This is known as the *Effective Address* (EA) of the instruction. The Effective Address field may require additional information to fully specify the operand. This additional information, called the Effective Address extension, is contained in a following word (or words) and is considered part of the instruction as shown in Fig. 15-8. The Effective Address modes are grouped into three categories: register direct, memory addressing, and special.

The Effective Addressing modes are shown in Table 15-2. They include these basic types:

- Register Direct
- Register Indirect
- Absolute
- Immediate
- Program Counter Relative

Included in the register indirect addressing modes is the capability to do postincrementing, predecrementing, offsetting, and indexing. Program Counter Relative (PCR) mode can also be modified via indexing and offsetting.

Some modes (those designated by 111 in the mode field) do not need to specify a register. In these cases the register field is used to further define the mode. Each of the addressing modes is considered in the following sections.

15	14	13	12	11	10	9	8	7	6	5	4	3	2	1	0
X	X	X	X	X	X	X	X	X	X	Effective Address Mode			Effective Address Register		

FIGURE 15-11 Single-effective-address-instruction operation—general format.

15-9.1 Register Direct Mode

The general format of a **68000** data instruction is

<Op code.X> <source>, <destination>

where X is the *length* of the instruction (B, W, or L). In Data Register Direct mode, the source or destination (or both) is a data register. For example, the instruction CLR.B D3 is a Data Register Direct instruction that needs only one operand. The .B specifies that it is a byte instruction. It clears bits 0–7 of D3.

15-9.2 Address Register Direct Mode

In Address Register Direct mode, the source or destination (or both) is an address register. These must be word or long-word operands; address registers do not work with byte operands. The instruction MOVE.W A3,D4, for example, uses Address Register Direct mode for the source and Data Register Direct for the destination; it copies the 16 LSBs of A3 into D4.

TABLE 15-2 Effective Address Mode Categories

Address Modes	Mode	Register	Data	Memory	Control	Alterable	Assembler Syntax
Data Register Direct	000	reg. no.	X	–	–	X	Dn
Address Register Direct	001	reg. no.	–	–	–	X	An
Address Register Indirect	010	reg. no.	X	X	X	X	(An)
Address Register Indirect with Postincrement	011	reg. no.	X	X	–	X	(An) +
Address Register Indirect with Predecrement	100	reg. no.	X	X	–	X	– (An)
Address Register Indirect with Displacement	101	reg. no.	X	X	X	X	(d_{16},An) or d_{16}(An)
Address Register Indirect with Index	110	reg. no.	X	X	X	X	(d_8,An,Xn) or d_8(An,Xn)
Absolute Short	111	000	X	X	X	X	(xxx).W
Absolute Long	111	001	X	X	X	X	(xxx).L
Program Counter Indirect with Displacement	111	101	X	X	X	–	(d_{16},PC) or d_{16}(PC)
Program Counter Indirect with Index	111	011	X	X	X	–	(d_8,PC,Xn) or d_8(PC,Xn)
Immediate	111	100	X	X	–	–	#<data>

15-9.3 Address Register Indirect

Address Register Indirect is a very popular addressing mode. It uses the contents of an address register as the memory address. Its Assembler syntax is (An), where n specifies the address register being used. If, for example, A5 contains $2004, then the EA in (A5) is $2004.

There are two other Address Register Indirect modes; *predecrement* and *postincrement*. In predecrement mode, the contents of the selected address register are first decremented and then used as an address. Although the **68000** does not contain PUSH or PULL instructions, this is essentially what happens during a PUSH instruction, as used in other μPs, when putting data on the stack. Its syntax is −(An).

In postincrement mode the selected register is used as an address and is then incremented. This is similar to a PULL instruction. Its syntax is (An)+. The equivalent of a PUSH from Data Register Dn can be obtained by the instruction MOVE.X Dn,−(An) and the corresponding PULL can be obtained by MOVE.X (An)+,Dn. This adds flexibility to the **68000** because any vacant address register can be used for PUSH or PULL functions or for setting up additional stacks.

EXAMPLE 15-4

What does the following program do?

```
MOVEA.L  #$2004,A4
MOVE.W   (A4)+,D2
MOVE.W   D2,(A4)
```

SOLUTION

The first instruction is an *immediate* instruction that moves the number $2004 into Address Register A4. The source mode of the second instruction is Address Register Indirect with postincrement and the destination mode is Data Register Direct. This instruction moves the contents of $2004 and $2005 into D2 and increments A4 to $2006 because it is a word length instruction. The third instruction writes the contents of D2 into $2006.

15-9.4 Address Register Indirect with Displacement

In the Address Register Indirect with Displacement mode, the EA is the sum of the contents of the designated address register plus a *displacement*. The operation of this mode is shown in Fig. 15-12. The displacement is a 16-bit word that is added to the instruction (a number larger than 32767_{10} or smaller than -32768_{10} cannot be used). The addition is a 32-bit addition of the contents of the address register and the *extended* displacement. The displacement is extended as follows.

If the MSB of the 16-bit displacement is a 0, leading 0s are added to fill out the 32 bits.

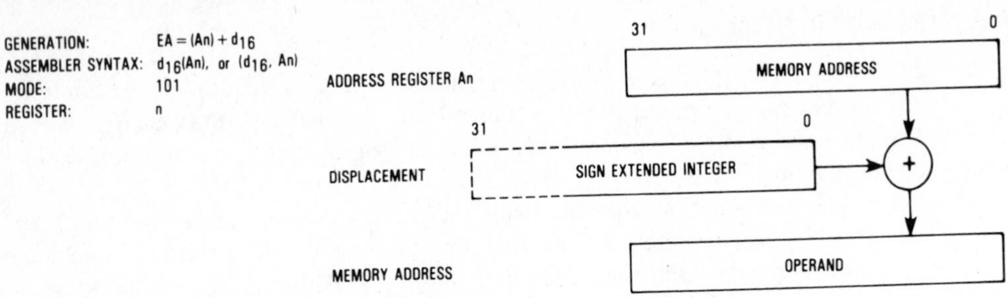

FIGURE 15-12 Address Register Indirect instruction with displacement.

If the MSB of the displacement is 1, leading 1s are added to fill out the 32 bits. This allows the displacement to be either a positive or a negative number.

EXAMPLE 15-5

If A4 contains 20004, what is the Effective Address of the following expressions?

a. \$1234(A4)
b. −2(A4)

(When testing with the ECB it will be found that the −2 must be replaced with the 32-bit equivalent, FFFFFFFE. Also, the Effective Address must be an even address or it will cause an error.)

SOLUTION

a. Here, the displacement is positive. The EA is

```
  $00020004
 +$00001234
  $00021238
```

The result is a higher address.

b. Here, the displacement is negative, because the MSB of the displacement is 1. The displacement is extended by adding leading Fs (1s). The EA is

```
  $00020004
 +$FFFFFFFE
  $00020002
```

The result is a lower address.

15-9.5 Address Register Indirect with Index

The Address Register Indirect with Index mode is the **68000** equivalent of the index mode in the **6800**. The way the EA is generated and the Assembler syntax are shown in Fig. 15-13b.

This mode uses an 8-bit displacement that is extended to 32 bits and then added to the sum of the selected Address Register and the selected Index Register. The size of the index register does not affect the execution time of the instruction.

A one-word extension to the instruction is required as shown in Fig. 15-13a. This extension word defines the register to be used as an index and whether the Index Register is to be taken as a word, in which case it is extended to 16 bits, or as a long word (extended to 32 bits). The extension word also includes the 8-bit displacement integer.

EXAMPLE 15-6

If A4 contains \$20004, A6 contains \$ABCD, and the displacement is −99, find the Effective Address of the expression −99(A4,A6.W).

SOLUTION

The extension word to the instruction is \$E080 (see Section 15-9), and the EA is the sum of the three numbers

$$
\begin{array}{rl}
\$00020004 & \\
\$FFFFABCD & = \text{32-bit sign extension of } \$ABCD \\
+\$FFFFFF9D & = -99_{10} \\
\hline
\$0001AB6E &
\end{array}
$$

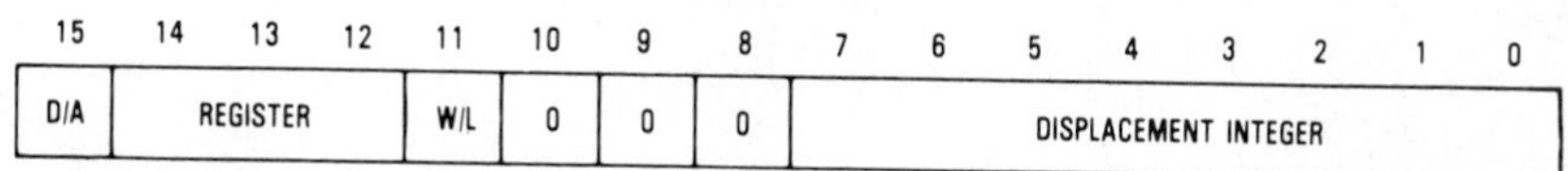

Bit 15 — Index register indicator
  0 — Data register
  1 — Address register
Bits 14 through 12 — Index register number
Bit 11 — Index size
  0 — Sign-extended, low order integer in index register
  1 — Long value in index register

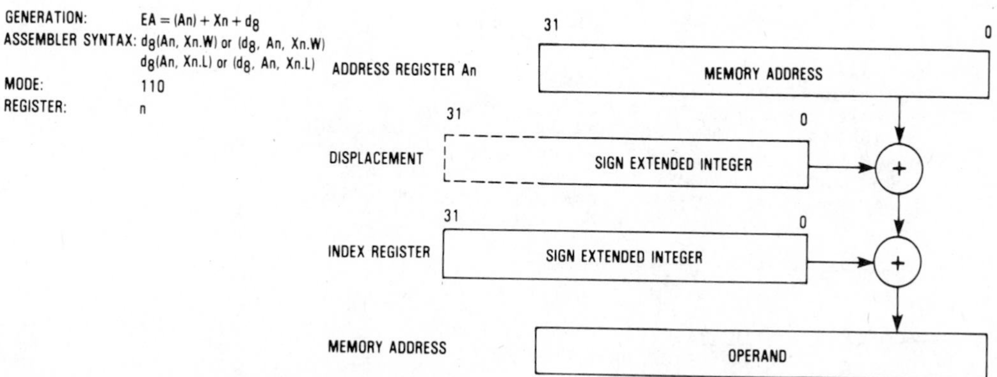

FIGURE 15-13 Address Register Indirect instruction with index. (a) Extension word. (b) Generation of effective address and assembly syntax.

Note that since A6 is defined as a word, the number entered in A6 can be $ABCD, which is sign-extended by the instruction to $FFFFABCD. If A6 is defined as a long word by specifying A6.L, the entry in A6 must be $FFFFABCD. The resulting EA is lower than the address in A4 because of the negative value in the index register (A6) and also because of the negative displacement.

EXAMPLE 15-7

If A4 contains an address of $3500, A6 contains −4, and the displacement is −128, find the EA for the expression −128(A4,A6.W).

SOLUTION
This can be solved as in Example 15-6 to give $347C. The EA can also be found without manual calculations by using the DC (Data Conversion) command of the ECB, as shown in Fig. 15-14. This figure shows the execution results using the ECB (described in Section 15-7).

To verify the results, a MOVE immediate instruction was created using the one-line assembler to place $222 into memory at the EA calculated by the expression. The instruction was entered using the command MM 2000;DI as shown on the top line. It created the machine language and mnemonics as shown in line 3 when the underlined part of line 2 was entered. The MM command was then exited by entering a period, as shown on line 4. The register values were then entered as

```
TUTOR  1.3 > MM 2000;DI
002000     00000000                      OR.B      #0,D0 ? MOVE #$222,-128(A4,A6)

002000     39BC0222E080                  MOVE      #$222,-128(A4,A6)
002006     00000000                      OR.B      #0,D0 ?.


TUTOR  1.3 > .PC 2000

TUTOR  1.3 > .A4 3500

TUTOR  1.3 > .A6 -4

TUTOR  1.3 > T
PHYSICAL ADDRESS=00002000
PC=00002006 SR=0000=..0..... US=00000782 SS=0001DC20
D0=00434E35 D1=00000000 D2=00004E75 D3=00000088
D4=00000030 D5=00000000 D6=00000008 D7=00000041
A0=00008902 A1=0000832C A2=00000414 A3=00000428
A4=00003500 A5=00000540 A6=FFFFFFFC A7=00000782
--------------------002006    00000000               OR.B     #0,D0

TUTOR  1.3 :> DC $3500-&128-4
$347C=&13436

TUTOR  1.3 > MD 3470
003470     00 00 00 00 00 00 00 00  00 00 00 00 02 22 00 00   ..........

TUTOR  1.3 >
```

FIGURE 15-14 ECB display results for Example 15-7.

shown on lines 5, 6, and 7, and the instruction was traced (by the T command—line 8). Normally the register display would have been examined using the DF command before executing the instruction and it would show that the registers involved have been set to the proper values and the instruction to be executed is displayed. (We skipped that step to save space.) After tracing one instruction, the registers were again displayed. It is not obvious from this that the instruction did what was intended, so the EA was calculated using the DC command. Note that the ECB creates a 32-bit value for −4. Also note that the ECB uses hex values for registers or addresses in the DC command but defaults to decimal for other numbers when it disassembles the instructions. It shows the EA to be $347C. When that address was examined, by displaying the line at $3470, it was seen to contain the $222.

15-9.6 Absolute Addressing

Absolute addressing uses a specific number to specify the address. This mode should be avoided when relocatable programs are being written, but it is necessary when addresssing peripherals, such as PIAs, that reside at fixed addresses. The instruction, MOVE.B $2004,D0 is an example of absolute source addressing and direct data addressing.

There are two types of absolute addressing, short and long. Short absolute addressing requires a one-word extension to the instruction and can specify any address from $0000 to $FFFF. Long absolute addressing uses a two-word extension, giving it a 32-bit address field, and can access any memory location. The longest **68000** instructions use one word of Op code, an absolute long source address, and an absolute long destination address. This is the worst case and results in a five-word instruction.

15-9.7 Program Counter Relative Modes

There are two Program Counter Relative modes in the **68000**. These modes are often used in relocatable programs because the Effective Addresses are relative to the PC and change when the starting address of the program changes.

The Program Counter with Displacement mode is shown in Figure 15-15. Its operation appears similar to that of the Address Register Indirect mode, except that the PC is used instead of an Address Register and the Assembler syntax is the reverse of what might be expected from the previous figures. The displacement is a sign-extended integer in an extension word to the instruction, and the address of that extension word is used as the PC component of the addition. When entering the mnemonic into a source program for assembly, into TUTOR's one-line Assembler, or into another similar debugger, the number in front of the parentheses is the *actual destination* address instead of the displacement. Typically, in an Assembly program, a *label* would be used to designate the destination address. When testing with TUTOR, it is therefore necessary to substitute the absolute

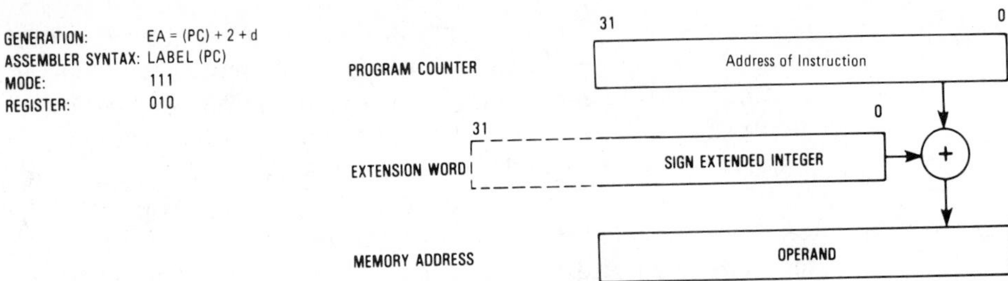

FIGURE 15-15 Program counter (with displacement) instruction generation and assembler syntax.

address that is equivalent to the label. This makes sense, because when testing loops or jumps, the absolute addresses must be used instead of the label.

Only data alterable addressing modes (see Section 15-9.9) are allowed for the destination EA field.

EXAMPLE 15-8

The machine language for the instruction MOVE $3002(PC),D3 is in memory starting at $3004. What is this Assembler-generated code and how is the displacement calculated?

SOLUTION

In the program counter relative mode, the reader must distinguish between the *Assembler syntax* and the *displacement* (or offset) calculated by the Assembler. In the instruction MOVE.W $3002(PC),D3, the Assembler interprets the $3002 as the Effective Address of the source of the data, or the *actual source address*. The (PC) tells the Assembler that this is a *Program Counter Relative* instruction. The Assembler then knows to calculate the *displacement* and includes it in the machine language.

In this mode each instruction consists of an Op code and an extension word. The Effective Address is the result of adding the displacement to the address of the extension word. In this example we have been told the EA ($3002) and we know the address of the extension word ($3006), so the Assembler calculates the displacement or difference between $3006 and $3002 or −4 ($FFFC). The Assembler Listing created for this instruction is

ADDR	CODE		INST.
003004	363AFFFC	MOVE.W	$3002(PC),D3

Here 363A (at location $3004) is the Op code for MOVE.W in the PC relative mode and the displacement, created by the Assembler of TUTOR or other Motorola Assemblers, is $FFFC (at location $3006). If MOVE.B had been used the Op code would have been 163A. The EA as calculated by the μP is

$00003006	Location of extension word
+$FFFFFFFC	displacement integer (extended)
$00003002	

The Program Counter with Index mode is similar to the Indirect Address with Index mode and is shown in Fig. 15-16. It also takes a one-word extension, as shown in Fig. 15-16a, which contains an 8-bit displacement byte. Again, the Assembler syntax requires the actual destination address (or a LABEL) to be entered preceding the (PC) rather than the displacement as in other instructions. (That is, MOVE.B $3008(PC,D6),D3 entered at location $3000 will generate 103B6006 where 06 is the displacement.) It adds this to the contents of the Index Register (D6, in this case) plus the PC address + 2 and the EA will be $3008 (if D6 is zero). Note that the address preceding the parenthesis in the Assembler syntax (or the label location) cannot be more than $7F (+127) bytes above the extension word's address or less than $80 (−128) below that address.

15-9.8 Immediate Mode

The Immediate mode uses either one or two extension words to provide the data for the instruction, depending on the size selected for the operation. The exten-

15	14	13	12	11	10	9	8	7	6	5	4	3	2	1	0
D/A	REGISTER			W/L	0	0	0	DISPLACEMENT INTEGER							

Bit 15 — Index register indicator
 0 — Data register
 1 — Address register
Bits 14 through 12 — Index register number
Bit 11 — Index size
 0 — Sign-extended, low order integer in index register
 1 — Long value in index register

(a)

Generation: EA = (PC + 2 + d_8 + (XN)
Where d_8 is the extended DISPLACEMENT INTEGER. (a 2s complement number)
Typical Assembler Syntax: $2480(PC,D3)

(for instruction at $24FE and maximum DISPLACEMENT INTEGER OF $80):
Where $2480 = (PC + 2 + d_8 (extended) or:
$2480 = $24FE + 2 + FFFFFF80
and EA = $2480 + (D3)
i.e.,

ADDR	CODE	INSTRUCTION
0024FE	303B3080	MOVE.W $2480(PC,D3),D0

MODE: 111
REGISTER: 100

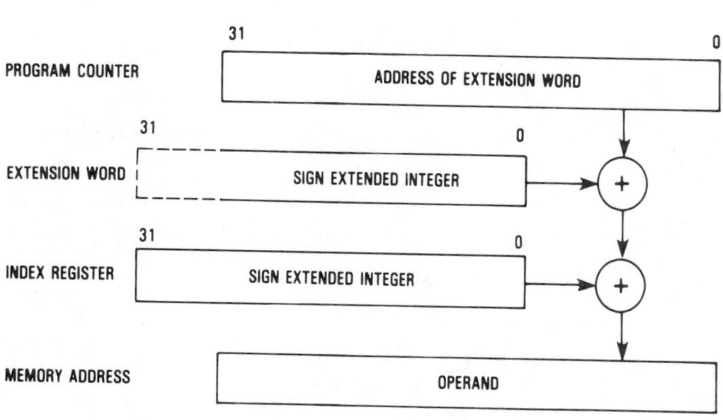

(b)

FIGURE 15-16 Program counter (with index) instruction generation and assembler syntax. (a) Extension word. (b) Effective address calculation.

sion word formats for byte, word, and long word are shown in Fig. 15-17. The Immediate mode can be a source but never a destination. For example, the instruction MOVE.W #$1234, −4(A4,A6) moves the first extension word (the hex number 1234) into the address that is the sum of the address in A4 plus the contents of A6 plus the displacement (second extension word), which in this case is also negative. This instruction has an Immediate mode source and an Address Register Indirect with Index destination.

The Immediate mode can be specified as byte, word, or long word, but the immediate extension to the instruction must be at least one word long. In byte-length mode, only bits 0–7 are used. Word sizes use the entire word and long-word sizes require two extension words to the instruction.

15-9.9 Address Categories

Effective Address modes may be categorized by the ways in which they may be used. Table 15-3 shows the various categories to which these Effective Addressing modes belong. Addresses fall into one or more of four categories:

Data. If an Effective Address mode may be used to refer to *data operands* (the contents of a Data Register), it is considered a *data addressing* Effective Address mode.

Memory. If an Effective Address mode may be used to refer to *memory operands,* it is considered a *memory addressing* Effective Address mode.

Alterable. If an address mode may be used to refer to alterable (writable) operands, it is considered to be an *alterable addressing* Effective Address mode. All addressing modes that do not involve the PC are alterable.

Control. If an Effective Address mode may be used to refer to memory

GENERATION: OPERAND GIVEN
ASSEMBLER SYNTAX: # xxxx or # <data>
MODE: 111
REGISTER: 100

The extension word formats are shown below:

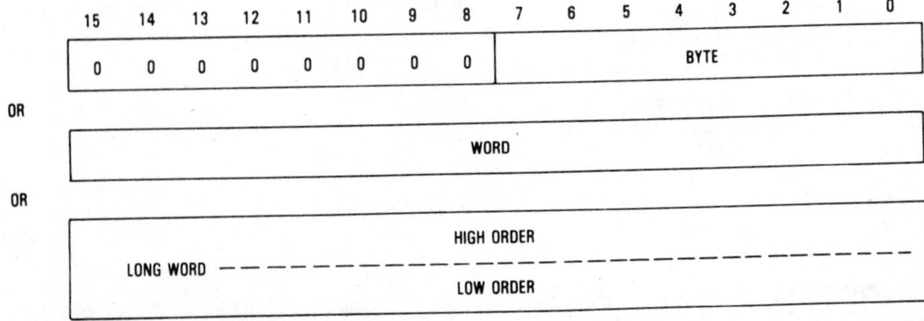

FIGURE 15-17 Immediate mode instructions.

TABLE 15-3 Effective Address Encoding Summary

Addressing Mode	Mode	Register
Data Register Direct	000	Register Number
Address Register Direct	001	Register Number
Address Register Indirect	010	Register Number
Address Register Indirect with Postincrement	011	Register Number
Address Register Indirect with Predecrement	100	Register Number
Address Register Indirect with Displacement	101	Register Number
Address Register Indirect with Index	110	Register Number
Absolute Short	111	000
Absolute Long	111	001
Program Counter with Displacement	111	010
Program Counter with Index	111	011
Immediate	111	100

operands without an associated size, it is considered a *control addressing* Effective Address mode. For example, the JMP instruction uses the control addressing modes, meaning those modes where the Effective Address is a memory location. The JMP instruction does not perform postincrement or predecrement. The allowed addressing modes are consistent with the nature of the instruction. The program should be allowed to jump to a location but not to a register.

To determine the allowed addressing mode for a specific instruction, determine the addressing category from the instruction set summary shown in Tables 15-7 through 15-15 in the following sections; then look up the allowed addressing modes in Table 15-3. The addressing modes that fall into each of these categories are defined with an "X" in the appropriate column. The *68000 Programmers Reference Manual* also shows the Condition Codes and the allowable modes for each instruction.

EXAMPLE 15-9

What address modes can be used with the instruction NEGX? (Create the 2s complement negative of a value with the sign bit extended).

SOLUTION

This instruction appears in Table 15-10 and the allowable addressing modes are "data alterable." This means that the addressing modes in Table 15-3 that have an "X" in both the data and the alterable columns are allowed. Looking at Table 15-3, we can see that the NEGX instruction can take all addressing modes except Address Register Direct, Immediate, Program Counter with Displacement, and Program Counter with Index. This allows the user to negate data registers and memory operands.

15-10 THE 68000 INSTRUCTION SET

A summary of the **68000** instructions is shown in Table 15-4. Some additional instructions are variations or subsets of these and appear in Table 15-5. Special emphasis has been given to the instruction set's support of structured high-level languages to facilitate ease of programming. Each instruction, with a few exceptions, operates on bytes, words, and long words and most instructions can use any of the 12 addressing modes. Combining instruction types, data types, and addressing modes, over 1000 useful instructions are provided. These instructions include BCD arithmetic, signed and unsigned, multiply and divide, "quick" arithmetic operations, and expanded operations (through traps). See Section 15-12.3. The following sections describe many of the **68000** instruction modes and illustrate their uses.

15-10.1 Quick Instructions

There are three instructions in the **68000** instruction set known as *Quick* instructions. A Quick instruction is a one-word Immediate instruction that deals with a small value in the operand. A Quick instruction uses a 3-bit field in the instruction word that contains the numbers 0–7. If a number from 1 to 7 is found in that field, it is the Immediate operand used by the instruction. If the field contains 0, the instruction uses 8 as its Immediate operand. The advantage of Quick instructions is that they require only one word in the program and thus save time and space.

TABLE 15-4 Instruction Set Summary

Mnemonic	Description
ABCD	Add Decimal With Extend
ADD	Add
AND	Logical And
ASL	Arithmetic Shift Left
ASR	Arithmetic Shift Right
Bcc	Branch Conditionally
BCHG	Bit Test and Change
BCLR	Bit Test and Clear
BRA	Branch Always
BSET	Bit Test and Set
BSR	Branch to Subroutine
BTST	Bit Test
CHK	Check Register Against Bounds
CLR	Clear Operand
CMP	Compare
DBcc	Test Condition, Decrement and Branch
DIVS	Signed Divide
DIVU	Unsigned Divide
EOR	Exclusive Or
EXG	Exchange Registers
EXT	Sign Extend
JMP	Jump
JSR	Jump to Subroutine
LEA	Load Effective Address
LINK	Link Stack
LSL	Logical Shift Left
LSR	Logical Shift Right

Mnemonic	Description
MOVE	Move
MULS	Signed Multiply
MULU	Unsigned Multiply
NBCD	Negate Decimal with Extend
NEG	Negate
NOP	No Operation
NOT	One's Complement
OR	Logical Or
PEA	Push Effective Address
RESET	Reset External Devices
ROL	Rotate Left without Extend
ROR	Rotate Right without Extend
ROXL	Rotate Left with Extend
ROXR	Rotate Right with Extend
RTE	Return from Exception
RTR	Return and Restore
RTS	Return from Subroutine
SBCD	Subtract Decimal with Extend
Scc	Set Conditional
STOP	Stop
SUB	Subtract
SWAP	Swap Data Register Halves
TAS	Test and Set Operand
TRAP	Trap
TRAPV	Trap on Overflow
TST	Test
UNLK	Unlink

TABLE 15-5 Variations of Instruction Types

Instruction Type	Variation	Description
ADD	ADD	Add
	ADDA	Add Address
	ADDQ	Add Quick
	ADDI	Add Immediate
	ADDX	Add with Extend
AND	AND	Logical And
	ANDI	And Immediate
	ANDI to CCR	And Immediate to Condition Codes
	ANDI to SR	And Immediate to Status Register
CMP	CMP	Compare
	CMPA	Compare Address
	CMPM	Compare Memory
	CMPI	Compare Immediate
EOR	EOR	Exclusive Or
	EORI	Exclusive Or Immediate
	EORI to CCR	Exclusive Or Immediate to Condition Codes
	EORI to SR	Exclusive Or Immediate to Status Register

Instruction Type	Variation	Description
MOVE	MOVE	Move
	MOVEA	Move Address
	MOVEM	Move Multiple Registers
	MOVEP	Move Peripheral Data
	MOVEQ	Move Quick
	MOVE from SR	Move from Status Register
	MOVE to SR	Move to Status Register
	MOVE to CCR	Move to Condition Codes
	MOVE USP	Move User Stack Pointer
NEG	NEG	Negate
	NEGX	Negate with Extend
OR	OR	Logical Or
	ORI	Or Immediate
	ORI to CCR	Or Immediate to Condition Codes
	ORI to SR	Or Immediate to Status Register
SUB	SUB	Subtract
	SUBA	Subtract Address
	SUBI	Subtract Immediate
	SUBQ	Subtract Quick
	SUBX	Subtract with Extend

The ADD Quick (ADDQ) and Subtract Quick (SUBQ) instructions allow the user to add or subtract the numbers 1 through 8 from a register or memory.

EXAMPLE 15-10

There is no decrement instruction in the **68000**. Show how to decrement register D4.

SOLUTION
The simplest way is to use the instruction

```
SUBQ   #1,D4
```

Note that a memory location could also have been decremented in this way by using the memory location as the destination of the instruction.

The MOVEQ instruction is discussed in Section 15-10.3.

15-10.2 Address Register Destination Instructions

Instructions that specify an Address Register as a destination are somewhat special. They may use only word or long-word operands, and most of them do not affect the Condition Codes. The four address destination words are MOVEA, ADDA, SUBA, and CMPA. Of these, only the COMPARE sets the Condition Codes; it subtracts the destination address register from the source, which can be a register, a memory location, or an Immediate value, and sets the Condition Codes accordingly without changing the registers.

15-10.3 The MOVE Instructions

The MOVE instruction uses another common format. The page of the manual for that instruction is shown in Fig. 15-18. The instruction format contains an Op code

MOVE — Move Data from Source to Destination — MOVE

Operation: Source → Destination

Assembler Syntax: MOVE <ea>,<ea>

Attributes: Size = (Byte, Word, Long)

Description: Move the content of the source to the destination location. The data is examined as it is moved, and the condition codes set accordingly. The size of the operation may be specified to be byte, word, or long.

Condition Codes:

X	N	Z	V	C
—	*	*	0	0

N Set if the result is negative. Cleared otherwise.
Z Set if the result is zero. Cleared otherwise.
V Always cleared.
C Always cleared.
X Not affected.

Instruction Format:

15	14	13–12	11–9	8–6	5–3	2–0
			Destination		Source	
0	0	Size	Register	Mode	Mode	Register

Instruction Fields:

Size field — Specifies the size of the operand to be moved:
01—byte operation.
11—word operation.
10—long operation.

Destination Effective Address field — Specifies the destination location. Only data alterable addressing modes are allowed as shown:

Addr. Mode	Mode	Register
Dn	000	reg. number:An
An	—	—
(An)	010	reg. number:An
(An) +	011	reg. number:An
− (An)	100	reg. number:An
(d_{16},An)	101	reg. number:An
(d_8,An,Xn)	110	reg. number:An

Addr. Mode	Mode	Register
(xxx).W	111	000
(xxx).L	111	001
#<data>	—	—
(d_{16},PC)	—	—
(d_8,PC,Xn)	—	—

Source Effective Address field — Specifies the source operand. All addressing modes are allowed as shown:

Addr. Mode	Mode	Register
Dn	000	reg. number:Dn
An*	001	reg. number:An
(An)	010	reg. number:An
(An) +	011	reg. number:An
− (An)	100	reg. number:An
(d_{16},An)	101	reg. number:An
(d_8,An,Xn)	110	reg. number:An

Addr. Mode	Mode	Register
(xxx).W	111	000
(xxx).L	111	001
#<data>	111	100
(d_{16},PC)	111	010
(d_8,PC,Xn)	111	011

*For byte size operation, address register direct is not allowed.

Notes: 1. MOVEA is used when the destination is an address register. Most assemblers automatically make this distinction.
2. MOVEQ can also be used for certain operations on data registers.

FIGURE 15-18 Manual page for the MOVE instruction.

field that declares it to be a MOVE instruction and specifies the size of the operand. It then has a 6-bit field to define the destination and another 6-bit field to define the source.

EXAMPLE 15-11

Figure 15-19 shows the location of data in memory for this example. What data ends up in Data Register D0 after executing each of the following instructions?

a. **MOVE.B $2004,D0**
b. **MOVE.B $2005,D0**
c. **MOVE.W $2004,D0**
d. **MOVE.W $2005,D0**
e. **MOVE.L $2004,D0**

SOLUTION

a. The instruction MOVE.B $2004,D0 moves the byte at $2004 to D0. The 8 LSBs of D0 become AA. The remaining bytes of D0 are unchanged.
b. The byte at $2005 is moved to D0. Its 8 LSBs become BB. The remaining bytes are unchanged.
c. This instruction moves the word at $2004 to D0. The 16 LSBs of D0 become AABB; the rest of the bits are unchanged.
d. This instruction is illegal. Word or long-word transfers cannot specify odd addresses.
e. This is a long-word transfer. The contents of D0 become AABBCCDD.

Space limitations preclude giving as thorough a description of each instruction as may be found in the *M68000 Programmers Reference Manual* (see Section 15-17). Each **68000** instruction is covered here, however, in Tables 15-7 through 15-15. Between the tables and the descriptions we will present in the following paragraphs, we hope to provide enough information so that the reader can use the instructions. The tables give the instruction, the allowable sizes of its operands, its operation, its notation, and its allowable Effective Address modes. Using the notation provided in the tables and the address notation provided in Section 15-8, the reader should be able to specify an assembler instruction for an Assembler or

Memory	
Byte Addresses	*Data*
2004	AA
2005	BB
2006	CC
2007	DD

FIGURE 15-19 Data for Example 15-11.

TUTOR. The effect of the instruction on the Condition Codes is not given in these tables, but Table 15-6 shows how the various instructions affect the codes.

Characteristics of the MOVE group of instructions in the **68000** are shown in Table 15-7. The MOVE instruction copies data from the source, which can be any of the modes, to the destination, which can be any mode except an Address

TABLE 15-6 Condition Code Computations

Operations	X	N	Z	V	C	Special Definition
ABCD	*	U	?	U	?	C = Decimal Carry $Z = Z \wedge \overline{Rm} \wedge \ldots \wedge \overline{R0}$
ADD, ADDI, ADDQ	*	*	*	?	?	$V = Sm \wedge Dm \wedge \overline{Rm} \vee \overline{Sm} \wedge \overline{Dm} \wedge Rm$ $C = Sm \wedge Dm \vee \overline{Rm} \wedge Dm \vee Sm \wedge \overline{Rm}$
ADDX	*	*	?	?	?	$V = Sm \wedge Dm \wedge \overline{Rm} \vee \overline{Sm} \wedge \overline{Dm} \wedge Rm$ $C = Sm \wedge Dm \vee \overline{Rm} \wedge Dm \vee Sm \wedge \overline{Rm}$ $Z = Z \wedge \overline{Rm} \wedge \ldots \wedge \overline{R0}$
AND, ANDI, EOR, EORI, MOVEQ, MOVE, OR, ORI, CLR, EXT, NOT, TAS, TST	–	*	*	0	0	
CHK	–	*	U	U	U	
SUB, SUBI, SUBQ	*	*	*	?	?	$V = \overline{Sm} \wedge Dm \wedge \overline{Rm} \vee Sm \wedge \overline{Dm} \wedge Rm$ $C = Sm \wedge \overline{Dm} \vee Rm \wedge \overline{Dm} \vee Sm \wedge Rm$
SUBX	*	*	?	?	?	$V = \overline{Sm} \wedge Dm \wedge \overline{Rm} \vee Sm \wedge \overline{Dm} \wedge Rm$ $C = Sm \wedge \overline{Dm} \vee Rm \wedge \overline{Dm} \vee Sm \wedge Rm$ $Z = Z \wedge \overline{Rm} \wedge \ldots \wedge \overline{R0}$
CMP CMPI, CMPM	–	*	*	?	?	$V = \overline{Sm} \wedge Dm \wedge \overline{Rm} \vee Sm \wedge \overline{Dm} \wedge Rm$ $C = Sm \wedge \overline{Dm} \vee Rm \wedge \overline{Dm} \vee Sm \wedge Rm$
DIVS, DIVU	–	*	*	?	0	V = Division Overflow
MULS, MULU	–	*	*	?	0	V = Multiplication Overflow
SBCD, NBCD	*	U	?	U	?	C = Decimal Borrow $Z = Z \wedge \overline{Rm} \wedge \ldots \wedge \overline{R0}$
NEG	*	*	*	?	?	$V = Dm \wedge Rm$, $C = Dm \vee Rm$
NEGX	*	*	?	?	?	$V = Dm \wedge Rm$, $C = Dm \vee Rm$ $Z = Z \wedge \overline{Rm} \wedge \ldots \wedge \overline{R0}$
BTST, BCHG, BSET, BCLR	–	–	?	–	–	$Z = \overline{Dn}$
ASL	*	*	*	?	?	$V = Dm \wedge (\overline{Dm-1} \vee \ldots \vee \overline{Dm-r}) \vee \overline{Dm} \wedge (Dm-1 \vee \ldots + Dm-r)$ $C = \overline{Dm-r+1}$
ASL (r = 0)	–	*	*	0	0	
LSL, ROXL	*	*	*	0	?	$C = Dm - r + 1$
LSR (r = 0)	–	*	*	0	0	
ROXL (r = 0)	–	*	*	0	?	C = X
ROL	–	*	*	0	?	$C = Dm - r + 1$
ROL (r = 0)	–	*	*	0	0	
ASR, LSR, ROXR	*	*	*	0	?	$C = Dr - 1$
ASR, LSR (r = 0)	–	*	*	0	0	
ROXR (r = 0)	–	*	*	0	?	C = X
ROR	–	*	*	0	?	$C = Dr - 1$
ROR (r = 0)	–	*	*	0	0	

– = Not Affected
U = Undefined, result meaningless
? = Other – See Special Definition
* = General Case
  X = C
  N = Rm
  $Z = \overline{Rm} \wedge \ldots \wedge \overline{R0}$
Sm = Source Operand – most significant bit
Dm = Destination Operand – most significant bit

Rm = Result Operand – most significant bit
R = Register Tested
n = Bit Number
r = Shift Count
LB = Lower Bound
UB = Upper Bound
= Boolean AND
V = Boolean OR
$\overline{Rm}$ = NOT Rm

TABLE 15-7 Data Movement Instructions

Instruction	*Operand size*	*Operation*	*Notation*	*Allowable effective address modes*
MOVE	8,16,32	(SOURCE) → DESTINATION	MOVE ⟨ea⟩, ⟨ea⟩	SOURCE ALL DEST DATA ALTERABLE
MOVE from SR	16	SR → DESTINATION	MOVE SR, ⟨ea⟩	DATA ALTERABLE
MOVE to CC	16	(SOURCE) → CCR	MOVE ⟨ea⟩, CCR	DATA
MOVE to SR	16	(SOURCE) → SR	MOVE ⟨ea⟩, SR	DATA
MOVE USP	32	USP → An or An → USP	MOVE USP, An MOVE An, USP	—
MOVEA	16,32	(SOURCE) → REGISTERS	MOVEA ⟨ea⟩, An	ALL
MOVEM	16,32	REGISTERS → DESTINATION (SOURCE) → REGISTERS	MOVEM REGISTER LIST ⟨ea⟩	ALTERABLE CONTROL AND PREDECREMENT
			MOVEM ⟨ea⟩ REGISTER LIST	CONTROL AND POST INCREMENT
MOVEP	16,32	(SOURCE) → DESTINATION	MOVEP Dx, d(Ay) MOVEP d(Ay), Dx	—
MOVEQ	32	IMMEDIATE DATA → DESTINATION	MOVEQ # data, Dn	—
EXG	32	Rx ↔ Ry	EXG Rx,Ry	—
SWAP	16	Dnhw ↔ Dnhw	SWAP Dn	—

Register with Displacement or a PC with Displacement (control) mode. The MOVE is the only instruction in the group that accommodates byte instructions. It sets the N and Z flags, clears C and V, and does not affect X. Most of the other MOVE instructions do not affect the Condition Codes at all. The MOVE instruction has been used in Examples 15-5, 15-9, and 15-11. The other instructions in the move group are described below.

MOVEA Used when an Address Register is a destination. Many assemblers will convert a MOVE to a MOVEA where appropriate.

EXAMPLE 15-12

Write a program to transfer the words in \$1000–\$11FE to \$2000–\$21FE. This is a block transfer program.

SOLUTION

The program is very short using **68000** instructions:

```
        MOVEA.L   #$1000,A1
        MOVEA.L   #$2000,A2
LOOP    MOVE.W    (A1)+,(A2)+
        CMPA      #$1200,A1
        BNE       LOOP
        ....      CONTINUE
```

where the CMPA and BNE are the basic *compare address register* and *branch if not equal* instructions.

MOVE to CCR This instruction specifies a 16-bit source moved into the 8-bit Condition Codes. The lower byte of the source is moved and the upper byte is ignored. Of course, this instruction affects all the Condition Codes.

MOVE from SR This instruction moves the contents of the Status Register to a Data Register or memory so that the program can examine and use them.

MOVE to SR The converse of MOVE from SR. This instruction alters both the Condition Codes and the system byte. It is a privileged instruction (usable only in the supervisory mode) because it can change the S bit.

MOVE USP (Move User Stack Pointer) This instruction moves the User Stack Pointer (USP) to or from another Address Register. It can be used only in supervisory mode. It allows the executive program to set the USP before turning control over to the user.

MOVEM (Move Multiple Registers) This instruction moves a group of Address or Data Registers to or from memory. It uses a 16-bit extension word to define which of the eight data and eight address registers are to be moved. Only word or long-word operations are allowed. Its syntax is

```
MOVEM.X   <list> source, destination
```

where <list> is the list of registers to be moved. In the list a slash (/) separates the registers; a dash can be used to specify a group of inclusive registers.

EXAMPLE 15-13

Write a program segment to move registers D1 through D5, D7, A2, and A3 into memory starting at location $1000. Assume register A4 is available.

SOLUTION
The instructions are

```
MOVEA.L   #$1000,A4
MOVEM.L   D1-D5/D7/A1/A2,(A4)
```

These two instructions move the contents of the eight registers into $1000–$101F.

MOVEP (Move to Peripherals) This instruction is designed to move data so it can be used with 8-bit peripherals such as a PIA. This is discussed in Section 15-11.12.

MOVEQ The Move Quick instruction must have a Data Register as its destination. It will move 8 bits into the selected Data Register and then *sign extend* it to 32 bits. As a result of MOVEQ, the Data Register will contain a number between $+127_{10}$ and -128_{10}.

EXCHANGE This instruction is used to exchange data between any two registers. Its syntax is

```
EXG  Dx,Dy
EXG  Ax,Ay
EXG  Dx,Ay
```

Only long word exchanges are permitted.

SWAP The SWAP instruction exchanges words in a register rather than between registers. For example, if D4 contains 1234ABCD, a SWAP D4 will change it to ABCD1234. The N and Z condition codes are set by SWAP, while C and V are cleared.

15-10.4 Logic Instructions

The logic instructions in the **68000** are given in Table 15-8. They are AND, OR, EOR (Exclusive OR), and NOT. Address Registers cannot be the source or destination in a logic instruction. An example would be

```
AND.W  D0,(A0)
```

which ANDs the 16 LSB contents of D0 and memory and puts the results in memory.

TABLE 15-8 Logic Instructions

Instruction	*Operand size*	*Operation*	*Notation*	*Allowable effective address modes*
AND	8,16,32	(SOURCE) ∧ (DESTINATION) → DESTINATION	AND ⟨ea⟩, Dn	DATA
			AND Dn, ⟨ea⟩	ALTERABLE MEMORY
ANDI	8,16,32	IMMEDIATE DATA ∧ (DESTINATION) → DESTINATION	ANDI # ⟨data⟩, ⟨ea⟩	DATA ALTERABLE OR [a]STATUS REGISTER
EOR	8,16,32	(SOURCE) ⊕ (DESTINATION) → DESTINATION	EOR Dn, ⟨ea⟩	DATA ALTERABLE
EORI	8,16,32	IMMEDIATE DATA ⊕ (DESTINATION) → DESTINATION	EORI # ⟨data⟩, ⟨ea⟩	DATA ALTERABLE OR [a]STATUS REGISTER
NOT	8,16,32	$\overline{\text{(DESTINATION)}}$ → DESTINATION	NOT ⟨ea⟩	DATA ALTERABLE
OR	8,16,32	(SOURCE) ∨ (DESTINATION) → DESTINATION	OR DN, ⟨ea⟩	ALTERABLE MEMORY
			OR ⟨ea⟩, Dn	DATA
ORI	8,16,32	IMMEDIATE DATA ∨ (DESTINATION) → DESTINATION	ORI # ⟨data⟩, ⟨ea⟩	DATA ALTERABLE OR [a]STATUS REGISTER

[a] *Source: M68000 Programmer's Reference Manual*, 4th Edition, courtesy of Motorola, Inc.

The AND, OR and EOR instructions each have three submodes:

Immediate. This can be byte, word, or long word.

Immediate to CCR. This byte instruction allows the user to set or clear various bits in the CCR.

Immediate to SR. This word instruction allows the programmer to control the entire SR. It is a privileged instruction because it can change the S bit.

EXAMPLE 15-14

Write an instruction to clear the V bit of the CCR. All other bits must remain unchanged.

SOLUTION
The V bit is bit 1 (see Fig. 15-5). The instruction is ANDI.B #$FB,SR.

The NOT instruction complements a Data Register or memory location. Byte, word, or long word may be used. The NOT instruction cannot be used with an Address Register.

15-10.5 Add and Subtract Instructions

The ADD and SUBTRACT instructions in the **68000** are shown in Table 15-9. The ADD instructions are

ADD

ADDA—Add to an address register

ADDI—Add Immediate

ADDQ—Add Immediate (Immediate value is between 1 and 8)

ADDX—Add with the extend (X) bit - Add 1 if the X bit is set.

The SUBTRACT instructions are similar to the ADD instructions. The subtraction operation is

Destination − Source > Destination

EXAMPLE 15-15

Write a program to subtract the 6-byte number in $4000 from the 6-byte number in $3000 and store the result in $5000. The LSBs of the numbers are in $3005, $4005, and $5005, respectively.

SOLUTION
The minuend is in $3000–$3005 and the subtrahend is in $4000–$4005. Because the

TABLE 15-9 Integer Arithmetic Instructions

Instruction	*Operand size*	*Operation*	*Notation*	*Allowable effective address modes*
ADD	8,16,32	(DESTINATION) + (SOURCE) → DESTINATION	ADD Dn, ⟨ea⟩	ALTERABLE MEMORY
			ADD ⟨ea⟩, Dn	ALL
ADDA	16,32	(DESTINATION) + (SOURCE) → DESTINATION	ADD ⟨ea⟩, An	ALL
ADDI	8,16,32	(DESTINATION) + IMMEDIATE DATA → DESTINATION	ADDI # ⟨data⟩, ⟨ea⟩	DATA ALTERABLE
ADDQ	8,16,32	(DESTINATION) + IMMEDIATE DATA → DESTINATION	ADDQ # ⟨data⟩, ⟨ea⟩	ALTERABLE
ADDX	8,16,32	(DESTINATION) + (SOURCE) + X → DESTINATION	ADDX Dy, Dx ADDX −(Ay), −(Ax)	— —
SUB	8,16,32	(DESTINATION) − (SOURCE) → DESTINATION	SUB Dn, ⟨ea⟩	ALTERABLE MEMORY
			SUB ⟨ea⟩, Dn	ALL
SUBA	16,32	(DESTINATION) − (SOURCE) → DESTINATION	SUBA ⟨ea⟩, An	ALL
SUBI	8,16,32	(DESTINATION) − IMMEDIATE DATA → DESTINATION	SUBI # ⟨data⟩, ⟨ea⟩	DATA ALTERABLE
SUBQ	8,16,32	(DESTINATION) − IMMEDIATE DATA → DESTINATION	SUBQ # ⟨data⟩, ⟨ea⟩	ALTERABLE
SUBX	8,16,32	(DESTINATION) − (SOURCE) − X → DESTINATION	SUBX Dy, Dx SUBX −(Ay), −(Ax)	—

LSBs are in the highest locations, it would be most efficient to use the auto-predecrement mode. Three pointers are needed: a minuend pointer, a subtrahend pointer, and a destination pointer. The program will run in word mode and the pointers are each set one word higher than the data because the addresses will be decremented before they are used. The program is assumed to start at $1000.

```
        MOVEA    #$3006,A3     Set minuend pointer.
        MOVEA    #$4006,A4     Set subtrahend pointer.
        MOVEA    #$5006,A5     Set destination pointer.
        ADDI     #0,D3         This instruction does not change D3,
*                              but it clears the X bit.
LOOP    MOVE.W   -(A3),D3      Move minuend to D3.
        MOVE.W   -(A4),D4      Move subtrahend to D4.
        SUBX.W   D4,D3         Subtract: the difference goes to D3.
        MOVE.W   D3,-(A5)      Place result in memory.
        CMPA.W   #$3000,A3     Done?
        BNE      LOOP          No if not equal to zero.
        . . .      CONTINUE
```

15-10.6 The BCD Instructions

To use Binary Coded Decimal (BCD), the data must first be in BCD form, with two BCD digits to a byte. There are three BCD instructions, as shown in Table 15-10. They all operate only on bytes, so a length specification is unnecessary.

TABLE 15-10 BCD Operations

Instruction	*Operand size*	*Operation*	*Notation*	*Allowable effective address modes*
ABCD	8	$(\text{SOURCE})_{10} + (\text{DESTINATION})_{10} + X \rightarrow$ DESTINATION	ABCD Dy, Dx ABCD −(Ay), −(Ax)	—
NBCD	8	$0 - (\text{DESTINATION})_{10} - X \rightarrow$ DESTINATION	NBCD ⟨ea⟩	DATA ALTERABLE
SBCD	8	$(\text{DESTINATION})_{10} - (\text{SOURCE})_{10} - X \rightarrow$ DESTINATION	SBCD Dy, Dx SBCD −(Ay), −(Ax)	—

They all use the X bit. The BCD ADD and SUBTRACT instructions (ABCD and SBCD) require that both the source and destination be in Data Registers or in memory. If in memory, they can be accessed only in the auto-predecrement mode. The negate BCD (NBCD) produces the 10s complement of the destination if X is 0 and the 9s complement if X is 1 (see Section 4-8.4).

EXAMPLE 15-16

If D3 contains 46 in its LS byte, what is the result of the instruction NBCD D3?

SOLUTION
If X is clear, D3 will contain the 10s complement of 46, or 54, and if X is set it will contain the 9s complement, or 53.

15-10.7 Other Arithmetic Instructions

The other arithmetic instructions in the **68000** are given in Table 15-11. Most of them are very simple, but the MULTIPLY and DIVIDE instructions are more complex.

The CLEAR instruction is used to clear a byte, word, or long word in a data register or memory. An address register cannot be used. It sets Z and clears N, C, and V of the Condition Codes. X is not affected.

The EXT instruction *extends* the sign of a byte in a data register to a word, or the sign of a word to a long word. To extend a byte to a word, for example, it places either 00 or $FF in the upper byte, depending on whether the MSB of the lower byte was 0 or 1.

The NEG instruction negates (2s complements) the contents of a data register or memory location by subtracting the contents from zero. The results affect all the Condition Code bits; the X bit is set the same as the C bit. The NEGX instruction is similar, but it subtracts 1 if X is set. It is used where multiple-word 2s complementing is required.

The MULTIPLY instructions multiply a word length source by a word in the destination register. The result is a long word that fills the entire destination register. The source word can be in a data register, memory, or an Immediate value. The destination must be a data register. The MULU instruction treats the words as unsigned, or positive integers, regardless of their MSB. The MULS (signed multiply) instruction treats the numbers as signed numbers.

EXAMPLE 15-17

The number in D4 is $FFFE. What number appears in D4 after the following instructions?

a. MULU D4,D4
b. MULS D4,D4

SOLUTION
This instruction squares the number. For part a, where the numbers are treated as unsigned integers, the result is FFFC0004. For part b, we simply have $(-2)^2$, and the result in D4 is 00000004.

The division instructions start with a long-word dividend in a data register. The divisor is the source word and can be in another data register, memory, or an Immediate. The division places the 16-bit quotient in the lower word of the destination register and the 16-bit remainder in the upper word. The DIVU treats the numbers as unsigned and the DIVS assumes the numbers are signed. There are two possible errors in a division operation:

1. The quotient may be longer than 16 bits.
2. The divisor may be zero.

The first condition sets the V bit and the second condition causes a *trap* (see Section 15-10.2).

EXAMPLE 15-18

If the number in D4 is $1D, what appears in D4 after a DIVU #4,D4 instruction?

TABLE 15-11 Other Arithmetic Instructions

Instruction	*Operand size*	*Operation*	*Notation*	*Allowable effective address modes*
EXT	16,32	(DESTINATION) Sign-EXTENDED → DESTINATION	EXT Dn	
MULS	16	(SOURCE) × (DESTINATION) → DESTINATION	MULS ⟨ea⟩, Dn	DATA
MULU	16	(SOURCE) × (DESTINATION) → DESTINATION	MULU ⟨ea⟩, Dn	DATA
NEG	8,16,32	0 − (DESTINATION) → DESTINATION	NEG ⟨ea⟩	DATA ALTERABLE
NEGX	8,16,32	0 − (DESTINATION) − X → DESTINATION	NEGX ⟨ea⟩	DATA ALTERABLE
CLR	8,16,32	0 → DESTINATION	CLR ⟨ea⟩	DATA ALTERABLE
DIVS	16	(DESTINATION) + (SOURCE) → DESTINATION	DIVS ⟨ea⟩, Dn	DATA
DIVU	16	(DESTINATION) + (SOURCE) → DESTINATION	DIVU ⟨ea⟩, Dn	DATA

SOLUTION
The results of dividing \$1D $(29)_{10}$ are a quotient of 7 and a remainder of 1. The number in D4 is therefore 00010007.

15-10.8 Compare and Test Instructions

The COMPARE instructions, shown in Table 15-12, all subtract the source from the destination and then discard the results. They do *not* change the contents of any memory locations or registers, but they do affect the N, V, Z, and C Condition Codes. They do not affect the X bit. The CMP instruction must have a data register as the destination or minuend for the subtraction. The CMPA instruction uses an address register for the minuend. The CMPA instruction has already been used in Examples 15-12 and 15-15.

The CMPI can be used to compare an Immediate value with memory or a register. The CMPM compares two memory locations, but each location must be specified in the auto-postincrement mode.

EXAMPLE 15-19

Write a program segment to compare the contents of \$1000 and \$2000.

SOLUTION
The segment is

```
MOVEA    #$1000,A3
MOVEA    #$2000,A4
CMPM.B   (A3)+,(A4)+
```

At the end of the segment, the contents of A3 and A4 will be \$1001 and \$2001. The C bit will be set if the absolute value of the contents of \$1000 are greater than the contents of \$2000.

TABLE 15-12 Compare and Test Instructions

Instruction	*Operand size*	*Operation*	*Notation*	*Allowable effective address modes*
CMP	8,16,32	(OPERAND2) − (OPERAND1)	CMP ⟨ea⟩, Dn	ALL
CMPA	16,32	(OPERAND2) − (OPERAND1)	CMPA ⟨ea⟩, An	ALL
CMPI	8,16,32	(OPERAND) − IMMEDIATE DATA	CMPI # ⟨data⟩, ⟨ea⟩	DATA ALTERABLE
CMPM	8,16,32	(OPERAND2) − (OPERAND1)	CMPM (Ay) +,(Ax) +	
TST	8,16,32	(DESTINATION) − 0 (DESTINATION) TESTED → CC	TST ⟨ea⟩	DATA ALTERABLE

The TEST instruction simply subtracts zero from a register or memory location and sets the N and Z bits accordingly. It can be used to determine the characteristics of the destination (is it positive, negative, or zero?).

15-10.9 Bit Test Instructions

The BIT TEST group of instructions is given in Table 15-13. The function of the BTST instruction is to test a bit in a data register or memory and set or clear the Z flag if the selected bit is 0 or 1. All other bits of the CCR are unaffected. There are two allowable forms of the BTST instruction:

BTST Dn,<EA>

BTST #<data>,<EA>

In either form <EA> is the Effective Address of the byte or long word being tested. If <EA> specifies a memory address, then only bits 0–7 can be tested. This is a byte length instruction. If <EA> is a data register, however, any of its 32 bits can be tested. This is the long-word form of the instruction.

The first form of the instruction is sometimes called the dynamic form. The number of the bit to be tested is contained in Dn. The second form is called the static form. The number of the bit to be tested is specified *immediately*.

The BSET instruction is identical to the BTST instruction except that it sets the bit after testing it. After a BSET instruction the bit is a 1, but the Z flag gives the status of the bit before it was changed. The BCLR works like the BSET instruction, except that the bit is cleared after the test, and the BCHG instruction also works the same way except that the bit is changed (inverted) after the test. These three instructions can also be used to set or clear a bit in a location, as Example 15-20 shows.

EXAMPLE 15-20

Bits 0–6 of location $2000 contain an ASCII character. Write a program to set bit 7, if necessary, so that the parity of the byte is odd (it contains an odd number of 1s).

TABLE 15-13 Bit Manipulation Instructions

Instruction	*Operand size*[a]	*Operation*	*Notation*	*Allowable effective address modes*
BCHG	8,32	~(⟨bit number⟩ OF Destination) → Z ~(⟨bit number⟩ OF Destination) → ⟨bit number⟩ OF Destination	BCHG Dn, ⟨ea⟩ BCHG # ⟨data⟩, ⟨ea⟩	DATA ALTERABLE
BCLR	8,32	~(⟨bit number⟩ OF Destination) → Z 0 → ⟨bit number⟩ OF Destination	BCLR Dn, ⟨ea⟩ BCLR # ⟨data⟩, ⟨ea⟩	DATA ALTERABLE
BSET	8,32	~(⟨bit number⟩ OF Destination) → Z; 1 → ⟨bit number⟩ OF Destination	BSET Dn, ⟨ea⟩ BSET # ⟨data⟩ ⟨ea⟩	DATA ALTERABLE
BTST	8,32	~(⟨bit number⟩ OF Destination) → Z	BTST ⟨Dn⟩, ⟨ea⟩ BTST # ⟨data⟩, ⟨ea⟩	DATA

[a] For memory operation, the data size is byte. For data reg. operation, the data size is long word.

SOLUTION
The following program will set the parity:

```
         MOVEA   #$2000,A4
         CLR.B   D3
         BSET    #7,(A4)      Set the parity bit.
LOOP     BTST    D3,(A4)      Test a bit in $2000.
         BEQ     CONT         If the tested bit is a 1,
         BCHG    #7,(A4)        change the parity bit.
CONT     ADDQ    #1,D3        Increment D3 to get the
                                next bit.
         CMP.B   #7,D3        Done?
         BNE     LOOP
         ....      CONTINUE
```

The program starts by setting the parity bit, bit 7 of $2000, to 1. It then tests bit 0 of the byte in location $2000 and changes the parity bit if the tested bit is a 1. It then increments D3, so it will test bit 1 of $2000 on its second time through the loop. This continues until the program has tested bits 0–6 and changed the parity bit each time it finds a 1. Note that the parity bit was originally set to a 1 because if all the bits tested were 0, there would be no changes. It should be a 1 in this case.

15-10.10 Shift and Rotate Instructions

The SHIFT and ROTATE instructions in the **68000** are shown in Table 15-14, and the diagrams in the table show what each instruction is doing. The Arithmetic Shift Left, (ASL) brings 0s into the vacated LSBs, while the Arithmetic Shift Right, (ASR) replicates the MSB to preserve the sign. The Logical Shifts, LSL and LSR, bring 0s into the vacated positions. All the SHIFT instructions put the last bit shifted out into both C and X.

The **rotate** instructions (ROL, ROR) simply rotate the operand, placing the last bit both in the other end of the operand and in the carry flag. The Rotate-with-Extend instructions (ROXL, ROXR) rotate the combination of the operand and the X flag. The last bit shifted out also goes into the carry flag.

The operand to be shifted or rotated can be in a data register or in memory. If the operand is in a data register, a single SHIFT or ROTATE instruction can cause it to be shifted several places, instead of just 1 place as in the **6800**. There are three forms of the SHIFT and ROTATE instruction:

> ASL.X Dx,Dy This is the dynamic form. The number of shifts is contained in data register x and the data to be shifted is contained in data register y. An example would be ASL.B D2,D3. If D2 contained a 4, the LS byte of D3 would be shifted left by 4 bits.

ASL.X #n,Dy This is the static or Immediate form. The Immediate number (n) specifies the number of bits to be shifted.

ASL.W <EA> This is the memory form. The contents of <EA> are shifted. This form is restricted to a 1-bit shift and to word size.

In the previous examples ASL was used for illustration only. Any SHIFT or ROTATE instruction operates similarly.

EXAMPLE 15-21

If data register D3 contains C5 and X is 1, what will D3 contain after each of the following instructions?

a. **ASL.B #3,D3**
b. **ASR.B #3,D3**
c. **LSL.B #3,D3**
d. **LSR.B #3,D3**
e. **ROL.B #3,D3**
f. **ROR.B #3,D3**
g. **ROXL.B #3,D3**
h. **ROXR.B #3,D3**

TABLE 15-14 Shift and Rotate Instructions

Instruction	*Operand size*	*Operation*	*Notation*	*Allowable effective address modes*
ASL ASR	8,16,32 16	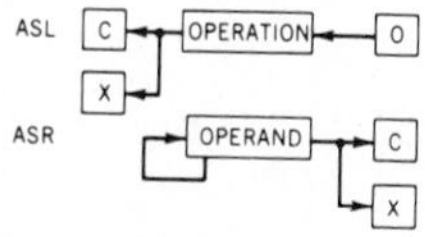 ASL: C ← OPERATION ← 0; X ASR: OPERAND → C; X	ASd Dx, Dy	—
			ASd # ⟨data⟩, Dy	—
			ASd ⟨ea⟩	MEMORY ALTERABLE
LSL LSR	8,16,32 16	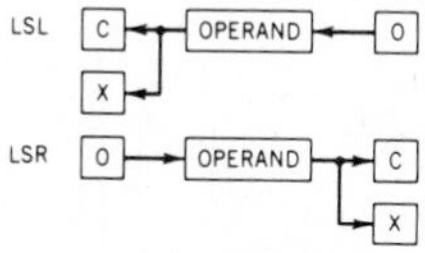 LSL: C ← OPERAND ← 0; X LSR: 0 → OPERAND → C; X	LSd Dx, Dy	—
			LSd # ⟨data⟩, Dy	—
			LSd ⟨ea⟩	MEMORY ALTERABLE
ROL ROR	8,16,32 16	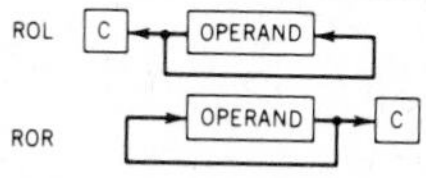 ROL: C ← OPERAND ROR: OPERAND → C	ROd Dx, Dy	—
			ROd # ⟨data⟩, Dy	—
			ROd ⟨ea⟩	MEMORY ALTERABLE
ROXL ROXR	8,16,32 16	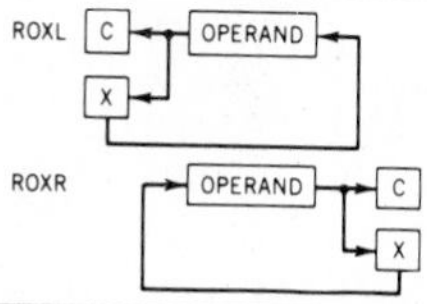 ROXL: C ← OPERAND; X ROXR: OPERAND → C; X	ROXd Dx, Dy	—
			ROXd # ⟨data⟩, Dy	—
			ROXd ⟨ea⟩	MEMORY ALTERABLE

SOLUTION
The results are

a. 28
b. F8
c. 28
d. 18
e. 2E
f. B8
g. 2F
h. 78

The results are best explained by referring to Fig. 15-20. It also shows the contents of C and X after each instruction.

EXAMPLE 15-22

There are two BCD digits in location \$2000. This is packed BCD. For example, the digits might be 57. The ASCII equivalent of these digits is to be put in locations \$3000 and \$3001 in order to be sent to a terminal. The ASCII equivalent of a digit is obtained by prefixing the digit with a 3, so in the example \$3000 and \$3001 will contain 35 and 37, respectively. Write a program to translate the packed BCD to ASCII.

SOLUTION
The program proceeds as follows:

```
                            C   5
                         11000101          Original Data

ASL.B   #3,D3   X=0      00101000            < 3 Bit Shift
                C=0

ASR.B   #3,D3            11111000    X=1   > 3 Bit Shift (sign preserved)
                                     C=1

LSL.B   #3,D3   X=0      00101000            < 3 Bit Shift
                C=0

LSR.B   #3,D3            00011000    X=1   > 3 Bit Shift
                                     C=1

ROL.B   #3,D3   C=0      00101110            < 3 Bit Rotate

ROR.B   #3,D3            10111000    C=1   > 3 Bit Rotate

ROXL.B  #3,D3   X=0      00101111            < 3 Bit Rotate Through X
                C=0

ROXR.B  #3,D3            01111000    X=1   > 3 Bit Rotate Through X
                                     C=1
```

FIGURE 15-20 Action of the C and X bits for Example 15–21.

```
MOVE.B   $2000,D3     Move data to D3.
LSR.B    #4,D3        Shift upper digit to lower.
ORI.B    #$30,D3      Add the prefix of 3.
MOVE.B   D3,$3000     Store data.
MOVE.B   $2000,D3     Move data to D3.
ANDI.B   #$F,D3       Zero upper byte. Keep lower byte.
ORI.B    #$30,D3      Add prefix.
MOVE.B   D3,$3001     Store data.
```

In this program we have chosen to use absolute addressing instead of data registers.

15-10.11 Program Control Instructions

The program control instructions are shown in Table 15-15. They will be discussed in order of simplicity, rather than the alphabetic order in which they are presented in the table.

The NOP (No Operation) instruction (4E 71) does nothing. After encountering it, the program simply goes to the next instruction. NOPs can be used to fill voids in programs, which might be left when an instruction is deleted. They can also be used to increase the time of a time delay loop (see Section 9-9). Some programmers deliberately write NOPs into their code at various places so that if an instruction has to be added during debugging it can replace the NOPs.

The Jump instruction is of the form JMP <EA>. It loads the PC with the Effective Address. Only the control addressing modes are allowed. The Effective Address may be in an address register or in the PC. Indexing and displacement are allowed, but predecrementing and postincrementing are not.

The Jump to Subroutine (JSR <EA>) is similar to the JMP. The addressing modes are the same. During a JSR the 4 bytes containing the address of the next instruction are put on the stack, and the stack pointer (A7) is decremented by four.

TABLE 15-15 Program Control Instructions

Instruction	*Operand size*	*Operation*	*Notation*	*Allowable effective address modes*
Bcc	8,16	If cc then PC + d → PC	Bcc ⟨label⟩	—
BRA	8,16	PC + d → PC	BRA ⟨label⟩	—
BSR	8,16	PC → −(SP); PC + d → PC	BSR ⟨label⟩	—
JMP	—	DESTINATION → PC	JMP ⟨ea⟩	CONTROL
JSR	—	PC → −(SP); DESTINATION → PC	JSR ⟨ea⟩	CONTROL
NOP	—	PC + 2 → PC	NOP	—
RESET	—	RESET EXTERNAL DEVICES	RESET	—
RTE	—	(SP)+ → SR; (SP)+ → PC	RTE	—
RTR	—	(SP)+ → CC; (SP)+ → PC	RTR	—
RTS	—	(SP)+ → PC	RTS	—
STOP	—	STOP PROGRAM EXECUTION	STOP # ⟨data⟩	—
TRAP	—	PC → −(SSP); SR → −(SSP); (VECTOR) → PC	TRAP ⟨VECTOR⟩	—
TRAPV	—	If V then TRAP	TRAPV	—

The Return from Subroutine (RTS) is the converse of the JSR. It pulls the return address off the stack, places it in the PC, and increments the stack pointer by 4 bytes. The JSR and RTS are similar to the **6800** instructions (see Section 5-5).

The ReTurn-and-Restore-condition-codes (RTR) instruction assumes the Condition Codes of the program were pushed onto the stack immediately after a JSR or BSR was encountered [i.e., MOVE CCR −(A7) is the first instruction of the subroutine]. The RTR first pulls the Condition Codes off the stack and then the PC.

The BRAnch instruction (BRA) operates like the **6800** BRA in that it adds a displacement to the PC and branches there. The displacement can be either 8 bits (short branch) or 16 bits (long branch). The Assembler form is BRA <label>, and Assemblers will calculate the value of the displacement. In TUTOR, one can use BRA <$address> because it cannot handle labels. Most of the previous examples used branch instructions.

The Branch-to-SubRoutine (BSR) instruction preserves the address of the next instruction on the stack before branching to a subroutine.

The Bcc is the Branch-on-condition-code instruction. Here cc represents a Condition Code as shown in Table 15-16. This is just a different way to represent the conditional branch instructions. They function as in the **6800** (BNE, BEQ, etc.) except that the instruction format allows for a 16-bit displacement, if desired. If the 8-bit displacement field is set to zero, an additional word (16-bit) is used to designate the offset.

The Set-according-to-condition (Scc) sets an entire byte to all 1s if the condition specified by cc is true and to all 0s if it is false. The condition table is the same for the Bcc instruction. The byte can be in a data register or memory location.

Other instructions in Table 15-15 such as RTE, TRAP, and TRAPV are discussed in Sections 15-12.4 and 15-12.6.

15-10.12 Other 68000 Instructions

Three other **68000** instructions do not fit conveniently into categories that have been discussed in this section.

The Test-condition-decrement-and-Branch (DBcc) is a powerful instruction for controlling loops. Again cc is a *condition* and Table 15-16 shows the conditions for this instruction.

The syntax of the DBcc is DBcc Dn,<label>. It uses a data register, Dn, that contains a loop count. The instruction operates as follows:

1. It first tests the condition. If the condition is true, the program falls through (does not branch).
2. If the condition is false it decrements Dn.
3. If Dn now equals −1 the program falls through. Otherwise it branches to <label> (loops back).

A program that uses the DBeq is given in Example 15-23.

TABLE 15-16 Conditional Tests

Mnemonic	Condition	Encoding	Test
T*	True	0000	1
F*	False	0001	0
HI	High	0010	$\overline{C}\cdot\overline{Z}$
LS	Low or Same	0011	$C+Z$
CC(HS)	Carry Clear	0100	$\overline{C}$
CS(LO)	Carry Set	0101	C
NE	Not Equal	0110	$\overline{Z}$
EQ	Equal	0111	Z
VC	Overflow Clear	1000	$\overline{V}$
VS	Overflow Set	1001	V
PL	Plus	1010	$\overline{N}$
MI	Minus	1011	N
GE	Greater or Equal	1100	$N\cdot V+\overline{N}\cdot\overline{V}$
LT	Less Than	1101	$N\cdot\overline{V}+\overline{N}\cdot V$
GT	Greater Than	1110	$N\cdot V\cdot\overline{Z}+\overline{N}\cdot\overline{V}\cdot\overline{Z}$
LE	Less or Equal	1111	$Z+N\cdot\overline{V}+\overline{N}\cdot V$

• = Boolean AND
+ = Boolean OR
$\overline{N}$ = Boolean NOT N

*Not available for the Bcc instruction

EXAMPLE 15-23

There is a block of 20 words of data starting at location $2000. Write a program to move them to a block starting at $3000 provided that none of the words is equal to zero. If a zero is found, terminate the block move.

SOLUTION

The list must be examined, a byte at a time, to determine whether a zero occurs. This suggests the use of a postincrementing register. The program is as follows:

```
        MOVE.W   #20,D2          Put count into D2.
        MOVEA.L  #$2000,A0       Put source address in A0.
        MOVEA.L  #$3000,A1       Put destination in A1.
LOOP    MOVE.W   (A0)+,(A1)+     Move word and increment pointers.
        DBEQ     D2,LOOP         Branch if not zero and D2 not = -1.
HERE    TST.W    D2              Does D2 = -1?
        BPL      FOUND           No; a word = zero was found.
        BRA      *               End of list. None found.
FOUND   BRA      *               Save it and exit.
```

The DBcc instruction works with byte- or word-sized operands. Therefore, the previous instruction must be selected to move bytes or words. After the byte (or word) is moved the DBeq instruction tests the Z bit, and if it is not set, and if D2 is not equal to -1, the program branches to LOOP. The label HERE is reached either because a zero value has been found or because D2 $= -1$. D2 is then tested to determine which condition exists. If D2 does equal −1, the list has been exhausted and no zero was found. Then the program drops through the BPL and continues.

To test this routine with the ECB, BRA * (branch to self) has been used. After stepping through the instructions, they can be allowed to execute by placing breakpoints at these branch addresses. Also note that this instruction has been improved in the **68010**, as discussed in Chapter 16.

The Load Effective Address (LEA) instruction calculates the Effective Address <EA> and stores it in an address register instead of using it as an address. The instruction is long word only (because it calculates a 24-bit address) and the destination must be an address register. The LEA can be used to preserve the results of a complex address calculation (such as address register indirect with indexing and displacement), which may be used more than once.

EXAMPLE 15-24

What does the instruction LEA AA(A2,D2.W),A3 do if address register A2 contains $22 and data register D2 contains ABCD0003?

SOLUTION

First the LEA calculates the Effective Address. In this example the index-with-offset address mode is used. The Effective Address is the sum of the offset (AA), the contents of A2 (22), and the word in D2 (0003). The result, CF, is placed in address register A3.

EXAMPLE 15-25

The proper use of the LEA can lead to more efficient coding. Suppose we are required to transfer a block of 100 words of data from a table located by using an address of $2000 in A2, with D1 as an index register, to location $3000 (in A1).

SOLUTION

One way to do this might be:

```
        MOVE.W   #4,D7              SET UP LOOP COUNTER
        MOVE.W   #$2000,A2          SET UP BASE ADDRESS
        MOVE.W   #$3000,A1          SET UP DESTINATION
LOOP    MOVE.W   (A2,D1.W),(A1)+    MOVE DATA
        ADDQ.W   #2,A2              INCREMENT SOURCE ADDR
        DBF.L    D7,LOOP            LOOP UNTIL DATA ENDS
        ...      ......
```

where the DBF is the Decrement-and-Branch-if-False instruction. (The way this operation works is not obvious; see Section 15-10.12.)

The same block transfer program might be written:

```
        MOVE.W   #4,D7          SET UP LOOP COUNT
        MOVE.W   #$2000,A2      SET UP BASE ADDR
        MOVE.W   #$3000,A1      SET UP DESTINATION
        LEA.L    (A2,D1.W),A3   PUT EFFECTIVE ADDR IN A3
LOOP    MOVE.W   (A3)+,(A1)+    MOVE DATA
        DBF.L    D7,LOOP         UNTIL COUNT = -1
        ...      ......
```

The second program is more efficient because it uses many less cycles. It only calculates the effective address once, using the LEA and stores it in A3. The first program has to calculate the effective address each time around the loop. The second program loop also includes one less instruction.

The Push-Effective-Address (PEA) instruction works like the LEA except that it pushes the Effective Address onto the stack instead of into an address register.

Figure 15-21 shows how the LEA and PEA instructions can replace three and four instructions respectively.

15-11 68000, 68008 AND 68010 PINOUTS AND SIGNALS

In addition to the programming aspects of the **68000** family that have just been described, it is necessary for an engineer interested in system design to understand the many new hardware features of the **68000**, **68008**, and **68010**. (The **68010** is included here because its pinouts are the same as those of the **68000** and **68008**.) The pin connections and signals can be functionally organized into groups as shown in Fig 15-22. The following paragraphs provide a description of these signals and a reference (if applicable) to other paragraphs that contain more detail. Readers are advised that this information is brief and they should refer to the Advance Information booklets listed in Section 15-17 for added details on each processor type.

15-11.1 The Address Bus (A1 through A23)

Although the Address Registers in the **68000** are 32 bits wide, only 24 bits are used, thus providing a bus capable of addressing 16 megabytes of memory. Because the memory is organized as words or long words, only even addresses are needed. Therefore, line A0 is not provided on the IC package and the address bus actually has only 23 lines. It is unidirectional and three-state and provides the addresses for bus operation for all cycles except interrupt cycles. During interrupt cycles, address lines A1, A2, and A3 provide information about the level of interrupt being serviced, while lines A4 through A23 are all set to a logic HIGH.

```
Motorola M68ØØØ ASM Version  1.9Ø BILL:Ø.   LEA.SA Ø8/Ø6/87 11:55:32

                                  LLEN     1ØØ
         ØØØØ1ØØØ                 ORG      $1ØØØ
                        *
         ØØØØØØØA       OFFSET    EQU      1Ø
                        *
                        * COMPARISON OF LEA AND PEA
                        *
                        * INPUT : (AØ.L) = ADDRESS OF TABLE
                        *         (DØ.W) = INDEX INTO TABLE
                        *         OFFSET = BYTE WITHIN ELEMENT OF PREDEFINED TABLE
                        *
                        * OUTPUT : (A1.L) = EFFECTIVE ADDRESS (LEA)
                        *
                        * OPERATION OF THE LEA TO LOAD THE ADDRESS OF AN ELEMENT
                        *
ØØØØ1ØØØ 43FØØØØA                 LEA      OFFSET(AØ,DØ.W),A1
                        *
                        * LOAD THE ADDRESS OF AN ELEMENT WITHOUT USING LEA
                        *
ØØØØ1ØØ4 2248                     MOVE.L   AØ,A1
ØØØØ1ØØ6 D2CØ                     ADDA.W   DØ,A1
ØØØØ1ØØ8 D2FCØØØA                 ADDA.W   #OFFSET,A1
                        *
                        * OPERATION OF THE PEA TO SAVE AN ADDRESS
                        *
ØØØØ1ØØC 487ØØØØA                 PEA      OFFSET(AØ,DØ.W)
                        *
                        * SAVE AN ADDRESS WITHOUT USING THE PEA
                        *
ØØØØ1Ø1Ø 2248                     MOVE.L   AØ,A1
ØØØØ1Ø12 D2CØ                     ADDA.W   DØ,A1
ØØØØ1Ø14 D2FCØØØA                 ADDA.W   #OFFSET,A1
ØØØØ1Ø18 2FØ9                     MOVE.L   A1,-(SP)
                        *
                                  END

****** TOTAL ERRORS      Ø--     ****** TOTAL WARNINGS     Ø--

SYMBOL TABLE LISTING

SYMBOL NAME      SECT   VALUE        SYMBOL NAME      SECT    VALUE

OFFSET                  ØØØØØØØA
```

FIGURE 15-21 Comparison of LEA and PEA instructions. From Thomas Harmon and Barbara Lawson, *The Motorola* ***MC68000*** *Microprocessor Family,* Prentice-Hall, 1985. Copyright © 1985 by Prentice-Hall Inc., Englewood Cliffs, New Jersey.)

15-11.2 Data Bus (D0 through D15)

The 16-bit bidirectional three-state bus is the general-purpose data path. It can transfer and accept data in either word or byte lengths. During an interrupt acknowledge cycle (see Section 15-13.3), the external device supplies the vector number on data lines D0–D7.

15-11.3 Asynchronous Bus Control

The **68000** address and data lines are not multiplexed and operate independently, which provides superior performance compared to multiplexed buses. A major innovation of the **68000** family is that the data bus is asynchronous. This eliminates the need to provide synchronizing signals around the system. The use of handshaking signals, such as Data Transfer ACKnowledge ($\overline{\text{DTACK}}$), allows devices and memories with large variations in response time to be connected to the processor bus. The processor can wait an arbitrary amount of time until the device or memory signals that the transfer is complete. This μP bus architecture is also convenient for connecting to system buses of varying lengths.

Asynchronous data transfers are handled using the following control signals:

- Address strobe.
- Read/write.
- Upper and lower data strobes.
- Data transfer acknowledge.

These signals (refer to Fig. 15-22) are explained in the following paragraphs.

15-11.4 Address Strobe ($\overline{\text{AS}}$)

This signal indicates that there is a valid address on the address bus. It is one of five lines that make up the asynchronous bus control function shown in Fig. 15-22.

15-11.5 Read/Write (R/$\overline{\text{W}}$)

This signal defines the data bus transfer as a read or write cycle. A write signal is a logic 0. The R/$\overline{\text{W}}$ signal also works in conjunction with the data strobes, as explained in the following paragraph.

15-11.6 Upper and Lower Data Strobe ($\overline{\text{UDS}}$, $\overline{\text{LDS}}$)

These **Data Strobe** lines control the flow of data on the data bus, as shown in Table 15-17. When the R/$\overline{\text{W}}$ line is high, the processor will read from the data bus as

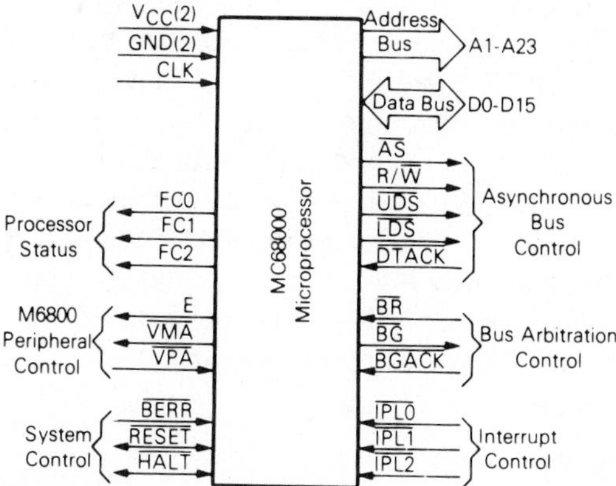

FIGURE 15-22 **68000** signal lines.

TABLE 15-17 Data Strobe Control of Data Bus

$\overline{UDS}$	$\overline{LDS}$	R/$\overline{W}$	D8-D15	D0-D7
High	High	—	No Valid Data	No Valid Data
Low	Low	High	Valid Data Bits 8-15	Valid Data Bits 0-7
High	Low	High	No Valid Data	Valid Data Bits 0-7
Low	High	High	Valid Data Bits 8-15	No Valid Data
Low	Low	Low	Valid Data Bits 8-15	Valid Data Bits 0-7
High	Low	Low	Valid Data Bits 0-7*	Valid Data Bits 0-7
Low	High	Low	Valid Data Bits 8-15	Valid Data Bits 8-15*

*These conditions are a result of current implementation and may not appear on future devices.

indicated. When the R/$\overline{W}$ line is LOW, the processor will write to the data bus as shown.

15-11.7 Data Transfer Acknowledge (DTACK)

This input indicates that the data transfer is complete. When the processor initiates a memory cycle it must wait for $\overline{DTACK}$ to terminate it. Each memory or peripheral in the system must have some means of generating $\overline{DTACK}$. Figure 15-23 shows the circuit used in the Educational Computer Board for the TUTOR ROMs. It is simply an **LS175** IC counter. It is wired to provide a delay sufficient for the data to be stable (based on the access time of the parts used). The counter is reset each time the ROMs are enabled and is clocked by the 8-MHz clock. When the processor recognizes $\overline{DTACK}$ during a read cycle, data is latched and the bus cycle is terminated.

15-11.8 Bus Arbitration Control

Another innovative feature of the **68000** family processors is *Bus Arbitration.* Only one μP can control the memory and peripherals in a typical system at one time. In a multiprocessor system some means is needed to transfer control when another processor or a Direct Memory Access (DMA) device such as a Disk Controller needs to access the common bus. Any number of μPs or DMA devices can be installed on the system bus provided bus arbitration is used to allow them to access the bus, one at a time, in an orderly fashion. **Bus Arbitration** is controlled by three signal lines. These signals—bus request, bus grant, and bus grant acknowledge—(explained below), are interconnected in a bus arbitration circuit to determine which device will be the **bus master** (the bus device that currently is transferring data to or from the data bus).

15-11.9 Bus Request ($\overline{BR}$)

The **Bus Request** ($\overline{BR}$) input is wire-ORed with all other devices that could be bus masters. When asserted, this input indicates to the processor that some other device wishes to become the *bus master*.

15-11.10 Bus Grant ($\overline{\text{BG}}$)

The **Bus Grant** output signal line, when true (LOW), indicates to all other potential bus master devices that the processor will release bus control at the end of the current bus cycle.

15-11.11 Bus Grant Acknowledge ($\overline{\text{BGACK}}$)

When the **Bus Grant ACKnowledge** ($\overline{\text{BGACK}}$) input is true (LOW), it indicates that some device has become the bus master. A device that is making a request to become bus master should not assert $\overline{\text{BGACK}}$ until the following four conditions are met:

1. A Bus Grant (BG) has been received.
2. Address Strobe (AS) is inactive, which indicates that the μP is not using the bus.
3. Data Transfer ACKnowledge (DTACK) is inactive, which indicates that neither memory nor peripherals are using the bus.
4. Bus Grant ACKnowledge ($\overline{\text{BGACK}}$) is inactive, which indicates that no other device is still claiming bus mastership.

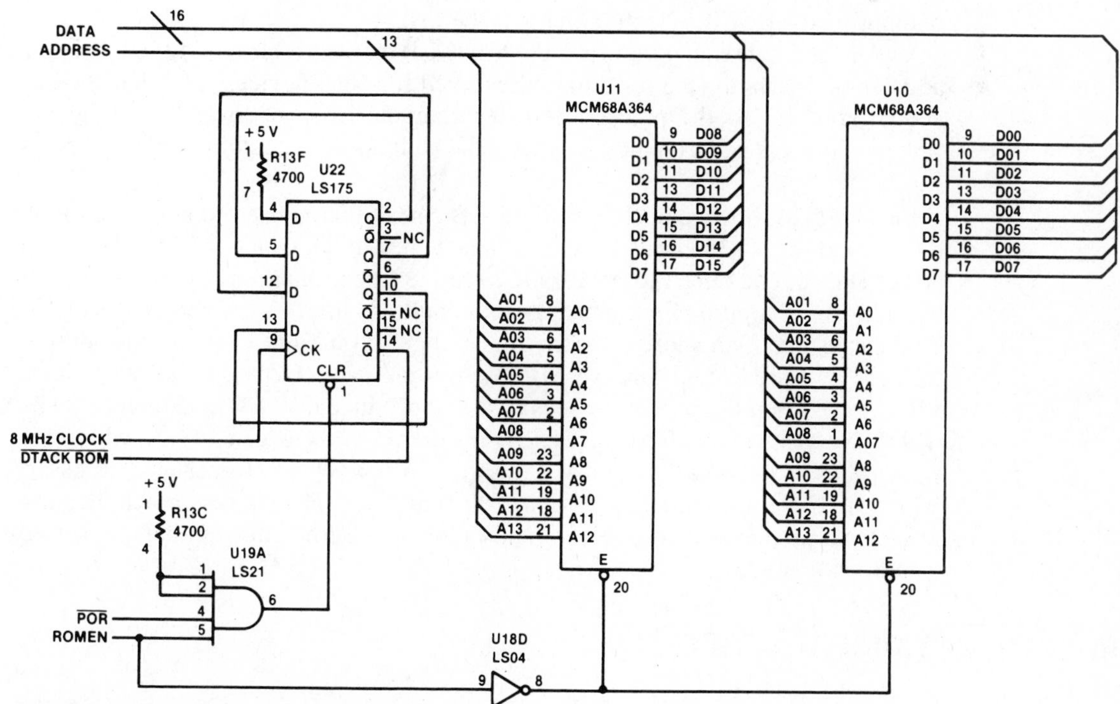

FIGURE 15-23 ROM DTACK schematic.

15-11.12 Peripheral Control

When the **68000** was first introduced, there were very few 16-bit peripheral ICs that could be used with it to make up a system. To avoid waiting for the development of other 16-bit devices, an 8-bit interface was included in the design. Devices such as the ACIA or PIA from the **6800** family, and the other **6800** peripherals described in previous chapters could then be used. The **68000**, **68008**, and **68010** μPs all have provisions for using 8-bit peripheral ICs. New 16-bit peripherals are continually being developed, however.

The interface is specifically designed to work with the **6800** family of peripherals, and three pins of the **68000** have been dedicated to provide the required signals. These are

- Enable (E)
- Valid Memory Address ($\overline{\text{VMA}}$)
- Valid Peripheral Address ($\overline{\text{VPA}}$)

Enable corresponds to phase 2 of the **6800** clock. The bus frequency is one-tenth of the incoming **68000** clock frequency. The timing of E allows 1-MHz peripherals to be used with 8-MHz **68000**s. Enable has a 60/40 duty cycle; that is, it is low for six input clocks and high for four input clocks.

The $\overline{\text{VMA}}$ signal is used by **6800** μP peripherals. It should be noted that the **68000** $\overline{\text{VMA}}$ signal is active LOW, in contrast to the active HIGH **6800** VMA. This allows the **68000** to put its buses in the high-impedance state on DMA requests without inadvertently selecting the peripherals.

$\overline{\text{VPA}}$ is an input signal that tells the **68000** μP that the address on the bus is the address of a **6800** device (or an area reserved for **6800** devices) and that the bus should conform to the phase 2 transfer characteristics of the **6800**. Valid Peripheral Address is derived by decoding the address bus, conditioned by Address Strobe.

Figure 15-24 shows a portion of the ECB circuit that is used to interface to the ACIAs and the **68230** Parallel Interface and Timer (PIT). Gate U45C is drawn like an AND gate, but since the signals are negative true it functions as an OR gate. If the address of a peripheral appears on the address lines, $\overline{\text{VPA}}$ should go LOW. This means that if an address for the ACIA appears on Y1 of U30, OR the address for the PIT is present, OR the $\overline{\text{VPAIRQ}}$ signal goes true (LOW), a true $\overline{\text{VPA}}$ signal will result. When the processor sees it, it will produce a $\overline{\text{VMA}}$ signal. Gate U33A will then generate the chip select (CS1) for the ACIAs OR gate U31A will do the same thing for the **68230** (PIT). When the $\overline{\text{VPA}}$ is asserted, the **68000** will assert $\overline{\text{VMA}}$ and thereby complete a normal **6800** read cycle. The processor will then use an internally generated autovector that is a function of the interrupt being serviced (see Section 15-12.7).

15-12 EXCEPTION PROCESSING

As mentioned in Section 15-4, the **exception processing** state is entered when the processor is reset, experiences an interrupt, executes a trap instruction, encoun-

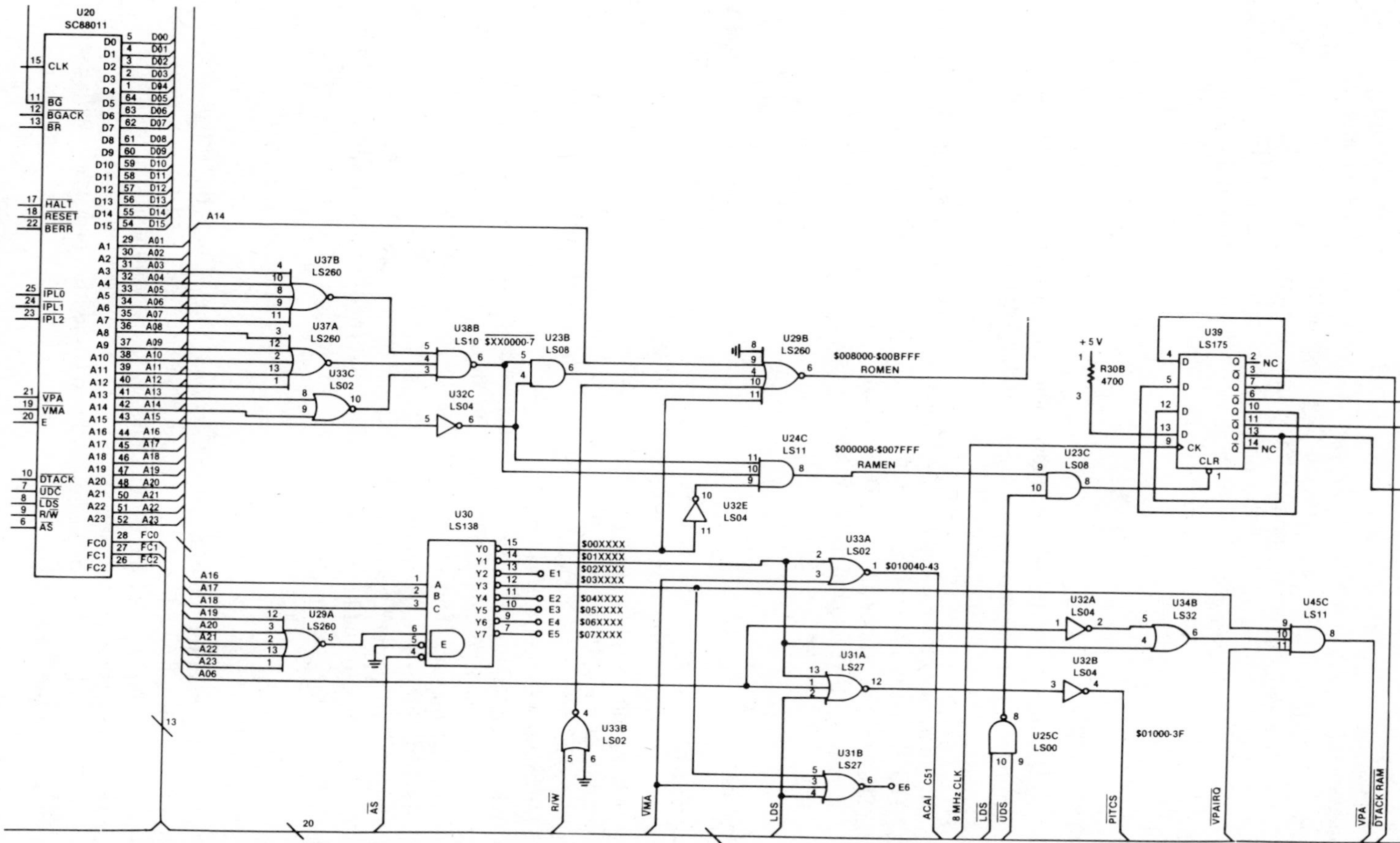

FIGURE 15-24 Schematic of the **68000** interface, showing address decoding.

ters a bus error, or has some other exceptional condition. Exception processing is designed to provide an efficient *context switch* so that the processor may quickly and gracefully handle unusual conditions. A **context switch** is the name given to the process of saving all the registers and flags that define the state of the system at the moment and replacing them with values that will cause the processor to process a different portion of the program. A context switch is caused by an exception, and another context switch occurs when returning to the main program after an exception. All of the causes of exception processing are described in the following sections.

15-12.1 Traps and Interrupts

Before discussing the details of interrupts, traps, tracing, and reset, a general description of exception processing is in order. After an exception is initiated, its processing occurs in four steps:

1. A temporary internal copy of the Status Register is made, and the *S* list is set.
2. The Exception Vector is determined.
3. The current processor context is saved.
4. A new context is obtained and the processor switches to instruction processing.

15-12.2 Exception Vectors

Exception Vectors are addresses of routines that will handle exceptions. They are kept in prescribed locations for each type of exception. Thus the processor can fetch the proper address to respond to a particular exception. Table 15-18 shows the table of exception vector addresses and Fig. 15-25 shows the vector format. All exception vectors are two words in length except for the Reset vector, which is four words (Section 15-13.8).

When an interrupt is caused by a peripheral, it provides an 8-bit vector number to the processor on data bus lines D0 through D7, as part of the interrupt acknowledge cycle. This is shown in Fig. 15-26. When multiplied by four (by left shifting two bit positions, and zero filling the upper-order bits to obtain a full 32-bit address), this number becomes the address of an exception vector as shown in Fig. 15-27. Vector numbers are generated internally or externally, depending on the cause of the exception, as explained in Section 15-13.3.

15-12.3 Instruction Traps

Traps are exceptions caused by *instructions*. They cause the program to depart from the normal sequence of executing instructions and go to a *trap handler routine*. The function of the trap handler is to respond to the abnormal condition or instruction that caused the trap. A TRAP instruction has a *vector* number associated with it that determines the routine the processor will execute in response to the trap.

TABLE 15-18 Exception Vector Assignment

Vector Number(s)	Address		Space[6]	Assignment
	Dec	Hex		
0	0	000	SP	Reset: Initial SSP[2]
1	4	004	SP	Reset: Initial PC[2]
2	8	008	SD	Bus Error
3	12	00C	SD	Address Error
4	16	010	SD	Illegal Instruction
5	20	014	SD	Zero Divide
6	24	018	SD	CHK Instruction
7	28	01C	SD	TRAPV Instruction
8	32	020	SD	Privilege Violation
9	36	024	SD	Trace
10	40	028	SD	Line 1010 Emulator
11	44	02C	SD	Line 1111 Emulator
12[1]	48	030	SD	(Unassigned, Reserved)
13[1]	52	034	SD	(Unassigned, Reserved)
14	56	038	SD	Format Error[5]
15	60	03C	SD	Uninitialized Interrupt Vector
16-23[1]	64	040	SD	(Unassigned, Reserved)
	92	05C		—
24	96	060	SD	Spurious Interrupt[3]
25	100	064	SD	Level 1 Interrupt Autovector
26	104	068	SD	Level 2 Interrupt Autovector
27	108	06C	SD	Level 3 Interrupt Autovector
28	112	070	SD	Level 4 Interrupt Autovector
29	116	074	SD	Level 5 Interrupt Autovector
30	120	078	SD	Level 6 Interrupt Autovector
31	124	07C	SD	Level 7 Interrupt Autovector
32-47	128	080	SD	TRAP Instruction Vectors[4]
	188	0BC		—
48-63[1]	192	0C0	SD	(Unassigned, Reserved)
	255	0FF		—
64-255	256	100	SD	User Interrupt Vectors
	1020	3FC		—

NOTES:

1. Vector numbers 12, 13, 16 through 23, and 48 through 63 are reserved for future enhancements by Motorola. No user peripheral devices should be assigned these numbers.
2. Reset vector (0) requires four words, unlike the other vectors which only require two words, and is located in the supervisor program space.
3. The spurious interrupt vector is taken when there is a bus error indication during interrupt processing. Refer to Paragraph 4.4.4.
4. TRAP #n uses vector number 32 + n.
5. MC68010/MC68012 only. See Return from Exception Section. This vector is unassigned, reserved on the MC68000 and MC68008.
6. SP denotes supervisor program space, and SD denotes supervisor data space.

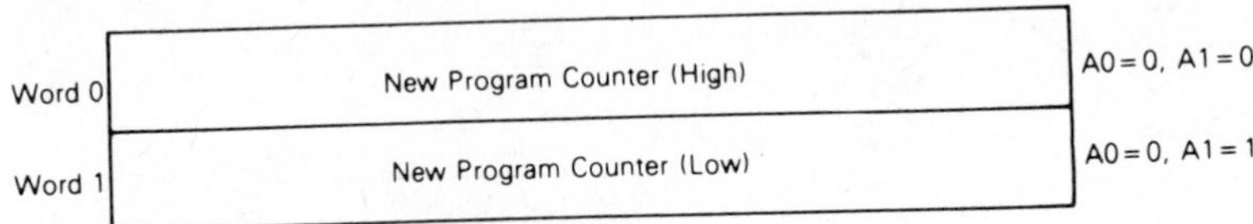

FIGURE 15-25 Exception vector format.

Exception processing for traps follows the steps outlined previously. A vector number is internally generated for the TRAP #n instruction. Part of the vector number comes from the instruction itself. The trap vector offset, the program counter, and the copy of the Status Register are saved on the Supervisor stack. The saved value of the Program Counter is the address of the instruction after the instruction that generated the trap. For all instruction traps other than TRAP #n, a pointer to the instruction that caused the trap is also saved. Finally, instruction execution commences at the address contained in the *exception vector*.

EXAMPLE 15-26

A program encounters a TRAP #1 instruction. What does the **68000** do in response?

SOLUTION

First the **68000** enters the Supervisor mode and stacks the address of the next instruction on the Supervisor's Stack. Note #4 of Table 15-18 says the address of the trap vector is in 32 + n, where n is the number of the TRAP (1 in this example). Thus the trap vector number is 33. This is multiplied by 4 to give an address of 132_{10} or 84_{16}. The system will go to location $84, where it will find a jump to the start of the trap handler routine. Certain instructions are used specifically to generate traps. The TRAP #n instruction always forces an exception and is useful for implementing system calls for user programs.

15-12.4 The Return from Exception (RTE) Instruction

Most trap handler routines end with a ReTurn from Exception (RTE) instruction. The RTE is a privileged instruction that can be executed only in Supervisor mode, but because traps place the μP in Supervisor mode this is usually not a problem. The RTE restores the Status Register and PC (the context) to their values before

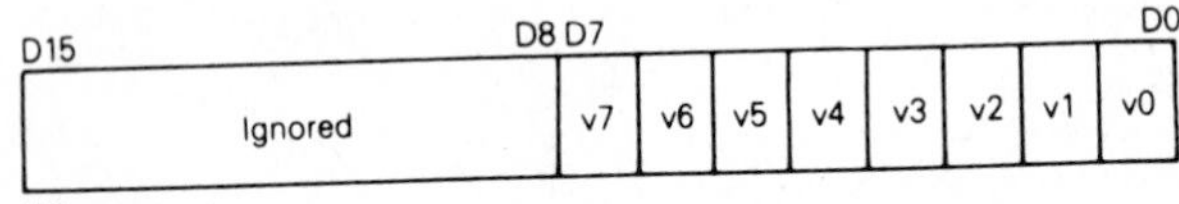

FIGURE 15-26 Peripheral vector number format.

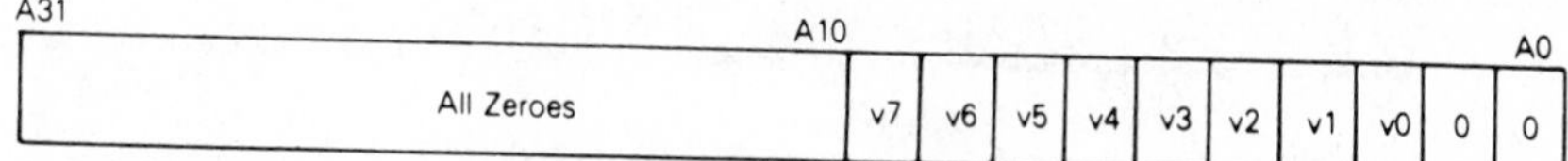

FIGURE 15-27 Address translated from 8-bit vector number **(68000/68008)**.

the trap occurred and allows the program to resume at the point where the trap occurred.

15-12.5 The TRAP #14 Handler in TUTOR

The monitor program in the Educational Computer Board, TUTOR, contains many useful functions. Users can access these functions for inclusion in their own programs by moving a function number into D7 and then executing a TRAP #14 instruction.

The TRAP 14 handler is a function contained within TUTOR that allows user system calls to access selected routines contained within the firmware, including ASCII/hex conversion, input routines, and output routines. Users need not reproduce these functions in their own programs. Table 15-19 is a summary of the available functions. They are used by including a calling sequence in the user's program as follows:

```
MOVE.B  #<function number>,D7
TRAP    #14
```

Where <function number> is a decimal number from 0 through 254 that represents the selected function. Calls to functions not defined result in the message "UNDEFINED TRAP 14"; program control is passed to TUTOR.

The appropriate function number is placed in the least significant byte of register D7 before executing the TRAP instruction.

EXAMPLE 15-27

Write a program to input a series of characters from the terminal into memory starting at $7000.

SOLUTION

Some of the details for this problem are contained in the *Educational Computer Board User's Manual* (see References Section 15-17). The function we need is PORTIN1—input string from port 1, which is #241 in Table 15-19. The User's manual shows that the buffer starting address must be in A5. At the beginning it must also be in A6. As each character is entered, A6 increments. A carriage return ($0D) terminates the TRAP. The program is as follows:

```
MOVEA.L   #$7000,A5     Set starting addresses in A5 and A6.
MOVEA.L   A5,A6
MOVE.B    #241,D7       Put function number in D7.
TRAP      #14
```

TABLE 15-19 TRAP 14 Function Summary

Function	Function Name	Function Description
255	—	Reserved function—end of table indicator.
254	—	Reserved function—used to link tables.
253	LINKIT	Append user table to TRAP 14 table.
252	FIXDADD	Append string to buffer.
251	FIXBUF	Initialize A5 and A6 to "BUFFER."
250	FIXDATA	Initialize A6 to "BUFFER" and append string to buffer.
249	FIXDCRLF	Move "CR," "LF" string to buffer.
248	OUTCH	Output single character to port 1.
247	INCHE	Input single character from port 1.
246	—	Reserved function.
245	—	Reserved function.
244	CHRPRINT	Output single character to port 3.
243	OUTPUT	Output string to port 1.
242	OUTPUT21	Output string to port 2.
241	PORTIN1	Input string from port 1.
240	PORTIN20	Input string from port 2.
239	TAPEOUT	Output string to port 4.
238	TAPEIN	Input string from port 4.
237	PRCRLF	Output string to port 3.
236	HEX2DEC	Convert hex value to ASCII-encoded decimal.
235	GETHEX	Convert ASCII character to hex.
234	PUTHEX	Convert 1 hex digit to ASCII.
233	PNT2HX	Convert 2 hex digits to ASCII.
232	PNT4HX	Convert 4 hex digits to ASCII.
231	PNT6HX	Convert 6 hex digits to ASCII.
230	PNT8HX	Convert 8 hex digits to ASCII.
229	START	Restart TUTOR; perform initialization.
228	TUTOR	Go to TUTOR; print prompt.
227	OUT1CR	Output string plus "CR," "LF" to port 1.
226	GETNUMA	Convert ASCII-encoded hex to hex.
225	GETNUMD	Convert ASCII-encoded decimal to hex.
224	PORTIN1N	Input string from port 1; no automatic line feed.
223–128	—	Reserved.
127–0	—	User-defined functions.

The computer now goes to the input routine to wait for data from the terminal.

15-12.6 Other Traps

The TRAPV and CHK instructions force an exception if the user program detects a run-time error, which may be an arithmetic overflow or subscript value out of bounds. The TRAPV instruction causes a **trap** (a jump to the exception processing routine pointed to by the TRAP vector) if the prior instructions cause an overflow to occur (setting the V flag).

The CHK instruction checks the low-order word in a data register against an upper *bound* (a number that should not be exceeded) or to see if it is negative. The upper bound is specified in the instruction as an Immediate value or in an operand. If the number in the data register is negative or exceeds the bound, a CHK trap will occur. For example, the instruction CHK D3,(A5) will cause a *trap* if the word in D3 is negative or if it is greater than the word in memory pointed to by A5.

EXAMPLE 15-28

Using the ECB, write a program to test the function of the CHK instruction.

SOLUTION

A program using the CHK instruction was written and is shown in Fig. 15-28. Execution of the program with an "out-of-bound" value in the D3 register causes the program to go to the CHK *exception vector*. A look at the vector table shows that vector to be in location 24 ($18). To illustrate how this instruction might be used, the TRAP 14 function #237 (PRCRLF) was used to print an "out-of-range" message on the printer when such a number was found in the D3 register. The upper bound was set to 16_{10} (or 10_{16}) by the CHK.W #16,D3 instruction, which also defines the register to be D3. The program writes a new vector to location $18 that jumps the program to the TRAP 14 routine located at $201C. The first two instructions are used to set the buffer pointers to the location of the message. The first command shown in Fig. 15-28 is MD (Memory Display), which shows the program after it was entered with the one-line assembler using the MM nnnn;DI command. Next, the PC was set to start at $2000. Breakpoints were previously entered and are shown by the BR comand. The DF (Display Formatted) command was used to show the contents of the registers prior to running the program. We can see that a value of $11 is in register D3, and the first instruction is displayed at the bottom of the register display. The contents of the memory from $3000 to $300F are shown next by the MD command.

When the G is entered, the program runs until it sees the breakpoint at $2022, and the message "Out of Range" will be printed on the ECB printer. If a value from 0 to $10 had been in D3, the program would have gone to the breakpoint at $2014 since the trap would not have occurred. If a value less than 0 is used, such as $FFFC (word length required), the "Out of Range" message would also be printed.

The TRAPV instruction can also be easily tested in the ECB by writing the one-line instruction (TRAPV) at $2500 (for example) and then tracing it. If the overflow bit (V) of the condition codes is set, it will trap, and the address in the PC for the next instruction will be $1C (the TRAPV vector). If the V bit was not set, the trap does not occur and the PC will be at the next instruction in sequence ($2502 in this case). The overflow bit (V) can be set or reset by entering a new number in the Status Register. For example, if the SR register contains $2004 and it is changed to $2006, the V bit will be set.

The DIVS and DIVU instructions can be tested similarly. They force an exception if a division operation is attempted with a divisor of zero.

```
TUTOR  1.3 > md 2000 29;di
002000      3A7C3000                MOVE.W   #12288,A5
002004      3C7C300F                MOVE.W   #12303,A6
002008      21FC0000201C0018        MOVE.L   #8220,$00000018
002010      47BC0010                CHK.W    #16,D3
002014      4E71                    NOP
002016      4E71                    NOP
002018      4EF82014                JMP.S    $00002014
00201C      3E3C00ED                MOVE.W   #237,D7
002020      4E4E                    TRAP     #14
002022      4E71                    NOP
002024      4E71                    NOP
002026      4EF82022                JMP.S    $00002022

TUTOR  1.3 > .pc 2000

TUTOR  1.3 > br

BREAKPOINTS
002014     002014
002022     002022

TUTOR  1.3 > df
PC=00002000 SR=2004=.S0..Z.. US=00000782 SS=0001DBF2
D0=00434E21 D1=00000000 D2=00014E75 D3=00000011
D4=00018000 D5=FFFFFFFF D6=00000008 D7=000000ED
A0=00008902 A1=0000832C A2=00000414 A3=00000428
A4=601A0000 A5=00003000 A6=0000300D A7=0001DBF2
--------------------002000    3A7C3000           MOVE.W   #12288,A5

TUTOR  1.3 > md 3000
003000     4F 75 74 20 6F 66 20 52  61 6E 67 65 21 0D 0A FF   Out of Range!...

TUTOR  1.3 > g
PHYSICAL ADDRESS=00002000

AT BREAKPOINT
PC=00002022 SR=2004=.S0..Z.. US=00000782 SS=0001DBEC
D0=00434E0A D1=00000000 D2=00014E75 D3=0000000A
D4=00018000 D5=FFFFFFFF D6=00000008 D7=000000ED
A0=00008902 A1=0000832C A2=00000414 A3=00000428
A4=601A0000 A5=00003000 A6=0000300F A7=0001DBEC
--------------------002022    4E71               NOP

TUTOR  1.3 >
```

FIGURE 15-28 Program to illustrate the CHK instruction for Example 15–28.

15-13 INTERRUPTS

External hardware devices can cause interrupts of the normal program processing by means of signals on the three interrupt lines. When these lines are encoded with a value greater than 000 that is not *masked* (see the following section), an interrupt is made pending. Pending interrupts are serviced between instruction executions. When this occurs, the interrupt vector is fetched and the **68000** enters an interrupt exception processing routine. There are two types of interrupts: *auto-*

vectored interrupts, discussed in Section 15-13.3, and *user* interrupts, discussed in Section 15-13.4.

15-13.1 Interrupt Priority Levels

Seven levels of interrupt priority are provided. They are numbered from one to seven, with level seven being the highest priority. The Status Register contains a 3-bit mask that indicates the current processor interrupt priority. Figure 15-29 shows how the interrupt mask bits in the Status Register determine the various priority levels. An interrupt request is made to the processor by encoding an interrupt level other than 000 on the interrupt request lines. Interrupt requests arriving at the processor do not force Immediate exception processing but are made *pending*. Pending interrupts are detected between instruction executions. If the priority of the pending interrupt is lower than or equal to the current processor priority, execution continues with the next instruction and the interrupt request is ignored. The recognition of level seven is slightly different, as explained in Section 15-13.5.

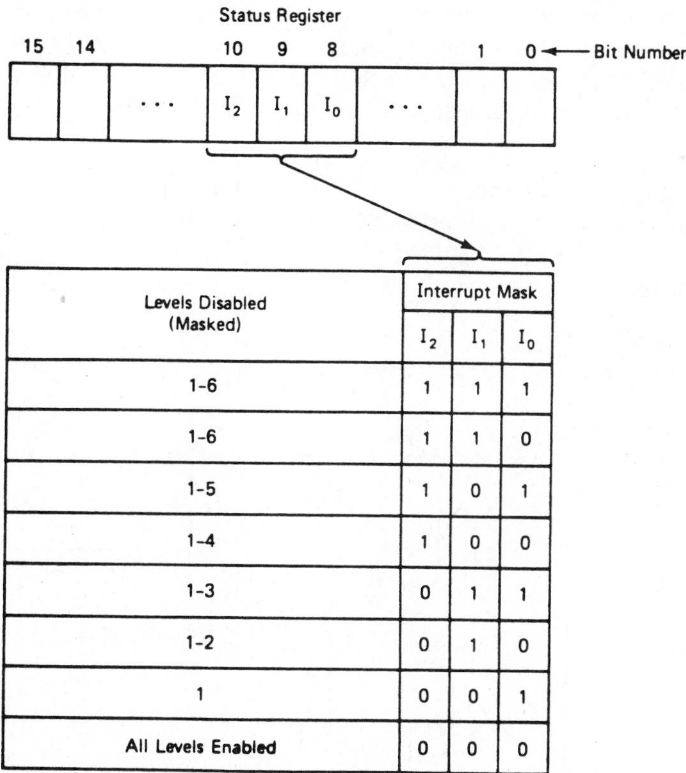

Levels Disabled (Masked)	Interrupt Mask		
	I_2	I_1	I_0
1-6	1	1	1
1-6	1	1	0
1-5	1	0	1
1-4	1	0	0
1-3	0	1	1
1-2	0	1	0
1	0	0	1
All Levels Enabled	0	0	0

FIGURE 15-29 Interrupt mask for the **68000**. From Thomas Harmon and Barbara Lawson, *The Motorola* ***MC68000*** *Microprocessor Family,* Prentice-Hall, 1985. Copyright © 1985 by Prentice-Hall Inc., Englewood Cliffs, New Jersey.)

Several devices may be assigned to interrupt at the same level by *daisy-chaining* them as shown in Fig. 15-30. If three devices are assigned to interrupt on line $\overline{\text{IRQ4}}$, for example, they will all be at a higher priority than those on lines $\overline{\text{IRQ0}}$ through $\overline{\text{IRQ3}}$, but there will also be priority among the three since the one closest to the μP has priority over all others on that line. By this means, an unlimited number of external devices can be connected to interrupt the processor.

15-13.2 Interrupt Processing

If the priority of the pending interrupt is greater than the current processor priority, the exception processing sequence is started. A flowchart of this process is shown in Fig. 15-31. The sequence is slightly different for user interrupts and auto-vectored interrupts, as described below.

15-13.3 Auto-Vectored Interrupts

An auto-vectored interrupt is caused by asserting an interrupt level on the IPL lines and generating an active $\overline{\text{VPA}}$ signal during the interrupt acknowledge cycle. Figure 15-32 shows a hardware configuration to generate both auto-vectored and user interrupts. In the figure, controller 1 connected to I/O_1 generates a user interrupt, and controller 2 connected to I/O_2 generates an auto-vectored interrupt.

To generate an auto-vectored interrupt, the following events must occur:

1. Controller 1 is not trying to generate a user interrupt.
2. Controller 2 generates a level 3 auto-vectored interrupt by taking its interrupt request line LOW. This forces one input of the **74LS32** LOW and brings the INT3 input to the **74148**[2] LOW. In the absence of other requests, the **74148** places a level 3 interrupt on the interrupt input pins ($\overline{\text{IPL0}}$, $\overline{\text{IPL1}}$, and $\overline{\text{IPL2}}$).

[2]The **74148** priority controller IC is discussed in Section 17-5.4 of *Practical Digital Design Using ICs*, Second Edition, by Joseph D. Greenfield, published by Wiley, New York, 1983.

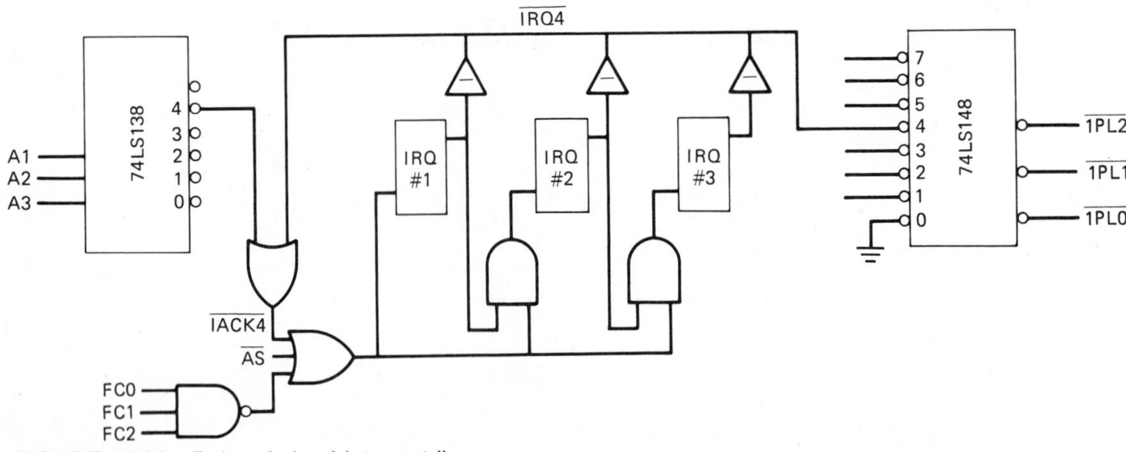

FIGURE 15-30 Daisy-chained interrupt lines.

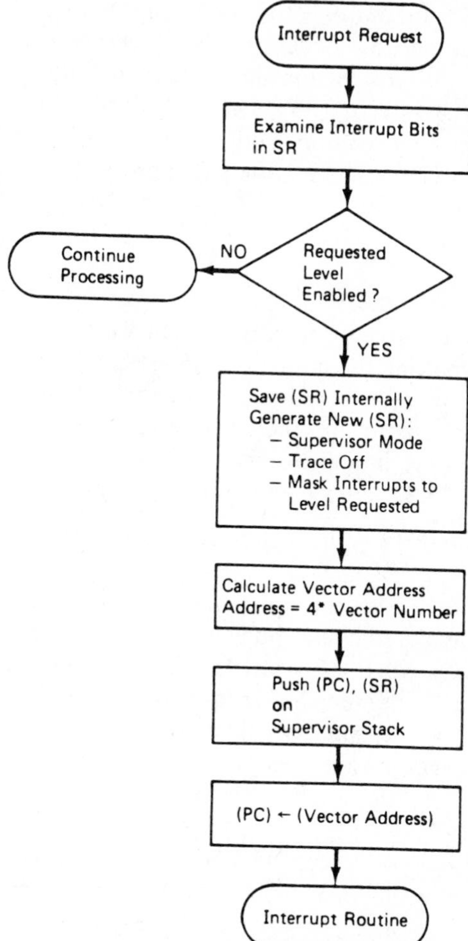

FIGURE 15-31 Interrupt processing. From Thomas Harmon and Barbara Lawson, *The Motorola **MC68000** Microprocessor Family,* Prentice-Hall, 1985. Copyright © 1985 by Prentice-Hall Inc., Englewood Cliffs, New Jersey.)

3. When the processor decides to honor the level 3 interrupt, it enters an interrupt acknowledge cycle by setting the three function control lines (FC0, FC1, FC2) to all 1s and placing the number 3 on address lines A1, A2, and A3. With the three FC lines at 1, the highest output of the first **74LS138** decoder goes LOW. This enables the second **74LS138**. Because the address inputs to it contain the number 3, the signal $\overline{IACK_3}$ (interrupt acknowledge 3) goes LOW.
4. When $\overline{IACK_3}$ goes LOW, both inputs to the **74LS32** are LOW and $\overline{VPA}$ goes LOW. The **68000** is now acknowledging a level 3 interrupt with $\overline{VPA}$ LOW. The fact that $\overline{VPA}$ is LOW during the interrupt acknowledge cycle tells the μP

that it is acknowledging an auto-vectored interrupt. The processor internally generates a *vector* number that is determined by the *interrupt* level number.

5. The μP goes to the level 3 interrupt auto-vector to find the address of the service routine for that interrupt. The vector allocation map (Table 15-18) shows that this vector is at memory address $6C.
6. After reading the auto-vector at $6C, the μP jumps to that address and starts executing the service routine.

15-13.4 User Interrupts

Figure 15-32 also shows the hardware required to generate a user interrupt. A user interrupt is generated by putting the interrupt request level on the IPL inputs and leaving $\overline{\text{VPA}}$ high. When the request is honored, the **68000** goes to one of the 192 user interrupt vector locations to find the address of the proper starting routine (the vector is put there by the initialization routine.)

Again referring to Fig. 15-32, a user interrupt is generated as follows:

1. Controller 1 brings the $\overline{\text{INT5}}$ input to the **74148** LOW. This puts a 5 on the IPL lines to the processor.
2. When the processor responds with an interrupt acknowledge cycle and address lines A1, A2, and A3 have a 5 on them, $\overline{\text{IACK}_5}$ is produced.
3. $\overline{\text{IACK}_5}$ gates the box labeled "ENABLE VECTOR NUMBER" to put the proper vector number (a number between $40 and $FF) on the data bus.
4. The μP knows this is a user interrupt because VPA is high. It multiplies the vector number by 4 to get the auto-vector address. It then goes to that address

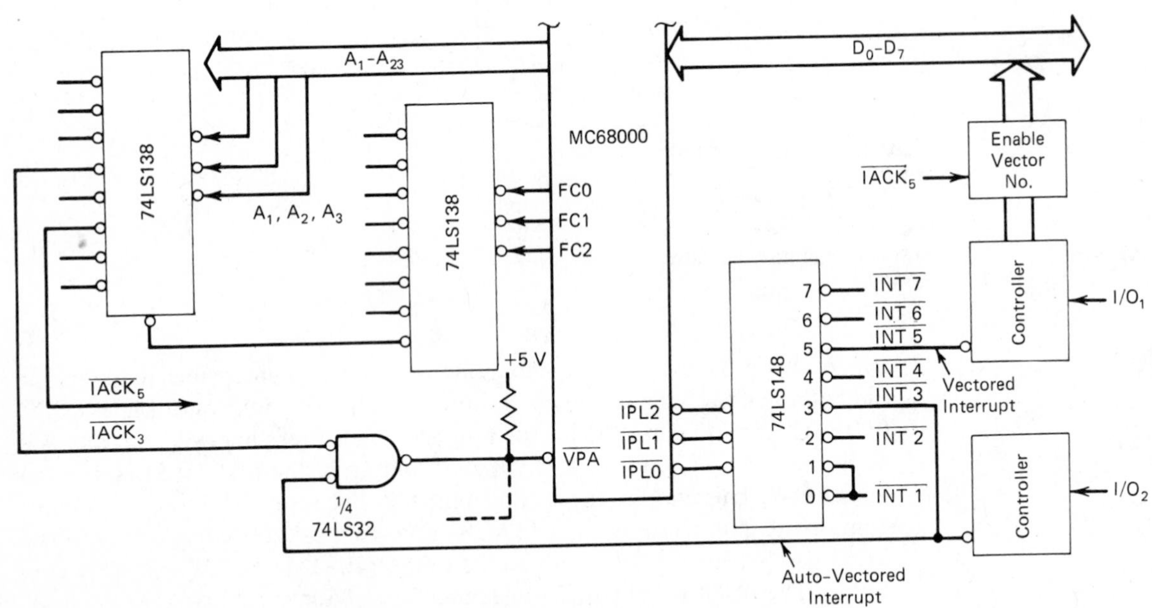

FIGURE 15-32 **68000** vectored and auto-vectored interrupt logic.

to get the starting address of the service routine. The controller must also generate $\overline{DTACK}$ to terminate the interrupt acknowledge cycle.

Table 15-18 shows that the seven auto-vectored interrupts are vectors 25 to 31 and the user interrupts are vectors 64 to 255.

EXAMPLE 15-29

A **6821** Peripheral Interface Adapter (PIA) is wired into a circuit similar to that in Fig. 15-32. It can interrupt on level 3 and is therefore assigned auto-vector number 27_{10}. The interrupt service routine for this PIA starts at location \$7000. Explain what happens when the PIA interrupts.

SOLUTION

The PIA's $\overline{IRQ}$ line is connected into an interrupt synchronizer circuit that places a 3 on the IPL lines when an interrupt is generated. External circuitry then monitors the FC and address lines until it detects an interrupt acknowledge cycle with the PIA's proper address on A1, A2, and A3. The processor then fetches the level 3 auto-vector (number 27_{10}) from location 108_{10} ($4 \times 27 = 108_{10}$ or \$6C), where it finds \$7000. It places this in the PC and starts the service routine, which ends with an RTE instruction. A flowchart for the interrupt acknowledge sequence is given in Fig. 15-33, a timing diagram is given in Fig. 15-34, and the interrupt processing sequence is shown in Fig. 15-35.

15-13.5 NonMaskable Interrupt (NMI)

The reader may have noticed in Fig. 15-29 that a level 7 interrupt cannot be masked by any setting of the Status Register. A level 7 interrupt is a **NonMaskable**

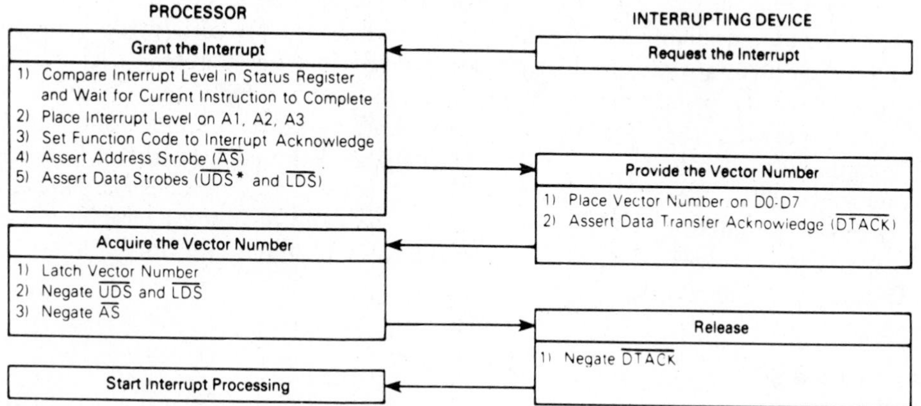

FIGURE 15-33 Vector acquisition flowchart.

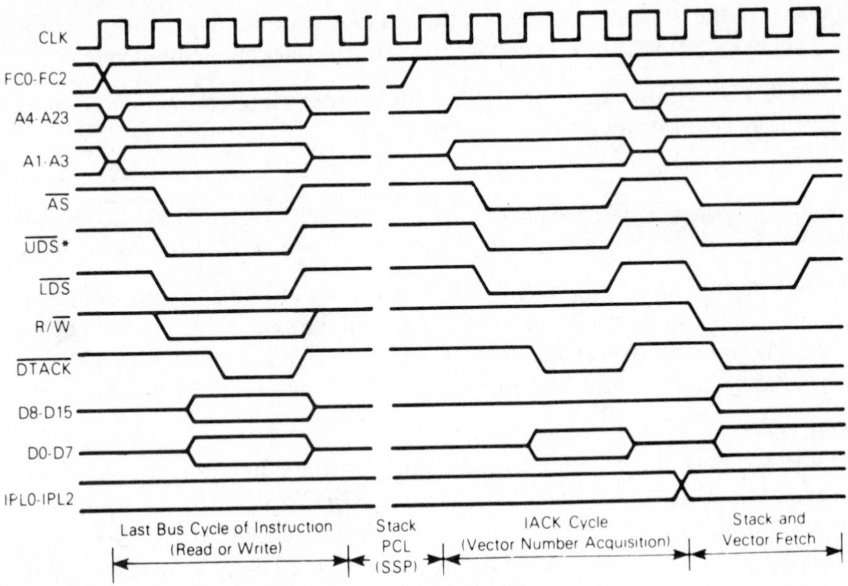

* Although a vector number is one byte, both data strobes are asserted due to the microcode used for exception processing. The processor does not recognize anything on data lines D8 through D15 at this time.

FIGURE 15-34 Interrupt acknowledge cycle timing diagram.

Interrupt (NMI) and should be used for things that cannot logically be interrupted, such as clock timing pulses, or emergency situations.

15-13.6 Uninitialized Interrupt

One of the **68000** family design rules states that the peripheral devices must have internal logic that initializes their internal vector register to a value of $0F when a Power-On-Reset (POR) occurs. It is the responsibility of the *system* initialization program to change that register value so that the correct vector can be fetched to point to the peripheral's interrupt service routine. During an **interrupt acknowledge cycle** an interrupting device asserts Valid Peripheral Address ($\overline{VPA}$) or a Bus Error (BERR), or provides an interrupt vector number and asserts $\overline{DTACK}$. If, however, an interrupt should occur before the initialization routine is done and the peripheral's vector register has not been updated (initialized), the $0F will be fetched and the vector from that location will be used by the processor. This is an **uninitialized interrupt**. The interrupt mask is set to 7 at the beginning of the initialization process, and if it is lowered as one of the last things done, this possibility is minimized.

15-13.7 Spurious Interrupt

If, during the interrupt acknowledge cycle, no device responds by asserting $\overline{DTACK}$ or $\overline{VPA}$, the Bus Error line ($\overline{BERR}$) should be asserted to terminate the vector acquisition. This is a **spurious interrupt**. The processor separates the processing of this error from bus error by fetching the *spurious interrupt vector* instead of the *bus error vector*. The processor then proceeds with the usual exception processing.

15-13.8 RESET

The $\overline{\text{RESET}}$ line is a hardware input very much like an interrupt, except that it uses only one pin on the μP. When it is taken LOW, it provides the highest exception level. The RESET signal is designed for system initiation (start-up) or recovery from catastrophic failure. Any processing in progress at the time of the reset is aborted and cannot be recovered. The processor is forced into the Supervisor state, the Trace state is forced off (see Section 15-14), and the processor *interrupt priority mask* is set to level 7 (see Section 15-13.1). The vector number is internally generated to reference the *reset exception vector* at location 0 in memory. Because no assumptions can be made about the validity of register contents, in particular the Supervisor Stack Pointer, neither the Program Counter nor the Status Register is saved. The reset exception vector contains four words that are fetched and placed in registers as follows. The address contained in the first two words of the *reset exception vector* is the initial Supervisor Stack Pointer, and the address in the last two words of the vector is the initial Program Counter. Finally, instruction execution is started at the address in the Program Counter. The power-up restart (system initialization) code should be pointed to by the initial Program Counter.

The reset *instruction* does not fetch the reset vector but does assert the $\overline{\text{RESET}}$ line to reset external devices. This allows the software to reset the system to a known state and then continue processing with the next instruction.

15-14 TRACING

As an aid to program development, the **68000** family of μPs includes a feature to allow instruction-by-instruction *tracing*. In the Trace state, an exception is forced

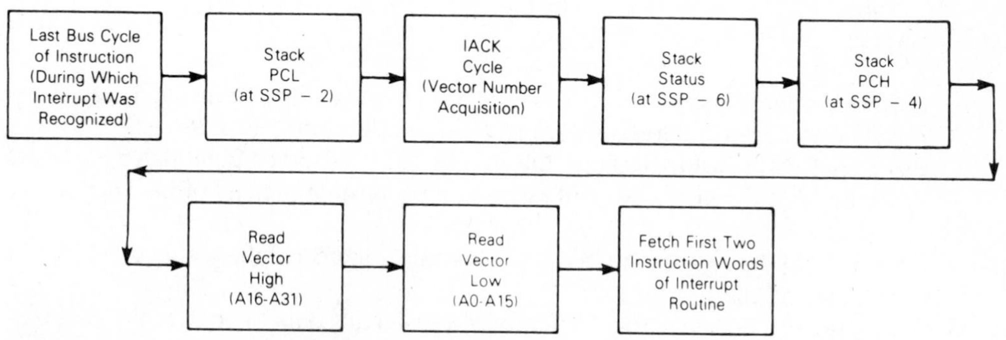

NOTE: SSP refers to the value of the supervisor stack pointer before the interrupt occurs.

FIGURE 15-35 Interrupt processing sequence.

after each instruction. This allows a debugger program to examine register or memory after each instruction and thus to analyze the user program's progress. This feature is used in the ECB's TUTOR program. The trace facility uses the T bit in the supervisor portion of the Status Register. If the T bit is clear (off), tracing is disabled and instruction execution proceeds as normal. If the T bit is set (on) at the beginning of the execution of an instruction, a *trace exception* will be generated as the execution of the instruction is completed. If the instruction is not executed, because an interrupt is taken or the instruction is illegal or privileged, the trace exception does not occur. The trace exception also does not occur if the instruction is aborted by a reset, bus error, or address error exception. If the instruction is indeed executed and an interrupt is pending on completion, the *trace* exception is processed before the *interrupt* exception. If, during the execution of the instruction, an exception is forced by that instruction, the *forced* exception is processed before the *trace* exception. This process is illustrated in the flowchart of Fig. 15-36. As an extreme illustration of the above rules, consider the arrival of an interrupt during the execution of a TRAP instruction while tracing is enabled. First the trap exception is processed, then the trace exception, and finally the interrupt exception. Instruction execution resumes in the interrupt handler routine.

15-15 SUMMARY

This chapter introduced the **68000** and explained the basic features. Differences between the **6800** and the **68000** were shown, and the merits of 8-, 16-, and 32-bit systems were explained. The register set within the **68000** was discussed first, followed by an explanation of the various addressing modes. A major part of the chapter was devoted to discussing the instruction set, and many programming examples were presented. The pinout and signal functions of the **68000** were described for the **68000** system designer. Finally, exceptions, traps, and interrupts were discussed. The more advanced features of the **68010**, **68020**, and **68030** are presented in Chapter 16.

15-16 GLOSSARY

Bus arbitration Use of three signals—Bus Request, Bus Grant, and Bus Grant Acknowledge—to determine which device will be the bus master.

Bus Grant ($\overline{\text{BG}}$) Output signal that indicates to all other potential bus master devices that the processor will release bus control at the end of the current bus cycle.

Bus Grant ACKnowledge ($\overline{\text{BGACK}}$) This signal indicates that some other device has become the bus master.

Bus master Bus device that currently is transferring data to or from the data bus.

Bus Request ($\overline{\text{BR}}$) Bus signal output by a device to indicate a desire to become the bus master.

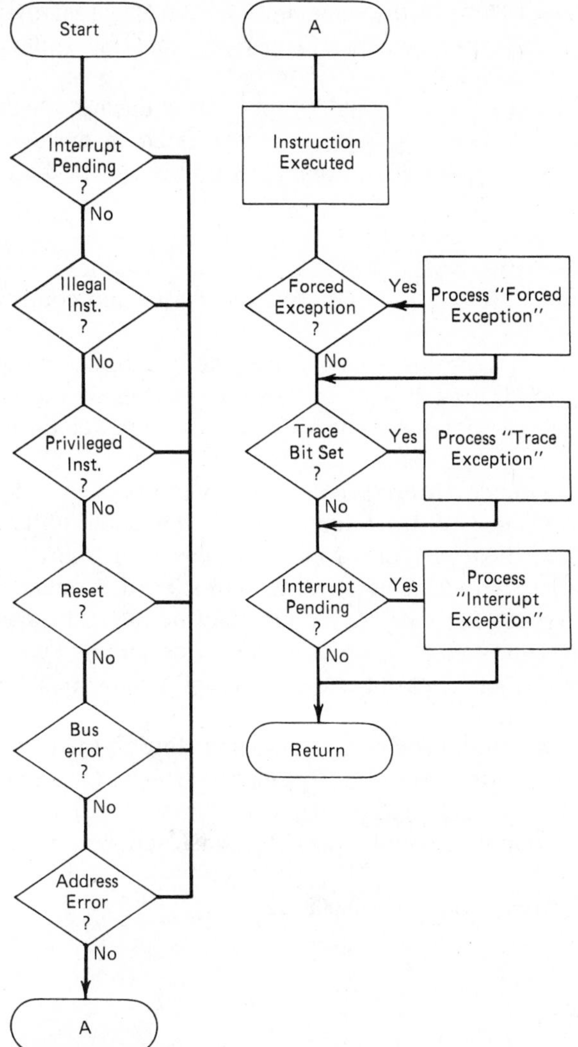

FIGURE 15-36 Flowchart showing trace exception.

Context switch Saving all the registers and flags that define the state of the system at the moment and substituting other values that will cause the processor to execute a different part of the program, such as an exception handler routine.

Data Strobes Signals that control the flow of data on the data bus. The **68000** μPs have Upper Data Strobe (UDS) and Lower Data Strobe (LDS), except the **68020**, which has only one DS signal line.

Exception processing Processing state associated with interrupts, trap instructions, tracing, and other exceptional conditions.

Exception Vector Pointer (address) used by the processor to fetch the address of a routine that will handle an exception.

Function code lines Three of the signal lines on the **68000** family μPs (FC1, FC2, and FC3) that indicate the state (Supervisor or User) and the cycle type currently being executed.

Interrupt acknowledge cycle Sequence of events during which the processor initiates interrupt processing beginning with fetching the interrupt vector. It then saves current conditions on the stack and executes the interrupt service routine.

Long word 32 bits.

NonMaskable Interrupt (NMI) Level 7 interrupt. Cannot be masked.

Operating system Software program that supervises and controls the operation of a computer.

Spurious interrupt Event that occurs during the Interrupt Acknowledge cycle. If no device responds, the bus error line is asserted to terminate the vector acquisition, and the μP fetches the spurious interrupt vector instead of the bus error vector.

Supervisor state or mode More privileged of the normal processing modes.

Supervisor Stack Pointer (SSP) Address kept in a register in the **68000** family μP and used to control storage of data in the Supervisor Stack area of memory.

System byte Most significant byte of the status word. Contains the Supervisor state (S) and Trace (T) mode status bits, and the interrupt mask bits.

Uninitialized interrupt vector Address of a service routine kept in Location $3C that is fetched when a peripheral's interrupt vector register has not been properly initialized.

User state or mode Less privileged processing state of the **68000** family μPs.

User Stack Pointer (USP) Address kept in a register in the **68000** family μP that points to the Users stack area of memory.

Trap Exception that is caused by the TRAP instruction and is useful for system calls.

Word 16-bits or two bytes in a **68000** μP.

15-17 REFERENCES

Greenfield, Joseph, Editor. *Microprocessor Handbook,* Wiley, New York, 1985.

Harman, Thomas L., and Barbara Lawson. *The Motorola MC68000 Microprocessor Family,* Prentice-Hall, Englewood Cliffs, NJ, 1985.

Motorola. *M68000 8-/16-/32-Bit Microprocessors Programmer's Reference Manual,* Fifth Edition, Prentice-Hall, Englewood Cliffs, NJ, 1985.

Motorola. *MC68000 Educational Computer Board User's Manual,* Second Edition, Motorola, Phoenix, AZ, 1982.

Motorola. *MC68000 16/32-Bit Microprocessor* ADI 814R6, Austin, TX, 1985.

Motorola. *M68000 Family Fact Sheet* BR249 REV 2, Phoenix, AZ, 1985.

Motorola. *MC68008 8/32-bit Microprocessor with 8-Bit Data Bus,* ADI 939R2, Austin, TX, 1985.

Motorola. *HDS-400 Microprocessor Hardware Development Station, User's Manual,* M68HDS4UM/D4, Phoenix, AZ, 1984.

Motorola. *MC68HC000 Low Power HCMOS 16/32-bit Microprocessor,* Technical Data Sheet BR275, Rev. 1, Phoenix, AZ, 1986.

Dataquest, *Technical Computer Systems Industry Service,* Dataquest Inc., 1986.

Note: All Motorola literature can be obtained from either Phoenix, Arizona, or Austin, Texas, at the following addresses.

Phoenix: P. O. Box 20912, Phoenix, AZ 85036.

Austin: Microprocessor Division, 3501 Ed Bluestein Blvd., Austin, TX 78721.

15-18 PROBLEMS

15-1 The following registers contain

(D1) = 1 2 3 4 A B C D
(D2) = 3 5 6 7 4 4 4 5
(A3) = 0 0 0 0 2 0 0 0

and the contents of \$2000 are \$1456. What are the contents of these registers and \$2000 after the following instructions?

```
a. MOVE.B    D1,D2
b. MOVE.W    D2,D1
c. ADDA.W    D2,A3
d. ADD.L     D1,D2
e. ADD.W     D2,D1
f. ADD.B     D2,D1
g. MOVEA.W   D2,A3
h. MOVE.L    A3,D1
i. MOVE.W    D1,(A3)
j. MOVE.B    D2,(A3)+
k. MOVE.B    A3,D2
```

15-2 The following registers contain

(D1) = 0 0 0 0 2 0 0 A
(D5) = 0 0 0 0 1 1 1 1
(A4) = 0 0 0 0 3 0 0 0

The PC is at \$5100. What is the Effective Address for the course of each of the following instructions?

```
a. MOVE.L    -(A4),D0
b. MOVE.B    -(A4),D0
c. MOVE.W    139(A4),D0
d. MOVE.B    AB(A5,D1.W),D0
e. MOVE.W    $F900(PC),D0
f. MOVE.W    $25(PC),D5.W,D0
```

15-3 What do the following machine language instructions do?

a. D 8 2 2
b. 3 1 1 5
c. 1 E 3 8
d. 1 0 0 8

15-4 Hand assemble the following instructions:

```
a. MOVE.B   D2,(A5)
b. ADD      (A6)+,D3
```

15-5 In Fig. 15-7, what are the contents of A2, A3, and the A7 register? Which stack is in use?

15-6 Data register D2 contains AAAABBBB. What does it contain after the following instructions?

```
a. ADD.W    #$1234,D2
b. ADDQ.B   #3,D2
c. ADDQ.B   #0,D2
```

15-7 Write a program to move the numbers in A0–A9 into registers D0–D2, D5, A1. Use word size transfers and only one instruction.

15-8 Use the register definitions of Problems 15-1. What are the results after the following instructions are executed?

```
a. EXG    D1,D2
b. EXG    D2,A3
c. SWAP   S2
```

15-9 Write a program to add the bytes in \$3000–\$3020. Place the sum in D3.

15-10 There is a 12-digit BCD number in \$2000–\$2005 and another one in \$2010–\$2015. Write a program to add them and put the results in locations \$2020–\$2025.

15-11 Multiply 3A by 2B using the **68000** MULTIPLY instruction.

15-12 If 1A2 is divided by 15, what are the results of using a DIVIDE instruction?

15-13 Write a program to test the byte in \$2003. Go to \$3000 if the parity is even and go to \$4000 if the parity is odd.

15-14 Write an assembly language program to subtract one multiple-word number from another. The number of words in each number is stored in the word at memory location \$002FF0. The first number is stored in memory, starting at location \$003000. The second number is stored in memory, starting at location \$004000. The result should be stored in memory starting at location \$005000. Both numbers and the results are stored MS word first. Subtract the second number from the first. Try your program with the following data:

002FF0	=	4
first number	=	10F3689400A16184
second number	=	09A2547400902071

15-15 There is a TRAPV instruction in location $2006. The overflow exception routine is to start at $4000. How must the vector table be altered to allow this to occur?

15-16 In Fig. 15-31 if both devices interrupt at the same time, which gets priority and why?

15-17 Modify Fig. 15-31 so that controller 2 can generate a second auto-vector interrupt on level 6.

After attempting to solve these problems, try to answer the self-evaluation questions in Section 15-2. If any of them seem difficult, review the appropriate sections of the chapter to find the answers.

CHAPTER 16

ADVANCED FEATURES OF THE NEWER MEMBERS OF THE 68000 FAMILY

16-1 INSTRUCTIONAL OBJECTIVES

This chapter continues the description of the **68000** family of microprocessors by discussing the newer and more capable μPs, the **68010**, **68020**, and **68030**. After reading this chapter, the student should be able to

1. Describe the new features that make the **68010** superior to the **68000**.
2. Explain Virtual Memory and Memory Management.
3. Discuss the methods used in the **68020** to increase its performance.
4. Discuss how the **68030** uses cache and memory management technologies to further improve performance.
5. Explain how the enhanced LOOP MODE instruction speeds table or block moves.

16-2 SELF-EVALUATION QUESTIONS

Watch for the answers to the following questions as you read the chapter. They should help you to understand the material presented.

1. How many words does the **68000** μP store on the stack when it is interrupted? How many for the **68010**?
2. What is the purpose of the Vector Base Register in the **68010**?
3. What added features does the **68020** have?
4. How does the **68020** execute instructions in zero time?
5. How does having the Memory Management Unit on-chip improve performance of the **68030**?
6. How does the data cache work to improve the performance of the **68030**?

16-3 INTRODUCTION TO THE ADVANCED 16/32-BIT μPS

Several references were made to the newer members of the **68000** μP family in the previous chapter. This chapter starts by describing the **68010** and then discusses the **68020** and **68030** in the later sections. Each of these μPs has substantial performance improvements over its earlier relative. The **68010** was introduced in 1983. It is pin- and software-compatible with the **68000**. It has several added features, such as the support of *virtual memory techniques* and *enhanced instruction execution timing,* that improve its performance.

The **68020** μP, introduced in 1984, has full 32-bit implementation of the ALU, internal data paths, and external address and data buses. It retains the virtual memory features of the **68010** and adds many new features such as the *internal instruction cache, the coprocessor interface,* and *pipelined internal architecture* that provide remarkable performance capabilities. All of these newer chips still qualify as members of the **68000** family because the software is upwardly compatible (i.e., **68000** programs will run on all of the newer μPs).

In September 1986 a still more powerful member of the **68000** μP family was added. This is the **68030**, and it also supports virtual memory operation. It is based on the **68020** core but has numerous enhanced performance features. Increased *internal parallelism* is provided by *multiple* internal data and address buses and a versatile built-in bus controller. An on-chip *Paged Memory Management Unit* (PMMU) reduces the minimum physical bus cycle time, and the *internal pipelining* provides this memory management with *zero* translation time for addresses. These features of the newer μPs will be described in Sections 16-7 and 16-12.

16-4 HCMOS TECHNOLOGY

The **68000** family of μPs were made possible by the continuing developments in semiconductor processing technology. Although the **68000** had processing improvements over the **6800** and **6809**, the **68020** required the newer features available in the HCMOS technology of 1984. By 1986, HCMOS had been made still smaller and faster, making the **68030** possible. With circuits as complex as those in the **68020** and **68030**, density, chip size, speed, power consumption, and manufacturability are all critical considerations.

Motorola's experience with High-density Complementary Metal Oxide Semiconductors (HCMOS) made it possible to design nearly 200,000 transistors into the **68020** chip and nearly 300,000 transistors into the **68030**. This process also provides the necessary combination of high-speed performance with very low power consumption. By using this advanced HCMOS process, production can be maintained at high volumes with proper yields. The resulting **68020** or **68030** μP provides many times the processing power of the **68000**, yet consumes less system power.

16-5 VIRTUAL MEMORY AND THE 68010

Virtual memory is memory that *appears* to be at an address different from the actual *physical* address. The virtual memory is said to be in the **logical address space**, whereas the real **physical memory** is in the **physical address space**. This is accomplished by *translating* the *logical* addresses put out by the μP to the *physical* addresses of the actual memory.

This technique has been used for several years in large mainframe computers and more recently in minicomputers. Improvements in semiconductor technology have made possible the inclusion of the additional registers and other hardware circuits required to support the advanced virtual memory features. The **68010** was one of the first μPs to provide this capability.

Because memory is expensive, most **68000** family μP systems provide physical memory for only a fraction of the 16 megabytes addressable by the 24-bit address bus. The *virtual memory* concept allows large programs to be written for the **68010** that exceed the physical memory size. With the help of suitable internal and external hardware, the full 16 megabytes of *virtual* space can be used successfully. This is possible because only a portion of a program need be in memory at a time. Virtual memory systems subdivide their memory into *pages*. One or more pages are in physical memory, while the rest of the program and data resides on secondary storage devices such as a large-capacity disk drive.

EXAMPLE 16-1

A programmer is writing a program that will require 16 megabytes of memory. Assume the memory is divided into 32K byte pages and that 1 megabyte of physical memory is available.

a. How many address bits does the programmer need?
b. How many address bits does each page have?
c. How many pages can be in memory and how many must remain on the disk?

SOLUTION

a. An address space of 16M bytes contains 2^{24} bytes and therefore requires 24 address bits.
b. Each page has 32K bytes of memory and will require 15 address bits. This leaves 9 address bits available for determining the page selected. This system contains 512 pages of 32K bytes each, to make up a total address space of 16M bytes.
c. Because there is only 1 megabyte of physical memory available, 16 pages can be in memory at any time. The other 496 pages will have to reside on the disk.

16-5.1 Page Faults

Virtual memory performs almost as well as physical memory because of the way programs operate. Statistically, it has been found that most memory references are nearby and thus they are usually made to a page that is already in physical memory. When the processor attempts to access a location in the virtual memory map that is not currently residing in physical memory, a *page fault* occurs. The access to that location is temporarily suspended while the necessary data (or instructions) are fetched from the secondary storage (usually a hard disk) and placed in the physical memory.

When a new section of the program or data is addressed, a page that is currently in the physical memory and has not been used recently must be returned to the disk to make room for the page from the disk that contains the newly addressed memory location. This return is necessary because the page may contain data changes that must be saved.

This process of writing an old page to the disk and bringing a new page into memory is called *swapping*. Program execution resumes when the swapping is completed. The **68010** provides hardware support for virtual memory operations such as these.

The **68010** uses *instruction continuation* rather than *instruction restart* to support virtual memory. With instruction restart, the processor must remember the exact state of the system *before* each instruction is started in order to restore that state if a page fault should occur during the execution. Then, after the page fault has been *repaired* (new memory page loaded), the entire instruction that caused the fault is reexecuted.

In order to utilize *instruction continuation,* the **68010** stores its internal state on the Supervisor stack whenever a bus cycle is terminated with a *bus error,* which indicates that a page fault has occurred. It then loads the program counter from *Exception Vector Table entry number two* (offset $008). This vector points to the bus error routine, and program execution begins again at that new address. When the bus error exception handler routine has completed execution, by swapping pages, an RTE instruction is executed that reloads the **68010** with the internal state previously stored on the stack, reruns the *faulted bus cycle,* and continues the suspended instruction.

To illustrate why *instruction continuation* is the necessary choice for the support of virtual I/O devices in memory-mapped input/output systems, assume that an instruction reads a register in a PIA (see Chapter 7) and when the data is being written to memory, a page fault occurs. It is *not* possible to restart the instruction since the status bits in the PIA have already been reset. Therefore the instruction *must* be continued after the page fault has been corrected so that the results will be proper.

Suppose also that a system is under development and will use I/O devices that are not yet installed. The registers in these I/O devices will occupy specific locations in memory. Again, the PIA can be used as an example. The **68010** and its program can be set up so that any attempted reference to these locations causes a page fault. The page fault will cause an exception, and the exception routine can be written to *simulate* the action of these registers. Thus the operating system program can be tested before the I/O ICs are actually installed.

16-5.2 Virtual Memory Processors

One typical use for a virtual memory processing system is in the development of software, such as an operating system, to work with hardware that is also under development and not available for programming use. In such a system, which typically has memory-mapped input/output devices [i.e., hardware registers for printers, disk drives, or Analog-to-Digital (A/D) converters], the governing operating system emulates this hardware and allows the operating system under development to be executed and debugged as though it were running on the new hardware. Such an emulated system is called a **virtual machine**.

Since the new operating system is controlled by the governing operating system, the new one must execute at a lower privilege level than the governing operating system. In the **68010** a virtual machine may be fully supported by running the new operating system in the *User* mode and the governing operating system in the *Supervisor* mode so that any attempts to access supervisor resources or execute privileged instructions by the new operating system will cause a trap to the governing operating system.

To fully support a virtual machine, the **68010** must protect the supervisor resources from access by user programs. The one supervisor resource that is not fully protected in the **68000** is the *System Byte* of the Status Register. In the **68000** and **68008**, the *MOVE from SR* instruction allows user programs to test the S bit (in addition to the T bit and interrupt mask) and thus determine that they are running in the *User* mode. For full virtual machine support, a new operating system must not be aware of the fact that it is running in the User mode and thus should not be allowed to access the S bit. For this reason, the MOVE from SR instruction *has been made privileged* in the **68010** to allow only supervisor programs unhindered access to the System Byte of the Status Register. By making this instruction privileged, a trap to the governing operating system will occur when the new operating system attempts to access the S bit, and the SR image passed to the new operating system by the governing operating system will have the S bit set.

16-5.3 Memory Management Units (MMUs)

In the μC systems that we have previously considered that used the **68000** or even the **6800** or **6809**s, the μP is connected directly to memory. Any program can therefore read or write to any part of the available memory. This type of system has many applications but is unsuitable for execution of *multiple concurrent tasks* since there is no mechanism to protect the memory of one task from interference by another task. It is also unsuitable for hosting virtual systems that are larger than the address space represented by the memory (or I/O) devices physically present.

The **68000** family processors and other *bus master* devices (i.e., DMA controllers or network controllers) provide an indication of the context in which they are operating on a cycle-by-cycle basis through the *Function Code* outputs. The Function Codes indicate the current privilege mode of the bus master (Supervisor or User) and the type of operand that is being accessed (program or data). These

Function Codes make it possible to designate portions of memory for specific uses and to *protect* them from unauthorized accesses.

A new family of devices has been developed to handle these problems. They are known as **Memory Management Units (MMUs)** or, as explained later, as *Paged Memory Management Units* (PMMUs).

The direction of sophisticated μP-based computer systems is toward *demand-paged* virtual memory. *Paging* means the subdivision of physical memory into equal-sized blocks called *page frames*.

The logical address space of a process is divided into *pages* that have the same number of bytes and therefore fit into the physical memory's *frames*. User processes can be completely unaware of this division. The operating system controls the allocation of pages to page frames (called *mapping*).

Paging is a desirable method for memory allocation because it means that the entire code of data segments (consisting of many pages) need not be resident in physical memory at the same time. Only those pages that are currently being used by the process need be assigned to frames. Since pages are all the same size, any page will fit into any frame.

The term *demand* means that a process does not need to specify in advance what areas of its logical address space it requires. An access to an address is interpreted by the system as a request to provide that memory. In a **demand-paged** system, new pages are loaded by the operating system when the processor addresses a location that is within one of them. This requires a processor with a virtual memory capability, as provided in the **68010/68020/68030** μPs, and in the first two cases it also requires external logic in one or more ICs to form a *memory management unit* or subsystem to control the memory allocations. One new IC that has been developed for this function is the **68851** PMMU described in Section 16-10.

In the early stages of development of these MMUs it was found desirable to build a Memory Management Board (MMB) using discrete components because the **68000** family MMU chips were not yet available. This MMB implemented a subset of the features of the **68851**. The MMB was targeted for relatively simple systems. Although it could be used in a more complex system, it was not expected to perform as well in that application as the **68851** would.

The MMU (or MMB) is inserted into the address bus between the Central Processing Unit (CPU), or μP, and memory, as shown in Fig. 16-1. Although the basic functions of an MMU also include memory protection/privilege selections by using the Function Codes, only the *memory mapping* or *address translation* function of MMUs is discussed here. (See Section 16-10 for the other aspects of MMUs.)

When an MMU is used, the address bus is divided into two parts: a *logical address bus* and a *physical address bus*. The μP drives the logical address bus that connects to the MMU. The physical address bus is the path that the MMU uses to communicate with the rest of the system.

An *Address Translation Cache* (ATC) is internal to the MMU. The ATC is a fast memory containing entries composed of *logical* information (logical address and Function Codes) and *physical* information (physical address and protection bits).

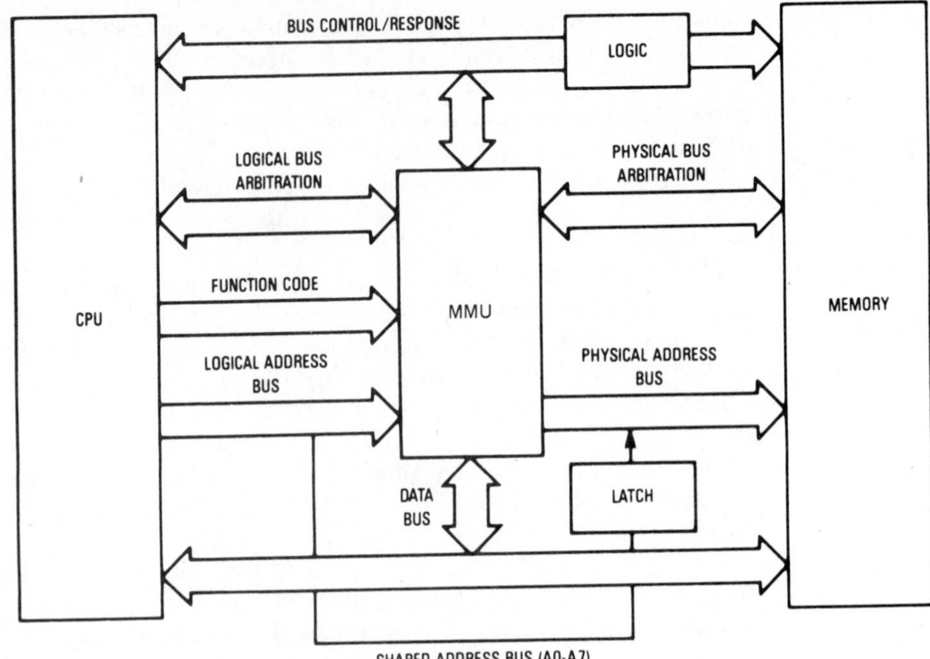

FIGURE 16-1 MMU block diagram.

During every cycle, the logical addresses and Function Codes are compared against the entries in the ATC. If one of the entries matches (*hits*), the stored physical address from the ATC is placed onto the physical address bus and access information is gated to *access checking* circuitry. If the MMB detects no exceptional conditions, it then asserts *Physical Address Strobe* (PAS). If the ATC entries do *not* match the bus status during an attempted access, a *page fault* has occurred, the pages containing the desired instructions or data are *swapped* into memory, and the ATC tables are updated.

The technique of memory management is used in conjunction with the chip hardware additions to make multiuser and multitasking systems possible. Programs can have different ranges of logical addresses and yet be swapped from a disk file into the same block of physical memory by having the memory management unit remap that block to the required addresses. In this way, only enough actual (physical) memory is needed to hold the code for processes that must be in memory at one time.

16-6 ADDITIONAL ENHANCEMENTS IN THE 68010

The **68010** contains several other new features not found in the **68000**. For one, a new register has been added, the **Vector Base Register** (VBR). In the **68000**, the *Exception Vector Table* must start at address 0. In the **68010** the VBR is used to determine the starting or **base address** of the Exception Vector Table in memory to support *multiple* vector tables (one must be at location 0). When an exception vector is fetched, the processor translates the 8-bit **vector number** to a full 32-bit **offset**, which is added to the contents of the VBR to get the **Vector table entry**. Since the VBR is initialized to zero during reset, the **68010** is fully compatible with **68000** programs.

A second new hardware feature is the inclusion of two small 2-bit registers: the Source Function Code (SFC) and Destination Function Code (DFC) registers. This allows the supervisor to use a new privileged instruction (MOVES) to move an operand from a specified general register to a location within the address space specified by the DFC register, or move the operand from a location within the address space specified by the SFC register to a specified general register.

If the destination is a data register, the source operand replaces the corresponding low-order bits of that data register. If the destination is an address register, the source operand is sign-extended to 32 bits and then loaded into that address register. The assembler syntax is

MOVES Rn,<EA> or

MOVES <EA>,Rn

where Rn is the specified general register and EA specifies the source or destination location within the alternate address space. See the *M68000 Programmer's Reference Manual* for complete details of the MOVES instruction. (see References, Section 16-15).

New instructions for the **68010** include

MOVEC	(move to/from control register)
RTD	(return and deallocate parameters)
MOVES	(move to/from address space)
MOVE from CCR	(move from the Condition Code Register)
MOVE to CCR	(move to Condition Code Register)

The reader should refer to the *Programmer's Reference Manual* for more details on these new **68010** instructions.

16-6.1 Loop Mode Operation

The **68010** has several features that improve the execution time of program loops. One of these is an enhanced DBcc looping instruction, where "cc" is one of the conditions shown in Table 15-16 of the previous chapter. The "cc" also has the same meaning as in the Bcc or Scc instructions that are described in Section 15-10.11. The DBcc instruction for the **68000** was described in Section 15-10.12. A new *loop mode* enhancement has been included in the **68010** that dramatically reduces the number of μP cycles required for the DBcc instruction and thereby speeds its execution. The following two examples illustrate the use of this instruction, but the enhancement will not be noticed in Example 16-2 since instruction cycle time is not displayed. Example 16-3 makes use of the HDS-300 μP Development System to show the improvement in performance.

EXAMPLE 16-2

There is a set of ASCII characters in locations \$2000–\$201F. Write a program to move all of them to locations \$3000–\$301F or move them until the table end is found (designated by a null byte).

SOLUTION
A program can be written using the ECB's Assembler/Disassembler as follows:

```
        LEA      ($2000),A0      Load pointer to source data.
        LEA      ($3000),A1      Load pointer to destination.
        MOVE.W   #$12,D0         Load the counter register.
LOOP    MOVE.B   (A0)+,(A1)+     Loop to move block of data.
        DBEQ     D0,LOOP         Stop if null found.
HERE    BRA      *               End of list or null found.
```

In this example, a character is moved into the new location and the program then loops back for the next character. In the process, each byte is tested for a value of zero. If a null byte (00) has not been found, Register D0 is decremented, and if it is not -1 the program loops back to move the next character. The program reaches the label HERE either because a null has been found or because D0 $= -1$. D0 can then be tested to determine which condition caused the termination.

The terminating condition may seem inverted, but should be thought of as similar to an UNTIL loop of a high-level language. For example, DBEQ can be stated as "decrement and branch *until* equal to zero."

Note: In order to test this routine with a debugger, such as the ECB, a branch-to-self instruction (BRA *) has been used. Also, since labels are not recognized in most debuggers, the equivalent address for LOOP (\$400C) should be entered. After stepping through the instructions (using *trace)* to verify that there are no errors, the program can be allowed to execute at full speed by placing a breakpoint at the address of the last instruction.

Loop mode operation is transparent to the programmer, with three conditions required for the **68010** to enter the loop mode.

1. The *condition* must be false.
2. The *count* must not be -1.
3. A branch displacement of *minus 4* must be specified.

(The last condition indicates that the branch must return to a one-word instruction that precedes the DBcc instruction.)

The unique feature of this **68010** loop mode is that the single-word instruction that precedes the DBcc instruction and the first word of the DBcc instruction (both within the loop) will only be fetched twice, when the loop is entered, and will not be fetched again until the DBcc loop conditions fail. (This will be made clear in Example 16-3.)

EXAMPLE 16-3

Show how a μP Development System (as described in Chapter 12) can be used to evaluate the DBcc loop mode instruction.

SOLUTION

An HDS-300 Development System with an **68010** Emulator Pod was connected to a terminal and used in the Stand-alone mode. Using the ASM command, the mnemonics of the program used in the previous Example 16-2 were entered. This command generates the machine language codes and loads them into the HDS memory, starting at location \$4000. Next, to verify that they were entered correctly, the DASM command was used to disassemble the codes and display the associated mnemonics, as shown in the top part of Fig. 16-2a.

This figure is a composite of two HDS-300 CRT screen displays that were printed using the PRINT command. The Memory Display (MD) command below the dotted line shows the hex machine language generated by the one-line assembler for the above program. For example, it can be seen that the code for the DBeq D0,\$400C instruction at \$400E is 57C8FFFC and for the last instruction (at \$4012), it is 60FE.

```
Env: DEBUG     As: SP   State: STOPPED  Bsm:  DISARMED  Coll: OFF  Macros: OFF

dasm 4000 4013
00004000            LEA        ($2000).W,A0
00004004            LEA        ($3000).W,A1
00004008            MOVE.W     #$12,D0
0000400C            MOVE.B     (A0)+,(A1)+
0000400E            DBEQ       D0,$400C
00004012            BRA.B      $4012
------------------------------------------------------------------------------
MD 4000 401F
00004000   41F82000 43F83000 303C0012 32D857C8   A. .C.0.0<..2.W.
00004010   FFFC60FE 00000000 00000000 00000000   .. .............

MD 2000 201F
00002000   31 32 33 34 35 36 37 38  39 61 62 63 64 65 66 67   123456789abcdefg
00002010   68 69 6A 6B 6C 6D 6E 6F  70 71 72 73 74 75 76 77   hijklmnopqrstuvw
==============================================================================
MD 3000 301F
00003000   31 32 33 34 35 36 37 38  39 61 62 63 64 65 66 67  123456789abcdefg
00003010   68 69 6A 00 00 00 00 00  00 00 00 00 00 00 00 00  hij.............
rd
 PC=00004012  SR=2700=.S7.....   SSP=00007FFF  USP=00000000
D0-D7 0000FFFF 00000000 00000000 00000000  00000000 00000000 00000000 00000000
A0-A7 00002013 00003013 00000000 00000000  00000000 00000000 00000000 00007FFE

>
To scroll:  ^Y-line up     ^B-line down     ^T-window up    ^V-window down
To edit command line: ^E-erase   ^H-left   ^K-right   ^I-insert   ^O-delete
```

(a)

FIGURE 16-2 HDS-300 display printouts for Example 16-3 for the case where no nulls were found. (a) DEBUG screen showing Disassembly of routine, Machine language, Original data, relocated data, and Register Display after looping terminated.

```
Env: BDIS      As: SP   State: STOPPED  Bsm:  DISARMED  Coll: OFF  Macros: OFF

                                 uds ber FC1 vpa ip2 ipØ bg  hit BRN ORG GRN
                               R/W lds FC2 FCØ vma ip1 br  bga rst RED YEL
 Cycle  Address Data
>ØØØØ   ØØØØ4ØØØ                  LEA      ($2ØØØ).W,AØ
 ØØØØ   ØØ4ØØØ   41F8          1 Ø Ø 1 1 1 Ø 1 1 1 1 1 1 1 1 1 1 1 1 1 1 1
 ØØØ1   ØØ4ØØ2   2ØØØ          1 Ø Ø 1 1 1 Ø 1 1 1 1 1 1 1 1 1 1 1 1 1 1 1
 ØØØ2   ØØØØ4ØØ4                  LEA      ($3ØØØ).W,A1
 ØØØ2   ØØ4ØØ4   43F8          1 Ø Ø 1 1 1 Ø 1 1 1 1 1 1 1 1 1 1 1 1 1 1 1
 ØØØ3   ØØ4ØØ6   3ØØØ          1 Ø Ø 1 1 1 Ø 1 1 1 1 1 1 1 1 1 1 1 1 1 1 1
 ØØØ4   ØØØØ4ØØ8                  MOVE.W   #$12,DØ
 ØØØ4   ØØ4ØØ8   3Ø3C          1 Ø Ø 1 1 1 Ø 1 1 1 1 1 1 1 1 1 1 1 1 1 1 1
 ØØØ5   ØØ4ØØA   ØØ12          1 Ø Ø 1 1 1 Ø 1 1 1 1 1 1 1 1 1 1 1 1 1 1 1
 ØØØ6   ØØØØ4ØØC                  MOVE.B   (AØ)+,(A1)+
 ØØØ6   ØØ4ØØC   12D8          1 Ø Ø 1 1 1 Ø 1 1 1 1 1 1 1 1 1 1 1 1 1 1 1
 ØØØ7   ØØØØ4ØØE                  DBEQ     DØ,$4ØØC
 ØØØ7   ØØ4ØØE   57C8          1 Ø Ø 1 1 1 Ø 1 1 1 1 1 1 1 1 1 1 1 1 1 1 1
 ØØØ8   ØØ2ØØØ   31C8          1 Ø 1 1 1 Ø 1 1 1 1 1 1 1 1 1 1 1 1 1 1 1 1
 ØØØ9   ØØ3ØØØ   3131          Ø Ø 1 1 1 Ø 1 1 1 1 1 1 1 1 1 1 1 1 1 1 1 1
 ØØ1Ø   ØØ4Ø1Ø   FFFC          1 Ø Ø 1 1 1 Ø 1 1 1 1 1 1 1 1 1 1 1 1 1 1 1
 ØØ11   ØØØØ4ØØC                  MOVE.B   (AØ)+,(A1)+
 ØØ11   ØØ4ØØC   12D8          1 Ø Ø 1 1 1 Ø 1 1 1 1 1 1 1 1 1 1 1 1 1 1 1
 ØØ12   ØØ4ØØE   57C8          1 Ø Ø 1 1 1 Ø 1 1 1 1 1 1 1 1 1 1 1 1 1 1 1
 ØØ13   ØØ2ØØØ   D732          1 1 Ø 1 1 Ø 1 1 1 1 1 1 1 1 1 1 1 1 1 1 1 1
 ØØ14   ØØ3ØØØ   3232          Ø 1 Ø 1 1 Ø 1 1 1 1 1 1 1 1 1 1 1 1 1 1 1 1
 ØØ15   ØØ2ØØ2   3332          1 Ø 1 1 1 Ø 1 1 1 1 1 1 1 1 1 1 1 1 1 1 1 1
 ØØ16   ØØ3ØØ2   3333          Ø Ø 1 1 1 Ø 1 1 1 1 1 1 1 1 1 1 1 1 1 1 1 1
 ØØ17   ØØ2ØØ2   B334          1 1 Ø 1 1 Ø 1 1 1 1 1 1 1 1 1 1 1 1 1 1 1 1
 ØØ18   ØØ3ØØ2   3434          Ø 1 Ø 1 1 Ø 1 1 1 1 1 1 1 1 1 1 1 1 1 1 1 1
 ØØ19   ØØ2ØØ4   3534          1 Ø 1 1 1 Ø 1 1 1 1 1 1 1 1 1 1 1 1 1 1 1 1
 ØØ2Ø   ØØ3ØØ4   3535          Ø Ø 1 1 1 Ø 1 1 1 1 1 1 1 1 1 1 1 1 1 1 1 1
 ØØ21   ØØ2ØØ4   B536          1 1 Ø 1 1 Ø 1 1 1 1 1 1 1 1 1 1 1 1 1 1 1 1
 ØØ22   ØØ3ØØ4   3636          Ø 1 Ø 1 1 Ø 1 1 1 1 1 1 1 1 1 1 1 1 1 1 1 1
 ØØ23   ØØ2ØØ6   3736          1 Ø 1 1 1 Ø 1 1 1 1 1 1 1 1 1 1 1 1 1 1 1 1
 ØØ24   ØØ3ØØ6   3737          Ø Ø 1 1 1 Ø 1 1 1 1 1 1 1 1 1 1 1 1 1 1 1 1
 ØØ25   ØØ2ØØ6   B738          1 1 Ø 1 1 Ø 1 1 1 1 1 1 1 1 1 1 1 1 1 1 1 1
 ØØ26   ØØ3ØØ6   3838          Ø 1 Ø 1 1 Ø 1 1 1 1 1 1 1 1 1 1 1 1 1 1 1 1
 ØØ27   ØØ2ØØ8   3938          1 Ø 1 1 1 Ø 1 1 1 1 1 1 1 1 1 1 1 1 1 1 1 1
 ØØ28   ØØ3ØØ8   3939          Ø Ø 1 1 1 Ø 1 1 1 1 1 1 1 1 1 1 1 1 1 1 1 1
 ØØ29   ØØ2ØØ8   B961          1 1 Ø 1 1 Ø 1 1 1 1 1 1 1 1 1 1 1 1 1 1 1 1
 ØØ3Ø   ØØ3ØØ8   6161          Ø 1 Ø 1 1 Ø 1 1 1 1 1 1 1 1 1 1 1 1 1 1 1 1
 ØØ31   ØØ2ØØA   6261          1 Ø 1 1 1 Ø 1 1 1 1 1 1 1 1 1 1 1 1 1 1 1 1
 ØØ32   ØØ3ØØA   6262          Ø Ø 1 1 1 Ø 1 1 1 1 1 1 1 1 1 1 1 1 1 1 1 1
 ØØ33   ØØ2ØØA   FE63          1 1 Ø 1 1 Ø 1 1 1 1 1 1 1 1 1 1 1 1 1 1 1 1
 ØØ34   ØØ3ØØA   6363          Ø 1 Ø 1 1 Ø 1 1 1 1 1 1 1 1 1 1 1 1 1 1 1 1
 ØØ35   ØØ2ØØC   6463          1 Ø 1 1 1 Ø 1 1 1 1 1 1 1 1 1 1 1 1 1 1 1 1
 ØØ36   ØØ3ØØC   6464          Ø Ø 1 1 1 Ø 1 1 1 1 1 1 1 1 1 1 1 1 1 1 1 1
 ØØ38   ØØ2ØØC   E665          1 1 Ø 1 1 Ø 1 1 1 1 1 1 1 1 1 1 1 1 1 1 1 1
 ØØ39   ØØ3ØØC   6565          Ø 1 Ø 1 1 Ø 1 1 1 1 1 1 1 1 1 1 1 1 1 1 1 1
 ØØ4Ø   ØØ2ØØE   6665          1 Ø 1 1 1 Ø 1 1 1 1 1 1 1 1 1 1 1 1 1 1 1 1
 ØØ41   ØØ3ØØE   6666          Ø Ø 1 1 1 Ø 1 1 1 1 1 1 1 1 1 1 1 1 1 1 1 1
 ØØ42   ØØ2ØØE   E667          1 1 Ø 1 1 Ø 1 1 1 1 1 1 1 1 1 1 1 1 1 1 1 1
 ØØ43   ØØ3ØØE   6767          Ø 1 Ø 1 1 Ø 1 1 1 1 1 1 1 1 1 1 1 1 1 1 1 1
 ØØ44   ØØ2Ø1Ø   6867          1 Ø 1 1 1 Ø 1 1 1 1 1 1 1 1 1 1 1 1 1 1 1 1
 ØØ45   ØØ3Ø1Ø   6868          Ø Ø 1 1 1 Ø 1 1 1 1 1 1 1 1 1 1 1 1 1 1 1 1
 ØØ46   ØØ2Ø1Ø   EE69          1 1 Ø 1 1 Ø 1 1 1 1 1 1 1 1 1 1 1 1 1 1 1 1
 ØØ47   ØØ3Ø1Ø   6969          Ø 1 Ø 1 1 Ø 1 1 1 1 1 1 1 1 1 1 1 1 1 1 1 1
 ØØ48   ØØ2Ø12   6A69          1 Ø 1 1 1 Ø 1 1 1 1 1 1 1 1 1 1 1 1 1 1 1 1
 ØØ49   ØØ3Ø12   6A6A          Ø Ø 1 1 1 Ø 1 1 1 1 1 1 1 1 1 1 1 1 1 1 1 1
 ØØ5Ø   ØØØØ4Ø12                  BRA.B    $4Ø12
E ØØ5Ø  ØØ4Ø12   6ØFE          1 Ø Ø 1 1 1 Ø 1 1 1 1 1 1 1 1 1 1 1 1 1 1 1
 ØØ51   ØØ4Ø14   ØØØØ          1 Ø Ø 1 1 1 Ø 1 1 1 1 1 1 1 1 1 1 1 1 1 1 1
 ØØ52   ØØØØ4Ø12                  BRA.B    $4Ø12
E ØØ52  ØØ4Ø12   6ØFE          1 Ø Ø 1 1 1 Ø 1 1 1 1 1 1 1 1 1 1 1 1 1 1 1
```

FIGURE 16-2 (*Continued*) (b) Printout of BDIS screen showing the Trace buffer contents for Example 16-3.

The next MD command shows the data (characters) that the program is designed to move. They were entered using the Memory Edit (ME) command. They are in a table at $2000 to $201F.

The program was first *traced* (one instruction at a time) to verify that it executes properly to move one word, and was then executed with a breakpoint at $4012 to move the whole table. The second MD command in the center area of the figure (below the double dashed line) shows how the table was relocated when no zeros were encountered in the data (i.e., DBeq is never true). The program looped until the count in register D0 became negative as shown in the bottom (RD) display in the screen window of Fig. 16-2a. This Register Display (RD) command, shows the values in the registers after the subroutine stopped looping. Note that the address register A0 and A1 have both been incremented to one more than the value in register D0.

The HDS-300 development system was then set up to capture the results in the *trace buffer* (a feature of the Bus State Monitor). The details of setting up this process will not be described here, except to say that the Bus COLlection (BCOL) and Bus EVent (BEV) screens of the HDS-300 are used.

The purpose in using the Bus State Monitor (BSM) of the HDS-300 system is to analyze the instruction flow on a *cycle-by-cycle* basis. The *trace buffer* is set up so that it will capture the state of each pin on the μP as each cycle of the instruction is executed. The breakpoint used previously is removed and the Bus EVent (BEV) screen used to set the "trigger" at the same address ($4012). (i.e., When the routine counts down to a negative value in register D0, the program *falls through* to the last instruction (at $4012), and the capture function is *triggered.)* This freezes all the trace buffer data.

The BDIS command is then used to display the buffer contents on the terminal screen. The μP status that existed after each cycle of the instruction can then be viewed by scrolling through the buffer, or the buffer contents can be printed by using the TYPE command. We chose to print 59 lines and this data is shown in Fig. 16-2b. This is a cycle-by-cycle printout of the status of the signals on the μP buses as the program is executed. In order to easily correlate the cycles with each instruction, the FD MIX command was used to show both the cycles and the instruction mnemonics. The *trace buffer* can save the status of up to 1024 execution cycles. It starts where the program begins execution and continues until the BSM is *triggered.*

There are many interesting things to be learned by studying this printout. Again the emulator status line is shown at the top, followed by the signal names for each column. It will be noted that the signal names correspond to the pins on the **68010** μP. Fortunately, the first 4 columns are the only ones we need to concern ourselves with now. They are: Cycle, Address, Data and R/W. The Data column is the main one to study.

It can be seen that the Op code for the first LEA instruction ($41F8) is fetched during the 1st cycle (cycle 0000), and the data source address is fetched during cycle 0001. Note the "1" in the R/W column indicating a *read* operation. The first 7 cycles show the fetching of the Op codes and operands involved.

Cycle 8 fetches the data word ($31C8) from address $2000. The first byte is really the only one fetched but since the data is shown in words, the last half of the word retains the value it had in cycle 7. The 9th cycle is the 1st *write* cycle (R/$\overline{W}$ = 0) and shows the $31 being written to location $3000. It is difficult to see how these overlapping words move the data, but a review of the MD display in the middle of Fig. 16-2a shows that they are properly moved. (See Fig. 16-4 for a more efficient way to move the data.)

Cycle 10 is a fetch of the displacement (FFFC) from location $4010 and is the second word of the DBEQ instruction. We next see that the program looped back to $400C and refetched the next two instructions (i.e., cycles 11 and 12 are repeats of 6 and 7). Thereafter, however, note that only data *reads* and *writes* are done until the program counts the D0 register down to −1. It then falls through to the last instruction at cycle 50.

Because the last instruction is a *branch-to-self* instruction, it keeps repeating this one instruction until interrupted. Note that the μP fetches the next word (cycle 51) but ignores it since the previous Op code was a branch.

This program was then repeated as shown in Fig. 16-3a with a null byte inserted at location $2006. This is intended to show the operation of the DBcc instruction when it encounters the condition it is testing rather than just to show it counting down to −1.

With the trigger still set at the last instruction (as previously set using the BEV screen), the ARM command was entered to *enable* the trace buffer, the PC was set to the start of the program at $4000, and the program was executed again.

```
Env: DEBUG      As: SP   State: STOPPED  Bsm:  DISARMED  Coll: OFF  Macros: OFF

DASM 4000 4013
00004000            LEA        ($2000).W,A0
00004004            LEA        ($3000).W,A1
00004008            MOVE.W     #$12,D0
0000400C            MOVE.B     (A0)+,(A1)+
0000400E            DBEQ       D0,$400C
00004012            BRA.B      $4012
--------------------------------------------------------------------------------
G
BSM TRIGGER STOPPED - PC=00004012
RD
 PC=00004012  SR=2704=.S7..Z..    SSP=00007FFF  USP=00000000
D0-D7 0000000C 00000000 00000000 00000000  00000000 00000000 00000000 00000000
A0-A7 00002006 00003006 00000000 00000000  00000000 00000000 00000000 00007FFE
MD 3000 301F
00003000   31323334 35000000  00000000 00000000   12345...........


>
To scroll:  ^Y-line up     ^B-line down     ^T-window up     ^V-window down
To edit command line: ^E-erase    ^H-left    ^K-right    ^I-insert    ^O-delete
```

(*a*)

FIGURE 16-3 HDS-300 printouts for the case where the program terminated when it found a null at location $2004. (a) DEBUG screen showing the program mnemonics, the BSM Trigger Stop, and the Register Display.

```
Env: BDIS        As: SP   State: STOPPED  Bsm:  DISARMED  Coll: OFF  Macros: OFF

                                  uds ber FC1 vpa ip2 ipØ bg  hit BRN ORG GRN
 Cycle  Address Data            R/W lds FC2 FCØ vma ip1 br  bga rst RED YEL
>ØØØØ   ØØØØ4ØØØ                  LEA     ($2ØØØ).W,AØ
 ØØØØ   ØØ4ØØØ   41F8           1 Ø Ø 1 1 1 Ø 1 1 1 1 1 1 1 1 1 1 1 1 1 1 1
 ØØØ1   ØØ4ØØ2   2ØØØ           1 Ø Ø 1 1 1 Ø 1 1 1 1 1 1 1 1 1 1 1 1 1 1 1
 ØØØ2   ØØØØ4ØØ4                  LEA     ($3ØØØ).W,A1
 ØØØ2   ØØ4ØØ4   43F8           1 Ø Ø 1 1 1 Ø 1 1 1 1 1 1 1 1 1 1 1 1 1 1 1
 ØØØ3   ØØ4ØØ6   3ØØØ           1 Ø Ø 1 1 1 Ø 1 1 1 1 1 1 1 1 1 1 1 1 1 1 1
 ØØØ4   ØØØØ4ØØ8                  MOVE.W  #$12,DØ
 ØØØ4   ØØ4ØØ8   3Ø3C           1 Ø Ø 1 1 1 Ø 1 1 1 1 1 1 1 1 1 1 1 1 1 1 1
 ØØØ5   ØØ4ØØA   ØØ12           1 Ø Ø 1 1 1 Ø 1 1 1 1 1 1 1 1 1 1 1 1 1 1 1
 ØØØ6   ØØØØ4ØØC                  MOVE.B  (AØ)+,(A1)+
 ØØØ6   ØØ4ØØC   12D8           1 Ø Ø 1 1 1 Ø 1 1 1 1 1 1 1 1 1 1 1 1 1 1 1
 ØØØ7   ØØØØ4ØØE                  DBEQ    DØ,$4ØØC
 ØØØ7   ØØ4ØØE   57C8           1 Ø Ø 1 1 1 Ø 1 1 1 1 1 1 1 1 1 1 1 1 1 1 1
 ØØØ8   ØØ2ØØØ   31C8           1 Ø 1 1 1 Ø 1 1 1 1 1 1 1 1 1 1 1 1 1 1 1 1
 ØØØ9   ØØ3ØØØ   3131           Ø Ø 1 1 1 Ø 1 1 1 1 1 1 1 1 1 1 1 1 1 1 1 1
 ØØ1Ø   ØØ4Ø1Ø   FFFC           1 Ø Ø 1 1 1 Ø 1 1 1 1 1 1 1 1 1 1 1 1 1 1 1
 ØØ11   ØØØØ4ØØC                  MOVE.B  (AØ)+,(A1)+
 ØØ11   ØØ4ØØC   12D8           1 Ø Ø 1 1 1 Ø 1 1 1 1 1 1 1 1 1 1 1 1 1 1 1
 ØØ12   ØØ4ØØE   57C8           1 Ø Ø 1 1 1 Ø 1 1 1 1 1 1 1 1 1 1 1 1 1 1 1
 ØØ13   ØØ2ØØØ   D732           1 1 Ø 1 1 Ø 1 1 1 1 1 1 1 1 1 1 1 1 1 1 1 1
 ØØ14   ØØ3ØØØ   3232           Ø 1 Ø 1 1 Ø 1 1 1 1 1 1 1 1 1 1 1 1 1 1 1 1
 ØØ15   ØØ2ØØ2   3332           1 Ø 1 1 1 Ø 1 1 1 1 1 1 1 1 1 1 1 1 1 1 1 1
 ØØ16   ØØ3ØØ2   3333           Ø Ø 1 1 1 Ø 1 1 1 1 1 1 1 1 1 1 1 1 1 1 1 1
 ØØ17   ØØ2ØØ2   B334           1 1 Ø 1 1 Ø 1 1 1 1 1 1 1 1 1 1 1 1 1 1 1 1
 ØØ18   ØØ3ØØ2   3434           Ø 1 Ø 1 1 Ø 1 1 1 1 1 1 1 1 1 1 1 1 1 1 1 1
 ØØ19   ØØ2ØØ4   3534           1 Ø 1 1 1 Ø 1 1 1 1 1 1 1 1 1 1 1 1 1 1 1 1
 ØØ2Ø   ØØ3ØØ4   3535           Ø Ø 1 1 1 Ø 1 1 1 1 1 1 1 1 1 1 1 1 1 1 1 1
 ØØ21   ØØ2ØØ4   B536           1 1 Ø 1 1 Ø 1 1 1 1 1 1 1 1 1 1 1 1 1 1 1 1
 ØØ22   ØØ3ØØ4   3636           Ø 1 Ø 1 1 Ø 1 1 1 1 1 1 1 1 1 1 1 1 1 1 1 1
 ØØ23   ØØ2ØØ6   ØØ36           1 Ø 1 1 1 Ø 1 1 1 1 1 1 1 1 1 1 1 1 1 1 1 1
 ØØ24   ØØ3ØØ6   ØØØØ           Ø Ø 1 1 1 Ø 1 1 1 1 1 1 1 1 1 1 1 1 1 1 1 1
 ØØ25   ØØØØ4Ø12                  BRA.B   $4Ø12
E ØØ25  ØØ4Ø12   6ØFE           1 Ø Ø 1 1 1 Ø 1 1 1 1 1 1 1 1 1 1 1 1 1 1 1
 ØØ26   ØØ4Ø14   ØØØØ           1 Ø Ø 1 1 1 Ø 1 1 1 1 1 1 1 1 1 1 1 1 1 1 1
 ØØ27   ØØØØ4Ø12                  BRA.B   $4Ø12
E ØØ27  ØØ4Ø12   6ØFE           1 Ø Ø 1 1 1 Ø 1 1 1 1 1 1 1 1 1 1 1 1 1 1 1
```

(*b*)

FIGURE 16-3 (*Continued*) (b) Trace buffer contents showing cycle-by-cycle status when null (00) found.

Figure 16-3a is a printout of the DEBUG screen after the program reached the null character. The line of characters across the top of the page is the status of the emulator. The mnemonics resulting from the DASM command are shown next. Below the dotted line, the G to start the program is followed by the message "BSM TRIGGER STOPPED" and then an RD is entered to see the registers after the program has stopped. It will be seen that the Status Register Z bit is set, Address Registers A0 and A1 were only incremented 6 bytes from their starting value, and the count in D0 was only decremented to $000C.

The bottom two lines of this figure are displayed on every screen and list the commands available. The scroll commands only affect the part of the screen that is below the dotted line. In this display the top part of the screen was *frozen* by the FRZ command.

Figure 16-3b is the cycle-by-cycle trace buffer for this execution of the program where the zero value caused the routine to terminate.

Figure 16-4 shows a similar trace buffer when the program was rerun again with a MOVE.W instruction used to move the data. The interesting thing about this printout is that if you eliminate the overhead cycles in each case only half as many cycles are required to move the same number of bytes. This is because the data is being moved a word at a time (two-characters). Note that a null *word* is needed to terminate the looping.

These figures all illustrate the functions of the *loop mode operation* of the **68010** using the DBcc instruction, and shows how easily the actual performance can be analyzed with a HDS-300 development system.

Note that this DBcc instruction will not behave this way, even in a **68010**, if the branch displacement is not a minus 4, which requires that a one-word instruction precede the DBcc instruction. This is explained in detail in the **68010** Advanced Information booklet referenced in Section 16-15.

A similar program (with the count set to 20 and moving data a word at a time) was then tested using a **68000** emulator pod with different results as seen in Fig. 16-5. Note that the first instructions (up to cycle 15) execute the same in both processors but in the **68000** version, the program loops back to fetch the Op codes again after each data word is moved. The total number of cycles needed to move 6

```
Env: BDIS        As: SP   State: STOPPED  Bsm:  DISARMED  Coll: OFF  Macros: OFF

                                uds ber FC1 vpa ip2 ipØ bg  hit BRN ORG GRN
 Cycle  Address Data          R/W lds FC2 FCØ vma ipl br  bga rst RED YEL
>ØØØØ   ØØØØ4ØØØ                LEA      ($2ØØØ).W,AØ
 ØØØØ   ØØ4ØØØ   41F8         1 Ø Ø 1 1 1 Ø 1 1 1 1 1 1 1 1 1 1 1 1 1 1 1
 ØØØ1   ØØ4ØØ2   2ØØØ         1 Ø Ø 1 1 1 Ø 1 1 1 1 1 1 1 1 1 1 1 1 1 1 1
 ØØØ2   ØØØØ4ØØ4                LEA      ($3ØØØ).W,A1
 ØØØ2   ØØ4ØØ4   43F8         1 Ø Ø Ø Ø 1 Ø 1 1 1 1 1 1 1 1 1 1 1 1 1 1 1
 ØØØ3   ØØ4ØØ6   3ØØØ         1 Ø Ø Ø Ø 1 Ø 1 1 1 1 1 1 1 1 1 1 1 1 1 1 1
 ØØØ4   ØØØØ4ØØ8                MOVE.W   #$2Ø,DØ
 ØØØ4   ØØ4ØØ8   3Ø3C         1 Ø Ø Ø Ø 1 Ø 1 1 1 1 1 1 1 1 1 1 1 1 1 1 1
 ØØØ5   ØØ4ØØA   ØØ2Ø         1 Ø Ø Ø Ø 1 Ø 1 1 1 1 1 1 1 1 1 1 1 1 1 1 1
 ØØØ6   ØØØØ4ØØC                MOVE.W   (AØ)+,(A1)+
 ØØØ6   ØØ4ØØC   32D8         1 Ø Ø Ø Ø 1 Ø 1 1 1 1 1 1 1 1 1 1 1 1 1 1 1
 ØØØ7   ØØØØ4ØØE                DBEQ     DØ,$4ØØC
 ØØØ7   ØØ4ØØE   57C8         1 Ø Ø 1 1 1 Ø 1 1 1 1 1 1 1 1 1 1 1 1 1 1 1
 ØØØ8   ØØ2ØØØ   3132         1 Ø Ø 1 1 Ø 1 1 1 1 1 1 1 1 1 1 1 1 1 1 1 1
 ØØØ9   ØØ3ØØØ   3132         Ø Ø Ø 1 1 Ø 1 1 1 1 1 1 1 1 1 1 1 1 1 1 1 1
 ØØ1Ø   ØØ4Ø1Ø   FFFC         1 Ø Ø 1 1 1 Ø 1 1 1 1 1 1 1 1 1 1 1 1 1 1 1
 ØØ11   ØØØØ4ØØC                MOVE.W   (AØ)+,(A1)+
 ØØ11   ØØ4ØØC   32D8         1 Ø Ø 1 1 1 Ø 1 1 1 1 1 1 1 1 1 1 1 1 1 1 1
 ØØ12   ØØØØ4ØØE                DEBQ     DØ,$4ØØC
 ØØ12   ØØ4ØØE   57C8         1 Ø Ø 1 1 1 Ø 1 1 1 1 1 1 1 1 1 1 1 1 1 1 1
 ØØ13   ØØ2ØØ2   3334         1 Ø Ø 1 1 Ø 1 1 1 1 1 1 1 1 1 1 1 1 1 1 1 1
 ØØ14   ØØ3ØØ2   3334         Ø Ø Ø 1 1 Ø 1 1 1 1 1 1 1 1 1 1 1 1 1 1 1 1
 ØØ15   ØØ2ØØ4   3536         1 Ø Ø 1 Ø 1 1 1 1 1 1 1 1 1 1 1 1 1 1 1 1 1
 ØØ16   ØØ3ØØ4   3536         Ø Ø Ø 1 1 Ø 1 1 1 1 1 1 1 1 1 1 1 1 1 1 1 1
 ØØ17   ØØ2ØØ6   ØØØØ         1 Ø Ø 1 1 Ø 1 1 1 1 1 1 1 1 1 1 1 1 1 1 1 1
 ØØ18   ØØ2ØØ6   ØØØØ         Ø Ø Ø 1 1 Ø 1 1 1 1 1 1 1 1 1 1 1 1 1 1 1 1
 ØØ19   ØØØØ4Ø12                BRA.B    $4Ø12
E ØØ19  ØØ4Ø12   6ØFE         1 Ø Ø 1 1 1 Ø 1 1 1 1 1 1 1 1 1 1 1 1 1 1 1
 ØØ2Ø   ØØØØ4Ø14                DIVS     (AØ),D2
 ØØ2Ø   ØØ4Ø14   85DØ         1 Ø Ø 1 1 1 Ø 1 1 1 1 1 1 1 1 1 1 1 1 1 1 1
 ØØ21   ØØØØ4Ø12                BRA.B    $4Ø12
E ØØ21  ØØ4Ø12   6ØFE         1 Ø Ø 1 1 1 Ø 1 1 1 1 1 1 1 1 1 1 1 1 1 1 1
 ØØ22   ØØØØ4Ø14                DIVS     (AØ),D2
```

FIGURE 16-4 HDS-300 display printout for a program using word-sized data.

```
Env: BDIS       As: SP   State: STOPPED  Bsm:  DISARMED  Coll: OFF  Macros: OFF

                              uds ber FC1 vpa ip2 ipØ bg  hit BRN ORG GRN
 Cycle  Address Data       R/W lds FC2 FCØ vma ip1 br  bga rst RED YEL
 >ØØØØ  ØØØØ4ØØØ              LEA       ($2ØØØ).W,AØ
  ØØØØ  ØØ4ØØØ   41F8     1 Ø Ø 1 1 1 Ø 1 1 1 1 1 1 1 1 1 1 1 1 1 1 1
  ØØØ1  ØØ4ØØ2   2ØØØ     1 Ø Ø 1 1 1 Ø 1 1 1 1 1 1 1 1 1 1 1 1 1 1 1
  ØØØ2  ØØØØ4ØØ4              LEA       ($3ØØØ).W,A1
  ØØØ2  ØØ4ØØ4   43F8     1 Ø Ø Ø Ø 1 Ø 1 1 1 1 1 1 1 1 1 1 1 1 1 1 1
  ØØØ3  ØØ4ØØ6   3ØØØ     1 Ø Ø Ø Ø 1 Ø 1 1 1 1 1 1 1 1 1 1 1 1 1 1 1
  ØØØ4  ØØØØ4ØØ8              MOVE.W   #$2Ø,DØ
  ØØØ4  ØØ4ØØ8   3Ø3C     1 Ø Ø Ø Ø 1 Ø 1 1 1 1 1 1 1 1 1 1 1 1 1 1 1
  ØØØ5  ØØ4ØØA   ØØ2Ø     1 Ø Ø Ø Ø 1 Ø 1 1 1 1 1 1 1 1 1 1 1 1 1 1 1
  ØØØ6  ØØØØ4ØØC              MOVE.W   (AØ)+,(A1)+
  ØØØ6  ØØ4ØØC   32D8     1 Ø Ø Ø Ø 1 Ø 1 1 1 1 1 1 1 1 1 1 1 1 1 1 1
  ØØØ7  ØØØØ4ØØE              DBEQ      DØ,$4ØØC
  ØØØ7  ØØ4ØØE   57C8     1 Ø Ø 1 1 1 Ø 1 1 1 1 1 1 1 1 1 1 1 1 1 1 1
  ØØØ8  ØØ2ØØØ   3132     1 Ø Ø 1 1 Ø 1 1 1 1 1 1 1 1 1 1 1 1 1 1 1 1
  ØØØ9  ØØ3ØØØ   3132     Ø Ø Ø 1 1 Ø 1 1 1 1 1 1 1 1 1 1 1 1 1 1 1 1
  ØØ1Ø  ØØ4Ø1Ø   FFFC     1 Ø Ø 1 1 1 Ø 1 1 1 1 1 1 1 1 1 1 1 1 1 1 1
  ØØ11  ØØØØ4ØØC              MOVE.W   (AØ)+,(A1)+
  ØØ11  ØØ4ØØC   32D8     1 Ø Ø 1 1 1 Ø 1 1 1 1 1 1 1 1 1 1 1 1 1 1 1
  ØØ12  ØØØØ4ØØE              DEBQ      DØ,$4ØØC
  ØØ12  ØØ4ØØE   57C8     1 Ø Ø 1 1 1 Ø 1 1 1 1 1 1 1 1 1 1 1 1 1 1 1
  ØØ13  ØØ2ØØ2   3334     1 Ø Ø 1 1 Ø 1 1 1 1 1 1 1 1 1 1 1 1 1 1 1 1
  ØØ14  ØØ3ØØ2   3334     Ø Ø Ø 1 1 Ø 1 1 1 1 1 1 1 1 1 1 1 1 1 1 1 1
  ØØ15  ØØ4Ø1Ø   FFFC     1 1 Ø Ø 1 1 1 Ø 1 1 1 1 1 1 1 1 1 1 1 1 1 1
  ØØ16  ØØØØ4ØØC              MOVE.W   (AØ)+,(A1)+
  ØØ16  ØØ4ØØC   32D8     1 Ø Ø 1 1 Ø 1 1 1 1 1 1 1 1 1 1 1 1 1 1 1 1
  ØØ17  ØØØØ4ØØE              DBEQ      DØ,$4ØØC
  ØØ17  ØØ4ØØE   57C8     1 Ø Ø 1 1 1 Ø 1 1 1 1 1 1 1 1 1 1 1 1 1 1 1
  ØØ18  ØØ2ØØ4   3536     1 Ø Ø 1 1 Ø 1 1 1 1 1 1 1 1 1 1 1 1 1 1 1 1
  ØØ19  ØØ3ØØ4   3536     Ø Ø Ø 1 1 Ø 1 1 1 1 1 1 1 1 1 1 1 1 1 1 1 1
  ØØ2Ø  ØØ4Ø1Ø   FFFC     1 Ø Ø 1 1 1 Ø 1 1 1 1 1 1 1 1 1 1 1 1 1 1 1
  ØØ21  ØØØØ4ØØC              MOVE.W   (AØ)+,(A1)+
  ØØ21  ØØ4ØØC   32D8     1 Ø Ø 1 1 1 Ø 1 1 1 1 1 1 1 1 1 1 1 1 1 1 1
  ØØ22  ØØØØ4ØØE              DBEQ      DØ,$4ØØC
  ØØ22  ØØ4ØØE   57C8     1 Ø Ø 1 1 1 Ø 1 1 1 1 1 1 1 1 1 1 1 1 1 1 1
  ØØ23  ØØ2ØØ6   ØØØØ     1 Ø Ø 1 1 Ø 1 1 1 1 1 1 1 1 1 1 1 1 1 1 1 1
  ØØ24  ØØ3ØØ6   ØØØØ     Ø Ø Ø 1 1 Ø 1 1 1 1 1 1 1 1 1 1 1 1 1 1 1 1
  ØØ25  ØØ4Ø1Ø   FFFC     1 Ø Ø 1 1 1 Ø 1 1 1 1 1 1 1 1 1 1 1 1 1 1 1
  ØØ26  ØØØØ4Ø12              BRA.B     $4Ø12
E ØØ26  ØØ4Ø12   6ØFE     1 Ø Ø 1 1 1 Ø 1 1 1 1 1 1 1 1 1 1 1 1 1 1 1
  ØØ27  ØØØØ4Ø14              ABCD      -(A2),-(A2)
  ØØ27  ØØ4Ø14   C5ØA     1 Ø Ø 1 1 1 Ø 1 1 1 1 1 1 1 1 1 1 1 1 1 1 1
  ØØ28  ØØØØ4Ø12              BRA.B     $4Ø12
E ØØ28  ØØ4Ø12   6ØFE     1 Ø Ø 1 1 1 Ø 1 1 1 1 1 1 1 1 1 1 1 1 1 1 1
  ØØ29  ØØØØ4Ø14              ABCD      -(A2),-(A2)
  ØØ29  ØØ4Ø14   C5ØA     1 Ø Ø 1 1 1 Ø 1 1 1 1 1 1 1 1 1 1 1 1 1 1 1
  ØØ3Ø  ØØØØ4Ø12              BRA.B     $4Ø12
E ØØ3Ø  ØØ4Ø12   6ØFE     1 Ø Ø 1 1 1 Ø 1 1 1 1 1 1 1 1 1 1 1 1 1 1 1
  ØØ31  ØØØØ4Ø14              ABCD      -(A2),-(A2)
  ØØ31  ØØ4Ø14   C5ØA     1 Ø Ø 1 1 1 Ø 1 1 1 1 1 1 1 1 1 1 1 1 1 1 1
  ØØ32  ØØØØ4Ø12              BRA.B     $4Ø12
E ØØ32  ØØ4Ø12   6ØFE     1 Ø Ø 1 1 1 Ø 1 1 1 1 1 1 1 1 1 1 1 1 1 1 1
  ØØ33  ØØØØ4Ø14              ABCD      -(A2),-(A2)
```

FIGURE 16-5 BDIS display printout for a similar program but using the **68000** μp.

characters in this case is 25 instead of the 18 used by the **68010**. Running the same program in a **68008** μP can be shown to require 51 cycles, which makes it almost 3 times as slow as the **68010**. If the program was allowed to move the full 32 bytes (no zero bytes), the differences would be even more dramatic.

16-6.2 The 68010 Exception Stack Frame

Exception processing was described in Section 15-12. One of the steps in this procedure is to save the *current* processor state, called the *context*, in the form of register contents, on the top of the supervisor stack. This context is organized in a format called the *exception stack frame*. The information in this frame varies with the type of exception and in the **68000** is three words in length as shown in Fig. 16-6a. It contains the Status Register contents (one word) and the Program Counter values (two words) that existed when the exception occurred.

One of the features added to the **68010** to provide for virtual memory was the use of a *long* and a *short* format in saving the *Exception Stack Frame*.

As shown in Fig. 16-6b, the short format for the **68010** contains four words. The added word includes a 4-bit field to define the format and the *vector offset* for the exception being processed.

The long format was needed to allow *instruction continuation*, which is used to recover from a *page fault* (see Section 16-5.1). When a long format exception occurs during a Bus Error, 29 words are actually written to the stack, although only 26 are used. Figure 16-7 shows the makeup of the long format Exception Stack Frame. The additional information describes the internal state of the processor at the time of the bus error.

The value of the saved program counter does not necessarily point to the instruction that was executing when the bus error occurred, but may be up to five words later. This is due to the prefetch mechanism in the **68010**, which always fetches a new instruction word as each previously fetched instruction word is used. Enough information is placed on the stack for the bus error exception handler routine to determine why the bus fault occurred. This additional information includes the address that was being accessed, the Function Codes for the access, whether it was a READ or a $\overline{\text{WRITE}}$, and what internal register was included in the transfer. The fault address can be used by an operating system to

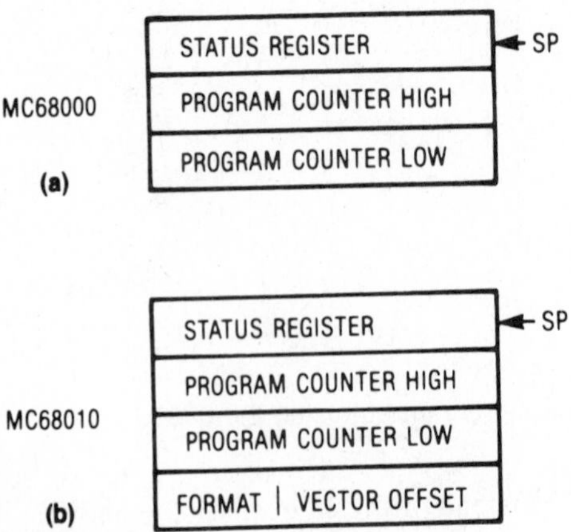

FIGURE 16-6 Exception stack frame. (a) of the **68000**. (b) short format of the **68010**.

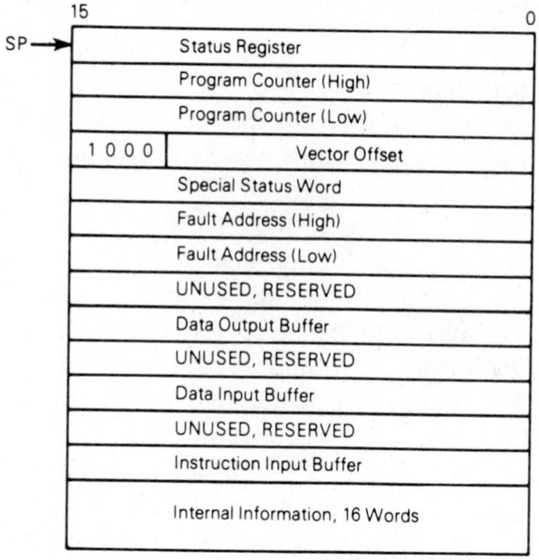

	15		0
SP→	Status Register		
	Program Counter (High)		
	Program Counter (Low)		
	1 0 0 0	Vector Offset	
	Special Status Word		
	Fault Address (High)		
	Fault Address (Low)		
	UNUSED, RESERVED		
	Data Output Buffer		
	UNUSED, RESERVED		
	Data Input Buffer		
	UNUSED, RESERVED		
	Instruction Input Buffer		
	Internal Information, 16 Words		

NOTE: The stack pointer is decremented by 29 words, although only 26 words of information are actually written to memory. The three additional words are reserved for future use by Motorola.

FIGURE 16-7 68010 Exception stack frame (long format) for a bus and address error.

determine what virtual memory location is needed so that the requested data can be brought into physical memory. The RTE instruction is then used to reload the processor's internal state at the time of the fault; the faulted bus cycle will then be rerun and the suspended instruction completed. If the faulted bus cycle was a read-modify-write, the entire cycle will be rerun whether the fault occurred during the read or the write operation.

In the **68010** there are only two valid stack formats: 0000 for the normal four-word format and 1000 for the long format. Additional format words are reserved for future use. Any other formats are identified as illegal by the **68010** and cause a *format error* exception.

16-6.3 The Return from Exception Instruction

The use of two formats when data is saved on the stack means that the ReTurn from Exception (RTE) instruction had to be expanded for the **68010** so that the type of exception associated with the Stack Frame could be determined and the appropriate action taken.

The execution of the RTE on the **68010** occurs as follows. The processor reads the Status Register, Program Counter, and stack format into the machine. The format bits are then evaluated. If the short stack format is present, the information needed for the return is resident in the machine and normal processing resumes at the address indicated by the restored Program Counter. If the long stack format is present, the remaining words of the processor state information must be read from the stack and restored to the appropriate location before execution can continue in the main program at the point of the exception.

16-7 THE 68020 MICROPROCESSOR

The **68020** μP was introduced in 1984. It retains all the features of the **68000** and **68010**, except that it does not have the special pins (signal lines) for support of 8-bit peripherals. It has several significant new features such as an on-chip cache memory and a coprocessor interface. The **68020** is the first full 32-bit implementation of a μP for the **68000** family with true 32-bit Address and Data Buses. The Arithmetic Logic Unit (ALU) and all internal data paths are also 32 bits wide. The functional groups of lines that make up the bus interface are shown in Fig. 16-8. The **68020** has a Pin Grid Array package (see Fig. 16-9) with 110 pins. The pinouts are identified in the **68020** *User's Manual* cited in Section 16-15.

The **68020** is compatible with the **68000** and **68010** in that their User mode instructions are exactly the same. (It will execute **68000** or **68010** programs.) Three new concepts that enhance the **68020**'s performance dramatically are the *instruction cache,* the *coprocessor interface,* and *pipelining*. They are explained in later paragraphs. An additional Stack Pointer (Master Stack Pointer) and two new registers for the *cache* have been added. Many new instructions are included and some are upgraded for 32-bit operation. New addressing modes and data types are also provided.

16-8 CACHE MEMORY CONCEPTS

The **68020** incorporates an on-chip **cache memory** as a means of improving the performance of the processor. This is a block of 64 long words of high-speed memory that is used to hold a small segment of a program within the μP so that instructions can be more quickly accessed. Studies have shown that typical programs spend most of their time in main routines or program loops. Therefore, once a program segment is loaded into the high-speed cache memory, many instructions can be executed without accessing the external memory. Thus the processor does not suffer many external memory delays, and the total program execution time is significantly improved.

Another major benefit of using the cache is that the processor's external bus activity is greatly reduced. Thus, in a system with more than one master (such as a processor and DMA device) or a tightly coupled multiprocessor system, more of the bus time is available to the alternate bus masters without a major degradation in the performance of the system.

16-8.1 Cache Organization

Figure 16-10 shows a diagram of the **68020** on-chip cache. Each cache entry consists of a **tag field** made up of the upper 24 address bits and the FC2 bit, 32 bits (two words) of instruction data, and 1 *valid* bit. The valid bit is set whenever new data is fetched from memory and written into a cache entry. It is cleared or reset by actions of the Clear Entry or Clear Cache bits, as explained in the following sections.

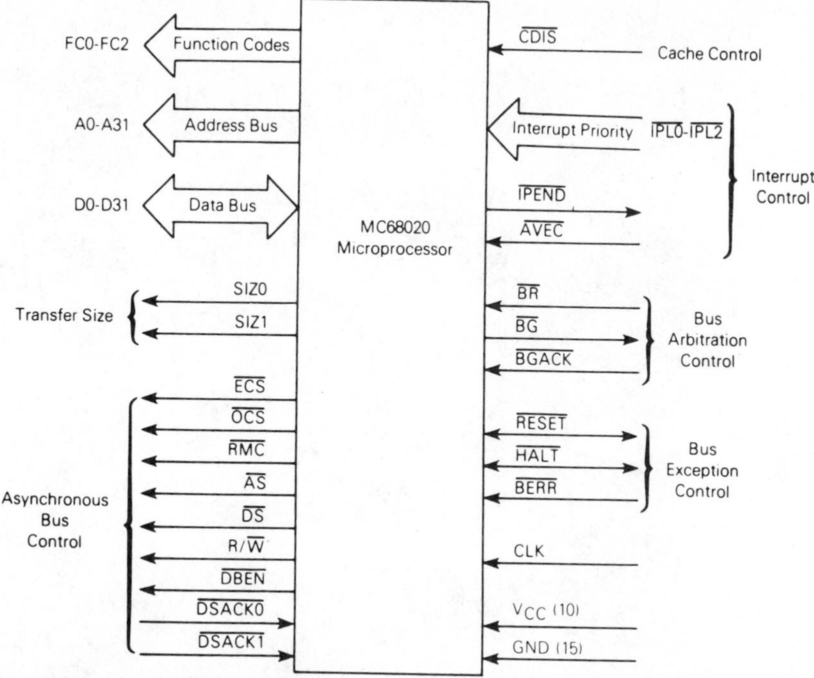

FIGURE 16-8 **68020** bus interface.

The cached instructions and associated data are accessible only by the internal **68020** control unit. The user has no direct way to read or write individual entries (e.g., tag, instructions, or *valid* bits); however, this data can be manipulated by a set of control functions available in a *Cache Control Register* (CACR).

16-8.2 Cache Control Register

The CACR is a 32-bit register that is organized as shown in Fig. 16-11. The unused bits from 8 to 31 (which are not shown) are always read as zeros. Before the operation of the cache can be understood, it is necessary to define the function of the bits in this register. Access to the CACR is provided by means of the privileged instruction *Move Control Register (MOVEC)*. The bits are defined as follows.

16-8.3 Enable Cache

The *cache enable* bit is necessary to permit *system debug and emulation*. This bit allows the designer to operate the processor with the cache disabled. Clearing this bit will disable the cache (force continuous misses and suppress fills) and force the processor always to access external memory. The cache will remain disabled as long as this bit is not set. The user must set this bit, which is automatically cleared whenever the processor is reset, to enable the cache.

FIGURE 16-9 The **68020** μP.

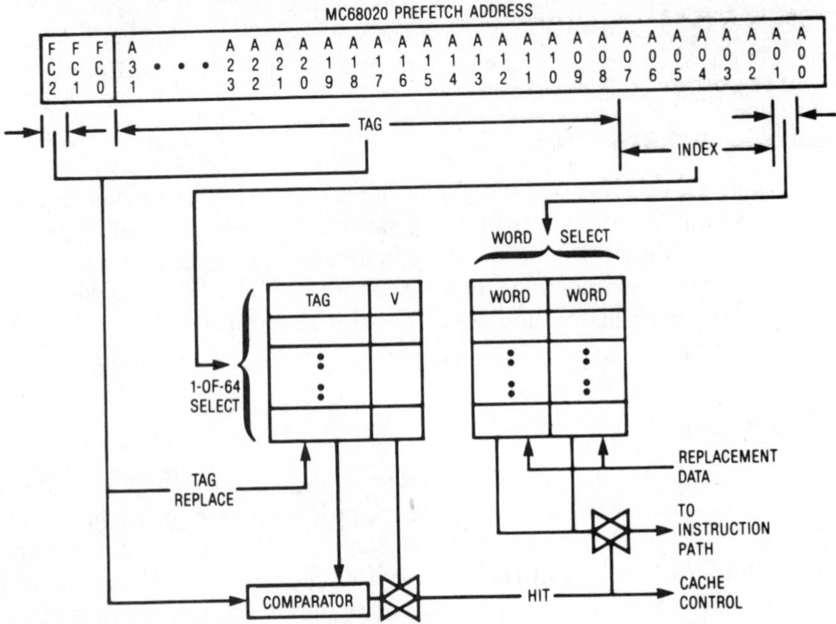

FIGURE 16-10 **68020** on-chip cache.

31	8	7							0
0	0	0	0	0	0	C	CE	F	E

C = Clear Cache
CE = Clear Entry
F = Freeze Cache
E = Enable Cache

FIGURE 16-11 The **68020** cache control register.

16-8.4 Freeze Cache

The *freeze bit* keeps the cache enabled, but cache *misses* are not allowed to replace valid cache data. This bit can be used by emulators to freeze the cache during emulation function execution.

16-8.5 Cache Address Register

The CAche Address Register (CAAR) is a 32-bit register that provides an address for cache control functions (see Fig. 16-12). The **68020** uses this register only for the Clear Entry (CE) function. Access to the CAAR is provided by the MOVEC instruction.

16-8.6 Clear Entry

When the Clear Entry bit is set, the processor takes the address (index field, bits 2–7) in the CAAR and invalidates the associated entry (clears the valid bit) in the cache, regardless of whether it provides a *hit,* that is, whether the tag field in the cache address register matches the cache tag or not. This function will occur only when a WRITE to the cache control register is performed with the CE bit set. This bit always reads as a zero, and the operation is independent of the state of the E or F bits or the external Cache Disable ($\overline{\text{CDIS}}$) pin.

16-8.7 Clear Cache

The *clear cache* bit is used to invalidate all entries in the cache. This function is necessary for operating systems and other software that must clear old data from the cache whenever a context switch is required. The setting of the clear cache bit in the cache control register causes all *valid* bits in the cache to be cleared, thus invalidating all entries. This function occurs only when a WRITE to the CACR is performed with the C bit set. This bit always reads as a zero.

16-8.8 Cache Disable Input

The *cache disable input* is used to dynamically disable the cache. The input signal on this pin is synchronized before being used, to control the internal cache. The

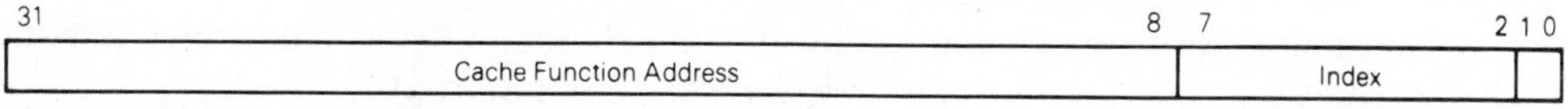

31 … 8	7 … 2	1 0
Cache Function Address	Index	

FIGURE 16-12 The **68020** cache address register.

cache is disabled on the first cache access after the synchronized $\overline{\text{CDIS}}$ signal is recognized as being asserted. The cache will be reenabled on the first cache access after the synchronized $\overline{\text{CDIS}}$ signal is recognized as being negated. This pin disables the cache independent of the enable bit in the CACR and therefore can be used by external emulator hardware to force the **68020** to make all accesses via the external bus.

16-8.9 Cache Functions

During processor reset, the cache is cleared by resetting all the *valid* bits. The CACR, enable (E), and Freeze (F) bits are also cleared.

Whenever an instruction fetch occurs, the *index field* (bits A2–A7) from the μP's program counter selects which of the 64 long words of the cache is being addressed. The other address bits (A8–A31) and Function Code 2 (FC2) are then compared to the *tag bits* and FC2 bit of the selected entry. If there is a match and the *valid* bit is set, a **cache hit** occurs. (The **valid bit** is set whenever a new entry has been placed in the cache.) The instruction that has just been found is then read into the instruction register, using address bit A1 to select the proper instruction word from the two-word cache entry, and the cycle ends.

If there is no match or the valid bit is clear, a **cache miss** occurs and the instruction is fetched from external memory. This new instruction is automatically written into the cache entry and the *valid* bit is set, unless the *freeze cache bit* has been set. (The freeze cache bit keeps the cache enabled, but cache *misses* are not allowed to replace valid cache data.)

The cache can also be inhibited by the enable bit of the CACR *or* by the disable pin on the μP. The cache disable input is used to dynamically disable the cache. This pin disables the cache independent of the enable bit and therefore can be used by external emulator hardware to force the **68020** to make all accesses from the external memory.

Since the processor always prefetches instructions externally with long word aligned bus cycles, both words of the entry will be updated, regardless of which word caused the miss.

16-9 COPROCESSOR CONCEPTS

A *coprocessor* is a special-purpose processor that is used *in conjunction* with the main processor to provide added capabilities. Coprocessors generally execute special-purpose instructions that are not recognized by the main processor. A math coprocessor such as the **68881** (see Section 16-9.1), for example, performs the mathematical functions of floating-point multiply and divide and includes a full set of trigonometric and transcendental functions. It uses an 80-bit word, which makes it highly accurate. The main **68020** processor could also provide these functions through subroutines, but it would take much longer to do them. Thus, in a system requiring much mathematical manipulation (number-crunching), a math coprocessor is very effective in reducing execution times.

The **68000** family of general-purpose μPs provides a level of performance that satisfies a wide range of computer applications. The coprocessor concept allows the capabilities and performance of a general-purpose processor to be enhanced for a particular application without unduly encumbering the main processor architecture. Coprocessors with different features can be designed and can be used separately or in combination. These features must typically be implemented in software when only a general-purpose processor is provided. Thus, the processing capabilities of a system can be tailored to a specific application by utilizing a general-purpose main processor and the appropriate coprocessor(s).

The interactions between the main processor and the coprocessor that are necessary for the coprocessor to provide a given service are transparent to the programmer in the case of the **68020**. No knowledge of the communication protocol between the main processor and the coprocessor is required of the programmer, since this protocol is implemented in the **68020** hardware. Thus, the coprocessor can provide capabilities to the user without appearing as hardware external to the main processor.

In contrast, standard peripheral hardware is generally accessed through the use of interface registers mapped into the memory space of the main processor. When coprocessors are used with the **68000** or **68010**, they function in this way. In this case, the programmer must use standard processor instructions to access the peripheral or coprocessor interface registers and thus utilize services provided by that device. While these units can conceivably provide capabilities equivalent to those of the built-in coprocessor interface for many applications, the programmer must provide the communication protocol between the main processor and the external hardware.

The coprocessor must be interfaced to the main processor so that the special instructions fetched can be communicated to the coprocessor. This **68000** family **coprocessor interface** is an integral part of the design of the **68020** and the various coprocessors. Coprocessors such as the **68881** Math Coprocessor or the **68851** MMU can be used. Each processor in a system has an instruction set that reflects its special function, whether it be floating-point math, memory management, or another unique purpose.

These special coprocessor instructions may be executed merely by placing the instruction Op code and parameters in the **68020** instruction stream. The **68020** detects the coprocessor instruction, initiates bus communication with the registers of the target coprocessor to pass the instruction, and tests for conditions requiring further action. The **68020** performs activity to support the execution of the instruction (e.g., address calculation or data transfer) at the request of the coprocessor.

The interchange of information and the division of responsibility between the main processor and the coprocessor are controlled by the coprocessor interface, and this process is completely transparent to the user. The addition of a coprocessing unit to a **68020** system supplements the instruction set executable by the processor. The register set of the coprocessor is perceived by system programmers to be a direct extension of the main processor registers.

16-9.1 The 68881 Floating-Point Coprocessor

The **68881** Floating-Point Coprocessor implements the IEEE Standard for Binary Floating-Point Arithmetic (P754) for use with the **68000** family of μPs. It uses Very Large-Scale Integration (VLSI) technology to provide remarkable performance in a physically small device.

Intended primarily for use as a coprocessor to the **68020**, the **68881** provides a logical extension of the main μP's integer data processing capabilities. It does so by providing a very high performance floating-point arithmetic unit and a set of floating-point data registers that are utilized in a manner analogous to the use of the integer data registers. The **68881** can be interfaced to the **68020** via a 32-, 16-, or 8-bit data bus configuration. These bus size differences are controlled by the connections to the A0 and SIZE pins of the **68881**. Diagrams are shown in the **68881** *Coprocessor User's Manual* cited in Section 16-15.

The **68881** instruction set is fully upward-compatible with all earlier members of the **68000** family and supports all of the addressing modes of the host μP. Because of the flexible bus interface of the **68000** family, the **68881** can be used with any of the μP devices of the family, such as the **68000**, **68008**, **68010**, or **68012**. In these cases the **68881** is connected as a peripheral via a 16- or 8-bit data bus, as shown in the User's Manual referred to above. It may also be used as a peripheral to non-**68000** processors.

The major features of the **68881** are

- Eight general-purpose floating-point data registers, each supporting a full 80-bit extended-precision real data format (a 64 bit mantissa plus a sign bit, and a 15-bit biased exponent).
- A 67-Bit ALU to allow very fast calculations, with intermediate precision greater than the extended precision result.
- A 67-bit **Barrel Shifter** for high-speed shifting operations (for normalizing).
- 46 instruction types, including 35 arithmetic operations.
- Full conformity with the IEEE P754 Standard (Draft 10.0), including all requirements and suggestions.
- Support functions not defined by the IEEE Standard, including a full set of trigonometric and logarithmic functions.
- Support of seven data types:
  - Byte, word, and long integers.
  - Single, double, and extended-precision real numbers.
  - Packed Binary Coded Decimal (BCD) string real numbers.
- Support of virtual memory/machine operations.
- Efficient mechanisms for procedure calls, context switches, and interrupt handling.
- Fully concurrent instruction execution with the main processor.
- Compatibility with any host processor on an 8-, 16-, and 32-bit data bus.

16-9.2 The 68882 Enhanced Floating-Point Coprocessor

The **68882** *enhanced* floating-point coprocessor was introduced in September 1986. It is pin-compatible with the **68881**, offers the same strict conformity to the IEEE 704 specification, and is software-compatible. The **68882** has a superior internal architecture that provides more concurrent operations. By simply removing a **68881** and replacing it with the **68882**, a 50% performance increase is obtained.

For designs that optimize the software, up to twofold improvement is possible. From the standpoint of applications software, the **68882** and the **68881** are functionally identical, right down to the results that are generated by calculations. The instruction set is also the same.

16-10 THE 68851 PAGED MEMORY MANAGEMENT UNIT

Another HCMOS coprocessor introduced in 1986 is the **68851** *Paged Memory Management Unit* (PMMU). It is a high-performance VLSI IC designed to efficiently support the **68020** 32-bit μP. The **68851** is optimized to perform very fast *logical-to-physical address translation,* to provide a comprehensive access control and protection mechanism for the installed memory, and to provide extensive support for *paged virtual systems.*

The **68851** functions as a coprocessor in systems where the **68020** is the main processor via the coprocessor interface. It can function as a peripheral in systems where the main processor is a **68010**, **68012**, or any other processor with virtual memory capabilities.

A powerful and complete memory management system is ensured by using the following **68851** features:

- 32-bit logical and physical addresses and 4 Function Code bits.
- Eight available page sizes from 256 bytes to 32K bytes.
- Fully associative 64 entry on-chip Address Translation Cache.
- Address Translation Cache support for Multitasking.
- Hardware maintenance of External Translation Tables and On-Chip Cache.
- **68020** Instruction set extension and instruction-oriented communication using the **68000** Family Coprocessor Interface.
- Hierarchical Protection Mechanism with up to eight Levels of protection.
- Instruction breakpoints for software debug and program control.
- Support for a logical and/or a physical data cache.
- Support for multiple logical and/or physical bus masters.

The primary system functions provided by the **68851** are logical-to-physical address translating (described in Section 16-5.3), implementing the protection/privilege mechanism, and supporting the breakpoint operations.

16-10.1 PMMU Protection Mechanism

The **68851** PMMU provides facilities to protect address spaces from access by the wrong user. This protects the supervisor from user tasks, user tasks from each other, and user tasks from themselves.

The **68851** also has two protection mechanisms that can be used either independently or together to provide a comprehensive memory protection scheme. The primary mechanism uses the Function Code outputs of the logical bus master to define address space based on the current operating mode of the master (Supervisor or User) and the type of operand (program or data) being accessed. The more comprehensive protection method subdivides the logical address space of user mode tasks into regions of privilege.

The **68851** completely supports the **68020** module call return functions (CALLM/RTM instructions), which include a mechanism for changing privilege levels during module operations. Details can be obtained in the *68851 PMMU User's Manual* cited in Section 16-15.

16-10.2 PMMU Instruction Set Extensions

The **68851** implements an extension of the **68000** μP family instruction set using the coprocessor interface. These added instructions provide control functions for

- Loading and storing MMU registers.
- Testing access rights and conditionals based on the results of this test.
- MMU control functions.

There are 16 additional instructions provided for the **68851**. Since we are limited in space, the reader is again referred to the *68851 User's Manual* cited in Section 16-15 for complete descriptions.

16-11 PIPELINED ARCHITECTURE

The concept of **Pipelined Architecture** inside a μP is not new. Internal connections that *pipe* the data directly to a register or part of the μP control unit where they can be processed at the same time as other data are the basis of the concept. The **6800** μP had the ability to fetch a new instruction while processing the previous one in the instruction decoder. It was not called pipelining at that time, but now that the idea is being expanded on, the name seems more descriptive. The **68020** has several pipeline mechanisms, but the primary one is a *three-stage instruction pipe* as shown in Fig. 16-13. Instructions are loaded from the on-chip cache or from external memory into stage B. The instructions are sequenced from stage B through stage C to D. Stage D presents a fully decoded and validated instruction to the control unit for execution. Instructions with *immediate data* or *extension words* will find these words already loaded in stage C, thus speeding up the execution.

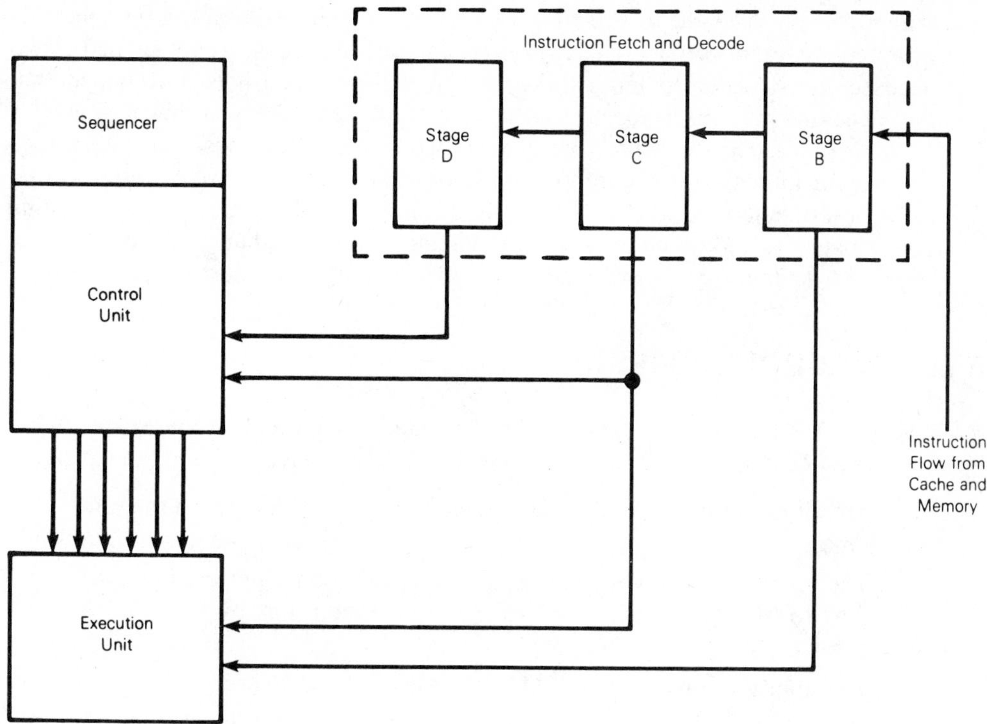

FIGURE 16-13 68020 pipeline.

The benefit of the pipeline is that it allows concurrent operations on up to three words at a time. They could be all part of the same instruction or could be three separate consecutive instructions. This technique is most efficient when dealing with instructions in normal program sequence. Since two short instructions can be processed concurrently even though they were fetched sequentially, it gives rise to the statement that some instructions are processed in *zero* time. When a change-of-flow instruction (i.e., a branch) occurs, however, the words following a jump or branch are fetched but must be ignored. Another three words must be fetched before processing can continue.

The depth of the instruction pipe was increased from two to three words on the **68020**, since it was observed that there is no performance penalty for the third element during a change-of-flow instruction on a 32-bit bus. This is true because it is always possible to fetch three words in two accesses. Because of the possibility of branching to an odd-word address, in which case two accesses are required to fetch either two or three words, the minimum number of accesses required to branch is two. A demonstration of the stubborn consistency of this principle is given by Fig. 16-14, which depicts two memory configurations for the instruction stream A, B, C, D, E. (These can be separate one-word instructions, five words of a single instruction, or, more likely, a mixture of one- and two-word instructions.)

If a branch is made to the first example (even aligned), only one access is required to fetch two words. However, in the other case (odd aligned), two accesses must occur to fetch the first two words. Once it is determined that two accesses must be made to fill the pipe, it can be observed that it is always possible to fetch the first three words with two memory accesses. Thus there is no penalty for increasing the depth of the instruction pipe from two to three words.

As described above, the greater depth of the instruction pipe, while improving performance of in-line code, has a detrimental effect on change-of-flow instructions. By using a three-word pipe, the **68020** optimizes the performance.

16-12 THE 68030 MICROPROCESSOR

The **68030** is a still newer, more powerful, and faster μP than the **68020**. It has many new features. Features of the **68030** over and above those in the **68020** are

- More internal buses so that address and data can be fetched at the same time.
- The *on-chip* PMMU, which reduces the minimum physical bus cycle time to two cycles and provides *zero* translation time by virtue of the parallel pipelining.
- The ability to enable or disable the PMMU by software.
- A 256-byte instruction cache and a 256-byte data cache that can be accessed simultaneously.
- An on-chip MMU that translates addresses in parallel with instruction execution.
- Two transparent segments that allow untranslated blocks to be defined for systems that transfer large blocks of data to predefined addresses, as in graphics applications.
- Pipelined architecture with increased parallelism that allows accesses from internal caches to occur in parallel with bus transfers and multiple instructions to be executed concurrently.
- An enhanced Bus Controller that supports asynhronous bus cycles, synchronous bus cycles that can operate in two clocks, and burst data transfers that can operate in one clock, all with physical addresses.

The functional signal groups of the **68030** bus interface can be seen in the diagram of Fig. 16-15.

EVEN ALIGNED

$00	A	B
$04	C	D
$08	E	

ODD ALIGNED

$00		A
$04	B	C
$08	D	E

FIGURE 16-14 Two memory configurations for the instruction stream A, B, C, D, E.

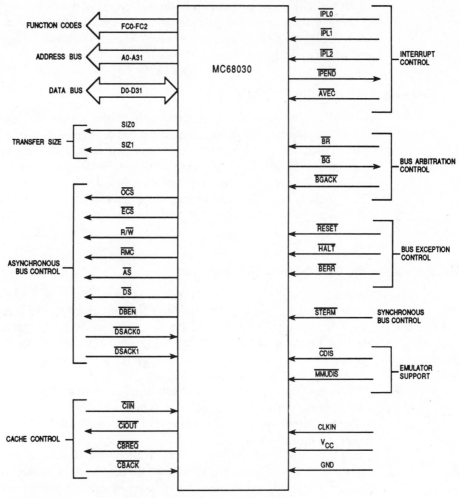

FIGURE 16-15 **68030** bus interface showing functional signal groups.

16-12.1 On-Chip Instruction and Data Caches

The **68030** is the first 32-bit μP to offer both an on-chip **instruction cache** and a **data cache**. A block diagram is shown in Fig. 16-16. Caches (high-speed temporary storage) are used to increase the performance by providing immediate access to instructions and data for the CPU execution unit. The two 256-byte on-chip caches serve to boost the data flow to the CPU, typically a major performance bottleneck, to enhance overall throughput. Operating from the caches not only reduces access times but also reduces the overall bus requirements since the μP spends less time on the bus accessing data. Bus access time is reduced further by the *burst-fillable cache mode,* which allows high-speed data fills of both the data and instruction caches. These features increase bus availability for other bus masters, including multiprocessor systems, Local Area Networks (LANs), and disks. Simulation studies on 17 million bus cycles of data captured from engineering workstations indicated that the combination of a 256-byte instruction cache and a 256-byte data cache is optimum when evaluating silicon die size, and performance increases.

16-12.2 On-Chip Harvard-Style Architecture

Harvard-style architecture has been used for many years in several super-computers and mainframe computers allowing parallel access of data and instructions. Two independent 32-bit address buses and two 32-bit data buses allow the CPU, caches, PMMU, and bus controller to operate in parallel. These parallel instruction and data paths give the processor an internal *bus bandwidth* of more than 80 Mbytes per second. The **68030** can simultaneously access an instruction from the instruction cache, data from the data cache, and instructions or data from external memory.

16-12.3 Dynamically Configurable Bus Interface

The **68030** is suitable for many types of systems from low-end ($2000–$3000) to high-performance (>$50,000) systems, with much of the difference due to the choice of memory configuration. Low-end systems typically interface directly to low-cost Dynamic RAM (DRAM) using only the internal caches, while high-performance systems use a multilevel hierarchy of memory that range from high-speed static to slow dynamic RAMs.

To support these features, the **68030** supports both a synchronous bus interface (with a minimum two-clock access), which allows maximum access time to a cache subsystem, and an asynchronous interface (such as that on the **68020**) for slower memories, peripherals, and other **68020**-compatible subsystems. This interface supports synchronous or asynchronous access on a cycle-by-cycle basis as determined by the memory subsystem used. As in the **68020**, compatibility is maintained by supporting the existing asynchronous dynamic bus sizing feature, which allows interfaces to 8-, 16-, or 32-bit devices.

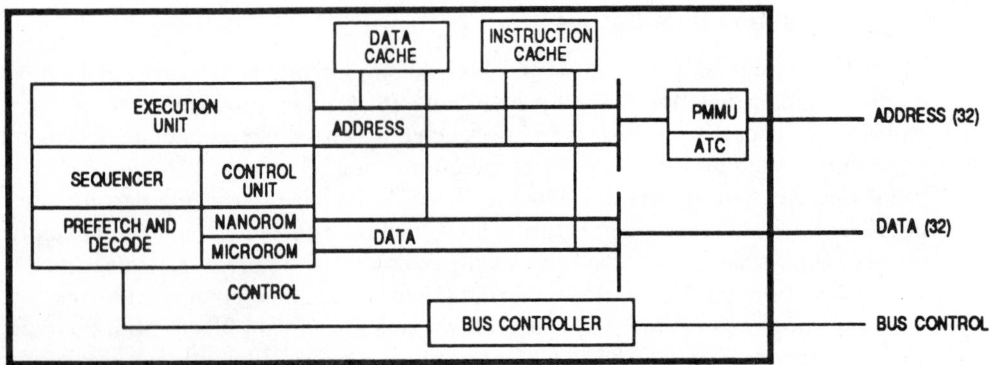

FIGURE 16-16 **68030** block diagram.

In addition, this bus interface offers the low-end system designer increased performance by taking advantage of the shorter access times offered by the paged mode, nibble mode, static column DRAM technology. Here, the **68030** can request a burst fill to the internal caches. Since data in the cache is organized in rows of four long words, up to three additional long words may be loaded during the access. The **68030** will request a burst fill and the system can then, in as little as one clock per subsequent access, supply the **68030** with the successive data obtained from the memory.

16-12.4 Summary of 68030 Performance Enhancements

The **68030**'s gains in performance are made possible by including the function of memory management on-chip and using a Harvard-style architecture (parallel address and data bus accesses). The relative performance increases of the **68030** over prior devices can be seen in Fig. 16-17. The dual bus structure offers 80 Mbytes of bandwidth and allows the MMU to be efficiently integrated on-chip. In doing this, the time to translate logical addresses to physical addresses can be hidden during cache access, so that the system will see no performance degradation due to MMU translations. In addition, the on-chip MMU is coupled to the instruction and data caches so that accesses to the on-chip caches are performed in parallel. Also, the MMU is not utilized unless required.

The MMU portion of the **68030** provides a high-powered set of functions that are a subset of those available on the **68851** PMMU. These include multiple page sizes, multilevel translation trees, on-chip Address Translation Cache (ATC), and automatic access history maintenance. The MMU on the **68030**, like the **68851**, will automatically search the main memory for address translations when they are not found in the ATC.

The on-chip MMU reduces the minimum physical bus cycle time to two clocks, half the time required by the **68020** and **68851**. Internal pipelining permits the MMU to avoid adding any translation time to any bus cycle, and physical accesses are just as fast as logical accesses. The 22-entry, fully associative, on-chip ATC helps maximize performance. ATC *hit* rates will be greater than 99% for 4K pages and about 98% for 1K pages.

The **68030** supports the powerful **68020** coprocessors: the **68851** PMMU, the **68881** Floating-Point Coprocessor (FPCP), or the new Enhanced FPCP, the **68882**. Unique dynamic disabling of the address translation provides for off-chip MMUs as well as when translations must be disabled for emulation support.

Occasionally, a system cannot afford the time required to search tables for a correct translation when referencing memory. For example, if the **68030** is sharing the graphics function in a low-cost system and if a translation in the ATC should miss, drawing a line may appear erratic as the tables are searched. To eliminate this problem, the **68030** provides the feature of *transparent memory windows* that can be used to bypass the MMU and thereby map the logical addresses directly through to the physical address space. In this way, no overhead is incurred for time-critical portions of the application. These windows can be as small as 16 Mbytes or as large as the entire 4-gigabyte address space supported by the **68030**.

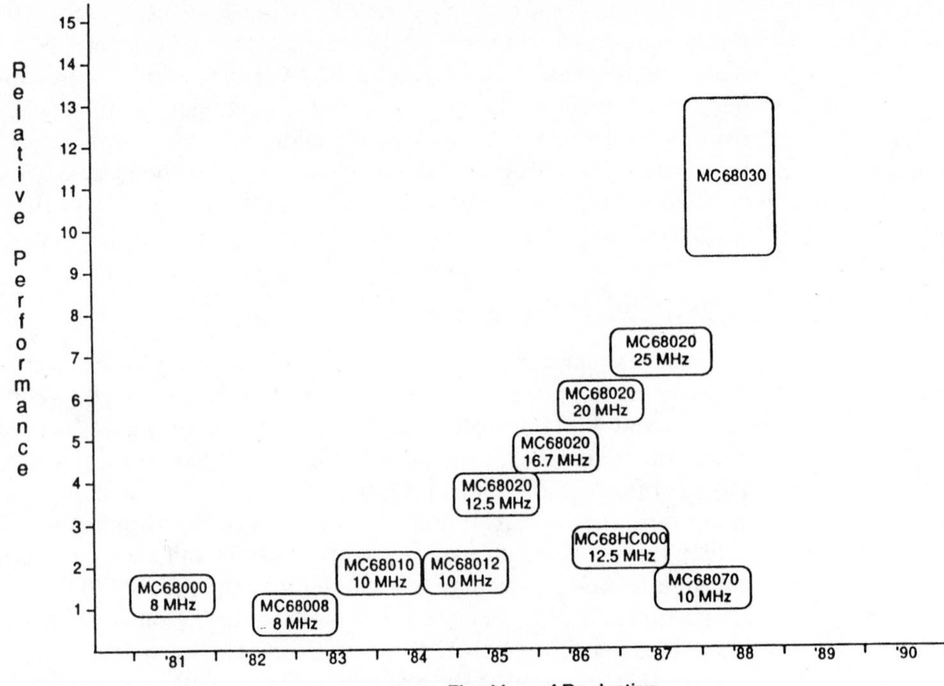

FIGURE 16-17 **68000** family relative performance.

16-13 SUMMARY

This chapter introduced the **68010**, **68020**, and **68030** members of the **68000** family of 16/32-bit μPs. The features supported by these μPs, such as Virtual Memory, PMMUs, Cache Memory, and Coprocessors, were described. These features and the μPs themselves are of such complexity that only a brief description has been possible in this single chapter. Students are referred to the manuals and data sheets listed in Section 16-15.

16-14 GLOSSARY

Addressable memory Memory that is accessible to the programmer.

Barrel shifter Hardware structure in the chip that will rotate or shift a 32-bit-long word any number of positions in one clock cycle. Used for normalizing.

Base address Beginning address of a table of addresses or a block of memory.

Cache hit Match between the parameters of a memory access and those of a cache entry when an instruction fetch occurs.

Cache memory Small high-speed memory that holds a group of instructions so that they can be sequenced through without the need to fetch them individually from main memory or from the disk memory.

Cache miss Instruction fetch that is not in the cache and must be fetched from external memory.

Context switch Process of saving the contents of all registers that represent the complete state of the machine and executing an exception, or of restoring the original conditions and resuming execution.

Coprocessor interface Provision to connect another specialized processor and communicate with it for enhanced overall performance. The coprocessor serves to add registers and instructions that are transparent to the programmer.

Demand-paged Paged without specifying areas of logical address space in advance. (See Paging.)

Instruction cache Cache memory used for storing a small group of instructions, as opposed to one used for data only.

Logical addresses Addresses put out by the μP that are translated by the MMU into the addresses of the actual physical memory.

Loop mode operation Special feature of the **68010** and **68020** μPs that provides efficient program loop operation.

Memory Management Unit (MMU) IC circuit or device that provides address translation in conjunction with the Function Code bits to implement virtual memory concepts. The Function Codes distinguish between the User and Supervisor address spaces and between data and program spaces within them.

Multiuser system μC system that can execute concurrent tasks by several users. Users may not be aware that other users are also present.

Paging Subdivision of physical memory into equal-sized blocks called page frames.

Physical addresses Addresses determined by the MMU with the aid of the Function Codes; the actual addresses of the memory ICs used by the MMU.

Physical memory Real memory that is located at the addresses on the physical address bus.

Pipelined architecture Bus structure within the μP that allows concurrent operations to occur.

Tag field Upper 24 address bits in each cache memory entry.

Valid bit Bit in each cache memory entry that is set when an instruction is entered into that cache entry.

Vector Base Register Register in the **68010** and later μPs that points to the base address of the 1K byte Exception Vector Table. It is initialized to 0 so that **68000** programs will work.

Vector number An 8-bit number that, when multiplied by 4, gives the offset of an exception vector.

Vector offset A 32-bit number, that, when added to the Vector Base Address, gives the Actual Vector Address.

Vector table entry Address pointer to the exception service routines.

Virtual machine Emulated μC that appears to have I/O and memory at virtual locations.

Virtual memory Memory that appears to be at a location different from that selected by the physical address bus.

Wired-OR Technique whereby open collector or open drain transistor circuits are paralleled and used with one pull-up resistor so that any one can provide the interrupt signal.

16-15 REFERENCES

Motorola - M68K2XSASM *M68020 Resident Structured Macro Assembler,* DS4040, Motorola, Phoenix, Arizona, 1984.

Motorola - M68KVMMB/D1 *Memory Management Board User's Manual,* Phoenix, Arizona, February 1985.

Motorola - *MC68020 32-Bit Microprocessor,* BR243/D, Austin, Texas, 1986.

Motorola - MC68881 *HCMOS Floating-Point Coprocessor, Technical Data Sheet,* BR265, Phoenix, Arizona, 1985.

Motorola - *Design Philosophy Behind Motorola's MC68000,* AR208, Austin, Texas, 1983.

Motorola - MC68451 *Memory Management Unit,* ADI 872 R1, Austin, Texas, April 1983.

Motorola - *Multiprocessing Capabilities of the MC68020 32-Bit Microprocessor,* AR220, Austin, Texas, WESCON 1984.

Motorola - *MC68020 32-Bit Microprocessor User's Manual,* Second Edition, MC68020UM/AD, Rev. 1, Motorola Phoenix and Prentice-Hall, Englewood Cliffs, New Jersey, 1985.

Motorola - *Second Generation 32-Bit Enhanced Microprocessor—The 68030,* Technical Data Sheet BR508/D, 1986.

Motorola - *MC68882 HCMOS Enhanced Floating Point Coprocessor,* Technical Data Sheet BR509/D, 1986.

Motorola - *M68000 Programmer's Reference Manual,* M68000UM/AD, Rev. 4, 1986.

Motorola - *MC68881 Floating-Point Coprocessor User's Manual,* MC68881UM/AD, First Edition, 1985.

Motorola - *MC68008 8/32-Bit Microprocessor with 8-Bit Data Bus,* ADI939R2, April 1985.

Motorola - *MC68010/68012 16-/32-Bit Virtual Memory Microprocessors,* ADI942R2, May 1985.

Motorola - *MC68000 16-/32-Bit Microprocessor,* ADI814R6, October 1985.

Motorola - *MC68851 Paged Memory Management Unit User's Manual,* MC68851UM/AD, 1986.

Motorola - *32-Bit Virtual Memory Microprocessor,* BR243/D, Rev. 1, 1986.

Motorola - *The MC68000 Family Seminar,* RBR-206, 1982.

Motorola - *MC68008 Minimum Configuration System,* AN897, 1984.

Motorola - *The MC68881 Floating-Point Coprocessor,* AR213, Motorola reprint from *IEEE MICRO,* Vol. 3, No. 6, pp. 44–54, December 1983.

Motorola - *The MC68020 and System V/68,* AR219, Motorola reprint from WESCON Professional Papers, Session 17/1, 1984.

Motorola - *Built-in Tight-Loop Mode Raises μP's Performance,* AR-211, Motorola reprint from *Electronic Design,* Vol. 31, No. 22, 1983.

Motorola - *Low Power HCMOS 16/32 Bit Microprocessor MC68H000,* BR275, Rev. 1, 1986.

Motorola - *Virtual Memory and the MC68010,* AR209, Motorola reprint from *IEEE MICRO,* Vol. 3, pp. 24–29, June 1983.

Motorola - *Memory Management Chip for 68020 Translates Addresses in Less Than a Clock Cycle,* AR238, Motorola reprint from *Electronic Design,* Vol. 34, No. 11, 1986.

Motorola - *020bug Resident Package,* M68K2RBBUG4, ADI 1109, 1984.

Motorola - *MC68000 Educational Computer Board User's Manual,* MEX68KECB/D2, Motorola, July 1982.

Motorola - *Tutor Program Assembly Listing,* Rev. 1.3, M68TUTOR/D4, Motorola Microsystems, Phoenix, Arizona, August 1982.

Note: These manuals, data sheets and article reprints are available from Motorola Literature Distribution, P. O. Box 20912, Phoenix, Arizona 85036.

APPENDIX A

POSITIVE AND NEGATIVE POWERS OF 2

TABLE A-1 Powers of 2[1]

2^n	n	2^{-n}
1	0	1.0
2	1	0.5
4	2	0.25
8	3	0.125
16	4	0.062 5
32	5	0.031 25
64	6	0.015 625
128	7	0.007 812 5
256	8	0.003 906 25
512	9	0.001 953 125
1 024	10	0.000 976 562 5
2 048	11	0.000 488 281 25
4 096	12	0.000 244 140 625
8 192	13	0.000 122 070 312 5
16 384	14	0.000 061 035 156 25
32 768	15	0.000 030 517 578 125
65 536	16	0.000 015 258 789 062 5
131 072	17	0.000 007 629 394 531 25
262 144	18	0.000 003 814 697 265 625
524 288	19	0.000 001 907 348 632 812 5
1 048 576	20	0.000 000 953 674 316 406 25
2 097 152	21	0.000 000 476 837 158 203 125
4 194 304	22	0.000 000 238 418 579 101 562 5
8 388 608	23	0.000 000 119 209 289 550 781 25
16 777 216	24	0.000 000 059 604 644 775 390 625
33 554 432	25	0.000 000 029 802 322 387 695 312 5
67 108 864	26	0.000 000 014 901 161 193 847 656 25
134 217 728	27	0.000 000 007 450 580 596 923 828 125
268 435 456	28	0.000 000 003 725 290 298 461 914 062 5
536 870 912	29	0.000 000 001 862 645 149 230 957 031 25
1 073 741 824	30	0.000 000 000 931 322 574 615 478 515 625
2 147 483 648	31	0.000 000 000 465 661 287 307 739 257 812 5
4 294 967 296	32	0.000 000 000 232 830 643 653 869 628 906 25
8 589 934 592	33	0.000 000 000 116 415 321 826 934 814 453 125
17 179 869 184	34	0.000 000 000 058 207 660 913 467 407 226 562 5
34 359 738 368	35	0.000 000 000 029 103 830 456 733 703 613 281 25
68 719 476 736	36	0.000 000 000 014 551 915 228 366 851 806 640 625
137 438 953 472	37	0.000 000 000 007 275 957 614 183 425 903 320 312 5
274 877 906 944	38	0.000 000 000 003 637 978 807 091 712 951 660 156 25
549 755 813 888	39	0.000 000 000 001 818 989 403 545 856 475 830 078 125
1 099 511 627 776	40	0.000 000 000 000 909 494 701 772 928 237 915 039 062 5
2 199 023 255 552	41	0.000 000 000 000 454 747 350 886 464 118 957 519 531 25
4 398 046 511 104	42	0.000 000 000 000 227 373 675 443 232 059 478 759 765 625
8 796 093 022 208	43	0.000 000 000 000 113 686 837 721 616 029 739 379 882 812 5
17 592 186 044 416	44	0.000 000 000 000 056 843 418 860 808 014 869 689 941 406 25
35 184 372 088 832	45	0.000 000 000 000 028 421 709 430 404 007 434 844 970 703 125
70 368 744 177 664	46	0.000 000 000 000 014 210 854 715 202 003 717 422 485 351 562 5
140 737 488 355 328	47	0.000 000 000 000 007 105 427 357 601 001 858 711 242 675 781 25
281 474 976 710 656	48	0.000 000 000 000 003 552 713 678 800 500 929 355 621 337 890 625
562 949 953 421 312	49	0.000 000 000 000 001 776 356 839 400 250 464 677 810 668 945 312 5
1 125 899 906 842 624	50	0.000 000 000 000 000 888 178 419 700 125 232 338 905 334 472 656 25
2 251 799 813 685 248	51	0.000 000 000 000 000 444 089 209 850 062 616 169 452 667 236 328 125
4 503 599 627 370 496	52	0.000 000 000 000 000 222 044 604 925 031 308 084 726 333 618 164 062 5
9 007 199 254 740 992	53	0.000 000 000 000 000 111 022 302 462 515 654 042 363 166 809 082 031 25
18 014 398 509 481 984	54	0.000 000 000 000 000 055 511 151 231 257 827 021 181 583 404 541 015 625
36 028 797 018 963 968	55	0.000 000 000 000 000 027 755 575 615 628 913 510 590 791 702 270 507 812 5
72 057 594 037 927 936	56	0.000 000 000 000 000 013 877 787 807 814 456 755 295 395 851 135 253 906 25
144 115 188 075 855 872	57	0.000 000 000 000 000 006 938 893 903 907 228 377 647 697 925 567 626 953 125
288 230 376 151 711 744	58	0.000 000 000 000 000 003 469 446 951 953 614 188 823 848 962 783 813 476 562 5
576 460 752 303 423 488	59	0.000 000 000 000 000 001 734 723 475 976 807 094 411 924 481 391 906 738 281 25
1 152 921 504 606 846 976	60	0.000 000 000 000 000 000 867 361 737 988 403 547 205 962 240 695 953 369 140 625
2 305 843 009 213 693 952	61	0.000 000 000 000 000 000 433 680 868 994 201 773 602 981 120 347 976 684 570 312 5
4 611 686 018 427 387 904	62	0.000 000 000 000 000 000 216 840 434 497 100 886 801 490 560 173 988 342 285 156 25
9 223 372 036 854 775 808	63	0.000 000 000 000 000 000 108 420 217 248 550 443 400 745 280 086 994 171 142 578 125
18 446 744 073 709 551 616	64	0.000 000 000 000 000 000 054 210 108 624 275 221 700 372 640 043 497 085 571 289 062 5
36 893 488 147 419 103 232	65	0.000 000 000 000 000 000 027 105 054 312 137 610 850 186 320 021 748 542 785 644 531 25
73 786 976 294 838 206 464	66	0.000 000 000 000 000 000 013 552 527 156 068 805 425 093 160 010 874 271 392 822 265 625
147 573 952 589 676 412 928	67	0.000 000 000 000 000 000 006 776 263 578 034 402 712 546 580 005 437 135 696 411 132 812 5
295 147 905 179 352 825 856	68	0.000 000 000 000 000 000 003 388 131 789 017 201 356 273 290 002 718 567 848 205 566 406 25
590 295 810 358 705 651 712	69	0.000 000 000 000 000 000 001 694 065 894 508 600 678 136 645 001 359 283 924 102 783 203 125
1 180 591 620 717 411 303 424	70	0.000 000 000 000 000 000 000 847 032 947 254 300 339 068 322 500 679 641 962 051 391 601 562 5
2 361 183 241 434 822 606 848	71	0.000 000 000 000 000 000 000 423 516 473 627 150 169 534 161 250 339 820 981 025 695 800 781 25
4 722 366 482 869 645 213 696	72	0.000 000 000 000 000 000 000 211 758 236 813 575 084 767 080 625 169 910 490 512 847 900 390 625

[1] George K. Kostopoulos. *Digital Engineering*. Copyright John Wiley & Sons, Inc., 1975. Reprinted by permission of John Wiley & Sons, Inc.

APPENDIX B

THE 6800 INSTRUCTION SET

TABLE B-1 Accumulator and Memory Instructions

		ADDRESSING MODES															BOOLEAN/ARITHMETIC OPERATION	COND. CODE REG.					
		IMMED			DIRECT			INDEX			EXTND			IMPLIED			(All register labels refer to contents)	5	4	3	2	1	0
OPERATIONS	MNEMONIC	OP	~	#	OP	~	#	OP	~	#	OP	~	#	OP	~	#		H	I	N	Z	V	C
Add	ADDA	8B	2	2	9B	3	2	AB	5	2	BB	4	3				A + M · A	↕	•	↕	↕	↕	↕
	ADDB	CB	2	2	DB	3	2	EB	5	2	FB	4	3				B + M · B	↕	•	↕	↕	↕	↕
Add Acmltrs	ABA													1B	2	1	A + B · A	↕	•	↕	↕	↕	↕
Add with Carry	ADCA	89	2	2	99	3	2	A9	5	2	B9	4	3				A + M + C · A	↕	•	↕	↕	↕	↕
	ADCB	C9	2	2	D9	3	2	E9	5	2	F9	4	3				B + M + C · B	↕	•	↕	↕	↕	↕
And	ANDA	84	2	2	94	3	2	A4	5	2	B4	4	3				A · M · A	•	•	↕	↕	R	•
	ANDB	C4	2	2	D4	3	2	E4	5	2	F4	4	3				B · M · B	•	•	↕	↕	R	•
Bit Test	BITA	85	2	2	95	3	2	A5	5	2	B5	4	3				A · M	•	•	↕	↕	R	•
	BITB	C5	2	2	D5	3	2	E5	5	2	F5	4	3				B · M	•	•	↕	↕	R	•
Clear	CLR							6F	7	2	7F	6	3				00 · M	•	•	R	S	R	R
	CLRA													4F	2	1	00 · A	•	•	R	S	R	R
	CLRB													5F	2	1	00 · B	•	•	R	S	R	R
Compare	CMPA	81	2	2	91	3	2	A1	5	2	B1	4	3				A M	•	•	↕	↕	↕	↕
	CMPB	C1	2	2	D1	3	2	E1	5	2	F1	4	3				B M	•	•	↕	↕	↕	↕
Compare Acmltrs	CBA													11	2	1	A B	•	•	↕	↕	↕	↕
Complement, 1's	COM							63	7	2	73	6	3				M̄ · M	•	•	↕	↕	R	S
	COMA													43	2	1	Ā · A	•	•	↕	↕	R	S
	COMB													53	2	1	B̄ · B	•	•	↕	↕	R	S
Complement, 2's	NEG							60	7	2	70	6	3				00 M · M	•	•	↕	↕	①	②
(Negate)	NEGA													40	2	1	00 A · A	•	•	↕	↕	①	②
	NEGB													50	2	1	00 B · B	•	•	↕	↕	①	②
Decimal Adjust, A	DAA													19	2	1	Converts Binary Add. of BCD Characters into BCD Format	•	•	↕	↕	↕	③
Decrement	DEC							6A	7	2	7A	6	3				M 1 · M	•	•	↕	↕	4	•
	DECA													4A	2	1	A 1 · A	•	•	↕	↕	4	•
	DECB													5A	2	1	B 1 · B	•	•	↕	↕	4	•
Exclusive OR	EORA	88	2	2	98	3	2	A8	5	2	B8	4	3				A⊕M · A	•	•	↕	↕	R	•
	EORB	C8	2	2	D8	3	2	E8	5	2	F8	4	3				B⊕M · B	•	•	↕	↕	R	•
Increment	INC							6C	7	2	7C	6	3				M + 1 · M	•	•	↕	↕	⑤	•
	INCA													4C	2	1	A + 1 · A	•	•	↕	↕	⑤	•
	INCB													5C	2	1	B + 1 · B	•	•	↕	↕	⑤	•
Load Acmltr	LDAA	86	2	2	96	3	2	A6	5	2	B6	4	3				M · A	•	•	↕	↕	R	•
	LDAB	C6	2	2	D6	3	2	E6	5	2	F6	4	3				M · B	•	•	↕	↕	R	•
Or, Inclusive	ORAA	8A	2	2	9A	3	2	AA	5	2	BA	4	3				A + M · A	•	•	↕	↕	R	•
	ORAB	CA	2	2	DA	3	2	EA	5	2	FA	4	3				B + M · B	•	•	↕	↕	R	•
Push Data	PSHA													36	4	1	A · M_{SP}, SP 1 · SP	•	•	•	•	•	•
	PSHB													37	4	1	B · M_{SP}, SP 1 · SP	•	•	•	•	•	•
Pull Data	PULA													32	4	1	SP + 1 · SP, M_{SP} · A	•	•	•	•	•	•
	PULB													33	4	1	SP + 1 · SP, M_{SP} · B	•	•	•	•	•	•
Rotate Left	ROL							69	7	2	79	6	3				M 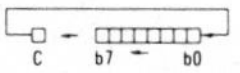	•	•	↕	↕	⑥	↕
	ROLA													49	2	1	A	•	•	↕	↕	⑥	↕
	ROLB													59	2	1	B C b7 b0	•	•	↕	↕	⑥	↕
Rotate Right	ROR							66	7	2	76	6	3				M 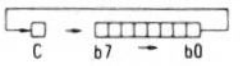	•	•	↕	↕	⑥	↕
	RORA													46	2	1	A	•	•	↕	↕	⑥	↕
	RORB													56	2	1	B C b7 b0	•	•	↕	↕	⑥	↕
Shift Left, Arithmetic	ASL							68	7	2	78	6	3				M 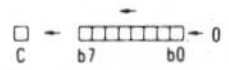	•	•	↕	↕	⑥	↕
	ASLA													48	2	1	A 0	•	•	↕	↕	⑥	↕
	ASLB													58	2	1	B C b7 b0	•	•	↕	↕	⑥	↕
Shift Right, Arithmetic	ASR							67	7	2	77	6	3				M 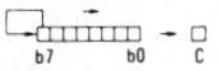	•	•	↕	↕	⑥	↕
	ASRA													47	2	1	A	•	•	↕	↕	⑥	↕
	ASRB													57	2	1	B b7 b0 C	•	•	↕	↕	⑥	↕
Shift Right, Logic	LSR							64	7	2	74	6	3				M 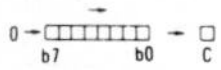	•	•	R	↕	⑥	↕
	LSRA													44	2	1	A 0	•	•	R	↕	⑥	↕
	LSRB													54	2	1	B b7 b0 C	•	•	R	↕	⑥	↕
Store Acmltr	STAA				97	4	2	A7	6	2	B7	5	3				A · M	•	•	↕	↕	R	•
	STAB				D7	4	2	E7	6	2	F7	5	3				B · M	•	•	↕	↕	R	•
Subtract	SUBA	80	2	2	90	3	2	A0	5	2	B0	4	3				A M · A	•	•	↕	↕	↕	↕
	SUBB	C0	2	2	D0	3	2	E0	5	2	F0	4	3				B M · B	•	•	↕	↕	↕	↕
Subtract Acmltrs	SBA													10	2	1	A B · A	•	•	↕	↕	↕	↕
Subtr. with Carry	SBCA	82	2	2	92	3	2	A2	5	2	B2	4	3				A M C · A	•	•	↕	↕	↕	↕
	SBCB	C2	2	2	D2	3	2	E2	5	2	F2	4	3				B M C · B	•	•	↕	↕	↕	↕
Transfer Acmltrs	TAB													16	2	1	A · B	•	•	↕	↕	R	•
	TBA													17	2	1	B · A	•	•	↕	↕	R	•
Test, Zero or Minus	TST							6D	7	2	7D	6	3				M 00	•	•	↕	↕	R	R
	TSTA													4D	2	1	A 00	•	•	↕	↕	R	R
	TSTB													5D	2	1	B 00	•	•	↕	↕	R	R
																		H	I	N	Z	V	C

LEGEND:

OP Operation Code (Hexadecimal).
~ Number of MPU Cycles.
# Number of Program Bytes.
+ Arithmetic Plus.
Arithmetic Minus.
· Boolean AND.
M_{SP} Contents of memory location pointed to be Stack Pointer.

+ Boolean Inclusive OR.
⊕ Boolean Exclusive OR.
M̄ Complement of M.
· Transfer Into.
0 Bit = Zero.
00 Byte = Zero.

Note: Accumulator addressing mode instructions are included in the column for IMPLIED addressing.

CONDITION CODE SYMBOLS:

H Half carry from bit 3.
I Interrupt mask
N Negative (sign bit)
Z Zero (byte)
V Overflow, 2's complement
C Carry from bit 7
R Reset Always
S Set Always
↕ Test and set if true, cleared otherwise
● Not Affected

TABLE B-2 Index Register and Stack Manipulation

		IMMED			DIRECT			INDEX			EXTND			IMPLIED				COND. CODE REG. 5	4	3	2	1	0
POINTER OPERATIONS	MNEMONIC	OP	~	#	OP	~	#	OP	~	#	OP	~	#	OP	~	#	BOOLEAN/ARITHMETIC OPERATION	H	I	N	Z	V	C
Compare Index Reg	CPX	8C	3	3	9C	4	2	AC	6	2	BC	5	3				$X_H - M, X_L - (M+1)$	•	•	⑦	↕	⑧	•
Decrement Index Reg	DEX													09	4	1	$X - 1 \rightarrow X$	•	•	•	↕	•	•
Decrement Stack Pntr	DES													34	4	1	$SP - 1 \rightarrow SP$	•	•	•	•	•	•
Increment Index Reg	INX													08	4	1	$X + 1 \rightarrow X$	•	•	•	↕	•	•
Increment Stack Pntr	INS													31	4	1	$SP + 1 \rightarrow SP$	•	•	•	•	•	•
Load Index Reg	LDX	CE	3	3	DE	4	2	EE	6	2	FE	5	3				$M \rightarrow X_H, (M+1) \rightarrow X_L$	•	•	⑨	↕	R	•
Load Stack Pntr	LDS	8E	3	3	9E	4	2	AE	6	2	BE	5	3				$M \rightarrow SP_H, (M+1) \rightarrow SP_L$	•	•	⑨	↕	R	•
Store Index Reg	STX				DF	5	2	EF	7	2	FF	6	3				$X_H \rightarrow M, X_L \rightarrow (M+1)$	•	•	⑨	↕	R	•
Store Stack Pntr	STS				9F	5	2	AF	7	2	BF	6	3				$SP_H \rightarrow M, SP_L \rightarrow (M+1)$	•	•	⑨	↕	R	•
Indx Reg → Stack Pntr	TXS													35	4	1	$X - 1 \rightarrow SP$	•	•	•	•	•	•
Stack Pntr → Indx Reg	TSX													30	4	1	$SP + 1 \rightarrow X$	•	•	•	•	•	•

TABLE B-3 Jump and Branch Instructions

		RELATIVE			INDEX			EXTND			IMPLIED				COND. CODE REG. 5	4	3	2	1	0
OPERATIONS	MNEMONIC	OP	~	#	OP	~	#	OP	~	#	OP	~	#	BRANCH TEST	H	I	N	Z	V	C
Branch Always	BRA	20	4	2										None	•	•	•	•	•	•
Branch If Carry Clear	BCC	24	4	2										C = 0	•	•	•	•	•	•
Branch If Carry Set	BCS	25	4	2										C = 1	•	•	•	•	•	•
Branch If = Zero	BEQ	27	4	2										Z = 1	•	•	•	•	•	•
Branch If ≥ Zero	BGE	2C	4	2										N ⊕ V = 0	•	•	•	•	•	•
Branch If > Zero	BGT	2E	4	2										Z + (N ⊕ V) = 0	•	•	•	•	•	•
Branch If Higher	BHI	22	4	2										C + Z = 0	•	•	•	•	•	•
Branch If ≤ Zero	BLE	2F	4	2										Z + (N ⊕ V) = 1	•	•	•	•	•	•
Branch If Lower Or Same	BLS	23	4	2										C + Z = 1	•	•	•	•	•	•
Branch If < Zero	BLT	2D	4	2										N ⊕ V = 1	•	•	•	•	•	•
Branch If Minus	BMI	2B	4	2										N = 1	•	•	•	•	•	•
Branch If Not Equal Zero	BNE	26	4	2										Z = 0	•	•	•	•	•	•
Branch If Overflow Clear	BVC	28	4	2										V = 0	•	•	•	•	•	•
Branch If Overflow Set	BVS	29	4	2										V = 1	•	•	•	•	•	•
Branch If Plus	BPL	2A	4	2										N = 0	•	•	•	•	•	•
Branch To Subroutine	BSR	8D	8	2										See Special Operations	•	•	•	•	•	•
Jump	JMP				6E	4	2	7E	3	3				See Special Operations	•	•	•	•	•	•
Jump To Subroutine	JSR				AD	8	2	BD	9	3				See Special Operations	•	•	•	•	•	•
No Operation	NOP										01	2	1	Advances Prog. Cntr. Only	•	•	•	•	•	•
Return From Interrupt	RTI										3B	10	1		⑩					
Return From Subroutine	RTS										39	5	1	See Special Operations	•	•	•	•	•	•
Software Interrupt	SWI										3F	12	1	See Special Operations	•	•	•	•	•	•
Wait for Interrupt*	WAI										3E	9	1	See Special Operations	•	⑪	•	•	•	•

*WAI puts Address Bus, R/W, and Data Bus in the three state mode while VMA is held low.

TABLE B-4 Condition Code Register Manipulation Instructions

		IMPLIED				COND. CODE REG. 5	4	3	2	1	0
OPERATIONS	MNEMONIC	OP	~	#	BOOLEAN OPERATION	H	I	N	Z	V	C
Clear Carry	CLC	0C	2	1	0 → C	•	•	•	•	•	R
Clear Interrupt Mask	CLI	0E	2	1	0 → I	•	R	•	•	•	•
Clear Overflow	CLV	0A	2	1	0 → V	•	•	•	•	R	•
Set Carry	SEC	0D	2	1	1 → C	•	•	•	•	•	S
Set Interrupt Mask	SEI	0F	2	1	1 → I	•	S	•	•	•	•
Set Overflow	SEV	0B	2	1	1 → V	•	•	•	•	S	•
Acmltr A → CCR	TAP	06	2	1	A → CCR	⑫					
CCR → Acmltr A	TPA	07	2	1	CCR → A	•	•	•	•	•	•

CONDITION CODE REGISTER NOTES: (Bit set if test is true and cleared otherwise)

1 (Bit V) Test: Result = 10000000?
2 (Bit C) Test: Result = 00000000?
3 (Bit C) Test: Decimal value of most significant BCD Character greater than nine? (Not cleared if previously set.)
4 (Bit V) Test: Operand = 10000000 prior to execution?
5 (Bit V) Test: Operand = 01111111 prior to execution?
6 (Bit V) Test: Set equal to result of N⊕C after shift has occurred.
7 (Bit N) Test: Sign bit of most significant (MS) byte = 1?
8 (Bit V) Test: 2's complement overflow from subtraction of MS bytes?
9 (Bit N) Test: Result less than zero? (Bit 15 = 1)
10 (All) Load Condition Code Register from Stack. (See Special Operations)
11 (Bit I) Set when interrupt occurs. If previously set, a Non-Maskable Interrupt is required to exit the wait state.
12 (All) Set according to the contents of Accumulator A.

APPENDIX C

TABLE OF CYCLE-BY-CYCLE OPERATION FOR EACH 6800 INSTRUCTION

Table C-1 provides a detailed description of the information present on the address bus, data bus, valid memory address line (VMA), and the read/write line (R/W) during each cycle for each instruction.

This information is useful in comparing actual with expected results during debug of both software and hardware as the control program is executed. The information is categorized in groups according to addressing mode and number of cycles per instruction. (In general, instructions with the same addressing mode and number of cycles execute in the same manner; exceptions are indicated in the table.)

TABLE C-1 Operation Summary

Address Mode and Instructions	Cycles	Cycle #	VMA Line	Address Bus	R/W Line	Data Bus
IMMEDIATE						
ADC EOR ADD LDA AND ORA BIT SBC CMP SUB	2	1	1	Op Code Address	1	Op Code
		2	1	Op Code Address + 1	1	Operand Data
CPX LDS LDX	3	1	1	Op Code Address	1	Op Code
		2	1	Op Code Address + 1	1	Operand Data (High Order Byte)
		3	1	Op Code Address + 2	1	Operand Data (Low Order Byte)
DIRECT						
ADC EOR ADD LDA AND ORA BIT SBC CMP SUB	3	1	1	Op Code Address	1	Op Code
		2	1	Op Code Address + 1	1	Address of Operand
		3	1	Address of Operand	1	Operand Data
CPX LDS LDX	4	1	1	Op Code Address	1	Op Code
		2	1	Op Code Address + 1	1	Address of Operand
		3	1	Address of Operand	1	Operand Data (High Order Byte)
		4	1	Operand Address + 1	1	Operand Data (Low Order Byte)
STA	4	1	1	Op Code Address	1	Op Code
		2	1	Op Code Address + 1	1	Destination Address
		3	0	Destination Address	1	Irrelevant Data (Note 1)
		4	1	Destination Address	0	Data from Accumulator
STS STX	5	1	1	Op Code Address	1	Op Code
		2	1	Op Code Address + 1	1	Address of Operand
		3	0	Address of Operand	1	Irrelevant Data (Note 1)
		4	1	Address of Operand	0	Register Data (High Order Byte)
		5	1	Address of Operand + 1	0	Register Data (Low Order Byte)
INDEXED						
JMP	4	1	1	Op Code Address	1	Op Code
		2	1	Op Code Address + 1	1	Offset
		3	0	Index Register	1	Irrelevant Data (Note 1)
		4	0	Index Register Plus Offset (w/o Carry)	1	Irrelevant Data (Note 1)
ADC EOR ADD LDA AND ORA BIT SBC CMP SUB	5	1	1	Op Code Address	1	Op Code
		2	1	Op Code Address + 1	1	Offset
		3	0	Index Register	1	Irrelevant Data (Note 1)
		4	0	Index Register Plus Offset (w/o Carry)	1	Irrelevant Data (Note 1)
		5	1	Index Register Plus Offset	1	Operand Data
CPX LDS LDX	6	1	1	Op Code Address	1	Op Code
		2	1	Op Code Address + 1	1	Offset
		3	0	Index Register	1	Irrelevant Data (Note 1)
		4	0	Index Register Plus Offset (w/o Carry)	1	Irrelevant Data (Note 1)
		5	1	Index Register Plus Offset	1	Operand Data (High Order Byte)
		6	1	Index Register Plus Offset + 1	1	Operand Data (Low Order Byte)

TABLE C-1 Continued

Address Mode and Instructions	Cycles	Cycle #	VMA Line	Address Bus	R/W Line	Data Bus
INDEXED (Continued)						
STA	6	1	1	Op Code Address	1	Op Code
		2	1	Op Code Address + 1	1	Offset
		3	0	Index Register	1	Irrelevant Data (Note 1)
		4	0	Index Register Plus Offset (w/o Carry)	1	Irrelevant Data (Note 1)
		5	0	Index Register Plus Offset	1	Irrelevant Data (Note 1)
		6	1	Index Register Plus Offset	0	Operand Data
ASL LSR ASR NEG CLR ROL COM ROR DEC TST INC	7	1	1	Op Code Address	1	Op Code
		2	1	Op Code Address + 1	1	Offset
		3	0	Index Register	1	Irrelevant Data (Note 1)
		4	0	Index Register Plus Offset (w/o Carry)	1	Irrelevant Data (Note 1)
		5	1	Index Register Plus Offset	1	Current Operand Data
		6	0	Index Register Plus Offset	1	Irrelevant Data (Note 1)
		7	1/0 (Note 3)	Index Register Plus Offset	0	New Operand Data (Note 3)
STS STX	7	1	1	Op Code Address	1	Op Code
		2	1	Op Code Address + 1	1	Offset
		3	0	Index Register	1	Irrelevant Data (Note 1)
		4	0	Index Register Plus Offset (w/o Carry)	1	Irrelevant Data (Note 1)
		5	0	Index Register Plus Offset	1	Irrelevant Data (Note 1)
		6	1	Index Register Plus Offset	0	Operand Data (High Order Byte)
		7	1	Index Register Plus Offset + 1	0	Operand Data (Low Order Byte)
JSR	8	1	1	Op Code Address	1	Op Code
		2	1	Op Code Address + 1	1	Offset
		3	0	Index Register	1	Irrelevant Data (Note 1)
		4	1	Stack Pointer	0	Return Address (Low Order Byte)
		5	1	Stack Pointer – 1	0	Return Address (High Order Byte)
		6	0	Stack Pointer – 2	1	Irrelevant Data (Note 1)
		7	0	Index Register	1	Irrelevant Data (Note 1)
		8	0	Index Register Plus Offset (w/o Carry)	1	Irrelevant Data (Note 1)
EXTENDED						
JMP	3	1	1	Op Code Address	1	Op Code
		2	1	Op Code Address + 1	1	Jump Address (High Order Byte)
		3	1	Op Code Address + 2	1	Jump Address (Low Order Byte)
ADC EOR ADD LDA AND ORA BIT SBC CMP SUB	4	1	1	Op Code Address	1	Op Code
		2	1	Op Code Address + 1	1	Address of Operand (High Order Byte)
		3	1	Op Code Address + 2	1	Address of Operand (Low Order Byte)
		4	1	Address of Operand	1	Operand Data
CPX LDS LDX	5	1	1	Op Code Address	1	Op Code
		2	1	Op Code Address + 1	1	Address of Operand (High Order Byte)
		3	1	Op Code Address + 2	1	Address of Operand (Low Order Byte)
		4	1	Address of Operand	1	Operand Data (High Order Byte)
		5	1	Address of Operand + 1	1	Operand Data (Low Order Byte)
STA A STA B	5	1	1	Op Code Address	1	Op Code
		2	1	Op Code Address + 1	1	Destination Address (High Order Byte)
		3	1	Op Code Address + 2	1	Destination Address (Low Order Byte)
		4	0	Operand Destination Address	1	Irrelevant Data (Note 1)
		5	1	Operand Destination Address	0	Data from Accumulator
ASL LSR ASR NEG CLR ROL COM ROR DEC TST INC	6	1	1	Op Code Address	1	Op Code
		2	1	Op Code Address + 1	1	Address of Operand (High Order Byte)
		3	1	Op Code Address + 2	1	Address of Operand (Low Order Byte)
		4	1	Address of Operand	1	Current Operand Data
		5	0	Address of Operand	1	Irrelevant Data (Note 1)
		6	1/0 (Note 3)	Address of Operand	0	New Operand Data (Note 3)

TABLE C-1 Continued

Address Mode and Instructions	Cycles	Cycle #	VMA Line	Address Bus	R/W Line	Data Bus
EXTENDED (Continued)						
STS STX	6	1	1	Op Code Address	1	Op Code
		2	1	Op Code Address + 1	1	Address of Operand (High Order Byte)
		3	1	Op Code Address + 2	1	Address of Operand (Low Order Byte)
		4	0	Address of Operand	1	Irrelevant Data (Note 1)
		5	1	Address of Operand	0	Operand Data (High Order Byte)
		6	1	Address of Operand + 1	0	Operand Data (Low Order Byte)
JSR	9	1	1	Op Code Address	1	Op Code
		2	1	Op Code Address + 1	1	Address of Subroutine (High Order Byte)
		3	1	Op Code Address + 2	1	Address of Subroutine (Low Order Byte)
		4	1	Subroutine Starting Address	1	Op Code of Next Instruction
		5	1	Stack Pointer	0	Return Address (Low Order Byte)
		6	1	Stack Pointer – 1	0	Return Address (High Order Byte)
		7	0	Stack Pointer – 2	1	Irrelevant Data (Note 1)
		8	0	Op Code Address + 2	1	Irrelevant Data (Note 1)
		9	1	Op Code Address + 2	1	Address of Subroutine (Low Order Byte)
INHERENT						
ABA DAA SEC ASL DEC SEI ASR INC SEV CBA LSR TAB CLC NEG TAP CLI NOP TBA CLR ROL TPA CLV ROR TST COM SBA	2	1	1	Op Code Address	1	Op Code
		2	1	Op Code Address + 1	1	Op Code of Next Instruction
DES DEX INS INX	4	1	1	Op Code Address	1	Op Code
		2	1	Op Code Address + 1	1	Op Code of Next Instruction
		3	0	Previous Register Contents	1	Irrelevant Data (Note 1)
		4	0	New Register Contents	1	Irrelevant Data (Note 1)
PSH	4	1	1	Op Code Address	1	Op Code
		2	1	Op Code Address + 1	1	Op Code of Next Instruction
		3	1	Stack Pointer	0	Accumulator Data
		4	0	Stack Pointer – 1	1	Accumulator Data
PUL	4	1	1	Op Code Address	1	Op Code
		2	1	Op Code Address + 1	1	Op Code of Next Instruction
		3	0	Stack Pointer	1	Irrelevant Data (Note 1)
		4	1	Stack Pointer + 1	1	Operand Data from Stack
TSX	4	1	1	Op Code Address	1	Op Code
		2	1	Op Code Address + 1	1	Op Code of Next Instruction
		3	0	Stack Pointer	1	Irrelevant Data (Note 1)
		4	0	New Index Register	1	Irrelevant Data (Note 1)
TXS	4	1	1	Op Code Address	1	Op Code
		2	1	Op Code Address + 1	1	Op Code of Next Instruction
		3	0	Index Register	1	Irrelevant Data
		4	0	New Stack Pointer	1	Irrelevant Data
RTS	5	1	1	Op Code Address	1	Op Code
		2	1	Op Code Address + 1	1	Irrelevant Data (Note 2)
		3	0	Stack Pointer	1	Irrelevant Data (Note 1)
		4	1	Stack Pointer + 1	1	Address of Next Instruction (High Order Byte)
		5	1	Stack Pointer + 2	1	Address of Next Instruction (Low Order Byte)

TABLE C-1 Continued

Address Mode and Instructions	Cycles	Cycle #	VMA Line	Address Bus	R/W Line	Data Bus
INHERENT (Continued)						
WAI	9	1	1	Op Code Address	1	Op Code
		2	1	Op Code Address + 1	1	Op Code of Next Instruction
		3	1	Stack Pointer	0	Return Address (Low Order Byte)
		4	1	Stack Pointer – 1	0	Return Address (High Order Byte)
		5	1	Stack Pointer – 2	0	Index Register (Low Order Byte)
		6	1	Stack Pointer – 3	0	Index Register (High Order Byte)
		7	1	Stack Pointer – 4	0	Contents of Accumulator A
		8	1	Stack Pointer – 5	0	Contents of Accumulator B
		9	1	Stack Pointer – 6 (Note 4)	1	Contents of Cond. Code Register
RTI	10	1	1	Op Code Address	1	Op Code
		2	1	Op Code Address + 1	1	Irrelevant Data (Note 2)
		3	0	Stack Pointer	1	Irrelevant Data (Note 1)
		4	1	Stack Pointer + 1	1	Contents of Cond. Code Register from Stack
		5	1	Stack Pointer + 2	1	Contents of Accumulator B from Stack
		6	1	Stack Pointer + 3	1	Contents of Accumulator A from Stack
		7	1	Stack Pointer + 4	1	Index Register from Stack (High Order Byte)
		8	1	Stack Pointer + 5	1	Index Register from Stack (Low Order Byte)
		9	1	Stack Pointer + 6	1	Next Instruction Address from Stack (High Order Byte)
		10	1	Stack Pointer + 7	1	Next Instruction Address from Stack (Low Order Byte)
SWI	12	1	1	Op Code Address	1	Op Code
		2	1	Op Code Address + 1	1	Irrelevant Data (Note 1)
		3	1	Stack Pointer	0	Return Address (Low Order Byte)
		4	1	Stack Pointer – 1	0	Return Address (High Order Byte)
		5	1	Stack Pointer – 2	0	Index Register (Low Order Byte)
		6	1	Stack Pointer – 3	0	Index Register (High Order Byte)
		7	1	Stack Pointer – 4	0	Contents of Accumulator A
		8	1	Stack Pointer – 5	0	Contents of Accumulator B
		9	1	Stack Pointer – 6	0	Contents of Cond. Code Register
		10	0	Stack Pointer – 7	1	Irrelevant Data (Note 1)
		11	1	Vector Address FFFA (Hex)	1	Address of Subroutine (High Order Byte)
		12	1	Vector Address FFFB (Hex)	1	Address of Subroutine (Low Order Byte)
RELATIVE						
BCC BHI BNE BCS BLE BPL BEQ BLS BRA BGE BLT BVC BGT BMI BVS	4	1	1	Op Code Address	1	Op Code
		2	1	Op Code Address + 1	1	Branch Offset
		3	0	Op Code Address + 2	1	Irrelevant Data (Note 1)
		4	0	Branch Address	1	Irrelevant Data (Note 1)
BSR	8	1	1	Op Code Address	1	Op Code
		2	1	Op Code Address + 1	1	Branch Offset
		3	0	Return Address of Main Program	1	Irrelevant Data (Note 1)
		4	1	Stack Pointer	0	Return Address (Low Order Byte)
		5	1	Stack Pointer – 1	0	Return Address (High Order Byte)
		6	0	Stack Pointer – 2	1	Irrelevant Data (Note 1)
		7	0	Return Address of Main Program	1	Irrelevant Data (Note 1)
		8	0	Subroutine Address	1	Irrelevant Data (Note 1)

Note 1. If device which is addressed during this cycle uses VMA, then the Data Bus will go to the high impedance three-state condition. Depending on bus capacitance, data from the previous cycle may be retained on the Data Bus.
Note 2. Data is ignored by the MPU.
Note 3. For TST, VMA = 0 and Operand data does not change.
Note 4. While the MPU is waiting for the interrupt, Bus Available will go high indicating the following states of the control lines: VMA is low; Address Bus, R/W, and Data Bus are all in the high impedance state.

APPENDIX D

PROGRAM FOR A CRT TERMINAL

```
PAGE  001   CRT

                          NAM    CRT
                   *  THIS IS A PROGRAM TO SUPPLY THE BASIC DRIVER
                   *  ROUTINES FOR A CRT TERMINAL USING THE 6845
                   *  AN EXECUTIVE IS PROVIDED TO PERFORM
                   *  THE FUNCTIONS OF A DUMB TERMINAL
                   *  OCT 29, 1978
                   *
                          OPT    O,NOG
B000                      ORG    $B000
                   *
                   *  ENTER HERE ON POWER SEQUENCE
                   *
B000 8E 00FF RESET  LDS    #STKADD  INITIALIZE STACK
B003 86 03          LDA A  #$03     RESET ACIA
B005 B7 0008        STA A  ACIACR
B008 86 15          LDA A  #$15     1 STOP BIT - NO PARITY
B00A B7 0008        STA A  ACIACR   INITIALIZE ACIA
B00D 4F             CLR A
B00E B7 0010        STA A  PIA1AD   PIA1A DDR INPUTS
B011 86 04          LDA A  #$04     CA1 NEG. INPUT
B013 B7 0011        STA A  PIA1AC   PROGRAM KEYBOARD PIA
                   *
                   *  ROUTINE TO CLEAR DISPLAY MEMORY
                   *
B016 CE 8000 CLEAR  LDX    #MEMSTR  GET STARTING MEMORY ADDR
B019 86 20          LDA A  #$20
B01B A7 00   CLEAR1 STA A  0,X      STORE A SPACE
B01D 08             INX             NEXT LOCATION
B01E 8C 87FF        CPX    #MEMEND  COMPARE WITH MEMORY END
B021 26 F8          BNE    CLEAR1
                   *
                   *
                   *  ROUTINE TO INITIALIZE CRTC
                   *  ADDRESS $4000
                   *
B023 CE B154 CRTIZ  LDX    #CRTTAB  POINT TO CRT INIT TAB
B026 4F             CLR A
B027 B7 4000 CRT1   STA A  CRTCAR   SELECT REGISTER
B02A E6 00          LDA B  0,X      GET VALUE
B02C F7 4001        STA B  CRTCDR   PROGRAM VALUE
```

```
PAGE  002   CRT

B02F 08               INX           NEXT VALUE
B030 4C               INC A         NEXT REGISTER
B031 81 10            CMP A  #$10   LAST REGISTER?
B033 26 F2            BNE    CRT1
B035 CE 8000          LDX    #MEMSTR INITIAL CURSOR POS.
B038 FF 0082          STX    CURPOS
B03B FF 0080          STX    STARAD  INITIAL START ADDR.
B03E FF 0086          STX    LINEAD  STARTING ADD. THIS LINE
B041 CE 0000          LDX    #0
B044 FF 0084          STX    CCOUNT  CLEAR CCOUNT & LCOUNT
                *
                * CONTROL LOOP
                *
B047 BD B0CF    CONTRO JSR   INCHP   SCAN KEYBOARD
B04A 24 02            BCC    CONT1   NO INPUT
B04C 8D 74            BSR    OUTCH   TRANSMIT CHAR
B04E 8D 63      CONT1 BSR    INCHS   CHECK SERIAL PORT
B050 24 F5            BCC    CONTRO  NO INPUT
B052 8D 02            BSR    DECODE  TEST CHAR.
B054 20 F1            BRA    CONTRO  GET NEXT CHAR
                *
                *  SUBROUTINE TO DECODE CHARACTER
                *
B056 85 60      DECODE BIT A #$60    CONTROL CHAR ?
B058 27 27            BEQ    DECOD1  YES - CONTROL CHAR
B05A F6 0082          LDA B  CURPOS  GET CURSOR POSITION MSB
B05D C4 1F            AND B  #$1F    MASK TO 8K
B05F F7 008C          STA B  CUTEMP  SAVE IN TEMP
B062 F6 0083          LDA B  CURPOS+1 GET LSB
B065 F7 008D          STA B  CUTEMP+1 SAVE IT
B068 FE 008C          LDX    CUTEMP  GET CURPOS MASKED TO 8K
B06B A7 00            STA A  0,X     WRITE CHAR.
B06D FE 0082          LDX    CURPOS  GET CURSOR POSITION
B070 08               INX            BUMP CURSOR POSITION
B071 FF 0082          STX    CURPOS  SAVE CURSOR POSITION
B074 7C 0084          INC    CCOUNT
B077 B6 0084          LDA A  CCOUNT  GET CHAR THIS LINE
B07A B1 B164          CMP A  CLINE   LAST CHARACTER?
B07D 2A 69            BPL    CRLF    YES -
B07F 20 1C            BRA    UPDATE  UPDATE CRTC
B081 CE B165    DECOD1 LDX   #DECTAB-1  POINT TO DECODE TAB
B084 5F               CLR B
B085 5C         NEXT1 INC B          COUNT ENTRY
B086 08               INX            NEXT ENTRY
B087 8C B16C          CPX    #DECEND
B08A 27 10            BEQ    DECOD   LAST ENTRY?
B08C A1 00            CMP A  0,X     THIS ENTRY
B08E 26 F5            BNE    NEXT1
B090 CE B16A          LDX    #DECADD-2  POINT TO ROUTINE TAB
B093 08         NEXT2 INX
B094 08               INX            NEXT ENTRY
B095 5A               DEC B          COUNT ENTRIES
B096 26 FB            BNE    NEXT2
B098 EE 00            LDX    0,X     GET ROUTINE ADD.
B09A AD 00            JSR    0,X     GOTO SUBROUTINE
B09C 39         DECOD RTS            BACK TO CONTROL
                *
                *  SUBROUTINE TO UPDATE THE CRTC
                *  A & X REGISTERS ARE DESTROYED
                *
B09D 37         UPDATE PSH B         SAVE B REG
B09E C6 0C            LDA B  #$0C    POINT TO CTRC START ADD.
B0A0 CE 0080          LDX    #STARAD POINT TO DISPLAY VAR.
B0A3 A6 00      UDATE1 LDA A 0,X     GET DATA
B0A5 F7 4000          STA B  CRTCAR  SELECT REGISTER
B0A8 B7 4001          STA A  CRTCDR  PROGRAM VALUE
```

```
PAGE  003   CRT

B0AB 08                INX                NEXT VALUE
B0AC 5C                INC B              NEXT REGISTER
B0AD C1 10             CMP B   #$10       LAST REG.?
B0AF 26 F2             BNE     UDATE1     NEXT VALUES
B0B1 33                PUL B              RESTORE B REG.
B0B2 39                RTS
                *
                *  SUBROUTINE TO SCAN ACIA
                *  IF CARRY SET, CHAR. IN A REG.
                *  B & X REGISTERS SAVED
                *
B0B3 37         INCHS  PSH B              SAVE B REG.
B0B4 F6 0008           LDA B   ACIACR     GET STATUS REG
B0B7 56                ROR B              TEST DATA READY BIT
B0B8 24 06             BCC     INCHS1
B0BA B6 0009           LDA A   ACIADR     GET CHARACTER
B0BD 84 7F             AND A   #$7F       MASK OFF PARITY
B0BF 0D                SEC                SET CARRY IF INPUT
B0C0 33         INCHS1 PUL B              RESTORE B REG
B0C1 39                RTS
                *
                *  SUBROUTINE TO OUTPUT A CHAR IN A REG.
                *  B & X REGISTERS SAVED
                *
B0C2 37         OUTCH  PSH B              SAVE B REG.
B0C3 F6 0008    OUTCH1 LDA B   ACIACR     GET ACIA STATUS
B0C6 56                ROR B
B0C7 56                ROR B
B0C8 24 F9             BCC     OUTCH1     DATA REG. EMPTY?
B0CA B7 0009           STA A   ACIADR     OUTPUT DATA
B0CD 33                PUL B              RESTORE B REG.
B0CE 39                RTS
                *
                *  SUBROUTINE TO SCAN PIA1A (KEYBOARD)
                *  IF CARRY SET, CHAR IN A REG.
                *
B0CF F6 0011    INCHP  LDA B   PIA1AC     GET STATUS REG.
B0D2 58                ASL B              CHECK FOR DATA
B0D3 24 07             BCC     INCHP1     NO DATA?
B0D5 B6 0010           LDA A   PIA1AD     GET DATA
                *  IF KEYBOARD IS NOT COMPLEMENTED REPLACE NEXT
                *     INSTRUCTION WITH A NOP.
B0D8 43                COM A              COMPLEMENT DATA
B0D9 84 7F             AND A   #$7F       STRIP PARITY
B0DB 0D                SEC                SET CARRY
B0DC 39         INCHP1 RTS
                *
                *  SUBROUTINE TO CARRIAGE RETURN
                *  ALL REGISTERS DESTROYED
                *
B0DD FE 0086    RTURN1 LDX     LINEAD     GET STAR. ADD THIS LINE
B0E0 FF 0082           STX     CURPOS     SAVE IT
B0E3 7F 0084           CLR     CCOUNT     CLEAR CHAR/LINE COUNTER
B0E6 20 B5             BRA     UPDATE     UPDATE CRTC
                *
                *  SUBROUTINE TO CRLF
                *
B0E8 8D F3      CRLF   BSR     RTURN1
                *
                * SUBROUTINE TO LINE FEED
                * ALL REGISTERS DESTROYED
                *
B0EA CE 0080    LFEED  LDX     #STARAD    POINT TO DISPLAY VARIBLE
B0ED A6 03             LDA A   3,X        GET CURPOS LSB
B0EF BB B164           ADD A   CLINE      ADD CHAR/LINE
B0F2 A7 03             STA A   3,X        SAVE IT
B0F4 24 02             BCC     LFEED1     CHECK CARRY
B0F6 6C 02             INC     2,X        ADD CARRY TO MSB
```

PAGE 004 CRT

```
                   *
                   *  ROUTINE TO ADVANCE LINE START ADDR
                   *
B0F8 A6 07   LFEED1 LDA A  7,X       GET LINEAD LSB
B0FA BB B164        ADD A  CLINE     ADD CHAR/LINE
B0FD A7 07          STA A  7,X       SAVE IT
B0FF B7 008D        STA A  CUTEMP+1 SAVE IT IN TEMP
B102 A6 06          LDA A  6,X       GET LINEAD MSB
B104 89 00          ADC A  #0        ADD CARRY
B106 A7 06          STA A  6,X       SAVE IT
                   *
                   *  ROUTINE TO CHECK FOR LAST LINE ON SCREEN
                   *
B108 CE 0080        LDX    #STARAD   POINT TO DISPLAY VARIABLE
B10B A6 05          LDA A  5,X       GET LINES THIS SCREEN
B10D B1 B165        CMP A  LSCREN    LAST LINE?
B110 26 04          BNE    LFEED2
B112 6C 05          INC    5,X       COUNT LINE
B114 20 05          BRA    SCROLU    SCROLL UP
B116 6C 05   LFEED2 INC    5,X       COUNT LINE
B118 7E B09D        JMP    UPDATE
                   *
                   *  SUBROUTINE TO SCROLL UP
                   *  A & X REGISTERS DESTROYED
                   *
B11B CE 0080 SCROLU LDX    #STARAD   POINT TO DISPLAY VARIBLE
B11E 6A 05          DEC    5,X       SUB1 FROM LINE COUNT
B120 A6 01          LDA A  1,X       GET STARTING ADD. LSB
B122 BB B164        ADD A  CLINE     ADD, CHAR/LINE
B125 A7 01          STA A  1,X
B127 24 02          BCC    SCROL1
B129 6C 00          INC    0,X
B12B 7E B09D SCROL1 JMP    UPDATE    UPDATE STARTING ADD.
                   *
                   *  SUBROUTINE TO SCROLL DOWN
                   *  A & X REGISTERS DESTROYED
                   *
B12E CE 0080 SCROLD LDX    #STARAD   POINT TO SCREEN VARIABLE
B131 6C 05          INC    5,X       ADD 1 LINE TO LINE COUNT
B133 A6 01   SCROD1 LDA A  1,X       GET STARTING ADD. LSB
B135 B0 B164        SUB A  CLINE     CHAR/LINE
B138 A7 01          STA A  1,X       SAVE IT
B13A 24 03          BCC    SCROD2    CHECK BORROW
B13C 7A 0000        DEC    0.X       SUB. BORROW FROM MSB
B13F 7E B09D SCROD2 JMP    UPDATE    UPDATE START ADD.
                   *
                   *  SUBROUTINE TO PAGE DOWN
                   *  ALL REGISTERS DESTROYED
                   *
B142 F6 B165 PAGEDN LDA B  LSCREN    GET LINE/SCREEN
B145 8D E7   PAGED1 BSR    SCROLD    SCROLD DOWN 1 LINE
B147 5A             DEC B            COUNT LINE
B148 2C FB          BGE    PAGED1    LAST LINE?
B14A 39             RTS
                   *
                   *  SUBROUTINE TO PAGE UP
                   *  ALL REGISTERS DESTROYED
                   *
B14B F6 B165 PAGEUP LDA B  LSCREN    GET LINE/SCREEN
B14E 8D CB   PAGEU1 BSR    SCROLU    SCROLL UP 1 LINE
B150 5A             DEC B            COUNT LINES
B151 2C FB          BGE    PAGEU1
B153 39             RTS
                   *
                   *  THIS TABLE CONTAINS THE CRTC INITIAL
                   *  CONDITIONS. TO CHANGE FORMATS THIS
                   *  TABLE MUST BE CHANGED
                   *
B154 67      CRTTAB FCB    103,80,86,06  HORIZONTAL SECTION
```

```
PAGE  005   CRT

B158 1A              FCB     26,00,24,25  VERTICAL SECTION
B15C 00              FCB     00,10     INTERLACE,MAX RASTER
B15E 00              FCB     00,10     CURSOR SIZE & BLINK
B160 01              FCB     1,0       CURSOR LOCATION
B162 01              FCB     1,0       START ADDRESS
              *
              *  THESE ARE TWO PARAMETERS THAT FORMAT
              *     THE SCREEN THEY ARE SET AT 80 BY 24
              *
B164 50       CLINE  FCB     80        NUMBER OF CHAR. LINE
B165 17       LSCREN FCB     24-1      LINES PER SCREEN-1
              *
              *  THIS TABLE IS SEARCHED FOR A CONTROL
              *   CHARACTER. TO ADD COMMANDS, ADD TO
              *     THIS TABLE. IF DIFFERENT CODES
              *      ARE REQUIRED CHANGE HERE.
              *
B166 0A       DECTAB FCB     $0A       LINE FEED
B167 0D              FCB     $0D       CARRIAGE RETURN
B168 05              FCB     $05       SCROLL UP - CONTROL E
B169 04              FCB     $04       SCROLL DOWN - CONTROL D
B16A 03              FCB     $03       PAGE UP - CONTROL C
B16B 02              FCB     $02       PAGE DOWN - CONTROL B
     B16C     DECEND EQU     *
B16C B0EA     DECADD FDB     LFEED
B16E B0DD            FDB     RTURN1
B170 B11B            FDB     SCROLU
B172 B12E            FDB     SCROLD
B174 B14B            FDB     PAGEUP
B176 B142            FDB     PAGEDN
              *
              *  THESE EQUATES DEFINE THE BEGINNING AND ENDING
              *  ADDRESSES FOR THE DISPLAY MEMORY CLEAR ROUTINE
     8000     MEMSTR EQU     $8000     DISPLAY MEM. START ADDR
     87FF     MEMEND EQU     $87FF     DISPLAY MEM. END ADDR
              *
              *  STACK INITIALIZATION LOCATION
     00FF     STKADD EQU     $FF       STACK INITIAL LOCATION
              *  THESE ARE THE I/O EQUATES THEY MUST
              *  MATCH THE HARDWARE USED
     4000     CRTCAR EQU     $4000
     4001     CRTCDR EQU     $4001
     0010     PIA1AD EQU     $0010
     0011     PIA1AC EQU     $0011
     0012     PIA1BD EQU     $0012
     0013     PIA1BC EQU     $0013
     0008     ACIACR EQU     $0008
     0009     ACIADR EQU     $0009
0080                 ORG     $0080
0080 0002     STARAD RMB     2
0082 0002     CURPOS RMB     2
0084 0001     CCOUNT RMB     1
0085 0001     LCOUNT RMB     1
0086 0002     LINEAD RMB     2
0088 0002     STEMP  RMB     2
008A 0002     CTEMP  RMB     2
008C 0002     CUTEMP RMB     2
                     END

TOTAL ERRORS 00000
```

APPENDIX E

ASCII CONVERSION CHART

The conversion chart listed below is helpful in converting from a two-digit (2-byte) hexadecimal number to an ASCII character or from an ASCII character to a two-digit hexadecimal number. The example provided below shows the method of using this conversion chart.

Example

		Bits						
		MSB ←						→ LSB
ASCII	**Hex #**	**6**	**5**	**4**	**3**	**2**	**1**	**0**
T	54	1	0	1	0	1	0	0
?	3F	0	1	1	1	1	1	1
+	2B	0	1	0	1	0	1	1

Bits 0 to 3 Second Hex Digit (LSB)	Bits 4 to 6 First Hex Digit (MSB): 0	1	2	3	4	5	6	7
0	NUL	DLE	SP	0	@	P		p
1	SOH	DC1	!	1	A	Q	a	q
2	STX	DC2	"	2	B	R	b	r
3	ETX	DC3	#	3	C	S	c	s
4	EOT	DC4	$	4	D	T	d	t
5	ENQ	NAK	%	5	E	U	e	u
6	ACK	SYN	&	6	F	V	f	v
7	BEL	ETB	'	7	G	W	g	w
8	BS	CAN	(	8	H	X	h	x
9	HT	EM	)	9	I	Y	i	y
A	LF	SUB	*	:	J	Z	j	z
B	VT	ESC	+	;	K	[	k	{
C	FF	FS	,	<	L	/	l	/
D	CR	GS	-	=	M	]	m	}
E	SO	RS	.	>	N	∧	n	≈
F	SI	US	/	?	O	—	o	DEL

APPENDIX F

MC68HC11A8 INSTRUCTIONS, ADDRESSING MODES, AND EXECUTION TIMES

Source Form(s)	Operation	Boolean Expression	Addressing Mode for Operand	Machine Coding (Hexadecimal) Opcode	Operand(s)	Bytes	Cycle	Cycle by Cycle*	S	X	H	I	N	Z	V	C
ABA	Add Accumulators	A + B → A	INH	1B		1	2	2-1	-	-	↕	-	↕	↕	↕	↕
ABX	Add B to X	IX + 00:B → IX	INH	3A		1	3	2-2	-	-	-	-	-	-	-	-
ABY	Add B to Y	IY + 00:B → IY	INH	18 3A		2	4	2-4	-	-	-	-	-	-	-	-
ADCA (opr)	Add with Carry to A	A + M + C → A	A IMM	89	ii	2	2	3-1	-	-	↕	-	↕	↕	↕	↕
			A DIR	99	dd	2	3	4-1								
			A EXT	B9	hh ll	3	4	5-2								
			A IND,X	A9	ff	2	4	6-2								
			A IND,Y	18 A9	ff	3	5	7-2								
ADCB (opr)	Add with Carry to B	B + M + C → B	B IMM	C9	ii	2	2	3-1	-	-	↕	-	↕	↕	↕	↕
			B DIR	D9	dd	2	3	4-1								
			B EXT	F9	hh ll	3	4	5-2								
			B IND,X	E9	ff	2	4	6-2								
			B IND,Y	18 E9	ff	3	5	7-2								
ADDA (opr)	Add Memory to A	A + M → A	A IMM	8B	ii	2	2	3-1	-	-	↕	-	↕	↕	↕	↕
			A DIR	9B	dd	2	3	4-1								
			A EXT	BB	hh ll	3	4	5-2								
			A IND,X	AB	ff	2	4	6-2								
			A IND,Y	18 AB	ff	3	5	7-2								
ADDB (opr)	Add Memory to B	B + M → B	B IMM	CB	ii	2	2	3-1	-	-	↕	-	↕	↕	↕	↕
			B DIR	DB	dd	2	3	4-1								
			B EXT	FB	hh ll	3	4	5-2								
			B IND,X	EB	ff	2	4	6-2								
			B IND,Y	18 EB	ff	3	5	7-2								
ADDD (opr)	Add 16-Bit to D	D + M:M + 1 → D	IMM	C3	jj kk	3	4	3-3	-	-	-	-	↕	↕	↕	↕
			DIR	D3	dd	2	5	4-7								
			EXT	F3	hh ll	3	6	5-10								
			IND,X	E3	ff	2	6	6-10								
			IND, Y	18 E3	ff	3	7	7-8								
ANDA (opr)	AND A with Memory	A•M → A	A IMM	84	ii	2	2	3-1	-	-	-	-	↕	↕	0	-
			A DIR	94	dd	2	3	4-1								
			A EXT	B4	hh ll	3	4	5-2								
			A IND,X	A4	ff	2	4	6-2								
			A IND,Y	18 A4	ff	3	5	7-2								

Source Form(s)	Operation	Boolean Expression	Addressing Mode for Operand	Opcode	Operand(s)	Bytes	Cycle	Cycle by Cycle*	S	X	H	I	N	Z	V	C
ANDB (opr)	AND B with Memory	B•M → B	B IMM	C4	ii	2	2	3-1	-	-	-	-	↕	↕	0	-
			B DIR	D4	dd	2	3	4-1								
			B EXT	F4	hh ll	3	4	5-2								
			B IND,X	E4	ff	2	4	6-2								
			B IND,Y	18 E4	ff	3	5	7-2								
ASL (opr)	Arithmetic Shift Left	← C b7 b0 ← 0	EXT	78	hh ll	3	6	5-8	-	-	-	-	↕	↕	↕	↕
			IND,X	68	ff	2	6	6-3								
			IND,Y	18 68	ff	3	7	7-3								
ASLA			A INH	48		1	2	2-1								
ASLB			B INH	58		1	2	2-1								
ASLD	Arithmetic Shift Left Double	C b15 b0 ← 0	INH	05		1	3	2-2	-	-	-	-	↕	↕	↕	↕
ASR (opr)	Arithmetic Shift Right	→ b7 b0 C	EXT	77	hh ll	3	6	5-8	-	-	-	-	↕	↕	↕	↕
			IND,X	67	ff	2	6	6-3								
			IND,Y	18 67	ff	3	7	7-3								
ASRA			A INH	47		1	2	2-1								
ASRB			B INH	57		1	2	2-1								
BCC (rel)	Branch if Carry Clear	? C = 0	REL	24	rr	2	3	8-1	-	-	-	-	-	-	-	-
BCLR (opr) (msk)	Clear Bit(s)	M•($\overline{mm}$) → M	DIR	15	dd mm	3	6	4-10	-	-	-	-	↕	↕	0	-
			IND,X	1D	ff mm	3	7	6-13								
			IND,Y	18 1D	ff mm	4	8	7-10								
BCS (rel)	Branch if Carry Set	? C = 1	REL	25	rr	2	3	8-1	-	-	-	-	-	-	-	-
BEQ (rel)	Branch if = Zero	? Z = 1	REL	27	rr	2	3	8-1	-	-	-	-	-	-	-	-
BGE (rel)	Branch if ≥ Zero	? N ⊕ V = 0	REL	2C	rr	2	3	8-1	-	-	-	-	-	-	-	-
BGT (rel)	Branch if > Zero	? Z + (N ⊕ V) = 0	REL	2E	rr	2	3	8-1	-	-	-	-	-	-	-	-
BHI (rel)	Branch if Higher	? C + Z = 0	REL	22	rr	2	3	8-1	-	-	-	-	-	-	-	-
BHS (rel)	Branch if Higher or Same	? C = 0	REL	24	rr	2	3	8-1	-	-	-	-	-	-	-	-
BITA (opr)	Bit(s) Test A with Memory	A•M	A IMM	85	ii	2	2	3-1	-	-	-	-	↕	↕	0	-
			A DIR	95	dd	2	3	4-1								
			A EXT	B5	hh ll	3	4	5-2								
			A IND,X	A5	ff	2	4	6-2								
			A IND,Y	18 A5	ff	3	5	7-2								
BITB (opr)	Bit(s) Test B with Memory	B•M	B IMM	C5	ii	2	2	3-1	-	-	-	-	↕	↕	0	-
			B DIR	D5	dd	2	3	4-1								
			B EXT	F5	hh ll	3	4	5-2								
			B IND,X	E5	ff	2	4	6-2								
			B IND,Y	18 E5	ff	3	5	7-2								
BLE (rel)	Branch if ≤ Zero	? Z + (N ⊕ V) = 1	REL	2F	rr	2	3	8-1	-	-	-	-	-	-	-	-
BLO (rel)	Branch if Lower	? C = 1	REL	25	rr	2	3	8-1	-	-	-	-	-	-	-	-
BLS (rel)	Branch if Lower or Same	? C + Z = 1	REL	23	rr	2	3	8-1	-	-	-	-	-	-	-	-
BLT (rel)	Branch If < Zero	? N ⊕ V = 1	REL	2D	rr	2	3	8-1	-	-	-	-	-	-	-	-
BMI (rel)	Branch if Minus	? N = 1	REL	2B	rr	2	3	8-1	-	-	-	-	-	-	-	-
BNE (rel)	Branch if Not = Zero	? Z = 0	REL	26	rr	2	3	8-1	-	-	-	-	-	-	-	-
BPL (rel)	Branch if Plus	? N = 0	REL	2A	rr	2	3	8-1	-	-	-	-	-	-	-	-
BRA (rel)	Branch Always	? 1 = 1	REL	20	rr	2	3	8-1	-	-	-	-	-	-	-	-
BRCLR(opr) (msk) (rel)	Branch if Bit(s) Clear	? M• mm = 0	DIR	13	dd mm rr	4	6	4-11	-	-	-	-	-	-	-	-
			IND,X	1F	ff mm rr	4	7	6-14								
			IND,Y	18 1F	ff mm rr	5	8	7-11								
BRN (rel)	Branch Never	? 1 = 0	REL	21	rr	2	3	8-1	-	-	-	-	-	-	-	-
BRSET(opr) (msk) (rel)	Branch if Bit(s) Set	? ($\overline{M}$)•mm = 0	DIR	12	dd mm rr	4	6	4-11	-	-	-	-	-	-	-	-
			IND,X	1E	ff mm rr	4	7	6-14								
			IND,Y	18 1E	ff mm rr	5	8	7-11								
BSET(opr) (msk)	Set Bit(s)	M + mm → M	DIR	14	dd mm	3	6	4-10	-	-	-	-	↕	↕	0	-
			IND,X	1C	ff mm	3	7	6-13								
			IND,Y	18 1C	ff mm	4	8	7-10								
BSR (rel)	Branch to Subroutine	See Special Ops	REL	8D	rr	2	6	8-2	-	-	-	-	-	-	-	-
BVC (rel)	Branch if Overflow Clear	? V = 0	REL	28	rr	2	3	8-1	-	-	-	-	-	-	-	-

Source Form(s)	Operation	Boolean Expression	Addressing Mode for Operand	Machine Coding (Hexadecimal) Opcode	Operand(s)	Bytes	Cycle	Cycle by Cycle*	S	X	H	I	N	Z	V	C
BVS (rel)	Branch if Overflow Set	? V = 1	REL	29	rr	2	3	8-1	-	-	-	-	-	-	-	-
CBA	Compare A to B	A-B	INH	11		1	2	2-1	-	-	-	-	↕	↕	↕	↕
CLC	Clear Carry Bit	0 → C	INH	0C		1	2	2-1	-	-	-	-	-	-	-	0
CLI	Clear Interrupt Mask	0 → I	INH	0E		1	2	2-1	-	-	-	0	-	-	-	-
CLR (opr)	Clear Memory Byte	0 → M	EXT	7F	hh ll	3	6	5-8	-	-	-	-	0	1	0	0
			IND,X	6F	ff	2	6	6-3								
			IND,Y	18 6F	ff	3	7	7-3								
CLRA	Clear Accumulator A	0 → A	A INH	4F		1	2	2-1	-	-	-	-	0	1	0	0
CLRB	Clear Accumulator B	0 → B	B INH	5F		1	2	2-1	-	-	-	-	0	1	0	0
CLV	Clear Overflow Flag	0 → V	INH	0A		1	2	2-1	-	-	-	-	-	-	0	-
CMPA (opr)	Compare A to Memory	A − M	A IMM	81	ii	2	2	3-1	-	-	-	-	↕	↕	↕	↕
			A DIR	91	dd	2	3	4-1								
			A EXT	B1	hh ll	3	4	5-2								
			A IND,X	A1	ff	2	4	6-2								
			A IND,Y	18 A1	ff	3	5	7-2								
CMPB (opr)	Compare B to Memory	B − M	B IMM	C1	ii	2	2	3-1	-	-	-	-	↕	↕	↕	↕
			B DIR	D1	dd	2	3	4-1								
			B EXT	F1	hh ll	3	4	5-2								
			B IND,X	E1	ff	2	4	6-2								
			B IND,Y	18 E1	ff	3	5	7-2								
COM (opr)	1's Complement Memory Byte	$FF − M → M	EXT	73	hh ll	3	6	5-8	-	-	-	-	↕	↕	0	1
			IND,X	63	ff	2	6	6-3								
			IND,Y	18 63	ff	3	7	7-3								
COMA	1's Complement A	$FF − A → A	A INH	43		1	2	2-1	-	-	-	-	↕	↕	0	1
COMB	1's Complement B	$FF − B → B	B INH	53		1	2	2-1	-	-	-	-	↕	↕	0	1
CPD (opr)	Compare D to Memory 16-Bit	D − M:M + 1	IMM	1A 83	jj kk	4	5	3-5	-	-	-	-	↕	↕	↕	↕
			DIR	1A 93	dd	3	6	4-9								
			EXT	1A B3	hh ll	4	7	5-11								
			IND,X	1A A3	ff	3	7	6-11								
			IND,Y	CD A3	ff	3	7	7-8								
CPX (opr)	Compare X to Memory 16-Bit	IX − M:M + 1	IMM	8C	jj kk	3	4	3-3	-	-	-	-	↕	↕	↕	↕
			DIR	9C	dd	2	5	4-7								
			EXT	BC	hh ll	3	6	5-10								
			IND,X	AC	ff	2	6	6-10								
			IND,Y	CD AC	ff	3	7	7-8								
CPY (opr)	Compare Y to Memory 16-Bit	IY − M:M + 1	IMM	18 8C	jj kk	4	5	3-5	-	-	-	-	↕	↕	↕	↕
			DIR	18 9C	dd	3	6	4-9								
			EXT	18 BC	hh ll	4	7	5-11								
			IND,X	1A AC	ff	3	7	6-11								
			IND,Y	18 AC	ff	3	7	7-8								
DAA	Decimal Adjust A	Adjust Sum to BCD	INH	19		1	2	2-1	-	-	-	-	↕	↕	↕	↕
DEC (opr)	Decrement Memory Byte	M − 1 → M	EXT	7A	hh ll	3	6	5-8	-	-	-	-	↕	↕	↕	-
			IND,X	6A	ff	2	6	6-3								
			IND,Y	18 6A	ff	3	7	7-3								
DECA	Decrement Accumulator A	A − 1 → A	A INH	4A		1	2	2-1	-	-	-	-	↕	↕	↕	-
DECB	Decrement Accumulator B	B − 1 → B	B INH	5A		1	2	2-1	-	-	-	-	↕	↕	↕	-
DES	Decrement Stack Pointer	SP − 1 → SP	INH	34		1	3	2-3	-	-	-	-	-	-	-	-
DEX	Decrement Index Register X	IX − 1 → IX	INH	09		1	3	2-2	-	-	-	-	-	↕	-	-
DEY	Decrement Index Register Y	IY − 1 → IY	INH	18 09		2	4	2-4	-	-	-	-	-	↕	-	-
EORA (opr)	Exclusive OR A with Memory	A ⊕ M → A	A IMM	88	ii	2	2	3-1	-	-	-	-	↕	↕	0	-
			A DIR	98	dd	2	3	4-1								
			A EXT	B8	hh ll	3	4	5-2								
			A IND,X	A8	ff	2	4	6-2								
			A IND,Y	18 A8	ff	3	5	7-2								
EORB (opr)	Exclusive OR B with Memory	B ⊕ M → B	B IMM	C8	ii	2	2	3-1	-	-	-	-	↕	↕	0	-
			B DIR	D8	dd	2	3	4-1								
			B EXT	F8	hh ll	3	4	5-2								
			B IND,X	E8	ff	2	4	6-2								
			B IND,Y	18 E8	ff	3	5	7-2								

Source Form(s)	Operation	Boolean Expression	Addressing Mode for Operand	Machine Coding (Hexadecimal) Opcode	Operand(s)	Bytes	Cycle	Cycle by Cycle*	S	X	H	I	N	Z	V	C
FDIV	Fractional Divide 16 by 16	D/IX → IX; r → D	INH	03		1	41	2-17	-	-	-	-	-	↕	↕	↕
IDIV	Integer Divide 16 by 16	D/IX → IX; r → D	INH	02		1	41	2-17	-	-	-	-	-	↕	0	↕
INC (opr)	Increment Memory Byte	M + 1 → M	EXT	7C	hh ll	3	6	5-8	-	-	-	-	↕	↕	↕	-
			IND,X	6C	ff	2	6	6-3								
			IND,Y	18 6C	ff	3	7	7-3								
INCA	Increment Accumulator A	A + 1 → A	A INH	4C		1	2	2-1	-	-	-	-	↕	↕	↕	-
INCB	Increment Accumulator B	B + 1 → B	B INH	5C		1	2	2-1	-	-	-	-	↕	↕	↕	-
INS	Increment Stack Pointer	SP + 1 → SP	INH	31		1	3	2-3	-	-	-	-	-	-	-	-
INX	Increment Index Register X	IX + 1 → IX	INH	08		1	3	2-2	-	-	-	-	-	↕	-	-
INY	Increment Index Register Y	IY + 1 → IY	INH	18 08		2	4	2-4	-	-	-	-	-	↕	-	-
JHP (opr)	Jump	See Special Ops	EXT	7E	hh ll	3	3	5-1	-	-	-	-	-	-	-	-
			IND,X	6E	ff	2	3	6-1								
			IND,Y	18 6E	ff	3	4	7-1								
JSR (Opr)	Jump to Subroutine	See Special Ops	DIR	9D	dd	2	5	4-8	-	-	-	-	-	-	-	-
			EXT	BD	hh ll	3	6	5-12								
			IND,X	AD	ff	2	6	6-12								
			IND,Y	18 AD	ff	3	7	7-9								
LDAA (opr)	Load Accumulator A	M → A	A IMM	86	ii	2	2	3-1	-	-	-	-	↕	↕	0	-
			A DIR	96	dd	2	3	4-1								
			A EXT	B6	hh ll	3	4	5-2								
			A IND,X	A6	ff	2	4	6-2								
			A IND,Y	18 A6	ff	3	5	7-2								
LDAB (opr)	Load Accumulator B	M → B	B IMM	C6	ii	2	2	3-1	-	-	-	-	↕	↕	0	-
			B DIR	D6	dd	2	3	4-1								
			B EXT	F6	hh ll	3	4	5-2								
			B IND,X	E6	ff	2	4	6-2								
			B IND,Y	18 E6	ff	3	5	7-2								
LDD (opr)	Load Double Accumulator D	M → A,M + 1 → B	IMM	CC	jj kk	3	3	3-2	-	-	-	-	↕	↕	0	-
			DIR	DC	dd	2	4	4-3								
			EXT	FC	hh ll	3	5	5-4								
			IND,X	EC	ff	2	5	6-6								
			IND,Y	18 EC	ff	3	6	7-6								
LDS (opr)	Load Stack Pointer	M:M + 1 → SP	IMM	8E	jj kk	3	3	3-2	-	-	-	-	↕	↕	0	-
			DIR	9E	dd	2	4	4-3								
			EXT	BE	hh ll	3	5	5-4								
			IND,X	AE	ff	2	5	6-6								
			IND,Y	18 AE	ff	3	6	7-6								
LDX (opr)	Load Index Register X	M:M + 1 → IX	IMM	CE	jj kk	3	3	3-2	-	-	-	-	↕	↕	0	-
			DIR	DE	dd	2	4	4-3								
			EXT	FE	hh ll	3	5	5-4								
			IND,X	EE	ff	2	5	6-6								
			IND,Y	CD EE	ff	3	6	7-6								
LDY (opr)	Load Index Register Y	M:M + 1 → IY	IMM	18 CE	jj kk	4	4	3-4	-	-	-	-	↕	↕	0	-
			DIR	18 DE	dd	3	5	4-5								
			EXT	18 FE	hh ll	4	6	5-6								
			IND,X	1A EE	ff	3	6	6-7								
			IND,Y	18 EE	ff	3	6	7-6								
LSL (opr)	Logical Shift Left	C ← b7 … b0 ← 0	EXT	78	hh ll	3	6	5-8	-	-	-	-	↕	↕	↕	↕
			IND,X	68	ff	2	6	6-3								
			IND,Y	18 68	ff	3	7	7-3								
LSLA			A INH	48		1	2	2-1								
LSLB			B INH	58		1	2	2-1								
LSLD	Logical Shift Left Double	C ← b15 … b0 ← 0	INH	05		1	3	2-2	-	-	-	-	↕	↕	↕	↕
LSR (opr)	Logical Shift Right	0 → b7 … b0 → C	EXT	74	hh ll	3	6	5-8	-	-	-	-	0	↕	↕	↕
			IND,X	64	ff	2	6	6-3								
			IND,Y	18 64	ff	3	7	7-3								
LSRA			A INH	44		1	2	2-1								
LSRB			B INH	54		1	2	2-1								

Source Form(s)	Operation	Boolean Expression	Addressing Mode for Operand	Machine Coding (Hexadecimal) Opcode	Operand(s)	Bytes	Cycle	Cycle by Cycle*	S	X	H	I	N	Z	V	C
LSRD	Logical Shift Right Double	0 → [b15 ... b0] → C	INH	04		1	3	2-2	-	-	-	-	0	↕	↕	↕
MUL	Multiply 8 by 8	AxB → D	INH	3D		1	10	2-13	-	-	-	-	-	-	-	↕
NEG (opr)	2's Complement Memory Byte	0 − M → M	EXT	70	hh ll	3	6	5-8	-	-	-	-	↕	↕	↕	↕
			IND,X	60	ff	2	6	6-3								
			IND,Y	18 60	ff	3	7	7-3								
NEGA	2's Complement A	0 − A → A	A INH	40		1	2	2-1	-	-	-	-	↕	↕	↕	↕
NEGB	2's Complement B	0 − B → B	B INH	50		1	2	2-1	-	-	-	-	↕	↕	↕	↕
NOP	No Operation	No Operation	INH	01		1	2	2-1	-	-	-	-	-	-	-	-
ORAA (opr)	OR Accumulator A (Inclusive)	A + M → A	A IMM	8A	ii	2	2	3-1	-	-	-	-	↕	↕	0	-
			A DIR	9A	dd	2	3	4-1								
			A EXT	BA	hh ll	3	4	5-2								
			A IND,X	AA	ff	2	4	6-2								
			A IND,Y	18 AA	ff	3	5	7-2								
ORAB (opr)	OR Accumulator B (Inclusive)	B + M → B	B IMM	CA	ii	2	2	3-1	-	-	-	-	↕	↕	0	-
			B DIR	DA	dd	2	3	4-1								
			B EXT	FA	hh ll	3	4	5-2								
			B IND,X	EA	ff	2	4	6-2								
			B IND,Y	18 EA	ff	3	5	7-2								
PSHA	Push A onto Stack	A → Stk, SP = SP − 1	A INH	36		1	3	2-6	-	-	-	-	-	-	-	-
PSHB	Push B onto Stack	B → Stk, SP = SP − 1	B INH	37		1	3	2-6	-	-	-	-	-	-	-	-
PSHX	Push X onto Stack (Lo First)	IX → Stk, SP = SP − 2	INH	3C		1	4	2-7	-	-	-	-	-	-	-	-
PSHY	Push Y onto Stack (Lo First)	IY → Stk, SP = SP − 2	INH	18 3C		2	5	2-8	-	-	-	-	-	-	-	-
PULA	Pull A from Stack	SP = SP + 1, A ← Stk	A INH	32		1	4	2-9	-	-	-	-	-	-	-	-
PULB	Pull B from Stack	SP = SP + 1, B ← Stk	B INH	33		1	4	2-9	-	-	-	-	-	-	-	-
PULX	Pull X from Stack (Hi First)	SP = SP + 2, IX ← Stk	INH	38		1	5	2-10	-	-	-	-	-	-	-	-
PULY	Pull Y from Stack (Hi First)	SP = SP + 2, IY ← Stk	INH	18 38		2	6	2-11	-	-	-	-	-	-	-	-
ROL (opr)	Rotate Left	C ← [b7 ← b0] ← C	EXT	79	hh ll	3	6	5-8	-	-	-	-	↕	↕	↕	↕
			IND,X	69	ff	2	6	6-3								
			IND,Y	18 69	ff	3	7	7-3								
ROLA			A INH	49		1	2	2-1								
ROLB			B INH	59		1	2	2-1								
ROR (opr)	Rotate Right	C → [b7 → b0] → C	EXT	76	hh ll	3	6	5-8	-	-	-	-	↕	↕	↕	↕
			IND,X	66	ff	2	6	6-3								
			IND,Y	18 66	ff	3	7	7-3								
RORA			A INH	46		1	2	2-1								
RORB			B INH	56		1	2	2-1								
RTI	Return from Interrupt	See Special Ops	INH	3B		1	12	2-14	↕	↓	↕	↕	↕	↕	↕	↕
RTS	Return from Subroutine	See Special Ops	INH	39		1	5	2-12	-	-	-	-	-	-	-	-
SBA	Subtract B from A	A − B → A	INH	10		1	2	2-1	-	-	-	-	↕	↕	↕	↕
SBCA (opr)	Subtract with Carry from A	A − M − C → A	A IMM	82	ii	2	2	3-1	-	-	-	-	↕	↕	↕	↕
			A DIR	92	dd	2	3	4-1								
			A EXT	B2	hh ll	3	4	5-2								
			A IND,X	A2	ff	2	4	6-2								
			A IND,Y	18 A2	ff	3	5	7-2								
SBCB (opr)	Subtract from Carry from B	B − M − C → B	B IMM	C2	ii	2	2	3-1	-	-	-	-	↕	↕	↕	↕
			B DIR	D2	dd	2	3	4-1								
			B EXT	F2	hh ll	3	4	5-2								
			B IND,X	E2	ff	2	4	6-2								
			B IND,Y	18 E2	ff	3	5	7-2								
SEC	Set Carry	1 → C	INH	0D		1	2	2-1	-	-	-	-	-	-	-	1
SEI	Set Interrupt Mask	1 → I	INH	0F		1	2	2-1	-	-	-	1	-	-	-	-
SEV	Set Overflow Flag	1 → V	INH	0B		1	2	2-1	-	-	-	-	-	-	1	-
STAA (opr)	Store Accumulator A	A → M	A DIR	97	dd	2	3	4-2	-	-	-	-	↕	↕	0	-
			A EXT	B7	hh ll	3	4	5-3								
			A IND,X	A7	ff	2	4	6-5								
			A IND,Y	18 A7	ff	3	5	7-5								

Source Form(s)	Operation	Boolean Expression	Addressing Mode for Operand	Machine Coding (Hexadecimal) Opcode	Operand(s)	Bytes	Cycle	Cycle by Cycle*	S	X	H	I	N	Z	V	C
STAB (opr)	Store Accumulator B	B → M	B DIR	D7	dd	2	3	4-2	-	-	-	-	↕	↕	0	-
			B EXT	F7	hh ll	3	4	5-3								
			B IND,X	E7	ff	2	4	6-5								
			B IND,Y	18 E7	ff	3	5	7-5								
STD (opr)	Store Accumulator D	A → M, B → M + 1	DIR	DD	dd	2	4	4-4	-	-	-	-	↕	↕	0	-
			EXT	FD	hh ll	3	5	5-5								
			IND,X	ED	ff	2	5	6-8								
			IND,Y	18 ED	ff	3	6	7-7								
STOP	Stop Internal Clocks		INH	CF		1	2	2-1	-	-	-	-	-	-	-	-
STS (opr)	Store Stack Pointer	SP → M:M + 1	DIR	9F	dd	2	4	4-4	-	-	-	-	↕	↕	0	-
			EXT	BF	hh ll	3	5	5-5								
			IND,X	AF	ff	2	5	6-8								
			IND,Y	18 AF	ff	3	6	7-7								
STX (opr)	Store Index Register X	IX → M:M + 1	DIR	DF	dd	2	4	4-4	-	-	-	-	↕	↕	0	-
			EXT	FF	hh ll	3	5	5-5								
			IND,X	EF	ff	2	5	6-8								
			IND,Y	CD EF	ff	3	6	7-7								
STY (opr)	Store Index Register Y	IY → M:M + 1	DIR	18 DF	dd	3	5	4-6	-	-	-	-	↕	↕	0	-
			EXT	18 FF	hh ll	4	6	5-7								
			IND,X	1A EF	ff	3	6	6-9								
			IND,Y	18 EF	ff	3	6	7-7								
SUBA (opr)	Subtract Memory from A	A − M → A	A IMM	80	ii	2	2	3-1	-	-	-	-	↕	↕	↕	↕
			A DIR	90	dd	2	3	4-1								
			A EXT	B0	hh ll	3	4	5-2								
			A IND,X	A0	ff	2	4	6-2								
			A IND,Y	18 A0	ff	3	5	7-2								
SUBB (opr)	Subtract Memory from B	B − M → B	B IMM	C0	ii	2	2	3-1	-	-	-	-	↕	↕	↕	↕
			B DIR	D0	dd	2	3	4-1								
			B EXT	F0	hh ll	3	4	5-2								
			B IND,X	E0	ff	2	4	6-2								
			B IND,Y	18 E0	ff	3	5	7-2								
SUBD (opr)	Subtract Memory from D	D − M:M + 1 → D	IMM	83	jj kk	3	4	3-3	-	-	-	-	↕	↕	↕	↕
			DIR	93	dd	2	5	4-7								
			EXT	B3	hh ll	3	6	5-10								
			IND,X	A3	ff	2	6	6-10								
			IND,Y	18 A3	ff	3	7	7-8								
SWI	Software Interrupt	See Special Ops	INH	3F		1	14	2-15	-	-	-	1	-	-	-	-
TAB	Transfer A to B	A → B	INH	16		1	2	2-1	-	-	-	-	↕	↕	0	-
TAP	Transfer A to CC Register	A → CCR	INH	06		1	2	2-1	↕	↓	↕	↕	↕	↕	↕	↕
TBA	Transfer B to A	B → A	INH	17		1	2	2-1	-	-	-	-	↕	↕	0	-
TEST	TEST (Only in Test Modes)	Address Bus Counts	INH	00		1	**	2-20	-	-	-	-	-	-	-	-
TPA	Transfer CC Register to A	CCR → A	INH	07		1	2	2-1	-	-	-	-	-	-	-	-
TST (opr)	Test for Zero or Minus	M − 0	EXT	7D	hh ll	3	6	5-9	-	-	-	-	↕	↕	0	0
			IND,X	6D	ff	2	6	6-4								
			IND,Y	18 6D	ff	3	7	7-4								
TSTA		A − 0	A INH	4D		1	2	2-1	-	-	-	-	↕	↕	0	0
TSTB		B − 0	B INH	5D		1	2	2-1	-	-	-	-	↕	↕	0	0
TSX	Transfer Stack Pointer to X	SP + 1 → IX	INH	30		1	3	2-3	-	-	-	-	-	-	-	-
TSY	Transfer Stack Pointer to Y	SP + 1 → IY	INH	18 30		2	4	2-5	-	-	-	-	-	-	-	-

Source Form(s)	Operation	Boolean Expression	Addressing Mode for Operand	Machine Coding (Hexadecimal) Opcode	Operand(s)	Bytes	Cycle	Cycle by Cycle	S	X	H	I	N	Z	V	C
TXS	Transfer X to Stack Pointer	IX − 1 → SP	INH	35		1	3	2-2	-	-	-	-	-	-	-	-
TYS	Transfer Y to Stack Pointer	IY − 1 → SP	INH	18 35		2	4	2-4	-	-	-	-	-	-	-	-
WAI	Wait for Interrupt	Stack Regs & WAIT	INH	3E		2	***	2-16	-	-	-	-	-	-	-	-
XGDX	Exchange D with X	IX → D, D → IX	INH	8F		1	3	2-2	-	-	-	-	-	-	-	-
XGDY	Exchange D with Y	IY → D, D → IY	INH	18 8F		2	4	2-4	-	-	-	-	-	-	-	-

* Infinity or Until Reset Occurs

** 12 Cycles are used beginning with the opcode fetch. A wait state is entered which remains in effect for an integer number of MPU E-clock cycles (n) until an interrupt is recognized. Finally, two additional cycles are used to fetch the appropriate interrupt vector (14 + n total).

dd = 8-Bit Direct Address ($0000 – $00FF) (High Byte Assumed to be $00)
ff = 8-Bit Positive Offset $00 (0) to $FF (255) (Is Added to Index)
hh = High Order Byte of 16-Bit Extended Address
ii = One Byte of Immediate Data
jj = High Order Byte of 16-Bit Immediate Data
kk = Low Order Byte of 16-Bit Immediate Data
ll = Low Order Byte of 16-Bit Extended Address
mm = 8-Bit Bit Mask (Set Bits to be Affected)
rr = Signed Relative Offset $80 (− 128) to $7F (+ 127)
(Offset Relative to the Address Following the Machine Code Offset Byte)

APPENDIX G

THE 6809 INSTRUCTION SET

TABLE G-1 Descriptors of 6809

MC6809

TABLE G–6 – PROGRAMMING AID

Instruction	Forms	Immediate Op	Immediate ~	Immediate #	Direct Op	Direct ~	Direct #	Indexed Op	Indexed ~	Indexed #	Extended Op	Extended ~	Extended #	Inherent Op	Inherent ~	Inherent #	Description	5 H	3 N	2 Z	1 V	0 C
ABX														3A	3	1	B + X → X (Unsigned)	•	•	•	•	•
ADC	ADCA	89	2	2	99	4	2	A9	4+	2+	B9	5	3				A + M + C → A	↕	↕	↕	↕	↕
	ADCB	C9	2	2	D9	4	2	E9	4+	2+	F9	5	3				B + M + C → B	↕	↕	↕	↕	↕
ADD	ADDA	8B	2	2	9B	4	2	AB	4+	2+	BB	5	3				A + M → A	↕	↕	↕	↕	↕
	ADDB	CB	2	2	DB	4	2	EB	4+	2+	FB	5	3				B + M → B	↕	↕	↕	↕	↕
	ADDD	C3	4	3	D3	6	2	E3	6+	2+	F3	7	3				D + M:M + 1 → D	•	↕	↕	↕	↕
AND	ANDA	84	2	2	94	4	2	A4	4+	2+	B4	5	3				A Λ M → A	•	↕	↕	0	•
	ANDB	C4	2	2	D4	4	2	E4	4+	2+	F4	5	3				B Λ M → B	•	↕	↕	0	•
	ANDCC	1C	3	2													CC Λ IMM → CC					7
ASL	ASLA													48	2	1	A	8	↕	↕	↕	↕
	ASLB													58	2	1	B } c ← b7 … b0 ← 0	8	↕	↕	↕	↕
	ASL				08	6	2	68	6+	2+	78	7	3				M	8	↕	↕	↕	↕
ASR	ASRA													47	2	1	A	8	↕	↕	•	↕
	ASRB													57	2	1	B } b7 … b0 → c	8	↕	↕	•	↕
	ASR				07	6	2	67	6+	2+	77	7	3				M	8	↕	↕	•	↕
BIT	BITA	85	2	2	95	4	2	A5	4+	2+	B5	5	3				Bit Test A (M Λ A)	•	↕	↕	0	•
	BITB	C5	2	2	D5	4	2	E5	4+	2+	F5	5	3				Bit Test B (M Λ B)	•	↕	↕	0	•
CLR	CLRA													4F	2	1	0 → A	•	0	1	0	0
	CLRB													5F	2	1	0 → B	•	0	1	0	0
	CLR				0F	6	2	6F	6+	2+	7F	7	3				0 → M	•	0	1	0	0
CMP	CMPA	81	2	2	91	4	2	A1	4+	2+	B1	5	3				Compare M from A	8	↕	↕	↕	↕
	CMPB	C1	2	2	D1	4	2	E1	4+	2+	F1	5	3				Compare M from B	8	↕	↕	↕	↕
	CMPD	10	5	4	10	7	3	10	7+	3+	10	8	4				Compare M:M + 1 from D	•	↕	↕	↕	↕
		83			93			A3			B3											
	CMPS	11	5	4	11	7	3	11	7+	3+	11	8	4				Compare M:M + 1 from S	•	↕	↕	↕	↕
		8C			9C			AC			BC											
	CMPU	11	5	4	11	7	3	11	7+	3+	11	8	4				Compare M:M + 1 from U	•	↕	↕	↕	↕
		83			93			A3			B3											
	CMPX	8C	4	3	9C	6	2	AC	6+	2+	BC	7	3				Compare M:M + 1 from X	•	↕	↕	↕	↕
	CMPY	10	5	4	10	7	3	10	7+	3+	10	8	4				Compare M:M + 1 from Y	•	↕	↕	↕	↕
		8C			9C			AC			BC											
COM	COMA													43	2	1	$\overline{A}$ → A	•	↕	↕	0	1
	COMB													53	2	1	$\overline{B}$ → B	•	↕	↕	0	1
	COM				03	6	2	63	6+	2+	73	7	3				$\overline{M}$ → M	•	↕	↕	0	1
CWAI		3C	≥20	2													CC Λ IMM → CC Wait for Interrupt					7
DAA														19	2	1	Decimal Adjust A	•	↕	↕	0	↕
DEC	DECA													4A	2	1	A – 1 → A	•	↕	↕	↕	•
	DECB													5A	2	1	B – 1 → B	•	↕	↕	↕	•
	DEC				0A	6	2	6A	6+	2+	7A	7	3				M – 1 → M	•	↕	↕	↕	•
EOR	EORA	88	2	2	98	4	2	A8	4+	2+	B8	5	3				A ⊻ M → A	•	↕	↕	0	•
	EORB	C8	2	2	D8	4	2	E8	4+	2+	F8	5	3				B ⊻ M → B	•	↕	↕	0	•
EXG	R1, R2	1E	8	2													R1 ↔ R2[2]	•	•	•	•	•
INC	INCA													4C	2	1	A + 1 → A	•	↕	↕	↕	•
	INCB													5C	2	1	B + 1 → B	•	↕	↕	↕	•
	INC				0C	6	2	6C	6+	2+	7C	7	3				M + 1 → M	•	↕	↕	↕	•
JMP					0E	3	2	6E	3+	2+	7E	4	3				EA[3] → PC	•	•	•	•	•
JSR					9D	7	2	AD	7+	2+	BD	8	3				Jump to Subroutine	•	•	•	•	•
LD	LDA	86	2	2	96	4	2	A6	4+	2+	B6	5	3				M → A	•	↕	↕	0	•
	LDB	C6	2	2	D6	4	2	E6	4+	2+	F6	5	3				M → B	•	↕	↕	0	•
	LDD	CC	3	3	DC	5	2	EC	5+	2+	FC	6	3				M:M + 1 → D	•	↕	↕	0	•
	LDS	10	4	4	10	6	3	10	6+	3+	10	7	4				M:M + 1 → S	•	↕	↕	0	•
		CE			DE			EE			FE											
	LDU	CE	3	3	DE	5	2	EE	5+	2+	FE	6	3				M:M + 1 → U	•	↕	↕	0	•
	LDX	8E	3	3	9E	5	2	AE	5+	2+	BE	6	3				M:M + 1 → X	•	↕	↕	0	•
	LDY	10	4	4	10	6	3	10	6+	3+	10	7	4				M:M + 1 → Y	•	↕	↕	0	•
		8E			9E			AE			BE											
LEA	LEAS							32	4+	2+							EA[3] → S	•	•	•	•	•
	LEAU							33	4+	2+							EA[3] → U	•	•	•	•	•
	LEAX							30	4+	2+							EA[3] → X	•	•	↕	•	•
	LEAY							31	4+	2+							EA[3] → Y	•	•	↕	•	•

LEGEND:

- OP Operation Code (Hexadecimal)
- ~ Number of MPU Cycles
- # Number of Program Bytes
- \+ Arithmetic Plus
- – Arithmetic Minus
- • Multiply
- $\overline{M}$ Complement of M
- → Transfer Into
- H Half-carry (from bit 3)
- N Negative (sign bit)
- Z Zero result
- V Overflow, 2's complement
- C Carry from ALU
- ↕ Test and set if true, cleared otherwise
- • Not Affected
- CC Condition Code Register
- : Concatenation
- V Logical or
- Λ Logical and
- ⊻ Logical Exclusive or

MOTOROLA *Semiconductor Products Inc.*

TABLE G-1 Continued

MC6809

TABLE G–6 — PROGRAMMING AID (CONTINUED)

Instruction	Forms	Immediate Op	~	#	Direct Op	~	#	Indexed[1] Op	~	#	Extended Op	~	#	Inherent Op	~	#	Description	5 H	3 N	2 Z	1 V	0 C
LSL	LSLA													48	2	1		•	↕	↕	↕	↕
	LSLB													58	2	1		•	↕	↕	↕	↕
	LSL				08	6	2	68	6+	2+	78	7	3					•	↕	↕	↕	↕
LSR	LSRA													44	2	1		•	0	↕	•	↕
	LSRB													54	2	1		•	0	↕	•	↕
	LSR				04	6	2	64	6+	2+	74	7	3					•	0	↕	•	↕
MUL														3D	11	1	A × B → D (Unsigned)	•	•	↕	•	9
NEG	NEGA													40	2	1	$\overline{A}$ + 1 → A	8	↕	↕	↕	↕
	NEGB													50	2	1	$\overline{B}$ + 1 → B	8	↕	↕	↕	↕
	NEG				00	6	2	60	6+	2+	70	7	3				$\overline{M}$ + 1 → M	8	↕	↕	↕	↕
NOP														12	2	1	No Operation	•	•	•	•	•
OR	ORA	8A	2	2	9A	4	2	AA	4+	2+	BA	5	3				A V M → A	•	↕	↕	0	•
	ORB	CA	2	2	DA	4	2	EA	4+	2+	FA	5	3				B V M → B	•	↕	↕	0	•
	ORCC	1A	3	2													CC V IMM → CC				7	
PSH	PSHS	34	5+[4]	2													Push Registers on S Stack	•	•	•	•	•
	PSHU	36	5+[4]	2													Push Registers on U Stack	•	•	•	•	•
PUL	PULS	35	5+[4]	2													Pull Registers from S Stack	•	•	•	•	•
	PULU	37	5+[4]	2													Pull Registers from U Stack	•	•	•	•	•
ROL	ROLA													49	2	1		•	↕	↕	↕	↕
	ROLB													59	2	1		•	↕	↕	↕	↕
	ROL				09	6	2	69	6+	2+	79	7	3					•	↕	↕	↕	↕
ROR	RORA													46	2	1		•	↕	↕	•	↕
	RORB													56	2	1		•	↕	↕	•	↕
	ROR				06	6	2	66	6+	2+	76	7	3					•	↕	↕	•	↕
RTI														3B	6 15	1	Return From Interrupt					7
RTS														39	5	1	Return from Subroutine	•	•	•	•	•
SBC	SBCA	82	2	2	92	4	2	A2	4+	2+	B2	5	3				A − M − C → A	8	↕	↕	↕	↕
	SBCB	C2	2	2	D2	4	2	E2	4+	2+	F2	5	3				B − M − C → B	8	↕	↕	↕	↕
SEX														1D	2	1	Sign Extend B into A	•	↕	↕	0	•
ST	STA				97	4	2	A7	4+	2+	B7	5	3				A → M	•	↕	↕	0	•
	STB				D7	4	2	E7	4+	2+	F7	5	3				B → M	•	↕	↕	0	•
	STD				DD	5	2	ED	5+	2+	FD	6	3				D → M:M + 1	•	↕	↕	0	•
	STS				10 DF	6	3	10 EF	6+	3+	10 FF	7	4				S → M:M + 1	•	↕	↕	0	•
	STU				DF	5	2	EF	5+	2+	FF	6	3				U → M:M + 1	•	↕	↕	0	•
	STX				9F	5	2	AF	5+	2+	BF	6	3				X → M:M + 1	•	↕	↕	0	•
	STY				10 9F	6	3	10 AF	6+	3+	10 BF	7	4				Y → M:M + 1	•	↕	↕	0	•
SUB	SUBA	80	2	2	90	4	2	A0	4+	2+	B0	5	3				A − M → A	8	↕	↕	↕	↕
	SUBB	C0	2	2	D0	4	2	E0	4+	2+	F0	5	3				B − M → B	8	↕	↕	↕	↕
	SUBD	83	4	3	93	6	2	A3	6+	2+	B3	7	3				D − M:M + 1 → D	•	↕	↕	↕	↕
SWI	SWI[6]													3F	19	1	Software Interrupt 1	•	•	•	•	•
	SWI2[6]													10 3F	20	2	Software Interrupt 2	•	•	•	•	•
	SWI3[6]													11 3F	20	1	Software Interrupt 3	•	•	•	•	•
SYNC														13	≥4	1	Synchronize to Interrupt	•	•	•	•	•
TFR	R1, R2	1F	6	2													R1 → R2[2]	•	•	•	•	•
TST	TSTA													4D	2	1	Test A	•	↕	↕	0	•
	TSTB													5D	2	1	Test B	•	↕	↕	0	•
	TST				0D	6	2	6D	6+	2+	7D	7	3				Test M	•	↕	↕	0	•

NOTES:

1. This column gives a base cycle and byte count. To obtain total count, add the values obtained from the INDEXED ADDRESSING MODE table, Table 2.
2. R1 and R2 may be any pair of 8 bit or any pair of 16 bit registers.
   The 8 bit registers are: A, B, CC, DP
   The 16 bit registers are: X, Y, U, S, D, PC
3. EA is the effective address.
4. The PSH and PUL instructions require 5 cycles plus 1 cycle for each **byte** pushed or pulled.
5. 5(6) means: 5 cycles if branch not taken, 6 cycles if taken (Branch instructions).
6. SWI sets I and F bits. SWI2 and SWI3 do not affect I and F.
7. Conditions Codes set as a direct result of the instruction.
8. Vaue of half-carry flag is undefined.
9. Special Case — Carry set if b7 is SET.

TABLE G-2 Descriptions of 6809 Branch Instructions

MC6809

TABLE G–6 – PROGRAMMING AID (CONTINUED)

Branch Instructions

Instruction	Forms	Addressing Mode Relative OP	~ 5	#	Description	5 H	3 N	2 Z	1 V	0 C
BCC	BCC LBCC	24 10 24	3 5(6)	2 4	Branch C = 0 Long Branch C = 0	• •	• •	• •	• •	• •
BCS	BCS LBCS	25 10 25	3 5(6)	2 4	Branch C = 1 Long Branch C = 1	• •	• •	• •	• •	• •
BEQ	BEQ LBEQ	27 10 27	3 5(6)	2 4	Branch Z = 1 Long Branch Z = 1	• •	• •	• •	• •	• •
BGE	BGE LBGE	2C 10 2C	3 5(6)	2 4	Branch ≥ Zero Long Branch ≥ Zero	• •	• •	• •	• •	• •
BGT	BGT LBGT	2E 10 2E	3 5(6)	2 4	Branch > Zero Long Branch > Zero	• •	• •	• •	• •	• •
BHI	BHI LBHI	22 10 22	3 5(6)	2 4	Branch Higher Long Branch Higher	• •	• •	• •	• •	• •
BHS	BHS LBHS	24 10 24	3 5(6)	2 4	Branch Higher or Same Long Branch Higher or Same	• •	• •	• •	• •	• •
BLE	BLE LBLE	2F 10 2F	3 5(6)	2 4	Branch ≤ Zero Long Branch ≤ Zero	• •	• •	• •	• •	• •
BLO	BLO LBLO	25 10 25	3 5(6)	2 4	Branch lower Long Branch Lower	• •	• •	• •	• •	• •
BLS	BLS LBLS	23 10 23	3 5(6)	2 4	Branch Lower or Same Long Branch Lower or Same	• •	• •	• •	• •	• •
BLT	BLT LBLT	2D 10 2D	3 5(6)	2 4	Branch < Zero Long Branch < Zero	• •	• •	• •	• •	• •
BMI	BMI LBMI	2B 10 2B	3 5(6)	2 4	Branch Minus Long Branch Minus	• •	• •	• •	• •	• •
BNE	BNE LBNE	26 10 26	3 5(6)	2 4	Branch Z = 0 Long Branch Z = 0	• •	• •	• •	• •	• •
BPL	BPL LBPL	2A 10 2A	3 5(6)	2 4	Branch Plus Long Branch Plus	• •	• •	• •	• •	• •
BRA	BRA LBRA	20 16	3 5	2 3	Branch Always Long Branch Always	• •	• •	• •	• •	• •
BRN	BRN LBRN	21 10 21	3 5	2 4	Branch Never Long Branch Never	• •	• •	• •	• •	• •
BSR	BSR LBSR	8D 17	7 9	2 3	Branch to Subroutine Long Branch to Subroutine	• •	• •	• •	• •	• •
BVC	BVC LBVC	28 10 28	3 5(6)	2 4	Branch V = 0 Long Branch V = 0	• •	• •	• •	• •	• •
BVS	BVS LBVS	29 10 29	3 5(6)	2 4	Branch V = 1 Long Branch V = 1	• •	• •	• •	• •	• •

SIMPLE BRANCHES

	OP	~	#
BRA	20	3	2
LBRA	16	5	3
BRN	21	3	2
LBRN	1021	5	4
BSR	8D	7	2
LBSR	17	9	3

SIMPLE CONDITIONAL BRANCHES (Notes 1-4)

Test	True	OP	False	OP
N = 1	BMI	2B	BPL	2A
Z = 1	BEQ	27	BNE	26
V = 1	BVS	29	BVC	28
C = 1	BCS	25	BCC	24

SIGNED CONDITIONAL BRANCHES (Notes 1-4)

Test	True	OP	False	OP
r > m	BGT	2E	BLE	2F
r ≥ m	BGE	2C	BLT	2D
r = m	BEQ	27	BNE	26
r ≤ m	BLE	2F	BGT	2E
r < m	BLT	2D	BGE	2C

UNSIGNED CONDITIONAL BRANCHES (Notes 1-4)

Test	True	OP	False	OP
r > m	BHI	22	BLS	23
r ≥ m	BHS	24	BLO	25
r = m	BEQ	27	BNE	26
r ≤ m	BLS	23	BHI	22
r < m	BLO	25	BHS	24

NOTES:

1. All conditional branches have both short and long variations.
2. All short branches are two bytes and require three cycles.
3. All conditional long branches are formed by prefixing the short branch opcode with $10 and using a 16-bit destination offset.
4. All conditional long branches require four bytes and six cycles if the branch is taken or five cycles if the branch is not taken.

MOTOROLA Semiconductor Products Inc.

APPENDIX H

THE 6805 INSTRUCTION SET

Mnemonic	Addressing Modes										Condition Codes				
	Inherent	Immediate	Direct	Extended	Relative	Indexed (No Offset)	Indexed (8 Bits)	Indexed (16 Bits)	Bit Set/ Clear	Bit Test & Branch	H	I	N	Z	C
ADC		X	X	X		X	X	X			Λ	●	Λ	Λ	Λ
ADD		X	X	X		X	X	X			Λ	●	Λ	Λ	Λ
AND		X	X	X		X	X	X			●	●	Λ	Λ	●
ASL	X		X			X	X				●	●	Λ	Λ	Λ
ASR	X		X			X	X				●	●	Λ	Λ	Λ
BCC					X						●	●	●	●	●
BCLR									X		●	●	●	●	●
BCS					X						●	●	●	●	●
BEQ					X						●	●	●	●	●
BHCC					X						●	●	●	●	●
BHCS					X						●	●	●	●	●
BHI					X						●	●	●	●	●
BHS					X						●	●	●	●	●
BIH					X						●	●	●	●	●
BIL					X						●	●	●	●	●
BIT		X	X	X		X	X	X			●	●	Λ	Λ	●
BLO					X						●	●	●	●	●
BLS					X						●	●	●	●	●
BMC					X						●	●	●	●	●
BMI					X						●	●	●	●	●
BMS					X						●	●	●	●	●
BNE					X						●	●	●	●	●
BPL					X						●	●	●	●	●
BRA					X						●	●	●	●	●
BRN					X						●	●	●	●	●
BRCLR										X	●	●	●	●	Λ
BRSET										X	●	●	●	●	Λ
BSET									X		●	●	●	●	●
BSR					X						●	●	●	●	●
CLC	X										●	●	●	●	0
CLI	X										●	0	●	●	●
CLR	X		X			X	X				●	●	0	1	●
CMP		X	X	X		X	X	X			●	●	Λ	Λ	Λ

Mnemonic	Addressing Modes										Condition Codes				
	Inherent	Immediate	Direct	Extended	Relative	Indexed (No Offset)	Indexed (8 Bits)	Indexed (16 Bits)	Bit Set/ Clear	Bit Test & Branch	H	I	N	Z	C
COM	X		X			X	X				●	●	Λ	Λ	1
CPX		X	X	X		X	X	X			●	●	Λ	Λ	Λ
DEC	X		X			X	X				●	●	Λ	Λ	●
EOR		X	X	X		X	X	X			●	●	Λ	Λ	●
INC	X		X			X	X				●	●	Λ	Λ	●
JMP			X	X		X	X	X			●	●	●	●	●
JSR			X	X		X	X	X			●	●	●	●	●
LDA		X	X	X		X	X	X			●	●	Λ	Λ	●
LDX		X	X	X		X	X	X			●	●	Λ	Λ	●
LSL	X		X			X	X				●	●	Λ	Λ	Λ
LSR	X		X			X	X				●	●	0	Λ	Λ
MUL	X										0	●	●	●	0
NEG	X		X			X	X				●	●	Λ	Λ	Λ
NOP	X										●	●	●	●	●
ORA		X	X	X		X	X	X			●	●	Λ	Λ	●
ROL	X		X			X	X				●	●	Λ	Λ	Λ
ROR	X		X			X	X				●	●	Λ	Λ	Λ
RSP	X										●	●	●	●	●
RTI	X										?	?	?	?	?
RTS	X										●	●	●	●	●
SBC		X	X	X		X	X	X			●	●	Λ	Λ	Λ
SEC	X										●	●	●	●	1
SEI	X										●	1	●	●	●
STA			X	X		X	X	X			●	●	Λ	Λ	●
STOP	X										●	0	●	●	●
STX			X	X		X	X	X			●	●	Λ	Λ	●
SUB		X	X	X		X	X	X			●	●	Λ	Λ	Λ
SWI	X										●	1	●	●	●
TAX	X										●	●	●	●	●
TST	X		X			X	X				●	●	Λ	Λ	●
TXA	X										●	●	●	●	●
WAIT	X										●	0	●	●	●

Condition Code Symbols:

H	Half Carry (From Bit 3)	Λ	Test and Set if True Cleared Otherwise
I	Interrupt Mask	●	Not Affected
N	Negate (Sign Bit)	?	Load CC Register From Stack
Z	Zero	0	Cleared
C	Carry/Borrow	1	Set

INDEX

Page numbers in *italics* are for defined words